CRIMINOLOGY

STEVE CASE, PHIL JOHNSON, DAVID MANLOW, ROGER SMITH, KATE WILLIAMS

With contributed chapters:

Chapter 10 by **Neena Samota**

Chapter 11 by **Pamela Ugwudike**

OXFORD
UNIVERSITY PRESS

OXFORD
UNIVERSITY PRESS

Great Clarendon Street, Oxford, OX2 6DP,
United Kingdom

Oxford University Press is a department of the University of Oxford.
It furthers the University's objective of excellence in research, scholarship,
and education by publishing worldwide. Oxford is a registered trade mark of
Oxford University Press in the UK and in certain other countries

Published in the United States of America by Oxford University Press
198 Madison Avenue, New York, NY 10016, United States of America

British Library Cataloguing in Publication Data
Data available

Library of Congress Control Number: 2016953995

ISBN 978-0-19-873675-2

Printed in Italy by L.E.G.O. S.p.A.

BRIEF TABLE OF CONTENTS

PART 1
JOURNEYING INTO CRIMINOLOGY   3

1. Becoming a student   5
2. What is the study of criminology?   29

PART 2
EXPLORING CRIME   53

3. What is crime?   55
4. What is justice?   81
5. Crime statistics   113
6. How does criminology 'know' about crime?   139
7. Crime and the media   165
8. Victimology and hate crime   199
9. Explaining youth crime and youth justice   227
10. Race, ethnicities, and the criminal justice system   263
11. Gender and feminist criminology   283

PART 3
EXPLAINING CRIME   313

12. Free will, classicism, and rational choice   315
13. Biological and psychological positivism   343
14. Sociological positivism   377
15. Critical criminology—part 1   417
16. Critical criminology—part 2   445
17. Right and left realism   479
18. Integrated theories of crime   503
19. Searching for the causes of crime   525

PART 4
RESPONDING TO CRIME   551

20. Criminal justice principles   553
21. Criminal justice—policy, practice, and people   577
22. Crime prevention   599
23. Crime control, policing, and community safety   631
24. Punishment and the idea of 'just deserts'   661
25. Rehabilitation of offenders   685
26. Alternatives to punishment   715
27. Critical perspectives on crime and punishment   743

PART 5
BECOMING A RESEARCHER OF CRIMINOLOGY   769

28. Becoming a researcher and knowledge producer   771
29. Applying your skills to employability or future study   805
30. Journeying into employability and careers   833

DETAILED TABLE OF CONTENTS

Preface xi
Acknowledgements xiii
Editorial advisory panel xiv
Message to students xv
Meet the authors xvi
Guide to the resources in this textbook xviii
Guide to the online resources xx

PART 1
JOURNEYING INTO CRIMINOLOGY 3

1. **Becoming a student** Tips, tricks, and tools for
effective learning 5
   Introduction 6
   Effective, engaged, employable: The E3 student 6
   Embarking on your journey at university 8
   Choosing your travel partners 11
   Developing a way to travel: Remember your ABC 25

2. **What is the study of criminology?** 29
   Introduction 30
   What does criminology look like as an academic
   subject? 31
   What is the nature of criminology? 33
   Studying criminology 34
   How will I study criminology at university? 36
   The independent learner 39
   How will your learning be assessed? 41
   What is the study of criminology?—revisited 50

PART 2
EXPLORING CRIME 53

3. **What is crime?** 55
   Introduction 56
   Crime as a social construct 57
   Crime and deviance 60
   Why are some actions criminalised? 62
   The harm principle 62

   Other reasons which might explain why some
   actions are crimes 70
   Do we need the criminal law? 73

4. **What is justice?** 81
   Introduction 82
   Justice—preliminary issues 82
   Definitions of justice 85
   Criminal justice models 88
   Philosophical ideas of justice 95
   Systems of criminal justice—adversarial and
   inquisitorial 102

5. **Crime statistics** 113
   Introduction 114
   Officially (police) recorded crime statistics 115
   Offence categories and patterns of offending 119
   Police recorded crime statistics and the 'justice gap'
   and Wales 120
   Surveying crime: The Crime Survey for England 126
   Conclusion 131

6. **How does criminology 'know' about crime?** 139
   Subjectivity, supposition, and study 139
   Introduction 140
   Approaching criminological knowledge with a
   critical eye 141
   Subjectivity, supposition, and study: The triad of
   knowledge creation 142
   Criminological theory as knowledge 143
   Supposition 148
   Study 150
   Reflecting on research as study: What can we know? 161

7. **Crime and the media** 165
   Introduction 166
   Traditional media criminology 167
   Newsworthiness and setting agendas 170
   The representation of young people in the media 175
   The representation of migrants in the media 178
   Crime novels, television, and film 182

Analysing crime film and the criminological imagination 184
Media classification and censorship 186
New technology, new media, and new fears 187
Cybercrime 189
The future of media criminology 193

8. **Victimology and hate crime** Evidence and campaigning for change 199
Introduction 200
Non-governmental organisations and pressure groups 201
Victims of crime and the victims movement 202
Theoretical approaches to studying victims 208
Hate crime 210
Disablist hate crime 215
Homophobic hate crime 218
Conclusion 220

9. **Explaining youth crime and youth justice** 227
Introduction 228
Why do we need to view youth crime differently? 228
Growing up—theories of childhood and youth 229
Theories of delinquency 232
Growing into crime: Culture and deviance 239
Responding to young people's offending behaviour 248
Progressive approaches to youth offending: Diversion and positive youth justice 254
Conclusions 257

10. **Race, ethnicities, and the criminal justice system** 263
Introduction 264
Critical race theory 264
Understanding race, crime, and the criminal justice system 266
Using CRT to understand crime and criminal justice in England and Wales 270
Conclusion 278

11. **Gender and feminist criminology** 283
Introduction 284
Feminist criminology: Key theoretical traditions 287
Gender and crime 299
Gender and criminal justice 303
Criticisms of feminist criminology 304
Conclusion 308

PART 3
EXPLAINING CRIME 313

12. **Free will, classicism, and rational choice** 315
The blame game 316
Introduction 316

What is a theory? 317
Testing a theory 318
Different types of theory 321
Criminological theory 322
Classical criminology 324
Conclusion and consideration of modern neo-classical theories 336

13. **Biological and psychological positivism** Determined to predetermine 343
Introduction 344
Positivism, punishment, and rehabilitation 344
Early positivism 346
Biological theories 351
Psychological theories 359
Learning 364

14. **Sociological positivism** Determined to predetermine 377
Introduction 378
Sociological theories 379
Key concepts in sociology 379
Social process/interaction theories 383
Social structural theories—macro-sociological theories 387
Culture and subcultural theories 397

15. **Critical criminology—part 1** Challenging the 'usual suspects' 417
Introduction: What do you see? 418
Social construction and power 421
Labelling perspectives: 1960s radicalism and humanising the deviant 422
The development of critical criminology in Britain 428
Conclusion 441

16. **Critical criminology—part 2** New and future directions 445
Introduction 446
A new era and a new 'ology': Enter the zemiologists 450
The greening of critical criminology? 454
Cultural criminology: Deviant subcultures, emotions, and the carnival of crime 460
Convict criminology 468
Conclusion 473

17. **Right and left realism** 479
Introduction: The emergence of realist perspectives 480
Right realism: Key ideas 482
Right realism: Policy implications 483
Evaluating right realism 488
Left realism: Key ideas 489
Left realism: Policy implications 492
Evaluating left realism 495
Conclusion 497

18. **Integrated theories of crime** 503
Introduction 504
Integrated explanations of crime 505
Evolving integrated explanations of crime 505
Integrated risk factor theories: Predicting, not explaining crime 511
The two sides of the integrated coin 520

19. **Searching for the causes of crime** 525
Introduction 526
Epistemology and the causes of crime 526
Operationalising the causes of crime 529
Exploring the causes of crime through scientific experiment 530
The rebirth of experimental criminology in the 21st century 536
Responding to crime 539
Chaos theory 542
Conclusion: Do we really search for the causes of crime? 545

**PART 4
RESPONDING TO CRIME** 551

20. **Criminal justice principles** 553
Introduction: The criminal justice game changers 554
The rule of law 555
Adversarial justice 565
Restorative justice 566
The police, the courts, and the CPS 568

21. **Criminal justice—policy, practice, and people** 577
Introduction 578
Criminal justice policies 578
Criminal justice practices 584
People in criminal justice 593

22. **Crime prevention** Ideas and practices 599
Introduction 600
What is crime prevention? 600
Alternative perspectives on crime prevention 608
Politics, interest groups, and crime prevention 613
Models of practice in crime prevention 616
What does prevention achieve? 619
Consequences of crime prevention 621
Limitations of crime prevention 624

23. **Crime control, policing, and community safety** 631
What is crime control? 632
Crime control and due process models 633
Objectives of crime control 635

The role of the police in crime control 638
Beyond policing: The place of other agencies and interests in controlling crime 642
Place, property, and people: The objects and technologies of crime control 645
What are the consequences of crime control? 647
Does it work? 651
The limitations of crime control 654

24. **Punishment and the idea of 'just deserts'** 661
Introduction 662
What is punishment? 662
What is punishment intended to achieve? 664
The delivery of punishment 668
Mind, body, soul: The objects of punishment 673
The organisation and impact of punishment 675
What are the consequences of punishment? 677
Objective or subjective considerations: Punishment, justice, and the public 680
What is wrong with the idea of punishment? 681

25. **Rehabilitation of offenders** 685
Introduction 686
What is rehabilitation? 686
What is rehabilitation for? 689
How is rehabilitation organised and administered? 693
Mind, body, soul: The objects of rehabilitation 695
Models and practices in the delivery of rehabilitative services 698
What are the outcomes of rehabilitation: How do we judge success? 701
What is the impact of rehabilitation? What does it achieve? 704
The limitations of rehabilitation 707

26. **Alternatives to punishment** Diversion and restorative justice 715
Introduction 716
Alternatives to punishment and offence resolution 716
The purpose of alternatives to punishment and offence resolution 720
Transformational goals 723
Alternatives to punishment: Structure, organisation, and operation 725
Delivering alternatives to punishment: Practices and challenges 728
The achievements of alternatives to punishment: Considering the evidence 732
Alternatives to punishment: The implications 734
The limitations of alternatives to punishment 737

27. Critical perspectives on crime and punishment 743

What are critical perspectives on punishment? 744

Unjust punishment 746

Punishment and hegemony: Justifications and
legitimacy 749

Crimes of the privileged 751

What is to be done about crime? 755

Limitations of critical perspectives on
punishment 763

Conclusion 765

PART 5
**BECOMING A RESEARCHER
OF CRIMINOLOGY** 769

28. Becoming a researcher and knowledge producer 771

Introduction 772

Why research? 772

Where to begin? 775

Planning your research 780

The importance of ethical standards ('The Only
Way Is Ethics') 786

Barriers for research 789

Writing up your research 793

Disseminating your findings 796

Where to next? 799

**29. Applying your skills to employability or
future study** 805

Introduction 806

Climbing the levels of your higher education 811

Future concerns for criminology 817

Future concerns for criminal justice 818

Campaigning in criminology 820

Seeing crime differently 823

30. Journeying into employability and careers 833

From university to the workplace 834

Introduction 836

Producing your own employability 836

Employers' perceptions of graduate
employability skills 837

Producing your 'RARE' employability framework 840

Getting a lift from work-based learning 840

Applying graduate employability to your career 842

People in criminal justice careers 846

Different types of career 859

Self-employability and social enterprise 862

Transferring your employability to your career 864

Glossary 869

Bibliography 879

Index 909

PREFACE

Developed in close partnership with lecturers and students across the UK, *Criminology* aims to be the most stimulating, critical, and applied textbook available in this subject area.

The book has been written for undergraduate criminology students with the intention of encouraging student engagement, facilitating effective study, and exploring the use of criminology in the real world. Our approach is informed by broad experience of undergraduate teaching, curriculum design, student engagement, and applied criminological research.

The overarching goal is to provide a dynamic framework for understanding and engaging with criminology as an academic subject and as an applied field of research, policy, practice, and employment. As such, we speak directly to the reader throughout, with the aim of challenging and motivating them to be an active participant in their own learning journey. This aim is reflected in the book's five-part structure: journeying into criminology (including pre-university guidance to students); exploring crime; explaining crime; responding to crime; and becoming a researcher of criminology (which focuses on the student as a knowledge creator and on post-university employability).

Every chapter includes a series of carefully developed pedagogical features (please see the 'Guide to the resources in this textbook' for a full description of each) that are designed to promote and enable close, critical student engagement with topics and debates.

Our aim has been to write a book that will help produce a new generation of active criminologists who carry their knowledge, enthusiasm, and newly-honed skills through their studies and into practice, research, policy, and/or other employment. We hope that we have achieved it.

Steve Case
Phil Johnson
David Manlow
Roger Smith
Kate Williams

ACKNOWLEDGEMENTS

The idea for an engaging, accessible, and student-friendly textbook came from our interactions with students over many years, so it is to these honest, forthright, and dedicated criminologists that we offer our thanks for raising the issues that brought our book to fruition.

We are grateful to Neena Samota (St Mary's University, Twickenham) and Dr Pamela Ugwudike (Swansea University) for contributing valuable chapters on race and gender, respectively, to the book. Further thanks must go to the diligent body of expert reviewers, both lecturers and students, whose invaluable feedback throughout the writing process has significantly enhanced the accessibility, quality, and scope of the work. We offer these reviewers our profound appreciation for giving up their time and energies to comment on the material, for constantly motivating us to improve, and for giving us confidence that our book is worthwhile.

We also owe a huge debt of gratitude to the talented staff at Oxford University Press. Without their expertise, support, and boundless enthusiasm, our project may have drifted aimlessly onto the rocks. However, they never lost faith, never stopped pushing, and never ceased encouraging. Particular thanks must go to our editorial team of Nicola Hartley and Tom Young—a nicer, more professional and talented pair of editors you could not hope to be given.

Steve would like to personally thank Nicola and Tom for their ceaseless support and the numerous coffees at our book meetings. Steve would also like to thank Professor Kevin Haines, who has guided him to this point and has always been a great mentor and friend.

Phil would like to particularly thank Belinda Child for all her assistance and support throughout his career—her constant advice and encouragement has inspired many of his new approaches to teaching and learning in higher education. Phil would also like to thank his UCBC colleagues Ian Ashworth, Gillian Dickinson, Dr Tass Hussain, and Mark Thistlethwaite for being major sources of help and expertise.

David would like to thank his many academic friends and colleagues, particularly those who contributed such excellent pieces for the feature boxes in his chapters. He would like to extend special thanks to Anita Hobson, Mick Fleming, Maggie Sumner, and Jax Freedman for their support and encouragement, and particularly to Zoe: without her unhealthy knowledge of crime fiction and storehouse of obscure facts, his chapters for this book would undoubtedly have been shorter and duller.

Roger would like to add his thanks to Nigel Hinks, Mike Payne, and all the other unsung heroes who have continued to try and ensure that criminal justice has a human face.

Kate would like to thank LJ, ME, AJ, SH, and DJ (they know who they are). Importantly, she also wants to thank all her students both for their interest and the questions they ask, each of which has helped to shape this work.

Steve Case
Phil Johnson
David Manlow
Roger Smith
Kate Williams

The publishers would like to acknowledge everybody who kindly granted us permission to reproduce images, figures, and quotations throughout this text. Every effort was made to trace copyright holders, but we would be pleased to make suitable arrangements to clear permission for material reproduced in this book with any copyright holders whom it has not been possible to contact.

EDITORIAL ADVISORY PANEL

The authors and Oxford University Press are immensely grateful to the following reviewers, who provided invaluable feedback at multiple stages throughout the writing of this text to inform its development and help us ensure that it fulfilled its aims. Thanks must also be extended to the many students who shared their views on the content and design of the book.

Dr Thomas D. Akoensi, University of Kent
Dr Ana Aliverti, University of Warwick
Dr Catrin Andersson, Sheffield Hallam University
Dr Linda Asquith, Leeds Beckett University
Dr John Bahadur Lamb, Birmingham City University
Dr Anette Ballinger, Keele University
Dr Charlotte Barlow, Birmingham City University
Dr Olivia Barnes, Ulster University (part-time tutor)
Dr Eric Baumgartner, Teesside University
Dr Sarah Charman, University of Portsmouth
Dr Helen Clarke, University of Derby
Dr Bill Davies, Leeds Beckett University
Dr Melissa Dearey, University of Hull
Dr Teresa Degenhardt, Queen's University Belfast
Dr Sarah Dubberley, Wrexham Glyndŵr University
Dr Marian Duggan, University of Kent
Dr Wendy Dyer, Northumbria University
Helen Easton, London South Bank University
Michael Fiddler, University of Greenwich
Dr Jennifer Fleetwood, University of Leicester
Dr Nick Flynn, De Montfort University, Leicester
Dr Anne Foley, University of the West of England
Elaine Genders, University College London
Dr Martin Glynn, Birmingham City University
Dr Paul Gray, Manchester Metropolitan University
Dr Tim Holmes, Bangor University
David Honeywell, University of York
Dr Elisa Impara, Kingston University
Dr Matthew Jones, Northumbria University
Dr Vasileios Karagiannopoulos, University of Portsmouth
Dr Anastasia Karamalidou, University of the West of England
Dr John Kerr, University of Roehampton
Dr Stephanie Kewley, Birmingham City University
Dr Anita Lavorgna, University of Southampton
Ross Little, De Montfort University
Dr Giuseppe Maglione, Edinburgh Napier University
Dr Andrew Mathers, University of the West of England

Dr Nikki McKenzie, University of the West of England
Dr Lynda Measor, University of Brighton
Dr Juan Medina-Ariza, University of Manchester
Tanya Miles-Berry, Sheffield Hallam University
Professor Andrew Millie, Edge Hill University
Dr Rachel Monaghan, Ulster University
Dr Catherine Morgan, Bath Spa University
Dr Rachel Morris, University of York
Dr Katrina Morrison, Edinburgh Napier University
Dr Nicholas Pamment, University of Portsmouth
Dr Donna Peacock, University of Sunderland
Dr Eleanor Peters, Edge Hill University
Jake Phillips, Sheffield Hallam University
Dr Helen Poole, Coventry University
Dr David Porteous, Middlesex University
Dr Hannah Quirk, University of Manchester
Dr Jason Roach, University of Huddersfield
Jon Shute, University of Manchester
Graham Smyth, Manchester Metropolitan University
Greta Squire, University of Brighton
Dr Alisa Stevens, University of Southampton
Dr Sundari Anitha, University of Lincoln
Dr Paul Taylor, University of Chester
Dr Maryse Tennant, Canterbury Christ Church University
Dr Hannah Thurston, University of Brighton
Professor Sandra Walklate, University of Liverpool
Dr Ian Walmsley, University of the West of England
Dr Julia Wardhaugh, Bangor University
Dr Robin West, University of Essex
Dr Paula Wilcox, University of Brighton
Dr Richard Wild, University of Greenwich
Professor Dean Wilson, University of Sussex
Dr Emma Wincup, University of Leeds
Dr Jonathan Wynne Evans, University of South Wales
Dr Suzanne Young, Leeds Beckett University
Dr Irene Zempi, Nottingham Trent University

MESSAGE TO STUDENTS

This book is written for you, the student of criminology.

When Oxford University Press approached me with their idea for a student-focused and engaging textbook that challenges students to think for themselves and to actively create criminological knowledge, I was immediately sold.

This comprehensive book breaks down criminology into a five-step learning journey, starting with understanding the basics of university study and criminology as an academic subject, through to exploring, explaining, and responding to crime, and ending with guidance on knowledge creation and how to enhance your employability. Throughout this learning journey, our aim is to demystify and animate criminology; to support you in becoming a more effective, engaged, and employable student (the 'E3' student).

We do this by speaking directly to you in every chapter and by encouraging you to explore, evaluate, challenge, and *Always Be Critical* (the ABC approach) towards everything you read and hear from your own perspective. We constantly ask 'what do you think?' about key issues. We highlight 'controversies and debates' and 'new frontiers' that challenge established, accepted knowledge in criminology. We offer 'conversations' with key academics and 'telling it like it is' accounts—these are personal perspectives from students and the authors that will give you valuable insights into the experiences and realities of research and knowledge production in criminology.

By the end of your journey through *Criminology*, the textbook, and also criminology, the academic subject, you will be a fully-fledged 'E3' student, capable of original critique and the creation of knowledge—you will be a true criminologist.

Steve Case, 2017

MEET THE AUTHORS

Professor Steve Case

I am a Professor of Criminology and Director of Studies in the Department of Social Sciences at Loughborough University, teaching modules on research methods and youth justice (this is the focus of my research and writing—good teaching is informed by research). In 2012, I led the team at Swansea University that won the British Society of Criminology's National Award for Excellence in Teaching Criminology for designing an undergraduate criminology degree programme that really engaged with students, linking its different elements together logically and effectively. I have conducted large-scale funded research projects for the Home Office, the Youth Justice Board, the National Institute for Health and Social Care, and the Welsh Government.

Dr Phil Johnson

I am the Academic Subject Leader for Criminology at the University Centre at Blackburn College and my main teaching and research interests are criminal justice, visual criminology, and employability. In 2014 I was appointed Senior Fellow of the Higher Education Academy in recognition of my work embedding both alternative approaches to employability and visual assessment methods into a range of undergraduate courses in the social sciences. I gained my PhD in Applied Social Science (Lancaster) in 2009 and have continued to research various aspects of community sentencing, policy, and practice.

David Manlow

I am Principal Lecturer in Criminology at the University of Westminster in London, where I also lead the BA Criminology programme. My main teaching and research interests are in the fields of youth justice, crime in the media, and critical criminological theory. I am currently researching the portrayal of crime in post-war British film and television, together with work on developing new forms of accessible and diverse pedagogy for undergraduate students. In 2016, I was proud to be the first individual to be awarded the British Society of Criminology's National Award for Excellence in Teaching Criminology.

Professor Roger Smith

I began my career in the probation service, and went on to work in an important diversion project with young offenders in Northamptonshire in the 1980s. After that, I worked for The Children's Society as Head of Policy, where I held a brief for promoting children's rights and challenging inequality. My horizontal career continued with a move into academia in 2000: I am currently Professor of Social Work at Durham University, where I teach, write, and research extensively at the interface between social work and youth justice. I have a particular interest in participatory research methods and I am still committed to children's rights.

Kate Williams

I am a Senior Lecturer in Criminology at Aberystwyth University and Director of the Welsh Centre for Crime and Social Justice. My recent research involves criminal justice services in rural areas, the treatment of women and young people who offend, and consideration of the work of the voluntary sector in resettlement of offenders. I support the Youth Justice Board Cymru's Practice Development Panel and have advised the Welsh Government on various subjects. My teaching is informed by research which keeps it fresh, interesting, and relevant, and I enjoy students' questions which often push me to think of things in different ways.

CONTACT THE AUTHORS

This textbook has been written with you, the student, in mind so why not get in touch with our author team and offer your feedback?

Twitter:

Steve Case: @SteveCaseCrim

Roger Smith: @rogerssmith37

Phil Johnson: @edupunk_phil

Facebook:

Steve convenes a *Positive Youth Justice* Facebook discussion group. Visit the group here:
https://www.facebook.com/groups/853804234630683/

We are always looking for ways we can improve the book so please do get involved and let us know what you think.

GUIDE TO THE RESOURCES IN THIS TEXTBOOK

The features in this text have been carefully designed, crafted, and reviewed to ensure that they deliver something truly meaningful and useful to you during your studies.

WHAT DO YOU THINK? 26.6

'Justice reinvestment' has become an i
ionable term to describe an emerging
development which emphasises the fina
made from pursuing less intrusive and i
punishment, especially custody.

The six Justice Reinvestment Pilots (Gre

REFLECT & CHALLENGE THROUGH WHAT DO YOU THINK?

Each and every one of us has preconceived ideas influenced by our upbringing, our peers, our family, and a whole range of other socio-economic and political factors. Reflect on and challenge your own viewpoints and preconceptions by engaging with the WHAT DO YOU THINK? boxes. Discussion questions are provided with each example.

CONVERSATIONS 25.1

**Arguments for rehabilitation: The ca
interventions and domestic violence
Professor Nicole Westmarland**

RS (Roger Smith): Fundamentally the
purposes of this conversation is 'Wha

LISTEN & ENGAGE THROUGH CONVERSATIONS

People make criminology, so take a moment to read through the CONVERSATIONS boxes provided throughout the text. There are contributions from a whole range of individuals including academics, students, victims, ex-convicts, employability experts, and practitioners in the field, such as probation and police officers. These personal accounts offer unique insights into many different facets of criminology and should help you understand academic concepts in 'real world' scenarios.

! **CONTROVERSY AND DE**

Realism and the 'Riots'

Drawing on the work of Jock Young (19
(2015: 147) has succinctly summaris
of similarity and difference between r
approaches. These are set out in **Tabl**

QUESTION & CRITIQUE THROUGH CONTROVERSY AND DEBATE

Consider alternative angles and provocative perceptions through the CONTROVERSY AND DEBATE feature. Use the information in these boxes to engage in discussions in key areas and critically evaluate the pros and cons of the topic or concept featured.

UNDERSTAND & ANALYSE THROUGH TELLING IT LIKE IT IS

Gain a personal and in-depth understanding of key areas through reading the viewpoints of the authors and students on key areas. The **TELLING IT LIKE IT IS** accounts are intended to provide practical, honest advice to help you navigate your way through your educational journey.

> **TELLING IT LIKE IT IS** 2.2
>
> **The criminology student's view of pres —with Emma Hurren and Amy Rowe**
>
> Emma Hurren, a recent criminology Swansea University, says, 'So you are s room full of people ready to listen to you presentation. Thinking about this filled

EXPLORE & PROGRESS THROUGH NEW FRONTIERS

Become a criminologist in your own right by exploring the thoughts, concepts, and initiatives at the forefront of criminology. Open up your mind to new ideas in this fast-changing field and offer progressive ideas yourself, inspired by the issues covered in the NEW FRONTIERS boxes.

> **NEW FRONTIERS** 6.1
>
> **The role of reflexivity in knowledge cr**
>
> It is crucial that criminologists reflect cri search decisions that they have made (e search method, how to create knowledg influenced these decisions (e.g. the soc and political contexts of the research) t

TEST & APPLY THROUGH REVIEW QUESTIONS

Use the **REVIEW QUESTIONS** at the end of each chapter to check your understanding of key topics and concepts before moving on. These are great resources to use when revising.

> **REVIEW QUESTIONS**
>
> 1. List and evaluate why, in the 21st centu
> 2. What does it mean to 'speak truth to pov
> 3. What are safety crimes? Are they really ⏎
> 4. Give three examples of issues which ar should we care about environmental pr

READ & RESEARCH THROUGH FURTHER READING

Annotated FURTHER READING suggestions are provided at the end of each chapter to help you select the best additional resources that are suitable either for gaining a more detailed general understanding of a topic, or for preparing for an essay or dissertation.

> **FURTHER READING**
>
> Rather than over-relying on the secondary theoretical criminology textbooks which h original authors wherever possible. In ter useful starting points.
>
> Hopkins-Burke, R. (2013) *An Introduction to Crim*
> Tierney, J. and O'Neill, M (2016) *Criminology; Theo*

GUIDE TO THE ONLINE RESOURCES

An extensive range of online resources to accompany this book can be found at:

www.oup.com/uk/case/

These resources have been developed to enhance your understanding of and engagement with the text, bring aspects of it to life, and help you stay up to date with changes within criminology—we hope you find them useful. From the resource centre you can also find and follow the **authors' social media accounts** to make sure you never miss a thing in this fast-moving subject area.

DECODE & DIGEST THROUGH ACADEMIC WRITING DEMYSTIFIED

Learn how to cut through formal, complex academic language to quickly zero in on what journal articles and monographs are really saying. Members of the author team show you how to translate their academic articles so that you can apply the same techniques in your own reading and research.

RECAP & REVISE THROUGH MULTIPLE-CHOICE QUESTIONS

This book takes the view that there's no 'right' and 'wrong' in criminology: it's about discussions, reasoned viewpoints, and critical analysis. But quick-fire questions can be valuable for checking that you've grasped the basics and jogging your memory ahead of exams, so the resources include over 100 of them, complete with answers and feedback, covering a wide variety of key topics from the book.

PROBE & DELVE DEEPER THROUGH FURTHER READING SUGGESTIONS AND USEFUL WEB LINKS

If you're particularly interested in a certain area and have already been through the further reading suggestions in the book, visit the online resources to find even more book and article suggestions and useful web links relating to every chapter.

COMPARE & CONTRAST THROUGH EXTRA CHAPTERS ON DEVOLVED JURISDICTION

Three additional chapters written by expert guest authors provide clear overviews of the distinctive aspects of the criminal justice systems (and their application and context) in Scotland, Wales, and Northern Ireland.

We've also provided a handy **checklist of key ethical considerations** to bear in mind when beginning a research project (summarising information covered in detail in Chapter 28) for you to print and consult.

Also available for lecturers are

- An edited collection of FREELY-AVAILABLE VIDEO RESOURCES from across the web, listed by topic, to help bring seminars to life, along with several author videos on teaching and learning in criminology.

- A bank of EXAM AND ESSAY QUESTIONS for key topics that can be used or adapted for teaching and assessment.

- TEMPLATE POWERPOINTS® ON KEY TOPICS that can be easily built upon and customised, along with downloadable versions of all the figures from the book.

PART OUTLINE

1. Becoming a student: Tips, tricks, and tools for effective learning
2. What is the study of criminology?

The opening part of our book focuses on your journey into studying criminology at university. In the first chapter, 'Becoming a student: Tips, tricks, and tools for effective learning', you are introduced to the skills required to become an effective, engaged, and employable student of criminology, or an 'E3' student as we will refer to it—a successful, capable, and committed individual who is attractive to employers. Your route to effectiveness, engagement, and employability is presented as a reflective journey that you embark upon at university in an informed, active, and critical way.

Central to your journey is the identification and utilisation of the 'travel partners' located at your university and in your department, subject area, programme of study, and classroom. Therefore, **Chapter 1** prepares you mentally and practically for your studies. The second and final chapter in this section, 'What is the study of criminology?', introduces criminology as an academic subject, what it looks like and how you will be expected to study it.

The chapter is underpinned by what is called the 'triad of criminology', a basic framework for understanding how criminology fits together through the study of definitions of crime, explanations of criminal behaviour, and responses to crime and criminal behaviour. As you will see, the whole book takes this structure by following the journeying into criminology discussion with parts focused on exploring (defining) crime, explaining crime, and responding to crime. Our final part, **Part 5** revisits **Part 1** with a discussion of how you can employ your new skills, knowledge, and understanding to become a researcher and producer of knowledge—a criminologist.

PART 1

JOURNEYING INTO CRIMINOLOGY

CHAPTER OUTLINE

Introduction   6

Effective, engaged, employable: The E3 student   6

Embarking on your journey at university   8

Choosing your travel partners   11

Developing a way to travel: Remember your ABC   25

1

Becoming a student

Tips, tricks, and tools for effective learning

KEY ISSUES

This chapter aims to:

- introduce and explain the learning journey at university;
- introduce and explore the role of travel partners who can help you with your learning journey;
- introduce and explore the 'way of travel' mindset you should develop, which is guided by being mature, dynamic, proactive, strategic, and critical.

Introduction

You will notice from the **Key Issues** that this opening, preliminary chapter introduces you to ideas for how to study and learn in the most effective ways in the university, higher education context. We will explore a series of learning tips, tricks, and tools that are intended to enable you to become the most *effective*, *engaged*, and *employable* student possible throughout your criminology studies and by the time you complete your student experience. Furthermore, these pointers should enable you to engage with and benefit from the contents of this book.

For those reasons, the chapter should be of value to new and existing students alike. Much of the information and practical advice could be considered common sense, but it is crucial that it is brought together in one place for you to draw upon as you begin your studies, and as you begin to find your way through this book. The information and advice here is a prequel to the academic content of the book;

preparatory reading to get you mentally and practically ready to study. Consequently, this chapter is more of an introduction to university study than an introduction to criminology, so existing students may prefer to start with the subject-specific introduction and guidance provided by **Chapter 2**. It is offered as an essential building block for your learning and subsequent engagement with criminology as an academic subject area. Once the basics are in place, you are in a stronger position to experience and learn whilst at university.

This chapter represents your studies as a learning journey: a process of embarking—preparing for your university experience and higher education (HE) study; choosing *travel partners*—from your university, department, programme, subject area, peer group; and developing a way to travel—being a proactive, strategic, constructive, focused and, above all, a critical learner.

Effective, engaged, employable: The E3 student

Making the most of your student experience involves dedicating yourself to becoming as effective in your studies as possible by completing academic work to the best of your abilities at all times, and aiming to make yourself as employable and attractive to potential employers as possible so that you can get the job that you want. These goals apply to you whatever type of student you are—undergraduate, postgraduate taught, postgraduate research, distance learner, international, mature; whatever subject you are studying and wherever in the world you are studying. In other words, throughout your studies, among other goals, you should be aiming to become effective, engaged, and employable. A determined pursuit of these goals can frame your way to travel on your learning journey at university, not simply serve as your destination. The study experience is a continual process of self-improvement. In criminology, it is crucial that we always operationalise key terms, so we should define what can be understood by the 3 Es (see **Figure 1.1**).

Effective

Studying effectively involves making yourself fully informed and aware of everything you need to do and everything and everyone you need to know to help you to succeed academically. It requires you to be motivated, dynamic, proactive, strategic, constructive, and critical in everything you do, with an understanding of *how* to study

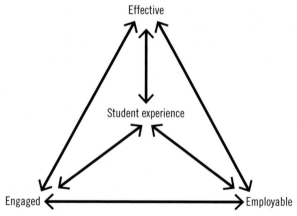

Figure 1.1 The E3 student

well (see Finch and Fafinski, *Criminology Skills*, 2016) and an awareness of *why* you are doing what you are doing at all times. Effective study is not limited to the goal of high grades; it could also apply, for example, to working productively with others and to maximising your enjoyment of your university student experience.

Engaged

Being engaged can mean a willingness and commitment to maximising your student experience, realised through full and active participation in, and dedication to, academic, work-based, extracurricular and social activities, and opportunities throughout your time at university. Engagement is a state of mind, an attitude, and a physical involvement in activities and opportunities. It is a key tool for fulfilling your potential and enhancing your student experience.

Employable

Enhancing your employability involves building your CV, gaining work experience, and developing personal transferable skills through your degree programme and extracurricular activities. These personal transferable skills are transferable to the world of work and specific occupations related to your area of academic study and beyond (see **Chapter 30**). There is an increasing focus on working constructively at university to become employable throughout and by the end of your studies.

Keeping it simple and straightforward (the 'KISS' principle), this book encourages you to make the most of your limited and busy time at university. You are an adult expending much time, effort, and money on enjoying the student experience in the short-term and on studying to give yourself a better life in the long-term. As authors, we sincerely hope that this chapter (and the rest of the book) goes a long way to helping you to do just that. From this point forwards, the chapter is divided into three inter-connected sections that represent different aspects of a learning journey at university and that map onto the key aims of the chapter.

Embarking on your journey at university

This opening stage on your learning journey explores how to most effectively prepare for your studies as soon as you have arrived. Emphasis will be placed on the importance of *reconnaissance*: finding out as much as possible in advance and from the outset of your studies about the university, your department, what you can expect from its staff (and what they can expect from you), the degree course, and the demands of university life, in and out of the classroom. Essentially, this section will cover the what, where, when, and who of university life and academic study. The central idea is that if you are informed and aware then you are able to be more effective and engaged.

Choosing your travel partners

It is really crucial to identify and select the best sources of support and guidance whilst at university—the people, places, and materials that will enable you to become effective, engaged, and employable. Once again, reconnaissance is key, as is being proactive and strategic in your learning. We will explore these sources of support; the travel partners on your learning journey, located at your university, in your department, in your subject area, in your programme of study and in your classroom. Furthermore, we will examine the support that you can offer yourself. This section addresses the who's and how's of university life and academic study. The key idea is that a focused, proactive, and strategic approach to learning increases your chances of becoming more effective, engaged, and employable.

Developing a way to travel

The final section of this chapter will prioritise how to most effectively apply and utilise the information and knowledge gained from your reconnaissance, fact-finding activities in the previous two sections. The focus will be on becoming a proactive and dynamic learner throughout your studies by adopting an appropriate critical mindset and attitude at all times, which will enable you to make the most informed study/learning choices and to get the most from your studies and university experience. It is here that you will be introduced to the guiding principle of this chapter and the book as a whole—*Always Be Critical* or ABC.

Take a look at **What do you think? 1.1**. With the answers to these challenging questions fresh in your mind, let us get started on your journey into studying at university.

WHAT DO YOU THINK? 1.1

Effective, engaged, employable

What are/were you expecting from your studies at university? In particular, consider:

- What factors increase/have increased your ability to be effective and engage whilst at university and to become employable by the time you leave?

- What differences do/did you anticipate experiencing between college or sixth form (further education) and university (higher education) study? How do you plan to manage them?

- Who and what can help you become effective, engaged, and employable?

- How can you help yourself? What exactly do you need to do?

Embarking on your journey at university

It is important to recognise that your learning journey begins much earlier than your first lecture or tutorial. It begins from the moment you decide on a university to attend and choose the academic subject that you'd like to study—in your case, criminology.

Identifying the answers to the questions in **What do you think? 1.2** is the first stage in the vital reconnaissance that you can conduct in order to become an informed, aware, and dynamic student. These reflective questions are the practical beginnings of your learning journey. Another, more significant element is identifying the appropriate mindset to adopt for university study—a positive, critical, responsible, and mature way of thinking and working towards becoming an E3 student. Key to developing this mindset is to identify and manage the potentially difficult transition that you will face when starting university. This transition may be from college into university, from a period out of study back into study, from the real world of work and family into HE, from another academic subject into criminology, from undergraduate into postgraduate study, etc. The most common and significant transition, the foundation for all of the other transitions, is the move from college into university study and the need to meet its associated academic requirements.

The expectations of university study are that you become far more independent and proactive in your learning than other forms of study earlier in life. You are responsible for shaping and directing your academic progress. You are responsible for developing an effective way to travel that increases your potential to succeed. You are responsible for identifying, seeking out, and working constructively with sources of support, and for making the most of your student experience. The university *will* help, your department and its staff *will* help—but *you* are ultimately responsible for the quality of your academic and student experience. For example, your attendance at university teaching sessions will not always be compulsory or monitored. This is more likely for lectures than for tutorials and seminars, although universities are tightening up their attendance expectations generally as a means of monitoring academic performance, identifying learning needs, and promoting student retention and progression. However, the majority of your study time will be independently driven by you outside of the classroom and other formal learning sessions. You will not be nagged, pushed, cajoled, encouraged, or disciplined as you may have been at school or college. You will be looked after, watched over, supported, and helped, but at the same time treated as a responsible, independent adult—the main partner in your learning and student experience.

WHAT DO YOU THINK? 1.2

Why did you choose your university and course?

This critical reflection exercise is aimed at those of you who are commencing an undergraduate programme at university, but current students may also find it informative, maybe even an eye opener. Your choice of university and department shapes a significant element of your study (of criminology). What questions did you ask yourself and others about where to study? Conducting critical reflection in this way will help you to develop a deeper understanding of what you are doing, why you are doing it and how to do it better, so consider:

- What were your reasons for choosing to study the course that you did at the particular university that you did?

- What was the most important influence of your decision: university or academic programme?

- What questions did you ask and to who about your chosen university and academic programme?

Arriving at university: Making your learning journey real

In order to develop a productive and constructive mindset whilst at university, one that energises and motivates you to become a dynamic learner in everything that you do, see, hear, read, and think, it is vital that you collect information. Everything you do should be intelligence-led and evidence-based, informed by your reconnaissance exercises to familiarise yourself with the what, where, when, who, and how of your studies. Once you have all of this information, you can turn it into usable knowledge (see **Chapter 6**) by answering the killer question of *why* you are doing what you are doing.

Focus on identifying the key sources of information, support, guidance, knowledge, and expertise related to your student experience, both in and out of the classroom. You can even start this process before you officially begin at your chosen university and you may have done so already. Conversely, some current students may not yet have commenced this fact-finding mission. Some of the information may have been made available to you during your pre-university induction. However, much of the

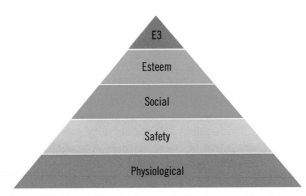

Figure 1.2 Maslow's hierarchy of needs with E3 (self-actualisation) at top

information relevant to your studies and your specific degree programme is made available or made clearer once you enrol and begin studying. So now that you have arrived at university, it is time to be systematic and focused about what you need to do, and how you need to do it.

The psychologist Abraham Maslow argued that human beings have a 'hierarchy of needs', as shown in **Figure 1.2** (Maslow 1943), that must be met if we are to learn to our maximum potential—a goal that he called self-actualisation. The most basic needs are physiological (health, warmth, food, drink), followed by safety (security, absence of danger), social (friendship, belonging), esteem (positive self-image and identity) and at the top of the pyramid, self-actualisation. In many ways, self-actualisation, or making the most of yourself and your abilities, is the true goal of our book. You will also find that much of your learning journey addresses the other needs in detail, as they are the foundations or building blocks of self-actualisation. Let us take a similarly hierarchical approach by identifying and encouraging you to research the what's, where's, when's, and who's of your university and department.

Your university

Embarking on your university journey into criminology requires you to carry out ongoing strategic reconnaissance about the location, university, department, and programme prior to choosing and arriving at your university, then again once you have arrived and throughout your period of study. Finding out the what, where, when, and who of university life is an essential starting point to becoming and being an E3 student. If you are an existing, experienced student who feels satisfied by your fact-finding in relation to university and department (skim the following sections first to check) then you may wish to jump ahead to the section titled 'Choosing your travel partners'.

For all students new to university and a (criminology) department, it is crucial that you familiarise yourself with the location, layout, services, and facilities at your university. This will help you to reduce your anxiety and uncertainty, whilst increasing your clarity of purpose and capacity to plan and structure your learning. For example, does your university have a single campus or multiple sites spread across locations? What services and facilities are available at the location(s) and where are they situated? The university and your chosen department should send you a campus map before you arrive, plus there will be maps on the university website and maps and guidance available on campus noticeboards, from the Information Office (or similarly titled office), and from security, porter, teaching, and administration staff. You can also find your bearings and identify services and facilities simply by walking around and about making a mental note of what's what and where.

What kinds of non-academic, pastoral services and facilities should you be looking for and can you expect to be in place when you start your studies? Remember that Abraham Maslow argued that if you are not happy and healthy, you cannot learn properly. These are the building blocks or basics for your learning. For example, what health and well-being services are available to you at your university? Is there a doctor's surgery, a nurse, a dentist, a chemist, a campus police officer, security staff? If so, where are they, when do they open, and how do you access them? Can you access them and still remain registered at your home doctors and dentist, for example?

What student well-being and support services are available to you, where are they located, and how do you contact and access them? For example, is there a Student Welfare Office that can help with any personal, psychological, emotional, physical or financial problems, disability issues (there may well be a university Disability Office too—see later), and learning support needs? If you experience any specific (unmet) needs, issues, or problems relating to your gender, ethnicity, background, or mature or international student status, is there a support office or officer dedicated to you? If you have a problem or are trying to avoid one emerging, go and ask them for help. If they can help, they will; if other services are better placed to help, they will put you in touch with them. Your health and well-being is a fundamental personal need that must be addressed before and throughout your student experience in order for you to 'achieve' at university, however you choose to measure this.

Beyond personal health and well-being, at the domestic and social level, what's available at your university to help you to survive and thrive? Think back to Maslow's physiological and social needs. Make it a priority to find out the location, extent, and nature of shops selling essentials such as books, food, drinks, clothes, stationery, sporting goods, and travel services. Also, seek out the canteens, cafes, restaurants, bars and pubs, nightclubs, banks and cash machines, and sporting/training facilities belonging to your university and located in the local area. It is also important to find out if these services and facilities (outside of university) are student-friendly in the sense of being welcoming and accessible, offering discounts, etc. With this final point in mind, whenever and wherever you give money for services whilst at university, always ask whether there is a student discount or loyalty scheme available.

Identifying and engaging with domestic and social facilities at your university can be a crucial building block for your goals of effective study and an enjoyable and fulfilling student experience. There are a number of useful practical 'survival' guides available for university students (e.g. Tobin 2015; Whichlow and Haskins 2011) and any of these are recommended if you require further information on reconnaissance and support. However, this book is more than this: whilst physical, pastoral, personal, social, and domestic facilities and issues play an increasingly pivotal role in the student experience and merit further discussion, this book focuses on the *academic* aspect of your study experiences and the foundational roles of these extracurricular influences in enabling and enhancing your studies. The priority is your 'self-actualisation' into a well-rounded E3 student of criminology.

In terms of academic support services, identify whether your university has any essay writing (assessment) and study skills support services, dyslexia support (if relevant), study support tutors for students with additional learning needs, etc. Attempt to familiarise yourself fully with the library and computing facilities and their associated resources (see 'Library and computing' section in this chapter). Another way to be financially astute in this area is to load up on the free pens, pencils, notebooks, paper, general stationery, and other goodies that are given out by enthusiastic students and staff during the week(s) before your official teaching starts—often known as 'Fresher's Week' (at university level) or 'Induction Week' (at programme level). Of course, some of these events may have occurred by the time you are reading this, and you may have already ticked many of these boxes; however it can still be a useful learning tool to reflect on what you have done, how it has helped you, and what more you could be doing in these areas to maximise your student experience.

Your department

In order to familiarise yourself further with what being a university student entails, find out the name of the department that runs your degree programme. Is it a department at all, or is it called a 'college', 'faculty', 'school', or some other label? These are often umbrella terms for groupings of subject teams/programmes and departments. For example, the current undergraduate programme at Swansea University, 'Criminal Justice and Criminology', sits within the Department of Criminology, which is within the College of Law—a grouping of the Law and Criminology programmes. However, the equivalent programme at Loughborough University is situated within the 'Criminology and Social Policy' subject group in the Department of Social Sciences at Loughborough University. Do not get too concerned about these structural and organisational details, but do try to find out the name of the 'body' that houses your programme and group of subject staff—if only so that you can find the right building and quote their name in relevant communications. Added to this, identifying the governing/coordinating body for your study programme can enhance your sense of belonging and identity and thus your engagement with the programme itself.

For the purposes of consistency and clarity, let's assume that your programme sits within a 'department'. Where is your department—in which part of the locality, campus, building? On which floor(s) and in which room(s)? What facilities does the department have—its own library resources and computing facilities, a common room (informal, communal meeting space for students and possibly staff too), office/study space for all students (or maybe just for postgraduates), lecture and seminar rooms, printing and photocopying facilities? If not the department, then does the college or school or faculty have these facilities? Where are they, how do you access them, how much do they cost, when are they open? For example, many institutions may not have bespoke criminology student common rooms, but they may have space for criminology students to use and mix with students from other subjects.

Arguably the single most important piece of information needed for an effective and efficient study experience is to identify your department's administration office—where it is, when it is open, who works there, what you can expect from the staff, and what they can expect from you. Develop a constructive relationship with your department's administration ('admin') staff. Be polite, respectful, clear, and regular in your communication with them. Admin staff can be the single most important source of practical-academic support in your time at university, particularly on the academic side of your student experience. They can help you with the practical details of study, learning, teaching, and assessment, such as timetabling, room locations, module selection, and assessment submission. Your programme may have more than one admin staff member—possibly with each one responsible for a different element of the programme, such as the different levels of study, assessment, student welfare, finance, computing, etc. These are vital pieces of information going forwards. You may not need support or advice now, but you may well do in the future. The expectation is not that you know everything, but rather that you can identify those people that do know what you need to know at any given time.

Another essential source of academic support at university is your personal tutor. You will be allocated a personal tutor, possibly one tutor for each subject if you are a joint honours student, on arrival at university. Your tutor will usually be a member of the department's teaching staff who is made responsible for monitoring and supporting your academic, pastoral (personal well-being), and employability progress. Find out who they are, where their office is, and when they have office hours for you to drop in without an appointment. Find out when your allocated tutorial sessions are and how to contact the tutor outside of office hours to ask for support or to arrange meetings. Much information regarding the admin staff and tutors should be available in departmental and programme documentation (see next section) and online materials (e.g. websites, social media sites). It may also be displayed on screens, posters, and office doors throughout the department (in the foyer, admin office, staff office doors, student noticeboards, etc.). It may even have already been sent to you before you arrived. If you cannot locate it, ask the admin staff.

Once you have gained a better understanding of the academic support services and facilities offered by your department and its staff, it is helpful on a practical level to familiarise yourself with the department's physical teaching resources. Look closely into the teaching/lecture rooms that your department uses—although these may only be identifiable once you are given your teaching timetable for the term. Does the department use (flat) classrooms or (tiered) lecture theatre rooms? Where are they located and how can you access them? What is the visibility of the display screens that will be used for teaching information? This information could be really important practically, especially if you have mobility, visual or hearing impairment, or learning support needs, which you should inform your personal tutor about as soon as possible so that you can receive appropriate support. The general point is that an early, basic reconnaissance into departmental learning and teaching facilities and resources can enhance the feelings of familiarity, comfort, and confidence that all contribute to more engagement with your studies.

Much of what we are covering in this chapter is common sense and may be already known to you, but it is hoped that it is a helpful learning resource to locate it all in one place. It is really the foundational and contextualising knowledge that can serve as a platform for your academic learning and student experience throughout your time at university. Much of this crucial departmental information is made available to you through university and departmental literature, online sources (e.g. virtual tours of the university and department, staff podcasts), and from students and staff. It is also likely that your department has or will run a programme of induction activities for new students and welcome back activities for returning students in the opening weeks of term. These activities can include introductory and welcome back lectures that explain the key 'need to know' departmental information such as the management, committee, and programme structures, staff roles and responsibilities, and what extracurricular services and facilities are available to you through the department. You may also be offered student or staff led tours of the department, campus, library, and other university facilities. There may be an informal welcome meeting or social event put on by the department and/or your academic, student-led society. As you can see, you will receive support with much of your reconnaissance and fact-finding. The information will be made available, but you must also make yourself available to receive it. Once again, *you* need to take responsibility from the very start of your studies to the very end. Work in partnership with staff and peers, but drive the learning process yourself.

Choosing your travel partners

Once you have identified the most important (re)sources of information, support, and expertise to help you to meet your learning needs and to guide your university studies, it is time to consider how you can make best use of these resources to facilitate your academic pursuit of the 3 Es of effectiveness, engagement, and employability. Being strategic in the sense of studying at and experiencing university in an informed, structured, organised, and motivated way will help you to improve your student experience. The key message of this chapter is that your best travel partners can be identified at a number of levels, several of which were identified in the previous section: university, department, programme, subject, peers, yourself. The objective of the advice in this section is to help you to turn the what's, where's, when's, and who's of your student experience and academic study into how's and why's. Both new and existing students may be familiar with several of these resources/travel partners already, so the following sections can help to consolidate this knowledge and help you to critically reflect on whether you are making optimal use of them. If a specific section doesn't apply to you, skip over it.

University travel partners

Previously, you were encouraged to identify and research the university-level support available to you—the services, facilities, and people that can help you to meet your health, well-being, domestic, social, and academic needs. Some of this support may only be required if you experience unforeseen difficulties and problems (e.g. welfare, accommodation, finance, crime, gender-specific issues), but others could be strategic essentials at any given point in your studies, albeit that they may only be essential to you.

Disability and additional learning needs

If you enter university with an existing (or diagnosed) disability or additional learning need, then please consider a visit to the university Disability Office and Learning Support Office to request support, advice, or even just a chat about your circumstances and what they may be able to offer you. Lecturers often hear students with existing issues saying 'I'll manage' or 'I do not like to ask for help' or 'I do not want an unfair advantage'. The lecturer will completely understand.

You have probably lived with and managed this issue for a long time and it is likely to have made you resilient and resourceful, maybe a little defensive, embarrassed, or insecure at times—any mixture of these. You have learned how to cope, to manage, to survive, maybe even to thrive. You do not want sympathy or special treatment. But the point is this: getting support with a disability or additional learning need should not be seen as special treatment or an unfair advantage, it simply levels the playing field so that you have the same opportunities as other students. If this means extra study support, funding for specialist equipment (e.g. a laptop, large print, or audio books), extra time in exams, or extensions on essay submission—ask for it and take it. Do not be too proud or stubborn to level up the academic playing field so that you can be judged on your own merits. That exemplifies a focused, mature, and responsible approach to learning. See the experience of a student with a long-term neurological condition in **Conversations 1.1**.

International student needs

If you are an international student living and studying away from home, do consider what support is available.

CONVERSATIONS 1.1

My experience of university studies with a long-term health condition—with a student who wishes to remain anonymous

I was diagnosed with a long-term neurological condition at the age of 14. This was terrifying and thinking about the impact that it would have on my life was extremely daunting. So, when I first applied to go to university, I purposely did not reveal on the UCAS form that I had a long-term health condition; I was too embarrassed and believed that if I admitted to having a problem I would not receive any offers. However, when I was offered a place at the University of Westminster, I was very happy and thought to myself that I was on the road to success. When I started the course, I still hid the fact that I had a health condition.

When I was about to enter my final year of studies, I decided to inform the university about my condition. I had been unwell over the summer and my doctor encouraged me to speak to the university. He suggested that there would be some support in place that could help me to reach the end of my degree. I approached Student Advice and underwent a disability needs assessment. This confirmed that I was eligible for the Learning Support Entitlement, which gave me an extra 10-day coursework extension. Having this entitlement has provided me with much needed extra time when completing my assignments as part of my condition means that I can get extremely tired and, as a result, I sometimes struggle to meet coursework deadlines.

I was also assigned a mentor whom I see every week to discuss any problems I face with my studies and my illness, and how I might overcome them. My mentor also helps me with planning my assignments and proof reads my essays with me to help with structure, syntax, and grammar. This additional support has allowed me to gain as much as I possibly can from my degree course and the opportunities it provides. It has helped me prepare for the changes and choices that are presented along the way. By having this support from the university, I feel it has removed barriers that may have previously restricted my ability to learn in the most effective way, considering some of my personal challenges.

I would encourage any student with health or disability problems to access support. University staff are well trained and sensitive so there really is no need to be embarrassed. This support really just levels the playing field so that you can be considered on your academic merits, just like other students.

Disabled student (who wishes to remain anonymous),
University of Westminster

This support may be in the form of guidance in the social, cultural, religious, or academic ways of your new country of residence, it may be free language lessons, it may be additional support with accommodation, finances, and welfare. It may be as simple and useful as putting you in contact with other international students (e.g. official groups and organisations) and/or people from your home country in your new locality so that you can meet up for domestic, social, cultural, religious, or academic purposes. You are likely to be facing some of the same issues as other international students, especially those of the same or similar cultures and religions, so why not meet up for a chat at least? They could help you with your international reconnaissance regarding where to stay, eat, drink, shop, socialise, worship, celebrate, study, etc. if any of these areas are not well-catered for in your host location of residence—your 'host culture', if you like. None of

this means that you should isolate yourself from 'home' students or from the indigenous culture. Do not self-exclude. Immerse yourself in the host culture, the facilities, the people, and the practices (where you can). It'll all add to your sense of participation, enrichment, and belonging (social and esteem needs) that contribute to your self-actualisation and your capacity to be an E3 student. You may even want to stay on after your studies. Engagement is crucial. See **Conversations 1.2** for an example.

Student societies

A key aspect of your extracurricular, social experience at university can be joining and participating in student societies of various kinds. Joining a student society enables you to better engage with student life, your location, your

---

CONVERSATIONS 1.2

My experience as an international student —with Cristian

My name is Cristian and I come from Rome, Italy. I am a full-time international student at the University of Westminster. I first realised I wanted to attend a university course in London when I was 14. I studied English in a private language school in Rome and took the English language exam because I was determined to fulfil my study ambitions. So, after my high school graduation and after meeting all the entry requirements, I enrolled on the criminology degree at the University of Westminster.

Since day one, everyone has been kind and helpful to me, offering support if I needed it. I remember going into my tutor's office during the second week of the first semester to ask for clarification about something. Because English is my second language, I struggled with it at the very beginning of my first year, because I wasn't used to all the specific language used in class (words such as 'probation', 'rule of law', and 'due process' were completely alien to me). Fortunately, my personal tutor helped me through the first few weeks. We would meet regularly and go through the vocabulary and the lectures that were quite confusing to me.

Another issue I faced during my first year was my writing style. Because English and Italian are two different languages, they have two different writing styles. Again, my personal tutor's support was incredible. We went through a few of my essay drafts and she explained to me what was different between the Italian and the English writing style and what I needed to change. After

those sessions my grades had a notable increase.

The academic support has really made the difference in my first year, and it is still giving me chances for improvement throughout my second. However, this is only one part of my experience. I also received great support from my classmates who encouraged me and worked with me. They didn't make me feel like 'the foreigner' but part of a group.

All universities have a wide range of clubs and societies, which are available to all students. My advice to any new undergraduate student would be to get involved in a society which interests you; they are a great way to make new friends from across the world and they can also give you a good network of support. For me the University's LGBTQI + society gives me constant help. The support, the encouragement, and the passion all these people have shown me made me work harder and made me realise who I really want to be. But most importantly, they made me feel accepted and special for what I am.

Moving to a new country and not knowing anyone can, at first, be scary, but get involved in all aspects of university life and do not be afraid to ask for help if you need it. For me, these three parts of my academic life—tutors/ lecturers/study support, classmates, and the LGBTQI + society—have made and are still making my university experience one of the best of my life.

Cristian, BA Criminology undergraduate and international student, University of Westminster university, the people in it and, ultimately, with your studies and future employers. Furthermore, experiencing the social side of university is highly enjoyable and rewarding in its own right.

Student societies can be academic in focus (e.g. your criminology student society), sporting (e.g. the Athletic Union/AU or an equivalently-named body), musical, artistic, dramatic, cultural, political, historical, etc. Find out what societies are available, what they do, how they might benefit you, where they are located, how you can sign up, and what they'll cost. You can usually find such information on the university website, in the university student newspaper, from existing students, and on posters scattered about campus, on noticeboards, walls, leaflets and t-shirts, not to mention them being heavily promoted during the opening week(s) of term at events often associated with Fresher's Week. If you haven't already joined a student society, there is still time this term, next term, whenever you choose.

It is common for these societies to be managed, coordinated, and even funded by a Students' Union (SU)—an organisation at your university that is run by students for students. The SU can be a valuable source of support and advice during your studies and can assist you in meeting your (Maslow-informed) needs for self-esteem (belonging, self-confidence, positive identity) and self-actualisation. The SU will consist of a President and a group of other SU officers, each elected by students and each of whom fulfil administrative/support roles similar to (and in addition to) those at university and departmental level—such as officers focused on welfare, education, societies, disability, women, international/overseas students, and so on.

A theme of this chapter is how your engagement can be key to effective study and to you ultimately becoming employable. Do not limit your engagement in university life just to your studies, even though this is obviously crucial. Consider engaging with as many social, extracurricular opportunities as you can or want to. At the university level, these are most likely to come from the SU and AU, although they can be organised by the university itself, by external organisations and sponsors, or by motivated groups of students such as housemates, halls of residence groups, or informal (non-SU) student groups. As discussed, there will be a huge range of student societies and clubs available to you, in all conceivable areas of interest; there's bound to be at least one group offering something that you are interested in, good at, or keen to learn. Find out more about the society you are interested in joining before you take the plunge and commit time and money to becoming a member. It can be intimidating to approach a pre-formed group and ask to join, even if they are sitting at a desk actively requesting that you join them. But in the spirit of taking a mature, responsible, strategic, and

brave approach to university life ... take a deep breath and go for it. The odds are that they will be really welcoming, friendly, helpful, and supportive. Moreover, you will make friends through joining a student society or club (in addition to those on your course)—friends who you will socialise with, learn with, support and be supported by throughout your university stay and beyond. It makes sense to identify something you enjoy and then to meet up with like-minded people who enjoy it too. Membership of a social group at university can offer you a strong sense of security and identity as you progress and learn. Security and identity are key to engagement in university life. Engagement is key to meeting your learning needs and becoming an effective student—informed, confident, proactive, and resourceful.

The key to your societies and socialising activities is not moderation, it is balance. Do not join so many societies that you cannot commit sufficient time, energy, or money to any specific one. Do not commit so much time, energy, and money to societies and socialising that your academic studies suffer. Achieving a balance at university between the academic and the social is critical; as must you be in achieving it. Consider the two different uses of 'critical' there. A healthy, balanced, and strategic engagement is the goal. This balance will offer you a breadth of university experience that will look strong on your CV, because:

- study > social life = all work and no play makes Johnny a dull boy;
- social life > study = all play and no work gets Johnny a poor degree.

Upon graduation, an employer is looking for a well-rounded individual who has engaged intensively and extensively in their academic studies and in constructive, enriching social activities that have developed transferable skills (e.g. organisational and communication skills, leadership, management, team-working, planning), life experience, and 'emotional intelligence'—understanding of the relationship between the emotions, thinking, and behaviour of yourself and others (Goleman 1996).

Employability services

Long gone are the days when employers would be satisfied with a 'good' degree and (if they were lucky) a healthy range of extracurricular and social experiences on their CV. The concept of employability is a priority area for university study, so much so that our book devotes its entire final chapter to it. A significant measure of how beneficial your student experience has been will relate to the value for money you get for your criminology course. Such value is increasingly measured in government and HE statistics in terms of universities producing students who obtain a well-paid job soon after graduating. To a certain extent, universities are judged and funded by this criterion; programmes are chosen by this criterion; student satisfaction is rated by this criterion. It is likely that among your other goals, you will be aiming to leave university as employable as possible; achieved by developing a wide range of personal transferable skills and experiences through your academic and social activities that will make you more attractive to potential employers. Of course, your university experience should be about much more than being consumer-minded, strategic, and selfish, to turn yourself into a marketable brand or product for an employer, but there is still an emerging emphasis on employability as an aspect of student life that must be developed. There is a rapidly growing employer expectation that you will complement your academic and social CV entries with a range of relevant and high-quality personal transferable skills, work experiences and career-enhancing activities. Many such experiences and activities will be made available by your department/programme (see 'Programme travel partners' section). However, do not neglect the more general academic (non-criminology) experiences, training, and opportunities made available at the university level—a general rule not just limited to employability concerns.

Your university will have a careers service or employability service, whether this be a physical office (or desk in another office) or an online portal or website. Either way, there should be a real person to speak to somehow, someway, somewhere. Your careers service can help you to become more employable and employed during your time at university and can increase your chances of being employed in a well-paid, fulfilling career once you have graduated. Use this valuable resource to complement the employability support you will receive from your department. Your

careers service can advise you about enhancing your employability—developing transferable skills, identifying suitable jobs and careers, gaining generic and subject-specific work experience and training, getting paid employment whilst studying, writing your CV, preparing for application processes and interviews, etc. Do not wait until you are about to graduate before you consider speaking to them. Engage with your careers service from the moment you start your studies. See an example of one of our authors' personal experiences in **Telling it like it is 1.1**.

We return to issues of careers and employability in much more detail in **Chapter 30**.

Library and computing

The library and computing facilities at your university are pivotal to effective study and a fulfilling student experience, most obviously because they are the home of the majority of the learning material/resources that you will draw upon when studying. By learning resources, we are talking primarily about printed resources such as books, journals, reports, newspapers, and dissertations; electronic resources such as e-journals, websites, social media sites, and recorded presentations; and staff resources such as criminology subject librarian(s), information desk staff, and computing and Information Technology (IT) support staff. (Explanations of each of these printed and electronic resources are provided in the 'Subject-specific learning resources as travel partners' section of this chapter.) The library and computing resources may not necessarily be in the same location. For example, the library building(s) may host computer facilities for all students, but subject-specific computer facilities may be available in your department. How do you find out? A good start would be to attend any advertised library induction or

TELLING IT LIKE IT IS 1.1

How careers can lead to careers—with author Steve Case

One of my smartest moves when I was a psychology undergraduate was to arrange an appointment with my subject-specific careers advisor to discuss my career plans (i.e. me needing to get some!). We set about diagnosing my strengths, what skills I could bring to a job, and therefore what my most suitable jobs/careers might be. We identified social researcher as an ideal job for me based on my profile of transferable skills, subject-specific skills (e.g. research methods training, statistical analysis experience), my knowledge, and my general

interests. Of course, this kind of job may not be for you, but hopefully you will follow my general point. When I received my first interview for a researcher post I re-visited my careers advisor, who helped me to prepare for interview in terms of what questions to expect and how best to answer them, how to research the organisation I was applying to, what questions to ask of them, how to prepare myself physically and psychologically, what to wear, body language, etc. I got the job and the rest is history. So in a way, this book began with my first visit to my careers service. Why not visit your careers advisor and see what begins for you?

Figure 1.3 Make the most of the available resources online before you start your course
Source: wavebreakmedia/Shutterstock.com

Figure 1.4 Physical library resources and facilities will be important to your undergraduate study
Source: Syda Productions/Shutterstock.com

familiarisation tours and talks in the opening weeks of the new academic year. Do this even if you are in your second or third year—what have you got to lose? You can always leave if you feel that you know everything already. When you locate the library, give yourself a little self-led, informal tour of the layout and facilities. Keep your eyes open for information on posters, leaflets, and signs such as library maps and directions to subject-specific sections, computer rooms, photocopiers, printers, and toilets. You will probably be spending a lot of quality time in your library or with online learning materials obtained via the library, so find your way around.

When this book's authors arrived at university we had to form a library survival plan—a hierarchy of library needs, if you like (cf. Maslow 1943). In order of priority: find a quiet, comfortable place to study, find the computers (no laptops in our days, but we did have the beginnings of the Internet), find out who to ask if guidance was needed, find out where to get coffee and other drinks, find out if you were allowed to drink coffee in the library. Nowadays, you are given far more sources of information, support, and guidance. Most (if not all) is provided to you before you arrive at university and can be identified outside of the physical library building(s) through websites and online support materials (see **Figure 1.3**). However, this is not an excuse to avoid utilising physical library facilities and resources as effectively and efficiently as you possibly can throughout your studies (see **Figure 1.4**).

Once you have familiarised yourself with your library buildings, progress your learning journey by identifying your online library access details (e.g. student/library number) and computing access (login) details and then logging onto the university computer system. There is likely to be an open access computer system in the library, but you will need your personal details for private browsing/searching in and out of the library (e.g. on your computer, laptop, tablet, or phone). If you do not know

what your personal access details are, ask the staff at the Information Desk or Help Desk. These staff can help you to locate your subject section and to find your way around the library, can advise you on the how, how long, and how many of borrowing learning materials, and can tell you the opening hours of different library services. Computing staff can guide you on how to access and use the online library catalogue of learning materials (or resources) and can help you with any computing problems—their support may be more technical than that of the information staff.

Your physical familiarisation tour around the library facilities can be consolidated by a virtual stroll around the university website and, perhaps more importantly, the library website that sits within it. The virtual tour will provide information on the physical and people (staff) services and facilities available through the library. The library website (it may be called a 'portal') may be accessible through the Internet or through your university's Intranet—the internal information system or network within an organisation. The library website will give you access to a broad range of learning resources, including software and learning support applications related to databases and data analysis, referencing, mind mapping, literature searching, personal organisation tools, and voice recognition software. The most important learning resource on your library website is the library catalogue. This site allows you to search for books, journals, and other available printed and electronic learning resources available in your library (and possibly other libraries). Find out how many of these resources there are, whether they are currently available, how long you can use them for, and where you can find them (indicated by a section label, a code, a number, a colour, etc.). You can identify useful resources for your programme by searching by category, title, keyword, by tracking down specific resources (e.g. references to books and journals) highlighted in your course materials, and from following up the references contained in other learning resources.

It is vital to get your head around how to research and access learning materials as soon as you can in your studies. Do not be afraid to ask information staff or your personal tutor (also see the 'Programme travel partners' section). You could and should also ask your criminology subject staff for support. Subject-specific staff are increasingly common in universities, yet hugely under utilised. They can help you with the practical and technical academic issues already highlighted, but also with programme-focused learning support needs such as identifying useful criminological resources, websites, blogs, social media groups, networks, databases, reports, study skills guidance, and careers/employability information. They should advertise their services to you at some point, which will help you with three standard reconnaissance questions: who are they, what do they do, and how can they help you (to help yourself)?

Programme travel partners

As discussed earlier, your physical criminology department and academic criminology programme will have a variety of staff, structures, strategies, and course materials (learning resources) in place to support you as travel partners on your voyage of discovery in criminology. It is really important to familiarise yourself with the what's, who's, and how's of these sources of departmental and programme support.

Starting with your department's *staff*, it is informative to identify what type of staff structure or hierarchy your department has. We have already identified just how important the admin staff can be for your smooth learning and student experience and how closely and constructively you should work with them throughout your studies. Teaching staff will also have certain admin roles that may be very useful to you at some point (see **Chapter 2**). So what else and who else? Start with the Head of Department—who is s/he, what does s/he do (teach? tutor? research? manage?), and could you meet with her/him if you get into difficulties or have issues or complaints that other staff cannot resolve? Who is the Undergraduate Programme Director? This person may be the second in command to the Head of Department and is likely to be the key authority figure for you as an undergraduate—the person you go to after teaching staff but before the Head of Department (see **Telling it like it is 1.2**).

TELLING IT LIKE IT IS 1.2

The Programme Director role—with author Steve Case

As the former Programme Director for Swansea University's Criminology and Criminal Justice undergraduate degree programmes (single and joint honours), my role was to make sure that the programmes ran effectively and efficiently. I worked with staff and students to design, evaluate, and redesign the programmes, structures, timetables, range of modules, the learning, teaching, and assessment methods used, the allocation of teaching to staff, and quality assurance.

I had to ensure that everything staff did met national standards/guidelines for criminology higher education programmes, met university and departmental policies, and continued to be innovative and cutting edge in educational terms. For example, I sat on the Steering Group (guiding committee) of the British Society of Criminology's Learning and Teaching Network, which develops and advises on effective practice for delivering criminology programmes across British universities. We also developed the Benchmark Standards (BCS 2014) that set the general expectations for the quality and content of undergraduate criminology programmes in British universities.

Alongside these roles and tasks, the Programme Director ensures that teaching staff are fulfilling their designated teaching and admin roles and that students are meeting their academic obligations to the department regarding attendance at learning sessions, appropriate behaviour, and timely assessment submission.

I monitored whether students and staff were satisfied with the programme, which I evaluated through chairing meetings, asking for feedback, dealing with problems, acting on recommendations, and trying to constantly improve every aspect of the programme. A final key element of my role was to work with staff and students from my department and across my university to develop strategies/policies (see 'University policies and strategies' later) and to lead departmental committees.

The Programme Director conducts constant reconnaissance, monitoring, and quality assurance of academic practices, policies, and developments inside and outside of their programme in order to inform improvements and to encourage student and staff satisfaction, fulfilment, and success. If you communicate with your Programme Director, you have a direct line to the person who designs your learning, teaching, and assessment experiences.

In addition to the Head of Department and Programme Director roles, who is responsible for learning and teaching issues, assessment, student progression and retention (keeping students on the course)? Who should you contact regarding student welfare, disability, learning support, the staff-student committee, or postgraduate issues? What is the extent and nature of the support that you can reasonably expect from each of these staff/roles, how can you access it, and when is it available? Familiarise yourself with the location of staff offices, staff office hours, and staff email addresses. Do the same for staff who coordinate the different modules that you are studying as part of your programme. These module leaders can be invaluable sources of learning support (your travel partners), particularly as they may know more about their module topic and the learning, teaching, and assessment requirements of the module than your personal tutor. Similarly, if postgraduate students in your department are given the responsibility to lead modules or learning sessions, they can be valuable sources of learning support; they may even be a little more approachable regarding certain issues (in your view, at least) than other teaching staff as they may be

that bit closer to your age. However, the rule of thumb should be to identify the extent and nature of the academic and pastoral support that you can expect from individual staff members, alongside what these staff members can expect from you in your role as a student partner in a developing learning relationship.

Personal tutors and other teaching staff

A constructive relationship with your personal tutor is absolutely crucial to your student experience and to your development as an E3 student—a relationship explored in detail in **Chapter 2**. The same can be said about your working relationship with other teaching staff, including module leaders and postgraduate students. With this in mind, communicate with teaching staff regularly and always with respect, clarity, and purpose (see **Telling it like it is 1.3**). Approach them with pre-formed ideas, explanations, and reasons, with specific, focused questions and requests for support, rather than adopting a passive and helpless 'what do you think?', 'tell me the answer' approach. This passive approach does not help you because

TELLING IT LIKE IT IS 1.3

Appropriate communication with staff—with author Steve Case

In my experience, it is important to maintain appropriate communication with staff. Start by finding out what to call them. Postgraduate students and admin staff are usually happy being addressed by their first names (do not forget to check), but lecturers may want you to call them by their professional, academic title such as Doctor (which comes with a PhD qualification) or Professor (given by a university in recognition of exceptional achievement in leadership, teaching, research or scholarship). Ask them. See if they sign off their emails to you using their first name—this gives you the green light to use it too. I much prefer being called Steve to Professor Case because the latter makes me feel really old! So please call me Steve when you email me to say how much you have enjoyed this book. Same goes for Phil, David, Roger, Kate, and our guest authors.

However, a staff member is not your mate—there is a professional relationship and distance that needs to be respected and maintained.

Which brings me to the communication danger zone of emails. Email etiquette is very simple; it is much like an

essay—introduction ('Dear recipient name'), main body (clear message with original questions and ideas using appropriate language), conclusion (sign off with 'Yours' or 'Regards' or 'Best wishes', etc. before your name). If you send an email without an appropriate introduction or conclusion, the recipient could consider it rude or careless. It seems minor, but it can come across like you do not care if these elements are missing. Similarly, make sure that the main body/message is clear and polite, not conveyed in an abrupt, colloquial, or misspelt way. Be patient when expecting a reply to an email, especially on the weekend or during the holiday period. Staff may be particularly busy at given times of the year too. If they are away from their desk for a prolonged period, they will usually tell you via an automatic response to your email. If you do not get a reply after a reasonable period of time, email again to politely remind them, and then speak to your Programme Director if you need to. If you need support by a certain deadline, send the email early enough that you can receive and act on the reply before the deadline. Email is an ideal way to miscommunicate, but if you get the etiquette right it can be a highly effective learning tool as part of your developing learning relationship with staff.

Figure 1.5 Interaction with your tutor will enhance your learning experience
Source: Micolas/ Shutterstock.com

you need to do the work, have the ideas, learn the topics, and experience the learning.

The tutee-tutor and student-staff relationships should be a partnership (see **Figure 1.5**), an ongoing and evolving dialogue, and the joint pursuit of common goals, such as developing your understanding of the subject area and enabling you to become an E3 student. Your tutor wears many hats—guide, support, mentor, counsellor, confidante, careers officer. They can also be a facilitator—helping you to identify and access services, facilities, staff support, academic and work-based opportunities, and so on. They can open doors, introduce you to the right people (e.g. subject experts, potential employers, useful networks), and ultimately give you a positive job reference. Make your tutor and other teaching staff your constant companions and partners. They can be far more than just an educational learning resource if you develop a consistent, constructive, and committed learning relationship with them.

So now that we have covered the who, what, and how of programme staff, what about programme structures and strategies as learning resources?

Student-staff committees

Your university and department will have student support structures in place to solicit and act upon student feedback regarding your course, student experience, and university facilities. One such important structure is the student-staff committee (or some such title)—a forum for students to communicate their programme-focused experiences, feedback, recommendations, complaints, and issues. If you want to offer your feedback in order to improve your programme, you need to find out who your student representative ('rep') is for your level of programme and how to contact them with your comments to take to the committee. The committee will include staff representatives such as the Programme Director, module leaders, admin staff, the subject-specific librarian(s), and your careers advisers. These staff are best placed to respond to and act on your feedback if the committee agrees that it is relevant, useful, justified, and/or feasible to do so. The student-staff committee is essentially a forum to identify and discuss programme issues, for staff to explain their programme-related decisions and what can influence these (e.g. resource issues, university policies, the HE context) and to reach agreement on how to move forwards—preferably together as a student-staff partnership, but at the very least a constructive working relationship.

It is helpful if you raise issues and feedback in a constructive and realistic way, such as in sufficient time for staff to act on them—do not wait until the final year of your degree. Make sure that you are not blaming or responsibilising staff for issues that may be more of your creation or your responsibility to resolve. Of course, certain problems and issues may be more the responsibility of staff, the programme structure or the university, but whatever their origin, it is important to recognise, accept, and work on these problems/issues in a mature and responsible manner and to work in partnership with staff to address them. If you are really motivated to improve the programme and your student experience, why not stand for election as a student rep? This position can be a valuable addition to your CV by demonstrating leadership, management, committee membership, team working, problem solving, taking responsibility, etc. Remember the employability 'E'.

Student reps may also be invited to attend the departmental (maybe even university-level) Board of Studies. This is a regular staff forum/meeting/committee that discusses programme monitoring and development issues such as feedback from students and external examiners; curriculum design; learning, teaching, and assessment methods; student outcomes data (e.g. grades, retention, progression); the minutes (written record of the discussions) of committee meetings; the implementation of departmental and university strategies. There may be a similar kind of department (and university) structure in addition to or instead of the Board of Studies called (something like) the Learning and Teaching Committee, which is a forum to discuss learning, teaching, and assessment structures, and methods and strategies (e.g. plans for improvement, student feedback). The minutes of all of these department/programme and university committees should be made available to you by staff as a way of keeping you informed, aware, and updated about your studies and broader student experience.

University policies and strategies

In the modern HE environment, with its emphasis on offering an enriching and satisfying student experience, alongside a more instrumental focus on providing students as consumers with high quality service and value for money, your university will have a range of policies and strategies in place to promote your learning needs—policies that your department must adhere to. There will be policies in place relating to pastoral issues such as behaviour, attendance, well-being, disability, and personal tutoring. These will be academic policies relating to (for example) programme design, module selection, learning, teaching, and assessment practices, expectations (of both students and staff), and quality assurance, malpractice, and complaints and appeals procedures. There may also be associated strategies (plans of action, proposals, ways of working) regarding any or all of these issues, such as explaining the rationale for the learning and teaching methods used on your programme and how they will be developed further during your studies. All of these university policies should be made available to you on the Internet and your university and/or department virtual learning environment (see specific section later). By 'made available', this means you should be guided towards them and have them explained clearly and simply. That is not to suggest that you read all of these documents, at least not straightaway, but find out where they are, what they are, and what they cover so they you can consult them (as travel partners) if you ever need them. The basic rule of thumb with what we are calling travel partners is not to feel as if you need to know everything yourself, which is impossible, but to *know who to ask* about them when you need them.

Programme handbooks

At the programme level, the support offered by staff, structures, policies and strategies will be complemented by programme-based learning materials—not to be confused with the subject-based criminology learning materials discussed in the following section. It is crucial that your department provides you with programme and module information, crucial that you read through it, that you understand it, and crucial that you are confident in how you should use it. If it is not provided or you do not understand it, ask staff for help. You should be given a programme handbook (or a course guide or scheme), which should outline the key programme information. It should set out the staffing structure in the department, the programme objectives (also known as 'learning outcomes'), the structure and content in each year of study which will list the available modules and their descriptions, compulsory and optional modules, and how many credits each module carries. The handbook should also contain learning, teaching, and assessment information including the methods used, any level-specific assessment criteria, assessment deadlines, and sources of support in the department and across the university. Each module within your programme should have its own handbook (if it does not, ask your tutor for this information) setting out the module's specific objectives, structure, and content (e.g. timetable, lecture, and seminar schedules); learning, teaching, and assessment methods; assessment deadlines; required/suggested readings (see 'Subject-specific learning resources as travel partners'); and other sources of learning support (e.g. social media sites, websites). All of these supports can help to progress your learning on the programme in a structured, focused, and guided way.

The Virtual Learning Environment

Your department may also provide you with additional learning support materials such as guides to developing your study skills, essay writing, presentations, referencing, and employability. These materials are likely to be emailed to you and made available on the programme and module Virtual Learning Environment (VLE)—an online portal on the university's Intranet that can be used to send programme and module messages, provide notifications, store course information, and encourage interaction with learning materials. The VLE can house university- and department-level documents such as course and module handbooks, assessment titles and deadlines, outline submission guidance, and staff office hours. The VLE may also store learning materials (e.g. handbooks, reading lists, Powerpoint and Prezi presentations), identify links to further sources of learning (e.g. websites, YouTube videos, blogs), and facilitate discussions through chat rooms and discussion groups. It is a useful learning strategy to get to grips with your programme's VLE system and use it effectively.

Programme learning expectations

In the spirit of ABC (*Always Be Critical*)—where critical means to be informed, aware, and focused—when you locate, read through, and evaluate programme and module learning materials, pay attention to the clear and consistent alignment (links, connections, progression) between the key elements of your learning. These key elements of learning on a programme or module within a programme include being aware of the nature and expectations of the learning outcomes (what you are expected to learn and be able to demonstrate that you have learned), the learning and teaching methods, module content, and the method of assessment. If any of these programme and module elements do not seem to fit together in your mind, you could constructively challenge this disconnect with the module leader or your tutor. You are not complaining; you are trying to make sense of the structure and content of your studies so that you can most effectively meet the programme and module requirements and expectations. In this way, you are being critical and strategic in your thinking in order to be effective in your learning processes and outcomes. To offer an illustrative example, on the single honours Criminology and Criminal Justice degree programme at Swansea, the learning outcomes are structured by year of study based on the identity and purpose of the learning and teaching in that year:

• **Year 1: Introducing criminology**—students are expected and supported to demonstrate that they can define, describe, identify, and outline key arguments, concepts, topics, and theories in criminology.

• **Year 2: Applying criminology**—students are expected and supported to be able to build on the year 1 learning outcomes by demonstrating that they can assess, discuss, explore, justify, and review key arguments, concepts, topics and theories in criminology.

• **Year 3: Advancing criminology**—students are expected and supported to be able to build on the year 2 learning outcomes by demonstrating that they can analyse, compare, contrast, and critically evaluate key arguments, concepts, topics, and theories in criminology.

Each of these sets of learning outcomes are linked or aligned in pedagogical terms to a glossary explaining their key terms (e.g. what it means to define, to assess, to analyse) and they are linked clearly to the assessment criteria for each module in a narrative explanation in module handbooks. The degree programme also has year-specific and assessment format-specific assessment/marking criteria, although this is not necessarily typical across all criminology departments, nor should it be expected. For example, the assessment criteria for essays and dissertations structured around specific marking categories: introduction, understanding and knowledge, quality of argument, conclusion, choice and use of source materials, focus and structure, written expression, and referencing.

It is important to stress that the extent and nature of learning outcomes, assessment criteria and the links between them will vary dramatically across departments within your university and between universities. Make sure to confirm what yours looks like so that you can tailor your learning and assessment preparation to them. For example, you may be graded against criteria that are not level-specific or specific to the assessment format, so

do not assume that learning expectations will be uniform across or even within different universities. What you *should* expect is that your learning resources/travel partners (e.g. staff, learning materials) make it very clear what the learning outcomes are for your programme and for the specific modules that form it, and that the assessment criteria and expectations match/align with those learning outcomes logically and fairly. If the learning outcomes on a module expect you to demonstrate the ability to define and describe, let us say, then the assessment criteria should also assess your ability to define and describe, not your ability to analyse or evaluate, for example. Many criminology departments internationally are well on top of the issue of alignment nowadays (we simply cannot afford not to be), but you owe it to yourself to assess and confirm that *your* programme and its modules are aligned across all areas, so that you can inform and shape your own learning going forwards, whilst gaining a better understanding of what is expected of you as a criminology student on your particular course.

In addition to the official programme learning materials already discussed, there are likely to be a number of less formal, extracurricular learning materials available to you at programme and module level. These range from physical learning materials; resources and sources of information such as departmental noticeboards, signs and posters; electronic learning resources such as in-house TV information screens; websites and social media sources such as Facebook module group sites and Twitter feeds; podcast collections; a department YouTube channel; and stores of recorded audio/visual learning sessions. There will also be social resources such as induction, familiarisation, and 'welcome back' events, meet and greet sessions with staff and current students, tours of the department and library, extracurricular seminars, talks and conferences organised by the department and students.

Much ground has been covered, so to reiterate—get engaged! The three Es reinforce one another, so engagement with extracurricular learning resources and opportunities will help you to become a more effective student and a more employable graduate.

Understanding the expectations of you as a learner and the expectations that you should have of staff can guide your learning—so it is possible to argue that expectations is actually the fourth E. Expectations can complement your pursuit of effectiveness, engagement, and employability.

Subject-specific learning resources as travel partners

Many of your programme learning materials will direct you towards the broader subject-level learning materials that will become essential travel partners on your learning journey. For ease of understanding, subject resources are split up into categories to be discussed in this section, largely based around course materials and support networks. Course materials are the subject-specific (printed and electronic) learning materials/resources identified in your programme learning materials. Much of the printed resources in our subject area are now available electronically, so you can pretty much see these as one and the same thing. It is important to recognise what they are so that you can better understand how to use them and how they can help you to become more effective and engaged as a student. As you progress through your learning journey, the chances are that your programme and its teaching staff will expect you to draw upon an increasing range of these learning materials. The main learning materials and resources you will come across in criminology are listed in the following sections. Developing an understanding about what these source materials are can inform you about what you can expect from them and how and when to use them most effectively over the course of your studies. So let us start with the most commonly-used learning materials, with a particular focus on our needs as students of criminology.

Textbooks

These are your starting points in criminology. A textbook gives you a general, broad, introductory, and often descriptive overview of the subject and/or specific topics within it. Most of the information and argument in a textbook is secondary (reporting the ideas of others), rather than primary (original commentary, opinion, research), although it is possible for a textbook to contain some original commentary and ideas, as this textbook does throughout. The introductory presentation of information in textbooks makes them ideal starting points for your learning journey in criminology. Excellent examples of criminology textbooks include *Textbook on Criminology* (Williams 2012), *An Introduction to Criminological Theory* (Hopkins-Burke 2009), and, of course, *Criminology* (Case et al. 2017).

Monographs (research-based books)

Once you have read a few textbooks and picked up the basics of the subject or topic area within it, you will be expected to put some flesh on the bones of your understanding by reading selected monographs. Monographs are specialist pieces of writing about an area of criminology, usually by a single author and/or printed just once (in Greek, 'mono' means single and 'grapho' means to write). Well-known research-based monographs in criminology

include *A View from the Boys*, Howard Parker's 1974 observational study of the delinquent activities and lifestyles of a gang of working-class young men in the UK, and *Crime in the Making*, Robert Sampson and Robert Laub's 1993 secondary data analysis (examination of data collected by someone else—see **Chapter 6**) study of the life course and pathways into/out of offending amongst a group of young men in the USA. Monographs are often based on the author's research and associated scholarship, their ideas, views, and writing. As such, a monograph can be classed as a primary source because the bulk of the information and argument is original and comes from the author(s).

Critical analysis texts

Your criminological learning and understanding can be extended beyond that enabled by textbooks and monographs by engaging with books that can be labelled 'critical analysis texts'. These are primary sources of original scholarship that take a topic area and subject it to a detailed and intensive critical analysis using evidence, (secondary) research data, and the author's academic perspectives and opinions. Critical analysis texts may present an entirely original argument or theory to develop an area of criminology—although this argument or theory will not necessarily be based on evidence generated through primary research. The arguments in these books may have greater elements of supposition and subjectivity (see **Chapter 6**) than a more objective and descriptive textbook—albeit presented in a reasoned way by an expert. Well-known examples of such texts in criminology are: *The New Criminology: For a Social Theory of Deviance* (Taylor, Walton, and Young 1973) and its sequels *The New Criminology Revisited* (Walton and Young 1998), and *The Criminological Imagination* (Young 2011)—each of which present original theories on how to understand crime and criminalisation from the perspective of radical/critical criminology (see **Chapters 15** and **16**). Examples of such texts from our author pool include *Contemporary Youth Justice* (Case 2017) and *Doing Justice to Young People* (Smith 2011). It is recommended that you read all of these texts at the appropriate time, namely once you have read a sufficient number of textbooks and once these critical analysis texts are identified as relevant to your learning on a specific module.

Edited texts

Some books on criminology or specific topic areas within criminology are collections of chapters from several authors who have written chapters separately (i.e. without the help of the other chapter authors); so they are not what

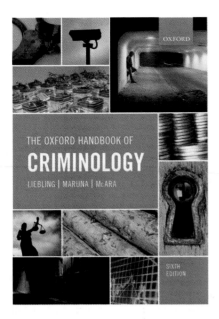

Figure 1.6 The front cover of *The Oxford Handbook of Criminology*, 6th edn
Source: Oxford University Press

you would call a 'multi-authored' book. The chapters in an edited text can be 'textbook-ish' in nature, or they can be more research–based and 'monograph-y', or more based on critical analysis—or a mixture of all three. It really depends on the nature of the edited text in general. Excellent examples of edited texts in criminology are the numerous edited handbooks that will give you a broad overview of a topic area, such as the *Handbook of Crime Prevention and Community Safety* (Tilley 2005), the *Handbook of Policing* (Newburn 2008), and the *Youth Justice Handbook* (Taylor, Earle, and Hester 2010). The most relevant example of an edited text for our learning purposes is the highly influential *The Oxford Handbook of Criminology* (Liebling, Maruna, and McAra 2017), our big brother. *The Oxford Handbook of Criminology* covers a wide range of criminological topics in depth via chapters written by world-leading experts—several of whom have made contributions to our book through various key features in different chapters. Frequent reference is made to the handbook throughout this textbook as it is a fantastic resource to help you deepen your knowledge, and further develop your critical mindset (see **Figure 1.6**).

Academic journals

Criminology as a broad subject area has a wide range of specialist *academic journals*: collections of (largely) research-based and critical analysis essays, reports, position pieces/statements—or journal articles, to give them their proper name. Academic journals may also feature book reviews and critical commentaries on their specialist area. Journal articles tend to be anywhere from 3,000–8,000 words long (it is up to the journal editors and publishers) and tend to be more specific and research-based than a chapter in an edited text (which may be of a similar length, but tend towards critical literature review and analysis). Journal articles will give you a more in-depth understanding of a specific topic or argument in criminology (which you can pin down further using a keyword search on the journal's website), enabling you to extend the knowledge you have gained from other learning materials. An example of a journal article is 'Children First, Offenders Second Positive Promotion: Reframing the Prevention Debate' (Case and Haines 2015), published in *Youth Justice* Journal.

Journals are quite like booklets in size when you see them in hard copy, although you are more likely these days to be accessing journals and articles online. New editions of a particular journal are released regularly (e.g. quarterly, every two months), unlike single edition monographs, textbooks, and edited texts, which may never be updated or are updated once every 3–5 years (e.g. *The Oxford Handbook of Criminology*).

An increasing number of academic journals in criminology are becoming multi-disciplinary (encompassing other subjects related to criminology, such as law, psychology, sociology, and social policy) and international in scope whilst some may focus on being accessible to professionals beyond the academic world. However, many criminology journals remain strongly academic in tone, content, style, and focus—written by academics for academics (rather than for students, for example). Consequently, it can be important that you commit to the (often difficult) process of translating their language and understanding their style. You can visit this book's online resources to see some examples of academic language 'demystified', but this is an area where your travel partners such as personal tutors and module leaders become invaluable. They may have written some of the articles themselves. Either way, they will be willing to facilitate your understanding of these learning resources. After all, a learning resource is useless to you if you cannot understand what it is saying: you can't learn from it and so it is not really a learning resource at all.

Reports

The final traditional or common learning material/resource in criminology is the report—a document containing descriptions, discussions, and evaluations of information, quantitative and qualitative data processes and practices in a particular area of criminology or criminal justice. This can be a report on a piece of research (e.g.

by an academic/group of academics or a research organisation), an evaluation of some aspect of criminology (e.g. a practice, process, project, programme or policy), the discussion of official statistics (e.g. crime and sentencing figures produced by government agencies), or a position/opinion statement from key stakeholders in criminology (e.g. government, pressure groups, charities, think-tanks).

Reports in their various forms are often held up as more objective (unbiased, scientific) than other academic learning materials, but as you will come to see later in the book, every author, organisation, and research sponsor/funder has an agenda and a particular way of looking at an issue, which can influence a certain type of finding or argument. The point to keep in your mind is that as long as you do not assume reports to be objective and factual, then they can be useful supplementary sources of information and argument to give you a broader understanding of a criminological issue. The most well-known criminological (research) report in the United Kingdom (UK) is the annual 'Crime in England and Wales' publication (formerly the 'British Crime Survey') produced by the UK Government Home Office. As indicated earlier, these reports are ideal supplementary reading to extend your understanding of a given topic area in criminology. Best of all, they are more likely to be written in clear, accessible English (not academic speak) and so be more comprehensible and easier to read than more academic sources. But these reports will often have agenda and bias. Read a few and see what *you* think.

Alternative learning materials

The expansion of alternative learning materials and resources in recent years has been motivated by at least two key factors—the rapid growth of the Internet and the rise of a more consumer-minded student body (and staff) who are dissatisfied with what they perceived as the complex and inaccessible nature of traditional learning materials. It is no coincidence, therefore, that alternative sources of information and learning support have increased in popularity amongst students of criminology all over the world. Two notable examples of such materials are blogs and social media.

Blogs

A rapidly-expanding form of alternative learning material is the blog, short for web log, a short opinion/thought piece on issues (in criminology), presented in an informal, engaging, and non-academic way. Blogs are a simple, quick, dynamic, and up-to-date way of getting your point across to a lay person—the novice or non-expert. Blogs can be an easy introduction into a complex subject before you jump into more academic literature. You know

yourself that if the first thing you read on a topic is impenetrable (impossible to get into or understand), then you are more likely to give up, so why not ease yourself in with a blog? For example, Wikipedia is essentially a blog—a forum for opinion and simple explanation presented as though it is academically rigorous. Although you really should not use Wikipedia as a reference in your assessments, precisely because it is so subjective and open to abuse, you could still engage with it as a useful starter to get your head around a topic before the main course of more academic literature/learning materials. You will find blogs located in subject and topic specific blogsites that can be found through Internet keyword searches, through social media, and through academic teaching staff. Blogs may even be included on your programme and module reading lists nowadays and you may even be expected to write a blog as a form of undergraduate assessment.

Social media

Social media houses an expanding range and depth of learning support in relation to criminology, from topic-specific Facebook groups (e.g. author Steve Case coordinates a group called 'Positive Youth Justice'), to podcasts (audio and video) accessible on different sites (e.g. iTunes, YouTube), to Twitter accounts and websites for academics, university departments and programmes, organisations, policy makers, practitioners, students, campaigners, criminology topics, and so on. These can all be really useful supplementary learning sources to give you an initial foundation or framework for understanding, to consolidate and expand your understanding in key criminological areas, and to network and converse with like-minded peers.

Visit the online resources and follow the links to access our authors' social media accounts.

Subject societies and networks

A source of learning support beyond your programme and department can be subject-specific societies and networks, all of which will have an online presence. The academic study and teaching of criminology internationally and in specific countries is monitored and guided by learned (expert, informed) professional organisations (e.g. the British, European or American societies of criminology, the Asian Criminological Society). Each of these subject societies guides and promotes the development of criminological knowledge in their region, supporting criminology professionals (academics, researchers, teachers, policy makers, practitioners) and students through a series of activities. Such activities can include editing an academic journal, organising conferences and seminars (events where professionals and students present and discuss their research and ideas via talks, debates and posters), managing regional or thematic networks (e.g. focused on serious crime, youth justice, substance use), or advertising jobs and producing support materials such as newsletters and ethical guidance for research. There is nothing to stop you joining these societies and networks (at a discounted student rate), receiving their publications and benefitting from attending and contributing to their events. Subject societies and networks are yet another expert travel partner for your journey to a heightened understanding of criminological issues.

As you can see, there is a myriad of learning material available to you, and at first it may seem overwhelming. Picture your learning journey to understanding your subject area as a funnel—start broad with general introductory textbooks, then progressively narrow down your focus and extend your understanding using edited texts, then monographs and critical analysis texts, followed up with journal articles that have been written to test, apply, generate, and evaluate the knowledge base in these topic areas. If you break down and tackle academic learning in this structured way, understanding of vast knowledge bases and complex arguments can become much more manageable and accessible. This textbook will consistently support your learning and growing understanding of criminology by providing you with informative lists of further reading. At the end of each chapter, we will identify additional learning materials for you to read, analyse, and critique, each related to the topics covered here.

Students as travel partners

So far, we have established that identifying and accessing the right support mechanisms to help you along your learning journey is vital for effective study. We have explored the issue of who and what you can work with and benefit from to progress your learning. Of course, a large part of becoming and being an E3 student and enjoying your student experience must be driven by you. However, a mature and focused approach would be to ask for help to go further, to do more. Who better to help and support you than your fellow students (your peers), especially those on your programme and in your year of study? It makes sense to choose your moments to join up with travel partners who are at the same stage on the same journey as you. Your fellow students can provide you with academic support in learning sessions (e.g. during group work and discussions) and perhaps even more so outside of them (e.g. offering and discussing ideas, explaining concepts and arguments, sharing notes and other learning resources, filling in missing information, acting as a constructive and productive group member). This dialogue and support should be reciprocal and equitable because partnership helps you to learn too.

The bigger picture is that it is crucial to develop and nurture constructive academic learning relationships with fellow students. The modern context of HE, for example, involves much more group working in learning sessions, as a learning/teaching/assessment tool, as a study skill, and as a way to develop key personal transferable/employability skills such as team-working. It is an essential soft learning strategy too.

Fellow students/peers not only offer you valuable academic support, but also vital practical and pastoral support. They can advise you of the what's, where's, when's, who's, how's, and why's when you are unsure, unable, or unwilling to get this information from staff or other learning resources. They can help you to learn from their academic, pastoral, and social experiences. They can provide you with essential practical support (e.g. give you a lift to class, take notes, and collect learning materials if you are late or unable to attend learning sessions, share books if these are limited or expensive), and offer you pastoral/emotional support if you need it (e.g. motivating you if you are depressed or feeling low, giving you a shoulder to cry on or an ear to vent into, encouraging you to persevere and succeed). Your department and/or your university may even run a mentoring or buddy scheme that links you up with older students who offer you academic, pastoral, and social support. Whatever form your interaction with peers may take, never lose sight of the notion that friends and classmates can serve as essential learning resources and travel partners throughout your learning journey at university.

Developing a way to travel: Remember your ABC

So you have embarked on your learning journey. You have begun the important reconnaissance process of identifying and familiarising yourself with the what's, where's, when's, and who's of your university and your department. Through your hard work so far, including starting to find your way through this book, you have begun to identify the travel partners (people, structures, learning materials) who can help you on your learning journey. These travel partners are the essential sources of support in your university, department, programme, subject, and student group. The main purpose of this chapter thus far has been to enable you to make yourself aware of the vast range of supports in place to guide you on your learning journey. However, there is a much bigger, more important, longer lasting learning support/travel partner that you simply *must* utilise to its fullest potential. Without this travel partner, all other travel partners are useless. It is *you*— you conduct the reconnaissance, you identify your travel partners, you ask for help with reconnaissance, and ask for help from travel partners. We have identified a series of positive attributes that can help you to become an E3, satisfied student—mature, responsible, independent, dynamic, motivated, proactive, professional, focused, strategic, and critical. These attributes are all ways to travel on your learning journey. They are not destinations, any more than being effective, engaged, and employable are destinations. They are attributes, learning characteristics, strengths, capacities, processes—part of a mindset that you should carry with you throughout your studies to guide everything you do. They are never completed or fully achieved; don't allow yourself to become complacent. They can always be improved.

Always Be Critical

Each of the ways to travel discussed are driven by the basic principle of our book—*Always Be Critical* (ABC). We need to start by clearly defining or operationalising our central concept so that we know what we are working with going forwards. The key term is 'critical'. By critical, this does not mean that you should criticise, complain, diminish, or reject everything that you see, hear, read, and do— there is a time and a place for this. Being critical is not an unconstructive exercise in negativity, it is a constructive exercise in being focused, deliberate, and analytical to enable you to move your learning and understanding forwards. ABC is a way of travel. It is not simply a mindset to use for reconnaissance and for identifying travel partners, although it is critical for these purposes. Strive to ensure that the information and support you gain along your learning journey complements the type of learner that *you* are, the E3 student that you want to become, and the student experience that you desire. Make sure that everything that you do academically focuses on moving you forward as a learner. Think critically about the quality and personal utility (usefulness to you) of the information and services you are receiving, the decisions that you are making and the work (e.g. study, assessment, employability-based) that you are doing—all of which are related to one another. *Always be critical* about whether you are making the most effective study choices. Ask yourself, are you:

- choosing the most suitable modules and research/ dissertation topics (e.g. to match your interests, skills, knowledge base, career plans)?
- engaging with the most useful learning materials and attending the most appropriate learning sessions (e.g. every formal lecture, seminar, workshop and tutorial, extracurricular talks and presentations)?
- taking the right study notes about the right content in the right way; planning, preparing, and executing your assessments in a painless, focused, strategic way?
- asking for support from the right people at the right times?
- always looking for opportunities to enhance your personal transferable skills and employability?
- organising your student experience (study, work placements, extracurricular activities, socialising) in a balanced and strategic way?

Try to adopt and apply a consistent ABC mindset about the how's and why's: how could I enhance my student experience and maximise my potential to succeed; why am I doing what I am doing in the way that I am doing it?

Using learning tips, tricks, and tools to shape your learning journey

The valuable processes described in this chapter of reconnaissance, identifying travel partners, and utilising learning supports are the tips, tricks, and tools that can shape your learning journey. Notably, the ABC mindset can equip you with the skills to use these tools to their full potential. As emphasised across the chapter, ABC means being mature, responsible, dynamic, strategic, critical, proactive, independent, and motivated. It means prioritising yourself, your goals, and your needs. ABC means that you choose to evolve from a passive recipient of information (a sponge who sits and soaks up knowledge) to an active learner, to a proactive producer of knowledge. ABC moves you from the reproduction of the information and arguments of others to reflection (critique, evaluation) on criminological knowledge to enlightenment in the form of creating your own ideas and producing your own knowledge. ABC means challenging yourself.

This mindset should be your constant travel partner as you journey through the following chapters of our book, where we will discuss how criminologists explore, explain, and respond to crime and criminals, before concluding with a reflection on you as an original researcher of criminology and producer of knowledge. Use ABC to engage with the content of these chapters, to ask yourself whether you understand or agree with it, to judge the quality and completeness of the information, to decide how it can help you in your studies and in your career. ABC is a positive, constructive mindset to drive your learning forwards and to enhance your student experience. Now let us begin.

FURTHER READING

Each chapter of this book will provide you with a list of key further reading material. For this chapter, however, additional sources are not as relevant. Instead, the recommendation is that you familiarise yourself with the **online resources** that accompany the book. They are free, accessible, and valuable resources with a number of complementary features to aid you on your journey. They should prove useful to consult as you make your way through this text.

 www.oup.com/uk/case/

CHAPTER OUTLINE

Introduction	30
What does criminology look like as an academic subject?	31
What is the nature of criminology?	33
Studying criminology	34
How will I study criminology at university?	36
The independent learner	39
How will your learning be assessed?	41
What is the study of criminology?—revisited	50

What is the study of criminology?

KEY ISSUES

After reading this chapter you should be able to:

- understand the objectives and key themes of this textbook;

- appreciate what criminology looks like as an academic discipline;

- be prepared for your journey through criminology; its objectives, structure, content, study methods, and uses;

- explore the type of criminology that you will consume, critique, and create throughout your engagement with this book.

Introduction

Welcome to criminology the academic subject. This is your first step on a personal and educational journey that will hopefully continue long after you graduate. Consider this book your guide and travel companion (one of many—see **Chapter 1**) to help you to find your way through the complexities of studying criminology. It is hoped that this chapter will be of use to students of criminology at all levels—providing new students with a guided introduction and route through the subject and enabling existing students to reflect critically on their framework for understanding criminology in the past, present, and future.

This is *not* a textbook that simply gives you facts, information, and arguments to remember and regurgitate later. As discussed at length in **Chapter 1**, this book encourages you to think for yourselves, to test, to manipulate, to criticise, to apply knowledge, to produce understandings that make sense to you; ultimately to create knowledge and understandings of your own. Too much of what has been written and spoken about in criminology, the literature and scholarship in course material (e.g. books, chapters, academic journal articles, reports), has been student unfriendly—unnecessarily complicated, taking too much prior knowledge for granted and not being critical or reflective enough. In other words, criminological literature can tend to be written by academics for other academics.

This book is written for you. As authors, we will not assume knowledge and understanding; nor will we patronise or condescend. What we *will* do is to challenge you to

be an *active learner*, to think, to critique, and to generate knowledge of your own (see **Chapter 1**).

The opening chapter introduced you to the tips, tricks, and tools needed for effective study at university. This chapter progresses and deepens your understanding of university study by introducing you to criminology as an academic subject, what it looks like, what you can expect to study, how you will learn, how this learning will be assessed, and how this textbook can facilitate these goals. It is intended to provide you with a route map through the subject area, through your developing learning in the subject, and towards becoming an effective, engaged, and employable student of criminology.

These aims all have a dual focus—to introduce criminology the academic subject area, whilst simultaneously introducing *Criminology* the book. These aims are clearly interconnected. The book is the tool that we will use to introduce and explore the subject area.

Our book has certain key objectives, which break down and will unpack your understanding of criminology into manageable parts, building on one another as you progress. They are:

- **to demystify**—explaining and exploring the subject of criminology in an accessible, practical, and student-focused way, rather than presenting arguments in the unnecessarily complex and unclear way that academics can do when they are talking to other academics;

- **to animate**—bringing the study of criminology to life by providing you with a framework for

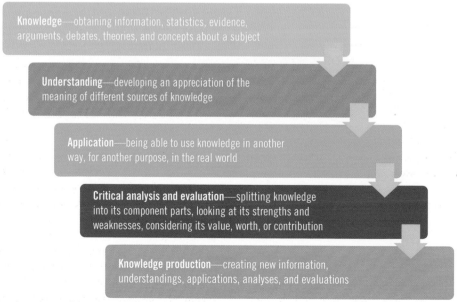

Figure 2.1 The evolution of student knowledge production

WHAT DO YOU THINK? 2.1

What is criminology?

The next two sections of this chapter will examine what criminology actually is. At this very early stage in your studies, the question of 'what is criminology?' is important to address as it provides both a context and a framework for your learning. Breaking this complex question down into more manageable sub-questions is helpful in this regard, so please consider:

* What do we study in criminology?

* How do we study criminology?

* Who studies criminology and who contributes to criminological knowledge?

* Why do we study criminology?

The most important question to ask yourself at this stage is: Why do/did you want to study criminology? What do/did you expect your studies look like and to gain from them? Perhaps most importantly, what do you expect yourself to look like as a learner, a potential employee, and an individual at the end of your studies?

---

understanding the subject in an engaging, motivating, stimulating, and invigorating way;

* **to guide**—supporting you as students as you take your first steps into learning about criminology and to guide you on your personalised and critical learning journey;

* **to transform**—challenging all students of criminology to take ownership of their academic learning journey through the subject, to learn in an active and dynamic way, to *Always Be Critical* (ABC) and to evolve from a consumer of knowledge into a creator and producer of knowledge.

Each of the book's objectives are a way to travel through your studies, not a final destination. Our learning journey in criminology is never over. That is what makes the study of criminology so fascinating, dynamic, and stimulating. By meeting these objectives, your personal and educational journey should evolve from obtaining knowledge to producing knowledge, a process illustrated in **Figure 2.1** and in **What do you think? 2.1**.

What does criminology look like as an academic subject?

Criminology is the academic study of crime. This apparently simple statement, however, is complex and contested, much like criminology itself. For example, it depends on what is meant by 'academic', what is meant by 'study', and in particular what is meant by 'crime'. The use of inverted commas indicates that concepts are ambiguous and debatable (typical in criminology), so please bear that in mind as we move forward. Understanding the meaning of crime is central to criminology and is a debate that shall be engaged with throughout this book (and is specifically discussed in **Chapter 3**). Criminology is an academic subject in that it produces knowledge and understanding through:

* **teaching and learning**—typically in educational institutions;

* **scholarship**—experts writing and arguing about the subject;

* **research**—for example observation, testing, asking, analysing;

* **debate**—for example the presentation, comparison, and contrast of reasoned and supported arguments;

* **critique**—for example the structured analysis and evaluation of academic scholarship, research, debate, and non-academic arguments, such as those presented by politicians, policy-makers and, especially, the media.

The lecturers, scholars, and researchers who create and impart criminological knowledge and understanding are known as criminologists. Students of criminology are rarely considered criminologists in this sense, but they could be and they should be. From the moment you begin to study criminology, you should consider yourself a criminologist.

The study of criminology can be divided into three interconnected areas that each contribute to our understanding and knowledge of crime: defining crime, explaining crime, and responding to crime. This is the *triad of criminology* (see **Figure 2.2**).

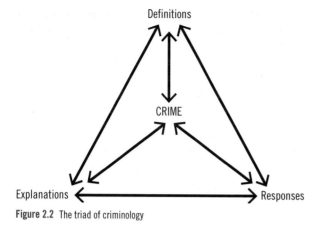

Figure 2.2 The triad of criminology

Defining crime

Defining includes describing, measuring, exploring, and debating issues such as what crime is, who decides what is considered crime, how much crime is committed, recorded or reported (the extent of crime), and which different types of crime are committed, recorded, or reported (the nature of crime). Of course, not all crime is recorded, reported, or even noticed. What is missed is known as the 'dark figure' crime. Think about this when you read about the crime statistics that supposedly represent the extent and nature of crime. Defining crime is also concerned with who commits crime and who is labelled as an offender (e.g. what is the age of criminal responsibility and the official difference between a young and adult offender?); when and where crime is committed, recorded, or reported; how the criminal law is enforced (e.g. the extent and nature of activity in the criminal justice system—arrest, sentencing, and punishment). Defining and exploring crime is often closely linked to discussions of what is (criminal) justice and what methods are used to better understand crime and justice.

Explaining crime

We *explain* crime by producing theories and arguments about what causes, influences, predicts, changes, increases, reduces, and prevents crime and associated behaviours (e.g. antisocial behaviour, substance use, social harm) of different types by different groups and individuals in different places at different times. As with defining crime, explanations incorporate the study of who is doing the explaining, an evaluation of the methods they employ to arrive at their explanations, and discussions of the historical and ongoing debates between different explanations and theorists. We cover these issues in **Part 3** of the book, '**Explaining crime**'.

Responding to crime

Responding to crime involves discussing how we do and should respond to crime and those who commit crime through policies (e.g. strategies) and practices such as law-making, law enforcement, criminal justice measures (e.g. sentencing and punishment), restorative justice, surveillance, control, treatment, rehabilitation, intervention, crime reduction and crime prevention programmes, service provision, relationship building, study, and research. There is often a focus on key criminal justice stakeholder organisations and staff such as police, courts, prison, probation and victim services. We cover these issues in detail in **Part 4** of the book, '**Responding to crime**'.

Criminologists often utilise diagrams to represent processes, structures, theories, and models such as the interconnected area just described (see **Figure 2.2**). It can be very helpful to be given a visual representation of complex areas or ideas, especially if you are a more visual type of learner.

Let us explore the key concept that is being represented in this diagram. The idea is that the definitions of, explanations of, and responses to crime are all interrelated and affect one another. They are what criminologists might call reciprocal, mutually-dependent, and mutually-reinforcing. For example, how we define crime (in a particular country or culture at a given point in history) shapes and influences how we try to explain it, because the definition determines the type of behaviour or concept we are trying to explain, namely what we call 'crime'. Consequently, how we explain crime determines or influences how we choose to respond to it (or at least should) because how we choose to understand the behaviour or concept of crime shapes our views of how it should be most appropriately punished, treated, reduced, and prevented. Do you see how these elements can be aligned? This alignment can work the other way around too. How we explain crime can influence how we choose to define it and re-define it in the future based on our new understandings, new information and evidence, technological advances, social changes, and so on. How we respond to crime may also bring us new evidence, understandings, and insights that affect our subsequent explanations and definitions of crime as a behaviour or concept.

Definitions of, explanations of, and responses to crime can all influence one another through the new knowledge and understandings that they create. Whether they always do in reality is debatable as there are many other influences on criminological knowledge construction. Definitions, explanation, and responses are dynamic or *socially-constructed* concepts—the constantly changing and evolving products of human understandings

(Williams 2012). These understandings are the creations of criminologists and others, presented as theories, practices, research methods, and societies that evolve and consistently change what we view as crime. The social construction of crime is a theme that runs throughout this book.

What is the nature of criminology?

What is the nature of criminology as an academic subject? What forms does it take? What does it focus on? Criminology is often seen as a 'social science' because it uses quasi (approximating) scientific methods (i.e. similar to those used in the natural sciences of physics, chemistry, and biology), particularly empirical research (see **Chapter 6**), to produce evidence, create knowledge, and progress understanding relating to crime. It is important to note, however, that the academic production of knowledge by teachers, scholars, researchers, and students is not the only product in criminology; nor are criminologists the only influencers of the crime-related definitions, explanations, and responses that are illustrated in the triad of criminology diagram. Criminological knowledge and understandings can be created, informed, and critiqued by a variety of non-academic individuals/stakeholders with a working interest in crime, including:

Figure 2.3 A police officer is perhaps one of the first professionals you consider when thinking about criminology

Source: © AskewNews/Alamy Stock Photo

- **politicians**—the Prime Minister, Home Secretary, and Justice Minister in the UK, the Attorney General in the USA;

- **policy-makers**—civil servants working in the Ministry of Justice, the Youth Justice Board, and local authority Committee Safety Departments in the UK, civil servants working in the Department of Justice, the National Institute of Justice, and the Office of Juvenile Justice and Delinquency Prevention in the USA;

- **practitioners**—judges and magistrates, prison and police officers (see **Figure 2.3**), lawyers and solicitors, FBI agents, youth justice workers, and the media (e.g. journalists, news columnists, TV and radio presenters).

The criminological knowledge and understanding produced by these non-academic stakeholders are typically intended to influence the general public's perception of crime (Jones 2013). In this case, 'perception' refers to their views of the most appropriate definitions, explanations, and responses to crime. This influence is often exerted to progress the agendas of those individuals and their organisations in some way, support for which is demonstrated by voting in elections, contributing to the operation and funding of crime-related programmes (e.g. community projects, CCTV), buying newspapers, and providing the audience for TV and radio programmes.

The general public's perception of crime (which can also be influenced by academic criminologists, but rarely to the same extent) can, of course, influence how politicians, policy-makers, practitioners, and the media discuss and portray crime (see **Chapter 7, Crime and the media**). After all, these individuals want to appeal to the general public in order to win votes, hearts, minds, customers, and audiences. Therefore, individuals outside of academia, especially politicians and those in the media, can be inclined to give the public what they think they want to see and hear in relation to crime. This may result in the perpetuation of a certain amount of spin, half-truths, and misinformation, rather than necessarily prioritising representations of crime that are valid (accurate, evidenced, honest, complete). So, it's possible to connect public opinion of crime with non-academic representations of crime using a double-headed arrow, as if they are reciprocal and mutually-reinforcing.

The primary focus of this book is the academic nature of criminology. We will explore throughout how academic knowledge and understandings in criminology interact with non-academic influences. However it is crucial to get the basics in place first, namely what criminology is and how we will explore it in this book.

Criminology is a hybrid (interdisciplinary) academic subject—very much the cuckoo of the social sciences. It has developed by adopting, adapting, and applying (using real-life situations) the main features, focus points, methods, theories, and arguments from other academic social science subjects, many of which are hybrid themselves, such as:

- **sociology**—the study of the behaviour of human beings, organisations and institutions in social settings (e.g. the study of crime and deviance);

- **psychology**—the study of the mind and individual human behaviour (e.g. the influence of psychological characteristics and illness on criminal behaviour);

- **law**—the study of law-making, legal systems, and legal processes and practices (e.g. the criminal justice process);

- **social policy**—the study of human well-being and needs, problems (e.g. poverty), and the political/governmental responses to them (e.g. the role of welfare systems and services in responding to crime);

- **anthropology**—the study of human beings, societies, and cultures in the past and present (e.g. how the law, criminal definitions, and legal systems have developed).

The interrelationships between these social science subjects and criminology are illustrated in **Figure 2.4**.

As a consequence of the hybrid nature of our subject, criminologists are interested in the sociological, psychological, legal, policy, and anthropological influences on defining, explaining, and responding to crime. These can also include historical, political, economic, and geographical influences. Criminologists use the knowledge and understandings gained from studying these definitions, explanations, and responses as a way of informing the development of academic theories and arguments They also inform government policies, and the practice of organisations and staff dealing with crime and people who come into conflict with the law (e.g. offenders, victims, families).

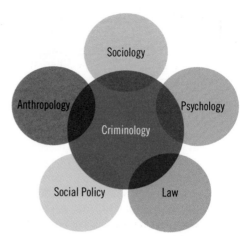

Figure 2.4 The interrelationships between criminology and selected other social sciences

Criminological knowledge is also used to inform the way that the media reports, represents, and discusses crime (see Hale, Hayward, Wahidin, and Wincup 2013); a highly contentious world, even more so than academia, politics, and practice combined. This will be explored in much more detail later in the book.

So what do we 'know' now about the nature of criminology? As an academic discipline, criminology is an interdisciplinary meeting point of older, related social science subjects like sociology, psychology, law, social policy, and anthropology. Criminological understanding and knowledge is produced by academic scholars and researchers, but is also subject to a host of non-academic influences from key stakeholders such as politicians, policymakers, practitioners, and the media. Therefore, knowledge in criminology is a dynamic product of the uneasy and complex relationship between academic and non-academic influences.

Studying criminology

When you become an HE student at university, you will be expected to study a number of different and exciting aspects of crime in a variety of stimulating ways, all of which can be situated within the *triad of criminology*. The typical content of an undergraduate criminology degree programme focuses on specific areas that help you to unpack the complexities of the subject into smaller and more manageable chunks. Whether you are a new student seeking to understand the structure and foci of criminology or an existing student reflecting critically on how the nature of criminology can inform your developing learning, it is useful to analyse the component parts of our subject as we do in the following sections.

Categories

It is commonplace for criminology courses to be broken down into modules and topics based around different types or categories of crime, reflected by the general content of this book. Courses can be divided into anything from general crime categories, such as serious, violent, property, youth, female, and ethnic, to more specific crime categories such as drug and alcohol-related, cyber, corporate/white collar, environmental, hate, organised, terrorism, sexual, homicide, art, political, economic, and animal crime, along with **victimology** (the study of crime victims), and **zemiology** (the study of social harms).

Theories

Central to any programme are the different explanations of frameworks for understanding the aetiology (origins, causes) and effects (e.g. on victims) of crime (Jones 2013). These theories include classical and rational choice approaches (crime is a product of choice); biological, psychological, and sociological positivism/determinism (crime is influenced by factors within the individual or their immediate environment); critical and radical theories (crime is a creation or label of the powerful that is imposed on the powerless); and realism (crime is a real phenomenon with real, damaging effects). Each of these theoretical frameworks will be covered in detail in the book. Theoretical debates also consider why and how organisations and systems should respond to crime (e.g. penology—the theory of why and how we should punish, sentence, and treat criminal behaviour) and the philosophies, principles, and ethical considerations of studying and working with crime and the people who commit crime (see Williams 2012).

People, organisations, and systems

Criminology involves studying the work of the staff/practitioners, policy-makers, and decision-makers in organisations relevant to criminology more broadly (e.g. universities, governments, research institutions, pressure groups, charities, support groups), as well as key stakeholders who work within criminal justice specifically (e.g. police, courts, probation, prisons, local authorities). Criminologists may also study how these people, organisations, and systems work together (or not) as part of the systems and structures seeking to understand and respond to crime (e.g. criminal justice systems, youth/juvenile justice systems, multi-agency partnerships, cross-national, and international agencies). University modules can also focus on the different groups of people who are affected by crime, such as victims, women and girls, black and ethnic minorities, young people, disabled people, etc., and the systems (e.g. communities, cultures, countries) that these people contribute to and live within.

Themes and issues

A series of critical concepts influence the extent and nature of understanding we can have about the categories, theories and people, organisations, and systems that form the focus of our definitions, explanations, and responses to crime. Across all undergraduate criminology modules at all levels of study, you are likely to examine themes and issues such as cross-cultural comparisons and differences between and within countries; differences between the extent and nature of crime at the local, national, and global levels; differences related to age, gender, ethnicity, and class, etc. (see Hale et al. 2013). You will note that these crucial themes and issues have been woven into discussions across several of the chapters in this book. You are also likely to study the growing influence of the media on our understandings and knowledge of crime, along with the increasing importance of social harm—a broader topic that studies damaging behaviours and actions that have not been labelled as crime through traditional, restricted definitions of it. A common critical theme is the social construction (creation, manipulation, exaggeration) of crime by powerful social groups (e.g. men, white people, the wealthy, adults, the Western world) over the history of criminology; in particular, the ways in which criminological study and knowledge is:

- androcentric—gender-biased—dominated by men, conducted by men on men for men; and
- ethnocentric—culturally-biased—dominated by white people (typically men) from the white westernised world; namely Europe, North America, and Australasia.

The critical theme of social construction is often compared and contrasted with the concept/theme of realism—a perspective that crime is a real-life, actual, measurable phenomenon with real consequences for real people, as opposed to an inflated creation or social construction by powerful groups.

In summary, the broad headline areas in criminology can be conceived of as definitions, explanations, and responses. These areas can be further broken down into categories of crime, theories of crime and justice, and the people, organisations, and systems who work with crime and the people who commit crime. A number of important critical themes and issues run across these areas, particularly concerning differences between and within countries, locations, and groups, the social construction of crime (versus reality), and the influence of androcentricism and ethnocentrism on our understandings and knowledge of crime. We will explore each of these fascinating areas as we journey through this book. They each contribute to making criminology the dynamic, stimulating, frustrating, and engaging subject that it is. With this in mind, let us consider how you might be expected to study on a typical undergraduate criminology degree programme. Current students of criminology may want to engage with this information as a means of consolidating their existing knowledge and learning, but they may prefer to move past this section and re-join the chapter at 'The independent learner'.

How will I study criminology at university?

Throughout your criminology degree studies at university, you will be exposed to a variety of learning experiences and teaching and assessment methods, both direct (e.g. face-to-face teaching) and indirect (e.g. distance-learning, virtual learning, independent study). The direct, face-to-face nature of the teaching and learning expected by students constitutes the formal, official learning, and teaching that you will experience at university. There is a simple but important distinction to be made between the direct, measured, monitored, formal contact you will have with teaching staff (e.g. lecturers, students, guest presenters) to progress your learning and the indirect, independent study and learning you will be expected to do outside of these official learning and teaching sessions—see **Figure 2.5**.

The extent of direct teaching you receive is typically measured in terms of contact hours—the number of hours on a course, over a year or across a module, where you are in direct, face-to-face contact with a member of academic teaching staff. The issue of contact hours is growing increasingly important in the modern age of HE, especially as students now pay tuition fees for their university courses and you finish your studies needing to find employment in a highly competitive and shrinking job market. Both the student experience (often measured through satisfaction) and employability are also hot topics for HE and are closely linked to the quantity of direct learning and teaching offered on degree programmes in the minds of students and their parents.

The direct and indirect learning and teaching you experience as part of your criminology degree can take a variety of forms, use a variety of tools, and be experienced in a variety of locations, the most common and well-known of which are explored in the following sections.

Lectures

The standard, traditional teaching method in HE more generally and criminology specifically is the lecture (see Finch and Fafinski 2016; Harrison, Simpson, Martin and Harrison 2012). Usually, a lecturer stands at the front of a classroom or lecture theatre and talks about the topic of the lecture (**Figure 2.6**). They may use PowerPoint slides, videos, recordings, Internet material, photos, handouts, etc. (these are collectively known as audio-visual aids or AVAs), they might write on a blackboard, whiteboard, interactive screen, or flipchart, they might just talk. This is really why the people who you learn from are called lecturers and not teachers—because we have traditionally talked *at* students rather than worked more closely *with* students to develop and check their understanding and learning. In the modern age, however, motivated by a focus on the student experience and informed by a better understanding of what type of teaching helps effective learning (Finch and Fafinski 2016), lecturers incorporate more interactive, individual and group activities, problem solving, electronic and social media, and employment-focused content into lectures. However, the traditional 'chalk and talk' approach may persist, with the lecturer talking and you writing down the key points. The trick is to be an active learner of criminology, *Always Be Critical* about everything you hear and read, and always think carefully about how your lectures and lecturers are helping you to understand course content and ultimately to produce new knowledge of your own. Helping you cultivate this mindset is very much key to this book.

Figure 2.5 Independent study, and therefore effective use of resources, will form a huge part of your degree

Source: wavebreakmedia/Shutterstock.com

Figure 2.6 In less interactive, more traditional 'chalk and talk' lectures it is particularly important to maintain an ABC mindset

Source: Syda Productions/Shutterstock.com

Seminars

Seminars are a smaller and more interactive version of a lecture, often with compulsory and monitored attendance, which may not be the case for lectures. Seminars are intended to help students to explore topics in more detail—ideally those already introduced in lectures and course materials. Seminars typically take place in classrooms (rather than lecture theatres) with smaller groups of students than you would usually find in a lecture. They often consist of individual and group activities that may be based on prepared readings and stimulus activities (e.g. engaging with academic criminological articles, problem-solving exercises, role-plays, simulations, debates, discussions, presentations, work-based scenarios, assessment preparation) using a variety of learning and teaching methods relevant to criminology (see Finch and Fafinski, *Criminology Skills*, 2016). So, the idea is that you as the student take more responsibility for your understanding, application, analysis, evaluation, and production of criminological knowledge (see **Figure 2.7**). Seminars may be led by a lecturer (e.g. the lecturer who convenes/leads the module), a postgraduate student, or an invited guest such as an academic expert or an experienced practitioner who works in the area under study. Seminars may also take place online—a format known as webinars. The most effective seminars (like all effective learning or teaching sessions) have a clear purpose that is linked to the learning outcomes, content, and assessment requirements of the module. Seminars are a great forum for knowledge sharing; they will provide you with the opportunity to listen to your fellow students' views on a topic, and communicate your own.

An increasingly popular adaptation of the seminar in the HE, university context is the workshop. These can be longer than seminars (e.g. half a day or a day long) and so give the opportunity for more contact hours and for more practical and applied group-based activities such as fieldwork (outside of the classroom), problem-solving, piloting research projects, discussions with guest speakers, assessment preparation, and developing and delivering presentations.

Tutorials

Once at university, you will be allocated a personal tutor for the duration of your studies—typically a member of the academic teaching team from your home department. You will be required to meet formally with your tutor at regular points throughout your studies (although you should of course always contact them whenever you need them outside of these formal contact points)—meeting them individually and/or as part of your tutor group (along with your tutor's other tutees). The frequency of this contact is dictated by your particular university and your department's personal tutorial policy (if they have one). Personal tutors are responsible for monitoring your academic progress and giving you generic and subject-specific academic advice and support relating to issues such as acclimatising to university education, study skills (general to HE and specific to criminology), assessment preparation, essay writing, exam technique, presentation skills, and clarifying criminology course content. Tutors also take a pastoral role, looking after your well-being, helping you to deal with personal problems (e.g. issues that may affect your ability to study to your full potential), directing you to appropriate support services in your university/department, and representing your views and interests in any committees where your progress may be discussed.

The third important role of the personal tutor in tutorial sessions is to offer guidance and support regarding your employability. For example, you could discuss with your tutor the transferable skills you are developing in your modules (skills that you can transfer from your degree to a job in the outside world), identifying suitable work placements and research internships for you, linking you with professional contacts in the workplace, helping you with your CV, and directing you towards modules or subject choices relevant to your planned career. Personal tutorials are usually held in your tutor's office or in a classroom (but they could be conducted by telephone or online) and consist of formal and informal discussions focused on one or more of the learning, teaching, assessment, and personal development elements discussed in this section—academic progress, pastoral care, and employability.

Figure 2.7 Seminar group discussion in a university seminar room—make sure you speak up too

Source: © Monkey Business Images/Shutterstock.com

Virtual and distance learning

Beyond your face-to-face learning and teaching experiences in criminology at university, it is also possible for learning and teaching to take place virtually (electronically, online) and/or at a distance. The increasing use of technology, online resources, and social media to facilitate and consolidate traditional learning and teaching methods in criminology has enabled a range of virtual learning contact opportunities for students and teaching staff, such as guided discussions and the posting of course-related content via websites, blogs, wikis, Facebook (Steve Case, one of our authors, convenes a 'Positive Youth Justice' Facebook discussion group), Twitter (our authors' handles are @SteveCaseCrim; @rogerssmith37; @edupunk_phil), Instagram, YouTube, podcasts, virtual learning environments, online discussion boards, video chat mechanisms (e.g. Skype, FaceTime), and other electronic communication tools (e.g. text, Messenger). Some universities also offer distance learning modules and courses, with limited or no face-to-face teaching contact. Instead, students study in their own time and space with their learning guided by specially-prepared study schedules and course materials provided online and (less so nowadays) in printed form, along with recommended criminological readings (e.g. books, chapters, journal articles) that can be accessed through the university's library. The online learning materials often contain stimulus activities and links to appropriate discussion boards and further reading. If you choose to take a distance learning course, you will normally be allocated a personal tutor who you can contact by telephone, email, and other electronic means. Criminology courses in HE can integrate formal teaching sessions such as scheduled online discussions or telephone tutorials, while some courses have face-to-face group tutorials and seminars built into the teaching schedule.

Work-based learning

An increasing number of undergraduate criminology courses are integrating employability-enhancing, work-based learning experiences such as work placements and research internships in relevant criminological and criminal justice organisations (e.g. the police, courts, prison and probation services, governmental agencies, crime reduction programmes and victim- and offender-support services). These placements can take the form of work shadowing (watching someone do the job, following them around), work experience (you conduct tasks related to the role), or research internships (you complete a small piece of job-related research for the organisation). Each of these may be formally assessed as a module or part of a module (such as through workplace activities, with a diary or log detailing what has been learned, why, how, when, etc.) or may be conducted outside of official contact hours (such as a year abroad or holiday scheme). For example, criminology students at Swansea University conduct work placements and research internships over the summer vacation following their second year of study, but draw upon their experiences and research for their final year dissertations, which are formally assessed. They are typically allocated a workplace mentor and a supervisor from their university department, who will usually visit them during the placement. Some criminal justice-heavy undergraduate programmes can be predominantly work placement- or practice-based and so are more like on-the-job study for existing criminal justice practitioners than traditional academic undergraduate study with elements of work-based learning.

Independent study

University students can tend to overlook that the majority of learning should take place informally and independently outside of timetabled teaching sessions and contact hours. There are only a limited and finite number of contact hours possible through formal lectures, seminars, workshops, and tutorials, so independent study and self-directed learning are absolutely essential to your university education and your student experience. This has always been the case at postgraduate level (especially for research students) and is increasingly the case for undergraduates. The formal, direct teaching events that you will experience (especially lectures) are intended to stimulate you, to motivate you, to encourage you to investigate a topic area in more depth in your own time. Formal teaching introduces you to key concepts, arguments, debates, issues, themes, and theories in time-limited, bite-sized sessions. Effective study at university relies on you exploring these elements further, independently of your teaching sessions, teaching staff, and tutors. You can do this on your own or in partnership with your classmates. Independent study requires you to engage with (work with, spend time with, explore) the course materials you are given and directed towards. These course materials can include university, programme/course, and module handbooks and guidance documents (e.g. essay writing guidance, referencing instruction, study skills advice), recommended sources of reading (e.g. books, chapters, journal articles, reports, policy briefings, blogs, websites—see **Chapter 1**), and suggested electronic/online supports.

The expectation for independent study has become increasingly demanding and formalised within criminology courses in HE. For example, a 20 credit module on the undergraduate Criminology and Criminal Justice degree at Swansea University carries with it the expectation that students will study for at least 200 hours—broken down into 40 formal contact hours (lectures, seminars, and workshops) and 160 independent study hours (100 hours of private study and 60 hours of preparation for assessment). Although independent study hours (like formal contact hours) vary within and between courses and universities, independent study is becoming an extremely important feature of the undergraduate student experience in criminology (and many other HE subjects), if not *the* most

important feature. Independent study is a skill that you must develop and a responsibility that you must embrace. However, the irony is that you should *not* be expected to develop this skill independently. You should be directed and guided towards effective independent study by your teaching staff and tutors—an essential support mechanism that is explored in more detail in **Chapter 1**. 'Independent' means working outside of formal contact hours and taking responsibility for your own learning; it does not mean being left alone to work out everything yourself.

The independent learner

A consequence of successfully completing your undergraduate course will be the formal qualification that verifies your abilities as a high-level independent learner. This feature is another clear marker of HE as all students are expected to independently manage and control their own learning. This means undergraduates should not be 'spoon fed'—i.e. be told how to do everything—instead they must develop the ability to learn for themselves from their own actions and experiences. This independence means you can direct and assess your own higher education learning experiences. Having this experience will not only benefit your studies in criminology, but also what you do after you have completed your course. Remember it is an aim of this book to encourage development of the attributes of an E3 student: the effective, engaged, and employable undergraduate discussed in **Chapter 1**. The opportunities in your student experience allow you to develop all three of these qualities; particularly with regard to your employability. In 'job-market speak', a competency is measured by achievement (i.e. it is based on things you have done in the past) and a capability is measured by potential achievement (i.e. it is based on what you could do in the future)—if you spend your time as an undergraduate wisely, you will be able to demonstrate high levels of both.

ABCs and the pedagogical power of patterns and prompts

Pedagogy (originally meaning to lead or guide a child) refers to the science of teaching and so seeks to explain how things can be taught and learnt. In recent decades it has been taken much more seriously in HE. A pedagogical approach is a method of teaching that aims, in undergraduate terms, to produce high-level independent learners. But, even though you are at this higher level, it is still important to do the basics right—so do not be afraid to use things you have learnt before. An ABC can be the first step in learning anything and so for this book, the prompt to *Always Be Critical* is a simple reminder of the rich learning potential from always questioning supposed criminological and criminal justice knowledge. It represents your first steps as an independent thinker and, as it is early in your studies, you should not be afraid of taking advantage of all available help from your lecturers and fellow students. These two basic points, if replicated enough, should become so natural that like any ABC you will become unaware you are actually doing it. Phil Johnson, one of our authors, explains further in **Telling it like it is 2.1**.

TELLING IT LIKE IT IS 2.1

Joining in with the teaching and learning game— with author Phil Johnson

This book has been designed in an attempt to help you extract maximum value from your course in criminology. Its use of clear thought prompts like 'ABC', 'Telling it like it is', and 'What do you think?' (also known as 'key features' in our book) have been intentionally crafted to help you overcome the challenging but essential parts of your studies. They seek to provide you with the strategies for managing the vast amounts of information you will encounter whilst studying criminology.

The patterns and prompts in this book are tips for organising and structuring your work as well as offering powerful aids for your memory. Clearly your degree course will not just be a test of memory, but there will be many times when memory is required (e.g. various forms of presentations and exams, etc.); so being able to break complicated issues down, in a memorable way, will be an invaluable skill. You probably have encountered memory prompts like mnemonics before—e.g. 'Richard Of York Gave Battle In Vain' for remembering the red, orange, yellow, green, blue, indigo and violet colours of the rainbow or 'My Very Easy Method Just Speeds Up Naming Planets' for always remembering the order of the planets from the sun: Mercury, Venus, Earth, Mars, Jupiter, Saturn, Uranus, Neptune and Pluto (despite the latter's recent demotion from planetary status). These can be very powerful weapons in assessments such as National Curriculum tests in schools but their use does not have to end there! Your current level of studies obviously requires more depth but by using examples such as the 'OUTSEX' formula for the due process of disputed confessions at a criminal trial (see **Part 4** of this book), it can be possible to break down complicated issues and tasks into manageable sections.

Of course they will not be enough on their own, but if you are struggling, such tricks can at least give reassurance when you first look at a blank piece of paper or computer screen that you know how you could begin. By breaking things down like this, you will have the basic structure, or content, of what is needed and these initial thoughts will help you with the deeper analysis for the required context. In addition to mnemonics, your creation of other patterns of letters and numbers could provide this structure. An example would be the '89' pattern which is an easy way of appreciating two major changes in the way criminal justice policy responded to offenders. It highlights '1789'—the year the French Revolution occurred (as did modern criminal justice) and '1989'—the year the Berlin Wall came down and anti-communist revolutions across Europe occurred (as did postmodern criminal justice). The words in parenthesis are clearly very blunt statements so please do not assume they are completely accurate, instead you should read **Part 4** of this book and 'ABC' them. Perhaps even do a **'SWOT'** analysis on them as once this method has been used it is difficult to forget its system for analysing **S**trengths, **W**eaknesses, **O**pportunities, and **T**hreats.

The autodidactic age

The autodidactic approach to teaching and learning holds self-education to be the most effective method for attaining understanding. It is a DIY approach to learning and has a contemporary position known as 'edupunk'. Some of the real possibilities for your future from having a 'degree of edupunk' are presented in **Part 5** of our book. Edupunk may sound like a joke because of its associations with the punk movement of the 1970s which usually emphasises the music and rebellious attitude of groups like the Sex Pistols, but these stereotypical images suppress the true heartbeat of punk that was founded on the growing numbers of self-taught musicians, record producers, and concert promoters who were simply having a go at doing things and seeing what happened. It was this spirit of independence that epitomised punk as a DIY movement and these 'ideals of access—which have been expanded by the Internet—have become one of Punk's enduring legacies' (Savage 2001: xv).

Although the recent interest in edupunk has been driven by both popular culture and the Internet, recognition for the power of autodidactical learning pre-dates these forces by an appreciable length of time. It is a Greek term beloved in classical times as a means of effective scholarship and learning and was later reaffirmed in Jacques Rancière's book, 'The Ignorant Schoolmaster: Five Lessons in Intellectual Emancipation' (1981). This text detailed the illustrious teaching career of Joseph Jacotot in the 18th century and, in his situation, an autodidactic approach to teaching and learning was effectively forced on Jacotot due to the language barriers between himself and his students. It resulted in standards far higher than was customarily achieved as his students produced 'sentences of writers not of schoolchildren' (p.4). This claimed superiority arose from the teaching and learning approach resting on the students independently recognising the different patterns in the two languages; following acquisition of this understanding, more original and higher quality work was produced.

Pedagogical patterns

The creation of your own pedagogical patterns and prompts has much use for surface learning but a different system is needed for deeper undergraduate learning. This can be advocated by teaching and learning experts who believe developing effective methods of learning is far more valuable than learning specific content. It has led to assertions that pedagogy for effective undergraduate learning can be 'captured' and transferred across any area of undergraduate study (Laurillard 2011). It is possible to take a transferable approach to your learning and clearly prove your independence and versatility for HE.

Your ability to learn anything as an undergraduate can occur when a structure of four key stages is

Topic	Learning Outcome	Summary
The water cycle	A clear understanding of the role of the critical factors in the system	Through preparing their own **animation** of **the water cycle**, to demonstrate the role of the critical factors, **using Open Educational Resources**; presenting it to their group; defending it against questions and comments
Using a search engine	A clear understanding of the role of the critical factors in the system	Through preparing their own **account** of **using a search engine**, to demonstrate the role of the critical factors, **using the Library guidelines**; presenting it to their group; defending it against questions and comments
The 4Ps of Criminal Justice	A clear understanding of the role of the critical factors in the system	Through preparing their own **report** of **the process of the 4Ps (principles, policy, practices, people) in criminal justice**, to demonstrate the role of the critical factors, **using Chapter 21 of Case et al. (2017)**; presenting it to their group; defending it against questions and comments

Table 2.1 Pedagogical patterns

Source: Inspired by Professor Diana Laurillard from the London Knowledge Lab at the Institute of Education

provided. This demonstrates how pedagogical patterns can offer much more than just revision cramming techniques (Laurillard 2011). The system provides a means for demonstrating your prowess as an independent learner so long as four different stages of activity (researching, presenting, defending, and revising) are appropriately addressed.

These stages represent the four core aspects of learning in HE and provide a sequence for producing the reflexive attitudes and actions expected from undergraduates. Examples of how it can be applied to different topics are in **Table 2.1** (adapted by Phil Johnson), which provides the examples from Professor Laurillard's outstanding presentation before illustrating how these stages can be employed to study the criminological topic of criminal justice as it has been broken down in this textbook. The text in bold type in Table 2.1 refers to content-specific information with the remainder being the required steps to effectively learn as an undergraduate (i.e. the pedagogy).

As you can see, you will develop your knowledge and understanding of criminology at university by experiencing a range of learning and teaching contexts (e.g. lectures, seminars, workshops, tutorials, virtual and distance learning, work placements, independent study). You will also develop knowledge and understanding through interacting with a variety of individuals (e.g. lecturers, seminar leaders, tutors, librarians, peers and classmates, practitioners) and course materials/learning resources (e.g. books, chapters, journal articles, policy reports, websites, blogs, virtual learning environments, online discussion groups). It is intended that you will come to look upon this book as your most valuable 'go to' learning resource (complemented by our more specialised academic big brother, *The Oxford Handbook of Criminology*—Liebling, Maruna, and McAra 2017) as you progress through your undergraduate studies and beyond. We would love for you to develop a strong academic relationship with this book, its online resources, and its authors as you embark on your journey of discovery through criminology the academic subject.

How will your learning be assessed?

Your knowledge and understanding of what you have learned and been taught, along with your ability to apply it to original questions and to manipulate it to support arguments, will be constantly tested and measured through *assessment*. These assessments will be formative (ongoing, informal, part-way through a module or course) and summative (formal, final). Your assessment grade/mark/score counts towards your progression through your course (e.g. passing a module or part of a module) and can count towards your final degree grade, typically in years two and three of your degree. Ultimately, every learning and teaching event that you experience should feed into and help you with the final, summative assessment on the module. So, for example, formative assessments conducted part of the way through a course are intended to enable teaching staff (and you) to assess what you know, what you do not know, and what you need to know in order to succeed with the final assessment.

Assessments in HE, particularly in qualitative, social science subjects like criminology, have been traditionally based on written essays and timed, essay-based exams—the formal description, discussion, explanation, application and (at higher levels of study) analysis, synthesis, and evaluation of course content in the context of a set question or statement relating to an aspect of criminology (see Finch and Fafinski 2016). Traditionally, these have been marked by the teacher/lecturer and completed by the individual student. However, in recent years, the range of assessment methods used in university social science subjects like criminology has expanded in line with the range of learning and teaching methods used, the increasing need for highly-skilled and employable graduates, and the increasing importance of a varied and diverse student experience. Consequently, traditional essay and exam assessment has been consolidated by alternative (written, spoken, visual, online) assessment methods completed individually and in groups, assessed not only by lecturers, but also by the individual student (*self-assessment*) and by their fellow group members (*peer assessment*). It is crucial to emphasise that all assessments will be marked/scored/graded/measured against specified *assessment criteria* that you should be provided with as part of the course and module information. Make sure that you have access to the assessment criteria for each of your assessments and ensure that you use it to inform your assessment preparation at all times.

This section will now go on to discuss the assessment methods/formats/types that you can expect to experience as part of your criminology degree.

Essay

An essay is a written or word processed response to a stimulus question, statement, quote or instruction, provided within a set word limit and submitted by a set deadline (Redman and Maples 2011). The stimuli (e.g. question, statement, quote, instruction) are usually given by the module leader/lecturer, although an essay stimulus can also be set by the student. This is known as an *independent essay*. An essay normally requires you to respond to stimuli with some combination of description, discussion, explanation, application, analysis, synthesis, and evaluation (usually dependent on the level of study) in order to demonstrate your knowledge and understanding of module and course content and (where appropriate) to demonstrate your ability to produce original critique, arguments, and knowledge (see **What do you think? 2.2**). For

---

WHAT DO YOU THINK? 2.2

Tackling essay questions in criminology

Here are some examples of differently worded essay stimuli requiring equivalent responses, based on the topic of female offenders:

- **Question**—What is the most effective way to respond to females who commit crimes?

- **Statement**—Females should be treated differently to males by the criminal justice system. Discuss.

- **Quote**—According to the former UK Government Home Secretary Michael Howard, 'prison works'. Assess this claim in relation to females who commit crime.

- **Instruction**—Explore the argument that we should treat females differently when they enter the criminal justice system.

What are your views on the essay stimuli above? How would you respond to the stimuli? What issues and themes would you introduce and explore in order to provide a detailed response and why?

---

example, in your first year, you may be asked to 'Describe the functions of the agencies in the criminal justice system' or to 'Consider the usefulness of official crime statistics'. In year two, you may need to 'Discuss the causes of crime' or 'Explore whether black and ethnic minority groups are treated unfairly by the police'. In your final undergraduate year, essay expectations might be to 'Analyse the ways in which sex work has been criminalised' or to 'Evaluate the effectiveness of the youth justice system'. These are very general examples of essay questions, but hopefully they give you a better idea of the kinds of stimuli you can expect and how expectations may increase as you progress through your studies.

Literature review

Recently, variations on the academic essay have been introduced into criminology degree programmes, for example, the literature review. Literature reviews are overviews of a topic area, such as a summary of the key debates, issues, theories, research findings, policies, and authors. They can be (any combination of) descriptive, critical, thematic, theoretical, and research-based. The key difference to essays is that literature reviews tend to be more focused on setting the context for and describing an area, rather than writing a detailed evaluation or critique in response to a stimulus question or statement (Redman and Maples 2011).

Dissertation

A dissertation is essentially an extended independent essay (often between 8,000 and 10,000 words) that is usually completed in your final year and focused on the topic of your choosing. Dissertations are supervised by a staff member (your personal tutor or an expert in your chosen area) and are intended to demonstrate your extended/elaborated understanding of the topic area (Arksey and Harris 2007). They will have chapters (unlike essays) and can be either desk-based critical literature reviews of criminological topics or research-based critical discussions of a piece of empirical research in criminology (i.e. based on a controlled study, observation, experiment, experience). The chapters of a desk-based dissertation tend to focus on the key themes that help you to unpack the title/question—much like you would break up an essay into themed sections, supplemented by introduction and discussions chapters. A research-based dissertation will have an introduction chapter outlining the dissertation structure, followed by a critical literature review chapter setting the scene/context for the research. There is then a methodology discussing the research method(s) used (see **Chapter 6** for a detailed discussion of the empirical research methods employed in criminology), a results/analysis chapter presenting the research findings, and a discussion chapter discussing the methods and results in relation to the set research question and the contribution of the dissertation to the topic area. It is also becoming increasingly popular for criminology programmes to formally assess a dissertation proposal prior to completion of the full dissertation—a structured plan of the chapters, questions, themes, debates and references that the dissertation will contain. This proposal may be a piece of formative (ongoing) assessment that does not count towards the final dissertation mark or it may be summative, counting as either part of the final dissertation mark or as a full module assessment in its own right.

Dissertations are very common forms of assessment in criminology at postgraduate level, such as in taught Masters degree courses and taught doctoral (PhD) courses. A research-based Masters degree such as a Master of Philosophy (M.Phil.) or a Master of Research (MRes.) can be assessed through an extended dissertation (often between 50,000 and 60,000 words) known as a thesis, whilst a non-taught, desk-based, or research-based PhD is examined through an even longer thesis of up to 100,000 words. A full-time Masters thesis can take up to three years to complete (usually between one and two years) and a full-time PhD takes three to four years to complete. For example, author Steve Case's MPhil in Psychology took two years to finish, whilst his PhD in Criminology took four years. Research-based theses at Masters and PhD levels are supervised by at least one member of academic staff and ultimately examined through a viva (see under the 'Presentation' heading).

Examination (Exam)

An exam is a written response to a stimulus question, statement, quote, instruction, or task that is completed under timed conditions (see **Figure 2.8**). Whilst it is possible to have a practical exam in criminology, where you conduct a physical activity or task (e.g. a role-play, a simulation of a practice scenario) in response to a stimulus, by far the most common form of exam in criminology is the essay-based exam (see Harrison et al. 2012). This format should be familiar to those of you who have studied broadly similar subjects in college, for example sociology, psychology, history, politics, philosophy, as well as others. Essay-based exams require you to respond to one or more stimuli (equivalent to essay stimuli) within a fixed-time period under controlled, supervised conditions. As you will probably know from your secondary school and further education studies, exams are usually written and take place in a large classroom or makeshift exam hall under the supervision of staff known as invigilators, who are there to ensure that you do not cheat, to give you extra answer sheets, to tell you how much time has elapsed, etc. Exam stimuli can be given in advance (the seen exam) or given to you once the exam begins (the unseen exam). You may also be allowed to take course materials into the exam with you (e.g. books, lecture and revision notes)—this is known as an open book exam. An increasingly popular alternative form of exam is the multi-choice question (MCQ) exam, where you are given a choice of possible

Figure 2.8 Essay-based exams are the most common form of assessment within criminology

Source: wavebreakmedia/Shutterstock.com

responses to questions/stimuli and you must choose the correct one(s). For example:

> Which school of thought in criminology uses 'scientific' methods to identify the causes of crime?
>
> (a) Positivism
>
> (b) Classicism
>
> (c) Critical criminology
>
> (d) Realism

The answer is (a) by the way, although subsequent chapters will provide you with arguments to enable you to challenge this uncritical acceptance of the term 'scientific'.

It is fair to say that exams give many students a great deal of anxiety, perhaps more so than any other form of assessment. However, keep in mind that essay-based exam questions and answers should look and read the same as normal essays. If you study effectively (i.e. read and engage with this book), execute your answers effectively (*Always Be Critical*), ask for the appropriate help and support (see, for example, **Chapter 1**), and practice writing exam answers, you can minimise this anxiety and maximise your chances of success. Remember your 5 Ps—**P**lanning and **P**reparation **P**romotes **P**ositive **P**erformance.

Presentation

The traditional preference for written essay and exam assessments in criminology is being challenged by the oral presentation assessment, which requires you to offer a formal presentation/talk on a topic, either individually or as part of a group. You may be given the topic/title/stimuli/specific question (a set presentation) or you may be permitted to choose your own focus (an independent presentation) linked to a programme or module topic area. You will most likely be allocated a time limit for your presentation and you may or may not be given a formal presentation structure to follow. Your presentation will be assessed by teaching staff (e.g. the module leader), but may also be assessed (in part) by the rest of your class and/or your presentation group—called peer assessment. You may also be required to assess your own performance—also known as self-assessment.

The assessment criteria for presentations may be similar to those for essays and exams, with your performance measured in terms of focus (on the question), understanding of content, clear and logical structure, and range and relevance of references used to support your arguments. You may also be graded against broadly equivalent assessment criteria such as the ability to keep within the time limit and clarity of delivery. There may also be presentation-specific criteria such as the use of audio-visual aids (e.g. handouts, PowerPoint presentations, multimedia) and non-verbal behaviour such as eye contact with your audience. Presentations are becoming more popular in criminology in part due to the growing emphasis within HE on employability and transferable skills—skills that you can apply to jobs and careers once you graduate. The diverse range of oral and written communication skills developed through presentations are perfect to meet these goals.

As with most forms of assessment, there are variations on the presentation method. For example, criminology and criminal justice courses have begun to introduce in-class individual and group discussions and debates around topics that may be set beforehand or may be unseen and introduced in class with minimal to no preparation time. At the PhD level, doctoral theses are assessed through a formal presentation known as a *viva*—an oral examination of the thesis by one or more examiners (who have not supervised the thesis), who ask the student searching and probing questions about the thesis and its contribution to knowledge, objectives, theoretical basis, key methods and findings, weaknesses and limitations, etc. The student is required to defend their work in the face of intense interrogation from subject experts regarding its content and value. Now *that* is an assessment experience to get anxious about, believe us!

Presentations can provide students with a learning journey that is unmatched by any other form of assessment. So many students have an intense concern, even a fear of presentations—anxieties about the demands and expectations of working in groups, being assessed as part of a group, being observed in the formal presentation situation, keeping to the time limit when presenting, etc.; these issues can induce unjustified levels of anxiety and panic, especially as presentations may be a new experience for some students, such as those coming to university from essay/exam-based college subjects or those who are new on the course. Dealing with such anxieties is a constant issue for those of us on the author team whose undergraduate courses involve presentations. However, presentations can be a constructive, rewarding, and enjoyable experience for students. (See **Telling it like it is 2.2** for two students' perspectives.) That is not to say that formal, assessed presentations are necessarily enjoyable or easy, although they get less painful and much easier the more you do them. What is being argued here is that compared to other forms of assessment (e.g. essays), presentations can be shorter, require less preparatory work, less time (especially if you are part of a larger group), and can have less demanding expectations in terms of detail, content, structure, and referencing. Better still, the assessment criteria for presentations can be more achievable, more forgiving, and more lenient, so you should be less anxious about them. Not only that, but the skills you develop and the experiences that you have look better and more relevant on your CV than anything you will get from essays and exams.

TELLING IT LIKE IT IS 2.2

The criminology student's view of presentations —with Emma Hurren and Amy Rowe

Emma Hurren, a recent criminology graduate from Swansea University, says, 'So you are stood there, the room full of people ready to listen to you and to see your presentation. Thinking about this filled me with dread and the majority of us found it very stressful. What if I say something wrong? What if they think I am stupid? Many of us let our anxieties take over and we worry about the idea of giving a presentation and forget about the reality. However, remember that presentations are often part of group work, so you have support, reassurance, and confidence from those around you. Also, remember who you are delivering the presentation to. Often it's your course mates, who will be giving a presentation too, so you are in the same boat. This takes off a lot of pressure.

'It is really important to remember how valuable presentations can be—it is an extremely beneficial tool for the learning process. Yes, you learn from writing essays, but having to freely discuss and explain a concept to others gives you a whole new understanding of the subject and increases your confidence in that understanding. This is an extremely useful skill to take into the working world once you've graduated. Some jobs require presentations as part of the interview process. With the experience of giving presentations in university, you can go to interview knowing you can talk with conviction and confidence. Presentations actually increase your self-esteem—it's such an achievement to overcome anxieties and do something you are truly proud of. Who knows, you might even find some enjoyment in it!'

Emma's course mate, Amy Rowe, added, 'I am not naturally confident talking to groups of people, particularly when there is the added pressure of being graded on various aspects including content and presentation. The prospect of group presentations was really daunting for me. Whilst I was as reluctant to speak as the rest of my group, I decided that the best way to deal with my nerves was to face them, so I volunteered to share the speaking role in the knowledge that doing this would leave me better equipped for future presentations. This gave me experience and confidence, so my next presentation went much more smoothly than the first and I actually quite enjoyed it in the end!

'The transferable skills I gained from presentations have been useful in so many ways. I am more confident to speak to large groups of people, such as when a friend asked me to propose her for a position within the Students Union to a group of 100 + people. Most importantly, I found the experience invaluable when I was asked to give a presentation as part of an interview for a job. I felt confident that I knew how to present information effectively and argue my case in a clear and persuasive way. It might be tempting to take a back seat in a group presentation and allow others to take on the speaking roles, but ultimately you will benefit much more from involving yourself as much as possible.'

Emma Hurren and Amy Rowe, BA Criminology
graduates, Swansea University

Research-based assessment

An increasing number of criminology degree programmes are integrating criminological research methods and evidence (see **Chapter 6**) to inform and shape their associated learning, teaching, and assessment, along with prioritising students' development of (transferable) research skills for learning and employability purposes. These research skills include team working, conducting critical literature reviews, understanding research methodologies, data analysis, and sharing research in presentations and reports (see Bryman 2015). With increasing amounts of bespoke research modules, research components within other modules (e.g. research-based dissertations), and research-informed teaching, has come an increasing range of research-based assessments. A common assessment method is the research report, which requires you (individually or in a group) to describe, discuss, and evaluate a research project that you have conducted. The standard assessment criteria focus on the background literature and research in that area, choice of question, the methods used, the results obtained, and what these mean (e.g. how they contribute to knowledge in the topic area, how they answered your research questions) and how you will disseminate (share, publicise) your study. There may also be some element of critical reflection required, where the individual or group looks back on the research process from a personal perspective and discusses (informally) what worked, what did not work, how the research could be improved, etc.

There are several associated research-based assessment formats. These include the research proposal, where you (individually or in a group) provide a report/plan regarding how and why you intend to conduct a piece of criminological research in the future. The research proposal basically has the same structure as the research report, except that it reports and discusses what you *will* do (it is *prospective*), rather than what you *have* done (which would be *retrospective*). The research proposal can discuss what literature you will examine, what method you will use, what form of results you will obtain (e.g. numbers, words, ratings), and how you will analyse and present them, etc. The research proposal (like the report) may include details of any pilot study—a much smaller scale, dry run of the research project conducted to test methods, practice the research process, and identify any issues to address in the main study.

Research posters

The research poster is growing in popularity as an assessment method, because it is efficient and it enhances transferable skills and employability. The poster involves the individual or group presenting their study details visually on a large poster-sized board or sheet of paper (see Bryman 2015) using a mixture of narrative and graphics (see **Figure 2.9**). Along with presentations, posters are the most common way for academic researchers to disseminate their research to others at conferences and they are a common research presentation format in the STEM subjects of (natural) science (physics, chemistry, biology), technology, engineering, and medicine.

You may also find that you will be given specific assessments focused on the individual elements of a research project. For example, you may be asked to complete a critical literature review as a formative or summative assessment. You could also be required to produce a methodology report or to conduct a piece of data analysis related to your proposal or completed research project. It may also be that different research-based assessments form part of a broader case study of a topic, organisation, practice, process, or community and that they are used in conjunction with other assessment formats. Case studies are likely to be conducted over a longer period of time than a typical cross-sectional (snapshot, at one point in time, one-off) piece of research.

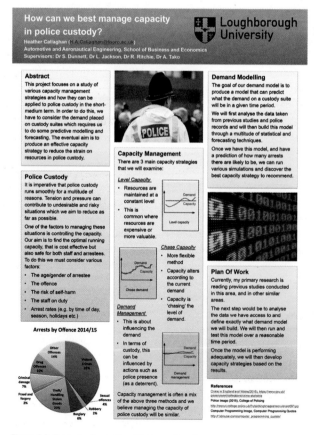

Figure 2.9 Example of a good quality research poster

Source: Heather Callaghan, Loughborough University

Review

It is possible that different forms of review will be part of the profile of assessments on your degree programme. We have already discussed the use of (critical) literature review as an alternative form of essay and as a vital volatile component of research-based assessments. Another common form of literature-based review is the book/chapter/article review, where you are asked to conduct a discussion and/or critical review of the content, structure, style, and value of a criminological text (not normally a textbook), a book chapter, or an article published in an academic journal, be it theoretical or research-based. The book, chapter, or article may be already chosen, you may be asked to select it from a list of options, or you will be required to select it independently without guidance. The common structure for the review is similar to that of an essay. It will consist of an *introduction* where you set out the key arguments or issues you will cover, a main *body* that contains your key arguments (the theoretical or political background to what has been written, the key issues covered, and how they compare and contrast with other issues in the same area), and a *conclusion* where you summarise the key themes you covered in the main body of the review. Like essays and other assessment forms, you will be offered anything from detailed guidance regarding structure, focus, content, and style to no guidance whatsoever.

Work-based assessment

The growing emphasis on employability as part of undergraduate criminology degree programmes (e.g. work placements, work experience, work shadowing, research internships, work-based learning) has necessitated an appropriate range of work-based assessments to measure the associated learning. One common format is workplace observations, with staff members (from the university, from the workplace organisation) assessing the student's performance against a set of assessment criteria. It is also common for students to conduct some form of self- and/or staff-assessed reflection during work placements, such as the completion of a reflective blog, diary, or journal, possibly in conjunction with other assessments such as essays, research reports, and presentations.

A major form of employability-focused assessment in criminology degrees is the curriculum vitae (CV), which can form a major part of careers-based modules. The beauty of the CV is that it is both formative and summative—it can be updated and enhanced throughout your studies, far beyond the duration of the module for which it is assessed; plus, you can take it with you when you've graduated.

Blog

A blog (shorthand for web log) is designed to assess your understanding and knowledge of a criminological topic by asking you to summarise and discuss it concisely (in about 500–1,000 words), using informal language (not technical jargon), and to explain it to a non-expert audience. The aim of the blog is to help you develop the ability to be flexible in your thinking so you can deal with new approaches. A major selling point for graduates on the job market is an ability to be creative and meet new challenges. Writing a blog uses similar skills to those required for an essay; it is just presented in a different way. Writing in this way can assist with the development of important skills that will help you use academic, 'scientific' literature more effectively in your studies; in particular, by encouraging you to think critically about your course materials. In the words of Dr Andy Whiting (a colleague of author Steve Case's) in his blog guidance to first year criminology students:

> There is no better way of demonstrating that you understand a concept or theory than being able to explain it to your house mate, parents or grandparents.

Presented in **Controversy and debate 2.1** is a clear and cogent example of a blog entitled 'Where next for youth justice?', kindly provided by Sean Creaney

---

! **CONTROVERSY AND DEBATE** 2.1

Where next for youth justice?

A guest blog by Sean Creaney, Trustee of the National Association for Youth Justice and Advisor to Peer Power, published on 15 October 2015 on http://www.no-offence. org/.

The Lord Chancellor and Secretary of State for Justice commissioned a review of the Youth Justice System in England and Wales on September the 11th https://www.gov.uk/government/speeches/youth-justice and

published the terms of reference on September 17th https://www.gov.uk/government/publications/youth-justice-review-terms-of-reference.

The review is timely and it is important to state that looking at more efficient and cost-effective ways of working is certainly sensible, especially in these difficult economic times. Indeed I hope that the review is meaningful and innovative.

However the review excludes the minimum age of criminal responsibility, courts and sentencing, leading to critics questioning whether it is a review at all. Some have argued it is a prelude to another Transforming Rehabilitation style service marketisation exercise. Such accusations have *not* been refuted.

It was suspected that the youth justice 'stocktake' was 'about privatisation' but interestingly this was refuted by government http://www.cypnow.co.uk/cyp/news/1148224/yot-stocktake-assess-services-evolve.

In the adult criminal justice arena there is a danger that such an exercise can result in private sector organisations engaging in gaming activities where maximising profit becomes the intention over enhancing the well-being of the individual. The government's flagship Payment by Results (PbR) schemes at Peterborough and Doncaster did not go to plan: the results appear disappointing for the Ministry of Justice http://www.russellwebster.com/disappointing-outcomes-for-peterborough-and-doncaster-prison-pbr-pilots.

I would like to respectfully remind Michael Gove and Charlie Taylor of the above issues and also that the rationale for payment by results in the youth justice system is largely rhetorical with few arguments of substance http://thenayj.org.uk/wp-content/uploads/2015/06/2011-Payment-by-results.pdf.

Payment by results

A PbR model of service delivery for children who offend that emphasises market mechanisms may be counterproductive as profit may take priority. Effectively, enhancing the welfare of the individual is of secondary concern. PbR is premised on the idea that organisations involved will receive financial reward for meeting prescribed targets. The focus is on short term reoffending (a simple yes/no indicator of criminal activity is used) at the expense of other longer-term developmental outcomes. Measuring success is very complex, especially as factors overlap and intersect as frequency and/or severity may reduce but offending may continue http://thenayj.org.uk/wp-content/uploads/2015/06/2011-Payment_by_results_and_the_youth_justice_system.pdf.

Although some young people who offend may be more receptive, resulting in success and in turn financial reward, others may be more difficult to engage where the securing of a successful outcome is problematic. Such children may not benefit then—arguably in any shape or form—if this was implemented.

Despite its flaws, PbR is a model that purports to innovate and make a 'real difference' to the hardest to reach. Ironically it is the 'hardest to reach' who suffer the most in PbR. Children with complex needs (who are also often the most marginalised and disadvantaged) may then be put aside as there will be no financial reward if the intervention fails and offending continues.

Persistent and serious 'offenders'

Some of the key successes of recent times include reduced numbers in custody and first time entrants to the Youth Justice System. However as Lord McNally recently said, such achievements 'have exposed a cohort of persistent and serious young offenders' https://www.gov.uk/government/speeches/lord-mcnallys-speech-to-the-criminal-justice-management-conference-2015'

Such children present very complex needs that the Youth Justice System currently struggles to address in the face of continual dwindling resources. Indeed the withdrawal of state support is evident in many areas of public life, not least universal services and in particular those available to young people. With the system not addressing such needs and PbR being arguably ineffective—at least where children are concerned—are Social Impact Bonds a better alternative?

Social Impact Bonds

Although there are perceived ethical and moral issues with PbR as a model of service delivery for vulnerable children, another model potentially associated with the work of Youth Offending Teams is social investment in the form of Social Impact Bonds (SIB). More specifically, SIB can help to alleviate financial pressures and could be a positive way forward in terms of engaging the 'hard to reach'—though this remains untested.

SIB could be another approach to deal with crime in these difficult economic times and a potentially viable solution to fill gaps in service provision left by reduced state support. Raising the capital from private companies, if positive outcomes are achieved investors see a sizable return on their investment. Although the government reward such providers financially for the achievement of such social goals, it can be cost-effective in the longer term for tax payers providing significant upstream savings.

Although the true impact will be determined by the length of time it would take to see a 'return on investment', SIB could prevent children and adult offenders entering the prison system and help to reduce health and social care spending over time.

Shared Decision Making

In contrast to youth justice practice that is often deficit-led and may increasingly become distorted by being profit-led, I believe the way forward is to re-think how to engage the 'hard to reach' through the utilisation of the Shared Decision Making model. There should be a commitment to working towards provision being user-led, where opportunities to co-design and shape service delivery are created.

Crucially, children's experiences of disempowerment need to be explored and solutions found fundamentally by involving children in assessment and decision-making processes—through their terms of reference—doing 'with' rather than 'to'.

Why not consult children on the proposed cuts?

I am *not* aware of any child who has offended being consulted about the proposed in year cuts to Youth Justice Services which will directly impact on them as service users. This is perhaps unsurprising as children are all too often seen and not heard in the youth justice context.

As service users, children are key stakeholders and have a unique insight into 'what works'.

Sean Creaney, Lecturer in Psychosocial Analysis of Offending Behaviour, Edge Hill University

from Edge Hill University. It was written for the 'No Offence' website (www.no-offence.org), which is an excellent user-friendly resource for criminal justice information, news, and views.

Visual assessments

As technology advances and becomes more accessible, there has been an increasing use of visual forms of assessment in HE generally and criminology specifically. A typical format is the use of photographs or videos to illustrate a topic (e.g. based on a statement, question, instruction),

supplemented by a narrative that is either written or spoken. So, for example, Phil Johnson, one of our authors, asks his students at the University Centre at Blackburn College to choose five photographs to illustrate a topic (e.g. 'The Environment and Corporate Crime') and to accompany each with a 250-word (written) description of how, when, and why the photograph was taken, an explanation of what it represents about the topic, and a justification of why it is appropriate as an illustration of the issues raised by the topic. See **New frontiers 2.1** for what Phil has to say.

As you've hopefully picked up from what you've read so far, you will experience a number of different forms of assessment during your study of criminology. These

NEW FRONTIERS 2.1

Using photographs as assessment in criminology—with author Phil Johnson

I have long been questioning the suitability of assessment methods in today's HE context and the sheer number of written words required from undergraduates over the course of a three-year degree. There are other concerns over our current assessment practices, such as the lack of relevance of writing skills in the world of work. Traditional essays may also discourage individual thought—the very thing HE is supposed to promote. Writing 'I think ...' can be so strongly disapproved of, in favour of more conservative approaches and formulaic essay structures. Consequently, the critically enthusiastic voices so often heard in seminars and workshops are replaced by answers that 'do the right thing' but do not reflect what a student actually thinks.

Many years ago, I was inspired to try a new approach. Kings College London advertised an unusual photography competition called 'Harm ... Crime ... Injustice ... What does it look like to you?' I adapted its requirements into a formal assessment and got validation from Lancaster University to use it as an alternative method. In my proposal to the university, I did not use the 'a picture is worth a thousand words' cliché, although for the purposes of word limits for modules, that is exactly what it can become. The general interest in crime photography meant that when I first ran this assessment method, there was a chance the students' assignments would end up on the front page of the national newspaper sponsoring the competition. My use of assignments has since moved online; this move has resulted in extra opportunities for e-learning as the assessment method can now include the students producing videos of their visual images hosted on an open access YouTube channel; this results in an audience far in excess of traditional assessment approaches, which generally only involves a student and a lecturer.

The number of words a photograph is deemed equivalent to varies with the detail in the assignment question and it can also be accompanied by tasks requiring written or verbal justifications for the taken images. So instead of writing *another* 2,500 word essay, students can choose *how* they present their work. A visual approach to assessing undergraduate criminology encourages the 'reading' of photographs; this can be done by paying close attention to all of the detail that is both *in* and *out* of this frame. This involves appreciating their connotations (what they suggest) and denotations (what they actually show)—this learning can result in the students' creation of photographs that express themselves in ways that may not have been possible through the conventional written word. The reading of photographs can be an effective way for using your ABC approach, as 'the source of the source' of photographs, like anything else (see **Chapter 6**), is fundamental to what they show. In addition to considering the possible truth in photographs this type of learning can also enhance ethical and legal awareness as by taking the role of a photographer in society, you are placed directly in a situation where these dilemmas occur.

Chapter 28 offers more information on visual ways of presenting your findings when you come to produce research of your own.

assessments could be written (e.g. essay, dissertation, exam, report, proposal, review, blog, CV, reflective diary), spoken/oral (e.g. presentation, viva), practical (e.g. work-based observation), or visual with accompanying discussion (e.g. research poster, photograph, video). Each form of assessment is intended to measure your knowledge and understanding of criminological topics, concepts, themes, and issues and should be closely linked to your course and module content, learning objectives, and learning and teaching methods.

What is the study of criminology?—revisited

This chapter has introduced you to criminology as an academic subject. We explored the question 'What is the study of criminology?', viewing criminology as the academic study of crime, with 'academic' referring to the production of knowledge through teaching and learning, scholarship, research, debate, and critique. We then divided the study of criminology into '*defining crime*', '*explaining crime*', and '*responding to crime*', which was represented by **Figure 2.2, The triad of criminology**. When exploring 'What is the nature of criminology?', it was explained that criminology is a hybrid subject influenced by a range of other social science subjects and by different academic and non-academic 'stakeholders'.

Studying criminology at university was broken down into smaller, manageable chunks: categories, theories, people, organisations and systems, and themes and issues. We then unpacked a typical undergraduate criminology degree programme as consisting of compulsory and optional modules, each containing a set number of credits, direct contact hours, and indirect independent study hours. The most common learning and teaching methods were outlined (lectures, seminars, tutorials, work-based, virtual and distance learning, independent study), followed by the typical assessment formats (formative, summative, written, spoken/oral, practical, visual).

FURTHER READING

Finch, E. and Fafinski, S. (2016) *Criminology Skills* (2nd edn). Oxford: Oxford University Press.
Before you move on to Chapter 3, delving fully into the more 'academic' content of this book, it will be worth your time to consult Part II of *Criminology Skills*. Aimed specifically at criminology students, this skills book elaborates on writing skills, essay writing, presentations, and many other skills you will need to complete your degree.

 Access the **online resources** to view selected further reading and web links relevant to the material covered in this chapter.
www.oup.com/uk/case/

PART OUTLINE

3. What is crime?

4. What is justice?

5. Crime statistics

6. How does criminology 'know' about crime?: Subjectivity, supposition, and study

7. Crime and the media

8. Victimology and hate crime: Evidence and campaigning for change

9. Explaining youth crime and youth justice

10. Race, ethnicities, and the criminal justice system

11. Gender and feminist criminology

Welcome to **Part 2**, our first critical explorations of crime.

The first two chapters focused on foundational issues with which all criminologists critically engage at the start of their criminological journeys; now we take things a stage further. Debates on how we conceptualise crime and justice are central issues which run throughout this book. By questioning the common-sense ideas that 'crime' is simply law violation, or that 'justice' amounts to little more than 'criminal justice', these chapters form the starting points for the ABC approach of our book.

We then pose two questions: firstly, what do we actually know about crime and secondly, how do we know this? We then go on to ask: how and why do governments construct and use crime statistics and victimisation surveys? How do criminologists bridge the gaps in official knowledge claims? The relationship between media and crime is then fully explored; from more traditional concerns of how printed and news media represent criminality, and whether these can actually be said to be a cause of crime, to a consideration of newer forms of media as a site of crime.

Next we consider the relationship between evidence and policy development. How do groups use evidence to push for policy change for victims of hate crime? The part ends by exploring how crime is experienced. Bringing together insights from previous chapters we focus on young people, race, and gender; however, these categories are interrelated. With the ABC point in mind, enjoy this part and your explorations of crime and criminology.

PART 2

EXPLORING CRIME

CHAPTER OUTLINE

Introduction	56
Crime as a social construct	57
Crime and deviance	60
Why are some actions criminalised?	62
The harm principle	62
Other reasons which might explain why some actions are crimes	70
Do we need the criminal law?	73

What is crime?

KEY ISSUES

After studying this chapter, you should be able to:

- identify what the criminal law is and what it is for;

- understand why the criminal law can be seen as a social construct that changes over time;

- consider the reasons why some actions are criminalised, and assess how well these reasons are applied;

- evaluate whether we need the criminal law in order to hold people to account and punish them, or whether a system designed to deal with any harm caused without apportioning blame would be more effective in ensuring safe and content communities.

Introduction

At one level the question 'what is crime?' is easy to answer. It is also an example of a very poor examination question. It is a poor examination question because it can be answered very simply and with no real discussion by saying what a crime is in legal terms. You could therefore answer it by saying: crime is any act or omission which a state at this time says is criminal, and to which the state attaches criminal consequences. That means that agents of the state such as the police and prosecutors can bring the person they believe is responsible to court to be prosecuted, to answer for their action or omission. If it is crime and they are found guilty then the court may decide they should be punished by the state so their money (if they are fined) or their liberty (if they are imprisoned), and, in some states even their life (if there is the death penalty), may be at risk.

To simplify it, in law a crime is:

- a norm or set of norms (rules);
- backed up by the threat of societal sanctions.

The answer just given is technically accurate, but it does not get us very far. For example, it does not tell us why societies criminalise some activities but not others, nor does it tell us what types of activities might be crimes. As criminologists, if we do not understand what activities are criminalised in our society, and why, then how can we try to discover why people offend? So what follows in this chapter is a rather longer and more detailed discussion about what sorts of activities are criminalised and why; what the criminal law may tell us about our society and what matters to it; and what we can learn about those who choose to break the rules and whether it matters what type of rule they break. So, whilst never forgetting the basic legal background let us look in more detail both at the content of the criminal law and what has to be proven in a criminal case, before considering why these are important.

Communities, societies, and international standards of human rights

There are some activities, such as murder, rape, and theft, that are prohibited in almost all societies. There are others that are less clearly included in the categories of crime such as fox hunting with dogs, smoking in public places, using certain drugs, dropping litter, swearing in public, not wearing a seat belt, etc. Even with serious, violent crimes such as murder and rape there is disagreement about exactly what should be banned, so how does society decide exactly which activities should be classed as crimes? Should you be able to help a person to die when that is their wish (an issue highlighted by the Campaign for Dignity in Dying, see **Figure 3.1**) or should such an act be murder or manslaughter? Should it be rape if a woman consents to sexual intercourse believing a man

Figure 3.1 Campaign for Dignity in Dying homepage
Source: Dignity in Dying: http://www.dignityindying.org.uk

is her boyfriend, when in fact the man has intentionally misled her and he is really a man she does not know? These are close to the facts of *R v Collins* [1973] QB 100, where Collins climbed up to a bedroom window and the woman in bed started to have sexual intercourse with him believing him to be her boyfriend. Should this be classed as burglary with intent to commit rape (the Court of Appeal thought it should)? Answers to these and similar questions give rise to animated political, legal, philosophical, academic, and public debates. This chapter will study some of these and, along the way, consider some of the difficult questions these debates pose.

Before we progress it is important to consider why the behaviour of individuals might need to be controlled. Each human being is an individual, and being able to express our individuality through choosing how we live is, for most of us, an important aspect of who we are. It is important to our dignity and happiness. That freedom to choose is often called autonomy. If we each lived alone we could, in theory, do anything we wanted. However, almost all humans live with other humans in (large or small) communities which often then group together into societies. We usually do this through choice as we are naturally sociable animals, but it is also easier to ensure that all our needs (physical needs such as food, and emotional needs such as happiness and well-being) are met if we can rely on others to help meet some of them. Living in a society with others is in our best interests.

Each individual is generally reliant on the community or some people within it to fulfil their needs and, often, to provide emotional support. This sets out two aspects of human life which are essential to most human beings: freedom (especially freedom of choice) and social living, including social interactions. In a group or community however, the choice of one person may interfere with the choice of another. For example, Charlie may have acquired some honey which Jo wants and then decides to try and take it. Jo and Charlie might fight over the honey and the strongest, or maybe the most cunning, would win. If nothing in the community stops Jo challenging and fighting each time she wants something then every member of that society will give up free choice. This will lead to a less happy and less healthy community because it will allow the strongest or most cunning to win, to take everything. This society would not value individual choice nor possibly social harmony; the strong would be happy and the weak not. In theory criminal law is supposed to deliver some justice or fairness into the community to level this playing field. How might it do that? In the modern world to prevent states (society) from interfering in individual freedoms the intersection between society and the individual is protected by international standards. These standards are usually referred to as human rights and they are designed to try to persuade states to protect and respect people's freedoms. In the modern world, the intersection between the society and the individual is protected by international standards of human rights which try to persuade states to protect and respect people's freedoms. This is in case a society oversteps the mark and interferes too much in individual freedoms. Therefore a community or society may set standards of behaviour they find acceptable, but they should do this whilst still respecting human rights, which form the limits of what a community should do and set the standards states or societies should uphold.

The international human rights standards set limits and values to be respected, but what each state decides to control through the criminal law is left to that particular society.

Crime as a social construct

Particular behaviours become controlled through the criminal law because a society decides that it wants to control them. Labelling a certain behaviour 'criminal' often happens because of a social response to the behaviour or towards those who take part in the behaviour. Overall, society considers this behaviour to be undesirable. Therefore, what we consider to be 'crime' is socially constructed. Thinking about crime as a social construct means that there is nothing in the acts or behaviours themselves which intrinsically means they *have* to be prohibited. Rather crime is what a society thinks it should be (or those in power in a society think it should be) at any one time. This means that each society sets different rules, and what is criminalised differs between different societies. For example, in some largely Arab states (such as Bangladesh) drinking alcohol is a criminal offence whereas other substances such as cannabis may be legal, but in the UK it is the other way around. What is criminalised therefore often depends on cultural values. This means that crime is a socially-bounded construct, a label used by a society in order to achieve certain aims. The powerful within a state may use the law to protect their own interests or those of other powerful groups at the expense of ordinary people, the powerless, or minority (see both labelling and critical criminology in **Chapter 15**).

What any one society considers to be unacceptable and criminal alters over time. Until the 1960s homosexuality was a criminal offence in England and Wales and people were prosecuted for practising it. Because homosexuality was a crime many people were blackmailed and consequently homosexuals were excluded (rather unsuccessfully) from certain occupations where blackmail might be a problem. Now homosexuality is legal in the UK and gay couples can legally be married. Each year parliament in the UK alters the criminal law by adding some activities, making them new offences, and removing others and therefore legalising some activities. So the activities which are prohibited and permitted in the UK are constantly changing. Furthermore, at one time in England and Wales suicide was a crime and those who attempted suicide were punished, those who succeeded could not be buried in consecrated ground, and often their families were shunned. Suicide (or attempted suicide) was legalised under the Suicide Act 1961 but even today families sometimes feel shame if a relative commits or attempts suicide. Despite this stigma there is now in England and Wales a social movement which is trying to legalise assisted suicide of those who are terminally ill; a number of states have already legalised this type of behaviour (Switzerland, Germany, Japan, Canada, and some states in the USA such as Washington). This proves that the criminal law alters over time. Societies alter over time and their values change; it is therefore important that the criminal law alters to ensure that it continues serving the needs of a particular society.

However, the malleability of the criminal law is not always advantageous to citizens. Possibly most damaging is the fact that because states choose which activities to criminalise and how to pursue those who offend, many activities are rarely criminalised. Therefore whilst laws, including the criminal laws, are socially constructed, the shape they take depends on the priorities of the law makers, often very powerful people in society. Today one of the activities most feared is terrorism and most states have laws which prohibit both acts which cause terror (such as murder) as well as specialist terrorist activities. In this way one would expect that our governments try their best to ensure that we are safe from terrorism. However, throughout history most of the very worst acts of terrorism have been carried out by people working for the state. State sanctioned terror of this sort is rarely illegal within a state.

Historical examples are the persecution and murder of Jews in Nazi Germany; the Cambodian genocide (often called the 'killing fields', where more than a million people were killed by Pol Pot's Khmer Rouge regime between 1975 and 1979, see **Figure 3.2**); the many human rights violations including killings committed by the state in Myanmar (Burma) since the 1960s; the mass killing of Tutsis by the Hutus in the Rwandan genocide of 1994 and then the expulsion of Hutus by the Tutsis when they regained power about 100 days later. None of these acts were considered criminal within the states at the time; the perpetrators were often following state orders. Occasionally the international community acts as in the Nuremberg trials of 1945–46 and International Criminal Tribunal for

Figure 3.2 Human skulls of victims of the Khmer Rouge at the Killing Fields of Choeung Ek Memorial, Phnom Penh, Cambodia.
Source: © khlungcenter/Shutterstock.com

Rwanda (ICTR), 1994. However, very often the international community fails to do anything because the acts of terror are considered an internal, state, matter as in the case of Myanmar and Cambodia. These are extreme examples, but they demonstrate that what is defined as a crime by a state is socially constructed and that this shaping of the rules generally serves those in power at the time. This means that not only is crime a social construct but it is shaped to fit the interests (cultural, political, and economic) of those in power. Very often their interests coincide with those of the wider population and then the areas controlled by the criminal law can be seen as acceptable to the broader population, but this is not always the case.

Outside state activity (and state atrocities), what becomes called a crime often turns on what the public wants—or more usually on what a strong or powerful social movement wants—to be prohibited or controlled.

Public perceptions of crime and how they shape the law

The criminalisation of many activities by the state is supported by most of the wider public, who disapprove of the people who participate in such activities. They talk negatively about this behaviour as being 'criminal', and this marks it out as being significantly worse than behaviour that is merely naughty or unpleasant. Those who participate are called criminals and are often excluded from 'good' society; they are stigmatised and unacceptable as friends and colleagues. This exclusion often arises when the activity has a clear victim such as violence or theft, especially if that victim is another individual. This sort of common-sense feeling that one should not harm other people is a deeply engrained ethos and is part of most societies, including ours in the UK. It is often discussed under the **harm principle** for criminal laws (this suggests that activities should only be crimes if they harm other people for more information—see 'The harm principle' section later). However, the exclusion of another person due to criminal activity may also arise where there is no clear victim but where the activity has become ingrained in society as being unacceptable. For example the use of illegal substances which, although no one is harmed apart from the user, might be seen as immoral or that criminalisation is necessary to protect the individual from themselves (this is known as paternalism). Exclusion and unacceptability can be taken even further. For example, parents may try to stop their children playing with other children whose parents are criminals as they are thought of as 'bad sorts' even though the children have done nothing wrong.

Whilst the public generally considers crime to be wrong and unacceptable, each crime will be seen as more or less heinous or unacceptable (see **What do you think? 3.1**). For example, if a worker steals pens and paper from their employer most would not vilify them in the same way as if they had done the same thing from a shop or an individual's home. Somehow we talk about theft from employers as a 'perk of the job' or as fiddling or pilfering, and this bending of the language allows us to refrain from thinking of people who do this as criminals and therefore from excluding them from society. This flexibility over what is acceptable often covers things we might have done (such as taking things from work) and allows us to still feel good about ourselves (we are not really bad, let alone actual criminals). For example, many think that lying on a tax form and so cheating HM Revenue and Customs (HMRC) is maybe not as bad as theft, and neither is bringing in more goods than

are permitted from abroad (cheating HMRC again). Similarly, many of us tell ourselves that everybody drives a little too fast sometimes so it is excusable even if a little unacceptable (while we know that it is actually illegal). Generally people who do these things are not excluded until someone is harmed, e.g. in a traffic accident caused by excess speed. Even when someone is injured in a driving accident and the speeding driver is at fault, quite often friends and family will not exclude the driver, they may remember the times they have exceeded the speed limit and consider the driver unfortunate. In fact the crime of death by dangerous (or reckless) driving which was introduced in the Road Traffic Act 1956 was only necessary because juries were reluctant to convict a fellow driver of manslaughter. By 1991 this law was focused almost entirely on the nature of the driving rather than the intent to cause harm, again increasing the likelihood that a jury would convict.

We have so far noted that the concept of crime can vary according to culture, the suggestion being that each state or society has a set of agreed standards. However, societies are more complex than that. Different groups in a society may have different standards or ideas of what is criminal or deviant. So a group of youths may applaud another youth who defaces someone's property with graffiti, whereas the owners of the property and others in the neighbourhood may want that person prosecuted and punished, and see them as bad or deviant people who should be excluded from society. In fact, the owner and the others in the neighbourhood may well wish to exclude not just the person who actually drew the graffiti but also those who applauded her, they may consider the whole group to be delinquent. Even if no crime is committed by anyone in the group, the adults may still consider the whole group as 'bad'. If the group of young people sit on a street corner or hang around a park others in the community may feel intimidated by them even if they do nothing wrong except to be a little noisy and call out to people on the street. We therefore also need to look at the intersection of groups within a society.

In summary, what makes up the criminal law and how those who break the law are treated are both very complicated areas of discussion. Each depends on the society you are considering and the period of history you are looking at. For most of the rest of this chapter we will focus on England and Wales today, in 2017. Our first journey will be to look briefly at the difference between crime and deviance. Our second will be to find out how a society may decide which actions to criminalise and our third will be to look at some of the legal requirements of criminalisation. Our fourth will be to briefly question whether we should have criminal laws at all, and whether criminalising activity may cause more harm than it solves.

WHAT DO YOU THINK? 3.1

- Can you think of any unlawful activities (such as stealing pens from a company in the example earlier) that are considered to be more acceptable than others?

- Think about yourself; have you ever done something that is technically against the law? How did you justify this?

- If that same activity was looked down upon by your immediate community or peers, would this be more of a deterrent against committing the act again than the fact it is illegal?

- If you knew that your parents would find out would that prevent you from participating in the activity?

Crime and deviance

Many criminologists discuss 'deviance' rather than crime. They construct theories which explain why people may be deviant rather than why they offend. Are deviance and crime different and, if so, how? Deviance is almost always a wider concept than crime. It includes behaviour that is different, out of the ordinary or not accepted but is not legally controlled. In general usage, to say that behaviour is deviant simply means that it is odd or unacceptable. In sociology, deviant behaviour is outside the acceptable standards of behaviour in a society, particularly the social or sexual standards of behaviour. It generally includes all kinds of crimes, from the petty, such as stealing a chocolate bar, all the way through to murder. So an act can break social rules (be deviant) and break legal rules (be a crime), but it also includes behaviour which is not criminal. Deviance is very much based on the cultural standards in a society, or even the cultural expectations of a part of a society.

Social rules and norms

Most societies have an unwritten though largely accepted set of norms (rules, standards, or values) which members of that society are expected to live by. These are social rules and not legally enforceable. The norms or rules are specific to each culture; what is deviant in one society may not be deviant in another. In some Islamic societies (or parts of societies) women may be expected to wear the hijab or the burqa and failure to dress correctly would be considered deviant. Whereas in some societies wearing the hijab or burqa may be considered deviant, in France to wear a burqa in public is a *crime*. It is often not the behaviour which is deviant but the behaviour *in that context*. For example: it is perfectly acceptable to tackle someone and take their legs from under them in a rugby match, but to do that to someone on the street would be both deviant and a crime; to shout at a rugby match might be acceptable but to do so at an orchestral concert is generally not (it is deviant); to have sexual intercourse in the privacy of your own home is acceptable but to do so on the central reservation of a motorway would be deviant, maybe even criminal.

Even the acts at the centre of the most serious crimes are sometimes allowed, and even called for by a society in certain situations. For example, killing is generally considered to be a very serious crime (murder or manslaughter) but governments condone killing in some circumstances such as to defend yourself (you can use appropriate force to defend yourself, even if that results in the death of another person) or where it is accidental (a failed operation to try to help the patient), and even call on people to kill others in the act of war (see **What do you think? 3.2**).

The rules governing each society are complex, never written down, and are finely balanced, often difficult for an outsider to understand and live by. The way in which the rules are applied is often perplexing. For example, the actions of many heroes might just as easily be defined as deviant. Some criminal acts are not thought of as deviant, driving over 60 mph on the open road in England and Wales is a crime but is often thought of as normal rather than deviant behaviour.

Societies and parts of societies (often referred to as 'sub-cultures' in criminological writing) use positive and

---

WHAT DO YOU THINK? 3.2

Killing is a complex issue and there is a lot of disagreement about its nature; the way in which it is viewed will depend on the perspective of the individual and the society. These two famous quotes give a flavour of some of the disagreements:

> To my mind, to kill in war is not a whit better than to commit ordinary murder.
>
> Albert Einstein

> Kill a man, and you are an assassin. Kill millions of men, and you are a conqueror. Kill everyone, and you are a god.
>
> Jean Rostand, famous French botanist

Intentionally killing another gives rise to many of the most difficult questions about where to draw the line concerning what should be considered illegal killing (murder or manslaughter) and what should be condoned, or even glorified.

- If Alison intentionally kills Brian painlessly because Brian, who has a terminal illness and is in constant pain, begs her to, should that be murder or mercy killing?

- If Claire, a doctor, allows Daniel, who is very elderly, to die by withholding medical treatment (e.g. by not treating him when he falls ill or by turning off his life support machine) should that be murder or mercy killing?

Consider where illegal killing (murder and manslaughter) should begin. You need to be able to explain why you make your choices. You might like to compare your choice with the criminal law of England and Wales.

negative reinforcements (encouragements or punishments) to try to ensure correct behaviour. This is called social control. It is a means whereby a society encourages people to conform to social norms. So a child will be praised for saying please and thank you in the right places; or a child will be told off and may have to stay late at school if they fail to do their homework. Similarly an adult who does as an employer asks/expects at work may get promotion, whereas one who is constantly late or fails to perform tasks correctly may lose their employment. None of these things is criminal but such means are used to enforce criminal laws. So if a person is violent to another they may be punished by imprisonment (the state punishment) and on release they may also be excluded from society, from getting a job, or from being accepted in certain groups (an outward display of societal disapproval which may feel like punishment).

Durkheim

Émile Durkheim (1858–1917) was a famous French sociologist who saw deviance as a normal and necessary part of people living together in social groups; he saw a certain level of deviance as an indication of a healthy society (Durkheim 1895). Durkheim considered that all groups of people had to set out certain agreed standards or values by which they should live and these boundaries allowed people to learn what was acceptable. Furthermore, there would always be someone in that group who would be tempted to break the expectation. However, within the group each person would set the boundaries in a slightly different place so there is always someone who is willing to break a particular rule. The fact that someone breaks the norm gives the rule a purpose: to try to prevent others from following suit and to allow the group to show what should happen in such circumstances, to show their idea of justice. It also allows the group to mark the deviant one out as different and as someone who should not be copied. If lots of people break one rule then the breach starts to become normal and the society may decide to change the rule: this deviance can lead to social change and renewal.

For example, as noted earlier, homosexuality used to be criminal. In 1967 it was legalised (for certain groups), however it remained a socially deviant behaviour. It has taken a long time for homosexuality to be accepted in England and Wales; it was only in 2013 that gay marriage was legalised (and the first marriages were not permitted to occur until March 2014). Some people still consider homosexuality to be deviant but the majority of society now considers this view itself to be deviant, and homosexuality to be as acceptable as heterosexuality. Furthermore, if a society treats certain acts as very deviant and punishes them very harshly then the frequency with which those acts occur reduces and then the society might notice people who break lesser rules. Durkheim argued that the society would become less tolerant of lesser infractions and treat them more seriously. For example, in many low crime areas people complain of very low level offences and will exclude people who maybe do not even break the criminal law but just fail to act in acceptable ways.

At this point, it is helpful to briefly summarise what deviance is:

- Deviance is any violation of social norms, values or expectations.
- It changes over time and is different in different cultures or societies.
- People who break the expectations are often called deviant.
- People who make the rules and decide who is deviant and how they should be treated have social power and can control others in the society.
- Possibly most important is to recognise that deviance is in the eye of the beholder—what one person classes as deviant another will not.

It is very important to remember this because many of the theories in this book try to explain why some people take part in deviant behaviour; they try to find the causes of deviance but if we fail to agree on what is deviant it becomes more difficult to explain or find causes for that behaviour (see **What do you think? 3.3**).

WHAT DO YOU THINK? 3.3

Consider which, if any, of the following is deviant:

- It is generally considered that people want to live and life is precious.
- If I am suffering a particularly unpleasant illness and want to end my own life am I deviant?

- If I ask someone to help me to achieve my goal of ending my life and they help me are they deviant?
- If I write a special scientific theory and win a Nobel prize I am clearly out of the ordinary but am I deviant?

- Alcohol is very common in our society, it is offered at almost all social functions and is used to denote celebration of success on many greetings cards. In such a society is:
    - an alcoholic deviant?
    - someone who does not drink deviant?

- In England and Wales the norm is to live as part of society. Does that mean that hermits are deviant?

- Is it deviant to cheat at cards? Is it deviant to chat when playing patience (card games against yourself)?

- Is it deviant to be rude to people?

- Is it deviant and/or criminal to become an eco-warrior?

- Is it deviant to fail to pick up after your dog fouls:
    - on the pavement?
    - in the park?
    - in the woods or the open countryside?

Why are some actions criminalised?

It is important to remember that crime is an activity that is prohibited by law in a particular state and for which the state can sanction you (punish you). It is also important to note that crimes in England and Wales differ from those in other countries (e.g. bigamy is criminal in England and Wales but permitted, and may even be the norm, in some other states) and that crimes in any state are constantly evolving: what was not criminal yesterday may be criminal today and vice versa.

Societies set out standards or boundaries for the behaviour of their members. Those who breach these are deviant. Not all deviant acts are crimes, many are just frowned upon. For example, in some societies it is thought to be deviant for a man to dress as a woman but this is not generally a criminal offence. Therefore crime is more than deviance so one needs to try to isolate the factor or factors that mark something out as worthy of criminalising. This is an important question as those in positions of influence need to have limits placed on their power. If members of a government could each choose things they merely did not like and have them criminalised then that would clearly be unacceptable. For example, burping might be criminalised and punishable with imprisonment, but most people would think that was absurd and unfair. What if the government decided to criminalise crossing the road, talking with your mouth full, showering or bathing or even breathing on Mondays? Need we go on? Without limits, without some guiding principles to decide whether an activity should be criminalised, justice would be left to chance.

The harm principle

Many suggest that the 'harm principle' might best serve as a standard by which to decide whether an activity should be criminal. By this principle any conduct or activity should normally be legal. It should only be made criminal if it harms other people. This was set out by John Stuart Mill (1806–73), an English philosopher. He stated the harm principle as:

> the only purpose for which power can be rightfully exercised over any member of a civilised community against his will is to prevent harm to others. His own good, either physical or moral, is not sufficient warrant. He cannot rightfully be compelled to do or forebear because in the opinion of others to do so would be wise or even right.
>
> Mill 1859: 6

If conduct is not harmful to others it should not be criminal even if we do not like it. For example, picking your nose does not harm others; people may find it disgusting and dislike it but it should not be criminal. Another example could be streaking (see **Figure 3.3**). Taking your clothes off does not harm anyone else. 'Harm' therefore needs to be a little more than something others dislike. The most complete discussion of the harm principle and where its limits lie was by Joel Feinberg (1984–88), who in four large volumes considers the issues in detail. Here we will only look briefly at some of the concerns and areas where there is still a lot of debate.

With any discussion of the harm principle there is always discussion about what constitutes harm. Does

Figure 3.3 Spectators look on as police attempt to restrain a streaker at an Australia v India cricket match, March 2008
Source: Duncan Yoyos, CC BY-SA 2.0

it need to be physical harm or will emotional or psychological harm count? And, if we include psychological harm, then what about actions which disgust me or offend my sensibilities? Each person who writes about harm disagrees about its limits (Mill 1859; Feinberg 1985). Is public nudity harmful or is it merely a moral issue? Does harm include acts of omission? If I fail to jump into a lake to save a drowning child or fail to stop to help someone injured in a car accident have I harmed them and, if so, should my failures be criminal? If you are a match as a donor should failure to donate a kidney be an offence?

These are very difficult questions which have concerned criminologists, lawyers, and philosophers for a long time. Sometimes understanding why the harm principle is important can help us to find answers to these questions. Many argue that applying the harm principle as the test for criminalising activities means that we are most likely to protect autonomy. Autonomy is the freedom to choose what you want to do free of external control. I should be able to choose to do lots of silly things. For example, I may choose to never step on the lines when I walk along the street, or to talk to myself all the time, to watch television for 15 hours a day, to lecture to students when they are hung over, to listen to advertising jingles, to only communicate through tweets: these choices may be a little strange to others but I am not harming anyone, so others should respect my right to make them. This is a sort of 'live and let live' policy; in any society there needs to be tolerance of others even if we find them a little odd. Just

because I find something odd or I dislike it does not mean that it causes me any harm.

If we only make actions criminal if they harm others then this protects for each of us the freedom to choose to act as we like. The harm principle also ensures that we are each also protected from the actions of others when they might harm us or might diminish our freedom of choice. As Isiah Berlin (1958) wrote, 'Freedom for the pike is death for the minnows' (at page 4, Berlin attributes the quote to Tawney though most people attribute it to Berlin); in other words the liberty of some must depend on the restraint of others. For example, if I save up money to travel to London (that is my autonomy or choice) and someone steals the money they not only steal my money but also my freedom to choose to spend it as I like and, in this instance, my freedom to travel to London. Society hopes that having a law against theft of this sort will make people less likely to steal from one another and so the law is intended to protect us all, to protect our autonomy.

Before progressing it is important to note that whilst the harm principle may allow a society to make an act criminal and to punish those who transgress, it does not require the society to make all harmful activities criminal. It is therefore a necessary (only things which are harmful should be crimes) but not a sufficient (not all things which are harmful must be made into crimes) test.

From this it is clear that the harm principle, as underlying why actions are made crimes, is attractive and few people argue against it. However, many consider that it is too vague to be of use in leading us to decide what to make criminal. It is therefore necessary to consider the limits of the idea in more detail. To do this we first need to look at what is included in harm.

Moral issues including offence and anxiety

Following on from what has been said earlier, the harm principle does not permit criminalising something just because it is immoral, just because it breaks the general norms of behaviour and others dislike it or find it offensive. To criminalise on moral grounds is usually referred to as legal moralism and involves prohibiting acts merely because they are offensive to the majority in that society, or because it is believed that if one fails to prohibit them they might destroy the very fabric of a society. In the past many acts were criminalised because they broke some of our moral codes, usually because they were against Christianity and performance of these acts might harm that religion or might question the divine authority, e.g. blasphemy, suicide, and many sexual practices.

However, as society in the UK has become more secular, more multi-cultural and multi-faith, it has moved away from the idea that the moral fibre of our society is fixed, is part of what defines our society and something which should be protected from change. One of the most famous arguments put forward on this was in the 1960s when England and Wales were first considering legalising homosexual acts between adults (then 21) in private and Lord Justice Devlin (1965) wrote a pamphlet arguing that it was important to retain homosexuality as illegal in order to protect the moral fibre of our society. For Devlin, the moral fibre of a society was essential to its existence and to fail to protect society against seriously immoral behaviour would lead to social disintegration and therefore prove harmful to society. Whilst this is a moral argument it might also have been seen as part of the harm principle by claiming that the moral standing of a society was necessary to a healthy society. Whilst few would now align themselves with Devlin we retain many criminal laws which might be seen as part of legal moralism; laws such as the prohibition against nudity in public or the use of illegal substances, laws against common prostitution or against brothels, and laws that prohibit sadomasochism among consenting adults (this arose from *R v Brown* [1994] 1 AC 212) are just a few examples. Many would wish to retain these as crimes but it is very difficult to argue for their retention on anything other than moral (or maybe paternal) grounds. Take a look at **What do you think? 3.4**.

The simple harm principle offers little in the way of resolving the issue put forward in **What do you think? 3.4**, however there are possible solutions. Feinberg (1985: Chapter 8) suggested that where something might cause serious offence then it is harmful and could be prohibited.

WHAT DO YOU THINK? 3.4

One day Ellen and Fred are enjoying a picnic in the local park. It is a very warm day and they decide to remove their clothes, to feel free. Other visitors to the park have different reactions: some find it amusing; others find it odd but are willing to tolerate it; many are offended, some even outraged by their behaviour. Ellen and Fred argue that they are getting a lot of pleasure from the feeling of freedom they get from not wearing clothes and allowing the sun to warm their whole bodies, that it does not harm anyone and that they should not be judged by the moral standards of others. Those who are offended by their nudity want them to put their clothes back on. Some of them say that they are so genuinely upset by the nudity that they will feel excluded from using the park unless such behaviour is prohibited, they will feel they have to curtail their freedom to use the park.

What do you think should happen? Should Ellen and Fred be free to go nude in the park? Should society make it clear that nudity is not acceptable, maybe even label it as deviant so that some in the community might treat them less favourably because they take their clothes off? Should it be made criminal so that Ellen and Fred will be punished if they remove their clothes when in the park?

This is a difficult case to decide. To force Ellen and Fred to wear clothes because others are offended is to criminalise the activity on largely moral grounds, because it offends some people and this goes against the harm principle. It interferes with Ellen and Fred's autonomy and does not harm others. Mill would argue that an individual 'cannot rightfully be compelled to do or forebear because in the opinion of others to do so would be wise or even right' (Mill 1859: 6). However, to fail to prevent nudity will lead those offended to feel their experience and feelings are less important. In this case they may also feel they have to exclude themselves from the park, and possibly even from other places too as Ellen and Fred might choose never to wear clothes.

He describes 'serious offence' as being more than causing squeamishness, disgust, or being unpleasant. He suggests that to qualify the activity should cause a psychological reaction or emotional trauma (shock, maybe) in someone of a normal disposition (not overly susceptible to offence) and to test for this one should consider the intensity, duration, and extent of the feeling.

The offence becomes more serious if a large proportion of the population find it more than just unpleasant. This is not really measurable and therefore he also suggests that even if there is such a reaction, if individuals can reasonably avoid the behaviour which causes them to feel that way it should not be criminal. They can avoid the park but is it reasonable to expect them to do that, especially if it is the only one in their area? Furthermore, Ellen and Fred might decide to wander around town with no clothes and then it would not be reasonable to expect others to avoid them. If sufficient numbers of people are seriously offended by public nudity and it is not something they can reasonably and easily avoid if it were to be legalised then Feinberg argues that it should remain criminal and he seems to argue for this outcome because serious offence is akin to harm. Clearly there would be a strong argument for setting aside part of the park for nudity. For Feinberg there is a two pronged test: is the activity seriously offensive; can it be reasonably avoided? Now try applying this test to the other crimes noted earlier: the use of illegal substances; laws against common prostitution or against brothels; laws that prohibit sadomasochism among consenting adults. Take a look at another example, in **What do you think? 3.5**.

In that example, there may only be a few people of that race in the society and others may not care. Today many

WHAT DO YOU THINK? 3.5

A young woman, Gwen, visits a local 24-hour shop late in the evening to pick up some small items for her family for the next morning. Just outside the shop she is verbally attacked by two young men, Huw and Joe, that she has never seen before and who have never seen her before. They are shouting racial hatred at her. She is very shaken by the events but was not physically attacked and no one in the shop thought twice about it, they see it as a bit insulting but nothing more.

- What do you think would/should happen in this type of case?

- What would be the outcome of applying Feinberg's rule to the situation?

would argue such speech should still not be permitted. Why? Because it offends some people or is there something more? How might this best be considered? Does hate speech differ from insulting speech or behaviour? In many ways it does not and is merely offensive; each is usually aimed at someone, Gwen in this example, and is intentionally used to hurt someone's feelings. However, many consider that hate speech goes further: it hurts or harms a whole race (or other group) so there is or may be a particular victim (Gwen) but there is also a whole race (or other group) which is attacked. The perpetrator(s) of such speech, in our example Huw and Joe, chose the victim (Gwen) because of what that person represents—here a racial group, but it might also be religion, sexual orientation, etc., or what the perpetrator thinks they represent and what he/she disapproves of or hates (what Huw and Joe hate). The harm is intentional or at least done knowing it is likely to offend. Furthermore, the victim or immediate target (as arguably the whole group is victimised) is chosen because of something they cannot change—their race or sexual orientation— or could only change by denying a core part of who they are—their religion—so they cannot really escape vulnerability.

These factors mark racial hatred out as different from other insults and actions which may cause offence. Feinberg (1985: Chapter 8) allows for this eventuality by calling on a society to take into account the personal importance of the behaviour to the actor himself and whether it serves any social value. Racial hatred may be important to the person espousing it, they may believe in the truth of what they say and wish to enjoy freedom of speech to express themselves; however, the social value of such speech is low, if not negative. Furthermore, Feinberg also calls on society to take account of two other things. Firstly, where and when the conduct took place; could the freedom to express these views have been enjoyed somewhere else or at a different time? Secondly, the extent to which there was a spiteful intention. These last two would often permit the normal freedom of speech to be interfered with in relation to racial hatred as it is most inflammatory when it takes place in public and/or is directed at those most likely to be offended.

What do you think? 3.6 provides examples of activities in which it is assumed that if there is consent there should be no crime. Without consent the first would be rape and the second actual or grievous bodily harm (ABH or GBH depending on the extent of the injuries). Therefore in the absence of consent both situations would be crimes because they would harm the non-consenting participants. However, if there is true consent there is no harm (except that consented to and welcomed) so the only reason to criminalise is, arguably, the protection of morals. Dempsey (2005) would disagree and argues that in the first example there is potential harm which is so great that we need to

WHAT DO YOU THINK? 3.6

Example 1: Olwen is 20 and a prostitute. Peter regularly visits her to pay for sex.

- Is there any crime in this scenario?
- Should it be possible to prosecute Peter for his behaviour?
- Is Peter's behaviour harmful?

Note: If Olwen willingly consents then arguably there is no harm—it is a victimless activity so should not be a crime at all. Many argue that morals provide the only reason for this being a crime.

Example 2: Kevin, Linda, Mary, and Nick are all adults and good friends. They are also sadomasochists who meet regularly to participate in sadomasochism for sexual gratification. They all consent to the behaviour and each of them enjoys it equally, no one is being exploited.

This behaviour is criminal.

- Should it be?
- Is it harmful?

Note: If they all consent and no one is exploited it would seem that there is no harm apart from harm to self (as assessed by others) or moral indignation that anyone should find this behaviour sexually gratifying.

These are both examples of activities which might be criminalised merely because some people find them immoral. Is that acceptable?

protect against it by criminalising all sale of sexual favours. She argues that when someone pays for sex they cannot be sure that the prostitute is willingly consenting. The prostitute may appear willing but may have been trafficked, been forced by a pimp to prostitute herself, or may be too young to consent. In the first two instances the central crime is by another person, the trafficker or the pimp, not Peter. In all three, without the consent Peter would be guilty of a sexual offence. Presumably the situation is similar in the case of the sadomasochists, where a third party may traffic or otherwise pressurise someone to participate to provide sexual gratification. Where, for example, Kevin and Linda have been trafficked and are being paid to inflict pain on Mary and Nick, there may be no harm to Kevin and Linda and the harm to Mary and Nick is consensual (paid for even) so still there should be no crime.

Under the harm principle it is only if someone does not fully consent that a crime is committed. To criminalise without direct harm and in case there is a harm (such as people trafficked for prostitution) is known as controlling due to remote harm. The decision in *R* v *Brown* [1994] 1 AC 212 (at 246) opened up another type of remote harm; the judges were concerned that others, particularly children, might be tempted to imitate and so participate in sadomasochistic acts. Many would argue that remote harm takes harm too far (see, for example, Baker 2007) and the law should seek to prosecute the direct wrongdoers (the trafficker and the pimp) rather than the person who buys the sexual favour. Husak (2007), for example, would suggest that no one should face criminal charges because of a remote harm unless:

they have some degree of culpability for the ultimate harm risked. It is not enough that the performance of the proscribed conduct just happens to make the occurrence of the ultimate harm more likely.

Husak 2007: 174

Therefore in our examples Peter's conduct should not be criminalised unless his actions make the conduct (the trafficking) more likely. Some might argue they do. However, in this sort of example remote harm is hiding a moral wrong—here maybe not the sexual morals but the exploitation of certain groups, particularly women. In some instances people are trafficked to work on farms or to clean people's homes (where they may work as slaves, unpaid, and unable to leave). Does that mean that we should outlaw the hiring of farm labourers or domestic cleaners? Is a proposition made in relation to prostitution partly on moral grounds and partly to protect a vulnerable group—women—from being exploited? Dempsey would recognise that where there is genuine consent buying sex involves no direct harm, but would find that potentially there is a very serious harm (rape); there is no social gain in selling sex so she would argue that criminalising Peter's activity should be acceptable. This is not the same in the case of farm labourers and domestic cleaners who provide what others see as a positive benefit to society, to get food on the table or have a clean house. This appears to ignore the moral dilemma until one asks why there is no social gain to selling sexual favours—surely it is because we consider it to have less worth (morally or ethically) than other occupations, though arguably it fulfils a sexual need. Why is this less valuable than a need for a clean house?

Harm to self

Where my behaviour harms someone else it clearly falls within the harm principle and is activity which may be criminalised. However, what about behaviour which only harms me? The harm principle does not normally protect people from themselves. Rock climbing may be dangerous and to do it without proper equipment may not be in my best interests, but it should not be a crime and I should be allowed to take part in rock climbing even if it is not very sensible, as long as it does not harm other people. Here the argument is that harm (or potential harm) to me should not be sufficient; this certainly falls in line with Mill's principle (1859) which refers to 'harm to others' and specifically states that 'His own good, either physical or moral, is not sufficient warrant' (Mill 1859: 6).

When something is designed to protect the actor from him- or herself it is generally called paternalism and can be defined as actions for the good of an adult (to protect their life, health, or safety) when they do not choose to be protected; the interference is at the expense of their liberty or autonomy. Generally paternalism should not be sufficient

to make an action criminal, though there are examples of paternalism in our criminal laws, e.g. requiring people to wear seat belts in cars or helmets on motorbikes. Each of these is paternalistic, although some suggest that each prevents greater reliance on the health service, so saving all taxpayers money, and that helmets have the knock-on effect of reducing theft of motorbikes. Whilst there may be harm elements to them when one searches for the reasons for their having been made into criminal laws (by looking at the parliamentary debates), there is no escaping the fact that they are paternalistic. Under the harm principle these criminal laws are difficult to justify. However, requiring the wearing of a seatbelt or helmet is a small infringement on freedom and autonomy and does not impinge one's life choices so some argue that these kinds of laws should be tolerated. Furthermore, it is argued that if one suggested seatbelts and helmets to rational people and explained all the reasons for using them, they would opt for them. These arguments may be true but do not prevent the requirement to wear a belt/helmet or face a criminal penalty being any less paternalistic. There are also other examples which may interfere more with real life choices or which rational people might well reject (**What do you think? 3.7**).

WHAT DO YOU THINK? 3.7

Quentin, Rachel, and Simon are all 18 and each of them uses illegal substances.

Quentin smokes cannabis regularly as he enjoys how mellow it makes him feel (see **Figure 3.4**). He does not drink alcohol as he believes this is more harmful. When his friends drink he notices that they become aggressive and attack other people and he does not want this to happen to him. Cannabis never makes him feel aggressive. He sometimes thinks about the law and about the

feeling of unease he gets from the people he meets to buy his drugs.

Rachel uses party drugs and sometimes some cocaine or similar substances. She is studying to be a lawyer and when she unwinds she likes the feeling drugs give her of losing herself and letting go of all her tensions. But Rachel is very worried that if she is caught using illegal drugs she will lose her chance of becoming a lawyer. She used to try to stay ahead of the law and to use 'legal highs', though she worried a lot about how dangerous these might be as their effects were still unknown. She knows that there is now no such thing as legal highs but she continues to buy her drugs over the Internet as she feels safer sourcing them that way. Now she worries both about what the chemicals are doing and that just by possessing the drugs she is breaking the law.

Simon is addicted to heroin. He would like to give it up but all his friends use and he cannot see a life beyond using. He craves the drug's effect but hates what it is doing to him.

Figure 3.4 Cannabis is a class-B illegal drug
Source: © Amihays/Shutterstock.com

- Should their drug use be criminal? Is it harmful?

- Is the harm caused by using the substance or by the fact that the substance is illegal?

In all three of these examples some people might argue that each individual is being harmed by the substance. However, it might be more accurate to say that they are being harmed by the criminalisation of the behaviour. See **Table 3.1** for a discussion about the relative harms caused by drug use and by trying to control its use.

Therefore whilst many substances (some of which are already legal) are harmful to individual users a lot of the harm from substances comes from their misuse and some of this is exacerbated due to the criminalisation of certain substances. There is also little proof that criminalisation performs useful functions. This is an argument made by many academics and some police officers for legalisation, or at least a more harm-based approach to the resolution of issues caused by substance misuse (Brunstrom 2007; see more generally Drug Equality Alliance and the Film Exchange on Alcohol and Drugs).

Harms from drugs	Hoped benefits of criminalisation	Harms at least partially caused by criminalising drugs	Harms better addressed through other means
Many of these drugs harm the health of users	Reduced use. Does this happen?	Criminalising may increase some harms. Individual harm to the user may be increased—addiction and other health problems. Harm to the community may increase—theft to pay for drugs	Would the harms be better addressed through health care?
Addiction	Reduced use. Does this happen?	Criminalisation renders it more difficult to request help	Better addressed through health care (for the addiction) and social care (to support reintegration of users into communities)
Death or health problems from the drugs. Some drugs are very dangerous to health, often only for some people. Some drugs cause temporary or permanent mental health problems for some people	Reduced use. Does this happen?	Dealers were constantly trying to beat the criminal law by inventing new legal highs but their effects on humans are unknown. In 2016 these were all criminalised as the state felt that was the best way to deal with the problem. However, the potential harm new drugs might cause could be reduced if drugs were legal but their purchase was regulated. Many people might wait for new substances to be tested	
Death or other health problems for added substances		Criminalisation causes a black market and increases the dangers. Many dealers add substances, often very dangerous substances, which may kill users	Legalise and sell by licence—these problems would not then arise as the content of each substance would be checked
Overdose		Adding even inert (non-dangerous) substances to drugs is dangerous as each dose has a different level of purity. Using the same weight each time does not provide the same amount of drug and an almost pure dose may lead to accidental overdoses	Overdose or other health problems can only be addressed through health care. Users and their friends are more likely to seek health care if they are not afraid of facing criminal charges. Accidental overdoses could be avoided if drugs were legalised and licensed as their strength would be checked and they would be carefully labelled

Harms from drugs	Hoped benefits of criminalisation	Harms at least partially caused by criminalising drugs	Harms better addressed through other means
Many illegal drugs interfere with the ability of users to work	Might reduce drug use and so reduce the effects on the economy		
These drugs interfere with the ability of users to safely perform tasks such as driving	Might reduce drug use and so reduce the risk of danger to the public		
Black market		Criminalising the behaviour causes a black market to arise	Legalise and sell by licence; the black market would shrink if not die out completely
		Otherwise law-abiding people who want to use drugs have to turn to criminals to obtain them. Users may (because of this association with offenders) be excluded from general society and find it harder to continue with their law-abiding life	Legalise and sell by licence. Law-abiding users would then not need to seek out offenders to obtain their drugs. Home Office estimates that about 11 million people have used illicit drugs (Brunstrom 2007); this is a lot of people to criminalise
		Drug prices are often higher because dealers take chances. People turn to crime in order to obtain the money necessary to purchase the drugs	Legalise and sell by licence—prices might reduce and fewer users would need to commit crime to obtain drugs
Some drugs such as cannabis are seen as trigger drugs leading people to try other substances		If users have to turn to dealers to obtain substances the dealers are going to try to sell them increasingly expensive and more addictive drugs to ensure they have a market	Legalise and sell by licence—if done intelligently, this escalation might be prevented though the licensing system; needs to be more carefully considered than that which covers alcohol
Call offenders to account		Uses large amounts of expensive police and court time. Could this money be better used in other ways? Also affects many people's lives: over half (52%) of all arrestees interviewed reported drug use in the month prior to arrest (30% were dependent on heroin or crack cocaine (Boreham, et al. 2007)). Would more health and social care be more effective?	
Some legal substances are as harmful (sometimes more harmful) than illegal substances	Criminal law cannot help to prevent harms from legal substances		Medical and social interventions would be better placed to deal with the harms of both presently legal and presently illegal substances (Nutt et.al. 2007)

Table 3.1 Harms caused by the use and control of drugs

Indirect harm

At a number of points in this chapter harm has been mentioned as something which does not directly hurt an individual but is more indirect, e.g. not wearing a seatbelt means more people will suffer serious injuries due to accidents and therefore the cost to the National Health Service will rise and cost the taxpayer more. There are many other examples such as non-payment of taxes or erroneous application for benefits. There may also be cases where there is the capacity to do harm but as yet no harm has been done and no harm may arise; examples include breaches of health and safety, carrying weapons such as knives or guns, acts preparatory to an offence (planning a robbery and starting to collect the items necessary to carrying it out), or acts which might lead to something like an act of terrorism.

These are an eclectic collection of crimes which are awkward to explain under the harm principle as there is no clear 'other' who is harmed. Von Hirsch (1996) argues that the harm principle can be extended to encompass at least some of these remote or indirect harms if there is a strong public interest which has been or might be breached, e.g. it is harmful to us all if too much money is spent on car accidents or too little collected via taxation or if our streets are made potentially more dangerous because people take potentially harmful items out with them and do not intend to do anything useful with those items—so a car is potentially dangerous but serves the purpose of moving people and things around whereas a gun is dangerous and rarely serves any useful purpose. Therefore it is possible to explain these offences using the harm principle but this needs great care as the argument could permit the state to interfere in our lives in many and surprising ways by claiming it is for the public good. Certainly Ashworth and Zedner (2008) have suggested that the way in which the criminal law is being used now is too broad and is used to manage social order, for easy governance and control, rather than to protect the public.

The limits of the harm principle

The harm principle has many limitations: just because something is harmful does not mean that it should be criminalised (Duff 2007). If I go to work with a cold I may be contagious and cause harm to my colleagues but that should not be a criminal act. So it is not logical to say 'actions should be criminalised if they are harmful to others'. You can say: 'the state should not criminalise activities which are not harmful to others'; or 'if an action is harmful then the state may be sensible to consider whether it should be criminalised'. In other words, harm to others acts as a gatekeeper. It should be necessary to show that an activity harms others before you criminalise it, but that alone should not be sufficient grounds to say an activity should be criminalised. As Gardner states:

> [t]he harm principle says that the law should not be used to restrict or punish harmless activities. ... it adds that the law should not restrict or punish harmful activities in ways which are disproportionate to the harm. But beyond this, it says nothing about how, or even when, harmful activities should be dealt with by the law.
>
> Gardner 1994: 213–14

In conclusion, the harm principle is useful to test which activities should *not* be criminalised but is not very useful in deciding which activities should be criminalised.

Other reasons which might explain why some actions are crimes

If we return to our starting point, setting out the need for criminal law as being an arbiter between individual freedoms and harmonious social living, including social interactions, then this provides both the impetus towards which acts to criminalise and the reason for limiting the actions which attract a criminal sanction. Basically criminalisation, especially when backed up with punishment, is designed to limit freedom of choice of citizens (to choose to do something they might want to do) and is harmful, so it should only be used if there is a very good reason which justifies a particular act being made criminal. If a state interferes with the rights and freedoms of an individual in cases where there is no harm to others or no acceptable reason for the intervention then it is an abuse of power and prevents individuals from enjoying their freedoms. (Henry and Milivanovic 1996). Clearly, some state interference is necessary to protect some people from the abuse of power or rights by others. Therefore many argue that some criminal law is necessary:

> Human beings are individuals, and being able to express that individuality in one's choices and actions is an essential component of human well-being. Alongside the individuality of human beings, however, their other most noticeable characteristic is sociability. ... If individual freedom is a precondition of human flourishing so, too, is membership of communities and groups, and a rich network of social interactions.
>
> Cane 2006: 23

Some even take this further arguing that the communal good should take precedence over individual freedom. So Cane goes on to say:

> individual freedom would have little or no value in the absence of external constraints. In this light, it seems hard to justify giving the individual's interest in freedom of choice lexical priority over the interest in social cooperation and coordination.
>
> Cane, 2006: 23

Cane is correct to note that without criminal law the freedoms of many might be reduced but does he go too far when he suggests that the group should be prioritised over the individual? In some situations the group interests may be strong. For example, earlier we considered the case for making racial hatred a crime where other verbal abuse should escape. The discussion was based on individual issues. Here the community or group interest will be considered. Marshall and Duff (1998) suggest that a community may need to protect its values because some of these:

> are so central to a community's identity and self-understanding, to its conception of its members' good, that actions which attack or flout those values are not merely individual matters ... but attacks on the community.
>
> Marshall and Duff 1998: 21–2

They do not indicate which values fall in to this category but in modern Britain racism may breach the value to respect each person equally. The question still arises as to whether this should attract a criminal level of control by that community; is the community permitted to harm the perpetrator because they breach that value? Presumably we only need to criminalise actions which are so dangerous to society as to necessitate the use of punishment if someone breaches the value. Marshall and Duff were silent on which values should be protected in that way. However, they argued it was an enquiry which should be made and they wanted to place community values at the centre of deciding which actions should be criminalised (presumably to replace or rival the harm principle).

There is certainly a need to look again at the harm principle. As seen earlier, many of our criminal laws permit punishment despite the absence of direct harms: dangerous driving, attempted robbery (attempted anything), selling firearms, selling or dealing in drugs or any other illicit substance, selling infected meat, controls to protect public hygiene, firing a gun (not on a firing range or at a gun club), almost all driving offences (speeding, no lights, on the wrong side of the road), health and safety at work, rules governing some professions (e.g. training for a doctor); one might also include Olwen and Peter's case in **What do you think? 3.6** (visiting the prostitute who may have been trafficked). None of these necessarily or directly involves any harm so why are they prohibited? They increase the possibility or risk of harm occurring. For example, all the driving offences may increase danger on the road and whilst one may be careful to speed (or break other rules) only when one can see there is no problem ahead and would not do so around bends, the risk is still there and it would not be sensible or possible to check in each case what the intention of the driver was. The sale of firearms does not cause harm unless and until the purchaser shoots someone but there is no other use for a firearm other than for shooting; therefore the seller needs to ensure that the gun is only to be used for sporting purposes. Crowbars are often used in burglary but their sale is not similarly restricted as they have legitimate uses in the building trade.

There is a need to look carefully at our criminal laws to ascertain whether each and every one of them should remain criminal or whether they could be dealt with through other processes. Most people would use the harm principle at the core of this test, some might use values as the core and some might use regulation. Some things need to be regulated for the smooth running of a society and sometimes this may require use of the criminal law. For example, we need to specify which side of the road cars should travel on. There is nothing safe about driving on the left and dangerous about driving on the right or vice versa. It is just that each state needs to specify which side they will use because if the decision is left to individuals the dangers of road travel would be immense. Road travel is, in many cases, a public good which needs to be facilitated but people also need to be protected from unnecessary harms or dangers, so regulation is used to deliver a safe mode of transport.

Others may rely on societal values (Marshall and Duff 1998) to decide what should be criminalised, i.e. whether there are any acts so awful as to offend against the values of our society. Many would argue that violent killing not only harms the victim but also attacks our view of the sanctity of life. This may be true but the real question is whether in the absence of harm (or only minimal harm) to an individual there should still be an offence (see the sadomasochist case of Kevin, Linda, Mary, and Nick in **What do you think? 3.6**). In some cases all three may come together but none be sufficient alone to argue for criminalisation. For example, what should happen about pollution by an industry? There may be some harm from each factory or other working unit, though the pollution by each alone may not be sufficient to harm anyone; however, when others in the industry behave in a similar manner the cumulative effect may be very large, e.g. the cumulative effect of substances farmers have put on their fields being washed into rivers. There may be a need to regulate the use of or disposal of certain substances by all in certain industries in order to prevent this cumulative problem of pollution which might adversely affect the health of many people. This might also affect a value of a community, respect for the environment. Should individuals then be criminalised if they dispose of their rubbish in a way which might be harmful, e.g. dropping litter in the street or failing to recycle rubbish, and if they breach societal expectations should they face conviction and punishment under the criminal law?

If we permit these ideas of protection from harm, regulation, and values to be used together are we allowing too much power to those who make the criminal laws? Might they use and abuse that power to restrict our freedoms in an illegitimate way? Later chapters will explore the way in which power can be used to protect certain parts of a society. Arguably, actions of the powerful (e.g. tax evasion) are less severely treated than those of the powerless (e.g. benefit fraud) for this reason. Some see this as necessarily underlying all criminal laws. It is always those in power who set the rules, e.g. following a revolution, if the revolutionaries win then the acts of the previous government are often criminalised and vice versa. Therefore, whilst academics may try to rationalise the extent and content of the criminal law, it may be power and the protection of vested interests which finally decides this. This is problematic because if we glibly apply the harm or value principles it may be the harms and values of the powerful elite which are protected rather than the interests of the larger number of less powerful people in society (Vold, Bernard, and Snipes 2002; Alvesto and Tombs 2002; Tombs and Whyte 2003; Green and Ward 2004). This need not always be true; some groups may manage to be heard by those in power and may achieve protection for some vulnerable sections of society. For example, some feminists fought hard for the legal definition of domestic violence to be broadened to encompass domestic abuse, others to ensure that the laws protecting against sexual violence remained largely gendered (Jones 2004: 62). So some vulnerable groups may be heard whilst others are not. There is no justice in the way this happens and it might still be considered an abuse of power (see discussions concerning critical criminology in **Chapters 15** and **16**). However, leaving things to politicians and the elite led, between 1997 and 2010, to over 3,000 new criminal offences being created. Not all can possibly pass the standards set out here, so why were they passed and whose interests did they serve?

If one is to avoid this some have argued that we should rely on a widely accepted standard such as human rights. This is a system based on individual rights and autonomy (as claimed by the harm principle) but which recognises that certain rights should always be protected. Certainly international human rights conventions suggest that states must protect their citizens against some conduct. The European Convention of Human Rights (ECHR, which applies in the UK at the time of writing) requires states, under Article 3, to protect their citizens from torture and inhuman and degrading treatment. Not only are states required to refrain from torture or from using inhuman and degrading treatment, but they are also expected to ensure that no one in their country is subjected to such treatment at the hands of anyone else.

It is important to remember that the ECHR is completely separate from the European Union (EU). The former regulates our rights whereas the latter is much broader. In June 2016 the British people voted to leave the EU. The Conservative government (appointed in 2015) have expressed the wish to withdraw from the ECHR without consulting the people.

In a case from Germany, the European Court of Human Rights decided that police officers who threatened the applicant with imminent (though brief) pain in order to get information they hoped would save the life of his victim (a child; unfortunately he had already killed the child) were breaching the article because this was 'inhuman treatment' (*Gäfgen* v *Germany* (2011) 52 EHRR 1). In a decision involving the UK the same court decided that Parliament had failed to protect children because the level of chastisement parents are allowed to use to control their children permitted 'inhuman treatment' (*A* v *United Kingdom* (1999) 27 EHRR 611). Here, therefore, the state is obliged, under international law, to ensure that individuals are protected and one of the most sure ways of proving the state is fulfilling that obligation is to criminalise the activity, especially as any breaches in the case of Article 3 of the ECHR are likely to harm the individual as well as break the values of European nations that no individual should ever face torture or inhuman treatment at the hands of the state or any other person or group. Other aspects of the ECHR are similarly protected. There is a general expectation that individuals feel sufficiently secure to enjoy the freedoms guaranteed under the Convention such as, under Article 8, a family life; failure to protect against racial hatred might make people feel so insecure as to undermine their Article 8 rights, so offences of racial hatred might legitimately be criminalised.

This reliance on human rights brings an important difference: a system based on rights recognises that states (or those acting for them, such as presidents) can be perpetrators of criminal wrongs. Human rights put responsibilities on states to ensure the rights of their citizens. Here, therefore, those acting on behalf of states can offend; this is important and was at the core of human rights conventions and declarations post-Second World War. It underlies the United Nations conventions and the ECHR and the idea can be seen most clearly in the International Criminal Court (set up in 2002 to try people accused of serious international violations such as genocide, war crimes, and crimes against humanity).

WHAT DO YOU THINK? 3.8

Which, if any, of the following is, or should be, criminal:

- Is prostitution a criminal offence in England and Wales? Should it be?

- Is the use of heroin illegal in England and Wales? Should it be?

- Is the use of cannabis illegal in England and Wales? Should it be?

- Is shouting racist abuse a crime in England and Wales? Should it be?

- Alcohol is very common in our society, it is offered at almost all social functions and is used to denote celebration of success on many greetings cards. In such a society is:
  – an alcoholic deviant?
  – someone who does not drink deviant?

- In England and Wales the norm is to live as part of society. Does that mean that hermits are deviant?

- Is it deviant to cheat at cards? Is it deviant to chat when playing patience (card games against yourself)?

- Is it deviant to be rude to people?

- Is it deviant to pay a worker less than the minimum wage when the worker is prepared to work for very low wages?

The discussion on a rights based system has, so far, been based on the rights guaranteed under the ECHR or other international conventions, but some authors suggest they need not be bound to such legal documents. For example, Von Hirsch and Jareborg (1991) have a broader scheme, intended to protect four types of interests: physical integrity, privacy, autonomy, and freedom from humiliation or degrading treatment. Schwendinger and Schwendinger (1970) would go further, claiming that all violations of basic human rights should be considered to be criminal violations whether included in the criminal law or not. In many instances it would be state actors who would be the perpetrators so that the powerful in the state would be called to account when they breached internationally recognised standards of human rights and this would mean the criminal law would be a tool of rights rather than of state control. This might go too far. Not all violations of rights are best addressed through the criminal law, some might be controlled through other means so that a criminal law based on rights violations might, like that based on harm, go too far, criminalising minor instances, and might indeed lead to an abuse of power under the criminal law in punishing when no punishment is warranted. Having read this section now consider the examples in **What do you think? 3.8**.

Do we need the criminal law?

One question not yet addressed is whether we need the criminal law at all. Many critical criminologists have questioned whether several aspects of the criminal law are really needed, and even whether we require a criminal law at all. Those who fall into the latter category are often known as zemiologists. Zemiologists focus on harm rather than crime. Having just spent much of this chapter considering the harm principle and its place in the criminalisation of activities this may sound strange and you may think 'So what, what is the difference?'. The difference is enormous.

The criminal law is only interested in some harms, generally those where an individual can be blamed. Here, the feeling seems to be that intentional acts are more deserving of punishment than acts of indifference, this is questioned by Box (1983) and Pemberton (2004). If Tim intentionally kills Umar is it worse than Vernon, acting as part of a company, choosing to make and sell a dangerous product knowing that it will kill some people but uncaring about who they will be or how many will die? Or than Waine, a dictator, choosing to spend state money on sending a rocket to space, knowing that many who could have been saved will die in his country due to starvation because the money was spent on the space race rather than on food? In the clearly criminal case one person dies, a clear victim, but in both the others more than one will die; however they may not be considered at all by the criminal law and are unlikely to be considered victims in the same way. A further example of this is explored in **Controversy and debate 3.1**.

! CONTROVERSY AND DEBATE 3.1

Consider the opening scenes of the film 'Fight Club' (see **Figure 3.5**), when there is a conversation about how a fictional major car company makes decisions around recalling cars.

Narrator: A new car built by my company leaves somewhere traveling at 60 mph. The rear differential locks up. The car crashes and burns with everyone trapped inside. Now, should we initiate a recall? Take the number of vehicles in the field, A, multiply by the probable rate of failure, B, multiply by the average out-of-court settlement, C. A times B times C equals X. If X is less than the cost of a recall, we don't do one.

Woman on plane: Are there a lot of these kinds of accidents?

Narrator: You wouldn't believe.

Woman on plane: Which car company do you work for?

Narrator: A major one.

Do you think the narrator committed a crime, if so what is it? Has he acted in a deviant way? Has the company committed a crime, if so what is it? Can a company or a state commit a crime? We can't imprison a company so how can we punish them?

Controversially, financial considerations like this can supercede the potential of harm in decisions made by large companies.

Figure 3.5 *Fight Club* film poster
Source: *20th Century Fox/The Kobal Collection*

Many critical criminologists and zemiologists often view criminal harms as less serious harms than other major forms of harm. The criminal law, they argue, ignores many of the more serious harms people suffer, such as poverty, inadequate housing, poor diet, poor education, inadequate health care, unemployment, pollution, inequalities of treatment, inequality of opportunity, inequality of outcome, unsafe working conditions, unsafe environments, and so on (Hillyard and Tombs 2004). They ask us to consider all harms suffered by individuals, families, groups, or communities, however caused, and whether the harm be physical, psychological, cultural (especially cultural safety), or economic (Hillyard and Tombs 2004). These theorists suggest that all harm causes suffering and that the suffering from non-criminal harms may sometimes be greater than that from crime; not all socially harmful acts are crimes. They therefore question the prioritising of criminal harms over other harms and suggest that we should have more sympathy for those who suffer other harms and be angrier about the causes

of these other harms. Consequently they argue that we should strive to both redress the harm (however caused) and prevent further harm (from whatever source). More money and energy should be spent on resolving other harms, such as poverty, rather than just focusing on blaming and calling criminals to account.

Many of the examples already considered in this chapter, such as poverty, may be considered to be outcomes of the capitalist economic model prevalent in Western societies, but there are also social harms caused by other types of system, such as communism (especially the limiting of autonomy). Using broader ideas of harms may serve to question the way in which some of our criminal laws are framed (see the earlier discussion of harms in relation to substance misuse). It may also make us think more carefully about what is important and how to make our society safer (see the earlier examples of Umar, Vernon, and Waine). Who are the true victims, only direct victims of crime or also others who suffer? What is harm and what is harmful to either an individual or a community is not self-evident and needs to be carefully discussed. Who takes responsibility, how, and to what extent also needs to be teased out. These last questions are immensely problematic. For example, the responsibility issue is important. Clearly we do not wish to criminalise all activities that cause all forms of harm but if we are to address the problem and change things for the better, we need to understand what needs to be altered and how making these changes will reduce overall harm (Reiman 2006 and Pemberton 2004). You may wish to read the section in **Chapter 16** where zemiology is discussed in more depth.

Put simply, most critical criminologists recognise that life will always involve problematic and potentially harmful situations. Problematic situations and harm are a natural part of social living, There will always be some times when certain people are harmed and others benefit from that harm but the ideal is to influence society, its structures, and the individuals who live in our communities to reduce those situations as far as possible. It is also important to remember that some situations:

- are seen as problematic for all those directly concerned (all those facing a gunman are likely to feel fear at the prospect that they may be killed);
- are problematic for some of those directly involved (if the gunman only threatens those with blonde hair the others may feel relieved and their fear may dissipate);
- may not be considered problematic by any of those directly involved but people viewing things from the outside may consider them problematic (if the gunman tells them all it is a toy gun then it is only a problem for those not directly involved).

In each of these situations the problem may arise from different sources. Hulsman calls these frames of reference and suggests that for each frame of reference the action and need may differ. In a natural disaster such as a flood all those immediately involved will feel harmed but the

extent of that feeling may vary. The frame of reference for the cause of the harm will generally be natural; no one could have prevented it so there is no directed anger, just a need for help and support. In an accident, someone may be injured and there may be some responsibility, e.g. in Hulsman's example of a road accident one driver may be injured and one may have suffered a problem at work and/ or had a drink (though not enough to really interfere with their driving). He then splits resolution of the problem down into a number of frames of reference:

- This is a natural part of life—an accident—and then the community needs to do all it can to help the injured party to heal.
- If the accident resulted from a structural problem, a problem with the community, or social structures such as the way traffic is managed in that spot, then we should work to change that so as to prevent future harms.
- If one person is more to blame then the other may want compensation or for the other to be punished. If the victim is willing to forgive, then should the compensation/punishment be reduced? If the injured party is the one to blame then should the compensation/punishment reflect the injury they've already suffered? Why?

Hulsman goes through a number of examples but the core of his message is that addressing the harm is the most important aspect and that this is rarely achieved through punishment, and therefore rarely through criminal law.

This perspective calls into question the need for criminal law and, by implication, the need for the study of criminology. Whilst this is an interesting way of thinking it is not one shared by everyone and therefore we will continue for the rest of this book to assume that criminal law will continue to exist and that some people will choose both to deviate from accepted ways of behaving and to commit offences.

SUMMARY

- Identify what the criminal law is and what it is for

At its most basic, the criminal law is a set of rules backed up by sanctions. The rules are designed to prevent certain behaviour which a state (or community) wants to control. The state also sets up a system including various institutions and agencies designed to prevent these actions and to ensure transgressors are convicted (see **Chapter 23**). People who break the rules face sanctions, often punishments which are designed to try to dissuade others from offending (see **Chapters 24**, **25**, and **26**). Criminal laws are generally used to try to prevent actions which threaten the security of the state or community or which threaten the security and well-being of people who live within its borders.

From this it is clear that crime is socially constructed—each state decides what should be prohibited at any particular time. This means that the criminal laws of one country are different from those of other countries and that therefore there is nothing about particular acts that of themselves means that they are always crimes, even the boundaries of laws such as murder differ from one state to another.

- Understand why the criminal law can be seen as a social construct that changes over time

Social construction underlies the activities which become criminalised in any particular state. What this means is that strong social movements, such as calls to legalise assisted suicide or to criminalise the smoking of cigarettes in the work place, often eventually manage to shape the criminal law—the law bends to the social conventions that society most wants. This is positive in that the criminal law is more likely to represent what people living within that society believe is right. However, it is also problematic as it may allow the criminal law to protect one (powerful) group at the expense of another, less powerful (or minority) group. The malleability permitted through the fact that the law is a social construction means that it may not be fair and it may not protect people; it is not required to follow any particular ethical or human rights standards. Therefore the criminal law is, at least to some extent, a social construct but there may be limits such as those central to the harm principle.

- Consider the reasons why some actions are criminalised, and assess how well these reasons are applied

In England and Wales most activities are only criminalised if they are harmful to other people—the harm principle. Under this principle if an activity is not harmful it should not be criminalised. Note that the harm principle does not mean that all activities that cause harm to other people must be criminalised—if this were the case many sports such as boxing would be criminalised. However, it does mean that people should be free to participate in activities that do not harm others.

Defending people from harm is supposed to protect their freedom to make choices without any negative consequences. Actions which are not as harmful and do not really curtail the freedom of others should not be criminal. These lesser issues may be unpleasant and be actions a community do not like, they may be deviant and the community might try to dissuade such deviant acts by treating people differently if they participate (e.g. looking down on those who pick their noses in public).

Although the harm principle underlies many offences states do not always stick to that principle. Those in power may use their position to prevent activities they dislike or that may interfere with their interests, or they may refuse to criminalise a behaviour that harms some people if it is useful to them. For example, they may refuse to criminalise factory owners who fail to put safety guards on dangerous machinery in the workplace. The refusal is dangerous and clearly likely to be harmful to some people but safety guards may slow down production and so reduce the profits of those in power. Therefore, although there is a general standard this is often breached to protect the interests of those in power at the expense of others, usually the poor or minority groups (see labelling in **Chapters 15** and **16**).

There are also many criminal laws which seem to protect moral interests rather than prevent harm to others. For example, laws such as those prohibiting nudity in public places are more about the protection of morals than about preventing harm.

Some criminal laws try to prevent people from harming themselves. For example, laws prohibiting the use of certain substances (drug laws) or requiring people to wear helmets on motorbikes or seatbelts in cars all protect individuals from harming themselves.

From this it is clear that the harm principle is something which is not always followed and that no one rule can explain how a state chooses which activities to criminalise.

- Evaluate whether we need the criminal law in order to hold people to account and punish them, or whether a system designed to deal with any harm caused without apportioning blame would be more effective in ensuring safe and content communities

The criminal law deals with problems by blaming individuals (sometimes they may blame a company or those who act for a company) and then punishing them for acting in ways which are unacceptable to everyone else. The reason states have such laws is that they consider that punishment is the best way of persuading most of us not to participate in what are often activities that harm other people. However, if you ask most people why they do not kill someone when they are angry, few will answer that they do not want to be punished. Most people either have internalised high moral standards so that they consider killing or stealing to be immoral and would not participate, or they do not want to disappoint loved ones by participating in activities they know are unacceptable to most people. Therefore the criminal law may not be only the tool through which societies control behaviour; education which includes moral standards may be as, or even more, effective at achieving this.

If the criminal law does not deliver safer societies then some thinkers, zemiologists, argue that we should stop blaming people and instead spend money on supporting victims, those who suffer harm, however that harm arises. These theorists note that the criminal law does not deal with all harm and they call on us to take a broader understanding of harm rather than always seeking to blame.

REVIEW QUESTIONS

1. What is the criminal law?
2. What can the criminal law be used for?
3. In what ways can the criminal law be considered a social construct?
4. What is the harm principle?
5. What are the main differences between crime and deviance?
6. Can you identify three reasons why certain actions may be criminalised?
7. What are the main differences between crime and social harm?

FURTHER READING

Downes, D. and Rock, P. (2003) *Understanding Deviance*. Oxford: Oxford University Press. Chapter 1.
Herring, J. (2012) *Great Debates: Criminal Law*. Basingstoke: Palgrave Macmillan. Chapter 1.
A useful, clear, and easily understood discussion of the subject. It is a brilliant place to start your extra reading and introduces the debates in an easily readable manner.

Williams, K. S. (2012) *Textbook on Criminology* (8th edn). Oxford: Oxford University Press. Chapter 2, especially pp. 20–39.

There are many textbooks which consider where we should set the limits of the criminal law. Most criminal law books have a brief section set aside to discuss these issues though many of these are overly legalistic for your use. However, the preceding books are particularly helpful and approachable.

Dorling, D., Gordon, D., Hillyard, P., Pantazis, C., Pemberton, S., and Tombs. S. (2008) *Criminal obsessions: Why harm matters more than crime* (2nd edn). London: Centre for Crime and Justice Studies. Especially Chapter 5, pp. 70–90.

A discussion of harm has been central to this chapter. For a clear and novel consideration of how to differentiate harm and crime it would be sensible to consult this book.

Lacey, N. and Zedner, L. (2017) 'Legal Constructions of Crime' in Liebling, A., Maruna, S., and McAra, L. (eds) *The Oxford Handbook of Criminology* (6th edn). Oxford: Oxford University Press.

A particularly incisive and analytical discussion. This book gives a more detailed consideration of the legal and contextual construction of crime. It introduces some of the more complex legal and criminological theories and guides the reader through the ways in which they might be analysed.

 Access the **online resources** to view selected further reading and web links relevant to the material covered in this chapter.
www.oup.com/uk/case/

CHAPTER OUTLINE

Introduction	82
Justice—preliminary issues	82
Definitions of justice	85
Criminal justice models	88
Philosophical ideas of justice	95
Systems of criminal justice—adversarial and inquisitorial	102
Drawing ideas together	105

What is justice?

KEY ISSUES

After studying this chapter, you should be able to:

- explain and appreciate why justice is so important;

- critically consider the criminal justice approaches to justice and evaluate how these help our understanding of the concept and its outcomes;

- describe the six criminal justice models and be able to critically assess each one;

- outline and evaluate the four philosophical approaches to justice that take a broad view of the concept and allow you to see how justice and injustice can impact on society, crime, security, and well-being;

- explain and critically compare the two main systems of criminal justice.

Introduction

As we will discover in this chapter, 'justice' is an abstract and fluid concept which is often used very loosely or imprecisely. It is an idea which most understand but few explain. We know injustice when we experience it, or, more commonly we recognise it when we feel aggrieved, and we assume other people think about justice in the same way we do, but this is often not the case. In studying criminology you will read and hear the term justice in countless different contexts, which is why it is imperative to better understand it.

This chapter will provide you with some definitions of justice, knowledge of criminal justice models, the philosophical underpinnings of justice as a concept and, finally, the systems of criminal justice. By considering both the theoretical notions and practical applications it is hoped that you will gain a more rounded view of this notion, and most importantly, a more nuanced understanding of justice and its importance across all your criminological studies.

To illustrate why justice is so important and the fact that justice may be approached from differing standpoints we will here look briefly at sentencing (something which will be further considered later in the chapter). Sentencing occurs towards the end of the criminal justice system: an individual commits a crime, is caught and found guilty, and then the state (often through judges or magistrates) has to decide what should happen, what sentence to pass.

Many people see equal treatment as essential to justice. If two cases are the same they should receive the same punishment, the same sentence; however, justice is not as straightforward as this. If two people are driving at 40 mph through a 30 mph speed restricted area it may seem fair to punish them in the same way, but this tendency to treat like cases alike may actually fail to deliver justice; it may lead to injustice. If one of the drivers was trying to get someone to hospital in order to save the life of a passenger that might be a reason to give them a different sentence. There are other reasons why one might give each a different sentence. For example, assume that both drivers would normally be fined £100. This sounds fair. However, should the sentence take account of their circumstances; one of the drivers might be very rich and £100 fine would be nothing to them, the other may be very poor and £100 would represent more than they have to feed their family in a month. Is a fine of the same amount still fair? Does it represent justice?

These types of dilemmas arise at every point in the criminal justice system. This chapter cannot give you definitive answers as to where justice lies: there is no final answer to that question. However, the chapter will introduce you to different facets of justice. It will encourage you to challenge your own ideas of justice through learning how criminologists, philosophers, and others have written about it. We will be exploring what a just criminal justice system might look like and you will be presented with frameworks called criminal justice models on which to anchor that understanding. In this way the chapter will suggest the types of questions you might like to ask in order to decide what might be just, both in a particular case and more generally. This will enable you to evaluate what a state does at each point in the system. By the end of this chapter you should have a nuanced understanding of this concept, be confident in explaining or writing about the various schools of thought concerning it, and be able to use justice to test other aspects of your criminological studies.

Justice—preliminary issues

Justice emerges as an issue throughout all areas of our lives. If we take a sporting example: what if in a football match a referee fails to give a penalty for what many see as a clear handball? Fans may see this as unjust or unfair. What is being claimed when someone says it is unjust? It could mean that it is unfair or unjust that:

- the referee (and presumably the linesmen) was looking the other way and missed the incident;
- the referee saw the incident but made the wrong decision, and may have believed it was unintentional, whereas others believe it was deliberate;
- there are lots of cameras there and the fans can see that the decision is incorrect; they feel the referee should listen to them;
- because there are lots of cameras, the game should use technology and the film should be watched by another referee to correct an incorrect decision (as happens in rugby).

So we can see that justice in any one situation is experienced differently depending on your perspective. In daily life we often accept when others use the terms just or unjust and do not think or ask exactly what they mean by using the term in that specific situation. However, despite their different reasons for believing it to be an unjust decision they still come to the same conclusion: that the decision was unjust. You may feel that their reasons do not matter. In football it may not be essential but if we are thinking of locking someone up for a long period of time it matters greatly whether the decision is just, and we need to understand exactly why it is just or unjust.

Many great philosophers have written about justice and each brings a slightly different approach. Some try to set out ideal systems of justice which, if applied, should give rise to justice in a society (see Rawls 1971). Others will put forward a more fluid idea of justice (see Sen 2010), again often useful in setting up or testing criminal justice systems or theories. Both Rawls and Sen are considered later in this chapter. Justice as described by these thinkers can be complex but read each section carefully, it is important to grasp the ideas and to be able to assess them for yourself.

Justice lies at the core of the whole criminal justice system—from deciding what activities should be controlled through to choosing how to punish (or otherwise react to) any crime. Justice also enters into some theories which purport to explain criminal behaviour. For example, justice is important in deciding:

- when and how an investigation should be conducted—what sort of rights should suspects enjoy, how and when police should be permitted to question them;
- what rights should the accused enjoy in court and how should victims and witnesses be protected;
- whether we should take into account the interests of victims and, if so, when;
- how much to punish people;
- how punishment should be administered and whether prisoners are justly treated whilst they are incarcerated;
- whether community punishments are justly administered;
- whether there is injustice in society. If so, whether injustice impacts on criminal behaviour and whether punishing such behaviour is just.

Justice is (or rather should be) guaranteed by the laws, especially the criminal laws, in any state. It should also be apparent in all decisions made by those working for the state, decisions about crime and social issues. Grasping the concept of justice is therefore central to all your criminological studies.

Justice as a social construct

In **Chapter 3**, you were introduced to the idea that crime is a socially constructed concept. In doing so you learnt that the activities a society chooses to label as crimes depend on both the cultural ideals of the society (so that what is crime in England and Wales may not be in Australia or India) and the time period you study (what is defined as crime alters as the society alters). Many academics, such as Scottish philosopher David Hume (1711–76), have argued that justice is very similar to crime in that it is a socially constructed concept. Hume argued that justice is important centrally as it has social utility and is malleable so can alter as communities and societies progress. For Hume, justice was therefore a set of standards used in a particular culture or society at a particular time to help to control self interest—it is a social construct.

Whilst a number of the theorists (who we discuss in this chapter) might disagree with this idea, at least in relation to social justice (the way in which all benefits and burdens are distributed within a society), there is certainly an element of social construction in relation to criminal justice. Criminal justice does not necessarily embrace all the elements of an absolute idea of justice. Criminal justice is the system of rules and practices under which government institutions and agencies act in order to prevent or control crime or deal with those who break the law. This system does change over time, as society changes. For example, today many people in England and Wales (though not necessarily a majority) consider the death penalty to be an unjust punishment (something we should not use) whereas 300 years ago few people would have had that view. The view of what is just and unjust for states to do within a criminal justice arena is therefore shaped over time and does alter as a society changes (it is socially constructed).

Justice issues within criminal justice

Justice is a powerful tool to use when assessing the criminal justice system. You need to learn to consider and critically analyse all aspects of the criminal justice system and to decide whether they are fair both in individual cases and more generally. To do this, the broader definitions of justice will be very useful. For example, as was seen in the speeding example (in the 'Introduction'), the criminal justice system is constantly tested against the ideal of equality (this will be discussed in more depth). To test the system you can look at individual types of case—as with the speeding example—or you can look more generally at the outcomes overall (all decisions) or from different perspectives (different types of groups). There is a lot of evidence (Skogan 2006; Macpherson 1999) that different groups of people have very different experiences of the criminal justice system. People might be treated differently depending on their: age; ethnicity; gender; religion; sexuality; the community they live in; whether they have or lack money, influence or power. etc.

To take ethnicity as an example, black people or those of Afro-Caribbean origin appear more frequently than expected at all levels of the criminal justice system (are arrested, cautioned, convicted, punished harshly, etc.) than might be expected from the numbers in the population. At one time it was assumed that the system was just and that therefore people in these ethnic groups offended more frequently than others, but more recently this has been heavily questioned (Skogan 2006; Macpherson 1999) and the system has been accused of operating unjustly. For example, after the Stephen Lawrence inquiry William Macpherson accused the system of 'institutional racism' (Macpherson, 1999) which he described as:

> The collective failure of an organisation to provide an appropriate and professional service to people because of their colour, culture, or ethnic origin. It can be seen or detected in processes, attitudes and behaviour which amount to discrimination through unwitting prejudice, ignorance, thoughtlessness and racist stereotyping which disadvantage minority ethnic people.
>
> Macpherson 1999: para. 6.34

Overall, Macpherson was claiming that the criminal justice system worked against certain racial groups, that it was unjust in its operation. It is important to note that in many ways the accusation that Macpherson was making was not necessarily that the system was unjust, and that the rules were necessarily wrong (though there were and are examples of this). Rather he was suggesting that those applying the rules, that the people working in the criminal justice system—from the bottom all the way to the top in all criminal justice organisations—tended to make decisions which were likely to go against certain racial groups and that this was unjust and needed to be tackled. Whilst things have improved since 1999 (see *Macpherson 10 years on*, 2009) there are still major problems, especially in areas such as stop and search (see the 'Drawing ideas together' section in this chapter and **Telling it like it is 4.1**).

TELLING IT LIKE IT IS 4.1

Below are a few quotes taken from a piece of research done into the causes of the 2011 riots in England. Whilst these quotes do not excuse the behaviour, they may explain how injustice makes people feel, that it frees them to take part in unacceptable activities which harm other people and communities—The Guardian and LSE (2012) *Reading the Riots: Investigating England's summer of disorder*. London: The Guardian and LSE (http://eprints.lse.ac.uk/46297/1/Reading%20the%20riots(published).pdf):

> These young people are coming out to prove they have an existence, to prove that if you don't listen to them and you don't take into account our views, potentially this is a destructive force.
>
> Man, mid-20s, north London, at page 13

> You see the rioting yeah? Everything the police have done to us, did to us, was in our heads. That's what gave everyone their adrenaline to want to fight the police ... It was because of the way they treated us.
>
> Man, 20, from London, at page 18

> The government needed someone to blame and [put] everything together under 'gangs'. I don't believe there was much planned gangland activity. I believe there was a lot of angry, very working-class, disillusioned young men that realised 'hang on a minute, it's going off'.
>
> Man, 21, Salford, at page 22

> All I can tell you is that me, myself and the group I was in, none of us have got jobs, yeah? I been out of work now coming up two years ... and it's just like a depression, man, that you sink into ... I felt like I needed to be there as well to just say 'Look, this is what's gonna happen if there's no jobs offered to us out there'.
>
> Man, 22, London, at page 25

> When I left my house ... it wasn't anything to do with the police ... I literally went there to say, 'All right then, well, everyone's getting free stuff, I'm joining in', like, 'cos, it's fucking my area. These fucking shops, like, I've given them a hundred CVs ... not one job. That's why I left my house. It's not like I haven't got GCSEs ... but I see people with no GCSEs nothing like that, and they're working in places. Like somewhere like Tesco. I'm not being funny like, I don't need any GCSEs to work in Tesco. But I've got them. So here's my CV. I don't need A-levels, but you know, here's my CV. Why haven't I even got [an] interview? ... I feel like I haven't [been] given the same opportunities and chances as other people ... If I had a job ... I honestly wouldn't have stolen nothing ... Like you could work in Tesco but ... Tesco could make you feel like you're a valuable worker, and you could be on £5 an hour. But it doesn't matter, yeah, cos you feel you're worth something you would never jeopardise that. Because that feeling's better than making £10 an hour. Do you see what I'm saying? And that's what I feel like: people are not worth anything in this area.
>
> Man, 22, from south London, at page 26

This illustrates how powerful justice is as a construct and how justice, or in the example of the Stephen Lawrence Inquiry, injustice, can be used to force organisations and the state to recognise when they need to change their behaviour or their systems. It can be used to improve the criminal justice system, to make it fairer.

Definitions of justice

Despite being a fluid, changeable concept (as discussed earlier), justice can be more formally or carefully delineated, and such a definition is useful if we are to use the term to help us think about criminology. In its simplest form, taking just a narrow view, justice can be said to have been served when the rules are applied. Injustice arises if the rules are either not applied or misapplied. The rules referred to here will differ depending on the situation. For example, if you are playing netball it is the rules (usually international rules) of that sport; if you are visiting France it will be the laws or legal rules of that country. In order to be just, the law (state rules) must be applied fairly, objectively, and correctly. In criminal law this happens when the guilty are convicted and punished, and when the innocent are acquitted. However, decisions are not always correctly made and injustice can result. We need to be able to recognise when this happens and to be able to explain why a decision is fair or unfair.

Is injustice justified: do the reasons matter?

In the earlier example about the handball in a game of football, which of the claims is really one of injustice and which is not? Does it matter? For example, is the first reason given (that the referee and linesmen were looking the other way) really a case of injustice? Presumably the referee and linesmen did everything possible to watch all material incidents in the game; it may be unlucky if they miss this one but is it really unjust? It would be if what is being claimed is that the referee deliberately looked away or was not paying due care and attention to the game (maybe using a mobile phone), but in other situations this is probably not a reason (alone) to claim that the decision is unjust.

Similarly, it is not unjust if lots of people are killed in an earthquake, although it is certainly very distressing and a major disaster. It is only unjust if something could and should have been done to prevent the deaths, e.g. if it was known that it was about to happen and nothing was done to evacuate people.

Do referees explain why they make that particular decision? Should they? In the 18th century, Lord Mansfield (a very famous judge) advised a colonial governor on his decision making by saying:

> consider what you think justice requires and decide accordingly. But never give your reasons; for your judgement will probably be right, but your reasons will certainly be wrong.

> Lord Mansfield as quoted in Sen 2010: page 4

Whilst failing to explain decisions protects the decision-maker (in our case the referee) from attack or question, it prevents us knowing whether decisions are based on acceptable reasoning. What if the referee sees the incident, but has decided that the handball rule is too difficult, so he gives a penalty on every alternate occurrence; last time he saw one he awarded a penalty, so this time he does not. The decision may be correct but the reasoning is clearly unjust. So, contrary to Lord Mansfield's advice it is very important to understand why the decision is made. The people involved and the community (in our example the player involved and the other players and fans) deserve to know. In football that rarely happens, the referee makes the decision and the players and fans are expected to accept it; the referee is seen as the independent arbiter with no reason to support one team over the other, therefore as someone who will make the right decision.

This is not the same in all sports. In rugby, for example, the referee generally (though not always) explains the decision made and also talks to the players in the game, warning them when they might be about to breach the rules so as to help them remain within their bounds and so keep the game moving. Here the referee acts as arbiter and advisor. Many feel this renders the game more just but it does not always lead to justice, as the referee may still make incorrect decisions. An example of this happened at the end of the Scotland v Australia quarter final match in the Rugby World Cup in 2015, when the referee controversially awarded Australia a penalty which led to a score that won them the game. Whilst examples drawn from games are interesting and useful to illustrate some points, you now need to be introduced to issues which are linked to decision making in the criminal justice context and those which are linked to criminological explanations.

The scales of justice—a visual depiction of justice

In England and Wales the scales of justice sit prominently above the Old Bailey, the Central Criminal Court of London (see **Figure 4.1**).

Figure 4.1 The scales of justice above the Old Bailey, London

Source: BasPhoto/Shutterstock.com

This iconography aims to symbolise that justice will be dispensed in the courts and is intended to depict the fact that law without justice is a mockery. The scales are supposed to suggest that in law, especially criminal law, there are two sides, two arguments. However, this is too simplistic.

Firstly, there may be more than two sides. In criminal law there may be the state, the accused, and the victim. Each of these might have a very different idea of where justice would lie. Members of the public and the communities in which the victim and offender live may also each have their own ideas of justice. So although only the state and the accused are represented in a criminal case, i.e. only they have a voice (see **Chapter 8** for more on the marginalisation of the victim)—they may not represent the only ideas which should be considered. The scales are too simple.

Secondly, the scales suggest that if they tip the right way justice is served but it may not be. Even if justice is done (that is, the side that is victorious has the most just case) the *reason* for the decision may be unjust. For example, an innocent person may be acquitted but if the reason for acquittal is that the magistrates were impressed by the defendant's overall appearance and demeanour then it is questionable as to whether justice was done.

Clearly, justice is more difficult than a simple set of scales. The examples of justice in sport and law which we have considered assume that if you apply the law equally to all then it delivers justice. This would mean that just application of the law will deliver justice. However, this is a very narrow, legalistic, and contained view of justice. If the law decreed that all people with blue eyes should be put to death by the state (or in Nazi Germany that all Jews should be put into concentration camps with many killed or in South Africa that all black people should be disadvantaged) then most would agree that putting those laws into operation could not be seen as justice. In that case the law itself would be unjust and therefore applying it could only lead to unjust outcomes.

Therefore, the narrow, legalistic concept of justice misses the wider and more important point that should be considered in order to test for justice. In order to analyse justice, we need, therefore, to look at whether the law itself is fair or good. This is an evaluative test—we are trying to test or evaluate whether one law would be fairer or lead to more justice than another. At this point ethical issues enter the equation and we are testing what the outcome ought to be, and therefore what the law should be in order to deliver that outcome. Much of what was considered in **Chapter 3** questioned where the criminal law should start; decisions on these questions should always take account of what would be just. Many theorists assume that the rules in our society are just and merely try to explain why some people obey or break those rules and discuss what should be done to punish them. Other theorists will question or attack the very foundations of the way in which the criminal law is formed (what actions should be criminal) or operates (what a state can legitimately do to enforce those rules), questioning some of the core principles on which our society builds its ideas of justice. In studying justice it is important to understand that there are many different perspectives about what is right or just and it is important to consider each of them.

Recognising that justice is at the core of many discussions in criminology, criminal justice and law opens up important issues. Those theorists who assume that the law is just and therefore who try to explain why some breach it (or obey it) can be questioned on their implicit acceptance of the status quo, their acceptance of the law. Those who question the law should be called to account in terms of their understanding of justice; how would their proposed change be an improvement? It is always important to recognise that justice in any one situation is experienced differently depending on perspective, as we have previously discussed. To illustrate this please listen to some of the brief video and audio links on the Howard League Justice website. Another way of illustrating the plurality of ideas of justice is to take an example such as that in **What do you think? 4.1**.

WHAT DO YOU THINK? 4.1

Let us assume that Amy stole food from Ben and Colin stole food from Debbie. What should happen to Amy and Colin, and should the victim's views be important in that decision? Does it matter why Amy and Colin stole the food? Should Amy and Colin's situations have anything to do with the decision about how we should react? What would be a just outcome?

Society often says that if someone commits a crime the state not only *can* punish that person but has an *obligation* to punish them. The argument is that they have disturbed justice in that society and therefore must be punished. They should not be permitted to gain by doing wrong. The crime is an affront to everyone in that society and needs to be marked out as such. The food was owned by one person and we all own things which we do not want others to take, so when the state punishes for stealing, in this case food, they are protecting the interests of everyone who owns something.

One of the victims, Ben, who owned the food, may also want to see the individual suffer and be punished. However, Ben may also want an apology, a recognition that the person has done him harm and regrets it. Ben might even want compensation or reparation to make up for his victimisation in some small way. Justice for Ben, the victim, is more personal. A victim has a different perspective from the rest of society.

Debbie, the other victim, may be forgiving. She may consider that it is only food and that she should be willing to share food. She may not want to see anyone punished for such a small breach. She may just hope for an apology but wish to be forgiving. Another personal, victim perspective, but very different from the last.

Amy, one of the offenders, may be very poor, even starving and feel that she deserved the food more than Ben, the owner, who is rich. In such a scenario Amy would feel that any punishment would be unjust, though she might be willing to apologise for having stolen the food.

Colin, the other offender, is not poor and stole the food for fun or just because he wanted to and could. Here punishment may feel more just, although it would depend on the punishment: a fine may be acceptable, but an extended prison sentence, loss of a hand, or death may all feel unjust and excessive.

Now, consider the scenarios above and think about how you would answer these questions:

- What is justice when someone does something wrong, and how do we discover justice?

- Should we use an objective societal view of wrongdoing and punishment and so punish both Amy and Colin for their wrongdoing?

- Should we give more weight to the views of the victims in deciding punishment? Remember that if we do that in this case Amy, the starving offender, will face punishment whereas Colin, the wealthy offender, will face none and merely need to apologise. The less deserving offender may face less punishment. Is that fair?

- Should we take account of why the offenders acted or of their situations in any decision about just outcomes?

- Whose justice should be given legal backing? Which of these should be able to impose their justice on the others?

- What would be the most just outcome in each case and why?

You will have noticed that these are very difficult questions, and often impossible to answer with certainty one way or another.

Justice is often a matter of perspective and relies on individual personal thought and on culture. The culture in which these events occur may be important but so too is the culture/sub-culture (part of society) in which the people (especially the victim and offender) are brought up. The expectations and understanding of justice may differ. In such a complex and uncertain world in which we are faced with such difficult choices how can we decide whether something is just/fair or unjust/unfair?

Why study justice?

As we have seen, the idea of justice matters in sport, in legal decision-making (it is important that the laws themselves are just), and it matters that decisions made by schools, universities, employers, or others who have authority over people are fair and just. The truth is that in all these situations and others each individual hopes to be treated justly. In the case of law, and particularly the criminal law, if the rules and their application are not just then the law loses all moral authority and loses its power so that justice is not merely an aspiration but a requirement. As so much of what criminologists study is tied up with the law and legal decisions, it is very important that we are able to assess justice and so assess the moral authority of the state in any particular situation. Justice is therefore a very good test of whether a particular law or a particular standard of behaviour as expected by a society is morally fair; when evaluating a law or standard, we need to ask 'is it just?'.

Social justice

As well as being essential when discussing law and rules, justice is also an issue in deciding who should have what within a society: *social justice*. Studying justice necessitates consideration of the way in which all benefits and burdens are distributed. It asks how they are distributed and how the distribution came about. How and why are some rich, others reasonably well off, while some live in poverty? It also asks whether that situation is fair. How and why are some people rewarded with almost limitless choices whilst others enjoy only some choices, and some are penalised, controlled, punished, and maybe even put to death or allowed to die? Whilst no one wants to be poor or penalised, deciding on whether that situation is just is not always merely a matter of equal distribution of everything but will often require an understanding of why the situation has arisen. Poverty will be unjust if it is the result of exploitation or of arbitrary factors such as race, but may uphold the justice of one person having burdens if they arise out of, for example, the criminal behaviour of that individual. Justice asks whether the situation is seen as just, once full and proper account has been taken of all relevant issues. For example, deciding on a just situation may require some analysis of whether the law and social rules are being manipulated (intentionally or not) to ensure that the interests of some groups are always protected.

This chapter will provide you with some tools you can use to discuss these issues. It will not provide a simple definition of justice which can be applied in all cases, or give any easy answers, but it *will* provide you with tools you can use to assess academic claims and real-life situations.

Why does justice matter to criminology?

Studying justice will serve you well in your study of criminology. Being willing to question everything and everyone is essential to sound criminological study (see *Always Be Critical*—**Chapter 1**); in academia we often call this analysis or consideration of the issues. This questioning, analysis, and consideration needs to be rational and founded on firm ground. A grasp of the ideas of justice can provide you with one tool to analyse or critique other people's ideas (those you read in studying criminology, those of your lecturers and fellow students, those you hear in the media, those you hear when you are discussing things with friends and family). This chapter will arm you with some ideas you can use in your discussions and challenges.

The discussion will begin with consideration of models of justice often used in criminal justice and then look more deeply at four more theoretical ideas of justice—Aristotle (384–322 B.C.), John Rawls (1971), Amartya Sen (2010), and communitarianism. Each of these will provide you with tools to consider and analyse much of what you study in criminology. Please remember that there are many other ideas of justice so this is merely an introduction. These models and the four types of justice (three theorists and communitarianism) represent some of the most famous ideas related to justice and are not intended to be directly political. You will come across other ideas of justice in later chapters. Many of these, such as feminist, critical, or radical criminologies, may not be represented as justice theories as such but, at their core, argue that something in our society is unfair or unjust and that the behaviour of individuals and the state cannot be properly understood or judged without an understanding and consideration of that issue. Many theories therefore require a consideration of justice and at their core is often the call to look at things from a different perspective. Therefore, throughout any consideration of justice, it is important to remember that different perspectives should be respected and considered.

Criminal justice models

In 1981, criminological theorist Michael King identified six models of criminal justice (King 1981: 13). He set out three which were **descriptive** and three which were **normative**. The descriptive models describe what researchers found when they studied the systems; no claim was made as to whether this was a just or unjust way of setting up the system. The advocates of the three normative models set them out as being an ideal, just, and moral basis for the criminal justice system. We will briefly look at some of these descriptive and normative criminal justice models, but also widen the consideration out to others which King does not include (for an overview see **Table 4.1**).

Name of model	Type of model	Characteristics	Benefits	Limitations
Bureaucratic model	Descriptive	Procedures, recording information, efficiency, cost limitation measures	This model has the potential to save time and money. It involves the management of crime and criminals	The rules do not need to be fair or just
Stigmatisation or status passage	Descriptive	Societal	Society gains strength through social cohesion	Does not always deliver a just outcome
Power	Descriptive	Accuses the law, especially criminal law, of allowing the domination of one group over another	Opens our eyes to the injustices that may be in our legal systems	Often it merely describes and questions what it sees the criminal justice system as doing without suggesting or building alternatives
Crime control	Normative	Driving aim is to deliver law and order—to punish offenders swiftly and harshly in order to deter and therefore to protect the public	Pulls law-abiding people together. May be a deterrence for others. Denunciation of crime and aims to make communities safer	Innocent people could be wrongfully convicted
Due process	Normative	Onus on the state to prove the defendant is guilty	By requiring the state (police, courts, etc.) to abide by laws and rules that curtail state power it protects individuals. Requires legal rights to be respected	Some guilty people could avoid conviction
Rights	Normative	Attempts to protect democratic freedoms	Requires rights to be respected even when not fully enshrined in state law. Curtails the way in which agents of the state (police and prosecutors) pursue offenders	Does not always balance the rights of victims and offenders

Table 4.1 Outline characteristics of the six models of criminal justice

Descriptive models

Weber: the bureaucratic model

The bureaucratic model is the first of the descriptive models. It derives from the work of the German sociologist and philosopher Max Weber (1864–1920) and is linked to what is often referred to Weberian sociology. Weber suggested that the systems operated on standardisation of procedures, and adhering to these was considered to deliver good practice. There were four elements to this model:

1. Adherence to procedures, rights, and powers.
2. Recording of information.
3. Resolution of cases as efficiently as possible.
4. Limitation of costs.

Firstly, in every criminal case there were procedures to follow to prevent arbitrary decisions. The procedures were there not to guarantee fairness but because they limited

discretion so delivered consistency and prevented political interference in cases. The procedures set out the rights and powers of the state and its citizens, and a central part of this was to ensure that each person was treated equally without political bias, favouritism, or discrimination.

The second element was to record all information. A criminal case then consisted of what was officially recorded and to decide on guilt or innocence the court read the contents of the file and decided where the truth lay. In this type of system written evidence is prioritised over oral evidence (this aspect is more relevant in continental systems and will be considered and analysed later in the chapter when inquisitorial systems are considered). Thirdly, these systems expected cases to be resolved as quickly as possible—justice should be swift and the result of efficient systems. Finally, these systems prioritised cost limitation, using cost/benefit analysis to decide whether something was worth doing.

The linking of cost limitation and swift justice meant that these systems prioritised diversion from costly trials by full use of guilty pleas. Weber was not advocating this as an ideal way of delivering justice but rather noting that complex organisations have a tendency to become bureaucratic. However, in modern systems certain of these elements are suggested as being something to which we should aspire. This approach can be seen clearly in England and Wales, starting with the Royal Commission on Criminal Justice 1993 (the Runciman Commission) and running through many policies up to today where systems, speed, and cost effectiveness are seen as positive. See, for example, policies such as managing the risks of known offenders. A central element of the bureaucratic model is that cases should be tried and sentenced (or acquitted) quickly and efficiently (such a system is more cost effective). A system may achieve these ends but using this model it is difficult to tell whether the system or any particular outcome is fair or just. It is difficult to decide issues or justice through the application of cost effectiveness. Indeed, whilst efficiency may call for a quick decision from reading what is in the file, justice may require the case to be tried and, if the accused is innocent, justice requires an acquittal whereas the bureaucratic model sees acquittals (at least a large number of acquittals) as a problem.

Durkheim: the stigmatisation or status passage model

Émile Durkheim (1858–1917), a French sociologist and philosopher noted that stigmatisation helped to reinforce social cohesion so making a society stronger; he saw this as being used by states to build stronger societies (Durkheim 1895). Stigmatising offenders (and maybe even defendants, on the basis that there is no smoke without fire) sets them apart from law-abiding members of the community. It makes the law-abiding feel good about themselves and appreciate the same goodness in others. Spreading information about offending behaviour (i.e. wide media coverage) is valuable as it allows the whole society to denounce the behaviour of the offenders, and often to denounce or reject the offenders themselves as being bad.

Durkheim saw states and communities using the broad dissemination of information about trial and punishment of criminals as positive, as helping to unite the good against the bad. Historically, this publication would have been by public punishments (e.g. public hanging or public flogging), more recently it is done through the media and the Internet (see **Chapter 7**). Here the trial and punishment express society's disapproval of criminal activity. Durkheim understood that any state, with any political bent, could use this to build social cohesion; it can therefore be used to uphold some very unjust regimes. A system which has stigmatisation and denunciation at its centre may not be just, it may make the victim feel their plight is taken seriously and so deliver part of a just outcome, but it does little to ensure a just outcome.

Power models—the maintenance of domination

As will be seen in **Chapters 15** and **16**, radical and critical theorists describe (and attack) the criminal justice system as something which maintains the domination of one group over another. Power models are based on this dynamic. Domination may arise from a number of factors: it might be class, social, gender, race, etc. or a combination of these. They analyse and assess the whole of the criminal justice system (from decisions about which activities are criminalised through to how to punish). Their analysis generally accuses criminal justice systems of being used as a means of a powerful group subjugating a less powerful group (and therefore not about social cohesion but about control). They often emphasise the historical role of the criminal justice system in maintaining political, social, cultural, and economic domination. It may be achieved by having rules which are then directed more at one group than another, for example, by more closely policing certain areas. When done most effectively, power theorists (such as Quinney 1970) remark that the powerless group accepts the perspective of the dominant group and may even ask for greater domination to resolve social problems they suffer. These theorists challenge systems of dominance, e.g. patriarchy, class systems, and colonialism, and see the punishment of offenders as proof of the domination, as they point to an over-representation of the dominated group among those being punished. These models are useful to ensure that in looking for justice we are aware of the way in which laws can be abused; they remind us to question and search for justice. However, they are very politicised and therefore do not necessarily help us to ensure or even evaluate just outcomes.

Normative models

None of the models discussed so far is intended as a blueprint for the formation of a criminal justice system, each merely describes or questions what they find. In some cases the description has later become advanced as something a system should aspire to, in others it is a negative evaluation. The last, the power model (radical and critical theorists), goes further; such theorists are attacking the system for being a tool of domination (see **Chapters 15** and **16**). The next three models, the normative models, are advocated as being a just way to run a criminal justice system; they are ideals. The first two, crime control and due process, are traditionally linked to the criminal justice system and each claims to be delivering justice. They were most famously compared by Herbert Packer (1968) in his work *The Limits of the Criminal Sanction*. The third is linked to international and theoretical ideals of human rights.

Crime control model

Crime control is often associated with ideas of utilitarianism (greatest good for the greatest number), a system which tries to ensure that most people are looked after. In terms of criminal justice, this means that offenders and maybe even suspects should be repressed and controlled to protect the good. This should happen through an efficient and accurate quest for truth, allowing society to express disgust and generally denunciate criminals and criminal activities.

The denunciation helps to strengthen moral standards and pulls law-abiding people together (it is therefore related to the status passage model advocated by Durkheim) but ensures that individuals are not tempted to take matters into their own hands. Crime control requires a strong criminal justice system, one which relies on professional judgement and does not control decision making. Ideally most of those who are tried should be found guilty (to show the professionals are doing their jobs properly) and then be swiftly and harshly punished. A few acquittals (findings of not guilty) can be explained due to technical problems in the evidence or the jury misunderstanding something. A significant number of acquittals, however, could be seen as a failure of the system.

The crime control model calls on people to trust the professionals so that if both the police and prosecutor think this person is guilty they probably are (a presumption of guilt). A strong and harsh system, one which efficiently catches, convicts, and punishes people, is thought to deter the person being punished, and also to deter other people, from choosing to offend. If this deterrence is real it would deliver something positive. It also makes people feel as if crime is being controlled, so law-abiding citizens feel free to enjoy their lives (if it really does reduce crime then they can also do so safely).

Crime control aims to guarantee social freedom to those who do not offend. The model sees legal controls to protect the defendant (suspect) as something which can be bent or broken in order to ensure a swift conviction and to protect the innocent. Those acquitted are often thought to 'have got away with it', rather than being innocent. Here the presumption of innocence only really rules the way in which the court process is conducted; the presumption of guilt is the factor which predicts the most common and expected outcome. The central element is the control of crime, which requires a high rate of apprehension and conviction of criminals, and results must be

seen to be met very quickly. If occasionally some innocent individuals are sacrificed by being wrongly punished this may be a necessary evil in order to deliver the good which crime control wishes to deliver. This model asserts the rights of victims and society over those of suspects and defendants. The bottom line is that punishment should be swift, punitive, and proportional to ensure that it is clearly linked to the offending and allows the law abiding to see justice done. It is also intended to demonstrate that crime does not pay—if you offend you are likely to be caught and punished.

Formal procedures are kept to an absolute minimum and their breach should never lead to the exclusion of evidence which is otherwise thought reliable; the guilty should never be acquitted on a technicality. This type of model would encourage the police to pursue someone they know to be guilty to ensure they are convicted and to bend or break rules, such as the need for a search warrant, in order to secure proof of guilt. Here the end of crime control—punishing the guilty—always justifies the means. Police collecting evidence with little respect for the rights of suspects (a crime control type of action) has led to police procedures being more carefully set out in rules such as those contained in the Police and Criminal Evidence Act 1984 and all its codes of practice that try to instruct the police on what is and is not acceptable. The crime control model can be juxtaposed to the next model—the due process model.

Due process model

Both crime control and due process consider that the state has a duty to protect the community from crime and criminals; they both expect the state to punish the guilty. However, due process places greater responsibility on the state to prove the guilt of the defendant beyond reasonable doubt. Some of the ideas of due process theorists might be seen as being embedded in the theories of Beccaria which are discussed in **Chapter 12**. To punish an innocent person is seen as a double injustice, firstly the guilty person goes free and secondly an innocent person is wrongly punished, their rights are violated by the state. To prevent this, due process requires a fair balance between the power of the state and the ability of individuals to defend themselves. When a crime occurs the state generally enjoys a lot of legal power to investigate and try a case; a suspect or the accused lacks power. Due process theorists set up rules to curtail the power of the state (often the police) and ensure that suspects are fairly treated. The limitations on the state are an attempt to ensure the individual and the state have more balanced and equal powers.

Due process theorists recognise that the police may have an honest belief that a suspect is guilty, but they might be mistaken or may be misled by witnesses and/or victims who are mistaken or lying to the police. Suspects may also confess because they feel under pressure: for that reason, due process theorists argue that formal rules and processes need to protect individuals from excessive use of power and the whole process should be tested in a court case and re-trials, and appeals in case of other errors. The processes are important to protect the individual. Central to this model is the presumption of innocence—every suspect is presumed innocent until proven guilty and no-one should have to incriminate him- or herself. In this model if breaking the rules leads to evidence, even irrefutable evidence, it should not be used to prove guilt. Allowing such evidence:

> would I believe encourage serious wrongdoing from some police officers who might be tempted to exert force or fabricate or suppress evidence in the hope of establishing the guilt of the suspect, especially in a serious case where they believe him to be guilty. ... The integrity of the criminal justice system is a higher objective than the conviction of any individual.
>
> Zander's 1993 dissenting opinion
> in the Royal Commission on Criminal Justice,
> Runciman Report, (Cm 2263), pages 234–5

If, within the process rules, the state proves a person guilty they can punish them. Of course there may still be an error and the person may not actually be guilty, but at least the state has done everything they can to ensure that the process and trial is fair (just). In ensuring that no (or very few) innocent people are convicted due process theorists recognise and accept that some guilty people will go free. They see this as being fairer or more just than convicting the innocent.

To be truly due process it is necessary not just to follow the rules but to ensure that the intentions underlying them are not ignored and ensure that the ethical intentions are preserved—this ideal is clear in the quote from Zander. This is procedural justice—it follows procedures and if the procedures are fair the outcome should be fair and just. By focusing on protection of suspects, however, there is a tendency to ignore the rights and interests of victims and of communities. It is important to note that the due process model does not guarantee rights, it merely sets up procedures to ensure that the criminal process is fair to the suspect and to prevent the state using its power unjustly, even if that state action would be popular.

Rights model

The rights model takes the procedural restraints set out in the due process model, chooses those that are most fundamental to the freedom of the individual, and declares them to be rights. Once protections are recognised internationally as rights, they should be respected even if they interfere with the criminal justice system or render it more difficult to obtain a conviction. A model based on rights is designed to ensure that the state and its representatives do not use their powers arbitrarily. Rights are there to ensure that the criminal justice system, especially the police, does not unacceptably interfere with the freedoms that are essential to democracy. The state is supposed to protect our democratic freedoms: things such as immunity from arbitrary arrest, detention, and exile; right to a fair trial; freedom of speech, demonstration, and association. Ideally the police and the criminal justice system are there to protect democratic freedoms. However, poor policing or a deficient criminal justice system can quickly undermine freedom and be used to repress people or parts of communities.

Rights set out standards below which no state should ever fall. They are generally basic standards and states in their liberties and due process are supposed to improve on them. Their real value lies in the fact that they are standards which sit above states; they can be used to test the actions of a state, to test the laws and the use of force (see the example of Edward in 'Applying the normative models'). Whereas each state can set its due processes or civil liberties, rights standards are above the state and can only be altered by agreement of many states. This is important because even where a state is under extreme threat (e.g. a threatened terror attack) it is important that it does not resort to human rights violations such as torture. At these times, rights set standards and limits to the use of power to try to ensure that a state does not overreach acceptable power just in order to deal with a terrorist threat. Some things one has an *absolute* right to, such as not changing the rules after the fact. In sport, this means that the rules are the same when the game starts as when it finishes. In life, there is an assumption that one cannot be guilty of a crime if the activity was not criminal when you participated. The rules can be altered for those who follow you but should not be altered for you.

Applying the normative models

Let us take one example and apply it to each of the normative models discussed to better understand what these mean in practice. For example, we may know that an individual, Edward, has vital information about a bombing which is to take place in the near future.

- Under the crime control model the ideal is to protect the people; this might permit Edward to be tortured to get the information.

- Under due process the state is not normally permitted to torture but some states may permit the police to *threaten* torture, hoping that Edward will tell them something. If there is time then under the due process model Parliament might choose to pass a law permitting extreme measures (maybe even torture) in certain very limited circumstances (with lots of checks and balances to its use), and again torture may be threatened and possibly even permitted.

- Under a rights model torture is absolutely prohibited and under no circumstances can the state or any of its agents conduct or threaten torture, even if it means that a bomb might go off and kill many people.

The example of Edward is loosely based on a real case, that of *Ireland* v *United Kingdom* (5310/71) [1978] ECHR 1. In the early 1970s there had been acts of terrorism committed by members of the Irish Republican Army (IRA). The authorities arrested and detained several members of the IRA. They were interrogated for hours at a time using tactics that included wall-standing, hooding, and deprivation of food and sleep. The European Court of Human Rights decided that the techniques did not quite amount to torture but were examples of 'inhuman and degrading' treatment which violated Article 3 of the European Convention of Human Rights. The rights set

out in Article 3 are protected absolutely: they can never be breached by any state which is party to the Human Rights Convention. It was unacceptable for any state to use either terrorism or cruel and inhuman treatment even if they thought that the tactics might give them information which would prevent an act of terrorism; some activities are never permissible. For discussion of another example see **Controversy and debate 4.1**.

Let us take another example which may be relevant in more cases: it was formerly the case that if a suspect remained silent no one could assume that they were guilty, even if most people thought that an innocent person would answer the question(s). How would each model consider this view?

- A crime control model is focused on conviction of the guilty. This model would always have permitted a judge or jury to infer guilt from silence in the belief that an innocent person would want to take every opportunity to defend themselves. Therefore this model would assume that silence would only be used by the guilty. In order to ensure the conviction of guilty people, crime control theorists would argue that it should always be acceptable to infer guilt from silence.

CONTROVERSY AND DEBATE 4.1

A young boy is abducted. His parents are asked for a ransom, which they then pay, but the child is not returned. The police arrest a man and all the evidence points to his having abducted the child; he even admits that this is what happened. The man refuses to tell the police where the child is. Should police officers be permitted to threaten to torture the suspect if they believe this may save the life of an innocent child?

These basic facts are from an actual case. The situation arose in Germany in 2002 and the police did threaten the suspect with considerable violence and suffering if he did not disclose the whereabouts of the child. The police believed the child was still alive and were worried he might die if they did not find him soon. The suspect, Magnus Gäfgen (now known as Thomas David Lukas Olsen, pictured in **Figure 4.2**), confessed to abducting and killing the boy and directed the police to where they could find his body. The court decided that the German police could not, under any circumstances, either torture or threaten to torture (as this was inhuman treatment) a suspect. They did, however, permit the court to use the finding of the boy's body and evidence found with the body to be used to convict the suspect (see *Gäfgen* v *Germany* (2011) 52 EHRR 1).

Part of the reasoning against the use or threat of torture is that we can never be certain that the suspect has the information. In this case the police threatened Gäfgen because they believed the child was alive and wanted to save him. But they were wrong; nothing could save the boy, he was already dead. This is proof that the authorities may get things wrong and to allow certain breaches of rights should never be condoned, it would be unjust.

However, would the threat or use of torture ever be justified if (using this case) the boy *were* in fact still alive?

Figure 4.2 Magnus Gäfgen, now known as Thomas David Lukas Olsen
Source: Boris Roessler/picture-alliance/dpa/AP Images

- A due process model believes in checks and balances to protect suspects from the abuse of power by the state and to ensure that the innocent are acquitted. This implies checks and balances which must be followed in each case but an acceptance that the rules may alter if the balance of power alters. The law in England and Wales on the 'right to silence' (the right to prevent people assuming guilt if one refused to answer questions) remained at the centre of the British criminal justice system until very recently. It was designed to protect suspects from undue pressure under questioning. Following the Police and Criminal Evidence Act 1984 all interviews were recorded (now they are often video recorded). These recordings meant that suspects were protected from unfair or oppressive questioning; as such due process lawyers thought that the power differential in the interview was now more equal. Once taping of interviews was the norm many due process lawyers argued that it was fair to allow the court to infer guilt in cases where a suspect refused to answer acceptable questions. Under due process protection against the drawing of inferences from silence

was not a right; it was only there to ensure a fairer balance of powers in the interview room.

- A rights model protects individual rights from state power. Whilst Article 3 is absolute most other rights in the Convention can be altered, but only if necessary for the protection of higher goals. The decision about whether a right or interest is protected does not depend on the whim of one state but is decided by judges drawn from all over Europe. Under a rights system if an individual should enjoy a particular right then they do not lose that protection just because the balance of power shifts a little, they enjoy it as of right. Therefore, if the right to silence was protected under the Convention it could not be jeopardised even if other things had altered.

Normative models—a conclusion

Table 4.2 is a summary of the three normative models, each of which sets out an ideal for the criminal justice system to follow. Each tends to prioritise the interests of

	Crime Control	**Due Process**	**Rights**
Aim	Keep law and order—punish offenders to deter criminal conduct and to control crime. Harsh sentences to try to protect the public	Administer justice in each case by using fair legal rules and procedures—the state and courts should be impartial arbiters	Ensure state power is fair and not arbitrary—to uphold democratic freedoms for everyone
Strategy	Police and courts guard law and order. They should not be over-controlled by rules	Checks and balances to protect suspects from abuse of power	Provide basic standards against which the actions of a state can be tested—rights for each person. These cannot be violated
Assumption	Guilt is implied—trust police professionalism	Presumption of innocence	Presumption of innocence. Guarantee that individuals enjoy their rights. Absolute right to a fair trial
Legal controls	Minimal—procedural rules should be kept to a minimum and if breached by the authorities that should not prevent evidence being admitted	Control on powers, especially police powers. These are checks and balances which must be followed in each case. If procedure is broken evidence may be excluded. Procedures may be legally altered	Individuals have rights which cannot be violated or altered. Evidence obtained in breach of rights should be excluded
Process	Speedy apprehension, conviction and punishment of offenders, what Packer (1968) calls a conveyor belt	Fair trial with complicated criminal processes (but can be compromised)	Right to a fair trial—absolute
Guilt/Innocence	Intent on convicting the guilty (even if some innocent people are convicted or some people's civil liberties are interfered with). Victim rights above those of the accused	Respect the civil liberties of everyone (even if some guilty people are acquitted)	Protecting individual rights—problem when victim and suspect rights collide
Idea of justice	Denunciation of crime. Community safety and crime control are paramount	Procedural justice—following the rules even if they deliver an unfair outcome	Justice which respects and seeks to uphold all rights—still not quite substantive justice, though closer to it

Table 4.2 Outline of the three normative criminal justice models

certain groups over others and will be used by people to make specific points. In evaluating the way a criminal justice system operates you need to consider all of these models, both normative and descriptive.

However, each of these models falls short of really getting to grips with justice. Some may deliver procedural justice but is that *real* justice? Procedural justice means that the procedures (often due process procedures) are correctly followed and applied equally in each case. It generally means that there is a system which is designed to resolve conflict or to divide burdens or benefits. If the procedures are unfair then the outcome will be unjust. What about substantive justice? Substantive justice is concerned with the way in which an individual evaluates important issues. It is more about the principle. What about a just outcome? This is a different question again—just outcome

is treatment that is fair and just, leading to a fair and just resolution of a situation, particularly as experienced by those who are involved. Ideally, process and substantive principles deliver just outcomes.

Justice is about public decision making regarding the distribution of goods and of negative things like punishment (distributive justice). It is also about trying to deliver moral outcomes and correcting problems which arise, e.g. deciding what should happen when A takes something from B (corrective justice). We need to look a little more closely at justice to study these more complex ideas. Therefore having looked at criminal justice models we will now delve deeper into the idea of justice. This chapter will now look in depth at four theoretical ideas of justice.

Philosophical ideas of justice

Many theorists have considered the concept of justice. Here you will be introduced to just four of these: Aristotle (384–322 B.C.), John Rawls (1971), Amartya Sen (2010), and communitarianism (e.g. Etzioni 1994). These have been chosen because they are the theorists or theories most commonly used when discussing justice in relation to the criminal justice system. They are also important because each also considers ideals of social justice and how these might be achieved. This is important in many theories of criminology.

Aristotle on justice

Since the time of ancient Greece people have been trying to define justice or identify what perfect justice might look like. Aristotle (a philosopher from ancient Greece 384–322 B.C., see web pages by Sandel) proposed that justice consisted of treating equals alike, and unequals differently in proportion to their inequality (their difference). Put more simply: some see this as meaning that all people should be treated equally, which is one of the main claims made by the law—the criminal law will be applied to everyone equally. However, there is a second part to this idea of justice: that those who are different deserve different treatment. This could have been used to say that rich and poor should enjoy different justice when faced with the criminal law, but that is not what Aristotle meant. For him, difference should only be considered when it is important to the decision being made and, in criminal decisions, wealth does not increase or decrease guilt. This second part of the rule is more concerned with what is known as distributive justice (or substantive justice),

which for Aristotle means that each person should enjoy or be given his or her desert (what someone deserves). The first part of the rule—to treat everyone equally—he saw as something the courts should ensure; the second part of the rule—to do with distribution of goods—should be done by the law makers, the legislature.

There is, however, a third aspect which needs to be decided both by the courts and the legislature. In all decisions it is important to decide when things are alike and different, such that it should be taken into account in decision making or law making. This looks reasonably simple until one tries to apply the rule. Think of the example earlier about food being stolen. A simple application of criminal law would lead to the perpetrator (the one who takes the food) being found guilty and punished. As noted, wealth or poverty are not issues which need to be considered when one decides whether someone is guilty or innocent. However, what about the punishment? There are a number of ways in which one might answer this question:

1. Many people (such as Judge Bazelon, 1976 and 1981) would not support punishing someone (Amy in our example in **What do you think 4.1**) who is hungry and steals food. Here they argue that this individual's need is greater than that of the owner and he/she whilst guilty should not face punishment, although we might ask him or her to apologise.

2. Others, such as Anthony Duff (2001), a British legal philosopher, would disagree. For Duff, applying the second part of Aristotle's rule—that the law maker in that country has a duty to ensure that goods such as food and money are fairly distributed (not necessarily

evenly but fairly)—is essential to a just and moral society. Where the law makers have failed to ensure such justice it means that the whole society has failed to ensure any justice. They have failed in their moral duty and therefore should not be permitted to punish others when they fail. By failing to ensure the second part of Aristotle's ideas they have lost the moral high ground and therefore lost the power to punish anyone. They cannot punish either the rich man or the poor man for stealing food. The victim cannot complain as he or she is complicit in the unfair distribution of goods, such as food and wealth.

3. A third group argue that the way in which food and wealth are distributed is immaterial to either the guilt or innocence or the decision to punish.

In many ways, therefore, Aristotle's idea drew out some important issues about justice: that it should take account of equality. This is useful, but only deals with one facet of the debate and whilst it is of some help in deciding difficult cases it does not provide answers. It is unable to guide us in deciding which inequalities should lead to different treatment so it is necessary to find other ideas which will take the analysis further.

John Rawls on justice

John Rawls (1921–2002) was an American moral and political philosopher. He worked for a time at Oxford University and was influenced by both Isaiah Berlin (1909–1997, political theorist and historian) and H. L. A. Hart (1907–1992, legal philosopher). Two major occurrences are also often thought to have shaped his ideas: the fact that he lost three brothers to illness when he was a child, and his experiences in the Second World War. Each of these instilled in him the idea that a civilised society was one which respected social justice. What this meant and how one might achieve social justice became the core of his professional work. Rawls wrote his most famous work, *A Theory of Justice*, in 1971 and it is still regarded as one of the foremost texts on political philosophy. His ideas have many followers and his position on justice is often referred to as Rawlsianism.

Rawls (pictured in **Figure 4.3**) argues that the first duty of any state or any group who rule others is to ensure that justice is respected. Without justice, he argues, nothing in a society can be seen to be truly good. Rawls wanted to find an ideal theory of justice with which to judge whether a society (or part of it) was just or not. Even more than that, Rawls wanted his ideal theory to be used to test whether actual policy choices are just or not, or to decide which policy choices would be most just. His theory is therefore intended to resolve all issues. He began

Figure 4.3 John Rawls
Source: Photo by Steve Pyke/Getty Images

with the idea that justice is not merely about equality but also about fairness. He assumes that the fairest society will be built on social justice.

To build his idea of justice, Rawls starts with what is called a social contract. The idea of a social contract is an agreement between all people in a society as to how that society should be run. Before the people in Rawls' state make their social contract he sets a few ground rules. Firstly, he says that everyone makes the contract from what he calls the 'original position', where each person is ignorant of what they presently enjoy before they contract with others to form the society. They do not know which sex, class, religion, or social position they belong to, they do not know whether they are rich or poor, powerful or powerless, etc. He calls this the 'veil of ignorance'.

Rawls says this 'veil of ignorance' is important because when each person makes the contract they do not know whether they stand to gain from the contract or lose by it. In that situation, he claims, they will choose what is fair and this will mean the contract will be just—for him that means it will be positive for everyone but be most advantageous for the least well off in society. He argues that each person in the 'original position' will make their choice using rational self-interest but as each person is ignorant of their present position they will set the contract so that it will give them the best chance of attaining the good life (whatever that person thinks of as necessary for their own happiness).

Rawls argues that any rational person in the 'original position' will always choose a contract (set of principles)

WHAT DO YOU THINK? 4.2

Freda has a cake which she has to cut up and share fairly between nine people. How would we ensure that Freda did this as fairly as possible?

Rawls argues that we should tell Freda that she would get the last piece. This places her in a sort of original position in that she might end up with the smallest piece. The idea is that each person would take the largest piece available when it came to their turn so that the only way

she can be sure to get her share is to cut the cake into nine equal parts.

- Do you agree with Rawls?
- Could this outcome be achieved any other way?
- Is it necessarily just for each person to get an equal sized piece?
- If one is starving would it be just to ensure that person got a larger portion?

which will be in their best interests should they turn out to be at the bottom of the social pile (for an example of how this might happen see **What do you think? 4.2**).

From this 'original position' Rawls says people will build a society based on two basic principles—liberty and equality:

1. First Principle (liberty):

   This refers to the fact that each person should have an equal right to as much basic liberty as is possible when making sure that everyone else enjoys the same amount of liberty.

   This is the most important principle and put simply this means equality of liberty for everyone. The liberties Rawls included here are sometimes referred to as political rights or basic rights, such as voting rights, freedom of speech and assembly, freedom of conscience, freedom from arbitrary arrest, etc. These he felt were so important no government should ever be able to interfere with them or take them away. Other rights or liberties, such as rights over property, he thought to be less important. Here Rawls is more interested in justice as something which can and should deliver fairness.

2. Second Principle (equality):

   This refers to the idea that social and economic inequalities are to be arranged so that:

   (a) ideally they are to be to everyone's advantage but where this is not fair they are to the greatest benefit of the least-advantaged, consistent with the just savings principle (the difference principle);

   (b) offices and positions must be open to everyone under conditions of fair equality of opportunity.

Rawls put (b), the right to equality of opportunity (including the opportunity to acquire skills necessary to advancement), as more important than and taking priority over (a), the difference principle (how to fairly distribute

difference). Equality of opportunity means that offices and positions such as jobs should be open to everyone and not depend on who you know or whether you are black or white, male or female. However, Rawls went further to note that everyone should have not just an opportunity, but an effective chance of success equal to others with similar talents no matter what their backgrounds. So, in any occupation there should be a percentage of people from rich and poor, etc. equal to the percentage of that group in the population. This wide idea of equality of opportunity may be adversely affected by application of the difference principle and therefore, to protect it, Rawls placed it as more important: it should come first.

The final part of his justice system is the difference principle, which decides what should happen when decisions have to be made about inequality. Put simply, the difference principle means that material differences can only be justified on the basis that they benefit the least advantaged, and that there should be fair equality of opportunity for everyone. This is designed to ensure that the worst off are properly provided for because here Rawls compensates for inequalities which may arise naturally or through the way society is formed, socially. Here the least well off (in all goods) are always to gain from the contract, so that there is some redistribution of all basic goods. This assumes that there should be some wealth distribution from the rich to the poor, however it does not expect that all goods should be equally distributed. Rawls therefore sees that inequality might be fair, as long as the inequality is not intrinsically unfair. The inequality should not be enough to interfere with the basic liberties. Furthermore, all decisions made by the society about this inequality tend to advantage the least advantaged.

Importantly, Rawls argued that people would see their liberty (the first principle) as more important than their equal right to goods and opportunities in society (the second principle). This is because no one would agree to risk their liberty, therefore this has to be guaranteed; it is all important to everyone. However, every intelligent and fully reasoning individual will agree to part (a) of the difference principle (or the equality principle) in case they are in the worst advantaged group, in which case all decisions have to be of most benefit to them as members of the least advantaged group. Rawls argues that liberty alone would be a form of total free market and does not distribute wealth nor interfere if you are lucky, e.g. to be born into wealth. For Rawls luck is not a just principle for the distribution of advantages. Rawls also rejects the idea of relying purely on equality of opportunity. This places the distribution of advantages on natural talent (plus a desire to exploit it). Whilst he considers this better than absolute liberty he considers that the luck of being born with talents that are, at the moment, thought to be good is not just or fair.

For Rawls it is very important to use these principles to set up just institutions, and establish just rules for the institutions to apply. Rawls put a lot of faith in the idea that just institutions would deliver justice. The constitution, institutions, and rules (laws) are set in stages where the veil of ignorance is slowly lifted, allowing the society to set up a scheme (constitution) to deliver justice and then institutions to give shape to that constitution, followed by rules (laws), and finally by an application of those laws in the society. At each stage, the individuals in the society learn more about their situation before they have to set up the next system. All decisions are to be guided by the basic principles. Rawls then places great faith in the institutions and systems which should only be questioned if they fail to apply the basic principles.

There are clear problems with Rawls' ideas. They are based on a contract so that non-contractors such as foreigners, future generations, nature, and the environment are not important (although there is a little protection for future generations in the just savings principle). This assumes that each society is cut off from others and that they do not affect each other; this is clearly not the case. It might, for example, mean that one society can create lots of pollution for the world and this would not be unjust as long as those within the society were justly treated. To take a criminal justice example, it would permit a state to decide that in the interests of protecting its law-abiding citizens and to punish all criminals, it could deport offenders and refuse to allow them back into the country. This action ignores the safety of people living in other states, the ones to which the deported offenders will be sent. It shows that Rawls' justice does not take account of people outside the contract, people who live in other countries. This happened in the 17th century when Britain transported many criminals to penal colonies in Australia. Most transportation occurred between 1788 and 1868 (about 160,000 people were transported). This type of treatment might be seen as unjust towards the offenders and their families (many never saw their families again) and was also unfair

on the indigenous population of Australia, whose interests and safety were never considered; at that time they were not of interest to the British Government.

Furthermore, many very intelligent and rational people in the 'original position' may choose to take a gamble and choose absolute liberty, hoping to be at the top of society (liberty over equality). Others may choose equality over liberty. There is no guarantee people in the 'original position' will choose this outcome nor that this outcome is fair or the fairest solution. If we take the idea that it is unjust for a person to take a large advantage just because they happen to be born with a talent which is prized, then Rawls' solution assumes that it is more just for everyone to gain from that talent, for it to be communally owned; is that fair? If the advantages which arise from talent are to be shared is it just to force the talented to use their talents so that we all gain?

Finally, the idea of just organisations giving rise to just solutions is never proven nor is it likely to be correct. Everything would depend on the rules being applied: if the rules are not just they would never deliver justice; if they are just for some situations but do not permit flexibility then they will be unjust in some situations.

If we return to the example given earlier in **What do you think? 4.1** about food being stolen, a simple application of the procedural rules would lead to the perpetrator (Amy, the one who takes the food) being found guilty and punished. Rawls' theory would agree that wealth and poverty are not issues which need to be considered when one decides whether someone is guilty or innocent. However, what about the punishment? Rawls accepts inequalities in wealth as being just so would not undermine the general right to punish simply because some people are less wealthy. However, in a particular case Rawls would accept that before deciding how to distribute punishment the decision maker should take account of all the facts and might mitigate the punishment in light of Amy's hunger.

Amartya Sen on justice

Amartya Sen (1933–) is an economist and a philosopher still working to refine his ideas (pictured in **Figure 4.4**). He was born in India and is particularly interested in real world and rational solutions. Like Rawls he aims to deliver social justice for everyone. He wants to improve well-being for all. He wants to free people from hunger, disease, indignity, and discrimination and to deliver real and greater positive freedoms and well-being by increasing their capacity or capabilities. He published *The Idea of Justice* in 2010.

Sen's central concept for justice is fairness. He questions Rawls' faith in institutions and processes as being capable of delivering justice. Whilst he recognises the importance of trying to set up just institutions and systems these alone, Sen argues, are not enough. Institutions will

Figure 4.4 Amartya Sen
Source: LSE Library@Flickr Commons/Public domain

not necessarily deliver good social outcomes. Importantly he questions the idea that there is any ideal theory of justice. He therefore questions the basis of Rawls' thinking. He argues that things are not clearly always just or unjust (it is not a binary idea). Justice exists on a continuum and whether something is just or not may depend both on circumstances and on who is assessing the situation, on different perspectives. He also argues that people can recognise justice (or injustice) without having clear theoretical guidance—you can recognise injustice without knowing what a perfectly fair society would look like or how it would justify itself. This almost sounds as if he is giving no concept of justice but that is not quite the case. Sen's passion for justice, individual and collective justice for all, is clearly evident in his writing. He also sees the need for justice to serve all communities across the globe and questions Rawls and other thinkers for only serving Western justice—he sees it as a global idea and something which should improve everyone's lives in all parts of the world.

Sen does not see people as driven by self-interest; they care for each other and generally observe social norms (rules or ethical or moral standards). He does not believe that they are always self-serving, seeking to improve their own lot, but rather sees that people question their own desires. For Sen well-being and happiness cannot be given cash value nor necessarily bought. The key to justice is complex, nuanced, and somewhat subjective. However, it is linked to the desire to counter evils such as hunger, disease, victimisation, indignity, discrimination, and lack of safety all of which are measurable. The key for Sen is that if one counters these negatives, one increases people's capacity or capabilities and also increases equality.

Sen draws on Sanskrit literature (Niti and Nyaya) which give him his two conceptions of justice:

1. Correct procedures and formal rules can give a starting point (Niti).

2. The decisions from these need to be tested by 'impartial spectators' to ensure they emerge with just results (social realisation).

Fairness and justice are therefore assessed by the 'impartial spectators' who view the decision from different vantage points to give a plurality of points of view—a complex assessment of justice. Impartial spectators are people who are separated from their own self-interest and can make a dispassionate assessment of justice, able to recognise justice and injustice. They are able to take a 'social choice' perspective—to combine individual preferences, interests, or welfare needs and reach a collective rational decision which will improve or uphold social justice. Each of these impartial spectators may come to a different decision on justice because motivation, rationality and well-being are complex and can be analysed in differing ways.

Sen sets out an example (Sen 2010: 13):

- Three children: Ann, Bob, and Carla, are quarrelling over the fate of a flute.
  - Ann claims the flute on the basis that she is the only one who can play it;
  - Bob claims it because he has no other toys to play with whereas the others do; and
  - Carla's claim is based on the fact that she made the flute in the first place.
- If one took a utilitarian approach (greatest good for the greatest number) or looked at the purpose of the flute and decided on that basis, then Ann would get the flute as she can play it (fit its purpose) and will bring joy to people who hear her play (utilitarian).
- If equality is brought to the fore then Bob will get the flute as he does not have anything else to play with.
- If it is all based on legal rights then Carla will get the flute as it belongs to her.

However, Sen argues that there is merit in all three answers as each outcome would increase the well-being of at least one person. He argues that there are many correct and just answers to any problem and we should embrace the fact that justice has many faces—pluralism. He suggests that we merely deal with situations that are clearly unjust in all cases, e.g. that the problem is difficult so we destroy the flute and no-one has it.

Well-being depends on constantly striving to increase people's entitlement and freedom, so increasing their capacity to engage in their communities. Justice and well-being are measured by the social outcome—the measurable increase in positive outcomes for people. There is no ideal formula, no one answer to a problem. In deciding on justice we should always take account of moral or ethical values and judgements but should recognise that they are value laden and there is a need to respect alternative values. In deciding on justice, rights are central and should never be ignored, but are not preeminent or paramount. However, other things are also important: sociability; moral constraint; respect for others; freedom; safety and security; distribution of goods; social and communal living; and equality. These are not always easy to interpret. So with equality there is always the question of 'equality of what'? Is it that we give each person an equal chance or that we look at the outcome and ensure that one group is not unfairly disadvantaged by decisions? If one group is disadvantaged then Sen argues that we need to advantage individuals from that group over others until the disadvantage is dealt with (maybe through use of positive discrimination). The only aspects which are always important and are essential are social justice, well-being, and capacity.

Therefore Sen recognises that any theory or idea about justice has something useful to say about the real choices we actually face and how we might resolve those choices. Almost any problem involving justice and resolution of social justice and freedom can have plural resolutions which may be incompatible but each may have merit, so each should be considered and respected. This means that justice will always be a work in progress (incomplete) and learning to compromise. Recognition that there is no ideal is an important aspect of life and justice. In any socially relevant decision, and certainly those involved in the criminal justice system, different individual and collective needs and priorities will vie for prominence and at each juncture there is a need to take account of social policy. Understanding and testing the decisions and outcomes will help to improve justice. Recognising and rationally debating conflicting just outcomes allows the nuances of problems to be fully considered and understood; it is likely to lead to better, more fully just, outcomes.

If we return to the example about food being stolen (**What do you think? 4.1**), Sen would not assume that criminal law would necessarily be the just way to resolve this dilemma. The issue might be resolved by a more restorative or community-based outcome, such as an apology to the victim and support for Amy to increase her financial capacity so that she would not need to steal. If criminal law were to be used he would admit that justice would be served if Amy, the one who takes the food, is found guilty. Once found guilty however, the issue of whether or not to punish would open up more conflicting outcomes, each of which might have a claim to be just. He would accept that there might be many just ways of punishing Amy; each would serve justice in some way but in so doing would prevent a different idea of justice being served. In such a situation Sen calls on decision makers such as the police and judges to become 'impartial spectators', willing and able to consider all outcomes and take both individual and collective perspectives into account before making a final decision.

Communitarianism—ideological and philosophical

So far we have discussed Aristotle and Rawls, who both focus on individualistic ideas of justice, as do the criminal justice models of justice. Communitarianism, which we will now explore, sees these ideas as being too focused on individual rights and freedoms, too inward looking and absorbed with self-interest. Despite Sen's calls for a multicultural and open approach to justice even he is seen, by most communitarians, as focusing too closely on the individual in his search for justice.

Communitarians consider that social order is best upheld by protecting and nurturing informal communal bonds. Communitarians see both left wing (welfare and rights) and right wing (the market) solutions to making society fairer as being wrongly focused because they ignore the social needs of human beings. They emphasise the connections between individuals and their communities, focusing on the fact that humans live in close communities and societies because we need each other. They see us as social beings, not separate individual beings, and argue that most ideas of justice, especially the individual and rights-based systems so far considered, ignore this social aspect of human needs. Communitarians focus on solidarity and belonging; they call on us to stop searching for liberty and individual rights and focus instead on cultural controls in small close-knit communities. The idea is that small, local communities should make their own decisions. Whilst ideas of social solidarity have a long pedigree and the word communitarianism has been used for at least 150 years, the ideas of communitarianism we will consider here have a fairly modern basis.

Amitai Etzioni

One of the best known modern conservative communitarians is the Israeli-American sociologist Amitai Etzioni (1929–). Etzioni (1994) does not reject individual rights but sees these as needing to be nested in and understood against a sense of community. He claims that through strengthening the community and its institutions, such as schools and local employers, each individual in that community is strengthened. At points he is very clear that he wants to recreate the more stable, law-abiding and orderly past experienced in America in the 1950s where there was a more culturally agreed moral consensus and widely agreed norms (1994: 22). This form of communitarianism focuses on ensuring that society and everyone in it behaves in a law-abiding and orderly fashion. The expectation is that individuals should respect each other and the whole community:

> communitarians call to restore civic virtues, for people to live up to their responsibilities and not to merely focus on their entitlements, and to shore up the moral foundations of society.
>
> Etziono 1995: ix

Individual rights (at least democratic and social) should be tempered by a call on community so that the right to free speech should be permitted as long as it does not damage others in the community (though note here that conservative communitarians do not question property rights which they generally wish to preserve). Etzioni questions the strong sense of entitlement that rights ideologies give rise to, at the expense of community responsibility, and calls for a strengthening of a sense of moral obligation owed, he argues, by each person to others in their society. In terms of criminal justice this leads to calls for close community policing and a use of strong, draconian ideas of shaming offenders and those who break other social mores. He sees that justice will be delivered through security which can only exist if there is a tight, homogenous community. This form of communitarianism ignores the racial, homophobic, and gendered nature of these homogenous communities in the past. It also goes counter to many modern ideas of justice as it rejects the multi-culturalism and globalisation agendas that are common today. Sen, for example, calls on us to take account of the way in which various individuals or groups might define justice before deciding how best to resolve a situation; for him there is not one just outcome but many and the secret is to choose the most valid in any particular situation. Sen would attack Etzioni and communitarianism for their protection of relatively narrow Anglo/American cultural mores and the fact that they ignore other perspectives. His thesis would argue that they miss the possibility of alighting on real just outcomes which take account of the wider perspective, seeing issues from the different perspectives of each person in each situation. Furthermore, Etzioni is rather vague about how justice within communitarianism will be assured.

Radical communitarianism

There are other forms of communitarianism which arise more from the left of politics and focus on solidarity and mutual respect or reciprocity: radical communitarianism. Radical communitarians suggest justice is better achieved in small-scale communities in which each member participates in democratic decision making. Radical communitarians recognise that there may be multi-cultural values (not homogenous values) in a community and that the plurality of values can be resolved into a just solution through discussion and full participation in decision making.

The ideas of radical communitarians are not linked to just one theorist but arise out of the ideals of socialist solidarity. However, the American criminologist Elliott Currie (1942–) is often strongly linked to radical communitarianism and his ideas, especially in relation to justice and criminal justice, will be briefly considered. Currie, and other modern proponents of radical communitarianism, recognise that democracy and community decisions do not always respect minority or individual interests and therefore they argue that individual rights and moral autonomy need to be guaranteed to protect each person in the community from the dangers of the powerful majority (Currie 1997). Radical communitarians embrace the multi-cultural and pluralistic nature of society and see community solidarity and respect for each other as the best way to guarantee tolerance and just decision making. They point to modern Western liberal states as allowing one section of the community (the rich and powerful) to exploit the others (the poor, largely disenfranchised, powerless, and excluded). Radical communitarians argue that democracy in these neo-liberal societies is unjust for large numbers of people and that the exploited have lost any real autonomy and quality of life; their individual and group moral authority has been silenced. For these theorists, like Currie, many of the ills in society arise due to the loss of solidarity within society. The absence of any idea of a common good or a common goal and the feelings of exclusion, marginalisation, and inequality release people to offend; the lack of solidarity is a root cause of crime and other ills in society.

Here justice involves redistribution of the goods in society and where problems arise there needs to be a focus on reintegration rather than shaming. Through redistribution and reintegration, radical or social communitarians argue that each individual will be better placed to participate in decision making and support the community; each will be more likely to choose a path that is supportive of both themselves and others in the community. Their first ideal of redistribution is based on social justice (fairer distribution of all goods) though often needs greater explanation of how to ensure that the new distribution is fair or just. The second assumes that reintegration is sufficient to right all wrongs but again fails to properly engage with justice as it often ignores the harm that might have been caused. There is in this radical communitarianism no concept of how these ideals might be delivered nor any real proof that their achievement would necessarily deliver safer, more just, more cohesive, and less crime-ridden societies. Whilst much of what is argued by this group may sound as if it might lead to greater justice, this is difficult to fully assess as there is not enough detail to analyse whether their ideals would lead to a more just society or more just outcomes.

One criminal justice resolution which is often strongly linked to or claimed by communitarianism is restorative justice (Braithwaite 2002). Certainly in its original Maori usage, where a whole community agrees on the outcome of a transgression and the whole community unites to support both the victim and offender to ensure a more positive outcome in the future, one can see aspects of communitarianism. However, most modern societies do not permit this whole community resolution nor are they as culturally homogenous or unified as the old Maori communities.

Restorative justice in most Western societies seeks to heal and put right the wrongs which arise from the offending; there is an appearance that the whole resolution is voluntary, though the offender often has the worry of a full criminal trial if they refuse to cooperate. Often the community or the state merely ensures that the victims interests are met but does not necessarily then mend the problem by supporting either the offender or the victim to build more positive lives, or at least if it does this it

is not usually a necessary part of the restorative justice process. The process of reintegrative shaming or restorative justice as used in many Western systems allows a community to stigmatise an offender for what they have done. This part of the process delivers the stigma called for by conservative communitarians. It is then restorative for the victim but often fails to fully restore the offender back into their community. Radical communitarians would argue that this failure prevents the systems being truly restorative; it is not restorative for the community as a whole because the offender may reoffend, and even if they do not they may still feel aggrieved and cause other problems for the community. In this situation it is questionable whether this is true justice. In radical communitarianism there would be a focus on using restorative justice to redistribute goods and the reintegrative element would be focused on the offender (without any stigma). This approach would sideline or ignore the position of the victim and again might not be truly just. True restorative justice gives equal weight to all three, it recognises the need to restore victims, offenders, and communities and that each has to support the needs of the other two (see Braithwaite 2002).

Systems of criminal justice—adversarial and inquisitorial

Most of what we have so far been considering revolves around the content of decision making rather than the process. Whilst Rawls set out a process for deciding how to achieve justice, even his ideas largely embraced ideals such as equality, rather than being practical. In the case of criminal justice there is a need for the state to intervene in what might once have been private matters; this requires very practical rules which Rawlsian justice, along with the other broad ideals, might fail to provide.

However, once we have a process or system these theorists' ideas can be used to test how just the system is. The criminal justice system needs practical and clear rules because serious wrongs need to be addressed. Serious wrongs, crimes, are ones in which the public shares: Duff stated, 'as members of the community, we should see them not merely as the victim's wrongs but as "our" wrongs' (2001: 63) and we should make it clear that we, as a society or state, are not willing to tolerate certain types of behaviour, that those who perpetrate certain wrongs 'should be called to account and censured by the community' (Duff 2001: 61). Here Duff is claiming that there are certain types of behaviour which are so unacceptable that the whole of society should be unwilling to tolerate them, that justice requires us to act.

Where this happens the state has to decide how to dispense such justice; how to decide when and why to censure someone and who to censure. Therefore each state or community where justice is dispensed needs to have a system or mechanism to decide what would be just, who should be punished; a mechanism to dispense justice. The criminal justice system in each jurisdiction is generally constituted of: control processes and agents such as the police, who investigate and channel people through to the rest of the system (maybe choosing to divert, reintegrate, or process through the full criminal justice system); court processes where decisions are made concerning guilt or innocence; agents and systems to punish, rehabilitate, or control. The whole criminal justice system should exist to empower rather than control a population: ensuring that as many people as possible live full and free lives and enjoy their rights as long as they respect the freedom and rights of others. In other words, the system should only intervene when necessary. To deliver on that ideal there need to be mechanisms to guide the criminal justice system towards the best outcomes. Each section of the system has rules and standards within which it needs to operate.

Clearly the criminal justice system is vast, in terms of its workings and processes, but here we will limit ourselves to considering the system which is used in court. Each state uses a system loosely linked to one of the central types of criminal justice system. In most Western states one of two central types of system is normally used: an adversarial or an inquisitorial system.

In the United Kingdom and in all common law countries, the system is largely based on an adversarial system. In most of continental Europe and many codified legal systems their criminal justice systems are largely based on the inquisitorial system. Whilst there was a time when these two systems were fairly pure in the areas in which they were used, modern criminal justice systems borrow from one another so that, as Tulkens states, 'nowhere is the model any longer pure; it is, for better or worse, contorted, attenuated, modified' (1995: 8). The two systems have some things in common: they are both designed to convict the guilty and each tries to protect against convicting the innocent; they both intend to protect the interests of wider society and so make their society safer and empower innocent people to live their lives free of fear. They disagree about how best to deliver on these ideals.

Adversarial systems

The adversarial system is based on a contest between the accused and the accuser (the victim and the state). The state has to draw together sufficient evidence to prove, *beyond reasonable doubt*, that the accused is guilty. This system is about the contest and it is not primarily designed to establish the *truth*. In an adversarial system the search for the *truth* (if it happens at all) occurs earlier; the police follow the evidence until they are sure that they have unearthed what happened and who is guilty. At that point the state uses all its powers to prove the guilt of the accused. Whilst the police might sift through all possible outcomes before finding their suspect, they are not required to do that. The police are not required to conduct an inquiry, they merely investigate an occurrence. The evidence they find is then tested in court. The state has to convince a magistrate(s) or a jury *beyond reasonable doubt* that the person they are accusing is guilty. It is important to remember that the accused does not have to prove that they are innocent, they merely need to raise sufficient doubt about their guilt; raise sufficient questions to throw doubt on the prosecution evidence.

When most people think of our system they picture a judge in wig and gown presiding over a court and 12 jurors (ordinary people) deciding whether they believe the accused is guilty; this is the Crown Court system. If the accused does not plead guilty, cases in the Crown Court generally take days if not weeks to conclude. However, the Crown Court is in fact only used for the more serious cases (only 3–4 per cent of all criminal trials); it is not

the normal arena for criminal cases. Most criminal trials (96–97 per cent) take place in magistrates' courts. In a magistrates' court the trial is heard by either a professional stipendiary magistrate (who sits alone) or by a bench of lay-magistrates (usually three), who are advised by the Clerk to the Court (a local solicitor) on legal matters. In the magistrates' court the magistrate(s) decide whether the case is proven beyond reasonable doubt. Cases in the magistrates' court tend to be over quite quickly, as many people plead guilty. Even in cases where the accused pleads not guilty, the magistrates' court will usually conclude the case in less than a day.

Regardless of which court hears the case, the trial is adversarial and the contest is led by the lawyers: prosecution lawyers for the state and defence lawyers for the accused. These lawyers present the evidence that they want the court to consider (not necessarily everything they know) and the lawyers only have to present the jury with the information that is most beneficial for their case, which is not always the same as the truth. The judge is there to make sure that the lawyers only use permitted evidence and to sum up the case to the jury, to explain some of the law (in magistrates' courts this is done by the Clerk to the Court). On the face of it the jury (or magistrate's bench) decides which set of facts they believe, whether a case has been proven beyond reasonable doubt. However, the jury (magistrate's bench) does more than that: if they think a law is unfair or unjust they can choose to acquit even if the proof is overwhelming. An example of this was the case of Clive Ponting in 1985. Ponting was accused of offences under the Official Secrets Act 2011. He was accused of leaking government documents to the press about the sinking of an enemy ship, the Belgrano, during the Falkland's war. The judge directed the jury that if they believed he leaked the documents the law required them to convict, they had a duty to convict. There was overwhelming proof that Ponting leaked the documents. Despite that the jury acquitted Ponting. It has always been assumed that they did this because they felt that it would be unjust to apply the letter of the law in that case. In England and Wales jury members are not permitted to discuss their work so we can never be sure of why they acquitted Ponting, but it seems to be the only logical explanation. The jury therefore are in a powerful position to make decisions they think are just, even if that does not follow the facts they are presented at trial. Juries are therefore very powerful and seen as bringing fairness and impartiality to the case. Whilst this makes the jury appear very positive there are problems with their position. Firstly, they do not have to explain their decision to anyone so the defendant does not know why he or she has been convicted. This lack of an explanation of the decision makes appeals against jury decisions very difficult as one does not know which aspect of the case one needs to undermine. Partly for this reason, appeals against convictions are very difficult in common law countries. In some jurisdictions, including England and Wales, the convicted person has to find new evidence before anyone will even consider an appeal or re-trial.

The core of an adversarial system is as follows: the trial is crucial; oral evidence (from the victim, witnesses, and accused) heard at trial is central to most cases; there are clear rules which determine what each person (judge, lawyers, jury) is permitted to do and to decide what evidence can and cannot be heard in court. This system originated in Britain and is something that has been exported to many other jurisdictions. Many argue that it allows the accused the best chance of justice. However, does it seek justice more broadly? What about truth? The main problem with the adversarial system is that it is a sort of game and may not be best suited to delivering truth and or justice in all cases. The outcome may depend on how charismatic and persuasive the lawyer is rather than the weight of facts in the case. Witnesses, particularly vulnerable witnesses who may be telling the truth, can be frightened by and become flustered by the experience of having to appear in court. They may forget things under pressure or appear to be less confident about the truth merely because they are nervous. Whilst some witnesses can use special measures (e.g. pre-videoed evidence) this is not available to all. The main advantage is that every accused person has a chance to prove their innocence to their peers; they have a chance of being acquitted.

The inquisitorial system

The inquisitorial system is completely different. This claims to be a search for *truth*. Whilst each inquisitorial system is slightly different, they generally turn around the building of a file. Everything that the police have done to investigate the case should be written up and be contained in the case file or *dossier*, containing all the investigative information. The dossier is then made available to all interested parties (or at least to their lawyers). In this way everyone knows all the evidence against the accused as well as any evidence which might point in other directions (at least that which the police have followed up and thought important enough to put into the dossier). In theory, the dossier contains everything of relevance to the case, but the police may choose not to include some things in the dossier; absence of information in the dossier might affect the outcome of the case. For this reason the police are tightly regulated about what they can and cannot do, and in many systems (e.g. France and Netherlands) they appoint a judge at the start of an investigation who oversees the investigation and may also be able to direct the police to follow up various lines of enquiry.

The dossier contains the evidence which will convict or acquit the accused. It is the contents of the dossier which is considered in court; often there is no confrontational trial of evidence in court. In some inquisitorial jurisdictions there is no jury at all and in others the jury and judge together decide on an outcome. Inquisitorial systems often see juries as unpredictable and capable of returning unjust verdicts so that they are not generally trusted to make the decision as to guilt or innocence alone. Decisions, and the reasons for them, are often given in open court, thereby facilitating any appeal.

The core of the inquisitorial system is the investigation and the dossier to which it gives rise. Witnesses are generally questioned in less stressful situations, often with just the inquisitorial judge present. The defence lawyers may be able to ask questions or to get the judge to ask questions for them, but the accused is often not present. The decision as to guilt or innocence is generally made either by one or more professional judges or by a judge(s) along with some lay-people (but not by just lay-people). The decision is therefore less likely to rely on a charismatic lawyer and be more likely to rest on the facts. Furthermore, as the dossier is available before the trial and can be studied at length, the decision as to guilt or innocence is more likely to be carefully considered and to rest on the information uncovered during the investigation rather than be affected by dramatic uncovering of evidence in court.

Evaluating the systems

For a full consideration of each of these systems and of others, such as Islamic justice systems, see Pakes (2004). The systems are very different and following major miscarriages of justice in England and Wales, such as those involving the Guildford Four and the Birmingham Six, there have sometimes been suggestions that we should look carefully at our adversarial system, and maybe adopt the inquisitorial system (see, for example, the Royal Commission on Criminal Justice, 1993). As noted at the start of this section, what has happened is that we increasingly borrow ideas from the inquisitorial system and alter them slightly to work in our adversarial system (such as requiring the defence to disclose their case to the prosecution before trial or permitting vulnerable witnesses to give evidence via video-link). These changes generally occur so as to better deliver justice though there are some, such as Michael Zander (see his dissenting opinion in the Report of the Royal Commission on Criminal Justice, 1993: 221–35), who see them as undermining that ideal. Recently, there have been suggestions for changes, particularly to the use of juries, which have occurred or been suggested to speed up justice and/or to save money rather than to serve justice (Cooper 2012).

Our system, like systems in other countries, is constantly evolving. Whilst retaining their fundamental differences the adversarial and inquisitorial systems of criminal justice are constantly converging and becoming more similar. Whether they are delivering more just outcomes as a result is not clear.

Drawing ideas together

At first sight it is probably difficult to work out exactly how the criminal justice models and philosophical writings about justice can fit with a chapter to consider justice, especially justice as it applies in criminology and therefore criminal justice. The models set out some of the important issues which have traditionally been attached to testing whether the criminal justice system is just. However, they leave much out, they do not fully consider the *need* for such a system—what just purpose it serves— nor do they always help in assessing justice in particular cases. The philosophical ideas about justice are generally interesting but it is often difficult to see how they link to justice within a corrective system such as the criminal justice system. It is particularly difficult to use them to resolve individual cases: this final section will therefore throw light on these issues and help you to apply some of the ideas.

To illustrate most of our points we will look at sentencing and punishment; these are often the end results of criminal actions. The offender commits a crime, is caught and found guilty, and then the state has to decide how to deal with the offender.

As noted in the 'Introduction', many see equal treatment as paramount to fairness. So where a crime is committed the punishment should be proportionate to the action (the crime and the harm caused by it). This idea can be seen to link into the scales of justice (discussed at the start of the chapter). Here the amount of punishment goes on one side and the seriousness of the offence and the harm caused goes on the other; to deliver justice the scales should balance. To illustrate the point—if Gabby steals a pint of milk and Helen murders someone it would generally be seen to be unjust if they both faced life in prison or the death penalty. In this example the scales would not balance in Gabby's case because the harm caused does not match the punishment. In such a situation Gabby would feel (quite rightly) that she had been unfairly treated and might even regret not having done something more serious—why not if you are to receive the same punishment? It would also be unjust from the societal perspective; it would fail to help to teach people moral standards—it would indicate that murder and theft are equal.

Treating like cases alike is seen by many as being just (see Aristotle and Rawls). It fits well with crime control as long as the punishment is also swift and punitive. It would also be seen as useful to Durkheim's stigmatisation model as each person can see clearly what is wrong and how important a transgression it is; how much people should be stigmatised for participating in that behaviour. The idea that punishment should fit the crime has been part of our system since the enlightenment thinkers such as Beccaria (1767) suggested it. More recently it has been part of the drive behind an increasing limit put on the discretion of judges and other decision makers by setting out sentencing guidelines and by increasing the number and type of offence for which there is a minimum sentence.

However, this tendency and call to treat like cases alike may also fail to deliver justice; it may lead to injustice. Let us return to Amy and compare her case with that of Colin (see **What do you think? 4.1**): each has stolen some food so on the equal treatment or proportionality argument they should receive the same punishment. However, to give them the same punishment would ignore underlying context and issues which may be relevant to why the crime was committed. Such a course of action may also ignore injustices and/or victimisations which may have been caused by the structure of society (e.g. a society that does not effectively prevent abject poverty). Amy was poor and very hungry, whereas Colin may well be neither of these things.

Both Rawls and Sen considered issues such as social justice (offending related to poverty or need) as relevant to an assessment of justice. Treating two cases in the same way, giving out the same punishment, may also ignore injustices and/or victimisations that society should have dealt with and has not (victimisation, that has possibly been ignored for years). Rawls and Sen each consider that justice requires a state to deal with injustices. Dealing with injustices is also relevant to communitarian ideas because if stigmatisation is intended to reinforce social cohesion then it needs to be seen to be just. Punishment needs to take account of and recognise the harm that a person has done in committing the crime, but they must not be too harsh. If punishments are too harsh, either generally or in individual cases, people will view the whole system as unjust and distrust it.

Under radical communitarianism and the power model, if punishment is more severe for certain groups (the poor) by failing to take account of their situation then it is unjust. Therefore many criminal justice models and philosophers consider that the underlying context in which crime is committed is at least important to some degree in ensuring just punishment. So whilst we work towards delivering social justice we may need to treat the disadvantaged more leniently. Duff (2001) would suggest that this does not go far enough and would question the state's right to punish at all unless and until it delivers social justice. Although many philosophers and theorists might agree that the severity of punishment should take account of injustices, few would agree that punishment cannot be used until a society delivers social justice. Furthermore, theorists are unlikely to agree about how punishment should take account of injustice. They are unlikely to agree on which differences or injustices are sufficiently serious to count as social injustices or how much to reduce punishment to take account of each injustice.

Should Amy and Colin's sentences differ in the following situations: if one has been sexually victimised as a child; if one is being abused now; if one is racially disadvantaged; if one is addicted to drugs; if one has dependent children, etc? If these differences should lead to different punishments then how do we decide how much to reduce a punishment? Rawls would answer that we take account of those differences which would be chosen in the 'veil of ignorance': i.e. the differences that everyone would agree were important if they did not know what their situation would be. Sen would recognise that justice might be served by many answers and that decision makers or 'impartial spectators' should openly discuss the outcomes and explain why one outcome would deliver more entitlement and well-being than another to ensure that they are seen to take justice seriously—one might then disagree but can respect the outcome. Conservative communitarians would argue that only those aspects important to the homogeneous community should be considered, whereas radical communitarians would respect the rights of the individual and take account of those elements which need to be corrected in order to redistribute goods or restore an equal and balanced community. Each of these makes a valid argument. You need to understand their arguments, work out what they would mean in practice and begin to play with the ideas and build your own concepts of justice.

Why does justice matter? Why should we try to make sure that our sentencing decisions and all other decisions in criminal justice and in wider society are just? Why is justice central to our subject? The criminal law and the criminal justice service impact most directly on certain groups. For some people the main way in which they relate to the state or experience the state is through the criminal justice system. If that system is experienced as

or seen to be unfair to them or to people like them (other poor people or people from their racial/sex group), they will learn to disrespect it. Still worse, if the state is seen to be violent or brutal towards them or people like them, they may learn that power, violence, and brutality are acceptable and effective ways of teaching people and of getting things done. In that situation criminal law and its enforcement may actually be the problem rather than the solution. In this way injustice causes more harm than it resolves—some of the models discussed may be more likely to lead to these consequences (see the examples in **Telling it like it is 4.1**).

We constantly need to search for resolutions to criminal conflict that are just to victims and offenders alike and that have a positive outcome overall, increasing well-being for everyone. To do that we must never be blind to contextual aspects of situations—what brings people to act the way they did. Issues of past victimisation, social injustice, and deprivation need to be addressed to increase the well-being of particular individuals, to support them to live more positive lives. However, on a broader idea of justice a state should seek to prevent or address injustices for all people. These ideals would be accepted by many theorists because many envisage at least some fair distribution of goods and burdens (e.g. the second rule of Rawls; Sen's broad writings about the importance of increasing the entitlement of each individual and radical communitarians).

We need to seek to uphold human rights of victims and offenders and where they conflict, the conflict needs to be resolved in a way which preserves as much of the rights for each group as possible, even if that is at the expense of the state. Here the justice of removing things like legal aid has to be seriously questioned—does it interfere with the ability of suspects to defend themselves and, if so, can a trial be just and fair?

Punishment and the criminal justice system generally need to operate justly; be felt to operate justly. They should empower, not control, people, communities, and society. If they are experienced as being about control they may be causing more of a social problem than is caused by crime (at least in some areas or for some groups) and may actually be adding to the likelihood of criminality. If the system and punishment are too harsh they cause social division rather than social cohesion.

All groups and sections of our society need to have a strong voice in the discussions about how our society should be shaped—where justice and fairness lie. We need to be open to cultural differences and to different ways of resolving a situation, especially if one of the parties to a situation comes from a different culture.

SUMMARY

- Explain and appreciate why justice is so important

From a very young age, children tend to almost instinctively understand that justice is important, that they should enjoy the same as others in their community. Why do children have this almost instinctive feeling that justice is important? It is generally accepted that any society or group of people—family, school, university, community, state, the world—is improved if it embraces justice as one of its core ideals because in a just society each person is valued equally. Justice ensures that no one person or one group enjoys more rights than another and that no person or group should be denied rights enjoyed by others. A fully just society calls on each person to respect the rights of everyone else, it is a standard to live up to. When people break standards of justice they should face consequences. Similarly, when they are good they should be appreciated.

- Critically consider the criminal justice approaches to justice and evaluate how these help our understanding of the concept and its outcomes

In relation to crime, a society expects people to refrain from breaking the law. So part of justice is that we should not—for example—kill each other or that we should drive carefully. If we all live up to the ideal of justice in relation to crime it should ensure that each individual in a society is safe both from other people and from the tyranny of the state or of the majority. In a just society, the offenders are punished (to prevent them gaining from their wrongdoing) and/or supported to change their behaviour in the future (to prevent future offending). Whether the punishment or intervention is experienced as fair or just may depend on the circumstances. A person driving over the speed limit on a road where others were driving faster may feel aggrieved if he or she is the only one punished but may see the fairness if everyone is punished. The amount of punishment in a just society should reflect the seriousness of what someone has done and the amount of harm they have caused. So a murderer should be punished more harshly than someone who steals a pen from a shop. If two people have committed the same offence (theft of the same amount of money) one would expect the same punishment, for example, the same level of fine, say £100. However, if one is rich and the other poor a fine of £100 will hurt the poor person more that the rich person. In that situation there are some who would argue the rich person should face a harsher fine. To decide what the most just outcome would be is a very complex consideration and people often disagree about what is just or unjust.

- Describe the six criminal justice models and be able to critically assess each one

Descriptive models:

There are three descriptive models: bureaucratic, denunciation and status passage, and power. None of these sets out what a system of justice should look like, rather they describe or critique the systems they find.

The function of the bureaucratic model is to manage crime and criminals in the most efficient and cost-effective way possible. It sets out clear processes to be followed by law enforcement officials, believing that these will lead to the right results and will cut down on subjective decision making.

The status passage model sees the function of criminal justice as being to draw the good together to denounce crime and criminals and so re-enforce societal values.

The power model accuses the criminal justice system of controlling the poor or other disadvantaged groups in order to benefit the wealthy or advantaged groups.

Normative models:

We covered three normative models: due process, crime control, and rights. Each of these sets out what they consider a system of justice should look like and which aspects of the system are most important.

The due process model seeks to deliver justice for suspects and offenders and believes this is the best way to ensure a more just community. The model recognises that in most criminal cases the state has more access to resources than does the defendant so it sets out rules which try to ensure that suspects and defendants are fairly treated. For due process theorists it is important that innocent people are not convicted even if some guilty people go free.

Crime control models are about ensuring that people are swiftly and harshly punished for wrongdoing and that all wrongdoing (or as much as possible) is punished. The crime control model believes that the professionals (like the police) should be trusted and reduces the controls on their powers. For crime control theorists it is important that all guilty people are convicted even if some innocent people are also convicted.

Rights theorists want to protect democratic freedoms and, in particular, want to protect individuals from the misuse of power by the state. This leads to real restraints on how state agents work. Rights theorists want to ensure all guilty people are convicted and all innocent people are acquitted, and that the state is proportionate and respectful in the way in which it deals with each individual.

It is important to be able to identify and describe the models as this will permit you to use them to evaluate and analyse criminal justice decisions you come across in your studies.

• Outline and evaluate the four philosophical approaches to justice that take a broad view of the concept, and allow you to see how justice and injustice can impact on society, crime, security, and well-being

To help us decide what would or would not be just, many philosophers and others have discussed at length how to achieve justice. In this chapter we have looked at four approaches.

For Aristotle the core of justice lies in equality. Generally, people should be treated equally. However, if they are different then they should be treated differently to the extent that they are different. To give rise to different treatment, the difference should be relevant to the issue being discussed. It would not be just to alter the amount of punishment someone should get because the judge likes or dislikes the colour of their eyes.

For Rawls justice will be guaranteed under a social contract—an agreement that underpins a society. The first principle of his agreement is that every person should enjoy equality in relation to the core rights. His second principle is that where there are inequalities, any decisions should benefit the least advantaged. As with Aristotle the difference in treatment should be pertinent to the issue being discussed. We noted that some would think it just to fine everyone the same amount when their crime is the same whereas others would fine poor people less so that their fine hurts them the same amount as it hurts the rich person. The difference here advantages the poor person (the least advantaged). Note that it might not, however, be just to increase the fine to the rich person as then they might have to pay more than would be fair for the harm they caused. Here the process of deciding what is just is trusted to deliver justice.

Sen, while agreeing with the general idea that everyone should be equal and enjoy equal rights and social standards, disagrees with Rawls that using the right process or rules will always deliver justice. For Sen one needs to take account of all the factors in each particular case. He also argues that we need to understand and embrace the idea that there is rarely one just outcome. There are likely to be a number of competing outcomes, each of which might be viewed as just; different people would view the situation differently. In deciding which outcome, he argues we should keep social justice, well-being, and capacity in mind; for Sen these are at the core of justice. He pleads for tolerance and for listening to the competing ideas of justice before finally choosing which to apply in each case.

Communitarianism emphasises solidarity with small units and/or informal community networks at the centre of society and of decision making. Conservative communitarianism is more about the way in which rules are made or decisions are imposed than about their content, whereas radical communitarianism is about the foregrounding of equality and the redistribution and restitution of justice without any method of deciding what is just. These are more about systems and types of political stances than about raw justice.

- Explain and critically compare the two main systems of criminal justice

The two main systems used in Western cultures are the adversarial system, used mostly in common law jurisdictions, and the inquisitorial system, used mostly in countries with a criminal code.

The adversarial system which is used in England and Wales requires the state to prove its case beyond reasonable doubt. The state investigates a crime and once they believe that they have correctly identified an offender they use their resources to prove their case. The accused uses information it has to prove innocence. This makes the system a contest between the state and the accused and the contest is led by the lawyers for each side, with the judge or magistrate making sure that they conduct a fair trial. Officially the jury or magistrate then decides which side it believes, but as they do not have to explain their decision they can make it on what they think is fair even if the fact (the truth) or the law might suggest a different outcome. The system does allow the accused to take control of their defence and present all the aspects they feel are important. There are problems with the adversarial system. To take a few examples: firstly, as the jury do not explain why they make a decision no-one can appeal their decision or test whether it is fair (they could even convict because they think the accused looks guilty or acquit if they think he or she looks innocent). Secondly, the system is not necessarily focused on finding the truth and can become more of a legal game so that the outcome may depend more on how charismatic the lawyer is than the facts of the case. Witnesses may be so worried that they may appear to be lying even when they are telling the truth. Overall, there are some strengths to the system but also some serious weaknesses.

The inquisitorial system, used in most of Europe, claims to be a real search for the truth. Core to this system is the file or dossier that is built up by the police and investigative judge. This dossier is then presented to all interested parties and it is generally the dossier which is assessed to decide upon guilt or innocence. The advantages are that everyone knows the facts as presented by the state as well as those claimed by the accused. The investigative judge is supposed to use their powers to test the case and to use the police to follow leads which may prove innocence as well as those which may prove guilt. Ideally this will lead to the truth being uncovered. However, the investigative judge (and/or police) may discount important information, fail to put it in the dossier, and then the decision makers will never be aware of it so that truth may be lost.

Clearly neither system is ideal and over the last 100 years or so each has borrowed from the other so that no system is entirely one or the other.

REVIEW QUESTIONS

1. Name and outline the key points of the three descriptive models and the three normative models outlined in this chapter.

2. Compare and contrast crime control and due process models of criminal justice and explain whether one of them is more likely to deliver just outcomes (with reasons).

3. What are the main differences between justice as set out by Rawls and that set out by Sen?

4. Why do well-being and justice matter in considering criminological theory?

5. Choose one of the quotations in **Telling it like it is 4.1** and discuss how and why it is important to criminological discussions.

FURTHER READING

Bix, B. (2006) *Jurisprudence: Theory and Context* (4th edn). London: Sweet and Maxwell.
Simmonds, N. E. (2008) *Central Issues in Jurisprudence* (3rd edn). London: Sweet and Maxwell.
There are many textbooks which consider justice, a concept which is generally discussed at length in all jurisprudence books. These two are particularly helpful and approachable. Each of them provides an accessible introduction to some of the important theories of justice. They are both well written, aimed at a legal audience, but as they address students directly they are also both still approachable.

Pakes, F. (2004) *Comparative Criminal Justice*. Cullompton: Willan
For a full consideration and evaluation of the adversarial and inquisitorial systems of criminal justice (as well as discussion of other systems, such as Islamic justice systems).

 Access the **online resources** to view selected further reading and web links relevant to the material covered in this chapter.
www.oup.com/uk/case/

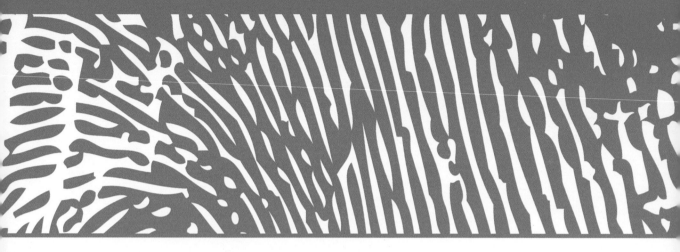

CHAPTER OUTLINE

Introduction   114

Officially (police) recorded crime statistics   115

Offence categories and patterns of offending   119

Police recorded crime statistics and the 'justice gap'   120

Surveying crime: The Crime Survey for England and Wales 126

Conclusion   131

Crime statistics

KEY ISSUES

After studying this chapter, you should be able to:

- appreciate why governments may want to collect data on crime and how they go about this;

- identify the main problems with police recorded crime statistics and understand what is meant by the 'justice gap';

- relate the collation of crime statistics to broader issues of politics and power;

- evaluate the main strengths and weaknesses of attempting to measure criminal behaviour through the use of social surveys;

- critically assess the Crime Survey for England and Wales (CSEW) as a way of measuring crime and its trends in those countries.

Introduction

In **Chapters 3** and **4** we looked at the complicated and disputed ideas around how both crime and justice are socially constructed and defined. You are probably still thinking about the difficulties these questions bring with them, and we hope you are developing your critical skills when you consider your own ideas and responses. However, in this section we are not going to be so concerned with the broader and more philosophical debates around what is 'crime' and what is 'justice'; instead, we will be looking at what we think we *know* about crime and how it is measured, and even more importantly, *how* we come by that knowledge. After all, whilst wanting to 'know' something might be useful in itself, the main logic of wanting to find out the scale of a perceived social problem and its trends is that this knowledge can enable 'society' and its state agencies to act on that particular 'problem'—whether this be in terms of attempting to eradicate the problem, control it, or simply to be seen to be addressing it and managing it in some way.

This chapter is going to look in more depth at why the government wants to know about crime and how it goes about collecting the information it wants. The question of whether that is the information it *needs* may also occur to us. This chapter will then move on to explore what is done with this knowledge once it is produced, and what this tells us about the key concept of power.

There are of course some well-known, obvious ways in which governments gather such information. It is usually presented in a very hard, mathematical format classed as 'official' figures. Such figures claim to give us proof of what's going on in the world—in this case, the criminal world. A simple enumeration of the types of crime being carried out, rates of increase or decrease, trends and anomalies—anything at all, in fact, may be described and set out in pie charts, frequency distribution graphs, percentages, and so on. We usually refer to these by the catch-all name *descriptive statistics* and you will often see them screaming out to you in newspaper headlines (see **Telling it like it is 5.1**) and in the interactive graphics on television bulletins.

Our scepticism about figures is nothing new; in 1891 the following phrase was in common use: 'there are three degrees of falsehood: the first is a fib, the second a lie, and then come statistics'. This scepticism also illustrates an important warning for us in terms of critically engaging with and understanding crime data. We are, from a very young age, taught that figures and so-called 'facts' are highly important. We place great value on information that we believe has been objectively collated, and that we can tell ourselves is 'hard fact'. Look at the number of television advertisements that claim to 'prove' that a particular shampoo/toothpaste/fruit drink is more popular or effective. Read the small print carefully and you will usually see that where a face cream claims that '75 per cent of women said their wrinkles had got smaller' the figures are fact based on a very small sample of 8 or 9 people testing the product. This is hardly a ringing endorsement.

Or take the health scare about bacon. Reports claimed that eating red or processed meat increased the risk of developing colon cancer by 20 per cent, which seems terrifying and was enough to make many people give up their favourite breakfast food. Yet, as the charity Sense about Science explains, the real issue is how likely you

---

TELLING IT LIKE IT IS 5.1

The headlines shown in this box reflect the growing media and public scepticism about the reliability and validity of officially recorded crime statistics, with one of them highlighting that they have recently lost their 'official' status.

How we can't trust the crime figures: After plebgate, now watchdog says police statistics are unreliable

- UK statistics Authority withdrew approval on UK crime figures
- Watchdog chair pointed to ONS warning that figures 'overstate the truth'
- Forces accused of downgrading crimes or erasing them altogether

- 'Rapes and child abuse disappearing in a puff of smoke' a senior officer said

Daily Mail, 16 January 2014

30,000 car thefts each year not investigated

New figures show forces up and down the country fail to look into cases involving stolen vehicles.

Daily Express, 22 December 2015

Crime rate to rise by 40% after inclusion of cyber-offences

Apparent surge is likely to reignite debate over whether there has been a long-term decline in offending in England and Wales.

Guardian, 15 October 2015

are to get colon cancer in the first place. On average, we have a 5 per cent chance of developing the illness (your 'absolute risk'); eating a bacon sandwich every day does not mean you have a 20 per cent chance. Instead, what it actually means is that your risk increases by 20 per cent of that original 5 per cent (the 'relative' risk). In other words, there's a 1 per cent rise to a less-than-scary 6 per cent. But no newspaper is going to print a headline explaining the concept of relative risk, even assuming that the journalist understands it in the first place. The alarmist headline is easier to digest, and sells more papers. Can the same be said of media reporting of crime statistics?

All of this goes to show that we need to think about statistics carefully when we consider the two most important questions which have underpinned much of criminological thought:

1. What are the causes of crime?

2. How much crime actually happens?

The first of these is covered elsewhere in this book (see **Part 3**), so we will not give it much time here. Our exploration will instead focus on the second question.

As we have seen, this is more than just how many robberies or car thefts have been counted; it also covers things like shifts in the type of crimes and perpetrators—more burglaries than assaults, more women committing violence—as well as broader concerns like a rise in the total numbers of offences or an increase in what we may consider to be more serious acts of deviance. That leads us to a second health warning: we need to remember, of course, that 'crime' is a social construction, so our consideration here will only be of acts that are defined as crime by the criminal law as this is what government claim they can meaningfully measure. Whether or not something actually should have been recorded as a crime (that is, be included on the notifiable offence list) is a debate for

elsewhere, but it is for this very reason that you should always keep your critical eyes and mind open when thinking about crime statistics.

In this chapter we will be looking at two main sets of data relating to crime in England and Wales: so-called 'official' statistics (which are collated by police forces from the crimes committed which they record), and mass victimisation surveys, principally the Crime Survey for England and Wales (the CSEW, formerly known as the British Crime Survey) which asks people to relate their experiences of crime as victims. It is worth bearing in mind that most industrialised countries today also produce such statistical measures, although making meaningful international comparisons with England and Wales is obviously fraught with difficulties given that different forms of crime are defined and measured differently across jurisdictions. We will be thinking about what these data tell us, but also we will need to ask ourselves what use they are, and how we can best assess and evaluate their findings.

Criminologists are social scientists and as such will use evidence to develop and support their arguments (see **Chapter 6**), but the crucial point here is that 'evidence' does not speak for itself. It has to be analysed and tested before it can be used. If you consider this in forensic terms it can be likened to the fact that a splash of blood is just a splash of blood until we have examined it. Only when we know if it comes from a stubbed toe or a dead body can we use it to help decide if a murder has taken place. We have to learn not to take 'facts' on faith or trust, but instead to use them to test our ideas, help us to ask challenging questions, and then evaluate the response. It won't surprise you to learn that this approach usually ends up with more questions and very few answers—which is why we shall be looking at statistics in more detail and asking critical questions of them throughout the rest of this chapter. So, firstly, let us think about the so-called 'official' (recorded) crime statistics.

Officially (police) recorded crime statistics

The historical development of statistics

The prison at Newgate in London was in use for over 700 years, and even today its site is still concerned with the delivery of justice as it is now the location of the Old Bailey (properly known as the Central Criminal Court of England and Wales). What is interesting from a statistical point of view is that from 1773, a monthly list of all the executions that had taken place at the prison was published. This gruesome 'Newgate Calendar' was hugely popular

and went on to become a book giving biographical details of such famous criminals as Dick Turpin and Moll Cutpurse, but in its original form it was probably one of the first examples of a statistical record relating to crime and criminals being kept and made public (see **Figure 5.1**).

More formal, and less sensationalised, figures began to be kept throughout the course of the 19th century. This was partly due to improved communications, making it possible for the central collection and storage of national or regional data, but it also reflects the Victorians' fondness for record-keeping and measurement. The first national census was held in 1801, and in 1836 it became

Figure 5.1 Front cover of the Newgate Calendar, published in London by E. Harrison—'Remarkable lives and trials of all notorious criminals past and present'

Source: Public domain

a legal requirement to register births, marriages, and deaths, creating significant amounts of data which needed analysis. Statistical techniques were developed in order to make sense of the information; in 1841, for instance, the census questions were worded in such a way that it helped to identify risks to public health, while the requirement to record causes of death on a death certificate meant that the dangers of particular occupations could be measured. One of the men responsible for this approach, William Farr (1807–83), redefined statistics as 'a *method of analysis* rather than a social discipline in itself' (Magnello 2011: 270) and that is a useful summary when we think about the use of figures in a criminological sense. You may be surprised to learn that Florence Nightingale, the 'Lady of the Lamp' herself, was in fact a hugely successful statistician and was one of the first people to use the pie chart!

Much of this new analytical work was put to use in the public health arena. For instance, over two weeks in 1854, an outbreak of cholera killed over 700 people in one London parish alone. Doctor John Snow and the Reverend Henry Whitehead used statistics to prove that the source was one particular parish water pump; the pair mapped the outbreak, showing how it clustered around the infected pump, helping

to save lives and to found the emerging science of epidemiology (the study of patterns in diseases and deaths in a given population). In this case, the Board of Guardians, the Medical Committee of the General Board of Health, and the Parish Paving Committee were also involved in investigating what had happened, a situation which reflected the growing trend for a bureaucratic and official response to public matters. It is no surprise therefore that an increasingly well organised state system, one which protected its people from polluted water, would also seek to protect them from the moral pollution of crime (and thus to control criminals), using the new tools of statistics and their analysis to help them do so.

At the same time that Snow and Whitehead were using data to improve public health, the social researcher and reformer Henry Mayhew (1812–87, see **Figure 5.2**) was publishing his vast survey on *London Labour and the London Poor* (1851). This work, which spanned four volumes, recorded Mayhew's interviews with an enormous range of characters from the poor of the city, giving details of their dress, habits, and even their accents and dialects. Some of his assumptions are questionable today, such as his beliefs that the human race could be split into two classes, the wanderers and the civilised, and that members of each group could be identified by the shape of their heads; however, his overall aim was to 'give the rich a more intimate knowledge of the sufferings, and the frequent heroism under those sufferings, of the poor.' (1861: li).

HENRY MAYHEW.

[*From a Daguerreotype by* BEARD.]

Figure 5.2 Henry Mayhew, the social researcher who published *London Labour and the London Poor*

Source: Public domain

The fourth volume of Mayhew's work, which came out in 1861, had a more detailed focus on crime and criminals. Again, he sought to classify his subjects, this time identifying a 'criminal class' such as beggars, thieves, and fraudsters, whose refusal to work was due to a moral defect. However, he also recognised a second group, people who committed 'crime' as a result of poverty or circumstances—for example, classifying as prostitutes the widows of service men who lived with their new partners because remarriage would mean the loss of their pensions. As part of this work, Mayhew and his collaborators mapped incidents of crime and correlated this data with other social concerns, such as illegitimacy or illiteracy, again using the results to highlight links between crime, poverty, and social deprivation. His ideas of what constituted crime are an early example of how difficult it is to define criminality, and to place it into clear offence types; it also highlights the way social context affects the public construction and perception of crime. It is unlikely that today we would recognise many of the criminal 'types' Mayhew described—for example, how many of us would know how a stock-buzzer, sawney-hunter, or Charley-pitcher broke the law? (A stock-buzzer stole handkerchiefs; a sawney-hunter stole bacon from cheesemongers; and a Charley-pitcher would run fraudulent gambling games.)

There was also the potential for such data to be used to influence positive social reform though public policy.

Despite his good intentions—using data to prove the need for change—it could be argued that Mayhew's work strengthened existing prejudices amongst the powerful by appearing to corroborate ideas about the powerless and the poor. It was perhaps the work of social reformers such as Mayhew and other pioneering figures such as Charles Booth (1849–1916) and Seebohm Rowntree (1871–1954) which highlighted the need for governments to collect more accurate data on a range of social issues and problems. The first British national criminal statistics based on data derived from the police and court records were published in 1876.

Statistics today

All of this means we today inherit a situation in which we are faced with a veritable explosion of knowledge about crime. Ways of manipulating and evaluating statistical data have become vastly more sophisticated; for example, we can easily now obtain data on how much crime there is, what types of offence are being committed, who is being sentenced by the courts, how many injunctions are issued, and the frequency with which various court disposals (community sentences, imprisonment, etc.) are being used. The Ministry of Justice, the Home Office, the Office for National Statistics (see **Figure 5.3**), and other agencies

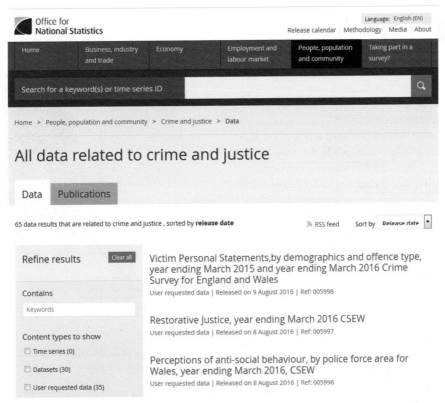

Figure 5.3 Page from the ONS website illustrating the types of reports available

Source: Office for National Statistics (www.ons.gov.uk), content available under the Open Government Licence v3.0

are now producing statistical bulletins on a monthly basis which are presented in a range of formats.

Other sources of information are available from the Home Office and the Office for National Statistics, both of which provide websites with links to many reports relating to the police and security. Indeed, you could spend hours perusing the thousands of graphs and tables on crime and its control which are now at your fingertips. You will find reports not just on criminal justice statistics, but also others which relate to civil justice, courts, race and the criminal justice system, gender and the criminal justice system, the prison population, the probation service, reoffending, sexual offences, youth justice, and much more. It is enough to make the head of any criminologist spin.

How much crime is there? The extent of offending

Suppose we simply wanted to find out how much crime had been recorded in England and Wales since the first set of data was published all those years ago. We could easily plot a graph (a frequency distribution) which would show us something like the one in **Figure 5.4**.

What, however, do such graphs actually tell us? Simply look at this one for a moment. Make a note of the sorts of stories it may tell.

Firstly, hopefully we can all agree that the graph's sinister-looking upwards line shows that crime has increased over this period. It might also reaffirm your worst fears confirming that crime in England and Wales is getting worse and is simply out of control. You could argue that it proves our era is more criminal (and by implication dangerous) than that of our forebears, who lived in more tranquil and peaceable times. What else can we say? Look carefully for the points of greatest increase. Where are these, according to this source? It would appear from the graph that crime in England and Wales is predominantly a post war (1945 onwards) phenomenon with significant increases each decade from 1955 to 1995 but with an odd dip around 1997.

If we were so inclined, we could infer many other tales from such a graph as shown in **Figure 5.4**. The big question is whether or not we would be fully justified in doing so. So let us think about what the graph does not tell us. First of all, we have to examine the chart's limitations. For instance, it does not tell us what types of crime are being committed. Would we look at it differently if it were a chart showing murder rates, or a chart showing incidents of failure to pay parking tickets? What sorts of crimes are being included, and which ones are being left out?

That last point is particularly important. As we said at the beginning of the chapter, recorded crime figures in England and Wales are reliant upon data collected by the police forces which report to the Home Office (not all

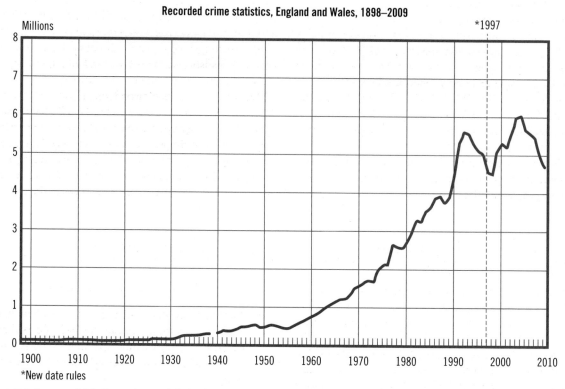

Recorded crime statistics, England and Wales, 1898–2009

Figure 5.4 Frequency distribution graph—recorded crime by the millions from 1900–2010

Source: The Home Office, content available under the Open Government Licence v3.0

do, such as the British Transport Police). They also only include what are called 'notifiable offences', so a whole range of offences ('summary offences') which are usually thought of as being of a less serious nature (and are heard at a magistrates' court) are not included. As we shall discuss further, the police do not record every type or incident of crime that is reported to them, so there will be some reported incidents which are not included in the statistics. Thus we can see that from the start, the data are incomplete and we are only getting part of the story.

Nor can we assume that the information collected in 1900 was consistent with that from 2000. It is crucial to remember that crime is a social construct. We have seen already that the criminal law changes over time and so does the 'notifiable offence' list, as well as Home Office rules on the counting and classification of crimes. So in 2000 an employer can be prosecuted for not providing health and safety equipment, whereas in 1920 nobody would have considered that to be an offence and it would not have been included in the crime data. Also, police counting rules change, something else we shall consider further later. Equally, we cannot assume that people living in 1950 would have had the same experiences as we do today. It's an old joke that nobody got burgled in 'the olden days' because they didn't have anything worth stealing, but there's a nugget of truth in it. Nobody in 1975 had their mobile phone stolen or their online bank account hacked, but the 2010 figures will almost certainly include that sort of crime. And something that might have been dealt with by the local policeman giving a naughty child the proverbial 'clip around the ear'—a version of police brutality which the older generation seems to look back on with extraordinary nostalgia—is almost certainly going to be recorded in some form by a modern officer. Also, as we saw in **Telling it like it is 5.1** when looking at newspaper headlines, in 2015 the recording of various cyber offences had the effect of increasing the overall crime rate by 40 per cent.

It is probably clear from this brief discussion that what is important for criminologists to think about is how such statistical representations can be interpreted. Put simply, there is more to crime, criminals, and criminal statistics than initially meets the eye. In short, we need to deconstruct and critically question such representations and not take them at face value. As we reminded ourselves a moment ago, 'crime' is a social construct; that is, it is constructed by human beings through sets of social processes. From those complex issues of definition, to when an act is committed and reported to—and recorded by—the police, 'crime' is both a social construction and an essentially contested (argued over) concept. So rather than provide us with a totally accurate and 'true' picture of crime (such a figure is unknowable) they can perhaps tell us much more about police practices, government priorities, public fears, and what the criminal justice personnel actually do.

This does not, however, mean that crime statistics are all unreliable or that they are totally useless indicators which tell us nothing whatsoever. We will consider further the trend towards crime mapping in particular areas and postcodes, and the potential uses this has in terms of making policy more 'evidence'—and 'intelligence'—led. From a more radical and critical position it could be said that such statistical indices tell us much about power and power relations. In other words, we will think about how particular 'crime waves' are created, together with the potential parts played in this by media reporting of crime statistics—it is they after all who play a central role in the dissemination and interpretation of the 'facts of crime'. This leads us to consider the impact of statistics on public fears (which may be a product of such reporting), political priorities (which may result from such public fears), and from there onto police targeting and resource deployment (which may be the result of political priorities and agendas). Statistical data leads to a web of interesting and important interconnected ideas and activity.

By now you are probably wondering if you can trust anything you see and take it at face value. Good! That's exactly the kind of critical response you need to have when dealing with this kind of simple timescale frequency distribution (in other words, a line plotting incidence over time), especially one which shows crime on an ever-upward march. Such a thing needs to be treated with great caution.

Offence categories and patterns of offending

This section of the chapter will consider what recorded crime statistics actually measure. For a start, we need to know how many different categories of recorded crime there are today in England and Wales. Would it surprise you to learn that there are over 100? For the sake of simplicity, these are usually reduced to down to nine broad, main offence categories, which are then used by the media in their reporting of crime. After reading this section look at **What do you think? 5.1**.

These nine offence categories are as follows:

1. **Theft and handling stolen goods**—which includes stealing items from cars and the theft of cars themselves, so stealing a handbag from the back seat of a car, and selling a stolen Ferrari fall under the same category.

2. **Burglary**—domestic and 'other'. There is also the category of 'aggravated burglary' which covers acts like

WHAT DO YOU THINK? 5.1

How much crime (by category) do you think there is?

Just like Florence Nightingale, we can look at this with a pie chart, shown as **Figure 5.5**. Each slice relates to an offence category, showing (by percentage) how many of each were recorded by the police at the end of March 2016 (you can look at and further analyse the full table at the end of this chapter). Judging by the size, can you decide which slice and which percentage relates to which crime category?

The crime categories for this exercise, in random order, are: bicycle theft; fraud; sexual offences; vehicle offences; violence against the person; public order offences; theft from the person; robbery offences; possession of weapon offences; shoplifting; drug offences; criminal damage and arson; burglary; other thefts; and all other offences (please note that some sources and reports list the various crime categories in slightly different ways to the nine-point list given). So, for example, do you think that the big blue slice (22 per cent of recorded crimes in 2016) represents burglary, or one of the other types of crime? Jot your answers down and think about why you made your choices. If I were to tell you that the overall figure for recorded crime in that year was 4,513,964 you might

also wish to convert these percentages into raw figures, i.e. a crime category which makes up 12 per cent of the total recorded crime would mean that approximately 540,000 different offences of this type had been recorded.

What, if anything, surprised you when doing this? Did you expect one crime to have a bigger slice than another? Can you list the reasons why you had these assumptions? You will find the correct figures and an updated pie chart (**Table 5.1** and **Figure 5.9**) at the end of the chapter but have a go at the exercise before you take a look at this.

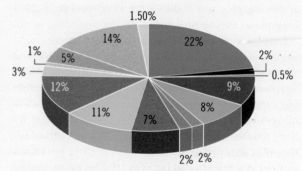

Figure 5.5 Pie chart showing police recorded crime in March 2016 (categories shown at end of chapter)

---

vandalising the premises or where the victim has been chosen because of their sexuality, race, or disability.

3. **Criminal damage**—this is subdivided into damage to a dwelling, damage to a building other than a dwelling, and damage to a vehicle.

4. **Violence against the person**—this one is really huge and covers everything from murder through to the Saturday night fracas.

5. **Sexual offences**—again, a very broad umbrella term which covers, as you might expect, rape and indecent assault but also includes having sex with a corpse or being a voyeur.

6. **Robbery**—this is distinct from theft or burglary in that it involves the use of force or fear. A good way to remember it is to think of highwaymen and their drawn pistols—hence the phrase 'highway robbery'.

7. **Fraud and forgery**.

8. **Drug offences**—this category includes the possession, distribution, and production of illegal drugs and is an area in which there have been many changes, particularly with regard to so-called 'legal highs' and the use of cannabis, which will affect statistical analysis of this field of crime.

9. **Other offences**—a useful catch-all category.

Police recorded crime statistics and the 'justice gap'
Reporting crime

This section focuses on police recorded crime statistics and, as with all statistics, it is vital to maintain a critical mindset when assessing them.

Firstly, we need to think about the problem of attrition. Put simply, attrition (in criminological terms) is where a crime takes place but the record of it somehow gets filtered out during the various phases of the criminal justice process(es). These are cases which may be reported, but which do not result in any formal court action like a sentence or fine; this is also sometimes referred to as the 'justice gap'. There are thus many cases which are reported and recorded, but which do not end up as a court disposal in terms of sentencing and convictions. This can seem shocking—how can a crime simply be ignored? To understand that, we need to think about how and why we consider a crime to have happened in the first place.

It is perhaps useful to think of the criminal justice system as a set of processes (as opposed to being a coherent, seamless system). The first process starts with the reporting of crime by the public and then moves on to the recording and investigation of it by the police. From there, we can move to the decision taken by the Crown Prosecution Service whether or not to prosecute a crime, before we end up with sentencing processes in the courts (see **Chapters 20** and **21** for more on the criminal justice system).

Seeing the system as this series of actions means that we can see all stages of the 'system' as a set of *social processes* in which all the agencies can exercise a degree of discretion. Decisions are also affected by other considerations, such as costs, the level of public interest in a case, and the likelihood of securing a conviction. We will go on to consider some of the reasons why the public may not report a crime and why the police may decide not to record it as such, but it might surprise you to learn that out of every 100 crimes committed, fewer than half are reported to the police. This figure roughly halves again in terms of police recording them as crimes. Furthermore, of all of these offences, fewer than 5 per cent end up with a caution or conviction. This gap between reporting and punishment sees significant variation for different types of offence. For instance, you may have read about concerns being raised about the high attrition rates for sexual offences such as rape.

Why else may statistics be skewed? Firstly, of course, we have to be aware that something has happened before it can be recorded. Crime writers and historians are often asked what they consider to be the 'perfect crime'. The answer is of course that we don't know, because if a crime has been recognised as such then it's not perfect. To be perfect, the crime must have gone undiscovered and certainly unsolved! We need to bear this in mind when thinking about crime statistics. If we don't know that there's been a crime, we can't report it.

Another factor that affects people's willingness to report a crime is one of complicity. If you make a claim on your insurance because you've lost your wedding ring, and you find it after receiving your pay out, you have a choice. You can keep quiet, wear your ring and keep the money; or you can send the cash back. If you choose the first course, you have committed a crime that nobody will ever know about. Whether or not you even consider yourself to have done something deviant will depend on all sorts of factors, such as your upbringing, your religious faith (or lack of one), your financial situation, and how much you trust your partner not to report you. All of which goes to illustrate something else we need to think about: how we choose to categorise something as a crime or otherwise can be a complicated and variable process that is not always straightforward. It is a series of social processes, which are rooted in our backgrounds, class, education, and personal beliefs.

We need to consider in more detail the vital distinction between reporting and recording. Crimes may be reported but not included in statistics for all sorts of reasons; people choose to withdraw their allegations or, as in our wedding ring example, they may find a lost item and realise that it hadn't been stolen after all. (It is, however, also worth mentioning here that in some cases one incident can lead to more than one crime; for example, the Home Office counting rules for incidents of violence against the person state that if a drunk driver kills his two passengers in one accident, it is recorded as two crimes, one for each victim). This means that there is no definite correlation between numbers of incidents and the resultant numbers of crimes that show up in the statistics. Changes in the counting rules can therefore result in an increase in the overall levels of recorded crime as well as for specific offences, and this can make attempts to draw comparisons over time meaningless. The same can be said with regards to the introduction of the National Crime Recording Standard (NCRS) which was introduced in 2002. This changed the ways in which all police forces recorded crime to ensure greater consistency between them. We shall explore this further later on in the chapter but it is worth noting here that police officers still have a fair amount of discretion when dealing with the public on the street. It is also important to consider that people may choose not to report crime for a variety of reasons which are explored further in **What do you think? 5.2**.

Police recording of crime

As we noted earlier there have been many important changes in the ways in which police officers record crime, not least the introduction of the NCRS. In **Telling it like it is 5.2** we hear from Detective Constable John Harbison, who is a police officer with 15 years' service with the Metropolitan Police Service. John spent four years in uniform in central London before transferring to various specialist units as a detective. Here he candidly reflects on some of the very real issues and problems he confronted when dealing with crime allegations and their investigation.

DC Harbison raises many important and interesting points, not least about the administrative and bureaucratic complexities involved in police recording processes and practices, together with the real pressures which police officers face in their day-to-day

WHAT DO YOU THINK? 5.2

To report or not to report...that is the question

Have you ever been the victim of a crime, or witnessed a crime tasking place? What did you do? Did you report it? Why—or why not?

Make a list of some of the reasons why you made the reporting choice you did.

Compare your response to the list below. It is taken from various British Crime Survey Reports on the main reasons why people choose not to report crimes. Would your response have been different if it had been a different category of crime you saw?

Reasons for not reporting (derived from Flately et al. 2010):

- it seemed trivial;
- the police will be impotent;
- the police would not be interested;
- nobody would believe you;
- I was too busy;
- I was embarrassed;
- I was too scared or fearful;
- I chose to deal with it in another way.

Now, consider the following list of crime categories:

- bicycle theft;
- vandalism;
- burglary with loss;
- wounding;
- theft from the person;
- theft of vehicle;
- assault with minor injury or no injury.

Which types of crime do you think are most likely to be reported to the police? Why do you think that this might be the case? Jot down your answers and then look at **Figure 5.10**, 'Reporting crimes for different offences', at the end of the chapter and compare your responses.

TELLING IT LIKE IT IS 5.2

A view from the police—with DC John Harbison

Not a day went by without a person rushing into the police station shouting that their car had been stolen. The first time this happened to me, I had fairly recently graduated from Hendon (the Met's police college). Eager to assist, I took all the relevant details and officially recorded the crime just as my training had taught me. It was only when I had finished this long and laborious task that I remembered something: before recording the allegation and circulating the car's details as stolen, I should check with the central car pound to see whether it had been towed away by the council for being illegally parked. That day, as is so often the case, the car had indeed been towed and was waiting safely in the council pound to be collected. This meant I had to spend another hour cancelling the stolen circulation, and writing a long report to justify why I had just marked up my report as 'no crime'.

Even though this is a very simplistic example, it is an excellent demonstration of how the recording of crime is not as straightforward as one might at first think. People will call the police, adamant they were a victim of crime, when actually no crime has actually been committed. Usually, it would be a civil dispute at most, such as a customer refusing to pay for a meal due to poor service, or a neighbour playing their music too loud.

Be that as it may, when an allegation of crime is made, an officer is duty bound to record it. Before recording it, however, the officer needs to understand what offence has been committed. Even though officers receive detailed training, they must assess very quickly what offence—if any—has been committed. We can sometimes get it wrong, and fail to understand what crime is being alleged. At the end of the day, police officers are human beings and like everyone can make mistakes.

However, this tends to be rare. Even if officers didn't get the right crime, they will often record something and leave it for more experienced officers to tidy up the report. In the case of a more serious crime, it will be for detectives to sort out the report and establish the correct offence. During my time as a supervisor in a busy CID (Criminal Investigation Department), I spent most of my day going through these reports and justifying why there was either no crime in the first place, or that an incorrect offence had been recorded. I would also look at the reports where there were no evidence or witnesses, and see if an investigation was even possible. Again, I would see if the report could be 'no crime'.

Saying this, it is extremely hard to have a report changed to a 'no crime'. Many just get 'screened out', which means that no further investigation would take place, but the recorded crime will still be counted and included in the statistics.

Nonetheless, in most cases where an investigation is started, the cooperation of the victim is crucial. If the victim refuses to assist with the investigation, often we cannot proceed. But what if no other evidence is available and there are no witnesses? Did the crime really happen? And what about fraud? It's common for people to lose or damage something but then report it as stolen in order to claim from their insurance. No crime of theft has occurred, but an offence of fraud has. Do they both get recorded, even though it would be hard to prove either?

The process of recording crime has changed many times and, over the years, new crimes have been added to the list of recordable offences. Furthermore, recording systems are much more automated than they were in the past. Today, you can report a crime online without even having to speak to an officer. If you do, however, phone the police to report a crime, a despatch message—a CAD—gets created. A CAD is a Computer Aided Despatch and it the most widely used system which has been in use for many years. It includes a comprehensive geographic information system which allows an operator to log a call, record the information, and use the latest mapping systems to see the location of the reported offence. It is impossible to close a CAD without an outcome, such as someone being charged with the offence. As well as the outcome, most CADs will require a crime reference number before they can be closed. As if things were not complicated enough, from an administrative point of view it is easier to create a crime report in order to close it than it is to justify why there is no report. This means that officers will always be more inclined to create a report in order to cover themselves and show that they have taken some action, however minimal, with the added benefit that this makes it easier to close the CAD too. It is therefore very unlikely that an officer will fail to record a crime out of laziness, as this involves much more work and carries a higher risk.

Even though it can be argued that crime figures are only used by the press and politicians to make headlines and push agendas, the statistics do serve a serious purpose. You will know that crime statistics can be taken out of context, and that you can read pretty much what you want to in all those numbers. However, one form of statistical analysis, known as crime mapping, can be important in terms of preventing crimes from occurring in the first place. Crime mapping is the use of accurate crime reporting, especially street crime and burglary, to pinpoint problematic areas and specific times at which such crimes occur (see **Figures 5.6** and **5.7**). It can be very useful to senior officers in planning how to effectively deploy hard-pressed police resources across their borough in order to get the greatest impact. In these times of budget cuts and shrinking police numbers, intelligence-led policing is key and crime statistics play a vital part in gathering this intelligence data.

[If you zoom in on one of the numbers on the map in **Figure 5.6**, you get a breakdown of the specific crimes committed there, as shown in **Figure 5.7**.] Here, next to Leicester Square, we are told that there was one instance of anti-social behaviour, burglary, other theft, and theft from a person reported in the month of June 2016.

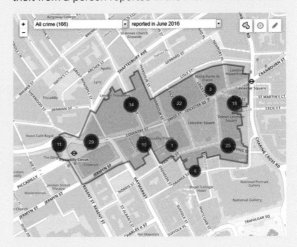

Figure 5.6 Area around Leicester Square, London

Source: The Home Office, content available under the Open Government Licence v3.0

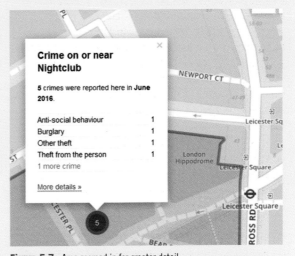

Figure 5.7 Area zoomed in for greater detail

Source: The Home Office, content available under the Open Government Licence v3.0

Even though senior officers will scrutinise recorded crime to make sure it is being reduced, at the end of the day, police officers who are out and about 'on the beat' will care more about helping the public and arresting offenders than about how crimes are being recorded. Failing to record a crime in order to manipulate the figures will certainly never cross their minds. Police officers are, however, under a lot of pressure to reduce crime and accurate recording is an essential tool in achieving this. But this comes at a price; we have to face the fact that pressure to reduce crime or detect more offenders can tempt a small number of individuals into making serious mistakes by tampering with reports to increase detection rates. If we put value on data, we need to make sure we protect it and help those who are compiling it to do so with integrity.

Detective Constable John Harbison, a police officer with 15 years' service with the Metropolitan Police Service

working lives. One of the important points he highlights, and which we should underscore here, is that not all crimes which are reported to the police will eventually be recorded by them. Although he argues that 'cuffing' (that is, an officer wilfully failing to record a crime to save themselves work and/or to artificially inflate police detection rates) is rare, it does still happen. The broader issues which are highlighted in his account are however worth briefly reiterating: that officers may not accept what is being reported to them or they may be unsure as to what offence has been alleged; that there simply may not be sufficient evidence for them to proceed with an investigation; and that victim non-cooperation will halt an investigation from taking place.

A 2014 report by Her Majesty's Inspectorate of Constabulary (HMIC) noted that the police failed to record one in five crimes which are reported to them. Perhaps the most controversial finding of this report was that it is victims of violent crime (33 per cent) and sexual offences (26 per cent) who are more likely not to have the offences committed against them investigated by the police. As DC Harbison noted, in some cases this is due to the victim's disengagement. The HMIC report however found that there were other reasons for not recording offences: to police practices with insufficient knowledge (21 per cent) and inadequate supervision (51 per cent) were cited as the main reasons. We will revisit and consider the main limitations of police recorded crime statistics at the end of this section.

One of the more recent developments which DC Harbison regards as being positive is the way in which police services now automatically record crime in the form of crime mapping. Here he argues that such technological developments can help to develop 'intelligence-led' policing approaches, and lead to ways in which police services can efficiently deploy police resources to prevent crime and stop people becoming victims. There is after all a simple logic to all of this. If the police can identify where certain types of crime take place (and, on average, when) they can identify 'hot spots' and marshal their resources accordingly. In doing so they can be (and be seen to be) doing something to prevent or, at the very least, to manage a particular crime problem.

Now, consider the points raised in **What do you think? 5.3**.

WHAT DO YOU THINK? 5.3

What are the crime problems where you live?

- Do you think that you live in a high crime area?
- What types of crime 'problems' occur where you live?
- Do you think, for instance, that there are a high number of burglaries in your neighbourhood?
- What about violent offences?
- Are such things increasing or decreasing?
- Think also about how you 'know' what you think you 'know' about these issues.

Jot down some notes on these questions. Having done this, now access a website such as www.crime-statistics.co.uk/postcode and enter your postcode. Here you will find all of the crimes which have been reported in the last month within a one-mile radius of a particular postcode. What, if anything, surprised you about your findings? Were your perceptions of crime levels and the types of crimes which occur where you live different from the 'official' statistical picture? How can you account for such disparities? Perhaps the most important thing for you to reflect on here is what all of this tells us about the broader issues involved in the reporting and the official recording of crime.

Figure 5.8 shows some crime statistics for three post-codes within the UK. What kind of impression do they give you about the area? If you had to choose, based on these details, which would you prefer to live in? Or what other information would you look for before making such a choice?

More details of each place are shown at the end of the chapter—they may surprise you!

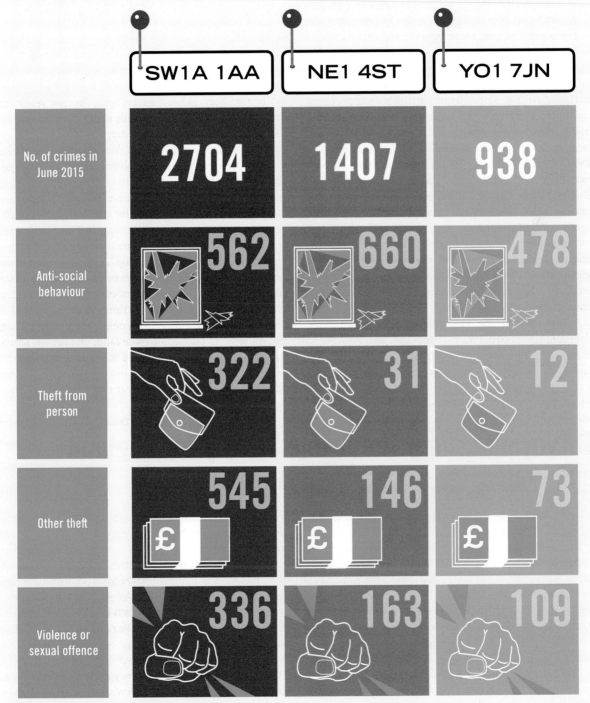

Figure 5.8 Selected postcode crime figures, June 2015
Source: Data taken from www.crime-statistics.co.uk/postcode

The uses and abuses of official statistics

The development of crime mapping is undoubtedly an interesting one. As we have seen, from a police perspective it is seen as a positive intervention, in terms of it leading to more proactive, intelligence-led (that is, based on statistical evidence) forms of policing which aim to prevent crime. In a managerialist way, it was argued that this can help the police to deploy their resources in more efficient and cost-effective ways. On the flip side, however, it could also be argued that there is the potential here for the police to target particular areas at particular times which, in turn, might lead to more recorded incidences of a particular form of crime, thus creating a particular 'crime wave'. It has also been argued by many criminologists, such as Mike Maguire (2002), that the resulting figures are often taken by both journalists and politicians as being an accurate reflection of what is happening, and that this can lead to responses of greater control, increased sentences for particular offences, a greater fear of crime amongst the public and so on.

It could be said that this policing strategy also highlights and reinforces the overall limitations of official recorded crime statistics. To re-cap the main points we have considered in this chapter, these limitations can be listed as follows:

- They only include 'notifiable' offences (and exclude 'summary' offences).
- They are based on returns of crimes recorded by police services which are responsible to the Home Office.

- The impact of legislative change; notifiable offence list and crime recording standards change too.
- Not all crimes which occur are reported to the police (and the reasons why this may be the case).
- The police do not always record incidences of crime which are reported to them (and the possible reasons for this).

So, overall, we can say that any picture of crime provided by official police recorded crime statistics is far from being a clear one; it is blurred, slanted, and incomplete, and could be described as being almost a very basic 'painting by numbers' rather than an accurate representation. We can see a clear picture but the depth of detail and the subtleties and nuances of it are absent.

As we noted at the start of this chapter, historically speaking, one of the reasons for generating statistical or any other kind of 'evidence' is to guide policy makers in enacting policy in ways which address a particular social problem. Such 'evidence' can also (mis)inform public perceptions. By the 1980s in England and Wales, the real limitations of police recorded statistics were widely recognised in government circles and a new attempt was made to develop a clearer and more accurate research and statistical tool. It was argued that this would help to uncover the so-called 'hidden' figure of crime as well as provide a more accurate guide for both policy makers and the general public. This was called the British Crime Survey and will be the focus of the next section of this chapter.

Surveying crime: The Crime Survey for England and Wales

In an attempt to address some of the shortcomings of the police recorded crime statistics, which we discussed in the last section of this chapter, in 1982 the British government introduced a national crime survey. This was called the British Crime Survey (BCS) but since 2002 it has been re-titled as the Crime Survey for England and Wales (CSEW). The main aims of the survey are to uncover the so-called 'dark' figure of crime and provide a more accurate picture in terms of the trends of the various types of crime which are being committed. This can then, in theory, feed into public policy to help to control, regulate, and prevent crime. It can help the state to provide appropriate support for victims of crime, as well as to respond to public perceptions of unfairness in the justice system as a whole. The survey asks respondents about their own victimisation as well as exploring their attitudes to issues related to crime, such as their general perceptions of

crime levels and their attitudes to the criminal justice agencies. For instance, respondents are asked to rate their overall confidence in the police and local councils and whether they think these agencies are doing a good, effective, and fair job in addressing local and national crime problems. Perhaps unsurprisingly, both sets of data tell us different things. For instance, in 2016 the police recorded 4.5 million offences (representing an annual rise of 8 per cent) whilst the CSEW estimated 6.3 million incidents against adults (a 6 per cent decrease from the previous survey year).

From 1982 the survey ran at (mostly) two year intervals but since 2001 it became a continuous annual survey. As a research tool is it now a large (in terms of its sample size) and methodologically sophisticated attempt to estimate a more accurate and realistic reflection of the extent of crime experienced by the population of households in

England and Wales. In short, it tries to overcome the very real problems and issues with the reporting and recording of crime which we explored in the last section of this chapter. The complex methodological issues need not concern us too much here (see **Chapter 6** on how criminologists research their subject matter and the use of sample surveys within this) but it is perhaps worth briefly mentioning the basic logic of social survey methodology. As we previously noted, arriving at a complete enumeration of crimes committed in a given area is an impossible task, especially given the problems of attrition and the number of crimes which are not even reported to the police in the first place. What a social survey does is to take a representative sample of a given population, in this case all households in England and Wales. It will ask household members to answer its questions and then, through various statistical techniques, it claims to make valid and reliable generalisations from the sample to the population as a whole. As you have probably realised, all research instruments (and research studies) are far from being perfect; that is, after all, why criminologists and other social scientists read and critically evaluate each other's work in order to critique, develop, and improve on it.

To be sure, large social surveys sometimes get it wrong and their findings are not borne out by what actually happens. A good, non-criminological example of this is to consider briefly is the work of psephologists (people who study political elections and electoral behaviour). During the 2015 general election in Britain, many opinion pollsters were predicting a hung parliament in which there would be no overall majority of seats in the House of Parliament for any individual political party. As we know, what actually happened in the final election results was that the Conservative party won the majority needed to form a government. In short, the vast majority of opinion and exit polls got it wrong. There is currently much debate on how the pollsters arrived at such erroneous conclusions, with many people now focusing on intricate methodological issues, such as how members of the public were sampled and selected for the various polls which were held. It could well also have been that the people questioned were unsure as to how they were going to vote, or perhaps that they even changed their minds before casting their votes. They could also possibly have been untruthful when answering how they had voted when the polls had closed.

In general, the CSEW works on the same basis as election polls, that of selecting a representative sample of the population in order to make meaningful, reliable, and valid generalisations. The first BCS survey questioned a representative sample of households (and the people living within them) numbering 10,000; by 2005–06 this sample size had increased significantly to over 47,000, and now it aims to achieve a sample size of around 35,000. This is still a significant number of people to question and, as we have noted, it is a technically sophisticated and large piece of social research. The survey attempts to respond to changing

social needs; for instance, in 2009 it was extended to examine the views of children aged 10-15. Although this allowed a greater level of awareness of children as victims of crime, the extension, like the survey as a whole, has some limits, notably in that parental or guardian permission is sought before a child is allowed to take part. Whilst this may help to support children who are being interviewed, there is a correlated risk that a child victim may be prevented from participating. This is particularly worrying given that children are most likely to be harmed by people in their own family. Nor are the voices of younger children heard.

Regardless of such complex methodological issues, most commentators, including the majority of criminologists, regard the CSEW to be a stronger and more robust indicator of national estimated levels of crime and trends in specific offences over time than most other measures. It simply cannot, however, cover everything in terms of the types of crime experienced across all groups in society. Difficult choices have to be made and clear parameters set for it to be meaningful.

Once you have worked through the **What do you think? 5.4** exercise on designing a crime survey for your university, you will realise that designing and carrying out any piece of social scientific research is very challenging, at both practical and technical levels. If you found the exercise a challenge, imagine trying to design a survey which covers crime throughout England and Wales.

We will end this section by covering some of the nuts and bolts of the CSEW as well as considering some of its strengths and weaknesses. We do not have space to cover all of these issues, especially the more technical issues, but the Office for National Statistics has produced a very useful and detailed *User Guide to Crime Statistics in England and Wales* (ONS 2015) which you can access from their website. This usefully covers police recorded crime statistics as well as the CSEW.

Many students are often sceptical about the claim that from a well-designed survey we can make valid and reliable generalisations from the sample that are applicable to the target population; in this case, all households in England and Wales (or in the **What do you think? 5.4** exercise, all students studying at your university). The mathematics behind it is very complicated but remember that the CSEW involves a large team of well-qualified and experienced research designers, researchers, and interviewers to ensure its rigour and credibility. In short, it is a very sophisticated research instrument and, as such, it is perhaps the best source of information (to date) we have when studying crime rates and trends in England and Wales. It is also constantly evolving to reflect changing times and concerns. But it is not without its limitations, in terms of both the types of households surveyed and the offence categories considered. The ONS are very clear about some of its potential limitations.

As we noted earlier, the CSEW aims to survey around 35,000 households every year. By focusing on

WHAT DO YOU THINK? 5.4

How much crime is committed at your university—and how will you find out?

As you will see in **Chapter 7**, the media can sometimes fuel public concerns about crime. Let us imagine that the following (fictitious) headlines have appeared in the national press:

* *Crime Soars at UK Universities*
* *Campus Crime on the Rise*
* *Fury at Student Safety—More Crimes at University than Ever Before*

Concerned by this, the Government is planning to carry out a national survey of campus crime, but also wants each university to initially carry out its own, internal research. As a result, your Chancellor has asked you and your fellow criminology students to design a survey that will give accurate information about crime rates for your own university. The Vice Chancellor has hinted that this data will be made available to future students and their families, as well as to the press, and will become part of the national survey.

What will your survey look like? There will be lots of things to consider: you will need to think very carefully about these and start to make some difficult decisions and choices. Let us suppose that you make the following decisions:

* you will be surveying all full-time students;
* you will ask about their experiences of theft, car theft, drug use, sexual assault, and violence (and use offence categories which mirror official police recorded crime statistics) whilst on campus;
* you will ask about incidents that took place within the last academic year;
* you will ask respondents to fill in an online survey, which they can access in the main library on campus through their main student account;
* the survey will use a simple yes/no format to certain question items and standard attitudinal scales (ranging from respondents being asked to strongly agree to strongly disagree with particular statements) for others;
* the results will be published on the university website.

Take a moment to write down what you consider to be the strengths and weaknesses of this approach. Be as honest as you can, and try to think about how you would use your format in future years—for example to measure trends.

Now let us imagine that having drafted the framework of your survey; you have issued it to your peers for their thoughts as a pilot test to gauge the overall clarity of your questions and the general survey design. They challenge your decisions with more questions. Have a look at this list and see how it compares to your 'strengths and weaknesses' ideas:

* If the survey is only for full time students, how will you justify excluding staff and visitors?
* How are you going to make sure you get a truly representative sample of the student body in terms of gender, ethnicity, and socio-economic status?
* What would you use as your sampling frame?
* Many students say that they would not simply take the time to complete an online survey—how could you increase your response rate? Would carrying out more time-consuming face-to-face interviews be more effective?
* Most mature students are part time. How will you seek their views?
* What about damage to the university itself—such as vandalism, arson, fraud?
* Very few students drive as there is limited parking on campus. Most use bicycles. Why are you not asking about crimes involving bikes?
* What is your definition of violence?
* To what extent are you confident that your questions (including the use of particular crime categories) are worded in a way that actually measures what you want them to measure?
* How will you make sure respondents are clear about the meaning of terms used in your survey—for instance, explaining the difference between an offence and an attempted offence?
* Why are you not examining incidents of hate crime?
* There are ethical concerns around surveys and how they are carried out. How will you protect anyone who is affected by discussing crimes they have experienced?
* Are you going to warn students that they are going to be asked about sensitive topics such as sexual assault?
* If students are going to use their personal logins to complete the survey, how can you reassure them about confidentiality? Will this also affect how people respond?
* The university has a significant number of disabled students who use assistive technology like screen

readers. How will you adapt the survey to ensure that they are able to use it?

- Similarly, how will you ensure that students with learning needs such as dyslexia are able to understand and complete the survey?

- We have a large number of foreign students here, as part of an exchange programme with universities in Europe. How will you check that they have been able to understand the survey?

- What about student attitudes to crime? How will these be measured?

The Vice Chancellor also has a few concerns that you will need to consider. Before reading on, try to anticipate what these may be. Write a short list, then think about how you will answer this memo from the VC:

Dear Students

Thank you for your proposed survey design. I would be obliged if you would consult with your tutors and provide me with the following reassurances:

We need to maintain public confidence in our university. Without a strong reputation for campus safety, we are less likely to attract new students. Without them, and the income they attract, we would see a reduction in our ability to offer financially-viable courses. Similarly, our capacity to carry out research would be impaired, which would affect our standing as a centre of international excellence in criminology.

I would ask you therefore to consider how you will carry out your research in such a way as to allow us to reassure students and their families that we do not have a crime issue on our campus. I would also ask that you identify a suitable way of publishing the findings without causing unwelcome and hostile publicity.

Now go back to your initial ideas. What will you change? Do you think that it is practicable to accommodate everyone's concerns? If not, how will you justify your decisions?

---

individual households it can ask questions about household crimes (such as burglary or criminal damage to a car) as well as personal crimes (such as any member of that household who has been the victim of assault). As its sampling frame it draws on the small users Postcode Address File (PAF). This is a very practical and pragmatic thing to do but, as a result, the survey will not include those people who live in other types of setting, such as care homes or university halls of residence. It is, however, thought that this does not hamper the survey or skew its results in any way, although given the rise in concerns about hate crime and elder abuse it could be argued that a valuable source of information is being overlooked.

This mass victimisation survey is administered by face-to-face interviews which are now carried out with the assistance of computer-assisted interviewing (this, as opposed to a paper-based questionnaire, is thought to give the survey results more consistency). The survey carefully tries to be representative of all household types in England and Wales (you may wish to read up further in the ONS guide mentioned earlier about how this issue is addressed) but it is openly acknowledged that it cannot cover every victim-based criminal offence and that, by necessity, there are some exclusions; currently these include fraud and so-called 'victimless' crimes (such as the possession of and consumption of drugs) as well as types of business crime. It does, however, attempt to use the main categories of crime as recorded by the police—the main survey covers crimes of violence, robbery, theft from person, domestic burglary in a dwelling, vehicle-related theft, bicycle theft, criminal damage to a dwelling, and criminal damage to a vehicle. In doing so it is argued that we can directly compare the incidence of specific crimes and various crimes trends (both at a general and more offence-specific level) between the police recorded statistics and the CSEW. Many official reports and newspaper articles now draw on both sources when reporting on crime.

As for the main findings, there is really no substitute for you perusing the most recent published report and bulletins which compare police recorded crime and CSEW data. These are a veritable treasure trove of information on crime-related matters, which all criminology students should get into the habit of dipping into from time to time. However, it is important to bear in mind that despite the obvious successes of the CSEW in highlighting and addressing some of the shortcomings of police recording statistics, as well as its usefulness in measuring peoples' perceptions on crime where they live and their attitudes to criminal justice agencies, not everyone agrees that is it the best method. Indeed, many criminologists are now beginning to critically question the use of carrying out such a survey in the first place.

In **Telling it like it is 5.3** we hear from Tim Hope. Professor Hope argues that the CSEW is simply not a very good or effective way to measure crime at all, and he calls for a new type of crime survey.

TELLING IT LIKE IT IS 5.3

Why we need a different crime survey—with Professor Tim Hope

The Crime Survey for England and Wales (CSEW) doesn't cover all types of crime, it doesn't include all victims, and it doesn't count all crime incidents.

When it started out, the British Crime Survey was really intended to reflect those crimes that were not reported to the police. Essentially, its purpose was to audit police crime recording so as to obtain more reliable official crime statistics. So, the CSEW was only ever intended as a *mirror* of police recorded crime (PRC). Not surprisingly, its findings are broadly similar to the data produced by the police, yielding similar types of crime, that are affecting similar types of victim. Where it differs is in the quantity of crimes described. People may also feel able to tell the CSEW about concerns that they would not want to bring to police attention.

Still, the CSEW/PRC mirror has been a very useful political device. In the past, it has been used to puff up government 'performance' in the 'War Against Crime'. Now, because the CSEW tells us that crime is dropping, it has been equally useful as evidence to reduce spending on the police. Additionally, the subjective elements of the CSEW, such as fear of crime and confidence in the police, have served very well as the Home Office's own public opinion polling on the public's apparent 'satisfaction' with its efforts to improve the criminal justice system.

It is instructive to see what has actually happened to the standing of PRC. As a result of a damning parliamentary enquiry that lambasted the police for fiddling the figures—especially for failing to record serious, sexual offences—the UK Statistics Authority has withdrawn national recognition of PRC. Unfortunately, the CSEW has been no help either; it is not large enough to shed any light specifically on local crime experiences, and it records very few serious sexual offences. Nevertheless, the mirror itself didn't crack: despite similar failures to record crime as PRC, the CSEW remains the *only* nationally approved measure of crime.

Yet we still don't know enough about the true extent of crime, especially about inter-personal violent crime amongst family members and people known to each other. We suspect that there is a huge amount hidden even beneath the tip of the CSEW iceberg.

Over the years, the CSEW has got progressively better at measuring the reporting of crime, and much worse at measuring crime victimisation, paradoxically because it has got better at representing the experiences of the general population and worse at representing the experiences of victims. We do know that the overall distribution of crime victimisation amongst the population is highly unequal: around 80 per cent of the population suffer only about 20 per cent of the crime, while about 20 per cent of the population take around 80 per cent of the burden of crime upon their shoulders. But despite this glaring inequality we don't know a great deal about the experiences of victims. While most who are vulnerable to crime may suffer only intermittently, there is a relatively small population who are chronically victimised (Hope and Norris 2013). These are the true victims.

Nevertheless, the politics of large numbers prevail. Politicians can relax because crime seems to be going down for the majority of their constituents, but this is only because they are experiencing less of what was always a rare misfortune. However, it *does* matter for the less fortunate; for them, crime victimisation is as it always has been, a constant and depressing concern of their everyday lives.

So, we need to reform the crime survey. We should:

- **try to find more victims**: when the CSEW took over from the BCS, it ceased to be a *crime* survey and became a police performance survey instead. The CSEW stopped looking so much at inner city, high crime areas and instead over-sampled suburban and rural areas. The CSEW became more interested in how the government's law and order policies were going down amongst ordinary citizens and became insouciant about the needs of people who experience crime on a daily basis. So we don't know how this has affected the typical profile of victims; particularly, we don't know how many more chronic victims are now being over-looked.

- **try to include the crime that is hard to reach**: we need to find ways of encouraging victims to talk to the survey frankly, safely, and openly. We should be as sensitive to interviewing in the CSEW (and find alternative ways of finding and interviewing victims) as we are now expecting the police to be, especially concerning sexual offences, domestic violence, bullying, harassment and grooming, Internet fraud, and indeed in any of the harms victims experience that cannot be compensated with new-for-old insurance.

- **try to contact the people that are hard to reach**: since the start, the BCS/CSEW has always failed to contact, or had refusals from, around a quarter to a third of its sample, and that just includes the residential population. It does not reach the homeless, the institutionalised, and the transient. Market research and opinion polling can always write this off since they tend to focus on the mainstream of society and want to cut costs (it is revealing that it is the market research industry that has always designed and run the BCS/CSEW). But non-response cannot be ignored in a crime victims' measurement survey: not only does every response count but the kinds of people who refuse or cannot be contacted are precisely the kinds of people who are most likely to be vulnerable to crime victimisation.

- **try to count crime accurately and truthfully**: the counting procedures themselves need to change. Usually, an arbitrary 'cap' is put on the number of victimisations that victims report in order to ensure that the national averages are not affected by a very small number of respondents who report extremely high numbers of incidents. But it is precisely these chronic victims to whom we need to listen. The

consequences are dramatic: when the capping is removed there are 60 per cent more violent crimes overall; violence against women, along with family and domestic violence, all increase by 70 per cent. In sum, violent crime becomes much less of a problem of 'stranger-danger' and much more a problem of intimate human relationships (Walby et al. 2015).

Obviously, much more needs to be done technically to implement a truly victim-oriented national survey but the issue goes beyond this. Politicians always talk like accountants and never talk about the moral purpose of their policies. We need very much to restore the moral dimension to our contemporary measurement of crime if we are to bring the moral dimension back to our criminal justice policies.

Professor Tim Hope is visiting Fellow at the Centre for Crime and Justice Studies, London, and a former Professor of Criminology at the University of Salford and Keele University

Source: Hope, T. (2015), 'We need a different crime survey', Centre for Crime and Justice Studies; London (www.crimeandjustice.org.uk/resources/we-need-different-crime-survey).

Conclusion

In this chapter we have explored some of the reasons why governments and state agencies have collected, collated, and disseminated statistics on crime as well as the various ways in which they have done (and do) so. We have also noted some of the uses and abuses to which such data has been put.

It is sometimes said that deconstructing official crime statistics is little more than a (dull) rite of passage which all criminology students must go through, before they can move on to study what might seem to be more interesting and dynamic areas of criminological study. The position adopted in this chapter is somewhat different. It argues that by carefully working through the processes of deconstructing and reconstructing official statistical representations of crime, we can raise many important and interesting questions, which should be at the forefront of your mind throughout the rest of your studies. Indeed, it could be said that these processes are central to your being able to develop your own critical criminological imaginations. The position we have adopted here has been one which will provide you with a critical lens through which you should view all claims to knowledge about crime, criminality, criminals, and crime control—not just those statistical claims generated by governments, but also those made by other interested groups (and indeed criminologists themselves). You should also be able to think about

the possibility that statistics can be used for the purposes of governance and control.

As part of this critical approach, we all need to remember that sets of official crime data are not the useless or meaningless constructions that some commentators and journalists would have us believe. Although, as we have seen in this chapter, they are far from being perfect and accurate (especially in terms of what is counted and how), if we carefully deconstruct them they can, and do, tell us a great deal. This is not just when considering issues of broader power and power relations. Data can also be highly suggestive in terms of certain crime trends and patterns, and how these may affect people who are the victims of crime. The quality, reliability, and use of data can only be improved if we all exercise our critical imaginations.

We will continue to develop our critical approach to statistical data in **Chapter 8** where we will begin to explore how some non-governmental organisations, pressure groups, and criminologists critically draw on government statistics (as well as generating their own knowledge claims based on both quantitative and qualitative data) to agitate for reform and change through public policies, which could lead to the creation of a fairer and more just society. Perhaps this, and the campaigning of these groups, is the start of what Professor Hope has called for in terms of a more 'moral dimension' to the way in which we generate and interpret the findings of central government surveys. As we shall see, by critically appraising the limitations of government surveys, we can perhaps design more focused and effective research tools.

The main focus of **Chapter 8** will be on how research can help us to re-centre the victims (who can also include offenders) of crime in our studies. A critical reading of official criminal statistics can perhaps start us on our journey into this particular area of criminology—sometimes referred to as victimology. Our central focus in developing this will be on the recent recognition of crimes which are motivated by hatred and prejudice directed at certain individuals or groups.

SUMMARY

- Appreciate why governments may want to collect data on crime and how they go about this

As we noted at the start of the chapter, the use of statistics can throw up some interesting and thought-provoking questions and issues. Statistics can also chart changes in social attitudes and lifestyles. However, statistical data have a wider usage in that they are often used to inform or justify policy decisions, sometimes in response to public pressure or social reaction, regardless of whether this is borne out by the actual data. From a critical perspective, it can be argued therefore that governments may gather and use data selectively. Governments use a range of techniques for gathering data, including surveys and the analysis of crimes as recorded by the police, but again, the critical response can be that these are of limited accuracy and can be skewed by political, social or economic factors both on behalf of state agencies and the public itself.

- Identify the main problems with police recorded crime statistics and understand what is meant by the 'justice gap'

Police recorded crime figures are of themselves incomplete and inaccurate, for many and complex reasons including problems of public perception towards an act of deviance, attitudes towards the criminal justice system, and the perceived power or powerlessness of victims. Likewise, the formal categorisation of incidents and the discretion afforded to criminal justice agencies means that not all crimes which are notifiable are always considered to warrant further action. The definition of crimes, and the actions of the criminal justice system, may be affected by political or social pressures which mean that outcomes vary over time. These factors influence the distinction between what is reported and what is actually recorded, forming the 'justice gap' and highlighting the associated issue of attrition.

- Relate the collation of crime statistics to broader issues of politics and power

It is uncontroversial to say that crime statistics do not paint an accurate picture of crime and its incidence. However, it does not automatically follow that the information gathered is useless; instead, it can be used to explore and evaluate the series of social processes that go on within the criminal justice system. Critical criminologists (see **Chapter 15** for a further discussion of this theoretical perspective) would go further and argue that data can tell us a great deal about the matrices of power involved with policing and policy, such as the way in which resources are allocated or particular problems prioritised. The data may also be used to inform changes to the notifiable offence list, which in turn may reflect public anxieties and political agendas. This can be related to the publicising and manipulation of selected data by powerful agencies as a form of governance and control.

- Evaluate the main strengths and weaknesses in trying to measure criminal behaviour through the use of social surveys

As illustrated by the **What do you think? 5.4** exercise on creating a campus-wide crime survey, there are significant concerns around the use of social surveys. To be effective, a survey must be designed to capture information from a carefully-selected representative sample population, and needs to ensure its questions are clear, unambiguous, and allow accurate interpretation of the findings. In some forms, surveys can be time-limited in that they are not designed to withstand social, political, or technological change. Whilst social surveys have the advantage of being able to reach large numbers of participants, they cannot be exhaustive and therefore it is possible that important areas of concern are not examined in the required depth.

- Critically assess the Crime Survey for England and Wales (CSEW) as a way of measuring crime and its tends in England and Wales.

Whilst generally regarded as the best statistical picture of crime we currently have (especially when taken together with police recorded statistics) the CSEW has important flaws. As noted by Professor Hope, the CSEW sample population does not reach those individuals who have a higher probability of being victimised; nor does it at present fully examine crimes such as bullying or sexual offences—perhaps because of reluctance on the part of respondents to reveal and discuss what are emotionally difficult topics. This, it could be argued, bears out Professor Hope's view that this or other crime surveys need to restore a 'moral dimension' to the examination of crime.

REVIEW QUESTIONS

1. List three reasons why governments collect and collate crime data.

2. What is meant by the term 'justice gap'?

3. Give three reasons why members of the public may decide not to report a crime to the police and consider how (and why) this varies between offence type.

4. Give three reasons why the police may decide not to record an incident which has been reported to them.

5. What is meant by 'attrition' in the context of the criminal justice system?

6. What are the potential benefits and drawbacks of the police developing crime mapping techniques?

7. In what ways is the Crime Survey for England and Wales (CSEW) thought to provide us with a more accurate picture of crime levels and does it manage to achieve this?

FURTHER READING

As we noted in this chapter, there has recently been a data explosion with regards to published 'facts' and figures on crime and criminality. Government ministries produce various monthly statistical bulletins on a range of issues of criminological concerns. There is really no substitute for you dipping into these from time to time. You will, for instance, find many such bulletins on the Ministry of Justice website (http://www.justice.gov.uk/), the website of the Office for National Statistics (https://www.ons.gov.uk/), and the Home Office web pages (https://www.gov.uk/government/organisations/home-office).

If you want to explore how criminologists have charted the various changes in how governments have collated crime data over the last 20 years or so, you could do far worse than to read the detailed scholarly discussions in *The Oxford Handbook of Criminology.* Taken together these now provide us with an interesting historical discussion and analysis of the development of official crime statistics since 1994. These are:

Maguire, M. (1997) 'Crime statistics, patterns and trends' in Maguire, M., Morgan, R., and Reiner, R. (eds) *The Oxford Handbook of Criminology* (2nd edn). Oxford: Oxford University Press.

Maguire, M. (2002) 'Crime statistics: the "data explosion" and its implications' in Maguire, M., Morgan, R., and Reiner, R. (eds) *The Oxford Handbook of Criminology* (3rd edn). Oxford: Oxford University Press.

Maguire, M. (2007) 'Crime data and statistics' in Maguire, M., Morgan, R., and Reiner, R. (eds) *The Oxford Handbook of Criminology* (4th edn). Oxford: Oxford University Press.

Maguire, M. (2012) 'Criminal statistics and the construction of crime' in Maguire, M., Morgan, R., and Reiner, R. (eds) *The Oxford Handbook of Criminology* (5th edn). Oxford: Oxford University Press.

Maguire, M. and McVie, S. (2017) 'Crime data and criminal statistics: a critical reflection' in Liebling, A., Maruna, S., and McAra, L. (eds) *The Oxford Handbook of Criminology* (6th edn). Oxford: Oxford University Press.

 Access the **online resources** to view selected further reading and web links relevant to the material covered in this chapter.
www.oup.com/uk/case/

ANSWERS TO EXERCISES

WHAT DO YOU THINK? 5.1

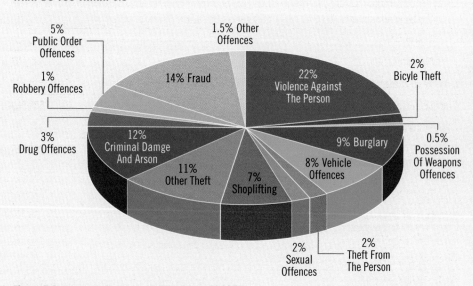

Figure 5.9 Answers to the exercise in **What do you think? 5.1**

Source: Office for National Statistics (www.ons.gov.uk). Content is available under the Open Government Licence v3.0.

Police recorded crimes, March 2016

England and Wales

Offence group	Number of offences
VICTIM-BASED CRIME	3,451,940
Violence against the person offences	994,444
Homicide	571
Violence with injury	431,258
Violence without injury	562,615
Sexual offences	106,378
Rape	35,798
Other sexual offences	70,580
Robbery offences	50,904
Robbery of business property	5,421
Robbery of personal property	45,483
Theft offences	1,760,305
Burglary	400,361
Domestic burglary	193,773
Non-domestic burglary	206,588
Vehicle offences	366,715
Theft of a motor vehicle	82,047
Theft from a vehicle	239,082
Interfering with a motor vehicle	45,586
Theft from the person	83,315
Bicycle theft	86,616
Shoplifting	336,708
All other theft offences	486,590
Criminal damage and arson	539,909
OTHER CRIMES AGAINST SOCIETY	441,007
Drug offences	147,557
Trafficking of drugs	25,402
Possession of drugs	122,155
Possession of weapons offences	25,502
Public order offences	204,616
Miscellaneous crimes against society	63,332
TOTAL FRAUD OFFENCES	621,017
TOTAL RECORDED CRIME—ALL OFFENCES INCLUDING FRAUD	4,513,964

Table 5.1 Answers to the exercise in **What do you think? 5.1**

Source: Office for National Statistics (www.ons.gov.uk), content available under the Open Government Licence v3.0

WHAT DO YOU THINK? 5.2

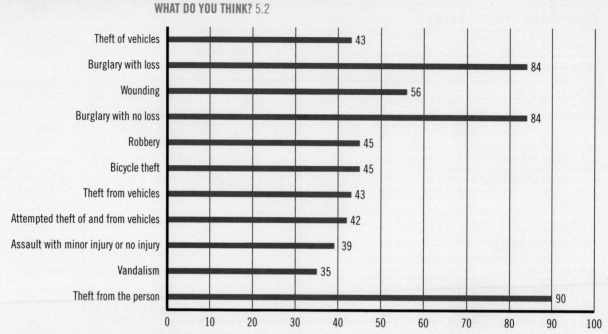

Figure 5.10 Reporting rates for different offences (derived from BCS, Flately et al., 2010)

WHAT DO YOU THINK? 5.3

SW1A 1AA is the postcode for Buckingham Palace, the London residence of Queen Elizabeth II

Source: Diliff/Public domain

NE1 4ST is St James' Park, the home of Newcastle United Football Club

Source: Joe89316/Public domain

YO1 7JN is the postcode for York Minster, one of the largest cathedrals in Europe

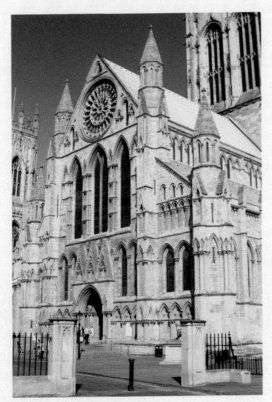

Source: Steve F.E. Cameron/CC BY-SA 3.0

CHAPTER OUTLINE

Introduction   140

Approaching criminological knowledge with a critical eye   141

Subjectivity, supposition, and study: The triad of
knowledge creation   142

Criminological theory as knowledge   143

Supposition   148

Study   150

Reflecting on research as study: What can we know?   161

How does criminology 'know' about crime?

Subjectivity, supposition, and study

KEY ISSUES

After reading this chapter you should be able to:

- consider from a critical viewpoint how knowledge in criminology is produced and what it means to know about crime;

- understand what is meant by subjectivity, supposition, and study (through research) in criminological terms;

- critically evaluate the benefits and limitations of different research study methods on the creation of criminological knowledge;

- explore how subjectivity, supposition, and study interact with, and impact on, understanding and knowledge production in criminology.

Introduction

In **Chapter 5**, you were introduced to the ways and forms in which government and non-governmental organisations produce evidence and knowledge, particularly regarding the extent and nature of crime in England and Wales. In this chapter, we will explore and evaluate the means by which different forms of knowledge are created in criminology by criminologists—the knowledge that we then learn about in lectures, seminars, textbooks, journal articles, research reports, policy documents, and so on. Particular attention will be paid to the complex and rarely acknowledged interplay between subjectivity, supposition (guesswork, assumption, conjecture), and study in the creation of knowledge. In particular, this chapter casts a critical eye over the empirical research methods used by criminologists.

'Empirical methods' refers to the generation of evidence through (sensory) experience, particularly using experiments and observations (Chamberlain 2013). However, this definiton will be expanded in this instance to incorporate survey methods, and we will move beyond it to incorporate secondary data analysis, which is non-empirical. This chapter will explore both the benefits and limitations of the multitude of ways through which we collect information in criminology. The second part of this chapter will then go on to consider the different research methods available to criminologists, covering both primary and secondary source material. All this will be useful to you as a knowledge-producing criminology student when you come to embark on your own research work.

Subjectivity and supposition guide and shape study in criminology, dictating the choices and arguments that researchers make when conducting research. That same subjectivity lies behind the choice of research method in the first place. This chapter is not intended as a series of damning criticisms of the quality of the knowledge generated in criminology; nor is it urging you to reject everything you read or hear. To do so would be counterproductive to the purpose of this book. Knowledge in any discipline can only be advanced by strong-willed, opinionated individuals who are committed to a particular viewpoint (over others) and who value the knowledge they generate. This is what makes us criminologists. In any case, as we will come to recognise, a degree of subjectivity is inevitable, even helpful in knowledge production, especially when human beings research the behaviour of other human beings in our complex social world. Indeed, we will use *our own* subjectivity to illustrate that all authors, even those who appear balanced, should be questioned about their preferences and prejudices.

It is crucial that we learn to reflect critically on the impact of our subjectivity on the validity of the arguments we make and on the nature of the knowledge we create—this process of critical reflection is known as reflexivity. A central argument of this chapter, therefore, is that subjectivity, supposition, and study (particularly empirical research methods) in criminology exert influence on the extent and nature of the knowledge produced; influences that we should acknowledge and factor into our evaluation of any knowledge we receive and produce. Adopting such a critical perspective is an essential tool in navigating your way through criminological knowledge, but this critical eye should only ever be used to move forwards, to progress knowledge in a more informed, realistic, and valid way.

When we study criminology, we are taught what we should know, what we need to know, and what we will be asked to show that we know. But every source of knowledge in criminology has been created by someone who has a degree of subjectivity and who may have an agenda: so knowledge may have an agenda bias. It is important to be aware that subjectivities, agendas, and biases produce certain types of knowledge and not others, even when they are based on evidence generated from research. Being subjective and exerting a personal or disciplinary perspective on the research decisions and interpretations that help us to create knowledge does not necessarily constitute bias in any negative, restricted, or partial sense. Subjectivity can guide, shape, and render transparent knowledge creation in the face of uncertainty, complexity, and practical constraints. Reflexive consideration of the influence of our subjectivities is key to the production of valid, realistic, and practical knowledge—important for keeping our perspective in perspective, if you like.

When knowledge is based on unsupported and unacknowledged opinion and/or guesswork rather than evidence emerging from study, then this is a greater issue. What we will come to know in this chapter is how subjectivity, supposition, and study create knowledge of certain kinds in criminology. Knowing this will enable us to better analyse and evaluate criminological knowledge in terms of its value and utility, motivating us to become thoughtful and reflexive criminologists in our daily lives (Stout, Yates, and Williams 2008). It should also help you to better understand your own research agenda and consider that from a critical perspective too. This heightened awareness will ultimately serve you well when evaluating criminological knowledge and when writing essays and conducting research projects or dissertations.

In order to explore the influences of the subjectivity, supposition, and study that underpin criminological research, this chapter will investigate two key questions:

1. **What does it mean to know about crime?** We will examine how our understanding and knowledge of crime can be developed through the application, analysis, synthesis, and evaluation of criminological information.

2. **What are the influences of subjectivity, supposition, and study on our understandings of crime?** The main focus of the chapter will be an exploration of the roles of academic and external subjectivity (personal and disciplinary perspectives), supposition (assumption and guesswork, often educated), and study (e.g. scholarship, conducting empirical and other research) in the creation of understanding and knowledge regarding crime.

Approaching criminological knowledge with a critical eye

The material that we read, hear, observe, discuss, and produce in criminology has been created or *socially constructed* for a purpose. It is knowledge, but of a specific and possibly limited kind. We should always ask questions about the knowledge we are asked to learn in criminology, such as:

- Who has created it?
- How have they created it?
- Why have they created it?
- Who have they created it for?
- Whose knowledge is it?

It is essential that we consider the source of all knowledge we engage with in criminology, particularly the objectives, perspectives, preferences, agendas, and biases of the producer of that knowledge. We should also consider the source of the source. This refers to the methods used to create or obtain knowledge (Westmarland 2011), what form of knowledge it is, the extent to which it is based on evidence, its strengths/benefits, and its limitations/weaknesses. Only by asking such critical questions can we begin to evaluate the quality of the knowledge we are learning and, perhaps more importantly, evaluate how it benefits criminology in general and us specifically.

A key issue here, therefore, is what is known as validity, which essentially means the accuracy, honesty, trustworthiness, and appropriateness of knowledge, of the methods we use to obtain it, and how it can be used to inform criminological theories, explanations, concepts, and arguments (the knowledge base). It is absolutely crucial to be able to judge the quality and value of the knowledge that we draw upon to help us understand crime. Not only that, but it is essential to be able to judge the amount of faith that should be placed in this knowledge, how it can be used, and whether we actually agree with it. Such questions are pivotal if you as a student are to move past simply existing

as a *consumer* of criminological knowledge towards operating as a critical *evaluator* of criminological knowledge and ultimately evolving into a *producer* of criminological knowledge (see **Chapter 2** and **Chapter 28**).

What does it mean to know about crime?

To know about crime means to receive, explore, manipulate, and create knowledge about it. By actively manipulating and owning information in these ways, you move beyond repetition and description into demonstrating your understandings as being critical, original, reflective, and knowing about criminology. However, knowledge is different to fact. Fact is a universal truth, accepted by everyone everywhere. Such facts often emerge from the STEM subjects (science, technology, engineering, mathematics) that study the natural world, physical structures, artificial processes, and numbers, not conscious human beings living in complex societies. Criminology contains facts, of course—the names of organisations and structures (e.g. the criminal justice system, the youth justice system, the police), the names of crimes (e.g. burglary, theft, criminal damage/vandalism) and illegal substances (e.g. heroin, cannabis) at a given point in time in a given country, etc., although such facts are often dynamic over time and vary between cultures. However, criminology and the knowledge that criminologists generate is shaped by debate, issues, and theories (Chamberlain 2015). These tend to be social constructions—the artificial creations of subjective human beings—rather than facts that can be taken for granted. The criminological knowledge base evolves through debate and disagreement, through opinion and perspective, through divisions and resolutions. Therefore, much of what we consider knowledge in our subject is more accurately defined as perspective, interpretation, and personal preference, rather than cold, hard fact. Why? Because criminology is a social science conducted by humans with humans for humans in a complex social word populated by humans.

The creation and evaluation of knowledge in the social sciences is guided by epistemology, which is 'a branch of philosophy which examines the concept of knowledge—what it is, where it comes from and whether absolute, true knowledge can be achieved' (Crow and Semmens 2008: 23). Therefore, the concept of epistemology examines what constitutes appropriate knowledge about the social world and how this knowledge is created (Robson 2015). The dominant epistemology/form of knowledge creation in criminology is *empiricism*, a position arguing that the only acceptable knowledge is that obtained through objective sensory perception and through research methods that measure this form of perception.

Within empiricism, the dominant epistemology is positivism, which asserts that the empirical research methods of the natural sciences (observation and experiment) can be employed to study and create knowledge about the social world—particularly in the form of univeral laws and cause and effect relationships between variables in the real world. As we will come to see, positivist epistemology is most commonly associated with the use of quantitative research methods in criminology and the creation of quantifiable, allegedly-objective, and value-free forms of knowledge about the reality of crime.

Across the social sciences more generally and within criminology specifically, the positivist epistemology has been challenged by interpretivism, which focuses on how individuals interpret, create, experience, and make meaning of their social worlds, for example, though their social interactions with others. Interpretivism argues that reality is a subjective, personal construction (Noaks and Wincup 2004). Interpretivist epistemology is most closely linked to qualitative research methods and their production of qualitative, subjective forms of knowledge, as we will discuss later in this chapter.

Traditionally in the social sciences, the positvist and interpretivist epistemologies have been viewed as dichotomous, incompatible, and conflicting—Oakley (1999) famously dubbed this conflict 'the paradigm wars'. Consequently, academics and researchers have tended to prefer a specific epistemology in their work to the exclusion of the other. However, since the 1990s, a third epsitemology has gained popularity as both a challenge to and a compromise between this unhelpful dichotomy (Tashakkori and Teddlie 1998). The epistemology of realism, also known as pragmatism, maintains that it is possible to study, understand, and create knowledge about an objective, externally-measurable reality through any combination of methods, including by combining methods with positivist and interpretivist leanings in order to fit the practical objectives of the research (cf. Bryman 2015; see also later discussion of mixed methods and **Chapter 19**'s discussion of realistic evaluation).

Realist/pragmatist epistemology is presented as a feasible, fit-for-purpose approach to knowledge creation that draws upon the essentially compatible values of positivist/quantitative and intepretivist/qualitative research. For example, quantitative and qualitative researchers can agree that reality is complex and (to some extent) constructed, and that single theories and methods offer only limited explanations of different social behaviours in the real world (see Reichardt and Rallis 1994). By extension, single epistemologies may not provide the most comprehensive and valid means of knowledge creation.

Subjectivity, supposition, and study: The triad of knowledge creation

As criminologists, we come to know about crime through (at least) one of three routes: subjectivity, supposition, and study (see **Chapter 2**). Any one of these may dominate knowledge generation at a given time for a particular person, but they are each ever present (Case, in Vaidya 2015). So, what is meant by subjectivity, supposition, and study—this triad of knowledge creation in criminology?

Subjectivity

This refers to the personal opinion, preferences, experiences, perspectives, and agendas (e.g. biases) that can shape the processes of knowledge creation in criminology and how criminologists understand, interpret, and present what they think and what they have found. Subjectivity is about the creation of personally meaningful information that enables a person to understand, discuss, explain, analyse, and evaluate the subject in a way that makes sense to them. Criminology often presents itself as an evidence-based and research-informed subject—a social science using scientific, empirical (largely positivist) methods to study social life and social phenomena (Davies, Francis, and Jupp 2011). However, that is only part of the story, as demonstrated in the previous discussion of epistemologies. If criminology is a science, then it is a subjective science—a healthy cocktail of individual perspective, educated guesswork, and empirical study.

Supposition

This term refers to the use of guesswork, imputation, assumption, estimates, speculation, and predictions to fill the gaps in our knowledge and understanding. Human beings have an overwhelming need to control and understand their lives, their surroundings, their experiences. We do not like uncertainty or the unknown, so when our knowledge is incomplete, we have a tendency to make it whole by inventing plausible stories and explanations based on common sense, expertise, experience, and subjectivity, generated from partial (related or unrelated) evidence and misinterpretations. Supposition in criminology is closely linked to extrapolation—an educated guess or prediction about the future based on available evidence, often moving beyond the limits or scope of the evidence and into speculation.

Study

Study is the process of reading, writing, talking, watching, and doing criminology, often (but not always) linked to some form of evidence generation through research (see Crow and Semmens 2008; King and Wincup 2008). A great deal of knowledge in criminology is created in this way. The methods, results, and conclusions of study are influenced by subjectivity and supposition, but it is study that is the main vehicle for knowledge production in our subject. Studying criminology is what criminologists do and what criminology students do. Examining knowledge and information with a critical eye (the ABC approach) is an essential part of studying criminology and key to becoming an effective criminologist (Chamberlain 2013). We are all forever students of criminology.

Criminological theory as knowledge

As an academic subject, criminology has developed in ways that exemplify the influence of subjectivity and supposition on knowledge generation, particularly in terms of their reciprocal relationships with theoretical explanations of criminal behaviour. The applied, real-world study of criminological issues, with its attendant subjectivities and suppositions (preferably accounted for via reflexivity), is inextricably linked to the development, refinement, and rejection of theories—explanatory frameworks for understanding and knowing about criminological behaviours, such as the causes of crime. Theories can be generated inductively—an original product of study. Existing theories can be tested, validated, improved, and falsified deductively through study. For example, theoretical developments can enhance the validity, applicability, and practicality of different research methods (e.g. informing suitable survey content) and different research designs (e.g. identifying appropriate sample groups). Similarly, theory itself can be used to fine tune study methods and to guard against the distorting (biasing) influences of subjectivity and supposition by providing a clear touchstone for applied study (Chamberlain 2015; Stout et al. 2008). In this way, theory and study (including study influenced by subjectivity and supposition) function in a virtuous circle with one another, each benefitting from, validating, and mediating each other.

The discipline of criminology grew from concerns about the levels of crime reflected by the creation of official crime statistics (themselves subjective social constructions—see **Chapter 5**) and the need to explain and respond to criminal behaviour in scientific, evidenced terms. However, the evidence behind the original theories and explanations of what causes crime and how to respond to it (i.e. the criminological knowledge base) was rarely underpinned, based far more on subjectivity and supposition than on applied, empirical study (see Case, in Vaidya 2015).

- **Classicism: Subjectivity and supposition**—The classical school of criminology (see **Chapter 12**) explained criminal behaviour as based on an individual's free will and rational choices, but these explanations were heavily criticised on methodological, evidential grounds as being based on 'armchair theorising' (Chamberlain 2015). This term implies the use of personal opinion (subjectivity), common sense, guesswork, and speculation (supposition) instead of collecting and analysing empirical evidence of real-life behaviour through applied research (study). Classicists were accused of being out of touch with reality; the phrase 'armchair theorising' refers to them sitting in their comfy armchairs and trying to explain real life from a distance. This embodies the practice of supposition—'guesstimating' realities and supposing what does, could, would, and should happen, without necessarily drawing upon the systematic collection of evidence.

- **Positivism: Study through research**—Positivism emerged in criminology to fill the evidential void of classicism with data gained from empirical study using methods adopted from the natural sciences (experiment, observation), adding other applied methods adopted from psychology and sociology, such as interviews, questionnaires, and the secondary analysis of data and documents. This was a much more satisfactory situation for criminology in its pursuit of 'social science' status as a marker of methodological legitimacy and credibility (Hagan 2013). However, positivists haven't always agreed on the best research methods to use or the most convincing theoretical explanations for criminal behaviour (e.g. biological, psychological, sociological, and variations of each of these—see **Chapters 13** and **14**). These major disagreements indicate that subjectivity has run throughout criminology, shaping the choice of methods used, the identification of suitable populations and behaviours to examine and understand, the results achieved, and the theories supported and rejected, but there has been only limited reflexivity within positivism regarding these subjectivities and their influence on validity and knowledge creation. What positivists *do* agree is that the concept of crime can be understood as an unproblematic, taken for granted, fact.

- **Critical criminology: The rebirth of subjectivity**—Critical/radical criminology came along in the 1950s/1960s to argue that positivism had it all wrong and that from an interpretivist perspective, crime and criminals were labels or social constructions applied by powerful groups (e.g whites, middle classes, adults) to less powerful groups such as ethnic minorities, the working classes, and young people (see **Chapters 15** and **16**). Therefore, it was argued that criminology should be focusing on who has the power to label—to define who is and is not criminal—not what causes crime (Williams 2012). However, critical criminologists tended to rely on subjectively criticising the evidence of others, rather than producing much evidence of their own through actual study and research. The inherent problem with this viewpoint is that it is dangerously close to the armchair theorising that criminology once rejected. However, the view that people who commit crime are somehow victims of being labelled criminal by powerful groups was itself criticised by realist criminology (see **Chapter 17**), working from the evidence-based perspective that crime is a real phenomena that is experienced negatively by victims, families, communities, and societies, so should be dealt with on this basis (Williams 2012).

None of these theories ever go away. They regenerate and redefine themselves based on a variety of academic influences, such as the creation of new evidence, new interpretations of old evidence, subjectivity based on no evidence, new research methods and new studies, along with non-academic influences such as political favour, media representations, and public opinion. Consequently, theory development in criminology is influenced by and in turn influences subjectivity, supposition, and study—combining in reciprocal and reflexive relationships to create and refine knowledge.

Subjectivity

Every step on the journey to understanding and knowledge creation in criminology is to some extent subjective, based on decisions, choices and the personal and professional reasons influencing them. The subjectivity that underpins knowledge generation in criminology is an inevitable and unavoidable element of a multi-faceted social science subject driven by human beings. It is also partly the product of criminology's history as a hybrid, synthetic subject (see **Chapter 2**), where academics tended to train in a cognate area such as sociology, psychology, or law, then move on to specialise in a criminological area, bringing to it their existing disciplinary preferences for particular theories and methods. This subjectivity plays a large part in making it such a dynamic, diverse, complex, and fascinating discipline. Criminologists have made a choice to study criminology, rather than to study a different social science subject. They have chosen the topics within criminology that they are interested in studying, learning about, reading about, writing about, hearing about, and researching. Subjectivity in and of itself is not necessarily a negative influence on knowledge production in criminology, as long as its role in the decision-making, assessments, explanations, and conclusions of criminologists is reflexively acknowledged and explored (Westmarland 2011; see also later in this chapter).

As students of criminology, we consciously and subconsciously decide what we think about the knowledge that we read about in the criminological literature, hear about in lectures, and choose to find out about through our own study and research. Our subjectivities lead us to make certain decisions and choices (and not others). These choices and decisions can be further manipulated and influenced by a number of subjective factors in our past and current lives, factors which can be categorised as external subjectivities, external-internal subjectivities, and internal subjectivities.

External bias

Your lecturers and the scholars and researchers whose work you read may have preferences and even biases (unconscious or deliberate, hidden or acknowledged) towards particular theories, explanations, topics research methods, policies, and practices (e.g. **Telling it like it is 6.1**). These subjective preferences—*professional subjectivity*—can direct and restrict the information you receive (and do not

TELLING IT LIKE IT IS 6.1

My biased academic journey—with author Steve Case

Let me offer you the best example of academic bias that I can—myself. I began my academic journey as an undergraduate student of psychology. Due to what I was taught and the ways I was taught it, I became committed to understanding human behaviour in specific ways that focused on the individual (e.g. thoughts, feelings, emotions). Studying psychology offered me micro-level understandings and explanations of human behaviour focused on and within the individual person. I was drawn in by the definite and technical nature of the conclusions psychologists made about human behaviour, often through using experiments and statistical tests. My developing disciplinary preference/bias for psychological methods and understandings fuelled a preference/bias for the study of memory, itself driven by a preference/bias for working with a particularly charismatic, expert professor. Consequently, I decided to study for a master's degree, generating micro-level, individual, experimental understandings of the eyewitness testimony memory of primary schoolchildren.

Sometime later, a research assistant post with a PhD attached to it was advertised in my university's criminology department. The PhD focused on the evaluation of a local youth crime prevention programme. Once again, I was lucky enough to be paired up with a charismatic, expert professor, only this time he was a criminologist, not a psychologist. He chose to examine the impact of this crime prevention programme in meso-level social ways, considering the influence of external factors such as neighbourhood characteristics, school processes, and family relationships alongside the individual's thoughts,

feelings, and psychological features. He also preferred a broader range of research methods than was typical from my experience in psychology, arguing that using experiments and generating quantitative, numerical data with human beings does not provide a valid representation of real-life behaviour and circumstances. What results instead is a restricted understanding of human behaviour that focuses far too much on the individual and not enough on external, macro-level influences such as social factors or relationships and interactions with other people. Simultaneously, these individual, psychologised explanations tend to ignore the views, experiences, understanding, perceptions, and perspectives of the people they are researching.

It took me a while, but once I opened up my world view, I committed to a criminological journey, just like you are doing now. I began to conduct multi-method research studies; always focused on soliciting the views of children and young people (a new bias that I had been given and readily signed up to) and I became increasingly critical of the reductionist (limited, superficial, over-simplified) research and understandings of human behaviour that in my view typified the discipline I had come from. Where had I picked up this critical, sociological form of criminological preference/bias? I had adopted it from my PhD supervisor, developed it in conversation with him (and other like-minded individuals), and consolidated it through my choice of research focus, methods, conclusions, and target audiences (see Case 2007; Case and Haines 2009). These biases shaped me into a critical youth criminologist and anti-positivist researcher. It has been a voyage of discovery that continues to this day.

receive) through your studies, the theories employed, the debates you engage with, the methods you use, and the knowledge you generate (see Case, in Vaidya 2015).

Every generation of criminology and topic within criminology has its own dominant theories and arguments (see 'Criminological theory' section above) known as *dominant subject viewpoints*. These theories are inextricably bound up with dominant research methods and the hot topic questions that the subject, politicians, and broader society wants answered (Chamberlain 2015; Hagan 2013). Prime examples of these hot topic issues are the recent emergence of substance use and the even more recent emergence of cyberterrorism in criminology, requiring urgent investigation and explanations to

inform laws, policies, and practices/responses. Consider, for example, the group Anonymous, famed for protesting in masks similar to that depicted in **Figure 6.1**, who hacked into (and subsequently brought down) more than 5,500 Twitter accounts under the banner of #OpISIS, allegedly belonging to the terrorist organisation, so-called Islamic State.

Of course, the dominant viewpoints that influence knowledge within our subject are themselves influenced by external dominant viewpoints in politics, different cultures, different societies, historical periods, economic climates, and so on. Criminology is influenced from the outside in, far more than it can ever influence the outside from within. In addition, criminological knowledge and

Figure 6.1 Anonymous, famed for protesting in masks similar to the one depicted here

Source: oneinchpunch/Shutterstock.com

Figure 6.2 Young Muslim men—unfair targets of modern day scaremongering by the press as a result of the rise in terrorist activity

Source: Naiyyer/Shutterstock.com

understanding has been influenced historically by the androcentricism and ethnocentrism of the individuals who study crime (see **Chapter 2**), such as academics, politicians, and criminal justice practitioners. In turn, these biases have influenced who has been studied (e.g. typically working class white boys) and what has been studied (e.g. typically the violent and property crimes associated with this group as a category of offender) in order to populate and evidence classical, positivist, and critical theories of crime (Chamberlain 2015). The preferences of those who have the power to decide the criminological knowledge agenda (i.e. middle class professionals in the western world) have tended to override and relatively-neglect (at least historically) issues of diversity in criminology's explanations of and responses to crime, such as the potentially differential experiences of the criminal justice system on the basis of ethnicity, gender, or disability (Pollock 2016).

It is argued that mass media and social media consistently (mis)represent the extent and nature of crime (King and Wincup 2008). These *media (mis)representations* are partly due to the misinformation and partial information that the media receives from criminologists and politicians, which can encourage misrepresentation through misunderstanding, exaggeration, and extrapolation (Williams 2012). A clear example here is the tabloid news media's (mis)representation of the threat to society posed by young people's behaviour since the 19th century, a phenomenon known as deviancy amplification (see **Chapter 9**).

Further examples are ever-present in modern day media scaremongering around the terrorist threat posed by young Muslim men (see **Figure 6.2**), itself a reincarnation of 1970s media (mis)representation of the epidemic of violent street robbery (labelled 'mugging' by the news media) supposedly caused by young black males (see Hall 1978). These representations have also been manifest in the USA, with stark differences between how white and black victims and suspects are portrayed (see **Controversy and debate 6.1**). The media's biased representations could be partly a product of ignorance (wilful or otherwise); they could be partly a product of the particular political leanings of the media organisation discussing crime. Obviously, media representations of crime are highly motivated by the desire to entice viewers, listeners, and readers (see **Chapter 7**). Whatever the motivation for media misrepresentations and preferences, the subjectivity and supposition of the mass media can seep into our psyche, can create or confirm our own suppositions and stereotypes (e.g. relating to the perceived criminal behaviours of young people and certain ethnic groups), and can fuel and shape our subjectivity going forwards.

External-internal subjectivity

Individual demographics (our broader personal and social characteristics) can influence our views, perceptions, the experiences and interactions that we have with our environment (e.g. with other people), and how we interpret and make meaning of these experiences and interactions (i.e. an interpretivist epistemology). How we behave, what we believe, how others behave towards us, and what others believe about us are all shaped by demographic characteristics (of us and those who interact with us) such as age, gender, ethnic group, social class, cultural background, religous orientation, sexuality, disability, locality, etc. (Gray 2013; Hagan 2013). Each of these demographic characteristics is a socially determined and constructed label (external) that can influence the personal experiences (see 'Internal subjectivity', next), interactions, and perspectives (internal) that shape us as human beings. For example, the demographic make-up of prominent academic criminologists and other criminal justice

CONTROVERSY AND DEBATE 6.1

Take a look at the following newspaper headings taken from news sources from around the US. They serve to exemplify how the media can spin a certain situation to evoke certain emotions. The role of the media is explored in full in **Chapter 7**, but these headlines serve to demonstrate how important it is to always look beneath the surface and question who has produced the knowledge and why. Take a look at the sources of each heading and have a think about the different agenda biases which may be at play (*Source: Huffington Post*, 14th August 2014).

Headlines covering white suspects

Santa Barbara shooting: 'Suspect was soft-spoken, polite, a gentleman' ex principal says.

Whitter Daily News, 25th May 2014

Oregon school shooting suspect fascinated with guns but was a devoted Mormon, his friends say.

Fox News, 12th June 2014

Headlines covering black victims

Montgomery's latest homicide victim had history of narcotics abuse, tangles with the law.

AL.com, 14th April 2014

Trayvon Martin was suspended three times from school.

NBC News, 26th March 2012

professionals (e.g. politicians, practitioners, journalists) in the history of criminology has been predominantly white, westernised, middle class, and male (although this gender disparity is diminishing professionally and most notably amongst the undergraduate student body). It is these very individuals who hold the power to decide who to study, who to target, and how to understand and respond to the behaviours of those they have decided to study and target. However, it's possible that the demographic characteristics of these powerful knowledge producers can bias the criminological agenda, creating understandings that are androcentric, ethnocentric, and otherwise neglectful of the diversity of perspectives and behaviours of any populations outside of their immediate focus of study (Mitchell Miller 2014).

The development of our own subjectivity can also be influenced by our *peer groups and social interactions*—the subjectivities of friends, family members, peers (e.g. fellow students), work colleagues, and team mates with whom we interact socially. Social interactions can provide us with validations of our own subjective viewpoints, often because we gravitate towards friends and peers with similar views to us. They may also provide new and improved perspectives by offering us new information or by challenging our own perspectives. Social interactions can also provide us with information about how a peer group or work team are expected to think (groupthink) and behave (group norms)—in other words, the group-level preferences and biases that members are expected to adopt (cf. Janis 1972). This is an essential element of group initiation and membership. The implication here is that we do not always fully commit to or believe in the biases we adopt—we

may simply be following others, fitting in, or trying to get ahead by choosing the most convenient or acceptable bias for our own purposes and goals. However, we do not always recognise external influences on the way we develop biases. As has been argued at length, it is crucial to be aware of your own subjectivity—where it comes from and the influence it can have on your study and application of the knowledge you produce from it—linking back to our previous discussion of reflexivity and positionality.

Internal subjectivity

Our past and current *personal experience* can colour and shape the ways in which we perceive and understand the world (an intepretivist epistemology once again). It is important that we do not confuse personal experience and anecdotes (personal stories about our experiences) with evidence to support our academic arguments (Stout et al. 2008). Personal experiences can offer useful illustrations of the arguments we are making, but they do not count as supporting evidence in any academic or empirical research sense, mainly because they are so personalised and subjective. That said, it is really useful to reflect critically on your experiences and how they may have influenced the stereotypes, preconceptions, values, prejudices, attitudes, and perceptions that we possess and how we understand different issues in criminology. A classic example of this is that victims of crime are likely to have a greater fear of crime than non-victims (Ferraro 1995), despite both groups (arguably) having an equivalent likelihood of experiencing crime in the future. However,

WHAT DO YOU THINK? 6.1

How should we respond to crime?

What do you think is the best way to respond to crime and why? Try to list the potential causes of and influences on crime that you can think of, then prioritise those that you see as most important or most likely, then consider how we can tackle these influences in the most effective ways. Then ask yourself:

- Is this an easy question to answer?

- Why do you think what you do about how to respond to crime?

- Where have your views come from and what has influenced them?

- To what degree are your views based on evidence or opinion?

- Do we need research evidence to support our views? Why? Why not?

- Are your views based on your personal opinion/perspective of particular evidence or just based on personal opinion?

this may not be a valid claim for certain types of crime, such as burglary and hate crime where the repeat victimisation effect has more evidence. Another example is that students who have had a specific negative or unsatisfactory experience of, and interaction with, the police may be more likely to express negative views of the police in general, even when they are required to offer a balanced, open-minded academic debate or perspective. This example seems to be the university student equivalent of research evidence suggesting that certain ethnic groups (e.g. young black males) hold more negative views of the police (than white males who have been in similar situations) if they perceive that they have experienced unjust treatment by the criminal justice system (Pollock 2016). A lesson here is to ensure that you acknowledge and evidence your internal, personal subjectivities as a student, but keep them in perspective so that they do not become bias and supposition. In your studies, you are expected to present all sides of an argument.

Part of your personal experience, of course, is the understanding and *existing knowledge* that you have developed through your discussions, interactions, and studies (e.g. through dominant subject viewpoints). Your subjective preferences develop in part due to what and how you learn at home, school, college, university, and work. You pick up a knowledge base of information, facts, understandings, perspectives, suppositions, and biases from external influences (e.g. books, teachers, peers) that you then reflect on, consolidate and extend through your study choices (Aronson, Wilson, and Akert 2010)—from the knowledge you choose to collect to the ways in which you choose to interpret it, to how you choose to (selectively, subjectively) present it. It is essential to maintain a reflexive approach to study and learning so that your knowledge base does not become a knowledge *bias*. An ABC method of maintaining reflexivity as a criminology student is to examine the (research) methods used to obtain knowledge for any instances of bias (e.g. relative to gender, ethnicity, class, age) and other failures to acknowledge and explore potential diversity (e.g. based on sexuality, disability, locality, religion) that could affect the validity of the knowledge production process.

Your choices and decisions as a student of criminology can be affected by any and all of these entirely subjective influences, just as the choices and decisions of each of the influencers (e.g. lecturers, scholars, researchers, politicians, criminal justice practitioners, journalists) has been influenced by these influences. The result can be a vicious circle of subjectivity if left unacknowledged and unchallenged, but engaging with and utilising this subjectivity and bias can create a virtuous circle of reflection and learning.

After reading this section it is worth considering the questions raised in **What do you think? 6.1**.

Supposition

A good story is often less probable than a less satisfactory one.

Kahneman, Slovic, and Tversky 1982: 98

Human beings have an innate need to understand and control their environment. When we lack sufficient information and knowledge to allow us to do this properly, it causes us anxiety. The solution is often to fill the gap in our knowledge using supposition, conjecture, prediction, estimation, assumption, guesswork, and common sense, often drawing on examples from history, personal experience, and subjectivity. Criminologists are not exempt from this. When knowledge is lacking, we may fill the gaps with plausible explanations and extrapolations, with the 'codification of commonsense' and with appeals to stereotypes and preconceptions (Hoefnagels 1973), rather than necessarily with detailed research and the generation of convincing evidence.

Supposition can help to bridge the knowledge gap between subjectivity and study (see Taleb 2001). It formalises and legitimises the illusion of control over understanding of our social worlds. It helps us to manage and deal with the uncertain, random, complex, and unknown. When we study criminology, we may overvalue supposition because it is presented so convincingly by experts such as scholars, lecturers, and politicians, etc. We may be beguiled into an uncritical acceptance of what we hear, read, and see because of the apparent legitimacy and credibility of the source. This is not to say that we should reject expert knowledge that is based on supposition, because this may be only part of what influenced

its construction; plus the supposition of experts may be informed, credible, and plausible. Nor is expert knowledge in criminology ever entirely based on supposition. Indeed, much knowledge is fully or predominantly based on study. But the existence of supposition does suggest that you should remember your ABC—*Always Be Critical*. Always evaluate the origins and validity of the knowledge being imparted. In this way, even if the author has not been (sufficiently) critical and reflexive (see later), you can introduce reflexivity into the creation and application of criminological knowledge.

The lesson from this section and **Controversy and debate 6.2** is, as always, to *Always Be Critical* in our study. Subjectivity and supposition, especially taken together, produce certain forms of knowledge (Taleb 2001; Hoefnagels 1973). This knowledge typically conforms to an interpretivist epistemology, but it is knowledge that is not necessarily grounded in research evidence and so it may have a limited validity and even certain biases that must be acknowledged and accounted for by reflexive criminologists. Subjectivity and supposition can reinforce one another, but on their own they can only produce a partial knowledge base for criminology.

CONTROVERSY AND DEBATE 6.2

The supposition of risk prediction—with author Steve Case

The dominant theoretical explanation used to understand and respond to offending by young people is known as the 'Risk Factor Prevention Paradigm' or 'RFPP' (Hawkins and Catalano 1992; see Case and Haines 2009 for a detailed critique). The RFPP considers 'risk factors' to be negative experiences, situations, and interactions. In particular, it states that exposure to risk factors from an individual's childhood, school, neighbourhood, and personal life predicts criminal behaviour in later life. Examples of these risk factors include having poor familial relationships, low academic achievement, living in close proximity to criminal gangs, and psychological issues. Therefore, these risk factors should be the logical targets for intervention and prevention work—it makes sense (Farrington, in Maguire et al. 2007; Baker 2005). Furthermore, supporters of the RFPP argue that identifying and targeting risk factors is a proven effective, evidence-based, and practical method of reducing current offending and preventing future crime (see Utting 1999; Youth Justice Board 2005). However, I disagree on methodological and analytical grounds (see Case 2006; Case 2007; Case and Haines 2009); not to mention because of the explanatory limitations placed on this research

due to its historical androcentricism and ethnocentrism (see **Chapter 9**).

Correlates are not causes

In my subjective opinion, born from my research experience and scholarly consideration of the evidence-base, the claim that risk factors predict or increase the risk of youth offending is based on supposition, which itself is born of subjectivity. The RFPP is supported by hundreds of studies, all measuring the presence of risk factors in early life and then statistically linking them to a measure of offending taken at a later point (see **Chapter 18— integrated theories**). This is what's known as identifying a statistical correlation/relationship. It simply shows that a person who has certain characteristics/ risk factors (e.g. has experienced their parents arguing in childhood) is more likely to possess another characteristic (e.g. offending behaviour in adolescence) than other people without those initial characteristics/risk factors (e.g. parents arguing). Supposition occurs when we extrapolate these findings by assuming that certain characteristics predict offending behaviour in the real world. Whilst a risk factor may be correlated with offending behaviour, there is no convincing evidence that this purported relationship has a definitive direction—such as the risk factor causing or influencing offending.

The proliferation of longitudinal designs containing complex statistical analyses and data modelling techniques has progressed criminological research beyond over-simplified and over-generalised claims that correlation does not equal causation. Our statistical methods are now so sophisticated and sensitive that this crude supposition cannot be sustained, notably across the range of longitudinal, qualitative multi-method risk factor studies that have adopted more focus on young people's constructions of risk over time and analysed their relationship with offending in statistically complex ways (cf. McAra and McVie 2010). However, the overwhelming majority of research studies have adopted an **artefactual risk factor theories** approach to converting risk into a factor/number and then examining its (correlational) relationship with offending (see Case and Haines 2009; Kemshall 2008). Artefactual risk factor research often measures risk factors and offending simultaneously in cross-sectional and repeated cross-sectional studies, making it much more difficult to conclude which comes first. So in our example, a young person may be experiencing parents arguing in their current life, alongside committing offences—they are both happening at the same time, along with exposure to a potentially huge range of additional risk factors/influences, so the direction of any relationship is extremely difficult to untangle in the absence of further longitudinal, qualitative research and more sophisticated statistical analyses.

Some studies have measured exposure to risk factors *before* they measure offending behaviour, then assume that young people experience risk factors before they offend (i.e. that risk factors have **temporal precedence** over offending behaviour), concluding that risk factors must be causing or in some way influencing the offending behaviour. However, the reality here is that the risk factor was simply *measured* first, not necessarily experienced first. To conclude that it predicts offending on this basis (other studies even extrapolate this conclusion into presenting risk factors as *causes* of offending) is supposition—a plausible explanation based on common sense rather than evidence. Until we can convincingly measure which actually occurred first in the young person's life, we cannot accurately assess the nature of the risk factor-offending relationship. It could be that risk factors predict or cause offending—we could at least be more confident of this if parents arguing first occurred at an age before offending behaviour began. Conversely, offending could predict or cause increased exposure to risk factors (e.g. if you commit crime, being caught and punished may cause your parents to argue), or even that other unmeasured influences (e.g. poverty, unemployment, sibling offending) predict or cause both exposure to risk factors and offending behaviour (Case and Haines 2009). If either of these alternative explanations are valid (accurate) then the label of 'risk factors' is surely misleading because the label would relate to factors that do not actually predict or increase the risk of a future behaviour. Here, supposition fills the gap in our knowledge of how (and even if) risk factors and offending are related.

Regardless of the methodological issues that pervade (artefactual) risk factor studies, the supposition that risk factors predict offending has attained uncritical acceptance amongst researchers, policymakers, and practitioners across the world (for further discussion, see **Chapter 9**).

Study

Subjectivity and supposition are important and much-neglected elements of knowledge production in criminology. However, they do not exist in isolation. They influence one another and each have an influence on (and are influenced by) the central vehicle for the generation, application, and critique of knowledge in criminology: study. We study criminology by reading about it, observing it, hearing about it, talking about it, examining it, and by actually conducting empirical research. Study can involve the collection and examination of secondary information and evidence and/or the creation of original, primary information and evidence by us (Chamberlain 2013). Creating primary knowledge can involve research, but may also be based on the original critique and application of the arguments of others. Study requires you to function as a criminologist and to fulfil the main goal of this book—to move from being a consumer of knowledge to being a producer of knowledge.

When academics, scholars, and researchers talk about studying criminology, they are more often than not implying systematic, controlled study, gathering data through some form of observation or experiment—otherwise known as empirical research (Crowther-Dowey and Fussey 2013). By study, criminologists are often talking about scientifically capturing information, analysing it so it becomes evidence, and the process of turning it into knowledge that progresses our understandings and informs our theories and explanations. The process of study underpins the arguments throughout this book due to our commitment to understanding criminology through discussion of the methods and findings of applied research conducted in the real world.

Research as study

Applied research is a key vehicle of study in criminology. As discussed in relation to reflexivity, (empirical) researchers are influenced by a degree of subjectivity at every step in terms of their decisions and choices regarding what research question to investigate, who to study, how to study (e.g. the research method used), how to analyse and interpret the data, what to conclude, who to tell about this, and how to share the information. These decisions do not invalidate or weaken the research, nor do they make the researcher/research wrong, because criminology does not really do right and wrong as much as it seeks reasoned opinion, but their influence on the research process, on the validity of findings/conclusions, and on the knowledge produced should be acknowledged and accounted for.

Criminology has traditionally presented itself as a legitimate, credible social science to rival its older sibling subjects of sociology and psychology. The traditional empiricist, positivist dominance of epistemology and choice of research methods has enabled academics to assert criminology's scientific credentials on the basis of having control over its subject matter, generating generalisable, non-biased, valid results, producing universal laws and basing study on independence and objectivity (Caulfield and Hill 2014). However, as we will go on to explore in more depth, applied (especially empirical) research can never be a perfect means of generating criminological knowledge—such a method does not exist. As discussed, all criminologists will have partialities for certain epistemologies and methods; these serve to inform and shape their arguments, whilst acting as a touchstone against which to reflexively evaluate their work (Savin-Baden

and Howell-Major 2013). All research methods have allegiances to a particular epistemology and specific strengths/benefits and weaknesses/limitations, all of which determine the types of knowledge they can and cannot create.

Earlier in the chapter, the concept of empirical research methods was introduced—research which obtains knowledge though sensory experience and experimental and observational methods (Bryman 2015). Empirical research methods can be quantitative (collecting and analysing numbers and statistics) or qualitative (collecting and analysing the written word and visual texts such as photographs, film, tattoos) or a mixture of both. The most common aims of empirical research in criminology are to describe, explore, explain, and evaluate criminological concepts, phenomena, issues, behaviours, and groups (see Gray 2013; Robson 2015). Empirical research can have a mixture of these aims. It can be used to generate brand new knowledge and understandings (inductive research), to test existing knowledge and understandings (deductive research), or to do both in the same study.

In an ideal world, the most valid forms of research would use the most appropriate research method for the question(s) that needs to be answered, to meet the objectives and agendas of the research, and to pursue the forms of knowledge (epistemology) that the research(er) wants to create. However, research does not take place in an ideal world untouched by external, non-academic influences. For example, a major influence on choice of research method beyond academic concerns is *practicality*. Research projects, such as funded evaluations conducted for government sponsors, are often short on time, money, and physical resources (people, rooms, equipment, etc.). Consequently, researchers must choose the most suitable research method under those circumstances (Chamberlain 2013; Hagan 2013), possibly regardless of their own research-based subjectivities and suppositions. In a way, practical requirements can encourage researchers to adopt a realist/pragmatist epistemological approach to the study of criminological topics. However, in the spirit of ABC/reflexivity, we should acknowledge that choice of research method is also guided by many subjective factors, including professional (disciplinary) training, professional experience of a particular method, personal preference, the preferences of the academic discipline or sub-topic within a discipline, theoretical standpoint, what the researcher feels has been effective in the past (however 'effective' is defined), perceived suitability of a method for a certain group of participants, in addition to the demands or (subjective) requirements of the research funders (see **New frontiers 6.1**). For example,

NEW FRONTIERS 6.1

The role of reflexivity in knowledge creation

It is crucial that criminologists reflect critically on the research decisions that they have made (e.g. choice of research method, how to create knowledge) and what has influenced these decisions (e.g. the social, institutional, and political contexts of the research) throughout a research study, because all research findings, conclusions, and recommendations are the consequences of these decisions (Davies and Francis, in Davies et al. 2011).

The process of evaluating research decisions, known as **reflection**, acknowledges that social research is a set of compromises actioned within complex, imperfect situations—compromises such as maximising the strengths and mitigating for the limitations of different research methods in the context of practical constraints (e.g. financial, resource, time) on the research (Davies et al. 2011). The extension of reflection is reflexivity, which is 'a process that helps researchers to consider their position and influence during the study ... to know how they have constructed and even sometimes imposed meanings on the research process' (Savin-Baden and Howell-Major 2013: 76). Reflexivity is an essential process to enable academics and researchers to critically assess the influence of their own subjectivities (constructed meanings) and suppositions (imposed meanings) on study (the research process). For example, **epistemological reflexivity** encourages researchers to critically examine

how their belief system has shaped research design and interpretation of findings (Willig 2001). Researchers may even wish to travel further back reflexively to consider how their own demographic characteristics (e.g. age, gender, ethnicity) and their experiences related to these may have influenced their belief system.

Reflexivity is closely aligned to the concept of **positionality**, the stance/position that the researcher has chosen to adopt within a specific study. Addressing their positionality involves researchers reflexively examining the influence of their own subjective position in relation to the subject matter being studied, the research context, and the research participants, including the influence of their chosen epistemology, disciplinary perspective, and preconceptions (Nightingale and Cromby 1999).

Reflexivity incorporating positionality should be employed by criminologists to assess the *validity* of the conclusions they draw as a result of research study (their own and that of others), notably how research decisions, subjectivities, and suppositions may have influenced these conclusions. 'Validity' in this case means the extent to which conclusions are plausible, credible, and generalisable to other contexts and populations (Savin-Baden and Howell-Major 2013). Furthermore, reflexivity should be employed to enable criminologists to reflect critically on what counts as knowledge in criminology (in their specific study), how this knowledge was produced, and why.

---

governments may have a preference for funding experimental evaluations of programmes and interventions, prioritising the measurement of differences between control and experimental groups, or before and after differences within individuals (the 'what works' model of evaluation). This preference may override an alternative approach of researching how the author of an intervention understands how its inputs (may) lead to outputs and asking recipients of intervention how it has influenced or changed them (the theory of change model of evaluation—discussed in more detail in **Chapter 19**).

See **New frontiers 6.1** for more on the role of reflexivity in knowledge creation.

The most common research methods used to generate empirical knowledge in criminology are experiment, survey, observation, and secondary data analysis, so let us critically examine these methods and the nature of the criminological knowledge that they produce.

Experiment—researching by doing and manipulating

The experimental method in criminology involves manipulating an aspect of a person's surroundings/environment, what they experience, or what they are subjected to, in order to see if it has an effect on their behaviour (Caulfield and Hill 2014). What is manipulated is called the *independent variable* (IV) and the behaviour that is measured as a result of this manipulation is called the *dependent variable* (DV). For example, a particular form of sentence, treatment, or intervention programme (the IV) could be given to offenders or substance users to see if it led to reductions in their offending behaviour or substance use (the DVs). A simple way to remember the difference between these two types of variable is that 'I' manipulate the IV and we get our 'd'ata from the DV. Variables are almost always measured in numerical/statistical form, which means that experiments are a quantitative research method).

Experiments typically take place in highly controlled situations (the laboratory) or in a—controlled—version of a real world environment (in the field). The objective of an experiment is to control all other possible influences on behaviour (extraneous variables) so that the researcher can conclude that manipulating the IV caused a change in a person's behaviour, or DV—the classic 'cause and effect' relationship that underpins the knowledge pursued by positivist epistemology. Experiments in criminology are often designed to provide a service, treatment, or intervention (IV) to a particular group (the *experimental group*) and to withhold this service or treatment or intervention from an equivalent group (the *control group*), in order to measure any differences between the two groups that result. Experiments can also measure the before and after behaviours of a group or individual to see if there was a change after the service or treatment or intervention was given, which can then be attributed to it (Robson 2015). In this way, experiments are the embodiment of positivist, scientific methodology in criminology. Experimenters in criminology claim to be able to exert such control over the research situation that they can identify the causes of human behaviours (e.g. crime, substance use, antisocial behaviour, and desistance). This claim is explored in **Chapter 19**. It is argued that the large amount of control over behaviour made possible by an experiment allows experimental processes to be standardised (conducted in the same way each time), which improves the reliability of the experiment. 'Reliability' in this instance refers to the replicability, repeatability, and consistency of experimental methods and results; a crucial benefit if researchers are seeking generalisable, universally applicable explanations for behaviour and recommendations for potentially effective responses.

An experiment in preventing shoplifting

In their 'Experiment on the prevention of shoplifting', Farrington et al. (in Clarke 1993) compared the effectiveness of different situational crime prevention methods on levels of shoplifting in nine shops from the same UK electrical goods chain. These shops were 'reasonably comparable' in size, sales, and shoplifting rates. Having taken a baseline level of shoplifting (number of missing items compared to number of items sold) in each shop in the pre-test week before the experiment, the experimenters allocated a crime prevention condition to each shop for the experimental week: electronic tagging of all items (two shops), shop redesign (two shops), uniformed guard (two shops), and no intervention/control

condition (three shops). The researchers then compared levels of shoplifting in the pre-test week, with levels measured in the post-test week immediately following the experimental week and a follow-up measure three to six weeks later. This is known as a before and after experimental design.

The results of the crime prevention experiment were that electronic tagging 'caused a lasting decrease in shoplifting' (Farrington et al., in Clarke 1993: 94), still evident six weeks post-experiment. Shop redesign demonstrated an immediate effect post-test that diminished after six weeks, whilst the uniformed guard and control conditions made no difference to shoplifting levels. The researchers did reflect on a series of experimental limitations regarding the generalisability and reliability of their results, including resource constraints, unforeseen reductions in pre- and post-test periods (so these were not actually a full week) and weather disruptions—all acting as potential extraneous variables. Having accounted for these, the researchers concluded that the experiment indicated the long-term effectiveness of electronic tagging as a shoplifting prevention method and implied a strong long-term preventative potential for shop redesign if this method was enhanced, as this was a less expensive option for the company.

Control in experiments

A significant issue for experiments in a criminological context relates to their need to exert control over variables in order to fulfil their measurement objectives. Controlling for all possible influences on behaviour in the real world could be seen as virtually impossible (see **Chapter 19**). Furthermore, control itself may render the measured behaviour less real and more artificial. The overarching criticism is that experiments in criminology can lack ecological validity—they do not produce results that are a complete and accurate reflection of real-life behaviour. Indeed, experiments could actually create forms of behaviour that are not realistic, which is problematic for a research method employed to study crime—a real-life, real-world behaviour committed by, created by, and experienced by real people. Not only this, but experimenters may rely on a degree of supposition when assuming the degree to which external influences can be controlled, when assuming how an IV effects a DV, and when assuming that any differences between control and experimental groups are necessarily the result of (caused by) their own manipulations (see **Chapter 19**). Changes in people's behaviour in an experimental context could be the result of a series of other influences, including existing differences between the control and experimental groups, chance, the influence of other unmeasured, uncontrolled, and unforeseen variables (e.g. bad weather at a specific shop's location in the shoplifting experiment), researcher measurement error, participants changing their behaviour due to the pressure and demands of the experimental situation, and so on (cf. Hope 2009). Consequently, experiments can encourage 'black box' understandings of crime (see Pawson and Tilley 2004). In other words, we have an input (the manipulation of the IV; a particular sentence, treatment, or intervention) and a measurable output (the DV; any changes in behaviour, such as crime reduction). However, we have very little knowledge and explanation of what goes on in the black box between these inputs and outputs (for further discussion, see **Chapter 19**).

In order to illustrate these arguments, let us return to the shoplifting prevention experiment. The IV was the type of crime prevention condition put into each of the shops. The DV was the difference between shoplifting levels in the pre-test and post-test periods. Any changes in shoplifting levels were attributed to the impact of the intervention. However, the reasons/explanations for any changes were impossible to identify from the intervention alone and no qualitative study was conducted to explore them further. Consequently, there is an explanatory black box sitting between the IV (interventions) and the DV (changes in shoplifting levels), along with no consideration or understanding of the influence of extraneous variables (EVs) such as context, location or customer demographics. By leaving the black box empty, the researchers were not in a position to explain to the company exactly *why* particular interventions may have worked, or to advise the company *how* these interventions should be applied and improved in the future.

Consider the issues above when experimental criminologists (many of whom work in the USA) proclaim (often unreflexively) that a programme or sentence or intervention 'works' or is 'effective' following an experimental study or evaluation. Also consider how the experimental preference/bias for converting behaviour to numbers/quantities artificially reduces the ecological validity of what is measured and can wash away its complexity and detail (Pawson and Tilley 2004). In criminological, methodological terms, this is called reductionism (see also **Chapter 9**). Experimental criminologists deliberately reduce and simplify/quantify variables to make them easier to analyse and understand using statistics. Arguably, such reductionism makes perfect sense as it makes our complex world more manageable and digestible and the research more practical and feasible. However, this process necessarily can disregard *qualitative* outcomes such as what participants think, feel, understand, experience, and perceive about their lives (Westmarland 2011). In other words, quantification on its own neglects to measure subjectivity and so does not represent the (subjective) reality of a real life situation

from a participant's perspective, rendering participants more like 'subjects' of a research experiment that is *done to* them rather than *done with* them (Case 2007). It can also be considered unethical to manipulate people's behaviour or (if they are in the control group), to deny them access to something helpful or vital such as a specialised treatment or support service, just to measure if their behaviour is harmed by not having it.

If they are not reflexive, experimenters in criminology can overlook these issues.

Surveys—researching by asking

Surveys in criminology involve researchers asking people questions about their attitudes, opinions, feelings, thoughts, memories, perceptions, and experiences relating to a specific issue. In this way, surveys facilitate an ethnographic approach—understanding the world from the perspective of the research participant, usually studied in their natural environment (see also **Chapter 29**). Questions can be asked and answered in written form (questionnaires) or spoken form (interviews, focus groups), and can be asked to individuals (questionnaires, interviews) or groups (focus groups). The main objectives of surveys are to measure participants' perspectives on a subject at a set point in time (cross-sectional research) or changes in these perspectives over time (longitudinal research), and to identify associations/correlations between specific elements of these perspectives and their behaviours (Crowther-Dower and Fussey 2013). For example, a survey questionnaire could explore whether young people who offend report higher levels of impulsive behaviour than young people who do not offend, or whether older people express a higher fear of crime than younger people. Here we look at each of these different types of survey and the knowledge they create in more detail.

Questionnaires

A questionnaire is a form of survey where participants provide written/typed responses to written questions (on paper or electronically/online), typically by reading the questions themselves (self-completion) or having them read by the researcher (face-to-face completion). The design of the questionnaire will determine the type and quantity of information the researcher receives back.

Questions can be:

- **closed**—with a set way of responding (e.g. a dichotomous yes-no scale or a ratings scale);
- **open-ended**—with participants able to elaborate on their responses at length.

Interviews

An interview is one-to-one survey where participants respond verbally to spoken questions from a researcher. Interviews may be conducted face-to-face and in-person, via telephone or online (e.g. via Skype).

Interviews may also contain closed and open questions and the interview design can be:

- **structured**—following a set list of questions in a rigid format;
- **semi-structured**—following a set list of questions, but supplementing and expanding upon these with extra questions that the interviewer feels might be useful at the time;
- **unstructured**—flexible, improvised, open-ended, not following a set of questions;
- **focus group**—a form of interview conducted with a group of participants (see **Figure 6.3**).

The epistemologies underpinning surveys are contingent on how that survey is designed and executed (e.g. how the data are collected and analysed). For example, questionnaires or interviews consisting entirely or predominantly of closed questions that require quantifiable responses (e.g. ratings scales, yes/no answers) can be categorised as quantitative methods with a positivist epistemology, as they produce quantified, numerical data that can be statistically tested to identify cause and effect relationships between variables. Conversely, surveys that contain open questions can be more qualitative in approach and interpretivist in epistemology because they explore how participants construct and make meaning of their experiences in the social world (King and Wincup 2008). Where surveys contain both closed and open questions and response formats (e.g. a semi-structured interview, a questionnaire with ratings and narrative sections), they offer perhaps the best example of a mixed methodology. Mixed surveys animate a realist/pragmatist epistemology that applies the respective strengths of quantitative and qualitative methods to practical research objectives in the real world.

Surveys afford specific benefits to knowledge in criminology. For example, structured surveys offer similar advantages to experiments in terms of the standardisation of methods and the consequent reliability and generalisability of methods and results. This is a particular advantage of quantitative questionnaires and more structured forms of interview. Certain forms of survey are cheap to administer (e.g. questionnaires, especially online versions) and can collect a large amount of information quickly (e.g. questionnaires, large focus groups). More flexible, qualitative versions of surveys can benefit knowledge further by identifying the personalised meanings, understandings, and interpretations the people have in relation to different behaviours, actions, interactions, perspectives, and other elements of their lives (Case 2006). Collecting such data can extend knowledge creation beyond the more restricted, reductionist understandings dictated by narrow,

Figure 6.3 Focus group under researcher observation
Source: Linda Nylind for The Guardian

quantitative responses to narrow, quantitative, closed questions.

As with all applied research in criminology, it is vital to reflect on the validity of the knowledge that can be generated by asking about it. Research participants (researchers themselves, in fact) may exaggerate, misrepresent, forget, even lie; questions can be biased or can mislead and confuse; interviewers can manipulate and lead participants, researchers can choose what and who to ask, how to ask, and how to interpret the answers (see **What do you think? 6.2**). These are the types of issues that reflexive researchers address through piloting—pre-testing the practicality and validity of their research methods and processes in order to refine them prior to full implementation. Therefore, surveys can have similar limitations in terms of ecological validity as experiments, in that the behaviour of participants (typically called 'subjects' in experiments) can be artificially manipulated by researchers, either deliberately (e.g. through leading questions) or inadvertently (e.g. through non-verbal behaviour in interviews) and participants may deliberately or inadvertently change their behaviour as a result of being part of the survey (Westmarland 2011; King and Wincup 2008). For example, participants may change their perspectives in surveys (just as they may change their behaviours in experiments) to fit in with what they perceive that the researcher, the research context, or other participants (in the case of focus groups) desires—thus displaying what are called demand characteristics (Gilbert 2001). Where demand characteristics result from the perceived needs of the researcher, this can reflect the differential power dynamics in the survey situation—the questioner/interviewer holds the majority of the power to determine the survey context, process, content, and outcomes. A typical demand characteristic in a job interview, for example, is to artificially present the best version of yourself possible—this is known as social desirability bias (Gray 2013). Take a look at **What do you think? 6.2** on the use of leading

WHAT DO YOU THINK? 6.2

Using leading questions to harass evasive politicians

In the 13th May 1997 edition of the BBC current affairs programme 'Newsnight', the bullish political interviewer Jeremy Paxman interrogated former UK Home Secretary, Michael Howard (the man who claimed 'prison works'). The interview became famous for Paxman's repeated attempts to lead Howard into admitting that he had threatened to overrule the Head of Her Majesty's Prison Service (Derek Lewis) regarding the dismissal of the Governor of Parkhurst Prison (John Marriott). Howard ultimately sacked both Lewis and Marriott. The implication throughout was that Howard had exceeded his powers as Home Secretary. The interview is equally famous for Howard's repeated attempts to evade Paxman's central question, yet all the while continuing to assert that he had not overstepped his authority. The crux of the interview was:

Paxman (P): Did you threaten to overrule him [Lewis]?

Howard (H): Mr Marriott was not suspended.

P: Did you threaten to overrule him?

H: I have accounted for my decision to dismiss Derek Lewis.

P: (overlapping) Did you threaten to overrule him?

H: (overlapping) ... in great detail before the House of Commons.

P: I note that you're not answering the question whether you threatened to overrule him

H: You can put the question and I will give you an answer.

P: It's a straight yes or no question and a straight yes or no answer. Did you threaten to overrule him?

H: I discussed the matter with Derek Lewis ... but I did not instruct him because I was not entitled to instruct him.

P: With respect, that is not answering the question of whether you threatened to overrule him.

H: It's dealing with the relevant point of what I was entitled to do...

You can view this interview clip on YouTube if you follow the link provided in the **online resources** that accompany this book **www.oup.com/uk/case/**.

What do you think about the validity and dynamics of this interaction? Specifically:

- Was Paxman using leading questions to get to the truth?

- Did Paxman's repeated use of the same question amount to one huge leading question or leading interview?

- What do you think of Howard's attempts to evade the question? Was he giving answers to 'lead' the interview in a different direction?

- Do you think that such aggressive questioning or evasive responding is justifiable in a political context?

questions by a political interviewer and consider whether they actually helped or hindered his pursuit of complete and valid information.

Survey participants may also damage the validity of a study by withholding or distorting information—a kind of inverted demand characteristic. This can be due to belligerence or mistrust of authority figures, for example, in a police interview—another power dynamic in an interview context. However, the provision of incomplete or misleading information can be due to unwillingness, apprehension, or embarrassment caused by power dynamics in a sensitive survey situation and/or interviewer characteristics that may be non-conducive to full disclosure of information. For example, there may be significant power differentials and issues of researcher credibility, trustworthiness, or suitability in interview contexts where an older male interviewer questions teenage girls about their experiences of sexual abuse by older men (gender and age issues), where adult professionals ask children about their illegal activities (age issues), or where a white interviewer explores negative experiences of the criminal justice system with black and ethnic minority participants (ethnicity issues). The problem is that demand characteristics and the influence of power can reduce the ecological validity of research results when surveys are employed.

It is possible for researchers themselves to facilitate demand characteristics in surveys through their own research choices/decisions and behaviours, which can reflect the differential power dynamics in the survey context. The power of the interviewer/questioner to construct and manipulate knowledge production can be animated by the questions that they choose to ask and to which groups of the population, by how they allow participants to respond (e.g. response categories in questionnaires, time allowed for answers in interviews), by how they ask questions and respond to the answers (including leading or intimidating non-verbal behaviour in interviews), and by how they choose to select and interpret the results. Indeed, the very choice of a particular form of survey as a research method illustrates a researcher's subjectivity (preference/bias) for certain forms of research (i.e. research by asking, either in written or spoken form). Choosing a survey in itself indicates a preference for the creation of particular forms of knowledge and for choosing a certain form of data. For example, questionnaires tend to collect large amounts of quantitative data from closed questions, whereas interviews and focus groups produce more qualitative data, which may then be quantified (Creswell 2013). An example of how the methodological preferences of a survey researcher have influenced knowledge production is provided by the *Cambridge Study in Delinquent Development* (West and Farrington 1973; see also **Chapter 9**). The researchers drew heavily on interviews and questionnaires to identify the best predictors of youth crime, and preventative interventions have targeted these predictors ever since. However, the study population was predominantly white and male, so subsequent understandings of and responses to youth crime based on this study, whilst suitably interpretivist and qualitative, may also be androcentric and ethnocentric. Any generalisation of the study's explanations and recommendations for intervention to girls or black and ethnic minority young people , therefore, are likely to be invalid without further examination of their applicability.

Each of the methodological choices a survey researcher makes can influence the scope and usefulness of survey methods and the knowledge produced, be it positivist, interpretivist, or realist/pragmatist. These are not necessarily criticisms/limitations of the survey method, unless researchers choose not to reflect critically on them.

If they are not reflexive, survey researchers in criminology can overlook these issues.

Observations—researching by watching

Conducting observations in criminology involves researching by watching—observing individuals or groups in real world settings (in the field) to examine different aspects of their behaviour (Creswell 2013). Observers may look for certain predicted behaviours to occur (deductive research) and then record these on an 'observation schedule' (a list of important behaviours to record) and/or be prepared to record new and unexpected behaviours, thus generating new knowledge (inductive research). An observation can be overt or open, with research participants fully aware that they are being observed, or the observation may be covert or closed, with participants being unaware that they are being observed, so not really being participants in any willing/consenting sense. Observers can become part of the individual or group environment that they are observing, which is known as participant observation. They can also observe without taking a direct part in proceedings, known as non-participant observation (Noaks and Wincup 2004). For example, a criminologist could observe the behaviour of a group or gang by joining them and recording (e.g. filming, tape recording, writing down) their behaviours with the group being fully aware (overt observation). Alternatively, the observer could watch the group from the outside (e.g. filming a documentary) without becoming part of the situation (non-participant observation—see **Figure 6.3**) and/or recording their behaviour secretly without their knowledge or consent (covert observation). As with surveys, the manner in which the data are collected and recorded determines the form of research conducted. If data are collected in numerical form (e.g. using a tick box or tally chart to record items on the observation schedule) then the research is quantitative/positivist, whereas if the data are recorded in written or spoken form (e.g. the observer looks for illustrative examples of observation schedule themes) then the research is qualitative/interpretivist (Davies et al. 2011). Similar to surveys, observations can incorporate both forms of research, which can accord with a realist/pragmatist epistemology that draws upon the benefits of both positivism and interpretivism to meet the specific requirements of the research project.

Observations offer researchers the potential for a degree of ecological validity beyond that possible with more controlling and artificial research methods such as experiments and surveys, because these observations tend to study real-world behaviour in real-world contexts (Noaks and Wincup 2004). This can be a particular benefit of unobtrusive observations; those that minimise the observer's interference (deliberately or inadvertently) with the research context (e.g. covert, non-participant observations) and therefore minimise the extent to which participants may react artificially and change their behaviour in some way because they are being observed. The embeddedness of the researcher in the research context and their proximity to the research participants can also enhance the researcher's ability to access and understand (empathise with) the meanings, perceptions, and experiences of those participants in their everyday lives (Crowther-Dowey and Fussey 2013). This richness of data can facilitate the production of knowledge from an interpretivist perspective and can enable a degree of first-hand experience and explanation of (rather than supposition about) behaviours that quantitative methodologies may not be able to achieve.

As with other types of researcher and research method, observers and observations are inherently subjective in terms of what and whom they choose to observe (cf. Howard Parker's inevitably androcentric observational study in 1974, 'A View from the Boys', perhaps the most famous and compelling observation study in criminology), what they choose to record and not record, and how they choose to understand what they see. However, observational research can go beyond subjectivity and into (inadvertent) bias if researchers also bias and change the behaviour of who and what they observe by their overt presence, whether the researcher is participating or not. For example, simply by involving themselves in the daily lives of a person or group, a researcher changes that situation by their very presence—known as the Hawthorne Effect (Chamberlain 2013)—along with changing the group dynamics and interactions that different people have in their lives. This may limit the ecological validity of the method and its findings, particularly if the observer does not reflect on and account for their influence. The completeness and accuracy of the data collected can

also be limited by the observer becoming physically and practically unable to record all aspects of the observation situation, for example, because there is too much behaviour to record at any one time, there are too many people in the observation group or situation (who may not all be in the same place at the same time), or because it is too dangerous to record behaviour in certain situations at certain times. In 'A View from the Boys', Parker used to write his observation records from memory after the event, but he acknowledged that this process was imperfect, often incomplete, and vulnerable to his own distortions and biases (see Parker 1974).

Observing people without their knowledge, as in the 'I.D.' example in **Controversy and debate 6.3**, raises ethical issues about invasion of privacy, lack of informed consent (agreement to participate in the study based on full understanding of the research processes, although not necessarily its aims), protection of participants from harm, and researcher safety. It is pretty much impossible to gain informed consent from participants if you do not tell them that you are conducting research (cf. Parker 1974). In the case of covert observations, participants do not even know that they are participants and they are actually more like the classic experimental 'subjects'. As a researcher, you need a really good reason *not* to obtain informed consent from the individuals who you are researching. The best reason is often based on a 'cost benefits analysis'—that the benefits to criminological knowledge that will come from the research and that cannot be obtained if participants are fully aware of the research processes or research aims, are greater than the potential costs to the research participants or subjects in terms of them being deceived, manipulated, or not fully informed in the short term (Davies et al. 2011). These costs can then be addressed after the research has been conducted by a process called debriefing, where the researcher explains the research aims and rationale for not obtaining informed consent initially and checks that participants have not suffered long-term harm. Participants could then give their consent retrospectively or withdraw it, as the right to withdraw is a key ethical consideration in our criminological research (King and Wincup 2008).

If they are not reflexive, observers in criminology can overlook these issues.

Secondary analysis—researching by analysing someone else's data

The most common alternative research method in criminology to the big three of experiment, survey, and observation is secondary data analysis, which involves the collection, review and analysis of secondary data (i.e. collected by someone other than the person conducting the

CONTROVERSY AND DEBATE 6.3

Observing football hooligans: the film *I.D.*

In the 1995 British film *I.D.*, a group of police officers go undercover to infiltrate a dangerous gang of football hooligans called 'The Dogs', who follow the fictitious London football club Shadwell FC. The officers pose as painter-decorators and begin visiting 'The Rock', a backstreet pub where the gang is based, in order to observe its members, analyse the gang's behaviours, and establish the group's hierarchy and leadership structure. The main character, John, is eventually accepted into the gang following several individual displays of violence against rival gangs and is then invited to accompany the group to matches and pre-arranged fights. This acceptance gives John a closer and more detailed insight into the group members' histories, motivations, personalities, and behaviours.

At set points (first daily, then weekly, then further apart), John joins his colleagues at the police station and other locations to record their observations. However, the validity of John's observations is increasingly weakened by a range of extraneous variables: extended lengths of time between recording episodes, an emerging alcoholism affecting recall during and after observations, and a growing affinity and identification with the characters and behaviours under observation. These extraneous variables lead to more subjectivity and ultimately to John 'going native' by becoming a real-life member of the gang, behaving how the gang members are expected to behave (i.e. demonstrating demand characteristics), and influencing the individuals and situations he is meant to be observing (i.e. exerting observer effects).

Life imitates art: This small screen scenario may not be as far-fetched as you'd think. Have a look at this online article (http://www.theguardian.com/uk/2011/jan/19/undercover-policeman-married-activist-spy): it covers a real-life example of an undercover police officer who married a woman he was observing as part of an investigation! Do you think that this compromised the validity of his observations and the ethics of the investigation?

analysis), rather than primary data (collected by you as researcher). Secondary data analysis, as its name suggests, is not strictly a research method—instead it is the analysis of the arguments of others or data collected through someone else's research method (Caulfield and Hill 2014). Neither is secondary data analysis empirical or applied research, although the original, primary research may have been.

Secondary data analysis can be conducted on data obtained from either quantitative or qualitative research. Numerical, statistical data can be collected (e.g. from a statistical database, official statistics, questionnaires completed by other researchers) and analysed statistically for causal relationships (i.e. positivism), differences between groups, and correlations between variables. For example, from 2011, the author was granted access to the youth offending data for England and Wales and analysed it for statistical differences between the reoffending rates of young people in each country, in order to evaluate any differences in the effectiveness of national youth justice policies (Haines and Case 2015; see also **Chapter 9**). This was an original analytical focus, but as the researcher did not collect the data that was analysed, the research method was secondary analysis of quantitative data. In addition, the data or information used in secondary analysis can be in qualitative, written, documentary form (e.g. in books, journal articles, policy documents, newspapers, diaries, blogs, literature reviews) and can be analysed for key themes (through thematic analysis and content analysis), arguments, and issues (e.g. common ideas, dominant perspectives, particular use of language) that allow the researcher to explore and explain a subject area. This method of secondary analysis is often known as documentary analysis. For example, a student conducting research for an essay or dissertation typically identifies and analyses relevant criminological literature for themes and arguments that address the question—this is documentary analysis using thematic analysis. Other studies have explored the use of exaggerated and sensationalist language in newspaper reporting of crime committed by certain groups such as young people and ethnic minorities—language that can contribute to the phenomena of 'moral panics'. It is also possible to collect and analyse qualitative data in the form of focus group transcripts, social network discussions, email/telephone/postal correspondence, or from observations of interactions. This is known as discourse analysis or conversation analysis. For example, criminologists examine the use of inflammatory language on a discussion forum in order to investigate the topic of cyber-bullying.

Secondary data analysis offers an alternative, flexible, and potentially innovative range of research methodologies to substitute for or supplement the traditional, primary, empirical research methods used in criminology. A key advantage of secondary data analysis over methods that collect primary data is that it is an unobtrusive methodological and analytical tool (Robson 2015), which may therefore minimise the influence of subjectivity on the part of the researched parties, although it is always possible that they displayed subjectivity during the original, primary research process. With secondary data analysis, however, there are no research subjects/participants to influence, to manipulate, or to react in artificial ways to the research situation. Secondary data analysis is relatively cheap and quick compared to other methods, as the main financial and resource costs are concerned with accessing statistics and documents, many of which are freely available electronically or can be made available through local data sharing arrangements and the Freedom of Information Act.

In respect of validity, secondary data analysis also enables researchers to deductively cross-validate data collected through other methods—a process known as **triangulation** (Robson 2015). In other words, research findings and conclusions can be tested, corroborated, extended, or contradicted through secondary data analysis, enabling the researcher to reflect on the validity of the original research conclusions. Of course, it is also possible to inductively generate new questions and understandings/knowledge existing issues by exploring existing data from new angles. However, we must always bear in mind that the original data has been collected, analysed, and presented for a different purpose (e.g. to answer another question) by a different researcher, which is a major challenge to the validity of any analysis and our interpretation of data, hence the importance of cross-validation/triangulation when using documentary analysis. Indeed, the data may not always be based on empirical research evidence at all, but instead generated through subjectivity and supposition, such as the data contained in certain government policy documents and position statements, pressure group websites, and personal blogs.

A major issue with secondary data analysis could be labelled 'double subjectivity'. The validity of the data collected (e.g. which data sets or documents were chosen), the analysis (e.g. the chosen method of analysis), and the interpretation of data (e.g. which findings we choose to present or reject) can be influenced by the subjectivity of the researcher who is conducting the secondary data analysis. However, because researchers rely on secondary data in the special case of secondary data analysis, this validity could be further influenced by the subjectivity of the original researcher—hence double subjectivity. It is difficult and painful enough for researchers to reflect honestly on the impact of their own subjectivity on their research. It is more difficult, even impossible at times, to fully know the subjectivity of others. The subjectivity, influences (external and internal—see earlier), and even the research methods of other researchers are not always documented, clarified, fully discussed, or acknowledged. For example,

how did the researcher collect, analyse, and interpret the quantitative statistics or qualitative literature and why did they make these decisions and not others? It can be difficult to discern the agenda of an author or contributor to discourse (Westmarland 2011), for example, unless it has been made explicit on the page, in the conversation, or identified at some other point via a survey—unless the researcher has fully disclosed their methods and been reflexive regarding their subjectivity, epistemology, and positionality. Certain documents, conversations and statistical datasets are authored anonymously, anonymized, or the product of multiple authors, so it is impossible to pin down who wrote what and why. Unless we are aware of the extent and nature of the subjectivity of other researchers when we analyse their work (e.g. if they have provided a 'positionality statement' reflecting on the different elements of their positionality—Savin-Baden and Howell-Major 2013), our capacity to judge the validity of the research is limited, as is what we can know about criminology from their data and our subsequent analysis of it (see Case, in Vaidya 2015).

If they are not reflexive, researchers who conduct secondary data analysis can overlook these issues.

Multiple and mixed research methods—researching by combining methods

Quantitative and qualitative research methods can be used alongside one another at different stages of a research project to answer different questions (multi-method models) or combined with other methods to produce more comprehensive and triangulated knowledge in answer to the same question (mixed methods). This can be a very useful research technique because, as you know by now, research methods used in isolation have certain limitations regarding what and how they can study, what they are able to conclude and the forms of knowledge they are able to produce, so combining them can allow methods to build on the strengths and to compensate for the limitations of one another (see Robson 2015). Researchers in the social sciences have developed a liking for multiple and mixed method designs in recent years and criminology is no exception (Creswell 2013). A particular appeal of multiple and mixed methods beyond the benefits of triangulation is the ability to explore several questions or the same question from different angles within the same study, thus producing a broader range and depth of cross-validated data and (hopefully) knowledge as a result. Multiple and mixed methods designs, therefore, are ideally suited to longitudinal research conducted over long periods, with multiple data collection points, as these designs have the objective

WHAT DO YOU THINK? 6.3

Using multiple and mixed methods to design a local crime prevention programme

Let us say that you become part of the team in your local authority Community Safety Department and you are asked to prevent crime in a socially deprived neighbourhood that has been identified as having a growing crime problem. How would you go about researching the issue? Specifically:

- How would you identify the most important targets (e.g. behaviours, areas, organisations, people, ages, ethnic groups, genders) for any interventions?

- How would you explore potential explanations for offending behaviour amongst these target groups?

- How would you establish how a particular intervention was meant to 'work' to prevent offending?

- Would you use a multi-methods or mixed methods design? Neither?

- Would this design give you advantages over using a specific research method in isolation?

of measuring trends and developments in behaviours and perspectives over time (Bryman 2015). For example, if you were interested in researching why people commit crime, you could start with a documentary analysis of relevant empirical research or theoretical publications in order to identify the most popular explanations for crime. You could then formulate these explanations into a questionnaire full of closed questions that measure the most common explanations across a certain population in a certain place. You could follow this with an interview asking a select group of people (e.g. those identified by the questionnaire as the most typical offenders) if any of the most common explanations apply to them and, if so, how and why they influence offending behaviour. See **What do you think? 6.3** which raises similar issues as well as questions specific to the example of a local crime prevention programme.

As noted previously, in the second half of the 20th century there was an ongoing debate between social science researchers regarding the relative merits of quantitative and qualitative methods and the (un)suitability of combining the two approaches—Oakley's (1999) 'paradigm wars'. Some researchers have opposed the idea of combining research methods with allegedly conflicting expectations for knowledge generation (cf. Lincoln and Guba 1985). In other words, it was once considered almost sacrilegious to merge quantitative positivist methods, focused on identifying cause and effect relationships with qualitative interpretivist methods, focused on identifying meanings and understandings. In the 21st century,

we are more concerned with realist pragmatism in criminology—what works practically to generate knowledge of our real, complex world (cf. Gray 2013). That said, as we now know, a big problem associated with using research methods to study and learn about criminology can be a lack of critical reflection/reflexivity—that researchers may ignore or neglect the limitations of their chosen methods and exaggerate the usefulness (utility) of their research projects, whilst also ignoring the influence of their own subjectivity, suppositions, and methodological principles on their choice of research topic, questions, methods, subjects/participants, analyses, and conclusions (Savin-Baden and Howell-Major 2013). Clearly, this could be even more problematic when attempting to use several methods in multiple or mixed methods models, with each model full of their own subjectivities, suppositions, and methodological principles. It is not unusual in criminology, for example, to find multiple and mixed methods employed for no obvious or stated reason other than that they seem fashionable or exciting. The rationale for choosing multiple and mixed methods and for conducting them in specific ways is not always discussed in detail; this could indicate that subjectivity (e.g. preference for particular methods) and supposition (e.g. assumption that the methods will complement one another) is driving research study choices in preference to pragmatism.

If they are not reflexive, researchers in criminology who choose multiple and mixed methods can overlook these issues.

Reflecting on research as study: What can we know?

Research is an imperfect, complex process with many external and internal influences on the methods chosen and the validity of the findings and conclusions

produced—that is, the knowledge created. Reflecting critically on the subjectivity, supposition, and study methods that guide the generation of knowledge in criminology can help us to become active and productive criminologists. Subjectivity is both inevitable and constructive—it guides and shapes the arguments that criminologists make to further knowledge in criminology. Subjectivity is itself guided and shaped by various external and internal influences that change over time and that we are either aware or unaware of—an issue that we must reflect on through a constant process of reflexivity. Subjectivity is also influenced by supposition—the conscious and subconscious filling the gaps in knowledge that humans rely upon so that we can retain the illusion of control over and understanding of our world. Reflecting critically upon and challenging the accepted knowledge base and the accepted means of knowledge creation is central to being a student of criminology and to becoming a criminologist. The need to challenge is a challenge in itself. Criminology is a multi-headed, multi-directional, unstable, fascinating subject. Just as you should challenge and question

established methods and knowledge (including your own), so criminology and criminologists constantly challenge accepted wisdom to push the boundaries of knowledge creation (e.g. to evolve theoretical explanations). As a student, indeed as a criminologist, you can contribute in a meaningful way to this dynamic enterprise. No other academic subject is as broad-minded, transparent, and open (even vulnerable) to criticism and enhancement as criminology. What is more, the knowledge to which you may contribute can make a real difference to real people. Criminology is not sitting on a shelf gathering dust. Criminology exists and develops in the real world—the world that you study and study within. Be brave and ambitious—value your potential to contribute to knowledge in criminology by analysing what exists and by producing new understandings. If we can 'know' anything from this chapter, it is that reflexivity is crucial in our study of criminology, so with this in mind, remember your ABC … *Always Be Critical*!

SUMMARY

- Consider from a critical viewpoint how knowledge in criminology is produced and what it means to know about crime

This chapter invited you to consider critically how we produce knowledge in criminology. It was argued that criminological knowledge is the product of theory and research guided by subjectivity (external and internal), supposition (educated guesswork, prediction), and study (research and scholarship), each of which can be enhanced by the producer's ability to be reflexive. Knowing about crime was presented not as a collection of facts, but as understanding how debates, issues, and theories are socially constructed products of subjectivity and the particular epistemology adopted by the researcher.

- Understand what is meant by subjectivity, supposition, and study (through research) in criminological terms

In criminological terms, subjectivity refers to the personal opinion, preferences, experiences, perspectives, and agendas of knowledge producers, whilst supposition refers to guesswork, imputation, assumption, estimates, speculation, and prediction. For our purposes, study mainly relates to the generation of evidence through research.

- Critically evaluate the benefits and limitations of different research study methods on the creation of criminological knowledge

The chapter outlined and reviewed the key methods used for quantitative and qualitative research study in criminology: experiment, survey, observation, secondary analysis, and mixed methods. The strengths and limitations of each approach were evaluated, with a particular focus on the importance of researcher reflexivity for minimising validity issues caused by subjectivity and supposition.

- Explore how subjectivity, supposition, and study interact with, and impact on, understanding and knowledge production in criminology

It was argued that subjectivity and supposition interact with and influence (research) study, notably the validity and applicability of the evidence and knowledge produced through different methods. Subjectivity and supposition were presented as largely inevitable—but not necessarily negative—elements of a practical and realistic research process that can lead to comprehensive and fit-for-purpose knowledge in criminology if the researcher is suitably reflexive.

REVIEW QUESTIONS

1. What do you understand by the term 'subjectivity' and can you provide examples of such?

2. What effect can supposition have on research?

3. What is meant by the term 'black box' supposition?

4. Outline the advantages and disadvantages of the different types of surveys: questionnaires, interviews, and focus groups.

5. How would you assess if an observational method of data collection is viable for your research requirements?

6. Why is it important to acknowledge your own subjectivity when conducting research?

7. What are the potential benefits of employing a mixed methods approach?

FURTHER READING

Chamberlain, J.M. (2015) *Criminological Theory in Context: An Introduction*. London: Sage.
A lively, concise and definitive guide to the historical development of criminology as an academic discipline. The book presents an overview of a range of different theories of crime and analyses the strengths and weaknesses of each theory discussed.

Chamberlain, J.M. (2013) *Understanding Criminological Research: A Guide to Data Analysis*. London: Sage.
A clear and accessible step-by-step guide to conducting criminological research and analysing data, illustrated by useful case studies.

Caulfield, L. and Hill, J. (2014) *Criminological Research for Beginners: A Student's Guide*. Abingdon: Routledge.
This is a comprehensive guide to understanding and undertaking research in criminology and will be a helpful aid for a third year project or dissertation.

Finch, E. and Fafinksi, S. (2016) *Criminology Skills* (2nd edn). Oxford: Oxford University Press.
This text covers practical, academic, and research skills for the study of criminology, including comprehensive coverage of research methods, ethics, and data analysis.

 Access the **online resources** to view selected further reading and web links relevant to the material covered in this chapter.
www.oup.com/uk/case/

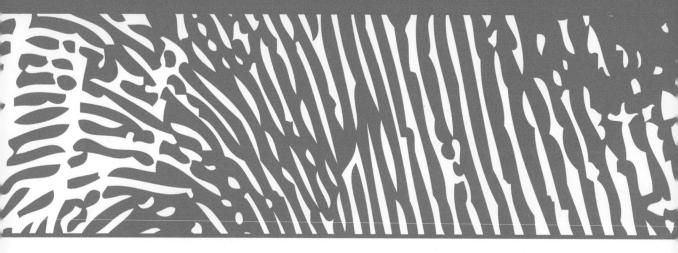

CHAPTER OUTLINE

Introduction	166
Traditional media criminology	167
Newsworthiness and setting agendas	170
The representation of young people in the media	175
The representation of migrants in the media	178
Crime novels, television, and film	182
Analysing crime film and the criminological imagination	184
Media classification and censorship	186
New technology, new media, and new fears	187
Cybercrime	189
The future of media criminology	193

7

Crime and the media

KEY ISSUES

After studying this chapter you should be able to:

- develop a critical and reflective view of media representations of crime and criminals;

- explain how criminologists have researched this through content analysis and discourse analysis, and the capacity of media to distort and shape public perceptions of crime, criminality, and the criminal justice system;

- relate a range of concepts to your own consumption of media;

- assess the importance of media in forming new narratives such as citizen journalism;

- compare and analyse differences between traditional and emerging branches of criminological research on the representation of crime across a variety of media.

Introduction

The public's fascination with crime

The Wellcome Collection's 2015 exhibition 'Forensics: The Anatomy of Crime' (2015) proved hugely popular, packing in crowds of people of all ages who wanted to learn more about how crimes are solved. There were films showing pathologists and anthropologists at work; crime scene sketches and photographs dating back to the days of Jack the Ripper; art works made from the bones of genocide victims; and even wounded human organs (see **Figure 7.1**).

The popularity of such exhibitions is part of a long-lived fascination with crime and its effects. Until recently, only strictly-vetted visitors were allowed into the Metropolitan Police's London Black Museum; nowadays, popular demand means that the collection of nooses, death masks, and murder weapons has been put on public display through the Museum of London. There are hundreds of thousands of books on 'crime', thousands of films with crime as a focus, and hundreds of video and computer games in which crime and violence are central themes. These could be regarded as a form of popular criminology. People love to look at crime, think about it, and read about it, as long as it's safely in a book, on a screen, or—in the case of the Wellcome exhibition—in a display case. For most of us today, crime, criminality, and its control have become mediated experiences.

Human beings have historically used all available media at their disposal to meet this urge to document crime. From the 13th century, when the printing press was invented, through the 1820s (the typewriter), 1840s (photography), 1930s (television), 1970s (America's first computer shop), and the 1990s (the launch of Google), we in the developed world have used media to record, discuss, and fantasise about crime and its effects. One of the most striking things about the Forensics exhibition was its use of multi-media; this ranged from the filmed discussion of a pathologist talking about the use of three dimensional imaging used in today's virtual autopsy to an ongoing electronic database logging victims of the Balkans war. The various types of media have become diverse, interconnected, and fragmented, and at the same time highly accessible to practically everyone.

Most of us, thankfully, have little personal experience of crime and its impact. Instead, we use media to tell us what is happening and what we should think about it. This takes place in an increasingly multi-mediated world. It is true to say, more than ever, that we rely on the media to give us information and to shape our reactions. At this point you might wish to consider the questions raised in **What do you think? 7.1**. Whilst fewer people now read a daily newspaper or regularly go to the cinema, the vast majority of houses in the UK have access to the Internet. Most households have at least one television set and can access hundreds of channels. There are even channels which focus solely on the committal and detection of crime,

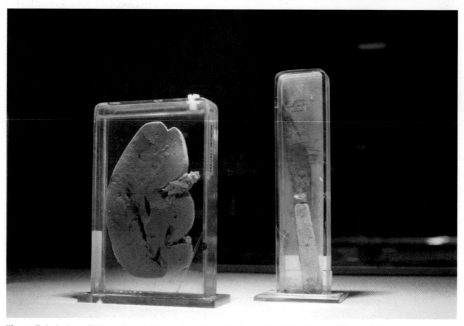

Figure 7.1 A piece of kidney with a knife wound and the offending knife exhibited at the Wellcome Collection

Source: Steve Parsons/PA Archive/Press Association Images

WHAT DO YOU THINK? 7.1

What media criminologists study

The relationships between crime and the media are far from straightforward. Criminologists have studied this over the last 50 years or so and have traditionally explored issues like:

- Does the media create and reinforce false and harmful stereotypes?

- Does the media exaggerate and distort particular forms of criminality?

- Does the media cause a fear of crime?

- Do media representations cause violence?

- Is the media itself criminogenic (a cause of crime)?

What do you think about these questions? Jot down your answers to them.

Are your responses the same for each form of media? Do they change when you look at a popular tabloid newspaper which traditionally has a generally right wing readership (like the *Daily Mail*) or a more liberal broadsheet paper (such as the *Guardian*)? Look at your local newspaper too. Does what you read about where you live match your own experiences?

---

such as 'Crime and Investigation' (which focuses on real crime) and 'Alibi' (which focuses on crime drama). However, we should also remember that stories of crime also regularly crop up in popular soap operas, and this leads to discussions about crime in school playgrounds, workplace canteens, on buses, and on social media.

As Reiner (1997: 376–77) has argued, there are two broad public anxieties around media representations of crime, criminality, and its control; he calls these 'the media as subversive' and 'the media as (a not so subtle form of) social control'. In other words, the first position regards media representations as being in some ways a threat to wider issues of morality, law, and order. Thus, for example, it could be argued that by portraying 'deviant' behaviour as glamorous or exciting, the media make it appear more attractive and therefore more people do it. The second position argues that the media exaggerates existing fears and anxieties and that, through this, forms of social control are implemented and legislated into existence—you may hear this referred to as 'knee jerk' legislation, often described as being fuelled by media concerns. Both of these positions, which can be seen to demonise the media, have been reflected in criminological research in the field, so do bear them in mind as you critically work through this chapter.

It could be argued that the challenges of living in a multi-mediated world have outpaced traditional criminological research, bringing instead new issues and problems with novel questions and concerns. This chapter will firstly consider the original research into various forms of media and their long, complicated relationships with crime. Firstly, we will examine some of the ways in which criminologists have traditionally examined the media and analysed the ways in which it has been used to represent—either directly or indirectly—'facts' and opinions about crime. We will also be looking at how this can reflect wider and less obvious considerations, such as social concerns and attitudes to different groups, like women or young people. This chapter then moves on to explore some of the newer strands of media criminology, and in examining these developments we will be looking at:

- **crime as fiction and popular entertainment**—novels, television dramas, music, and films;

- **new technology**—the Internet, games, and how these are used by young people, together with the risks they face, such as exploitation;

- **positive outcomes from new developments in media**—how evolution in technology means that we can blog, vlog, and commentate, giving us each the chance to be a citizen journalist or to share views and thoughts with others (whether that is for good or ill).

Ultimately this chapter will encourage you to critically consider media representations of crime.

Traditional media criminology

Before delving into media representations of crime, it is firstly essential that you better understand how criminologists measure the reporting of crime. There are two main methods traditionally used: content analysis and discourse analysis. We will look at both of these in turn.

Content analysis and counting crime

Watch a news programme and count the number of times that crime is mentioned or look at the amount of time taken up by crime stories as measured against the length of the whole broadcast. What other categories or elements might you be interested in counting and why? This depends on what it is you want to research. For instance, you may wish to count the types of crime reported (violence, theft, robbery, for example), who the offenders are (male, female, young, old, black, white), or who the victims are.

Did you find it difficult to clearly distinguish between different types of crime? What did you do if a story involved more than one crime category? There are clearly complications with such types of research and it is important to understand and consider these when you read the statistics or research of others. Content analysis can be a very useful research tool in your own project or dissertation, but it is important to bear these considerations in mind.

Content analysis

Media criminologists have traditionally used a research method known as content analysis to examine and critically analyse the extent and patterns of crimes in the news, how often they are reported, and which crimes are focused on. This mainly quantitative research strategy focuses simply on counting the frequency of particular things. In other words, it calculates how many times a particular word (like 'crime') or theme (such as violence) is used in a news report or in other documents such as diaries or magazines. By using this method we can therefore count the number of headlines which focus on a particular form of criminality and the number of articles which report on it. We can also count the average number of words used in these articles and study precisely where on a newspaper page they are placed. Furthermore, we can develop a similar basic research schedule to cover a given time period, as well as studying crime reporting across more than one newspaper.

It has been argued that content analysis is both systematic and objective (see the section on empirical research in **Chapter 6** for a further discussion of these important issues). The claim for it being systematic is important. When researching crime stories we must do more than simply look at or read a document, otherwise the claims which we make would be subjective and therefore not reliable or valid. We must also be very clear as to what we are counting and that our categories are clearly stated or coded. The reason for this is that if other researchers should wish to replicate, or build on, a piece of research it is important that they are able to do so with ease and accuracy. Being clear and specific can only strengthen and verify the findings of the research.

It is by using this strategy that researchers of media criminology have been able to justifiably make claims such as: newspapers allocate more than 60 per cent of all crime stories to reporting crimes of interpersonal violence (Williams and Dickinson 1993), or that whilst crimes of a violent or sexual nature make up 2.4 per cent of recorded crime, newspaper coverage devotes 45.8 per cent to it (Ditton and Duffy 1983). It is important to understand the process and methods undertaken to produce such statistics so that you can appreciate the work behind them and critically evaluate those you come across in your own studies. With this in mind you should now approach the exercise in **What do you think? 7.2**.

Discourse analysis

Whilst claims from the content analysis method are interesting and suggest all sorts of patterns of crime in the news, its critics point out that it does not really consider deeper meanings and interpretations of events. This is where discourse analysis, as a more qualitative research tool, is helpful. Discourse analysis concentrates on the language and meanings of texts, speech, and documents. It can offer a more nuanced picture when compared with content analysis. Discourse analysis can also pay attention to what is *excluded* as much as *included* by examining events in their broader contexts. For example, it will look at questions such as who says what about a particular subject, why they feel they have the authority to make their claims, and who their intended audience is.

Discourse analysis is therefore an altogether very different and more difficult research methodology to understand. Mayr and Machin (2012) explore its use in detail, providing some fascinating examples of how language is used in media and popular culture to discuss the ways in which crime, criminality, and its control are portrayed; amongst other things, they look at the use of language in the media discussions on young people and the criminal justice system. Jewkes (2015) pays attention to what she calls 'media misogyny' in her analysis of the portrayal of female offenders, thinking about the way their physical attractiveness, motherhood, or mental health are foregrounded in ways which do not happen when men are under scrutiny (see **further reading** at the end of the chapter for details).

Discourse analysis therefore gives us another layer of understanding but for now, let's see what the available research on the extent and pattern of crime in the news actually tells us.

In their thorough review of research carried out over the last 30 years in this area, Greer and Reiner (2015: 255–56) come to the following six conclusions:

(a) that news and fiction stories about crime are covered extensively by all media;

(b) that within news and fictional representations of crime there is an over-concentration on crimes of violence and that this (as we have seen in **Chapter 5**) is very different from the picture we get from official statistics;

(c) the media tend to focus on older and richer victims and offenders, but are also more likely today to give greater attention to children who are victims (or perpetrators);

(d) the risks of becoming a victim or becoming affected by crime are portrayed as being far higher than official sources tell us, but the chances of suffering property crime (burglary or theft, for example) are under-reported by media;

(e) that there has been a recent focus on individual victims and their suffering;

(f) that the news generally paints the police and the criminal justice system in a positive light, although there is some movement towards criticism, for example in the way that miscarriages of justice or police racism are reported.

From this brief overview a picture slowly begins to emerge: that crime is a staple across all media; that it focuses more on crimes of violence over property crimes; and that it overplays our risk of becoming a victim of crime, something which perhaps makes us all more fearful. As a result, certain types of crime and offender are more likely to result in 'front page outrage', controversial tweets and soundbites, and we are left with the impression that we live in riskier and more dangerous times (see **Figure 7.2**). But how exactly are news stories on crime produced? This next section of the chapter will focus on the concept of newsworthiness.

Figure 7.2 This is how you stab someone: Images from police film, *Daily Mail*, 15 February 1997

Source: Daily Mail

Newsworthiness and setting agendas

Let us for a moment consider what actually gets reported in the press. Do we have different expectations of different types of media? Are we startled when a broadsheet publishes an April Fools' joke? Do we think it's odd if a redtop tabloid (such as *The Sun*) features a campaign on behalf of female victims of domestic abuse on the same page as a picture of a topless woman? The point is that we think our media will do a certain job, depending on how it presents itself. So, if we consider this further we need to think about why things are reported (or not) and why they end up being shown in the way and place that they are. This is the process whereby editors decide what is newsworthy—what deserves a place in their publication, whatever form that may take. Criminologists will often use the terms 'newsworthiness' and 'news values' to explore how such choices are made. Take a look at **What do you think? 7.3** and put yourself in the shoes of a news editor.

News values and criminology

The first detailed criminological study of the construction of crime news in the printed press was Chibnall's *Law and Order News* (1977). In it, Chibnall lists what he

perhaps rather grandly calls eight 'professional imperatives' (which you can think of as being news values) which he argues guide journalists' decisions on what they think ought to be in the news. As you read the list below think about whether, and if so, how, these news values link with the lists you made when considering our four scenarios in **What do you think? 7.3.**

The eight professional imperatives are:

1. immediacy (speed/the present);
2. dramatisation (drama and action);
3. personalisation (cult of celebrity);
4. simplification (elimination of shades of grey);
5. titillation (revealing the forbidden/voyeurism);
6. conventionalism (hegemonic ideology);
7. structured access (experts, power base, authority);
8. novelty (new angle/speculation/twist).

This analysis will now explore the extent to which these eight guiding imperatives, albeit with some development, fit with today's rapidly changing mediascape. In short, are they still of relevance and importance in the construction of crime news today?

WHAT DO YOU THINK? 7.3

Newsworthiness and news values

The perceived attraction of particular stories to particular readers or viewers is often a guiding factor in whether or not they are reported. Even on a quiet news day, editors have an almost unlimited supply of events which they could cover.

Imagine that you are the news editor of a national newspaper or rolling 24 hour television news programme. You have owners to please, reader or viewer targets to maintain, advertising revenue to earn. All of these things mean you have to choose your stories carefully, especially your headline. Today, out of all the thousands of events and occasions happening all over the world, you need to select from these four:

- A report states that poor children with special needs are four times more likely to be excluded from school than richer classmates.

- A pretty blonde child has gone missing from a park which is also being used as a traveller site.

- A stockbroker is found guilty of evading the payment of enough tax to fund 12 National Health Service (NHS) nurses.

- The firm employed to monitor safety at a nuclear power plant is accused of using unqualified staff.

Which story do you choose? Why? Would your choice be different if, for example, you were working for a tabloid rather than a broadsheet newspaper? Would a TV news programme go for a different story because of the images that could be used? Make a list of the sort of things which would guide your decisions as to the potential newsworthiness of a particular event. You could even design your own front page cover story, write your headline, and note what sort of images you would like to use. In short, editorial decisions have to be made, and quickly. Doing this exercise should help you understand the complexity of the decisions behind media coverage of crimes, and the matrix of choices editors are faced with.

1. **Immediacy (speed/the present)**—It perhaps goes without saying that the 'news' is all about what is new. By its very nature, news is orientated to the here and now, and not the past. Journalists undoubtedly work under enormous (and increasing) institutional and time constraints. Working in a progressively competitive and expanding marketplace means that journalists are under increasing pressure to submit 'copy' quickly and work to very tight deadlines. As we shall see later under the 'simplification' professional imperative, one possible consequence of this is that what are often important parts of a crime story are often absent in initial crime news reports, especially in those cases where the story unfolds and develops slowly, as most do. With the developments in new technologies events today can be in the public domain within literally seconds, together with speculation, theorising, and what are often inaccurate statements.

2. **Dramatisation (drama and action)**—Peaceful political protests rarely make it on to the front page of newspapers or form the lead story on television news reports. Political protests with a hint of violence, however, do. Can you think of any recent events, be they political protests, animal export protests, anti-immigration protests, which carried that edge of danger and force? Do you think that the reporting of these events is fair and unbiased, or does it bracket off and exclude broader issues which are perhaps worthy of a more considered and serious debate and discussion? Another relevant and changing development to this particular news value is the increasing importance of the visual, often moving, image over the written word. As Greer (2010) has noted, the digital revolution has meant that dramatic action can quickly be filmed and uploaded to news websites. Indeed, having an online presence is today seen as being essential for most large media companies and public figures. Through this, the spectacular can become even more of a spectacle, especially when accompanied by graphic moving images of car chases, police raids, shootouts, and violence. This can now be done either by professional film crews or ordinary citizens. The film *Nightcrawler* (Dir. Gilroy, 2014) takes us in to the word, albeit in a highly exaggerated way, of a Los Angeles stringer (or nightcrawler)—these are freelance 'journalists' who, armed with police radio scanners and camcorders, race to crime scenes to video the action, the footage of which they then sell to the highest TV company bidder. This film raises many interesting and broader ethical issues but for our purposes in this chapter it highlights nicely the point made by Greer (2010) of the increasing importance of the visual in crime reporting today.

3. **Personalisation (cult of celebrity)**—This news value can perhaps work on three different levels. Firstly, the modern world is one where, it would seem, people like to read about the rich and famous, especially more so when they transgress the criminal law or social norms and conventions. Secondly, the media can often personalise crime victims to the extent that people think they know them personally and come to refer to them by their first names. This is something which so-called 'reality' crime shows such as *Crimewatch UK* do well. Through its use of faded family photographs and home videos we are taken into the intimate, personal world of the victim, seeing them in altogether happier times. Finally, the media can also help to recreate notorious criminals as celebrities. For instance, the Kray twins, the notorious East End London gangsters who were once described as the most dangerous men in Britain, have been the subject of many films, the most recent of which is *Legend* (Dir. Brian Helgeland, 2015). Thousands of people lined the roads at both of their funerals (which themselves became media events).

4. **Simplification (elimination of shades of grey)**—There is usually more to acts of criminality than initially meets the eye. Even mundane volume crime is often far more complex than it first appears. With the pressure to produce quick copy and a shrinking set of news sources, journalists often over-simplify what turn out to be complex events. Crime stories are often represented in black and white, with a clearly identifiable victim and offender and with the story presented as a confrontation between good and evil, right and wrong. For example, the English Collective of Prostitutes complained in 1981 about the way sex-worker victims of the Yorkshire Ripper were portrayed as somehow deserving their fate, whereas non-sex workers he attacked were described as 'innocent'. This can go to the extent of suggesting that some people contribute to crimes carried out against them through their own negligence or life style choices.

5. **Titillation (revealing the forbidden/voyeurism)**—In short, sex and drugs and rock and roll sells. Drunken celebrities, 'wardrobe malfunctions', or famous chefs having marital fights in restaurants are good examples of how papers use our sense of curiosity to encourage us to read on. For instance, the Forensics exhibition we described at the start of the chapter graphically displayed the front pages of popular Mexican newspapers reporting the various drugs wars. The editors of these publications were happy to show colour photographs of decapitated bodies next to separate images of half-naked young women in provocative poses.

6. **Conventionalism (hegemonic ideology)**—This refers to the idea that the media frame events within

conventional patterns of meaning; in other words, the common sense understandings of the social world and crime which we, as criminologists, seek to unpick, unravel, and go beyond. For instance, thanks to popular news reporting, we all 'know' that all prisoners are highly dangerous people who live lives of luxury of which many a pensioner would be envious. What, however, do we really know about the day-to-day lives of those who are incarcerated, or the pains of such imprisonment? This theme will be developed later on in this chapter with our discussion of prison films.

7. **Structured access (experts, power base, authority)**—Today very few newspapers have as many specialist crime correspondents as they used to. Also, like the rest of us, journalist and television reporters have little direct experience of, and access to, crime. So where do you think that most of the information relating to the story of a crime initially comes from? The answer is press releases and various press agencies. A careful reading of various newspapers on just one day would highlight the fact that many news stories are very similar in both style and content, which is perhaps due to an increasing over-reliance on such sources. Most police forces now have dedicated press offices which issue press releases, as does the Ministry of Justice. Beyond the official voices of governmental organisations, most non-governmental organisations (NGOs) in the sphere of penal reform and policy (such as the Howard League for Penal Reform and the Prison Reform Trust) are also more media-savvy than they have been in the past. However, the extent to which they can set or influence media agendas on such things as prison conditions is highly debatable (see Colbran 2015 for a fuller discussion of these issues). Why do you think that this might be the case? Would an NGO press release meet any of the eight imperatives discussed in this section? Would a report highlighting poor and overcrowded prison conditions, rates of self-harm—especially amongst female prisoners—and diagnosed mental health conditions amongst young offenders, for instance, be deemed newsworthy by a journalist working in the mainstream media? We will return to the issue of media representations of prisons and prisoners in our section on crime film, but it appears to be very difficult for such reform organisations to get sustained media coverage and to use it in order to influence wider debate and policy.

8. **Novelty (new angle/speculation/twist)**—In keeping a particular story going, a newspaper may seek to find a new angle. This can often be at the victim's expense. For instance, there have been cases where the sex lives of a murder victim's parents were discussed in court and splashed all over the tabloid headlines, even though this was in no way connected to the death of their child.

News values today

Whilst Chibnall's (1977) list of imperatives still retains a certain relevance, Jewkes (2015) revisits his work, bringing it into a 21st century context (although inevitably there is some clear overlap in focus). As we saw with our discussion of discourse analysis, the intended audience for a piece of news reporting will have an influence on the way a story is presented; recognising this, Jewkes points out that we are today in a very different social, political, and economic environment to the one in which Chibnall was writing in the 1970s. Ask anyone over the age of 35 how many television channels they remember from their childhood, and you will get a vivid illustration of the different landscape in which media criminologists are now operating. In short, there are far more media outlets reporting on the same crime stories, in very different ways, 24 hours a day.

This change in landscape, according to Jewkes, means we need to reconsider the elements which were previously thought to mark out a story as newsworthy—although it is worth noting that different communities and countries will have different values, which in turn mean that a story can receive wide coverage in one place but generate little attention in another. Jewkes does not consider crime, negativity, and novelty as separate factors, but rather as ideas that run through all aspects of newsworthiness; for example, as she points out, any crime is broadly negative in and of itself.

Thus Jewkes suggests that there are now 12 'news structures' which are behind the shaping and reporting of today's crime news. These are included here to show how criminological concepts can be updated, developed, and expanded to reflect the rapidly changing worlds in which we live:

1. **Threshold**—Is the story important or dramatic enough? (There are supplementary thresholds, such as the grotesque, the unusual, or the involvement of a celebrity.)

2. **Predictability**—Some aspects of crime reporting can be planned in advance. For instance, during a general election it is certain that every political party will make policy statements on dealing with crime. However, as we shall see in the section on **folk devils** and **moral panics**, once a newspaper has decided that something is criminal, they will very rarely backtrack and say that is it not; therefore, they will seek out aspects of the story that confirm their initial approach. As Jewkes describes it: 'once the media expect something to happen, it will' (2015: p 51).

3. **Simplification**—Like Chibnall (1977), Jewkes (2015) recognises that for an event to become newsworthy, it must be possible to break its story down into separate

themes or conventions. It must be brief, have relatively few possible interpretations, and it must be unambiguous. That way, the audience is more likely to respond uncritically, and to join with the journalist and their editors in following a particular point of view.

4. **Individualism**—This structure encourages us to see and interpret crimes in terms of the personal (sometimes called 'human interest') context instead of within a wider political or social context. Thus we may see a skewed number of reports where the victim of crime is young and female (someone likely to look good in a press photograph). In other words, some types of victim may be more newsworthy and ideal than others (see the discussion in **Chapter 8** on the hierarchy of victimhood).

5. **Risk**—The news media can exacerbate fears about the risk of crime, making us believe that we are in far more danger than is actually the case. The idea that we may be killed by a random stranger generates more drama and excitement than the reality, which is that we are more likely to be killed or assaulted by someone we already know.

6. **Sex**—Chibnall (1977) identified titillation as a theme and this is continued here. Media are likely to over-report sex offences and to focus on crimes committed against women and girls; however, as Adrian Howe (1998) argues, we should really consider the question of sexed crimes, where the gender of either victim or perpetrator is a key factor in the commission of the offence.

7. **Celebrity**—As Chibnall (1977) noted, this structure seems to be an ever-growing feature of all media; the connection of a famous person to an incident practically guarantees that it will receive coverage. In other cases, the status of an alleged perpetrator can mean they are not

exposed by the press; this is what happened in the case of the BBC radio and television presenter Jimmy Savile, about whom there were suspicions and allegations many years before he was finally exposed as a predatory sex criminal.

8. **Proximity**—The location of a crime can affect its newsworthiness. This can be on a local or national basis; a story has to feel relevant to the audience. Despite living in an increasingly globalised world with increasing global crime problems, most outlets will focus predominantly on the relatively local and national rather than international.

9. **Violence or conflict**—The levels of acceptability as to what can or cannot be shown are constantly changing, with an increasing tendency for media to use content which would earlier have been thought too shocking or graphic for publication. An example would be the use by European press outlets of images showing the body of Princess Diana in the wreckage of her car; British newspapers declined to show the pictures, which again highlights the importance of proximity as a news structure.

10. **Visual spectacle and graphic imagery**—As with violence, there is an increasing use of such imagery in news outlets; so much so that at least one UK newspaper website (www.dailymail.co.uk) now precedes some stories with a warning that they contain graphic content. (See **Controversy and debate 7.1**.)

11. **Conservative ideology and political diversion**—Stories which either champion the so-called 'traditional way of life' or which highlight perceived threats to it are likely to gain news coverage. Such stories may focus on deviant activities of 'others', for example immigrants, the unemployed, or the young.

! CONTROVERSY AND DEBATE 7.1

The ethics of immediacy

Instant communication means that images and sounds from disasters, accidents, and acts of terrorism are sent around the world within moments of the incident taking place. We have become accustomed to seeing pictures of wounded people, shattered streets, and burning cars, and to hearing the often emotional testimonies of those who have been affected. In some cases, a particular image has become so closely associated with the event that it becomes iconic—for example, the film shot by Abraham Zapruder which captured the assassination

of President Kennedy. Yet how do the people shown in these pictures feel about being used to illustrate a news story? Do we care enough about them and how they have been affected? Or does the need to document and record what is happening override personal considerations?

Let us consider the two points of view involved in this debate. Imagine that you are the first to arrive on the scene of a violent attack. You take several clear shots of the aftermath—particularly of the injured people who are waiting for medical help to arrive. Now put yourself in the position of one of those injured victims. You are lying on the ground, bleeding and in pain, when a stranger appears and photographs you and your surroundings.

Jot down how you feel about the following statements from two perspectives, victim and photographer:

• The pictures could provide vital evidence for the police.

• The pictures are voyeuristic and show no respect for victims.

• It is important to show the impact of such events to a wider audience.

• People have the right to earn money from their photos if they get a chance.

• People only take photos like this so they can sell them to the media.

• Both photographer and victim should be credited whenever the picture is shown and share any royalties.

• Victims should have the right to ban the use of their images.

• Television channels should only show the images after the watershed.

• Television channels should not show the images as they involve real people.

Did your answers differ according to the person you were thinking about? Or could you see both sides?

Now think about the reaction of a television news editor. What do you think their views would be about using the images? What would influence their decision on whether or not to use the images?

You may also have thought about whether or not the photographer should have stopped to help the injured, rather than photographing them. In some countries, this would be a criminal offence—a breach of so-called 'Good Samaritan' laws, such as section 323c of the German Penal Code, which makes it illegal to fail to assist someone in danger where this can be done safely. There is no such law in the United Kingdom, despite politicians over the years saying that something similar would be introduced. You may want to think about why this has not become UK legislation.

Ketevan Kardava's images, taken immediately after the bombing of Brussels airport on 22 March 2016 (see **Figure 7.3**), were widely distributed across all forms of media. There has since been a debate about whether this was ethical or offensive. Should they have been used in newspapers, television reports, and websites? Should they even be in this book?

Figure 7.3 One of Ketevan Kardava's images of the aftermath of the Brussels airport bombing

Source: Ketevan Kardava/AFP/Getty Images

Figure 7.4 Police arresting youths on Brighton beach
Source: PA Archive/Press Association Images

12. **Children**—This is perhaps the most important revision to Chibnall's list. Whether as innocent victims or evil, monstrous, and feral (or should that be simply neglected?) offenders, stories about young people have become increasingly newsworthy (see **Figure 7.4**). Why do you think this may be the case? It is worth spending some time on considering this further.

The representation of young people in the media

The findings of a survey about youth crime, youth justice, and public opinion (Hough and Roberts 2004) found that people are generally not very well informed about trends in youth offending or the workings of the youth justice system. Indeed, it would appear that there are many misperceptions about levels of youth offending (that it is continually rising) and the types of crime committed by young people (that they are increasingly becoming more violent). Overall, people seem have a very negative and pessimistic view of young people. Interestingly, when asked how they know what they know, 64 per cent of people in this survey said the media was the main source of these generally poor perceptions. So, how do the media portray young people? One example is a 2012 *Daily Mail* article that was published with the title: 'Truth about Britain's feral youth: Small core of youngsters commit staggering 86 crimes by age 16' (*Daily Mail*, 24 June 2012, Rebecca Camber).

The criminological 'evidence' on all of this mirrors some of the points made earlier in this chapter in the discussion of content analysis. In analysing the media output of 2,130 news items across all major television channels in 2006, Wayne, M., Henderson, L., Murray, C., and Petley, J. (2008) argue that young people are increasingly being demonised in the media; that they are portrayed as not quite being full citizens and as being people to be feared. (See **What do you think? 7.4**.) Some of the findings they draw on to support this argument are that of the 2,130 stories that were analysed:

- 286 had young people as the main subject;
- 90 per cent of these stories focused on violent crime;
- 82 per cent of these focused on young people as being either the victims or perpetrators of crime;
- 42 per cent of offenders or suspects were young people;
- 1 per cent of sources gave young people the chance to voice their opinions or to tell their stories.

The fear, loathing, and demonisation of young people is, perhaps unsurprisingly, nothing new. In an excellent example of how social history can inform the criminological imagination, Geoffrey Pearson's book *Hooligan: A History*

WHAT DO YOU THINK? 7.4

The demonisation of young people

Do you think that young people get a good press? What kinds of stories do we hear about young people? Do we get to hear their voices in mainstream media at all?

In a piece of analysis conducted for Children & Young People Now, Ipsos MORI, a leading market research company, examined 493 articles about young people across 17 national and local newspapers between 2–8 August 2004. They categorised the main coverage of each article into one of seven subject areas, as well as according to whether the tone was positive, negative or neutral. The results are partially represented in **Table 7.1**—some boxes have been left (deliberately) blank.

Look at the upper section of the table, which shows the percentage of coverage for each of the seven subjects. Bearing in mind that the seven rows in each column will add up to approximately 100%, have a go at guessing the missing percentages for the other subject areas.

Now look at the lower section of the table, where just the percentages of articles considered to be neutral in tone are provided. Given that the three figures in each of these columns will again add up to approximately 100%, what would you estimate the remaining percentages to be?

Finally, compare your notes to the complete table at the end of the chapter. Did anything surprise you about the reported findings, and if so, why? Did your estimations roughly match the true percentages?

		Tabloids (281) %	Broadsheets (159) %	Locals (53) %
Subject	Violence/crime/anti-social behaviour			
	Child abuse/neglect			
	Lifestyle	16	9	7
	(Mental) Health			
	Accident	14	8	15
	Education/parenting	6	22	17
	Achievement	8	6	9
Tone	Negative			
	Neutral	8	36	9
	Positive			

Table 7.1 Newspaper articles about youth, by newspaper type, subject and tone.
Source: Ipsos MORI, www.ipsos-mori.com, 2–8 August 2004

of Respectable Fears (1984) shows us how such fears about young people have a very long history. If you were to look at the digitised archives of a newspaper such as *The Times*, you would find many examples of headlines stretching back well over two centuries which could perhaps have been written today. Even Aristotle, writing in Ancient Greece, complained that young people 'overdo everything; they love too much, hate too much, and the same with everything else' (Aristotle, *Nichomachean Ethics*).

The presence of absence

We will end this section by thinking about what is often referred to as the 'presence of absence'; in other words, the broader issues behind youth crime stories which the

news does not always report. Remember what was said above on discourse analysis and the importance of what is *not* said in news reporting. To be sure, young people do commit crimes which can affect local communities and cause serious harm. Some of it is of a violent nature. But to what extent does news reporting exaggerate and distort youthful offending? What is missing from a lot of the headlines, the front page outrage, and the bad press which young people get?

As previously discussed, most people think that the bulk of the 'crime problem' in England and Wales is a youth crime problem and that youth offending is continually rising (see **Chapter 9** on youth crime and justice). If you were to access the Youth Justice Board for England and Wales' annual statistics 2014/2015 (available at www.gov.uk) you would see that this is not in fact the case. For instance, it is reported that in the year ending March 2015 there were around 950,000 arrests for notifiable offences in England and Wales, of which 94,960 were of people aged 10–17 years. The arrests of 10–17 year olds accounted for 10 per cent of all arrests; this is the same as the proportion of young people in England and Wales of offending age. Overall, the number of arrests of young people has fallen by 13 per cent between the years ending March 2014 and March 2015. This continues the downward trend seen since the peak in arrests in the year ending March 2007. Since this peak it has fallen by 73 per cent.

Whilst statistics should always be critically assessed it is clear that the media play a crucial role in both interpreting the official data on crime and in disseminating it to the general public. As noted in **Chapter 5**, 'evidence' (especially official statistical 'evidence') certainly does not speak for itself and needs to be carefully interpreted and evaluated. We should always wonder whether certain issues are being neglected, ignored, or filtered out. Perhaps they are just not thought to be newsworthy enough? So, what exactly is not being reported and why is it perhaps being left out?

The profile of young people in custody shows some very clear and shocking patterns in terms of their education and health backgrounds. According to an official report, *Transforming Youth Custody: Putting Education at the Heart of Detention* (2013: 9), half of 15–17 year olds entering public sector young offender institutions were assessed as having the literacy levels expected of 7–11 year olds. The report also found that 18 per cent of sentenced young people in custody had a statement of special educational needs, compared to 3 per cent of the general population, and 27 per cent of young men aged 15–17 in custody felt they had emotional or mental health problems. A study into the background and circumstances of 200 sentenced young people who had been locked up showed that 39 per cent had been on the child protection register or had experienced abuse and neglect.

These broader issues tell us much about the problems and difficulties modern societies face across a range of public policy areas such as education and health. Do you think that such issues get the amount and type of media coverage that they perhaps deserve? If one of the main aims of criminology is to understand criminal behaviour (remember that this is very different from condoning it) then perhaps the answer is a resounding no. Fears about young people in the media are indeed nothing new, but as John Muncie succinctly puts it:

> The recurring fears directed at young people probably tell us more about adult concerns for morality, national security, unemployment, leisure, independence, imperialism and so on than they do about the nature and extent of young offending.
>
> Muncie 2015:81

The mainstream media continue to present young people as folk devils about whom there are periods of moral panic. These two important concepts of media criminology will be the focus of our next section.

The folk devils and moral panics of today

The concepts of moral panic and folk devils have been with us for over 50 years now. Perhaps ironically, it is not unusual to hear both of these terms used by media commentators and the general public alike when referring to perceived threats and fears of 'dangerous people' today. Put simply, the idea of a moral panic concerns an aggressive over-reaction to an event, person, or group of people who appear to threaten the 'moral fabric' of society—that is, society's ideas of right and wrong. The people who present that 'threat' are termed the folk devils and the public reaction is a 'moral' one rather than a general societal or financial panic. The role of the media in creating, maintaining, and perpetuating such panics is often seen as being pivotal in their reporting of events. This reporting, it is argued, is often stereotyped and distorted. The last and often neglected part of this process is the public reaction to such news coverage, which is often to demand that governments do something about a 'problem'. This, in turn, can lead to the government passing tougher laws, meaning that a chain reaction ensues.

Leslie Wilkins (1964) used the term '*deviancy amplification spiral*' to describe the processes through which rather than controlling crime, media reporting, together with police, public, and political reactions, can actually increase it. For instance, an event or form of behaviours is reported in an exaggerated and sensationalised way by the media. The public demand that something be done and governments react accordingly, sometimes giving the police new powers to deal with this perceived 'dangerous' situation. This in turn leads to more sensationalist reporting and the whole spiral continues to whirl.

Stan Cohen and the mods and rockers

Over the years there have been many studies which draw on these concepts, but the most famous (and certainly the first detailed one) was Stan Cohen's (1972) study of the social reactions to the youth subcultures of the Mods and Rockers in 1960s England. In it he charts and analyses the exaggerated and distorted press coverage of the so-called violent mobs marauding through tranquil south coast seaside resorts over bank holiday weekends (see **Figure 7.4**). His book also describes the press and public reaction to all of this. In carrying out his research, Cohen did many things. As he used to recount it, in the evening he stayed out all night partying on the beach and in the morning he would get up and read the tabloid headlines. Then he would put on a suit, sit in a magistrates' court, and listen to how the cases of 'wanton destruction and vandalism' were presented in there. This reconciliation between competing versions of reality is the very stuff that sociological criminology is really

all about. As Cohen warned, this was not about competing versions of reality in the literal sense but more a case of reconciling how the world looked to, and was experienced by, the young people involved, the newspaper readers, and middle class magistrates. Indeed, his book is now, rightly, regarded as being a criminological 'classic' which all criminologists should read at some point (details on the publication can be found in the **further reading** section).

The representation of migrants in the media

A pertinent question now is whether the concepts of folk devils and moral panics still retain their value and power for today's criminologists in trying to understand and explain post millennial crime. We shall consider this through examining the current and recurring fear over immigration and 'immigrants'.

Once you have completed the exercise in **What do you think? 7.5**, it should be clearer to you that a single word or phrase can totally skew our perception of a news story. Again, this harks back to discourse analysis in which the impact of vocabulary and grammar is seen to be of great importance in terms of the consequences of how readers and viewers may come to form their opinions. Consider the recent example of how the *Daily Mail* reported in 2015 about a boatload of mixed-faith migrants caught in

a storm. The story was couched in terms of 'Muslim migrants throwing Christian refugees overboard'—the implication being that migrants of one faith were bad, but refugees of another were good.

Migration is nothing new. People have always feared the outsider; Victorian newspapers warned against Jews, Lascars (sailors from India), and the Irish. Consider **Controversy and debate 7.2** and think a bit more about immigration, the human tragedies which it can cause, and its place in a globally reported world.

In **Conversations 7.1** we hear from Lea Sitkin. Dr Sitkin, who is a lecturer in criminology at the University of Westminster, tells us about her current research which focuses on the media's role in shaping immigration politics in the UK today.

WHAT DO YOU THINK? 7.5

The fear of the 'deviant migrant'

Consider the following newspaper headlines:

EU Ministers meet for crisis talks after hundreds of tourists drown in Mediterranean.

Guardian, 20 April 2015

Towns in the UK are 'swamped' by obese, Cabinet Office Minister warns.

Daily Telegraph, 26 October 2014

Managers who plunder Britain's free health care cost the NHS up to £300 million a year.

Daily Express, 8 April 2015

NHS 'deterring' pregnant students from seeking care.

Huffington Post UK, 28 March 2015

How do you feel about them? Do you feel a sense of outrage or a sense of agreement and acceptance? Now, let's replace a few words. In the first headline replace the word tourists for migrants, in the second, obese for EU migrants, the third, managers for migrants and in the fourth, students for migrants. If we do so, you will see the *real and actual* headlines as they appeared in the tabloid, middle-brow, and broadsheet press. (You can find examples of many similar newspaper headlines relating to migration in the archived media section of the MigrationWatchUK website www.migrationwatchuk.com.)

Do you feel differently now? Why? What is it about the issue of migration and migrants which is so emotive (that is, something which produces an intense feeling)?

CONTROVERSY AND DEBATE 7.2

Migrants and crime

The UK census is a complete count of all people and households which is carried out by the Office for National Statistics every ten years. It provides a substantial amount of interesting information—such as how many people claim their religion to be that of Jedi Knight. But on a more serious note, we can look at it to examine the changing make-up of the UK's population.

Migration to the UK has a long and complicated history. The first census was in 1801 but it did not start to count the birth places of people until 1851. This would indicate that whilst migration to the UK is not new, the pace and the scale of migration has increased dramatically since the second world war (1945 onwards) and particularly since the 1990s. As **Table 7.2** shows, the percentage of the total population of England and Wales that was born abroad has increased by nearly 50 per cent between 1991 and 2011 (the date of the last census). (Figures derived from mediawatch.com, accessed 29 April 2015.)

People have come to the UK from all over the world (Africa, Ireland, South Africa, New Zealand, Europe, the Indian Subcontinent, China) at different periods in history for a variety of reasons, but social reactions are the main focus here.

Certainly since the 1950s, these reactions have ranged from hatred, racial discrimination, and violence to outright fear. Recent fears (and media reports) have centred on the notion that the country is becoming overpopulated, which is unsustainable, and that this will put a strain on a range of public services, as well as causing unemployment and the general decline of the economic well-being of the country. This was a key plank of the 'Leave' campaign during the 2016 EU referendum in the United Kingdom; prominent politicians, such as Michael Gove and Boris Johnson, publicly supported a statement which argued that:

Class sizes will rise [in schools] and waiting lists [for seeing a GP and housing etc...] will lengthen if we don't tackle free movement. As the euro crisis continues, more people from southern Europe will want to escape unemployment and austerity in their countries by coming to the UK. Their arrival will put further strain on schools and hospitals. Last year, 77,000 jobseekers from the EU came to the UK. ... The Government failed to achieve this during the renegotiation of our membership. If we vote to remain in the EU then continued free movement for jobseekers will place considerable pressure on the wages of low paid British workers.

http://www.telegraph.co.uk/news/2016/06/04/michael-gove-and-boris-johnson-tell-david-cameron-youve-deceived/

Imposing limits on immigration certainly seems to have public support. A recent Social Attitudes Survey Report (2014) states that 77 per cent of the population want to see a reduction of immigration into Britain. This includes support for the idea from people who are themselves second or third generation migrants into the UK.

Let's look at the issue from a criminological perspective and consider what you understand by the term migrant. The over-simplification of this category masks a diversity of different groups of people. The UK census uses the term 'foreign born', but even this is perhaps too simplistic; people migrate for many reasons. They may be economic migrants, they may be asylum seekers, they may be legal or illegal migrants, or they may be family members of previous generations of (now settled) migrants.

One of the main fears over migrants has focused on crime. We often read that there is a migrant crime wave. See, for example, **Figure 7.5** where the first image displays a headline using a sensationalist statistic. The second image is a table of the ten 'worst offenders' by

Year	Foreign born population	Total population	Percentage of total population that was born abroad
1851	100,000	17,900,000	0.6
1951	1,875,000	43,700,000	4.3
1991	3,625,000	49,900,000	7.3
2001	4,600,000	52,500,000	8.8
2011	7,500,000	56,000,000	13.4

Table 7.2 The foreign born population of England and Wales, the total population, and the percentage of the population that was foreign born
Source: Figures derived from www.mediawatch.com

Figure 7.5 Screenshots taken from *Daily Mail* Online.

Source: Daily Mail online

nationality, *accused* of crime in London, not necessarily convicted. Are such arguments and popular fears supported by evidence?

It is just not the raw figures of reported crime that media commentators have focused on in constructing the image of the dangerous, criminal migrant. They have also concentrated on the prison population figures with such headlines as:

> Immigrant crime soars with foreign prisoners rising; SHOCK new figures today reveal an increase of nearly 40 per cent in the number of Romanian criminals in Britain's jails.

> *Daily Express,* 17 February 2013

Although such headlines are misleading (many will perhaps read this as 40 per cent of the prison population being Romanian rather than there being an increase of 40 per cent of Romanian people being incarcerated;

over what time period?) the Ministry of Justice (2013) confirms that the number of foreign nationals in prison has indeed increased over the last 10 years. In thinking about the so-called 'facts' of crime, such as that migrant groups represent over 14 per cent of the total prison population in England and Wales—and are alleged to commit more crime—we need to ask more searching questions and do some more detailed research. We have to go beyond the headlines and stories. What sorts of questions do you think are relevant here? Here are a few to get you started:

- What is the general age and gender of most migrants? Why might this be important?

- What are the unemployment rates amongst different migrant communities?

- What are the offending rates for different migrant groups?

- What are the different offences which different migrant groups commit?

- Are migrant groups policed differently?

- Are there sentencing differences for different migrant groups?

In researching the answers to some of these questions you may just find that migrant groups are perhaps not more likely to be criminals.

CONVERSATIONS 7.1

Immigration politics and the media—with Dr Lea Sitkin

Although my DPhil focused on irregular immigration and the different methods that countries use to control irregular immigrants, I have recently moved away from analysing the role of the state and instead am focusing on the media's role in shaping immigration politics in the UK today. It's a funny thing: whenever I tell people that I work on issues around immigration, they always say something like 'that's a hot topic!' and 'you'll never be out of a job!' Pick up any newspaper today, and it's very likely that there will be at least one article about immigration; it may even be the topic of a front page headline or a double page spread. Immigration is, in other words, big news; it has been for a very long time and it is likely to be for some time yet. The key questions I'm looking at are: how are immigrants being represented in the media, and how important is the media

in stoking public fears around immigration?

The first thing to say is that media representations of immigrants in the UK range from the negative (focusing on illegality of entry, economic burden to the country, criminality, and the challenges of expulsion) to more positive coverage (focusing on immigrants' plights, their abilities and contributions to the country, and solutions to humanitarian crises) (Picard 2014: 3). While certain newspapers (the *Guardian*, the *Independent*) are more likely to give positive accounts of immigration than others (such as the *Daily Mail*), there are times when a sympathetic consensus is reached across different media outlets. This was the case around the death of Alan Kurdi, a 3 year old Syrian child who drowned in the Mediterranean Sea as his family

Figure 7.6 Body of Alan Kurdi, a 3 year old Syrian child who drowned in the Mediterranean Sea as his family attempted to travel to Greece
Source: AP Photo/DHA

attempted to travel to Greece. His image was used in newspapers across the globe; a surge in donations to refugee charities soon followed (see **Figure 7.6**).

Overall, however, you will be unsurprised to hear that media portrayals of immigration are pretty negative (Gabrielatos and Baker 2008). KhosraviNik (2009) found that the representation of immigrant issues in newspapers in Europe largely emphasised economic burden and criminality. Will Allen and Scott Blinder (2013) found that the term 'illegal' is by far the most common word associated with 'immigrant' in British newspapers; other words that also regularly feature in such stories include those which emphasise the large number of immigrants to this country ('thousands', 'millions', 'influx'), as well as water-metaphors, which evoke fears of being overwhelmed by immigration ('floods', 'waves', 'swamp'). Most recently, a study by Alex Balch and Ekaterina Balabanova in 2015 found that UK press coverage of immigration is becoming increasingly 'dehumanised'. The main change was that liberal newspapers like the *Guardian* and the *Independent* are increasingly reporting about immigration in a fashion similar to that normally associated with the right-wing or tabloid press: that is, focusing on migrants as security threats and burdens on the welfare state.

The way that crimes are reported is also influenced by whether the perpetrator is a member of an immigrant community. One of my undergraduate dissertation students compared articles on two sex abuse cases—the Rotherham and the Derby cases—in which the perpetrators were of Pakistani-British and White-British origin respectively. She found that 'offenders of Asian ethnicity are framed in a more negative light than offenders of white ethnicity'. In addition, there were far fewer articles about the Derby case to begin with. Thus we can see that the study of media representation must look both at what is reported and how it is reported, and what is not reported in the first place.

The extent to which the media does actually have an influence on public opinion is, however, open to debate. Agenda setting theory describes the ability of media to influence the salience (or prominence) of a topic within the public agenda. Media influence studies show that topics given significance and prominence gain salience with the general public—in other words, the public thinks the issue is important. However, if the media omit a topic, it reduces in importance in the minds of the public (Picard 2014): literally out of sight and out of mind. There is strong evidence to support the notion that media coverage is a key factor in influencing people's views on immigration. A US-based study in 2010 found that 'individuals are most likely to identify immigration as an [important problem] as the media's attention to the issue increases … simply put, the degree to which people are concerned about the issue varies with media coverage of the issue, not with real-world patterns relevant to opinion formation about immigration (i.e., changes in immigrant populations, terrorist threat level, or immigrant crime statistics)' (Dunaway et al. 2010: 374). A recent experimental study by Scott Blinder, which involved a representative sample of just under 2,000 British respondents, showed that subtle changes to news frames significantly impact on individuals' estimates of the size of the immigrant group, perceptions of who immigrants are, and immigration policy preferences. A cross-national study in 2015 found a positive relationship between exposure to news about immigration and crime and the likelihood to vote for an anti-immigrant party (Burscher et al. 2015).

However, agenda setting does not address the fundamental issue of how the topic becomes part of the media agenda in the first place. As Stuart Hall commented in his seminal work, 'Policing the Crisis' (1978 [2013]), 'the media do not themselves autonomously create news items; rather they are "cued in" to specific news topics by regular and reliable institutional sources … ' (p.60). Further, the narratives used by the media need to have cultural resonance with the audience. As I told my students in a recent lecture, a newspaper article on

immigrants eating a lot of broccoli does not have cultural resonance because people would not care; it would seem, somehow, to come out of the blue and to be a pointless report. By contrast, the topic of immigration and crime, or immigration and terrorism, does have cultural relevance; it fits in with pre-existing anxieties and discourses; it, somehow, makes sense to the audience.

Thus, while the media undoubtedly have an effect on public opinion, it would be a mistake to see the relationship between the two as unidirectional. The relationship between media and public opinion is, instead, a complex one, involving both the production of ways of seeing the world, and a reproduction of previously held values, beliefs, and attitudes. Much as we might wish that the media reported on immigration in a more measured and responsible fashion, we also face the uphill and personal struggle of consuming media in a critical and reflective manner.

Dr Lea Sitkin, Lecturer in Criminology, University of Westminster

Dr Sitkin succinctly summarises some of the most important themes of this chapter so far. For instance, she discusses the operation of news values, how newspaper agendas are set, the creation of folk devils, the highly complex relationship

between the printed media and its influence on public opinion, and so on. We will now move away from our discussion and analysis of newspaper representations of crime, criminality and its control, to consider other forms of media.

Crime novels, television, and film

Name a detective.

Unless you happen to know a member of your local CID (or have a criminal record yourself!) the chances are that the name you came up with will belong to someone who doesn't exist: Sherlock Holmes (see **Figure 7.7**), Lord Peter Wimsey, Inspector Morse, Vera, Hercule Poirot, Miss Marple … The solving of crime as entertainment has been a feature of crime media for over 150 years and it would seem that we are nowhere near getting tired of it yet.

Take the case of Inspector Jonathan 'Jack' Whicher. A real-life Victorian detective, he was involved in the notorious Road Hill House case of 1860, in which a three-year old boy called Francis Saville Kent was found murdered. Inspector Whicher was convinced that the boy's half-sister, Constance Kent, had killed him, but at the time society could not face the idea that a middle-class girl of 16 could do anything so dreadful and the case against her was dropped. The inspector was seen as having disgraced the newly-formed detective branch of the police, which was already struggling against the idea that a working man could ask questions of a gentleman in his own home, and his personal reputation suffered greatly. However, in 1865, Constance confessed to the killing. Having been

proved right all along, Inspector Whicher went on to be involved in several other high-profile cases and finally died a successful and respected man.

This example illustrates the way that the idea of a detective was being formed in the public imagination. The 19th century novelists Charles Dickens and Wilkie Collins both based characters on Inspector Whicher, and the solitary, often misunderstood figure of a crime-solver went on to be central to most of our well-known detective fiction. But Inspector Whicher's story goes even further. In 2008, Kate Summerscale wrote a best-selling book about the Road Hill House murder, which was televised as a drama in 2011. Following this, a further set of stories were filmed in which the real Inspector Whicher solved cases that had never actually happened and arrested people who never actually existed. Genuine crime (let us not forget Francis, who died at the start of all this) has blurred into fiction, and it can sometimes be hard to see which is which. We now have crime fiction in which the detective is Jane Austen or Oscar Wilde, in books by Stephanie Barron and Giles Brandreth respectively. The boundaries of fact and fiction are loosening and our attitudes to crime in the written word are also shifting.

however bad—and state sponsored murder made an uneasy blend of justice and entertainment, just as public hangings and beheadings did.

The study of crime fiction by literary scholars is something which some more culturally attuned criminologists are now beginning to explore and study. For them, this popular form of criminology does not only offer us another way of analysing the importance of cultural representations of crime, criminality, and its control; it can also help us to critically engage with broader issues such as how crime fiction (in its classic, modern, and postmodern forms) can act as socio-political critique, as well as allowing a discussion of themes of violence, urban decay, and changing identity politics (for some good overviews of the field by literary scholars see Horsley 2005, Knight 2010, and Priestman 2012).

This early form of sensationalist literature has evolved into the groaning shelves of any 'True Crime' section in high street book shops. Titles can range from the scholarly and academic, such as studies on applied criminal psychology, to the lurid and shocking 'misery lit', in which victims tell their stories and are inevitably described as 'inspirational'. Of course we hope that the authors find some kind of healing and peace from writing these books, but they do raise an important question: how do books about true crime alter our opinions? Do we learn more about suffering, or do we assume that all such victims will rise above their past and therefore see the crime itself as less horrifying? How do we feel about people who remain deeply affected by what has happened to them—are we less sympathetic or supportive?

Figure 7.7 A Sherlock Holmes film poster (Dir. Albert Parker 1922)

Source: Goldwyn Pictures/Public domain

It is often argued that the first crime story is that of Cain and Abel in the Bible, and the use of text to record crime and our reactions to it has remained enduringly popular over the following 2,000 years. Stories of Robin Hood are essentially about a forest-dwelling 'mugger', after all. From the 1700s onwards, confessions of criminals on the gallows were printed and sold as souvenirs for a penny a time to the crowds which gathered to watch public executions, often including moral verses to instruct and warn the reader:

Comfort and peace affrighted fled

From our accursed place

The spectres of the Murdered Dead

Grinn'd daily in our face …

This was the grim message to anyone attending the execution of Margaret Joyer in 1836 (she had poisoned eight people, including her father; she confessed to the crimes after seeing a victim's ghost, and for killing her father she also had her hand cut off before being hanged). Poetry—

Criminology in film

Perhaps one of the most popular ways in which stories of crime and punishment are told is through film, both fictional or factual; sometimes a mixture of both. Since the days of first silent and then 'talkie' pictures, people have used crime as a theme in fiction, documentaries, and (as with books and TV), sometimes a mix of both.

Surprisingly, it is only in fairly recent times that crime films have been studied and analysed by criminologists—for example in the work of Rafter (2006) and Rafter and Brown (2011). Films are undoubtedly a rich source of material for the criminologist.

The popular criminology that arises from crime film is something that has a serious and thought-provoking side which may inform our attitudes and knowledge (including those of people who work in the criminal justice system). By examining films over time, we can chart the shifts in public attitudes and expectations, and changes in the limits of what is acceptable viewing. It also gives us a chance to reflect on the concerns and anxieties that were relevant to the film-makers and their intended audience. For instance, the first film to receive an X-rated certificate in Britain was *Cosh Boy* (1953, Dir. Lewis Gilbert). From the opening reel of the film we get an unambiguous statement of the central focus of the plot which reflected the fears at the time. In a very serious, almost 'public service broadcast' tone we are told that:

> By itself, the 'Cosh' is the cowardly implement of a contemporary evil; in association with 'Boy', it marks a post-war tragedy, the juvenile delinquent. 'Cosh Boy' portrays starkly the development of a young criminal, an enemy of society at sixteen. Our Judges and Magistrates and the Police, whose stern duty it is to resolve the problem, agree that its origins lie mainly in the lack of parental control and early discipline. The problem exists –and we cannot escape it by closing our eyes. This film is presented in the hope that it will contribute towards stamping out this social evil.

Similarly, the opening lines of a very popular and award-winning police drama released in the same decade, *The Blue Lamp* (1950, Dir. Basil Dearden), warn us that:

> To this man until today, the crime wave was nothing but a newspaper headline. What stands between the ordinary public and this outbreak of crime? What protection has the man in the street against the armed threat to life and property? At the Old Bailey Mr. Justice Fidmore in passing sentence for a crime of robbery with violence gave this plain answer; 'This is perhaps of another illustration of the disaster caused by insufficient numbers of police. I have no doubt that one of the best preventives of crime is the regular uniformed police officer on the beat.'

The focus and the intentions of both films are hardly subtle. Both are perhaps good examples of early 'traditional' crime films. Indeed, in its opening credits, *The Blue Lamp* thanked for Metropolitan Police for its input and advice,

and the screenplay was written by an ex-policeman. Interestingly, *The Blue Lamp* inspired a popular television series, *Dixon of Dock Green*, which ran from 1955 to 1976. The central character, the avuncular PC George Dixon, was a very different creature to subsequent television police detectives such as Detective Inspector Barlow (*Z-Cars*, 1962–78) or Detective Inspector Jack Regan (*The Sweeney*, 1974–78). Both of these later television series had a grittier realism and dealt with issues such as police corruption and violence, and the criminal was not always 'bang to rights' but could instead be framed or beaten into confession. There were also three films based on *The Sweeney*, the last being in 2012 (Dir. Nick Love) and staring popular rap artist Ben Drew (also known as Plan B).

It is also worth remembering that at the time, films were made in the belief that they would only be viewed in a specific social setting (a local cinema) by people who would experience them as part of a group. DVD or VHS technology was not available at the time when *The Blue Lamp* and other classic films were made, so watching them in the cinema was the only option. This gave studios the chance to put across a message that they knew would be seen by dozens of people at a time who, probably, would all be from the same community and have the same kind of outlook. The targeting of films to a certain type of audience was therefore always going to influence content and distribution. Having said that, as with other forms of media we have discussed in this chapter, crime films can be looked at in many different ways. After all, if we were all to sit down and watch the same film and then discuss it, the chances are that we would pick up on different themes and issues, some of which may be controversial or ambiguous. Thus the study of crime films also gives us a chance to compare the messages they put across and to assess them in the light of more conventional criminological knowledge, as well as to contrast them with other types of media content.

Analysing crime film and the criminological imagination

It is helpful to take a quick view of a theoretical analysis at this point. The American criminologist Nicole Rafter (2006) makes a basic and broad distinction between two main types of crime film: the traditional and the radical.

Traditional crime films (such as *The Blue Lamp* discussed earlier) are usually simple tales of goodies and baddies, in which the goodies (usually the police) always catch their man—and it is indeed normally a man. The criminal justice system triumphs and fair punishment is seen to be handed out. Criminals are guilty and are seen

to get their comeuppance. In Britain, until the 1950s, such films generally supported the class system and indeed characters who didn't 'know their place' were either there for comic relief or else got into trouble, as we have seen with *Cosh Boy* and *The Blue Lamp*.

Most of the films we talked about in the previous section are fairly conventional. Bad guys get caught by good guys and justice prevails; the pretty girl who has been led astray may be allowed to find a good man who is prepared to forgive her past.

Radical films, on the other hand, aim to question the established order and its attitudes. How many of you have watched a film and ended up identifying with, or feeling sympathy for, a main character who had actually done dreadful things (instead of merely being falsely accused)? A good example is Uma Thurman's professional assassin in *Kill Bill* (2004, Dir. Quentin Tarantino). The plot essentially centres around a small child being taken away from her father, the only parent she has ever known, by a mass murderer. And yet the film manipulates our sympathies so we are pleased when Thurman's character manages to finally *Kill Bill* and ride off with her daughter.

Radical films are also more critical of the workings of the criminal justice system and the people who work within it, not hesitating to portray corrupt police and prison officers or flaws within the jury system. Indeed, in some films the corrupt becomes the hero, or the flaws are exploited to the criminal's advantage. A more radical approach to studying crime film therefore foregrounds the potential ideological functions of the genre. Yar (2010) provides a good introductory discussion of how criminologists can theoretically understand and analyse the cinematic constructions of crime.

Crime film as a distinct genre is a very broad category and we need to remember that crime can also feature in films where it is not the main focus of the story. However, if we look at films in which the main narrative thread is connected to crime or criminals, we can start to break the genre down into various components or sub-types: courtroom dramas, gangster films, police procedurals, heist films, serial killer films, prison break films, and so on (for a fuller discussion of these see Rafter 2006). However, the one we will concentrate on in this part of the chapter is the prison film.

The prison film

What do we really know about prisons and the lives of the people within them? Prisons are, after all, a sealed-off world hidden behind high walls and only inhabited by certain groups, and so most people probably have very limited factual knowledge about them. But if we pause for a moment and think about prison as described by the tabloid press, we can build a picture of places full of scary and dangerous inmates, living in pleasant and easy conditions. They have easy access to phones, the Internet, and drugs, and are pampered because of their 'human rights'. This all gives an impression that prison conditions should be made harsher, or at least not exceed the lifestyle of the poorest members of free society, and that crime can actually pay (see Mason 2006, 2007 for an interesting analysis of these issues).

Similar memes (a way of spreading of ideas and concepts) can be found in some prison films, which often feature generic elements such as the nervous new inmate, the old lag with a heart of gold, someone who has been wrongly convicted, an unfaithful spouse, naked shower scenes, and violence in the exercise yard. Obviously such films are watched for entertainment rather than as factual studies, but the point is that they, like the tabloids, deserve deeper analysis. Prison films can contain more than meets the eye—can they actually be used to inform and even to reform?

According to Wilson and O'Sullivan (2004: 9), prison films do indeed have the potential to function as a way to get broader messages across. Indeed, they argue that prison films have five such functions. These functions are:

1. A *revelatory* function—bringing to light practices which are or should be disapproved of.
2. A *benchmarking* function—helping to set standards of decency for what is and what is not acceptable practice in prisons.
3. A *defence of gains* function—attempting to combat backsliding by penal authorities on gains established by functions (1) and (2).
4. A *'news'/memory* function—spreading the news that certain events happened and keeping alive a memory of them, e.g. prison riots and massacres.
5. A *humanising/empathy* function—representing prisoners as people in an attempt to counter processes of de-personalisation and de-humanisation.

These themes and ideas can then lead to wider awareness of realities within the prison system, and to campaigns for change. *Starred Up* (2013, Dir. David Mackenzie) is a film about a violent teenager who is sent to an adult prison from a young offenders' institution and who for the first time is able to form a relationship with his father, who is also an inmate there. Many reviews of the film commented positively on the way that the young man was shown as having been damaged by his upbringing: Emma Simmonds, for example, describes it on the website www.film.list.co.uk as a film that 'manages to highlight the consequences of confinement, staff corruption and the power structures that exist between inmates and officers', and Chris Bumbray on www.JoBlo.com commented that the lead character was clearly violent: 'although they keep him sympathetic in that it's clear that his rage is a by-product of a vicious upbringing'. So while the film is on one level simply a story about a young man who has committed crime, it also brings into focus the impact of multiple forms of disadvantage, domestic violence, and the importance of supportive relationships in a child's life. The harsh brutality of day-to-day life for many prisoners is also portrayed; none of which would be immediately apparent from the film's title or the cover of the DVD box.

Media classification and censorship

Popular entertainment and public anxieties

Anyone who has heard Frank Sinatra singing *Mack the Knife* will be listening to a modern(ish) take on an aria from the *Beggar's Opera*, a play written by John Gay and first performed in 1728. The original opera features highwaymen, prostitutes, debtors, and thieves, using them to mock the upper classes. Needless to say it was hugely popular, but even in its own day the piece was considered scandalous for the way it satirised the elite and made criminals into heroes (Mullison 2009).

Throughout history there have always been concerns and panics about the possible harmful effects that media and forms of popular entertainment are thought to have on people. These concerns far outweigh any ideas that there may actually be some benefits. Even Shakespeare was affected when in 1818 an English doctor called Thomas Bowdler published a version of the plays with all the rude and violent bits cut out so they could be read by genteel women and children without causing offence.

Such fears reached their heights with the rising popularity of cinema-going in the 1920s and 1930s. During this era, film studios were governed by a Production Code which forbade certain things from being shown. Some of these would still be considered problematic today, for example showing a child's genitals, or scenes of drug-taking, but others give us an indication of the values of the era: the use of words such as 'damn' or 'hell' were forbidden and 'God' could only be used if it was being said as part of a religious service.

By the 1930s most towns had at least one cinema, many had several, and film-going hit its peak in the 1940s. There was an obvious use of film for propaganda during the Second World War, and in some cases, films such as *Mrs Miniver* (1942, Dir. William Wyler) are credited with having had a direct impact on the direction of the war itself. By the end of hostilities, the power of film had not waned; films showing Nazi atrocities were shown to bolster the morale and resolve of a tired and bankrupt Britain. Newsreels usually ran for three days, but the film showing the liberation of the Belsen concentration camp ran for a week; with over 30 million cinema tickets being sold in a week in 1945, this meant that the appalling images reached a huge audience (Reilly 1998: p.61). Interestingly, some US states would not show the films as they were felt to be in breach of the Production Code's veto on showing other countries in a poor light.

Although cinema-going declined in the 1950s and 1960s, the fears did not subside, and instead transferred themselves effortlessly to the new technology that was finding its way into people's living rooms: television. By 1964 there was a Clean Up TV campaign, which was aimed at women who were felt to be the natural guardians of family values. The campaign was run by the formidable Mary Whitehouse who, with her National Viewers' and Listeners' Association, accused the BBC of corrupting the nation's morals and failing to ensure that programmes were sufficiently religious in tone. Similar campaigns continue today with organisations such as MediaWatch-UK who work for 'socially responsible media and against content which is potentially harmful'. This group and others like it have extended the concerns about harm and social responsibility into new areas, such as social media and computer games.

Crime and music

As well as visual media, music too has been a cause of concern, ever since a dance called the waltz brought public indecency into the ballroom (men and women dancing within six inches of each other caused outrage all over 19th century Europe). We may laugh, but in recent years the Aliso Niguel High School in California has asked students to accept 'dancing guidelines' that ban 'lewd and lascivious dancing such as "freaking"' (school website, 2016). The riots in London in 2011 were blamed by some politicians and media commentators on gangsta rap, hard core hip-hop, and a resulting thuggish youth culture (and there are perhaps legitimate concerns about the sexual violence in some bands' lyrics). In the aftermath of the so-called London riots, the *Daily Mirror* journalist Paul Routledge (2011) posed the question: 'Is rap music to blame for encouraging this culture of violence?' For him the solution was an obvious one: 'I blame the pernicious culture of hatred around rap music, which glorifies violence and loathing of authority (especially the police but including parents), exalts trashy materialism and raves about drugs … I would ban the broadcasting of poisonous rap'.

Forms of popular music have, throughout history, excited strong opinions and often caused controversy. For example, going back to the 1920s and 1930s, it was not just Nazi Germany where governments banned the public broadcasting of jazz (see **Figure 7.8**). This was not because of any debate on its musical merits, but simply because as an art form it has clear associations with artists who were black or Jewish, such as Louis Armstrong or Benny Goodman. Jazz was therefore portrayed as degenerate, obscene, and racially alien. It was banned in Soviet Russia, where many regarded it an expression of

Figure 7.8 A catalogue image from a Munich Exhibition organised by the official Nazi cultural watchdog in 1937. The offensive beliefs about race, Judaism and 'Entartete Musik' or 'degenerate music' as illustrated here need no explanation

Source: Public domain

bourgeois individualism (with its focus on improvisation or instant composition), which ran counter to the ideals of Soviet communism, as well as in a racially divided US.

In America, it was argued that jazz came out of the Southern states, where older generations and religious groups worried that it led to such dangerous habits such as drinking and smoking. Perhaps even more worryingly for them, jazz could lead to black and white men and women coming together to enjoy daring dances such as the lindy hop. Such integration would eventually, it was argued, lead to a decline in the 'racial purity' of the nation. Similar debates over the perceived 'dangerousness' of musical styles continue; most recently within the 'grime scene' and Form 696, a risk assessment process which allows local authorities to cancel gigs at a moment's notice. Questions on the form relate to what are perceived as being 'risky genres' of music, such as grime, garage, rap, reggae, or R&B. A number of MCs have argued that this amounts to a form of racial profiling and police associations with music, race, and violence (see Hancox 2009).

All of this is very interesting, but there is a more serious note: the clear historical continuities we have been thinking about here should lead us to consider broader questions over whether media forms and popular entertainment should, due to their potentially dangerous (and criminogenic) consequences, be regulated and censored.

New technology, new media, and new fears

Playing with violence through gaming

Let us now apply these ideas to the 21st century by considering one current fear and panic: the popularity and perceived dangerousness of playing video games. The development of these games in terms of content and graphics (and the ways in which it is possible to play them now through gaming consoles, a personal computer, smart phones, and online) has been staggering. The mainstream popular video games of the 1970s (such as *Pac Man*, *Asteroids*, and *Pong*) were usually only encountered in games arcades and now seem very, very tame in comparison to some of today's most popular products, such as *Call of Duty*, *Manhunt*, *Warcraft*, or *Mortal Kombat*. Most of the biggest-selling games are not of a violent nature—the most popular of all time include *Tetris*, *Wii Sports*, and *Super Mario* (http://www.techtimes.com/articles/32614/20150213/15-best-selling-video-games-of-all-time.htm)—but societal concerns (and media panics) have focused on the increasingly violent content of other games.

There are also fears about the possible effects that playing them may have on a gamer. Of course, there are legitimate concerns about some aspects of these games, ranging from sleep deprivation in children who play them into the early hours to the potential for abusive contact between adult and child online players (not to mention fears of computer game addiction). The point to note here is that video games are now a global multi-billion pound industry. They give all other forms of media popular entertainment (including the Hollywood film industry) a run for their money in terms of the time people invest in interacting with them and in total sales and profits made.

The game on which we will focus here is the *Grand Theft Auto* (GTA) series. Since the first GTA game was released in 1997 it has become one of the most popular games ever made. It has been estimated that the series as a whole has sold in excess of 150 million copies. This particular game is infamous both for the controversy it has generated and for its clear criminal themes: gang wars, murder, drug dealing, coercive sexual relations, prostitution, drunk driving, and torture are all there for you to 'play' with.

The game, which is set in slightly fictionalised American cities, is essentially one in which gamers adopt a character and attempt to negotiate their progress through a violent criminal underworld. GTA has proved to be controversial, not least in terms of accusations of it being sexist and racist; the game does indeed contain many examples of sexualising women and racially stereotyping particular ethnic groups (see Garrelts 2006 for a collection of scholarly essays on the contested cultural product that is GTA). More importantly, for our purposes here, several law suits have been filed against the makers and distributors of the game on the grounds that it has caused people to behave violently and even that it has driven players to murder, such as a case in Bangkok in 2008 where a youth killed a taxi driver, which led to the game being banned in Thailand (Nopporn Wong-Anan 2008) (although it could be argued that this too is nothing new, as in the 1970s there were fears that playing certain records backwards could reveal a message that incited suicide). After considering the discussion in this section, now look at the questions raised in **What do you think? 7.6**.

The problem of media effects— are media criminogenic?

How many times have you read in the press that the perpetrator of some awful crime regularly watched 'video nasties' or regularly played particularly violent video games? For example, the Norwegian killer Anders Breivik is alleged to have played violent games before carrying out his shootings (Pidd 2012 (www.theguardian.com/world/2012/apr/19/anders-breivik-call-of-duty)) and even threatened to go on hunger strike unless he was allowed access to better games in prison (Saul 2014 (www.independent.co.uk/news/world/europe/anders-breivik-demands-better-video-games-and-

threatens-hunger-strike-over-jail-hell-9130592.html)). This argument seems to chime with many people. It seems self-evident and intuitive that there is a link, but are the popular imagination and such common sense understandings correct? Even if it could be proved for an individual case, would the same conclusions apply to everyone who watched that particular video or played that particular game? Psychologists (and others) have long been interested in finding out what effects (if any) may arise from watching a violent or pornographic film, listening to music with aggressive, sexist, and racist lyrics or playing violent shoot 'em up—or 'Shmup'—video games.

Imagine that we all sat down together to watch a particular news item, read a lead story in a paper, listen to the same piece of music, or watch the same crime film. Do you think that we would all interpret it in the exactly the same way? The answer is probably not. The fascinating thing about watching crime films, for instance, is that they spark debate and conversations. In short, we all decode media messages in (often very) different ways; just eavesdrop conversations on buses and trains. You can learn a lot about a popular soap opera's tale of a murder, and who may have done it, without even watching.

Early experimental research by behavioural psychologists in the 1950s and 1960s argued that people somehow learned behaviour (including violent and aggressive behaviour) through watching television and interacting with other media forms. Is it as straightforward and simple as all of this? Can we really separate media effects from other possible influences such as the parental, cultural, or psychological factors in our lives? How long do such effects last for? Can consuming media even have positive effects, or can watching routine atrocity deepen our abhorrence of it? The amount of research carried out over the years on this subject would probably fill several books as big as this one.

In a review on the continuing problems of media effects research, Sonia Livingstone notes that the evidence from available research is contradictory in nature (Livingstone in Curran and Gurevitch, 1996). She argues that it would be sensible to agree with Huesmann and Malamuth's (1986: pp. 1–2) conclusion over 25 years ago that:

> it seems fair to say that the majority of researchers in the area are now convinced that excessive violence in the media increases the likelihood that at least some viewers will behave more violently.

while:

> a significant minority of dedicated researchers have remained unconvinced that media violence significantly influences real life behavior.

Another way to express this would be to paraphrase the much quoted conclusions of Schramm et al. (1961); for some in some conditions it could be harmful, for others it could even be beneficial, but for most it might be neither of these things. In short, we simply do not know.

Cybercrime

It would be true to say that the development and use of media technology since the 1990s has been staggering. Indeed, for many people today, it's hard to imagine a world without Facebook, even though it wasn't launched until 2004. Until relatively recently, the day-to-day use of the Internet, something we now take for granted, was something that the vast majority of people simply didn't do. Estimates vary, but it is fair to say that in 2000, around only 4 million people worldwide had access to the Internet, as opposed to approximately 3 billion in 2014. Historically, developments in media technology have always resulted in new fears. Fears of crime, fears of subversion—usually fears held by the rulers and the elite, who see technology (rightly) as being a way in which the population can organise itself, and probably get up to no good whilst they are about it. This fear is deep-rooted in our past. For example, people in Tudor England risked death for owning a printed prayer book in English; the London riots of 2011 were widely reported as being coordinated via BlackBerry Messenger. Today we have fears and anxieties around new technologies and developments in social media and we continue to experience this same (over) reaction.

The term cybercrime is an extremely broad one that refers to any criminal activity which involves, or takes place within, a technological network. The term 'cyberspace' is usually used to describe this environment. In this chapter we will be mostly focusing on the Internet, but you should bear in mind that cybercrime can involve a multitude of technologies, such as text or telephone services. You also need to consider the impact of the so-called digital divide, which refers to the fact that access to the Internet is not globally equal, whether due to poverty or the lack of the necessary infrastructure. It can also be affected by political ideologies, like China's restriction of access to search engines such as Google.

The Internet is a prime example of how crime and criminals (and perhaps, at a slower rate, policing and regulatory agencies) have adapted to technology. Our fears and reactions have adapted too. Cybercrime is indeed a huge issue and concern which cannot be covered in detail here, however recent fears have been linked to the Internet and include issues such as those listed below:

- **Identity theft**—There are many news stories which warn people to protect their personal information such as banking details and when making online transactions.

- **Hacking**—Recent scandals involving journalists listening to messages mean that the crime reporter has become accused of being the criminal.

- **Fraud**—We now have subtle (and the not-so-subtle) methods in use, like the exploitation of lonely men and women who fall prey to fraudulent 'lonely hearts' adverts; there is also fraudulent activity of a financial nature like 'phishing', where criminals try to gain personal information to use in online thefts.

- **Hate crime**—Extreme religious, disablist, homophobic groups all find a voice online; this can be general or focused on an individual, such as the recent Twitter threats against women who campaigned for a female face on English banknotes.

- **Pornography**—Not always strictly illegal and damaging, but you might want to think about how consuming adult porn may become addictive. There are growing concerns about how it can affect people's real life sexual expectations and relationships, particularly amongst the young, who may see it as a form of sex education.

- **Civil unrest**—As we mentioned earlier, technology can be used to organise specific actions, but can also be used to co-ordinate wider insurgency. Groups of so-called 'hacktivists' claim to be able to lead mass hacking of other sites to cause disruption, or to release sensitive information. Others, such as the website 'Guido Fawkes' and the group 'Anonymous', have even been accused of hacking in order to discredit politicians and controversial campaigns.

- **Cyber-terrorism**—The recruitment, radicalisation, and instruction of those who wish to commit criminal or terrorist acts.

One of the biggest fears connected with all of these issues is the problem of control and policing. Some web content is hard to trace, using encryption or so-called 'dark' Internet networks to conceal authors or to hide the origin of content. In other cases, a site is owned in one country where laws and standards are different to those of the people using it—who may be exposed to content which is technically illegal in their country of residence. The pace of the growth of technology often means that policing agencies are playing a game of 'catch up' both in terms of resourcing and expertise.

As you are probably beginning to realise, cybercrime is a huge subject and one which could fill several books on its own (see the collection of papers edited by Jewkes and Yar (2009) for fuller discussion of forms of cybercrime). In **New frontiers 7.1** we will explore one aspect of it—young people's use of technology and the potential risks and dangers it may involve.

Young people's use of the Internet

Risk, e-safety, exploitation, and the digital tattoo

Consider for a moment your own use of technology and consumption of media in your everyday lives. For instance, are you an active member of a social networking site? If so, what do you use it for? Do you own a smart phone? Do you illegally download films or music? Do you play online games, alone or with others? Do you use platforms such as Skype to stay in touch with friends and family members? Have you ever used a different name or constructed a different identity when using social media or gaming sites? The questions we can ask are almost endless.

One thing we can be sure of: people, especially young people, are using media forms in very different ways from the past. Whilst this undoubtedly offers new opportunities and brings its own excitement, it would be naïve to pretend that different ways of using media technologies do not have a potential dark side. Recent threats which have emerged concerning young people's online presence include the proliferation and harvesting of self-generated explicit images, revenge porn, and cyberbullying in all of its forms. There are also worries about so-called lifestyle sites which have been accused of promoting anorexia, bulimia, self-harm, and suicide.

Such threats are complex, and growing by the day. It is certain that they are not going to go away—educators in the field of e-safety are even now having to warn six year-olds that anything they say online will still be there decades later. This has been called the 'digital tattoo'; as the case of Paris Brown proves, our digital past really can come back to haunt us. Paris' case is a good place in which to start our exploration of how young people use the new technological platforms, and how they can as a result be affected by (or inadvertently involved in) these new forms of criminality.

Paris was a 17 year old chosen to be the Youth Police and Crime Commissioner, appointed to the £15,000 per year role by Kent Police in 2013. Naturally interested in a young person who had been given this kind of prestigious and lucrative role, the press went digging and found tweets she had sent three years earlier. Paris found herself accused of racism, homophobia, and violence, and whilst it was later ruled that her messages did not reach the standard required for prosecution, she resigned from her job. Even today, any web search of her name results in over 700,000 hits, which will include personal attacks and comments in amongst the more traditional reporting of her story. She will be followed by this online presence—her 'digital tattoo'—for the rest of her life.

Young people who grew up with the Internet are often being referred to as the digital natives—unlike the older digital migrants—and the net gen(eration). They take for granted the use of integrated technologies in their everyday lives. It would also seem that the introduction to new and developing technologies begins at a very early age. Whilst all of this transforms the ways in which people communicate and spend their leisure hours and offers many benefits, it also has a darker and more sinister side. Do young people face new dangers which previous generations did not? In **Conversations 7.2** we hear the views of Zoe Barkham, a practitioner in the field of education and emotional well-being, who has a particular focus on e-safety training for children and their parents.

Zoe makes many interesting points and raises some interesting issues in **Conversations 7.2**. The Internet is also one area where the mainstream news media are beginning to focus more on young people as being victims of crime instead of offenders. But what is the evidence? Is this a real and growing problem, or is it—as some might have it—another example of a media-inspired panic? Consider the available evidence and see what you think.

According to a recent survey by EU Kids online (Livingstone et al., 2011), 12 per cent of 11–16 year old Internet users have received sexual messages, but only 3 per cent admit to sending them. Also, 'sexting' (the sending of a sexualised photograph, which is technically a criminal offence, carrying a potential prison sentence of up to 10 years) appears to be less common in the UK than other parts of Europe. Similarly, CEOP (2013), which is a command of the National Crime Agency, states in its

NEW FRONTIERS 7.1

Social media and the dark net

Throughout history, change and technological innovations have caused anxiety that they will lead to increased crime and disorder, a trend that continues today with widespread concerns about the development of web-based communications; in particular, the use of social media and the so-called 'dark web.'

Social media is an umbrella term for websites and apps that allow users to talk, make new connections, share images, and to play games. The boundaries of such sites are shifting, with an increasing number of platforms featuring at least some elements of social media—for instance, games such as Minecraft relying on social media sites like YouTube to teach new players and to allow the spread of tips, cheats, and new elements of play. Some users such as Dan TDM (Dan Middleton) have built lucrative careers on producing social media content explaining how to get around a particular part of the game, or sharing ways to get a higher score.

Whilst users like Dan are legitimate, various forms of social media have been linked to a range of different crime and deviant behaviours, which have required new responses from law enforcement agencies. Young people who take, share, or receive nude images of themselves and their boyfriend or girlfriend are guilty of making and possessing an indecent image of a child—but if this is done consensually as part of a romantic relationship, does it merit a criminal sanction that will show up on records checks for the rest of the young person's life? The resulting compromise has been the introduction of a new Home Office Crime Code, Outcome 21, which acknowledges that an offence has technically taken place, but which takes no further action and does not feature on future checks.

In other areas, legal responses have been slower and less definite. In 2016 it was reported that the Sentencing Council is drafting guidance for judges in England and Wales, advising them to take into account the use of social media in cases where young people have posted films or boasts about their crime online and to see this as aggravating the offence. Coercive and controlling behaviour became an offence in December 2015; the offence can include messages sent via social media or the use of social media to track, monitor, or stalk a victim. On the other side of the debate, some civil liberties groups are concerned that the police or security agencies can use social media as a cheap, easy way to monitor individuals or groups. Of course, it can be argued that in some cases this is an effective and efficient way to identify potential causes of harm—for instance, finding people who post hate messages or indicate support for extreme and radical organisations—but there are questions to be asked about ethical boundaries, and respect for individual privacy.

One response to such concerns about privacy and online identities has been the growth in use of the dark net (also sometimes referred to as the dark web)—that part of the Internet where sites and users take advantage of sophisticated encryption techniques to disguise their Internet protocol (IP) identity (in other words, their Internet 'address'). The most well-known of these is Tor, which is readily downloaded to a home computer. Tor disguises a user's IP so they can browse the Internet anonymously, a benefit that is clearly of use to people for whom revealing their identity may be dangerous; for example, during the 2016 attempted coup in Turkey, the authorities attempted a news blackout by shutting down social media, so Tor and other anonymous services were used to make contact with the outside world and to share images and films of what was happening.

Many of the 2.5 million people using Tor every day do so simply for reasons of personal security, to protect their privacy, and to reduce their risk of falling victim to online criminals. However, some have realised that the secrecy of the service can be used to cover illegal activity such as the promotion of terrorism, as well as the sale of guns, stolen credit card details, Class A drugs, or images of child abuse. It is this exploitation of the Internet by criminals that raises significant questions and challenges for users, law enforcement, and criminologists. As a society we will need to debate where the boundary lies between personal privacy and the detection or prevention of crime; how far we should allow the freedom of speech to extend into cyberspace; and how we can best respond to the changing behaviours that the Internet brings.

latest threat assessment that, every year, approximately 1,000 children in the UK report suffering online child exploitation, such as being coerced into sending images of themselves. The largest victim group here is 13 and 14 year olds (at 35 per cent). 11 and 12 year olds (26 per cent) and 15 and 16 year olds (22 per cent) are also being victimised by sexual predators using the Internet (http://ceop.police.uk/Publications/). Some of the most recent research into the sending of self-generated images was carried out by the University of Edinburgh and European

CONVERSATIONS 7.2

A view from the classroom—with Zoe Barkham

Recent research by Ofcom (2015) has shown that children today struggle to tell the difference between the online and offline worlds. Their friendships, social development, and self-esteem are increasingly played out through a strange blend of the digital and the personal, where an online comment can have far greater impact than a face-to-face insult, and where an offer to send nude images in exchange for help with homework is seen as nothing out of the ordinary.

In my work, I rely on the threat assessment published by the CEOP (Child Exploitation and Online Protection) command of the National Crime Agency for quantified intelligence about the biggest risks faced by children in their digital lives. This means I can shape my training materials accordingly. At present, CEOP's judgement is that the most significant risks are less about contact abuse (although that is still a very real threat) and more from the taking and sharing of indecent images of children. These images are often taken and passed on by young people themselves. (An indecent image is one showing the child naked or engaging in sexual behaviour.) Sometimes it's innocent enough—like children through the ages, they are experimenting with their maturity and learning about their sexuality, and the only difference is that they do this electronically instead of behind the bike sheds. Sometimes it's romantic, images shared between boyfriends and girlfriends, although this in itself is dangerous, as the use of pictures as 'revenge porn' is now a common feature of relationship breakdowns. In other instances images get stolen, perhaps when a password is leaked or a phone is lost. However they end up online, in a high number of cases the images are then harvested by remote programmes and placed on so-called 'parasite' websites from where they cannot be retrieved, which can include pornographic websites dedicated to these pictures of young people.

More worryingly, in other cases the images have been taken as a result of an abusive online relationship in which the offender has moved away from the long-term building up of trust that signified old-style grooming. Today, offenders are more likely to have a scatter-gun approach, using chat rooms and messaging services to contact as many children as possible. Sometimes they pretend to be another child, or a celebrity. Once contact has been made, they move quickly into sexualised conversation or ask the child for a nude photograph. As soon as the child has engaged in this type of interaction, the offender uses blackmail to encourage the child to send other images ('I'll tell your mum/put this on your Facebook/hack into your computer if you don't send me a new picture'), and this forms a pattern of abuse which can go on for months or years. The psychological impact can be appalling, with children describing their sense of helplessness, guilt, and shame as well as their fear that anyone they meet may have encountered the pictures. Young people also feel complicit in the abuse as they may have taken some of the images voluntarily.

The taking of nude images is now a widespread behaviour amongst young people, partly due to the popularity of image-sharing apps such as Snapchat or Instagram. As long ago as 2009, research indicated that 40 per cent of 11–18 year olds knew someone who had sent a nude image; in a recent classroom session with 14 year old girls, I found that at least 75 per cent of them said they had friends who send pictures. Yet although these young women were shocked to learn that taking such photographs, even consensually, is illegal, and they were aware of the potential problems that could arise, most said they would only ask for help as a very last resort. The reason they gave was that their fear of losing access to the online world was greater than their fear of exposure, blackmail, or shame.

At the end of the day, children are children. Their technological skills outweigh their social and emotional abilities, so when they are online they think that they are cleverer, smarter, and more sophisticated than they really are. They usually believe they will be able to spot a liar online with ease or that they will be able to deal with a problem without the need to involve an adult. When asked what worries them about being online, their responses are often exaggerated and unrealistic—for instance, fears about kidnap, murder, and drug dealers are common, whereas knowledge of grooming or the importance of privacy is scant.

If we are to successfully educate and support children in the digital age, we need to acknowledge and accept that their relationship with the Internet is now so integral with their day-to-day lives that it must be part of the solution and not part of a punishment. We must not allow our own anxieties or distaste to prevent us from delivering a frank and open education programme about sex, relationships, and growing up that will help children and young people negotiate their online and offline lives. Most of all, however, we need to give them the tools and knowledge they need to grow up safely in the digital world into which, whether we like it or not, they have been born.

References

Sharing Personal Images and Videos Among Young Peoplehttp://www.blackpoollscb.org.uk/contents/documents/sextingdetail.pdf 9

Internet Watch Foundation (2015), 'Emerging Patterns and Trends Report #1 Online-Produced Sexual Content'

Ofcom (2015) Children and Parents: Media Use and Attitudes Report

Zoe Barkham, practitioner in the field of education and emotional well-being

partners, as part of the SPIRTO project (Jonsson et al., 2015) which gives further and more detailed analysis of the motivations and implications connected to the sharing of such pictures. You may want to think about this in the context of wider media coverage, such as that around the actress Jennifer Lawrence, who had nude images of herself stolen and placed on the 4chan website (see, for example, Kashner 2014 (www.vanityfair.com/hollywood/2014/10/jennifer-lawrence-cover)); or the way that newspapers respond when the images are of a middle-aged man, such as the Tory MP Brooks Newmark who in 2014 sent photos of himself to a young woman posing as a supporter.

Another point for you to consider here is the extent to which online abuse contrasts with contact abuse—that is, abuse which involves physical contact—in terms of the abuser being known to the victim (often being a friend or family member) rather than a complete stranger.

Whatever we make of this 'evidence', the point remains that new media forms and young people's use of it can put them at risk of exploitation.

The future of media criminology

We will end this chapter by briefly considering some recent developments in the fascinating and broad field of media criminology, and leave you thinking about some of the ways that the reporting of crime may go in the future. There is no doubt that the rapidly changing and fragmenting digital mediascape has opened up new (often virtual) spaces for crime stories to be reported and told, whether these be factual or fictional. Almost anyone and everyone can today get involved with mainstream and alternative media platforms, and you do not need to have had journalistic or literary training to do so. Anyone who has access to the Internet can post a comment on a web log (blog) and anyone with access to a smart phone can make a video blog (vlog). And remember that such content is now truly global in its reach.

Mainstream printed and television news media now also rely, to some extent, on new technology. Often, news channels that are otherwise conventional will ask people to send in their photographs, films, and opinions. Many respected journalists (and indeed some criminologists) now blog or tweet to their followers, and you will notice that opinions from politicians and others are often presented on news bulletins via Twitter tweets rather than filmed interviews. If we think back to some of the more controversial areas covered in this chapter (such as media representations of prisons and prisoners or immigration) and search the digitised version of an established newspaper for stories relating to them, you will find that often 'ordinary' people have posted comments and their reactions. Literally anyone can do this and know that their views will

be seen, unlike in the past when all that could be done was to post a written 'letter to the editor' and hope that it would be published. These online comments may be supportive of news stories, but sometimes they challenge conventional understandings and others may border on the defamatory and abusive. In other words, they can highlight and challenge the types of media distortion and exaggeration we have been talking about throughout this chapter, but they do not always do so; sometimes they can in fact add to the distortion, stereotyping, and hate. This is an interesting (and sometimes scary) thing to look at, although criminologists are yet to fully study these developments in terms of the extent to which such comments reflect and inform broader public opinion. Remember also that such things as online comments sections are not 'scientific' surveys of attitudes and opinions. They are, however, still an interesting and novel way for us to try to get in touch with 'public opinion' about an issue.

Citizen journalism

One of the most interesting recent developments here is the rise of the so-called citizen journalist. These are ordinary people (citizens) who blog, tweet, and upload moving images to image-sharing network sites such as Instagram or YouTube. The importance of this development cannot be overstated, although the full implications are as yet far from clear. It could be argued that such developments have the potential to democratise news production and to

Figure 7.9 Taksim Gezi Park protests, 15 June 2013
Source: Fleshstorm/CC BY-SA 3.0

reinvigorate debate in the public sphere. It may even lead to increased political engagement and activism which could, in turn, bring about real social change and reform. Citizen journalists can, after all, often be 'on the scene' well before professional news crews turn up, and there are even cases where they can broadcast information in politically sensitive situations where professional journalists have been banned. Such things can also challenge the dominance of the shrinking number of news sources (for instance, official press releases) and can often critically question official stories and narratives. In terms of crime, one such issue which has 'hit the news' has been the racist and violent nature of policing in parts of America. Shocking and disturbing video footage has been uploaded for all to see of police officers beating up, shooting, wounding, and even killing people. It is also evident that since 2010, forms of citizen journalism have been important in capturing moments of civil unrest and political demonstration in response to perceived human rights abuses and state corruption across the globe; for example, across the Middle East and North Africa (Arab Spring), in Turkey (Gezi Park Protests, see **Figure 7.9**), in the Ukraine (Euromaidan protests), and the civil war in Syria. All of this has to be a good thing—or is it? After all, such things can challenge power relations and state corruption and cover-ups. Unlike the written word, the camera never lies. Or does it? As with all media reporting, the main issues here are the trustworthiness and reliability of the actual sources. These developments are very interesting and they have undoubtedly transformed the ways in which the story of crime is told. As you progress through your degree studies, all of this will continue to develop and change. Happy media watching!

SUMMARY

- Develop a critical and reflective view of media representations of crime and criminals

We have seen how media have, throughout history, been used to inform and govern social attitudes, for example by promoting the 'hegemonic ideology' of a particular time and place. However, the chapter also examines the ways in which the media themselves can be influenced by external social factors such as 'newsworthiness' and the over-riding need for media to be sold to a reading or viewing public. This is changing in the light of citizen journalism and the rise of independent news sources such as social media.

- Explain how criminologists have researched this through content analysis and discourse analysis, and the capacity of media to distort and shape public perceptions of crime, criminality, and the criminal justice system

Media tend to focus on particular elements of a news story, and in doing so can perpetuate stereotypes and prejudice. This is particularly true in the reporting of certain types of crime and criminality; for instance, when considering the reporting of crimes involving young people, we assessed the discrepancy between actual statistics and the differing impression given by news stories. Media representations also reflect, and in some cases add to, social anxieties of the era. Criminologists use a variety of methods to research this phenomenon and in this chapter we have briefly examined two of these: content analysis and discourse analysis.

- Relate theoretical concepts to your own consumption of media

Key theoretical concepts covered in this chapter include discourse analysis, the social and ideological construction of crime reporting, moral panics and folk devils, and the caution with which we need to treat statistics. The chapter also examines the blurring of fact and fiction in the shaping of public views about crime and how such fictitious representations can be used by government to reinforce social norms. You should be able to think about the functions of crime media in promoting key messages and to consider the question of whether media are themselves criminogenic or a cause of violence.

- Assess the importance of media in forming new narratives, such as citizen journalism

Just as new media have always been used to discuss and describe crime, so it is now evolving into new forms. Whereas in the past the use of media was generally confined to the rich and powerful (those who could afford to buy books or who were actually literate), since the development of mass media like cinemas more and more people have been able to witness and comment upon news and ideas. The most visible examples of this are the use of media to either encourage action against perceived offenders (such as newspapers naming alleged paedophiles) or to be personally active in the reporting of news stories, often offering an alternative and sometimes controversial stance to that given in mainstream accounts. It is argued that some of these new narratives can inform and even change public policy, such as prison films that highlight the true nature of life behind bars.

- Compare and analyse differences between traditional and emerging branches of criminological research to the representation of crime across a variety of media

You may wish to think about this question in the light of other chapters in this book, such as **Chapter 15** on critical criminology. However, the chapter here does highlight the different environment in which criminologists find themselves working when considering crime and the media; the vastly more varied news sources, the greater access to global media, and the use of crime reporting of all types in shaping public opinion.

REVIEW QUESTIONS

1. Give three examples of how the media exaggerate or distort crime.

2. What are the two research methods criminologists predominantly use to record the reporting of crime? What are the main differences between these?

3. Name four of the eight 'professional imperatives' that Chibnall identified.

4. What are today's moral panics and who are the folk devils? What is moral about a moral panic?

5. Give two arguments for and against the proposition that it is acceptable for 'true crime' to be portrayed as popular entertainment.

6. Identify three crime films which can be said to challenge dominant discourses about crime, criminality, and its control, and list the ways in which they do so.

7. List ways in which young people are thought to be at risk from being exploited online.

8. How does citizen journalism affect the future of crime reporting? Give a current example of how this can happen.

FURTHER READING

Cohen, S. (2011 [1973]) *Folk Devils and Moral Panics: The Creation of the Mods and the Rockers*. London: Routledge.

The 'classic' study of folk devils and moral panics. This 2011 reprint in the 'Routledge Classics' series includes the revised introduction written by the late Stan Cohen in 2003.

Jewkes, Y. (2015) *Media and Crime*. London: Sage.

This book offers a thorough review and critical examination of much that is covered in this chapter (and more). It is a very good place for you to start if you want to develop your knowledge and understanding of this subject.

Greer, C. (ed.) (2010) *Crime and the Media*. London: Routledge.

A comprehensive collection of edited articles, both classic and new, which covers a broad range of issues. Some are higher level than others but well worth dipping into.

Moore, S.E.H. (2014) *Crime and the Media*. London: Palgrave Macmillan.

A good, broad coverage of the field which has particularly useful introductory chapters on analysing the media in terms of content analysis, narrative analysis, and discourse analysis.

Rafter, N. and Brown, M. (2011) *Criminology Goes to the Movies: Crime Theory and Popular Culture*. New York: NYU Press.

This is an interesting collection of essays which attempt to teach criminological theory through (mainly American) crime films. If you want a greater understanding of the criminological theories explored in **Part 3** of this book then this text would be the best place to start.

Thompson, K. (1998) *Moral Panics*. London: Routledge.

A short introduction to this key idea which applies it to areas such as youth, 'mugging', sex and Aids, female gangs, and family violence.

Yar, M. (2013) *Cybercrime and Society* (2nd edn). London: Sage.

This offers a very clear introduction to the issues of hacking, cracking, virtual piracy, hate speech online, and all things cyber (including the problems of policing and regulating cyber space).

 Access the **online resources** to view selected further reading and web links relevant to the material covered in this chapter.
www.oup.com/uk/case/

ANSWERS TO EXERCISES

WHAT DO YOU THINK? 7.4

		Tabloids (281)	Broadsheets (159)	Locals (53)
		%	%	%
Subject	Violence/crime/anti-social behaviour	35	26	33
	Child abuse/neglect	12	17	8
	Lifestyle	16	9	7
	(Mental) Health	10	11	12
	Accident	14	8	15
	Education/parenting	6	22	17
	Achievement	8	6	9
Tone	Negative	82	50	71
	Neutral	8	36	9
	Positive	11	15	20

Table 7.3 Newspaper articles about young people, by newspaper type, subject and tone (2004)

Source: Ipsos MORI, www.ipsos-mori.com, 2–8 August 2004

CHAPTER OUTLINE

Introduction   200

Non-governmental organisations and pressure groups   201

Victims of crime and the victims movement   202

Theoretical approaches to studying victims   208

Hate crime   210

Disablist hate crime   215

Homophobic hate crime   218

Conclusion   220

Victimology and hate crime

Evidence and campaigning for change

KEY ISSUES

After studying this chapter, you should be able to:

- critically assess why only some types of criminological evidence (derived from both governmental and non-governmental sources) are drawn on to inform policy making processes;

- appreciate the changing role of the victim in criminal justice processes and why it has been argued that the victim has become marginalised from these;

- develop an awareness of why some victims of crime are regarded as being more 'deserving' than others and how this relates to broader issues of power;

- distinguish between positivist and radical/critical approaches to victimology;

- critically discuss the main features of hate crime and evaluate the need for hate crime legislation;

- identify forms of hate crime and analyse the underlying social and political issues which affect both public and policy responses to the affected groups;

- explain the broader notions of structural inequalities which are at the heart of a critical victimology in relationship to the concept of hate crime.

Introduction

The sub-discipline of victimology has become a growing area of importance in criminology. It was often said that the impact of criminal victimisation was an area of study neglected by criminologists and that in the criminal justice process the victim stood in the shadows: it was the criminal who took centre stage. Much has already been achieved in placing the victim in a more central role in the criminal justice process (see **Chapter 26** on restorative justice as one example) and taking their needs into consideration. More recently criminal acts which are thought to be motivated by hate have also risen in prominence as an area of public debate and criminological analysis.

This chapter will explore these two issues in a new way. As well as considering the main theories surrounding each, we will also be exploring these concepts combined with statistically-based evidence and the work of various pressure groups who draw on such evidence to transform what are often thought of as private issues into public problems. It is hoped that this approach will help you better understand how different types of criminological evidence related to victimology and hate crime can actually impact on policy making processes. This applied approach is vital if you are to truly understand the issues around victimology and hate crimes as well as how they can affect legislation.

The relationship between social science evidence and policy reform is a complicated one, and it is something which we shall explore in greater depth as the chapter progresses through a consideration of victimology and hate crime. Understanding how research can impact upon and influence public policy is a clear way of making the link between theory and practice.

As we saw in **Chapter 5**, police services and government agencies produce crime statistics for many, varied reasons. Despite the obvious and inherent problems associated with them, the collation and dissemination of such claims to knowledge are not, as is often thought, totally meaningless and without use. Taken together, police recorded crime statistics and the CSEW (Crime Survey for England and Wales) can inform us not least about power relations in terms of government priorities and police resource deployment but also, at a more practical and fundamental level, they can show trends in specific forms of crime over time and within given locations. Such figures are not simply generated to fuel what often become alarmist newspaper headlines and to create a fear of crime amongst the public; they have a broader purpose. As we saw in Detective Constable Harbison's reflections (see **Chapter 5**), crime statistics often inform both policing and government policies in that they provide 'leading intelligence' for crime prevention initiatives which are aimed at preventing the public from becoming victims of crime.

Indeed, the prevention of crime and disorder through policing by consent has been one of the main principles of policing since the Metropolitan Police was set up in 1828 (see **Chapter 21**). Continuing this tradition, most police authorities and individual police boroughs now publish their broad aims and objectives as well as their overarching missions and values. Although there are slight differences in emphasis, most of these 'mission statements' will include common aims such as the protection of the public as well as the intent to reduce crime in line with agreed targets (note, again, a statistical measure is deemed to be of importance here—in this instance to measure 'success').

Of course, it is not just police authorities and government agencies that generate and use crime data. In this chapter we will be exploring how non-governmental organisations and pressure groups also collate and analyse data on crime-related issues. The key focus for us will be to examine their reasons for doing so, not least because the desire of pressure and campaign groups to drive changes to policy has been a key factor in the explosion of the knowledge about crime and criminality. This link between the production of knowledge claims, and how they can be drawn on to influence policy in the hope of creating a fairer and just society is crucial, and one which is often overlooked by students beginning their journeys into criminology.

For now, let us think about the range of non-governmental organisations and pressure and campaign groups, and the outcomes that they were set up to achieve. They vary in size and in terms of their influence and access to government officials, but there are many such groups which seek both to inform the public and put pressure on governments to change the direction of criminal justice and social policies. Indeed, the role of independent pressure groups (that is, their aim is to put pressure on governments 'from below' to achieve policy change) has a long history in British policy-making that goes back to the 19th century. The list in the next section is far from exhaustive, and you are encouraged to search beyond these for yourselves, but have a look at the websites of the following national (that is British) campaign and pressure groups and consider precisely what it is they do and why they campaign for particular sectional interests.

Non-governmental organisations and pressure groups

Inquest

(http://www.inquest.org.uk/)

Founded in 1981, this small charity monitors and gives advice on deaths in custody (that is, in police custody, prisons, and immigration detention centres). Its overall objective is to reduce the number of custodial deaths and improve the treatment and care of those within the institutions where the deaths occur. Through the use of official data sets (such as Home Office statistics) and its own independent monitoring and casework, it aims to create clear policy proposals as well as undertaking further research that enables the group to lobby for changes to the inquest and investigation processes.

The Howard League for Penal Reform

(http://www.howardleague.org/about-us/)

This national charity was established in 1866 and is named after one the first prison reformers, John Howard. Its broad remit is to work towards a society in which there is less crime, safer communities, and fewer people in prison (see **Figure 8.1**). It campaigns on a wide range of criminal justice issues; at the moment they are focusing on the reform of sentencing, investing in communities, campaigning for justice for children and young people, and for change inside prisons. As well as their research they work with parliament, the media, criminal justice professionals, and the public, aiming to inform debate which leads to changes in government policy.

Stopwatch

(http://www.stop-watch.org/about-us/)

This charity describes itself as being a coalition of legal experts, academics, citizens, and civil liberty campaigners. Through its research strand it seeks, amongst other things, to inform the public about the use of police stop and search powers. It also aims to develop and share research on stop and search and its alternatives, with a view to promoting more effective, accountable, and fair policing.

Figure 8.1 A poster from the Howard League for Penal Reform
Source: The Howard League: http://howardleague.org/

The National Association for Youth Justice

(http://thenayj.org.uk/)

Formed in 1995, this organisation lobbies for the rights of children and young people who are in trouble with the law. It promotes the belief that the rights and welfare of children must be central to the youth justice system.

StopHateUK

(http://stophateuk.org)

This group was founded as a response to the murder of the black teenager Stephen Lawrence in 1995. In 2007 it took on a wider remit of supporting victims of all forms of hate crime, including racist, disablist, religiously-motivated, and homophobic offences. It offers a support line

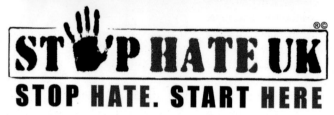

Figure 8.2 Poster from a campaign run by StopHateUK

Source: Stop Hate UK: http://www.stophateuk.org

for victims, works to improve local responses, and collates statistics to inform and monitor its work. See **Figure 8.2** for an example of their work to raise awareness of hate crime.

Other groups

Pressure groups do not only operate at a national level. It is clear that international organisations such as Amnesty International (https://www.amnesty.org.uk/) have become crucial at a global level for highlighting abuses of human rights, support for indigenous peoples, and opposition to torture and the death penalty. Other groups have joined together and formed collectives. A good example of this joint working would be the Criminal Justice Alliance (http://criminaljusticealliance.org/). Founded in 2007, the CJA is a coalition of 90 organisations who together aim to influence governments to introduce fairer and more effective criminal justice policies.

Beyond their campaigning zeal for a more just criminal justice system (and society), these groups also share

a common practice of actively monitoring existing policies and critically interpreting government data. In addition, many carry out their own, independent research. Why should this be so important? We will develop our responses to this this throughout the chapter.

It is important to bear in mind that many campaigning groups seek to champion victims of crime whose powerlessness means that their voices would otherwise go unheard. We should ask ourselves why this happens; why do some crime stories disappear within the statistical patterns or receive less attention? You may want to look back to the media chapter (**Chapter 7**) for some related concepts on how some victims and crimes can come to be overlooked, dismissed, or constructed as being unimportant. However, the groups' work illustrates one way in which statistics and data can be used for a purpose other than the prevention or control of crime; by analysing and interpreting such information, they can highlight the need for progressive reform and change to policy, policing, and practice and to work towards justice for both victims and offenders, although, as we shall see in this chapter, this distinction is not always as clear-cut as it at first may seem.

Victims of crime and the victims movement

Dispute resolution and the changing role of the victim

In the most basic sense, two things need to come together in order for any crime to occur: a perpetrator and a victim.

Of course, in reality things are rarely as clear cut as this—for example, as we saw in **Chapter 4**, a perpetrator may be an organisation rather than an individual, or a victim may themselves also be an offender. However, one thing that we can say with certainty is that there have always been disputes between people, and that some of these conflicts are viewed as deviant or unacceptable. We can study *dispute resolution* across history and between cultures through cultural and legal anthropology, which encompasses all forms of social structure, including small, non-industrial societies where people are hunter-gatherers or farmers, as well as large, urban and apparently more sophisticated groups. Legal anthropologists remind us that the 'law way' of resolving disputes—in other words, a system that relies on codified rules, the legitimate power of constables, and the rituals of a courtroom—is actually of relatively recent origin, however well-established it may seem to be.

Indeed, the development of the legal system that we are used to in the UK, with its police officers, solicitors, barristers, wigs, judges, courts, and prisons, can be traced back to 1750; it was not until 1856 that judges from the Central Criminal Court were given permission to hear cases outside their own jurisdiction in order to prevent local prejudice affecting a trial's outcome, and Courts of Assizes, which had been in existence since mediaeval times, only closed in 1971 when they were replaced by Crown Courts. Conversely, however, the Anglo-Saxon model of trial by combat was not formally removed as a legal option until 1818—although, in 2002, a 60 year old man in England attempted to revive this ancient right. After receiving a £20 fine for a minor motoring offence he challenged a 'champion' nominated by the Driver and Vehicle Licensing Authority (DVLA) to a fight to the death, involving samurai swords, Gurkha knives, or heavy hammers. Needless to say, despite his belief that this was a 'reasonable way' to settle the matter, his offer was rejected by the courts!

Anthropological studies in other parts of the world provide us with fascinating details of how pre-industrial societies resolved disputes and ruptures to their social fabrics. The use of oracles, song duels, moots, and the offering of compensation in the form of livestock and cattle and so on are all ways in which such peoples seek to restore justice and harmony to their communities; methods which may seem quaint to us but which are as meaningful to them as our courtrooms and archaic legal costumes and language—the insistence that we call a judge 'my lord' for example (see Roberts 2013 for a good review of the legal anthropological literature).

By looking at other ways to deal with crime and conflict we are also encouraged to think more deeply about the 'law way' of dispute resolution, and how we have come to regard it as being natural, inevitable, and right. As well as opening up our minds to the possibilities that 'justice' can be (and indeed often is) done differently, considering other models also makes us think about the role of the 'key actors' in the story of crime. For instance, we can look at the role of the victim, the offender, the wider community, and so on. As this is a book on criminology, we shall be considering the use of the legal system to resolve 'crimes' but it is useful to bear in mind that there are similar systems in place for civil cases too—divorce, property disputes, and similar—and you may want to consider whether there are points of similarity between the criminal and civil processes.

Victims in a criminal trial setting

If you have ever visited a magistrates' or Crown Court and observed a criminal trial taking place you would have observed the full pomp and regalia of the British criminal justice system unfold before your eyes. You may well have thought that the 'law way' of doing things can appear confusing, arcane, and rather mysterious—as well as sometimes being rather dull and boring (unless, of course, you were there to be tried for an offence or to give witness evidence, in which case it may have been traumatic and nerve-wracking).

Let us pause for a minute to think about the impressions that you received during your visit. Firstly, reflect on the spatial lay out of a court room, who sat where and what that told you about their status. Where was everyone's attention directed? Were there any regalia or special clothing on show? Then think back to what (and who) you saw and, perhaps more importantly, on what (and who) you heard. If you visited a Crown Court you would, no doubt, have seen the accused standing at the back or side of the courtroom, perhaps flanked by security guards and behind a glass shield. You would also have seen people wearing wigs and robes, and speaking in a very specific and occasionally complex legal language, debating the finer points of the law and using phrases in Latin. In doing so they may have been deferring to the judge who presides from literally above everyone else, looking down on the proceedings from a throne-like seat that is framed by the Royal Coat of Arms. As well as hearing legal language, you may also have seen expert witnesses called upon to give evidence who spoke in a highly technical language, discussing points of forensic science or medicine. Now ask yourself whether or not you saw or heard the victim. See **Figure 8.3**—where would you see the victim of crime in the court room depicted?

The Norwegian critical criminologist Nils Christie wrote an influential paper in 1977 which he called 'Conflicts as Property'. In it, amongst other things, he argues that the state and legal profession has 'stolen' the conflict or dispute away from the main protagonists in any criminal trial, but he especially suggests that the system has stolen it from the victim. As he writes:

> the party that is represented by the state, namely the victim, is so thoroughly represented that she or he for most of the proceedings is pushed completely out of the arena, reduced to the triggerer-off of the whole thing. She or he is a sort of

Figure 8.3 Layout of a standard Crown Court room
Source: kenny1/Shutterstock.com

double loser; first, *vis-a-vis* the offender, but secondly and often in a more crippling manner by being denied rights to full participation in what might have been one of the more important ritual encounters in life. The victim has lost the case to the state.

Christie 1977: 3

Many interesting points are raised for our purposes here, especially the idea that victims should have '*rights*', but it does seem strange that, for many commentators, the place of the victim in the criminal justice system is a marginal one and that their voices are to some extent silenced.

It is possible in the court room example that the victim was called upon to give witness evidence, or you may have heard their words in the form of a victim impact statement (sometimes called a victim personal statement), which can be made by a victim themselves or be read by their legal representative. Victims may choose not to make such a statement at all. However the statement is made, it has an important role to play in foregrounding the experience and emotions of the victim—although it will not affect the sentencing process.

The impacts of victimisation

The marginalisation of the victim becomes even more apparent if we consider the possible impacts which being a victim of crime may cause; not just in terms of possible material and financial effects, but also the potential physical, behavioural, and emotional ones. Given that the harm caused to victims can be so substantial, it could be argued that they should instead be at the very centre of the process. Many observers and criminologists (not just critical ones) have been making similar points in terms of how victims' needs are often *neglected* throughout the various stages of the criminal justice process for many years. And

yet the place and role of victims in justice process has not always been a marginalised one.

In their historical overview, Godfrey and Lawrence (2015) have charted how from the mid-18th century, victims were often central to the justice system, even unofficially; for example, the use of physical violence as a form of retribution was often tolerated in society. Thus for example victims could throw rubbish, dung, and even stones at offenders who were imprisoned in stocks or pillories. Throughout the 19th century, however, the court and legal profession became more organised and developed, and the police became the main prosecutor of crime on behalf of the victim and of society at large—to the extent that by the mid-20th century it was argued that the victims of crime had effectively disappeared from the courts. Recently there have been calls to 're-centre the victims of crime' throughout the criminal justice process (in particular through forms of restorative justice—on which see **Chapter 26**) and through the introduction of the 'Victims' Commissioner'—but let us think about what it precisely means to be a victim of crime.

Identifying and relating to victims

Defining a 'victim' may not be as straightforward as it may first appear. This section will examine some of the complexities around this contested and controversial aspect of victimology.

We shall start with the view of victimhood that is commonly presented and understood in popular culture. Arguably there are two possible interpretations of what it means to be a victim: someone who is entitled to financial recompense as a result of what has happened to them, or (perhaps as well) a victim is someone who seeks and deserves both justice and practical protection from the state. These broader issues of justice and care are of more interest to criminologists, although they hold differing views. Firstly, however, we will consider how the United Nations (see **Figure 8.4**) defines what it means to be a victim of crime.

The United Nations on victims

At the moment there is not any binding United Nations document which sets out to protect the rights of victims. Although the study of victimology now has an increasing presence in social science scholarship and in university courses, its definition remains problematic not least because the study of victims of crime has developed to encompass victimisation at both local and global levels. If you look at some of the recent editions of one of the main academic journals in the field—*The International Review* victim. The term 'victim' also includes, where appropriate, the immediate family or dependants of the direct victim and persons who have suffered harm in intervening to assist victims in distress or to prevent victimization.

After reading these paragraphs you should consider the questions and issues raised in **What do you think? 8.1**.

The UN declaration certainly raises some important issues. Firstly, you may have been struck by how it uses the word 'harm' and not crime (we will consider this further in **Chapter 16**). Similarly, you may have picked up on the idea of 'secondary' victimisation as outlined in the second paragraph with regards to the impacts which crime may have on the immediate family members of the direct or 'primary' victim.

As we seen throughout this book, definitional issues for some of our key concepts are rarely as clear-cut as we might at first think. We can perhaps take the ideas contained within the UN Declaration a bit further. Are the distinctions between victims and offenders always as straightforward as they might appear, or are these constructed boundaries often fuzzy? For instance, we 'know' that many offenders/perpetrators also suffer victimisation. An example of this is the evidence that suggests some people who inflict domestic abuse upon their partners themselves suffered abuse whilst growing up in violent or anti-social households (Simons et al. 1995). We could also argue that many young offenders who end up in young offenders institutions also suffer from multiple forms of deprivation.

Figure 8.4 United Nations Headquarters, New York City, USA
Source: blurAZ/Shutterstock.com

of *Victimology*—you will find cutting edge research on victimisation as it relates to various groups: these include the elderly, travelling communities such as Roma people, British Muslim women, and Ghanaian women; it also examines types of crime such as terrorism, cyber fraud, female prostitution, dating violence, genocide, and so on. You will also find research which reflects on broader issues in terms of the development of new laws and protocols which are thought to adequately and effectively protect the needs and rights of victims. Is such a thing possible or even desirable? Are the boundaries between the perceptions of and recognition for different types of victimhood equal or, are some victims deemed to more worthy and deserving than others? After all, an individual's responses to becoming a 'victim of crime' may well differ across and within different offence categories. For example, we would probably react in one way to having our car scratched by a vandal and in quite another to being physically attacked. For now, we will consider how the notion of how being a 'victim' is reflected internationally.

The following two paragraphs are taken from the 1985 United Nations Declaration of Basic Principles of Justice for Victims of Crime and Abuse of Power:

1. 'Victims' means persons who, individually or collectively, have suffered harm, including physical or mental injury, emotional suffering, economic loss or substantial impairment of their fundamental rights, through acts or omissions that are in violation of criminal laws operative within Member States, including those laws proscribing criminal abuse of power.

2. A person may be considered a victim, under this Declaration, regardless of whether the perpetrator is identified, apprehended, prosecuted or convicted and regardless of the familial relationship between the perpetrator and the

WHAT DO YOU THINK? 8.1

What makes a victim?

Having read the two points taken from the 1985 United Nations Declaration of Basic Principles of Justice for Victims of Crime and Abuse of Power, write down *your* perceptions of what it means to be a victim of crime. How would you define it?

Next, jot down some illustrative examples of what might make someone a victim. Once you have done this, carefully read the two points again and compare your ideas with what the UN has to say.

• How did you get on?

• How do both of your lists compare with each other?

• Were there any glaring discrepancies between them or, having read what the UN has to say on the matter, did your ideas change as you were doing this exercise in any way?

For instance, the charity Young Minds quotes published official statistics that show 95 per cent of imprisoned young people have at least one form of mental illness (Office for National Statistics 1997) and the Prison Reform Trust cites further evidence that a quarter of adult prisoners have an IQ under 80. Could it therefore be argued that these offenders are the victims of broader forms of social exclusion and injustice? Also, as we shall see in **Chapter 11** (when we look in more detail at the victimisation of women in terms of intimate partner violence and abuse) that some people may reject the label of being a 'victim' as it implies passivity and a lack of human agency. These mask the real problem, which in this case is male violence.

We shall develop such arguments further later in the chapter when we look in greater detail at theoretical approaches to studying victimisation which are known as 'radical' or 'critical' victimology. Before we move on to this however, we will end this section of this chapter by asking ourselves whether societal reaction and public perceptions mean some victims appear to be more deserving of public sympathy and their place as a 'true' victim than others. Consider the examples provided in **What do you think? 8.2**.

The idea of victimhood can be a complex and controversial one that is affected by a wide range of dynamics. In an attempt to analyse this further, Nils Christie developed the concept of the 'ideal victim', (1986) which sought to assess what factors make a victim appear to be legitimate and valued, at least from an ideological and social policy perspective. In Christie's work, the ideal victim is one who:

- is weaker than the offender—so likely to be elderly, female, or a child;
- is going about their normal day to day business (even where this may not be entirely legitimate);
- is not to blame in any way for what happened to them;
- is not known to the offender—in other words, the offender is a stranger (and an individual person, rather than a company or organisation);
- is the victim of someone who is clearly deviant;
- is not a threat to the dominant social norms and values.

WHAT DO YOU THINK? 8.2

A hierarchy of victims? 'Deserving', 'undeserving', and 'ideal' victims

On a scale of 1–5, where 1 is 'none' and 5 is 'full', rate your level of support for the following victims of crime. Jot down your score and reasons as you do so:

- A two-year-old child run over by a careless driver:
  ....
  ....
  ....

- A man who stays with an abusive and violent civil partner:
  ....
  ....
  ....

- A husband with a debilitating and terminal disease who is given a lethal overdose by his wife:
  ....
  ....
  ....

- A woman who is so drunk she cannot remember getting into a cab with a strange man who later attacks her:
  ....

- A heroin dealer beaten up by a rival:
  ....
  ....
  ....

- A prisoner who suffers violence within prison:
  ....
  ....
  ....

- An elderly woman who has £4,000 in cash stolen from her home by an unscrupulous tradesperson:
  ....
  ....
  ....

Were some of these easier to score than others? Would your ideas have changed had the circumstances been different—for instance if the heroin dealer had been selling drugs to pay for her child's medical care? How would the way you heard about the crime affect your view—if it had happened to someone you knew or if you heard it being gossiped about in the student bar?

We see from this how some victims may come to be seen as less important or valuable than others—even when it is clear that they have suffered harm at the hands of another person in a way that the law classifies as criminal. Thus we may see examples of so-called 'victim blaming and shaming' where someone is thought to be at least indirectly blamed for what has happened to them. This is discussed in greater detail later on. In other cases, such as in crimes involving children (some of whom are generally perceived as being innocent and fragile) there is greater outrage and shock than if the same offence had been perpetrated against an adult who may be regarded as being less vulnerable.

The idea of an ideal victim being one who does not challenge social values is particularly important when we consider hate crime later in the chapter. In some areas of some societies, certain groups may be seen as a threat—women who are sexually liberated, people from religious or ethnic minorities, young people who appear to be out of control—and in a crude sense, they may be seen as deserving of the crime they have suffered. We shall also see how the sense of threat is linked to that of a group's powerlessness and oppression and the extent to which their claims are recognised and their voices heard and reflected in policy making debates.

Measuring victimisation and its impact

Since 1982, our knowledge of victimisation in terms of its extent and its distribution amongst the population has increased significantly. As we saw in **Chapter 5**, 1982 was when the first 'sweep' of the British Crime Survey (now called the Crime Survey for England and Wales—CSEW) was published. As you will recall, the CSEW is a large scale victimisation survey which asks a significant number of people (the target sample size is now 35,000) about their experiences of crime. Not only does it act as a corrective to the more limited statistical picture of crimes as recorded by the police, it also offers us more information about the nature and scale of potential victimisation. For instance, for the period ending September 2015, the CSEW indicates there were an estimated 6.6 million incidents of crime against households and resident adults (aged 16 and over).

However, it is important to note that victimisation rates vary considerably across the population and by geographic area. You can find out more by visiting two important websites, the Office for National Statistics (http://www.ons.gov.uk) and the Crime Survey (http://www.crimesurvey.co.uk/index.html). As well as providing us with user-friendly infographics on what is measured by the survey, you can also download and peruse detailed

Age	%	Ethnic Group	%
All adults	4.1	White	3.9
16–24	8.4	White or Black Caribbean	11.3
45–54	3.6	Asian/British Asian	4.0
75+	1.3	**Marital Status**	
Men	4.7	Married/Civil partnered	2.6
16–24	10.6	Single	6.8
45–54	3.5	**Employment Status**	
75+	0.9	In employment	4.7
Women	3.5	Unemployed	8.3
16-24	6.1	Full-time student	7.0
45-54	3.8	**Number of visits to a nightclub in the last month**	
75+	1.6	None/Once a week or more	3.4/13.2

Table 8.1 Percentage of adults who were victims of personal crime by personal characteristics, year ending March 2015, CSEW

spreadsheets which detail the proportion of adults who were the victims of crime overall. You can also study rates of personal crime—that is crimes of violence, robbery, and theft from the person. Let us focus down a little more on these personal crimes and look at some of the statistics as they relate to some particular factors: the respondent's age, gender, ethnic group, marital and employment status, and lifestyle.

The figures in **Table 8.1** show us the risks of becoming a victim of personal crimes (which, it should be noted, are about five times lower than the risks of becoming a victim of all household crime). It is clear from looking at the table that, to some extent, becoming a victim of personal crime is patterned. For instance, it appears that some things make you more likely to become a victim than other people: being male, white or Caribbean, unemployed or a student, and enjoying visiting nightclubs. We do need to sound a note of caution: being a black student does not of itself mean you are more likely to become a victim, but it's not hard to see why young men who go out to places that tend to sell cheap alcohol are more likely to get into a fight.

Whilst such statistics are of interest in themselves (as are the further analyses of the geographical spread of victimisation and the issue of repeat victimisation) we should also take time to briefly consider the extent to which they can inform policy and, perhaps more importantly, what they can tell us about the impact that being a victim of crime can have on a person.

To be able to inform policies on addressing victims' rights and needs, we need more qualitative information about their lived experiences and emotional and behavioural reactions. In short, victimisation surveys will only take us so far when considering this empirical problem. As we noted earlier in the chapter, the various effects of being a victim of crime will vary between the type of crime experienced. Similarly, individual victims of similar crimes will react to their victimhood in different ways. For instance, some people whose houses are burgled may cope and be more resilient, whilst others may feel vulnerable, unsafe, and fearful of it happening again. Personal reactions can have a real impact on how victims live their lives after the offence.

We can also distinguish between the immediate and longer term needs of victims. The independent national charity Victim Support, which was set up in 1972 to offer help, advice and support to victims, now helps over a million victims of crime every year (see https://www. victimsupport.org.uk/homepage for more details of their work). Much of their activity focuses on the immediate effects of becoming a victim and so they offer practical help and advice such as assisting people to fill out forms (such as claims for compensation), helping to get broken windows and doors fixed, arranging medical treatment, and offering advice on how to deal with the often complicated and confusing criminal justice process if a case comes to trial.

As well as these more practical issues, becoming a victim of crime can have longer lasting and deeper effects, both physical and emotional (see Spalek 2006: 68–80 for a fuller discussion on the potential psychological, emotional, behavioural, physical, and material impacts that becoming a victim of crime may have on a person). We will consider some of the possible practical and psychological impacts of being a victim of crime below when we explore forms of hate crime and the groups affected by this form of offending.

Theoretical approaches to studying victims

Although victimisation has been the subject of academic study over the last 50 years or so, it could be argued that a coherent theoretical framework for it has not yet been developed—if this were at all possible given the diversity of the subject matter which could fall under the broad umbrella of 'victimology'. Social scientists have developed different typologies through which they seek to understand the diverse experiences that victims of crime may have (see, for example, Mendelson 1956 and Karmen 1990). Here we will consider a more straightforward narrative by identifying two very broad approaches. These might be better thought of as being frames of reference rather than being fully worked out theoretical perspectives. These are the positivist approach and the more critical/radical approach. Let us briefly sketch out what the focus of such approaches are.

Positivist approaches

The paradigm of positivism has been a dominant one for much of the history of criminology (see **Part 3**, specifically **Chapters 12, 13, 14** for defining tenets and critiques). At its most basic, positivism, as a generic social science concept, is concerned with the scientific (that is impartial, neutral, and objective) study of aspects of social life—in this case victimisation. The key focus of positivist approaches is aetiology; in other words, the quest to find out the causes of things. This frame of reference informs both large scale surveys which attempt to measure the extent of victimisation as well as studies which focus on the relationships between a perpetrator and an offender.

Early proponents of this approach to the study of victims of crime—such Von Hentig (1948) and Wolfgang (1958)—argued that the relationship between a perpetrator and victim is not a totally random one but is, in some ways, socially patterned. It is argued that if we can delineate such patterns and therefore understand the interaction between offender and victim, then crime prevention initiatives could be designed to prevent someone becoming a victim in the first place. Such work continues today in many forms—for instance, the government encourages us to remove opportunities for crime by heeding the 'common sense' advice we receive, such as remembering to lock our windows when we go out or to avoid taking a short cut home down a dark alleyway.

However, the early approaches are now largely discredited because of some of their more extreme assumptions. By fixing their gaze on psychological and social circumstances in the dyadic (i.e. involving two people) relationship between the perpetrator and victim, positivists tended towards victim-blaming and, in doing so, argued that the victim had 'precipitated' (that is, that they were somehow responsible for) their victimisation. An example of the more extreme work in this field was Amir's (1971) study of forcible rape, where he argued that around 20 per cent of the cases he studied could be attributed to the fault of the victim.

Despite years of feminist critique (which we will consider further in **Chapter 11**) it is worth asking if such ideas (or rape myths) totally disappeared? A poll carried out in 2005 by Amnesty International suggested that one in three respondents thought that a woman was partly or wholly responsible for being raped if she acted flirtatiously. Furthermore, one in four of the respondents said the same if she wore 'sexy' or 'revealing' clothing. The idea of 'contributory negligence' is relevant here; for instance, in the oft-cited case in 1982 when a judge fined a rapist £2,000 due to the victim's contributory negligence; she had been hitch-hiking. In other words, the assumption was that by hitch-hiking she had in some way contributed to her being a victim of rape, which was one reason why the sentence imposed was a fine rather than a prison sentence. By focusing on issues of power (in this case patriarchal forms of power) and broader forms of structural inequality, work such as Amnesty's research led to calls for a more radical and critical form of victimology to be developed.

Radical and critical approaches

These approaches to victimisation draw on the foundational critical traditions, which are discussed in more detail in **Chapters 15** and **16**. By drawing on insights derived from labelling perspectives, such as the power to label—in this case the label of a being a 'deserving' or 'undeserving' victim—and the broader concerns of the 'new criminology' (in terms of the role of state power in these labelling processes) the critical approach to victimisation re-focuses our attention on issues of vulnerability, power relations, structural inequalities and the notion of the rights, as well as the needs, of victims. Such approaches also consider victims of corporate and state power; see for example the conversations with Steve Tombs and Phil Scraton in **Chapter 16**.

In **Conversations 8.1** we hear from David Baker. Dr Baker, who is a senior lecturer in Criminology at Coventry University, tells us about his recent research into deaths which occur after police contact. He is also interested in issues of police accountability and in the search for justice by the families who have had family members die after police contact.

Although Baker's (2016) research is informed by a more socio-legal approach we can see from his very powerful piece in **Conversations 8.1** that it dovetails with the critical approach to victimology. Hopefully you will have picked up what he says on the role (and power) of state agencies in constructing the status of particular victims, in this case the role of the police and coroners' courts in labelling a victim as being either a 'deserving' or 'underserving'

CONVERSATIONS 8.1

Death after police contact—with Dr David Baker

I began researching this subject after the death of Ian Tomlinson during the G20 protests in London in 2009. He had committed no crime; he was simply walking home. Ian was moving away from police with his hands in his pockets when he was hit from behind by a police baton and shoved to the ground. He died shortly afterwards. In the immediate aftermath of this incident, it was obvious that the story the police constructed about his death was very different to the story told by eye-witnesses and Ian's family. Ian was constructed as being a homeless alcoholic, as though that would be sufficient to explain being struck and knocked down by a police officer. A pattern of smearing the deceased in these cases became very apparent to me the more I looked at this issue. It was a way of distracting attention from the police and focusing it on the 'undeserving' victim: portraying the incidents as a death, yes; a tragic death, yes; but ultimately, just one of those things, the sort of thing that happens to 'other' people. I wanted to understand how the families of people who died after police contact got justice in these cases, and this led me to do a PhD on this issue.

In the period 2004–15 a total of 1,539 citizens died after contact with the police in England and Wales. Very few police officers are successfully prosecuted in court in relation to these cases. You might find this shocking. In the United States, it became apparent in 2015 that authorities did not even count how many citizens die after police contact, a situation the Director of the FBI called 'embarrassing'. Embarrassing, shocking, or business as usual? In England and Wales the annual number of deaths has remained relatively unchanged since the turn of the century, suggesting that to some degree these deaths might indeed be seen as a case of 'business as usual'.

In the UK, Australia, and the US we know enough to be able to state that if you are from a black, minority, or ethnic (BME) group, or have mental health issues or substance dependency problems, you are disproportionately more likely to die after having contact with the police than other citizens are. Time and again, relatives of those who have died, together with pressure groups such as Inquest, have asked why lessons cannot be learned that prevent future deaths, why people with mental and physical health issues end up in police custody, and why police use of force cannot be held more to account.

The people who die leave behind a family who often experience a sort of double victimisation. Not only has their loved one died, but the deceased is often constructed as being someone who is either 'unfortunate' (for example, being homeless) or dangerous (for example, having mental health issues), and who is seen as being on the edges of society. The dead cannot defend themselves. Whilst families want to grieve for their loved one, they also want to get the truth of what happened: how exactly did they die? The truth tends to be elusive, if it appears at all. The machinery of state justice means that investigations into these cases can go on for years, as is the case with Sean Rigg who died in a police station in Brixton, South London in 2008. In 2016 his family are still pursuing the truth in his case, and it is unclear when this pursuit might end. In a way, the families themselves become victims of a justice system that seems to be set up to obstruct and deflect attempts to get at the truth. This seems some distance from the state pursuit

of justice, as in, for example the 2011 riots, when special night courts were set up to deal with 'rioters and looters' as quickly as possible. It seems that justice works one way for some, another way for others.

In 2011 Ian Tomlinson was found to have been 'unlawfully killed', in a verdict recorded by a coroner's court. This means that criminal liability could not be ascribed for his death. So we have a situation where somebody has been killed, but in law there is effectively no killer. This appears to sum up the state justice response to citizens who die after police contact: these cases are investigated in the coroner's court rather than being treated as potential crimes from the outset. It seems like there is one sort of justice system for victims of police force and another system for victims of force by other citizens. This suggests that the state protects its own, and in order to do so uses distraction techniques to suggest that the victims of such incidents are 'undeserving', and consequently so are their families. We need to think about how the state dispenses justice and why, and how this affects victims and their ability to get justice when their loved one dies after police contact.

Dr David Baker, Senior Lecturer in Criminology, Coventry University

one. It is as if a victim's vulnerability and status in society can lead to them being denied their claims to citizenship and their rights. The piece also clearly highlights the notion of secondary victimisation; the impact which having a loved one die after having contact with the police can have on their families, and the denial of their needs and rights; in these cases, a right to justice. We will return to the issues of the role of state power in constructing various 'crime problems' (and their victims) later in the book (in **Chapters 15** and **16**) when we fully consider the development of critical criminological perspectives.

We will however continue this theme of a radical/critical victimology in our next sections on hate crime and, in particular, our focus on disablist and homophobic hate crimes. These are both relatively new forms of hate crime—courts were not given the powers to enforce additional and tougher sentences for offences which were motivated or aggravated by the victim's sexual orientation or disability until the 2003 Criminal Justice Act—and are, as we shall see, linked to the broader notions of structural inequalities which are at the heart of a critical victimology.

Hate crime

Definitions of hate crime

When considering hate crime, it is important that we have a clear understanding of what is meant by the term. This is far from being unproblematic. As with the concept of 'crime' (considered in **Chapter 3**) the term 'hate crime' is also a social (and perhaps ideological) construct which covers a wide range of behaviours, such as property damage, physical attacks, written threats, bullying,

verbal threats and, more recently, the use of the Internet to spread hate speech. The key, and problematic, difference, is that these behaviours are motivated by forms of prejudice against people for simply being who they are. In other words, hate crime is related to broader issues of identity politics.

In its collation of hate crime figures, the UK government defines hate crime as 'any criminal offence which is perceived, by the victim or any other person, to be motivated by hostility or prejudice towards someone based on a personal characteristic.' This common definition was agreed in 2007 by the police, Crown Prosecution Service, Prison Service (now the National Offender Management Service), and other agencies that make up the criminal justice system. In its 2012 paper 'Challenge it, Report it, Stop it—The Government's Plan to Tackle Hate Crime' the government uses this definition and identifies five centrally monitored strands of hate crime. These are:

- race or ethnicity;
- religion or beliefs;
- sexual orientation;
- disability;
- transgender identity.

Other agencies have slightly different interpretations; for instance, the Metropolitan Police include domestic violence within their classification, whereas the national organisation StopHateUK defines hate crime as any crime that the victim believes to have been caused by hatred of their race, disability, sexual orientation or gender, or their religion. Some police forces also recognise hate directed at alternative sub-cultural groups, but any list is far from being exhaustive. It could be argued that there are other groups in society whose vulnerability and relative powerlessness might mean that their experiences of crime are not recognised; such as the elderly or the homeless perhaps? This issue of perception is important, and one we need to explore, because it affects how we interpret an offence. It also influences the impact of such offences, which we shall consider further on in the chapter. For now, let us imagine that someone has been physically assaulted because of their race; whilst the injuries received may be beyond dispute, should we treat the attack differently if the victim does not feel themselves to have been the subject of hate? Alternatively, if the victim feels that hate was a motive, but there is no evidence to support this, should the offence be treated as a hate crime or not? With this in mind consider the issues and questions raised in **What do you think? 8.3**.

WHAT DO YOU THINK? 8.3

Do we need hate crime legislation?

As we have seen, crimes which are said to be motivated by hate started to receive public and government recognition in the UK from the late 1990s. They are thought to be inextricably linked to broader issues of institutional and structural inequalities, as well as to identity politics.

- Is there however really a need for such a 'stranded' legal response to these issues?

- Should courts be given the powers to impose an enhanced sentence on the perpetrators of such crimes, if they are found guilty?

- How do we decide which groups are 'worthy' of such 'extra' legal protection?

- What if a victim who is black is also gay and/or disabled?

- Do we even really need such legislation in the first place?

Let us imagine that we are in a position to decide such issues.

As a junior minister working in the Ministry of Justice you have two important meetings scheduled in your diary for today. The first is with a national homeless charity who are going to lobby you on the need for current hate crime legislation to be extended to cover crimes committed against homeless people. You are also due to meet with senior officials from the Police Service and the Crown Prosecution Service (CPS), who will advise you on some of the broader and more practical issues related to you introducing such legislation.

In your first meeting the homeless charity points out to you that:

- Homelessness is an increasing national problem and that in terms of social isolation, life expectancy and physical and mental health issues the homeless are a very vulnerable group of people who need protection and assistance.

- All crimes committed against the homeless have increased over the last year but especially crimes of violence which, when compared to the levels experienced by the general population, are around 13 times higher.

- Your party was elected on a manifesto which stressed issues of tolerance, equality, and social justice.

- Crimes committed against the homeless compound their sense of isolation and exclusion and are particularly harmful in terms of their feelings of vulnerability and the levels of fear and anxiety they experience.

- By extending hate crime legislation to include this group you would send out an unambiguous message to the general public that such crimes are unacceptable, and the introduction of an enhanced sentence for hate crimes committed against the homeless would act as a real deterrent. As a result, such crimes would decrease which, in the long run, would result in a clear reduction in the government spend on the criminal justice system; the reduction of public expenditure and efficiency gains was also an election pledge made by your party.

In your opinion, has the charity made a convincing case? Do you think that you would consider extending hate crime legislation to include homeless people? At this stage, however, you decide to keep an open mind on the issue as you go into your second meeting with the senior officials from the Crown Prosecution and Police Services. They argue that:

- The crimes committed against homeless people (such as theft, violence, and so on) are already covered adequately by existing legislation.

- Policing the issue would prove to be very problematic for many police officers, especially if the victim were also black or disabled. Which part of a victim's identity should they prioritise when investigating

an allegation of such a crime? This would slow down investigations and make the CPS's job more complicated.

- Prosecutors would have a very difficult job in a court of law arguing for an enhanced sentence to be imposed in these cases—it is one thing to be able to secure a successful prosecution according to the clear guidelines relating to crimes of violence for instance, but another to argue that such violence was motivated by hate. This would make the prosecution of crimes more time consuming and costly.

- If the Minster were to introduce legislation to cover hate crimes committed against homeless people, you would be inundated by other campaign groups arguing that the legislation be extended to cover their particular interest group. In short, the government would be seen to prioritising some groups at the expense of others, which might be perceived by the general public, and the excluded groups, as being exclusive and simply not fair.

Which set of arguments do you think are more convincing, and why? It is a very difficult and complex task balancing out the arguments here but what you do think? What would you decide to do?

Theoretical approaches to studying hate crime

Some important studies of hate crime have considered this issue of definition from an academic, rather than an enforcement or campaigning, perspective. Phyllis Gerstenfeld (2013: 11) describes hate crime as 'a criminal act that is motivated at least in part by the group affiliation of the victim'. For her, there is no actual need for the offender to have personal hatred of the victim for the act to be classed as a hate crime. Building on this, Carolyn Petrosino (2003) expanded the definition, again considering the nature of the victim as a key factor. In her words, for a crime to be a hate crime, the victim is not only a member of a distinct group but is also someone who has less political or economic power than the majority; plus, they will be someone whom the offender perceives as posing a threat to their way of life, security, or identity. You may want to look back to Christie's list of characteristics of the 'ideal victim' which was set out earlier in this chapter—what were his views about the threat posed to society

by a victim, and how does this alter when the victim is part of an ostracised minority?

The notion of power being at the root of much hate crime is built on further by other writers, many of whom tackle the subjective and emotive topic of the impact of such crime upon victims, their families, and communities. Barbara Perry (2001) uses the term 'sprees of violence against the Other' to introduce the idea of how hate crimes emphasise and reinforce difference and segregation; she goes on to describe how 'racial, gender, ethnic and religious violence persist as mechanisms of oppression.' For Perry, a hate crime is one that takes place within a system of social processes that allow the restriction of oppressed groups and leave them vulnerable to exploitation and violence, particularly when those groups take any action which may seem to threaten the dominant (usually white, heterosexual and male) hierarchy of their environment. A hate crime is thus one which is committed in order to send a clear message that the victim is and will remain an unacceptable outsider. The victim is almost nameless and faceless, but also represents, at some level, his or her entire group or community.

Thus we can see that the concept of hate crime is one of those ideas which may seem straightforward—A attacks B out of hate—but is in reality a contested and complex one that needs to be examined critically and with sensitivity.

We will discuss the rates of hate crime further on in this chapter, but we do need to consider here some of the limitations that these data can have and how they may affect our understanding of this topic. You may also wish to look back to the statistics chapter (**Chapter 5**) to refresh your memory about some of the more general issues and controversies around the use of figures and information in the understanding of crime.

Limitations in examining hate crime

Firstly, there are some important barriers to examining hate crime and its victims. The government's hate crime page provides a link to report-it.org.uk, a site where victims can report hate crime online, and may choose whether or not to give their name or contact details. Reports are made to the police force for the area in which the crime took place. Victims or witnesses can report, and are asked to describe in their own words why they think the crime was motivated by hate. They are also asked if they wish to have their details passed onto support agencies.

Report-it.org.uk also gives advice on how to report online hate crime, which in the virtual world is generally related to the creation and distribution of material designed to incite hatred on the grounds of race, religion, and sexual orientation. However, the site does point out that there is no similar offence with regard to disability or gender transition.

The Crown Prosecution Service has issued guidance for lawyers prosecuting cases involving social media; this is largely connected with the nature or content of the material being sent, and whether it constitutes a credible threat targeting an individual or group. Sending grossly indecent or offensive material may also result in prosecution, but none of these issues are related to hate crime as a specific issue.

These may seem to be relatively small and insignificant issues, but in reality they pose serious barriers to our understanding and analysis of hate crime. For instance, if a witness or a victim chooses not to give their details, the police will be unable to take a more detailed statement or to link the incident to others that may be related. Similarly, online hate crime committed against the transgender community may well go unreported due to the lack of a legislative framework allowing its prosecution. The emotional component of a hate crime—the possibility that a victim may feel persecuted without there being any physical or circumstantial evidence to back up their perception—is similarly a factor which we need to consider when analysing and critiquing both the rates and effects of hate crime.

Rates of hate crime

Hate crime rates are analysed by statisticians working for the Home Office Crime and Policing Analysis Unit and the Office of National Statistics. You can view full reports on the gov.uk website but there are some key points which are worth highlighting here:

Over the period 2015–16, the police (in England and Wales) recorded 52,465 incidents of hate crime. Of these:

- 49,419 (79 per cent) were related to race;
- 7,194 (12 per cent) concerned sexual orientation;
- 4,400 (7 per cent) were faith-related;
- 3,629 (6 per cent) were related to disability; and
- 858 (1 per cent) were committed against transgender people.

All five of these 'monitored strands' have seen an increase from 2015 (see also **Figure 8.5**) and in fact there was an overall rise of 19 per cent in hate crime. You may have noticed that the figures quoted here do not add up; they total more than 52,465 and more than 100 per cent. As the report points out, this is because some incidents were related to more than one factor—so for example a victim could have been targeted because of both their race and their religion. Given the sensitivity in reporting such issues (even online), such figures are likely to be under-estimates. Following the EU referendum in June 2016, there was a sharp rise in the number of reported hate crimes in the UK. The National Police Chief's Council estimated that there was an increase of 57 per cent following the 'leave' vote: the vast majority of these reports related to anti-immigration forms of hate.

How do the figures reported by the Home Office compare to those collated by other organisations? StopHateUK publishes data on the reports it receives, including the calls made to the organisation's helplines and on the number of cases it refers on to local authorities or other agencies. As well as its research, this national organisation provides a range of services which include training, education, and consultancy. Its core activities are however focused on awareness-raising, campaigning, and delivering projects on a variety of issues relevant to hate crime and equality. Rather than taking a purely quantitative approach, they also invite victims to explain how the incident has made them feel and to describe the impact on them and their families.

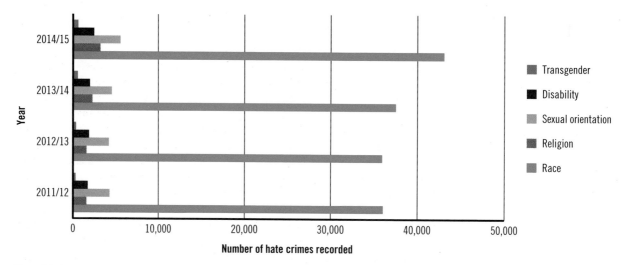

Figure 8.5 Police recorded hate crimes from 2011/12 to 2014/15 divided into race, religion, sexual orientation, disability, and transgender

Source: Home Office. Content is available under the Open Government Licence v3.0

Hate Crime	Total
Age	15
Disability	310
Gender Identity	39
Race	315
Religious/Faith/Belief	52
Sexual Orientation	122
Other*	201
Non-Hate Crime**	176
Number of Calls Reporting Two or More Hate Crime Strands	93

Table 8.2 Hate motivated crime 2014–15, as recorded by StopHateUK

*Recorded incidents that are perceived by the victim to be motivated by hate, but which do not fall into one of the monitored strands i.e. alternative subculture hate.

**Incidents where the victim does not believe there was a hate motivation involved.

(*Source: http://www.stophateuk.org/wp-content/uploads/2015/08/Stop-Hate-UK-Stats-Report-2014-15-Final.pdf*)

As with the government figures, StopHateUK record all factors involved in an offence; however, they also include strands which are not recognised by the Home Office, such as hate related to sub-cultures. The overall number of cases covered by their report is smaller than the government data, which may be due to all sorts of factors, not least a lack of awareness of the organisation and its reporting procedures; equally it may be linked to the fact that the evidence which they generate is reliant on self-reports rather than the use of a random sample survey of a particular population: however, through its overall contact methods (email, helpline, etc.) the organisation received 2,185 reports throughout 2014–15 (see **Table 8.2**).

Some organisations focus solely on statistics relating to their particular campaigning interest. Stonewall, the pressure group campaigning for lesbian, gay, bisexual, and transgender (LGBT) people, has carried out research into various issues affecting these communities; for example their experiences of mental health services or bullying in school. This report is considered in greater detail later.

What of other types of hate crime? There are ongoing concerns that some hate strands crimes are not taken seriously or investigated thoroughly. In 2014, a former Director of Public Prosecutions called reaction to disability hate crime a 'scar on the conscience' of the criminal justice system (http://www.bbc.co.uk/news/uk-29277363). If crimes are not reported, or reports are not followed up, then there will be problems in assessing the scale of the issue and the effectiveness of possible responses. Although the official statistics cited so far clearly show that, in terms of reported incidents, hate related to race is reported more than any other strand of hate, this chapter will consider two forms of hate crime which are perhaps less debated and discussed; disablist and sexual orientation. (For racist hate crime see **Chapter 10**, and for gender-specific hate crimes see **Chapter 11**.)

Disablist hate crime

A 'scar on the conscience' of the criminal justice system?

For many disabled people, state benefits such as Disability Living Allowance (which are due to be replaced by Personal Independence Payments) are an important source of financial support. These, together with many other benefits, have been subject to review as part of the current Conservative government's austerity programme. As a result, many disabled people have had their conditions or impairment reassessed by government agencies in order to determine whether or not they remain eligible to receive the payments. The media has reported many cases of so-called 'scroungers' being found out through this or other forms of scrutiny, resulting in headlines such as 'Shameless benefits scrounger who says he is too disabled to work is caught lifting 17-STONE mobility scooter up the stairs to his flat' (*Daily Mail*, 12 July 2015) and 'Benefits scrounger who "couldn't walk" filmed RUNNING with her pets at dog show' (*Daily Express*, 29 April 2015).

We may feel that it is legitimate to protect public money by preventing fraudulent claims: however, this approach has led to other, more disturbing stories. In 2007 Edward Bright, then aged 7, lost all four limbs to meningitis; in February 2016 he was told he needed to attend a meeting with the Department for Work and Pensions to prove that he was still disabled and entitled to benefits (*Daily Mirror*, 18 February 2016). In the same month, Denise Haddon who has bilateral femoral focal dysplasia and cannot walk without severe pain was told that her condition is not severe enough to allow her continued entitlement to her specially adapted car.

Examples such as these illustrate one of the key barriers to understanding disablist hate crime: the complex and sometimes unrealistic social attitudes towards disability and impairment. This has its roots in historical beliefs, particularly in Christian cultures where the Church struggled to reconcile the idea that man was made in God's image with the visible fact that some people were born with obvious impairments or illnesses; this, added to the economic problems caused when a disabled person could not make a full contribution to the community, created a troubled environment in which people with differences in their mental or physical condition came to be viewed with anxiety and even suspicion. This continued, in some forms, well into the present era.

In the US, the Supreme Court ruled in 1927 that it was not unconstitutional to forcibly sterilise learning disabled adults (a ruling that has never been overturned). In Britain, the 1944 Education Act meant that children with learning or physical disabilities were categorised according to their medical needs, and given educational placements that took little account of their intellectual or social abilities. Such children were often placed in residential schools or even hospitals, and it was not until the Warnock Report in 1978 that the concept of inclusive education was introduced, bringing disabled and non-disabled children together for the first time. This approach is now itself being reviewed, with a debate about whether it is effective for all children with 'Special Educational Needs' (SEN) to be placed in mainstream schools, and an examination of the links between SEN and social deprivation (*House of Commons Education and Skills Committee Special Educational Needs Third Report of Session 2005–06*, Volume I).

So what does this mean when we consider hate crimes directed at people with disabilities or, as they are sometimes known, disablist crimes? Firstly, we need to ascertain what we actually mean by 'disablist'. The College of Policing, in its operational guidance on dealing with hate crime, defines it as crimes directed towards a person because of their physical disability, learning disability, or mental ill health. As we saw in the figures from government and StopHateUK sources it is a very real and growing crime problem, the neglect of which is only now really starting to be addressed in both academic and policy circles.

Understanding 'disability': medical and social models

We also need to think about what we mean by the term 'disability' in itself, which is a more complex question than it might seem. In some ways, of course, it may seem obvious—when a person has, for example, a missing limb or a sensory loss, they are clearly facing challenges that are not shared by people who do not have these problems. This interpretation is known as the medical model of disability, in which the person is seen as disabled by their physical or mental limitations. However, for many disabled people, the medical model is not helpful, and instead they campaign for a different approach, the social model, to be adopted (see Shakespeare 2013, for a critical discussion of this model).

The social model of disability says that it is society's response to disabled people and their needs which creates their challenges, rather than their physical or cognitive issues. When the social response is changed, people are able to achieve independence and dignity. For example, the medical model might make the statement that because a

"As far as I'm concerned it's neither public nor convenient."

GENTLEMEN

THE SPASTICS SOCIETY
It's not that people don't care, it's just that they don't think.

Figure 8.6 A poster published by the Spastics Society, now known as Scope.
Source: Scope: www.scope.org.uk

wheelchair user cannot climb steps into a bank and a blind person cannot read printed information about setting up an account, their disability excludes them from managing their own money. The social model of disability, however, would take the view that there is no reason why the person could not take charge of their finances, and would instead seek to improve accessibility to the bank's services through the provision of practical measures like ramps, signs in braille, and so on. This is illustrated in the poster in **Figure 8.6** from the organisation known as Scope (formerly known as the Spastics Society).

We can therefore see how the two models could influence the public perception of disabled people, particularly if they are the victims of crime. If the medical model is the dominant discourse, then there may be a different response than if the social model had been foregrounded. This in turn may influence the policy and legal framework that surrounds disabled people and their relationship to the criminal justice system, particularly with regard to the way that the police deal with incidents of disablist crime. **What do you think? 8.4** examines these perceptions further.

Because the medical model has until recently been the most prevalent view of disability, there is still a simplistic view of disabled people; particularly when a disability is visible (for example, physical rather than cognitive) the assumption can be that it is the only factor to play a part in the offence. The idea that someone may suffer hate crime

WHAT DO YOU THINK? 8.4

Write down your immediate reactions to the following questions:

Imagine that a young man leaves a pub late one evening. He has had a lot to drink and is taking a short cut home down a dark alley when he is 'mugged'. He loses his wallet, containing £300, and suffers cuts and bruises when his attackers punch him. As a result, he develops anxiety attacks and depression. The local police do not catch the muggers, and simply advise him to be more careful in future.

- Do you feel sympathy?

- Was the man to blame for his own misfortune?

- Was the police response adequate?

Now read the story again.

Imagine that a young man with cerebral palsy and learning disabilities leaves a pub late one evening. He

has had a lot to drink and is riding his electric wheelchair down a dark alley when he is mugged. He loses his wallet, containing £300, and suffers cuts and bruises when his attackers punch him. As a result, he develops anxiety attacks and depression. The local police do not catch the muggers, and report the case to social services. The man is reassessed and it is suggested that he move into a residential home.

- Do you feel sympathy?

- Is the crime a hate crime or were the 'muggers' simply seeking an easy target?

- Is it reasonable to suggest that the man move into a home?

This example illustrates some of the further complexities of analysing hate crimes against disabled people.

because they also belong to another group may not be considered—so if someone is gay, lesbian, elderly, and so on as well as being disabled, these elements may not be recognised or reported and thus elements of hate crime—and elements of people's lives—remain hidden.

Other factors may also affect our understanding of hate crime. An immediate issue is one of accessibility—can the disabled person actually access the reporting mechanisms? The principal pathway for the reporting of hate crime is the report-it.org.uk website, to which many police forces provide links, whereas others operate their own online systems. Yet how useful is this to someone who cannot read, or type, or whose family deny them access to the Internet? How can a disabled person report an offender if that person is their sole carer? In the case of people with learning disabilities, we may also need to ask if they are personally aware that they are the subject of an offence, or even if they are being manipulated into committing offences themselves. And even if someone is not the victim of a crime, their family's anxiety about their perceived vulnerability may also impact on their life and opportunities.

In **Conversations 8.2** we hear from Sir Thomas Shakespeare. Sir Thomas is a sociologist, broadcaster, and campaigner for disability rights. He has achondroplasia and is a wheelchair user. Following the death of David

---

CONVERSATIONS 8.2

The cruel toll of disability hate crime—with Sir Thomas Shakespeare

The death of David Askew, who had an intellectual disability, in Manchester, after suffering years of harassment, is a sickeningly familiar story. For years, I have been sceptical about the notion of disability hate crime. While acknowledging occasional grotesque crimes such as the death of David Askew, I refused to believe that this was a common problem. As a person with restricted growth, all my life I have faced stares and mockery from people. Every day, children stare and laugh at me. If I'm in a city at night, some drunken stranger is sure to hurl abuse. But I have always shrugged my shoulders and followed my father's advice—'just ignore them'.

Two things changed my attitude. One night, coming home from Newcastle on the Tyne and Wear metro, a group of young women came and sat around me at the front of the train. As they started to harass me, asking facetious questions and making lewd comments, the encounter became increasingly humiliating. For the first time, I felt scared as well as hurt. These girls were probably 14 or 15, they had almost certainly been drinking or taking drugs, and they had no compunction at all about making me the butt of their games. Nobody on the train intervened. I felt very shaken by the time I got off the metro, and very relieved indeed that my abusers decided not follow me into the deserted car park.

Deeply unpleasant though this episode was, I classed it as bullying, rather than hate crime. From my research with disabled children in schools, I was well aware that bullying was a constant feature of their lives, in both mainstream and segregated settings. Later research with people with restricted growth confirmed that nasty

words and harassment were a common experience. My response was to argue for better disability equality education in schools, so as to challenge negative attitudes. I still felt that the term 'hate crime' was overstated and that violence was rare. The research evidence was scanty, and I thought the problem was exaggerated.

It was only when I was interviewed by a group of media students who were making a documentary film about hate crime, that I realised how wrong I was to downplay the seriousness of this very British problem. They challenged my complacency and forced me to question my attitude. I heard from them about the everyday stories of hate crime that they had investigated. I realised that these forms of violence were mostly directed towards people with intellectual disabilities.

Later, I asked several colleagues who work as advocates and supporters of people with intellectual disability about what they knew. They confirmed immediately that harassment was a constant feature of the lives of every person they worked with. They told me about conferences and gatherings where people had shared horrific experiences, which to them were commonplace. People being sellotaped to trees while people laughed, people being urinated on, people who had dog faeces put through their letter boxes, people who were beaten up. Faced with this constant exposure to the risk of abuse and violence, people with intellectual disability remained stoical and uncomplaining. Sometimes they were unable to make a complaint. Often, they were disbelieved, or were not taken seriously as witnesses. In most cases, the police were unwilling or unable to take effective action.

David Askew's tragedy follows the deaths of Raymond Atherton, Rikki Judkins, Steven Hoskin, Barrie-John Horrell, Kevin Davies, Fiona Pilkington, Christine Lakinski, and Christopher Foulkes over the last few years. Each of these individuals was targeted because they were vulnerable and disabled, exploited, humiliated, and finally killed. Looking again at the evidence, and thinking more deeply about the problem, I realise how mistaken I was to trivialise hate crime. It's not just

a matter of bullying. It's not something that people can just ignore or laugh off. It is a scourge on our society. We are members of a community where the most vulnerable people live in fear of their lives and where they are being terrified on a daily basis by the bored or the loutish or the dispossessed. I think my mental block arose because I did not want to believe that human beings could be so vile. I was wrong.

Sir Thomas Shakespeare, sociologist and broadcaster (*Guardian,* 12 March 2010; http://www.theguardian.com/ commentisfree/2010/mar/12/disability-hate-crime-david-askew)

Askew in 2010 he wrote an article (reproduced here) for the *Guardian* newspaper. In it he reflects on the issue of whether hate crimes directed at disabled people are really motivated by hate and whether or not they should be regarded as being criminal.

The study and analysis of hate crime against disabled people is a complex and emotive one. As with other groups who were previously hidden or stigmatised, we are still developing a theoretical understanding of their relationship to crime and deviance, not least in terms of our own social reactions to difference and the anxieties it causes. We shall look at this again in the light of another group which has been the target of hate: those people whose sexuality is outside what has traditionally been considered normal or acceptable—the lesbian, gay, bisexual, and transgender community.

Homophobic hate crime

The charpering omi was often to be seen in his regulation kaffies and capello. He got paid bona metzas, but was still glad to finish at chinker so he could go for a drink, maybe with a dolly Betty Bracelets.

This is not, as it might first appear, an extract from a fantasy novel or a book of Cockney rhyming slang but is in fact an example of the now almost-forgotten language of Polari. Sometimes spelled Palare or Palyaree, it was a slang-based form of speech used by gay men during the 20th century; the actors Kenneth Williams and Hugh Paddick used it to great effect when playing the two 'camp' characters Julian and Sandy in the BBC comedy series 'Round the Horne'. Hugely popular during the time in which it was broadcast to 15 million listeners (1965–68), Julian and Sandy were portrayed as being overtly gay, almost to the point of caricature, with a script full of innuendo and double entrendres. The affection in which they were held by listeners is perhaps surprising when we consider that the programme was being broadcast at a time when to be a male homosexual was illegal, punishable by a prison sentence—and only five years after explicit 'straight' sex in a novel like *Lady Chatterley's Lover* had caused the publisher to be prosecuted for releasing an 'indecent publication'.

Sexual activity between men had long been considered deviant by both the church and the state. It was classed as 'gross indecency' according to the 1861 Offences Against the Person Act; anal sex or 'buggerie' had already been prohibited, first by the church and then by Henry VIII in 1553, who made it a capital offence. It is worth noting that in 2016 the US state of Michigan nearly endorsed legislation that was worded in such a way as to make oral and anal sex illegal—bizarrely as part of an animal rights campaign—although this may be averted now that the problem has been noted. In other cultures, homosexuality is still actively persecuted, perhaps most notably in sub-Saharan Africa, India, and in the Middle East, with extreme examples being the grotesque killings of allegedly gay men by the so-called Islamic State.

Back in the 1960s, Williams and Paddick (both of whom were attracted to men in real life) were using comedy to expose something of the difficulties experienced by gay men at the time. Their use of Polari, whilst engaging and entertaining—especially when delivered in a highly comic manner that is still amusing today—also reflected the gay community's adoption of the language as a means whereby they could communicate with each other with less risk of being understood and persecuted. (In case you are wondering, the example at the beginning of this section translates as 'the searching policeman [i.e. one who might be looking for gay men to arrest] was often to be seen in his regulation trousers and hat. He got paid good money but was still glad to finish at five so he could go for a drink, maybe with a pretty policewoman.')

Whilst Julian and Sandy were so outrageously exaggerated that they were funny, and therefore acceptable, other gay men struggled in a society that deemed their sexuality to be perverse and dangerous. At best, homosexuality was viewed as an illness and something to be pitied; at worst, an unnatural character defect.

As the linguist Paul Barker (2002) has argued, these popular radio characters reflected society's attitudes to homosexuality at the time in terms of there being an acceptance of it as long as it was at a distance (through the medium of radio) and firmly within the limits of camp humour. As he concludes:

> While it is easy to dismiss Julian and Sandy as unfortunate, unsympathetic stereotypes who contributed to homophobic prejudice, I do not believe that it is useful to pass such a judgement (today). At a time when media representations of gay men were shrouded in shame, they cheerfully refused to be cowed by society's perceptions of them, paving the way for more challenging and realistic constructions.

The situation was slightly different for gay women, as lesbianism has never in the UK been illegal. Legend has it that Queen Victoria could not accept that ladies could indulge in such practices and so never signed the legislation; the truth is more likely to be bound up in legal definitions of sex being connected to a penetrative act, and the creation of a family line whereby property can be handed down.

Be that as it may, the social position of gay people in the UK has, until fairly recently, been a precarious one. This was certainly true for the working classes, who needed to maintain social acceptability in order to keep jobs, housing and status, although for the wealthy it was rather different. By the 1930s—amongst the aristocracy at least—it was possible to be gay and popular. The Honourable Nancy Mitford (daughter of Lord Redesdale) portrayed in her novels several characters who were clearly gay, basing them on her own gay friends such as the eccentric Lord Berners and the socialite Stephen Tennant (Hastings 1986).

However, there was still an overall atmosphere of mistrust and hostility towards gay people, who, we must remember, were breaking the law every time they expressed their sexuality and desires. By the end of 1954 there were 1,069 men in prison in England who had been sentenced for committing gay sex acts. The end of the second world war in 1945 had brought about an understandable desire to get life back to 'normal', a prevailing social attitude that further challenged attempts at social reform, and high profile cases such as the gay spies MacLean and Burgess, who defected to the then USSR in 1951, did not help to calm public unease and anxiety. Even war heroes such as the mathematician Alan Turing were tainted by homophobia;

Turing, who had undergone voluntary chemical 'treatment' for his homosexuality in 1952, lost his security clearance and was barred from entering America. He was granted a posthumous pardon in 2013—but it is not clear how someone without such a background would fare if they requested similar forgiveness, even today.

The Wolfenden Report of 1957 became the first formal attempt to civilise the UK's attitude to homosexuality. Interestingly, it specifically challenged the equation of crime with sin, pointing out that the law had no business interfering in the private lives of consenting adults. However, it was not until the passing of the Sexual Offences Act of 1967 that it finally became legal to be gay. There were some caveats: partners had to be over 21, they could only have sex in private, and if you happened to be in the Merchant Navy or the Armed Forces you were still vulnerable to legal action. (As late as the 1980s, some parts of the UK Civil Service still barred homosexuals from applying for positions.) In 2000, the law in England was changed to bring the age of consent for gay people down to 16, in line with that of their 'straight' peers, a move that was met with protest from religious and social leaders who complained in a letter to the *Daily Telegraph* that the new law failed to protect 'the young of both sexes from the most dangerous of sexual practices' (http://news.bbc.co.uk/1/hi/uk_politics/1047291.stm).

Finally, in 2003, the Criminal Justice Act allowed for sentences for offences against gay people to be enhanced if it were proven that the offender had been motivated by (or had been presumed to be motivated by) hostility towards the victim based on his or her sexual orientation. Further equalities legislation is also in place which seeks to protect the LGBT community from other forms of discrimination, although this can still lead to controversy in a way that other equalities rulings do not; for example, it is hard to imagine much public sympathy for a baker who refused to make a wedding cake for a couple with disabilities, yet when a Belfast cake shop owner cited his religious beliefs as grounds for refusing to make a cake for two gay men, there resulted a fierce debate on freedom of speech and the right of a business to refuse custom (http://www.theguardian.com/commentisfree/2016/feb/01/gay-cake-row-i-changed-my-mind-ashers-bakery-freedom-of-conscience-religion).

LGBT people as victims of hate

Alongside government collection of data on hate crime related to sexual orientation (which were cited in the section titled 'Rates of hate crime' in this chapter) there are other sources that seek to capture accurate information on the rates and reactions to this form of offence. The campaign group Stonewall carried out The Gay British Crime

Source	Number of hate crimes described	Reporting rates amongst respondents	Did victims report to the police?	Conviction success rates
Stonewall; Gay British Crime Survey, 2013	1 in 6 of LGB respondents said they had experienced hate crime or incident over the past 3 years	Two-thirds of respondents did not report the incident	Three quarters did not report to the police with 31% believing the police would take no action	Fewer than one in ten victims said their case resulted in a conviction Two in five said the incident was not recorded as homophobic
Galop; Hate Crime Report, 2013	1,008 homophobic crimes reported in London 2012–13 1 in 3 LGB* people report being a victim compared to 1 in 4 of the general population 1 in 14 LGB people report being victims of violence compared to 1 in 33 of the general population	76% of the general population report satisfaction in their experiences with the police compared to 67% of LGBT people	Confidence in the police has dropped in the LGBT community, from 78% in 2008–09 to 58% in 2012–13. This compares to 60% amongst the general population	Average success rate in UK courts (Crown and Magistrates) is 86% compared to 79% for homo/transphobic trials
Office of National Statistics, statistical bulletin 05/15	Aggregated figures for 2012–13 and 2014–15 are 29,000 sexual orientation hate crimes	59% of people reporting homophobic hate crime said they had been treated fairly by the police compared to 81% of the general population		

Table 8.3 Compares figures from the Galop report and the Stonewall survey

not all figures include specific data about people who are transgender—for example the Crime Survey of England and Wales does not question respondents about their gender history

Survey, which questioned 2,500 LGBT people in 2013 about their experiences; as we have seen, StopHateUK also records incidents of hate crime against LGBT people.

Galop is a London based and focused LGBT anti-violence and abuse charity which was set up in 1982 and works to prevent violence and abuse involving the LGBT community. They also support those who feel that they have been treated unfairly by the police and criminal justice system. In 2013 they commissioned a report into hate crime against the LGBT community in London (this can be viewed on their website at www.galop.org.uk).

The Galop report introduces some interesting new dimensions to our consideration of hate crime statistics, such as differences between London and the rest of the country. Its author, Nick Antjoule, is a hate crime specialist working on behalf of the National LGBT Hate Crime Partnership—a coalition of 33 charities focused on ending

homophobia, biphobia, and transphobia—who collated figures from Freedom of Information requests and data from other sources such as the Crime Survey of England and Wales.

Table 8.3 compares figures from the Galop report and the Stonewall survey. They give an overall picture of some of the key points that inform our understanding of hate crime directed at LGBT people in the UK.

Antjoule notes that whilst less hate crime generally is being reported, the proportion that relates to homophobic crime is in fact rising, from 9 per cent in 2009 to 11 per cent in 2011. Whilst this may be in part due to the government's belief that more LGBT people are willing to come forward, and that police forces are improving their recording of such incidents, we do need to ask ourselves whether there is in fact a related rise in levels of violence and prejudice towards this group of 'others'.

Conclusion

Throughout this chapter we have been exploring the relationships between 'official' and 'non-official' forms of 'evidence' and how these can raise public awareness of

a particular issue which, in turn, might lead to positive legislative and attitudinal changes. We have done this through a consideration of the important area of study which has become known as victimology, and our main focus has been on the victims of certain hate crime offences. As we have seen, victimology is a growing area of study that is contentious in terms of its definition and theoretical underpinnings. We also saw that the area of hate crime is not without its problems. For instance, we analysed some of the difficult issues involved in implementing hate crime legislation. Furthermore, some researchers, such as Mason-Bish (2014), also question the government's current 'stranded' (that is, the identification of the five strands of hate crime which are currently monitored) approach to such legislation. For her, this can lead to a silo mentality where issues of intersectionality are ignored, leading to an over-simplification of how the lived realities of being a victim are perceived and responded to.

In our discussion at the start of the chapter we noted the range of pressure and campaign groups which monitor government research as well as carrying out their own research studies. To be sure, some have greater (and more effective) access to the media and governmental policy-making circles than others, but potentially they remain an important part of the policy making process and of our criminological imaginations. By framing issues in particular ways, and in raising awareness of the various areas on which they focus, they can (and sometimes do) make a real impact.

From the first chapter of this book we have encouraged you to *Always Be Critical*. To this we could also add, *Try To Get Involved*. As a dynamic subject area there is much more to studying criminology than attending lectures, reading books, perusing websites, and doing assignments. If you have a passion for a particular area of study (such as victimology), see what you can do on a practical level. Many organisations (and there will be many more local ones where you are studying) offer opportunities for volunteering. Who knows, you may even end up working for such an organisation when you have graduated and you might be the ones who, in your campaigning for a more tolerant and just society, can make a difference.

SUMMARY

- Critically assess why only some types of criminological evidence (derived from both governmental and non-governmental sources) is drawn on to inform the policy-making process

As we saw in both this and **Chapter 6**, 'evidence', from a variety of sources, is often used to drive changes in criminal justice and social policies. In this chapter we looked at the important role that non-governmental organisations and pressure groups which have an interest in issues related to crime and justice can play in the policy making process. We also touched on their part in lobbying for change around, and raising public awareness of, their specific issue or interests. As we noted, some of the groups which focus on sectional interests have closer and more sympathetic links with both the media and government officials and are more effective and influential in achieving their aims than others; this may be due to their having better press coverage, resources, and connections. In other words, the nature of the social problem, the government in power, and the broader socio-political climate are all important variables when considering how policy decisions are reached. This can sometimes reflect on the issue involved and the amount of public sympathy it receives. Through our examples of how the LGBT and disabled communities have struggled to achieve recognition for hate crimes committed against them, we illustrated that it can sometimes take a long time to establish effective and lasting legislative change. This is especially true in areas which the public and government perceive as controversial and contentious. Having said that, as we have seen, there have been significant developments in dealing with hate crime in recent years, although clearly much still needs to be done. The research and campaigning of these groups is an important part of the democratic process in terms of informing the wider public of an issue and in attempting to monitor government policy, as well as holding them to account. Governments do however still retain a high degree of power in terms of which groups get listened to and in steering the overall direction of policy. In many ways it would appear that Christie's notion of the 'ideal' victim is still reflected in some policies, given that it can be argued that some victims are even today seen as being more ideal than others.

- Appreciate the changing role of the victim in criminal justice processes and why it has been argued that the victim has become marginalised from these

Early in the chapter we noted that many commentators have highlighted the issue of the virtual absence of the victim in the criminal justice process. We also noted that this however has not always been the case. Through a consideration of a brief history of the role of the victim in criminal justice processes, we examined how the visibility of the victim has fluctuated over time. Indeed, they once played a significant and central part in terms of initiating the prosecution of offenders. As the 19th century progressed the police took on this greater role to a much greater extent; this, combined with the growth of the legal system and its personnel, meant that the victim's role diminished. Whilst some positive changes have been achieved through the setting up of organisations such as Victim Support, recent calls to 're-centre' the victim have been questioned as there is controversy over the degree to which such a re-centring could ever be achieved in what is an adversarial justice system. Indeed, such appeals to victims' rights can often led to more punitive policies, such as tougher sentencing for offenders. This is also an important point to consider when recognising that the boundaries between the perpetrator and victim are not always as clear cut as they may seem.

- Develop an awareness of why some victims of crime are regarded as being more 'deserving' than others and how this relates to broader issues of power

As illustrated in **What do you think? 8.2** on 'deserving' and undeserving' victims, we noted that some victims elicit more sympathy than others. Drawing on the work of Christie and his notion of the 'ideal' victim, we were able to further analyse social, political, and media constructions of victimhood. Christie's work is perhaps particularly helpful to us with its highlighting of the ideological factors which are often involved in such processes. It is clear from this that power and power relations are linked here, especially in terms of his point regarding those victims who are perceived as being a threat to the dominant societal norms and values—for instance, sex workers, the homeless, travelling communities, and so on.

- Distinguish between positivist and radical/critical approaches to victimology

Although victimology lacks a strong and coherent theoretical underpinning, two broad frames of reference have been identified in this chapter. Positivist approaches focus on the scientific study of victims to find out the extent and patterns of victimisation, as well as concentrating on aspects of the relationship between the victim and the perpetrator. Early examples of the latter are often accused of encompassing a form of 'victim blaming' and have now mostly been rejected. The radical critique of the positivist frame of reference led to calls for a more critical form of victimology to be developed. This focuses more on relatively powerless groups and the forms of oppression which they are said to suffer.

- Critically discuss the main features of hate crime, the evidence of its occurrence, and evaluate the need for hate crime legislation

The ideas of hate crime and legislation aimed at tackling it are of relatively recent origin. As with the concept of crime itself, the term 'hate crime' is also a social construct which covers a wide range of criminal behaviours. The key, and problematic, difference is that hate crimes are described as being motivated by forms of prejudice against people for simply being who they are. Having considered the evidence of its occurrence (through both governmental and non-governmental sources) it is clear that the reporting of such crimes is often problematic, and it is very likely that some forms of hate crime (such as disablist and sexuality and gender identity-based crimes) are under-reported. As to whether there should be specific hate crime legislation with increased penalties being imposed on those found guilty of such offences, we have acknowledged that this is a keenly debated issue.

- Identify forms of hate crime and analyse the underlying social and political issues which affect both public and policy responses to the affected groups

At the moment there are officially five centrally monitored strands of hate crime, which are: race or ethnicity; religion or beliefs; sexual orientation; disability; and/or transgender identity. There has been some debate as to whether these strands adequately reflect the range of potentially vulnerable and relatively powerless groups who could become victims of crimes that are motivated by hate. In this chapter we focused our discussion primarily on the strands of sexual orientation and disability as these tend to get less coverage. You were encouraged to critically evaluate the case for increasing the number of strands which are monitored. For instance, should crimes committed against homeless people be included as a recognised strand? What about expanding hate crime categories to also include misogynistic incidents, as the Nottingham police force has recently done? It is clear that issues of social and political power are important here in terms of what is recognised as constituting hate crime and what is neglected. We also noted the issue of intersectionality which further complicates public and policy responses and perhaps oversimplifies the lived realities of this complex issue.

- Explain the broader notions of structural inequalities which are at the heart of a critical victimology in relationship to the concept of hate crime

This chapter has highlighted how victimology moved away from focusing on individual perspectives on the process of victimisation to focus more on broader structural factors and inequalities. The work by Mawby and Walklate (1994) took this further and argued from the point of view that victimisation represents a form of structural powerlessness. It was this more critical position which informed our discussions of hate crime directed against disabled people and the LGBT community.

REVIEW QUESTIONS

1. What precisely does it mean to be a victim of crime?

2. What are the various impacts that being a victim of crime can have on an individual?

3. What does it mean to say that criminal victimisation is socially patterned and not evenly distributed?

4. Why are some victims regarded as being more 'deserving' of their victim status than others?

5. Can an adversarial criminal justice really achieve justice for both victims and offenders?

6. Choose a recognised and officially monitored form of hate crime and list three reasons why victims may decide not to report it to the police.

7. Is disablist hate crime really a form of crime? Why, or why not?

8. List three arguments for and against there being hate crime legislation.

FURTHER READING

Chakraborti, N. and Garland, J. (2015) *Hate Crime; Impact, Causes and Responses*. London: Sage.
This is a good accessible book which covers the areas in this chapter as well as those which, for reasons of space, were not. For instance, you will find discussions of racist and religiously motivated hate crime as well abuse and violence targeted against the elderly, sex workers

and the homeless. It also has important discussions on responses to hate crime and international perspectives.

Chakraborti, N. and Garland, J. (eds) (2015) *Responding to Hate Crime: The Case for Connecting Policy and Research*. Bristol: Policy Press.
A solid edited collection for those of you who wish to explore the hate crime research-policy nexus in greater depth.

Hall, N., Corb, A., Giannasi, P., and Grieve, P. (eds) (2014) *The Routledge International Handbook on Hate Crime*. Oxford: Routledge.
The Routledge Handbooks series are pitched at a high level and contain a range of original essays from leading academic and practitioner experts. Well worth dipping into for higher level further study.

Spalek, B. (2006) *Crime Victims; Theory, Policy and Practice*. London: Palgrave MacMillan.
Regarded as a good introductory textbook to the general area of victimology. It includes concise overviews of the main areas such as: theoretical perspectives, researching victimisation, official responses, and the victims' needs and rights.

Access the **online resources** to view selected further reading and web links relevant to the material covered in this chapter.
www.oup.com/uk/case/

CHAPTER OUTLINE

Introduction   228

Why do we need to view youth crime differently?   228

Growing up—theories of childhood and youth   229

Theories of delinquency   232

Growing into crime: Culture and deviance   239

Responding to young people's offending behaviour   248

Progressive approaches to youth offending:
Diversion and positive youth justice   254

Conclusions   257

Explaining youth crime and youth justice

KEY ISSUES

After reading this chapter you should be able to:

- outline how 'childhood' and 'youth' have been socially-constructed;

- critically explore the key criminological explanations for youth crime;

- promote understanding of the cultural influences on offending by young people;

- explain the dominant role of early intervention and risk management approaches in responding to youth crime;

- interpret contemporary progressive models for responding to youth crime, notably diversion and positive youth justice.

Introduction

This chapter focuses on youth crime and youth justice: offending behaviour committed by children and young people and the subsequent treatment of young people in the justice system. Youth crime and youth justice are central issues in criminology; in particular the need to explore and explain offending behaviour by children and young people, and to respond to that offending in ways that are differentiated from adult offending.

In this chapter, we discuss the argument for a bespoke understanding and response to youth and crime as distinct from offending behaviour committed by adults. Our starting point is to look at how the concepts of 'childhood' and 'youth' have been theorised and socially constructed over time (cf. Hendrick 2015). This will lead into discussion of how youth crime and 'delinquency' have been explained in individualised, developmental, and agentic terms.

This chapter will then examine how young people may grow into crime, with a critical focus on the cultural and media influences that may help adults to better understand the youth crime problem as constructed by 'us' rather than as the sole responsibility or fault of 'them' (young people). As undergraduates, you may be uniquely placed to evaluate these from the perspective of age, as you are likely to have only recently moved from the category of youth (aged 10–17 years) into adult (aged 18 and over) in criminal justice terms. We move on to explore and evaluate the dominant formal responses to youth crime (i.e. youth justice), which are wedded to pseudo-positivist early intervention and risk management approaches. Finally, we introduce progressive, contemporary approaches to delivering youth justice/responding to youth crime via emphases on diversion and positive, children-first models. The chapter concludes by revisiting the over-arching question of 'who is the problem: them or us?', which contrasts the individualisation of explanations for youth crime with the potential for adult-led systemic and structural influences to socially construct youth crime and justice.

Why do we need to view youth crime differently?

Since the mid-1700s and the onset of the industrial revolution and compulsory schooling (in the UK), the notion of childhood has become quite clearly distinguished as a separate life stage, with its own very specific characteristics (Hendrick 2015). Before that time, children were thought of as essentially little adults, working and socialising with older adults. This distinction, based on identified differences in relation to biological, psychological, and social development and behaviour, led to a whole range of special provisions and institutional arrangements reserved for children in the criminal justice context. Thus, for example, there is a clear understanding that children are not to be subjected to the same expectations as adults in terms of their legal responsibilities or their obligations to provide for themselves through paid work. Their position in family life is clearly marked out as one of dependency and they are seen in terms of their relative immaturity and developmental growth towards a fully completed (and responsible) adult state. In the present day, indeed, international consensus on this issue has reached the point where nearly

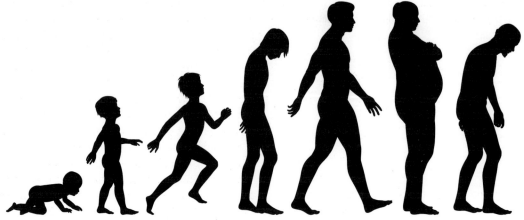

Figure 9.1 At what point does a child become an adult?
Source: © Robert Adrian Hillman/Shutterstock.com

all the nations of the world (the exception being the USA) have signed up to the United Nations Convention on the Rights of the Child, which marks out a series of state and public obligations defining the appropriate treatment of those members of the population defined as children—that is, everyone under the age of 18. That being said, there remain broad international variations in the age of criminal responsibility for a child or young person (see **Figure 9.1**).

All of these beliefs and expectations involve a series of assumptions about what it means to be a child, what should be expected in terms of children's development, and at the same time how they should be expected to come to terms with increasing levels of responsibility and social obligation. This, in turn, clearly flows through into a set of assumptions about their behaviour, and how this is to be managed. However, such assumptions can be problematic, and are associated with wide-ranging debate and disagreements about exactly what we should expect from our children; and how we should respond if they do not match up to these expectations. As we shall see, these contentious issues flow through into arguments about how we should hold children responsible for their actions, and what we should do to ensure their compliance with conventional standards of behaviour.

Growing up—theories of childhood and youth

Childhood has long been the subject of wide-ranging academic interest, not least because of widespread concerns about the problems associated with children and the sense of threat sometimes associated with the idea of young people being out of control. Indeed, this sort of fear has been around for a very long time, as Shakespeare's lines show:

> I would that there were no age between ten and three-and-twenty, or that youth would sleep out the rest; for there is nothing in between but getting wenches with child, wronging the ancientry, stealing, fighting.
>
> Shepherd, *The Winter's Tale*, Act III, Scene 3

It is important to understand how theories of childhood and youth have developed to provide context to the issues we will consider in later sections. We will now take a look at how the definition and concept of childhood has evolved through history and what it means today. You may wish to look at the questions raised in **What do you think? 9.1** before continuing.

Childhood in history

The concept of childhood is not as straightforward as you might think. So how then has this period in the lifespan been viewed by those who have tried to make sense of it? When we investigate this we find commentators who have taken contrasting perspectives on the matter. Philippe Ariès (a French medievalist and historian of the family, 1914–84), for instance, believed that childhood was effectively a modern invention, and that it was only effectively discovered in the Middle Ages. Recognising that children were virtually absent from artistic works before this time, he suggested that this, along with the absence of any distinctive form of dress, indicated: 'a marked indifference … to the special characteristics of childhood' (Aries 1962: 73). Children were accordingly treated in the same way as adults, with the same expectations of them, and the same social standing. This hypothesis may help to account for the apparent liability of children in pre-modern times to the same, often extreme, forms of punishment as their elders.

Only recently, argues Ariès, has childhood begun to be seen differently, with families beginning to 'coddle' their young, as they became both more sentimentalised, and more highly valued for their potential economic contribution. Accordingly, too, children's ignorance, weakness, and innocence began to be emphasised, and they were viewed now as 'fragile creatures … who needed to be both safeguarded and reformed' (Ariès 1962; 133).

The implications of this argument are that childhood itself has only come to be seen as a separate life stage in

WHAT DO YOU THINK? 9.1

Defining the 'child'

The age ranges ascribed to childhood have fluctuated greatly historically and between and within countries. Consider your views on these issues:

- What is the appropriate age range over which someone should be considered to be a child?

- Across what ages should they be considered to be a young person or youth?

- Should these age ranges be different for specific forms of behaviour such as offending or attending school or leaving home or voting?

- What are the main historical, social, political, public, and academic influences on how these categories are socially constructed and decided?

tandem with, and as a result of, wider social changes, such as industrialisation, the specialisation of labour, and the associated need for longer periods of education and preparation for work (cf. Case 2017). Although this account does seem to fit well with our recent history of increasing levels of distinction between children and adults within the justice system, Ariès has come in for substantial criticism, so it would be unwise to accept his portrayal simply at face value. Pollock (1983) for example, thinks that Ariès may have been inclined to take a relatively narrow Western perspective on childhood, and she comments that just because children have been treated differently by other cultures, this does not mean that they were not seen as children. Indeed, the Anglo-Saxon king, Athelstan, is believed to have promoted a policy of leniency to young offenders on the basis of their age and status.

Heywood (2001) has also criticised Ariès's position that somehow previous eras and cultures were times of depravity and lack of civilisation, in contrast to contemporary enlightenment and more humane treatment of those who offend. Cunningham (2005), on the other hand, has suggested that there has been persistent evidence of a divergence of views about how to bring up children, and evidence of recurrent tensions between advocates of punishment or nurture. What we can discern from these debates is that there has been a persistent concern historically over the ways in which children are seen and treated, but these have not reflected any substantial level of agreement as to shared understandings or common approaches to their upbringing; there have been contrasting perspectives on this issue throughout history (see **What do you think? 9.2**).

Constructing childhood

This lack of agreement throughout history has led some to the view that childhood is essentially a social construction, being dependent on prevailing norms and the expectations and requirements of the wider society for its specific qualities (Hendrick 2015). It is a changeable concept. Thus, for example, different stages of development and competence are not fixed but vary according to the assumptions we make about children's place in the world and their relationships with adults. Hence, for example, formal constructions of children's legal status vary quite significantly between different countries, and this in turn reflects differing assumptions about when they should be seen as becoming responsible for their behaviour (Case 2017). The age of criminal responsibility is relatively low in the countries of the United Kingdom, whereas elsewhere in Europe it is found to be much higher. **Figure 9.2** sets out the ages of criminal responsibility across countries in western Europe, illustrating that the lowest ages

lie in England and Wales and Northern Ireland, followed by Scotland and Ireland (the closest neighbour of the UK countries).

These variations are striking, but they are also illustrative of a significant cultural variation in the way we define childhood, and how we understand the process of development and maturation. Further complexities arise when we consider the differing ages at which children assume legal rights and responsibilities across other aspects of their lives. So, for example, across the UK the age of sexual consent is 16, and the age at which voting rights are acquired is 18 (except in Scotland, where it was lowered to 16 in 2015), suggesting a rather more restrictive view of children's civil rights as compared to their criminal responsibilities.

Aside from the material effects of these variations, it seems that they represent differential processes of conceptualising and constructing childhood (Smith 2010), so that it becomes difficult to see this as a life stage with many common or constant underlying features. James and James (2004: 58), for example, draw attention to the tensions between structure and agency and the corresponding implications for the ways in which children's attributes and actions can be understood—are they the product of inherent and deterministic forces, on the one hand, or the expression of rational calculations and free will, on the other, for instance? Importantly, for them, is the point that these are contested explanations, leading to different conclusions and different strategies for approaching the children's upbringing.

By implication, understandings and explanations of the problem behaviours of the young are also grounded in differing beliefs about the origins and causes of childhood misdemeanours.

WHAT DO YOU THINK? 9.2

Nature or nurture?

The argument has raged long and fiercely over whether children are predominantly driven by biological, instinctive urges that need to be contained and controlled in order to produce socially adjusted adult citizens (nature; see **Chapter 13**) or whether they are essentially products of their environment (e.g. social deprivation, poverty) and the influences around them (nurture; see **Chapter 14**). This in turn introduces questions as to whether children who offend are deprived or depraved; whether they are in need or at risk; whether they require care or control.

Which explanations seem more plausible to you, and what are the implications for policy and practice?

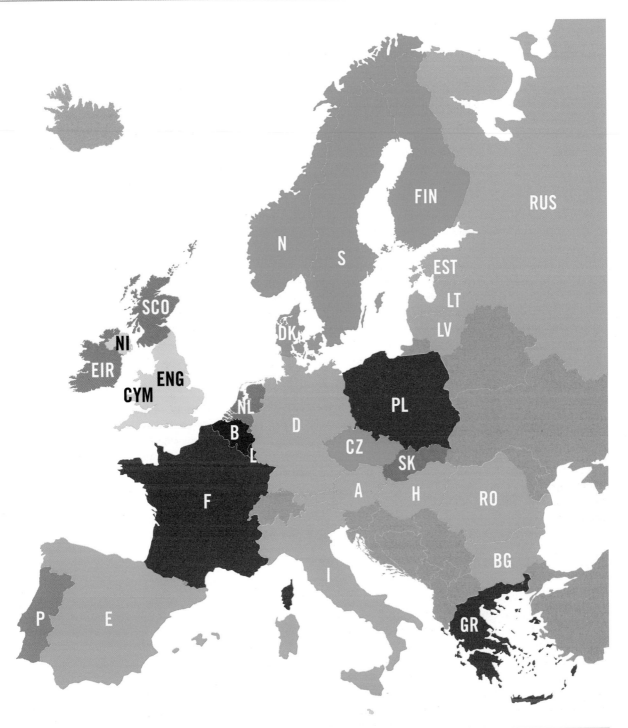

10	England, Wales, Northern Ireland
12	Scotland, Ireland, Netherlands
13	France, Greece, Poland
14	Bulgaria, Estonia, Germany, Hungary, Italy, Latvia, Lithuania, Romania, Russian Federation, Spain

14/15	Slovakia
15	Czech Republic, Denmark, Finland, Norway, Sweden
16	Portugal
18	Belgium, Luxembourg

Figure 9.2 Ages of criminal responsibility for young people in western European countries

Source: Adapted from Goldson 2013: 18

Developmental explanations of childhood

While the social construction of the 'child' can be explained in terms of the complex social processes which shape their experiences and their views of the world, 'childhood' has no essential form or structure. Conventional accounts tend to see it more as a developmental life phase, during which a series of identifiable biological, psychological, and psychosocial processes lead towards a mature state of adulthood.

Physical growth, and biological and hormonal changes are thus correlated with certain recognised stages in child development, such as puberty. Moving into the 21st century, such physiological features of childhood have been found to have parallels in neurological developments, too. In fact, children's brains have been found to be more highly organised than those of adults in some respects, purely to facilitate the pace of learning that they demonstrate: 'The number of connections in a baby's brain greatly exceeds adult levels. Many of these excess connections have to be cut back' (Blakemore and Frith 2005: 18).

In the same way as biological milestones are mapped out, so developmental psychology has also become an influential lens through which childhood has been evaluated. Piaget (1959: 55), for instance, articulated a number of stages in children's linguistic development, thought to reflect increasing levels of sophistication and social integration as they move from an 'ego-centric' and concrete form of thinking towards more abstract and other-oriented forms of expression. Vygotsky (1986), too, has constructed a detailed analysis of the processes of young children's learning and development; but he differs from Piaget in that he attributes this much more to the social dimensions of interaction and acculturation than to internal and innate qualities of the individual.

Others who have strongly shaped this 'ages and stages' model of child development have included Freud (1977) whose analysis of sexuality adopted this kind of framework; and Erikson (1995) whose work is seen as important to the extent that it provides an explanatory framework for the tensions and conflicts associated with adolescence. In Erikson's depiction, adolescence is a period characterised by 'ego-identity versus role confusion'; where a growing sense of self and one's individual qualities is mirrored by the challenge of finding a place and an accepted role in society. Failure to negotiate this divide can result in increasing uncertainty, and a corresponding need to experiment with different lifestyles and activities.

This conceptualisation of the changes associated with the transitions of youth finds echoes elsewhere in concepts such as 'storm and stress', a term originated by G. Stanley Hall in 1904 and exerting considerable subsequent influence (Arnett 1999). Such analyses have helped to cement in place the idea that conflict and disruption are more or less 'normal' features of making the transition from childhood to fully developed adulthood (Smith 2011: 12). While this portrayal of youth as inevitably experiencing conflict has been questioned to an extent (cf. Rutter et al. 1976), there is no doubt that adolescence is characterised by certain types of 'events' which may have an effect on young people. It is as important though, to think in terms of a range of factors that might have an impact rather than according primacy to any one source, such as biological drives or psychological phases. Some have suggested, for example, that it may be more helpful to think in terms of **critical moments** or **turning points** when the combination of individual characteristics and social influences shaping young people's experience is exposed to specific influences of forces which may lead to significant changes in their lives (Thomson et al. 2002; Sampson and Laub 1993, 2005).

So where are we now? Linking back to the key issues for this chapter, we have explored how the concepts of childhood and youth have been socially constructed—subject to historical, social, political, and academic influences in relation to how they have been categorised, contested, explored, and understood.

Theories of delinquency

Given the varied, complex, and clearly unresolved array of alternative accounts of childhood and youth, it may not be too surprising to find that when we turn to the subject of youth crime and deviance, explanations are similarly diverse.

Broadly, the origins and causes of young people's offending can be categorised under one of three headings (although in some explanatory accounts these may be combined) (based on Rutter at al 1998):

- individual attributes;
- psychodynamic factors;
- social and structural influence.

Each of these, too, can be understood as being to a greater or lesser extent to interact with young people's *agency*, that is, their capacity or otherwise to make rational decisions and choices about whether or not to behave in a particular way.

Individualised causes of delinquency

As we have seen in relation to understandings of childhood, individualised accounts (i.e. locating explanations and causes within the individual young person, not external influences) can be grounded in positivist biological and/or psychological explanations (see **Chapters 13** and **14**). It may be thought, for example, that young people are born with natural urges that are inherently self-centred, destructive, and antisocial. Jenks (1996), for example, portrays this as a centuries old preconception, which sees the untamed child as an inevitable threat to discipline and social order. As we have seen, this perception may well chime with ideas of the child as naturally unprepared for the demands and responsibilities of later life, and therefore in need of schooling and shaping in order to meet these expectations. Where these objectives are not achieved, crime is the inevitable consequence, it would seem.

Similarly, there may be other, innate or genetic characteristics that predispose some children more than others to wilful and deviant behaviour. So, there are purported to be certain inherited conditions that may be associated with such behaviour patterns, such as may be associated with ADHD, for example. Evidence to support such hypotheses is provided by twin studies, for example, whereby monozygotic (shared egg) and dizygotic (non-shared egg) twins are compared subsequently to evaluate the contribution of heredity to their attributes and behaviour. Such studies have consistently claimed to find a heredity effect whereby those with more genes in common are also more likely to demonstrate shared criminal traits as well (Hopkins-Burke 2013). On the other hand, it has also been pointed out that it is very difficult to separate out hereditary and environmental influences in such cases. Nonetheless, one twin study has come up with a very precise calculation of the proportionate effect of different factors on delinquent behaviour:

> The best fitting model suggested that 18%, 56% and 26% of the variance in delinquency among both boys and girls is associated with additive genetic, nonshared environment, and shared environmental factors, respectively.
>
> Taylor et al. 2000: 433

This quote illustrates the essential nature-nurture debate—assigning varying degrees of influence to genetics (nature) and environment (nurture).

Youth and gender

Of course, one strong and apparently indisputable biological factor that appears to have an influence on subsequent criminality is gender, with girls variously reported to be about half as likely to commit offences as boys (Arnull and Eagle 2009). This, in turn, prompts a challenging series of questions to do with the influence of genetic make-up and hormonal differences between genders, as compared to different patterns of socialisation and life events (Rutter et al. 1998). It is noted, for example, that 'greater male involvement in crime is a universal finding that applies across cultures and over time' (Rutter et al. 1998: 276), suggesting that there may be a biological basis for this pattern. On the other hand, the nature and extent of such disparities has also 'varied markedly over time and among ethnic groups' and 'the male:female difference varies greatly by both pattern of antisocial behaviour and by age' (Rutter et al. 1998: 276). Thus, males are much more likely to be responsible for certain types of violent behaviour, but only slightly more likely to engage in minor theft, and no more likely at all than females to be involved in shoplifting, it is observed. From this example, then, it seems impossible to single out one explanation of crime or antisocial behaviour, or even one type of explanation, that fits consistently. Biological differences might contribute, but these seem to be modified by cultural differences, and life experiences also appear to play a part—perhaps in amplifying exposure of boys to conflict and discord in light of innate tendencies towards greater levels of aggressive behaviour (Rutter et al. 1998: 277). For a more detailed discussion of gender issues in the youth justice context, you are recommended to read *Offending Girls. Young Women and Youth Justice* by Gilly Sharpe (2011)

Explaining youth crime developmentally

The second key issue of our chapter focuses on a critical exploration of the key criminological explanations for youth crime. Recognition of the likely complexity of the process of becoming delinquent has led to the emergence of a strand of criminological thinking which tries to account for youth crime as the product of interlocking developmental processes. The interaction between individual characteristics, personal experiences, and social and cultural influences peculiar to late childhood and adolescence is held to be specifically responsible for the types of antisocial and criminal behaviour which manifest themselves principally at this life stage. Explanations may be complex, but this framework establishes a coherent theoretical model for accounting for youth crime, both in general and in its specific manifestations. The observation that the peak period of offending falls in the teenage years offers potential validation for developmental theories. In fact, the peak age of offending (in England and Wales) appears to have been increasing in recent years, standing at 19 for males, and 21–24 for females in 2013 (Bateman 2015).

Crime and criminality can thus be thought of as following a particular pattern, depending on the factors which comprise the individual's personal life course. Adolescence in particular is a period of transitions with important potential triggers or turning points. This period allegedly establishes the pre-conditions for young people's involvement in criminal activity. However, of course, it is their specific impact on particular individuals that determines their propensity to become offenders, or in due course to desist from crime. Such events can be distinguished and enumerated to some degree, and Coleman and Hendry (1999: 210) have formulated a typology that helps us to distinguish between potential influences of young people's pathways into or out of crime (see also **Chapter 18**):

- **Normative events**, such as biological and physiological changes or school transfers will affect all young people.

- **Non-normative events**, such as low income, family change, illness, or being excluded from school affect particular groups to varying degrees, in varying combinations and at different times.

- **'Daily hassles'** are persistent experiences which may have a cumulative but largely hidden effect, such as isolation, bullying, or other forms of oppression.

Sampson and Laub (2005: 43) account for the development of young people's involvement in crime by way of 'the concept of *emergence*' [their emphasis], which tries to account for the interplay between different influences and different types of influence (to be discussed later in this chapter), which may be largely unpredictable and rely on chance combinations of factors, alongside individual characteristics, such as group dynamics, 'time-varying events', and 'human agency' (Sampson and Laub 2005: 43). Thus, outcomes that may be difficult to anticipate or predict with any degree of confidence can be reliably explained, albeit after the fact. Interestingly, too, this kind of account leaves room for individual freedom of action, so that although social structures and contingent events set the terms, it is the situated choice exercised by the young person which determines whether or not s/he will engage in offending behaviour.

Explaining delinquency empirically

The development of empirical, research-based (largely developmental) explanations of youth offending has been dominated by positivist theories, which are discussed in detail elsewhere in the book (see **Chapters 6, 13, and 14**). These theories have been criticised in a number of ways,

notably due to positivism's widespread reductionism in its methodology, explanations, and conclusions—reducing complex systems and behaviours to fixed statistical quantities and overly-simplistic and often exclusive biological, psychological, or sociological categories and explanations (see **Chapters 13** and **14**). Another purported limitation of positivist theories has been that the identified causal influences on crime can be more accurately described as correlates with, rather than causes of, criminal behaviour, so the extent of their explanatory utility has been overstated (see **Chapter 19**). Notwithstanding these criticisms, positivist theories have attained explanatory dominance within criminology since the turn of the 20th century (Case and Haines 2009). This explanatory dominance has been largely based on empirical research with young males, which has provided positivist theories with a significant evidence base compared to other explanatory models. Consequently, the relevance of these theories to explaining offending by young people is clear, as the majority young offenders are young (obviously) and male (Case and Haines 2010). Therefore, any attempt to explore and explain youth crime must consider positivist theories closely.

In the past 20 or so years, positivist explanations have begun to receive a significant challenge from critical theories offering alternative explanations of youth offending. Radical and critical theories of criminology (see **Chapters 15** and **16**) have tended to explain youth offending as a social construction resulting from differential power relations in Western society (Case 2017). The result is that young offenders are viewed (to a large degree) as victims of differential control over the creation and application of laws in youth justice systems, based on factors such as socio-economic status, gender, ethnicity, and (latterly) age (i.e. adults exerting power over young people). Critical theorists have posited that young people who offend have become stigmatised by explanations and responses to youth offending due to:

- positivist explanations privileging individual factors as causes of youth offending over wider social, economic, and political influences (Goldson and Muncie 2015), which can lead to labelling and blaming young people, rather than adopting a broader explanatory view of their behaviour;

- the harmful and criminalising use of custody for juveniles across western Europe and North America in opposition to the ethical and principled use of rehabilitation and adherence to basic human rights (Muncie and Goldson 2006);

- the neglect of the universal human rights of young people in trouble with the law in the UK, western Europe, and North America, which stigmatises and labels these young people as offenders first rather than as children who have offended (Haines and Case 2015; Case and Haines 2010);

- the excessive interventionism of youth justice systems internationally—increasingly interfering in young people's lives across an ever-expanding age range for an ever-expanding range of (not always criminal) behaviours, thus increasingly labelling young people as risky, problematic, and in need of adult control (Muncie and Goldson 2006).

Despite critical theories bemoaning the theoretical, ethical, and practical weaknesses of modern youth justice, pseudo-positivist, developmental theories (pseudo due to their focus on predictors rather than causes—see **Chapters 18** and 19) continues to dominate explanations of and responses to youth offending in the industrialised western world due to its common sense explanation, vast evidence base, and practical nature—all of which appeal to politicians, policy makers, and practitioners (Case and Haines 2009). The 'Risk Factor Prevention Paradigm' or 'RFPP', the practical animation of artefactual risk factor theories, has become the go-to explanation of youth offending, largely motivated by a perceived need to respond to the risks that young people supposedly present to themselves and others (Goldson 2005). The basis of the RFPP is straightforward:

> Identify the key risk factors for offending and implement prevention methods designed to counteract them … identify key protective factors against offending and implement prevention methods designed to enhance them.
>
> Farrington 2007: 606

Artefactual risk factor researchers have employed positivist, empirical methods (see **Chapter 6**) to quantify different aspects of young people's behaviour into 'risk factors', which they then statistically-manipulate in order to conclude predictive relationships with later offending. The paradigm incorporates a range of developmental explanatory theories, which suggest that risk factors can be identified in the family, school, neighbourhood, lifestyle, and psychological domains of a young person's early life (e.g. childhood, early adolescence), which (statistically) predict the development of offending in later life (e.g. late adolescence, adulthood).

The UK government's preferred explanations of, and responses to, youth offending have privileged the RFPP as the vehicle to animate an early intervention and risk management approach to youth justice (discussed later in this chapter; see also Youth Justice Board 2003). This approach has been shaped by and evidentially-grounded in two particular developmental, artefactual risk factor studies: *The Cambridge Study in Delinquent Development* (West and Farrington 1973) and *Crime in the Making* (Sampson and Laub 1993).

The Cambridge Study in Delinquent Development

The much-respected 'Cambridge Study' began in 1961 at Cambridge University (hence its common nickname) under Donald West, who was later joined and then replaced by David Farrington. Its theoretical and methodological origins can be traced to the *Unraveling Juvenile Delinquency* study (Glueck and Glueck 1930) in the USA, which 'pointed to the strong and continuing influence of early upbringing and family circumstances in determining who became delinquent' (West 1982: 3). In the seminal *Present Conduct and Future Delinquency*, West (1969: 1) set out the central aim 'to trace the influence of community, family and individual factors, as seen at this early age, on personality, performance and social adjustment in later years'. The prospective longitudinal study design was intended to enable the study to trace the development of individual offending over time, to explore the key features of the 'criminal career' (i.e. onset, duration, continuity, desistance), and to investigate the extent to which offending in adolescence could be predicted by early life experiences. Consequently, the Cambridge Study adopted a 'developmental' approach to explaining youth crime, locating its causes in individual characteristics that developed from early childhood—with these influences typically seen as predictors of, and 'risk factors' for, offending.

Methodologically, the Cambridge Study investigated 'a traditional White, urban, working class sample of British origin' (Farrington, in Thornberry and Krohn 2003: 139), all of whom were born in 1953–54 in South London, England. The majority of the all-male sample of 411 boys (97 per cent) were from state primary schools, with the other 12 boys sampled from a local school for the 'educationally subnormal'. The boys were interviewed in school at ages 8–9, 10–11, and 14–15, then re-interviewed in the study research office when aged 16, 18, and 21 years and in their homes at age 25, 32, 46, and 50 years. The early interviews explored a variety of psychological and social factors in childhood and adolescence, supplemented in the adult interviews (aged 18 years and over) by gathering data on employment histories, adult relationships, and the children of the sample (Farrington, in Rutter 1988). A variety of additional research methods were employed to gather information to complement the interview data, including: in-school tests of individual characteristics (e.g. intelligence), annual parent interviews, teacher questionnaires, peer ratings, and official statistics of delinquency of parents and siblings (see Farrington, in Thornberry and Krohn 2003).

In *Who Becomes Delinquent*, West and Farrington (1973) made statistical comparisons between delinquents and non-delinquents to identify so-called explanatory risk factors that were measured when the boys were aged 8–10 years and which allegedly were able to statistically predict future offending (official and self-reported) at age 14–15 years. The 50-year review of the Cambridge Study located the 'most important predictors' of later offending at age 8–10 years within six categories (Farrington, in Thornberry and Krohn 2003):

- **antisocial behaviour in childhood**—including 'troublesomeness', dishonesty, aggressiveness;
- **hyperactivity-impulsivity-attention deficit**—including poor concentration, restlessness, risk-taking;
- **low intelligence** and low school achievement;
- **family criminality**—including convicted parents, delinquent older siblings, siblings with behaviour problems;
- **family poverty**—including low family income, large family size, poor housing;
- **poor parenting**—including harsh discipline, poor supervision, parental conflict.

The Cambridge Study utilised a highly innovative methodology for its time—a prospective longitudinal design (that is a method whereby information is collected over a long period of time) to measure the development of behaviour and the use of multiple data forms (official and self-reported, quantitative and qualitative) obtained from multiple sources (children, parents, teachers). This enabled the study findings to be triangulated—validated against one another for a more holistic and accurate understanding of young people's behaviour. However, several methodological criticisms remain, which seriously question the validity of any findings, explanations, and conclusions: urban-bias, class-bias, outdated, psychosocial bias, androcentricism, and ethnocentrism (see **Figure 9.3**).

The *Cambridge Study in Delinquent Development* is still being replicated with the children of the original sample after over 50 years. It has been the theoretical and empirical inspiration for artefactual risk factor theories and the RFPP for over 50 years. The predictive risk factors identified (in childhood) have exerted a powerful influence over virtually all subsequent risk-focused research with young people and have found their way into the policy making of politicians and senior government policy makers, who have been attracted by the longevity of the Cambridge Study, the common sense nature of its findings, and the confidence with which their replicability and apparent validity has been asserted (see later in this chapter).

Crime in the Making

In 1985, Robert Sampson and John Laub obtained access to the raw data from the Gluecks' developmental risk factor study *Unraveling Juvenile Delinquency* (Glueck and Glueck 1930; see also Case and Haines 2009), upon which the Cambridge Study had been based. From there, they embarked on the extensive process of restoring, rebuilding, validating, and re-analysing this data. The challenge

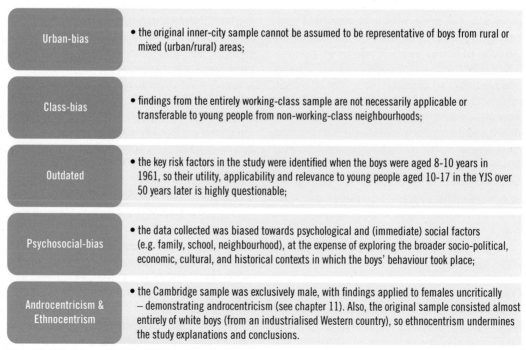

Urban-bias	• the original inner-city sample cannot be assumed to be representative of boys from rural or mixed (urban/rural) areas;
Class-bias	• findings from the entirely working-class sample are not necessarily applicable or transferable to young people from non-working-class neighbourhoods;
Outdated	• the key risk factors in the study were identified when the boys were aged 8-10 years in 1961, so their utility, applicability and relevance to young people aged 10-17 in the YJS over 50 years later is highly questionable;
Psychosocial-bias	• the data collected was biased towards psychological and (immediate) social factors (e.g. family, school, neighbourhood), at the expense of exploring the broader socio-political, economic, cultural, and historical contexts in which the boys' behaviour took place;
Androcentricism & Ethnocentrism	• the Cambridge sample was exclusively male, with findings applied to females uncritically – demonstrating androcentricism (see chapter 11). Also, the original sample consisted almost entirely of white boys (from an industrialised Western country), so ethnocentrism undermines the study explanations and conclusions.

Figure 9.3 Methodological criticisms of the Cambridge Study

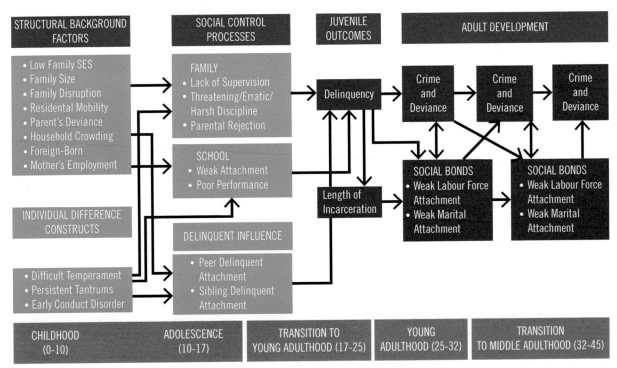

Figure 9.4 Sampson and Laub's (1993) Age-graded theory of informal social control

Source: Sampson and Laub (1993), pp. 244–5, Harvard University Press

Sampson and Laub set themselves was to construct and test a theoretical model of individual development in childhood, adolescence, *and* adulthood to expand the Gluecks' developmental focus (not to mention that of the Cambridge Study) on childhood experiences and to explore the possibility of stability and *change* in offending behaviour over the life course. Following their extensive re-analysis, Sampson and Laub formulated the 'age-graded theory of informal social control' in their ground-breaking book *Crime in the Making* (see **Figure 9.4**), a theory that explained youth offending in relation to three key influences (Sampson and Laub 1993: 7):

- **Structural context** (e.g. social class, ethnicity, gender, poverty, broken home, household overcrowding, parental employment) mediated by informal family and school social controls explains offending in childhood and adolescence.

- **Strong continuity** in criminal behaviour from childhood to adulthood in a variety of life domains.

- **Informal social bonds** to the family and employment in adulthood explain changes in criminality over the lifespan despite early childhood propensities.

According to this theory, a young person's offending behaviour is met with a range of formal and informal responses (e.g. conviction may result in official sanction, parental discipline, approval/disapproval of peers). The nature of these responses interacts with existing risk/

protective factors to shape the individual's future behaviour. For example, incarceration could damage educational opportunities by removing the young person from school, whilst a community sentence could set the young person on a prosocial pathway by making education compulsory. Therefore, the interaction between risk/protective factors and formal/informal responses to the behaviour can form either vicious or virtuous circles. Sampson and Laub added the notion of individual agency into their theory, so risk factors and formal/informal responses to offending behaviour were not the only influences on future behaviour (unlike in the Cambridge Study), but were said to provide the context which shapes the decisions an individual makes about how to behave (Sampson and Laub 1993, 2005). A more complex version of the full model is presented in **Figure 9.4**, but if you understand the three central points above, that is good enough.

The 'age-graded theory of informal social control' introduced the notion of measuring risk factors across the life course, extending the focus on early childhood risk factors perpetuated by the developmental criminology of the Gluecks and Farrington. As such, it is considered a 'life course' developmental theory/explanation of youth offending. Sampson and Laub identified life events that could be demonstrated to interrupt the supposedly pre-determined criminal career path and which questions the idea of a stable path of criminal development and the stability of the offending *trajectory*—the popular focal point of developmental criminology in the early 1990s due to Farrington's

Cambridge Study research (Farrington 2007). Sampson and Laub argued that offending trajectories could change in times of *transition*—important, influential periods in an individual's life (e.g. leaving school, getting a job). Thus, transitions and/or exposure to short-term, often abrupt, life events could promote offending or desistance from offending—labelled *turning points*. Re-analysis of the Gluecks' data identified employment, marriage, and military service as the key turning points, which motivated choices/decisions to desist from offending. In this way, the life course model moved developmental risk factor explanations of youth offending forward from an over-reliance on quantitative (artefactual), developmental, and deterministic understandings of the impact of childhood risk factors (see France and Homel 2007a). This progressive move could be seen as an evolution of risk factor theory. The evolution/improvement in this case is towards constructivist explanations of the individual's ability to actively influence their pathways into and out of crime (see **Chapter 18**)—albeit an ability shaped and constrained by existing risk factors and societal responses to previous behaviour.

Patterns of crime vary, though, and so developmental explanations have had to adapt to this recognition. Offending is not simply a function of age, for instance, as Smith (2014) demonstrates with widely varying peak ages for different types of offence. This observation has prompted some developmental theorists to suggest that there are alternative pathways, and that it is important to distinguish between what might be seen as 'life-course persistent offending' and 'adolescence-limited offending' (Smith 2014: 675), with gender differences much more likely to be evident in the former than the latter grouping.

The differential effect of the range of factors identified is also problematic in the context of developmental explanations, with some accounts appearing to identify a greater role for antisocial behaviour, which originates in later childhood or adolescence rather than at an earlier stage. There appears to be a complex interplay, too, between individual risk and protective factors and wider neighbourhood influences. So, for certain specific groups social circumstances may be decisive, it seems: 'findings suggest that there is a direct effect of neighbourhood disadvantage on well-adjusted children influencing them to become involved in serious offending as they reach adolescence' (Wikstrom and Loeber 2000: 1133).

Mediated choice and agency

As Wikstrom and Loeber (2000: 1134) recognise, it is possible that neighbourhood disadvantage may have variable effects, notably as what they term 'well-adjusted children' (i.e. those having a good school motivation, adequate guilt feelings, etc.) move into adolescence; at which point, they will probably become increasingly aware of the disparities between their circumstances and those of others who are better off. This observation, in turn, certainly provides some potential support for those theories, which see youth crime as perhaps a predictable response to perceptions of unfairness, or restricted opportunities associated with disadvantage. Therefore, young people are active agents capable of making rational choices and decisions (in line with classical and rational choice explanations of crime), but it is possible to consider that external influences such as neighbourhood disadvantage can mediate (intervene in, stand between) their ability to make and act on these choices and decisions.

Here, perhaps strain theory and anomie take a meaningful place in the explanatory frame. Agnew's (1992) important contribution is widely viewed as providing a plausible account of the mechanisms underlying young people's decisions to offend. Drawing on Merton's (1938) argument that crime can be understood as the product of frustrations generated by the dominant competitive social structure, Agnew argued that a multi-level model of strain could help to explain deviant choices. As he puts it, 'the general strain theory … focuses on three categories of strain or negative relationships with others: 1) the actual or anticipated failure to achieve positively valued goals, 2) the actual or anticipated removal of positively valued stimuli, and 3) the actual or anticipated presentation of negative stimuli' (Agnew 1992: 74). By this, Agnew means in effect that crime becomes more likely in a context where legitimate social aspirations are not achievable; where there are no socially acceptable sources of enjoyment or fulfilment available; and where these appear to be offered, on the other hand, through undesirable activities. This, in his view, helps to establish a framework for understanding the dynamics of the development of delinquency, as these stages illustrate the combined effect of different forms of adversity, and the necessity for all three to be in place before young people become involved in offending. At the same time, this model also offers a potential explanation for those cases where negative experiences or 'failures' of one kind or another may not lead to delinquency, where, for example, positive personal relationships remain in place.

However, the use of terms such as stimuli indicates a deterministic view of criminality, in the sense that young people's actions are shaped and driven by factors outside their control, and the notion of choice, situated or otherwise, does not seem to play a part. Matza (1964, 1969), by contrast, seeks to reinsert the notion of freedom and self-determination into the process of 'becoming deviant':

An alternative image of the delinquent can be developed by accepting the implications of soft rather than hard determinism. One effect of restoring choice … is to render feasible a joining of classical with positivist assumptions.

Matza 1964: 27

Arguing that the 'general conditions' of social organisation are best represented by a continuum from freedom to constraint, he suggests that adolescence is a peculiar period in which the individual may drift in and out of criminal activity depending on immediate circumstances: 'The delinquent *transiently* [his emphasis] exists in a limbo between convention and crime, responding to the demands of each, flirting now with one, now the other, but postponing commitment, evading decision' (Matza 1964: 28). This portrayal does sit more readily with our earlier observation that certain types of crime, in particular, are associated with youth, and that becoming an offender does not signal a lifelong commitment, or an unbreakable pattern of behaviour.

Instead, it might be more appropriate to think in terms of delinquency as a product of predisposition, circumstances, and opportunity. Indeed, the notion of differential opportunity was first advanced some time ago by Cloward and Ohlin (1960), who argued that delinquent acts might in fact represent the same kind of decision-making process exercised in different contexts: 'if goal-oriented behavior occurs under conditions in which there are socially structured obstacles to the satisfaction of these drives by legitimate means, the resulting pressures, we contend, might lead to deviance' (Cloward and Ohlin 1960: 151). As we shall see, this points towards the need for explanations of youth crime which are contextualised, and seek to understand the kind of choices and decisions available to young people, where it is the nature of the behaviour or opportunity which is significant from their point of view, rather than its legal status.

Indeed, some have taken this kind of argument further, to suggest that the contextual nature of the choices made by young people means that much of what is defined by law as criminal behaviour is actually typical, and is the result of situated decisions which take no account of the legal status of the activity in question. Pitts (2008: 17) points out that youth offending is 'statistically "normal": self-report studies consistently show that between 40 and 98 per cent of adolescents admit to having broken the law in the preceding 12 months'.

This section demonstrates that the key criminological explanations of youth crime have been largely individualised and developmental versions of positivist theory. Whilst some studies have moved beyond the traditional psychosocial and individualising biases of positivism by considering agentic, contextual, socio-structural, and situational influences (cf. Case 2017), fewer have sought to address the androcentricism and ethnocentrism of explanatory models. Accordingly, there remains a degree of reductionism in explanations of youth crime—a tendency to only explain offending by white males and only in psychosocial ways.

Growing into crime: Culture and deviance

Following the exploration of dominant criminological explanations of crime from a developmental perspective, we move now to our third key issue—promoting understanding of the cultural influences on offending by young people. The subtitle of Cloward and Ohlin's (1960) book refers to 'delinquent gangs', and one of the recurrent questions for youth criminology has been the role of peers and culture in shaping allegiances and patterns of behaviour amongst young people who offend. The idea of 'delinquent subcultures' is based on the assumption that their members 'have withdrawn their attribution of legitimacy to certain of the norms maintained by law-abiding groups of the larger society and have given it, instead, to new patterns of conduct which are defined as illegitimate by representatives of official agencies' (Cloward and Ohlin 1960: 19). In effect, members of these groups have reassigned their commitment to ideas and groupings that lie outside those associated with conventional norms and the prevailing moral order (e.g. truancy from school, substance use, antisocial behaviour, offending). Conventional expectations and routes to achievement thus no longer apply, and status and reward become associated with an alternative value system, operating outside (or regardless of) the given legal framework. Cloward and Ohlin (1960: 20) suggest, too, that such deviant subcultures can, themselves, be subdivided into three categories: one which draws its justification from purely 'criminal values', and is based on seeking material rewards by illegitimate means; a second populated by those whose status is earned by exercising force and the perpetration of domination through violent means; and a third represented by alienation and retreat from conventional roles, as may be evident in drug cultures, for instance.

These categories seem somewhat schematic and certainly may not be mutually exclusive, but what they do appear to have in common is an explicit and conscious rejection of mainstream norms, values, and behavioural expectations. In the manner outlined by Agnew, and before him, Merton (1957), the denial of regular opportunities or status and the attractions of alternative routes to some sort of social standing apparently combine to offer pathways into criminality, and even an alternative rebel identity for young people should they choose to follow this course.

Gang culture

Pitts' (2008) study of gangs in a UK context attempts to steer a path between sensationalised and over-simplified accounts on the one hand, and the realities of life and life choices in difficult circumstances. This leads to recognition of the contextual and structural influences which seem to underlie the emergence of a certain type of outsider group with its own sense of identity and embedded meaning. This may notably be the case for young people from black and minority ethnic (BME) communities, for whom, as Pitts (2008: 64) puts it, social conditions may be significantly worse than for their white counterparts, and for whom: 'the effects of structural youth and adult unemployment and family poverty were exacerbated by negative experiences in school and confrontations with the police in the street'. Associated with these experiences is what he describes as a bleaker alternative worldview that generates a sense of threat and readiness to resist and respond. The end result may be that these young people 'only feel at ease in the gang' (2008: 65).

As Pitts (2008: 102) goes on to argue, though, gang affiliation may represent quite a complex series of motivations rather than a relatively straightforward and linear process of exclusion and commitment to an alternative lifestyle. 'Reluctant gangsters' are those who become associated through a concern to minimise risks to themselves, for instance, whether these take the form of threats from other gangs, or pressure from within one's own gang leaders:

> So he tells 'em to 'fuck off'. Anyway, the next thing he knows, someone's shot up his mother's flat. There's lots of families round here can't use their front rooms because of this sort of thing.
>
> Local resident (quoted in Pitts 2008: 102)

Set alongside other less direct and obvious motivations, such as the lack of access to legitimate future prospects (cf. strain theory) and the positive attraction of 'belonging' to a recognised social group (cf. subcultural theory), these factors create a complex, interlocking and persuasive set of reasons for establishing criminal allegiances. Behaviour which is outlawed at the societal level becomes relatively 'normalised' in the context in which such choices are made. It is noted, for example, in the context of one major research project that young people 'tended to live in areas of high crime' (France and Homel, 2007a, p. 20). Crime was therefore an everyday feature of their lives and most of the young people in these areas had regular encounters with criminal activity, as witnesses or even as victims. As a consequence, it would form a normal part of their lives to be engaged in 'managing their relationships' with deviance. Take a look at **Telling it like it is 9.1** for the first hand explanations of two young men who joined gangs,

explored through interview in Young et al.'s (2013) qualitative study of the role of family in gang formation. What do you think were their motivations for joining a gang and how could these be explained theoretically?

Thornberry et al. (2003: 184) have somewhat similarly argued that young people joining gangs can be attributed to a combination of 'push' and 'pull' factors: 'street gangs—populated by friends and families, offering a ready source of fun and action, as well as protection from a hostile world—may be a viable response to the bleakness often confronting these urban, generally poor adolescents'. These characterisations of situated decision-making have parallels in 'pathways' models of youth crime (France and Homel, 2007b). According to this perspective, we should not expect to find fixed and linear explanations for young people's involvement in crime. Instead, human development 'is always contextualised and constructed in dynamic, interactive processes. ... The person's life is not preformed, but rather, its dimensions emerge, are built up, become refined, and either persist or are superseded as the person engages with ... others persons and institutions' (Lawrence 2007: 32). So, we may not just think in terms of multiple influences, but of factors working in parallel, sometimes mutually supporting, sometimes in conflict, and with different degrees of strength and persuasiveness; and at the same time, contingent events and opportunities may in turn alter the landscape of risk and opportunity from the young person's perspective.

TELLING IT LIKE IT IS 9.1

Why I joined a gang

I was thinking to myself, obviously, this is the only way I could get money. I'm not working and what else can I do? Signing on money ain't going far enough; that couldn't even support a sixteen-year-old much less me ... One of my friends from a long time ago. He used to go to my secondary school, he kind of, not told me to, but he said I should do it ... [he said] like it's quick, easy money.

When you maybe reach fourteen or thirteen or fifteen, you just feel, "I'm free!". You just want to go out now, and you just want to enjoy, you just want to mingle with friends, whatever they're into you're just gonna get into it. It's only when you start growing up you realise what you've done when you're young.

Young men, quoted in Young et al. 2013

Further development of this sort of argument leads to a consideration of 'contexts' (Goodnow 2007), and their role in establishing the conditions in which young people make choices. Such ideas are perhaps theoretically derived from concepts such as 'habitus' (Bourdieu 1977), which tries to capture the sense of all the factors in combination (social, material, cultural, personal experience) which act as the context and preconditions for our decisions and actions.

Radicalisation and youth criminality

In the contemporary period, the issue of radicalisation and its links with youth crime has emerged as one of pressing concern (Christmann 2012, for example). This concern has, of course, arisen in the aftermath of a series of concerted attacks on communities in western and European cities, which have been linked to 'Islamic extremism' (Christmann 2012: 6). The search for explanations, though, has followed a similar explanatory model to those focusing on more established 'pathways' into crime: 'which contextual features interact with which individual factors through which mechanisms…' (Christmann 2012: 6). Particular attention has been accorded to those social groupings which are believed to act as a catalyst for radicalisation—again, analogous to the association of youth criminality with deviant subcultures posited by Cohen (1955) and others. The subculture, it is argued, provides a source of validation and fulfilment for those who are either alienated or unable to achieve according to conventional expectations. With nothing to gain from affiliation to mainstream society and norms, they can be expected to turn to alternative means of expression and to give allegiance to oppositional belief systems.

Echoes of this kind of perspective can be found in proposed models of the radicalisation process identified by Christmann (2012: 12), one of which proposes a four-stage progression:

- **Pre-radicalisation**—defined in terms of the person's 'vulnerable' life situation.
- **Self-identification**—where the individual begins to associate with new ideas and new social groups, possibly in response to particular alienating trigger events.
- **Indoctrination**—intensification of beliefs and commitment to the group which represents an alternative value system.
- **'Jihadisation'**—where membership of the group involves complete rejection of conventional society and the submergence of individual interests to the commitment to radical social change (in which violence is seen as playing a legitimate part).

In some cases, this sort of process is articulated as a pathway model (Gill 2007), exemplifying its apparent consistency with the routes into 'normal' crime set out by France and Homel (2007a). So it is that radicalisation, like youth crime in general, comes to be explained in terms of a combination of biological, psychological, and societal theories (Christmann 2012), with emphasis being placed on a number of risk factors (as well as being male; Bakker 2006), including: emotional vulnerability; dissatisfaction or disillusionment; identification with the suffering of other Muslims; the conviction that action—including violence—against the state is legitimate; gaining benefits from being part of an identifiable group or cause; reinforcement through valued and meaningful social links (Christmann 2012: 33). Portrayed in this way, the process of radicalisation seems to follow a similar trajectory as that mapped out by earlier scholars, with, once again, both 'push' and 'pull' factors in operation:

> The group members begin to exhibit a greater cohesiveness and sense of mutual dependence. They learn to define more closely those who are friendly or hostile to their activities. The experience of arrest, court adjudication of some members of the group casts a new light on the meaning and consequences of their activities.
>
> Cloward and Ohlin 1960: 142

Pitts (2008: 112), however, cautions us against the risks of applying what is essentially a 'deficit model' to the behaviours of those whose criminality takes the form of challenging state power. Not only does this overlook the political dimensions of their actions, but it also denies them agency, with the result that interventions to address their behaviour tend to be misconceived and ineffective. Indeed, Pitts (2008: 112) suggests that we should perhaps instead consider developing 'politicised responses which aim to establish solidarity with these embattled young people, rather than ones which simply aim to cure or suppress them in equal measure'.

Constructing young criminals?

As we have implicitly recognised, much criminological endeavour focuses on young people and their behaviour with the aim of teasing out what it is about them that makes some of them turn to crime. There is, however, another way of asking the question; and this is to turn the spotlight on the social structures and processes which, it could be argued, criminalise young people. The concept of crime itself is a social construction (a theme running throughout this book), so definitions of what is legal, what constitute infractions, and who are defined as offenders are all dependent on the way in which that concept is operationalised (Case 2017). In this sense, then, notions of crime and delinquency become problematic, since they depend on the perspective and power of those who create and enforce the distinctions between legality and illegality. These processes, in turn, operate at a number of levels, from the initial definitional action of determining what is or is not an offence, through the decisions about how to implement and prioritise enforcement action, to the enactment of encounters between criminal justice workers and young people which themselves contribute (or not) to their eventual criminalisation. Viewing young people who offend as (to some degree) *victims* of the criminalising, stigmatising, and marginalising processes of the youth justice system (e.g. labelling, excessive intervention, targeting of 'at risk' populations) is an increasingly popular way of exploring youth crime and justice.

A vociferous group of youth justice academics and researchers with a critical criminology agenda (such as John Muncie, Barry Goldson, John Pitts, Tim Bateman, Jo Phoenix, and the authors of this chapter, Steve Case and Roger Smith) have vigorously challenged the negative, individualising, and criminalising nature of dominant positivist explanations of youth crime and the individualised (youth justice) responses to youth crime that tend towards placing excessive responsibility on young people and their families for the causes of this behaviour and the success of any responses to it—what Muncie (2004) dubbed **responsibilisation**.

A concrete illustration of this argument is provided by the experience of young people from BME communities who have been consistently over-represented amongst those being drawn into the justice system and being made subject to criminal sanctions. One major study commissioned by the Youth Justice Board found a series of inconsistencies in the way certain ethnic groups were treated, including (Feilzer and Hood 2004: 27):

- a higher (than the average) rate of prosecution and conviction for mixed-parentage young people;
- a higher (than average) proportion of black and Asian males remanded in custody;
- a slightly greater (than average) use of custody for Asian males;
- a much greater proportion (than average) of mixed-parentage females being prosecuted.

Similar patterns were observed in a subsequent study: 'Taking offence and criminal history into account, mixed race offenders and suspects were more likely than whites to be prosecuted than to be reprimanded or warned. Black and mixed race defendants were also more likely to be remanded in custody than white defendants' (May et al. 2010: vi).

The *Young Review* (Mullen 2014) reiterated many of these findings, albeit in relation to the 18–24 age group.

Notably, the review drew attention to the over-representation of both 'black and Muslim' young people in the custodial population (Mullen 2014: 19), with a notable rise in the numbers of young Muslim prisoners from 2002 onwards. But in addition to the numerical imbalance, both groups 'report being perceived through racialised stereotypes'; and so young black prisoners are identified with gangs or drugs, and young Muslim prisoners with violent extremism. Criminalisation then could be said to be taking place by two distinct mechanisms: the first being the disproportionately punitive treatment of these groups, and the second being the attribution of narrow and prejudiced identities to both.

In this sense, then, we might be led to the observation that material injustices are compounded by additional social processes which ascribe certain criminalised identities to certain groups, almost irrespective of their own life histories and characteristics. Historically, this kind of mechanism was first articulated in the form of **labelling theory**, which was associated with a number of leading criminological theorists of the 1960s, including Becker (1963), Lemert (1967) and Kitsuse (1962); and perhaps a more contemporary version of this can be found in the concept of 'othering' associated with Garland (2001), in particular. Labelling theory has sought to articulate a twofold process, so that the initial commission of an offence (primary deviance) is subsequently compounded by the experience of being processed and formally identified as an offender (leading to secondary deviance, as the ascribed identity becomes self-fulfilling).

Becker's (1963) argument was that a wide range of behaviours could be said to deviate from conventional expectations, and that in itself such behaviour might have no particular consequences for the individual. It is only through the process of the societal response to the initial behaviour that secondary 'deviation' arises, according to Lemert (1967: 17). For him, primary deviation can arise in a range of social settings, and in itself it has only 'marginal implications … it does not lead to symbolic reorganization at the level of self-regarding attitudes and social roles'. In other words, the choice of a marginal infringement of social norms does not, of itself, lead to the adoption of a criminal identity. On the other hand, he suggests, secondary deviance arises precisely as a reaction to society's response to perceived primary deviation. Thus, the initial causes of the outlawed behaviour become less influential, and the effects of society's disapproval and punitive interventions become relatively more important in shaping the offender's future behaviour. Of course, as McNeill and Barry (2009) point out, it is not just that the attribution of a label might enhance the likelihood of further deviant activity, but it also contributes to the **stigmatisation** of young people in trouble, so that they are more noticeable, and perhaps more likely to come to official attention again, and so be further criminalised, even in respect of behaviour that is unexceptional.

Research has demonstrated that such suggestions are more than just speculation. McAra and McVie (2007), drawing on findings from the *Edinburgh Study of Youth Transitions and Crime* (see also **Chapter 18**), have been able to specify the effect of system contact in some detail. Their analysis shows that criminalisation of young people depended extensively on selective police responses; such that 'boys and disadvantaged children' were found to be discriminated against by beat police officers in terms of the initial decision whether or not to bring charges (McAra and McVie 2007: 326). More dramatically, however, their analysis found that children 'who reported that they had been charged in previous years were *over seven times* [their emphasis] more likely to be charged at age 15' than those who had not been charged previously (2007: 327).

Furthermore, this labelling effect appears to operate completely independently of young people's actual level of involvement in criminal behaviour. According to McAra and McVie (2007: 337), these observations suggest that there is in effect a recruitment process in operation such that certain young people become identified as the 'usual suspects', and become repeatedly reprocessed by the justice system, irrespective of their actual levels or pattern of offending or need. By contrast, they note, where decisions are taken to divert young people from formal interventions, their levels of serious offending appear to decline. In this respect, then, perhaps these findings support the earlier arguments of Lemert (1967) in particular; but they also throw into question the suggestion that it is system contact that escalates deviancy. Once the system has formed a judgement, it seems, it will continue to treat young people as offenders (or not) regardless of their behaviour. Nowhere is this phenomenon animated more clearly than when young people are given custodial sentences for offending.

Custody: experiencing life inside

For those young people who enter the youth justice system (YJS), and particularly those who go into custody, the experience has been documented as problematic in a number of ways. Concerns have repeatedly been expressed about the effects of being detached from family and community life and becoming subject to institutional regimes; on the grounds that their rights are compromised and their life chances are significantly adversely affected. Although there had been a substantial reduction of the number of children (under 18s) in custody between 2007–08 (average number 2,932) and 2015–16 (average

number 969), substantial evidence persists of negative experiences whilst in custody.

As Goldson (2015: 179) points out, it is internationally the case that children and young people who are made subject to custodial sentences are from 'the most disadvantaged, distressed and impoverished communities'. Repeated evidence provided by the same author (Goldson, 2002; 2005), by official bodies such as the prison inspectorate, and by lobby groups such as the Howard League and the Prison Reform Trust, has shown that the experience of custody is damaging and unpleasant for many children. Although in principle children and young people may be detained in children's homes whilst serving sentences, most are instead held in prison department institutions (Goldson 2015: 180), where the conditions of their detention are essentially unsuited to their status as children, with notional rights as children afforded to them by the UN Convention on the Rights of the Child (UNCRC). Successive reports by the UN Committee on the Rights of the Child (which monitors international implementation of the UNCRC) have castigated the UK for continually placing too many young people in custody and for failing to use custody as a last resort sentencing measure—in direct contravention of the principles of the UNCRC (cf. UN Committee 2016).

So, as Her Majesty's Inspector of Prisons and the Youth Justice Board (2013) found, when surveyed, a considerable number of young people reported that they had been victimised by other young people or by staff (22 per cent in each case); and at the same time, they are routinely subject to restraint, a legitimate form of intervention applied by staff, supposedly as a 'last resort' (House of Commons Justice Committee, 2013). In a considerable number of such cases, the use of restraint itself results in injury to the child concerned. At the same time, the reported outcomes of custodial sentences are poor, with the Prison Reform Trust (2013) reporting that 72 per cent of children and young people released from custody reoffended within a year. Consequently, serious questions then have to be asked about what locking up children is supposed to achieve and how systems which are obliged still to afford them their general rights as children apparently fail to do so in so many cases.

As we have seen, one of the perennial concerns of academics, policy makers, and practitioners in relation to youth justice is the use of child imprisonment. I discussed the extent and nature of this issue with Dr Tim Bateman, Principal Policy Advisor for Youth Justice to the Children's Commissioner for England (see **Conversations 9.1**). Tim has written widely on youth custody and is commissioned by the National Association for Youth Justice to produce their annual report on the *State of Youth Justice* (Bateman 2015).

CONVERSATIONS 9.1

The problem of child imprisonment—with Dr Tim Bateman

SC (Steve Case): What is the extent and nature of youth custody in England and Wales?

TB (Tim Bateman): The number of children who are locked up for offending fluctuates dramatically over time. So for example, while the use of child incarceration fell sharply during the 1980s, the decade from 1992 onwards was characterised by a rapid increase: in 2001, the number of children sentenced to custody was 90 per cent higher than in 1992. Although there are genuine problems of comparison, it has been estimated that, at its peak, the proportion of the overall child population imprisoned in England and Wales was four times that in France, 10 times that in Spain and 100 times that in Finland (Nacro 2003). More recently, the tide has turned again leading to a considerable decline in youth custody. In April 2016, the population of the child custodial estate was 70 per cent below that in April 2008 (Youth Justice Board 2016). This fall notwithstanding, the use of detention remains high by international standards as the United Nations Committee on the Rights of the Child (2016) has recently noted. Moreover, while the overall custodial population has contracted, the over-representation of children from minority ethnic communities has risen to account for 45 per cent of the total (Youth Justice Board 2016).

Turning to the second question, custodial regimes are also subject to change over time (Hagel and Hazel 2001). Since 2000, the secure estate for children and young people has consisted of three distinct types of establishment. Young offender institutions (YOIs) are managed by the prison service. They are large scale institutions that hold up to 350 boys aged 15–17 years and closely resemble adult prisons. Secure training centres (STCs) are privately managed custodial facilities that detain up to 80 children of both sexes aged 12–17, including vulnerable boys aged 15–17. Secure children's homes (SCHs), by contrast, are managed by local authorities, have a child care, rather than a custodial, ethos and offer provision for children secured on welfare grounds as well as those subject to penal detention. They accommodate girls and boys, aged 10 to 17, deprived of their liberty for offending who are assessed as being particularly vulnerable. SCHs are considerably smaller than the other two types of establishment with capacity ranging from eight to 42 children. Staff to child ratios also vary considerably across the different sectors: from an average of one to 10 in YOIs to around one to two in SCHs (Children's Commissioner for England 2015).

Children's experience of detention is determined largely by the nature of the establishment in which they are placed. Research conducted by the HM Inspectorate of Prisons indicates that while less than a quarter of those in STCs report having felt unsafe at some point, one third of children in YOIs do so; 97 per cent of children in STCs consider that staff treat them with respect compared with 70 per cent in YOIs; and a higher proportion (62 per cent) of those in the former establishments believe that they done something while in custody that will reduce the likelihood of reoffending when they return to the community than those in YOIs (52 per cent) (Redmond 2015). It is deeply disappointing, however, that the large majority of children in prison are locked up in facilities least suited to their needs. In April 2016, of the 906 children in custody, more than 71 per cent were placed in YOIs, 18 per cent were in STCs and just 11 per cent were accommodated in SCHs (Youth Justice Board 2016). It is hard to escape the conclusion that this configuration is driven by financial considerations: placement in a SCH costs more than three times that in a YOI.

SC: What are the implications of putting young people into custody?

TB: The social costs of imprisoning children are enormous. Research indicates that children deprived of their liberty derive from the most disadvantaged communities and are among those with the highest levels of need and vulnerabilities. An analysis of the child custodial population published in 2010 established that more than half (51 per cent) lived in a deprived household and/or unsuitable accommodation, almost half (47 per cent) had run away from home at some point, and more than a quarter (27 per cent) had previously been in care. Twelve per cent had experienced the death of parents or siblings compared with four per cent in the general population. Almost half (48 per cent) had been excluded from school, one in five had self-harmed, and 11 per cent had attempted suicide (Jacobson et al. 2010). In summary, 'around three-quarters of the sample are known to have three or more indicators of home/family disadvantage, and more than two-fifths to have five or more' (Jacobson et al. 2010: 52). As the number of children in custody has fallen, in the interim period, the extent of need within the secure estate has increased.

The glaring chasm between the welfare needs of children whose offending is sufficiently serious to result in deprivation of liberty and the ability of custody to deliver a service that meets those needs constitutes the tragedy of child imprisonment (Goldson 2005). Child prisons are places of violence and are deteriorating in this regard. Between 2010 and 2015, the number of assaults rose from 9 per 100 detained children to 16.1; over the same period, the rate of physical restraint per 100 children increased from 17.6 to 28.2. In this context, it is perhaps unsurprising that episodes of recorded self-harm (presumably many lesser incidents go unrecorded) also expanded, from 5.3 per 100 to 7.7 (Ministry of Justice/Youth Justice Board 2016). Sixteen children have died in custody since the Youth Justice Board took over responsibility for the secure estate in 2000 (Youth Justice Board 2014).

Successive inspection reports demonstrate that provision of high quality education, appropriate support within custody and on release is lacking (Bateman et al. 2013). The evidence that incarceration is criminogenic, increasing the risk of further offending is clear, with reconviction rates within a year of release standing at more than two thirds. The lifelong barriers for children who have experienced imprisonment to reintegrating fully in society are considerable (Goldson 2005).

SC: Can you suggest a way forward?

TB: There are, it seems to me, two priorities. The first is to reduce substantially the number of children behind bars. The recent fall in youth imprisonment, while obviously welcome, is simply insufficient. It is moreover relatively easy to identify measures that would achieve this aim (although implementing them may prove more challenging). As outlined above, the use of child imprisonment is in part a product of the level of prosecution; further expansion of diversionary mechanisms would be likely to generate a contraction in custodial outcomes. Within the court arena itself, the existing custodial threshold for children is largely the same as that which applies to adults. It allows imprisonment for relatively minor, persistent property offending. Ensuring compliance with the UNCRC's obligation that custody should be used only as a measure of last resort would require a tightening of the criteria that must be satisfied before a child can be imprisoned. Statutory provisions should mandate a non-custodial response other than in cases:

- involving violent or sexual offending;
- where the child poses a serious risk of harm to the public; and
- non-custodial options have been fully explored.

Once a child is sentenced to prison, existing arrangements for release are relatively inflexible. Children remain within the secure estate in most cases until they have served half of their sentence (with some provision for early or late release). Reform of these rigid mechanisms might permit transfer to some form of non-secure provision at an earlier point, as soon as children no longer pose a serious risk of harm to the public. The custodial term would, in this scenario, constitute an upper limit on detention rather than dictating the release date in automatic fashion. As well as reducing the numbers incarcerated at any one time, such a system would provide tangible incentives for children to engage with programmes of rehabilitation within the custodial environment.

The second priority concerns the nature of custodial facilities themselves. Where incarceration is absolutely necessary, children should be accommodated in small child care establishments, with high staff to child ratios, and a therapeutic environment. Most existing custodial provision could be replaced by a network of 'secure schools' that would be smaller than YOIs and would have a focus on education. While such a model would no doubt constitute an improvement over current arrangements, the National Association for Youth Justice (NAYJ) has convincingly argued that the principle of 'placement in a secure child care establishment with high quality education provided on the premises, rather than a school that provides secure accommodation … would better reflect the complexities of need experienced by this cohort of children and would reinforce the importance of healthy development and emotional support alongside education' (NAYJ 2016: 3). SCHs would appear to fit the bill nicely. There would appear to be no need to reinvent the wheel.

Dr Tim Bateman, Reader in Youth Justice,
University of Bedfordshire

Amplifying deviance

What we seem to have detected here, at least in this one example of empirical research, is a manifestation of the 'amplification of deviance' thesis (Wilkins 1964); that is, the suggestion that the justice system does not merely react to manifestations of youthful indiscretion, but plays a significant part in escalating it, both directly and in the way in which it is dramatised and represented.

Alongside the responses of the formal representatives of the justice system, we must also take account of the role of the media and the part this plays in problematising young people and their behaviour. Classically, of course, this process has been captured by Cohen's (1972)

'Folk Devils and Moral Panics'. With all the elements of a dramatic confrontation available, the media are shown by Cohen to have been responsible firstly for portraying a massively overblown and over-problematised picture of a confrontation between two groups of young people, the Mods and Rockers; and secondly, for escalating the situation by acting as a sort of rallying call, inviting young people to take part in further re-enactments of the supposed 'battles' that had taken place previously. See **What do you think? 9.3** for further examples and discussion.

In Cohen's (1972) terms, the media response was effective partly because of its interaction with other agents of control, repeating what the courts said about the deviant behaviour, rather than the extent and nature of the behaviour in itself. In other words, stories were told about stories, which over time came to constitute the truth of the matter, and to be self-sustaining. In fact, as Cohen (1972) reports it, a relatively minor incident in Clacton (i.e. a series of scuffles on the seafront between Mods and Rockers) became the focal point for a mass of headlines which in turn created an expectation of further disruption and violence and a demonisation of large groups of young people. Further studies have reached similar conclusions about the media's role in orchestrating reactions to what might be termed signal events, and in the process contributing to the formulation and sustenance of stereotyped views of threatening or dangerous youth. In the case of 'mugging' (the media constructed label for violent street robbery), graphically illustrated by Hall et al. (2013), it is notable that the threat was also racialised, helping to support and, indeed, amplify another stereotypical assumption, locating criminality amongst black young people (Hall et al. 2013: 324).

The 1990s was a particularly significant period in terms of reconstructing children who offended as 'youth offenders' who were irresponsible, immoral, evil, and dangerous (cf. Case 2017). This radical reconstruction of youth offenders was in part based on the desire of the new government to stamp its authority on law-making and distinguish itself as different from its predecessor. However, the necessity and urgency for a new approach to youth justice policy and practice, animated by reconstructing youth offenders as dangerous, was largely precipitated by a single horrific event in England—the murder of Jamie Bulger (see **Controversy and debate** 9.1).

WHAT DO YOU THINK? 9.3

Deviancy amplification in the media

The print media have historically represented young people as problematic, risky, dangerous, and out of control, along with a persistent view that the youth crime 'problem' is both new and worse now than it is has ever been. What do you think about such mis/representations? Take a look at the selected headlines, photographs (**Figures 9.5–9.8**), and printed social commentaries from newspapers in this box and see if you can spot a pattern in the representation of youth; a pattern that arguably challenges the view of problem youth as a contemporary social construction.

19th century

Morals are getting much worse. When I was young my mother would have knocked me down for speaking improperly to her.

Newspaper editorial, 1843

Early 20th century

The passing of parental authority, defiance of pre-war conditions, the absence of restraint, the wildness of extremes ... are but a few characteristics of after-war conditions.

Boy's club leader, 1932—referring to World War I 1914–18

1950s/1960s

The adolescent has learned no definite moral standards from his parents, is contemptuous of the law, easily bored.

British Medical Association, 1961

There has been a decline in the disciplinary forces governing a child. Obedience and respect for law have decreased.

The Times, 1952

21st century

British youths are 'the most unpleasant and violent in the world': Damning verdict of writer as globe reacts to riots.

Daily Mail headline, 10 August 2011

... people nationally are sick of kids making their life hell ... it never happened in the 1950s.

Letter to provincial newspaper, 2005

Figure 9.5 Youth over the years: 19th century
Source: Gavin Wilson (Flickr)

Figure 9.7 Youth over the years: 1950s/1960s
Source: © Roger Mayne/Mary Evans Picture Library

Figure 9.6 Youth over the years: 20th century
Source: Nationaal Archief @Flickr Commons/Public domain

Figure 9.8 Youth over the years: 21st century
Source: © Andy Sewell

! CONTROVERSY AND DEBATE 9.1

Jamie Bulger and the abolition of *doli incapax*

On 12 February 1993, two year old Jamie Bulger was abducted, tortured, and murdered by two 10 year-old boys in Bootle, England. The moral panic that ensued in the news media motivated the reconstruction of children who offend as representing 'evil', where previously 10 year olds were considered closer to innocent children requiring welfare and protection. With one horrific act, the perception of children who offended became one of wicked, immoral, and rational individuals who should be assigned full responsibility for their actions (responsibilisation) and as such should be punished as if they were adults (adulterisation).

The Bulger murder motivated 'the politicization of juvenile crime' and significantly influenced the way in which child 'offenders' were socially constructed from that point (Goldson 2013). A climate of 'institutionalized intolerance' emerged (Muncie 2004) and any debate regarding raising the age of criminal responsibility above 10 years old was quashed. Five years later, the Crime and Disorder Act 1998 abolished *doli incapax*—the legal presumption that children aged from 10 to 14 years old were not necessarily capable of discerning between right and wrong and so could only be convicted of an offence if this presumption was refuted in court. In a sense, *doli incapax* represented the presumption of innocence in childhood and provided for children up to the age of 14 to be kept out of the formal youth justice system. However, the abolition of *doli incapax* represented 'an effective lowering of the age' of criminal responsibility (Bateman 2012: 5) and led to the 'statutory construction of the 10 year-old child "offender" as a fully responsibilised and adultified agent (which) confirms England's and Wales' status as the jurisdiction of the lower stage of (unmitigated) criminal responsibility in Europe' (Crofts 2009: 268).

The Crime and Disorder Act 1998 abolition of *doli incapax* exacerbated the contradictory views of children and young people in England and Wales. In particular, the Act contrasted with the more welfare-based Children Act 1989, which assigned the status of 'child' to individuals below 18 years of age. Both of these parliamentary Acts accorded with Article 1 of the United Nations Convention on the Rights of the Child (UNICEF 1989) by distinguishing a child as 'every human being below the age of 18 years', yet there are stark differences in how the 'child' should be understood and treated if they demonstrate problematic behaviour—in terms of punishment, control, and the prevention of risk (Crime and Disorder Act) versus vulnerability, need, and protection (Children Act).

Explaining youth crime: promoting a them and us mentality

As discussed, the adult-constructed explanations of youth crime in the western world have evidenced a positivist dominance in how youth crime has been theorised and researched empirically, producing a series of explanations focused on the *individual* young person, their biology, psychology, exposure to developmental (psychosocial) risk factors, and their experiences of critical life events/turning points. Consequently, explanations for youth crime offered by academics, politicians, the media, and stakeholders from the YJS have typically 'othered' young people who offend (Kelly 2012) and marked them out as a problematic, dangerous, irresponsible, and risky population in need of control and punishment (Haines and Case 2015). Thus, the source of youth crime according to these explanations is clearly 'them'—young people.

However, alternative explanations have emerged that explore young people's individual choices to offend as mediated and mitigated by external, structural, and systemic influences that are both criminogenic and constructed by adults—for example, neighbourhood disorganisation and social deprivation. This interplay between individual choices and (largely) structural issues suggests a similar interplay between 'them' (young people) and 'us' (adults, agents of the state, society) as contributing to explanations of youth crime. This less individualising and more holistic explanatory trajectory has been advanced by cultural explanations focusing on the criminalising role of contextual and structural factors beyond the individual young person's control (e.g. socially deprived neighbourhoods, the activities of the YJS) and that can perpetuate criminogenic outcomes such as gang membership, radicalization, and deviancy amplification by the media. In this respect, the emphasis of explanations turns 180 degrees towards 'us'—the adult key stakeholders and decision-makers who create/socially-construct these criminogenic contexts and structures.

To summarise this ever more complex issue, given that youth crime may be (at least in part) either the fault or creation of 'them', the product of an interaction between 'us' and 'them', or the social construction of 'us', how should we respond to offending behaviour by young people?

Responding to young people's offending behaviour

In the previous section we explored how criminality in the young develops, and how reactions to youth criminality have also developed. In this part of the chapter we will explore responses to young people's offending behaviour, particularly the dominance of early intervention and risk management approaches in shaping responses to youth crime (key issue four for this chapter).

Despite the emergence of a critical youth justice movement in academia and practice that challenges the traditionally negative depictions of young 'offenders' and individualised explanations of offending, positivist and

Figure 9.9 The triad of risk-based crime reduction and prevention

developmental risk-based theories have attained dominance when politicians, policy makers, and other key stakeholders construct youth justice responses to youth crime in England and Wales (along with many other westernised countries) due to their common sense, evidenced, and practical nature (see Case and Haines 2015, 2009). As discussed previously in the 'Explaining delinquency empirically' section, the RFPP has attained hegemony as *the* model for explaining and responding to youth offending, to the extent that 'the risk-factors and prediction paradigms have taken hold of criminology' (Laub and Sampson 2003: 289). A major consequence of governmental support for the RFPP across the UK, western Europe, North America, and Australasia has been a widespread utilisation of risk assessment instruments within youth justice systems to quantify risk factors and to determine appropriate responses to offending (see Kemshall 2008). What constitutes 'appropriate' and 'effective' responses to youth crime have therefore been predominantly risk-focused, aiming to identify, measure, and tackle young people's exposure to risk factors prior to them offending (i.e. early intervention) or once they have offended (i.e. risk management). The guiding objective here is the *prevention* of youth crime.

After the Labour Party took power in the UK in 1997, their first major piece of legislation was the Crime and Disorder Act 1998, which, as discussed, abolished the presumption of *doli incapax*. Under this Act, the prevention of offending through early intervention and risk management became the focus of the YJS. Previous soundbites about being 'tough on crime, tough on the causes of crime' and needing to 'nip offending in the bud' were to be realised by an emphasis on prevention that superseded all previous system concerns with addressing the welfare needs of young people or delivering justice based on the offence committed—an emphasis that has persisted since the Coalition Government replaced Labour in 2010:

It shall be the principal aim of the youth justice system to prevent offending.

Crime and Disorder Act 1998, section 37

Prevention is the cheapest and most effective way to deal with crime.

David Cameron, UK Prime Minister, 2012

Shaped largely by the dominant RFPP and its associated developmental and life course explanations of youth offending, prevention and early intervention activity with young people within and outside of the YJS since that time can be located at three points of what we have represented as a triangle of risk-based crime reduction and prevention—each point in some way negative, risk-based, and targeted on crime reduction and prevention, as demonstrated by **Figure 9.9** (Case and Haines 2015):

1. Targeted reduction of established negative behaviours/outcomes for (convicted) children within the YJS.

2. Targeted reduction of risk factors for negative behaviours/outcomes for

3. (convicted) children within the YJS (e.g. the 'Scaled Approach'—see later).

4. Targeted early intervention into established behavioural trajectories of children outside of the YJS considered 'at risk' of negative behaviours/outcomes.

Each of these approaches is popular in contemporary youth justice in England and Wales and each claims to be wedded to prevention goals, despite often focusing more on the reduction of existing problems rather than the prevention of new problems (Case and Haines 2015). The majority of youth justice prevention work, therefore, takes place with identified offenders (or those deemed to be 'at risk' of offending) and is situated within the formal YJS—thereby reflecting definitional confusion over what should be classified as the prevention of offending, compared to early intervention and the reduction of reoffending.

Risk-focused early intervention

> If we are not prepared to predict and intervene far more thoroughly then the children are going to grow up ... a menace to society and actually threats to themselves.
>
> Tony Blair, UK Prime Minister, 2006

In practice, much early intervention in the YJS takes place once a young person has been officially identified as 'at risk' of offending. Typically, this intervention is risk-focused, preventative, and developmental (in accordance with the RFPP) and deals with the young person as an offender, employing a range of offence- and offender-first interventions. Supporters of risk-focused early intervention argue that it offers a sensible, logical, purportedly effective, efficient, and economical preventative approach (Farrington 2007); especially when animated by rigorously-evaluated, evidence-based 'what works' intervention programmes (Sherman et al. 1998; see also **Chapter 19**). The UK government has been so enamoured by the RFPP since 1998 that it has underpinned youth justice policy and practice from that time with risk assessment and risk-focused interventions. The Youth Justice Board or 'YJB', the body that monitors and manages the Youth Justice System of England and Wales, has produced a series of 'Key Elements of Effective Practice' (KEEPs) to promote a consistent, evidence-based approach to working with young people (YJB 2003), with the pivotal KEEP being the practical realisation of the RFPP. Each KEEP focuses on a key area of youth justice practice and have variously consisted of: education, training and employment, mental health, substance use, young people who sexually abuse, offending behaviour programmes, parenting, restorative justice, mentoring, targeted neighbourhood intervention, final warning interventions, swift administration of justice, intensive supervision and surveillance, custody, and resettlement (Stephenson et al. 2013; Case and Haines 2009). The central KEEP is 'Assessment, Planning Interventions and Supervision' (APIS), which outlines 'foundation activities which guide and shape all work with young people who offend' (YJB 2003: 6) and which are crucial to the successful execution of each of the other KEEPs. These foundation activities are basically to assess levels of risk (factors) in young people's lives and to target effective services and interventions on this assessed risk through 'dependable methods'—methods that are synonymous with the YJS risk assessment tool *Asset*.

Asset: structured risk assessment

> All children and young people entering the youth justice system should benefit from a structured assessment ... to identify the risk factors associated with offending behaviour and to inform effective intervention programmes.
>
> YJB 2004: 27

In April 2000, the YJB introduced the *Asset* tool for use by practitioners from multi-agency youth offending teams (YOTs) with all young people aged 10–17 who enter the YJS (Baker 2005). *Asset* measures risk factors in different psychosocial developmental domains of a young person's life in order to explain offending and thus inform service development and intervention planning. *Asset* is a risk factor questionnaire completed by YOT practitioners during interviews with a young person, based around a series of questions relating to their current or recent exposure to 'dynamic' (able to be changed) risk factors in 12 psychosocial domains:

(a) **living arrangements** (living with known offenders);

(b) **family and personal relationships** (family/carers involved in criminal activity);

(c) **education, training, and employment** (regular truancy);

(d) **neighbourhood** (signs of drug dealing)

(e) **lifestyle** (associating with delinquent peers);

(f) **substance use** (detrimental effect on daily functioning);

(g) **physical health** (physical immaturity);

(h) **emotional and mental health** (concerns about the future);

(i) **perception of self and others** (difficulties with self-identity);

(j) **thinking and behaviour** (impulsivity);

(k) **attitudes to offending** (reluctance to accept responsibility for behaviour);

(l) **motivation to change** (understanding of problematic behaviour).

The 'core profile' of *Asset* is supplemented by four additional sections (see YJB 2007):

- **positive (protective) factors** (positive attitudes);
- **indicators of vulnerability** (vulnerability to physical or emotional harm);
- **indicators of serious harm to others** (evidence of actual harmful behaviour);
- **what do you think**—the young person reports their thoughts and feelings regarding issues about their life and offending.

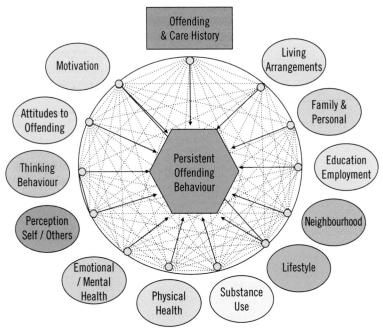

Figure 9.10 Purported complexity of interrelationships between risk factors and youth offending

Source: Centre for Youth and Criminal Justice 2016

The supposedly complex interrelationships between *Asset* risk domains and (persistent) offending behaviour are depicted in **Figure 9.10**.

When practitioners have completed responses to the multiple (risk factor) questions in each domain (i.e. yes/no is a given risk factor present?), they complete an explanations box in which they provide narrative evidence of the adjudged influence of these domain-specific risks. This narrative is the evidence base for subsequent decisions and judgements regarding how to respond to that young person. Finally, practitioners must make a generalised quantitative judgement on a five-point scale about the extent to which they feel the group of risk factors in each domain when taken together are associated with 'the likelihood of further offending': 0 = no association, 1 = slight or limited indirect association, 2 = moderate direct or indirect association, 3 = quite strong association, normally direct, 4 = very strong, clear and direct association. The ratings for each psychosocial domain are totalled to give the young person an aggregate risk score from 0–64 (16 domains, each scored 0–4). This aggregate score determines whether the young person is assessed as being a low, medium, or high risk of being reconvicted in the 12 months following the assessment.

In 2009, the UK government consolidated their commitment to the RFPP by introducing the 'scaled approach' to assessment and intervention. Under this new framework, YOT practitioners tailor or scale the frequency, duration, and intensity of planned interventions to levels of risk assessed by the young person's *Asset* score, with

intervention categorised as: standard/low likelihood of reconviction (*Asset* score of 0–14), enhanced/medium likelihood (15–32), and intensive/high likelihood (33 +). The scaled approach elaborates the risk-based approach to assessing, explaining, and responding to offending by young people in England and Wales.

Onset: pre-offending risk assessment

The YJB has pursued prevention with young people outside of the formal YJS through a committed early intervention agenda, exemplified by the creation of two large-scale preventative programmes—Youth Inclusion and Support Panels (YISPs) and Youth Inclusion Programmes (YIPs). Both programmes have been underpinned by a pre-offending risk assessment tool called *Onset*, which was introduced in April 2003 for use with young people aged 8–13 years (despite 10 years being the minimum age of criminal responsibility) to identify them as 'at risk' of offending in the future. *Onset* focuses on risk factors for the onset of offending (hence the name) rather than for reoffending or reconviction (the focus of *Asset*). It facilitates risk-focused early intervention, with early taken to mean pre-offending and the prevention of offending onset, rather than risk-focused interventions seeking to prevent the continuance or exacerbation of existing offending behaviour (Case and Haines 2009). The *Onset* assessment is divided into sections that broadly correspond in content and structure to those in *Asset,* with risk rated by practitioners in a similar way. For example, sections with ratings of 3–4 are considered by the YJB to be 'more closely linked to offending' than sections with lower ratings and therefore, these risk sections should become the priority for *Onset*-informed interventions. *Onset* is used to identify 'at risk' young people for referral to YISPs or YIPs by key stakeholder agencies such as the police, social services, education and health.

YISPs and YIPs: *Onset* in action

The *Onset* process was developed specifically for use by YISPs for use with young people considered to be pre-crime and 'at risk' of offending. YISPs began in April 2003 in 13 pilot areas and have expanded into over 220 areas across the country. They are multi-agency panels with representatives from different agencies working with young people, in particular the statutory agencies of police, education, health, and social services. The aim of these panels is to prevent offending and antisocial behaviour by 8–13 year olds (or 14–18 year olds in the case of the YISP + programme) who have been identified by referring agencies (using *Onset*) as 'at risk' of offending and to ensure that these young people and their families can access mainstream services at the earliest possible stage (although participation is voluntary).

Neighbourhood-based YIPs were established by the YJB in 2000 in response to demands for further investment in targeted preventative activity with young people living in deprived, 'high risk' neighbourhoods. YIPs are tailor-made programmes for 8–17 year olds (Junior YIPs for 8–12 year olds, Senior YIPs for 13–17 year olds) living in any of over 100 of the most socially deprived/high crime and therefore most high-risk neighbourhoods in England and Wales (YJB 2006). The YJB has outlined a series of key objectives for YIPs:

- to engage with those young people considered to be most at risk of offending and reoffending in a particular neighbourhood;
- to address the risk and protective factors identified by *Onset* assessments;
- to prevent and reduce offending through intervention with individuals, families, and communities (YJB 2006).

The reductionism of risk management

The assessment and intervention frameworks used with young people in the YJS (*Asset* and the scaled approach)

and outside/on the brink of the system (*Onset* and YISPs/YIPs) are underpinned by a risk management approach to prevention and early intervention—the need to identify and manage 'risk factors' that could lead to future and further offending. Risk-based explanations of, and responses to, youth offending have been critiqued at length in this book elsewhere for their *reductionism* (see **Chapter 6**; see also Case 2017; Case and Haines 2015, 2009). What is meant by this is that these explanations and responses (e.g. the scaled approach) operate a staged process of incrementally moving understandings of youth offending further and further away from the young person's own interpretations, understandings, and experiences of their own lives (see France and Homel 2007a). For example, the assessment of risks in each dynamic (psychosocial) domain in *Asset* is removed/distanced from the realities of young people's lives by requiring (adult) practitioners to simplistically reduce them to a generalised rating for each domain regarding its association with the likelihood of further offending. The very act of oversimplifying potentially complex and dynamic aspects of young people's lives, experiences, perceptions and thoughts into readily quantifiable and targetable risk factors is arguably an exercise in reductionism; the results of which do not necessarily represent the 'lived realities' of young people (see Kemshall 2008; France and Homel 2007a), so it could be difficult to utilise this data to inform meaningful responses to their lives: but what do you think?

Risk assessment may further reduce and restrict measures of risk by individualising the explanations of, and responsibility for, offending. The identified bias of risk assessment tools towards measuring psychosocial risk factors, it is argued, places the responsibility (blame) for offending with the young person and their inability to resist these risk factors, rather than examining the possible (less controllable) influence of broader issues. Such broader issues could include socio-structural factors (e.g. social class, poverty, unemployment, social deprivation, ethnicity), the absence of support mechanisms or the external influence of others (e.g. youth justice agencies, schools, youth provision) on their offending (France and Homel 2007a, 2007b). This *responsibilisation* (Muncie 2004) is incongruous when applied to a demographic group (young people aged 10–17) who are typically assigned few other social responsibilities or capabilities such as being allowed to vote, drive a car, own a house, have sex, or marry. Therefore, it could be argued that young people are viewed as lacking the responsibility to fully engage in society but possessing full responsibility for committing a complex, subjective, and socially constructed act that is influenced (at least in part) by factors outside of their control (Case and Haines 2009).

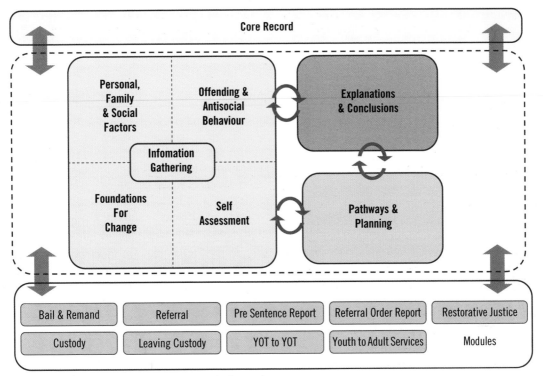

Figure 9.11 The *AssetPlus* assessment and intervention framework

Source: Youth Justice Board 2013, content available under the Open Government Licence v3.0

The reductionism of risk management and its associated early intervention also has ethical implications. Critics have asserted that scaling intervention in response to assessed, quantified levels of risk is unethical (and ineffective) because it is pre-emptive and disproportionate (Case 2017; Bateman 2011):

1. **Pre-emptive**—risk-based early intervention (e.g. the scaled approach) intervenes in the lives of young people on the basis of what they are predicted to do in the future rather than what they have done. Youth justice responses are based on predicting what might happen and responding to this prediction, rather than responding to the actual offence—thus subverting the criminal justice principles of due process, proportionality, and evidence-based practice.

2. **Disproportionate**—scaling intervention based on predicted risk levels could lead to the YJS visiting excessive intervention on a 'high risk' young person who may never have actually offended in the future (a 'false positive') or providing insufficient intervention to a 'low risk' young person who may actually go on to offend (a 'false negative'). In other words, young people may get too much intervention (i.e. interference) or not enough intervention (i.e. support).

The YJB has recognised and responded to criticism of its risk-based approach to explaining and responding to youth crime (animated by *Asset* and the scaled approach) with the introduction of *AssetPlus* (YJB 2013). This revised assessment and intervention framework (see **Figure 9.11**) focuses on enhancing children's strengths rather than prioritising risks/deficits; addressing needs alongside risks, promoting desistance from offending, accessing children's voices rather than privileging adult prescriptions and understandings of 'risk' and children's lives, enabling more practitioner discretion in assessment and intervention planning, and focusing on achieving positive outcomes for children.

AssetPlus looks and sounds like a contemporary, progressive, and practical evolution of assessment and intervention in the YJS. It introduces a framework for explaining and responding to youth crime and represents an evolution beyond artefactual risk factor theories and the RFPP towards more enhanced and constructivist ways of exploring risk and explaining offending. Indeed Professor Kevin Haines, longtime research and writing collaborator of Steve Case, argues that *AssetPlus* is a rejection of risk-based explanatory models. Let me explain why you might disagree with this view and instead harbour doubts about the extent of progression and evolution evidenced by *AssetPlus* (see **Telling it like it is 9.2**).

TELLING IT LIKE IT IS 9.2

A subjective critique of *AssetPlus*

The basis of *AssetPlus* is an assessment completed through interview between youth justice practitioners, a young person, and significant adults in their life, which populates an 'information gathering and description' section. Here, the youth justice practitioner collects information about 'personal, family and social factors' in the young person's life that might influence their offending: family and environmental factors (e.g. living arrangements, community influences, significant life events), parenting, care and supervision (e.g. young person's experience as a parent/carer), and personal development (e.g. mental, emotional and physical health, lifestyle, peer group, education). These factors are rated (albeit not numerically) in an explanations and conclusions section in terms of their influence on the likelihood of reoffending. Therefore, the reality is that they are risk factors. They are all psychosocial (basically merging the *Asset* risk sections into broader sections) and are used to assess the risk of future offending. They may not be given the label of 'risk factors', but they fulfil the same function. So in this sense, *AssetPlus* is a rebranded asset. But it's actually more than that—it is a rebooted explanatory framework that evolves explanations of youth crime beyond these original risk factors and into new areas in new ways. *AssetPlus* intends to explore contextual information (mainly situational influences) and the dynamic interactions between context and personal, family, and social factors. *AssetPlus* has also committed to expanding the explanatory focus beyond the predictors of offending and into a consideration of the factors that influence resilience and desistance (resisting risk

and stopping offending—similar to social control theory), along with focusing on young people's strengths and the influences in their lives that promote positive behaviours and outcomes (see Haines and Case 2015). Perhaps most importantly, *AssetPlus* has a specific section for 'self-assessment' by the young person—enabling practitioners to access the much-neglected voices and perspectives of young people and to examine how they construct, experience, and negotiate their exposure to different (risk) factors at different points in their lives. This is an enhanced (constructivist), pathways form of risk factor theory by another name (see **Chapter 18**).

If we accept the critique of artefactual risk factor theories and their animation in *Asset* risk assessment, then *AssetPlus* is a step in the right direction as a tool for explaining crime. It integrates more sensitive modes of explanation (e.g. context, interactions, constructions) and moves away from the quantified reductionism of its predecessor. However, in its current form, it is still vague and limited. The vagueness is around what and how it will attempt to explain. What contextual information? What positive behaviours? How will interactions be identified? How will young people's voices be accessed and integrated? It's all a bit ambiguous and ambitious. The limitations are standard risk factor theory limitations—the lack of consideration of socio-structural, economical or political influences, psychosocial biases, the inevitable reductionist threat of individualising explanations of crime, the obsession with measuring the 'likelihood of reoffending'—then using all of these limitations uncritically to dictate responses to offending (cf. Case 2017; Case and Haines 2009).

Progressive approaches to youth offending: Diversion and positive youth justice

Having explored the dominance of early intervention and risk management in official responses to youth offending, the previous section concluded with a discussion of a potentially more progressive approach—*AssetPlus*. As discussed, the introduction of *AssetPlus* evidences an arguably more positive approach to understanding young people's lives and to delivering youth justice than has been pursued through negative-facing risk-based approaches. Moves are afoot in contemporary youth justice to evolve more progressive, less criminalising methods of working

with young people who come to the attention of the YJS. Whether motivated by financial necessity, political imperatives, practical concerns, academic advances, or ethical issues (or a mixture of these), these positive approaches mainly seek to reduce the numbers of young people entering the YJS for the first time and the number who reoffend after entry. These objectives are pursued via more future-orientated perspectives that prioritise promoting positive behaviours and outcomes rather than simply targeting the reduction of previous negative behaviours (e.g.

offending) and outcomes (e.g. exposure to risks). Broadly speaking, progressive youth justice models have focused on two key areas: diversion from the formal YJS and delivering a positive youth justice in promotional, child-friendly ways.

Diversion from the formal YJS

Diversionary models go beyond acknowledging that the system may have criminogenic and iatrogenic (damaging) properties (cf. McAra and McVie 2007) such as labelling, stigmatising, and marginalising effects that could exacerbate criminality. Supporters of diversion within youth justice argue that young people who demonstrate problems and problematic behaviour (e.g. low level offending, antisocial behaviour, substance use) should be worked with by practitioners offering supportive services. Therefore, young people should be simultaneously diverted away from the potentially damaging influence of contact with the formal YJS and diverted into positive and supportive interventions (cf. Smith 2014; Richards 2014).

There has been a significant change in the direction of youth justice since the Coalition Government came to power in the UK in 2010 and since the Conservatives took full control in 2015. This change ushered in what Creaney and Smith (2014: 83) termed 'a new age of diversion'. The UK Coalition Government were heavily critical of the hierarchical approach to out-of-court disposals introduced by the previous Labour Government. They recommended changes to the out-of-court disposal system in the Legal Aid Sentencing and Punishment of Offenders Act 2012 (also known as LASPO), which replaced the escalating out-of-court disposal process of Reprimands to Final Warnings to Court (in other words, three strikes and you're out) with a more flexible, discretionary system of disposal—No Further Action, Community Resolution, Youth Caution, and Youth Conditional Caution—which young people could move in and out of without inevitable escalation into the court process. Accordingly, LASPO made space for 'dialogue around costly, net widening, criminalising, counterproductive, and damaging institutional practices' (Yates 2012: 5). Subsequent guidance given to YOTs regarding the implementation of the new out-of-court system alongside existing diversionary measures (MoJ and YJB 2013) recommended that their assessments of young people focus not just on risk, but also on the appropriateness of the intervention and of the agency seeking to meet the child's needs, and on young people's engagement with interventions (e.g. their motivation to participate, likelihood of family support). These revised pre-court processes were to be underpinned by the new *AssetPlus* assessment and intervention framework.

The government's diversionary pre-court system is interventionist in that it promotes diversion from the formal YJS through informal, out-of-court contact with that same system. Such 'interventionist diversion' (Kelly and Armitage 2015) raises the issue of whether support mechanisms could lead to the child acquiring a criminal label through risk-based assessments—counter-productive to the non-criminalising and supportive aims of diversion. It could even be argued that the 'improved' system actually offers little to improve children's access to the range of non-offending based services that could benefit them, as the focus on intervention and restorative justice could unintentionally compound the young person's negative identity (NAYJ 2012) and embroil them within the very harmful system they are being protected from (Haines et al. 2013).

Recent diversionary trends in the YJS indicate a re-emergence of a government commitment to moving away from restricted, criminalising, punitive, and controlling justice-based approaches. However, that is not to say that this 'new age of diversion' is the principled, needs-led, holistic, and universal model that the political rhetoric may claim. Instead, the government's priority for diversionary schemes appears to be a form of 'fast track' justice, rather than a considered, consultative, and evidenced diversionary approach (Haines et al. 2013). Therefore, the Coalition Government's diversionary commitment may represent more of a practical drive for cost-effectiveness (following a re-examination of costly and counter-productive institutional practices—see Yates 2012), a 'minimum (cheapest) intervention' (Smith 2014a: 110), rather than a principled or progressive commitment to re-orientating how children who offend are perceived and responded to.

Positive youth justice

The newly emerging (re)emphasis on diversion from the formal YJS indicates a less stigmatising/labelling approach to working with young people who offend; an approach that deliberately seeks to avoid the negative outcomes associated with system contact. However, diversion is one way of challenging the negative, risk-based, and interventionist forms of youth justice visited upon young people since the Crime and Disorder Act 1998. A broader model of positive youth justice known as Children First, Offenders Second (CFOS) has been developed in the child-focused and rights-facing social policy context in Wales, where national government decision-making is partially devolved from England (e.g. in relation to health, education, social care, but not criminal justice). CFOS emphasises diversion, but coheres around a broader set of progressive principles for delivering youth justice (Haines and Case 2015):

- **Child-friendly, child-appropriate practice**—Young people who offend should be viewed primarily as children (hence the model's title), rather than offenders becoming their primary status or label just because they have entered the YJS. All system responses should therefore be child-friendly, child-appropriate, and should engage in child sensitive ways, not by treating children as mini-adults (adulterisation) in a mini-adult criminal justice system.

- **Positive promotion**—CFOS rejects the negative-facing, risk-focused prevention practice of the YJS in favour of promoting positive behaviours (e.g. educational success, involvement in constructive activities) and positive outcomes (e.g. employment, ability to access their rights) for children in the YJS. Children are viewed as agentic (able to make decisions) and as part of the solution to their problems, not part of the problem itself.

- **Systems management**—The YJS is an inter-connected series of decision-making points (e.g. decisions to arrest, bail, remand, sentence, divert, imprison, punish) that can be targeted to meet positive goals for children. The principles of CFOS should give direction to all decision making.

- **Diversion**—CFOS systems management is animated by child-appropriate diversion that is holistic, inclusionary, and applied to all children, not simply those deemed to have committed low-level offences and those at an early stage in the YJS. CFOS normalises offending as an everyday behaviour, so responsive intervention is the minimum necessary level.

- **Engagement**—CFOS aims to be engaging and inclusionary—accessing children's perspectives by encouraging their meaningful participation (not simply consultation) in decision-making, assessment, and intervention (Haines and Case 2015), in accordance with the UNCRC (UNICEF 1989).

- **Legitimacy**—If children consider the authority of, and their treatment by, the state and the agents of the state (e.g. police, YOT staff, teachers) to be legitimate (fair, just, moral, right), they are more likely to engage with crime prevention interventions and to live crime-free lives (see Tyler 2007; Hawes 2013; both in Haines and Case 2015).

- **Evidence-based partnership**—Genuine partnership between children, families, communities, and key stakeholder staff (e.g. YOTs, police, teachers, researchers) that is evidence-based can shape and guide interventions that are more likely to be meaningful, engaging, and legitimate to children (Haines and Case 2015).

- **Responsibilising adults**—Children cannot (fully) make their own independent decisions about their behaviour or lead their own independent lives (Freeman 2007)—so much about a child's life is decided by adults and is the responsibility of adults. Recognising the responsibilities of adults for decision-making in respect of children and outcomes for children is a central feature of CFOS.

The progressive principles of the CFOS positive youth justice approach have been animated in different areas of England and Wales, but perhaps the best example thus far is in Surrey, England. The approach is explored further in **Conversations 9.2**.

CONVERSATIONS 9.2

Positive youth justice in Surrey—with Ben Byrne

In conversation, the head of Surrey Youth Support Service, Ben Byrne explained what makes their approach to youth justice both positive and different to traditional models.

What makes Surrey's approach different?

Over recent years, Surrey has tried to develop an approach to youth justice, which draws upon the criminological evidence base and better reflects commitments from the United Nations Convention on the Rights of the Child (Byrne and Brooks 2015). Two key reforms have been central to the development of Surrey's model.

The first of these reforms was the abandonment of the YOT model in 2012 and the development of an informal,

restorative, and integrated response to supporting young people who have offended within a broader Youth Support Service. Underpinning this change was a desire to move away from reliance upon discrete services for 'offenders', thereby avoiding labelling and prolonged systems contact (cf. McAra and McVie 2007), and to develop a bespoke response to vulnerable and marginalised adolescents. This means that older children receive essentially the same services and opportunities, coordinated and delivered through one key relationship with their youth support officer, regardless of whether their entry route to the service is through offending, homelessness, mental health, unemployment, or 'child in need' status.

The second change in Surrey with respect to the delivery of youth justice services was the development from 2009 of the Youth Restorative Intervention (the YRI). This is the default response to all young people's offending that is too serious to be dealt with through a simple community resolution and is not so serious that it would be indictable only for an adult. The YRI is restorative in that it seeks active involvement of the victim and young person who has offended in order to address the harm that has been caused. It is also restorative in the sense that it recognises that children who offend (particularly those who repeatedly offend) themselves often require restoration and repair because of their own experiences, because of fractured family, peer or school relationships, or because of environmental factors which mean they are at risk of missing out on the opportunities available to the majority of children and young people. The YRI separates work to be done to appropriately deal with the offence from work which needs to be done to support the child's participation, safeguarding, and well-being.

What has been the result of your changes?

The combination of the dampening down of the formal youth justice system with the integration of youth justice into a broader approach to support for older children in Surrey has seen a 93 per cent reduction in the numbers of first time entrants to the youth justice system and 70 per cent fewer court orders. This means youth justice in Surrey costs far less than it used to and much of the savings have been used to develop homelessness services, mental health provision, and employment services with the YSS [Youth Support Service] meaning a virtuous cycle has been created as these are the types of approaches, available to all young people who need them, that are most likely to prevent youth crime.

What next for youth justice in Surrey?

We recognise that in spite of the reforms undertaken in Surrey which have gone some way to improving the prospects for children in conflict with the law this still could not be described as a child first approach. Too many children still get arrested and detained in police custody for behaviour that is symptomatic of safeguarding needs, those in the formal system are still assessed and supervised according to offender first national requirement, and for those who go to custody this is to institutions which are not safe or suitable to accommodate vulnerable children. As part of Surrey's positive youth justice pilot all these areas are being reformed from a starting point of the needs of the child in accordance with internationally established rights, our responsibilities towards them as children, and practice informed by what we know works with older children at risk (Hanson and Holmes 2014).

Ben Byrne, head of Surrey Youth Support Service

The contemporary focus on diversion and positive youth justice explored in this section provides progressive and allegedly 'positive' models for responding to youth crime. These approaches are considered progressive and positive by their advocates because they prioritise child-friendly and children first (not offender first) understandings of young people's lives that normalise typical youthful behaviour (as opposed to labelling and stigmatising children and their behaviours). Consequently, the approaches inform and recommend less formal and negative responses, grounded in the promotion of positive behaviours and outcomes for young people (see Haines and Case 2015). Privileging young people's meaningful participation in youth justice processes and decisions, along with the importance of researching how they construct their lives is considered progressive and positive in its own right and a healthy, principled contrast to the negative, positivist, individualised, developmental, and risk-led ways in which young people have been typically understood and responded to.

Conclusions

In this chapter, we've explored the ways in which perceptions of children/childhood and young people/youth have been socially constructed through historical, political, social, media, public, and academic influences. The chapter has critically explored the key criminological explanations of youth crime and identified the explanatory dominance of positivist, developmental theories that individualise causation. We also sought to understand the potential cultural influences on offending by young people, such as gang culture, radicalisation, the ways that young people are constructed and criminalised (e.g. through use of custody), and the related issue of deviancy amplification. This was followed by a discussion of the hegemony of early intervention and risk management approaches within official responses to youth crime by the YJS, leading into a concluding review of contemporary, arguably more progressive, positive versions of youth justice, notably diversion and CFOS.

The development of social constructions of childhood and youth, the hegemonic explanations of youth crime and responses to it, have been represented as an evolution or trajectory—an ongoing 'them or us?' debate. This has involved theorising and constructing youth crime as a problem located within the helpless, out of control child/young person ('them'), rationalised and promoted by positivist, developmental explanations, contrasted with views of youth crime as a problem socially-constructed by adult-led structural, cultural, and contextual influences. Consequent debates around the most appropriate and effective responses to youth crime have often been presented as dichotomies: deprived or depraved?; care or control?; in need or at risk? The YJS of England and Wales has tried to some extent to address both sides of these dichotomies in its responses, but has tended to fall into positivist, individualised, and developmental responses that privilege control through early (risk-based) interventions and expanding levels of risk management. From the outside looking in, the predominance of developmental explanations and risk-based youth justice responses strongly indicates that key stakeholders, be they academic, political, or media, prefer to view youth crime as the problem of 'them' that can only be fixed by 'us'.

SUMMARY

- Outline how 'childhood' and 'youth' have been socially constructed

The chapter began with a discussion of how, since the mid-1700s and the onset of the industrial revolution and compulsory schooling (in the UK), the notions of childhood and youth have become quite clearly distinguished as a separate life stage, with their own very specific characteristics. Previously, children were thought as essentially little adults, working and socialising with older adults. Distinctions have been based on identified differences in relation to biological, psychological and social development, and behaviour, leading to a whole range of special provisions and institutional arrangements reserved for children and youth in the criminal justice context. The constructions of childhood and youth have been dynamic and contested over time and place such that formal constructions of children's legal status vary quite significantly between different countries, and this in turn reflects differing assumptions about when they should be seen as becoming responsible for their behaviour.

- Critically explore the key criminological explanations for youth crime

The explanatory section began with an exploration of developmental theories of childhood, which hold that the social construction of the 'child' can be explained in terms of the complex social processes, which shape their experiences and their views of the world. Developmental theories tend to view childhood as a developmental life phase, during which a series of identifiable biological, psychological, and psychosocial processes lead towards a mature state of adulthood. Physical growth, and biological and hormonal changes are thus correlated with certain recognised stages in child development, such as puberty. Moving into the 21st century, such physiological features of childhood have been found to have parallels in neurological developments too.

We then explored theories of delinquency, categorising and discussing the origins and causes of young people's offending under three broad headings: individual attributes, psychodynamic factors, and social and structural influences. Each of these sets of theories were understood as being, to a greater or lesser extent, about interacting with young people's agency, that is, their capacity of otherwise to make rational decisions and choices about whether or not to behave in a particular way.

Finally, we addressed the issue of explaining delinquency empirically, noting that the development of empirical, research-based (largely developmental) explanations of youth offending has been dominated by positivist theories. These theories were criticised in a number of ways, notably due to positivism's widespread reductionism in its methodology, explanations, and conclusions—reducing complex systems and behaviours to fixed statistical quantities and overly-simplistic and often exclusive biological, psychological, or sociological categories and explanations.

- Promote understanding of the cultural influences on offending by young people

The cultural influences discussion focused mainly on the role of peers and culture in shaping allegiances and patterns of behaviour amongst young people who offend. It was suggested that young people who join certain groups or 'sub-cultures' or 'gangs' have reassigned their commitment to ideas and groupings that lie outside those associated with conventional norms and the prevailing moral order (e.g. truancy from school substance use, antisocial behaviour, offending). The cultural discussions were illustrated with the examples of gang membership and radicalisation.

- Discuss the extent to which young criminals have been socially constructed

The chapter identified how adult-constructed theories of youth crime in the western world have evidenced a positivist dominance, producing a series of explanations focused on the individual young person, their biology, psychology, exposure to developmental (psychosocial) risk factors, and their experiences of critical life events/turning points. Consequently, explanations for youth crime have typically 'othered' young people who offend and marked them out as a problematic, dangerous, irresponsible, and risky population in need of control and punishment—creating a 'them' (young people) and 'us' (adults) mentality. The experiences of black and ethnic minority youth and young people in custody were used to illustrate these arguments.

- Explain the dominant role of early intervention and risk management approaches in responding to youth crime

Negative depictions of young 'offenders' and individualised explanations of offending, positivist and developmental risk-based theories have attained dominance when politicians, policy makers, and other key stakeholders construct youth justice responses to youth crime in England and Wales. In particular, the RFPP has become the hegemonic model for explaining and responding to youth offending in the YJS. A major consequence of this hegemony has been a widespread utilisation of risk assessment instruments within youth justice systems to quantify risk factors and to determine appropriate responses to offending. What constitutes 'appropriate' and 'effective' responses to youth crime have therefore been predominantly risk-focused, aiming to identify, measure, and tackle young people's exposure to risk factors prior to them offending (i.e. early intervention) or once they have offended (i.e. risk management), with the guiding objective being the prevention of youth crime.

- Interpret contemporary progressive models for responding to youth crime, notably diversion and positive youth justice

The chapter concluded by presenting more positive alternative models for responding to youth crime. Particular focus was giving to diverting young people away from the formal YFS and diverting them into constructive, less formal interventions. We also explore the concept of positive youth justice as animated by the CFOS model, which is asserted to be child-friendly, promotional, diversion-based, engaging, legitimate, and founded in evidence—with a focus is on partnership, systems management, and making adults responsible for positive outcomes for young people.

REVIEW QUESTIONS

1. What do you understand by the social construction of childhood and youth?

2. Can you identify and outline three key categories of theory used to explain delinquency?

3. What cultural factors may influence youth offending?

4. What is the relationship between developmental theories of offending and the dominance of risk management and early intervention?

5. In what ways are diversion and children first approaches progressive models of youth justice?

FURTHER READING

Case, S.P. (2017) *Contemporary Youth Justice.* Abingdon: Routledge.
The most up-to-date and comprehensive youth justice textbook available. The author of this textbook Steve Case has attempted to transfer the writing style from this current *Criminology* text into a detailed exposition of the definitions and explanations of youth offending and an examination of the youth justice responses to this behaviour. In essence, the *Contemporary Youth Justice* textbook is an elaboration of this chapter.

Smith, R. (2014) *Youth Justice: Ideas, Policy and Practice.* London: Routledge.
A very popular, comprehensive, and expertly written textbook that explores the key issues from the current chapter in much greater depth and breadth. Highly recommended.

Case, S.P. and Haines, K.R. (2009) *Understanding Youth Offending: Risk Factor Research, Policy and Practice.* Cullompton: Willan.
This dynamic and highly critical book will give you a comprehensive overview of the different forms of risk factor theory that have been used to explain youth offending and to inform youth justice responses. It also covers the main theoretical, methodological, and ethical criticisms of these explanations in detail.

Goldson, B. and Muncie, J. (2015) *Youth Crime and Justice.* London: Sage.
A highly accessible edited text authored by an impressive group of international youth justice experts. This book covers a wide range of important themes related to youth crime and justice and is a must read for students interested in the topic. Of particular interest to us here is Harry Hendrick's superb chapter on the social construction of youth crime.

Haines, K.R. and Case, S.P. (2015) *Positive Youth Justice: Children First, Offenders Second.* Bristol: Policy Press.
An evidence-based text providing a clear and critical context for progressive, child-friendly approaches to youth justice. Reading this will provide you with much more detail to complement the final section of this chapter.

Youth Justice Journal
For students wishing to expand their knowledge of youth crime and justice still further, we recommend exploring the website of *Youth Justice Journal*, an international, multi-disciplinary publication containing articles that are accessible to a wide range of key stakeholders in the area.

 Access the **online resources** to view selected further reading and web links relevant to the material covered in this chapter.
www.oup.com/uk/case/

CHAPTER OUTLINE

Introduction   264

Critical race theory   264

Understanding race, crime, and the criminal
justice system   266

Using CRT to understand crime and criminal justice
in England and Wales   270

Conclusion   278

Race, ethnicities, and the criminal justice system

Neena Samota

KEY ISSUES

After studying this chapter you should be able to:

- explain what is critical race theory and reflect on the salience of race in the criminal justice system;

- develop a critical view of official and policy responses which aim to address institutional racism and ethnic disproportionality;

- recognise and comprehend the key decision making points in the criminal justice process that potentially increase or decrease ethnic disproportionality;

- apply critical race theory to analyse disparate outcomes for ethnic minority groups involved in the criminal justice system;

- comprehend why people from ethnic minorities feel they would be treated worse than people from other races by the criminal justice agencies;

- apply critical race theory framework to your own research or essay questions.

Introduction

Race and ethnicity are enduring concepts which continue to animate broader discussions about justice and injustice. In assessing fairness and equality within multi-ethnic and multicultural societies, portraits of race inequality in housing, employment, education, and health are common features (Equality and Human Rights Commission (EHRC) 2011). By far the worst portrait of inequality emerges in the criminal justice system. Racial disparities in policing, sentencing, and imprisonment have become a common feature in the criminal justice systems of diverse societies like the United States, Canada, and the UK. (NB the focus of this chapter is on the criminal justice system in England and Wales.)

Criminological literature is saturated with references to race and ethnicity in describing the nature and extent of the crime problem. Positivist theorists such as Cesare Lombroso claimed direct links between criminality and race (see **Chapter 13** on biological positivism).

Although such claims have now been rejected and discredited, links between race and crime continue to fuel the popular imagination and media interest. Is it true that some groups do simply commit more crime? While this may be a good starting point for you as a criminology student, there are more significant lines of inquiry that need to be opened for further discussion. The assertion that justice is 'colour-blind' is too simplistic and tends to focus exclusively on the outcomes, while ignoring the disparities in processes of operation that lead to those outcomes.

This chapter invites you to critically examine such processes of operation, for example, those associated with labelling and implicating certain groups with criminality on grounds of race, and ethnicity. Critical race theory will be introduced as a new perspective that helps to further our understanding of race inequality in the criminal justice system and why it persists.

Critical race theory

Critical race theory (CRT) is an interdisciplinary movement that developed in the United States to study and theorise the relationship between race, racism, and power. CRT is set within a broader socio-economic and historical perspective and seeks to challenge racial hierarchy and subordination in all its forms. Its intellectual and activist attributes aim to transform unequal societal structures. This section attempts to locate CRT within the critical criminological theoretical tradition. It proceeds to uncover how and why a CRT perspective can help challenge established legal and social norms that help perpetuate conditions of oppression and disadvantage. Within social structures that are defined by race, CRT helps to examine the nature of institutionalised racial oppression; where intentional and unintentional racism is not only prevalent but also subtle, making some forms of racism unresponsive to legal remedies such as race equality legislation. CRT helps to examine the dominant ideology, assumptions, and discourse that shape racial oppression. It helps understand the dynamics of structures and institutions such as the criminal justice system and key concepts of race, crime, and justice that characterise it. More specifically, it helps to ask questions like: why are racial minority groups over-represented in the criminal justice system? Why do institutions, such as the police, profile and target specific groups disproportionately when using tactics like stop and search? Why, despite several official responses to racial violence in England and Wales, does the victimisation of racial minority groups persist? More specifically,

CRT is a useful tool to understand critical issues such as racial profiling and the over-representation of ethnic minorities in the criminal justice process and official responses to racial violence.

Mainstream criminological perspectives are inadequate in challenging dominant ideas about crime and deviance. Critical criminological perspectives help to understand how inequalities within society and the unequal distribution of power tends to criminalise and victimise those who are less powerful (see **Chapter 15**).

The development of CRT

Key foundational perspectives in critical criminology emerged through the 1960s and 1970s with the works on labelling by Howard Becker and conflict perspectives (including Marxist criminology) as explored by William Chambliss, Richard Quinney, and Jock Young. Criminologists on the Left offered perspectives on how inequality based on class affected crime and deviance whereas Right leaning criminologists overlooked structural factors and focused on the individual instead.

Contemporary critical criminologists in the late 1980s reasserted the foundational perspectives of critical criminologists and focused on how power shaped the construction of crime and the operation of criminal justice. The works of Steven Box, Steve Tombs, Paddy Hillyard, described as zemiology, expanded the remit of criminal

CONTROVERSY AND DEBATE 10.1

The entrenched notion of 'black' criminality—with contributor Neena Samota

A young black male, travelling home with his three friends after college, found my mobile phone on the train. I rang my phone hoping someone would answer it. The young man answered and said he had noticed my phone on the seat as the train doors were closing. So he decided to get off at the next station. I was simply impressed by the goodness of the young man and thanked him profusely for waiting for me to collect my phone. In narrating this experience to my local station officer I was left with much more to think about. Although he was pleased I got my phone back he asked me if the person was 'black'. Upon confirming that the young man was indeed 'black' he expressed further surprise that despite being 'black' the young man did such a good deed.

How did you react to reading that and what were your initial thoughts? Would you have thought the same as the station officer?

Labelling is commonplace and such race consciousness further rejects and excludes individuals on grounds of race and ethnicity. This sort of racial profiling is a critical issue because it touches the core of the orientation we have towards certain groups in our society. It is important for us to consider how, for example, young black men are perceived and how society responds to them. The example in this box illustrates that leaping to conclusions and conceiving of a young black male as a potential opportunist for criminal acts informs our public and private lives.

(For a full discussion of 'black' criminality and views about their family structures, values, and culture, see Paul Gilroy (1987) *There Ain't No Black in the Union Jack*. London: Hutchinson.)

justice to incorporate acts that cause social harm and undermine social justice. Cultural criminologists like Jeff Ferrell and Mike Presdee further added to our understanding of factors that sustain criminal activity; not only background factors such as socio-economic disadvantage but also foreground factors such as emotion and thrill seeking leading to criminal activity (Ugwudike 2015).

Critical race theory, a relatively new movement that emerged in the 1970s, brings together insights from critical legal studies and radical feminism (Delgado and Stefancic 2012). In the absence of literature that critically evaluated race and the law, CRT scholars made the treatment of race central, not only to the law and policy of the United States but also to the expression of racism and power in wider society. Early proponents of CRT, such as Derrick Bell, Alan Freeman, Mari Matsuda, Kimberle Crenshaw, Patricia Williams, and Richard Delgado aimed to pursue new theories and strategies to address more subtle forms of racism that were becoming common.

CRT shares in the ideas of critical legal studies to engage in the deconstruction of ideologies that support social hierarchies and law reform. CRT challenges 'the very foundations of liberal order, including equality theory, legal reasoning, Enlightenment rationalism, and neutral principles of constitutional law.' (Delgado and Stefancic 2012: 3). The relationship between power and the construction of social roles and the hidden patterns and habits that support patriarchy and other forms of domination were insights borrowed from radical feminism.

According to Ugwudike, CRT theorists study how society constructs race and attributes certain traits to groups thereby constructing ideas about racial difference (Ugwudike 2015). The concepts of intersectionality and anti-essentialism are also important to CRT theorists. Rather than having fixed identities individuals are constitutive of an accumulation of identities. How different features of individual identity intersect to produce different experiences for minority ethnic groups is key to critical race theory. For CRT theorists, racism is not an aberration but a normal feature of social relations, prevalent but insidious. They also believe that race equality laws work only on the most blatant forms of racism. Consider the example in **Controversy and debate 10.1**.

In their rejection of legal liberalism, CRT scholars assert that both procedural and substantive American law, including anti-discrimination law, is structured to maintain white privilege. In bringing together a review of the key writings that informed the CRT movement Bennett Capers (2014: 26) identifies the following five recurring themes and tenets:

1. Formal equality laws often serve to marginalise and obscure social, political, and economic inequality.

2. The principle of 'interest convergence' emphasises that legal reforms that seemingly benefit ethnic minorities happen only when such reforms benefit the interests of the white majority.

3. Race is biologically insignificant and, to a large extent, socially and legally constructed.

4. CRT scholars reject crude essentialism and recognise that oppression and subordination operate on multiple axes.

5. Reference to race is often omitted in the law and therefore CRT tries to make race visible by incorporating personal narratives or 'legal storytelling' in their methods.

CRT also recognises that racism is not simply embedded in individual prejudices and biases but is also embedded and reproduced within social structures and within political and legal institutions. A robust deconstruction of procedures and laws helps eliminate racialised hierarchies. Since CRT emerged as a challenge to US law, critical race theorists use the concept of 'legal indeterminacy' to suggest that in a legal case the court has the power to determine a different outcome. According to Ugwudike, the court can select different legal arguments or legal doctrines to create different outcomes which opens room for potentially discriminatory decision making on racial or other grounds. Critical theorists also explore how 'deficit thinking' can further put minority ethnic groups at a disadvantage as it involves construction of negative narratives which suggest certain groups possess inherent deficits that can be linked to their pathology or biological constitution (2015: 227).

Although CRT developed in the US it is a useful tool to challenge racial inequality wherever it occurs. As a body of scholarship in the UK context CRT is mostly used in the field of education. According to Rollock and Gillborn, CRT exposes how race and racism represent social thought and power relations and maintain racial inequality in ways that 'appear normal and unremarkable' (2011: 1). In an attempt to understand ethnic disproportionality and unequal outcomes in the criminal justice system, CRT presents a very useful framework.

Criticisms of CRT

CRT is not without its critics. According to Capers, CRT is criticised for being separatist, insufficiently prescriptive in offering solutions to structural problems, and even described by Richard Posner as a 'lunatic fringe' (2014: 26). Ugwudike also offers a useful summary of criticisms levelled at CRT. These include playing the race card, playing the victim that deserves better treatment, propounding irrational ideas, sacrificing objective theoretical analysis for subjective storytelling, and implying that black people think alike. The CRT movement has also faced internal criticisms such as the inability to offer alternatives to social arrangements CRT criticises. Others have questioned why CRT focuses on theoretical work and challenges civil rights laws. Some have accused CRT scholars of abandoning their focus on the materialist issues that impact disenfranchised groups in society and turning to matters such as 'microaggression' that interest middle-class members. Microaggression refers to the minor, spontaneous but hurtful acts of unkindness that black people experience due to the colour of their skin. In response to these criticisms critical race theorists are combining theory and practice and developing alternatives to social injustices that disadvantage black groups (Ugwudike 2015: 229–31).

Despite criticisms, the influence of CRT is growing in law to challenge substantive criminal law and procedure. As a discipline it is now being widely taught at law schools and CRT scholarship is now evident beyond the United States. According to Capers, CRT has spawned other critical approaches to the law such as LatCrit theory, Asian-American jurisprudence, queer critical theory, critical race feminism, and critical white studies (2014: 26).

Understanding race, crime, and the criminal justice system

Having outlined the key ideas of critical race theory this section evaluates how knowledge of race and ethnicity is constructed in a socio-political context and then applied within public institutions by policy makers.

State response to rising social inequality and racial discrimination

In their authoritative account in *Racism, Crime and Justice*, Bowling and Phillips provide a useful overview of a social and political context that defined how different ethnic groups experienced policing, offending, and victimisation.

The British government ignored the fact that racist violence at the end of the 1970s was on the rise. That racism in policing and criminal justice practices adversely affected the safety and liberty of ethnic minorities was simply denied by the British state. The police as an institution did not come under the scope of the Race Relations Act 1976 (2002: xv).

Parliamentary Acts

The politics of race and immigration from Commonwealth countries on the one hand, and the politics of race and crime on the other, simultaneously victimised and criminalised African and Asian people in Britain. The Commonwealth Immigration Act 1962, the Commonwealth Immigrants Act 1968, and the Immigration Act 1971 were passed by Parliament as a response to restrict 'coloured' immigration. A 'moral panic' concerning fears that Britain was becoming a 'coffee-coloured' nation (Bowling and Phillips 2002: 7) infused political speeches. Further legislation in the form of the British Nationality Act 1981 consolidated the discriminatory basis of the previous nationality legislation and removed the automatic right of citizenship.

As people from the Caribbean, Africa, and the Indian sub-continent arrived and settled in Britain they experienced rejection both politically and socially. Perceived as a problem and viewed as 'bad stock' that would pollute the 'British race', anti-immigrant views became popular and fuelled hostility and racist violence towards these groups (Phillips and Bowling 2012: 372). Policing practices singled out minority communities for special attention as they were increasingly perceived as disorderly. Stuart Hall et al.'s seminal work, *Policing the Crisis*, illustrated clearly how police believed black people to be criminal and therefore sought actively to police, control, and punish them. These beliefs were further legitimised and gained currency through the media, politicians, and criminal justice agents. In these ways the black population was demonised and constructed as a 'social problem'. The new 'folk devil' and inherently criminal, were some of the new ways to describe and define black young men through the 1970s and 1980s.

The Scarman Inquiry 1981

By the end of the 1970s political promises of 'more law and order' and 'an end to immigration' (Bowling and Phillips 2002: 8) empowered the police and immigration services. Inner-city disturbances, riots, and public disorder that followed set the tone of policing ethnic minorities in British society. As a direct response to the collapse of social order following the 1981 riots in Brixton (see **Figure 10.1**), the then home Secretary William Whitelaw appointed Lord Scarman to head a public inquiry. Similar riots, between 1980 and 1981, in other English cities of Birmingham, Manchester, Bristol, and Liverpool brought young African-Caribbean and Asian men in direct confrontation with police. Scarman identified many issues through his inquiry around policing ethnically diverse communities, racial prejudice and discrimination, inequality, racial disadvantage, accountability, fairness, and justice. The report focused on flawed policing methods use by Operation Swamp such as deployment of special patrol groups, use of the infamous 'sus' law and the statutory power to stop and search. The Scarman inquiry

Figure 10.1 11 April 1981, during the Brixton riot, police with riot shields line up outside the Atlantic Pub, on the corner of Atlantic Road and Coldharbour Lane
Source: Kim Aldis/CC BY-SA 3.0

report concluded with a call to address racial disadvantage through positive action and to enforce existing law on racial discrimination with no further recommendations for new legislation.

Despite noting the fact that not all people involved in the riots were black, Scarman placed race at the centre of his analysis and depicted events in racialised terms. In official commentaries, including Scarman, the actions of the young African-Caribbean and Asian men involved in the riots were depicted as 'something new and sinister'. Scarman himself noted 'the rioters … found a ferocious delight in arson, criminal damage to property, and in violent attacks upon police, the fire brigade, and the ambulance service. Their ferocity, which made no distinction between the police and the members of the rescue services is, perhaps, the most frightening aspect of this terrifying weekend' (cited in McGhee 2005: 18–19).

While the Scarman report received enthusiastic support from politicians and police it received mixed reactions from the black community. For scholars like Paul Gilroy, Lee Bridges, and Darcus Howe, the Scarman report was flawed and reinforced racist pathologies of black people. The problematic areas of policing such as use of stop and search powers, the investigation of complaints against the police, and police accountability were not addressed by Scarman. The fact that policing as an institution still remained outside the purview of the Race Relations Act 1976, and the inability of the state to recognise this omission and bring the police under democratic control, further exacerbated frustration and anger amongst black and Asian communities. Racial discrimination and inequality persisted and the disproportionate criminalisation of black communities accelerated. According to Bowling and Phillips (2002), between 1985 and 1999 the number of white males in prison increased by 31 per cent whereas it increased by 80 per cent for Asians and by 101 per cent for black groups.

As the Scarman report was discussed in the House of Lords, Lord Anthony Gifford, who chaired inquiries into the Broadwater Farm and the Toxteth riots in Liverpool, put in a strong note of dissent.

> the Scarman Report amounted really to no more than tinkering in the face of the failure to face up to the one historical factor which above all caused the Brixton disorders, which is that the police force in Brixton and other inner city areas have again and again and again abused the rights and freedoms of black citizens. They have abused them without their superiors or their political masters or the courts making the efforts which are called for to stop them. That was the charge that was made and which has been made by responsible leader after responsible leader of the black community.
>
> Hansard 1982: 1435–37

Lord Gifford rightly pointed out that Scarman failed to treat this serious occasion of harassment with the seriousness it deserved. By pinning down social deprivation as the cause of the riots Scarman blurred the issues, as riots were provoked through experiences of injustice that were not heard and not redressed. Gifford also pointed out that the most unpleasant form of injustice was racism by those in authority. When the Scarman report was presented to Parliament, the suggestion that Britain was an institutionally racist society and that the Metropolitan Police Service was a racist force were both flatly denied.

Inadequate responses by the state to social inequality and experiences of racial discrimination in inner-city areas of the country prompted the riots. The conclusion of the Scarman Inquiry should be viewed as the first missed opportunity to recognise that black communities were experiencing racism at the hands of the police and yet nothing substantive was done by the state to address it.

Official responses and policy developments to address race issues in the criminal justice system

The Lawrence Inquiry 1999

The tragic murder of Stephen Lawrence, on 22 April 1993, in an unprovoked racist knife attack by a group of five white youths was a turning point in the examination of race relations in Britain. After tedious and persistent campaigning by the Lawrence family, Jack Straw (then Home Secretary), announced a formal inquiry into the circumstances that led to the death of Stephen Lawrence. The inquiry, headed by Sir William MacPherson, produced its report titled the Stephen Lawrence Inquiry in 1999.

Eighteen years on from the Scarman report, it emerged that attitudes of fear, suspicion, distrust, and hostility towards police remained strong as ever.

While the Scarman Inquiry focused on constructing the social problem around race, the Lawrence Inquiry in contrast viewed racism as the social problem to be addressed. Race relations had deteriorated in the intervening years between Scarman and MacPherson. Attempts were made by the Commission for Racial Equality to make racist violence a criminal offence and recommended new legislation to strengthen the provisions of the Race Relations Act 1976. Despite condemning racism and xenophobia as morally unacceptable John Major's conservative government rejected both recommendations.

Scholars like McLaughlin and Murji noted that the Lawrence Inquiry was a matter of great public importance for three reasons. Firstly, the Metropolitan Police force was subjected to an unprecedented public scrutiny. Secondly, the established view of the police that young African-Caribbean men were street criminals and drug dealers was challenged; previous campaigns for justice were reconnected to the public debate (cited in McGhee 2005: 17). In contrast to the Scarman Inquiry, the Lawrence Inquiry recognised and acknowledged the existence of **institutional racism** not simply in the police force but also in a wide range of institutions including housing and education. The evidence presented to the inquiry identified institutional racism in relation to four areas: firstly, the police investigation and treatment of witnesses in relation to the murder of Stephen Lawrence; secondly in the disproportionate application of the police powers to stop and search on the African-Caribbean community; thirdly, under-reporting of racist incidents due to lack of trust in police; fourthly, the lack of police training in racism awareness. The Lawrence Inquiry diagnosed a problem of racism that was systematic and institutional and proceeded to define the term:

> The collective failure of an organisation to provide an appropriate and professional service to people because of their colour, culture, or ethnic origin. It can be seen or detected in processes, attitudes and behaviour which amount to discrimination through unwitting prejudice, ignorance, thoughtlessness and racist stereotyping which disadvantage minority ethnic people.
>
> MacPherson 1999: 6.34

In addition, the Lawrence Inquiry offered a victim-oriented definition of racist incidents and made specific recommendations for the criminalisation of such incidents. Just before the Lawrence Inquiry report was published the Crime and Disorder Act 1998 came into force which included new offences under sections 28–32 that dealt with racially aggravated offences. The Lawrence Inquiry concluded with 70 recommendations for openness, accountability, and the restoration of confidence. The first recommendation was to make it a ministerial priority for all police services 'to increase trust and confidence in policing amongst minority ethnic communities' (MacPherson 1999).

The Lawrence Inquiry was followed by a significant change in race equality legislation. With the Race Relations (Amendment) Act 2000, Parliament made it unlawful to treat persons less favourably than others on grounds of race, colour, nationality, and national or ethnic origin. Direct and indirect discrimination and victimisation were outlawed in public authority functions. The Act placed a general duty on the police and other public authorities to promote race equality and good race relations as well as a specific duty for public sector organisations to produce race equality schemes.

Zahid Mubarek Inquiry 2006

Within a year of the Lawrence Inquiry report and in yet another tragic incident a young Asian teenager, Zahid Mubarek, was murdered in Feltham Young Offender Institution in March 2000. He was attacked by his cell mate who had a history of violence and racist behaviour. A public inquiry into his murder was led by the Honourable Mr Justice Keith who presented the Zahid Mubarek Inquiry to Parliament in 2006.

The circumstances that led to the Zahid Mubarek Inquiry were remarkably similar to the Lawrence Inquiry. Two individual families beset by personal loss and tragedy persisted to get justice in the face of strong resistance by the state and the criminal justice system. In both cases individual family campaigns led to an inquiry. There were three different investigations before Justice Keith led his inquiry; the Butt investigation led by a senior Prison Service Investigating Officer, the investigation by the Commission for Racial Equality, and the investigation of the Metropolitan Police. Zahid's family was unable to involve itself in any meaningful way in any of the investigations that followed his death. They persisted and moved the House of Lords for instigating a public inquiry. The House of Lords ruled in their favour and required a public inquiry to fulfil requirements and obligations under the European Convention of Human Rights. In April 2004, the then Home Secretary, David Blunkett, announced a public inquiry into the death of Zahid.

The starting point for Justice Keith was racism and this issue was at the heart of the inquiry.

> This was not simply because Zahid's killer was himself a racist, and because his racism may have played an important part in his selection of Zahid as his victim. It was also because of the need to explore whether *explicit* racism on the part of individual prison officers had been the reason either for Zahid sharing a cell with Stewart in the first place or continuing to share a cell with him. There have been lurid allegations about prisoners of different ethnic origins being put in the same cell to see if violence would ensue.
>
> Zahid Mubarek Inquiry 2006: 3.2

To explore the extent to which unwitting racism led to Zahid's death the context for the inquiry was to uncover if the vice of racism was endemic and whether Feltham and the Prison Service as a whole was institutionally racist. The Zahid Mubarek Inquiry highlighted numerous issues pertaining to racism and religious intolerance and specified 13 failings in race relations at Feltham. It made 88 recommendations for change to the Prison Service, 10 of which related specifically to race and diversity. The Director General of the Prison Service, Martin Narey, never sought to deny that the Prison Service had failed in its duty of care towards Zahid and that his death was preventable.

These two tragic racist murders of a black and Asian teenager reveal the nature of official responses to allegations of racism as well as the collective and institutional failures to prevent it.

Continuing self-interrogation

The Stephen Lawrence Inquiry and the duties imposed on public sector institutions under the Race Relations (Amendment) Act 2000 propelled criminal justice agencies into a self-interrogation exercise. Ten years later, with the passage of the Equality Act 2010, the specific focus on race diminished as duties relating to equality now covered nine protected characteristics including race.

In the last 15 years, numerous reports and reviews have been undertaken to tackle race issues in the operation of the criminal justice system. A handful are listed below:

- **Denman Inquiry**—A review of race discrimination in the Crown Prosecution Service, led by Sylvia Denman (2001).
- **Young Black People and the Criminal Justice System**—A Home Affairs Committee report, chaired by John Denham MP, to understand the reasons for the over-representation of young black people in the system (2007).
- **The Race Review**—Implementing race equality in prisons, five years on from the formal investigation of the Commission for Racial Equality which was led by the Prison Service Race and Equality Action Group with the help of an independent advisory group (2008).
- **The Young Review**—A review into improving outcomes for young black and Muslim men in the

criminal justice system supported by an independent advisory group (2014).

- **The Laming Review**—An independent review chaired by Lord Laming to challenge and change the over-representation of looked after children in the youth justice system in England and Wales (2016).
- **The Lammy Review**—A review to investigate evidence of possible bias against black defendants and other ethnic minorities. It will scrutinise charging decisions, courts, prisons and rehabilitation. Led by the Labour MP, David Lammy and is due to report in 2017.

Other reports such as the Cantle Report of 2006, preceded by the Ritchie Report of 2001, are also noteworthy despite their focus on broader social problems. Both reports were made on understanding the causes behind the ethnic conflict that sparked rioting between Asian and white groups in Oldham in May 2001. They were followed by similar riots in Leeds, Bradford, and Burnley. While these reports were a detailed commentary on the state of deteriorating race relations, polarisation, and segregated communities living in these areas, they also shed light on widespread perception, based on experience, that police were racist in their attitudes. Those arrested during the violent disorders and riots were given harsh and long sentences. In Bradford, for example, 282 individuals were arrested of whom 134 individuals, mainly Asian males, were given sentences ranging between 18 months to five years (McGhee 2005: 59). Both reports attempted to reconcile the tension between punishment of criminal acts and addressing cultural tensions between communities and between communities and the police. The effects were quite the opposite and all too familiar. The labelling of violent disorders as riots, under the Public Order Act

WHAT DO YOU THINK? 10.1

Look up these reviews and inquiry reports to critically evaluate policy and practice on race equality in the criminal justice system.

- Explore what has changed since Scarman and identify what are the key drivers for change?
- Discuss what hasn't changed and why?
- What are the possible explanations?
- How should broader debates about justice and injustice incorporate a sensible discussion of race and ethnicity?

1986, allowed ratcheting up the sentences for those caught up in the disturbances. Despite petitions by campaigning groups to lessen the sentence for first-time offenders and to avoid the criminalisation of many Asian young males, the then Home Secretary, David Blunkett, supported the tough sentencing policy. Discourses in the media and amongst policy makers about Asian communities had all the signs of a reaction to a 'dangerous other' and their criminalisation further intensified through legitimised surveillance techniques in the form of Operation Wheel (McGhee 2005: 60). This further illustrates how public discourses and media reports on 'black criminality' and 'Asian gangs' as violent and disorderly reinforced an image of racial and ethnic minority groups as a security threat and thus a legitimate target of policing activity.

Following on from this section you should look at the discussion and questions raised in **What do you think? 10.1.**

Using CRT to understand crime and criminal justice in England and Wales

In her book, *The New Jim Crow*, Michelle Alexander describes mass incarceration as 'a well disguised system of racialized social control' (Alexander 2010: 4). In the US context this appears to be the case given the stark racial disparities in prison numbers. In discussing CRT and criminal law in the United States, Bennett Capers notes that racial and ethnic minorities comprise 60 per cent of the prison population and when expressed as a percentage of the general population implies that one in every 10 black men in his 30s is in prison (2014: 27). The explanation offered by Alexander demonstrates how 'a tightly

networked system of laws, policies, customs and institutions' (2010: 13) work collectively to subordinate racial groups in the US context. Now consider the Scarman, Lawrence, and Mubarek Inquiry reports. Doesn't the discourse and treatment of race, racism, and social control seem familiar?

The development of CRT is based on the US experience where it is now taught within the higher education sector, its ideas infused in advocacy work, and is also used to challenge discrimination in the legal system. Ugwudike notes that there are criminologists in other western jurisdictions who study the impact of race in criminal justice but don't necessarily describe their work as CRT. In the case of England and Wales, Bowling and Phillips (2002, 2012) offer a comprehensive and useful account of the relationship between race, ethnicity, and crime. Despite lack of reliable evidence linking ethnicity to criminality, Phillips and Bowling suggest that people who are 'darker-skinned' tend to be over-represented in the prison populations of many western countries. While right-realist criminologists may disagree, Phillips and Bowling (2012: 370–75) suggest that socio-economic marginalisation and the discriminatory practices found in the criminal justice process may help to explain the over-representation of certain groups in the criminal justice system. The concept of race does not shed much light on crime which is socially constructed. The tendency to associate people with dark skin to criminality based on racist stereotypes leads individuals working in criminal justice institutions to discriminate. Racial discrimination, including all its subtle forms, increases the likelihood of individuals from ethnic minorities of being suspected, arrested, convicted, and imprisoned. Like the Lawrence Inquiry, Phillips and Bowling suggest that the criminological problem is not 'race' but racism (2012: 370).

Inequality and the criminal justice system in England and Wales

The criminal justice system in England and Wales investigates, tries, punishes, and rehabilitates people who are convicted or suspected of committing a crime. The system comprises police forces, the Crown Prosecution Service, Her Majesty's Courts and Tribunal Service (includes magistrate and Crown Court), Prison Service, Probation Service, and Youth Offending Service. This system has evolved over time and is situated across two different government departments, namely the Home Office and Ministry of Justice. The system is subject to regular change and reform based on government policy priorities. A wide range of other bodies with different functions and accountabilities form part of the infrastructure delivering justice and include HM Inspectorates of Constabulary, HM Inspectorate of Prisons, HM Inspectorate of Probation, Youth Justice Board, Independent Police Complaints Commission, and Victim Support. To ensure justice is delivered fairly to all, criminal justice agencies not only need to work independently of each other but also depend on each other to deliver justice in a timely and efficient manner. Conflicting objectives such as the tension between punishment and rehabilitation or crime control and crime prevention make it difficult to achieve competing objectives at once (see **Chapters 20** and **21** on the criminal justice system for a more in-depth explanation).

Despite availability of this vast system and a criminal justice process that should be transparent and responsive to victims, witnesses, suspects, defendants, and offenders, inequality remains a core feature of the criminal justice system. Barbara Hudson's work (cited in Phillips and Bowling 2012: 384) explores the claim that the criminal justice process is dominated by white males. As such these male practitioners may view individuals from ethnic minority groups through stereotypical, imperialist myths, and representations. Through direct and indirect racial discrimination, empirical research in relation to police detention and court processes is now beginning to show evidence for the over-penalisation and criminalisation of racialised subjects.

Statistics on race and ethnic backgrounds

To understand the nature and extent of inequality and racial disparities in the criminal justice system, comprehensive data are required which is further broken down with details of race and ethnicity. The first official statistics on racial and ethnic background of the prison population in England and Wales were produced in 1984. It was only after the Criminal Justice Act 1991 was passed that statistical data on race and gender was systematically collected and published. The Act required the Secretary of State to publish data and information annually so as to facilitate performance of those engaged in the administration of justice to avoid discrimination against any persons on grounds of race or sex or any other improper ground. This data set was published for the first time in 1992 and has developed incrementally. It is one of the main sources of information available on black and minority ethnic groups' involvement and experiences across the criminal justice system and is available as a report *Statistics on Race and the Criminal Justice System* published by the Ministry of Justice. Since 2010 this report has been published every two years.

An infographic containing the key statistics from the 2014 report is reproduced in **Figure 10.2**.

Limitations of statistics

It is important to note that statistics on crime can equally be problematic due to variations in reporting and recording of crime, and also due to the operation of discretion on the part of different criminal justice agencies (see **Chapter 5** for further discussion). For instance, not all criminal justice agencies record and monitor information on suspects, victims, witnesses, defendants, offenders, and prisoners based on race and ethnic background in a consistent manner. Data from courts disaggregated

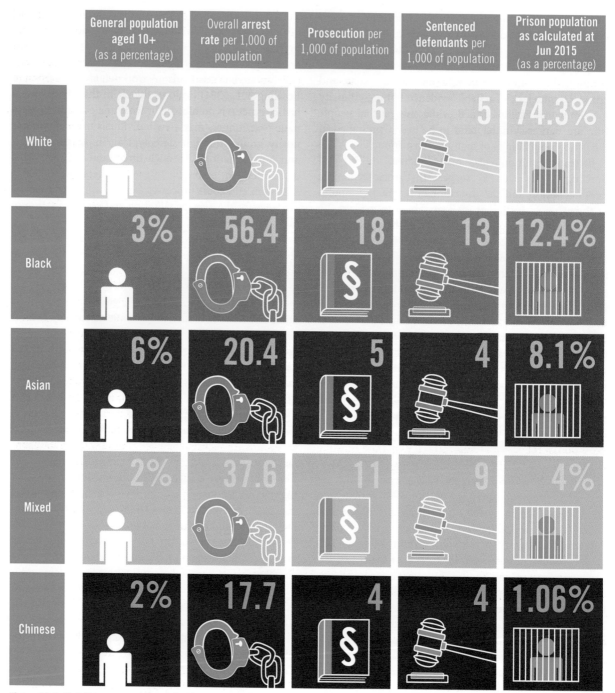

	General population aged 10+ (as a percentage)	Overall **arrest** rate per 1,000 of population	**Prosecution** per 1,000 of population	**Sentenced** defendants per 1,000 of population	**Prison population** as calculated at Jun 2015 (as a percentage)
White	87%	19	6	5	74.3%
Black	3%	56.4	18	13	12.4%
Asian	6%	20.4	5	4	8.1%
Mixed	2%	37.6	11	9	4%
Chinese	2%	17.7	4	4	1.06%

Figure 10.2 Statistics on race and the criminal justice system 2014
Source: Ministry of Justice, content available under the Open Government Licence v3.0

by race, ethnicity, and at different stages of decision making during the sentencing process is not easily available. As Bowling and Phillips (2002) note, these statistics are problematic as they focus only on a small proportion of individuals who get involved in the different stages of the criminal justice process. There are definitional and conceptual problems that fail to adequately reflect more nuanced detail on race and gender. Statistics on race present data and information on ethnic minorities in contrast to their white counterparts and does not present data informed by intersectionalities such as race and gender. *Statistics on Women and the Criminal Justice System*, published by the Ministry of Justice every two years now, reports data exclusively on outcomes for women in contrast to men in the criminal justice process without detailing the experiences of black women.

In evidence presented to the Home Affairs Committee (2007) the causes of over-representation of young black people in the criminal justice and youth justice estate were described as multiple, complex, and interrelated. In one piece of evidence related to causes of over-representation, the Home Office told the Committee:

> Due to the complexity of the relationship between race, ethnicity and crime and the lack of reliable data, we are unable to say with confidence whether people are being treated differently by the system because of their ethnic group or why disproportionality occurs.
>
> Home Affairs Committee 2007: 29, para. 95

While the over-representation of ethnic minority groups in the criminal justice system is a reality the meaning of statistics which show disproportionate representation is deeply contested. Data over the years may well have proven a variation between different ethnic groups on patterns of offending. For instance, offences related to fraud and forgery, drug offences, and robbery are commonly associated in arrest figures with black people. Asians are over-represented in arrests for sexual offences and for fraud and forgery. For burglary and criminal damage offences, both groups are under-represented and this is a pattern consistent since 1985. There is no empirical evidence, with the exception of robbery and homicide (Phillips and Bowling 2012: 376), to suggest that ethnic minority groups specialise in different types of offending.

Interpreting the statistics

So, if figures show that more black people enter the criminal justice system and remain there for longer periods does it imply a greater proportion and level of offending? The causes of over-representation are more complex. The Home Affairs Committee report, distilled from the evidence presented, indicated three causes of over-representation. Firstly, social exclusion both past and current; secondly, factors specific to the black community such as family patterns and culture fuelled by socio-economic deprivation; and, finally, the operation of the criminal justice system, including reality and perception of discrimination.

Explanations and arguments about data complexity and reliability ultimately appear to benefit those in power; officials who make policy and decisions in the criminal justice system. As explained in this section, the criminal justice system is a vast system of processes and is run predominantly by white males. When challenged by campaigners and scholars to account for decision making processes to prove any form of discriminatory practices in operation, conscious or unconscious, a typical response of criminal justice practitioners is the claim that reliable data are not available, is incomplete, or is not nuanced enough. For several decades now, attempts to methodically, systematically, and comprehensively uncover points of discretion in the criminal justice process that enhance opportunities for racial bias have been frustrated due to limitations of data availability and the inability to acknowledge ethnic disproportionality as a problem in the first place.

What does the data tell us about over-representation in England and Wales?

The data shown in **Table 10.1** shows proportions and rates (per 1,000 of the population) at which different groups are represented at specific stages of the criminal justice process. Data have been compiled from *Statistics on Race and the Criminal Justice System* and refer to the year 2014. This by no means is meant to be a comprehensive representation of all the stages, but an indicative one to demonstrate the journey of minority ethnic groups as suspects, defendants, and prisoners.

According to the 2011 census, black and minority ethnic groups, aged ten years and over, constitute 14 per cent of the general population in England and Wales. Compared to their proportions in the general population some ethnic groups are disproportionately represented in the criminal justice statistics. Black people comprise only 3 per cent of the general population but account for 12 per cent of those who are stopped and searched under section 1 of PACE. They are also three times more likely to be arrested compared to white groups.

Policing
Stop and search

Fairness is a key principle underpinning the concept of policing by consent and any unfair practices or unlawful discrimination significantly undermines this principle. The power to stop and search is an example that undermines the core principles of fairness and policing by consent. According to Delsol and Shiner, stop and search is a form of adversarial contact between the police and public, 'bringing citizens face-to-face with the coercive power of the state' (Delsol and Shiner 2015: 1). The police have the power to stop and search under many different pieces of legislation: but the controversy around the use of such powers was established in the use of 'sus' law (since abolished) which was evidenced in the Scarman and Lawrence inquiries as a racist and abusive policing tool and which also triggered much unrest and rioting at the time.

	White	Black	Asian	Mixed	Chinese
General population aged 10 +	87 %	3 %	6 %	2 %	2 %
Stop and search section 1 PACE	75 %	12 %	9 %	3 %	2 %
Arrests as a result of section 1 PACE	11.5 %	16.4 %	11.5 %	15 %	15.4 %
Stop and search—section 60	52.9 %	30.1 %	10.5 %	5 %	1.5 %
Arrests as a result of section 60	5.2 %	5.9 %	3.8 %	4.3 %	4.1 %
Overall arrest rate per 1,000 of population	19	56.4	20.4	37.6	17.7
Out of court cautions	84 %	8 %	6 %	—	2 %
Prosecutions per 1,000 of the population	6	18	5	11	4
Conviction ratio	82 %	77 %	74 %	76 %	80 %
Sentenced defendants per 1,000 of the population	5	13	4	9	4
Prison population (calculated as at Jun 2015)	74.3 %	12.4 %	8.1 %	4 %	1.06 %

Table 10.1 Different stages of the criminal justice process by ethnic group: England and Wales

Source: Statistics on Race and the Criminal Justice System, Ministry of Justice 2015

Nothing has been more damaging to the relationship between the police and the black community than the ill-judged use of stop and search powers. For young black men in particular, the humiliating experience of being repeatedly stopped and searched is a sad fact of life, in some parts of London at least. It is hardly surprising that those on the receiving end of this treatment should develop hostile attitudes towards the police. The right to walk the streets is a fundamental one, and one that is quite rightly jealously guarded.

Bernie Grant MP, quoted in Nacro 2002: 3

The most commonly used powers are those under section 1 of the Police and Criminal Evidence Act 1984 (PACE), section 23 of the Misuse of Drugs Act 1971, section 60 of the Criminal Justice and Public Order Act 1994, and section 47A of and Schedule 7 to the Terrorism Act 2000. There are other powers too and together these provisions and their over-use against ethnic minorities continues to provoke tension and political conflict. The history, experience, and impact of policing black communities has resonated in David Muir's phrase 'over policed and to a large extent under protected' (Macpherson 1999: 45.7).

As a gateway to the criminal justice system policing activity, particularly the use of stop and search, fuels the disproportionate entry of ethnic minorities into the criminal justice system. Recent research and statistical data on suspicion-based stop and search activity, such as section 1 of PACE, have consistently shown that black people are subjected to it at around five to six times the rate of white people and Asians at two to three times the rate of whites (Delsol and Shiner 2015; Ministry of Justice 2015; EHRC 2013). Stop and search is intrusive, coercive, and a humiliating experience for those subjected to it. It constitutes an invasion of individual liberty and privacy and has been subject to many judicial challenges in courts.

A big controversy surrounding stop and search is about its effectiveness. Is stop and search an effective tool in combating crime? In purely statistical terms, when considering the data in **Table 10.1**, it would appear that the proportion of arrests as a result of stop and search has been minimal. If over a million stops and searches are recorded every year and only one in every ten leads to an arrest then (the then Home Secretary) Theresa May, was right in calling for a review of these powers following an inspection of Her Majesty's Inspectorate of Constabulary (HMIC) in 2013. Consider the issue in more detail using the sources covered in **What do you think? 10.2**.

WHAT DO YOU THINK? 10.2

The question of effectiveness can be a good seminar activity. To explore this further read Bowling and Phillips (2002 and 2012); Delsol and Shiner (2015); HMIC report on *Stop and Search Powers: Are the police using them effectively and fairly?* (2013) www.justiceinspectorates.gov.uk/hmic/publications/stop-and-search-powers-20130709/ to study the inspection report for your own region; visit the campaigning organisation StopWatch www.stop-watch.org to explore activities, publications, tell your story if you have experienced stop and search and to learn about your rights.

Figure 10.3 Police undertaking traffic stops
Source: Rob/Alamy Stock Photo

There are new and emerging controversies around the use of stop and search such as traffic stops (**Figure 10.3**), strip searches, use of Tasers, and the stops of children. Section 163 of the Road Traffic Act 1988 is the most widely used stop power and its deployment does not depend on reasonable suspicion or explicitly on road traffic violations. There is also no requirement to record these stops. Data derived from the Crime Survey of England and Wales (previously the British Crime Survey) estimates 5.5 million vehicle stops in 2010–11 and suggests that people from black and minority ethnic groups are disproportionately subject to such stops. According to a StopWatch (2013, 2016) submission to the Home Office on the review of stop and search powers, traffic stops are being abused and misapplied, with individuals being stopped under this power for matters unrelated to traffic violations (see Roberti 2016). There is limited guidance on the use of this power and very little external oversight in contrast to other stop and search powers. The recent inspectorate report (HMIC 2015) reveals how black and minority ethnic drivers are more likely to be pulled over although they are not likely to be arrested or fined. They are treated less professionally and are not provided with a reason for the stop. This led to the then Home Secretary, Theresa May, announcing in early 2016 that all traffic stops will now be recorded and monitored by ethnicity.

Similarly, strip searches are also an area of concern in policing black and minority ethnic groups. Currently there is no data available on the use of strip searches across police forces and there is no clear way of distinguishing an intimate stop and search from a standard stop and search. The power to strip-search is so intrusive and yet it does not form part of the PACE recording framework. As the threshold for subjecting an individual to such an intimate search is one of arrest then the power to strip search should have no basis in the law.

Prosecution

When individuals are arrested by the police it is simply a demonstration of an outcome regarding police activity; it does not follow automatically that the person arrested is guilty as charged by the police. As the agency responsible for establishing the charge, and in deciding whether an arrest and subsequent prosecution is in the public interest, the Crown Prosecution Service (CPS) plays an important part in delivering justice. As seen previously in the case of stop and search activity, there are areas of great discretion and criminal justice agents have power over individuals through this decision making process.

The examination of the CPS

The CPS begins a review process when police bring forward a case. The process includes decisions to reduce or increase the charge, whether to grant or oppose bail, on mode of trial, whether to discontinue a case, and acceptance of plea. The first ever examination of racial bias in the CPS decision making process was undertaken in 2003 by Professor Gus John. He examined case files access to which was facilitated through the CPS Equality and Diversity Unit. The study (Race for Justice 2003: 16–18) showed that in an overwhelming majority of case studies the victim was a black or Asian person and the perpetrator white. In relation to the charging process there was a general failure to acknowledge and record racial aggravation and this failure further amplified the acceptance of a lesser charge by both the CPS and police. It also emerged that in almost 24 per cent of cases the CPS downgraded racially aggravated charges brought forward by the police. The statistical analysis showed that African Caribbean and Asian defendants were brought to trial on a less sound basis than white defendants. In light of this study better monitoring was recommended with respect to mode of trial, discontinuance, failed cases, acquittals, and sentence.

Evidence of direct discrimination emerges from a handful of studies. A 1998 study of 1,175 defendants found that being from an ethnic minority predicted an increased chance of case termination by the CPS. This was the case after controlling for previous convictions and type and seriousness of offence. Mhlanga's study of young suspects showed that police officers were charging black and Asian suspects without sufficient evidence (Phillips and Brown and Mhlanga cited in Phillips and Bowling 2012: 385). The Denman Inquiry concluded that as the CPS failed to correct the bias in police charging decisions the agency itself could be accused of discrimination on racial grounds.

A recent study by Eastwood, Shiner, and Bear (2013), *The Numbers in Black and White*, showed that policing and prosecutions of drug offences in England and Wales is focused on black and minority ethnic communities. Data studied from 2008–10 showed that black people were 6.7 to 6.3 times more likely to be stopped and searched for drugs compared to white people and were arrested for drugs offences at six times the rate of white people. Black people are also likely to receive a harsher police response for the possession of cannabis. Subjected to court proceedings for drug possession offences at 4.5 times the rate of whites, black people are also subject to immediate custody following prosecution and sentencing at 5 times the rate of white people. The report suggests significant harms associated with drugs policing and prosecution, particularly drugs possession offences. The report findings provide clear evidence that black groups are at greater risk of criminalisation and harsher sanctions through the policing, prosecution, and sentencing stages.

Sentencing

Research and statistics from the 1980s and 1990s proved that ethnic minority groups in England and Wales were disproportionately victimised and criminalised. Debates within criminology were concerned with the increasing numbers of African-Caribbeans appearing before courts and ending up in prison. This over-representation was explained in two ways. Greater numbers of African-Caribbeans were in prison as they were more likely to be guilty of criminal behaviour. Alternatively, this was the result of racial discrimination at various stages from policing to sentencing. Both these explanations proved simplistic till Roger Hood's study on *Race and Sentencing* was published in 1992. Using a large Crown Court sample of 2,884 cases this major study revealed a complex and disturbing pattern of racial differences in decision making on custody, sentence length, and choice of alternative punishments. Detailed analysis showed that black males had a 5 per cent greater probability of being sentenced to custody compared to their white and Asian counterparts, with the difference being particularly marked in one of the five Crown Courts in the study. In addition, black males received longer custodial sentences, largely on account of their propensity to plead not guilty reducing the likelihood of receiving a discount in the sentence.

In relation to the youth justice estate Feilzer and Hood's (2004) analysis of over 31,000 YOT records found substantial over-representation of young black people and under-representation of young Asians in caseloads (Phillips and Bowling 2012). Another study found that young people from minority ethnic groups were more often subject to proactive arrests mostly for drug and traffic offences.

Feilzer and Hood showed that in several key stages black, Asian, and mixed race youths were disadvantaged in the criminal justice process; pre-court disposals, case termination, remands, acquittals, committals to Crown court, pre-sentence reports, and higher tariff sentencing.

There have been other peculiarities in relation to statistics on first-time entrants in the youth justice estate. Following the Home Affairs Committee report the Youth Justice Board introduced diversion and out-of-court disposal schemes to reduce the first-time entrants into the criminal justice system. While this conscious choice of using alternatives such as diversion worked for keeping white young people away from the formal justice system this wasn't the case for black and minority ethnic young people. From 2007–08, the percentage fall in the numbers of black and minority ethnic children in custody was 16 per cent compared to 37 per cent for white groups (Allen 2011: 7). Whether this adverse outcome is due to types of offences committed by black and minority ethnic children, geographical variations in the rates of custody reduction, or other reasons needs further exploration. The Laming Review (2016) noted that young people in care are significantly over-represented in the criminal justice system particularly in prison where many have poor experiences. Another striking fact is that in the care system 9 per cent of children are from a mixed background and 7 per cent are black. Lord Laming notes that looked after children and young people who are black or from other minority ethnic backgrounds, and those of Muslim faith, are over-represented in the criminal justice system. These young people also feel discriminated against particularly by police (2016: 14).

Prisons and probation

As Phillips and Bowling point out, at the end of the criminal justice process the cumulative effects of social exclusion, direct, and indirect discrimination are made visible through disproportionate rates of imprisonment by ethnicity. Recent statistical data on custody (Ministry of Justice, 2015) show that relative to their population, rates of sentencing were three times higher for black offenders and two times for mixed race offenders. The average length in custody for black and Asian groups is currently 25 months. There are more black and mixed groups in prison compared to other groups. According to the Young Review (2014: 10), there is now greater disproportionality in the number of black people in prisons in the UK than in the United States. 13.1 per cent of prisoners identify themselves as black despite comprising just 3 per cent of the general population aged 18 and over. Muslim prisoners account for 15 per cent of the prison population compared to 4.2 per cent of the general population. The figure in 2014 has risen sharply since 2002 when Muslims comprised 7.7 per cent of the prison population.

What factors explain the over-representation of black, Asian and minority ethnic offenders in prison? In relation to sentencing outcomes many statistical reports show that black, Asian, and minority ethnic defendants are more likely to receive a custodial rather than a community sentence in England and Wales. Using data from 2011, a recent Ministry of Justice analytical report demonstrated associations between police-recorded ethnicity and the likelihood of being sentenced to prison. The data showed that when police-recorded ethnicity was black, Asian, and minority ethnic, there were 39 per cent higher odds of receiving custody compared to those the police recorded as white. Despite the effect being small the result was statistically significant. The report also considered ethnicity and gender outcomes in relation to sentencing outcomes. The analysis showed, males and females from minority ethnic groups were least likely to have previous convictions or cautions compared to their white counterparts and yet the relative odds of receiving custodial sentence were 40 per cent and 30 per cent higher than their white male and white female counterparts. Using logistic regression to show the probability of imprisonment the report found that given similar circumstances in 'theft/handling stolen goods' cases, black, Asian, and minority ethnic male offenders were twice as likely to be sent to custody compared to white females. For 'robbery' offences, under similar circumstances, the predicted possibility of receiving a custodial sentence was 74.5 per cent for black, Asian, and minority ethnic males compared to 53.5 per cent white females and 67.7 per cent white males (Hopkins, 2015). Offence group strongly predicted imprisonment for offenders convicted of violence against the person offences, sexual offences, burglary, and robbery the most likely to be imprisoned. Having previous convictions, recorded cautions, and having a non-UK nationality increased the likelihood of punishment. Black and minority ethnic prisoners are also serving indeterminate sentences for public protection which means they remain in prison for a longer period. New research by Williams and Clarke, demonstrates that individuals convicted under the joint enterprise doctrine serve longer sentences and also consider their sentences to be illegitimate. Currently 37.2 per cent of black British prisoners are serving custodial sentences for joint enterprise. Their proportion in the prison population is 11 times greater than their proportion in the general population which is 3.3 per cent, challenging notions of 'procedural fairness' and 'moral legitimacy' (Williams and Clarke 2016: 7).

While in prison, statistical evidence also shows that people from minority ethnic backgrounds have a more negative perception of race equality in prison. Prison regimes and the discretionary decisions about incentive and earned privileges, discipline, information, and requests were key to perceptions of fairness: the 'informal partiality' in prison (observed by Edgar and Martin cited in Phillips and Bowling 2012: 387) where the use of discretion by officers had no managerial oversight or monitoring. Similar themes were uncovered by the Race Review undertaken by the National Offender Management Service. The Review further noted that black prisoners were 30 per cent more likely than white prisoners to be on basic regime without privileges, 50 per cent more likely to be held in segregation, and 60 per cent more likely to have force used against them. The Mubarek Inquiry had already highlighted a string of 'systemic shortcomings' that existed in prisons at the time of Zahid's murder. These included an over-burdened prison service, lack of resources, poorly administered race relations strategy, as well as poor procedures to tackle racist incidents and complaints. A 'culture of indifference and insensitivity to black people and people from ethnic minorities which institutional racism breeds' (Mubarek Inquiry report, 2006: 413) demonstrated the prevalence of racism in the prison. Legislative and policy changes intended to improve race equality have not been entirely successful and despite the passage of the Equality Act 2010 there is evidence that racism still fuels violence and abuse in prisons.

In relation to probation services that supervise offenders in custody and in the community, the experiences of minority ethnic groups were recognised from the 1980s but policy development was inconsistent. Probation inspectorate reports on racial equality noted poor quality supervision and shorter contact periods at later stages of probation orders for black offenders. As noted by Phillips and Bowling, a key issue, yet again, has been the experience of racism. Calverley et al. (cited in Phillips and Bowling 2012: 388) found that while minority ethnic offenders had similar socio-economic disadvantage to their white counterparts, one-fifth had experienced racism in school and that racial discrimination limited opportunities to engage legitimately in the labour market.

In both the policing and prison context the ability to make complaints and have faith in the process is paramount to maintaining trust and confidence in the system. Research evidence and literature so far show that black and minority ethnic groups tend not to use the complaints processes. The following example is taken from the Independent Police Complaints Commission, *Guidelines for Handling Allegations of Discrimination* (2015: 44).

Mr S, a young black man, alleges that he and his friend were subjected to racist abuse on a bus and then beaten in a racist attack by a group of eight young white men. The police arrive on the scene. Mr S told them that he had been the victim of a racist attack. He was the only injured party and had received a serious head injury. The police treated the incident as a fight where both groups were seen as equally responsible and told them all to go their separate ways. No crime was recorded. Mr S complains that the failure of the police to treat him as a victim of hate crime was racist and that his attackers should have been arrested.

In this case both parties were treated in the same way (i.e. no one was arrested). However, this does not disprove discrimination. The complaint is that they should have been treated differently but were not. An investigation would need to assess whether it was reasonable for the officers to decide *not to* treat Mr S and his friend as victims and the white group as suspects and to not record a race hate crime.

The comparison the investigating officer should consider is:

If police encountered two white men, one with a serious head injury, surrounded by a large group of black men who had caused the injury, would the police treat them as equally responsible and not see the white men as victims?

What do you think? When deciding on such a case, should decision makers engage in race-switching exercises in order to foreground racial biases? CRT scholars suggest that foregrounding racial biases helps to neutralise them. This approach can also be applied to train other criminal justice practitioners.

Conclusion

CRT offers a tool to understand, question, and challenge racially discriminatory practices within substantive law and policies that operate in the criminal justice system. With all the data reviewed so far it is clear that inequality has become a core feature of the criminal justice system in England and Wales (see **Telling it like it is 10.1** for the views of Mark Blake from BTEG). Much like its US counterpart, the criminal justice system in England and Wales has also become a system of racialised social control. Ethnic minority groups comprise 14 per cent of the general population of England and Wales but 26 per cent of the prisoner population at the end of 2015. One in ten prisoners are black British. At the gateway to criminal justice system disparities informed by race and ethnicity continue in stop and search and other forms of policing activity. Criminalisation of young black men continues through the discourse shaped around gangs. Williams and Clarke, reveal 'dangerous associations of a series of negative constructs, signifying racialized stereotypes that endure and underpin contemporary policing and prosecution strategies' (2016: 3). While this research was in relation to serious youth violence in England and Wales similar strategies and negative constructs disproportionately punish and criminalise black groups at all stages in the criminal justice system.

CRT allows further exploration of how crime categories are constructed and helps uncover new forms of discretion such as the use of stop and search to gather intelligence on gangs and joint enterprise. This social construction of threat and the construction of 'black' criminality allow the system to focus its energies and resources on policing and control strategies at the expense of criminalising other white-collar crimes subject only to ethical or civil sanctions. Bennett Capers suggests that the definition and ranking of crimes is dependent on race which has also informed critiques of grading crack cocaine offences as opposed to other drug offences such as possession of powder cocaine (Capers 2014: 29). Data findings from

The Numbers in Black and White report show that in the Metropolitan Police force area in 2009–10, 56 per cent of white people caught in possession of cocaine received cautions, the remaining 44 per cent were charged. In the case of black people caught in possession of cocaine 22 per cent received cautions and 78 per cent were charged for the offence (Eastwood, Shiner, and Bear 2013: 35).

The extent to which discretion is informed by implicit bias is becoming a popular scrutiny tool to examine how decisions are made and by whom: the questioning of discretion in police officers' decision to stop based on reasonable suspicion and in the judge's decision to sentence and for what lengths of time. According to Angela Davis, a prosecutor may choose to prosecute a defendant more aggressively in cases where white victims are involved but may decide to be less aggressive when prosecuting a similar case when the victim is from a racial minority. The decision making may not be transparent or available to review but Davis suggests such differences are rarely the product of direct discrimination but has more to do with implicit biases we all share about race, worth, and crime (cited in Capers 2014: 30). A vast amount of research on implicit bias has been shaped in the US context. The implications of the research using implicit bias are a matter of debate but it does show how implicit racial bias can operate in judgements made on bail, pre-trial motions, evidentiary issues, and witness credibility in a way that has a cumulative effect on statistics, on imprisonment rates, and sentence length. **What do you think? 10.3** offers a way to consider this further.

It is ironic that despite legislation and good policies ethnic disproportionality remains in the justice system. CRT opens new areas of scrutiny and allows scholars to examine the construction and operation of criminal law, policy, and practice; to address systemic inequalities that are hardwired into a punitive system that treats black people, albeit implicitly, inequitably and keeps them longer in

WHAT DO YOU THINK? 10.3

Access the online implicit association project test available at https://implicit.harvard.edu/implicit/takeatest. html note the results of the test and discuss your findings and observations in the classroom. Now apply the key tenets of CRT to explore and understand the results.

the system once in it. While it is no longer legal or socially acceptable to discriminate, exclude, and condemn explicitly on grounds of race it is acceptable to continue using labels and language to make associations between race and criminality. As in the US, Alexander astutely observes racial caste has not ended but merely been re-designed.

CRT opens a window to understand how policies are designed and should operate for the benefit of all groups in society: as in the case of criminal justice in England and Wales it is increasingly becoming clear how policy is being used as a means to legitimate, extend, and create distinctive groups some of whom deserve to be protected more than others. The racial disparities, created by laws and policies of stop and search, prosecuting race-hate crime, rape, and domestic violence show clearly which groups are demonised, excluded, and pushed to further socio-economic marginalisation—young black and Muslim suspects, defendants, and offenders with criminal records. The same groups also disproportionately suffer as victims of crime and perceive that the different criminal justice agencies will treat them unfairly compared to white groups. As social constructions of crime, race, gender, and other minorities gain legitimacy, narratives of difference become amplified and institutionalised along social, political, and economic divides. Public perception and treatment by state agencies, of children leaving care, and those black and mixed race groups among them, who end up in the criminal justice or mental health systems is a good example of marginalisation made worse by institutionalisation.

It has taken several decades for state and society in the UK to recognise and understand the shape of inequality, the portrait of which in relation to criminal justice is the worst. The Race Relations (Amendment) Act 2000 and the Equality Act 2010 have proven to be equally ineffective remedies for reducing and reversing inequalities. Key tenets and themes of CRT are instructive in making sense of the entrenched inequalities that the criminal justice system presents. Recent high level strategic reviews in the criminal justice system, namely the Young Review and the Lammy Review, are being led by black individuals who have acknowledged the centrality of racism in the criminal justice system. This is an important departure from previous inquiries and reviews that failed to acknowledge this. In working closely with organisations and agencies dominated by the majority white groups the Young and Lammy Reviews have the potential to challenge (consciously or unconsciously) white privilege. In seeking and accessing the views of racial and ethnic minorities the Young Review offers an insightful counter-narrative that empowers the voice and experience of those who have experienced racism and understand how they have been racially minoritised in the criminal justice system. In England and Wales, the high rates of stop and search, arrest, and imprisonment of young black males are variously attributed to problems associated with family structure or black culture. In reviewing the evidence and statistics over-representation is seldom satisfactorily explained simply by racial profiling, joblessness, or the operation of gang laws and policing activities that unfairly target black young people in groups. The state response through inquiry reports and reviews sheds light on a contradiction between the ideal of equality and fairness and the reality of the so-called 'dangerous' groups that are marginalised, disadvantaged, and undeserving. Using the CRT framework, policy analysts can actively look for over-representation in social policy indicators and then address the failings of criminal justice. With current levels of ethnic disproportionality the criminal justice system appears to have become less equal and less just.

TELLING IT LIKE IT IS 10.1

Can we talk about racial inequality?—with Mark Blake

My son is a rather talented footballer signed to a Premier League academy and because of his talent I have spent a great deal of my spare time driving him around the country to play and train over the past few years. Football dominates the national conversation; it's one of the few topics, apart from the weather, that the British can strike up instant conversation around. It cuts through the barriers of class, region, religion, wealth, or ethnicity.

But, of course, there are issues that as a society we find it much more difficult to talk about, and these are often the most divisive issues in our society. A few weeks ago I was watching my son play football and noticed something out of the ordinary about the coaching staff of the opposing team. I shared my thought with another parent and she looked at me with a blend of shared exultation and annoyance. My observation was simply that the opposing team had two black coaches. The parent with whom I shared the observation was also black. Would I have made this comment if she had been white? In all likelihood, the answer is probably not.

I use this anecdote because it resonates with themes in my work for BTEG (Black Training and Enterprise Group), where I have led on trying to address the over-representation of black and minority ethnic groups in the criminal justice system. That conversation on the touch-line relates to my day job on a number of levels. Firstly, it neatly illustrates the difficulties and social anxieties we face in talking about race, discrimination, inclusion, and racism. These are issues that affect all parts of our society and its institutions, which have on the one hand become more visible, but conversely are now more difficult to raise with statutory bodies than at any time over the past decade or so. Acknowledging and breaching the barriers to such discussions have been the biggest challenge for me in my work over the past five years.

But the football analogy is also interesting because the football industry has, over the past few years, developed into what is arguably the one theatre in British society where there has been a really informed and open debate about race, inclusion, and racism. [...] In an attempt to broaden diversity within the game, the National Football League (NFL) in the US has brought in the 'Rooney rule' which requires the National Basketball Association (NBA) and the NFL clubs to shortlist black and minority ethnic candidates for coaching positions, a policy which has also recently been agreed for English football academies. These innovations should be seen in the light of some statistics: fewer than 3 per cent of coaching positions in professional football are held from people from BME groups yet in the Premier League more than 25 per cent of the players are of a BME background. I can count on the fingers of one hand the number of black coaches I have seen in more than three years of observing academy football, so it will be interesting to see how English academies take the Rooney rule forward in this country.

All of this means that within the 'beautiful game', race and inclusion have been a constant source of debate. Football undoubtedly has a long way to go, but you could argue that it is miles ahead of some of our institutions, both in its practical reactions and its willingness to engage in a wide-ranging and open debate on the challenges we face if we are to bring about full inclusion and equality.

In contrast, we could be forgiven for thinking that within the criminal justice system, discussions around race and discrimination are uncomfortable and to be avoided. This is certainly the impression that the institutions of law give to anyone who investigates or researches questions of inclusion and diversity in the context of crime and punishment. Such institutions acknowledge that there is a challenge around equality, but it is hard to find evidence of anything being done to overcome it. It is fair to ask: is any action actually being taken to improve the situation?

In an attempt to answer this question, we can look to a report published in December 2014 by BTEG and Clinks. This set out the findings of the Young Review into improving outcomes for young black and/or Muslim young men in the criminal justice system. [...]

Since the launch of the report, an independent advisory group has been established to work with MOJ/NOMS on implementing the report's recommendations. [...] Following on from this, the then Prime Minister (David Cameron) launched his own review into the over-representation of black and ethnic minority groups in the criminal justice system. He laudably attempted to develop a bipartisan approach to what has been such a protracted issue through appointing Labour MP David Lammy to lead it. At the launch of the review, David Cameron said:

> If you're black, you're more likely to be in a prison cell than studying at a top university. And if you're black, it seems you're more likely to be sentenced to custody for a crime than if you're white. We should investigate why this is and how we can end this possible discrimination.

I firmly believe that successful progress on this and other aspects of equality—in both the criminal justice arena and wider society—can only take place in a context where there is commitment to reform the system that includes an emphasis on rehabilitation. At BTEG we also passionately believe that the voice of people who have been through the system needs to be utilised more effectively if we are to change things for the better. [...]

The road to equality will be a long one, but like any journey it will begin with one step; in this case, that step is the pressure that has been put on our institutions to openly discuss the issues and challenges, a debate which is the precursor to action and change. The justice system can learn something from what has been happening in the football industry, so that these difficult conversations can be embraced with a clear sense of purpose and a passion for lasting change.

Mark Blake, Project Development Officer, BTEG.

REVIEW QUESTIONS

1. In which decade and where did critical race theory first gain prominence?

2. In his review of the key writings that informed the CRT movement, what five recurring themes or tenets did Bennett Capers identify?

3. What are the main criticisms of critical race theory?

4. In the context of England and Wales, consider the factors that explain over-representation of black, Asian, and minority ethnic groups at each stage of the criminal justice process.

5. Two recent reviews focusing on race issues in criminal justice have been led by Baroness Lola Young and member of parliament for Tottenham, David Lammy. Using CRT discuss why these reviews stand out and what makes them significant.

FURTHER READING

Equality and Human Rights Commission (2011) *How Fair is Britain? The First Triennial Review* (www.equality-humanrights.com/sites/default/files/how_fair_is_britain_-_complete_report.pdf).
This review, the first of its kind, contains important information about the progress made on equality, human rights, and good relations. It offers a comprehensive picture of critical issues, findings, and challenges in relation to fairness across different areas of public life in Britain.

Delsol, R. and Shiner, M. (eds) (2015) *Stop and Search: The Anatomy of a Police Power*. London: Palgrave Macmillan.
This book is an important read to understand the key controversies around the police power to stop and search. It provides important insights into the history of policing black communities and the up to date developments, including regulation and reform, in assessing the effectiveness of these powers.

Bowling, B. and Phillips, C. (2002) *Racism, Crime and Justice*. Harlow: Pearson Education Limited.
A key textbook that offers rich analysis of racism in the criminal justice process and accounts for experiences of criminalisation of ethnic minority groups.

Ugwudike, P. (2015) *An Introduction to Critical Criminology*. Bristol: Policy Press.
Important text that examines and brings together critical criminological perspectives including critical race theory to understand inequalities and power dynamics in society.

 Access the **online resources** to view selected further reading and web links relevant to the material covered in this chapter.
www.oup.com/uk/case/

CHAPTER OUTLINE

Introduction	284
Feminist criminology: Key theoretical traditions	287
Gender and crime	299
Gender and criminal justice	303
Criticisms of feminist criminology	304
Conclusion	308

11

Gender and feminist criminology

Pamela Ugwudike

KEY ISSUES

After reading this chapter, you should be able to:

- identify the origins, definition, and key principles of feminist criminology;

- understand the main theoretical traditions that underpin feminist criminology, namely liberalism, radicalism, Marxism, and socialism;

- recognise feminist epistemologies such as feminist empiricism, standpoint feminism, and postmodern feminism;

- appreciate the intersections between gender and other structures of disadvantage;

- identify relationships between gender and crime by considering feminist explanations of female crime and masculinities studies of male crime;

- consider the role of gender in the criminal justice system; and,

- critically evaluate the criticisms of feminist criminology.

Introduction

This chapter explores the origins, definitions, and principles of feminist criminology. Although feminist criminologists accuse mainstream criminological theories of gender blindness, and seek to bring gender issues to the fore of criminological debates, they have generally focused mainly on researching women and their experiences as offenders or victims. The study of masculinities is a notable exception that is covered in this chapter. The chapter also analyses feminist criminologists' criticisms of what they describe as the androcentricism of mainstream criminological theories. Mainstream criminology's androcentricism manifests as a tendency to focus on men whilst ignoring or misrepresenting the experiences of women as offenders and/or victims. In addition, mainstream criminological theories are criticised for generalising theories of crime that are based on the experiences of men, and overlooking the gender gap in offending. This gender gap is reflected by the greater representation of men in official crime statistics compared with women. The chapter explores these issues and it also examines the theoretical traditions that have informed feminist criminology.

Furthermore, this chapter provides an account of the **epistemological** orientations that influence feminist research on gender and crime. In social science research, a researcher's epistemological stance reflects that researcher's philosophical position on what constitutes valid knowledge of the social world, and how such knowledge should be generated. Therefore, feminist epistemologies reflect feminists' views about what constitutes valid knowledge of the beliefs, experiences, and behaviour of women, and the best means of generating such knowledge. The concept of epistemology is underpinned by questions such as:

- What constitutes valid knowledge?
- How can we generate valid knowledge of aspects of the social world?

Having examined the epistemological orientations of feminist research on gender and crime, the chapter moves on to analyse key debates in feminist criminology. Some of the key debates revolve around explanations of female offending and victimisation. There is also an exploration of the study of masculinities which focuses on the links between socially constructed notions of the male gender (masculinity) and crime. In addition, the chapter analyses some of the key criticisms feminist perspectives on gender and crime have received. In its conclusion, the chapter highlights feminist criminology's key contributions to the field.

Origins of feminist criminology

The origins of feminist criminology have been traced to the second wave of feminism that originated in the United States in the 1970s (Daly 2006), and proliferated across other jurisdictions such as the United Kingdom and the United States (Heidensohn 2012; Heidensohn and Silvestri 2012). Gelsthorpe and Morris (1988) note that the British scholar, Carol Smart's (1976), seminal text *Women, Crime and Criminology*, initiated the advent of feminist criminology in Britain and highlighted the discriminatory treatment of female offenders, particularly in England and Wales. Daly (2006) has since described Carol Smart as a 'pioneering feminist critic of criminological theory'. It is however worth noting that Frances Heidensohn (1968), who is now one of the key writers in the field, had earlier drawn attention to the lack of interest in the study of female deviance, and the sentencing practices targeted at female offenders.

Smart's (1976) text highlighted the male-centredness of criminological theories and the lack of adequate scholarship on female offending and victimisation. The fundamental critique of mainstream criminology's tendency to overlook the role of women as 'producers and subjects' of criminological knowledge is now a recurring theme within feminist criminology (Gelsthorpe and Morris 1988: 225; Heidensohn and Silvestri 2012). As Chesney-Lind and Morash (2013: 287) put it: 'the founders of criminology almost completely overlooked women's crime, and they ignored, minimized, and trivialized female victimization'. Gelsthorpe and Morris (1988) note that some of the early feminist criminologists integrated theories of female offending and victimisation within existing theories of crime, to redress the gender imbalance in criminological theorising. Others found the existing criminological theories male-centred, and argued that the few theories that did address female offending and victimisation (albeit cursorily) were riddled with stereotypical portrayals of women and their behaviour (Smart 1976). We shall explore these theories later. For the moment, it is worth noting that the theories attributed female crime to predisposing attributes that were supposedly unique to women. See, for example, Lombroso and Fererro (1895) and **Figure 11.1**. The text surrounding the image in Lombroso and Fererro's (1895) *The Female Offender* identifies physical facial features such as 'projecting cheek-bones', 'enormous lower jaw', and 'over-jutting brows' as potential indicators of female criminality (1895: 77).

Indeed, the few theories that existed before the advent of feminist criminology refuted the ability of women to exercise their rationality or self-determination (Smart 1976).

PHYSIOGNOMY OF RUSSIAN FEMALE OFFENDERS.

PLATE I.

Figure 11.1 Image taken from a plate section in Lobroso and Fererro's *The Female Offender* (1895)

Source: Lombroso, C. and Ferrero, W. (1895) The Female Offender. New York, D. Appleton & Co./Public domain

Defining feminist criminology

Feminist criminology comprises several theoretical and epistemological strands. Perhaps unsurprisingly, it lacks precise definition. However, some scholars have offered definitions that capture its unifying themes. Gelsthorpe and Morris (1988: 224) state that: 'the essence of feminist perspectives is that they reflect the view that women experience subordination on the basis of their sex'. Daly and Chesney-Lind (1988: 502) go on to define feminist criminology as: 'a set of theories about women's oppression and a set of strategies for change'. As these definitions indicate, feminist criminologists emphasise that gender inequality exists in society and it disadvantages women. This gender inequality informs women's experiences in society, including their experiences as victims and offenders. It should be noted, however, that feminist criminologists do not all agree on the precise source or sources of gender

inequality and the effective mechanisms of gender equality (Flavin 2001).

Principles of feminist criminology

There are several feminist perspectives in criminology but amongst these it is possible to identify what might be described as the key unifying principles of feminist criminology. One key theme is that feminist criminology places gender (particularly the female gender) at the core of its analysis of crime and criminal justice (Chesney-Lind and Morash 2013).

Reversing gender blindness by theorising the concept of gender

Mainstream criminology has historically overlooked gender, and has consequently been accused of 'gender-blindness' (Chesney-Lind and Pasko 2013; Gelsthorpe and Morris 1988: 98). However, scholars inspired by feminist theories have sought to address the gap created by criminology's gender blindness by theorising the concept of gender and its impact on crime and criminal justice. For example, the early feminist criminologists sought to reverse existing stereotypical accounts which conflated gender with innate biological sex, and attributed female offending to purportedly innate gender abnormalities.

The early feminist criminologists rejected this approach and highlighted the conceptual difference between gender and biological sex (see for example, Oakley 1972); mirroring the broader field of feminist theory in the 1970s. Smart (1995) notes that by the 1970s, feminist criminologists began to argue that sex refers to the biological constitution of an individual, while gender embodies socially constructed connotations that do not necessarily relate to the biologically-determined sex of an individual (Oakley 1972; Daly 2010). In the specific context of criminological theorising, differentiating gender from biological sex meant that feminist criminologists could counteract the prevailing tendency to apply gender-based norms to the biological sex of the female offender. According to the theoretical orthodoxy at the time, women who contravened gender norms (society's expectations of them) by, for example, committing crime, were deemed to possess an abnormal sexuality. Their criminality was portrayed as evidence of biological (sex) abnormality (Lombroso and Ferrero 1895). This supposed abnormality was, at the time, ascribed to women who offended, because of the tendency to assign gender norms of femininity to the female biological sex. Key examples of the gender norms that were cited at the time were the docility and passivity that according to some, predisposed women to conformity

(Lombroso and Ferrero 1895). This, and other similarly stereotypical accounts of female offending prevailed before the advent of feminist criminology and are explored in more detail later.

The problem of gender dichotomy

Scholars inspired by feminism such as Smart (1990) have also theorised the concept of gender by highlighting problems with the traditional tendency to dichotomise gender. They reject the historical and cultural construction of gender as a binary concept that comprises two substantively different social categories; the male gender and the female gender. They argue that the binary conceptualisation of gender invokes spurious notions of difference that benefit men, and expose women to adverse differential treatment. According to Daly (2010), such a conceptualisation is fundamentally essentialist; and implies that each gender (male or female) comprises a homogenous group of people who share the same identity, subjectivity, and other attributes.

Later, we shall explore the arguments feminists have put forward to challenge the tendency to homogenise gender. For the moment, it is worth noting that as we shall see in the section on feminist explanations of female crime, those who study gendered pathways into crime highlight the merits of homogenising the female gender. In their view, there are socio-structural conditions that affect women specifically, and these conditions underpin women's offending behaviour (Belknap 2015; Chesney-Lind and Pasko 2013; Daly 1992). The studies suggest that overlooking the universal experiences women share exposes them to adverse treatment within societal institutions that are designed mainly for men (for example, the criminal justice system) (Daly and Chesney-Lind 1988). In these institutions, and in wider society, women's treatment and experiences are said to be shaped by male-defined and male-centred rules and norms. From this perspective, viewing men and women as distinct groups and emphasising that women share certain universalising qualities, is necessary. It justifies the need for women-centred or gender-responsive policies and services (see also, Flavin and Artz 2013).

Challenging androcentricism

It is argued that another key unifying principle of feminist criminology is the rejection of mainstream criminology's androcentricism (or male-centredness) (Daly and Chesney-Lind 1988; Heidensohn and Silvestri 2012). Some early feminist criminologists such as Carol Smart (1976; 1990) and Maureen Cain (1986) described the discipline rather pejoratively as 'malestream' or male-centred criminology (Gelsthorpe and Morris 1988: 96). Criminology was accused of promoting a male-centred view of the world or an 'amnesia' of women' (Gelsthorpe and Morris 1988: 98).

In their effort to reverse this criminological status quo, feminist criminologists theorise and research the concept of gender. As already noted, they integrate the concept within their study of crime and criminal justice. Some who are influenced by feminist theories, for example Messerschmidt (1993), have explored possible connections between the male gender and criminality. However, feminist criminologists and others influenced by feminism bring to the fore of their analyses, the nature and extent of female victimisation, offending, and punishment (see generally, Brownmiller 1975; Dobash and Dobash 1979; 1998; Gelsthorpe 2006; Eaton 1986; Russell 1975; Stanko 1990).

Theorising the gender gap

Added to their rejection of criminology's androcentricism, some feminist criminologists criticise criminology for failing to theorise the gender-gap in offending statistics (Heidensohn and Silvestri 2012b). The term gender-gap refers to the over-representation of men in crime statistics compared with women. Thus, the gap indicates that men commit more crimes than women (Chesney-Lind and Morash 2013). Heidensohn and Silvestri (2012b: 348) point out: 'That men and boys are responsible for the majority of offending behaviour remains an uncontested feature within criminology and debates about gender and crime.' As we shall see in the section that explores liberal feminists' theory, it is argued that since the 1970s, rates of female crime have increased steadily and orchestrated a narrowing of this gap (Heidensohn and Silvestri 2012b).

The latest statistics on women and criminal justice in England and Wales reveal that between 2014 and 2015, women represented 18.45 per cent of all arrests (see **Figure 11.2**), 5 per cent of the entire prison population (see **Figure 11.3**) (for context, as of 18 December 2015 there were a total of 85,641 individuals in prison), and 15 per cent of all those undertaking community-based orders (Ministry of Justice 2014).

These statistics reinforce the notion that a gender gap in crime statistics exists and it deserves criminological attention. Later on in this chapter, we shall explore the efforts that have been made by some scholars influenced by feminist theory, for example some liberal feminist theorists and masculinities scholars, to theorise the gender gap.

So far, we have seen that feminist criminology emerged in the 1970s. We have also seen that the early feminist

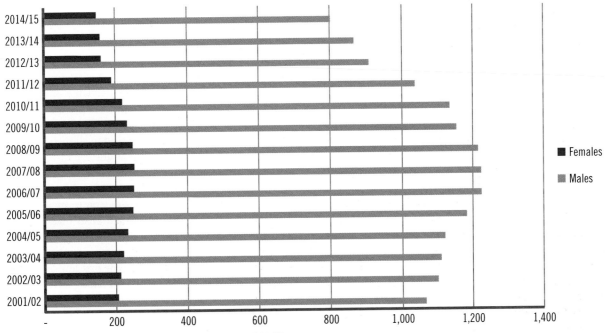

Figure 11.2 The number of persons arrested by sex 2001–02 until 2014–15.

Source: Arrests Collection, Home Office. Content is available under the Open Government Licence v3.0

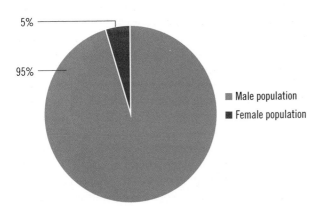

Figure 11.3 Significant difference between the number of males and females currently in the prison population, UK 2015

Source: https://www.gov.uk/government/statistics/prison-population-figures-2015, content available under the Open Government Licence v3.0

criminologists criticised the mainstream theories of the time for overlooking how gender intersects with crime.

Feminist criminologists and others influenced by feminist theories have since striven to theorise gender, with some differentiating it from biological sex to counter the stereotypical explanations of female criminality that pervaded mainstream criminology before the emergence of feminist criminology.

As we have also seen, the early feminist criminologists accused mainstream theories of *androcentricism* for being male-centred and ignoring or misrepresenting female offending and victimisation. Furthermore, feminist criminologists have criticised mainstream criminology for failing to theorise the documented gender gap in offending. Below, we explore the alternative approaches to understanding female criminality and victimisation, that feminist criminologist have since proposed. These alternative approaches are rooted in theoretical traditions that locate the experiences of women within the wider socio-structural contexts of their lives.

Feminist criminology: Key theoretical traditions

It is beyond the scope of this chapter to outline all the different theoretical traditions that have inspired feminist perspectives in criminology. Therefore, the chapter focuses on the key feminist traditions: *liberal feminist theory*; *radical feminist theory*; *Marxist feminism*; *socialist feminism*; and *postmodern feminism*. These are key traditions because they are recognised as the 'the best known of the early theoretical influences on criminology' (Chesney-Lind and Karlene 2001; Chesney-Lind and Morash 2013: 290). They emphasise the aforementioned unifying principles of feminist criminology. They also subscribe to the view that gender inequality, which disadvantages women, exists in society and should be addressed. However the traditions offer differing accounts of the source of gender inequality and the best means of eradicating it or alleviating its harmful impact on women in the criminal justice system, and wider society.

Liberal feminist theory

A key tenet of liberal feminist theory or liberal feminism is that although men and women are naturally equal, gender inequality pervades society. This gender inequality disadvantages women by exposing them to gender-based discriminatory treatment within social institutions, including the criminal justice system. Liberal feminism proposes that to achieve gender equality, it is necessary to alter the existing socialisation process. This is because in their view, the process indoctrinates and perpetuates culturally determined gender roles, which in turn, fuel the gender inequality that disadvantages women. Men are accorded high-status roles that empower them; being 'competitive and aggressive' are examples of attributes that are associated with the male gender, and they are deemed to be socially acceptable male attributes (Burgess-Proctor 2006). By contrast, women are expected to be 'nurturing and passive' and are such relegated to lower status roles that disempower them (Burgess-Proctor 2006: 29). Therefore, liberal feminism is associated with the view that sociological factors, primarily the sexist socialisation of women into gender roles that are associated with passivity and conformity, explain the limited extent of female offending (Adler 1975, 1977; Simon 1975).

From this perspective, the gender gap in offending is considered to be the upshot of the socialisation process through which individuals internalise the perception that criminal activity is more consistent with the aggressiveness and other attributes of the male gender (masculinity). Alongside this, the socialisation process imbues in individuals the perception that criminal activity is inconsistent with the conventional gender roles ascribed to the female gender (femininity). In addition, as they undergo socialisation and go through requisite developmental phases, women are subjected to stricter social controls than men. Taken together, these factors are said to limit the occurrence of female crime. (Some scholars contend that the gap is narrowing, for reasons we shall explore later.)

As we shall see when we explore the experiences of female defendants or offenders in criminal justice settings, some feminist criminologists and others argue that gender role expectations may also impact on the treatment of women in these settings. Women who offend may be vulnerable to gender-based discriminatory treatment. They could receive severe court sentences for their offence *and* for violating gender role expectations.

Liberal feminism advocates alterations to the socialisation process to inculcate gender equality, and ameliorate the adverse impact of gender inequality on women. Furthermore, liberal feminism proposes the dismantling of barriers that circumscribe equality of opportunity for women in all aspects of social life, and in all social institutions, from educational institutions and the institution of marriage, to legal institutions. Indeed, from a liberal feminist perspective, lack of opportunity is at the root of the gender inequality that disadvantages women in society.

In the 1960s and 1970s, liberal feminists made significant progress in their quest for gender equality and for women to have greater access to opportunities previously foreclosed to them. Some of the first few studies on women and crime suggested that, in taking advantage of these opportunities, women acquired attributes that were traditional associated with masculinity (the male gender), notably aggressiveness and even criminality (Adler 1975; Simon 1975): indeed some put forward a range of theses and hypotheses to explain this phenomenon.

Key examples are the liberation hypothesis and emancipation theory, both of which proposed that a narrowing of the gender gap, characterised by a rise in female offending rates, had occurred (Adler 1975; Simon 1975). The rise in rates of female offending was said to be a consequence of the progress towards greater gender equality, particularly equality of opportunity (Adler 1975). Proponents of the liberation hypothesis for instance, claimed that the emergence of the feminist movement in the 1960s (see **Figure 11.4**), and the accompanying trend towards greater gender equality, led to an increase in the economic and social opportunities available to women, including employment opportunities (Adler 1975, 1977; Simon 1975). These developments amplified the extent to which women became able to engage in activities that were previously dominated by men, and deemed expressive of attributes associated with the male gender (Adler 1975). Criminal activity in the workplace (or elsewhere) was identified as one example of those activities (Adler 1975), as was 'boisterousness' after excessive alcohol consumption which was subsequently depicted by the media as emblematic of a 'ladette culture' (Heidensohn 1996; Silvestri and Crowther-Dowey 2008; Worrall 2004). The newspaper article discussed in **What do you think? 11.1** exemplifies how the news media sensationalised the so-called 'ladette culture' by portraying it as a social malaise that was rising at a rather alarming rate.

Articles such as the one cited in **What do you think? 11.1** lent credence to the view that women's increasing involvement in behaviours traditionally associated with masculinity, such as criminal behaviour, demonstrated that men

Figure 11.4 Women's liberation march from Farrugut Square to Layfette Park, Washington D.C., August 1970

Source: Warren K Leffler/Public domain

WHAT DO YOU THINK? 11.1

There was an article published by the *Telegraph* in 2009 with the headline 'Rise of ladette culture as 241 women arrested each day for violence'.

The article alludes to the advent of a 'ladette culture' which, according to the article, is characterised by an increase in the number of teenage girls arrested daily for engaging in acts of violence. The article estimates that approximately 241 women are arrested daily for these acts and implies that the sole factor which explains the rise in rates of violent attacks by teenage girls are the girls' increasing tendency to engage in binge-drinking. (See **Figure 11.5**.) The article goes further to cite a politician and government official who echo the view that the involvement of women and girls in acts of violence is increasing and the so-called 'ladette culture of binge drinking' is the key trigger.

What do you think? Follow the link provided at the end of this box. Do you agree with the concerns raised in the article and the implicit proposition that a 'ladette culture' is to blame for the increase in the number of teenage girls arrested for violence? (http://www.telegraph.co.uk/news/uknews/law-and-order/5251042/Rise-of-ladette-culture-as-241-women-arrested-each-day-for-violence.html)

Figure 11.5 'Ladette' culture?

Source: Edw/Shutterstock.com

and women did not possess different abilities or propensities to commit crime. The gender gap had only existed because women lacked the opportunities required for occupying roles or engaging in activities reserved for men (Adler 1975). They were socialised into roles that disempowered them, and opportunities to occupy the powerful roles reserved for men were blocked to them.

Some have since rejected these claims, and have adduced empirical evidence which suggests that the purported rise in female crime after the 1960s occurred before any gains could have been made from liberal feminism and the women's liberation movement it spawned (Chesney-Lind and Pasko 2004). Others point out that the rise in female offending could be attributable to other factors such as the adverse economic and other circumstances that affect women's lives (Batchelor 2009; Box and Hale 1983; Carlen 1988). The increasing involvement of women in property crimes rather than serious violent crimes is cited as evidence of this (Carlen 1988). Furthermore, there is evidence in the UK that far from any increase in rates of violence among young women, the increasing exposure of young women who do not appear to conform to the socially constructed ideals of femininity to harsh penal policies and sanctions, explains their increasing representation in criminal justice statistics (Batchelor 2005).

Radical feminist theory

Similar to liberal feminism, radical feminism asserts that gender inequality exists in society, and it impinges on the experiences of women in the criminal justice system and wider society. However, a key difference between liberal feminism and radical feminism is that the latter identifies patriarchy as the fundamental factor that drives the gender inequality that oppresses women regardless of their ethnicity, social class or other attributes (MacKinnon 1989). Broadly conceived, patriarchy manifests as the oppression and subordination of women by men. It is defined as a 'set of social relations between men, which have a material base, and which, though hierarchical, establish or create interdependence and solidarity among them that enable them to dominate women' (Hartmann 1981: 175). Radical feminism proceeds on the premise that in patriarchal societies, men construct gender roles and notions of femininity that are beneficial to them but oppressive for women (Brownmiller 1975). Furthermore, this feminist tradition asserts that gender relations in patriarchal societies are characterised by men's efforts to control women's sexuality and capacity to reproduce; men resort to violence and abuse to achieve their objectives (Brownmiller 1975).

Consequently, unlike liberal feminism, radical feminism posits that, to achieve better outcomes for women, a complete overhaul of the existing social order is required.

Rebalancing the existing social order to achieve gender equality as the liberal feminists propose is insufficient. Dismantling the patriarchal order should obliterate the endemic patriarchy that empowers men to oppress women.

The tenets of radical feminism are evident in the findings of studies that highlight the violent victimisation men perpetrate against women, and the limited protection the criminal justice system offers the victims (Brownmiller 1975; Dobash and Dobash 1979; 2004; Maidment 2006). Indeed, the criminal justice system has been described as a patriarchal institution within a wider 'patriarchal social structure' (Renzetti 2012: 134).

Through their seminal studies of female victimisation by intimate male partners, Rebecca Dobash and Russell Dobash (1978; 1979; 1983) for instance, have highlighted the role of men as the main perpetrators of domestic violence. They have also drawn attention to the nature of domestic violence as an instrument of male control over women in a patriarchal society, in line with the principles of radical feminist theory (see also Brownmiller 1975; Hanmer 1978). In addition, Dobash and Dobash (1979) and others have highlighted the social conditions that render women vulnerable to male control and abuse in patriarchal societies. For example, Dobash and Dobash (1979) argue that male dominance over women is inscribed in normative conceptualisations of the family. The latter is depicted as a setting where men, having undergone a socialisation process that teaches them to be domineering husbands, control their wives, who have in turn, been socialised into submissiveness (Dobash and Dobash 1979). Alongside this, existing socioeconomic arrangements enable men to secure high status and more lucrative employment but relegate women to low status low paid positions. Consequently, women are more likely to become financially reliant on men, exacerbating their subordinate status in the home, and rendering them more vulnerable to male domination and abuse (Dobash and Dobash 1979).

The work of the Dobashes and others who have highlighted the high rates at which men inflict violence on their intimate female partners, has reinforced the tenets of radical feminism that the acts of violence are expressions of patriarchy (see also Brownmiller 1975; Rafter 1990). The violence is motivated by men's quest to control women and reinforce male dominance. Reinforcing this in a text that explored the dynamics of rape in diverse jurisdictions, Brownmiller (1975: 15; emphasis in original) described the violent sexual assaults perpetrated by men against women as: 'nothing more or less than a conscious process of intimidation by which *all* men keep *all* women in a state of fear'.

Thus, the early radical feminists uncovered the vulnerability of women to male violence and domination.

Added to this, official crime statistics and local victimisation studies also revealed the high extent of violent victimisation women experience through the actions of the men with whom they shared intimate or other types of relationships (Mirrlees-Black 1999; Walby and Myhill 2001; Walby and Allen 2004; Myhill and Allen 2002).

The 1998 and 2000 British Crime Surveys found that:

> Women are most likely to be sexually attacked by men they know in some way, most often partners (32%) or acquaintances (22%). Current partners (at the time of the attack) were responsible for 45% of rapes reported to the survey. Strangers were responsible for only 8% of rapes reported to the survey. Less than two-thirds (60%) of female rape victims were prepared to self-classify their experience as 'rape'.
>
> Myhill and Allen 2002: 1

In 2012–13 the same pattern emerged: for the majority of female victims of a serious sexual assault the offender was a partner or someone who was known to them (41 per cent and 39 per cent respectively) with a fifth reporting the offender as a stranger (20 per cent, see **Figure 11.6**). This contrasts with the findings for less serious sexual assaults where strangers committed 53 per cent of these crimes (see **Figure 11.7**).

Other studies have revealed similar findings. For example, a study of the criminal justice system's response to sexual offences in the North East Region of England found that almost all of the perpetrators were known to the victims (Hester 2013). These studies, statistics, and the work of radical feminists (particularly their research studies) have helped to dispel the myth of the 'safe home', or the 'stranger danger' myth. This myth is underpinned by the notion created by earlier crime statistics which

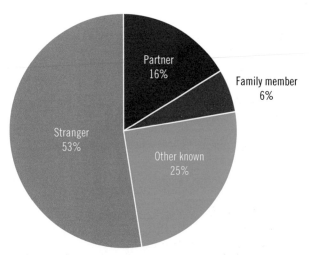

Figure 11.7 Victim-offender relationship less serious sexual assault 2012–13
Source: Crime Survey for England and Wales, published by the Office for National Statistics, content available under the Open Government Licence v3.0

ignored the victimisation of women by their intimate partners, and claimed that violent victimisation consisted mainly of random acts perpetrated outside the home by strangers (Myhill and Allen 2002).

The studies have also helped to repudiate the myth that men are more vulnerable to violent crimes (particularly violent street crimes) (Myhill and Allen 2002). There is now greater awareness of the high extent of so-called 'hidden' domestic crimes that affect women's lives. These crimes are often unreported by the victims or unrecorded by the police. This is because they are often classed as domestic incidents, and are perhaps viewed by some police officers as not serious enough to warrant criminal justice intervention (Dobash and Dobash 1992; Hester 2013). **Controversy and debate 11.1** sets out some of the reasons why victims are unwilling to report these crimes, and why the response of the police is often inadequate.

Insights from the work of radical feminists and others who campaign for women's rights have prompted legislative changes which seek to protect women from domestic violence and sexual assaults that are perpetrated by intimate male partners. Examples of these changes are the laws that prescribe mandatory criminal justice intervention in domestic violence cases in the United States and the United Kingdom.

Before the late 1970s, the laws were not as robust as they are today. In the United States for example, in cases of domestic abuse classed as misdemeanours (which tended to represent the majority of such cases), the police were required to have witnessed the incident before they could arrest the suspected perpetrator without a warrant. In felony cases, they could make an arrest without a warrant at their discretion. However, it is argued that many male police officers and prosecutors

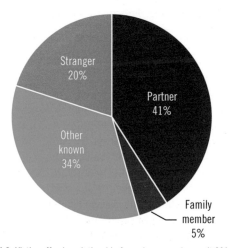

Figure 11.6 Victim-offender relationship for serious sexual assault 2012–13
Source: Crime Survey for England and Wales, published by the Office for National Statistics, content available under the Open Government Licence v3.0

CONTROVERSY AND DEBATE 11.1

This feature considers an article published by the BBC which highlights the inadequacy of the police response to incidents of domestic violence.

Domestic abuse: Police 'nearly overwhelmed' by increase

'They take everything away'

Lexy Godden told BBC 5 live she was married to a man who subjected her to domestic violence.

'I was in a relationship for 13 years, the violence got really bad when I got pregnant with my daughter. He tried to strangle me.

'He said he wasn't going to do it again. He threw a battery at me just before I gave birth, and abused me again when I had my son.

'Eventually I thought "this isn't right, I need to leave. I want to live a normal life". I was worried about my son and daughter as well. You're in your own little bubble and they've taken everything away from you.

'When I went back to pick up my clothes the police weren't very compassionate and kept telling me to hurry up, in case he comes back. So I forgot half the clothes that I wanted to take.

'I would always say get out of the relationship. Just go, because it's not worth it.'

Sussex Police, which dealt with Ms Godden, says it will not comment on individual cases but did say 'stopping domestic abuse remains a priority'.

But it highlights problems including:

- 'Limited evidence' of forces engaging with victims for feedback
- 'Mixed' attitudes among officers, sometimes leading to victims 'losing trust and not being willing to report subsequent abuse'

- Some forces not monitoring their domestic abuse data for 'insight', meaning they 'do not have a good understanding of their performance'
- 'Wide variation' between forces on arrest rates for domestic abuse call-outs, suggesting victims are subject to a 'postcode lottery'
- Forces using a 'range of different and therefore inconsistent practices' when assessing risk
- 'Inconsistent awareness'—especially among response staff—of coercive and controlling behaviour
- 'Over-reliance' on e-learning training packages
- 'Extremely varied' use of Domestic Violence Protection Orders, which can protect victims immediately after abuse incidents

The report notes the 'enormous' number of people affected by domestic abuse—with 900,000 calls to police in England and Wales in the 12 months to March 2015.

Louisa Rolfe, of the National Police Chiefs' Council and temporary deputy chief constable of Avon and Somerset Police, said many police forces were working 'really hard' to prioritise domestic abuse cases.

'New officers are being trained, many forces are investing more in their specialist teams, but also fundamentally we're making sure that every frontline officer has the right skills and the right tools available to them to deal with this effectively, because not every case will go to a specialist team.'

'So I think we're stretched but not overwhelmed.'

BBC News Online, 15 December 2015,
http://www.bbc.co.uk/news/uk-35093837

---

harboured sexist views and often exercised their discretion in favour of men. This contributed to the limited progress that was made in arresting and prosecuting male perpetrators of abuse against women, and protecting the female victims of these crimes (Houston 2014). Another explanation for the lack of sufficient criminal justice intervention in these cases was, and still is, the issue of case attrition that stems from the reluctance of many victims to testify in these cases (Houston 2014; Smith and Skinner 2012).

Court delays, the risk of exposing one's sexual history, the risk of re-victimisation, and lack of information about

the progress of the case, have been cited as key reasons why many victims are reluctant to testify (Houston 2014; Smith and Skinner 2012). Nevertheless by the late 1980s, and in the 1990s and 2000s, as a result of the work of scholars such as Dobash and Dobash (1979), and the work of others who were advocating for state intervention to protect the female victims of male violence, almost all the states in the US had enacted 'pro-arrest and mandatory arrest' laws. These laws permitted the police to arrest suspected perpetrators of domestic violence without a warrant even if the police had not witnessed the incident (Houston 2014: 262).

Similar to their counterparts in the US, the scholarly work of feminists and others inspired by feminism in the UK such as Stanko (1990) and Walklate (1991), moved domestic violence from its hitherto private setting to the public domain. Their efforts, alongside the work of campaigners, for example, the charitable organisation now known as Women's Aid, activated policy and legislative changes. Laws such as the Domestic Violence and Matrimonial Proceedings Act 1976 which empowered the police to arrest those suspected of breaching injunctions in cases involving domestic violence, were introduced. In 1991, marital rape became a crime and the previous presumption that marriage implied consent was abolished. In 1996, changes were made to the Family Law Act, Part IV to give police automatic powers to arrest suspects in domestic incidents where violence, or threats of violence, had occurred. In 2004, the Domestic Violence, Crime and Victims Act empowered the police

to arrest a person suspected of common assault without a warrant. The document: 'Domestic Violence: A National Report' which was published by the Home Office in 2005 signified the government's commitment to propounding policies that deal with domestic violence, and in 2010, the government expressed its plans to commit funding to support 'rape crisis' centres for female victims. In 2013, the UK government expanded the definition of domestic violence to include not only physical domestic abuse but also non-violent domestic abuse such as behaviour that amounts to controlling the victim or coercing them in some way (Home Office 2014). New laws were enacted in 2015 to criminalise such behaviour (see **Controversy and debate 11.2**). Furthermore, Clare's Law was introduced in 2015 across England and Wales to enable people to request information form the police regarding their partner's history of domestic abuse. For more on women as victims, and a powerful account given

---

 ## CONTROVERSY AND DEBATE 11.2

This feature considers an article published by the BBC which describes changes to domestic abuse legislation.

Emotional abuse to become illegal under new domestic abuse law

A new offence of emotional abuse and controlling behaviour has been announced by the government.

The Home Office is giving police in England and Wales new powers in a drive to crack down on domestic abuse.

At the moment the government's **definition of domestic violence** recognises the impact of threatening behaviour but it has never been a law.

...

It means that now for the first time people who control their partners through threats or by restricting their personal or financial freedom, could face prison in the same way they do if they're violent.

The new offence, which will come into force in late 2015, will mean abusers could face up to five years behind bars if found guilty of domestic abuse.

The victims

Alison—we've given her another name to protect her identity—was in an abusive and violent relationship for around 12 months.

'It started with name calling, "You're fat", "You're lucky that I love you because no-one else would".'

She says after he'd isolated her from her family and friends the abuse became physical.

'I was flung across the room, hit, punched, kicked, head butted and strangled.

'I felt numb, scared. I didn't know whether he was going to carry on. I didn't know if I was going to see tomorrow.

'He apologised but the abuse continued, five days a week.

'Police never prosecuted him and I still get a recurring dream of not being able to breathe and I see him with his hands around my throat.'

BBC News Online, Nomia Iqbal and Elaine Doran, Newsbeat reporters, 18 December 2014, http://www.bbc.co.uk/ newsbeat/article/30098611/emotional-abuse-to-become-illegal-under-new-domestic-abuse-law

Figure 11.8 Woman in fear of domestic abuse
Source: Lolostoc/ Shutterstock.com

by Eve McDougall (a victim of domestic abuse) please see **Chapter 15** on critical criminology.

Alongside these legislative developments, policies have been introduced to prevent 'victim blaming' which involves apportioning blame to the victim of sexual assaults rather than the perpetrator. These policies seek to protect the rights of female victims and to alleviate the impact of negative prosecutorial processes that could stigmatise and revictimise them (Coyle 2007; Mawby and Walklate 1994). Victims of sexual abuse are now permitted to give evidence in private so they are not exposed to potentially distressing interactions with the perpetrator in court. Furthermore, policies have been introduced to improve the proficiency of the police in responding to the violent victimisation of women by their intimate partners (Matczak, Hatzidimitriadou, and Lindsay 2011). Indeed, the effort to highlight the harmful impact of male violence on women has been so extensive that domestic violence is now generally recognised as an obstacle that prevents the female victims from exercising their citizenship rights (Westmarland 2015).

That said, despite the policy and legislative developments cited earlier, in the UK, studies and official inspections of policing activity in this field, continue to reveal that the police do not respond to incidents of domestic violence as vigorously as might be expected. For example, a recent inspection of how the police responds to domestic abuse cases across England and Wales found that only eight out of the 43 police forces in England and Wales responded effectively to such incidents by bringing perpetrators to justice (Her Majesty's Inspectorate of Constabulary 2014). There is also statistical evidence that in 2012–13, out of the 91 fatal victims of violence perpetrated by an intimate partner or ex-partner, most (75) were female (Office for National Statistics 2014; Westmarland 2015). As Westmarland (2015) rightly observes, these are conservative estimates given that some of the fatalities associated with the behaviour of abusive male partners occur through other means such as substance misuse and suicide. Furthermore, it has long been recognised that many incidents of domestic violence are under-reported, under-recorded, and under-prosecuted (Coy et al. 2008).

The situation appears to be similar in the United States. Perpetrators of domestic violence against women still enjoy greater impunity than other violent offenders. Demonstrating this, Nelson's (2014: 1) study of police and prosecutorial discretion in domestic violence cases found that 'there is substantial room for investigative improvement by police' and substantial work has to be done to improve prosecution rates; approximately 97 per cent of cases that were taken to court were resolved through plea bargaining.

These findings reinforce radical feminism's contention that female victimisation does not attract adequate criminal justice intervention, because gender inequality that disadvantages women permeates the system. In sum, radical feminism asserts that a patriarchal order in the form of an oppressive status quo that sustains male dominance and breeds the oppression and subordination of women, exists and should be dismantled.

Marxist feminist theory

Unlike radical feminism, Marxist feminist theory does not attribute female victimisation and offending solely to gender inequality and the patriarchal structures that are said to sustain it. Instead, Marxist feminist theory identifies the capitalist mode of production (and the social class inequality it breeds), as the primary factor that provokes the oppression of women (Schwendinger and Schwendinger 1983). This strand of feminist thought is influenced by Marxist analyses of class dynamics in capitalist societies. From a Marxist perspective, in capitalist societies, an individual's position in relation to the production of the goods and services that are vital for human sustenance, determines his or her social class and ability to exercise power. The wealthy ruling class capitalists are said to control the means of production in these societies. Marxist feminist theory holds that men are often the ruling class capitalists and they also often occupy high-level positions in the production process. Consequently, men enjoy a high social status and possess substantial power.

In contrast, women contribute to the production process at the lower end of the occupational ladder. They are primarily relegated to low paid domestic and caring roles which reflect the dominant view that women are naturally programmed to perform nurturing roles in society. Their typically low occupational status corresponds with their relatively low social status and powerlessness in wider society compared with men. These unequal gender arrangements are said to shape gender relations. The latter, it is argued, is characterised by male domination because, given their respective positions in relation to production in capitalist societies, men are able to dominate and oppress women, rendering them fundamentally vulnerable to male violence (Chesney-Lind and Morash 2013). Furthermore, female offending is considered to be the product of the exploitative class structure of capitalist societies that consigns women to economic marginality and a correspondingly low social status (Carlen 1988). Therefore, the crimes women typically commit such as shoplifting and other property crimes reflect their economic marginality (Burgess-Proctor 2006). Marxist feminists consequently believe that capitalism is a mode of production that gives rise to exploitative gender relations which disadvantage women. To redress this unfair status quo, Marxist feminists propose a transformation of the economic system to replace capitalism with socialism. The latter mode of production, they argue, should engender more egalitarian production processes and equitable distribution of societal resources, which should in turn, give rise to egalitarian gender relations (Schwendinger and Schwendinger 1983).

To summarise, Marxist feminist theory identifies capitalism as the key factor that fuels male domination of women in capitalist societies. It is a mode of production that gives rise to unequal gender relations. The primary reason for this is that those who control the means of production, and who invariably tend to be men, are able to dominate and control women whose contribution to production is typically relegated to low status, low paid employment, for example, domestic labour. These inequitable gender relations also contribute to female offending.

After reading the previous sections you could go on to consider the questions raised in **What do you think? 11.2**.

Socialist feminist theory

Social feminist theory combines dimensions of radical and Marxist feminist theories. As such, similar to Marxist feminist theory, socialist feminism identifies class difference as an endemic feature of capitalist societies that underpins female crime and victimisation. Furthermore, in line with radical feminism, socialist feminism asserts that patriarchy or male domination is a factor that impacts on women adversely. But socialist feminism also posits that patriarchy intersects with class inequality in capitalist societies to disadvantage women. Thus, those inspired by socialist feminism believe that gender relations (typified by patriarchy or male domination) *and* the class relations generated by the machinations of capitalism, are factors that shape women's lived experiences (Acker 1990, 1992; Messerschmidt 1986).

In summary, proponents of socialist feminist theory trace the experiences of women as victims and offenders to the oppressive gender relations orchestrated by the intersection of patriarchy and capitalism (Hartmann 1981).

WHAT DO YOU THINK? 11.2

- Are you convinced by Marxist feminist theory's focus on economic structure, or do you find the arguments of liberal feminist theory and radical feminist theory more compelling?

- What arguments can you develop to critique each of these approaches?

Consequently, as Chesney-Lind and Morash (2013) note, socialist feminists advocate egalitarian gender relations to reverse patriarchy, *and* economic reforms, particularly a shift away from capitalism to socialism, to achieve gender and social class equality.

Feminist epistemologies

Added to the aforementioned theoretical positions, in their study of gender and crime, feminist researchers are also influenced by several epistemological positions, which reflect their views about the appropriate means of generating valid knowledge of the social world. The main epistemological orientations that are associated with feminist research on gender and crime are: feminist empiricism; standpoint feminism; and postmodern feminism (Comack 1999; Harding 1986). Key features of these epistemological positions are explored below.

Feminist empiricism

Feminist empiricism is an epistemological position which presumes that by using scientific methods of enquiry, it is possible to produce unbiased, gender-neutral knowledge of the nature of crime (Harding 1991; Naffine 1997). According to Smart (1995), liberal feminism presumes that scientific methods of enquiry can be used to generate objective knowledge (or the causes and effects) of female crime. This is particularly the case if the methods are applied effectively. The prevailing ontological basis of this epistemological position is that objective knowledge of social reality exists and is discoverable. (In social science research, the term ontological position refers to the subject matter of ontology which is the study of what exists in the social world. It concerns itself with issues to do with whether or not concepts such as gender and crime are realities that exist objectively without prior description, and have unique qualities, or whether they are social constructs.) Translated in the real world of social research, the epistemological assumption is that the researcher is a neutral observer who is capable of engaging in the scientific processes of data collection, analysis, and dissemination of value-neutral knowledge, with detached objectivity (Harding 1991). These ideas that the ideal approach to the study of the social world is the scientific approach, and researcher objectivity is vital, dominated criminology before the advent of feminist criminology. According to Smart (1995), feminist empiricists, who have been described as the earliest feminist criminologists, endorsed the approach. They believed that 'scientific' studies of women's experiences were required to redress the imbalance created by the focus of scientific enquiry on men. Comack (1999: 288; emphasis in original) points out that:

> Feminist empiricists, by and large, left the scientific enterprise intact and called for more studies "on" women in order to fill the historical gap which had been created by the exclusion of women as research subjects.

It is argued that feminist empiricists perhaps accepted the utility of so-called 'scientific' methods without question unlike the standpoint feminists whose position is explored next, because they (the feminist empiricists) focused on their broader aim which was to generate empirical insights that would aid the emancipation of women (Carrington 2008).

Standpoint feminism

Standpoint feminism is an epistemological stance that prioritises the experiences of women as articulated by women (Cain 1990a, 1990b; Hartsock 1987; Harding 1987; 1991). This departs from feminist empiricism's commitment to the 'scientific' approach of researcher objectivity in the search for value-free knowledge. Standpoint feminism is underpinned by the belief that women suffer marginalisation, and those who are marginalised are more likely to offer accurate accounts of their experiences in the social world (Flavin 2001). Women, for example, are said to occupy a unique vantage position (given their shared experiences of oppression) from which they can provide accurate accounts of social reality within a patriarchal society (Harding 1987). Unlike the dominant group (men) who may wish to sustain the unfair conditions that help them maintain their privileged position, marginalised groups do not have any vested interest in concealing the adverse conditions that affect them (Harding 1991). Thus, those whose approach to the study of women's experiences reflects the tenets of standpoint feminism, describe the knowledge produced from women's accounts of their experiences as 'epistemologically privileged' or more authoritative (Cain 1990b: 126). Women's views, or 'stories' (Comack 1999: 296) which are likely to be informed by their struggle for emancipation, are said to represent more accurate reflections of reality that should inform criminal justice policy reform and indeed wider policy changes.

Scholars inspired by standpoint feminism therefore propose the use of empirical methods that can in their view, produce knowledge from the standpoint of women with the overall aim of promoting women's interests (Cain 1990b; Harding 1987; 1991; 2004; Hartsock 1987). Smart (1995) notes that they reject the scientific methods of social enquiry which the feminist empiricists endorse, and the underlying assumption that objective, gender-neutral 'facts' are discoverable. They also believe that scientific methods are male-centred. They argue that women are best placed to conduct research that seeks to study the experiences of women (Smith and Skinner 2012). Smart (1995: 43) observes that 'the epistemological basis of this form of feminist knowledge is experience'. Female researchers, by virtue of their personal experiences, are said to possess unique insight and a clearer perception of the experiences of female research participants.

Several scholars who contributed to the early development of standpoint feminism, for example Maureen Cain (1990a, 1990b), have subsequently revised their earlier position that women share similar experiences of oppression. According to Smart (1990a: 204, 1990b), they still maintain that women's views or perspectives constitute more authoritative knowledge of social reality than androcentric accounts. However, they have come to acknowledge that women experience 'multiple realities' or have diverse experiences of oppression; and these experiences are relative to the contexts from which they emerge (Cain 1990a, 1990b; Comack 1999).

Some of the studies conducted by scholars who reinforced radical feminism's theoretical insights by exposing the extent of male violence against women, were influenced by standpoint feminism (see for example, Dobash and Dobash 1992). The studies produced knowledge of domestic violence that were based on the constructions of the female victims themselves and revealed the power dynamics that underpin domestic violence.

Postmodern feminism

Postmodern feminists seek to deconstruct the dominant language or discourses that are used to infuse social categories, such as gender, with meaning (Butler 1990; Comack 1999; Howe 1994; Young 1996). They believe that this exercise can help unmask structures of power that fuel the gender inequality which disadvantages women (Smart 1995). Similar to the feminist empiricists and standpoint feminists, postmodern feminists explore the epistemological question of how best to produce knowledge of social reality. They also seek to uncover what they consider to be the power dynamics that underpin knowledge production (Carrington 2008). However, unlike some standpoint feminists who focus on women's experiences and describe women's accounts of their experiences as definitive knowledge of the social world, postmodern feminists view all accounts, whatever the source or sources, as culturally constructed and biased (Howe 1994; Smart 1995; Young 1996).

Postmodern feminists also reject empirical feminists' contention that scientific methods of enquiry produce an objective, universal 'truth' of social reality. Instead, they argue that truth is relative to context and interpretation.

Therefore, knowledge or 'what we know' about the things that exist or occur in the social world, including our knowledge of gender issues, is situated in the contexts from which it emerges. It is also the value-laden product of definitions constructed by the powerful. Unlike other feminist perspectives that emphasise the androcentric situatedness of power, postmodern feminists believe that power is 'ubiquitous' and resides in diverse groups and contexts in society (Smart 1995: 46).

Postmodern feminists are influenced by post-structural theory, particularly Derrida's (1976) notion of 'deconstruction', which is a technique for studying the social world. It is based on the belief that the language or discourse that is used to construct what is accepted as knowledge of the social world lacks objectivity and reflects the values and biases of those who have the power to produce such knowledge. Influenced by these themes, postmodern feminists challenge the idea that a discoverable universal 'truth' about social reality exists. From this perspective, knowledge that is produced and accepted as the 'truth' about gender does not reflect any objective truth. Rather, postmodern feminists view key social categories such as gender, crime, and so forth, as concepts that are culturally constructed by those who have the power to transform their subjective definitions into what is subsequently accepted as 'truth' (Young 1996). Equally, the language that is used to define gender difference reflects the values and preferences of the knowledge creators. The more powerful in society preside over knowledge production and it is their subjective constructions of social categories which represent dominant knowledge of these categories. Indeed, postmodern feminists argue that the normalisation of binary conceptualisations of gender stems from the language and discourses of the powerful. They hold that gender (both male and female) has no inherent qualities or essence but that homogenising characteristics are assigned to gender, which benefit men, disadvantage women, and fuel gender inequality.

Consequently, postmodern feminists seek to develop discourses that can uncover women's 'realities' (Maidment 2006). This implies that, as Flavin (2001) points out, unlike the early standpoint feminists, postmodern feminists assert that multiple realities exist. Therefore, in contradistinction to feminist empiricists who search for scientifically generated 'truth' or standpoint feminists who depict women's viewpoints as the definitive 'truth', postmodern feminists contend that no universal 'truth' exists. Rather, multiple realities exist, including the realities of groups who lack the power to propagate their views as 'truth'. These groups typically comprise those affected by racial, social class, and gender inequality. As Comack (1999) points out, according to postmodern feminists, for these groups, their realities reflect the truths of their particular social, economic, and political circumstances, and are valid sources of knowledge. This view is very much in line with arguments of feminists who as we shall see later when we examine the concept of intersectionality, draw attention to how intersections of gender, and sociostructural factors such as ethnicity and social class, affect women differentially. Smart (1995: 44–5) notes that:

> It would be a mistake to depict feminist postmodernism as the third stage or synthesis of feminist empiricism and standpoint feminism … The core element of feminist postmodernism is the rejection of the one reality which arises from 'the falsely universalizing perspective of the master' (Harding 1987: 188). So the aim of feminism ceases to be the establishment of the feminist truth and becomes the aim of deconstructing Truth and analysing the power effects that claims to truth entail.

Therefore, postmodern feminism's agenda is to deconstruct accepted universalist claims made about social categories, particularly gender and female criminality. For postmodern feminism then, deconstructionism is a useful means of interpreting the language knowledge producers employ and to unmask power structures of knowledge production. Deconstructionism involves analysing texts and discourses in criminology (and other social sciences) that are used to define and categorise human beings and social occurrences. The objective of these analyses is to uncover and challenge underlying myths of female attributes, behaviours, and experiences in society that disadvantage women. As already noted, postmodern feminism asserts that these myths are constructed by the powerful and held out as 'truth' (Smart 1995). Daly (2010) argues that a key example is the tendency to homogenise gender. Another example is the binary conceptualisation of gender. It is argued that this conceptualisation is based on spurious, socially constructed gender differences that benefit men and disadvantage women.

Following on from this summary of some of the differing feminist theories that exist, see **Telling it like it is 11.1** to read contributor Pamela Ugwudike's opinion—hopefully it will help you to formulate your own thoughts and opinions.

Highlighting intersectionality: the influence of social categories that coexist with gender

In the 1980s and 1990s some began to argue that white, middle class women dominated feminism and had overlooked how racial, social class, and other societal structures rendered the experiences of other women, for example black women, qualitatively different (see for example, hooks 1981; Baca Zinn and Thornton 1996).

TELLING IT LIKE IT IS 11.1

My views on feminist approaches to criminology—with contributor Pamela Ugwudike

You are, of course, free to decide which of the feminist approaches to criminology you find most convincing. For my part, although I do not identify myself wholly with any of the approaches, I would say that postmodern feminism is closest to my epistemological position on what constitutes the appropriate means of generating knowledge of the social world. I believe that the interpretations and meanings social actors apply to their experiences represent valid sources of knowledge. Therefore, research studies that seek to document women's experiences should elicit women's descriptions or interpretations of their experiences. It should also be recognised that in many instances, women's experiences are likely to be diversified rather than universally shared. Therefore, I agree with the intersectionality scholars who argue that women do not necessarily share the same experiences in society. Social, racial, and other differences are factors that can impact differentially on women. The importance of accounting for these differences when we try to analyse how gender relations affect women is explored further in the 'Highlighting intersectionality' section.

The debates surrounding these issues heralded what is now described as the third wave of feminism (Burgess-Proctor 2006). It was a development in feminism that was rooted in the work of African American feminists such as bell hooks (1981, see **Figure 11.9**), and Hull and Colleagues (1982), who produced texts that were respectively titled: *Aint I a Woman?* and *All the Women are White, All the Blacks are men, But some of Us are Brave.*

These scholars and others, highlighted the gap created by white middle-class feminism which dominated feminist analyses at the time. It was described as a brand of feminism that did not, and could not, effectively portray or represent the interests of other women whose ethnicity, social class, and other aspects of their identities interacted to compound their disadvantage. White middle-class feminism promulgated universalising perspectives which could not capture the interactive impact of the multiple identities some women (for example, black women) possess. Indeed, it was argued that the conceptualisation of 'womanhood' within early feminism conjured up the image of the 'white, middle class, Anglo-Saxon' woman (Smart 1995: 45). This definition of womanhood was not broad enough to encompass the lived realities of those who did not belong to that category (Crenshaw 1994).

Reinforcing this, Comack (1999: 288) remarked that:

> For feminists in both criminology and elsewhere, the task of producing feminist knowledge initially appeared to be straightforward one. There was a broad consensus, which emanated from the point that we knew what we were rejecting: the androcentrism of the traditional research enterprise. However, as feminists began to respond to this common problematic, cracks in the consensus began to appear.

Debates about these issues relate to the subject matter of intersectionality which is defined as the 'interaction of multiple identities and experiences of exclusion and subordination' (Davis 2008: 68). Coined by Kimberlé Crenshaw (1989), the concept of intersectionality in this context refers to the impact of attributes such as race and class, which can, alongside gender, exacerbate some women's exposure to discrimination in the criminal justice system, and wider society. For example, there is evidence that compared with white women, black and other minority ethnic women on both sides of the Atlantic (the UK and the US), receive more punitive court sanctions such as longer prison sentences (Chigwada-Bailey 1997; Seitz 2005). With respect to their experiences as victims of domestic violence, it is also argued that they are disadvantaged by the racial, class-based, and sexuality-related considerations that inform

Figure 11.9 bell hooks

Source: Alex Lozupone (Tduk)/CC BY-SA 4.0

stereotypes of what constitutes normative gender behaviour in domestic violence incidents. Women involved in these incidents are expected to conform to the socially constructed feminine ideal of passivity associated with the white middle-class heterosexual female (Dasgupta 2002, cited in Romain et al. 2016). Ethnic minority women who do not exhibit this quality could be labelled as masculine and excessively violent, and consequently denied adequate protection (Romain et al. 2016).

In a seminal text that was published in 1981, the African American author, bell hooks, highlighted these issues and rejected the dominant presumption of the feminist orthodoxy at the time, which was that all women share similar experiences of disadvantage. hooks persuasively argued that the extreme marginalisation and deprivation of African American women is markedly and qualitatively different from the social experiences of other women (see also Davis 1983). In her view, black women were doubly disadvantaged by inequalities that stemmed from their gender *and* their ethnicity. It was therefore misleading to present a universalising view that depicted women as a homogenous group, with a shared social reality, and who could as such, advocate change with one voice. Chesney-Lind and Morash (2013: 293) have since stated that: 'African American scholar and activist bell hooks' book, Ain't I a woman? (1984), highlighted and forever invalidated the sole focus on gender'.

In the 1980s, additional African American feminists and others echoed this critique. Their contention that women's experiences differ along racial, social class, and other lines, inspired more comprehensive accounts of gender relations and women's experiences in patriarchal societies. As Daly (2010: 229) put it: their critique challenged any simple idea of a 'woman's perspective' and any unified feminist politics for change'. Accurate knowledge of women's lived *realities* required much broader evaluation of intersectionality, that is, how gender interacts with age, race, class, sexual identity, disability, and other categories to produce disadvantage (Potter 2006). In a paper that seeks to advance 'a black feminist criminology', Potter (2006: 107) argues that 'traditional feminist criminology is built on mainstream feminism, which historically placed issues of race as secondary to gender'. She notes that:

> For Black women, and arguably for all women, other inequities must be considered principal, not peripheral, to the analysis of women. This includes incorporating key factors such as race and/or ethnicity, sexuality, and economic status into any examination.

According to Potter (2006: 110), a black feminist criminology, which explores the nature of crime and victimisation among African Americans (and 'other groups of colour'), and responses to it, would also countenance the societal, familial, and other circumstances of black women. In Potter's (2006) view, these circumstances shape their victimisation. Added to race and social class, age and disability are examples of attributes that are said to interact with gender to expose those affected to qualitatively different forms of oppression (Crenshaw 1994; Daly 2006; Maidment 2006; Potter 2006).

Although intersectionality now represents a conceptual tool that is often employed to explore how identity interacts with oppression, it has since been argued that women might possess multiple identities and experience diverse realities, but they nevertheless share certain universalising qualities (Flavin and Artz 2013). In their study of women's experiences of violence in South Africa which comprises multiple cultural groups and in which the social stratification of women is quite diverse, Flavin and Artz were able to identify shared experiences of violence that affected the women's lives. They found that the unfortunate legacy of apartheid is visible in the 'indiscriminate violence, including sexual violence' many women experience, and the far from responsive criminal justice system that exists in the country (2013: 23). They subsequently argued that their findings highlighted the importance of remaining alert to the universalising inequalities that are endemic in many societies across the world, which disproportionately disadvantage women.

Gender and crime

The foregoing reveals that feminist theories and epistemologies have drawn attention to gender relations that shape women's experiences in wider society generally, and in the criminal justice system specifically. The theories and epistemologies also highlight feminists' responses to criminology's androcentrism. What follows is an account of the limited explanations of female crime the early feminist criminologists rejected. The explanations are based on stereotypical notions that still have some influence on the treatment of women in the criminal justice system.

Some early explanations of female crime

Smart (1976) who, as noted earlier, is recognised as one of the key scholars whose work prompted the emergence of feminist criminology, argued that the limited explanations of female offending that existed before the advent of feminist criminology were entrenched within the positivist paradigm (see **Chapters 13** and **14**). The explanations were deterministic because they attributed criminality to predisposing factors and embodied stereotypical characterisations of the female gender. According to Smart (1976), women were portrayed as a homogenous group whose behaviour was driven by biological and psychological forces beyond their control. Wider structural factors that tended to affect women differentially and impact on their experiences and behaviour, such as cultural expectations, class, and power inequality, were disregarded, as was their ability to exercise their rationality (Klein and Kress 1976; Carlen 1983). Instead, as Klein and Kress (1976) observe, female offending was attributed to their sexuality or unique biological constitution.

Illustrating this stereotypical approach to explaining female offending, some of the earliest criminologists contended that women were not biologically programmed to commit crime (Lombroso and Ferrero 1895). The reason proffered for this claim was that the biological constitution of the female sex controlled their personal attributes such as their perspicacity and disposition, and diminished the prospect of criminality (Lombroso and Ferrero 1895). It was also argued that women were genetically averse to criminality because they are less evolved beings compared with men, and were innately passive and committed to domesticity (Lombroso and Ferrero 1895).

An upshot of these accounts of female offending is that such behaviour was deemed anomalous, and women who went on to commit crimes were assigned unique (primarily negative) characteristics by the early positivist theories (Lombroso and Ferrero 1895). For example, as Smart (1976, 1977) observes, the theories implied that female offenders lacked the biologically-determined essence of female sexuality which would otherwise ensure female conformity. It was believed that they possessed anatomically masculine features and traits (Lombroso and Ferrero 1895). Thus, traits associated with the male sex were imputed to female offenders. Indeed, Lombroso and Ferrero (1895) argued that the absence of attributes conventionally associated with the female sex, such as a maternal instinct, is indicative of criminality.

Smart (1976) notes that attributing female offending to biological and psychological abnormality was tantamount to pathologising female offending. Depicting female offending as a pathological condition justified the imposition of court sentences that had the stated objective of treating female offenders in criminal justice institutions to 'cure' their condition. As already noted, the rationality of female offenders and the wider structural contexts of their offending were overlooked.

Others also subsequently proffered explanations of female offending that were also based on their biological sex, and overlooked their rationality. Pollock (1950) for example, characterised women as inherently criminal by nature. Dalton (1961) argued that hormonal changes due to menstruation or menopausal development catalysed female offending.

The cases covered in **Controversy and debate 11.3** provide a useful example to consider the points raised so far.

Feminist explanations of female crime

By the 1970s, feminist perspectives on female offending emerged, incorporating elements of the theoretical traditions cited earlier. Liberal feminists for example, argued that there was a gender gap in offending (typified by low rates of female offending) because women were socialised into roles that restricted the opportunities available to them to commit crime. In addition, it was argued that women were not as involved in criminality as men were, because unlike men, they were subject to greater supervision and social control. They were also socialised into internalising and exhibiting certain characteristics that were by their nature, more likely to encourage conformity.

Some of the subsequent analyses of female crime that emerged in the 1980s reveal the influence of radical, Marxist, and socialist feminist theories. Some, for example, offered socio-structural accounts that depicted female offending as the product of rational decisions based on economic adversity (Carlen 1988). Aligned to this was the view that economic marginalisation characterised women's status in patriarchal, capitalist societies. This economic marginalisation fueled their subjugation in society, and explained their resort to criminality as a means of survival (Box and Hale 1983; Chesney-Lind and Pasko 2004).

Some have gone on to analyse women's pathways into crime and have identified additional socio-structural factors that contribute to female offending. Key pathways are said to include: violent victimisation of women by men in patriarchal societies; history of childhood abuse; having intimate relationships or friendships with those involved in drug offences; and mental health problems (Belknap 2015; Belknap and Holsinger 2006).

Further developments in the study of gender and crime: the study of masculinities

We have already seen that the early feminists criticised the mainstream theories for overlooking the impact of gender on criminality, particularly given the gender gap in recorded crime statistics. In the 1990s, some perspectives on masculinities and crime emerged and extensively

CONTROVERSY AND DEBATE 11.3

The depiction of women in the criminal justice system

The objective of the exercise is to consider how women who kill are depicted in the criminal justice system. Critically compare the depiction of Beverley Allit with the portrayal of Benjamin Geen. Both are nurses who were convicted of killing their patients. Although the specific facts of both cases are somewhat different, the two nurses were convicted of the same crimes. Identify the differences in the judges' sentencing remarks in the two cases and possible explanations for the differences. Did the judges accord similar levels of rationality to both offenders during sentencing? What do the judges' remarks tell us about the portrayal of female offenders compared with the depiction of male offenders?

The case of Beverley Allitt

https://www.theguardian.com/uk/2007/dec/06/ukcrime.health

The serial killer nurse Beverly Allitt must serve a minimum of 30 years in jail for the murder and abuse of children in her care, the high court ruled today. A high court judge ruled that Allitt, dubbed the 'Angel of Death', should serve a minimum sentence of 28 years and 175 days, taking into account the one year and 190 days she spent in custody before being sentenced.

Allitt was given 13 life sentences in 1993 for murdering four children, attempting to murder another three, and causing grievous bodily harm with intent to a further six at Grantham and Kesteven hospital in Lincolnshire.

Allitt will be 54 before she will be considered for parole.

The former nurse was diagnosed as suffering from Munchausen syndrome by proxy (MSbP) when she carried out the attacks between 1991 and 1993.

The 39-year-old is now being held at the Rampton high-security hospital in Nottingham. Allitt murdered the four children by injecting them with high doses of insulin.

The judge made the following statement:

I have found that there is an element of sadism in Ms Allitt's conduct and her offending. But that sadism is itself, if not the result, certainly a manifestation of her mental disorder, and it would be unduly simplistic to treat it in the same way as one would if the offender were mentally well.

The case of Benjamin Geen

https://www.theguardian.com/society/2006/may/10/health.crime

A nurse who killed two of his patients 'to satisfy his lust for excitement' was jailed for life today. Judge Mr Justice Crane told Benjamin Geen, 25, that he would serve a minimum of 30 years for a 'terrible betrayal of the trust of others in the medical profession and his patients'.

Geen received life sentences for two counts of murder and 15 counts of grievous bodily harm. The staff nurse injected 17 victims with drugs including muscle relaxants, insulin, and sedatives to stop them breathing.

Although doctors revived 15 of his victims, two did not survive. Mr Justice Crane told Geen at Oxford Crown Court:

Your purpose was to cause a collapse of the patient in order that you could take part in the revival of the patient. It seems that you relished the excitement of that feeling of taking control but you must have known quite well that you were playing with their lives.

This was a terrible betrayal. You betrayed your nursing and medical colleagues and the vital profession of which you had been a member. Most of all, you betrayed the trust of the patients. They were in your care and you intentionally caused them huge damage.

During the trial, the jury heard how Geen 'came alive' and looked 'elated' as his patients went into respiratory arrest. During his closing speech, prosecutor Michael Austin Smith QC said that Geen must have known the fatal consequences of what he was doing but that toying with patients' lives was a 'price he was willing to pay in order to satisfy his perverse needs'.

---

theorised the links between the male gender (**masculinities**) and crime. Masculinities theorists believe that there is no singular 'masculinity' that can be ascribed to all men. Instead, multiple 'masculinities' exist and these are structured around a social constructed hierarchy which comprises the highly-valued **hegemonic masculinity** and other masculinities including subordinated masculinities. This section of the chapter explores these issues.

They also theorised the gender gap in offending (Messerschmidt 1993; Messerschmidt and Tomsen 2012). The study of masculinities and crime is influenced by several theoretical traditions, particularly femininist criminology. Its origins have been traced to feminists' analyses of gender, the work some men have done on feminist issues, and studies of gay and lesbian issues (Flavin 2001; Heidensohn and Silvestri 2012).

Masculinities theorists integrate gender identities, particularly masculinities which can be defined as expressions of normative or culturally constructed beliefs about the male gender. In their study of crime and victimisation, Messerschmidt and Tomsen (2012) explore the gender gap in offending. As they see it: 'Male offenders commit the great majority of crimes … and men have a virtual monopoly on the commission of syndicated, corporate and political crime' (2012: 190). Naffine (1997) notes that, in their analyses of the gender gap in offending, masculinities theorists argue that the gender gap exists because there is a close link between masculinities and crime, but they believe that the link is often taken for granted, or in other words, overlooked by mainstream criminologists (see also, Messerschmidt 1993).

Masculinities theorists such as Messerschmidt and Tomsen (2012) advance the view that masculinities intersect with crime, and men commit more violent crime than women. This is because male crime is sometimes attributable to the pressure on men to attain the socially prescribed 'masculine status and power' associated with hegemonic masculinity (Messerschmidt and Tomsen 2012: 151). This form of masculinity symbolises heterosexuality, toughness, power, authority and competition' in (Connell 1995; Heidensohn and Silvestri, 2012: 348). It is located at the top of a hierarchy of masculinities (Connell 1995; 2000). It is also emblematic of socially approved maleness and it ideologically legitimises male dominance in patriarchal societies (see also, Messerschmidt and Tomsen 2012). Men are socially conditioned to aspire to this form of masculinity but only few men in positions of power can attain it (Connell 1995). As we shall see in this section, masculinities theorists argue that those who fail to attain hegemonic masculinity might resort to crime as a means of obtaining the resources required for attaining it (Messerschmidt 1993).

According to masculinities theorists, Connell and Messerschmidt (2005), the notion that a hierarchy of masculinities exists was in part informed by the violent attacks and prejudices that were targeted at homosexual men by heterosexual men in the 1970s when homophobia emerged as a socially accepted male role. Heidensohn and Silvestri (2012: 348) note that in light of these developments, scholars began to postulate that some men possess 'subordinated masculinities'. Men with subordinated masculinities lack the attributes associated with hegemonic masculinity such as heterosexuality, toughness, and power, or lack the resources required for attaining the privilege and high social status that hegemonic masculinity embody (Heidensohn and Silvestri 2012: 348). Examples of the resources required for attaining hegemonic masculinity are academic achievement and the opportunity to engage in legitimate leisure activities (Messerschmidt 1993; Messerschmidt and Tomsen 2012). Some masculinities theorists argue that men with subordinated masculinities might resort to crime to obtain these resources and attain hegemonic masculine status (Messerschmidt 1993). Therefore, for some men, crime serves as 'a means of accomplishing gender' (Renzetti 2012: 135).

To summarise, during the 1970s, some feminist criminologists highlighted the gap in knowledge created by mainstream criminology's androcentricism and neglect of gender. Since then, several scholars have explored the factors associated with female crime whilst others have also demonstrated how gender intersects with other adverse social structures to disproportionately disadvantage some women more than others. Furthermore, masculinities theories of male criminality have theorised the gender gap in offending by emphasising that crime is typically an expression of some men's effort to attain a highly valued form of masculinity. See **New frontiers 11.1** which highlights new developments in the field of feminism following on from the study of masculinities.

NEW FRONTIERS 11.1

Queer, trans, and disability feminism

Since the advent of feminist criminology in the 1970s, and its expansion through the 1980s and 1990s to include the theoretical frameworks and epistemological positions described earlier, additional feminist perspectives have emerged. Added to the study of masculinities, examples of additional developments in the field are queer feminism (typically associated with Lesbian, gay, bisexual, transgender—LGBT feminism),

transfeminism, and disability feminism. These theoretical frameworks integrate intersectionality into their analyses of gender issues. Therefore, they explore how constructions and intersections of identities, such as sexual orientation, disability, race, social class, and other social categories, affect the experiences of groups whose identities do not conform to normative gender identities.

They study these groups' experiences as offenders in the criminal justice system where they are likely to be exposed to harsh treatment (for example, inadequate police protection from hate crimes, and punitive court sentences) because they do not conform to gender norms (see, Knight and Wilson 2016; Wolff and Cokely 2007). They also explore the groups' experiences as victims who are particularly vulnerable to hate crimes, again because their identities contravene normative identities including culturally constructed gender identities (see generally, Ball 2016; Balderston 2013; Butler 1990; 1999; Jauk 2013; Koyama 2003; Knight and Wilson 2016). The emergence of these perspectives demonstrate that feminist criminology is a growing field of study that has taken on board the intersectionality debates of the 1980s onwards. Consequently, it has expanded to accommodate the diversity of identities that could expose people to victimisation, and adverse treatment in the criminal justice system (see **Figure 11.10**).

Figure 11.10 A human rights demonstration for the transgender community, Halifax Pride Parade, Canada, July 2012
Source: ©istock.com/ tomeng

Gender and criminal justice

Two key interrelated theses have emerged from feminist criminologists' empirical analyses of women's experiences in the criminal justice system, namely the chivalry thesis and the double deviance thesis. Underpinning both theses is the idea that stereotypical notions of ideal femininity determine women's treatment in the system. Therefore, quite apart from the offence in question, gender is perceived to be the key factor that influences women's experiences in the system. In the following section we explore both theses and their implications.

Women as offenders: the chivalry thesis

According to the chivalry thesis, women receive more lenient treatment in the criminal justice system because of the chivalrous attitudes and behaviour of the predominantly male criminal justice workforce (Crew 1991). Chivalrous treatment in this context is more likely where the demeanour and circumstances of female offenders, and their offences, are not considered to be incongruent with stereotypical notions of conventional femininity.

The chivalry thesis is associated with Otto Pollak's (1950) account of female offending, in which he problematised the gender gap in offending. According to Pollak (1950), women are inherently more prone to criminality but their adeptness at avoiding apprehension or manipulating men into committing crimes on their behalf, explains the gender gap. He believed that women were innately reticent and deceitful and were, as such, able to conceal their crimes. In his view, women's ability to accomplish fake orgasms (unlike men) and to conceal their menstruation despite the discomfort associated with the condition, demonstrated their predisposition to reticence and deception.

His assertions have been criticised as uncritical, unsubstantiated (Smart 1977), and, perhaps consequently, ideological (Heidensohn 1985). Nevertheless, his work informed the chivalry thesis; he argued that although women were inherently more criminal than men, their crimes were often undetected because of their deceitfulness, and adeptness at hiding their crimes. Even when women's crimes were detected, male criminal justice officials, influenced by prevailing but misleading depictions of women as unassertive and gentle, offered them lenient treatment. Pollak (1950) believed that in a male-dominated criminal justice system, this tendency to treat women more leniently than men could also explain the gender gap in offending; many women escape criminal justice intervention because of the leniency of chivalrous officials.

Although chivalrous treatment might be beneficial to some women, it has been argued that the very notion of chivalry reinforces negative stereotypes of women as passive, inferior, and reliant on men for their protection (Steffensmeier, 1980; Gilbert, 2002; Rodriguez et al., 2006). By contrast, men are portrayed as independent, and as such, inherently more powerful. Critics of the chivalry thesis also note that what appears to be chivalrous leniency towards women is primarily paternalism (Chesney-Lind and Shelden, 2004). This is because lenient treatment is more readily granted to women who occupy what men identify as acceptable feminine roles or statuses, such as submissiveness and being sexually conservative, as might be exemplified by, for example, being married with children (Chesney-Lind 1988; Chesney-Lind 1999; Daly 1987).

Women as offenders: the 'evil woman' hypothesis

The evil woman hypothesis is another conceptual framework that has been employed to articulate the experiences of female offenders in the criminal justice system. Similar to the chivalry thesis, the evil woman hypothesis suggests that gender is a key dimension of the treatment of women in the criminal justice system (Belknap 2001; Rodriguez et al., 2006; Simon 1975). Both theses imply that decisions in the criminal justice system are not based solely on the offence; they are also influenced by gender. According to the 'evil woman' hypothesis, those whose lifestyles or circumstances appear to fall short of the normative standards of femininity set by men are deemed doubly deviant. Consequently, they are doubly condemned and punished; first for violating socially defined gender norms and secondly for violating the law (Carlen 1983; Heidensohn 1985; Worrall 1981). Those who are particularly vulnerable to more severe punishment include: homosexuals; those convicted of sexual misconduct; single mothers; those labelled as 'bad mothers'; and others whose circumstances and lifestyles do not fit in with the ideal gender role that is socially prescribed for women (Eaton 1986; Heidensohn and Silvestri 2012: 351; Mellor and Deering 2010). We have already seen that black feminism, queer feminism, transfeminism, and disability feminism are developments in gender studies which emphasise that groups whose identities appear to violate normative identities, including normative gender identities, are vulnerable to harsh treatment in the criminal justice system.

Some studies have explored the validity of the chivalry and the evil woman hypotheses, and they have produced mixed findings. While some suggest that women receive more lenient treatment (Curry et al. 2004; Hood 1992; Jeffries et al. 2003), others refute this, and indicate that women receive similar sentences to men, particularly when they are convicted of serious crimes (Farrington and Morris 1983; Daly 1994; Mellor and Deering 2010). Indeed, Mawby (1977: 42) found in his study that: 'when previous record is taken into consideration, females are more likely to be imprisoned than males'. These findings counter the assumption that women receive more lenient treatment than men (see also, Carlen 1983; Eaton 1986; Pearson 1976; Worrall 1981).

Added to the studies of women's experiences at the early stages of the criminal justice process (during interactions with the police, and whilst in court) other studies have examined the experiences of women in the penal system. These studies have not explored whether practitioners such as prison officers or probation officers offer some women chivalrous treatment and treat other women harshly because they are considered to be doubly deviant. But, the studies have documented the unsuitability of the system for female offenders. In England and Wales, the much-cited report by Baroness Corston revealed that most of the existing prisons are unsuitable for women, and geared towards men's needs (Corston Report 2007). Similar findings have been recorded by studies that highlight the unsuitability of existing probation services for women. For instance, the risk assessment methods employed in probation settings are said to be tailored to suit men's needs, and are as such inadequate for identifying the needs that could be targeted to address female offending (see for example, Martin et al. 2009).

Criticisms of feminist criminology

Feminist criminology has sustained several criticisms, some of which are explored here. First, the criticisms leveled at the key feminist traditions cited earlier are examined. Then, the criticisms targeted at the feminist epistemologies covered in this chapter are also explored. In addition, there is a brief reference to the advent of intersectionality as a key concept in feminist theorising, and the criticisms that were offered by those who argued that greater attention should be paid to the concept.

Criticisms of liberal feminist criminology

A key criticism is that those who advocate gender equality in line with liberal feminism for instance, do not challenge the patriarchal status quo; they are accused of accepting without question the supposition that men's views and experiences represent the norm or the yardstick for measuring appropriate standards of gender equality. Smart (1995: 42) puts it that:

> Basically the equality paradigm always affirms the centrality of men. Men continue to constitute the norm, the unproblematic, the natural social actor. Women are thus always seen as interlopers into a world already organized by others.

For the critics of liberal feminism, it is necessary to challenge male dominance and to advocate for gender-specific provision for women in the criminal justice system and in wider society. From this perspective, gender equality that facilitates the inclusion of women in existing androcentric systems, disadvantages them. As already noted, some of the studies that have explored the experiences of women in the criminal justice system, and the provision available to them, reinforce the importance of gender-specific policies that can accommodate the unique needs of female offenders (Corston Report 2007; Martin et al. 2009).

Critics of the liberation hypothesis which is also associated with liberal feminism, reject the claim made by the proponents of the thesis that the emancipation of women, and their access to opportunities previously foreclosed to them, have contributed to the narrowing gender gap in offending. According to the critics, the rise in female offending rates is attributable to the economic marginality that affects women, and the rise has been in relation to crimes that are associated with poverty and disadvantage, for example larceny, rather than women's liberation (Burman and Batchelor 2009; Daly 1989; Box and Hale 1983). These crimes are said to constitute rational reactions to adverse socio-economic circumstances (Batchelor 2005). It is also argued that the rise in rates of violent crime among women is a function of the harsh penal policies that have been targeted at women who appear to contravene feminine ideals (Batchelor 2005).

The findings of several studies that have explored the reasons for female violence, further repudiate the premises of the liberation and emancipation theses. For example, in a study that explored why women in prison committed violent crimes, Batchelor (2005) found that the tendency of some women to resort to violence as a means of empowerment and protection demonstrated that far from being liberated, these women, particularly those who were socio-economically marginalised, felt disempowered and vulnerable to violent victimisation (see also, Batchelor 2009; Burman and Batchelor 2009). Importantly, the studies also revealed that far from the stereotypical portrayal of women by the early positivists, as being unable to exercise a degree of rationality (unlike men), the women actively exercised their agency. In addition, they utilised their rationality to *choose* violence as a protective strategy. In **Conversations 11.1**, two discussants also draw attention to the agency and rationality with which some vulnerable women engage in activities that expose them to violent victimisation such as sexual assaults. The discussants note that the women's experiences of victimisation could in turn prompt them to 'act out' by committing crime. However, the discussants also allude to the continuing tendency to overlook women's agency and rationality, particularly in criminal justice contexts. This poses implications for the self-identities of the women and the effectiveness of interventions intended to address their victimisation and offending behaviour.

Criticisms of radical feminist criminology

According to Renzetti (2012), radical feminism has been criticised for presenting a one-dimensional account that portrays all men as predatory oppressors whilst overlooking female criminality. Studies that highlight the violent victimisation of women by men are accused of implying that women are passive and incapable of exercising

---

CONVERSATIONS 11.1

Victimisation, offending, and agency—with Jo Phoenix

This discussion between Roger Smith (one of the authors of this book) and Professor Jo Phoenix revolves around the victimisation of women when they enter the criminal justice system, or the experiences of victimised women who enter the criminal justice system.

JP (Jo Phoenix): Let's begin by discussing child sexual exploitation, and girls' involvement in gangs. Now, you can see how, sociologically, a girl of 15, 16 years old will, allow herself to be 'passed around'

a gang to be brutalised, or at least misused sexually for 'the gains', of being the object to be consumed, within a consumer society. So you can see how that identity, that subject position begins to make sense.

When you translate this into the world of policy, law and practice, the only thing that the people [in the criminal justice system] have at their disposal to deal with is the offender. Sexual agency or not. And the discourses around girls and victimisation and sexuality are so big that they, in a sense, override all the other potential possibilities.

RS (Roger Smith): And the problem is, it always seems to me, is that you don't then have an easy route towards solutions and ways out for young people who necessarily have perhaps ambiguous perceptions of themselves and need to resolve that. So in terms of being able to offer them an insight for response, that classification doesn't work at all.

JP: No, because it is tough to go up to a 16 year old and say, yes, you may have been enjoying yourself, or maybe you weren't. Maybe actually you were really hurt. But the law knows you as a victim. And that's a very difficult label to carry. Particularly if you're a victim of child sexual exploitation.

RS: And you thought you were exercising agency and now you're told you weren't, and you don't know what to do. You lose that one thing that you felt you had control over, in a way.

JP: Yes, so whether the interventions happen through the courts or whether they happen through social work, it's a very difficult subject position for the girl to operate. And then when you actually combine, and pull the lens a little bit back from just the girl and her subject positions and what are possibilities and what aren't, and you start looking again at some of the complex realities of the girls, who really are being harmed. That's not to say that that other category [who believed they were exercising control over their situation] aren't, but then there's a whole other category, isn't there, really?

RS: Yeah, who are coerced, directly coerced and feel powerless, and feel and are completely vulnerable, and the term victim works for them.

JP: Yes, absolutely. And for them they may be in situations where they're being offered the same solutions that they were offered before they got into that situation. More social work.

RS: Yes, and something that apparently didn't work previously?

JP: Yes. And they then may choose, because you and I both know people in extreme situations are resilient. They make choices. Not in conditions of their own choosing, and often those choices are so constrained that the only choices they have are between very toxic or extremely toxic choices. So in some circumstances, as we know, these girls may act out. They may commit crime. Because what they're actually experiencing is more equivalent to rape than it is the other category of girls. And what do we know about rape? We know that very few people will disclose rape. So they get caught up in the justice systems for the other crimes that they're committing, rather than the crimes that are being committed against them, and they don't disclose what's actually happening to them.

RS: No. And similarly, I wonder if some of the drugs offences, the large scale arrests for carrying large amounts of drugs through customs in countries which have very severe penalties, may be partly a product of getting into a situation where you're trying to exercise and buy, if you like, a little bit of space to be able to exercise some freedom. That bigger picture never really gets detailed. You just think about somebody who is a serious drug offender but what they're probably doing is trying to buy themselves a little bit of space.

JP: Yes, and I mean what do we know from feminists, criminology, and feminist studies generally? We know that those who report rape are only the tip of the iceberg. And so why should we assume that somebody who's caught up in the criminal justice system is going to be more likely to report rape? In fact, there's a whole series of arguments to say they would be less likely. So that link between their victimisation and their criminalisation, I mean, you know, methodologically, it's a minefield of a study. But those are the things that I don't think we as critical scholars have really fleshed out very much empirically.

Roger Smith, one of the authors of this book, and Professor Jo Phoenix, Chair in Criminology at the Open University, gender and crime expert, and contributor to The Oxford Handbook of Criminology *(Liebling, Maruna, and McAra 2017)*

their agency, although it is worth noting that some feminists also study female offending (Gelsthorpe 2004). Furthermore, radical feminism is accused of overlooking the progress that has been made to protect women from oppressive patriarchal social arrangements (Renzetti 2012). As already noted, laws and policies have been introduced to address domestic violence perpetrated by men against women in intimate relationships.

Criticisms of Marxist feminist criminology and socialist feminist criminology

Marxist feminism has been criticised for elevating the importance of economic class inequality (in which men enjoy greater economic power), and the gender oppression it breeds, over other forms of oppression that occur when gender inequality intersects with other inequalities (Maidment 2006). Socialist feminist criminology has also been accused of presuming that both genders comprise homogenous groups. Aligned to this, they are accused of identifying social class as the only factor that differentiates one group from the other. It is argued that this account overlooks the impact of other attributes such as race (Sudbury 2005).

Indeed, early versions of the key feminist traditions were generally criticised for homogenising women by identifying one social category (or a combination of social categories) as the key factor that explains the oppression of all women. For example, radical feminists were accused of focusing on gender inequality fuelled by patriarchy whilst overlooking other inequalities that also oppress women (Walby 1990). Racial and social class inequality were identified as examples of these inequalities. As already noted, this relates to the issue of intersectionality.

Criticisms of feminist epistemologies

This section considers additional criticisms of feminist criminology, and it focuses on the criticisms leveled at the feminist epistemologies that were explored earlier.

Criticisms of feminist empiricism and standpoint feminism

Feminist empiricism has been criticised for endorsing and adopting male-centred 'scientific' methods which presume that objective, gender-neutral 'facts' are discoverable, and consider scientific methods to be male-centred (Smart 1995). Some scholars, for example those influenced by early standpoint feminism, emphasise the role of women in producing knowledge of their subjective experiences (Smith and Skinner 2012).

Standpoint feminists are however, criticised for prioritising women's perspectives over others. Furthermore, early standpoint feminists were accused of wrongly depicting women's views as definitive knowledge of social

reality (Comack 1999; Smart 1995), and portraying the knowledge that is produced by academic researchers who adopt the standpoint epistemological stance, as superior knowledge.

It has also been argued that standpoint feminists depict women as a homogenous group (Smart 1995). They are accused of seeking to 'impose: a different unitary reality' on women (Smart 1995: 95), and women are portrayed as a group that can, with one voice, speak of the adverse experiences they share in an unfair androcentric social world (Smart 1995). This conceptualisation of women and their experiences discounts the racial, cultural and other structures of disadvantage that peculiarise the identities and experiences of some women (Carrington 2008). Again, this relates to the subject matter of intersectionality and the view that scholars should recognise how intersections of gender and other structures, impact differentially on the lives of those who are ascribed the same gender.

Criticisms of postmodern feminism

Postmodern feminism has been accused of relativism because it discounts knowledge as social constructions (Flavin 2001). It is argued that their dismissive perspective on knowledge could preclude them from studying and challenging dominant discourses. The objective should be to challenge these discourses, and replace them with accounts that highlight women's experiences (Cain 1990a; 1990b). As Smart (1995) notes, the critics maintain that leaving dominant accounts unchallenged amounts to an apolitical approach that is inconsistent with the feminist agenda of placing gender and the adverse experiences of women at the core of analyses. In addition, some allude to the impracticality of translating the theoretical tenets of postmodern feminism in the contexts of real world social research (see, for example, Flavin 2001). Principally, postmodern feminists describe all social categories as social constructions. They would therefore describe efforts to study how gender intersects with categories such as race and social class to oppress women, as tantamount to essentialising (or accepting as pre-given), social categories that are nothing more than social constructions (Comack 1999). It is argued that dismissing social categories such as gender and crime as social constructions does not mean that the categories automatically disappear; they still affect women's lives. As such, they deserve empirical scrutiny; it is necessary to explore how women give meaning to the social categories that oppress them and generally affect their lives albeit somewhat differentially (Comack 1999).

Furthermore, by presuming that multiple realities exist, postmodern feminists imply that striving for gender equality in order to alleviate the adverse experiences of women in androcentric societies is futile. This is because, in their view, both outcomes would impact on the target population (women) differentially; the outcomes will not produce any universal impact on women given their qualitatively different realities (Comack 1999).

In sum, a recurring theme that underlies most of the criticisms feminist perspectives have sustained is the contention that feminist theorising in criminology, particularly in its early development, focused primarily on the impact of culturally constructed notions of gender on women's experiences in society. Apart from postmodern feminism, the early feminist theories and epistemologies did not pay sufficient attention to other social categories that interact with gender to impact on women's lives. Instead they portrayed women as a homogenous group. They believed that although women might possess different attributes such as ethnicity, class, and political orientation, their gender exposes them to the same type of oppression. Smart (1995: 45) argues that a presumed 'sisterhood' prevailed in early feminist discourse. There was an implicit assumption that feminist scholarship and activism could be considered a joint enterprise embarked on by women who are unified by their shared ideals and shared struggle against androcentrism and patriarchy. We have seen that in the 1980s some began to challenge these presumptions by arguing that for some women, gender intersects with other structures of disadvantage to impinge on their wellbeing.

Feminist criminologists have also examined the impact of intersectionality on men's experiences in society. In their view, essentialising the male gender (the concept of masculinity) by ascribing inherent qualities to the concept (for example, privilege and power) overlooks the reality that some men do not possess those qualities. We have already seen that the concept of subordinated masculinities suggests that some men do not have access to the privileges associated with ideal masculinity in patriarchal societies (Connell 1995; 2000).

Conclusion

The advent of feminist criminology helped to redress the androcentricism that historically pervaded traditional criminology (Daly and Chesney-Lind 1988). Feminist criminologists sought to rebalance criminology's skewed focus on male offending (Gelsthorpe and Morris 1988: 98) and as a result of their work, several feminist perspectives on female crime and victimisation now exist. Additionally, feminist criminologists adopt diverse epistemological positions. These positions reflect their views about the most appropriate means of generating knowledge of women's experiences in the social world. Therefore, feminist empiricists prioritise forms of knowledge that emerge from scientific enquiry. Some standpoint feminists privilege women's views as the authoritative source of knowledge (Cain 1990b). Meanwhile, postmodern feminists problematise all sources and forms of knowledge, arguing that deconstructing what is depicted as authoritative knowledge is necessary to uncover the power structures that underlie knowledge production (Smart 1995). It is clear from the preceding description of key feminist epistemologies that feminist criminologists disagree over the precise constitution of authoritative knowledge, and the appropriate means of generating such knowledge: however, they are similarly motivated to generate forms of knowledge that can advance the welfare of women.

Furthermore, by advocating approaches to knowledge production that bring women's perspectives to the fore, feminist criminologists seek to generate knowledge that can help dispel the myths about gender and its relation to crime and criminal justice (Cain 1990b; Smart 1995). Through their analyses of the processes of knowledge production, feminist criminologists illuminate power structures that underpin these processes. As their study of gender and its impact on crime and justice has evolved, feminist criminologists have gone on to highlight how gender intersects with other social categories to expose those affected to even greater disadvantage. In doing so, they have moved away from the prevailing tendency to homogenise gender (Daly 2010; hooks 1984; Potter 2006).

Furthermore, studies conducted mainly by those whose ideas reflect the propositions of radical feminism have drawn attention to the hitherto largely ignored experiences of women as victims of violent crimes that are perpetrated by their intimate male partners (see for example, Dobash and Dobash 1998). They have highlighted the plight of women whose violent victimisation might be hidden or minimised because of their low social status and powerlessness in a male-dominated society.

SUMMARY

This chapter has been designed to help you:

- Identify the origins, definition, and key principles of feminist criminology

The key principles of feminist criminology are: the rejection of mainstream criminology's gender blindness and androcentricism; and the effort to address these by theorising gender and its links to crime and criminal justice.

- Understand the main theoretical traditions that underpin feminist criminology, namely liberalism, radicalism, Marxism, and socialism

Although the traditions differ in important respects, they share in common the belief that gender inequality that disadvantages women exists in society, and should be dismantled.

- Recognise the different strands of feminist criminology, such as feminist empiricism, standpoint feminism, and postmodern feminism

Together, the epistemological positions provide insights into feminists' views about the nature of knowledge, and how best to generate knowledge of women's experiences. Whilst feminist empiricism subscribes to orthodox methods of social science enquiry, standpoint feminism and postmodern feminism propose alternative methods that can be used to highlight women's lived realities.

- Appreciate how gender intersects with other structures of disadvantage

Some of the key positivist explanations overlooked female rationality and attributed female offending to predisposing biological and psychological deficiencies. The feminist accounts of female crime that emerged from the 1970s and 1980s onwards differed from the positivist explanations and reflected the tenets of the key feminist traditions. Feminist criminology has since expanded in several different directions and now incorporates insights from feminist perspectives that explore how intersections between gender and a range of identities affect people's lives. Examples of these perspectives are black feminism, queer feminism, transfeminism, and disability feminism.

- Identify relationships between gender and crime by considering feminist explanations of female crime and studies that explore links between masculinities and crime

Feminist criminologists have drawn a range of feminist traditions to provide accounts of women's experiences, including their experiences as perpetrators or victims of crime. The key feminist traditions that have influenced feminist criminologists are liberal feminist theory, radical feminist theory, Marxist feminism, socialist feminism, and postmodern feminism. Feminist criminologists have also adopted several epistemological positions in their study of gender and crime. These are: feminist empiricism, standpoint feminism, and postmodern feminism. In the 1990s, some perspectives on masculinities and crime emerged and extensively theorised the links between the male gender (masculinities) and crime.

- Consider the role of gender in the criminal justice system

Two key theses that have emerged from feminist criminologists' exploration of the experiences of women in the criminal justice have also been discussed in this chapter. Both theses illuminate the role of gender in the criminal justice system, and posit that women are exposed to discriminatory treatment that disadvantages them. Quite apart from their offence, the stereotypical notions ascribed to their gender inform their treatment in the system.

- Critically evaluate the criticisms of feminist criminology

The chapter has drawn together the key criticisms of feminist criminology. There has been an analysis of the criticisms that have been levelled at the key traditions in feminist criminology. Criticisms of feminist epistemologies have also been explored. The feminist traditions and epistemologies have received disparate criticisms, but a unifying criticism is that, apart from postmodern feminism, they homogenise women. They do not pay sufficient attention to the wider social categories that intersect with gender to adversely affect certain women. Race and social class are examples of these categories.

REVIEW QUESTIONS

1. What is meant by the term 'gender blindness'?

2. What are the main similarities and differences between liberal feminist theory and radical feminist theory?

3. How did positivism seek to explain female criminality?

4. What is the 'chivalry thesis'?

5. Outline the main criticisms of standpoint and postmodern feminism.

FURTHER READING

Burman, M. and Gelsthorpe, L., (2017) 'Feminist criminology: inequalities, powerlessness, and justice' in Liebling, A., Maruna, S., and McAra, L. (eds) *The Oxford Handbook of Criminology* (6th edn). Oxford: Oxford University Press.

This chapter has hopefully provided you with enough grounding knowledge to build on. An ideal next step would be to consult this chapter in *The Oxford Handbook of Criminology* to broaden your understanding.

Belknap, J. (2015) *The Invisible Woman: Gender, Crime, and Justice* (4th edn). Stanford, CT: Cengage Learning.

Renzetti, C.M., Miller, S.L., and Gover, R.A. (eds) (2013) *Routledge International Handbook of Crime and Gender Studies*. London: Routledge.

These are comprehensive texts that cover the experiences of women as offenders, victims, and professionals in the criminal justice system. Some jurisdictions, particularly the US, are given wider coverage, but an effort is made to present international perspectives.

Brownmiller, S. (1975) *Against our Will: Men, Women and Rape*. New York: Simon and Schuster.

Dobash, R.E. and Dobash, R.P. (1979) *Violence Against Wives*. New York: Free Press.

Both texts are notable examples of the scholarly work of the 1970s which reflected the tenets of radical feminism and improved awareness of the violent victimisation of women by their male partners.

Burgess-Proctor, A. (2006) 'Intersection of race, class, gender, and crime: Future directions for feminist criminology'. *Feminist Criminology* 1: 27–47.

This article offers an insightful account of the Intersectionality debates that instituted the so-called third wave of feminism.

Smart, C. (1976) *Women, Crime and Criminology.* Abingdon: Routledge.
This is a seminal text that provided the impetus for the emergence of feminist criminology, once again, we encourage you to read the original. It is a clearly written text that sets out the context from which the need for studies of gender and crime emerged.

 Access the **online resources** to view selected further reading and web links relevant to the material covered in this chapter.
www.oup.com/uk/case/

PART OUTLINE

12. Free will, classicism, and rational choice: The blame game

13. Biological and psychological positivism: Determined to predetermine

14. Sociological positivism: Determined to predetermine

15. Critical criminology—part 1: Challenging the 'usual suspects'

16. Critical criminology—part 2: New and future directions

17. Right and left realism

18. Integrated theories of crime

19. Searching for the causes of crime

Welcome to **Part 3**, which focuses on the aetiology of crime, its origins and causes. Here the causes of both criminal behaviour and state control are considered.

The section starts with a chapter of two parts. **Chapter 12** first explains the purpose of theory and how to interpret, test, and critically consider ideas, then moves on to discuss classical theories which assert that people freely and rationally choose to offend and therefore can, and should, be punished or have their choices prevented (by, for example, reducing offending opportunities).

The following chapters, **13** and **14**, take a positivist stance, using scientific methods to study crime and its causes. Crime is seen as determined (made more likely) due to biological, psychological, or sociological causes, meaning we should rehabilitate offenders or alter our society to reduce the likelihood of criminal behaviour.

Chapters 15 and **16** consider critical criminology which questions everything that has gone before: the idea of crime and the positivist and classical explanations of its causes. Indeed, it questions aspects of our society, such as state definitions of crime, which are assumed to be 'true'. **Chapter 17** then pulls together two very different responses to this critical tradition, left and right realism, which consider real problems faced by society and then suggest solutions.

The part closes with two chapters designed to identify certain explanatory themes and question others. **Chapter 18** considers grand theories which draw on central tenets from other ideas and combine them to build new, integrated theories. Finally, **Chapter 19** questions criminology's obsession with the causes of crime, especially in light of problems in defining crime.

Overall, this part will give you insight into the many aspects of human beings and societies which either move us to control each other or explain why some participate in 'unacceptable' behaviours.

PART 3

EXPLAINING CRIME

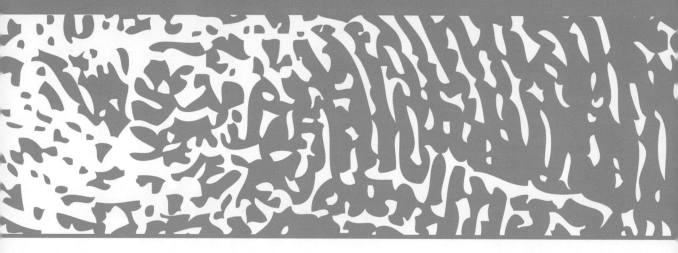

CHAPTER OUTLINE

Introduction	316
What is a theory?	317
Testing a theory	318
Different types of theory	321
Criminological theory	322
Classical criminology	324
Conclusion and consideration of modern neo-classical theories	336

Free will, classicism, and rational choice

The blame game

KEY ISSUES

After reading this chapter you should be able to:

- define the concept of theory and understand the purpose of it in the context of criminological study;

- evaluate different theories by understanding how to test the different elements;

- consider the main theoretical schools in criminology including classicism, positivism, interpretivism, and critical criminology;

- critically consider classical criminology; both the key thinkers that shaped it, and the policies to which it gave rise;

- appreciate the importance of free will and rational choice and demonstrate how these ideas in the 16th and 17th centuries underlined the building of the modern new criminal justice system;

- assess modern classical thinkers (neo-classical criminology) to discover how since the 1960s there has been a re-focus on the idea that criminals choose to offend and how, when, and where that might occur.

Introduction

Understanding criminological theories is essential if you are to identify, interpret, and assess criminal activities and why we control them. Grasping these theories will play a vital role in your degree; they underpin this entire subject, and you will be expected to know and make reference to different theories throughout your degree. You should not worry about this because learning these theories should not be difficult.

If theory is introduced gently and with the proper guidance and encouragement most students come to value its use in drawing together a logical narrative (story or set of ideas) from disparate information. It serves as a bridge between the real world, the research, and your learning. Reading a theory is to travel into someone else's mind and perceive reality the way they do. In fact sometimes all of us work with theory. Theories are the assumptions that allow us to make sense of the world; it allows us to make choices that work for us and to protect ourselves. We sometimes call this common sense—choosing not to walk alone at night down a dark alley is something that many choose because they have learnt that going down the alley might be dangerous (see **Figure 12.1**). We have taken data and built an understanding of our world—a theory about danger and dark alleys. That is all criminological theorists do. The theorist takes you on a journey and explains what they are thinking and how you might better understand parts of the world. They show you the evidence on which their ideas are based and explain how they are interpreted in order to build their hypotheses. They enable us to make sense of parts of the world that we have not got firsthand knowledge about and explain things outside our experiences. They also explain how they fit into other ideas or theories that already exist. The theorist:

(a) takes a complicated part of our lives or our world;

(b) takes information from lots of observations or from asking lots of people about that activity;

(c) draws out important conclusions that helps us to understand the activity;

(d) through this, also allows us to predict when the phenomenon might recur; and,

(e) if it is something negative then the theory should throw light on how to prevent it.

Figure 12.1 Formulation of everyday theories: walking through an alleyway, at night and alone, could be dangerous

Source: Atmosphere1/Shutterstock.com

A useful theory therefore helps us to understand part of what is going on around us and may also help to predict when certain events may happen. Theory therefore allows people to unravel and understand things which are otherwise very complicated, such as the nature of unacceptable offensive and criminal behaviour, societies, desire to control it, and the means they use to alter, punish, and prevent such damaging behaviour. A theory synethsises a substantial amount of information collected from observing the real world and tries to discern patterns so making sense of what might otherwise be just lots of independent pieces of information. Criminological and social science theories therefore look for general truths; a useful theory might explain the circumstances or conditions under which a particular behaviour or outcome is likely and why those conditions are important to the outcome. It should therefore allow us to prevent it from happening (see **Figure 12.2**). Ultimately, a theory enables us to identify and name a problem, understand and predict it, and plan a means to deal with it.

The example in **What do you think? 12.1** shows you that there is no reason why you should find studying theory difficult, it just requires different ways of looking at ideas and information.

Theorising about the world around us opens up a wealth of stimulating insights into the whole area of criminology. It affords a much fuller understanding of

Identification Observations Conclusions Predictions Prevention

Figure 12.2 The theoretical process

WHAT DO YOU THINK? 12.1

You live in a house with four other students and you have very little money and you are very careful not to overspend. Every Saturday you go shopping and buy a packet of digestive biscuits. There are 21 biscuits in each packet and these are your treat, you allow yourself three biscuits a day.

You start to notice that biscuits are going missing but no-one will own up to taking them. They all dismiss you as petty, why would you care—you should be willing to share with your friends.

You become obsessive and watch the kitchen all the time, noting when people go in and then checking your biscuits. Over a few weeks you note that every time one of the biscuits is missing Karin, one of your flatmates, has been in the kitchen by herself.

This is a theory—you believe that Karin has been taking the biscuits. Is this definite? Is it proof? Is it enough to confront her?

If you are sure you then believe that you know—but it is still a theory. There is no hard proof. However, the knowledge, the theory, allows you to make choices about how to deal with the problem. In order to try to resolve things you may not need actual proof, your theory may be enough to give you some options about how to resolve the issue:

- You could confront Karin, maybe get cross and have an argument. However, she may deny it. Also she is a friend and, as your flatmates say, it is only biscuits. Is it worth losing a friend over, even if she has been underhand and lied?

- If Karin is very short you could now just put the biscuits on top of a high cupboard and the problem would be sorted without needing to have an argument, and without losing a friend.

The theory gives you an idea of how you may solve the problem. If you think things through there is usually more than one way to deal with any problem and a theory may help.

our world, our society, and peoples' behaviours. Theories help us to understand how and why things happen so they can help to show us where we need more research or how we might tackle problem behaviour in a way that might prove to be effective. So although some people have a perception of theory as something that does not do anything useful, theories in criminology are generally very practical.

This chapter will consider what a theory is, how to assess a theory, and explain some of the overarching ideas in criminology in a way that can be understood by you even if you are new to the field. It will simplify and explain theorists' ideas without distorting the core of the theory. It will thereby afford you the opportunity to read and better understand those theorists and so assist you to use the theories in your studies and to be willing to open your mind to other theories that will be introduced in other parts of this book. It is *not* meant as a substitute

for reading the primary texts but to help you understand those texts when you do go to read them (see Newburn 2009 for excerpts from original criminology texts, the key readings for most of the theories covered in **Part 3** or you can, of course, read the originals in full).

Each core theory will be presented through an initial explanation, then an analysis of its strengths and weaknesses. Introduced in this way a study and consideration of core theory can be very valuable throughout your studies. It can help you to develop analytical and critical skills which will serve you well long after your degree (see also **Chapters 29** and **30**). Looking at theory allows you to think logically and to find weaknesses and strengths in your own and other theories and ideas. It may even give you the confidence to think creatively about some of the issues you study in criminology. Please remember that all learning is a tool you can use when you approach new questions.

What is a theory?

Criminology and the real importance of theory is maybe best understood once you recognise that the subject is all about questions. Instead of thinking about theory, it is probably sensible to think about answers to questions. There are many theories in criminology and students often ask which is correct—they want to know which theory gives the right answer, but this is the wrong way of looking at things. It is the wrong question. The important thing to remember is that most theories have an element of truth in them and most have areas where they do not hold true at all. That does not mean that one theory is right and another wrong, rather it means that one theory (Theory A) is a more useful answer to a particular question than another (Theory B). Once you understand that each theory is answering a slightly different question or wants to give an answer which will be useful to a different audience, you will understand that they are each discussing slightly different aspects of the same puzzle, and therefore that each may have something to offer. So far from being competing claims they may each be adding a useful facet to an understanding of a very complex issue (see **Chapter 18** on integrated theories). Each therefore is of use but each needs to be considered alongside the question it was trying to answer. In trying to understand or assess a theory it is sensible to consider some basic questions:

- Why is this theorist making this claim—what questions are they trying to answer?

- What is the significance of the claim, what does it say that might be important, useful, or worthwhile?

- What is the problem with the theory, what does it assume, and are those assumptions acceptable?

- What is controversial in the theory and is that controversy useful, does it challenge policy or practice and make you think again?

- Who or which theories seem to disagree with this theory? What are the points of disagreement and which is better argued? Do the disagreements arise because each is answering a slightly different question or intended for a different audience?

Once you understand that the subject is best approached through questions it is easy to see that often our understanding or reading of criminology is not shaped by theory or answers but by which questions we choose to ask. For example, most people first ask: why do people offend? But is that the right question? Before there can be a breach of rules or an offence there has to be a rule that one is expected to obey. So an important early question might be why are certain behaviours unacceptable—this was something discussed in **Chapter 3** which asks the question—'what is crime?'. Other questions one might ask include:

- In what sense, if at all is a general theory of criminology either possible or desirable?

- What is the point of conceptual claims (claims based on ideas) and how can one evaluate them?

- In which sense can one speak of the relative merits of different criminological theories or ideas?

The important thing to remember throughout your studies is that you must be an active learner which means that you do not just accept and learn what you are told and what you read but rather that you think and think critically about all that information. This does not mean that you have to criticise everything but rather that you consider it all and learn to discern what is good or useful from what may be bad, of little use, or may even be damaging. On top of coming to these conclusions it is imperative that you are able to explain why something is useful or something else may be damaging—that you support your claims with reasoned argument.

Testing a theory

In criminology as in all social science a theory needs to be relevant to the real world. If it has been developed with care it should illuminate or help one to understand situations, feelings, human behaviour, or human interactions. When reading theories or explanations of behaviours you may want to assess the following issues and ask some or all of the questions in **Figure 12.3**.

Therefore a theory should provide a simple explanation of the observed relations relevant to the phenomenon. It should be consistent with the observed relations; that is

the interpretation of information found in the research should be true to the data. It should clarify how it relates to an already established body of knowledge. A theory should provide the means for verification and revision. It should stimulate and highlight areas where further research and investigation are needed. In short it should be simple (or as simple and clear as possible), testable, novel, supportive of other theories, internally consistent, and predictive.

Logical consistency	• Is the theory clear and **does it make sense**? This might be called *logical consistency*. Here, you are here trying to decide whether it is clear which questions the theory is trying to answer and whether it manages to answer them. Do all the parts of the theory hold together, or are there contradictions?
Coverage	• Linked to the question of whether it makes sense is the question of **whether everything included in the theory is necessary**. A good theory should explain complex ideas relatively briefly (though it may not always feel brief). This is often referred to as Parsimony. • As well as asking if everything covered is necessary, does the theory **ignore aspects which are essential** and should have been included or at least explained? For example, much criminological theory fails to consider whether age or gender might make a difference to its utility as an idea.
Breadth of claims	• Does the theory **try to explain all criminal behaviour or only certain types of crime**? Does it apply in all places and at all times or does it only explain e.g. crime in the night-time economy or crime in rural areas? Does it explain the criminal activities of all different types of people or should it be seen as explaining only, for example, youth crime or male crime? It is always worth considering whether a theory is limited by individual characteristics such as race, gender or age or by situational characteristics such as urban or rural or a particular country. Often theories do not state they are limited in these ways, they are often written as if they apply to all people, as if they are generally applicable. However, if all the data supporting a theory is from particular groups (male, the young, a particular ethnic group or a particular type of environment) then there is good reason to question its more general applicability. If the theory comes from abroad or is based on data collected in one state its findings may not apply in other countries as parts of it may depend on local cultural or ethical values. Theories should clarify all of these aspects and if they fail to do so then that is one aspect that you can question about the theory but **please remember that failing to confine a theory does not mean that the ideas have no worth, merely that their worth is confined to a particular time, place, type of behaviour or type of person**.
Verification	• Ideally one should be able to test (**verify or falsify**) a theory. In science a theory is usually an idea that can be tested in a controlled experiment—once you control everything except what you are testing the results will hold true (verify) or not (falsify) the theory. In social science the ability to replicate findings exactly is unrealistic as people are less predictable than objects. One cannot 'control' for important aspects but the overall theory should be capable of being tested. Note that even if the theory is 'verified' it does not mean that it is 'true', no idea or generalisation can ever be proven to be entirely true (Popper 1994). Because of this one often says that it is important that a theory is able to be tested and disproved. However, even if a theory is 'falsified' it may not mean that the theory has no use. It may be that the theory was written about behaviour in one country or place and that it may still hold true there but it may not hold true in another place; in this case it would need to be altered to note the fact that its claim should be narrowed.

Figure 12.3 Useful questions to ask when testing a theory (*continued*)

Empirical validity

- Is it **supported by research evidence**—empirical validity? If there is supporting research then you need to consider how the research was collected—look carefully at the methodology and methods for each of its supporting sets of data. To see how well supported it is one needs to know whether the evidence comes all from one place and one time or whether there were multiple sites and the evidence was collected over time. If there is no supporting evidence is it just making grand claims based on ideas alone (see some of the ideas from early classical theorists later in the chapter) or is it making a suggestion—setting out a hypothesis that needs to be tested (and can be tested)? Just because it has not been tested yet or the tests are limited or flawed or even question the theory does not necessarily mean that it has no merit.

Relation to other theories

- Is it **supported by, or does it relate to, an already existing body of knowledge**? It is important for theorists to indicate how their ideas fit together with what we already think we know. It may be that it will question some ideas we think are 'true' or will support others. It is important for the theory to indicate how and why it questions or supports other theories.

Accuracy

- How **accurate** is it? How effective is it at predicting new phenomena (new or future happenings)? Also may ask **how useful is it**? Is it sufficiently clear and well supported to be able to use it to design new policy and practice to deal with offending behaviour? Even if it appears to be both accurate and useful there may be reasons, other theories, ideological problems, cultural issues or political or economic reasons why it cannot or will not be put into operation. For example no-one can dispute that once a person is dead they do not pose any further crime threat but there would be ideological reasons for not having a policy which would execute all convicted offenders.

Critical evaluation

- There are then things which you might ask to help you to critically evaluate the 'truth' that the theory purports to uncover. In all your criminological studies you should watch out for certain things such as: where the **power** lies to define and control behaviour; whether there is an underlying inequality which the theory should, but does not consider; is the theory or are the behaviours of individuals it purports to describe shaped or controlled by social background (e.g. **class**) which is not recognised; does the theory ignore underlying **discrimination** which may affect the situation; does it ignore underlying **political, economic, or ideological** issues that may affect the way in which we should interpret the data; are there issues of **justice** (see **chapter 2**) that should be but have not been considered? In fact each of these is a very valuable tool in evaluating and considering almost any question in criminology.

Counter claims

- Finally, what are the counter claims? Many theories are or can be juxtaposed to other ideas/ theories and these should be recognised.

Figure 12.3 (*continued*)

Different types of theory

Criminology is a very wide subject; its only real connecting feature is that it is the study of crime (as defined by law) or deviance (breach of: a moral code; a social norm (or rule); a basic human right; or something which a powerful group does not like and can prevent a powerless group from doing, which may also be criminal). Under this linking element one finds multidisciplinary approaches each trying to explain and predict criminality or its control. Because it relies on many disciplines, you will need to be able to work with concepts and ways of thinking drawn from a number of different disciplines, e.g. political science, law, social science, sociology, human geography, psychology, etc. Each of these approaches will offer a different, and possibly conflicting, answer as to how and why crime occurs and what should be done to prevent it. Some appear to be common sense but this does not make them right, nor does it mean they are too simple and therefore wrong. Others appear to be farfetched or to challenge the way in which you have so far understood something; their strangeness does not make them wrong nor does the fact that you find them clever make them correct. Each needs to be tested against the list in **Figure 12.3** but most importantly against the evidence of human behaviour.

The multidisciplinary nature leads to diverse theoretical ideas, different theories which purport to explain a situation from a different perspective. Although they may be very different they may each add something useful to the puzzle of explaining crime, criminality, and control. This makes criminology a complex and sometimes frustrating discipline. It is a contested and fought over area so there is always an interesting and disputed discourse. This means that it is always possible to use one idea to question or validate another and therefore to build a convincing and intelligent critical discussion. It also means that there are opportunities for new cross-disciplinary research and theoretical ideas.

Before moving on to try to give shape to some of the theoretical complexity it is important to look at different types of theory. First we will consider what different types of theory are trying to do and then look at what different types of theory are trying to explain.

Some theories are known as **hypotheses**, suggestions about what will happen in particular situations or that certain things are linked. These theories might be seen as speculative in that they think about the world as they know it and then attempt to explain what is happening or what might happen. A hypothesis has not yet been tested, it is an educated guess about what will happen.

Normative and descriptive theories

Others are normative and set out ideal standards about the way in which things should, in that theorist's opinion, happen. These theories may set out beliefs or values and might attack what others set out as real occurrences as being set on unacceptable or unfair systems. Marxist theory often falls into this category.

A lot of criminological theory is based on empirical data and might be thought of as descriptive theory. The researcher chooses an area of study and gathers data (what the researcher hopes is typical data) and describes what is happening. It uses the data to build categories and predict and explain behaviour (see **Chapter 4** for definitions of descriptive and normative in relation to criminal justice models).

Many researchers use their data to revise old theories or to question and expand what we think we know and understand. So a researcher may take an old theory or a general theory and apply it in a particular situation, discover that parts of the theory do not hold true and so suggest alterations to the theory for that situation. For example, one theory may have been built on data from an urban environment and it may need to be altered to take account of a rural environment.

Grand theories or integrated theories

Grand theory is a different type of explanation. Only a few criminological and sociological theories fall into this category. A grand theory, sometimes referred to as integrated theories (see **Chapter 18**), offers an explanation to a problem which is applicable in most situations. It is generally fairly abstract, based on formal theorising by one person or a group of people rather than growing out of measured phenomena. It often draws together other ideas or theories which are based on observed and measured facts and often draws together different disciplines. Most grand theories are so broad that they are not really capable of being tested: though theoretical concepts based on them may well be open to testing.

You will come across many grand theories in your study of criminology. It includes very broad ideas. For example, structural functionalism sees society as a complex system, each part of which works together to build a solid and workable society. It assumes that the ideas, common values, common understandings of symbols and customs are shared by most in a society and are necessary—the glue that helps to bind the individuals together to form a healthy society. They are almost more important than each individual (for an example and a full consideration see Durkheim 1858–1917 ('Durkheim and functionalism') in **Chapter 14**).

Grand theories often draw on many disciplines and are important to criminology and to sociology more broadly. There are also theories which are wholly criminological such as Tittle's control balance theory which will be briefly considered in **Chapter 18**. A useful grand theory will organise materials in ways that people can use to illuminate their area of study. They offer an understanding usually based on generalised assumptions about what they consider to be the important problems facing the discipline. For example, **rational choice** theory assumes people think rationally before they act, it assumes that we are all quite calculating and want to ensure the best outcomes for ourselves, it assumes an inward looking and basically selfish approach or rationality. One drawback is that grand theories are difficult to verify (see **Figure 12.3**) due to their sheer breadth.

Particular theories

There are then smaller theories, particular theories which either try to explain one thing or a few contained questions. These tend to be simpler, more focused, and are more likely to be capable of being tested or verified. They may form a part of or sit beneath the general or grand theories. For example, deterrence theory might be seen as part of rational choice theory. Deterrence theory suggests that rather than punishing after someone offends we should structure our world and our punishments to deter future offending. This fits well with rational choice theory

and will be discussed in the classical criminology section to follow.

To aid your understanding of the building blocks of a theory we will now consider some of the things which often constitute one.

- To begin with, there are items called concepts which are often part of the theory. They draw together a class of data by some characteristic or set of characteristics which marks them out. A concept is a representation (a word) for a thing, e.g. offender, building, chair, etc., which is used as a shorthand to call together all other things which share its characteristics or as many of its characteristics as possible. Naming a concept or a group of like things or occurrences allows us to talk about them.

- An abstract concept or construct is a word for concepts with no physical characteristics and may be thought of as ideas, for example, free will, freedom, social class, democracy, undeserving. Often a construct forms from concepts that are linked in some way. It is important that the theory specifies or explains what is meant by each term (concept or construct) so that the reader is sure that he or she is understanding the theory correctly, interpreting it in the way in which the theorist meant it to be understood.

- The third part of a theory is the principles or propositions which explain the relationship between two or more concepts or constructs. They explain how the concepts and constructs interrelate and so permit us to understand how specific outcomes arise. So when all these parts are fitted together they form a clear theory.

When fitted together these make up a theory. Each aspect should be clear to permit the theory both to be used to predict future occurrences, given the circumstances necessary to the theory and to be tested.

Criminological theory

Theory allows us to name what we observe, to describe and explain what is going on in the world. Criminological theory improves our understanding of why laws are made, how and why we enforce rules and punish those who transgress, what the effects of crime control are, how and why people choose to break or obey rules, and what the effects of rule breaking may be. It allows us to explain what we see and experience and so provides a platform from which we can try to alter things. It supports us in identifying and understanding problems and so permits us to suggest policies and practices which might alter the situation and resolve the problem.

Criminologists ask very diverse questions:

- Why do we control (declare illegal) one type of behaviour and not another, and who chooses?

- When, why, and how do we enforce those rules and is that enforcement legitimate?

- Why do some people in certain situations break societal rules and why do others conform? This may ask why certain classes of people offend, e.g. why most crime involves males rather than females, or it might look more closely at individual situations—why some individuals in very similar circumstances offend when others do not?

Note that a theory which explains group behaviours, e.g. why men offend more than women, may be based on individual difference (biological differences between men and women). Whereas a theory which purports to explain individual difference may be based on a social, structural problem such as unemployment or poverty.

There are so many different questions and approaches that it helps to draw similar ideas together. Here we will briefly consider four types of theory: classical, positivism, interpretivist, and critical.

Classicism

Classical criminology originally arose in the enlightenment period in the eighteenth century and is based on arguments about the causes of crime and how it should be dealt with. It was not based on research or evidence, but instead focused on ideological considerations about how to control and punish. Classical criminologists focus on the offence and how to deal with it; they tend to see offending arising out of free will or rational choice because they calculate that they will gain something. Classical thinkers portray offenders as rational and calculating. Because they choose that behaviour they can be held responsible for any offences they commit and they can therefore be punished. Once the state has proven their guilt they should be punished proportionate to their wrongdoing.

Originally, the theorists who suggested classical thought argued that their work was designed to fight against arbitrary use of power which gave rise to unfair outcomes and inequality. However, many critics of classical theory argue that the system to which it gave rise is about the continuation of present power and authority and gives rise to inequality. They argue that it is about the preservation and protection of social elites. Classicism will be considered at greater length later in this chapter.

Positivism

Positivist criminology began to emerge through the 19th century and was heavily influenced by the power of science that was emerging in other fields. Positivists strove to collect knowledge about the social world in the same way that scientists collect information about the natural world—through the collection of facts. They tend to study the offender or society, rather than the crime. This group of theorists believed that the social world could be measured and by collecting information we would uncover an objective external reality to explain behaviour. They considered that they could be value neutral when conducting research, that is that the research would not be influenced by their own values or opinions so any findings would be true.

Positivists collected information about the social world and when they found links they often drew causative conclusions. Therefore many positivists took (and still take) their factual results, they may find that two things are related and assume a causal link. For example they may find that there is more crime in unlit streets, a useful finding which could lead to more lighting in order to prevent offending. However, many take findings like this too far and suggest that the lack of lighting causes criminality instead of realising that the cause is something else and the lack of lighting merely provides an opportunity to offend with impunity.

At its heart positivism finds that two things are related. It often claims to explain that relationship but rarely collects the data to permit a full explanation—it is usually merely descriptive. Despite the descriptive nature of their findings they often attribute behaviour to biological, psychological, or social influences and see the behaviour as determined by one of those factors. If this is the case the behaviour is pathological and one should not really blame the offender as their behaviour was determined by something outside their control. In this case the offender is not really responsible for their actions and should be treated or rehabilitated rather than being punished. Treatment or rehabilitation may be very invasive and the necessary intervention will not be limited by the seriousness of the crime but rather by the underlying problem as discovered in the research. Most positivist ideas are largely based on quantitative research and it is often used to test a hypothesis.

Interpretivism

Interpretivist criminology rejects the idea that complex social and human interactions can ever be fully measured. They feel that science can never measure the subjective thoughts and feelings that give rise to human behaviour and human interactions. We cannot treat people as objects and their behaviour cannot be explained by merely taking simple measurements. Interpretivist criminologists reject the idea that there is any measurable objective reality because they argue that social reality is constructed and negotiated. They argue that it is only through a study of the whole persona and the world they inhabit that one can begin to interpret their actions. Key to these theorists is a desire to interpret or understand behaviour or a situation through the eyes of those participating, so that the individuals would recognise themselves as interpreted by the researcher. It seeks to give meaning to situations and is subjective, opinion based, and founded on qualitative research.

Critical criminology

Critical criminology emerged in the 1960s and challenges the classical, positivist, and interpretivist epistemologies. Critical criminologists accept that reality is constructed and recognise the differences of place, time, and approach. It argues that one needs to question the accepted understandings or constructions of society and test them from different perspectives. Here it is often necessary to study how power and authority are constructed and how inequality and discrimination is experienced and frequently accepted. It is often about conflicting conceptions of how and whether society should be controlled. It is also about how the apparent consensus which exists in our society today should be questioned, what holds it together. They reject the idea that there is any measurable objective reality or true consensus because they argue that social reality is constructed and negotiated. These theories often critique social construction from a particular perspective—Marxist, feminist, racist, etc. Critical criminology focuses on and is critical of the way in which society is structured and the effect this has on the way in which people behave and the way that their behaviours are judged (for a full consideration see **Chapters 15** and **16**).

In considering each theory and theorist it is sensible to remember that no theory comes into being in a vacuum and no theorist's ideas appear out of nothing. Each theorist will have been influenced by certain types of theory, certain ways of interpreting the world, and will have used particular methods or ways of interpreting data. When reading a theory it is useful to be aware of these broad influences—such as those discussed here—it may help to both understand and critique the ideas. The remainder of this chapter will consider classical criminology and the modern ideas with which it is associated. It will, therefore, consider the place of free will, risk assessment, and rational choice. Other chapters in this Part of the book will introduce you to positivism (biological and psychological theories in **Chapter 13** and sociological theories in **Chapter 14**), critical theories (**Chapters 15** and **16**), left and right realism (**Chapter 17**), and grand or integrated theories (**Chapter 18**). The Part will close with a discussion of the causes of crime in **Chapter 19**.

Classical criminology

As noted earlier, classical criminology is traditionally believed to be born out of Enlightenment thinking in the 18th century. The Enlightenment was the first time crime and criminal justice were seriously considered by theorists and it is from this time that the early criminological theories arise. Many modern systems of crime investigation, procedure, and punishment can be traced back to these ideals. Before the Enlightenment, problem behaviour (if dealt with) was solved by the use of power, often an arbitrary use of power. The state and those in authority often used fear to control the people and torture might be used in order to elicit a confession (see **Chapter 24** for early forms of punishment). The punishment was harsh and openly used to back up the power of the state (monarch) and the large land-owners or the church. The old systems were feudal—power came with land ownership (and wealth) which were concentrated and held by a few people, nobles. Ordinary people enjoyed very few rights and were expected to obey their feudal lords. When someone broke the rules how they were dealt with often depended on who they were and whether they could protect themselves. Justice was unpredictable. Punishment was, by today's standards, cruel and often physical—public flogging until someone bled, burning hands, death, and banishment were all common punishments. Punishment in continental Europe was particularly severe. These

sound barbaric to us but many then believed they were justified and necessary to retain order. In some instances they were less severe than what had been used in earlier times, death would normally be faster rather than protracted; there might be fewer lashes of the whip than had been the case in previous times. Many thought they were already living in a less unforgiving world than their parents and grandparents.

Key thinkers in classical criminology

John Locke

Enlightenment thinkers, what we now call classical thinkers, challenged the arbitrary use of barbaric punishment and questioned how it could be thought of as justice. They also questioned the absolute power of monarchs and noblemen and some hid their identity and their writing for fear of being punished by those in power. They argued that societies should be run on fairer grounds. One of the early general enlightenment thinkers was the English philosopher John Locke (1632–1704, see **Figure 12.4**). In very simple terms he argued that all nations and all societies should be run so that each person only gives up a

Figure 12.4 English philosopher John Locke (1632–1704)
Source: Sir Gottfried Kniller/Public domain

portion of their liberty, that necessary to a fair and functioning society. Each person should then be able to rely on the state to protect their interests from those who are greedy or unfair, a form of social contract (Locke 1690). He was also one of the first thinkers to argue that each and every person in a society enjoyed conscious thought and was capable of making choices based on previous experience or knowledge.

Locke's revolutionary ideas helped to form the basis of classical criminological thought which encouraged every man to think for themselves, make their own choices and not be controlled by either the fear of arbitrary state punishment or religion. Classical criminologists argued that each person should retain the right to choose how to live and behave; the state should only rarely intrude on and limit that choice. So at its heart, the Enlightenment saw each individual as someone who exercised free will and used rational thought to decide how to make their choices and how to act. They saw each individual as reasonable and assumed that before a person chose how to act he or she would weigh up the possible benefits and costs of that action for themselves. They would then decide which action would be most beneficial for them, which one made sense and then and only then they would act.

Cesare Beccaria and Jeremy Bentham

The two theorists most commonly linked with classical criminological thought are Cesare Beccaria (1738–94) and Jeremy Bentham (English philosopher, 1748–1832). Both believed passionately that each person should make rational decisions and that the state should get rid of barbaric punishments. They recognised the potential for criminality in each person—everyone is capable of greed and bad behaviour—but called on people to refrain from criminal behaviour, and to respect each other. These two thinkers agreed that: the barbaric and unpredictable forms of punishment then used needed to stop; and that each individual had rational choice and should be expected to make choices sensibly (rationally). However, they disagreed on many other details.

For Beccaria, an Italian criminologist and philosopher, when people failed to live up to this ideal the state needed to protect them from each other; it is only with such protection that everyone can live freely and without fear. In this situation state power should be permitted to protect one citizen from the unacceptable behaviour of another. Beccaria in his short treatise (a theory) entitled *Dei Delitti e Delle Pene* (1764) or in English *On Crimes and Punishments* (see its front cover in **Figure 12.5**) argued that unacceptable behaviours (crimes) should be clearly set out and the punishment for breaking the law should be clear and proportionate to the harm. He said that only then could people rationally choose to respect the law. He went on to argue that when a crime is committed no punishment should be allowed until the incident is investigated (only touched on by Beccaria) and the perpetrator was found guilty in a court of law following evidence to prove that guilt (legal and rational proof of guilt).

All the way through this process, Beccaria argued that the accused had rights which should be respected. Once

Figure 12.5 The frontispiece of Beccaria's *Dei Delittie e Delle Pene*
Source: Public domain

this situation was reached then Beccaria argued that punishment should follow. Where this happens punishment is not only acceptable because they have chosen to infringe the rights of others but is expected in order to protect others, to redress the harm inflicted by the crime. Although punishment is deserved it should not be excessive. Punishment should only be as much as is necessary to mark the harm caused, any more or less would be unjust.

Beccaria believed the process of investigation, proof, and punishment should be swift in order to keep the link between the act and the punishment and to help to prevent criminality. He argued that with clear legal and just systems rational men would see the punishment and not choose to transgress. He saw a just system which caught and punished real offenders as likely to deter others and he considered that it was more important to prevent crimes than to punish once they happen. A fair system that made sure that only the guilty were punished and punishment was only as much as was necessary to redress the harm caused by the offending and so deter others. For Beccaria the system needed four things:

1. **A just and fair process**—if the wrong person is punished or the system is believed to be arbitrary or corrupt it would not deter.

2. **Exactly the right punishment**—too little punishment and it might fail to meet the seriousness of the harm and also fail to deter; too much punishment would be an unjust act of violence and reduce respect for the law so it will fail to deter. Beccaria argued that to have maximum deterrent effect punishment should be just a little worse than the harm inflicted. He also stated that the death penalty should be removed and never used.

3. **Speedy justice**—essential in order to retain the link between the crime and the punishment in the mind of both the offender and of others.

4. **Certainty**—that people believe that offenders will be both caught and punished. Beccaria argued that deterrence only works if people are certain that they are going to be punished. If they believe they will get away with something then they will offend.

All of this assumes that people are rational and that they always consider what the outcome will be before they participate in any activity. This should all sound very familiar; Beccaria was one of the founders of modern criminal justice systems in many countries. The theory is very legalistic (Beccaria was legally trained) and draws out many modern ideas such as justice for all, rights for those accused in court, and fair and just punishment. The call for the punishment to reflect the harm done in each case was the start of what is called retribution or retributive justice (see **Chapter 24**, for detail on retribution). Beccaria suggested

a particularly pure form of retributive justice whereby one could not increase punishment for repeat offending as each time a person transgressed the punishment should meet the harm done on that occasion. There were a number of problems with Beccaria's ideas, for example, he assumed that all people had the ability to reason and therefore should be called to account. Children and the mentally ill were assumed to be rational and able to choose not to offend so could be punished if they transgressed.

The English philosopher Jeremy Bentham added other aspects to the classical school (Bentham 1789, reprinted 1907). He suggested a slightly different form of classical theory, that based on utilitarianism or the greatest good for the greatest number. Bentham believed that everyone wants to maximise pleasure and minimise pain or unpleasantness. Law breaking occurred, he argued, when someone thought they would be happier if they offended than if they did not. The state therefore has to ensure that the pleasure or happiness which the crime will bring is outweighed by the punishment or unpleasantness. He argued that punishment usually only needed to be a little bit more unpleasant, just enough to deter criminal behaviour and ensure the law was not broken.

Whereas Beccaria strongly bound the level of punishment to the level of harm committed, Bentham would permit more severe punishments if they would prevent offending. Beccaria believed that to deter offending and for justice to be served the punishment should fit the crime. However, for Bentham conformity to the law was paramount for the greatest good of the greatest number. Therefore punishment should just outweigh any pleasure that would be gained by offending and that would ensure compliance. If compliance required more punishment than was necessary to redress the harm done he would argue that the greater punishment should be inflicted in order to prevent future offending. Bentham would embrace greater punishment for repeat offenders in an attempt to convince them not to reoffend. That being said, if conformity could be guaranteed without punishment, through education or rehabilitation, then that lesser intervention in the offender's freedom should be used rather than punishment. This is punishment based on what one aims to achieve—deterrence or the prevention of offending—rather than based on what someone has done—retributivism, as suggested by Beccaria.

Bentham argued that as little punishment as necessary should be used. He considered the death penalty was generally too severe. However, where Beccaria would not use it at all Bentham accepted its use in cases of murder. Bentham firmly believed in prison as a form of punishment and even designed a prison, called the Panopticon (see **Figure 12.6**), in which each prisoner could be constantly watched from a central point. Bentham had a more sophisticated concept of reason and recognised that the

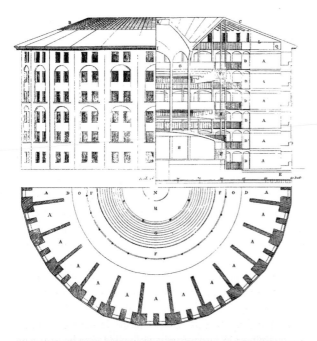

Figure 12.6 Bentham's classic Panopticon design, and a modern incarnation; the Presido Modelo Prison, Cuba

Source: Jeremy Bentham and Friman/CC BY-SA 3.0

mentally incapacitated should not be punished. He also rejected punishment if the victim consented, which is interesting when one considers that sadomasochism is still illegal (see **Chapter 3**) in England and Wales.

Classical criminology in a historical context

Classical criminology and the Enlightenment thinkers are generally credited with the changes to the criminal justice system which ensued. They were credited with the building of what is now seen as a modern system of criminal justice, though this view should not go unchallenged. The Enlightenment thinkers and classical criminologists were operating in a society already facing problems, one looking for new ways of dealing with offending. The industrial revolution was under way and beginning to build in western European states. These societies' traditional ways of operating were therefore already under threat. The ruling classes were being challenged, first in the American revolution of 1776 and later, closer to home, in the French revolution of 1789. These revolutions challenged the authority of the state and the supremacy of monarchs. Other European states also experienced upheavals through the changes to land use.

The control of the poor through the feudal system was breaking down as the working poor chose to migrate to cities to seek factory labour. This was the start of a fully waged economy needing new forms of control. Industrial systems, property ownership, and the newly emerging population bases all needed to be legally regulated. The ruling classes were unsettled by these changes and wished to retain their power even if that meant relinquishing previous systems of control and at least paying lip service to the instigation of more humane and just systems. Therefore the adoption of classical systems might be seen as resulting from the social upheaval rather than from classical criminology or the Enlightenment theorists. The ideas were a product of their time, were successful, preserved, and widely disseminated because they served a purpose—the continuation of the power systems even if in a somewhat altered form and more rigidly answerable to law.

For whatever reason, states were willing to alter their systems of governance and chose generally those suggested by the classical school. Therefore classical criminology was an idea shaped by the surrounding upheavals which also shaped the likelihood that states would accept the ideas. New states such as America and France were particularly strongly influenced; their constitutions are based on Enlightenment principles. However, other states also adopted classical theorists' ideas.

The influence of classical criminology

Throughout Europe, classical ideas shaped the law and jurisprudence including the criminal justice system, from suspicion through arrest, and trial to punishment. The authorities had (and still have) to prove guilt through a trial based on due process (see **Chapter 4**—What is justice?) which respects the rights and interests of suspects. Torturing people into confessions was replaced by investigation and fair trial. Once guilt was proven states treated offenders as rational actors and ensured that punishment reflected the crime. This was generally done through retributive justice, punishment shaped by the harm done. The more severe punishments of the body such as corporal punishment and the death penalty declined and are no longer used in England and Wales. Despite this focus on punishment reflecting the crime many modern criminal justice systems (including England and Wales) embrace a complex idea of deterrence which leads to more severe punishment of repeat offenders than might be expected as a result of the harm done. Two central aspects of classical thinking and their influence on criminal justice require closer consideration.

Firstly, the centrality of free will and choice is reflected in one of the core legal aspects at a criminal trial: *mens rea*. In almost every criminal trial two things need to be proven: *actus reus* and *mens rea*. *Actus rea* are the factual actions that need to be proven, the actions that are prescribed by law. It is *mens rea* that is affected by classical thought. Almost all criminal offences require the prosecution to prove a guilty mind (*mens rea*; there are some crimes, such as driving without brake lights, which do not require proof of a guilty mind). *Mens rea* is the intention to act in a way which is proscribed by law, it is the fact that a person chooses to do something which is illegal. Therefore to convict a person of most crimes the prosecution needs to prove beyond reasonable doubt both that they performed the proscribed acts (did what they are not permitted to do, *actus reus*) and that they intended to do those acts (that they chose to act illegally, *mens rea*). The guilty mind is about choice not motive. There may be some criminal acts that are done for love and compassion but are still crimes. I might intentionally kill someone because they are in pain and they beg me to do it. This is still murder because of my intention; my motive is not taken into consideration in decisions as to whether to convict, although, in some cases, it may be a reason for a less severe punishment (more recently it is something taken into consideration in deciding whether to prosecute, although on strict legal grounds it should not be). Therefore, the choice to act illegally is central to being able to call an individual guilty and being able to punish them for their choice.

Secondly, classical theorists considered deterrence to be the core aim of the criminal law: it should deter future unacceptable behaviours. For this to occur the punishment needed to be sufficiently severe to ensure that the criminal did not gain from their crime and yet not so severe as to allow it to be seen as unjust. This is known as proportionality in sentencing and in many states (including England and Wales) it is central to the sentencing of each and every offender. It is also central to the setting of the maximum sentences when acts are prohibited (when prohibiting a particular act Parliament considers how harmful the act can be and sets the maximum punishment in line with the possible harm). Without this proportionality, if murder had the same sentence as theft, criminals might choose to kill witnesses (to a theft) in order to prevent the authorities from discovering that they committed the crime.

Proportionality deters this type of decision as if they do kill witnesses their punishment will be far more severe than it would be just for theft. The idea is that proportionality of sentencing prevents criminals from gaining from their crime and so should deter them from choosing to offend in the future. For deterrence to work in this way punishment needs to be both fairly swift (happen soon after the offence so that they link the punishment and the choice to act) and certain; the rate at which the authorities solve crimes and punish offenders needs to be high (if not people will continue to offend and take the chance that they will get away with it). In sentencing each individual the level of harm done indicates the upper limit of punishment. However, the actual punishment may be reduced to take account of mitigating circumstances, to take account of good behaviour, or of reduced guilt.

These two aspects of modern systems of criminal justice display the important way in which the theories have had a real, lasting, and important impact on modern justice. However, modern systems also embrace ideas such as rehabilitation and restorative justice which do not fit with classical theories. Therefore whilst many core aspects of justice are based on the ideals of the classical thinkers other ideas can also be found in modern criminal justice systems. The embracing of classical ideals also gave rise to problems, however.

Limitations of classical criminology

Over reliance on every person enjoying rational thought led to the full punishment of children and the mentally ill or impaired as if they possessed full mental capacity and were able to make fully rational choices. Rigidly punishing each person for the harm done prevented judges being able to take account of different factors and might lead to injustice. For example, **Chapter 4** suggested that justice would be better served if one could take circumstances into account, e.g. when a starving person steals food one should treat them less severely than other such thefts. Strict adherence to classical ideals would have prevented many of the advances in our systems:

> There would have been no ... adjustment of fines to the means of offenders, no suspended sentences, no probation, no parole, no special measures for young offenders and the mentally ill.
>
> Radzinowicz, 1966: 123

Of course classical thinking has not stood still. Theorists such as H.L.A. Hart (1907–92) have re-evaluated classical thinking and taken it into what is known as neo-classical (literally, new classical) thought. Through their work the concept of justice and how it should work has been refined over time so that capacity and responsibility are now more carefully considered. Today we recognise that children and those with mental impairment should be treated differently as they may not be fully capable of rational thought. We also recognise that malicious intent (intending to wrong someone with no justification) should be treated more severely (shows more responsibility) than acting under necessity or error. So, stealing out of greed may be worse than stealing in order to eat. These neo-classical thinkers have recognised complexities in behaviour and so argued for more complex sentencing decisions, ones which can take into account differences in responsibility. Neo-classical approaches tend to try to temper the core classical ideals with seeking either just outcomes or outcomes that may be more likely to achieve a particular aim such as prevention. However, the changes have never interfered with the basic classical link between the need to call people to account when their choices (their free will and rational decisions) are unacceptable to others. Even with these modernisations of the theory there remain issues.

Culpability

Whilst neo-classical thinking has allowed some issues such as capacity and more complex sentencing decisions, it still leaves the basic problem of its rigidity. Classical criminology and court and punishment systems based on it have problems dealing with differences between defendants. To treat people differently interferes with the core idea that conviction and punishment should be based on free will. Classical criminology assumes that if you are capable of rational decision-making then you always make rational decisions. However, in reality many of us act on impulse, without thinking things through; then to be punished as if we had considered all eventualities appears a little unjust.

Intentions

It also has problems with taking into account differences in crimes. It sees one case of assault or murder the same as another and yet both for the victim and offender they may be very different. For example, intentionally killing someone in order to rob a bank is murder but so too is intentionally killing someone you love, who has repeatedly asked to die in order to be put out of extreme pain and misery. To classical thinking and therefore to our legal system both are murder and both require life imprisonment (more recently 'mercy' killing is something taken into consideration in deciding whether to prosecute though on strict legal grounds it should not be). Whilst overall the system may be just it cannot deal with nuance and subtlety and this leads to injustice in some cases.

Timing

Classical theory believes that it is important that punishment happens very soon after the crime is committed so that people can see and understand the connection between the two. In practice there is always a conflict between the speed in obtaining a conviction and the fairness/justice of the process (also important to the classical ideals). In practice ensuring that the correct procedures are followed and being just is often time-consuming so resulting in a delay in convicting anyone. Classical theory cannot resolve this conflict.

Power structures

An issue that is often overlooked is its relationship with power. Classical approaches tend to ensure that the present power structures remain largely unchallenged. Those in power tend to make criminal laws that protect their interests. Furthermore, reliance on free will and rational decision making as the underlying basis of crime fails to explain why the poor tend to be accused and convicted of crimes more frequently than the rich. It suggests that rational decision making is more likely if you are rich. Can this really be the case? An alternative explanation might be that those in power (generally the rich) make laws they are less likely to break. For other discussions concerning the complex and often unjust relationship between classical criminology and power see **Chapters 16** and **17** (and **Chapter 10** where race is considered and **Chapter 11** which discusses gender).

However, the core of classical thought has always been this calling to account and the idea that it should prevent bad choices both by that individual in the future and by others who see what happens, that it has a preventative aspect. This preventative use of classical thought has been taken further in ideas such as rational choice theory.

Neo-classical criminology

For many years classical ideas took a back seat in criminological work and became more of a tool used by lawyers and jurisprudence. Because it was the core of the criminal justice system classical ideas were generally used to discuss processes and punishments. The core of criminological thought for most of the 20th century was to consider why crime occurred and what we should do about it. As noted by Garland (2000) from about 1890 through to the 1970s there was confidence that through a combination of improved social conditions and rehabilitation one might reduce crime by altering the offender's disposition or likelihood to reoffend or by softening the worst problems caused by structural problems like poverty and unemployment. However, the end of the 1960s saw a loss in faith that this would occur and the beginning of an era in criminology where 'nothing works' or 'penal pessimism' took over and led policy making.

For offenders this led a move away from welfare and rehabilitation towards punishment as the underlying factor in the way in which they would be treated—a move back to a purer form of classical decision making in court. Of course, if during the punishment someone might also be rehabilitated this was seen as a bonus. In case pure punishment failed there was a resurgence of neo-classical thinkers intent on using classical ideals to reduce crime in ways that did not rely on working directly with offenders. Most of these theorists do not see crime as arising out of a disposition in certain individuals to offend but rather out of choices and argue that policies should be adopted that make the criminal choice less likely, so reducing offending. They therefore focus on reducing the opportunities for crime or increasing the risk of being caught if you do offend. Most work by altering the environment to reduce criminality. The core of these theories is that altering the environment means that potential offenders will be less likely to choose to offend; the change influences people's choices. Neo-classical criminological theories such as rational choice theories and the others in the rest of this chapter were born out of this movement.

Classical criminology is at the core of modern neo-classical criminological theories as they both start from the idea that offenders want to gain an advantage from their offending behaviour. They want to maximise pleasure with minimum pain. It ignores any other motivations and focuses on this cost/benefit analysis to explain everything. It therefore assumes that people weigh up the benefits and disadvantages of particular actions and make choices based on that assessment. So the core assumptions are that:

- each human being is rational;
- rational consideration involves weighing up gains against possible dangers;
- rational assessment decides how each person will behave (both their legal and illegal behaviours);
- before acting each person weighs up the likely pleasure against the possible pain;
- the choice will depend on which will give the person most individual pleasure;
- possible future punishment (if it is sufficiently swift, severe, and certain) may reduce the likelihood that illegal behaviour is chosen.

Here the offender is a rational actor with power to make decisions. Punishments available if they are caught doing something wrong may act as a prevention (classical theory) for some people in some situations, or at least may reduce the number of times they choose to offend. However, neo-classical theorists in the 1980s wanted to take this further and look at rational choice in the shaping of crime prevention policy.

Rational choice theory

At the heart of rational choice theory are Cornish and Clarke (1986 and 2014) who argued that for most people even quick decisions, based on minimum data, would follow a pattern of self-interested rational choice. Rational choice, they claim, is at the core of whether to offend and when, where, and with whom to offend. Offending would occur if there was a suitable target which was not protected. The idea was therefore suggested that if one made something harder to offend against (protected it) then the potential offender would move on to something else.

Rational choice theorists study why some people in some circumstances decide to behave in criminal ways and how one can change those choices. In 2006 Cornish and Clarke set out a refined consideration of their rational choice theory. Basically an individual will only choose to participate in any particular act if they will benefit from it. A crime indicates that the individual thinks that they will benefit from that offending activity; it does not indicate that they think they will benefit from other criminal acts. When deciding whether to participate in a crime each individual has to weigh up many issues. Not all aspects of a situation are clear and each potential offender has to weigh up risks and uncertainties and try to arrive at the decision which is most likely to benefit them. There is no blueprint to the decision making. The way in which decisions are made and outcomes arrived at differs in each situation. There is no pattern which always works, it depends on the situation and the type of crime they are considering participating in. There are generally two layers of decision making—involvement decisions and event decisions and each is a complex set of choices that occur at different times.

Involvement decisions

Involvement decisions are those about whether to engage in crime as opposed to other types of activity. They generally concern the values, attitudes, and personality traits that lead a person to be more likely to accept criminal, or particular types of criminal, behaviour. So someone may believe that substance use should not be regulated and so be open to involvement in that activity, and may have friends who participate but that does not mean that they necessarily offend themselves. However, it lays them open to doing so if they so choose.

These involvement decisions are depicted in **Figure 12.7**. This figure notes aspects which may lead someone towards or away from crime. For example, a young man who lives in an area where crime is common and whose father offends: (1) may have learnt some criminal techniques from

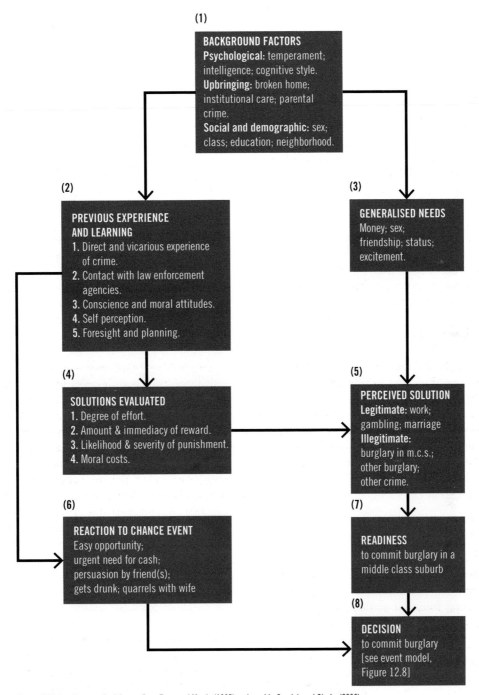

(1)
BACKGROUND FACTORS
Psychological: temperament; intelligence; cognitive style.
Upbringing: broken home; institutional care; parental crime.
Social and demographic: sex; class; education; neighborhood.

(2)
PREVIOUS EXPERIENCE AND LEARNING
1. Direct and vicarious experience of crime.
2. Contact with law enforcement agencies.
3. Conscience and moral attitudes.
4. Self perception.
5. Foresight and planning.

(3)
GENERALISED NEEDS
Money; sex; friendship; status; excitement.

(4)
SOLUTIONS EVALUATED
1. Degree of effort.
2. Amount & immediacy of reward.
3. Likelihood & severity of punishment.
4. Moral costs.

(5)
PERCEIVED SOLUTION
Legitimate: work; gambling; marriage
Illegitimate: burglary in m.c.s.; other burglary; other crime.

(6)
REACTION TO CHANCE EVENT
Easy opportunity; urgent need for cash; persuasion by friend(s); gets drunk; quarrels with wife

(7)
READINESS
to commit burglary in a middle class suburb

(8)
DECISION
to commit burglary [see event model, Figure 12.8]

Figure 12.7 **Involvement decisions**—From Tonry and Morris (1985) and used in Cornish and Clarke (2006)

Source: Tonry and Morris (1985) Crime and Justice Volume 6, University of Chicago Press

his father; (2) so when he needs money; (3) he sees the easiest way to get it to be burglary (4 and 5); he sees his chance (6 and 7); and so offends (8). By inserting different facts **Figure 12.7** can also explain why or how a person may choose not to offend (either not commit this burglary or never commit a burglary). Furthermore, the factors noted in **Figure 12.7** may alter over time so the factors that opened someone up to become involved (such as their temperament or upbringing or the fact that they need money, see in **Figure 12.7**) are different from those which may make such involvement a normal part of their life— they realise they are good at offending, it brings them money or happiness or escapism, it may result in a change of peer group which supports the offending (see **Figure 12.7** again). Other factors may lead them to stopping their involvement: they may become more settled, e.g. with a

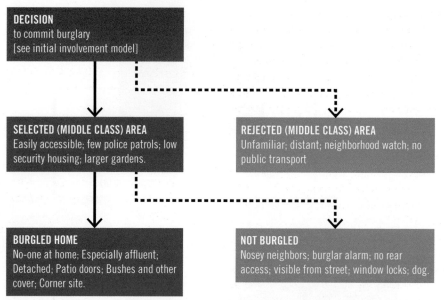

Figure 12.8 **Event decisions**—originally from Tonry and Morris (1985) and used in Cornish and Clarke (2006)

Source: Tonry and Morris (1985) Crime and Justice Volume 6, University of Chicago Press

partner and not want to chance being caught; the security may be increased so that opportunities are no longer available; they may get caught or almost get caught; they may secure a job; and some or all of these may lead them to stop offending, to desist. It is important to note that involvement decisions are specific to each separate crime so that just because someone may be willing to or open to committing burglary does not mean that they are open to committing murder or rape.

Event decisions

Event decisions are those factors which influence the decision about whether to commit a specific crime, e.g. to commit a burglary from this particular house now. This decision involves all sorts of aspects. There is the decision to commit a burglary (see the involvement decision in **Figure 12.7**) but then one has to select the area in which it will be committed—this is the event decision which is depicted in **Figure 12.8**. As noted in **Figure 12.8** the first part of the decision will take account of how easy (or difficult) an area of housing (an estate or a particular road) is to access, whether it is overlooked, and what level of security is available. **Figure 12.8** also notes that the next level of decision making is to select an exact house to target – target selection. This could be chosen by asking the following questions: Is it empty? Is there a dog or a security system? Is it possible to enter without being seen? etc. Following target selection one has to decide how to enter, when to commit the crime, how to escape, and then how to get rid of the stolen property. As the individual

becomes a more skilled burglar they may choose more lucrative areas and houses to enter, they are becoming more professional.

In rational choice theory crime always serves a purpose; it is not pointless. Originally many thought the idea of purpose was very limited—an economic advantage. However, purpose for Cornish and Clarke (2006 and 2014) is a broad concept and includes greater happiness, prestige amongst one's peer group, excitement, and sexual or other gratification. This takes account of benefits and punishments that might accompany offending, but also recognises that the way in which these benefits and punishments are viewed and rationally weighed up may alter over time or as peer group, learning, and professionalism alter.

The discussion about decisions taking place suggests that people sit down and consider all the options at length before deciding to offend. That is not what Cornish and Clarke (2006) are suggesting. They recognise that in many cases the decision is made quickly or with reduced capacity to be rational (they may be drunk, very young, or mentally impaired). However, even in these instances they still argue that there is a rational choice even if that choice may be bounded or conditional. They argue that criminals, like everyone else, are making the most rational or sensible decision for them in the time, with the information and with the capacity they have at that moment. Even a quick decision is a decision. In many instances the decision to commit a particular crime is made fairly quickly. Even if the crime is planned (and many are not) the offender is likely to encounter unexpected problems and need to decide how to deal with those; for this many rely on experience and instinct.

Whilst the original classical criminologists considered that offenders would weigh up benefits (often long term) and punishments, Cornish and Clarke (2006) suggest that offenders tend to focus on the immediate risks and benefits, what the crime will give them now compared to the immediate likelihood of being caught. Other factors that are often considered are frequently referred to as situational variables such as their skills, the tools available to them (cannot commit computer crimes without a computer), their personality and background, whether they need or are motivated to offend, whether they have the opportunity, and whether something triggers the actual event. The punishment they see as less relevant to the immediate decision.

Using all these elements Cornish and Clarke then began to build crime scripts which are accounts of how the decisions leading up to a crime and following the crime (getaway and selling the stolen goods) might be taken. Most human activity can be broken down into a script, a logical sequence of events which when together describe and possibly explain an activity. For example the crime script for eating in a restaurant might be: enter the restaurant; get shown to a table; study the menu; order; be served; eat; get the bill; pay; and leave the restaurant. Crime scripts are similar, they walk us through what might happen and consider and explain the rational choices included in the activity. They often explain and answer the questions as to who, what, when, where, why, and how. For example the crime script for a pickpocket might be:

Preparation	Select a general area in which to pickpocket; Dress and behave appropriately for that setting.
Pre-activity	Arrive at the location; Loiter and watch the crowd but ensure that one blends in; Identify a suitable target; Move in close and create an opportunity e.g. bump into them.
Activity	Take hold of the target goods—wallet, purse, mobile phone, etc.
Post-activity	Move away from target; Do not draw attention; Find a more private location; Secure important items such as cash and cards; Dispose of unwanted items such as the wallet or purse; Pocket immediately useful items e.g. cash; Sell other items such as cards and phones; Spend money.

WHAT DO YOU THINK? 12.2

Create a crime script for one of these offences:

- bank robbery;

- house burglary;

- shoplifting.

Consider what aspects need to be present for this crime to be committed. Classify each aspect of the crime into: preparation; pre-activity; activity; and post-activity.

Using your script consider what might be done to prevent the activity.

This script might be used to suggest that people should be more careful to keep valuable portable goods, cash, and credit cards in zipped pockets within bags or zipped pockets inside clothes to ensure that they are not available to pickpockets.

Theorists have constructed these scripts for many types of crime in an effort to try to prevent or predict such offences (take a look at **What do you think? 12.2** to have a go yourself). Rational choice theory does not explain why certain people or types of people offend; rather it explains why crime happens. It is interested in the situations and circumstances in which crime is likely to be chosen. It focuses on the situations and opportunities which make crime possible or more likely and suggests policies which might deal with those possibilities.

Rational choice theory has been used by some policy makers as a reason to increase the severity of punishments. The argument goes:

(a) if offenders make rational choices about whether to offend or not; and

(b) they choose to offend because they will gain more by offending than they will lose by being punished; then

(c) the punishment is too lenient.

To use rational choice theory in this way is understandable but displays a lack of understanding of its finer points. A more serious limitation of the theory lies in its almost complete disregard for what it terms 'background factors' (see **Figure 12.7**). These are individual and structural aspects linked to crime. They are mentioned but then largely ignored by rational choice theorists. They are not intending to look for ways in which policy might alter these underlying elements/causes of crime, they even claim that policies such as rehabilitation programmes have failed to prevent criminality.

Despite these shortcomings the theory is important as it reminds criminologists and policy makers that merely relying on individual and structural underlying causes of crime is to miss the fact that people do make choices. People's behaviour is not determined purely by other forces, they are active decision makers and we should search for ways to alter their decision making processes.

Routine activity theory

Cohen and Felson (1979) added aspects to rational choice theory and suggested routine activity theory. They argued that for crime to occur there were three things necessary: a motivated offender; a suitable target (it might be a human victim or an object such as a car or a house); and the absence of guardians (as well as the police this includes other people who might see what happens and also surveillance systems such as CCTV). All three had to be present at the same time and in the same place before a crime would occur (the chemical reaction would take place). This is a wonderfully simple idea which can help understand crime and so suggest simple ways to prevent it. The theory is now most closely associated with the American criminologist Marcus Felson. He argues that a motivated offender, a suitable target, and the absence of guardians will tend to converge in the routine patterns of people's lives. As with rational choice theory, crime is here at the centre supplemented by the motivated offender. Here people's routine activities add the predictive element as to where, when, and against whom crime might be committed. When looking at victims and trying to predict victimisation a similar theory comes to the fore—this is lifestyle rather than routine activity theory but it is used in similar ways to predict personal victimisation. Routine activity theory is wider than rational choice theory, although each is focused on similar aspects of the problem. It is termed routine because it studies the everyday activities or patterns of activities that people follow. However, routine also means the normal rather than the unusual. For routine activity theory, crime is therefore linked to normal things that occur in society, not to abnormal or pathological aspects of life. Here the opportunity to offend arises because of what happens normally in a society.

Felson was interested to explain changes in crime rates over time. He noted that post Second World War when welfare provision was increasing and poverty was being tackled crime was increasing. From this he argued that crime was not explained by weighty and pathological problems such as poverty, inequality, unemployment, or social exclusion which had been at least partially tackled by the welfare system. Rather crime was to be understood in human frailties such as temptation which led people to be motivated to do things they should not. This, along with

increased opportunities due to a large number of houses being empty during the day and therefore lacking people to watch over them, meant that crime would increase. Motivation, a suitable target such as a growing number of portable and high value goods in peoples' homes, and lack of a capable guardian because both adults in a house frequently worked all day all came together so crime increased. There were other factors which also fed the crime wave such as increased access to private transport to travel to and from the crime scene. Here social prosperity actually opens up more opportunities for crime rather than acting as something which will reduce offending.

A large part of their theory was that people's routine activities had altered in ways that made offending more likely. The labour market routinely took people out of the home leaving houses empty and so good targets. As more people were out and about there were more people available to be victimised. Adults more frequently lived alone and therefore spent longer outside the home both to work and for companionship, so leaving their homes empty for long periods of time. The rise in car ownership both provided means to carry goods away from the crime scene and were themselves targets of crime both to steal the cars and to steal goods left in cars.

From this it would appear that routine activity theory only explains acquisitive crime and the early versions of the theory did just that. However, more recently Felson has suggested that similar analysis can be made of every crime type. He claims that each crime has its own chemistry. Meaning that for each crime one just needs to work out what encourages or discourages a motivated offender, a target (often a place where one can offend), and an absence of capable guardians to come together in time and space.

As with rational choice theory there are important truths here. However, despite a focus on a motivated offender as one of the three necessary ingredients of crime, there is insufficient consideration of what this might mean. The theory does not really link with other work that focuses on motivation, rather it sees offenders as motivated by a desire to gain pleasure immediately and to avoid imminent unpleasantness.

Some theorists have used the ideas of routine activity theory which focus on the activities of everyone, all those who might be potential victims to study offenders—they consider the routine activities of offenders. They have tried to understand normal decisions made by offenders and to map these into routine activities so that they can better understand their behaviour. They argue that typically offenders have mental maps of where they are comfortable and will offend in spaces familiar to them. Familiar areas may include areas: they live in (or have lived in); where they work; near where they go to a sports centre or a pub; near a school they used to attend; or a place they used to take holidays. The routine activities of offenders then need to be layered onto those of other people and where there are overlaps are areas most in need of work to reduce the attractiveness of offending. Therefore the logical outcome of routine activity theory is to work to reduce criminal opportunities by making targets more difficult to offend against. This leads into situational crime prevention and ideas of defensible space.

Situational crime prevention

Out of rational choice theory and routine activity theory, situational crime prevention arose. Under situational crime prevention the environment and particularly possessions should be managed so as to reduce opportunities for crime or to deter criminals. By removing the opportunity for criminal behaviour one makes the costs of crime outweigh the benefits and so individuals will not choose to offend. This might be done by:

- designing goods which are harder to, for example, steal (e.g. better car locks);
- persuading people to be more responsible about their own goods and their person;
- using locks on property, cars, etc.;
- installing CCTV to make it harder to steal something or more likely that you will be seen and so more likely that you will be caught.

Here crime is seen as a sensible choice in certain situations; it is therefore a normal part of social living and the only way of dealing with crime is to reduce the situations in which crime might occur. Situational crime prevention expects everyone: state; local authority; health service; education; voluntary services; and individuals all to work together and take responsibility for reducing criminal opportunities. **What do you think? 12.3** provides some examples of situational crime prevention and shows that there may be some unexpected and unplanned outcomes; it shows that one needs to be careful when employing situational crime prevention.

Hardening the targets or situational crime prevention might have partial success but may only displace offending to another place, another time, or to another crime type. Situational crime prevention may therefore only be a partial answer because it says nothing about the offender. However, because of this lack of focus on the offender, rational choice theory views offending and offenders as normal people, not monsters or people with a problem. They therefore argue that one should tackle the target (make it less attractive or less available) or increase the risk of being caught (increase guardianship). **Table 12.1** suggests a number of techniques commonly suggested as means of target hardening.

WHAT DO YOU THINK? 12.3

- If there is a problem with thefts from shops in one area of town and CCTV was installed in that area what do you think the outcome might be?

- You need to think about what the outcome might be both for that area and for other areas of the town.

- If buses were being vandalised late at night on some routes it was thought that introducing conductors would protect the buses. What do you think might happen?

- Installing CCTV might help to prevent offending in that area but the criminality might move from that area of town to another area.

- Employing conductors to work on buses might reduce vandalism but the conductors may be attacked—the crime is altered, not stopped.

- Can you think of any examples of other situational crime prevention strategies and consider what their unintentional outcomes might be?

The approach of situational crime prevention can be used to alter whole areas. For example Alison Coleman (1990) building on the work of Newman (1972) and his defensible space theory argues that through careful design of spaces to live, shopping centres, and towns one could decrease the likelihood of crime. She suggested three aspects which needed to be addressed:

1. Fewer anonymous spaces—by allocating space to a home (or business) the residents (or owners and workers) would be more likely to care for it.

2. Increasing surveillance—design buildings so that they overlook each other and so that shared spaces are all able to be seen and so guarded; this might mean removing hedges and other impediments to guardianship.

3. Remove the possibility of easy escape without being seen.

Coleman suggested that public housing should return to building more houses or low rise flats rather than high rise blocks of flats. She also suggested that things such as walkways and subways should be avoided as they could not be overlooked (see **Figure 12.9**). She produced a table of design suggestions which should be taken into account in all public space development and even in deciding on planning applications for large private developments.

Increasing the effort	Increasing the risks	Reducing the reward	Removing excuses
Target hardening Steering locks Anti-robber screens	*Entry/exit screening* Baggage screening Merchandise tags	*Target removal* Keep car in garage Removable car radio fascia	*Rule setting* Customs declaration Hotel registration
Access control Entry phones Computer passwords	*Formal surveillance* CCTV Automatic number plate recognition	*Identify property* Product serial numbers Vehicle licence plates	*Stimulating* Roadside speed displays Drink-drive campaigns
Deflecting offenders Cul-de-sacs Routing away fans at soccer matches	*Employee surveillance* Park wardens Club doormen	*Removing inducements* Rapid repair of damaged property Removing graffiti	*Controlling* Drinking age laws Parental controls on Internet
Controlling means Weapons availability Photographs on credit cards	*Natural surveillance* Street lighting Windows	*Rule setting* Tenancy agreements Software copyright agreement before installation	*Facilitating compliance* Fine deduction from salary Ample litter bins

Table 12.1 Target hardening techniques

Source: Pease (2002) who summarised Clarke 1997

Figure 12.9 Building high rise blocks of flats (Trellick Tower, London pictured here) and using pedestrian subways (St Dunstan's Subway, Cranford, London) are discouraged by Coleman's designs for decreasing the likelihood of crime

Sources: Steve Cadman (Flickr)/ CC BY-SA 2.0 and Shirokazan (Flickr)/ CC BY 2.0

Conclusion and consideration of modern neo-classical theories

As with the original classical criminology, neo-classical theories have had a profound effect on modern life. They have an appeal that renders them likely to be attractive to policy makers in that they sound sensible and suggest policy changes that are relatively simple and do not undermine modern social structures. They each treat crime as normal and produced by the normal routines of modern life. An offender is not then different or problematic, just someone who is motivated and assumes they will avoid consequences for their offence. These theories largely ignore the offender and concentrate on making the targets less appealing and decreasing the risk of offending. As with the early classical criminology they are products of their time. In many western states the 1980s and 1990s saw a loss of faith in the provision of welfare to resolve social problems, including crime. This was the Thatcherite era in Britain where there was a general move to empower the individual, to withdraw the state, and allow people more room to make choices for themselves. Along with this came the idea that if they made the wrong choices they should face the consequences. If they invested sensibly they would become wealthy, if they invested unwisely they would lose money. Similarly, if they behaved appropriately society would respect their freedom and allow them to live lives largely uncontrolled by the state. However, if they behaved unwisely, if they offended, the state would step in and blame and punish them harshly, exclude them from society. In this political environment a theory based on conservative principles which saw crime as a product of improperly focused free will was clearly a theory of its time. These ideas are very closely related to the right realism discussed in **Chapter 17**.

Summary

- We started the chapter considering what is theory?

Theory is a way of explaining parts of our world. In criminology most theories try to answer a particular question or set of questions. That means that although theories may appear to be in conflict they may just be answering a different set of questions. Most criminological theories have elements in them that are useful to our understanding of crime. However, no theory answers all the questions.

- Evaluating theories

To assess a theory it is sensible to make sure you understand which questions it is trying to answer and then you might consider:

- Why this theorist is making this claim—what questions are they trying to answer?
- What is the significance of the claim, what does it say that might be important/useful or worthwhile?
- What is the problem with the theory, what does it assume and are those assumptions acceptable?
- What is controversial in the theory and is that controversy useful, does it challenge policy or practice and make you think again?
- Who or which theories seem to disagree with this theory? What are the points of disagreement and which is better argued? Do the disagreements arise because each is answering a slightly different question or intended for a different audience?

And then to test the theory you should ask:

1. Is the theory clear and **does it make sense**?
2. Is **everything included in the theory necessary to explaining things**?
3. Does the theory **cover all necessary aspects**?
4. **How broad are the claims it makes**?
5. Can one test (**verify or falsify**) the theory?
6. Is it **supported by research evidence**?
7. Is it **supported by, or does it relate to, an already existing body of knowledge**?
8. How **accurate** is it?

9. You should also always consider questions about:
   (a) **power**—such as where the **power** lies to define and control behaviour;
   (b) **inequality**—does the theory address inequality? If not, should it?
   (c) **discrimination**—are there hidden issues of discrimination and does the theory apply to e.g. men and women, to all races etc.;
   (d) **political, economic or ideological** issues—are these addressed? Are there any that it should but does not address?
   (e) **justice**—is this fully considered?

10. What are the counter claims—what do other theories say?

- Consider the main theoretical schools in criminology including classicism, positivism, interpretivism, and critical criminology

There are many types of theory, some focus on the individual, others on society or the control system.

Classical criminology arose in the late 17th and early 18th centuries out of a desire to introduce a fairer system for all people living in a state. Classical, Enlightenment theorists saw the system then operating as arbitrary and unfair. They therefore suggested a system of clear legal rules to be applied in every criminal case. This system was to punish (proportionately) those who chose to offend. Classical thinkers believed a system of sure and proportionate punishment of those who chose to offend would prevent future offending. Modern, neo-classical thinkers embrace the ideas about choice and extend the theory by suggesting various interventions which aim to reduce the likelihood that people will choose to offend.

Positivists used (and continue to use) science to study what led people to offend. They collected a lot of information about their societies and where they find something is related to criminality they suggest a link, often a causal link. Positivist theorists may find links between a person's biology or psychology or between them and their environment, society, community, or friends which increases the likelihood that they will offend. All of these theories reduce (though generally do not preclude) the extent of free will as they suggest that where the link arises the likelihood is that someone will offend. Some argue that this interferes with the punishment suggested by classical thinkers as the individual is not entirely to blame. Many positivists suggest rehabilitation to help the individual.

Interpretivism suggests that the links suggested by positivist thinkers are too simplistic. They also argue that to blame and punish the individual for wrong choices is too simplistic. Interpretivists argue that each person's social reality is constructed and negotiated through the many interactions of their daily lives. They seek to describe a reality that the person him or herself would recognise.

Critical criminology challenges all other ideas. Whilst they accept social realities are constructed they challenge all accepted understanding or descriptions of our society and posit different interpretations and means of constructing our societies and communities. They often argue that the present social realities are structured to favour the more powerful at the expense of the less powerful (whether the power be financial, political, gender, racial, etc.). This leads to a deep questioning of the basis upon which our society stands and thereby of the controls and criminal justice systems designed to enforce those controls.

Each of these types of theory contain many competing individual theories and the criminologist needs to learn to assess and consider each with care and objectivity.

- Classical criminology and the policies to which it gave rise

Enlightenment thinkers encouraged every man to think for themselves, make their own choices and not be controlled by either the fear of arbitrary state punishment or religion. Classical criminologists argued that each person should retain the right to choose how to live and behave; each individual exercises free will and uses rational thought to decide how to make their choices and how to act. Before acting each individual decides which action would be most beneficial for them, if they choose something which harms others it should be criminal and should be punished for their choice but only after a fair trial. These ideas arose at a time when other events such as the start of the industrial revolution meant that the old systems of governance were already being challenged. Community and family ties were being stretched as were feudal systems of control, these ideas which placed the individual at the centre of systems such as the criminal justice system were seized on as new ways of governing and controlling the new industrialised communities.

Many critics of classical theory argue that the system to which it gave rise is about the continuation of power and authority and gives rise to inequality (something Enlightenment thinkers claimed to be fighting against). They argue that it is about the preservation and protection of social elites.

- Appreciate the importance of free will and rational choice and demonstrate how these ideas in the 17th and 18th centuries underlined the building of the modern new criminal justice system

The reliance on free will and rational choice was pivotal to Enlightenment thinkers. These two concepts were at the centre of reforms to the criminal justice system and other legal reforms in the 17th and 18th centuries. Classical theories are very legalistic and draw out many modern ideas such as justice for all, rights for those accused in court, fair and just punishment to reflect the harm done (Beccaria) or to ensure compliance and so protect non-offenders (Bentham). These can all be seen in modern criminal justice systems throughout the world. However, modern criminal justice systems have also been shaped by new ideas many of which are neo-classical (new classical). Ideas such as:

(a) the recognition that some people have limited capacity to choose (children and the mentally impaired) and these facts should be taken into consideration;

(b) the idea that whilst two acts may appear the same—killing a person—they may differ in important respects. The differences may affect either the guilt or the justice of punishment—death on an operating table as against a mercy killing as against killing for pleasure.

- Assess modern classical thinkers (neo-classical criminology) to discover how since the 1960s there has been a re-focus on the idea that criminals choose to offend and how, when, and where that might occur.

Starting in the 1980s new theories based on the classical tradition began to be considered: rational choice theory and routine activity theory. These two re-focused our understanding of crime onto the event and to choosing to offend (both classical ideas). Rational choice theory looks at intervening in the decision making process that may lead to offending behaviour being chosen. Here crime may be a normal and rational choice and policy makers need to intervene to render that choice less attractive. Routine activity theory encourages us to think of crime from the perspective of: motivated offenders; suitable targets; and capable guardians. Crime patterns mirror fundamental and normal patterns of behaviour in all areas of a life.

Both rational choice theory and routine activity theory have a common sense appeal to policy makers. Policy makers embrace them because they focus reasons for criminal behaviour away from social structural problems which would be expensive to address and might involve changes to power structures. These theories have suggested practical and more manageable changes to: e.g. harden targets, increase surveillance, increase punishments or increase the likelihood of being caught. However neither theory fully explains why the changes might succeed (how the link works). Their popularity is explained partly due to the rise of conservative ideals (Thatcherite policies) across the full political spectrum. Right wing policy makers would be likely to embrace conservative or neo-classical explanations of criminality.

REVIEW QUESTIONS

1. Describe what theories do and how they can be tested.

2. Explain the main aspects of classical criminology and consider to what extent they are valid in the modern world.

3. Explain the term 'bounded rationality' and give examples of how it might operate.

4. What is a 'crime script'? Choose a crime type and construct a crime script for it.

5. In routine activity theory explain the three things necessary to the commission of a crime.

6. How could you use both routine activity theory and situational crime prevention to reduce crime on a university campus?

7. Is situational crime prevention a theory or merely a tool through which rational choice theory and routine activity theory can be made relevant to policy makers?

8. How do the neo-classical ideas or modern classical theories link to the traditional classical school of thought?

FURTHER READING

Cornish, D. B. and Clarke, R. V. (2014) *The Reasoning Criminal: Rational Choice Perspectives on Offending*. London: Transaction Publishers.

This is a reprint of their 1986 book but with a new introduction by Clarke. The whole book offers detailed consideration of each aspect of neo-classical thought. It is a very good primary text as it is a collection of contributions by leading proponents of these theories and it provides a critical and analytic introduction to what was, in 1986, a ground-breaking new direction of criminological thought.

Williams, K. S. (2012) *Textbook on Criminology* (8th edn). Oxford: Oxford University Press. Chapter 2 especially pp. 20–39.

Most criminological textbooks also have useful chapters which consider both classical and neo-classical ideas. This text considers the subject from a broad perspective—both legal and criminological perspectives.

Dorling, D., Gordon, D., Hillyard, P., Pantazis, C., Pemberton, S., and Tombs, S. (2008) *Criminal Obsessions: Why Harm Matters More Than Crime* (2nd edn). London: Centre for Crime and Justice Studies. Especially Chapter 5, pp. 70–90.

A useful questioning of societies' focus on crime as being particularly important to resolve rather than seeing other social problems which cause harm as being equally important. This challenges the commonly accepted ideas about why and when a society should control behaviour and pushes the reader to think differently or to develop answers to the different solutions and ways of thinking which the text suggests.

Newburn, T. (2009) *Key Readings in Criminology*. Abingdon: Willan Publishing.

For excerpts from original criminology texts, the key readings for the theories covered in this Chapter see Chapter 5, 5.1 (Beccaria) and all the readings in Chapter 14.

 Access the **online resources** to view selected further reading and web links relevant to the material covered in this chapter.
www.oup.com/uk/case/

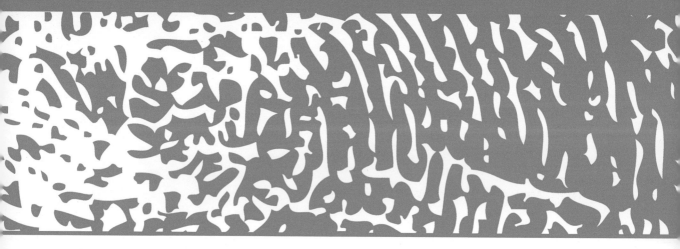

CHAPTER OUTLINE

Introduction	344
Positivism, punishment, and rehabilitation	344
Early positivism	346
Biological theories	351
Psychological theories	359
Learning	364

Biological and psychological positivism

Determined to predetermine

KEY ISSUES

At the end of this chapter you should be able to:

- recognise the contribution of both biology and psychology to our understanding of crime;

- identify the main biological theories relating to criminology;

- identify the main psychological theories relating to criminology;

- relate each of the main concepts and strands of thought to the scientists and criminologists who are centrally connected with them;

- analyse and critically assess each of these ideas and the contribution it makes to our understanding of crime and criminal behaviour.

Introduction

Chapter 12 discussed a number of classical theories which locate the fault for criminal behaviour in the individual primarily through free will, classicism, and rational choice. For classical criminologists criminality is connected to the decisions and choices people make. If criminality results from a choice this means that society can:

- blame and therefore punish the individual for the bad choices they make on the assumption that the individual is responsible for their action(s) (this requires fair criminal justice systems so that punishments are legitimate and likely to make people think twice about offending);
- support the individual in learning why that choice was wrong and how to make better choices in the future;
- help potential victims to better secure their property and think of their own safety and thereby hopefully reduce the likelihood of future victimisation.

Through these mechanisms classical theorists believe crime can be reduced and possibly even eliminated.

This chapter moves away from classical thinking and away from looking to blame the individual for incorrect choices, although the individual remains at the centre of the explanations that follow. Here we will be studying individual positivism: that is those aspects of positivist criminological explanations that look for differences between criminal and non-criminal populations. Positivist criminology surfaced during the 19th century when scientific study was coming to the fore. Scientists, such as Charles Darwin, were collecting information and facts about the natural world in order to better understand it. At the same time information about both people who offend and about the social world was also being collected. Positivists believed that they would be able to discover patterns in society or certain types of people which would explain crime (for a critical examination of positivist methods, see also **Chapters 6** and **19**).

Biological and psychological positivists believed that by measuring medical and psychological differences between offenders and non-offenders they would discover a clear explanation of criminal behaviour, a truth that explained criminal actions. Early positivists such as Cesare Lombroso (1835–1909), a famous Italian criminologist, collected large amounts of information and when physical or biological differences were discovered between offenders and non-offenders they tended to assume that those characteristics were causative and explained the behaviour. However, as we will see there is a large step between finding differences which one reports as factual truths and taking things further by assuming that the difference explains behaviour. Correlation does not equal causation. One famous example of this was a graph produced which plotted two things: the divorce rate in Maine (USA) and the consumption of margarine per capita from 2000–09. On the graph, these two lines fluctuate in tandem, but it would be ridiculous to suggest that the amount of margarine you consume is linked to the likelihood of you getting divorced. Whilst everyone can see that this example is extreme, many people do not question other such findings in the same way.

Positivists, particularly early positivists, found differences between offenders and others, assumed that the difference caused the criminal behaviour (predetermined the individuals to act in a criminal way) and so tried to design ways to counter the problem and thereby to reduce crime. This chapter will study the journey of biological and psychological positivist thinking from its roots in the 19th century through to more modern approaches in the 21st century where these biological and psychological traits are merely seen as one factor which may increase the likelihood of criminality rather than causing it. In this chapter we will only consider positivism in relation to people, biological and psychological factors. The next chapter (**Chapter 14**, Sociological positivism) will look at whether crime can be explained from the perspective of society, or the social world.

Positivism, punishment, and rehabilitation

Classical theories (see **Chapter 12**) focused around free will and therefore suggested punishing people for incorrect choices. If a person chooses to offend then they should face punishment which is proportionate to the harm they do. Positivism is very different, it tends to suggest that people offend when aspects of their lives which they cannot control make offending more likely. If this is

the case it is questionable whether a society should punish to meet the harm done as the behaviour is at least partly out of the control of the offender. Positivists consider what that might mean in terms of how a society or state should respond: punishment or rehabilitation.

We can take an historical example which careful research has refuted but which still resonates with many people. For many years there was a claim that black people were more likely to commit crime than white people, in other words something in their racial make-up caused their bad behaviour. This claim arose partly because there was a greater ratio of black people arrested and punished than one might expect compared with the ratio of black people in the general population. This argument assumed that the criminal justice system (being stopped by police, charged, convicted, and punished) was objective, and therefore black people must be offending at a higher rate than other groups. This has since been proven to be incorrect and it is in fact a result of how the criminal justice system operates rather than the behaviour of one race (for a full discussion of the link between ethnicity, crime, and criminal justice agencies see Bowling and Phillips 2002 (also **Chapter 10**)). However, if it were true, if black people were more likely to offend because of something in their biological or psychological make-up then surely they should not be punished, or at least not punished as severely as suggested by the harm caused. Therefore, if true, positivism suggests that something in the biological (or psychological) make-up of black people renders them more likely to offend—this is something over which they have no control—the offending is not the result of free will and so punishment to fit the harm caused would be unjust.

In cases where a person is more likely than others to offend, that behaviour is pathological so positivists question the use of punishment and instead suggest using treatment or rehabilitation to support them to resist the biological (or sociological, see **Chapter 14**) draw to offend. If one does that, the treatment or rehabilitation needs to continue until the pathology is overcome; therefore the length of treatment and the seriousness of the treatment may bear no relation to the seriousness of the offence. It is now clearly understood that the colour of one's skin does not affect the rate of offending. What is now suggested is that people living in similar social situations and who are treated in similar ways (discriminated against) are likely to have similar rates of offending. Where problems such as discrimination may be the intervening causative factor, full (or any) punishment may be unjust; the individual was acting at least partly due to things outside their control. Here again rehabilitation may be necessary but arguably society should change to reduce discrimination and so reduce offending related to it (for a discussion concerning sociological positivism see **Chapter 14**).

Whilst rejecting the idea that whole racial groups are pathologically more or less inclined to offend, biologists and psychologists still point to specific differences that may mean some individuals are more likely to offend than are others. If these theories are correct such individuals should not be punished, rather they should be treated or rehabilitated.

The examples in the **What do you think? 13.1** indicate that rehabilitation, removing the problem, or requiring assessment is not necessarily less severe, sometimes it is more invasive and more unpleasant for the offender. I remember once talking to a group of prostitutes who said they would far rather pay a fine or serve a short prison sentence than face a sentence of 'rehabilitation'. They had chosen to sell sex for money, had done this after weighing up the alternatives open to them such as working in a factory and decided that prostitution was their best option. They did not feel they harmed anyone though they recognised that many prostitutes had not made a similar free choice and might need protecting. The point here is that punishment, rehabilitation, treatment, and other responses to offending (other sentences) or other interventions all involve interfering with someone's free will and all need to be justified. If the claim is that crime results from a biological or psychological trait this needs to be proven and care taken to ensure that the subsequent intervention is both proportionate and legitimate. For a full discussion of moral reasoning in relation to crime and criminal justice interventions, especially the use of rehabilitation see Palmer (2003).

Theorists who suggest biological and psychological theories today tend to accept that no single theory can ever explain all criminality (see **Chapter 18** for discussions of integrated theories of crime). No one theory is able to explain murder, speeding, insider dealing, and computer fraud. Therefore, modern biological and psychological positivists usually claim that the science is only a partial explanation; environment and societal situations also influence choices and behaviour. Biological or psychological explanations may influence behaviour, but they do not determine what is going to happen. For example, people who have an increased psychopathic (or sociopathic) element to their personalities are often associated with criminal or antisocial behaviour. They tend to be antisocial, lack empathy and remorse, lack respect for the social expectations and social controls (they do not feel so bound by the rules), and are impulsive. Whilst it is true that many offenders display these characteristics, so too do many of our top sports personalities or athletes and many of those who excel in business or in the financial markets. From this it is clear that an individual with an enhanced psychopathic (sociopathic) aspect to their personalities has a choice. The personality trait does not determine whether they become a chief executive or an offender. At best the personality trait is a partial explanation, a background factor.

The prior discussion suggests that although the theories in this chapter are useful to our understanding of behaviour they should be studied as part of a much broader explanation which will include social and other factors as well. Recognition of the fact that any theory is at best

WHAT DO YOU THINK? 13.1

How far should treatment go?

- Abigail steals a pencil from a shop. She is found to have a problem with her brain that is believed to cause such behaviour. In that situation, her behaviour is out of her control so justice suggests that she should not be punished. Is it acceptable to force her to undergo invasive brain surgery to prevent her offending in the future?

- Barnaby kills his wife. He is found to have a minor vitamin deficiency that causes him to become violent. Again, the behaviour is not his fault so maybe he should not be punished. His problem can be rectified through giving a vitamin supplement. He is merely given the vitamin supplement and sent on his way. Is that acceptable?

- Cameron is 30, he has been offending since he was 10. In his teens he (and his friends) tended to participate in a mixture of petty offences, anti-social behaviour, and substance misuse. In his 20s he moved on to more serious crimes such as burglary. Recent studies claim to have discovered that specific gene structures are clearly associated with persistent offending. Cameron is now in a permanent relationship. Justice Devon, the judge sentencing Cameron following his most recent burglary, has decided that Cameron should be sterilised so that he does not pass on this genetic problem to any offspring. Justice Devon is determined to protect future generations from this type of persistent offender. Is that acceptable?

- Building on the scenario in Cameron's case assume that the findings linking specific gene structures with persistent offending have led the government to consider mandatory testing of all people to locate these genetic structures with a view to adopting one or more of the following laws:

  – sterilising all people with these gene structures to prevent them being passed on;

  – genetic engineering of all people with these gene structures to eradicate the unwanted genes;

  – laws specifying legal and illegal breeding groups; and/or

  – execution of all people with these gene structures.

- Would these policies be acceptable, would they be fair and just?

- You need to consider your reaction to each of these cases very carefully and reflect on why you answer them in a particular way. Reading the rest of the chapter will help in collecting your thoughts.

only a partial truth is good reason to be careful of any intervention in the life of an individual. It is reason not to use extreme treatments or extreme punishments as specific responses to any specific explanation of crime (see also in **Chapter 2** the discussion of the 'triad of criminology').

Early positivism

Cesare Lombroso

Biological positivism arose out of the growing interest in science in the 19th century and as a backlash against the harsh effects of classical criminology. As classical ideals became more widely applied they were being used to control many types of social problems. People were being ever more closely monitored, not only for their actions but also for their attitudes (to protect the moral fibre of society). Many different types of people and activities were being controlled—drunkards, the mentally ill, the poor, immigrants, those moving from one parish to another, prostitutes, those suffering from sexually transmitted diseases, petty offenders, blasphemers, and hardened criminals. Control in the 19th century usually meant being incarcerated. Despite growing levels of imprisonment the problems were still increasing—control was failing so people looked for other answers. Positivism offered different solutions. If people could not be controlled then the problem might lie inside them—there might be something biologically or psychologically wrong with them. The idea of biological or psychological problems causing criminality—the born criminal (see **Figure 13.1**)—began to emerge at the beginning of the 19th century but really took hold towards the end of that century.

Figure 13.1 Illustration of some 'physical defects' which Lombroso believed indicated a criminal tendency
Source: Lombroso 1876/Public domain

Figure 13.2 Physiognomy of criminals
Source: Lombroso 1876/Public domain

Cesare Lombroso (1835–1909), was an Italian criminologist and is often referred to as the father of criminology. His work was the turning point for the discipline to move away from a legalistic focus on the crime towards a scientific study of the criminals. Classical theorists concentrated on the crime and responsibility: biological and psychological positivists focused on the criminal, the crime being the backdrop to the study. Lombroso considered crime something that normal people would not participate in so he searched for a pathological explanation, something different about criminals which made them break the law. In 1876, he published *L'Uomo Deliquente* (The Criminal Man) and in 1899 he published *Le Crime, causes et Remèdes* (*Crime, Its Causes and Remedies*). He replaced the legal and moralistic approach to crime with one based on a scientific stance which used the careful analysis of empirical evidence. He is most remembered for claiming that criminals were atavistic throwbacks, people whose genetic make-up was from a more primitive stage of human development. In sum, they were more 'savage' than non-criminals. Lombroso also claimed that this primitive aspect of their genetic make-up was evident not only in their criminal behaviour but also in physical anomalies which he called stigmata (for an illustration see **Figure 13.2**). On a basic level, Lombroso's early claims were that one could pick out a criminal from their appearance.

Thieves (see number 5 in **Figure 13.2**, bottom left hand corner) and murderers (see number 3 in **Figure 13.2**, middle left) are characterised by:

their expressive faces and manual dexterity, small wandering eyes that are often oblique in form, thick and close eyebrows, distorted or squashed noses, thin beards and hair and sloping foreheads. … habitual murders have a cold, glassy stare and eyes that are sometimes bloodshot and filmy, the nose is often hawk-like and always large; the jaw is strong, the cheekbones broad; and their hair is dark, abundant, and crisply textured. Their beards are scanty, their canine teeth very developed, and their lips thin … nearly all criminals have jug ears, thick hair, thin beards, pronounced sinuses, protruding chins and broad cheek bones.

Lombroso 1876: 51

Lombroso measured skull size and found anomalies among the criminals. He also noted asymmetrical facial features and marked facial bone structures. All of these were later rejected as markers which might be useful in detecting those likely to offend, in fact his whole thesis claiming that there is a 'born criminal' type has largely been discredited (see Rock, 2007). However, it is not his findings for which he is remembered, rather it is for the methodology he used in building his evidence. Lombroso did not just posit a theory: rather, he collected data to test it. He used scientific methods to collect empirical facts which would confirm (or disprove) his ideas.

Although others before him had used this methodology his was the first major work which might be said to be entirely based on the scientific collection of information. He was also the first to apply Darwin's theories to explain his findings. It is therefore his methodology rather than his findings that make him the father of modern criminology. His retention of the title possibly arises from the fact that he recognised the importance of collecting empirical data to either discover or to test theories, and from his willingness to be flexible and amend his theories. So, whilst his earlier work is focused on the individual alone, his later work (Lombroso, 1906 *Crime: Causes et Remèdes*) whilst still holding physical factors at the centre also includes all sorts of social and psychological factors. His later work includes factors such as climate, grain prices, sex and marriage customs, education, moral and mental strength, and so embraces and measures aspects of the three disciplines which underpin positivist criminology: biology, psychology, and sociology (Morrison 2004). It is the links to the need for a scientific approach to explaining crime through collection and measurement of data that is his real legacy; theories and assumptions should be tested or verified. Since Lombroso's time this scientific approach has been at the centre of criminology, especially positivist criminology. The positivist tends to suggest that either an individual has a predisposition to offend or that aspects of the environment close down choices and so, in effect, make it more likely that he/she will offend and they search for proof as to which aspects are linked in this way to crime.

Before moving on it is sensible to at least recognise what acceptance of Lombroso's theory might look like. If one accepts both that some people are born with a predisposition to offend and that this can be seen in their features from a young age, then it might influence the way in which a state chooses to control crime. In this type of scenario, the state might move away from punishing people for the crime they committed (making the punishment fit the crime) towards controlling some people (the 'born criminals') to protect the rest of society. In this circumstance, following a crime, a state might:

- permit a sentencing judge to choose to incarcerate people for longer to protect society from them;
- permit a judge to require them to undergo treatment to teach them to control their natural urges;

- require them to take drugs or undergo operations in order to cure them;
- permit sterilisation to prevent them passing on their substandard genes;
- even put them to death.

Assuming one could locate a 'born criminal' a state might also argue that it could legitimately intervene even before a crime is committed. On the back of this and other theories based on genetic and/or biological explanations of offending most of these punishments or treatments have been tried somewhere in the world. It was partly what the eugenics movement (this began in the late 19th century but really took hold in Europe and North America from about 1925 to 1950) was based on and it was at least partly behind the rationale for the Nazi concentration camps. Therefore, despite being largely discredited (see Rock 2007) these types of theories have underpinned some appalling state policies designed to protect society. They stand as a warning to the awful consequences that arise when theories are misused.

William Sheldon

The types of ideas which surround the 'born criminal' underpinned other famous criminological ideas. For example, those arising out of the work of William Sheldon (1898–1977), an American psychologist who related behaviour to body type. This area of study is referred to as somatotyping. Sheldon (1949) identified three main body types—endomorphs who are physically soft and round, often fat and have friendly and sociable temperaments; mesomorphs who are physically muscular and athletic, and have assertive and active temperaments; and ectomorphs who are physically thin and rather weak and temperamentally focused on privacy and restraint and are very self-aware (see **Figure 13.3**). Sheldon suggested that mesomorphs were most likely to be criminals whereas others have suggested that the somatotypes are linked to particular types of offending. This type of theory, like that of Lombroso, was largely discredited (Sampson and Laub 1991 accredit that to Sutherland). However, more recently whilst the details of their work relating to body type remain discredited some of their findings such as that linking offending to types of personality has been revived and used in developmental criminology and life-course criminology (Sampson and Laub 1991, 2005; McAra and McVie 2017; see also **Chapters 9** and **18**).

Francis Galton

Regardless of the point made in **What do you think? 13.2**, it is important not to dismiss outright these early theories.

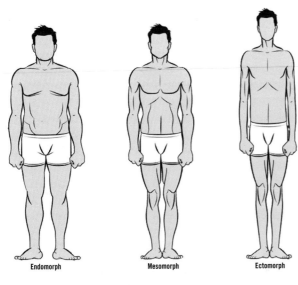

Figure 13.3 Sheldon's three somatotypes
Source: www.slimguyfitness.com

Galton searched for facial features which were common to people who were successful in certain types of profession, or ranks within a profession. He recorded different features for soldiers and commanding officers and he argued that one could pick out a criminal from facial features alone (Galton 1883). He also built composite images of these types. Whilst his ideas have been largely discredited it is interesting that when shown computer generated images of various facial types it is possible to construct faces that most people find more attractive than other faces. More sinister is the fact that some evidence suggests that physical appearance (including facial features) may affect outcomes in court. Berry (1988) found people were more likely to believe that those with baby faces, rounded faces with large eyes and small chins, can be involved in crimes of negligence because they are seen as naïve. However, people were less likely to believe that people with baby faces could be involved in crimes involving mental intent or those of violence because they are perceived as more honest and gentle (Berry 1988).

Despite thinking of them as ludicrous, there may be a link: this link between crime and physical appearance is still important, though far more complex, than so far discussed. To understand it better we need to look at the work of Francis Galton (1822–1911), a 19th century English researcher with a particular interest in sociology and anthropology. Galton's idea was that one could predict and read behaviour from facial features; he even suggested that these might determine a person's fitness for a particular profession.

If true, this evidence would suggest that decision makers in court may be partially swayed by looks. This would be worrying for law, criminal justice, and for society, although it may tell us nothing about any link between behaviour and looks—merely that others may assume one. Baumeister (1982) suggested that these assumptions can be proved wrong by the use of strong proof one way or the other. That is the assumption concerning facial features was only important in cases where the proven facts were unclear. In cases where either the prosecution

WHAT DO YOU THINK? 13.2

- Most of you have recently started at university and have had to start to build up new friendship groups. When you have walked into a room full of people you do not know, how have you decided which to talk to? How have you chosen your friends?

- Some of you may have tried to narrow down the field by joining clubs and so trying to find people who enjoy the same things you do. Even if you have done that you still need to decide who to talk to when you go to the club or participate in activities. Most of us do this based on appearance—facial appearance and the way others are dressed. Be honest about what you do and how you choose to talk to people.

- Now look at the images in **Figure 13.4**. Which, if any, of these people would you choose to befriend if you

knew nothing about them but were merely placed in a room with them?

- Do you ever judge people or think of them differently depending on their facial features? Be honest, it might merely be when you are watching television programmes. If this does ever happen, which facial features might lead you to feel differently about an individual? Which might be enough to make you treat them differently?

- In your experience, are people treated differently by you or others dependent on their facial features (think about school and all the other environments where you encounter or have encountered people)? If people *are* treated differently depending on their facial features does this influence their behaviour and their personality? Do you think it might have

Figure 13.4 Selection of faces

Source: SFIO CRACHO/Shutterstock.com, racorn/Shutterstock.com, and Dean Drobot/Shutterstock.com

an effect on how they feel about themselves and therefore, maybe on how they behave? If so, what is affecting their behaviour—their looks or the way people treat them because of their looks—is it biology or environment?

- There are countless recognisable figures that have been convicted of crimes, but who do not fit into Lombroso's idea of the 'born criminal'. Take a look at this list and as you do, envision the celebrities faces:

  - Tim Allen convicted in 1978 (age 25) for possessing more than 650 grams of cocaine. He served two and a half years in prison.

  - Martha Stewart in 2004 was convicted of felony charges of conspiracy, obstruction of an agency proceeding, and making false statements to federal investigators (related to the ImClone stock trading case). She was sentenced in July 2004 to serve a five-month term in a federal correctional facility and a two-year period of supervised release.

  - Mark Wahlberg (at age 16) attacked two Vietnamese men with a wooden stick, leaving one of them blind in one eye. He was convicted of assault and was sentenced to two years in prison, he served 45 days.

  - In 1999 Jay Z was convicted of assault (he stabbed a record executive in the stomach) and was sentenced to three years on probation.

  - In 1994 50 Cent (aged 19) was convicted of selling heroin and crack cocaine. He served six months in a boot camp prison.

  - In 2003 Cheryl Cole (then Cheryl Tweedy) was convicted of assaulting a bathroom attendant at a nightclub. She was sentenced to 120 hours of unpaid community service and had to compensate her victim.

  - Stephen Fry (aged 17) was convicted of credit card fraud and sentenced to probation (he had already served three months in prison on remand).

- Having looked through this list and thought about the faces of these people, do you now think it is straightforward to gauge criminal predisposition from looks alone?

or defence had hard proof, factual evidence, the assumption (prejudice) would not stand and the decision-maker would follow the evidence (Baumeister 1982). What is interesting is that the assumptions (prejudices) may *need* to be proven wrong. When people are introduced to the theories of Lombroso and Galton most consider them to be ridiculous, but what more recent research suggests is that many people are affected by the way someone looks (Berry 1988; Baumeister 1982 and Eberhardt et al. 2006). Our prejudices about looks and behaviour are likely to be learned and their existence shows how people may believe the link between biology and crime might be present. However, these assumptions (prejudices) do not mean that the links are real, they only show that people believe in them or use them. If there is any link between biology and crime it is very complex. Acceptance of its existence or an unwillingness to question one's prejudices can lead to very serious outcomes; for example in the US, assumptions about appearance linked to crime have been found to affect whether someone faces the death penalty. Eberhardt et al. (2006) found that having black features made one more likely to face death row:

> male murderers with stereotypically black-looking features are more than twice as likely to get the death sentence than lighter-skinned African American defendants found guilty of killing a white person.

Therefore, despite our rejection of the theories of Lombroso, Galton, and others we all still use their ideas in our daily lives, in our interactions with other people. Generally, our prejudices are relatively harmless but when they affect justice in police or jury decision making they cause serious problems. We therefore need to be more aware of our prejudices and try to resist them at least in situations where their use may cause injustice. Finally, it is important to recognise that the lasting legacy of Lombroso is the understanding that the collection and analysis of data are essential to criminological work.

Biological theories

Brain structure and function

Each person has a certain degree of choice over the way in which they react to things or behave. This choice emanates from the decisions a person makes, which in turn come from within the brain. It is clear that the way in which the brain functions may have a strong influence on our behaviour. Anything which alters brain structure, or functioning, will similarly affect behaviour. A basic understanding of the structure and function of the brain (and the rest of the nervous system) is therefore very important and useful to understanding some aspects of behaviour.

There are two parts of the nervous system and of decision making: the central nervous system and the peripheral nervous system (see **Figure 13.5**):

1. The central nervous system (CNS) which is made up of the brain and spinal cord.

2. The peripheral nervous system (PNS) which is made up of all the nerves running through the body that carry signals from the senses and communicate through the spinal cord back up to the brain. They also carry instructions from the brain to other parts of the body, the effectors (muscles and glands) and these allow a person to react. In turn, there are two aspects to the PNS—the somatic and automatic.

Central Nervous System

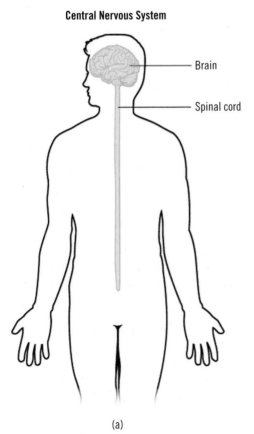

(a)

Peripheral Nervous System

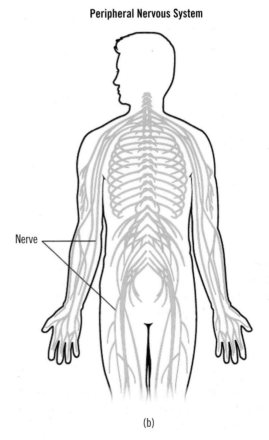

(b)

Figure 13.5 The central and peripheral nervous systems
Source: OpenStax/CC BY 4.0

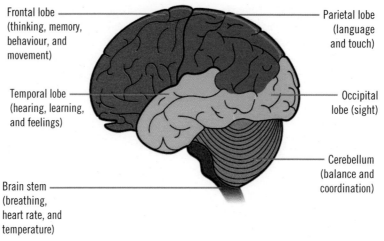

Frontal lobe (thinking, memory, behaviour, and movement)

Parietal lobe (language and touch)

Temporal lobe (hearing, learning, and feelings)

Occipital lobe (sight)

Cerebellum (balance and coordination)

Brain stem (breathing, heart rate, and temperature)

Figure 13.6 Illustration of the different sections of the brain and their functions
Source: Public domain

The CNS has two main parts, the spinal cord and the brain. The spinal cord is the communication system between the body and the brain. If this is damaged, messages fail to get through and so the senses can't tell the brain what they see or feel and the brain can't tell the muscles and glands how to react. The brain logs and sorts the information it receives, decides what to do, and sends messages to the rest of the body telling it how to respond. It is a command and control centre—it interprets the information the senses pick up from the external environment and from the internal environment (the rest of the body), analyses all the data, decides how to respond, and sends instructions to the rest of the body. It is also the centre to store memories and it allows people to reason and think.

The brain is separated into different areas and each part of the brain performs a different function (see **Figure 13.6**). Whilst each part is important, it is the frontal lobe (thinking and behaviour), parietal lobe (language), and temporal lobe (feelings) that are most important to behaviour and to communicating with the outside world. The frontal lobe is particularly important as it is the site of thinking, reasoning, social behaviour, planning, and cognitive decision-making.

The famous case of Phineas Cage (**Figure 13.7**) illustrates what happens if this area of the brain is damaged. Phineas was a railway worker who in 1848 was involved in an accident where an iron bar was shot through his skull. It entered his head behind his left ear and travelled through his frontal lobe out of the top of his head. He survived and functioned normally except that his personality altered completely. Before the accident, he was a normal, pleasant, and well-adjusted family man. Following the accident, he became rude, impatient, reckless, and unpleasant. This was one of the incidents that led scientists to recognise that different parts of the brain were responsible

Figure 13.7 Portrait of Phineas Cage
Source: Public domain

for different functions. Whilst this science has come a long way there are still many things we are discovering about brain function and structure.

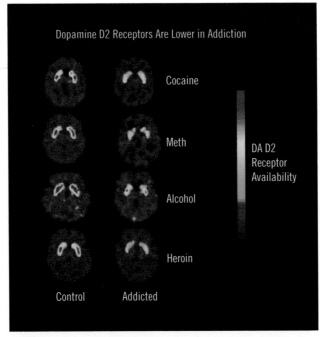

Figure 13.8 Brain scans showing effect on brain of Dopamine D2 receptors
Source: Science Source/SCIENCE PHOTO LIBRARY

Problems with the structure and/or functioning of the frontal lobe are very frequently linked to negative behaviours (Adverse Childhood Experiences Study starting in 1997; Dube et al. 2003; Kolb et al. 2009; Kolla et al. 2013; and Reavis et al. 2013). Damage to the frontal and prefrontal lobes is likely to: impair a person's ability to understand the consequences of their actions or their ability to learn from previous experience; their concentration will be reduced; their self-control will be reduced; their feelings of empathy will be reduced; and they will also be less able to feel shame or guilt. Each of these has been linked to criminal behaviour. However, damage to other parts of the brain may also cause behavioural difficulties. Furthermore, more recently it has been recognised that the brain does not need to be physically impaired to cause it to function less effectively. Such problems can occur through maltreatment, neglect, or even lack of love shown to children when they are young, when their brain functions are still forming.

It is now well recognised that maltreatment alters the way in which the brain develops; it tends to inhibit the formation of the communication network within the child's brain and this can have an effect on behaviours in later life: so that the environment in which a child is reared may affect the way in which the brain develops which has a knock on effect on the way in which the child experiences the world, their ability to feel emotions and the behavioural choices they make, their ability to think rationally and to learn from their mistakes. These inabilities which may be

caused by brain development (or lack of development) may be one of the factors that make criminal behaviour more likely, especially in adolescence. It might also be one of the factors that prevents individuals from maturing out of or learning not to offend; it may be a factor leading to a life-course of offending, a persistent offender.

Even once the structure of the brain is largely formed it can be affected, or at least the way in which it functions can be affected by behavioural choices made later in life. **Figure 13.8** illustrates that the use of certain substances affects the way in which the brain functions. The brain scans show the effects on the brain of dopamine D2 receptors when a person uses the substance occasionally, compared with an addiction. Yellow to red colouring shows greater dopamine receptors, but you can clearly see that those who are addicted to the substances listed in the figure have a lower number of dopamine receptors compared with those who use occasionally. This clearly illustrates that environmental and behavioural choices can affect the structure of the brain and its ability to produce the normal hormonal balance of neurotransmitters like dopamine or serotonin. Neurotransmitters support the transmission of signals between neurons in the brain and, in the right levels, assist in the healthy functioning of the brain so that too much or too little may well affect emotion and behaviour.

The links to behaviour (crime) and the structure and functioning of the brain are therefore clear. What is less clear is:

- whether they are caused by genetics, biology or environment;

- the extent to which the individual's ability to control their behaviour might be impaired; and,

- the extent to which the damage to the brain and its functioning can be reversed or repaired and would this then prevent or help to prevent further offending.

Having considered the main effects of the structure and development of the brain on behaviour and how that might affect criminality, this chapter will now move on to look at another theory, namely chemical and biochemical influences and then genetics and how these might affect behaviour and therefore increase criminality.

Chemical and biochemical influences

Every chemical taken into the body affects an individual either physically or mentally. Many foods and other substances merely affect the body physically, providing strength and nutrients. However, others will also affect the biochemical balance of the mind and therefore may have an effect on behaviour. Clearly alcohol and all illegal drugs have this effect, it is partly why they are either illegal or, in the case of alcohol, its sale is controlled and once under the influence users are limited in their use of potentially dangerous activities such as driving.

From **What do you think? 13.3** it is clear that many substances which we drink or eat, such as chocolate and coffee, affect our minds and therefore may also affect our behaviours. Behavioural changes may also be associated with low blood sugars (hypoglycaemia), food allergies, and excesses or deficiencies in vitamins. Therefore, many substances which are introduced into the body (or their deficiency) can affect the way in which the brain functions and therefore influence behaviour. However, here we will focus on the effects of testosterone which is one the internal chemicals or hormones produced by the body.

Testosterone

In almost all parts of the world, official statistics suggest that men commit far more crime than women. Researchers seeking to explain the difference began to suspect that it might be caused by testosterone, the hormone which is related to characteristics often associated with men and such aggressiveness (Olwens 1987; Schalling 1987; and Raine 1993). Many of the early scientific studies involved

WHAT DO YOU THINK? 13.3

In this box you will see a list of symptoms, try to work out which substance has the effects listed.

Symptoms

- **Drug A:** Whilst often unpleasant to start with, once people become accustomed to this drug they usually get addicted and find it hard to stop. Most users find it difficult to get though the day without this substance, they often need it as soon as they wake, and multiple times through the day. If they don't get the drug they can become irritable, inattentive, and moody. This drug probably kills more people than any other drug. This drug is unpleasant and risks causing serious harm to non-users—every year a number of innocent people are killed.

- **Drug B:** This depressant drug can affect mood and behaviour negatively. It is physically addictive and withdrawal is particularly unpleasant—in some of the worst cases drug users suffer epileptic seizures and hallucinations when withdrawing. This drug is strongly linked to aggression and violence.

- **Drug C:** This stimulant drug is psychologically addictive. These drug users feel that they can't face life unless they have their fix. Most of these drug users have to take the drug at least once a day. If they can't get hold of their drug these users become edgy, irritable, depressed, and restless. Heavy users suffer palpitations, dizziness, headaches, migraine, and insomnia.

Think carefully before looking at the following answers.

Answers

- **Drug A = Tobacco:** This drug acts as a stimulant and is quite addictive but it is very harmful to the user. When you smoke tobacco you inhale tar, nicotine, carbon monoxide and other gases. Many smokers find it releases anxiety and helps them to concentrate. However, it is harmful and each year in the UK about 120,000 die prematurely through smoking related diseases (see Drugwise at http://www.drugwise.org.uk). However, smoking is also harmful to other people. Passive smoking is believed to cause about

600 cancers and 12,000 other deaths (from heart disease) in the UK each year (see Drugwise). Cigarettes have caused many deaths through fires in people's homes but have also caused mass deaths, e.g. when Bradford football club stadium caught fire 56 people were killed and in Kings Cross tube station 31 people died; both of these are thought to have been caused by dropped cigarette ends.

- **Drug B = Alcohol:** It's a depressant drug that most adults use. It is toxic to our bodies and damages the heart, liver, brain, and other major organs. Alcohol Concern records that it is linked to crime in a number of ways (see www.alcoholconcern.org.uk):

  - Alcohol-related crime in the UK is estimated to cost between £8bn and £13bn per year.

  - A fifth (29 per cent) of all violent incidents in 2013–14 took place in or around a pub or club. This rises to 42 per cent for stranger violence. Over two thirds (68 per cent) of violent offences occur in the evening or at night.

  - There were 8,270 casualties of drink driving accidents in the UK in 2013, including 240 fatalities and 1,100 people who suffered serious injury.

  - Victims believed the offender(s) to be under the influence of alcohol in over half (53 per cent) of all violent incidents, or 704,000 offences.

  - Male and female prisoners who reported drinking daily drank an average of 20 units per day.

- Alcohol has been related to harm more widely than this. Alcohol Concern estimates that alcohol related harm costs England around £21bn per year, with £3.5bn to the NHS, £11bn tackling alcohol-related crime, and £7.3bn from lost work days and productivity costs. Alcohol related deaths have increased every year since 1979, direct deaths are now 5,543 per year in the UK whereas those where alcohol is a factor are as many as 22,000 (Drugwise). Despite these figures alcohol is part of our culture, it is offered at most celebrations or parties. We demonise other substances (many of which are less harmful) and yet alcohol is promoted and advertised. Why is that?

- **Drug C = Caffeine:** Caffeine is found in chocolate, lemonade, tea, coffee, pills (e.g. Pro-plus) and energy drinks (e.g. Red Bull). Caffeine is a stimulant drug and increases the heart rate and blood pressure, it can counter tiredness and increase brain activity. People who drink more than about six cups of coffee a day start to become dependent. In large quantities caffeine may make people irritable and it can cause headaches. Caffeine is a relatively harmless stimulant.

References:

http://www.drugwise.org.uk
http://www.alcoholconcern.org.uk/help-and-advice/statistics-on-alcohol/
This What do you think? box was inspired by Professor Julian Buchanan's Inaugural lecture   http://www.academia.edu/181097/Inaugural_Professorial_Lecture_Questionnaire_Powerpoint_Lecture_Notes_preview_and_download_below_

primates, but we will consider those which studied the relationship between testosterone and human behaviour, particularly aggression (Olwens 1987; Schalling 1987). Dan Olwens (1987) found a link between testosterone and both verbal and physical aggression especially when the male was provoked. While he suggested that provoked violence (verbal and physical) was directly correlated to testosterone, he noted that unprovoked aggression had a more complex connection with testosterone. Olwens concluded that while there was a clear relationship between testosterone and aggression this link was complex and many other factors also affected aggression. Daisy Schalling (1987) suggested that testosterone was only associated with verbal aggression, not physical aggression. Testosterone increased when young men felt that their status was threatened. Boys with low testosterone avoided conflict but those with high testosterone were more assertive, extrovert, and social but tended to become angry when they were questioned or threatened. As with

Olwens' work, Schalling suggests that the link between testosterone and aggression is complex and many other factors also play a part; no direct causal relationship was found.

More direct links between testosterone and crime have been found by Ellis and Coontz (1990)—who linked testosterone to high crime rates across many societies and across time—and Dabbs and Dabbs (2000) who linked high testosterone to criminal aggression, violence, delinquency, substance abuse, and other unacceptable or challenging behaviours. Ellis and Coontz (1990) suggest that the explanation for the causal link between testosterone and behaviour lies in the fact that it affects the developing brain of the foetus; however, this is not yet clear and even if the substance does affect the developing brain it is unclear what the effects of this would be on later behaviours. Therefore, it is unclear whether testosterone causes unacceptable behaviours. Hollin (1992) suggests that the claimed links arise partly because young males show many challenging behaviours (including heightened aggression, antisocial behaviour, and criminality) and also experienced high levels of testosterone but that the way in which testosterone causes behaviour change is far from understood; the two may have a different cause or link.

Overall, whilst the empirical evidence suggesting a link between testosterone (and many other substances) and unacceptable behaviours is strong, the evidence does not always prove a causal link. Explanations as to how or why the substances cause the change in behaviour are still often far from clear.

Genetics
Family studies

From very early on in the development of positivist explanations of crime (cf. Sheldon 1949) there have been theories that the body and mind are related. Following Darwin's findings many suggested that types of behaviour such as criminal behaviour were somehow inherited (Dugdale 1877; Goddard 1912; and Goring 1913). To prove this some (Dugdale 1877 and Goddard 1912) studied 'criminal families'. The most famous such study was of the Juke family and was conducted by an American sociologist, Richard Dugdale (1841–83). Dugdale (1877) found that a high proportion of the family were either criminals (males) or prostitutes (females). From this he postulated that criminality and prostitution were related and ran in the family, were somehow inherited, and would be passed between generations. However, remember that finding the link does not mean that the behaviour is genetic, it might result from being in the same environment or from learning social behaviours from each other. However, as well as Dugdale, other theorists, using similar correlations (finding crime within families) also claimed a genetic link.

Charles Goring (1870–1919), a British criminologist, discovered that there were many fathers and sons in prison as outlined in his work *The English Convict: A Statistical Study* (1913). He claimed the correlation was too close to be explained by environmental factors and it occurred even if the father was removed from the family when the child was very young. He therefore concluded there must be a genetic link. He argued that criminality was passed on in the same way as eye colour so there must be a criminal gene and therefore a born criminal. Similar close family links in relation to criminality are found today. In a group of 397 children from 344 families studied since the 1960s (a longitudinal study) half of the convictions were found in just 23 families and three-quarters of convicted mothers and fathers have a convicted child (see Rowe and Farrington 1997). The modern study recognises the possibility that the links may be environmental or learnt rather than genetic.

Adoption and twin studies

To study the possibility of inherited behavioural characteristics scientists have used two other methods—adoption studies and twin studies. Adoption studies are important because the environment for the twins or siblings (brothers and sisters) is different, so similarities are more likely to be explained by genetics. Studying identical twins is an attractive prospect because they are genetically identical—both have the same genetic make-up so any differences in behaviour will clearly be due to environment whereas similarities should be explained by genetics. There are two types of twins—monozygotic (MZ) twins who are genetically identical because they are from a single egg and a single sperm (identical twins), and dizygotic (DZ) twins who are formed from two eggs simultaneously fertilised by two sperm (non-identical twins who share only about 50 per cent of their genes, like any brother or sister). Twin studies tend to compare the behaviours of these two types of twins. There have been many such studies and some have included twins separated at birth (adoption studies) so that similarities would be assumed to be explained by the genetic similarities.

There is a lot of disagreement amongst criminologists about the strength of findings from these studies. Few today suggest that there is a criminal gene, rather they suggest that certain types of behaviour often related to criminal tendencies (such as extraversion) may be genetically passed on. Many believe there is a strong suggestion that genetics play a part in forming these broader behavioural traits. For example, Loehlin (1992) suggests that MZ (identical) twins are at least twice as likely to share behavioural traits as are DZ (fraternal) twins (see **Figure 13.9** which shows that in his study MZ (identical) twins tended to behave the same far more often than did DZ (fraternal) twins. The conclusion from this and other work is that both genetics and environment play a part in the formation of any behavioural traits—both nature and nurture are important to eventual behaviour (Fishbein 2001 and Joseph 2000).

So, there is likely to be some family connection in terms of criminality, but exactly what this is or how it operates is difficult to assess. If it is genetic how does it manifest itself in the genetic code? The gene code has now all been mapped and there have been no individual genes found for any behaviour, certainly no criminal gene. Is this even possible if we consider crime to be a social construction (see **Chapter 3**)? Most geneticists predict that what will be found in the future is that certain places on the genome will be identified which may be linked to personality

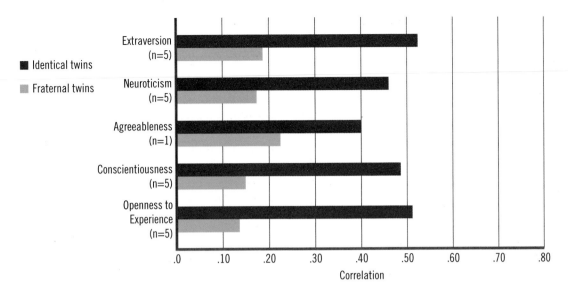

Figure 13.9 The extent to which twins share behavioural traits

Source: Loehilin, J.C. (1992) 'Genes and environment in personality development' in European Journal of Personality 7(3), 139–210

types. Some of these personality types may be more common among criminals than others, but this is a long way from a criminal gene. For example, a heightened drive or aggression might be useful in sport, for physical labour, for competitive financial or business practices, or for violent crime, etc. Therefore, such drives do not lead to criminality but may make it more likely. If a genetic link is found to such personality traits then it may lead to certain policy changes:

• It may be decided that we should not fully punish these individuals—they could not help their criminal behaviour, it resulted at least in part from their genetic make-up. They should therefore be helped to find more positive outlets for their personality traits or be given drugs to control the trait.

• If people cannot be controlled or redirected then they should be removed to protect everyone else. If people are to be removed for the benefit of everyone else they should presumably enjoy very comfortable surroundings. To an extent this is used today as we extend punishments to protect the public, although the policy is not related to genetic or to environmental factors merely to an acceptance that this person is somehow more dangerous than another and needs to be removed for as long as the law permits. These people are generally contained in prisons and do not enjoy better conditions.

• There might even be renewed calls for selective breeding or genetic manipulation, although as there are always legal outlets for these behavioural traits this would be more difficult to argue.

Therefore, if we were to find or accept that the personal choice of an individual is interfered with because their mind/body is predisposed to certain types of behaviour then one of the above outcomes (which accept determinism) would be logical. However, scientists tend to agree that it is not possible to ascertain whether (and to what extent) behaviour is affected by genetics (nature) and whether (and to what extent) it is affected by environment and upbringing (nurture) so it is almost impossible to quantify how much of any individual's behaviour results from free choice. In this circumstance, it is difficult to agree to what extent a state can justly punish. Most believe that behaviour is a combination of:

> gene and environment acting together. It is impossible to sort them into convenient compartments. An attribute such as intelligence is often seen as a cake which can be sliced into so much 'gene' and so much 'environment'. In fact, the two are so closely blended that trying to separate them is more like trying to unbake the cake.
>
> Jones 1993: 171

From this it is clear that both nature and nurture are involved in behaviour. The most that can be claimed for biology or genetics is that some people may be more physically or psychologically prone to certain types of emotions which may be linked to criminal behaviour (but also to perfectly legal behaviours). Some of these may be affected by their genetic make-up. From this it is clear that there is no strong or direct link between genetics and criminal behaviour. The possible link is made even more complicated when one adds in a study of evolutionary psychology.

Evolutionary psychology

Evolutionary psychology is a fairly new and emerging field. It applies Darwinian ideas to the development of the human psyche. There are aspects of this which apply to the evolution of humanity and aspects that apply to small groups of people, often families. The idea is that in order to understand modern humans and their behaviours, one needs to consider the environment in which our ancestors lived. This helps us to understand some aspects of our behaviour and our preferences and how these have evolved. Some of our likes and behaviours are left over from our evolution. Take two examples used by Toates (2007).

> Firstly, despite rising diabetes, obesity and dental decay humans generally have a love of sweet food, something which was an advantage in hunter gatherer communities in the past where sweet foods were uncommon (so people would not get fat) and unlikely to be poisonous (so they would not kill those who ate them).

> Secondly, the discussion about the attractiveness of symmetrical faces is explained because they tend to be both younger and reflect a strong developmental history so be good gene pools and therefore good people to mate with (natural selection of the fittest).

Evolutionary psychology recognises that the mind has evolved various methods or mechanisms to process information in a way which permits us to resolve problems which humans often meet. Therefore behaviour or characteristics which have over time benefitted a group of people will tend to be selected, people with those traits will be chosen as possible mates. In this way our thoughts and feelings have evolved to enhance those found to help humans survive:

- caring and protecting our children helps their survival and the survival of our genes;
- social living enhances the safety of the group and is therefore encouraged so that respecting and protecting others in one's group is a natural way of enhancing our own likelihood of survival so it is selected;
- aspects of social living such as religion which might tie people more closely to each other might also be evolutionary positives; and
- distrust of those not in one's group also enhances survival in a world where resources are limited—the them and us attitude is therefore rational and more likely to guarantee survival.

Whilst recognising that most behaviour is learned and based in our culture, what is being suggested is that aspects of how well ideas are learnt may partially depend on this underlying evolutionary psychology. They suggest that our behaviour when under extreme stress is probably partially explained by this underlying and natural psychology. The lines between the cultural/learned and the evolved psychology are not really understood and are constantly moving. Most people view learning and cultural aspects as strongest (except in extreme situations). The argument seems to be that evolutionary psychology sets the background for likely behaviours but learning and culture shape how those will normally become real and so which aspects of those evolutionary possibilities are brought to the fore.

Some evolutionary psychologists (Ridley 2004) even suggest that these background elements alter through a persons' life. Until recently (the end of the 20th century) it was believed that genes were completely set at the time the sperm and egg join. However, evolutionary psychologists question this idea; they believe that genes alter through a person's life and these changes arise in response to external stimuli. These theorists recognise that whilst genes largely shape or predetermine the structure of the body and the brain these are also affected by external factors. For example, the basic brain structure is moulded by genes but will develop differently depending on the way in which it is stimulated. Formative experiences, especially those at important developmental stages of the brain will affect the physical structure of the brain (see the 'Brain function and structure' section in this chapter). Although the physical boundaries of the way in which a particular brain can develop may be set at birth, the way in which it actually develops and which of its potentials it reaches depends on experience, opportunities, and life choices: free will, cultural opportunities, and family upbringing (especially the amount of affection) may well shape the brain. Therefore, nature gives us the building blocks but environment and nurture decides how these are finally shaped (Ridley 2004). This area of science is called *epigenetics*—it studies the genetic changes which might result from environment or upbringing. These changes do not alter the basic genetic material or DNA, rather they are changes to the way in which the genes can be interpreted or expressed. So if the DNA is the computer hardware, the epigenetics is the software. Some epigenetic material has always been necessary—it is what tells a cell to become a brain cell or a toenail, etc. so without it the DNA could not build the complexity necessary to become a human. Epigenetic elements are sort of tags attached to the genes which help the body to decide how the gene should be interpreted, which bits should be enhanced or suppressed. Recently it was recognised that these *tags* can be altered by environment. Many of these epigenetic *tags* are stripped off when DNA is passed on to the next generation. However, scientists are now finding that many of these *tags* get passed on to children and grandchildren, so that a health problem or a liking for, e.g., smoking might get passed down through the generations. Therefore aspects of behaviour and traits that were thought to be entirely nurture or environment based are increasingly found to be associated with these *tags* or epigenetics: they are inherited. This is beginning to further blur the lines between natural and environmental determination and may well have scientific and policy implications as more is understood about this area.

This evolutionary psychology or epigenetics renders it more difficult to ascertain which aspects of behaviour are inherited and which result from the environment. This means that it is difficult to determine whether a predisposition for criminal behaviour is caused by nature (genetics) or nurture (environment). However, what the theorists clearly agree on is that some people are more likely to choose criminal behaviour than are others. They also agree that this predisposition has implications for how much punishment would be just and how frequently and to what extent one should intervene in other ways (especially to rehabilitate).

Biological positivism: concluding remarks

This section of the chapter has considered the effects of physical attributes on behaviour: the genetic make-up or *tags* on genes which affect behavioural choices; the physical development of the brain and its effect on emotion and behaviour; and the production of substances such as testosterone or serotonin which affect the functioning of the brain and so alter behaviour. Whilst it is clear that biological factors have some role to play in determining behaviour, including criminal behaviour, the extent of their effects may be fairly minor and exactly how their effects might intervene to cause particular behaviours is far from understood. What all theorists agree is that the effects of these substances and physical attributes are altered or enhanced by broader social and environmental factors. Therefore, modern claims made by biological positivists are much less powerful than those made by Lombroso and other early positivists and even these limited claims need to be more carefully assessed before being finally accepted. We will now move on to explore psychological theories.

Psychological theories

Psychology suggests an alternative scientific basis for criminal behaviour. In contrast to biological theories, psychological explanations focus more directly on the workings of the mind and how that affects behaviour. Here we move away from the physical make-up to deal directly with individual characteristics such as personality, reasoning, thought, intelligence, learning, perception, imagination, memory, creativity, and how they may give us some insight into human behaviour.

There are many aspects of psychology, many theories which have been associated with criminal behaviour. Some of these are cognitive and place the issues clearly in the mind of the individual. These theories see behaviour as the result of thought processes, compelling mental forces or drives (the result of anger, frustration, desire, despair, etc.). Others, often referred to as behavioural psychologists, consider behaviour to arise out of both internal factors and external social or environmental factors, which may reinforce or discourage the behaviour. Each of these approaches has many different ideas about how psychology and criminal behaviour may be linked. Some theorists are closely linked to biological explanations and related ideas such as genetics and neurological factors. Others work more closely with some of the sociological theories such as social bonding. Here we do not propose a full consideration of all possible ideas nor how they are linked to other aspects covered in this volume. Rather we will present a brief introduction to two areas of psychology which often form a part of other theories: psychoanalytic perspectives and learning theories.

As with biological theories of crime, psychological theories are grounded in positivism—they claim that crime is the result of some mental or behavioural construct and is not entirely the result of free will or human choice (although psychological factors can influence and interact with free will).

Psychoanalytic perspectives

In psychoanalysis, the forces within an individual explain their behaviour. These inner forces are usually a mix of drives to fulfil their desires. The desires arise in an unconscious part of the brain and are merely experienced as strong needs or wants. The desires or base instincts grapple with reason and feelings of right and wrong to decide whether the desire will be met. The mental conflict is therefore often between reason and standards of behaviour on one side and fulfilling the desires of base instincts on the other. This mental conflict is experienced by everyone. Some people control their desires quite well. Others fail to control themselves and their behaviour then often causes concern. Crime and other unacceptable behaviours often arise when someone fails to control their desires.

Sigmund Freud and psychoanalysis

The mental conflict, how it arises and is resolved, is the core of psychoanalysis. These ideas are strongly associated with Sigmund Freud (1856–1939), an Austrian neurologist and psychologist whose theories have had a profound effect on psychology, literature, philosophy, and on the way in which we understand our world. In fact his influence is so complete that psychoanalysis is often referred to as Freudian (Freud 1935; and for information about application of his ideas to crime, Kline 1984). Psychoanalysis breaks the workings of the mind into three levels of awareness: conscious thought, preconscious thought, and unconscious thought.

- **Conscious thought**—current thoughts and experiences are held in this part of the mind and the individual is always aware of these. This is where the three aspects of the personality (see next list) are resolved and where reason and conscience either control or fail to control the desires. If desires are not controlled in line with social expectations then crimes occur.

- **Preconscious thought**—ideas, thoughts, and functions are held just outside your conscious mind but close enough to allow your conscious mind to decide to pull them to the fore when they are needed. Some of these are memories that are partially triggered by something in the conscious mind.

- **Unconscious thought**—thoughts, memories, feelings, and wishes that are safely stored in your mind but which, at the moment, you are wholly unaware of. This is also where natural instincts and drives are held and where there will be repressed memories. For the most part things held in your unconscious mind are not available to the conscious mind, or not without considerable help. These may be used by the mind unconsciously as when a smell invokes a memory.

Alongside these (though not perfectly mapped onto them) Freud singled out three constituents of personality: Id, Ego, and Superego.

- **The Id** is the pleasure-seeking part of the personality. The Id is basically in the unconscious part of the mind and is the most primitive portion of one's personality. We are born with our Id. It is driven by desire and operates on a pleasure principle—it knows what the person likes and seeks to deliver the most pleasure possible. The Id houses the drives to eat, drink, excrete, be comfortable, enjoy sexual pleasure, etc. The Id has no control or restraint (no reason or ethical or moral standards) and seeks to deliver as much pleasure as possible as soon as possible. Freud argued that in order to live with other people the Id needs to be repressed or controlled so that people do not harm each other.

- **The Ego** acts as a break on the Id. One is not born with an ego, it has to be learnt. The ego recognises what happens in the real world and reasons with the Id. If April likes chocolate the Id will require her to take it from the shelf in a shop and eat it immediately. The Ego recognises that taking chocolate from a shop (without paying) leads to punishment. The Ego tries to prevent the Id from taking the chocolate but the Id is strong so the Ego also wants to ensure that April gets her chocolate. So the Ego will take the chocolate to the counter and pay before eating it. This delays the pleasure and ensures that what happens relates to the real world—the necessity to pay. The Ego uses the 'reality principle' and tries to ensure that the desires are met in the most appropriate way possible. This may mean delaying fulfilment of the desire or only fulfilling it after another action has happened (paying). The Ego learns both how to control and how best to serve the Id in the real world. For example, the Ego learns that we are more likely to get what we want if we say please or that we will not be punished if we pay. The Ego tries to provide as much pleasure as possible whilst staying within the expected boundaries—the reality.

- **The Superego** controls the Ego. This is the conscience and it begins to develop at about two years old. The Superego exists in both unconscious (guilt) and conscious (moral or ethical codes) parts of the brain. Whilst there is a conscious element it is largely unconscious in the way in which it operates—feelings of guilt or pride rather than consciously working out where the right lies. However, it is where societal values reside, where the rules of a society (family, community, country) get stored. The Superego tries to ensure the individual is a perfect social being. It has an ideal image of the perfect person and constantly measures actions against that image. Of course, perfection looks different to each person, each of us learns from different people and learns slightly different rules, etc. The Superego is where we internalise rules so that if we live up to what is expected we feel pride—we have come close to the perfect social being—if we break the rules we feel guilt or shame—we are a long way from perfection. In this way it is the Superego which allows us to feel pride, guilt, or shame and it is through these feelings rather than conscious thought that the Superego often operates. The guilt and shame are remembered as unpleasant so the next time the person considers the action they experience anxiety that the bad feelings will return, the person represses the action and controls their desires. Often the Superego goes further by actually repressing the thought or desire before it comes to being a conscious thought. In this way thoughts and desires may also be repressed.

Those who use Freudian analysis to explain negative or criminal behaviours often claim the individuals have underdeveloped Superegos (Aichhorn 1936). That means that the person is likely to be a persistent offender as their internal moral code is not developed. Just as the biological theorists claimed that neglect or other problems with upbringing caused the brain to fail to develop connections so the psychologists claim that it fails to develop the Superego. However, what is different here is that people may fail to develop what society would class as an adequate Superego if the parents are overindulgent and do not set boundaries and/or if the parents or others close to the individual have a different, more permissive, moral code. It may be that they are from a different culture or that their immediate community is otherwise different from that of the wider society. For example, a person who has been groomed by terrorists might possess a normal, fully developed Superego with respect to the rules of the terrorist organisation. They therefore obey the rules of the terrorist organisation: however, they may have inadequate or underdeveloped Superegos with respect to the rules of society. Or they might repress the Superego they developed as part of the wider society and supplement it with this new Superego. However this happens the individual will be free to break some of the most fundamental rules of the wider society.

Freud also set out five stages of development for the personality. Each is associated with a particular age and any problems experienced at that age cause problems for that stage of development.

• **Oral Stage**—this occurs at ages 0 to 17 months and affects the mouth (sucking, biting, and chewing). Freud believed that because at birth the mouth is the pleasure centre babies are born with a sucking reflex and with a desire to suckle on their mother's breast. If a child's oral needs are not met during infancy, he or she may develop negative habits such as nail biting or thumb sucking to meet this basic need. Freud claims that the mouth is the pleasure centre at this age.

• **Anal Stage**—this occurs at ages 18 to 35 months and affects the anus, children begin to play with urine and faeces and are fixated on bowel and bladder control. The control they learn to exert over their bodily functions is important. Problems at this stage, such as parents toilet training their children too early, can result in a child who is uptight and overly obsessed with order.

• **Phallic Stage**—this occurs at ages 3 to 6 years and affects the genitals—masturbation. During this stage

children begin to enjoy their genitals and to struggle with sexual desires toward the opposite sex parent. Boys get attracted to their mothers (Oedipus complex) and want to replace their fathers who are seen as rivals for the mother's attention. However, they also feel guilty and worry the father will punish them by removing the penis. The fear of castration forces the child to control his desire for his mother. Freud believed that it is through resolving this conflict that the Superego (his restraint and conscience) is developed. Failure to resolve the conflict leads to problems in the Superego and serious behavioural problems may arise. Girls get attracted to their fathers (Electra complex—proposed by Jung) and want to replace their mothers. Freud argued that the resolution of this conflict is more complex and less complete with problems for the Superego—often leading to an over-developed Superego.

• **Latency Stage**—this occurs in children of over the age of 6 until just before puberty and is associated with the repression of sexual feelings. Sexual instincts reduce. Children focus on developing their Superego or conscience. They begin to behave in morally acceptable ways and adopt the values of their parents and other important adults.

• **Genital Stage**—this occurs at puberty and beyond and is associated with the maturation of sexual orientation. Sexual desires and impulses re-emerge. If other stages have been successfully met, adolescents engage in appropriate sexual behaviour.

Each of these stages helps to shape the personality and the resolution of each stage involves a progression in the development of the Superego and of its ability to persuade the Id to seek satisfaction through means which are acceptable to the Superego. Basically the Ego sits between the powerful forces of natural, biological urges on one side (the Id) and reality and social requirements (the Superego) on the other.

Freud posited that there were a number of defence mechanisms that were used to build an acceptable balance between desire and repression. When a conflict between Id and Superego arises the Ego feels overwhelmed and gets anxious; in order to resolve the anxiety a range of defence mechanisms are used. The defence mechanisms generally operate at the unconscious level but have an effect on the conscious decision about how to resolve the conflict. The balance, once it is reached, is mostly kept by the Ego. The perfect personality balance is reached when the desires of the Id are satisfied but that satisfaction is achieved by means which are acceptable to the Superego so allowing the person to enjoy what they want but also feel good about themselves. As part of the building of a Superego the mind uses a number of defence mechanisms, examples of which are provided in **Table 13.1**.

Defence Mechanism	Description	Example
Repression	This was the first mechanism Freud discovered. It is a mechanism which arises in the unconscious part of the mind and prevents threatening or disturbing thoughts getting to the conscious mind. This is done unconsciously so people have no control over it and are unaware that it has been done	Repression is used to stop an individual becoming conscious of thoughts that would result in guilt. For example, in the Oedipal stage it prevents thoughts about harming the same-sex parent reaching the conscious mind. Repressed memories have been blocked for the conscious mind and often contain things which are damaging to the person or that they cannot face
Projection	Where an unacceptable thought, motive, or feeling reaches the conscious mind it is attributed to somebody else. This arises when someone is not able to acknowledge their own feelings or is unaware or not conscious of them	Often aggressive or inappropriate sexual thoughts and desires are dealt with in this way. Strong feelings of dislike or hatred are unacceptable so when they arise you tell yourself the other person hates you and you are merely returning the feelings. Or you may be angry at your partner for not listening when it is you that is not listening
Denial	Refusing to accept reality. Here someone acts as if a nasty fact, feeling, thought, motive, etc. is not real. This is one of the most dangerous and primitive defence mechanisms and is often used by young children	People use this to deal with truths in their lives that they cannot deal with. For example, an alcoholic may deny the problem and state that they can hold down a job or keep a relationship going so they can't be an alcoholic
Regression	When a person is faced with unacceptable thoughts, impulses, or realities they merely move backwards to an earlier stage of development. Stress moves them backwards	A teenager who becomes overwhelmed by the changes in their feelings (anger) and desires (especially sexual) may move back to problem childhood behaviours such as thumb sucking or bedwetting. People may also refuse to get out of bed and face the world
Acting out	Performing an extreme behaviour in order to express or release thoughts or feelings they cannot otherwise deal with. Taking the action releases tension and stress	Children often have temper tantrums when they feel they cannot control something or cannot express themselves to let people know how they feel. As an adult, instead of telling someone they are angry they break something, punch an object, or self-harm
Displacement	This mechanism causes thought feelings and impulses about a person or object to be directed at another person or object. This mechanism can be helpful if redirected to a useful purpose but generally causes more problems when it is directed towards an innocent person	The classic example is someone who is angry with a boss or someone else who has power over them and who then comes home and takes things out on the family or on pets. The anger is redirected from the person who caused the problem to others who are not to blame. This causes guilt whilst not resolving the anger
Sublimation	Channelling unacceptable impulses, thoughts, and emotions into acceptable ones	In the example under 'displacement' above if the anger is redirected into driving the person to do better in a sport then whilst still not resolving the anger it does not increase the problem by adding guilt. Sexual frustrations and other problems may be usefully dealt with in this way. Another example is the use of humour to defuse tension

Table 13.1 Examples of the mind's defence mechanisms

Very often the desires of the Id are channelled into more acceptable behaviours. For example, a person may be persuaded that they should satisfy their sexual desires only in a relationship, or destruction and violence might be satisfied by taking apart toys and learning to rebuild them or through competitive sports. However, as is evident from **Table 13.1**, sometimes the mechanisms cause unacceptable or criminal behaviours or store problems up for the future.

Freud used these ideas to treat people who were experiencing problems, he never specifically used them as a tool to analyse the criminal mind though he recognised that they might underlie odd or unacceptable behaviours. Therefore psychoanalysis may be useful to explain criminality. For example, if a criminal has no personality problem (no conflict between the Superego on the one side and the Id and Ego on the other) then Freud might explain the behaviour as arising out of a complete criminal personality. Here the Superego is fully formed but is very permissive of behaviour others find unacceptable or criminal. Here the offender's cultural and social upbringing taught them to regard certain types of offending as acceptable and so they do not see it as wrong. For example, they may consider theft from a company as acceptable whilst still condemning theft from individuals. Along with the rest of society they may condemn many other acts; they merely feel free to commit particular offences. Furthermore, some of the defence mechanisms can also be connected to particular types of criminal act; see displacement in **Table 13.1** where anger at a boss and frustration about not being able to resolve it is displaced to a family member. Other defence mechanisms may provide an offender with a way of coping once they do offend, for example, someone who has been violent or attacked someone sexually may project the problem on to the victim so claiming they caused the violence or sexual attack.

Freud set out most of this analytical psychology though others have added to it (many defensive mechanisms have been added by others). It was Freud who first set out a well-organised and reasonably complete theory to untangle the human personality. Inspired by Freud other theorists such as Carl Jung (1875–1961), a Swiss psychologist who worked with Freud, extended or altered his ideas.

Extroversion, neuroticism, and psychoticism

Karl Jung diverted from Freud on several points but most importantly for the study of crime was the addition of the introvert and extrovert personality types. According to Jung, extroverts love people and love being surrounded by people. They are most energised when others are with them because they love an audience. They are often the life and soul of the party and other people find them very engaging, charming, good company, and likeable. However, they can be a lot of work because they always like to be centre stage, they get easily bored, and do not like repetitive tasks. They tend to have a short concentration span and do not like solitary tasks. They will happily invest in people. Extroverts talk and act without properly considering things. They are sociable people who can be impulsive.

Introverts, on the other hand, like some people, often have a few close friends and prefer to know when people will come around. Introverts do not like attention unless they know everyone. They may not be shy but are more reserved and are happy to listen, to be part of the group but not at the centre. Introverts focus on their world at that time so can read a book in a busy room, they can shut the world out and focus on a task, they are happy doing just that. Introverts are often more lonely in a crowded room than when they are alone. They often choose not to engage with people but when something or someone interests them they have a lot of concentration. They make friends for life. Introverts think things through before they speak or act. They are private people, defend their territory, and think before they act. Jung said that there

was a continuance from introversion to extroversion, and that everybody could be placed somewhere along the spectrum.

Whilst Jung applied the spectrum to criminality the main work in this area is that of Eysenck (1959, 1977, and 1987), and Eysenck and Gudjonsson (1989). Eysenck argued that the personality one develops is partly explained by genetics and partly by social factors. He said that people learn societal rules (develop a Superego) through conditioning: punishment for bad acts and reward for good ones. However, their capacity or ability to learn is set by their genetic make-up; how well they are able to learn through conditioning is part of who they are. He used Jung's extroversion-introversion spectrum (the E scale) as one part of this. Each person is born somewhere on that spectrum. However he added in another spectrum for neuroticism which runs from neurotic or unstable to stable (the N scale) (see **Figure 13.10**). Neurotics tend to be anxious and moody and are often overly emotional whereas stable people are emotionally calm and tend not to react. He argued that everyone lies somewhere on each of these scales; most fall somewhere in the middle but some people are placed at the extremes of each scale. The positioning of people on the scales set their ability to learn social norms, Eysenck's hierarchy of conditionability:

(a) stable introverts (low N low E) are the easiest to condition;

(b) stable extroverts (low N high E) and neurotic introverts (high N low E) are less malleable but do not encounter great difficulty in social learning;

(c) neurotic extroverts (high N high E) experience most difficulty in social learning.

In his later theories he added a third dimension—psychoticism (the P scale, see **Figure 13.11**) which runs from low impulse control (psychoticism) to high impulse control. A person with low impulse control (psychoticism) lacks empathy and can be cruel, aggressive, and sensation seeking whereas a person with good impulse control is empathetic, gentle, and caring. Neurotic, psychotic extroverts (High N, High E, High P) are the least likely to learn societal norms and so most likely to offend. Later, he also suggested that in order to enhance the predictability it was necessary to split the extrovert scale (E scale) into sociability and impulsiveness and it is only impulsiveness (lack of thought before acting) that is linked to criminal behaviour. There is some support for his ideas. For example, McGurk and McDougall (1981) found that neurotic extroverts and psychotic neurotic extroverts were only found in delinquent groups (stable introverts were only in the non-delinquent groups) and the link between offending and impulsiveness has been supported (Farrington

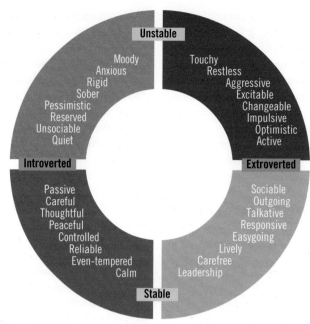

Figure 13.10 Extroversion and neuroticism (based on Eysenck's ideas)

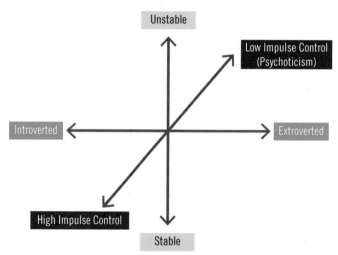

Figure 13.11 Extroversion, neuroticism, and psychoticism (from Eysenck's later works)

1994). However, there is still quite a bit of controversy both about the extent to which these underlying and broad personality traits may be linked to delinquency and whether the personality traits are genetic or learned as part of an individual's socialisation.

Here therefore the underlying personality renders a person more or less likely to offend. Whether they do offend is not governed by their personality trait; they have other choices, but offending behaviour is made more likely as a result of it.

Learning

Whilst desires may be innate, most activities and behaviours need to be learned. Often learning includes the physical elements of what to do; the results to which those actions will give rise; why and how those results may be

beneficial; and whether the activity is encouraged and valued by others, permitted, tolerated, or banned. Learning theories see most criminality to be a product of learned behaviour. Some behaviours may be innate (one is born with them); this would include behaviours such as swallowing or making vocal noises. However, most are learned either through studying others or through experience (trial and error), such as learning to train the vocal noises to produce words and verbal communication.

There are many different ways of learning and different aspects to learning which are important to unacceptable behaviours and crime.

Learning theories

People learn in various ways. However, the environment in which a person is raised and lives is thought to have the strongest impact on what they learn and therefore on how they learn to behave. Young children are most affected, first by their family, particularly parents, and then by teachers. As a child grows the influence of their peer group increases until in adolescence the peer group is probably the strongest influence on social learning. Whoever is the strongest influence or whatever the learning environment there are four main ways in which behaviour, attitudes, and skills are learnt: classical conditioning (classical learning); operant conditioning (operant learning); and cognitive learning. We will consider each of these and also briefly look at social learning.

Classical conditioning or classical learning

This is strongly associated with Ivan Pavlov, a Russian physiologist (1927) who found that behaviours can be learned by association. Pavlov noticed that some stimuli caused an animal to respond in a particular way, e.g. dogs salivate (unconditioned response) when they are fed (unconditioned stimulus) (see **Figure 13.12**).

Unconditioned here merely means that it happens naturally and is not learnt. He then set out to make them salivate even when they were not fed. He started to ring a bell (neutral stimulus) when feeding the dog. Eventually the dog salivated (conditioned response) when the bell rang (conditioned stimulus). This is a learned or conditioned response. He had taught the dog that the sound of a bell meant food; the dog associated bell ringing with being fed. If these behaviours are firmly embedded it is difficult to unlearn them. These are learned responses to our environment, so they often arise without feeling as if they are being learned; the learned responses are often strongly attached to emotions and are therefore very powerful.

Most people associate some sounds or smells with happy or sad occurrences and the mere sound (for example, of a voice) or smell may bring on powerful feelings of fear or joy. It is how most phobias arise; a strong emotional response to a stimulus and the emotional response is generally far more powerful than logic would suggest is sensible. The response arises due to something experienced or learnt from someone else. However, the emotional response is sometimes rather inexact, arising outside the exact and expected learned reaction, e.g. abused children often associate an angry face with violence and can experience extreme fear when others would merely feel uncomfortable (Pollak et al. 1998 and Pollak and Tolley-Schell 2003).

This learning is used in training animals and small children. Punishment is often used to teach people not to behave in certain ways. By punishing them they relate the punishment to the unacceptable behaviour and learn not to participate. Here behaviour is shaped not just by the inner forces (like the Id) but by the environment, so increasing the extent to which the environment punishes unacceptable behaviour should reduce that behaviour. It is often referred to as avoidance learning. Treatments based on classical learning are limited because the person who is learning is passive. However, useful treatments include exposure therapy (flooding is where a person is exposed to their painful memories and learns to deal with them using knowledge they now have) and systematic desensitisation (exposing someone to their phobia and teaching them to relax rather than react). These are mostly used to treat phobias or post-traumatic stress disorders (PTSD) so are little used in criminal justice.

Operant conditioning or operant learning

Skinner (1938) used the operant chamber (sometimes called a 'Skinner box', see **Figure 13.13**). Rats were given food if they pressed a lever. They learnt that pressing the lever gave rise to being fed so they pressed the lever frequently. This is an example of positive reinforcement—a reward stimulates more of the activity. Sometimes when the rat was put in the box the floor of the box had a low level electric current running through it (unpleasant for the rat). The rats soon learnt that pushing the lever turned off the electric current through the floor. This is an example of negative reinforcement—an action removes an unpleasant stimulus.

The individual interacts with the environment to either increase or decrease a particular behaviour. It operates through rewards and punishments. If a person is rewarded that behaviour is reinforced, they learn it is good and that nice things happen when they participate so they perform more of this type of behaviour. Through use of negative reinforcement people learn that to prevent something nasty they need to participate in a particular activity.

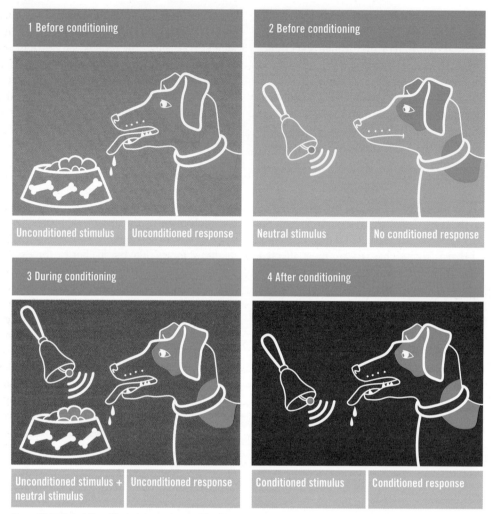

Figure 13.12 A depiction of Pavlov's learned or conditioned response

Bad behaviours are dealt with through punishment. Positive punishment is the use of something nasty to persuade people that they should not participate in that behaviour any more. For example, having to pay a fine might persuade someone that it is not worth parking on a double yellow line. Negative punishment is the removal of a desired activity in order to persuade that person and others not to act that way again. For example, the removal of a driving licence for speeding or the removal of the right to be a company director for breach of regulations. Here the person learns not just what happens when certain types of behaviour occur but also how to increase positive outcomes, e.g. to continue with the bad behaviour when no-one is watching.

Each individual tries to maximise rewards whilst minimising unpleasantness. The techniques of positive and negative reinforcement and of positive and negative punishment are used to try to shape behaviour. However, there is little detail as to how the conditioning works. Here the changes in behaviour are a reaction to the environment and the learning does not include any element

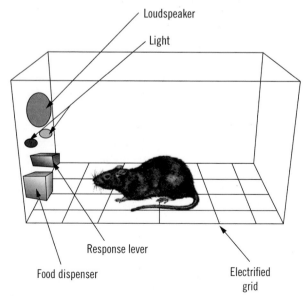

Figure 13.13 A depiction of Skinner's operant conditioning
Source: Andreas1/CC BY-SA 2.0

explaining why the behaviour is unacceptable or why it should be avoided.

To alter behaviour, one needs to manipulate the environment to either encourage or discourage a particular activity. Systems such as Antecedent-Behaviour-Consequence (A:B:C) are used. An antecedent is something that happens before behaviour and may trigger the behaviour. Behaviour is just something someone does. Consequence is something that follows the behaviour. So, if a peer group persuades a young person to misbehave and then the peer group applauds the behaviour and society and possibly their family punishes that misbehaviour: if the fun or the approval of the peer group is stronger than the punishment the behaviour will be repeated but if that is not the case it will not. For each individual one finds out why that behaviour is encouraged or worth participating in and then try to counter that to find ways in which the behaviour might be discouraged in the future.

Social learning theory

Social learning theory suggests that humans learn through social interactions and tend to mimic behaviours of others. Bandura (1961) argued that one could learn any human behaviour and that all behaviour was learned rather than inherited. He claimed that the learning happens through imitating and copying others. The Bobo doll experiment was designed to test these ideas. There are different variations of the experiment but here we will consider just one. Bandura put some children into a room with an adult who verbally and physically attacked a large doll. They hit the doll with a mallet put in the room for that purpose. He put others in a room with an adult who was neither verbally nor physically aggressive towards the doll and just played quietly with other toys in the room. A third group were in a room with no adult present. All the children were then exposed to a mild stimulus which might increase their feelings of aggression—as soon as the child started to play with toys they were told that they could not. Each child was then taken to another room with a variety of toys (including the Bobo doll and the mallet). Children who witnessed the aggressive behaviour tended to either be verbally or physically aggressive (or both). Boys were three times more likely to be physically violent towards the doll than were girls (society is more tolerant of male aggression). Both boys and girls had the same rates of verbal aggression. Those who witnessed no aggression or where there was no adult in the room (the control) were less likely to show any aggression (see **Figure 13.14**).

The experiment supports the ideas set out in social learning theory—that people learn social behaviour, even aggression, through observation and learning. Some believe that this has important implications for child rearing and for the showing of things such as aggression in the media. That at least is one interpretation of the findings.

Figure 13.14 Pictures from Bandura's Bobo doll experiments
Source: Okhanm/CC BY-SA 4.0

Another way of understanding the findings is to say that people have the urges to be aggressive and far from learning aggression they learn to control aggression. When they see aggression by others (particularly if it is not punished) they feel free to be aggressive so they imitate the levels of aggression they have witnessed. This would mean that the showing of aggression does not cause the problem. There is therefore disagreement about the effects of showing aggression and some argue that it is therefore unacceptable to curtail the freedom of the media, others that such freedom should be curtailed in the hope that it might prevent violence by others whether that is social learning or merely imitation. This is a complex issue and one with conflicting evidence on each side.

What is important here is that it suggests that through this and the other behavioural learning theories (such as classical and operant learning) it may be possible to retrain offenders to avoid certain unacceptable behaviours.

Each of these theories is, however, limited. It fails to take account of the individual and how their brain works, how they think.

Cognitive learning

Cognition is very important as it adds understanding to the activities of humans. The early learning theories are known as behavioural psychology and treat the learner rather like a container, you put certain things in and know you will get something out. So if someone is exposed to positive reinforcement it will encourage the behaviour they are participating in at the time. This does not explain why they learn to perform or not to perform certain activities. It does not consider what goes on inside the brain of the person who experiences the stimulus.

Cognitive learning is different from behavioural learning. It is based on cognitive psychology and understands that all aspects of, and processes of, the conscious mind are engaged in choices about how to behave. It is therefore necessary to interact with many aspects of learning to fully alter behaviour. The idea is that an informed learner is more likely to retain the positive activity because it becomes part of what is important to them. Learning, especially cognitive learning, involves learning not only the behaviours and skills but also the attitudes and moral standing. Cognitive learning requires a focus not just on external experiences as affecting behaviour but also the way in which each of us processes those experiences. Cognitive learning focuses on how we can alter the internal processes which affect behaviour and thought. The idea is that morals and attitudes are learnt from others in the environment. Cognitive theorists argue that one of the strongest protections against criminal behaviour is a moral standing that rejects such behaviour

as unacceptable so that the person chooses not to offend. This is not just a response learning. This requires an individual to understand, to give meaning to what they experience in the world. Here individuals learn about the physical world and the skills necessary to interact as well as learning meaning, attitude, and beliefs. It includes learning to: control impulsive desires and behaviours; develop powers of moral reasoning; solve interpersonal problems; respect others; take responsibility; make rational choices about behaviour.

The tenets of cognitive learning are often used to try to alter the behaviour of offenders. Here it is necessary to use multimodal learning which teaches a person about various aspects of their behaviour. For example, it might teach them how and why to process information or to problem solve as well as teaching practical skills, social skills, and moral reasoning. If only one of these is taught the learning might not be complete. Many aspects of probation or youth justice work use cognitive behavioural therapy (CBT) to address particular behaviours.

Cognitive learning is based on a broader school of cognitive psychology. This makes it clear that learning, like any other part of brain processing, is complex and may affect each person differently. Cognitive psychology studies (or gets to know) an individual's mental processes such as their attention, language use, memory, emotion, perception, creativity, and problem solving. It studies these processes and their effects on how people think, feel, and behave. It seeks to understand how things such as memory, attention, problem solving, and language work. How do people process information? How do we remember things? Why does one person focus on one aspect of a story or an occurrence whereas another focuses on other aspects? They are therefore interested in the processes that occur from the time someone experiences something (a stimulus) until there is a response. The core processes studied are things like perception, attention, language, memory, and thinking.

Cognitive psychology asks questions such as:

- How do different people perceive the world around them? How do they perceive colour or shapes? In criminology and criminal justice we might want to understand how they perceive what they witness at a crime scene and why one eye-witness account may differ from another.

- Why do people remember some facts and not others? Why does one person remember faces better than another? Why do eye-witnesses remember different things even if they experience the same crime scene?

- Why do some people learn from a particular input and others do not? This is very important if a state wishes to alter or regulate behaviour.

If you have taken the tests in **What do you think? 13.4** it should be clear that what is in the world and what we *see* as being in the world may be different. Each of us selects, organises, interprets, and responds to information in the outside world. We do this very quickly and constantly and we organise the information we take in in such a way that it makes sense (the triangles in **Figure 13.16**). We may also not see things which we do not know or understand. This

happens particularly if we are watching a play, reading a story, or watching a film. We will tend to try to make the story fit what we know so we will enhance things that make sense and might ignore or see as less important things which are difficult to understand or which we have been taught are less important. We also do that when we witness things in real life such as a crime and therefore eye-witness accounts may differ, but each may be true as our minds

WHAT DO YOU THINK? 13.4

- Would you believe eye-witness testimony would be accurate? Do you believe your eyes?

- What we see and how we see it is complex. Take some of the tests below.

- Look at **Figure 13.15**, what do you see?

- Did you see faces or a vase?

- What shapes do you see in **Figure 13.16**?

- Most people answer that they see a triangle and a square, but that is not correct. In fact there is neither a square or a triangle; your eyes see the potential for these shapes and your brain fills in the gaps.

- Which of the circles turns most quickly in **Figure 13.17**?

- None of these is turning—it is a still photograph. Your eyes see the shapes and your brain perceives movement where there is none.

Figure 13.15 Test 1
Source: Public domain

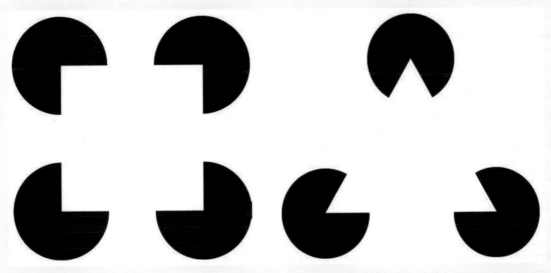

Figure 13.16 Test 2
Source: Public domain

Figure 13.17 Test 3
Source: Public domain

are not like a camera. Also, one person may learn from a particular input whilst another does not, one may understand and empathise with a victim whilst another may not and sometimes it may be due to differences in what they have already learnt or understood. True cognitive learning takes all of this into account and tailors the learning to fit the individual, to make sure that this person understands and fully learns about a particular type of behaviour. The need for this learning of understanding and moral stance as well actions in trying to control behaviour explains why punishment alone often fails to alter behaviour.

Cognitive learning could influence some or all of the following behaviours relating to criminality or the absence of it: law-abiding attitudes and emotions; greater interactive or social skills; acceptable types of behaviour; acceptable reactions to certain stimuli which they may encounter; and life skills so they are more able to cope with everyday problems such as finding and keeping a job. The effectiveness of such learning depends on a number of factors, including the skill of the teacher and the willingness of the criminal to learn, also how far the learning takes account of the psychological processes and ways of thinking of the person who needs to learn new controls. Cognitive learning uses skills-based approaches

to address problem-solving and social interaction while also challenging belief structures and attitudes. For real success it is necessary for the individual's understanding and attitude to change not just the behaviour in relation to a particular response (see Vennard and Hedderman, 1998; and Hollin, 1995). One of the problems with cognitive learning is that if it is not properly and fully effective it may teach people how to avoid detection, make them more effective offenders so great care needs to be taken with the use of CBT to ensure that attitude, values, and moral reasoning have also altered (Hollin 1995 and 2002). With serious offences this often requires a lot of one-to-one work with a specialist. With less serious offences group work can be effective. Cognitive group work is often used to teach those who drive over the speed limit or to reduce aggression in cases of lower level violence.

Cognitive psychology is very important to understanding how best to obtain reliable testimony from victims, witnesses, and from suspects or the accused. This is used in most modern police work but still needs to be adopted by courts. The problems involved in how we perceive and remember things is also not explained to jurors and this may interfere with justice. Cognitive psychology and what it tells us about learning and behaviour is central to

	Closely associated with	Core of the idea	Application to human learning	Relationship to criminology
Classical Conditioning Or Classical Learning	Pavlov (1927)	Behaviours can be learned by association. In humans this type of learning is often associated with strong emotions	Here behaviour is shaped not just by the inner forces (like the Id) but by the environment	Punishment is often used to teach people not to behave in certain ways
Operant Conditioning Or Operant Learning	Skinner (1938)	Behaviours can be encouraged through positive reinforcement or discouraged through negative reinforcement	It operates through rewards and punishments. There is often little detail as to how the conditioning works	The techniques of positive and negative reinforcement and of positive and negative punishment are used to try to shape behaviour
Social Learning Theory	Bandura (1961)	All human behaviour is learned rather than inherited	He claimed that the learning happens through imitating and copying others	Humans learn from each other so it is important to receive positive social inputs
Cognitive Learning Or Cognitive Behavioural Theory (CBT)	Most modern learning theorists	Cognition is very important as it adds understanding to the activities of humans. Cognitive learning is not just a response, it requires an individual to understand, to give meaning to what they experience in the world	Learning the interactive skills as well as meaning, attitude and beliefs all of which is necessary to social living. It includes learning to: control impulsive desires and behaviours; develop powers of moral reasoning; solve interpersonal problems; respect others; take responsibility; and make rational choices about behaviour	An informed learner is more likely to retain the positive activity because it becomes part of what is important to them. Many aspects of probation or youth justice work use CBT to address particular behaviours

Table 13.2 A precis of learning theories and their contribution to understanding criminal behaviour

much rehabilitative work being done by probation and youth justice. Cognitive behavioural therapy (CBT) is routinely used to alter behaviour in the hope of teaching people to be more law abiding.

Table 13.2 sets out a precis of learning theories, their core ideas, application to human learning and relationship to criminology. From all of this, the impact of learning theories on criminology are clear: they can throw light both on why some people learn to offend and what we could do to counter that problem.

Conclusion of learning theories

Behavioural learning, especially classical and operant learning are each affected by social setting, social interactions, personal associations, and the environment. Whilst they do not take account of how each person processes the information they do lay out ways in which people learn which behaviours are acceptable and which are not. They also display human capacity to understand when and where particular behaviours may be appropriate as they are firmly linked to the environment in which the learning takes place. Clearly cognitive learning goes further as

it involves interacting with the attitudes, values, and moral reasoning of an individual in order to alter their behaviour not just in that environment but in all environments.

Learning, especially cognitive learning involves learning not only the behaviours and skills but also the attitudes and moral standing. The morals and attitudes are learnt from others in the environment. One of the strongest protections against criminal behaviour is a moral standing that rejects such behaviour as unacceptable so that the person chooses not to offend. From this it is clear that learning theories have a powerful input to rehabilitation and make a positive contribution to the problem of criminality—to our understanding of how crime might be learnt and how society can alter that learning. It is important to recognise that this is not about treatment for offenders but rather about increasing their learning so that they can live in society without harming others. However, learning will not always be able to prevent future offending, to equip people to make more socially constructive (or less destructive) choices in the future.

If criminal behaviour and social behaviour are both learnt, then the earlier biological theories in this chapter suggesting that crime is innate or genetically passed from one generation to the next, are questionable.

SUMMARY

- Critically discuss Lombroso's ideas and then consider his most important contribution to criminology

Working at the end of the 19th century Lombroso collected large amounts of data. He took measurements from many offenders and from this information he suggested that certain facial and body characteristics were indicative of particular types of criminal behaviour. He described people with these characteristics as throwbacks to an earlier evolutionary stage, they were dangerous and less civilised. People with those characteristics were therefore thought to be likely to offend than were others. From these ideas and others like them grew the eugenics movement which wanted to rid society of these dangerous and less civilised people. The eugenics movement suggested either controlling the breeding of those described as evolutionary throwbacks or killing them so as to prevent their genes being passed on to future generations. The idea was to create a more positive, crime free society. Nazi Germany adopted these theories and some other states tried to prevent certain people from reproducing. We now understand that Lombroso's theory (and others which claimed to discover a 'born criminal') were too simplistic and their ideas have been discredited (Rock 2007). The actions undertaken in the name of theories like Lombroso's should remain as a warning against relying too heavily on ideas which offer easy solutions; at least one should not interfere with people's liberties based on these sorts of ideas. However, Lombroso remains important because of the use he made of scientific methodology to collect information from which he tried to build an explanation of human behaviour. Whilst the methodology he used was seriously flawed, his recognition of the importance of detailed data is still used today.

- Briefly explain how brain structure is formed and altered and then consider its effect on behaviour

The central nervous system is made up of the brain and the spinal cord. The spinal cord takes communications from the body to the brain and back. The brain is a complex structure which sorts and retains information and makes decisions about how to act, etc. The brain is separated into a number of different areas each of which performs a different function. The areas which are most important in the study of criminology are the frontal lobe (thinking and behaviour), parietal lobe (language), and temporal lobe (feelings). Of these the frontal lobe is most central to deciding how to behave.

The way in which and the rate at which the brain develops affects our ability to process information. An under developed brain impairs concentration and self-control. It also impairs a person's ability to: make rational decisions; understand the consequences of their actions; solve problems; feel empathy; sorting of and access to information; learn from previous experiences. Each of these might make criminal behaviour more likely. Similar problems in the structure of the brain can result from life choices such as the misuse of alcohol or drugs or as a result of life experiences such as maltreatment especially while the brain is developing (up to the age of about 25). The difference in development of the structures of the brain is likely to be a factor, but only one factor, that makes criminal behaviour more likely, especially in adolescence and that prevents individuals from maturing out of or learning not to offend.

- How does Eysenck suggest that personality impacts on criminal behaviour?

For Eysenck development of the personality depends on both a person's genetic make-up and the environment or social context in which he or she lives, social factors. He noted that each person had a different capacity to learn, remember, and live by rules. He claimed that three scales impact on learning capacity: the extroversion-introversion spectrum (the E scale, first suggested by Jung); the neurotic (unstable)—stable scale (the N-scale); and the high impulse control—low impulse control (P scale or psychotic scale). Each person is placed somewhere on the continuum for each of these scales. For each scale a high score impedes a person's ability to learn social norms. Therefore a neurotic, psychotic extrovert (High N, High E, High P) is the least likely to learn societal norms and so most likely to offend. Later he also suggested that in order to enhance the predictability it was necessary to split the extrovert scale (E scale) into sociability and impulsiveness and it is only impulsiveness (lack of thought before acting) that is linked to criminal behaviour.

There is some support for his ideas. For example, McGurk and McDougall (1981) found that neurotic extroverts and psychotic neurotic extroverts were only found in delinquent groups (stable introverts were only in the non-delinquent groups) and the link between offending and impulsiveness has been supported (Farrington 1994). However, there is still quite a bit of controversy both about the extent to which these underlying and broad personality traits may be linked to delinquency and whether the personality traits are genetic or learned as part of an individual's socialisation.

- Compare and contrast the various learning theories and consider which is most useful to reduce criminal behaviour

There are four main learning theories: classical conditioning (classical learning); operant conditioning (operant learning); social learning theory; and cognitive learning (cognitive behavioural theory or therapy/CBT). The simplest learning (classical) is often associated with strong emotions and therefore is strongly embedded. However, the classical learning is fairly limited in its ability to teach social norms, using only punishment through which to alter behaviour. Operant learning uses both positive and negative reinforcement to teach correct social behaviour but again is limited as a means of teaching social norms. Classical and operant learning are both behavioural learning theories and therefore depend on social settings and environmental factors. However, they do not take account of how people process information; nor do they inform learners why rules are chosen or should be followed. Bandura explained how social learning works and emphasised the need for positive social inputs for a child to copy. Finally, cognitive learning theory (or therapy, CBT) is the most sophisticated as it embeds meanings, attitudes, morals, and beliefs as part of the learning theory. The idea is that an informed learning is more likely to be remembered, understood, and accepted by the individual, and therefore more likely to be followed. If learning includes moral or ethical rules it also allows the learner to apply the rules to new situations. Learning theories may hold the key to understanding both why people offend and how we can counter that to bring someone back to acceptable behaviour patterns. Ideally they teach sound social norms so that individuals avoid criminality in the first place, but they can also be used to alter behaviours once someone has offended.

It is important to note that the learning theories put in doubt the idea that crime is innate, whether that is genetically passed on or the result of brain development etc.

FURTHER READING

Newburn, T. (2009) *Key Readings in Criminology.* Abingdon: Willan Publishing.
For excerpts from original criminology texts and the key readings for the theories covered in this chapter relating to biological positivism and psychological positivism.

Bernard, T. J., Snipes, J. B., and Gerould, A. L. (2015) *Vold's Theoretical Criminology* (7th edn). Oxford: Oxford University Press. Chapter 4 Biological and Chapter 5 Psychological.

Hollin, C. (1992) *Criminal Behaviour: A Psychological Approach to Explanation and Prevention*. London: Falmer Press.

Chapter 3 of this text discusses criminal behaviour in relation to biological aspects but the rest of the volume is of interest in its discussion of psychological aspects.

Hopkins-Burke, R. (2013) *An Introduction to Criminological Theory*. Abingdon: Routledge.

Chapters 5 and 6 of this text provide a clear and accessible introduction to biological (Chapter 5) and psychological (Chapter 6) theories.

Polaschek, D. (2017) 'Psychology of Violence' in Maguire, M., Morgan, R., and Reiner, R. (eds) *The Oxford Handbook of Criminology* (5th edn). Oxford: Oxford University Press.

These texts all have excellent discussions of biological and/or psychological positivist theories.

Access the **online resources** to view selected further reading and web links relevant to the material covered in this chapter.
www.oup.com/uk/case/

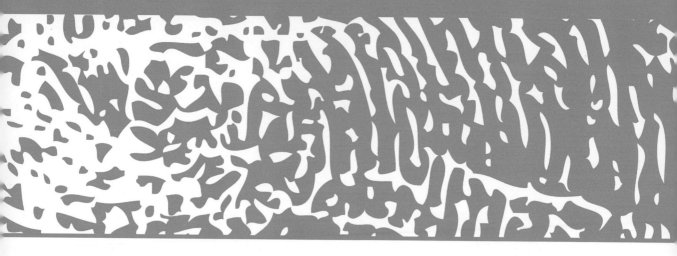

CHAPTER OUTLINE

Introduction	378
Sociological theories	379
Key concepts in sociology	379
Social process/interaction theories	383
Social structural theories—macro-sociological theories	387
Culture and subcultural theories	397

Sociological positivism

Determined to predetermine

KEY ISSUES

At the end of this chapter you should be able to:

- recognise the contribution of sociology to the making of criminology as a subject in its own right;

- identify the main strands of sociological thinking and distinguish their differing contributions to the subject;

- appreciate the contribution of the Chicago school to the study of criminology;

- understand the basic concepts of anomie, strain, subculture, and social learning and relate each of these concepts to the criminologists who are most often connected with them;

- analyse and critically assess the ideas discussed and the contribution they make to our understanding of crime and criminal behaviour.

Introduction

In this book, we have been looking at various theories of criminology to help us understand criminal behaviour. The theories studied so far have focused on individuals, their choices and how their differences might impact on their likelihood to offend. In many of these chapters the individual was seen as problematic, either because they made poor choices for which they needed to be punished or because there was something inherently wrong with them.

Firstly, in **Chapter 12** we studied theories based on classical thinking; these theories assert that criminality is explained by the choices people make. From these theories come the ideas that if we can alter those choices, making people less likely to opt for criminal behaviour, we can reduce or eliminate crime. Classical theorists put this into action by devising fair criminal justice systems leading to punishments aimed at preventing people from gaining from criminal behaviour. For neo-positivists, a branch within classic theory, the outcome of this action often involved and continues to involve manipulating the environment to render it harder to successfully gain anything from criminal behaviour, therefore making it less likely that people will opt to offend (see 'Situational crime prevention' in **Chapter 12**).

Secondly, in **Chapter 13**, we considered the ideas of early positivists and theories based on biological or psychological ideas. These theories study the individual and suggest that criminals are biologically or psychologically different from everyone else. They assume that if we could identify a difference between offenders and the rest of the population we could design a way to counter it. In most of these (biological and psychological) theories the 'difference' identified is deemed pathological, a term denoting disease, either physical or mental. In this way, positivists assume that there is something wrong with offenders, claiming that there is something about the person which predetermines them to act in a criminal way. In early theories this was taken almost literally—so that there was a drive to rid societies of people with criminal characteristics; criminals were seen as less civilised or less evolved than other people (atavistic throwbacks); and it was thought that they should not be allowed to breed. Note that if this were true then—as a consequence—punishment would be wrong as these offenders would not be in control of their actions. More recently theorists have accepted that, whilst these biological or psychological traits may make a person more likely to offend, they do not predetermine behaviour and lots of other factors are also involved.

In this chapter we will be moving away from locating the explanation for criminality in the individual and instead studying how society or social processes might affect behaviour. We will be asking why there might be more known offenders in some geographical areas than in others and why more people from a certain background might become offenders than those from other backgrounds.

Psychological theories suggest that a person with an enhanced psychopathic or sociopathic element to their personality is more likely to turn to crime (though they might also become sportsmen or work in high finance, Dutton and McNab 2014). Whether that person turns to crime or chooses a law-abiding life may depend on decisions taken by government about economic issues or by companies about where to locate or how to operate. The choices made by governments and companies may open up law abiding choices (removing the need for criminality) or close down law abiding opportunities (making offending more likely). Decisions by governments and companies and sociological issues (such as poverty) affect individuals but may also affect whole communities; they may influence the likelihood of many people to choose to offend or be law abiding. Therefore, the health of the economy or the rate of unemployment, for example, may influence the behaviour of an entire population, not just one individual and so may lead to a rise or fall in criminal behaviour (the crime rate may be affected).

Sociologists often study the underlying social conditions in which people may be more likely to choose to offend, such as, for example, if they lose their job. Sociologists are therefore suggesting that individual behaviour may be affected by broader social conditions or political decisions, and that all the individual decisions added together may cause other effects, e.g. high crime rates. As with the biological and psychological theories discussed in **Chapter 13**, many sociological theories are also positivist and suggest that the behaviour of each individual is, to an extent, predetermined. This means that offenders are at least partially (often almost wholly) directed by forces outside the control of the individual. For example, offenders have no control over the economy though it may cause them to become unemployed and that may propel them towards criminality.

Like the biological and psychological theories, sociological theories are not absolute—not everyone who loses their job will offend, though that state may increase the likelihood of offending. What sociological theories most often suggest is that particular social or societal changes or factors may *influence* criminal behaviour. Here tangible and measurable aspects of society can be scientifically recorded and the information obtained can be used to understand criminal activity. Criminology is concerned with studying and identifying these sociological determining factors as it may then be possible to alter those social factors and so increase or decrease criminal behaviour. Before we begin to consider some of these theories it is probably sensible to remember that because crime encompasses many activities (graffiti, murder, burglary, blackmail, substance misuse, etc.) no one theory will ever be able to explain all crime. There are therefore many theories and it is important not to disregard the biological and psychological ideas (from **Chapter 13**) nor to try to choose any single sociological theory to explain criminality.

Sociological theories

Sociological theories are often split into three distinct types: social interaction or social process theories; social structural theories; and social conflict theories. Each will now be briefly described (see also **Figure 14.1**).

Social interaction theories

Firstly, there are social interaction or social process theories; here they will be referred to as **social interaction theories**. These are micro-sociological theories—they look at elements close to the individual and explain crime in terms of the immediate social situation an individual finds him-/herself in and how that impacts on choices and behaviours. Interaction theories focus on small groups and individuals and consider the way in which people behave and how they interact with each other, which then creates the society they live in. They are called interaction theories because they accept that the choices made by an individual impact on their immediate social situation and on that of others around them, so affecting the micro-sociological environment in the immediate future. The effect is reciprocal in that the social situation around a person affects the way in which they behave and their behaviour, in turn, affects their social environment. Social interaction theories include: differential association theories; social control theories; and labelling perspectives.

Social structural theories

Secondly, there are social structural theories, often referred to as structuralism. These are macro-sociological theories—they stress the impact of broad social conditions (such as unemployment rates) on the behaviour of individuals. Structuralism looks at how society makes us what we are—they look at the way in which the structure of a society has an influence on our daily lives. These theories assert that the way in which the big social picture affects the individual's behaviour may have more of an effect than their immediate social situation (their home, upbringing, school, etc.). Social structural theories include: social strain theories; social disorganisation theories; and subcultural theories.

Social conflict theories

The social conflict theories are generally macro-sociological theories stressing the impact of the way in which societies are structured. Conflict theorists consider that those in power pass laws (including criminal laws) and use the legal system and other state organs to ensure both that they—the leaders—remain in power and at the top of society and that they also keep the powerless controlled and on the bottom. They argue that the poor, the disadvantaged (sometimes including women) and minorities, such as non-dominant racial groups, are more likely to be closely controlled, arrested, convicted, or imprisoned, simply because of their poverty, gender, and/or race. These theorists therefore study the distribution of power and of other goods in society and see these factors as associated with what behaviours we choose to control (and how we control them), and with why some transgress at all.

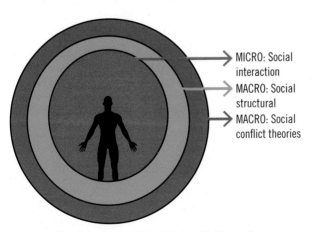

Figure 14.1 The relation between the individual and the three main sociological theories

Key concepts in sociology

There are a few concepts which are always important to sociological study. Whilst different theorists may view them and weigh them up differently, they are always significant in sociological discussions and need to be understood.

Status and role

Every person in a society inhabits various positions or states associated with a status. Status may be largely given or ascribed, for example, gender, race, and age. Ascribed status is generally thought of as fixed. Status may also be earned and be more transient, such as, class, professional or marriage status, which may change throughout a person's life. Being a student is an earned status, and so too is being a criminal. In each society there are expectations which will be linked to each status and, even before we meet someone, their status will affect the way in which we view them. Each status will have a different meaning or connotation in different societies. For example, in some societies (especially Asian cultures) the elderly are respected and valued; in others (many western cultures) they are considered more of a burden or at least in a more negative light (Giles et al. 2003). Similarly roles (such as a type of job), which are generally earned rather than ascribed (though people may be born into a particular role, e.g. a King), bring with them certain expectations.

From knowing a person's role or status one expects certain things to follow and certain behaviours. So, one expects something different from a mother, a doctor, a teacher, a builder etc., and if an individual acts outside their expected role/status then it can make us uncomfortable. To give an extreme example, one expects a lecturer to teach you but not to take your blood pressure whereas a doctor might be expected to take your blood pressure but not lecture you. So if a lecturer is teaching students then they are living up to the expectations placed on that role and, if they teach well, they will be respected. If that same lecturer suddenly starts to touch students (especially if they touch them in intimate and private ways) he or she has moved outside their expected role and students will react against them. Many sociological theories revolve around roles and statuses, how they are 'earned' or changed, and the meanings given to each.

Rules/norms

Social rules or norms are the standards by which people in a society are expected to live. Many are just types of behaviour which are expected or frowned upon. Some have existed for a long time, such as the expectation that it is not polite to pick your nose in public or that one is expected to wear clothes and cover one's genitals in public. Others may be newer, such as the expectation that people should walk on the left (in the UK) in busy buildings. Some change frequently and come into and fall out of fashion. Some, often referred to as social mores are taken more seriously; people may get angry if they are broken or

some people in society might act negatively towards you if you breach them (a social sanction). For example, in some societies it is not considered acceptable for a woman to be highly sexually promiscuous and such women may be looked down upon or even excluded from parts of that society. Some social mores may even become criminal laws and will be enforced by the state through the use of sanctions if they are broken (see **Chapter 3**).

If the state gets the criminal law right, then most people will obey them and accept that those who transgress should be punished. If the state is wrong about making something illegal (in that they make laws that most people disagree with) then people may protest or may feel free to break that law whilst still respecting other laws. For example, from 1920–33 the federal government in the USA made it illegal to make, transport, import, or sell alcohol; this was known as prohibition (see **Figures 14.2** and **14.3**). It was not illegal to own or to consume alcohol and doctors could also prescribe it. Many people disagreed with this law and many broke it. Some people

Figure 14.2 Headline from *The American Issue* at the start of prohibition
Source: The American Issue/Public domain

Figure 14.3 Removal of liquor during prohibition
Source: Public domain

illegally made alcohol (moonshine), others opened underground bars (speakeasies) and/or smuggled alcohol into the USA. The manufacture, transportation, and selling of alcohol was taken over by crime rings and organised crime fed the desire for alcohol and made a lot of money from it. To avoid being detected the gangsters often paid off public servants (especially, though not only, the police) to turn a blind eye. Police were willing to be bribed to ignore breaches of this law because, like many other Americans, they thought the law was incorrect and should not be enforced. So this little-supported law helped to build organised crime and rendered the corruption of public servants a frequent occurrence. It helped to forge strong connections between organised crime and public officials, something which was very difficult to break and caused officers to 'turn a blind eye' to practices they disagreed with (harmful crimes) because they were concerned their earlier corruption would be discovered. The prohibition of alcohol clearly caused many problems and in 1933 the federal government transferred the power to decide issues concerning the sale of alcohol to States; it made laws about the sale of alcohol a local rather than a federal matter. Some states still control and/or prohibit alcohol, as demonstrated by **Figure 14.4**:

The majority of Kentucky's 120 counties are still dry or partially dry, despite the state being home to some of the world's best-known liquor brands, such as Jim Beam and Maker's Mark bourbon.

Wheeler 2012

However, some (especially large corporations) are now pushing for the laws concerning the making, distribution, and using of alcohol to move back into federal hands. In 2015 Wal-Mart (a multi-national retail organisation) challenged the laws in Texas because they were not permitted to sell alcohol in their shops. Furthermore Wal-Mart is petitioning for the sale of alcohol to become a federal issue, this time to force states to adopt 'acceptable' alcohol retail legislation.

This is an example of almost a 100-year battle over the content of the criminal law in respect of alcohol in the US. Similar discussions and disagreements over the content of the criminal law take place from time to time in all states. The US example demonstrates the importance of understanding the accepted standards or *mores* in a society before making criminal laws and being careful not to curtail people's freedom by passing criminal laws merely because a strong and vociferous group pushes for the change.

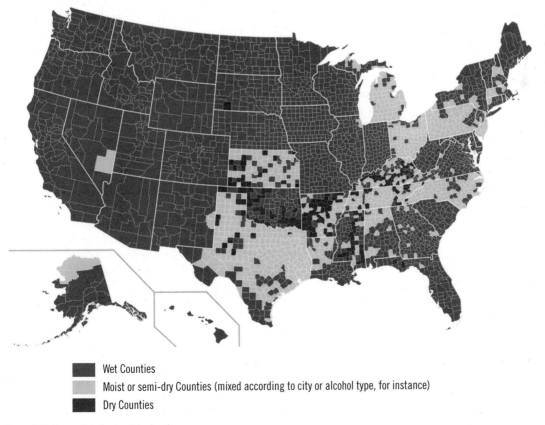

■ Wet Counties
■ Moist or semi-dry Counties (mixed according to city or alcohol type, for instance)
■ Dry Counties

Figure 14.4 A snapshot of wet and dry America
Source: Mr. Matté/Public domain

Therefore, whilst mores are important as guidance for people within a society they should not always be used as the basis for a criminal law.

Socialisation

Socialisation is another key concept in sociology—it refers to the way in which we all learn the norms and rules of our society, learn what is expected of us, and learn how to behave in order to live up to those expectations. Psychologists look at the mechanics of the process of socialisation (reward and punishment). Sociologists look at where the learning happens and study what is likely to be learnt in that environment. For sociologists there are two levels at which socialisation occurs—informal and formal.

Informal socialisation takes place within organisations such as families or groups of friends or peer groups. In a family, children learn how to distinguish between right and wrong and how to behave. The family helps people to fit in to the family and to the wider social groups that the family interacts with; ideally it teaches members how to live pro-socially (positively, not breaking the norms of behaviour) within a society. However, some families may have different values from those of the wider society. Some immigrant or religious families may have different cultural or moral standards which, while they do not breach the norms of the broader society, may be misunderstood by that wider society. Other families who participate in crime may teach values which permit certain forms of crime, which does cause problems for others in society.

Families and peer groups may transmit different expectations; the peer group may expect certain clothing to be worn and may expect some rule breaking, whereas the family may expect people to obey the criminal laws. Each of these will also influence the way in which their members think about certain laws. The family often helps the individual work out who they are, what their role or status is, and what is expected of them. These expectations may differ from those of the peer group which may encourage an individual to break out of their 'expected' status to build a different view of themselves, one which embraces different behaviours and may lead to different statuses being adopted.

Formal socialisation takes place within organisations such as schools; education transmits social values of an organisation and of the society. Every organisation tries to socialise people into their ways of working or operating but many also help socialise individuals into society. Again, there may be conflicts. For example, a corporation may socialise some of its employees into bending or breaking laws to advantage the company; these employees may be otherwise very conforming members of society but are socialised by the firm and its corporate expectations into different behaviours. Some of these behaviours may be illegal, others merely unacceptable. See, for example the manipulation of

company structures by some multi-national organisations to avoid paying taxes (Google, Amazon, and Starbucks: Bradford and Holt 2013). The criminal justice agencies, on the other hand, will use sanctions and coercion to try to force or persuade people to abide by societal rules.

Conflict and consensus

Consensus theorists often believe that society is held together or 'works' because the people in that society share a set of key values and beliefs, and agree on the same norms or rules. Consensus theorists emphasise harmony, integration, and stability within a society. They also often view these values as largely set and something that will be passed from one generation to another as each generation teaches the next to abide by the same values and rules. Here social order, stability, and social regulation are emphasised and social order is considered to be in the best interests of all its members. They are generally supportive of societal organisations and institutions, seeing them as working for the society, for the consensus. Whilst they recognise that no healthy society should be preserved for all time without change they argue that any change should be incremental and follow an agreed direction for development. Any change should be based on and reflect the shared norms and values which are seen as fundamental. The main consensus theory we will be considering (later in this chapter) is Durkheim's functionalism (see the 'Durkheim and functionalism—the normality of crime' section in this chapter).

Conflict, on the other hand, sees society as being organised to benefit some groups over others. They argue that members of the favoured groups almost always do better. Members of favoured groups tend to help to set the values or make the rules and laws so they can ensure that their ideals and ways of life are protected at the expense of other people. In the eyes of conflict theorists, dominant groups and individuals have the control and power to decide how everyone lives their lives. These theorists believe that all societies are basically built on disagreement, conflict, and struggle but that the secret to hiding that fact is to convince or socialise everyone to believe that the society is to benefit everyone.

Traditionally Britain is seen as a society in which certain social classes do better than others, but in which those in power spend considerable time convincing the middle and lower classes that the society is fair and designed to work best for them. For example, education is designed to socialise the young into accepting the society as it is presently constructed, teaching them the morals and ethics necessary for their control so that they adopt the view of a fair and just society as that in which they live. Conflict theorists argue that the basic institutions in a society (religion, education, government, law, media) help to maintain this unequal situation, keeping some groups in a privileged situation whilst others suffer or are less fortunate. The conflict theorists study the way in which conflicts of interest between certain groups are resolved to protect the privileged. Theorists such as Karl Marx and those based on his original ideas clearly depict this type of thought (see **Chapter 15**) as well as feminist or racist critiques of society (see **Chapters 10 and 11**).

Power

The way in which power is distributed and what it means for a society is vital to many sociological theories. Power is part of consensus and conflict but is so integral to sociological explanations of crime that it deserves to be considered separately. In sociological terms, power is by and large the ability to influence people's behaviour or to have the authority to set standards and rules to be followed by others. It often means that you or your group manages to enjoy freedom to participate in activities of your choice, regardless of whether or not other groups approve, and even when others may suffer as a result.

Most effective uses of power are authorised, made legitimate, or at least appear to be authorised in democratic societies; however, sometimes power is forced or coercive, in authoritarian societies for example. Power can accrue through many means. It may arise, for example, due to authority vested through some accepted institution or organisation, through social class (often material wealth), through knowledge, through social status, or through charisma. However power is achieved, it permits one individual or group to control their own destiny but also often to shape the way in which others think and act in order to ensure the well-being of those in power (maybe also of others). The powerful therefore shape society, or parts of it, to suit themselves or their group. As noted earlier in the consideration of conflict, those in power may also try to manipulate others into believing the society is being run to serve the needs of the powerless, through education, the media, and/or employment.

Clearly where one person or group has power, others are powerless and this means there are likely to be inequalities. Many conflicts in society are struggles over power because the authority a group or individual enjoys determines how effectively they can impose their wishes and values on others. Sociology has many theorists who study power (Galbraith 1983 and Foucault 1975). It will become central in the study of radical theories in **Chapter 15** though you should search for it and be aware of it in discussion of all sociological theories. Many sociological theories rely on decisions being made by those in power; law makers or those applying the rules such as police. These decisions result in inequalities which can cause problems for those who lose out. Often the way in which this is done is not considered by those theorists and this may well be a weakness to the theory; it is often something worth exploring or considering.

Having considered some of the key parameters and concepts in terms of society's effect on criminal behaviour, the rest of this chapter will be used to consider some of the most important and influential sociological theories. We will begin by those focused on the close social environment (micro-social theories) and then move on to those associated with broader sociological issues (macro-social theories, see **Figure 14.1** for a reminder).

Social process/interaction theories

Micro-sociological theories

Social process theories are micro-social theories which look at how particular social processes impact on individuals. In particular they study social interaction between individuals in a society. Rather than looking at broad social categories they consider social factors in an individual's immediate social situation and how these impact on their behaviour generally and criminal activity in particular. They study how individuals and groups interact; they might consider social interaction within a family or school to understand its impact on behaviour and how that behaviour impacts on the group or social setting. There are a number of these theories but only one will be considered in this chapter: differential association. Other chapters will consider other examples of social interaction/process theories: social control theory will be discussed in **Chapter 18** and labelling perspectives in **Chapter 15**.

Differential association—crime as a learned behaviour

Edwin H. Sutherland (1883–1950) was an American sociologist and part of the Chicago school of sociology and criminology in the 1930s (see 'The Chicago school—Social disorganisation' later in this chapter for a discussion of this school of thought). Whereas much of the Chicago school were concerned with explaining the physical distribution of crime, Sutherland (1939a) was more interested in social distribution, arguing that crime existed and was committed by people at all levels of society (1939a and 1939b).

He studied white-collar crime, that is offences which are committed by those in a position of responsibility and respectability (Sutherland 1949). In his studies he sometimes included activities which 'ought' to be criminalised because they are as socially or individually damaging as other offences. The focus of his study was to consider how

WHAT DO YOU THINK? 14.1

John, is a 45 year old man who was brought up in a traditional middle-class home. He went to school where he fitted in well, achieved academic success, and never really got into any trouble. He studied law and business at university, achieving a 2:1 in his degree. Following graduation, he trained as a solicitor and also did his accountancy examinations. He obtained a job working as a company lawyer for a multi-national company called Moonpounds and did very well for himself. His clear understanding of both law and business allowed him to rise through the company ranks quite quickly. He also learned very quickly the company mantra of 'keeping the customers happy whilst also ensuring large profits for shareholders'. He became director of law and finance at the age of 35 and has spent the last 10 years shaping the company structure to ensure that the organisation globally makes the highest profits possible.

Is this likely to lead to criminality and/or deviant activity in any aspect of his life?

The company may expect all its employees to be willing to stretch the rules so as to maximise profits. In this environment he might lead a decision to structure the multi-national company so as to avoid taxes in countries where they take large profits. Whilst this may not be illegal, its customers in countries where it is avoiding taxation may see the activity as immoral, as breaching the social expectations. John might be very surprised by the reaction to him. He clearly sees himself as law abiding and conforming. However, conforming too strictly to the company expectations may have led him to breach the expected standards of the broader society even if no laws have actually been broken.

What has led John into this position? Do you think he will continue to see himself as good and law abiding? If he does do you think that he will accept that the avoidance of tax was immoral or is he likely to continue to look at the legality and see nothing wrong?

those in upper or middle classes might turn to crime and demonstrate that they are affected by the same processes as are individuals from the working or lower classes. To demonstrate this he therefore looked at processes and interactions in the individual's immediate social situation. In particular he looked at differential association. See **What do you think? 14.1** for an example which clarifies and discusses these ideas.

Differential association is a learning theory (1939b: 4–8). Whereas some behaviours are natural—breathing

or swallowing—and depend on biology, not all behaviours fall into this category. Sutherland argued that most behaviours are learned and therefore depend on the knowledge, skills, habits, and recognition of opportunities that result from experience. For example, whilst swallowing may be natural, what to swallow is something parents and others we are close to teach us; similarly, it is not natural to purchase a ticket before travelling on a train, it is something society expects us to do and we are taught through social interactions. Sutherland argued that crime was no exception, it needed to be learned. For Sutherland criminal behaviour is normal learned behaviour and arises when someone is in an environment where it can be absorbed. He considered the way in which criminal behaviour might become part of an individual's normal behaviour is that it would be learnt, as with all other behaviours. Sutherland argued that crime is discovered through association with other people. Note that this is a social learning theory so it discusses the social circumstances in which the behaviour might be learned but does not consider *how* the learning occurs (that would be a psychological learning theory).

There are two parts to Sutherland's theory. He argues that people learn both to imitate and replicate behaviours by learning the techniques to perform that behaviour and the motives, rationalisations, values, and reasons for committing it (the reasons behind the crime). For Sutherland this learning occurs through direct interaction between individuals; he thought that the media had less impact. Some individuals might come into direct contact with criminal activity but not learn or adopt that behaviour. Whether a person adopts the behaviour is dependent on the amount of contact they have with such behaviour compared with law abiding behaviour and whether the individual's main contacts (or those they most admire) support that activity or not.

Sutherland's basic thesis can be, and often is, set out in nine propositions:

1. Criminal behaviour is learned.
2. The learning happens in interaction with other people.
3. Most learning of criminal behaviour occurs within close groupings.
4. The learning includes:
   (a) the techniques necessary to commit the crime (may be fairly simple);
   (b) the motives, drives, and attitudes necessary to the offending.
5. The direction of motives and drives is learned from understanding the legal codes as being favourable or unfavourable.
6. A person becomes delinquent because of an excess of definitions favourable to violation of law over definitions unfavourable to violation of law.

7. Differential associations may vary in frequency, duration, priority and intensity. People are more likely to offend if they are exposed first (*priority*), more *frequently*, for a longer time period (*duration*), and with greater *intensity* (importance which can include the importance of the person or of the behaviour, attitude, or values) to law-violating than to law-abiding associations.

8. Learning criminal behaviour involves all the same mechanisms that are used to learn any other behaviour.

9. The needs and values expressed or satisfied through criminal behaviour often also explain or underlie law-abiding behaviour: therefore, those needs and values do not explain the behaviour.

Sutherland recognises that each direct contact a person has with someone else may be partially criminal and partially law-abiding. He took account of the effects of both the behaviour and the attitudes and values others display and the effects these have on other people. Whilst people generally believe, for example, that those who kill should be punished, they may not want to punish those who take the life of someone who is dying in pain and who asks to be euthanised (mercy killing). Each of these is technically murder but many would take a different attitude to each behaviour and might pass on that way of thinking to others.

Every individual will be exposed to some criminal behaviours and attitudes and some law-abiding behaviours and attitudes, as well as many that are not clearly one or the other. These experiences will only lead to criminality if an individual has more personal contact (with people they admire) who support and participate in criminal behaviour than those who are law-abiding. The learning is affected by the frequency, duration, and intensity of the definitions either for law-abiding or law-breaking behaviour. They are also affected by how early in a person's life (or their experience in a particular environment) the interaction occurs; the respect for the other person and how close their relationship is; as well as whether the behaviour resulted in positive or negative outcomes.

Sutherland—a critique

Differential association is based on the *assumption* that all behaviour, including criminal behaviour, is learned. To an extent, therefore, it is claiming that criminality is both a 'normal' and learned behaviour. This idea challenges two claims made in earlier chapters: that it is fully chosen (**Chapter 12**) or that something in the individual's pathology causes the criminality (**Chapter 13**).

Firstly, the normality challenges the idea that the behaviour itself is necessarily unacceptable (even killing is sometimes condoned—mercy killing or killing in war). If the behaviour is intrinsically normal and merely made

unacceptable in certain social situations it then becomes necessary to consider why some behaviours are controlled and others are not (even though both behaviours may be equally harmful). Sutherland was interested in this as he noted that many practices carried out by the upper and middle-class, often whilst at work, were damaging but not criminalised. He suggested that the power structures were benefitting these basically privileged groups.

Secondly, claiming that behaviour is learnt undermines the idea that criminality is somehow biologically or psychologically predetermined. Remember, in sociological learning theories the way in which the learning occurs is not central, it is the context in which this happens that is of interest. The theory is therefore of great interest and importance as a counter to other ideas: it questions the often claimed objectivity of the criminal law; and the idea that some people are predisposed to criminality.

Differential association cannot explain all crime but it is a very wide-ranging idea and it is true that the learning process must clearly be a factor in most behaviours. It has certainly been supported by some researchers; see, for example, McCarthy (1996). Clearly, being a theory based on learned behaviour it cannot explain how crimes first arose or how new forms of crime arise. Nor can it explain the crimes of those who offend despite never being subjected to direct interpersonal experiences of offending. It does not explain why some youths will learn offending or deviant behaviour from a peer group despite very strong and close interpersonal family relationships which are law-abiding (or vice versa). Nor can it explain impulsive, opportunist, or angry behaviour committed on the spur of the moment, without any real thought or planning; these may be closer to 'natural', non-learned, behaviours.

Despite these shortcomings, the idea of differential association certainly has some merit, at least to explain what types of offending a person may be involved in. However, it is not possible to test the theory because it is not possible to measure whether someone has more inputs favourable to criminality than to law-abiding behaviour. This is particularly difficult to evaluate given that it is not merely a matter of counting inputs but also of gauging how strongly they might affect an individual and why. It is impossible to assess whether motives and values existed before a particular set of interactions or only arose as a result of those interactions. One might, for example, question whether someone becomes a member of a delinquent peer group because they want an outlet for their already existing delinquent tendencies or due to the need for friendship and, once a member, they then learn the deviant behaviours. Of course, for some individuals it may be the former and for others it may be the latter. Even for the former, they may have learned those deviant tendencies in previous interactions. It is often very difficult to tease out the effect of any particular interaction on the behaviour of an individual. However, in more closed areas of interaction this may sometimes be possible.

Sutherland started out trying to both prove that the upper and middle-classes offended and/or were deviant and to explain that deviance (1939a). His suggestion was, in essence, that law abiding people might learn to breach the rules (societal morals or ethics and criminal laws) whilst at work. He suggested that each working environment may set up certain standards and expectations. Whilst in many cases these might fit in with or even be stricter than those of the wider society, sometimes they might be in conflict with those broader expectations. Where they are broader, obeying the expectations of the workplace and the employer might well breach the standards set by wider society.

Other theorists, for example Steven Box (1983), agree that law-abiding people may learn criminality at work. Box and others argue that such behaviour, conflicting with societal expectations, seems nonsensical unless the offending behaviour, along with the reasons why it should be committed, are learnt at work; the behaviour may well not be fully considered criminal but just one of the 'realities of business', necessary in order to ensure the firm survives and prospers (Box 1983 and Bauman 1994). The firm may even reward those who participate in such activities by promoting them so that the behaviour becomes considered respectable or necessary to an extent that it is not really condemned by either those working in the field or wider society (Slapper and Tombs 1999; Croall 2001). Complying with these workplace expectations is then understandable though still in breach of societal expectations (see the reaction to tax avoidance by large multi-national corporations such as Google, Amazon, and Starbucks discussed in Campbell 2014). Therefore in areas of life which might be seen as somewhat separated from broader society—areas which set their own expectations for individuals—such different behaviour may be both understandable and explicable based on interactions within that environment.

What is more difficult to explain is that even where someone has the knowledge, values and morals which would support criminality they nonetheless spend most of their time in law-abiding behaviour. Even if within their working environment these people may be willing to and learn to breach a few rules, they are basically law-abiding; Sutherland does not really address this underlying conforming existence. Sutherland's theory also fails to explain why two people from very similar backgrounds, with very similar interpersonal and learnt experiences may behave very differently. In addition, his theory ignores most individual aspects—it assumes that all people learn in similar ways, as long as one allows them to personally experience a behaviour and the values that support it they will adopt it. Apart from a lack of respect for the person conducting the behaviour, little will interfere with the learning;

if there are more facets supporting criminality than law-abiding behaviour, this will give rise to criminality. In reality, it is unlikely to be quite this simple but Sutherland allows no real room within his theory for free will or different personalities.

Despite these problems, some theorists have adopted part of Sutherland's theory in expounding their own (see Cloward and Ohlin in the 'Differential opportunity' section later in this chapter). Others have conducted empirical research which partially supports the thesis (McCarthy 1996) though finding that differential association only partly explained the behaviour, other important factors being lax supervision within the family, coming from a 'broken' home, and insecurity. What his theory can help to explain is why some people who suffer these or other structural problems offend whilst others do not; only some will have been exposed to the learning necessary for them to offend. It also helps to explain why someone who is law abiding in most aspects of their life may be willing to offend in one area; a very honourable and upstanding member of society may, for example, be willing to offend at work. It is not surprising that these are the conclusions we draw, given that this is the aspect of criminality which Sutherland started out trying to explain; white-collar offending especially by those who are basically law-abiding (see **What do you think? 14.1** and the discussion associated with it).

Another outcome of Sutherland's theories has been that they have provided a foundation for some resolutions to offending. Reintegrative shaming, for example (Braithwaite 1988 and Fisse and Braithwaite 1993), relies heavily on the interpersonal opinions of those law-abiding individuals who are important to the offender; it is these individuals who can awaken guilt within the offender at the offending behaviour, whilst also supporting a change to more law-abiding behaviour. The theory might also be seen as the impetus behind mentoring services. By giving an offender a mentor it is hoped that the mentor's pro-social behaviour will have a positive impetus to future conforming behaviour. The mentor can guide the offender's values so helping them adopt a conforming outlook and can be an example of how to behave and the benefits which might flow from conformity.

Others have tried to use social learning to support controlling practices such as media censorship. They argue that the media can teach 'unacceptable' values and practices. However, Sutherland rejected the media as a tool through which people learnt, insisting that direct interpersonal connections were more important. This would call into question any media censorship on the basis that it might lead some to copying the values or actions seen on the screen. Of course, if someone is intending to offend, and has already learnt the values which would support offending, he or she may learn how to offend from watching the media, using it to pick up the mechanics of the activity. So, before censorship is used people should be clear exactly why it is intended to be imposed and be realistic about whether these considerations are really likely to affect behaviour.

Overall therefore, differential association and other social learning theories may be useful in altering future behaviour. This does not mean individuals are not responsible for their offending; they are. What it does mean is that it may be more fruitful to spend time and money on altering future behaviour through mentoring, for example, rather than blaming wrong choices, seeking punishment, or claiming the behaviour is caused by something inherently 'wrong' with the individual and therefore trying to 'cure' them. Differential association calls for taught-behaviour patterns that will encourage positive behaviour and values and so lead to more conforming and socially beneficial decisions in the future.

Social structural theories—macro-sociological theories

Social structural theories are much broader than the interaction or process theories. They are macro-sociological theories and focus on whether (and how) broad, societal issues such as poverty or unemployment might have an effect on our daily lives and on individual behaviour. It considers how the wider social picture affects both individual behaviour and shapes the more immediate, micro-social environment in which inter-personal interactions occur. Social structural theories include: anomie; social strain theories; social disorganisation theories; subcultural theories; and social exclusion theories. Each of these will be considered below.

Durkheim and functionalism—the normality of crime

Emile Durkheim (1858–1917) (see **Figure 14.5**) was a French academic in the late 19th and early 20th century. Whilst he trained as a biologist he is most famous as a sociologist, criminologist, and philosopher. He is thought of as one of the founders of modern social science and sociology. Durkheim's aim was to understand what made societies operate and keep their members integrated and cohesive. To achieve this he observed societies and took particular care to gain an insight into social institutions, to understand them and how they helped preserve a society. He understood beliefs and behaviours as part of a collective, rather than a merely individual, aspect of society. Instead of studying the acts of individuals he tried to understand behaviours such as suicide, crime, and deviance at a societal level. So, rather than looking at the individual behaviour and blaming individuals for the ills of the world he looked at the society as a whole. To do this, he studied rates of crime, suicide, or deviance in a society, compared rates in different societies and sought to explain differences in terms of either institutions or aspects of society or of social rules and regulations.

Durkheim was a structuralist. He was a consensus theorist who adopted a functionalist approach; a functionalist

sociology. This is a sociological approach which sees society as a system of interconnected parts working together to ensure that the balance and equilibrium of a social group is not interfered with. He used his scientific, biological background to help his understanding of societies, seeing them as organic structures. He studied various institutions and aspects of the society such as family, education, and the legal system, trying to ascertain what function each served. He wanted to understand how societies functioned and how they succeeded in curbing the most powerful

Figure 14.5 Emile Durkheim (1858–1917)
Source: Public domain

needs and drives of the individuals who lived within them in order to allow people to live together in relative harmony. He viewed society as a delicate system whose separate parts (or institutions) worked together for the good of all its members. Here, according to his perspective, society was more than all the individuals who were a part of it. A society was important of and for itself and needed to be preserved, even if some of its members may be damaged, to achieve that goal. Its healthy survival would ultimately benefit the common good. Durkheim recognised that the healthy survival of society benefited everyone and argued that the function of institutions, practices, values, and norms (rules) should be to help to ensure society as a whole functions properly, for the good of all.

Durkheim argued that to understand a society, and especially to understand any phenomenon which happened within a society, it was necessary to understand both the cause which produced it and the function it fulfilled. For Durkheim both cause and function were essential to understanding each aspect of society and its relation to social harmony. Here, cause takes on its normal meaning but function needs more explanation. Function, for Durkheim, includes all the objective consequences (of an aspect of society) which were capable of being observed (whether intended or not). Intended consequences he refers to as 'manifest' whereas unintended consequences are known as 'latent'. If we take punishment as our example: the cause of punishment is generally something negative happening, a crime; but the function of punishment is more complex. At an individual level punishment ensures the criminal does not gain and so it will tend to deter that individual. However, more broadly it serves to maintain social order by deterring others and maintaining 'social solidarity'. It is this broader function which particularly interested Durkheim. Crime is the element which triggers punishment and the positive effects of punishment—social solidarity and maintaining social order—are important to society, so crime is also functional and important to a healthy society.

Simple, ancient, and pre-industrial societies tend to be very close-knit. Its members share the same culture, religion, attitudes, and values so that each individual and the whole are mirrors of each other and as a result social solidarity is mechanical and can almost be taken for granted. Each member is similarly linked to all others by close obligations and responsibilities. In modern, more complex, societies each person serves a different function, there are many cultures, many religions, many attitudes. Links are not obvious nor are they always strong; they have to be worked on. In complex societies the basic collective values and ideas (like democracy, human rights, the rule of law. etc.) are agreed on and represent the collective consciousness. For Durkheim this collective conscience ties people together and is the basis of the social order. Institutions such as punishment serve to unite people and strengthen this social conscience.

Durkheim makes two very important contributions to criminology: seeing crime as necessary to a healthy society; and his consideration of **anomie**, a dysfunctional society in which the rules have broken down.

Crime as normal and healthy

Durkheim noted that crime and deviance existed in all societies. From this he decided that they must be 'normal' aspects of a society. He argued that it would be impossible to have a society with no crime or deviance. All societies have some rules (criminal laws) and provide sanctions (punishments) if they are broken. These sanctions and rules would not be necessary if people did not naturally want to participate in those criminal activities. Furthermore, given that they are part of every society at all times, crime and deviance must, he argued, serve a positive function or a useful purpose: therefore, he argues that a certain, fairly low, level of crime is normal and functional; necessary to the good order, health, and function of a society.

Durkheim cited two main reasons for believing that crime is a social good. Firstly, because crime attracts punishment and serves as the catalyst for an expression of collective indignation against the crime (deviance) that has been committed and against the criminal/deviant who committed it. This collective moral outrage serves to build and strengthen the bonds between law-abiding members of society and so strengthens that society's solidarity. Secondly, crime sometimes acts as a catalyst for social change, helping to display problems with the present rules and preparing people for the change, thus helping any change in rules to be accepted as part of the collective values and rules.

In recent years there has been an ongoing discussion around whether helping someone to die when they have asked to die should be illegal (for a populist account see Purdy with Paul 2010, and for a round-up of European laws see BBC News, 2009). A strict application of the criminal law would consider helping someone to die to be murder, but public opinion is slowly altering and many now believe this should not be illegal (see **Figure 14.6**), at least where the 'victim' is already ill and is explicitly asking to end their lives. Today, in these circumstances, perpetrators are less likely to face murder charges than was the case in the past. In the future it seems likely that assisted suicide (within particular carefully defined circumstances) may move from being murder to being legal, partly because many people are outraged that relatives and doctors face prosecutions when they help someone who is already very ill to achieve their desire to die (in the UK there is already an understanding that such cases should not normally be prosecuted). In these cases bonds have been strengthened in sympathy for the perpetrators rather than in moral outrage at what they have done and the law is slowly following suit. So whilst outrage at crime

Right-to-die

If you were suffering from a painful and incurable illness, and assisted dying was legal, would you consider it?

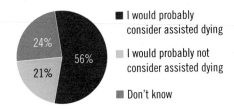

- ■ I would probably consider assisted dying
- ▨ I would probably not consider assisted dying
- ▨ Don't know

Do you think the law should or should not be changed to allow someone to assist in the suicide of …

... someone suffering from a terminal illness?

.... someone suffering from a painful. incurable, but NOT terminal illness?

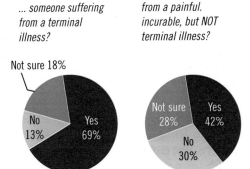

Figure 14.6 Popular opinions concerning the right to die

Source: YouGov, July 2014

generally strengthens bonds and draws people together in moral outrage, where this ceases to be the case there is an impetus to change the law, to preserve the powerful social solidarity that moral outrage against crime provides. This is modern proof that Durkheim's analysis of the positive effects of crime are evident today.

Durkheim notes that the need for this communal outrage is so strong that in societies with no crime they use unacceptable behaviour to produce the same moral outrage:

> Imagine a society of saints, a perfect cloister of exemplary individuals. Crimes, properly so called, will there be unknown, but faults which appear venial to the layman will create there the same scandal that the ordinary offense does in ordinary consciousness. If, then, this society has the power to judge and punish, it will define these acts as criminal and will treat them as such.
>
> Durkheim 1895, from the edition edited by Lukes 2014: 100

So in a religious society, such as a nunnery, there may be no real crimes but the members would find small transgressions which they can treat as unacceptable. They may be things such as being late for prayers which would be seen as deviance and those who are late may be shunned. The deviance would bring the others together to enjoy 'moral anger' and 'righteous indignation' which in turn

allows them to develop a tighter bond of social solidarity. When something unacceptable happens in society people get together to talk about it, they gossip about how unacceptable it is and so the deviance or crime draws together those who are indignant and makes them feel good about themselves and each other, it encourages their feeling of being 'one of the good in society'.

Societies need to have conformity and values and those values need to be agreed. Individuals in a society need to be reminded of the values and of their agreement to them. Crime permits society to show all its members what will happen if they break the rules. For Durkheim the functional aspect of crime happens through the ritual or moral indignation provided by trials and punishment; these are essential to crime being seen as functional. In the past this was done by public punishments (stocks and public hanging) while we now use local gossip, the media, and social media to publicise unacceptable behaviour and what is being done about it. Durkheim therefore found that a limited amount of crime is useful or functional for society in reinforcing its collective values and that a society would suffer if the crime rate was either too high (that would be destructive) or too low (some crime is needed to fuel the moral outrage). Here crime serves a function because it helps people feel that they have something in common and that they really belong to a particular group or a particular community; it supports social integration.

Others academics such as Albert Cohen (1966) and Kai Erikson (1966) have added to the positive functions of crime as identified by Durkheim and claim that deviance and crime:

- unite the broader society against the deviants (criminals) and promote solidarity around shared values;
- help societies locate their 'boundaries' through apprehending and punishing deviant and criminal individuals;
- help to define and point out the virtue in conformity and normality;
- can help to point out problems in society, things which may need to be changed (Cohen 1966);
- provide jobs for many people as police officers, prison guards, probation officers, social workers, youth justice workers, workers in many charities, criminology lecturers, and researchers;
- clarify the rules and serve as a reason to remind people about the rules and why they are there (Cohen 1966);
- act as a safety valve for societal pressures, when people are stressed or under strain they might find an outlet in criminality (Cohen 1966); and
- act as an educating process (Erikson 1971).

There are a number of very interesting examples of the application of Durkheim's functionalist theory. One by

Kai Erikson (1966) applies these ideas to an historical setting. Erikson studied the Salem witch trials in colonial Massachusetts (1692–93), distilling Durkheim's ideas down to three elements which he wanted to test: 1. all communities set their boundaries for acceptable behaviour through the process of punishing deviants; 2. rates of deviance remain fairly steady over time; and 3. each community has its own way of defining and dealing with deviants. He therefore studied the new settlers who were cut off from their old societies in Europe and were in the process of building new communities, with new values which required building new bonds of social solidarity. He discovered that they were a fairly closed community with a powerful shared culture and strict religious and moral codes and found some low-level crime and breaches of the strict moral code but little real crime. In this atmosphere, minor transgressions were focused on. When the behaviour of a few young girls fell into question and they faced exclusion from the group they accused others in the community of bewitching them. The women they accused were tried, convicted, and punished. The trials were one way of expressing and displaying how important religion and strong moral codes were to the group. However, when the young women started to accuse others, including trusted elders in the community, their stories were no longer believed. At that point the prosecution and punishment would serve no purpose, rather than uniting the community against transgressors it would destroy the community by undermining those intent on its protection.

The second example is more contemporary. Kingsley Davis (1971) analysed prostitution which he noted had existed in society through time; he wanted to discover whether this criminal activity could be seen as beneficial for the community. He noted that prostitution exists and had always existed despite it being almost universally denigrated. He argued that it exists because it provides a positive function in society—the prostitutes (a small number of women) take care of the sexual needs of a lot of men, including those who are not physically attractive. Furthermore, he argued that by providing a safety valve for married men to enjoy their more perverted sexual appetites it actually serves to support married life allowing it to be more harmonious, successful, and functional. He also suggests that the prostitutes benefit by earning more money than other employment might provide. From this he suggested that the provision of sexual activities for money was functional and would always exist, though this, of course, is not universally accepted by others.

You can take your consideration of these ideas further by looking at the questions raised in **What do you think? 14.2**.

WHAT DO YOU THINK? 14.2

Are any of the following functional? If so, explain how.

- Drug taking
- Rioting
- Public punishment—putting people in the stocks or publishing their punishment in newspapers
- Being drunk and disorderly in a public place

Anomie

Durkheim (see the 1933 and 1970 editions of his works) is one of the earliest theorists to write about anomie. As a reminder, anomie refers to the breakdown of social standards or controls. As was the case when we discussed functionalism, it is also instructive here to remember that simple societies are largely homogeneous and 'mechanical'; they are held together because each individual is similar to the others, therefore each has similar values, aims, and roles. In these societies law is used to ensure any areas of diversity fit together harmoniously and is generally not heavily used. With modern industrial, technological, and economic complexity the interrelationships in any given society have become more complex and diverse resulting in largely 'organic societies' coming into being. Whilst there is still some overlap (some mechanical aspects) most individuals fulfil different roles. This means that each individual depends on the others to support an aspect of their lives. Whilst being more different we are also more interdependent so that we need greater social cohesion to ensure that we can rely on each other.

Durkheim viewed the change from largely 'mechanical' to largely 'organic' societies as inevitable and as positive, bringing greater freedom because individuals can enjoy goods produced by others. When this transformation is gradual it is likely to lead to a healthy society. When it is too fast the society might well become unhealthy. In an unhealthy society the laws would be inadequate to regulate the diversity of the society and that society would collapse into anomie. One of the results of anomie is an excess of criminality. For Durkheim if a society changed too quickly anomie was likely to arise. The change might arise out of a financial crisis and a resultant industrial conflict; an overly rigid class or other societal division which might lead the oppressed to rebel; and an abnormal division of labour which might well mean many would be unemployed and thereby alienated as feeling dysfunctional and not a part of 'normal' society. For Durkheim any major upheaval of this sort might give rise to anomie. For other writers anomie is possible without these large economic and political upheavals.

Durkheim viewed anomie as a collapse of social solidarity, a state in which the fundamental bonds that generally unite individuals into a collective social order break down. He argued that this occurred when there was a major upheaval and people no longer felt regulated by the rules of a society; their desires and aspirations were no longer controlled by the social order. For Durkheim a functioning society, in which individuals could be happy, had to control or set moral standards, that is, set out what people could reasonably expect to enjoy. Where these moral limits and expectations were absent he argued the situation was always miserable for a society and for all those within a society and brought with it unhealthy levels of ills such as suicide and crime. Like crime, he viewed suicide as a natural phenomenon and as generally functional—all societies have some suicide and this was to be expected. He explained suicide from four perspectives, set out in **Table 14.1.**

Anomie has a profound effect on criminality and deviance. Durkheim never clarified what level of crime and deviance would be functional for a society. However, too little crime and deviance was indicative of an over-regulated society which was too intolerant. On the other hand, too much crime was indicative of a society in which there was insufficient trust and people could not depend on each other so that social solidarity would collapse, the ties that bind people to conformity would be broken and many would feel free to offend.

Durkheim therefore viewed anomie as existing when a society lacked norms (laws and rules) and common shared values. He argued that this occurred when there had been a profound and abrupt change such as that resulting from the technical revolution, the breakdown of the modern state as a socialising force, or globalisation. Some, such as Bauman (2001) suggest that in the modern era there have been many changes and people are less unified and so feel released to offend, whereas another way of looking at this is that the modern world with its stronger calls of national identity in fact may be delivering shared values and norms so helping to control crime. Over the modern era there have been a number of instances of crime increases during periods of recession and unemployment and these might be seen as upheavals sufficient to lead to anomie and therefore increased criminality and increased suicides. If Durkheim is right, then to prevent these one needs to strengthen social controls and strengthen people's commitment to shared values.

Durkheim—critique

Durkheim powerfully questions the blaming of individuals for criminality. He shows clearly how individual behaviour is affected by social forces and might, in turn, affect those forces. However, there are weaknesses in his approach.

Running through Durkheim's work is a recurring ambiguity. He suggests many functions but none of these is essential. Therefore, whilst his ideas may help us understand some fundamental aspect of our society and certainly provide information and ammunition to question other theories, they also leave too many questions unanswered. How much crime is healthy and how do we know? Does society deliberately create deviance and crime to ensure its members bond to the culture? Is deviance necessary before we can say that a society exists and functions? Are some crimes and acts of deviance so destructive as to be unhealthy and, if so, which are they?

Whilst through analysis of some real-life situations authors, such as Erikson (1966) and Davis (1971), have applied some of Durkheim's ideas, generally they are too vague and ambiguous to be carefully validated and tested. It is unclear how much crime is functional or when a society is in anomie or enjoys healthy social bonds. There are too many unanswered questions for this to be the only explanation of criminality.

Merton and strain

The American sociologist and criminologist Robert K. Merton (1910–2003) borrows and develops some of Durkheim's ideas to build a strain theory built on his own concept of anomie. His theory is macro-sociological, explaining crime in terms of social structural issues. Merton sought to explain the crime problem in the US in the 1930s and 1940s when crime rates were increasing very quickly. As with Durkheim's theory, Merton puts anomie at the centre of his explanation. However, anomie as described by Merton is rather different. For Durkheim, in a healthy society the moral norms regulate the individual's desires—each person knows what he or she can legitimately expect and accepts their place in society. However, for Merton, the norms regulate the means of achieving the goals. For Merton if the goals of a society are limitless there is no problem if most of its members only or largely use legitimate means to achieve those goals (it's not winning that matters but how you play the game'). For Merton the society only becomes anomic if its members use illegitimate means to achieve their goals ('it is winning that matters not how you play the game'): it is the relationship between desires and the means of achieving those desires which is fundamental (Merton 1938 and 1949). Therefore, for Merton there is no need for social upheaval to occur for a society be anomic. Rather anomie arises when people's desires, which they honestly feel they should be able to attain, go beyond what they could possibly achieve through legitimate means. For Merton there

Durkheim's Types of Suicide	Description	Examples	Type of social issue
Egoistic	The individual is insufficiently integrated into the social group. They feel alienated, separate	Those with mental or physical illnesses or the bereaved who feel they are not supported by society and cannot continue	Egoistic and Altruistic suicides are connected to the level to which individuals are integrated into a society. Egoistic suicides are under-integrated
Altruistic	Individuals who are overly integrated and who put the group or society before themselves, before their own well-being	Here an individual may perform suicide out of a sense of duty to the group. Their action serves a greater good—social cohesion and the success of a community. Here the action is not selfish, it is altruistic. This might include actions we do not immediately consider to be suicides such as heroism in war, or someone who undertakes a seemingly impossible task for the benefit of the group. It would also include the actions of a suicide bomber who sacrifices him or herself for the greater good of the group—to promote the political group	Altruistic suicides are over-integrated
Anomic	Suicides that occur due to an upheaval in society. Durkheim argued that: 'No living being can be happy or even exist unless his needs are sufficiently proportioned to his means' (*Suicide*, original 1897, reprinted 1970: 246) Where the society is in a state of flux or upheaval people lose their way, the society fails to regulate either what they could legitimately desire or how they could legitimately achieve it. In such a situation some turn to crime, others to suicide. Here the increased suicides result from the sudden change in society which undermines the collective order and leads to high levels of uncertainty and unhappiness about what is going to happen	For example, suicide rates often increase when there is an economic crisis such as the Wall Street crash in the 1920s and even the less catastrophic crash in 2008–09	Anomic and Fatalistic suicides are connected to levels of regulation and effective setting of social values and standards in a society Anomic suicides result when the norms and values are lax or non-existent
Fatalistic	Individuals who are heavily over-controlled feel they have no life. Durkheim did not discuss this type in depth	This might include slaves	Fatalistic suicides occur when individuals feel they have no individuality, no self

Table 14.1 Durkheim's types of suicide

are two parts to take into account to decide whether a society is anomic:

1. The culturally defined goals of a society—the things which the whole or most people in a society value. These are elements that the society considers it is important for all its members to achieve or enjoy. For some in the UK it might include a good education to get a good job and a certain standard of living, perhaps by owning a house. For others it might include the enjoyment of rights.

2. The institutional means by which the goals can be achieved. For example, it might be ensuring good educational opportunities for everyone or a legal and political system which guarantees rights are enjoyed.

His theory is therefore about means and ends. For Merton anomie occurs, or a state is anomic, where there is a mismatch between these two concepts, where the generally accepted goals (or ends) cannot be achieved through the legitimate means available to individuals. Where the society encourages individuals to achieve goals which are not attainable by legitimate means the society is anomic and individuals will be under strain to achieve or deal with the conflict in other ways. This may occur if people are led to believe that they deserve a lot, for example that they deserve the 'American dream' (that everyone is capable of succeeding and becoming wealthy) but there is no way for most people to achieve that. If, for example, the educational and employment systems are biased and discriminate against certain groups or it is unlikely that many will actually achieve the 'American Dream', there may be discontent. Some people start further up the ladder, already enjoying better lives and having enhanced opportunities. Others will start lower down, with few opportunities and may even be discriminated against (so climbing the ladder with one hand tied behind their backs so to speak). These latter groups and individuals will feel unfairly deprived relative to others in the society. In that situation these deprived groups may be dissatisfied and feel disaffected, which might lead them to being no longer bound by the rules. If this happens these individuals and groups are in a state of normlessness or anomie. Merton used this to explain the higher rates of criminality of the lower classes in the criminal statistics, for these groups criminality was a 'normal' and rational response to their situation. However, he suggested that people in these anomic groups might respond in various ways. There are five ways they might respond, as illustrated in **Table 14.2**.

For Merton, fundamental flaws in a society arise if the goals and means are not realistic; if they are not in accord with each other. His theory depends, therefore, on there being a 'strain' between the means and the ends; it is thought of as a social strain theory even though Merton himself did not accept that analysis of his theory (Cullen and Messner 2007). Merton argued that a healthy society emphasises and rewards conformity, whereas an anomic society emphasises reaching the goals by any means. If *how* the goal is achieved is unimportant, problems arise. So if being wealthy brings with it power, social status and prestige, even if the wealth is achieved through drug dealing or bank robbery (or no-one asks how it is achieved), then there are problems.

Merton, like Sutherland (see the 'Differential association' section of this chapter), argues that all people are basically trying to achieve similar goals but may choose different ways of achieving them, not because they learn different ways of achieving success (as suggested by Sutherland) but rather because of strain due to blocked opportunity.

Merton—critique

Merton's ideas may be useful in explaining lower class crime and, if the official statistics were a true reflection of crime, the ideas might be useful. However, Merton only really explains acquisitive crime committed by those who feel relatively deprived through social structural problems. He fails to explain crimes committed by middle and upper class groups or crimes which have no basis in the means/end dichotomy. In a more recent interview, however, Merton stated that he intended for the theory to apply more widely (Cullen and Messner 2007); and

Type of response	Culturally prescribed goals	Institutionally available means
Conformity	Accept the goals	Acceptance of the legitimate means of achieving them
Innovation	Accept the goals	Rejection of societal means and substitution of new means. Instead of getting a job an individual might turn to crime to make money
Ritualism	Rejects the goals because of an awareness that they can't be achieved. These individuals just accept that limitation	Acceptance of the legitimate means of achieving the ends. Work hard but with no real aspiration
Retreatism	Reject the goals, drops out of the usual intentions and aspirations	Rejection of accepted societal means of achieving the accepted goals. In fact these individuals generally reject almost everything about the society but are not destructive of the society (a homeless person)
Rebellion	Rejection of societal goals and substitution of new goals	Rejection of societal means and substitution of new means. These individuals physically live in the society but do not accept anything to do with the society and suggest an alternative way of living, e.g. new age travellers. In some cases they may turn against the society and try to substitute their own ideas—they might even use violence to force their interests

Table 14.2 Responses to anomie

elsewhere he did apply it to aspects of white-collar crime (Merton 1957). However, the criticism still holds true: generally the theory is not useful on a wider scale, even if he did intend for it to apply more broadly. Furthermore, even for acquisitive crime in the lower classes Merton relies too heavily on statistics which do not take account of how crime control agencies operate. The statistics on which Merton relied are therefore disputed and this places his theory into question.

Moreover, Merton does not fully explain what causes the strain and his theory of structural strain fails to locate a causative link between the strain and the type of action. Is the strain different for the rebel than for the innovator and, if so, is that what explains the different reactions? Furthermore, it is not clear what is cause and what effect. Does rebellion cause the social strain or does the social strain cause the rebellion and how does the causation work in practice?

Like Durkheim, Merton accepts society as it is and merely tries to explain the crime levels. He does not question why society is constructed the way it is. He does not even really criticise the inequalities and why social disparities exist. There is no critique of the political or social systems that lead to this situation or that allow it to continue.

The Chicago school—social disorganisation

The Chicago school is an example of another social structural theory. The Chicago school was a group of sociologists who studied various aspects of life in Chicago at a time when the city was undergoing considerable economic, industrial, and demographic changes. Their work is often referred to as social ecology because they studied how the city changed and developed over time and how each area had its own characteristics. They conducted a systematic analysis of the geographic distribution of the rates of various factors such as infant mortality, illness, adult crime, and juvenile delinquency. They mapped the rates for each factor in each area and searched for statistical correlations between these and specific characteristics of the areas. Alongside this they conducted ethnographic work, learning about people's everyday lives. They studied these elements because:

> it is assumed that People living in natural areas of the same type and subject to the same social conditions will display, on the whole, the same characteristics.

> Park 1929: 36

Robert Ezra Park (1864–1944, an American sociologist) and Ernest Burgess (1886–1966, a Canadian-American urban sociologist), part of the Chicago school, studied what they referred to as 'natural areas' which they described as geographical areas which were physically very similar and whose inhabitants shared certain social and cultural features. They argued that these 'natural' areas had distinct physical boundaries such that one would be aware when moving out of one area into another. Building on this they developed one of the Chicago school's most famous ideas, the zonal theory. In this they split the city into concentric circles and argued that each of the zones represented a distinct type of 'natural' area (see **Figure 14.7**).

In the centre was the business district made up of high value properties mainly used for commercial and economic transactions. This zone had very few residents. The next zone was the transitional zone, so called because its inhabitants were moving through and constantly changing. This zone had a large population living in crowded and inadequate accommodation; properties were run-down and in need of repair. The residents were poor, often immigrants. Outside this were zones 3, 4, and 5. These were all largely residential areas whose inhabitants became more affluent as one moved out from the centre: poor working families lived in zone three; the better off working classes and middle classes in zone 4; and the affluent in zone 5. The population in zone 2 tried to move on as quickly as possible and, in the early 20th century, altered from being largely new immigrants from northern Europe to being new immigrants from southern Europe and then predominantly African Americans. These populations were transient and, as soon as they were able to, they moved into zone 3 to more stable accommodation paid for from a more stable income.

One of the most famous pieces of criminological work conducted by the school was carried out by Clifford Shaw (1922–91) and Henry McKay (1899–1980) who studied the way in which juvenile delinquency rates were distributed. They conducted their study at three different time periods: 1900–06; 1917–23; and 1927–33. They were particularly interested in whether there was a causal correlation between the way in which different neighbourhoods were socially organised and their rates of delinquency, wanting to know whether the delinquency was caused by a breakdown in social integration. They thus developed the social disorganisation theory, building on the zonal theory to explain delinquency. It is important here to recognise that the Chicago school never claimed that the physical elements of an area caused the behaviour of the inhabitants. Rather, the claim is that these physical manifestations are an outward illustration of the type of community living within the areas and it is therefore the social communities, their levels of organisation, cultural features, and how rules and values are accepted within the communities which causes these manifestations. Healthy natural areas or communities were socially cohesive, with their own values and social order. However, others were not socially cohesive, divided on ethical, racial, cultural, religious, inter-generational, or political grounds. These communities were fragmented and dysfunctional. Shaw and McKay were interested in levels of social organisation

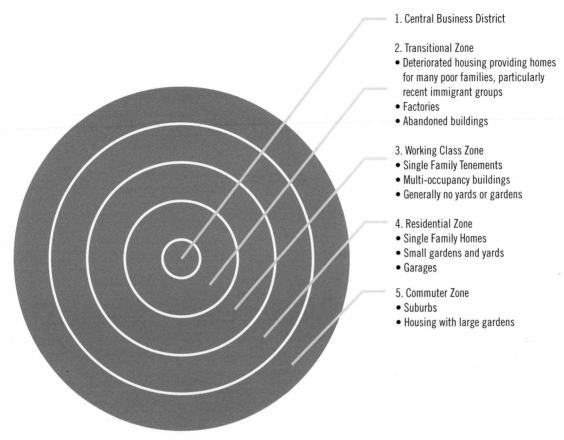

1. Central Business District

2. Transitional Zone
- Deteriorated housing providing homes for many poor families, particularly recent immigrant groups
- Factories
- Abandoned buildings

3. Working Class Zone
- Single Family Tenements
- Multi-occupancy buildings
- Generally no yards or gardens

4. Residential Zone
- Single Family Homes
- Small gardens and yards
- Garages

5. Commuter Zone
- Suburbs
- Housing with large gardens

Figure 14.7 The concentric zone model

and their link to negative outcomes such as crime and deviance, as illustrated by **Table 14.3**.

Shaw and McKay discovered that the highest rates of delinquency could be found in zone 2 and that these rates decreased as one moved out through zones 3 and 4 to zone 5. The highest rates of delinquency were found closest to industrial or commercial areas. This pattern of delinquency rates mapped onto the rates for social disorganisation so zone 2 had very high social disorganisation (low social organisation) whereas zone 5 had high levels of social organisation. They also discovered that the same areas that manifested high rates of delinquency areas also suffered from other negative social factors, such as high levels of mental and physical illness, high infant mortality, high rates of suicide, and high rates of adult involvement in crime, as well as being associated with negative economic conditions such as high unemployment, and poverty.

Interestingly, because they conducted their study at three separate times they could consider delinquency rates over time and discovered that low delinquency rate areas remained low over time and high delinquency rate areas remained high over time. High rates of delinquency in zone 2 survived changes in the population, and could not, therefore, be associated with the individuals living there. In their first time period, zone 2 was largely populated by immigrants from northern Europe and had high

rates of delinquency and was very socially disorganised. In their second time period, zone 2 was largely populated by immigrants from southern Europe; it still had high rates of delinquency and was very socially disorganised. In their third time period, zone 2 was largely populated by African Americans; once again it had high rates of delinquency and was very socially disorganised. This was a very important finding as it proved that the ethnic mix of the community did not affect the rate of delinquency nor did it affect the levels of disorganisation. Delinquency was, however, the result of social conditions such as the social disorganisation of a community; it was a facet of the community not the culture and values of a particular type of person or group.

Shaw and McKay found that the links between delinquency and the communities was strong but they did not claim that it was causative. These findings have been replicated in work by, for example, Sampson and Groves (1969) whose work probably provides the strongest support for social disorganisation theory. Like Shaw and McKay they included structural factors (such as ethnic heterogeneity, family disruption, and residential mobility) as well as measures of social disorganisation (such as the strength of friendship groups and participation in community organisations). For Sampson and Groves structural elements might themselves be linked to criminality and

Type of measure	Socially organised natural areas with high levels of cohesion	Socially disorganised natural areas lacking cohesion
Formal social controls—provided by organisations such as schools, churches, and the police	The formal mechanisms work effectively to teach individuals acceptable forms of behaviour and positive values. There is mutual respect between the community and the formal social control mechanisms such as school and police	A breakdown in the operation of these formal control mechanisms. For example, schools being unable to engage the young people and failing to teach social mores (standards of behaviour) or the police acting to contain problems within an area rather than enforcing and protecting from within
Informal social controls—provided by the family and peer groups, etc.	Families, peer groups and other informal social mechanisms work effectively to socialise members of the community into the cultural expectations, rules, and values of their communities so producing cohesive and socially sound communities. High levels of respect and support for formal groups such as the police	A breakdown in informal control mechanisms. For example, these informal groups fail to teach the generally accepted social values. They may even socialise into alternative, unacceptable rule-breaking mores. Low levels of social cohesion around conformity
Levels of social capital and internal supports	High levels of social capital—people participating in activities and groups within the community. Showing pride in their area, caring for their homes and for their streets. Also, caring for and about others in their community. People come together to volunteer or to happily participate in activities with others and with groups that help conformity such as religion, sports activities, etc. Citizens are willing to participate in informal and semi-formal groups	A lack of social capital—people being unwilling to participate in groups in the community. Not showing any pride in their area so letting the physical surroundings deteriorate and not connecting with or caring about others in the community. Children are likely to encounter conflicting moral standards and negative adult role-models (adult crime and involvement in drugs)
Values	Accepts and embraces the conventional values of the wider society	No real commitment to the values of the broader society. Wide diversity of norms and values

Table 14.3 Types of control and their effects by type of area

delinquency or might lead to social disorganisation which in turn would be linked to crime and delinquency, as shown in **Figure 14.8**.

Critique of social disorganisation

At the centre of Shaw and McKay's work is the belief that one could only understand juvenile delinquency if one first understood the social context in which it arose. They accepted that the social context was linked to structural factors such as transient populations, poverty, and unemployment but considered that the more important connector was with social disorganisation. Offenders lived in areas where the official and informal institutions were weak and/or dysfunctional, which left them uncontrolled and free to offend or to be delinquent.

From this, Shaw and McKay suggested that efforts should be made to strengthen community ties in these areas and to support the inhabitants to build a more organised social setting. They set up the Chicago Area Project (CAP) which used community leaders to try to tackle problems, provide activities for young people and encourage residents to take pride in their area. Whilst these efforts have never been

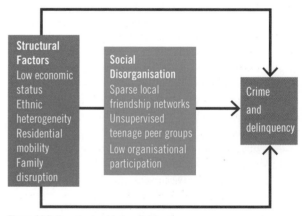

Figure 14.8 How structural factors link to crime
Source: Adapted from Sampson and Groves 1989: 783

carefully evaluated it is believed that they had limited success (Schlossman et al. 1984).

Despite being replicated and being a respected theory some serious critiques of Shaw and McKay's work might be made:

• Firstly, the researchers accepted and relied heavily on official statistics to assess rates of delinquency and crime.

However, these were unlikely to be correct; they probably better reflected the way in which areas are policed than the crime rates of those areas. Self-report studies on rates of juvenile delinquency show that rates of self-reported delinquency are not very different when one compares the different areas. Most young people transgress and rates of self-reported delinquency and crime remain fairly constant even as between socially organised and disorganised areas though the type of deviance might differ.

- Secondly, the zonal theory does not work particularly well for other cities. All cities have neighbourhoods with high and low levels of social organisation and in many cities the most socially disorganised areas attract the highest levels of officially recorded juvenile delinquency. However, most cities' deprived areas cannot neatly be placed in zones or concentric circles.

- Thirdly, it predicts too much delinquency and fails to explain why some young people in socially disorganised areas do not transgress.

- Finally, whilst it proves that race does not explain the differences in rates of juvenile delinquency it does not consider whether within these communities there might be differences based on ethnic, religious, or other differences.

Therefore although the theory is important in linking crime and other ills in a neighbourhood to lack of community cohesion, the details of the theory, such as the zonal nature of city layouts, are questionable.

Culture and subcultural theories

Culture is the sum of everything which a community invests into its members; sitting under its umbrella are knowledge, beliefs, morals, law, habits, expected standards of behaviour, all forms of art, and customs. All the theories discussed so far in this chapter have, to one extent or another, considered how effectively a community has passed on its culture. They have then linked high levels of crime and/or delinquency to communities where there is no real shared culture (anomie), or where one aspect fails to ensure legitimate behaviour is effective (strain and anomie), or where the community is ineffectively built and/or passed on (social disorganisation). Each of these theories indicated that delinquency and crime might be rational solutions to particular social situations and that therefore one could, in these situations, expect high rates of criminality. However, these theories seem to suggest too much criminality and fail to explain why not everyone living in a situation of anomie, strain, and social disorganisation offends or commits act of deviance. Subcultural theory offers some answer to this.

A subculture is a division of the broader culture with some of its own values, customs, and expectations to which individuals feel committed and which influences the way in which they think and behave. Many subcultures expect certain types of behaviour, styles of dressing, music, and other preferences, values, opinions and/or ways of expressing themselves. Displaying some or all of these allows an individual membership to the group. Subcultures may be built on class, ethnic origin, religion, music, or other unifying elements. Every complex society supports many subcultures. Some, such as many religious groups and professional groups (such as judges, parliament, the police, and the British Medical Council), are welcomed and embraced. Whilst each of these largely serves the greater good, aspects may occasionally be questioned or be damaging (see recent issues with parliamentary expenses and some aspects of police culture) but they are accepted as being necessary for the good functioning of the society. However, some cultures are viewed and treated negatively by the dominant elements of society; much youth culture falls in this category and even when it is not criminal it may be seen as deviant. The most studied subcultures are these juvenile subcultures each of which generally has a very distinctive image, style, behaviour, appearance, demeanour, values, and their own figures of speech or jargon. Many are also associated with particular types of music and often embrace excitement, power, and freedom.

There are many examples of youth cultures over time in the UK. First are mods and rockers in the 1960s and 70s—these were two British youth subcultures who were in conflict. The mods often rode scooters and were interested in fashion (often setting fashion), they wore suits and looked 'clean cut' with short hair. They often listened to soul, rhythm and blues, and beat music. The rockers generally rode motorbikes so needed protective clothing, their group got linked to wearing black leather jackets (often with slogans), they listened to rock and roll and often had their hair swept back from the face into 'big' hairdos. The two groups were in disagreement and there was always tension between them. This tension sometimes resulted in violent clashes. Reports of their conflicts in the media led to 'moral panic' about these two groups which led to them being labelled 'folk devils'. Many adults considered the members of these groups to be dangerous and called for them to be controlled.

Punks came next in the 1970s and 80s—The punks were a subculture that grew out of punk music (see **Figure 14.9**). This subculture was fractured and had a number of ideologies and fashions. For most punks it was important to allow individuals to express themselves through their bodies, clothing, music, and dance. The main unifying

Figure 14.9 European punks
Source: Roger Tillberg/Alamy Stock Photo

idea was probably negative—that they were against the controlling nature of the establishment. However, they also promoted individual freedom. Punk music is loud and both in its nature and the lyrics it is often confrontational or even aggressive. Because their appearance was often challenging, sometimes even aggressive, and the music they listened to was loud and aggressive many adults wanted punks to be controlled.

'Road' Life and 'Bad Boys' appeared from 2000 onwards. These young black Caribbean young men are deviant, commit crime and build a style, lifestyle and set values which revolve around badness (see Gunter 2008).

However, many of the gangs and peer groups who may cause trouble today do not necessarily belong to a particular, recognisable national gang. According to government, antisocial behaviour and group violence have been a central issue from the 1990s onwards (Squires 2006). Groups of youths may well be involved in antisocial behaviour, and though they may not be a national phenomenon and/or a visually recognisable group, the behaviour is still often believed to be from groups of youths, maybe because they are visible on the street. This belief and the

visibility of these groups led politicians to try to control young people. The Crime and Disorder Act 1998 first tried to curb and control these groups by making provision for antisocial behaviour. The controls were strengthened in the Anti-Social Behaviour Act 2003 (relates to adults and children though has been used most frequently to control children) and in later legislation. In no legislation is antisocial behaviour defined; it is a subjective feeling experienced by victims who complain to the authorities. Part 4 of the Policing and Crime Act 2009 (as amended by the Crime and Security Act 2010 and the Police Reform and Social Responsibility Act 2011) provides for injunctions to control those who participate in gang related activities (a gang is a group of three or more who have a 'style' by which they can be identified) and for punishment if the injunction is breached. These controls have had mixed success but have led to the criminalising of many young people who first have injunctions against certain behaviours and then are criminalised when they breach those injunctions (Burney 2009). Whilst antisocial behaviour is not only focused on young people they have been the group most controlled by the provisions.

Riots can act as indicators of youth problems; they break out occasionally and are often indicative of major discontent. That was the finding by Lord Scarman (1981) writing about the 1981 riots which started in Brixton but soon spread to cities around the country (these riots were caused by distrust of the police and were related to racial tension and inner city deprivation). It was also a strong feeling coming out of the riots of August 2011 which broke out in a number of cities in the UK and lasted a number of days. The joint *Guardian* and LSE (2012) research which followed pin-pointed the discontent of young people in British society:

These young people are coming out to prove they have an existence, to prove that if you don't listen to them and you don't take into account our views, potentially this is a destructive force.

Man, mid-20s, north London. *Guardian* and LSE 2012: 13

There's a massive police station there, and they couldn't do anything. It was ours for a day. Salford was more like a party atmosphere. Everyone was stood around, drinking … smoking weed, having a laugh. People weren't threatening the public.

There was people there to get on a rob [loot], there for the spectacle, there to have a go at police. And then people there for all of the above. We hate the police, hate the government, got no opportunities …

These aren't gangs. The kids just did what they wanted to do 'cos they wanted to do it, not because some gang boss orchestrated it to get back at the police.'

Unemployed man, 22. *Guardian* and LSE 2012: 20

The government needed someone to blame and [put] everything together under 'gangs'. I don't believe there was much planned gangland activity. I believe there was a lot of angry, very working-class, disillusioned young men that realised 'hang on a minute, it's going off'.

Man, 21. *Guardian* and LSE 2012: 22

When I left my house … it wasn't anything to do with the police … I literally went there to say, 'All right then, well, everyone's getting free stuff, I'm joining in', like, 'cos, it's fucking my area. These fucking shops, like, I've given them a hundred CVs … not one job. That's why I left my house.

It's not like I haven't got GCSEs … Why haven't I even got [an] interview? … I feel like I haven't [been] given the same opportunities and chances as other people … If I had a job … I honestly wouldn't have stolen nothing …

And that's what I feel like: people are not worth anything in this area.

Man 22 from London. *Guardian* and LSE 2012: 26

In all of the examples discussed thus far (mods and rockers; punks; road life and bad boys; the riots; and a lot of anti-social behaviour) young people group together most often to help them solve the problems they face. Even in riots there is a sense of belonging to a group which is united to reveal or solve a problem. In the case of gangs (better defined than loose, rioting groups), to get them through their lives, they adopt values and behaviours different from those of the general population. Whilst adults often accuse these youths of intentionally challenging the broader culture or trying to undermine it, this is not generally what underlies the youth subculture—most often they are just trying to deal with the social environment they inhabit.

Whilst all subcultures are 'deviant' by the standards of the broader culture, many only 'breach' conventions concerning relatively minor issues such as style, music, and speech patterns, remaining otherwise quite conforming. Some, however, do encourage and/or condone crime and damaging forms of delinquency. It is these subcultures which generally interest criminologists, partly because these young people often become the adult offenders of tomorrow and partly because the rate of juvenile offending is higher than for other age groups (almost one third of officially recorded crimes). Policy makers are constantly seeking new ways to tackle this youth criminality which often seems to serve no purpose and yet is very destructive for others, especially if it involves violence. Juvenile subcultures largely revolve around peer group or even gang delinquency which is generally considered to be a lower-class and male pursuit. This is important because since the 1960s academics have increasingly accepted that poverty is not the result of individual failure but rather it is the fault of the system, the society and the way it is structured. This

has also been accepted by many politicians and some aspects of the media. This acceptance of poverty as a social structural problem brought to the fore ideas based on Merton's idea of anomie—one in which everyone was told they could achieve 'the American dream' and were encouraged to strive for this goal but many of the poor could never legitimately attain this goal. The next few gang subculture theories draw heavily on this idea. Before considering them take a look at the contents of **What do you think? 14.3** for a real life example which may provide some context.

Cohen and delinquent subcultures

We will start with a consideration of Albert K. Cohen (1918–2014). Cohen was a prominent American criminologist who drew heavily on Merton's concept of anomie to suggest that young people used delinquency to resolve social problems. He also drew on Sutherland's differential association (see earlier in this chapter) believing that associating with a criminal or delinquent subculture would lead a young person to offend. In his major work *Delinquent Boys: The Culture of the Gang* (1955) Cohen argued that juvenile delinquency could be largely explained by the adoption of the values of their peer group. The core of his thesis was that to resolve the problems caused by the strains a society placed on certain young people they turned to each other to form a 'subculture' in which they could succeed and feel comfortable. However, he needed to explain where the delinquent subculture came from, how it arose, and why it persisted over time.

Cohen suggested that gangs provided a vehicle to allowing young people to belong and grow, and to solve the problems caused by the broader culture. The gangs that had values which were likely to lead their members into delinquent behaviour were concentrated in urban, lower-class areas and were largely the preserve of young men angry at the constraints of middle class culture which prevented them from succeeding. Whilst Cohen refers to middle class culture and values he means the values of the dominant culture in America:

Though we refer to them as 'middle class' norms, they are really manifestations of the dominant American value systems and even working class children must come to terms with them.

Cohen 1955: 87

He considered that the problems started to arise very early because working class boys faced a conflict once they went to school—the socialisation at school was different from and often clashed with that in their homes. This confused the boys. At school they were faced with values such as ambition, responsibility, rational behaviour, control of aggression (physical and verbal), and respect for others.

WHAT DO YOU THINK? 14.3

- This was a real letter sent out to many people in a particular area. Do you think that this is a positive way of tackling serious crimes of violence?

- How would you feel if you received this letter?

- What does it tell us about the way in which the police view these 'gangs'?

- Remember this letter as you read what follows.

 **METROPOLITAN POLICE**   Working together for a safer London

TERRITORIAL POLICING

Brent Borough
603 Harrow Road
Wembley
Middlesex
HA0 2HH

19th August 2015

Dear

You may be aware of an incident on the Kilburn High Road on Sunday 16th August during which a 24 year old man received serious stab injuries. This is being treated as an attempted murder.

Our intelligence suggests you are linked to gang related criminal activity in the South Kilburn area. We are determined to bring the cycle of violence affecting this area to an end. We are not suggesting you were directly involved in the latest incident but we believe that you are involved in criminal behaviour that puts you at greater risk of becoming a victim or a perpetrator of violent crime yourself.

We would like to invite you to take the opportunity to meet with Brent Police, Brent Council and other agencies to discuss the events of 16th August, possible risks to yourself, and ways we can help you move away from criminal behaviour.

This meeting will take place on **Thursday 27th August at 3pm at the Marian Centre 1 Stafford Road NW6 5RS.**

If you choose not to attend we will see this as a clear message that you intend to continue with a criminal lifestyle. As such, we will work hard to disrupt your activities utilising every legitimate means available to us.

Yours Sincerely

Borough Commander

At home there was recognition that the ambition was unlikely to be rewarded with success. In this confusing atmosphere they sought a way of resolving the conflict or of coping with their situation. Cohen suggested that they would adopt one of three solutions:

College Boys—these young men wholly accept the values of the wider culture and compete for success on those terms—they conform and compete. Cohen argued that only a minority of boys chose this solution.

Street Corner Boys—accept their limitations and live within them—they conform, lose any real ambition and just make the most of what legitimately they can attain. This solution is considered deviant but not problematic for the broader society.

Delinquent Corner Boys—are angry at their situation and hit out against what they see as the problem. These working class young males see middle-class values and ways of achieving success work unfairly against them. The way they choose to resolve this problem is to join with others and engage in negative and malicious behaviours, things destructive to the middle-class values they see as causing the strain and the problem. These boys want what the society says is valuable, they want success, but feel that it is being unfairly blocked which leads to strain. The means of coping with the situation is an anger focused on the dominant middle-class culture which is vented through the youth subculture which sees delinquency as attractive partly because it is 'non-utilitarian, malicious and negativistic' (Merton, 1938: 25).

To break this down, we can explore each of these terms:

- non-utilitarian—this delinquency is done for themselves, for fun or to vent anger, not for gain. If property or money is stolen this is done for 'kicks', for the excitement, and the 'profit' would be given away or 'wasted';

- malicious—to harm or undermine other people, authority or middle-class values. Here destructiveness is intentional not a by-product. They might well scrawl graffiti all over a property they broke into for no other reason than they could and it would upset others;

- negativistic—the behaviour is good because it is unacceptable to the dominant culture, the values are not accidently at odds but intentionally in opposition to the dominant culture.

One might add that he viewed this gang delinquency as short-term and hedonistic (the main reason for the delinquency is pleasure, excitement and immediate gratification) and included acquisitive, destructive and aggressive behaviours as well as causing problems or 'hell-raising'. Importantly, for these young people loyalty was to the group or gang rather than to society or family.

Therefore, for Cohen the style, music, culture, argot, and behaviour chosen are attractive to the subculture partly because it is in conflict with or undermining of the standards and norms of the wider culture. Many of the juvenile subcultures value aspects such as excitement, toughness, and

immediate gratification whereas those of the wider culture, particularly the middle classes prioritise responsibility, drive and ambition, individual responsibility, achievement and success, postponement of gratification, respect for others and for their property, control of both physical and verbal aggression, and respect for others and for their property. They therefore engage in delinquency which is irrational and disrespectful of conventional, middle-class culture, activities such as truanting from school, fighting, being disrespectful or rude to others, or vandalising or destroying property.

Here the strain caused by a class-based system, which excludes some from the success it claims and teaches (in schools and other institutions) is available to everyone, is the catalyst for delinquent subcultures; these will exist over time as long as this class-based strain persists. This theory of class-based strain claims to explain why delinquent subcultures arise, why they are in conflict with mainstream culture, and why they persist over many generations. Cohen also claims that the feeling of inclusion, friendship, and excitement that is offered by these delinquent subcultures (gangs) may attract some boys who do not feel the strain but merely wish to be a part of something which is 'fun'.

Cohen assumes, though he never really proves it, that working-class boys, and particularly those involved in gangs, first try to succeed by middle-class values and when they fail they become hostile to those values. Cohen suggests that it is frustration at failure which leads to the gangs and the delinquency (crime). However, Box (1981: 150) suggests that it may be that these young men never really try to succeed but feel resentment and anger at being called a failure and that it is this labelling which leads to the delinquency and crime. However, they may be both frustrated and resentful; a mixture of both of these theories.

Cloward and Ohlin and 'Differential Opportunity'

Richard A. Cloward (1926–2001) and Lloyd E. Ohlin (1918–2008) were famous American sociologists and criminologists who worked together in the 1950s and 1960s. They also drew on Merton's anomie. Cloward and Ohlin (1960) recognised that crime and delinquency existed throughout society. They argued, however, that for middle-class youths it arose as part of an individual struggle, whereas for working-class youths it was part of a lack of opportunity leading them to form peer groups or gangs to react against the problems this caused. Like Cohen, they concentrated on the delinquency of these lower-class youths because it permitted insight into the subculture of the peer group or gang. They also argued that these strong groupings were possible in lower-class neighbourhoods because they met with less disapproval from adults within their neighbourhood than would be the case for middle-class delinquency.

Cloward and Ohlin drew on both Merton and Sutherland. From Merton they recognised the pressure and strain that these young people were placed under because of:

> the disparity between what lower-class youths are led to want and what is actually available to them.
>
> Cloward and Ohlin 1960

This disparity caused the young men problems that needed to be resolved. Their strain theory is much closer to that of Merton than that of Cohen, in that it depends on failures in society, particularly economic failures, rather than the conflict caused by school. Whilst Cloward and Ohlin recognised that this anomie and its resulting strain was necessary to understanding the behaviours, they also recognised that it was not, alone, sufficient to explain the delinquency of young people because:

> it does not sufficiently explain why these pressures result in one deviant solution rather than another.
>
> Cloward and Ohlin 1960: 34

Cloward and Ohlin were critical of Cohen, believing he relied too heavily on the middle-class values in saying that these applied to 'college boys' but may not apply to others struggling in the lower-classes. Cloward and Ohlin add to the discussion of juvenile gang and peer delinquency by taking strain theory further, using it to explain why one delinquent solution is chosen over another.

From Sutherland they learned that whatever role a person chooses (legitimate or illegitimate) they need access to the means of succeeding in that role. If one were to become a teacher one might need education, training, and opportunity. To succeed as a burglar one might need some training and also access to people willing and able to fence the goods. Cloward and Ohlin therefore suggest that the type of gang or peer group depends on access to these opportunities.

Therefore, in brief, the background social situation necessary to this criminality is a blocking of legitimate opportunities. The blocking of opportunities is experienced as unfair because it is based not on merit or need but on subjective criteria such as speaking with the 'right' accent, coming from the 'right' background, or 'who you know'. The legitimate institutions such as schools and employers therefore fail the working-class youths who are then 'free' to choose other ways of achieving some sort of success and to do so without feeling any guilt about how they achieve 'success'. However, to explain the type of criminal activity one needs to consider the type of alternative opportunities available in their area. They suggest three types of solution to the strain, depending on opportunities available to youths: criminal subcultures; conflict subcultures; and retreatist subcultures, as set out in **Table 14.4**.

Cloward and Ohlin therefore embraced Merton's idea of strain theory and considered that the perceived unjust denial of access to legitimate opportunities to 'succeed' in society was a powerful pressure which explained why someone might be willing to commit acts of deviance or crime. However, they recognised that this theory was limited and could not explain why some people chose one way to resolve this strain and others another. They therefore added in a focus on the availability of illegitimate opportunities, a form of differential association theory, to explain why certain solutions were chosen to resolve the strain of restricted opportunities to succeed. Whilst they applied their theory to juvenile subcultures (peer groups and gangs) they also considered that differential opportunity theory would be relevant to explaining how and why adults resolved similar conflicts.

Neutralisation and drift

Gresham Sykes (1922–2010) and David Matza (1930–), American sociologists and criminologists, worked on the concept of 'neutralisation'. The original idea of 'neutralisation' arose out of work by Matza and Sykes in 1957 and 1961 but was refined, extended, and more fully considered by Matza (1961, 1964, and 1969) when he added the concept of 'drift'. For a shorthand all of this work is now often referred to as Matza's, presumably because he built on and refined the ideas but it is important that you recognise that the original concept of 'neutralisation' was conceived by Matza and Sykes together.

Matza argued that strain theory and Merton's concept of anomie predicted too much crime and delinquency. Strain theorists and other subcultural theorists could not explain why most people were law abiding and adhered to conventional values most of the time and why most offenders stop offending in their early 20s. He started from the premise that most people of all ages (including youths) are basically conventional and likely to conform to most of the rules most of the time. He also questioned the idea that subcultural values of gangs and youth peer groups were set up in opposition to the values of the broader society and in doing so rejected these elements of the subcultural theories of Cohen and Cloward and Ohlin. He did not accept the idea that young people in certain surroundings would face so much 'strain' that they would be forced into an otherwise unattractive coping strategy (a delinquent/criminal strategy).

However, he does not totally reject strain as an aspect of the formation of the offending group and he does include factors such as desperation as parts of some parts of his theory. His theory seeks to explain:

1. Why people who face this overwhelming strain are nonetheless law abiding most of the time?

2. Why, despite remaining in the areas where strain is strongest, they tend to grow out of deviant and

	Type of adaptation: Criminal subculture	Type of adaptation: Conflict subculture	Type of adaptation: Retreatist subculture
What is involved	Generally this gang or peer group is involved in the illegal taking of property or other means of making money	Young men who lack purpose in life, who then become angry because society has let them down. They use power and violence to give vent to this negativity. They come together to use power and violence in a conflict gang	This is a drug-oriented gang
Where	In organised slum areas where there are opportunities for offences like burglary and for fencing any goods which are stolen	In disorganised slum areas. These areas are transient or unstable due to shifts in population or because of lack of pride in the community. These areas lack both criminal and legitimate role models so the youths turn to using conflict	In any areas or neighbourhoods where drugs can be obtained
What is necessary	Adult offenders to serve both as role models and as people who can facilitate such behaviour or an established gang who can support in these ways It also often requires a wider community which is at least tolerant of this way of making money so that there is some respectability associated with succeeding in criminal endeavours	Absence of both legitimate and illegitimate (criminal) opportunities. With no supportive criminal opportunities the youths form gangs which use violence to build a reputation for themselves. Fear gives them an identity and a social standing	For those who fail in legitimate, illegitimate (criminal) and illegitimate (conflict or status) spheres retreatism is the only deviant coping strategy open to them. For Cloward and Ohlin this retreatism involves a retreat into drug use to blot out the reality of their lives. Note this drug use is different from the occasional use that may be a part of all these subcultures, it is more all-consuming Some of these young people may conform but give up any hope of achieving any goals—see Cohen's 'Delinquent Corner Boys' (1955) Whether they become part of a retreatist gang or peer group or conform depends partly on their own personality but also on the availability of drugs and a drug culture
Types of individuals involved	Those on whom the group can rely, unpredictable individuals will not be accepted as they will place the whole criminal endeavour in jeopardy	Mostly disorganised people who are seeking status and willing to participate in violence to achieve it. They are often angry because they lack both legitimate and illegitimate opportunities. This gives rise to a desire to prove their worth and status	Could be drawn from any area. This can involve almost anyone (no particular personal traits are involved). However, membership is a personal choice and clearly requires an opportunity, a drug culture, which can arise in any type of area
Legitimate goals and means	Accepts the traditional goals of the broader society Rejects legitimate means of achieving them	Rejects the traditional goals of the broader society Rejects legitimate means of achieving their ends Rejects the 'conventional' illegitimate means of succeeding which might lead to financial success	Some may accept the goals of society but generally this group rejects all legitimate and illegitimate goals Generally—though not in every case—members of this group reject both legitimate and illegitimate means of achieving goals
Illegitimate goals and means	Adopts illegitimate means of succeeding	Adopts destructive goals, linked to achieving personal and gang (peer group) status, often through fear Adopts violence and activities which lead to fear to achieve status	Generally this group rejects both legitimate and illegitimate goals Generally—though not in every case—members of this group reject both legitimate and illegitimate means of achieving goals

Table 14.4 Cloward and Ohlin's solutions to strain

criminal behaviour and become more conventional and law abiding?

He noted that most people's behaviour was not always or even usually delinquent or criminal. Instead he discovered that even in fairly prolific offenders such unacceptable behaviour was at best intermittent (i.e. they did not behave unacceptably all the time); people were largely conforming. So, instead of totally relying on strain, Matza suggested that all people retain free will and that delinquency and crime, like all other behaviour, is largely chosen; it is the outcome of free will. He called this aspect of his theory 'drift'. No individuals are totally committed to criminal or delinquent lives; people are basically law-abiding and merely offend occasionally. To explain this Matza suggested that they were in a state of drift—they were able to drift between commitment to conventional behaviour and unacceptable behaviour, never wholly committed to either.

Matza suggested that young working-class males did not reject conventional culture in order to form delinquent and criminal subcultures—this predicted too much crime. Instead they were in a state of 'drift'. This state of drift arises because the dominant values are fluid and have no real hard requirements. So, for example, dominant culture allows people to have fun (through enjoying pastimes) and to be aggressively competitive (to get a promotion or to win at sport) or to enjoy excitement and adventures (in extreme sports, by travelling or at funfairs). In the dominant culture these norms are 'subordinate' to the more important aspects of hard work and earning the right to enjoy oneself. People in a state of drift take these 'subordinate values' and extend or distort them so that excitement, aggression, violence, and others become more dominant and become used in inappropriate ways. Violence and aggression are supported if channelled into winning in sport or doing well at work, when the violence is not done for and of itself. Those in a state of drift extend the acceptable use of violence to include, for example, fighting to protect your reputation or credibility with a subgroup or to get a purse or wallet in order to get the money you need. Each person in a state of drift may extend rules in slightly different ways but they all generally retain aspects of the rule they do not feel it is legitimate to breach (it may be that violence towards other gangs is acceptable but towards elderly people is not); they do not become rule-less.

Furthermore, in every rule-based culture there are exceptions and defences to every activity; every rule is qualified. Intentional killing is generally illegal—murder—but might be excused if committed in self-defence or mercy killing, or might even be glorified if committed in war. Again, those in a state of drift extend these grey areas at the edges of rules; the area of permissible behaviour is widened. From the dominant culture they learn that no rule is absolute and therefore use the permissiveness which is part of the dominant culture, extending it to include permissions which are favourable to delinquency or crime. They, therefore, are simultaneously bound to the dominant culture and free to violate if they choose. Matza sees this as a subculture of delinquency—a subculture that permits delinquency and will excuse it if an individual chooses to break rules. He therefore rejects Cohen and Cloward and Ohlin's ideas of delinquent subcultures which depend on and positively encourage rule-breaking.

The other part of drift involves 'neutralisation'. Here people (including juveniles) generally accept and live within conventional values but learn ways of explaining their lapses into delinquency and crime. They use 'techniques of neutralisation' which would release them from the conventional rules and allow them to break the rules without feeling guilt. Part of this is the extension of the normally accepted defences used by officials and those who view themselves as entirely conforming. Matza found that the authorities often blamed parents for the actions of their children or accepted some transgressions as accidents and, as noted, these are extended to allow transgression without guilt. So, therefore, young people might see that society treats, for example, homeless people very badly and take that negative feeling further by becoming actively violent towards them. They might see big businesses being attacked for avoiding taxes and then decide that stealing from these big shops whose shareholders can afford the loss and would anyway be insured is acceptable. They suggested five techniques of 'neutralisation' which might be used as justifications before the act or excuses after they had transgressed, set out in **Table 14.5**.

All of this 'drift' and 'neutralisation' frees the individual to choose to offend but Matza recognises that not all individuals will choose to offend; some will lack 'the position, capacity or inclination to become agents in their own behalf' (Matza 1964: 29). Matza saw these people as permanent drifters. Just being free to offend does not mean it will happen; it does not explain the offending itself. Matza's theory is often thought of as a control theory. However, it differs from other control theories because here merely having controls removed does not mean offending will occur, it has to be both possible and chosen.

For Matza, before offending is chosen there is a combination of 'preparation' and/or 'desperation'. For Matza 'preparation' means that the individual:

(a) is aware that a particular type of offending is possible, that it can be done;

(b) knows how to commit the crime;

(c) is able to perform all aspects necessary to the crime and has all the tools and the opportunity to commit that offence; and

(d) can cope with the fear of being discovered and feels confident that they can perform the task.

Type of neutralisation	What it entails	Examples
Denial of responsibility	'It is not my fault'. Here offenders may claim that: • they had no choice and could therefore not be blamed; • it was the fault of someone or something else—a result of parental neglect or of poverty or being led astray by friends; or • the transgression was unintended and was an accident—'I didn't mean to do it'	Following the Second World War those who committed war crimes tried to claim that it was not their fault because they were 'only following orders' Claims such as: • 'I only wanted to steal her purse but she wouldn't give it to me so I had to hit her, I didn't want to'; • 'He was disrespecting me so I had to hit him'; and • 'If only you kept house properly I wouldn't have to hit you', would fall into this category. Claims which deny responsibility are very common
Denial of injury	The offender may claim that no-one was harmed—for example, the victim was insured They might also claim that the victim knew what they were letting themselves in for and therefore has no right or justification to complain about their injuries; it is a private affair Here very often the perpetrators are law abiding and genuinely believe that their extended view of what should be legal is what should be the law	If an individual starts a fight or disrespects someone or participates in a gang fight then any injuries are accepted and therefore there is no real victim Claims such as: • 'I stole a car but the victim will be insured so they have not lost out—what is the problem?'; • 'They have so much they will never miss it'; and • 'We enjoy it and no-one else is involved or those involved all consent' (e.g. sadomasochistic behaviours or drug taking or a gang fight)
Denial of victim	Offenders might claim that the victim is bad or a lesser person so has no right to complain. They may claim that the victim deserved their victimisation, or even that all those involved participate so there is no victim and it is no business of broader society	Examples of such claims might be: That the 'victim' started the fight so only got what was coming to them In domestic violence the offender might tell the victim that if they would only do things properly he would not need to punish them, it is for their own good. Other examples would be claims such as: • 'We were all enjoying taking drugs, it didn't harm anyone so what is the problem?'; • 'We had a fight but no-one really got hurt, it was just a bit of fun so what is the problem?'; • 'You can't rape a prostitute; it is just a matter of negotiating the price'; and • 'She was dressed provocatively and chose to come back for a coffee so can't complain of rape'
Condemnation of condemners	Offenders might claim that 'we have all offended so no-one can take the high ground and condemn others' They might take a 'everyone is doing it so why pick on me' stance Finally, they might claim that police and judges are corrupt or don't punish their friends or those who are rich	Examples might involve: 'everyone speeds so you should not just punish me; if you don't punish all of them it is not fair. You are unjust' Pointing out that those who evade taxes can merely pay them back whereas making a bogus benefit claim will be treated as a crime Claiming police corruption or brutality so seeing them as 'bad' and criminal so unable to call others to account

Table 14.5 Techniques of neutralisation (*continued*)

Type of neutralisation	What it entails	Examples
Appeal to higher loyalties or a mood of humanism	This subsumes some that deny responsibility The claim here is that one is acting on a 'higher' calling, something that is more important than obeying the laws or expectations of society. So it may be to redress a balance or for humanistic reasons	The example of 'only following orders' would fit here as well as above. Other claims which might fall under this head: • 'I was hungry' • 'I was taking it to feed my family' • 'The system is so unfair and I was trying to redress the balance and make things fairer' • 'My friends expect me to do it and I can't let them down' • 'It is a gang (peer group) ritual or necessary to support the gang (peer group) and I can't let them down' • 'The law is unjust and I am bound to and answerable to a higher and more important standard' • 'I acted because "god" expects me to' • 'It is being done to protect the faith' • 'It is necessary to free my people'

Table 14.5 (*continued*)

'Desperation' occurs when there is a very strong feeling of despair or hopelessness and a need to offend in order to prove that you can take control and show that you are a person, an individual.

Critique of 'neutralisation' and 'drift'

There are difficulties here. Some are internal; the claim to be answering a higher calling rarely fits with the action being taken. Also all the techniques of neutralisation are very 'convenient' as they let the offender off the hook, removing the need to feel guilty, looked at objectively one might even wonder whether they are explanations or excuses. In particular it is often difficult to decide whether something such as the denial of responsibility 'I had to, I was being pushed around and I had no choice' exists: before the offence is committed and 'frees' the offender to act; or is used to avoid feeling guilty and to avoid condemnation from accusers once he/she is found out. Clearly this is difficult to unpick and cannot be proven. What is, however, clear is that these techniques could both act to free someone from conventional bonds and assist the offender to escape full blame and censure either from themselves (guilt) or others.

Another issue arises from the ability of the theory to explain certain 'facts' recorded by officials. Matza's theory clearly deals with the problems of over predicting crime. However, his theory probably under predicts crime and may fail to adequately explain serious offending. Furthermore, it cannot explain why some people do not grow out of offending or only take to offending later in life. It does not explain the 6–10 per cent of offenders who are prolific and persistent. It therefore seems to solve one problem but ignores other aspects of the crime problem that do not fit with the theory.

It is also important to recognise that Matza is not really a subcultural theorist, but rather is often seen as a control theorist. This is because, for Matza, delinquency is an individual choice which occurs when someone is in a state of drift. However, it is a subculture theory because some of the forces that move someone into drift or that prepare someone for or place them in a position of desperation arise out of youth subculture. The difference for Matza—as opposed to other subcultural theorists—is that the subculture permits and facilitates delinquency and offending but these activities are not a required element of the subculture.

Social exclusion and the underclass

So far in this analysis we have concentrated on the social environment which arises due to different economic conditions and the impact it has on offending. At this point we will move away from environment to concentrate directly on external factors such as poverty, unemployment, and general despair. These factors have existed in all cultures over time but became particularly important to studies of crime once societies became industrialised and people tended to live in large conurbations where communities were less connected and more diverse. Migration, population growth, and rapid urbanisation led to the concentration of population in smaller geographic areas which rendered offending easier—there was 'more' close at hand (more property to steal or destroy and more people towards whom one might be violent)—and this made it more of a problem for the law abiding—there was more to fear. In these concentrations of population there emerged—over time—large differences between the rich and poor. The differentials gave rise to large areas of slums in which, 19th century commentators feared, dangerous sub-groups formed, commonly referred to as the 'Residuum' or the 'underclass' (see Phillips 1977; Tobias 1972; and Jones 1982).

In western cultures (similar concepts may apply in other parts of the world) the existence of an underclass which causes society problems is not a new idea but rather persists over time:

In 1844, Friedrich Engels (1820–95), a German philosopher, stated:

> If the demoralisation of the worker passes beyond a certain point, then it is just as natural that he will turn into a criminal—as inevitably as water turns into steam at boiling point.
>
> Engels 1844, from 1971 translation: 145

In 1850, Henry Mayhew (1812–87), an English social researcher, stated that the dishonest poor man was:

> distinguished from the civilised man by his repugnance to regular and continuous labour – by his want of providence in laying up a store for the future – by his inability to perceive consequences ever so slightly removed from immediate apprehensions – by his passion for stupefying herbs and roots and, when possible, for intoxicating fermenting liquors
>
> Henry Mayhew, *Morning Chronicle* in 1850

In 1982, Ken Auletta (1942–), American writer and media critic, stated:

> among students of poverty there is little disagreement that a fairly distinct black and white underclass does exist; that this underclass generally feels excluded from society, rejects commonly accepted values, suffers from *behavioural*, as well as *income* deficiencies. They don't just tend to be poor; to most Americans their behaviour seems aberrant.
>
> Auletta 1982: xiii

In 1990, Charles Murray (1943–), an American political scientist, said this of the 'underclass':

> They were defined by their behaviour. Their homes were littered and unkempt. The men in the family were unable to hold a job for more than a few weeks at a time. Drunkenness was common. The children grew up ill-schooled and ill-behaved and contributed a disproportionate share of the local juvenile delinquents.
>
> Murray 1990: 1

In 1990, Runciman (1934–), a British historical sociologist, stated that the term underclass:

> stand[s] not for a group or category of workers systematically disadvantaged within the labour market but for those members of British society whose roles place them more or less permanently at the economic level where benefits are paid by the state to those unable to participate in the labour market at all … They are typically the long-term unemployed.
>
> Runciman 1990: 388

In 2002, Jock Young (1942–2013), a British sociologist and criminologist, set out what the way in which others had described the underclass as:

> an underclass left stranded by the needs of capital on housing estates … those who because of illegitimacy, family pathology, or general disorganization were excluded from citizenship, whose spatial vistas were those of constant disorder and threat, and who were the recipients of stigma from the wider world of respectable citizens. The welfare 'scroungers', the immigrants, the junkies and crack heads: the demons of modern society. … an underclass of despair.
>
> Young 2002: 465

In 2011, Kenneth Clarke (1940–), a British conservative politician and the then Justice Secretary, following the riots (see **Figure 14.10**) of that year stated:

> I've dealt with plenty of civil disobedience in my time, but the riots in August shocked me to the core. What I found most disturbing was the sense that the hardcore of rioters came from a *feral underclass* cut off from the mainstream in everything but its materialism.
>
> Kenneth Clarke, *Guardian*, 5 September 2011

Figure 14.10 Hackney, London, during riots in August 2011
Source: Henry Langston

Looking briefly at the 19th century writers (Engels and Mayhew) we have just considered, two very different narratives emerge. Engels (1844) wrote about the iniquities of the unfair social system and saw crime as the start of a rising up against that system. This is a conflict concept of crime and social systems. Mayhew (1861–62), on the other hand, whilst recognising that many people were being driven into poverty and thence to crime, recognising crime as caused by social factors, did not argue for dramatic social change or revolution. Overall and generally he did not blame individuals though he recognised certain lifestyles as dangerous to the fabric of the rest of society—these lifestyles formed an underclass. This concept of an underclass, separate from the 'honest' poor still exists today. It can be seen in the writings of Murray (1990) and Young (2002) and of some politicians (Clarke 2011).

As with the writers of the 19th century Murray and Young take very different views of the underclass. Murray views the underclass as a danger, something which needs to be dealt with by removing welfare support and applying strong punishments and controls (for a fuller discussion see the consideration of right realism in **Chapter 17**). Young, on the other hand, studies it in order to discover how best to move to a more inclusive and just social order.

Charles Murray (1943–) is an American political scientist who stigmatises various aspects of modern society as the 'new underclass' (see Murray 1984, 1990, and 2001). As was the case for many 19th century authors he considers welfare dependency as the seat of this 'evil'. Welfare used to support people for a brief period while they get themselves back on their feet is, to Murray, acceptable as supporting the deserving poor. However, he is less tolerant of what he sees as the underclass or the undeserving poor. He argues that welfare supports some people's lives outside the legitimate job market for far too long so that they become dependent and stop taking responsibility for themselves. He even accuses young women of becoming pregnant in order to claim benefits and housing. In parts of society where this happens he argues that children are not being properly socialised and lack pro-social role models, so leaving them to expect to be kept and not need to provide for themselves. He argues that they learn to depend on the state and become unwilling to work, preferring state support supplemented by the proceeds of crime. These are the undeserving poor and—according to him—they are a danger to society and a danger to their communities; as these problems proliferate he argues that crime begins to take over and through the victimisation of some, by others in the neighbourhood, these communities tend to fragment and are destroyed or altered. The

victimisation and offending build up and as more people participate in crime so the norms of that community alter, leading them to tolerate more crime (the nature of the divide alters and the community is permanently altered).

Murray draws together a number of the common 'demons' within criminology such as dysfunctional families (particularly single mothers), welfare dependency, inconsistent discipline, and the negative effects of gangs and peer groups and ties them to a *moral* deficiency. For Murray crime and other social ills are not the result of poverty, rather they arise out of the moral depravity of some people. The morally deprived are, for him, those undeserving in society who take advantage of others and who need to be properly controlled and appropriately punished. Murray therefore sees the 'underclass' as the problem; the people and the choices they make cause the difficulties. Murray states that it is not a structural problem caused by the economic choices of the society, it is not lack of work or low pay which is the problem but rather that it is the people who are the problem, the immoral choices they make; the lack of a willingness to work is the problem. He considers societal structure to be a side issue except that welfare may help to sustain rather than control this group.

Jock Young (1942–2013) was a British sociologist and criminologist who approached discussions of an 'underclass' from a very different perspective. He would see the actions of the group that Murray defines as the 'underclass' as an understandable reaction to the appalling inequalities some face in our society. In particular, Young (1999, 2002, and 2007) and others like him such as Taylor (1999) see massive structural unemployment (especially that which is long term) and inequalities which some face due to our social structures as destroying the lives of some in society who are made poor, homeless, and desperate. Here the 'underclass' are not criminal but people who lack hope and choices, and in this situation they may fall back on criminality (Young 1999 and Taylor 1999). These commentators see lack of work, not lack of a willingness to work as the issue. Here the problem is structural not individual.

The problems faced by some in society were recognised by 'New Labour' when they came to power in 1997 and set up the Social Exclusion Unit to work towards reintegrating socially deprived individuals and communities and to deal with the issues of long-term unemployment, welfare dependent single mums, truanting young people, and unpleasant housing estates. The idea was to set out policies to counter the problems faced by those whom society had failed: one of its most important strategies was entitled *A New Commitment to Neighbourhood Renewal: National Strategy Action*

Society at large	The underclass
The unproblematic	The problem
Community	Disorganisation
Employment	The workless
Independence	Welfare dependency
Stable family	Single mothers
The natives	The immigrants
Drug free	Illicit drug use
Victims	Criminals

Table 14.6 Young's binaries of social exclusion

Source: Young, J. (2002) 'Crime and Social Exclusion' in Maguire, M., Morgan, R., and Reiner, R. (eds) The Oxford Handbook of Criminology (3rd edn). Oxford: Oxford University Press

Plan 2001. The action plan aimed to increase employment in areas hit by unemployment, increase work-based skill levels, reduce burglary in the areas most blighted by that problem, reduce health inequalities, and raise the standard of housing in deprived neighbourhoods. The idea of the action plan was to tackle some of the structural problems in society that led to the social exclusion of some groups. However, alongside this, 'New Labour' asserted that there was also a section of the socially excluded who breached the norms of the wider society. These they viewed as individual and moral breaches and so they set policies to deal with what they saw as unacceptable choices made by these people and groups—they brought in controls to deal with problems such as antisocial behaviour (Crime and Disorder Act 1998, Anti-social Behaviour Act 2003 and Part 4 of the Policing and Crime Act 2009 (as amended by the Crime and Security Act 2010)). These individual controls were used most commonly for the working/lower classes and particularly the young and the underclass (Squires and Stephen 2005). Young (2002) viewed this solution as setting up the illusion of a binary problem and of actually exacerbating the issue, as demonstrated in **Table 14.6**.

> The underclass, although in reality a group heterogeneous in composition and ill-defined in their nature, is a ready target for resentment. ... Re-constituted, rendered clear cut and homogenous by the mass media, they became a prime focus of public attention in the sense of stereotypes: 'the undeserving poor', 'the single mother', 'the welfare scrounger' etc., and an easy focus of hostility. ... the very opposite of the 'virtues' of the included, thus casting the social world into the binary mould.
>
> Young 2007: 36–37

He argues that seeing the problem as two separate groups, one conforming and the other delinquent is too simplistic. Whilst recognising that some areas and some people belong more to one group than another, there is a lot more intermingling of problems than often acknowledged and 'society at large' has its share of issues generally associated with the underclass and *vice versa*. His point is that the borders of behaviour are permeable so that people in the wider society participate in negative and damaging behaviours. Furthermore, the physical borders are also permeable, people move across them and there are no clear and 'real' splits in the population. Moreover, he suggests that by asserting that there are differences and trying to target the problems a clear differentiation is created where there may never have been one, or at least not one that was so clearly defined. Therefore the provision of social exclusion units placed some inside the wider 'good' society and others outside. Naming or labelling (see **Chapter 15**) that divide made it more real and actually caused greater exclusion, increasing the problems rather than dealing with them. He also talks of a 'bulimic' society; one in which inclusion and exclusion occur at the same time and alongside each other. He argues that cultural inclusion sits beside systematic and structural exclusion. In this situation society and those living in it are constantly unclear about what is happening and there can be claims that inclusion is working when in fact people are still experiencing clear social exclusion.

Bearing in mind what you have just read you may like to look at **What do you think? 14.4** and consider the questions raised.

Subcultural theories focus on the effect of groups on individuals; these are groupings chosen by the individual. Their choices of subculture may be constrained by those available in their neighbourhood but there is a choice. Consideration of social exclusion and the underclass concerns groups into which people are fitted rather than those into which they choose. Although Murray suggests some fault on their part (they might have moved into the honest poor rather than the underclass) these are still groupings that the individual might not even recognise let alone choose to inhabit. For Young the underclass is a structural creation of the powerful, for critical criminologists this group is important to society as it is a grouping into which others in society do not want to sink so it helps to control the honest poor. What they share in common is that both the underclass and subcultural criminology largely apply to the lower classes. In the case of much subcultural theory and of Murray's underclass they seek to explain criminal statistics which are seriously flawed and may explain more about the agencies of control than about those who offend.

WHAT DO YOU THINK? 14.4

This is a real letter sent to certain people last year. Previously you were asked how you would feel about receiving a letter like this and what it told you about the way the police were operating. Now you need to consider whether the letter should be seen as a positive move by the police. Different people in society might view it very differently. Here you also need to think about whether it is singling certain people out for different treatment and, if so, whether you think it is likely to cause greater problems as Young claimed would be the case with the social exclusion units?

METROPOLITAN **POLICE**   Working together for a safer London

TERRITORIAL POLICING

Brent Borough
603 Harrow Road
Wembley
Middlesex
HA0 2HH

19th August 2015

Dear

You may be aware of an incident on the Kilburn High Road on Sunday 16th August during which a 24 year old man received serious stab injuries. This is being treated as an attempted murder.

Our intelligence suggests you are linked to gang related criminal activity in the South Kilburn area. We are determined to bring the cycle of violence affecting this area to an end. We are not suggesting you were directly involved in the latest incident but we believe that you are involved in criminal behaviour that puts you at greater risk of becoming a victim or a perpetrator of violent crime yourself.

We would like to invite you to take the opportunity to meet with Brent Police, Brent Council and other agencies to discuss the events of 16th August, possible risks to yourself, and ways we can help you move away from criminal behaviour.

This meeting will take place on **Thursday 27th August at 3pm at the Marian Centre 1 Stafford Road NW6 5RS.**

If you choose not to attend we will see this as a clear message that you intend to continue with a criminal lifestyle. As such, we will work hard to disrupt your activities utilising every legitimate means available to us.

Yours Sincerely

Borough Commander

SUMMARY

- Recognise the contribution of sociology to the making of criminology as a subject in its own right

Sociologists suggest that individual behaviour is affected by broader social, structural, or cultural conditions. Many sociological theories are positivist in that they suggest that behaviour is, to an extent, predetermined. Criminal behaviour is therefore at least partially attributed to forces outside the control of the individual. For example, an individual may be born into a poor community where many people offend and through a peer group, or learning from others, or merely to survive and acquire money or food something (or a combination of things) may propel them towards criminality. Sociologists do not claim that these external factors absolutely cause crime but rather that they are an environment in which that behaviour becomes more likely, they *influence* some people to offend.

Sociologists measure aspects of society, collect and record large amounts of data and use that information to ascertain the environments which are most likely to encourage or support criminality. Their contribution is therefore to guide policy makers towards aspects of our social environment which, if altered, may reduce the likelihood of offending.

- Identify the main strands of sociological thinking and distinguish their differing contributions to the subject

In criminology there are three main strands of sociological thought: social intervention or social process theories (micro-sociological theories); social structural theories or structuralism (macro-sociological theories); and social conflict theories (generally macro-sociological theories).

Social interaction or social process theories search for explanations of criminality in an individual's close social situation or environment. They consider how and to what extent the groups and individuals with whom they socialise (their immediate social situation) impacts on their behaviour and the choices they make—hence interaction theories. Clearly the effect is reciprocal as the choices made by one person or group will rebound on others with whom they socialise. Social interaction theories include: differential association theories; social control theories; and labelling perspectives.

Structuralism considers the way in which broad social conditions such as poverty impact on the way in which people behave. Their argument is that the way in which a society chooses to structure itself opens up or closes down the choices people enjoy. Social structure and culture influence our lives in many, often unexpected, ways. The argument made by social structural theorists is that these broad building blocks of society and the large policy decisions made for us on the part of politicians have a powerful effect on an individual's social situation. For example, policy may shape what sort of home an individual lives in, the type of school they attend and the types of work available to them. Each of these will open up or close down various opportunities and therefore influence the direction of a person's life. Structuralism sees the policy building blocks of society as shaping people's choices and the types of interactions that will be open to them and thereby shaping their likelihood of participating in criminal behaviour. Social structural theories include: social strain theories; social disorganisation theories; and subcultural theories.

Conflict theorists consider that society is weighted in favour of certain groups of people—the powerful, those who pass laws. The core of their argument is that societies revolve around relationships of conflict and domination where those in power use their authority to ensure that they retain control and that others, the powerless subjects, are carefully controlled. Their power may arise due to their class, gender, ethnicity, etc. or because they have money or knowledge but they use that power to shape society and control others in ways which are beneficial to them. These theorists therefore study the distribution of power and of other goods in society and see these factors as associated with what behaviours we choose to control (and how we control them), and with why some people choose to transgress.

- Appreciate the contribution of the Chicago school to the study of criminology

The Chicago School is about social disorganisation and is significant for criminologists because it places the cause of offending squarely within the ecology surrounding the offender. For Shaw and McKay social context, linked in to broader structural factors such as transient populations, recession, poverty, unemployment, was of central importance. However, the most crucial factor was the social disorganisation within a community or neighbourhood, leading to weakened informal social controls leaving young people free to offend and be antisocial. Whilst the theory is attractive, as with the earlier theories in this chapter the theorists relied heavily on official statistics and their theory is weakened if these are not reliable (because they reflect policing rather than offending). Furthermore, the theory predicts too much delinquency in areas with high disorganisation and one would then need to explain why many people, often most people, in those areas remain law abiding. In spite of differing opinion, however, no one can deny its influence has been and remains strong as a factor to explain juvenile crime and was heavily drawn on in some of the subcultural theories. Furthermore, the Chicago project which added stability to neighbourhoods did have some success in reducing offending and improving other social indicators (such as improved health) in the areas in which it operated.

- Understand the basic concepts of anomie, strain, social learning, subculture, and social exclusion and relate each of these concepts to the criminologists who are most often connected with them

Durkheim and functionalism

Durkheim argues that far from being a negative occurrence crime is actually necessary for a healthy society; a certain level of crime is functional and helps to make law abiding citizens feel more connected. However, he views high levels of crime as dysfunctional, as an indication of a society in which the rules have broken down; an anomic society. Durkheim does not indicate how much crime is healthy and exactly how we know when a society is anomic.

Merton and strain

Merton uses the concept of anomie but alters it to take account of social structural problems. Merton sees no problem with a society that does not have limits on what people should expect as long as they only use legitimate means of achieving those goals. For Merton a society becomes anomic when people are willing to use illegitimate means to achieve what they desire. Here anomie arises when people's desires cannot be met through legitimate means. For Merton anomie is about means and ends. In an anomic society many people will continue to conform but some will choose one of the other ways of coping: innovation; ritualism; retreatism; and rebellion. His ideas are most useful in explaining lower-class crime where the desires may not be met through legitimate means and they may therefore be more likely to turn to crime. Merton does not really explain what causes the strain nor why it leads to a particular type of response.

Differential association (social learning)

This theory is strongly associated with Sutherland (1939a, 1939b, and 1949). He argued that, as with almost all other human activities, crime is a learnt behaviour. He argued that crime is learnt in a similar way to other activities. If crime occurred in the environment in which someone lived or worked then Sutherland considered that they would learn that behaviour along with other behaviours which occur in that environment, in that way he saw crime as normal behaviour. If at work criminal activity is normal it will be learnt but may not be transferred into other social environments. For Sutherland people learn both how to offend (the activities necessary for a particular type of crime) and the motives and values that release them to offend. Many also learn how to rationalise their behaviour as being acceptable. He argues that the learning happens in the social environment a person finds him-/herself in. However, his theory says little about how or why one a person learns criminal behaviour when someone else in the same environment does not. His theory cannot explain all crime and is of little use in explaining why some people are open to crime and others are not but may be useful to explain why certain offences are committed (a person commits offences for which they have the requisite skills). Because the learning involves both the values (values loose enough to permit, or even expect criminality) and the skills (the abilities necessary to commit a particular crime) the theory suggests that by undermining the values or teaching an individual why the activity is wrong one might be able to persuade them not to reoffend; this idea forms the basis of some resolutions to offending such as mentoring and reintegrative shaming.

Culture and subculture

Each of the theories above suggests that delinquency and crime might be rational solutions to problems in a society (strain, disorganisation, etc.). However, each of these suggests too much crime. Subcultural theories offer some solutions to this problem. Theorists such as Cohen; Cloward and Ohlin; Matza and Sykes; and Matza offered various answers based on subcultures within society. Cohen suggested that young people adopted the looser values adopted by their peer groups and therefore felt free to offend, these looser values allowed them to deal with the problems they faced in their societies and communities. For Cloward and Ohlin the young people were again under strain and offending was one coping strategy where legitimate opportunities were blocked. Matza and Sykes add the idea of neutralisation and Matza adds drift. Matza argued that other subcultural theories suggested too much offending and began with the idea that most people, even those who offend are generally mostly law abiding, the criminality does not define them. He argued that all people drift between being law abiding and offending, that most people most of the time choose to conform but in certain situations, especially when there is a supportive subculture they may offend. He argues that many feel free to offend in particular situations because they feel that offending is the only real solution at the time, the offending is therefore 'not their fault'. It is unclear whether this explanation of it being 'not their fault', arises before the offending and explains why they feel free to offend or is merely a mechanism used to assuage any feelings of guilt.

In all subcultural theories the explanations, to a greater or lesser extent, free the offenders from guilt, their criminal activity was explained by something outside their control. These theories have been very useful in showing some ways in which it is sensible to intervene with young people, helping them to build more law abiding lives. They have also been important in the emergence of cultural criminology which offers very different explanations for offending, ones often based on subcultures but not seeing the subculture juxtaposed to the wider culture but rather as a distinct entity with few points of reference back to mainstream culture.

Social exclusion

Finally, in this section the concept of social exclusion and its effect on offending behaviour was studied. There are a number of sides to this. Some, such as Murray, who see the 'underclass' or those who are socially excluded as being the problem, as dangerous, people everyone else needs to be protected from. Others see this group as suffering the problems of poverty and unemployment and who wish to help them (New Labour's social exclusion units). A third group, including Young, consider that while one might intervene to relieve problems for an individual or a family any blanket official differentiation will exacerbate the divide and thus cause more problems, more exclusion.

These subcultural or group theories are very varied. While most may be of some use in furthering our understanding of society and what affects levels of criminality in it each is too blunt a tool to be of wide use in this area. They may help in the design of group interventions such as the Chicago project or individual interventions but do not necessarily offer any broader understanding of offending in general.

- Analyse and critically assess the ideas discussed and the contribution they make to our understanding of crime and criminal behaviour

Each of the theories studied in this chapter has aspects which are useful to understanding crime but they are each also seriously flawed. Collectively their most important strength is that they draw our attention to the fact that the individual is not a totally separate actor making decisions without any input from others. They clearly illustrate that social, environmental, economic, and cultural aspects impact on each and every one of us and help to shape who we are, how we think and therefore play a part in whether we are likely to participate in criminal activities. They draw attention to particular aspects of our social architecture (physical, structural, cultural, human) which make it more or less likely that we will offend. Each theory draws attention to a different aspect of society as being important. In doing this they draw attention away from both our ability to fully blame an individual for the choices they make and our blaming behaviour on flawed individuals (individual physical or psychological flaws which may be associated with criminality). They awaken a realisation that the society which complains of the crime may be part of the problem, may be partially complicit or flawed such that crime is more likely.

Collectively they also have problems. Many of these theories rely too heavily on official statistics as a true indicator of who offends, where they live, and what types of laws are being breached. Many of these theories conveniently forget that many offences are committed by others (the wealthy and powerful or the middle classes) but that they are not caught or prosecuted. Anomie, strain, subcultural, and social exclusion theories all have this flaw. Some of these theories are accused of being atheoretical—too descriptive and not based in real theory. So, for example, social disorganisation is not a real theory, it is more a description of the problem. Most theories in this chapter also focus on men, they fail to really consider how these same social and structural issues impact on women and why there is such a large difference in the rate at which women resort to crime compared to men when they live in the same circumstances. Of course, maybe male and female criminality is, in fact, a lot more similar than suggested by the official statistics but if that is true then the statistics are problematic and, again, many of these theories lose much of their credibility. Many of these theories also use simplified ideas of e.g. culture or subculture, they do not always fully engage with the deeper sociological literature and they select the aspects of society, culture, structure they wish to highlight and collect data which will or might appear to throw light on its effects.

Overall, these theories are important to our wider understanding of the causes and effects of crime, they certainly ensure that we take account of social as well as individual facts. None of these theories alone, explain criminality generally nor in any individual case, neither do they together offer a full explanation of criminal behaviour. However, each throws light on certain aspects of criminality and therefore may offer a way of countering criminal activity.

Therefore, you need to read all of these theories with care and with a critical eye, looking for both strengths and weaknesses. You need to consider exactly how far it is sensible to use any one theory to explain criminality and to prevent offending or deal with those who transgress.

REVIEW QUESTIONS

1. Name and discuss three key concepts in the sociology of crime.

2. Explain the extent to which the following offences/acts of deviance might be explained by differential association and consider the limitations of that explanation:

   - Stealing the secrets of a rival company for use by your company

   - Burglary

3. How does Durkheim suggest that crime is functional for a society?

4. Explain the differences between Durkheim's and Merton's concepts of anomie.

5. How useful are the subcultural theories to explaining youth offending in the UK?

6. What are the main differences between Cohen's subcultural theory and that of Matza?

7. What is meant by the term 'underclass' and why does Young see it as divisive to deal with the issue through social exclusion?

FURTHER READING

Downes, D., Rock, P., and McLaughlin, E. (2016) *Understanding Deviance* (7th edn). Oxford. Oxford University Press.

This book has excellent chapters on each aspect of this sociological positivism (Chapters 3, 4, 6, and parts of 9). These chapters provide challenging and often radical consideration of the classical texts. The section about 'Culture and Subculture' (Chapter 6) is particularly useful.

Rock, P. (2012) 'The Sociology of Crime' in Maguire, M., Morgan, R., and Reiner, R. (eds) *The Oxford Handbook of Criminology* (5th edn). Oxford: Oxford University Press.

Williams, K. S. (2012) *Textbook on Criminology* (8th edn). Oxford: Oxford University Press. Chapters 11 and 12.

These discuss the issues in detail and provide more examples and references.

Lilly, J. R., Cullen, F. T., and Ball, R. A. (2011) *Criminological Theory: Context and Consequences*. Thousand Oaks, CA.: Sage Publications. Especially Chapters 3 and 4.

Provides clear analysis of the classical texts, though it is written from an American perspective.

Bernard, T. J., Snipes, J. B., and Gerould, A. L. (2015) *Vold's Theoretical Criminology* (7th edn). Oxford: Oxford University Press.

Chapter 6—Durkheim and anomie, Chapter 7—Chicago school, Chapter 8—Strain theories including Merton and parts of Chapter 9—Social learning.

McLaughlin, E. and Muncie, J. (2013) *Criminological Perspectives: Essential Readings* (3rd edn). Especially readings 6, 9, 10, 14, 15, 16, 21, 23, 24.

Newburn, T. (2009) *Key Readings in Criminology* (2nd edn). Cullompton: Willan Press. Especially sections 8 and 9.

It is very important to read the original texts written by these theorists. Whilst you may not be able to read their whole texts it is essential to read the essential or key extracts.

 Access the **online resources** to view selected further reading and web links relevant to the material covered in this chapter.
www.oup.com/uk/case/

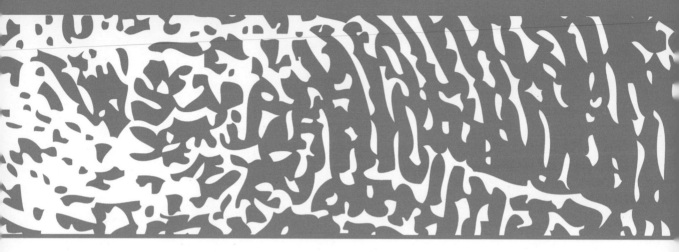

CHAPTER OUTLINE

Introduction: What do you see?   418

Social construction and power   421

Labelling perspectives: 1960s radicalism and
humanising the deviant   422

The development of critical criminology in Britain   428

Conclusion   441

Critical criminology—part 1

Challenging the 'usual suspects'

KEY ISSUES

After studying this chapter, you should be able to:

- appreciate the philosophical and political arguments that underpin critical criminologies;

- understand the different foundational strands within critical criminology, and their development within a cultural and historical context;

- relate theoretical ideas to the real world, and appreciate the flaws and strengths within the various approaches we shall cover;

- develop an awareness of how important the ideas of power and power relations are to critical criminology;

- discuss the problems of 'deviance' and its interpretation and control.

Introduction: What do you see?

In this and **Chapter 16** we will be looking at a range of criminological perspectives which are collectively known as critical criminology. There are many such related and diverse theories which criminologists draw on in their work, and here we shall consider what are regarded as historically being the three most important strands in the development of critical criminology, all of which arose in the 1960s and 1970s. These are: labelling perspectives, **Marxist inspired critical theories**, and **feminist perspectives**. As we shall see, the ideas and insights contained within these theories inspired and prepared the ground for more recent developments in the field; or in other words, variations on critical themes. These variations are the 'new horizons' of zemiology (the study of social harm), green criminology, cultural criminology, and an emerging convict criminology, and we will move on to consider these further in **Chapter 16**.

But first go and look at yourself in a mirror. Ask yourself these questions and think about the answers:

- Where did you get your clothes and why did you choose them?

- What sort of jewellery and make-up are you wearing?

- How many different toiletries have you used today?

- Were you so taken by your appearance that you took a selfie on your mobile phone?

All of this is, no doubt, a very welcome excuse to avoid reading a chapter on criminological theory, but there is a serious point to be made. Theory underpins all aspects of the study of crime and its control, and in this chapter we will be thinking about the ideas and the concepts which make up 'critical' theories themselves, as well as relating them to real life; because, of course, people and their behaviour are at the root of all humanities and social sciences. Theory may at first seem a bit dry and dull, but as we shall see, it is something we can think about in, and apply to, all aspects of our daily lives.

Theory for its own sake can also be academically challenging but as Kurt Lewin, the American psychologist once wrote, there is 'nothing so practical as a good theory' (1952). Although all of this can seem daunting, once you begin to understand it, you will be able to see how it works 'in real life' and it will all make sense. The whole point of this book is to make complex ideas accessible and understandable and to help you to see the relevance and practical uses of theory with regard to current political and social concerns. To prove this, let's go back to the questions posed above and examine your thoughts on these in a bit more detail.

First of all, did you think about your clothes? Do you know where they were made and under what conditions? Was your jacket a genuine bargain, or was it cheap because it was made by an exploited worker in an unsafe factory or sweatshop? If you are thinking smugly that your trousers came from a charity shop, have you ever questioned why, in the 21st century developed world, people with illnesses and disabilities still have to rely on charity for help and medical research, or why there are still starving populations?

We choose our clothes for many reasons—sometimes cultural or spiritual, but sometimes to make a point or to identify ourselves as belonging to a particular group. These choices tell other people something about us—for example, a yarmulke (or kippah, see **Figure 15.1**) tells us that the man next to us on the bus is Jewish—but these signifiers can also allow prejudice and disapproval. We are constantly exposed to the opinions of others about how we should and should not look; a skirt is too short, a hoodie hides a face, and we are judged accordingly. Muslim women are pressured to take off their scarves and veils (**Figure 15.2**), little girls complain to shoe shops because they want dinosaurs and not fairies on their new trainers, we have to be beach-body ready for the summer months ... but why does all of this matter when the disabled are often unable to use public buildings, are less likely to be able to find employment, and are more likely to be victims of abuse (see **Chapter 8**)?

Likewise with our jewellery. Are you lucky enough to be wearing any gold or diamonds? How were they mined? You may notice now that some high street jewellers offer 'ethical gems'—does the average shopper know what makes an 'unethical' one? Do you know if the make-up, hair products, or other toiletries you have used were tested on animals?

Figure 15.1 Boys wearing yarmulkes
Source: Gimas/Shutterstock.com

Figure 15.2 Young women wearing headscarves

Source: Amir Ridhwan/Shutterstock.com

As we saw in **Chapters 13** and **14**, the mainstream, traditional, and conventional criminological perspectives of classicism and positivism have over the years been subject to trenchant criticism. This is the first common theme—and indeed the starting point—of critical criminologies; that they were developed, in part, from a thorough, critical review of both classicism and positivism. We will set our sights on positivism here if only because it was, in many ways, the dominant and mainstream paradigm of viewing crime in the 20th century. Many would argue that perhaps it still is today. Indeed, as one of the foremost critical criminologists (Jock Young) has argued, the hubris of positivism, with its increasing use of sophisticated mathematical formulae which attempt to accurately measure our subject matter, has almost effectively 'closed down' the criminological imagination (Young 2011: 10–21).

Challenging positivist orthodoxy

As you will remember from **Chapters 13** and **14**, the perspective of positivism (in either its biological, psychological, or sociological forms) can be reduced down to four main ideas. These are:

- determinism;
- scientism;
- consensus;
- treatment/rehabilitation.

Before we see how critical theorists challenged these ideas, let's briefly re-cap what they mean.

In general, positivist theories argue that our behaviour is *determined* (or driven) through forces which are, to a great extent, beyond our control. These forces may be biological or psychological, such as through having a specific genetic predisposition (as in the individual variant of positivism) or social, such as where we live or who we associate with (as in the sociological variant). By speaking the powerful language of numbers and statistics, the 'holy grail' of much early criminological research was to *scientifically* find out the causes of crime (or aetiology). There is a logic to all this: if you can scientifically, in an *objective, neutral* and *value-free* way (see **Chapters 5** and **13** for a further discussion of these ideas) prove that A causes B, then it follows that you will be able to prevent B if you do something about A (for instance, treat or improve it). We can still see the logic of such arguments today. For instance, it has been argued that antisocial behaviour in young people (ASB) is a 'syndrome' (note the use of a medical language here) which can be 'treated' pharmacologically—that is, through the use of prescription drugs (see Viding et al. 2005). Similarly, if it is thought that crime is caused by poor living environments, then

And if you did snap a selfie, how much do you know about the precious and toxic metals that are used to make your handset? Where did they come from, who mined them, what happens to the old phone when you upgrade?

Countries which allow the exploitation of workers, which do not enforce equality, which breach human rights or international treaties, are examined through the lens of state crime, an example of crimes of the powerful (which some critical criminologists are very interested in studying).

The thoughts and opinions of others, and the effect that these may have on how we see ourselves and may behave, form the basis of labelling perspectives. Race and gender are important strands of criminological study (and are discussed further in **Chapters 10** and **11**), as is green criminology which considers the impact of human activity on the environment. That one short look in the mirror raised all these questions (and probably more) and so we shall look at the some of the theoretical approaches which are generally regarded as being 'critical' in more detail throughout this chapter. But first we need to analyse what it actually means to be critical.

What is critical about critical criminology?

What is actually *critical* about critical criminology? Perhaps the best way to answer this is to explain what critical criminology is not, as there is no standard or agreed definition of what it actually is. Nor is there one critical criminology. Instead there is a range of diverse perspectives, all of which have some features and themes in common (so it is probably more accurate to talk about critical criminologies, plural) and we shall be exploring some of these further in this and the next chapter.

these can be addressed through a range of social policies which focus on environmental design, such as improving housing standards and the areas in which people live. The last and most important foundational idea of positivism is that there is a general agreement (a *consensus*) not only on what 'crime' is, but also on who the 'criminals' and our 'public enemies' are. So what, according to critical criminologists, are the main problems with all of this?

Firstly, for the critical criminologist, it makes little sense to argue that our behaviour is totally determined through forces over which we have no control. To be sure, our behaviour may, in part, be driven or influenced by internal and external influences and social structures. For instance, the world and lived realities of an 18 year-old, single parent, black woman living in poverty are very different to those of a wealthy, white, middle-class male of the same age—race, class, and gender are, as we shall see later in the chapter, very important. But we all have degrees of choice. Indeed, it could be said that some forms of 'criminal' behaviour can be logical and very meaningful and cannot simply be the result of faulty reasoning or defective genes or where we grow up. However, the idea that we can 'scientifically' study all of this so that the 'criminal' can be treated in some way can also be questioned. As we saw in **Chapter 6** when we considered self-report studies, most of us, at some point in our lives, will have done something which has transgressed the criminal law and which have could have warranted a criminal sanction. In other words, to quote the late Sir Terry Pratchett (a novelist), 'everyone's guilty of something'. But even if we do think about ourselves with this much honesty, do we really see ourselves as 'criminals' who need to be 'treated' or do we see ourselves as somehow different, whose actions don't count as being *deviant* (something which is not the norm)? How do we and society draw these boundaries?

As well as helping and curing, we need to remember that treatment in its various guises can also be used as a form of control. Imagine, for a minute, the possibility that scientists discovered *the* criminal gene or that neuroscientists, through sophisticated brain imaging techniques, could clearly show us a 'criminal mind'. What do you think the logical conclusions and 'treatments' could be? Whilst advances in medical science have been incredible over the last 60 years (since the discovery of penicillin to treat disease) and have the potential for doing good in terms of the identification and treatment, prevention and management of various diseases, we should not forget that there is also a potential dark side to all of this. For instance, if a 'criminal gene' could be 'discovered' then the logic, when pushed to extremes, could result in the compulsory sterilisation of those carrying the gene or even worse—their complete eradication. This all may seem a little over the top, but history tells us otherwise; there are many historical examples of states implementing policies of eugenics and pseudoscientific forms of racism, with Nazi Germany being the obvious one. More recently, in 2012 a UKIP council candidate's personal manifesto proposed that any foetus with a disability be aborted, in order to prevent it being a 'burden' on the state (*Independent*, 2012).

All of these questions are raised by the critical criminologist. For this branch of criminological theory, the very idea that there could be a consensus on what is crime, and what causes it, is something that is in itself open to debate (see **What do you think? 15.1**). We often hear the word *law* coupled with the word *order* as if 'law and order' were one and the same thing. But, if you think about it, we can only really have a conception of 'order' if we have a clear picture of what 'disorder' might look like, and such things are rarely as clear-cut as they may, at first, seem.

WHAT DO YOU THINK? 15.1

What is antisocial about antisocial behaviour?

- We often read in the press about the idea of antisocial behaviour (ASB) but what does it actually mean?

- Try to jot down a precise definition of it and list forms of behaviour which you regard as being antisocial.

- What images come in to your head as you do so?

- Did you find this an easy thing to do or was it trickier than you initially thought?

- Why might this be the case?

- Do you think if you were to do this as a seminar exercise that you would find a general agreement (a consensus) across your class?

ASB hit the headlines in the late 1990s. It remains a cause for concern, to the extent that most local authorities now have multi-agency partnerships which work with the police and other agencies to try to deal with it. The Crime and Disorder Act 1998 defines ASB as:

> Acting in a manner that caused or was likely to cause harassment, alarm or distress to one or more persons not of the same household as (the defendant).

As you can see, this is a rather broad and even vague definition. What is antisocial to one person may well be acceptable to another. The main point of all of this is that terms such as ASB (and even the very concept of crime) are *socially constructed*; that is, they are constructed through a series of social processes and are essentially contested concepts about the ways through which human beings arrive at a shared belief or understanding of something. According to the critical criminologist, the same can be said of the concept of crime. This is seen through the fact that what counts as a crime is constantly changing: it is a dynamic concept (see **Chapter 3** for a more developed discussion and analysis of this crucial point). As we shall see in this chapter, laws do indeed change and they are far from being carved in tablets of stone. One of the reasons for this is to do with the final and perhaps most important and central concepts which inform critical criminology; that of *power*.

Social construction and power

The concept of power is crucial to critical criminologists, who argue that rather than being based on an agreed consensus, society (and the social order) is perhaps best viewed as being made of a variety of groups who do not always agree with each other and have different values; this is usually called *pluralism*, although you may wish to think of it in terms of diversity. After all, we live in diverse societies which have diverse norms and values. Can we really speak in terms of there being 'moral absolutes' today? In a stronger form, it could be argued that people rarely agree and are in constant *conflict* with each other. This is where the concept of power comes in. Here it is argued that the important thing for us to study is how particular versions of social reality are constructed in the first place; particularly the questions of who has the power to help define what is actually crime, and to declare what the crime problem is. In short, critical criminologists argue that power is distributed unequally in societies and that inequality in terms of social class, as well as race and gender, can lead to 'crime problems' and to distinct and often harsh penal policies in terms of policing and sentencing. Critical criminology can therefore be said to be a 'political project', as one of its key aims is to demystify how 'crime' itself is defined and to question the very nature of *justice*. In doing so it aims to somehow change society at a structural (social and cultural) level to bring about a more socially just society (see the discussion of the concept of justice in **Chapter 4**).

It could therefore be argued that the most important criticisms in terms of this particular chapter are that the orthodox and mainstream criminologies (such as positivism) didn't pay nearly enough attention to the crucial concept of *power* and the resulting *power relations* which characterise society. The very idea of power is a central one to all social sciences and is vital to critical criminological perspectives. In general, critical criminologists draw on this concept of power and foreground it in two particular ways:

1. **The power of some groups to criminalise (and decriminalise) forms of behaviour** Here it is argued that certain people in society (the powerful) have the authority to at least partially define what counts as 'crime' and what makes up the 'crime problem'. It follows that there are thus certain groups (the powerless) whose behaviour is sometimes defined as crime. A good way to think about this is to look back through history. You will see how things we now consider to be perfectly okay were once illegal—homosexuality, for instance. To be gay was against the law in the UK until 1967 and it was not until 1982 that it became legal in Northern Ireland. Homeless and starving children in the 18th century could be hanged for stealing food, whereas today we would be prosecuting the family that had neglected to feed and house them. The idea of who decides who and what are acceptable (and what causes the shifts in these beliefs) is something critical criminologists are very interested in.

2. **The power of some groups to evade being criminalised** This refers to the idea that the acts and behaviours of powerful groups are sometimes not defined as being criminal, even when these acts cause enormous harm and even deaths. For example, until relatively recently, only direct employees were able to claim compensation from companies who were negligent in their handling of asbestos—a fibre which if you breathe it in can cause illness and death. Nobody else affected was able to seek compensation for the effects of asbestos, regardless of the fact that women washing their husbands' work clothes were also inhaling the harmful fibres and suffering from the associated diseases. We have also read stories of large multi-national corporations avoiding the payment of corporation tax. For example, three large multinational companies and household names (Starbucks, Google, and Amazon) have all had the ways in which they sought to reduce their overall tax burdens scrutinised by the British government. In other words, millions of pounds which could

(and should) have gone into the public coffers to pay for things such as health care, schools, libraries, and housing and so on have been withheld through what are considered as being 'legitimate' tax avoidance schemes.

The obvious form of power that springs to mind when considering these issues is political power, closely followed by the economic power (although these often merge and become blurred), but it can also be seen in terms of race, class, and gender, where certain types of people are able to exercise power over others—for example, in a patriarchy where older men have a power over women, girls, and younger boys which may be reflected in the law. We will be looking at how critical criminology considers all these groups later on in the chapter. For now, though, it's important that we give the question of power more attention (see **What do you think? 15.2**).

WHAT DO YOU THINK? 15.2

- If power were a shape, what would it look like? Quickly draw your ideas and ask your classmates to do the same. Why have you all chosen to represent it in the way that you have?

- Many of you will have chosen to draw a triangle, with the point (apex) representing the 'top of the tree' with power being situated at the top and trickling downwards. Some of you may have drawn a triangle pointing downwards, suggesting that although power is in the smallest part, it supports the greatest area. How many of you drew a constantly moving spiral or changing shape? This is perhaps more accurate and interesting as it captures the idea that power can ebb and flow. For instance, it reflects the way that we as individuals experience differing levels of power throughout our lives—being powerless as children, more powerful as adults, and losing power again as we age. This supports the idea there is no one single powerful group in society but that there are many who have varying degrees of power at different times.

- Power is indeed a tricky and slippery concept but, as we have seen, critical criminologists draw on it to highlight how an individual or group of individuals utilise power to achieve acceptance and compliance, or to persuade people to behave in ways in which they would not ordinarily do and which may not even be in their interests. A key issue for you to think about here is how does power become legitimised? In other words, how do powerful groups gain, exercise and maintain their control over others? These questions are at least partly examined by the first perspective we shall look at, that of 'labelling'.

Labelling perspectives: 1960s radicalism and humanising the deviant

Although there has been a long history of critical thinking around issues of crime, criminality, and its control (dating back to the late 19th and early 20th centuries), this never really had a huge influence on the way in which the majority of people thought about these subjects. Such ideas therefore had very little impact on governmental responses to crime and never really successfully challenged and changed mainstream, powerful ideas. Indeed, many of the earliest critical thinkers were marginalised voices at the time they were writing. They included Prince Pyotr Kropotkin (1842–1921), a Russian aristocrat who believed society did not need government but thought instead that it should be based upon ideals of mutual co-operation and support between the workers, and Willem Bonger (1876–1940) who was a Dutch criminologist heavily influenced by Karl Marx and who formed the view that crime was a result of the capitalist system. Whilst the legacy of these writers should not be ignored (we will return to Bonger a little later) things started to really change in the 1960s.

This decade undoubtedly witnessed a huge amount of social change. As I am sure that you are aware from your reading of **Chapters 13** and **14**, we often need to consider the broader context of the times in which theoretical perspectives develop—after all, they rarely emerge fully-formed from thin air. It is perhaps worth briefly mentioning here that in the United States in the 1960s (where and when the labelling tradition emerged), many people started to question the very social order in which they lived and the power relations which structured their lives. The civil rights movement, the gay rights movement, anti-war

Figure 15.3 Vietnam War protestors march at the Pentagon in Washington, D.C. on 21 October 1967

Source: Frank Wolfe/Public domain

For instance, who has the power to define crime and deviance in the first place? How might people react to being labelled in a particular way and what are the possible societal and individual consequences of this? By shifting the focus of enquiry towards the very processes of how crime becomes defined in the first place, and subsequently the social and individual reactions to it, this critical perspective literally revolutionised the development of criminology. The main line of argument of these perspectives is that it is the social reaction to certain behaviours which actually creates deviance. Or, as Lemert (1967) sums it up; that whilst the 'older sociology' … (that is positivism):

> tended to rest heavily on the assumption that deviance leads to social control. … (T)he reverse idea – i.e. that social control leads to deviance – is equally tenable and the richer premise for studying deviance in modern society.

As such, criminal behaviour was beginning to be characterised as often being meaningful, and the driven, pathological criminal 'other' of positivism was becoming humanised. This perspective is however often misunderstood, so before we start to talk about the theoretical niceties in more detail let's take a step back and start to think about what it may actually mean to label something or someone:

> Labels are devices for saving talkative persons the trouble of thinking.
>
> 1st Viscount Morley of Blackburn, 1838–1923

In the developed world, we use labels all the time. Adverts for anything from cough mixture to pimple cream tell us sternly to 'always read the label'. We have labels on food to tell us how much sugar is in a pudding and our clothes contain tags to tell us how they should be washed. A label, in this sense, gives us a lot of information very quickly, and in a way that is instantly visible. And yet how accurate are these labels? Why do we believe things because of the way they are presented to us and why do they make us behave in certain ways (usually, why do they make us spend money)? In the world of retail, this kind of marketing trick is studied and researched with great care because it makes profit. Manufacturers know that they can charge a premium for something that is labelled in a certain way. One classic example of this is the packaging of painkillers; the branded (more expensive) painkillers often contain the exact same, or at least very similar, ingredients to the supermarket or pharmacy own brands. Similarly, there is little difference in the tablets marketed as being specific to migraines, period pain, or muscle aches—other than the price of course.

We are taught from a very early age to decode signs and symbols. As a result, we unconsciously associate certain colours and shapes with particular aspects of life. Human beings are visual creatures, and we are drawn to how things look. We instinctively know what different labels each signify. Likewise, and through a similar process, we

movements (**Figure 15.3**), and alternative (hippie) subcultures all emerged with a sceptical and questioning attitude towards power and authority. Perhaps more importantly, critical sociologists such as Howard Becker (1928–), David Matza (1930–), and Edwin Lemert (1912–96) began to develop concepts which challenged the prevailing positivist orthodoxy. Such ideas began to take hold in the UK, as higher education was expanding, and these radical and critical ideas were being discussed by young people taking sociology degrees. Eventually they came together to form the basis of what became known as 'labelling' perspectives.

The development of these labelling perspectives in many ways did more than simply challenge the prevailing orthodoxy of positivism. By posing more challenging and different ethical questions it could be said that they turned the problem upside down. For instance, instead of merely seeking to answer the questions of who were the criminals and why did they behave in the ways that they did, and then looking for ways in which they could be punished and controlled more effectively, labelists began to tentatively ask questions about definition and process.

think we know what is right or wrong about a person or group because of the way we (as individuals and as a society) decode and interpret them.

The nature of deviance

At this point it is worth taking a few moments to think about the nature of deviance and why certain acts are labelled as such. In its broadest sense, deviance means an act which goes against what society considers to be normal, but this needs to be unpicked a bit. We need to take into account the social context before deciding if an act is deviant or not—as we saw earlier on, ideas about deviance and acceptability change through time and only a few things (murder, theft and so on) are more or less constantly disapproved of—although even this is argued about, such as whether killings by soldiers in times of war can be considered murder or whether stealing food to feed a starving child should be regarded as being a form of 'social crime'. We also need to bear in mind that there are degrees of deviance. Pinching an envelope from the office stationery cupboard is theft. So is embezzling vast sums from a pension fund and leaving millions of people without financial support in their old age.

Very few of us can hand on heart say we have never, ever committed any kind of deviant act. Which brings us to an important question: if we are all (at least to some degree) deviant, then why is it that only a minority of us is labelled? If we have all stolen something at some time or another—even if it is just that we stole a toffee from the corner shop when we were six—why are relatively few people defined as thieves and treated as such? Think about celebrities accused of tax avoidance—are the actions of the labelled really any different to the things the rest of us do? You are probably saying that to steal a toffee is not as important or meaningful as the theft of millions of pounds, but we need to think about why we make that assumption; if we swap 'toffee from the shop' for 'diamond ring from my granny' does it make any difference? Where do we draw the line between the important and the unimportant deviance?

Primary and secondary deviance

Edwin Lemert, in his book *Social Pathology* (1951) proposed that there are in fact two kinds of deviancy, which he simply called *primary* and *secondary deviance*. The primary kind is that which is temporary, unwitting, and often 'secret'. It causes no long term harm for the offender because either the act does not cause a social reaction or, if it does, then the reaction is not particularly strong or *stigmatising*. The offender does not get labelled, or—and this is where the personal reaction is important—he does not end up seeing himself as an offender.

Secondary deviance has deeper long-term consequences. In these cases, the offender's act is caused by the way she (and others) may come to think about herself. The impact of socially being labelled may well have an individual psychological impact on her self-identity. Having internalised the label, she may than act deviantly because she sees herself as deviant, or as part of a group that is viewed that way. As Howard Becker (1963), who is widely regarded as being the founder of the labelling tradition, would argue, the label has had a transformative effect on how she perceives herself. Think back to where we discussed how we are taught to view signs and symbols in the supermarket; we are also taught to think in certain ways about ourselves (and other people), either by our family and community, or the wider world, media, and education we are exposed to and interact with. These ideas were brought together in the work of George Herbert Mead (1934), who developed the sociological theory of *social interactionism* which influenced writers such as Becker, in which the reactions of others teach us what is 'normal' and what 'isn't'. We learn these ideas and in our turn pass them on to others who want to be accepted. Frank Tannenbaum, in his 1938 book *Crime and the Community*, had already proposed the idea that those who break the norms—the ones we have been learning to call the labelled—are placed in groups with names like 'junkies', 'troublemakers', and so on. Once in a group, it is harder for the labelled to be accepted back into the wider community. After all, would you want a convicted drug dealer or sex offender living next door to you?

The impact of stigma

We should also remember that it is human nature to seek companionship and support from others who are like us and share similar interests—for example a genre of books such as fantasy (like The Lord of the Rings), or a particular sport like football. You almost certainly will avoid places where you will be mocked or *stigmatised* for your passion, but instead will stick to places and people—and actions—where you feel accepted and understood. You are thus illustrating labelists' views that we live up to our own internal labels and by doing so may reinforce them. You feel better amongst other Tolkien or Crystal Palace fans and so your behaviour as such a fan can become more visible—you buy a scarf in your team's colours, you learn Elvish, and so on. Now imagine that the label you have is 'car thief'. You can't get a job because of it and nobody will lend you any money to get a vehicle, so you can't travel to work and are therefore unemployed. Or your label is 'immigrant' and you are shouted at in the street by a middle class supporter of a far-right movement. Or, your label is 'teenage mother' and you are not allowed to return to school to take your A levels. How are things like this likely to affect you and your actions?

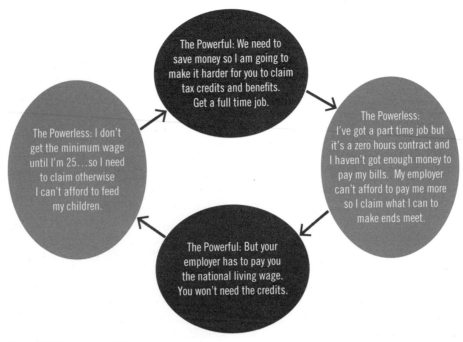

Figure 15.4 The 'welfare cycle'

Stigma is therefore a pivotal factor when we consider the potential impact of labelling and its usage as a criminological perspective. Many of the writers considered in this section on deviance (all writing in the 1960s) gave a lot of thought to the ways in which deviancy is created by social reactions.

By accepting the importance of stigma to the creation of deviance, we can of course move on to look at how the removal of such stigma can prevent crime in the first place. Labelling proposes that instead of asking why someone committed an offence, we should instead be asking ourselves: 'Why do we consider this action to be wrong? Who says it is unacceptable?'

It can thus be argued that labelling is a process whereby we undertake two unconscious actions: we classify what we see, which makes us have expectations, and we react accordingly when those expectations are met (or we think they are met). In criminological terms, the argument is that this process relates to how groups or individuals classify and categorise other people's actions, behaviour, and appearance. The people doing the classifying (who are usually the more powerful) stereotype the people who are classified (the powerless) and expect them to behave in a certain way. When that happens, the powerful have their expectations confirmed, and react accordingly.

Recently in the UK, in the name of austerity measures, the Coalition and Conservative governments have attempted to cut welfare spending budgets. The welfare state and its associated policies were intended to alleviate poverty, which people may find themselves in through no fault of their own; however, it can be argued that the impact of the cuts can itself lead to the criminalisation of the people that welfare was actually intended to support. The basic cycle can be summed up in chart form—see **Figure 15.4**.

This is a rather basic example, but it is a good illustration of the process of how the powerless comes to be labelled as deviant and how the powerful react accordingly. Once a label is applied it is very hard to remove: you can have what is often referred to as a *spoilt identity*. If you have ever applied for a job (and even on your university application) you may well have been asked to declare any criminal convictions; think for a moment about why this might be something employers (and even universities) are interested in. Sometimes it's obvious—a bank isn't going to want to employ a convicted forger—but if you were convicted of something irrelevant a long time ago, should that make any difference to your chances of getting the job or a university place? (This is something that is becoming increasingly important in the light of our 'digital tattoo'—see **Chapter 7** for more on this).

Bearing in mind the issues raised so far see the discussion in **What do you think? 15.3**.

Labelling according to race and ethnicity

One of the most visible ways in which labelling can be observed is in terms of race and ethnicity (see **Chapter 10** for fuller discussion of these issues and critical race theory). Someone's physical appearance is the first thing we

WHAT DO YOU THINK? 15.3

Have you ever been labelled or been a labeller?

- If you have ever been labelled, stop for a moment and think about how it made you feel and react.

- Have you ever labelled somebody else? Perhaps you called them a punk, emo, nerd, gangsta, stoner, teenage parent, educational failure, autist, wheelchair user …

These may not all be obviously connected to criminology—until we think about Muslim women having their veils torn off in the street, or women in short skirts 'asking' to be assaulted, or the murder of a young woman (Sophie Lancaster in 2008—**Figure 15.5**) who was beaten to death for her Goth clothes and lifestyle, or the high rate of hate crime against the disabled or gay people (see chapter 8)—the stories go on and on.

You might also want to think about how the media represent and label various groups, and the extent to which this influences public perceptions and our general 'social constructs'. So, for instance, something like gender is a social construct, in that societies have broadly agreed ways in which males and females are supposed to look and behave—despite the fact that medical science is now showing that biologically speaking, things are far less definite. Transgressing expected and emphasised gender expectations can often result in bullying, harassment, and violence.

WEIRDO. MOSHER. FREAK.

If only they'd stop at name calling.

Figure 15.5 Sophie Lancaster was murdered in 2008 for no other reason than her appearance as a 'goth'

Source: Propaganda/Johnny Green/PA Archive/Press Association Images

notice, so before we have even said our first hello we will have registered that another person is black, Asian, Chinese, white, or whatever. This can bring its own baggage in terms of our attitudes and prejudices, which in turn will have been shaped by our personal experience and the messages to which we have been exposed. Let's try to apply this to an area of current criminological concern; the controversial policing practice of stop and search.

Stop and search; an important police power or tool of discrimination and labelling?

It is often argued that in today's high crime and high risk societies that the police stop-and-search tactics are a good and effective method of crime prevention and crime control. Is there however any evidence to support this claim? STOPWATCH is an independent research-led charity, made up of academics, activists, young people, and lawyers, which carries out research in order to inform the public (and public debate) about how the police use such powers; it also aims to promote effective, fair, and accountable policing. There are a number of laws which give the police powers to stop and search people, and to stop and ask them to account for their actions, behaviours, or even why are they are where are (this is known as stop and account). You can perhaps find out more about these by researching your local crime commissioner's webpages. The important point to make here is that by collating data reported to the Home office by police forces, the figures show a clear trend of a disproportionate use of such tactics against specific ethnic groups (see www.stop-watch.org for their published reports). In 2013–14 a total of 332,036 recorded stop and searches were carried out by the Metropolitan Police. Black

Ethnic groups	Ratio
White: Black	1 : 2.9
White: Asian	1 : 1.1
White: Mixed	1 : 1.3
White: Other	1 : 0.7

Table 15.1 Ratio of stop and searches undertaken by the Metropolitan Police in 2013–14

people were stopped and searched at just under three times the rate of white people across London, whilst people from mixed or Asian backgrounds are stopped and searched at just over the same rate as whites (www.stop-watch.org). **Table 15.1** outlines the ratios by ethnicity.

What is perhaps just as interesting to us is that the charity is also interested in researching individual experiences (just like the early labelists); in other words, what does it feel like to be stopped and searched? What impact do forms of policing actually have on the individuals involved, and on their families and communities? **Controversy and debate 15.1** explores one personal account of this.

Kwabena's testimony in **Controversy and debate 15.1** highlights some of the things which we have been talking about in this section on labelling. Questions he echoes include 'where do labels come from' and 'what does it feel like to be labelled' and 'what are the potential consequences of this'. He does not adopt a 'deviant identity', as not all labels stick, but it clearly shows how such practices can make a difference to how the world is viewed; in this case, his attitude towards the police. His experiences also highlight some the potential pitfalls and problems with this approach. We will conclude this section with some thoughts on why labelling perspectives, even though they ask more searching questions about the social construction of crime and deviance and the individual or social reactions to it, only take us so far on our journey into critical criminology.

Beyond the label

As we said at the beginning of this section, the impact which labelling perspectives had on the study of crime and deviance cannot and should not be over-stated. At the time that they were forming their ideas, the key authors certainly started to ask a set of more penetrating questions and to raise many interesting and important issues which were neglected by more traditional criminologists. For instance: how are crime and deviance socially constructed? Who may have the power to pin a label on another? How might societies and individuals react to a particular label? And so on. We also began to see the human being behind the label. The driven, pathological evil monster of positivist criminologies became a person who made meaningful choices. This is however far from being the final word on critical criminological theorising. What are some of the problems with it?

You are probably thinking that some acts are obviously more serious than others, and in doing so you are raising one of the key criticisms of labelling theory. The ideas of labelling have some significant shortfalls, principally that the prime focus is on so-called 'victimless' crime and the 'underdog'. It's easier to think about labelling for offences

! CONTROVERSY AND DEBATE 15.1

Being stopped and searched by the police—with Kwabena Oduro-Ayim

Kwabena Oduro-Ayim is an accountancy student who lives in Tottenham, North London. He is a founding member of a youth-led group that works to combat knife and gang violence in London. Below he talks about his experience of being stopped and searched by the police how this made him feel.

There is a kind of feeling of us against them. There's been various generations that have had negative experiences with the police. And when you've got so many fragmented stories of negative experiences with the police, it really does give a negative mosaic of the police. I mean, if you're an 8-year-old child and you go to play football, and the police officer stops and searches you. If you experience that from the age of 8, all the way through your secondary school career, then you're not going to have a positive view of the police. You will not invest faith in the police if something happens to you. You start to feel you have to take the law into your own hands. Being stopped three times in the same day, that's bound to mess up your psyche. You're criminalizing people who are already in an environment where it is extremely easy to slip into crime anyway. You don't want to give them a motive to engage in crime. For my entire childhood I would never have turned to the police for any assistance. If someone tried to rob me, my mind frame would be to phone members of my community to help me go and get back my stuff.

Open Society, Justice Initiative, and Stopwatch (nd) *Viewed With Suspicion; The Human Cost of Stop and Search in England and Wales*. Available at www.stop-watch.org

that have less impact on us; most of us couldn't care less about whether the person who burns down our house or murders our friend has been labelled or not; we will probably see the act as deserving of stigma and punishment. Labelling also does not really give enough explanation of why only some behaviours get stigmatised, nor provide answers to questions of whose law and order is being imposed on the labelled. Lastly, we need to bear in mind that, as with all other criminological perspectives, definitions and contexts remain fluid and that this will always affect what is 'normal' and what is 'unacceptable.'

It is also often argued that labelling has little practical application in terms of broader criminal justice responses to crime. This link between theory and policy implications is a very important one when studying theory; often, once such links are made all of the other bits of the theory fall into place! For instance, as we saw in the last three chapters, the logic of classicism plays out in policy terms in the form of deterrence and punishment, whilst that of positivism does so in terms of treatment and rehabilitation. The logic of labelling would be that crime is caused by processes of labelling and that in order to do something about the 'crime problem,' society should simply not label. This is perhaps

not as ridiculous as it might first sound. Indeed, the idea of 'radical non-intervention' (that is simply not responding to certain forms of behaviours via the criminal justice system) which was proposed by Schur in 1973, informs, in part, current responses to youth crime in the form of what is known as *restorative justice*; a form of justice which aims not to stigmatise young 'offenders' and then reintegrate them back into their communities. (You will get the chance to consider this in more detail in **Chapter 26**.)

Perhaps the most telling criticism of labelling perspectives is that by concentrating mainly on small scale, mainly dyadic (that is between two people) interactions, it fails to contextualise the interactions within the broader contexts of power (why are police stop and search powers and practices as they are now?) or really analyse crimes committed by powerful groups; remember we noted the power to evade criminalisation earlier on in this chapter? In short, it can be argued that its analysis of power and power relations was merely suggestive rather being fully developed. This leads us to our next section where we will consider some Marxist-inspired critical criminologists who developed the insights derived from labelling perspectives in a very particular and even more critical way.

The development of critical criminology in Britain

Jock Young and the 'naughty schoolboys'

At the University of York, in July 1968, the first ever National Deviancy Conference (NDC) was held; this was the first of 14 such conferences which took place between 1968–73. It was a meeting of like-minded critical criminologists who wanted to challenge the prevailing academic (that is positivist) and official (that is Home Office) views about crime and its control which we outlined at the beginning of this chapter. They included some now legendary figures—such as Stan Cohen, Jock Young, and Mary McIntosh. Perhaps we should note that Mary was the only woman involved, and the only one of the founding members of the movement who was not later awarded a post as Professor anywhere, which suggests that academic institutions are not exempt from discrimination, although she did go on to do some very important work in the study of gender and feminism. These critical thinkers were part of a new wave of British criminologists and sociologists, benefiting from wider access to higher education; traditionally, something only available to the rich and privileged.

Described by one rather disapproving academic of the day as 'naughty schoolboys' (Radzinowicz 1999: 229)—presumably Ms McIntosh was gallantly exempted—the

leaders of the deviancy conference wanted to think about why society considers some acts to be deviant, why it reacts to deviancy in the ways it does, and to highlight the experiences and opinions of the deviant (who are of course often the powerless too). The critical movement argued that labelling didn't give enough consideration to issues of power, and instead attempted to develop a *fully social theory of deviance*, which drew on insights derived from both labelling perspectives and neo-Marxist theories of the state. This is all perhaps sounding a little bit complex so let's take a step back for a moment to consider what inspired them and, in particular, the writings of Marx.

The philosopher and political economist Karl Marx (1818–43) actually wrote very little about crime and criminality in his vast body of work; his concerns were far grander. Over the years, however, some of his ideas relating to the inequalities which he regarded as being inherent and inevitable in capitalist societies have been drawn on in different ways by many criminologists attempting to explain the constructions of crime and societies' responses to it. At its most basic, the main point to make here is about the *political economy*; in other words how economics, law, and politics in society interact and how particular types of society—such as capitalism or socialism—develop different institutions which create public policies on things such as health, education, and crime.

Figure 15.6 'Pyramid of Capitalist System' from the *Industrial Worker*
Source: International Pub. Co., Cleveland, Ohio/Public domain

As an economic system, capitalism has often been represented as a pyramid, such as the one published by the *Industrial Worker* in 1911 (see **Figure 15.6** and also **What do you think? 15.4**).

In terms of our journey through criminology, the argument is that in capitalist societies there is a distinct *mode of production* which is linked to 'crime' and how those

with power (the state and its agencies) respond to it. Such societies are characterised by the existence of a class of capitalists (who own the *means of production)* and a working class (who do not). You will often read of these two classes being referred to as the *bourgeoisie* who are the ruling or capitalist class, and the *proletariat* or working class; although many writers influenced by Marxism today will, more often than not, simply use the terms the 'powerful' and 'less powerful'.

The basic argument is this: the powerful produce the goods and services we all consume, and do so for profit. In doing so they employ workers who, in turn, sell their labour power for a wage, and are thus exploited because they need the money to buy the goods they have themselves made. This results in there being a conflict in society between capital and labour, which is, in part, resolved through law. The law in turn reflects and encourages the capitalist system and the power relations it involves, because of course it is the powerful who make the laws in the first place. The argument goes on to say that it is this very economic system and its fundamental unfairness which produces conflict and crime.

The links between money and crime go back a long way—the poison arsenic, for example, used to be known as 'inheritance powder' due to its popularity as a means of killing people who had left their not-so grieving relatives a little something in their will! But it's the wider implications of power and money that have concerned critical criminologists, for what may seem a surprisingly long time. So, let's take a moment to think about how economics are intricately related to crime and punishment.

Willem Bonger: capitalism and crimes of the powerful

Perhaps the best way to answer this would be to turn to the Dutch criminologist Willem Bonger (1876–1940) to whom you were introduced earlier on in the chapter. Bonger is widely regarded as being the first person to really apply Marx's ideas in terms of how it is that the social, political, and economic structures of a society (in this case a capitalist one) can actually create 'crime' and form social responses to it. In arguing that capitalism is criminogenic (that is, that it actually causes crime) he came up with the following six propositions (or statements of opinion) (Bonger 1916, from Muncie 2015: 128). They are:

1. That ideas of immorality and criminality are socially and historically variable.

2. That the criminal law exists to protect the interests of the powerful.

3. That capitalism is held together by coercive exploitation rather than co-operative consensus.

WHAT DO YOU THINK? 15.4

Developing the pyramid of capitalism

Look at the reproduction of the 1911 poster in **Figure 15.6**, noting the clear power relations between power and wealth at the top, and poverty and labour at the bottom. Obviously, capitalism has developed since 1911. If you were to draw this poster today what would it look like? What would you include? For instance, where you place global conflict and inequalities, an economy changing from manufacturing to services based on short term contracts and zero hours contracts, consumerism and crime?

4. That capitalism encourages egoism and greed. In the pursuit of such 'pleasures' both the proletariat and bourgeoisie become prone to crime as the mutual sense of responsibility towards each other is diminished.

5. That poverty prompts crime to the extent that it creates a desperate need for food and other necessities.

6. That crime also results when there is a perceived opportunity to gain an advantage through illegal means and/or when opportunities to achieve pleasure are closed off by a biased legal system.

Here Bonger is raising many important and interesting critical issues. For instance, he suggests that capitalist societies are based primarily on exploitation, greed, and conflict. He also holds the view that, as we have argued earlier in this chapter, 'crime' is something which changes over time but that under capitalism the criminal law comes to reflect the interests of powerful groups and so on (so we hang the child for stealing the bread instead of punishing the person who allowed it to go hungry in the first place).

Perhaps the most interesting points noted by Bonger relate to points 4 and 6. Here he argues that both the powerful and powerless groups commit crime through greed and when they have the opportunity to do so. Studying 'crimes of the powerful' gives us a chance to look at the way that such actions (or omissions) can cause great harm, but are often not even classed as crimes at all (see **What do you think? 15.5**).

The 'New Criminology'

Since Bonger's work over 100 years ago many critical criminologists have re-visited the work of Karl Marx and developed some of his ideas in novel ways with regard to the of analysis of crime and its control—see for instance, the work of the American critical scholars Quinney (1974) and Chambliss (1975). In Britain, the most ambitious and influential ideas came out of the work of three criminologists who were at the centre of the NDC. They were Ian Taylor, Paul Walton, and Jock Young. In 1973 they published what was to become almost a manifesto for critical criminology which has influenced and inspired generations of critical criminologists. Whilst their book was very much a product of its time in that it reflected a social and political backdrop of discrimination and social injustice, it was the first text to offer a thorough and rigorous critique of both classicist and positivist thinking. It however goes much further than this. In the last chapter the authors, by integrating elements of interactionism, labelling, and neo-Marxism, call for the development of a *fully social theory* of deviance. Let's see what they argued are the requirements for this.

The *New Criminology*

In the *New Criminology* (1973) the authors set out seven core and formal requirements for a *fully social theory* of crime and deviance. These formal requirements are

---

WHAT DO YOU THINK? 15.5

Crimes of the powerful

2015 saw the 800th anniversary of Magna Carta. This 'Great Charter' is perhaps the most famous document setting out restrictions on power—in this case, that of the King of England. However, Magna Carta, like any similar document over the years, is a reflection of its time and context.

The examples below are all taken from Magna Carta or other legal frameworks. Which do you think are genuine pieces of law-making? Which are modern, which are mediaeval? Which do you think are still in force? And what do they tell us about the power relations of the time and place in which they happen?

- A woman may not accuse a man of murder or manslaughter, unless the case involves her husband.

- Only men who are members of the Church of England can stand for Parliament.

- Companies responsible for the environmental disasters in the developing world can avoid liability for cleaning operations or compensating the victims.

- The British police may cut off food supplies to people in protest camps.

- The UK Foreign Secretary can issue secret warrants allowing phone tapping.

- American secret services hid evidence of war crimes to allow Nazi scientists to work in the US after the war.

All of the above examples are, or were, genuine. (In case you are wondering, the first is from Magna Carta and has long since been superseded; the second was true until the so-called Jew Act of 1858. All the others are modern). We will return to issues concerning crimes of the powerful in **Chapter 16** when we consider *zemiology* and *green criminology,* as it is such an important part of critical criminology today.

(Taylor et al., derived from Mooney in DeKeseredy and Dragiewicz 2012: 18):

1. The wider origins of the deviant act—'in other words to place the act in terms of its wider structural origins'.

2. The immediate origins of the deviant act—to 'be able to explain the different events, experiences and structural developments that precipitate the deviant act'.

3. The actual act, to explain the relationship between the behaviour and the causes—'a working class adolescent for example, confronted with blockage of opportunity with problems of status frustration, alienation from the kind of existence offered out to him in contemporary society, may want to engage in hedonistic activities or he may choose to kick back at a rejecting society (eg through acts of vandalism)'.

4. The immediate origins of the social reaction—that is how the act is responded to.

5. The wider origins of deviant reaction—that is 'the position and attributes of those who instigate the reaction against the deviant'.

6. The outcome of the social reaction on the deviants' further action.

7. The nature of the deviant process as a whole; how 1–6 connect.

Let's apply these ideas to a real example using the story of Eve McDougal (Eve's experiences will be considered further in the section on intimate partner violence later in the chapter). When Eve was 15 years old she was sent to an adult prison in Scotland for attempting to steal food, although her 'real' crime was criminal damage. Can we connect what happen to Eve with the complicated list of formal requirements for a *fully social theory* of deviance and crime as set out Taylor et al. back in 1973?

1. **The wider origins of the deviant act**—Eve grew up in a poor part of Scotland characterised by poverty and a sense of hopelessness. She did not meet her father until she was 17 (although he was pointed out to her by a school friend long before she actually met him) and her mother suffered from physical disabilities for which the family received no support and which were not, at that time, recognised by the state in terms of her receiving appropriate social security benefits.

2. **The immediate origins of the deviant act**—Eve wanted to escape her background and to have all of the things which she saw others having. She felt excluded. The absence of her father, and her mother's disabilities, meant that she did not have effective support to help her deal with the family's situation. By the age of nine she was stealing food and clothes and getting drunk on cheap wine. Her birthday and Christmas were ignored by her father and her mother's disabilities meant that the family had little money.

3. **The actual act, to explain the relationship between the behaviour and the causes**—Eve was hungry. She saw what she thought were buns and cakes in a shop window and broke it, in order to steal something to eat; however the food was fake and she was shocked to be arrested.

4. **The immediate origins of the social reaction**—Eve was seen by the 'authorities' only as a thief and as someone who had committed criminal damage, rather than as a socially vulnerable young woman. She was believed to be behaving in a way not thought of 'suitable' and 'appropriate' and deserving of punishment to teach her a lesson. Eve was assaulted by police officers after her arrest, who failed to treat her as the child she was.

5. **The wider origins of deviant reaction**—Eve had challenged society's expectations and it was felt that she needed to be made an example of. As a result she was treated as an adult rather than as a child (although she was only 15) and no attention was paid to her poverty, hunger, or social exclusion which could have been viewed as causing her act. The only question was how she should be punished, rather than how she could be helped to overcome her family's problems.

6. **The outcome of the social reaction on the deviant's further action**—In the first instance, Eve was taken to a police cell where she was hurt by officers who had a duty of care towards her. After her sentence she was sent to an adult prison where she encountered offenders who treated her with either kindness or harshness; she learnt more criminal behaviour from them but did not receive any help for her feelings of anger or for the poverty and frailty of her family's background.

As for point 7, if we think of Eve as a young person with particular thoughts and feelings who was living in a particular context—socially and economically—we can see how the factors all interlinked to form what the new criminologists would call a *fully social theory* of how she came to be imprisoned. Removing any one of the factors—for example, if Eve had not been hungry or if her father had been a supportive presence in the family—would perhaps have influenced the outcome.

Feminist perspectives

This chapter has so far said very little about women and the possible relationships between women and crime. If you hadn't given that any thought, you might want to ask yourself why this might be … do you automatically assume that all criminals are men? And if you have asked yourself 'where are the women'? maybe you should ask yourself similar questions, such as why the female absence speaks so strongly to you.

The rest of this section will seek to redress the balance—rather as feminist criminologies do. Once you have read it, it might be interesting to choose one of the other chapters and re-read it with the feminist perspective in mind and see if this raises any new ideas or concerns for you (see also **Chapter 11** for a chapter-length discussion of gender and crime).

We should pause for a moment here to give a small 'health warning'. This book is very much an introduction to the vast and ever expanding field of criminological study and as such it can't cover everything. For that reason, this section will itself have a general focus on women and the links with crime, victimisation, and criminal justice in the developed westernised world, and on women who are in heterosexual relationships. There is important work to be done in the field of women who don't fall into these broad categories, especially on a global level such as women as victims of trafficking and smuggling; the fact that we don't have space to consider their experiences and lives here does not mean that they are being sidelined or are less important.

For most of its history, criminology has focused almost exclusively on male actors in the criminal justice world, such as offenders, victims, judges, and police officers. Any study that involved women tended to look on them as weak, feeble creatures who were unable to control themselves or their actions, so the female criminal was seen in terms of her biology and sexuality. The ancient Greek word for 'womb' is 'hystera' and it was believed that a woman's uterus would actually detach itself from its normal position and go wandering all over her body, causing illness and—literally—'hysteria'. It was not until the 19th century that the number of women being diagnosed with 'female hysteria' declined, but until then many were incarcerated in insane asylums and were forced to undergo hysterectomies. The trope of the 'Madwoman in the Attic' found in 19th century literature (such as *Jane Eyre*) encapsulates this well.

Daft as such ideas can seem, they took a long time to die. Indeed, Cesare Lombroso and his collaborator Guglielmo Ferrero, in their 1893 book *Criminal Woman, the Prostitute and the Normal Woman*—a telling title if ever there was one—pictured women as being slaves to their biology, as you would perhaps expect from such early positivist approaches. The chapter on female criminals was accompanied by a section on criminal behaviour in animals; in dealing with prostitutes, the authors considered women who sold, or enjoyed, sex to be pretty much the same thing. Their view was that 'some female born criminals and prostitutes have more sexual sensitivity than normal women' (171) and that by measuring heads, feet, and other physical characteristics it was possible to determine the naturally occurring signs that a woman was going to be in some way 'wrong'. The concept that a person's character or personality can be determined through analysis of outer appearance, or physical composition, is known as the pseudo-science *physiognomy*. So, much early criminology reflected male criminologists' sexist assumptions that the majority of women were biologically pre-disposed to be conformist and law-abiding, whilst those who transgressed the criminal law were somehow mentally unstable beings who often displayed masculine traits.

In the 19th century there was great social anxiety about women in general, their changing role in society and their demands for greater freedom and visibility. The fight for women's rights was a campaign which can be traced back to Mary Wollstonecraft's 1792 book *A Vindication of the Rights of Women*, via the Suffrage campaign of the late 19th and early 20th centuries (it was not until 1928 that all women over the age of 21 were allowed to vote in general elections), and which reached its heights in the late 1960s and throughout the 1970s with the development of what has become known as second-wave feminism.

This latter feminist movement challenged obvious inequalities such as the way men and women could be paid at different rates—or how access to certain jobs was restricted to men. The legal framework was slow to respond, with the Equal Pay Act being passed in 1970; the Sex Discrimination Act did not include issues of education or employment until 1975 (it was not extended to cover transgender people until 2008). But as well as these day-to-day aspects of feminism there has been an expansion of academic interest in issues surrounding gender, particularly feminism, and this has been a very visible movement within criminology. The resulting perspective, which is considered to belong to the 'critical' school, has come to be known as feminist criminology.

As with critical criminology itself there is not just one feminist criminological perspective but many. These have different ideas and points of view, and include specific areas of interest such as black feminist or lesbian criminologies. Some feminists don't even agree that there can be such a thing as a feminist criminology in the first place! Taken as a whole, however, feminist criminological perspectives can be regarded as being critical whether they are based on liberalism or Marxism or indeed any other 'ism', because, despite their differences, they have definite characteristics in common. The principal ideas they share are the importance of social construction (in this case, the social construction of gender) and power relations (the focus being here on patriarchal power).

A major influence in the development of feminist perspectives within criminology is the work of Carol Smart. The first major study of women and crime was her 1976 book *Women, Crime and Criminology*. In it she criticises not only orthodox (positivist) criminology but also interactionist and radical studies for not fully considering female criminality and victimisation. Since then many further studies have been produced by feminist scholars—see Ugwudike (2015) for an overview of these. Much recent work, including that of Smart (1995) raises an important point which we need to bear in mind when exploring this arena: the way that feminism itself can be a divided movement which some groups of women (particularly the socially excluded, black, or poorly educated) feel does not speak for them or promote their interests.

However, even if we acknowledge the fact that feminism means different things to different groups (especially groups of women) we can argue that there are, nevertheless, strands of common thinking that remain. At the root of all feminisms is the idea and problem of equality—although, as you will probably expect by now, we need to remember that there are different views on what 'equality' means.

Smart (1976), and other feminist writers, put forward the idea that criminology was what they term 'malestream'—that like the criminal justice system and wider society as a whole, the focus is on males and maleness and that the female experience is ignored or belittled. Smart (1995: 71) uses the idea that the law, having power to establish the 'truth', is a major force in silencing women both by its stereotyped views of them and by the ways it projects certain expectations on to them. Feminist criminologies seek to challenge this 'gender blindness', and it is this which shall underpin the rest of this section on the gender blindness of much criminology.

In discussing this, the themes that we will cover are:

- the 'gender gap' in offending behaviours;
- women as victims (especially in terms of domestic abuse, family crime, and sexual crime);
- research on masculinities (as scholarship has moved on to consider gender as an issue rather than solely 'women').

The gender gap

As we have just seen, the idea that equality between the sexes should be protected by law is relatively recent. It's sobering to think that any woman we meet who is over the age of about 60 would almost certainly, in her youth, have been paid a lesser rate than a male colleague—if indeed she had been in employment. We still have justifiable concerns about equality in terms of female representation at the highest level of organisations. The so-called 'glass ceiling' is still very much in evidence when we look, for example, at women in the police force; in 2014, 27.9 per cent of police officers were women, but only 19.5 per cent of senior ranks were female; in North America in 2015, only 9 per cent of Chief Executive roles in business were held by women (Home Office police workforce statistics, July 2014; *Financial Times*, 23 March 2014).

How much of this is due to the way women are taught to think about themselves? How much is due to how society sees women and their opportunities? How much is due to discrimination and direct—or indirect—prejudice? (See **What do you think? 15.6**.) Criminologists have generally focused on the 'fact' that men commit far more recorded crime than women. Also, their offending behaviours appear to be of a more serious and violent nature, and there is a tendency for men to be reconvicted; both facts which can skew our perceptions.

Two further explanations have been put forward for these statistical 'truths': the so called *chivalry hypothesis* and the *double deviancy thesis*. These approach the issue in different ways but both share a focus on stereotyped notions of what a 'normal' woman is and how she should

WHAT DO YOU THINK? 15.6

How does gender impact on your life?

- Think about your family and friends. If you are female, consider your own experiences and upbringing compared to that of your female friends or relations, then see how they match those of your male circle. (If you are male, then of course do the same but in reverse!)

- Think about the things that you may have had in common, and the differences—for example, as girls, were you taught to think of yourself in a different way to the boys? Did you have restrictions placed on you that boys didn't whilst the boys were

given greater freedoms—or did they suffer greater anxieties?

- How do you all respond to adverts and media pressure about your gender, and what controls—formal and informal—do you all experience on your lives and actions?

- Were the reactions to your behaviours different from those in 'authority' such as your parents, carers, school teachers?

- Do you think your socialisation processes in terms of gender can account for the statistical patterns in offending behaviours described above, and if so, how?

behave. The idea of 'chivalry' argues that women who project an image of acceptable femininity (whatever this might mean) to the criminal justice system tend to get more lenient treatment.

Secondly, the idea of 'double deviancy' argues that women criminals are not just thought of as having broken the actual law, but also the unwritten social law of how women 'should' behave, and that this results in some women being treated more harshly by the penal system. This means that they are, in effect, punished twice. For instance, a poor black woman is likely to be seen differently to a wealthy white woman, who will in turn be viewed differently to a lesbian, who is likely to be portrayed as a bad mother or defective woman. Studies of sentencing practices by courts would certainly support that they are far from being consistent. Although inconclusive, the criminological evidence which is available to us would suggest that not all women have the same experiences and that class, race, and poverty have impact as well as gender. This is often referred to *intersectionality*.

The idea that courts do not respond adequately to the needs of women has been extended to cover policing and probation practices and the prison (see the Corsten Report 2007 for a fuller discussion of some of these important issues).

Women as victims of violence

Perhaps unsurprisingly, research in this area has been a principal focus of feminist research and has had significant impact on both public opinion and policy making. It is important to bear in mind, of course, that overall men are more likely to be victims of violence in the public sphere, and that women can themselves be perpetrators. However this section is focusing on women as victims of violence at the hands (and minds) of male offenders mainly, though not exclusively, in the private sphere behind closed doors. It is inevitable that we shall have to consider the distressing and sensitive subjects of sexual assault and domestic abuse; please make sure you have good support available if you feel that these topics will affect you.

One area of concern for feminist researchers has always been the inadequate responses of the criminal justice system to women who come forward as victims of male violence. This is not a new problem; in 1982 there was a public outcry at a documentary entitled *Police: A Complaint of Rape* which showed three male officers bullying a woman into withdrawing her allegation. Police training and procedures were changed as a result but was there a lasting impact? Possibly not as much as we would like; in 2015, a young woman was awarded a £20,000 compensation payment for the way Hampshire Police failed to adequately investigate when she was raped; having had a

previous police record and mental health issues, she was assumed to have been lying and forensic tests—which subsequently convicted her attacker—were not carried out until after she had herself been arrested on suspicion of perverting the course of justice.

Stories such as these bring victims to the forefront of the criminal justice arena, and cause huge public outrage. The concept of a 'victimology' is relatively new in this context. The term really refers to a radical strand of thought which concentrates on the way that power (especially male power) and the patriarchal state create victims and treat them as either deserving or undeserving. A good example of this is a justice system in which a prosecuting barrister could describe a 13 year old girl, who had been groomed for sex by a 41 year old man, as being a 'sexual predator'. These comments were accepted by the presiding judge, during a hearing in 2013 (http://www.bbc.co.uk/news/uk-23597224).

The very notion of being a 'victim' has also been questioned and alternatives, such as the idea of being a 'survivor', have been put forward by groups working with anyone who has suffered trauma as the result of a crime. Organisations such as Victim Support and domestic abuse shelters work to empower those affected by crime and to reduce its impact as far as possible. There are also grass-roots movements such as 'Reclaim the Night' (see **Figure 15.7**) which are women-only marches to protest against street violence, and so-called 'Slut Walks' in which women wear 'provocative' clothes in order to make the point that what we wear should not mean we are open to attack or assault.

All of these organisations and movements are a response to the positivistic concept of *victim precipitation*—that the victim somehow caused or deserved whatever happened. The obvious example of this is the notion that women 'ask for it' when they wear short skirts or low-cut tops. Colleges and schools in the US and UK have been challenged for dress codes which require female students

Figure 15.7 Image of a Reclaim the Night march in Wales
Source: Matthew Horwood/Alamy Stock Photo

to wear discreet, modest clothes because shorts, strapless tops, and yoga pants 'distract male teachers' and 'make men uncomfortable', but there is no mention at all about reviewing male attitudes to the female body.

Ideas about what is acceptable have also (slightly) shifted when considering other aspects of violence, such as domestic or intimate relationship abuse. This too has been a topic which historically was not seen as a crime requiring a criminal justice response, but rather as a private matter which requires a 'welfare' response. The actor Sir Patrick Stewart who now campaigns against violence, recalls his mother being beaten by his father, only to be told by the police that she must have done something to provoke it (see **Figure 15.8**).

As Sir Patrick has pointed out, perpetrators of domestic abuse may well have their own mental or emotional issues which may be at the root of their behaviour. However, this does not detract from the emotional, physical, and financial implications of domestic abuse; the charity Women's Aid estimates that domestic abuse costs the UK economy £23 billion a year. When we consider the issue of domestic abuse and intimate violence, we can see that it is a huge factor in the overall cost—in every sense—of crime.

Intimate personal violence and partner abuse

Obtaining reliable evidence in this area is fraught with difficulties (why do you think that this might be the case?). The various surveys which have been carried out over the last forty years or so would indicate that such crimes are far more numerous than you might expect. In short, as many of you will know, family life and intimate relationships, which are thought to provide us with a nurturing haven in an otherwise heartless world, can often be places of danger and violence. The Crime Survey for England and Wales (CSEW) (which we looked at in chapter 5) now

regularly asks its sample of respondents questions on their experiences of such violence and abuse. The UK government now defines domestic violence and abuse as:

Any incident or pattern of incidents of controlling, coercive, threatening behaviour, violence or abuse between those aged 16 or over who are, or have been, intimate partners or family members regardless of gender or sexuality. The abuse can encompass, but is not limited to:

- psychological
- physical
- sexual
- financial
- emotional.

Such a definition in many ways indicates the success and impact of feminist scholarship in this area, especially in terms that the definition includes the notions of psychological and emotional abuse. This was a point graphically made in a recent series of posters and adverts which are still available online (http://thisisabuse.direct.gov.uk/, see **Figure 15.9**). The poster makes clear that abuse is not always physical.

Figure 15.8 The actor Sir Patrick Stewart campaigns against violence against women

Source: Ian West/PA Archive/Press Association Images

Figure 15.9 Poster from a UK government campaign highlighting the psychological and emotional form that domestic abuse can take

Source: The Home Office, content available under the Open Government Licence v3.0

Indeed, psychological and emotional abuse is often ongoing and can impact on the victim very deeply indeed. This may be particularly true if there are social or cultural factors thrown into the mix—for example, do we feel differently about men who are abused by women? Do we see violence in gay or lesbian relationships as somehow different or less important? It is this definition—including non-physical abuse—which now informs the CSEW, and by using a self-completion survey (as opposed to a face-to-face one) it perhaps provides us with a more accurate picture than officially recorded police statistics, although there will still be obvious problems of under-reporting; would you be willing to report such things even in a self-completion and confidential survey? But what does the survey show us? See **What do you think? 15.7**.

One of the things which graphs and tables in **What do you think? 15.7** do not tell us about are the emotional and psychological impacts of being abused by an intimate

WHAT DO YOU THINK? 15.7

Evaluating the evidence

- This is where we have to look at the CSEW evidence. We can often get valuable information from statistical tables or graphs and they can quickly tell us much more at a glance than reading many pages of text. Also, being able to interpret and analyse graphs is an important transferable skill that you will be able to put on your CV to enhance your employability (see **Chapter 30**).

- Look at **Figure 15.10** and jot down three things which concern you or you think are of interest. This is a graph taken from the 2012–13 CSEW and shows the percentage of adults aged between 16 and 59 who have experienced some form of intimate violence since the age of 16.

- Were the headline figures higher or lower than you expected?

- What about the clear gender differences?

- In many ways, what the graphs confirm to us is that such crimes are not isolated incidents and that they show clear gendered patterns, for instance, that 30 per cent of women and 16.3 per cent of men had experienced domestic abuse since the age of 16. This is equivalent to an estimated 4.9 million women and 2.7 million men. It can also be seen that twice as many women as men have experienced some form of non-sexual partner abuse since the age of 16 (23.8 per cent compared to 11.1 per cent).

- The CSEW has been collecting data in this area since 2004–05 so it is interesting to also have a quick look at the trends in terms of yearly changes, in **Figure 15.11**.

- Whilst there are clear downward trends here, should that make us complacent?

- What would be 'acceptable' levels of intimate crime and abuse in your opinion?

- Also, are there any problems with such 'evidence'?

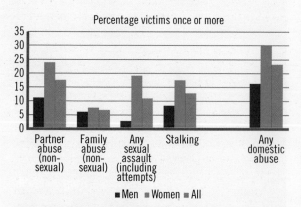

Figure 15.10 Percentage of adults aged 16 to 59 who experienced intimate violence since the age of 16, by sex and headline category, 2012–13 CSEW(1)

Source: The Home Office, content available under the Open Government Licence v3.0

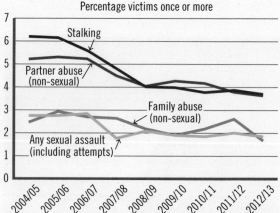

Figure 15.11 Percentage of women aged 16 to 59 who experienced intimate violence in the last year, by headline category, 2004–05 to 2012–13 CSEW(1)

Source: The Home Office, content available under the Open Government Licence v3.0

partner. Obviously different kinds of abuse will impact on different people in different ways, but we should perhaps reflect on how it might feel to be abused and also to be on the long and often painful journey to becoming a survivor. (See **Telling it like it is 15.1**.) Remember, we already know that this is not an uncommon experience for many

---

TELLING IT LIKE IT IS 15.1

A personal journey through intimate abuse—with Eve McDougall

Eve McDougall was sent to an adult prison at the age of 15 for stealing food and criminal damage (as we saw earlier in the chapter). The psychological and mental damage that followed her for 25 years afterwards was horrific and led her into an abusive marriage. She is now a successful writer, campaigner, and artist. You can read more about her journey in her book *A Wicked Fist: A True Story of Prison and Freedom* (1999). Below she candidly and bravely tells about some her experiences of being a victim of male violence and the impact this had on her whole family.

'When I got married I thought it would be a special day, I thought I knew him, thought he was the man for me, but how wrong was I. I was punched, kicked, and battered all over the place, that very evening. It was unbelievable; this man told me he loved me, he had taken special vows to take care of me, and this is how he showed his love. The days ahead were the most traumatic nightmare anyone could endure, daily beatings, rape, and hours of psychological and mental abuse. I was in shock and traumatised.

'I couldn't understand how someone you think you know could do all of these things to you and didn't even blink an eye, or that he was also injuring our unborn baby. It was extremely painful and shocking that my own husband was raping, beating, and traumatising us, hard to take in, even harder to accept this man who says he loves us and will do anything for us can then switch rapidly into a person I don't know anymore, behaving like a psychopath. He would always say it was my fault, that "I made him do it" and that I deserved to be taught a lesson. When I would ask him what I had done, he would attack me and abuse me kicking, punching, strangling, and raping me all over again, then he would get on his hands and knees begging forgiveness saying he didn't know what came over him and he would never do it again. He would even cry real tears, tears I would believe and give him another chance.

'It was degrading, humiliating, and all trust had flown off into the wilderness. How could I trust or believe this man who was injuring me, physically and emotionally scrambling my brains to the point of wanting to take my own life? I would run to my Mum and siblings but he always found me in the end. I felt I had nowhere to run. He battered me in front of my Mum and even strangers in public. It had a terrible effect on all of my family especially my Mum having to watch helplessly as her own child was being hurt by the husband who claimed to love and protect her daughter. Mum told me how hard it was to watch her daughter being harmed. She would break down crying, saying he was so nice to us all, promising to take care of you. She would tell me "you have to get away to a place of safety, he will end up killing you, I don't know this man anymore he's not the same guy who made all those promises, just shows how you think you know someone but you really don't."

'I felt injured, betrayed, and so depressed by someone I thought I loved and knew so intimately, a supposed loving husband who could intimidate and inflict such brutality on the woman and child he says he loves. Any little thing that he didn't like, for instance, if the dinner wasn't to his liking, he would be like the trigger of a gun and blast all his anger and frustration at me and his unborn child, the child he said he longed for and would do anything to protect and keep safe from the dangers that he acted out and possessed.

'The future years ahead didn't have any meaning in this world that I was existing in, I feared every second, minute, hour. I really didn't know this man I had married, he was a time bomb full of destruction and not the loving caring man I first met and the man who spoke of a future of happy marriage and children. This guy was the total opposite of every promise he had ever made. I didn't understand any of it, I was only 18 years old and I actually believed every "sorry" and that he would never do it again.

'It was a long journey back to reality when I finally did get away from him. I had no understanding of the trauma and disorder that it caused and it took 20 odd years to finally get on a healing path to a place of safety, where I could finally thaw out and work on the disorder that it had caused me. Now I look at what I want to do and what can I do, and I ignore the way he always told me I would amount to nothing, that I was worthless, illiterate, thick, and stupid. I had believed that. But now I am not a victim, I am a survivor.'

people, even though it is rarely talked about. Also, the statistical evidence also highlights that many of you reading this book now will have, at some point, in your lives, been abused in these ways.

The abuse of children and young people

Another glaring gap in the survey evidence presented in **What do you think? 15.7** is that (and some of you might have noticed this) the sample of respondents to CSEW does not include anyone under the age of 16. This is perhaps important as experiences in our formative years can often desensitise and normalise things for us. Although there are ethical reasons for this gap in the CSEW data, the National Society for the Protection of Children (NSPCC) carried out their own survey on partner exploitation and violence in teenage intimate relationships in 2009. This was the first study of its kind in Great Britain and it surveyed 1,353 young people, between 13 and 17 years old from England, Scotland, and Wales. In terms of physical, emotional, and sexual partner violence the results were startling. For instance:

- a quarter of girls and 18 per cent of boys reported some form of physical partner violence;
- one in nine girls and 4 per cent of boys reported severe physical violence;
- nearly three-quarters of girls and half of boys reported some form of emotional partner violence;
- one in three girls and 16 per cent of boys reported some form of sexual partner violence;
- the majority were single incidents. However, for a minority of young people, sexual violence was a more regular feature of their relationships.

Reflect on society's attitudes to these issues by reading and considering the questions in **Controversy and debate 15.2**.

Masculinities and crime; men behaving manly (and badly)?

We will end this section of the chapter by going back to have another look at the first theme of feminist criminologies which we discussed earlier; the so-called 'gender gap'. As you will remember, this refers to the different rates of offending between men and women rather than other 'gaps' such as those which relate to pay or job opportunities, although these are obviously important.

As you will have seen, there are two main ways of looking at the issue of female versus male offending—the chivalry hypothesis and the idea of double deviancy. Developments in gender studies (the study of gender as a whole, covering issues relating to men, women, gay men, lesbian women, and so on, as opposed to research that is solely concerned with matters relevant to heterosexual women) have, since the 1990s, pushed this on a bit. This more culturally informed work by authors such as Connell (1995) (also see Tomsen and Messerschmidt (2011) for a good discussion of these issues) which is being done in this area has fixed its gaze firmly on some of the potential links between our gender and our gendered identities and crime. By gendered identity, of course, I mean the way that we think of ourselves in terms of being a woman/man/transgender or whatever, rather than any other aspect of our life. This aspect of our identity is obviously affected by our ideas of masculinity (what it is, and means to be, male) and femininity (the same questions about being female). Indeed, these newer pieces of research have perhaps posed more searching questions about some of the possible reasons why men commit more (and different types) of crime. What does all of this really mean? Let's take a step back for a moment and consider the issues as raised in **What do you think? 15.8**.

The authors working and writing in this area are now talking about masculinities (and femininities) in the plural form. Whilst they recognise that there is variation amongst and between men, they talk of there being a *hegemonic* form of masculinity (as well as there being *subordinate* and *marginalised* ones). What this basically means is that there is a particular form of masculinity which is exalted and dominant—hegemonic—which is held to be of a higher value in some societies by some people. In some ways, the main traits which are thought to make up this form of masculinity are not far away from things such as being competitive, tough, powerful, competent, and so on. So how does all of this connect with the 'gender gap' and the higher crime rates for men?

What is being argued here is both interesting and suggestive. The basic idea is that some male crime may be the result of some young men simply 'doing gender'; in other words, their crimes are committed as a result of them trying to achieve masculinity in its hegemonic form. For instance, it could be argued that in the case of young men who have been excluded from formal and legitimate pathways of achieving 'success' (through the lack of employment opportunities, for example) they may attempt to assert and re-assert their masculinity and masculine status in criminal ways. A young man, angry and humiliated at being kicked out of school, makes himself feel better by stealing a fast car or getting into a fight; a man who is belittled at work and overlooked for promotion (or not being able to find legitimate employment) may take out his frustrations by beating his wife when he

CONTROVERSY AND DEBATE 15.2

Our attitudes to domestic violence and partner abuse

In 2002 the BBC commissioned a survey on domestic violence, the results of which were published as a report called *Hitting Home*. Below are some of the questions the survey asked 1,020 people aged over 18. Answer the following questions in terms of whether you agree, do not agree, or simply do not know. Be honest, answer what you genuinely think.

1. If you knew someone was kicking and mistreating their dog would you intervene by calling the RSPCA or police?
2. If you knew someone was kicking and mistreating their partner would you intervene by calling the police?
3. Domestic violence is not acceptable except if one partner has been unfaithful.
4. Domestic violence is not acceptable unless one person has nagged the other.
5. Domestic violence is not acceptable under any circumstances.
6. The police should always be called to incidents of domestic violence.

Table 15.2 shows the actual responses to the survey. Read these carefully and make note of anything which surprised or worried you.

Were you, for instance, shocked that more people (78 per cent) would report the mistreatment of a dog over that of a human being (53 per cent) or that nearly three out of 10 people thought that it was acceptable to violate their partner if they had been unfaithful with slightly more women thinking that this would be okay? What about the fact that nearly two thirds of people think that partner abuse should be dealt with as a 'private matter' and should not be a concern for the police and the criminal justice system? Finally, what does all of this tell us about the general attitudes to these important issues? Why do you think that this is the case?

Question	1			2			3			4			5			6		
	All	Men	Women	A	M	W	A	M	W	A	M	W	A	M	W	A	M	W
Yes	78%	74%	81%	53	53	53	30	30	31	27	28	25	60	57	63	29	26	32
No	8%	9%	6%	18	20	17	64	62	65	67	68	69	24	27	22	62	64	60
Don't know	5%	17%	12%	29	27	30	6	8	4	7	8	5	16	16	15	8	9	7

Table 15.2 Responses to BBC 'Hitting Home' survey

gets home. Crude examples as these may be, they illustrate the social and psychological processes going on; the release of rage and fear through an action which usually involves adrenaline, danger, or risk.

It is also helpful at this point to consider the way that these men may have learned what a real man is or does from their father, who is usually the dominant male role model in a young boy's life. Did they suffer repeated male abandonment as their mother had multiple failed relationships? Was their father himself a violent, angry man? If he was absent, did they find a substitute figure in a gang leader? What views of maleness are they passing on to their own sons? And why do we so rarely ask similar questions about mothers and women?

Similarly, recent work on young people's identity (both male and female) focuses on the so-called night-time economy and how for many of them a good night out on a Friday and Saturday often involves the importance of consumerism—wearing the right clothes, being out with the right people, drinking the right drinks in the right bar. The pre-loading and constant uploading of alcohol, part of our cultural acceptance of binge drinking, is a good example of gender identities which have changed over time; if you look back even 20 years, there was very little public female drunkenness; previously, getting drunk was very much a man's pastime, which could often end up with violence, a visit to an accident and emergency department of a hospital, or a night at the local police station. Following on from this, can you also think of any potential connections between hegemonic masculinities and the rise of racial and homophobic hate crime?

WHAT DO YOU THINK? 15.8

What does it mean to be a 'real man'?

- Consider your own responses to this question (whether you are male or female) and jot down your honest responses.

- When you have done this reflect on these and consider where your ideas and thoughts have come from. How are accepted 'masculine' (and 'feminine') traits defined by societies and cultures?

This is a question students are asked and whilst their responses do of course vary, every year some clear themes emerge and remain constant. Often young men will talk about the pressures they feel to look a certain way, not to show any signs of perceived 'weakness', to be supremely confident and to compete to achieve their goals in life. On the other hand, many young women will often say that their idea of a 'real' man is someone who is confident, and who 'knows what they want' but they also say that their 'ideal' man (in relationship terms) is someone who will also 'protect' them as well as having a 'sensitive' side.

The point to make here is that all of these traits are not biologically specific but that they are, in many ways, culturally constructed and maintained. In other words, such things are perhaps learnt culturally and that we internalise (accept them as being 'common sense' and rarely question them) in various ways. This happens through the signs and symbols we decode, often being taught their meanings via the media, and the general cultural expectations that are placed on us by our parents, teachers, friends, and so on.

There are other questions we can ask—for example, what in your opinion is the worst thing you can call a young boy in a playground? How could you offend most teenage girls? Why is there still a need for Stonewall (the LGBT organisation) to run campaigns against homophobic bullying?

More interestingly perhaps, it is not just to the 'usual suspects'—young men—that the concept of hegemonic masculinity can be applied. There are also potential links to the crimes of powerful groups—usually made up of white, wealthy, and middle-aged men. The ideas of real maleness are reflected in the ways we think of leadership and power. Go back to your answers to the 'what is a real man' questions and see how many of your answers can also be used to describe the traits which are thought to make a good business leader or captain of industry. In the award-winning documentary on Enron (2007: Dir. Gibney) we see how a particular corporate culture of hyper-masculinity flourished. The traits of aggressiveness, risk-taking, competitiveness, ruthlessness, playing hard, winning at any cost and so on, which were encouraged in the organisation, may have been at least partially responsible for fostering a climate in which fraud came to be seen as just another way of achieving business goals—success through an increased profit margin and so on. Enron's fraudulent activities eventually left many of its investors and employees penniless through what has been referred to as the corporate crime of the century; hundreds of people with no income, savings, or pensions as a result of one company's actions. You might also want to think about how, especially at election times, our (mainly) male party leaders will talk tough and try to out-tough each other with their macho posturing; for a few days

following the 2015 election in the UK all the major parties except one were led by women, but this fact received little media attention. Could this be because we still see politics as a male activity even though the UK now has its second female prime minister?

As we can see, there is much potential for the development of these ideas in terms of thinking about both crimes of the powerless and the powerful. Next time you read about large-scale corruption, tax evasion, riots, benefit fraud, and so on, try thinking about it as an indicator of power and the way it is used.

Despite the various general criticisms that can be made of feminist perspectives, this section has highlighted that, taken as a whole, they have contributed much to our understanding of crime and its control. They have also, more importantly, led to very real changes in some of the ways in which the criminal justice system (CJS) responds to female offenders and victims, and led to widespread calls for greater gender equality within the whole system. For instance, police forces now have dedicated domestic violence units; victims of rape are now allocated to a Sexual Offences Investigative Techniques (SOIT) Officer; there are now 'havens' (Sexual Assault Referral Centres which ensure that victims of rape and sexual assault get the help they need in a safe and supportive environment) and so on. These are all very real and important changes—it is sobering to think that such things certainly did not exist in the 1970s when Carol Smart was penning her critique of 'malestream' criminology. As we have also seen, however, there is still a very long way to go with regard to the ways in which female offenders and victims are treated by the CJS. Feminist, and feminist inspired, criminologies will undoubtedly continue to be a crucial strand of critical thinking and will be at the forefront of informing policy debate to result in change and the struggle for justice.

Conclusion

In this chapter we have explored some of the foundations of critical criminology in the form of labelling perspectives, the 'new' criminology, and feminist perspectives. It could be said that these were a powerful agenda for a criminology which was politically engaged and which sought to change the world and to challenge forms of injustice. Although it is not perhaps the dominant paradigm within criminology today, it retains a vital presence in today's criminological landscape. Despite the drift towards a narrow and empirically based 'crime science' and the recent revivals of classicist ideas (see **Chapter 12** on this) many would argue that the need for critical criminological perspectives is crucial to understanding today's rapidly changing, globalising, and fragmented world. To be sure, we have witnessed enormous and far-reaching social, economic, and political changes since the times in which the likes of Becker, Taylor, Walton, Young, and Smart were writing. For many, critical criminologies remain an important part of the criminological imagination, if for no other reason than they broaden our horizons to include acts and behaviours which are not normally regarded as being crime and, to echo Becker's rallying cry in the 1960s, encourage us to stand up and to advocate on behalf of the 'underdog'. The precise nature of these social changes and how critical criminologists have responded to them will be the focus of **Chapter 16**.

SUMMARY

- Appreciate the philosophical and political arguments that underpin critical criminologies

The chapter examined the way that critical criminologies challenge the more traditional, positivist and classicist approaches to the study of crime. It considers the critical view that differences in lifestyle, background, and social inequalities affect reactions to crime and its control, as well as placing the origin of the critical movement within the context of the social and political upheavals of the 1960s.

- Understand the different strands within critical criminology, and their development within a cultural and historical context

We have seen how critical criminology is a multi-faceted approach which embraces a wide range of issues and arguments (more of which will be covered and developed in **Chapter 16**). This chapter described some of the major ideas that concern the critical criminologist, in particular its discussion of how different groups have different experiences, needs, and reactions when it comes to the issue of crime and social control, and how there needs to be an appreciation of those differences to ensure equality and fairness within the criminal justice system and society. Key areas examined are feminism, the changing views of masculinity, and the notion of deviance.

- Relate theoretical ideas to the real world, and appreciate the flaws and strengths within the various approaches we shall cover

The chapter has asked you to consider various aspects of theory and to analyse how these are experienced in your own personal context. The chapter introduced the concept of 'labelling' and discussed how this basic human behaviour can be used to influence social reactions and expectations, often through the use of media and the positive or negative coverage received by various groups. The reaction of individuals to such labelling has also been discussed, with a focus on how ideas of deviance are formed and amplified by reaction to any breach of the social norms accepted within a particular group of people; the chapter also looked at the ways in which concepts such as feminist criminology have affected public discourse, particularly in the arena of domestic abuse, and the fresh arguments which such new approaches have raised.

- Develop an awareness of how important the ideas of power and power relations are to the study of critical criminology

Power and power relations are key to understanding the critical approach. Critical criminology argues that the underpinning issue for any study of crime is that of power; how it is used, by whom, and how the powerful maintain their position of authority over the powerless.

- Discuss the problems of 'deviance' and its interpretation and control

The chapter looks at the ways in which deviancy is ascribed to certain people and certain acts more than others, and the way that people who are thus 'labelled' may react by amplifying that deviance within their own psychological framework. The chapter looked at how power is a key function in the criminological perspectives examined, such as the impact of patriarchal power on women and children, and how the use of power (for example by the police) can be interpreted and experienced by different groups.

REVIEW QUESTIONS

1. What are the four defining ideas of positivist perspectives and how are critical criminologies critical of them?

2. To what extent can it be argued that the 'rich get richer and the poor get prison'? Why might this be the case?

3. In what ways can labelling someone be said to have a transformational effect on their self-identities?

4. Critically apply Taylor et al.'s (1973) notion of a 'fully social theory' of crime and deviance to a real world example of criminality.

5. Define the concepts of double deviancy and hegemonic masculinities and apply them critically to the study of gender and crime.

6. Should the police respond to domestic and intimate violence? What does the evidence on the number of people who think that such violence can be justified tell us about social attitudes to gender relations?

7. Give two examples of crimes of the powerful. Why should criminologists study these?

FURTHER READING

Ugwudike, P. (2015) *An Introduction to Critical Criminology*. Bristol: Policy Press.
This book offers a clearly written introductory account of both the foundations and contemporary theoretical positions of critical criminology.

DeKeseredy, W.S. and Dragiewicz, M. (eds) (2011) *The Routledge Handbook of Critical Criminology*. London: Routledge.

A good, although more advanced, collection of original essays which cover a range of critical perspectives and contemporary issues at both national and international levels.

Becker, H. (1997) *Outsiders; Studies in the Sociology of Deviance*. New York: Simon and Schuster.

Taylor, I., Walton, P., and Young, J. (2013) *The New Criminology: For a Social Theory of Deviance* (40th Anniversary Edition). London: Routledge.

Smart, C. (2014) *Women and Crime; A Feminist Critique*. London: Routledge.

There is no substitute for reading original classic texts in the raw. The preceding three titles are all therefore recommended.

 Access the **online resources** to view selected further reading and web links relevant to the material covered in this chapter.
www.oup.com/uk/case/

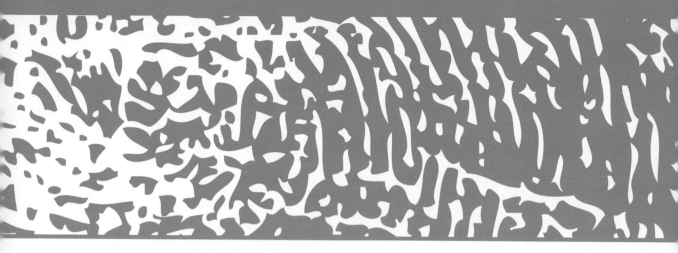

CHAPTER OUTLINE

Introduction   446

A new era and a new 'ology': Enter the zemiologists   450

The greening of critical criminology?   454

Cultural criminology: Deviant subcultures, emotions,
and the carnival of crime   460

Convict criminology   468

Conclusion   473

Critical criminology—part 2

New and future directions

KEY ISSUES

After studying this chapter, you should be able to:

- discuss some of the recent social, political, and economic changes that have occurred as we move into the 21st century, and appreciate how critical criminology has responded to these;

- show an understanding of the four key strands of critical criminology today (zemiology, green criminology, cultural criminology, and convict criminology) and explain what their common features are;

- develop an awareness of what it means to say that critical criminology is a 'political project';

- critically assess the argument put forward by zemiologists that the main weakness and limitation of traditional criminology is that it focuses too much on notions of 'crime' rather than of 'social harm';

- develop an understanding of basic economic concepts and ideas, and how these fit into the world of critical green criminology when studying crimes of the (economically) powerful;

- discuss how and why the features of subcultures and emotions are important to cultural criminologists;

- evaluate the claim made by convict criminologists that the prisoner voice should be a central one when considering prison reform and change.

Introduction

Since the 1960s and 1970s, when the critical perspectives we discussed in **Chapter 15** were first coming into criminological fashion, there have undoubtedly been enormous social, economic, and political changes. In trying to understand these changes, social and criminological theorists have characterised them in a variety of ways. For some, such as the British criminologist Jock Young (1999; 2007), the period from the last two decades of the 20th century to date has witnessed the transformation of society from being a period of *modernity* to one of *late modernity*. This new epoch, he argues, has heralded a period of greater uncertainty and insecurity in all areas of life for many people. According to him, most advanced western societies, and in particular the UK, have witnessed a shift from there being a stable, *inclusive*, and caring society to a more precarious, *exclusive*, and less forgiving one. For instance, the post war settlement of 1945 was very much a social democratic one, based on the values of equality of opportunity, fairness, and welfare. Social problems, whether these were in education, housing, or health—as well as crime—were seen to be the responsibility of the government and the state. It was thought that the political process could help to ameliorate (that is, reduce) inequalities through social and economic policies; for instance, welfare and taxation policies.

In terms of crime control this period between 1945 until the late 1970s is often regarded as representing the high point of welfarism and rehabilitation; this is characterised by a criminal justice system focused on the 'needs' as opposed to the 'deeds' of offenders, and one which attempted to rehabilitate criminals and return them to society rather than simply locking them up in prisons. This caring and restorative approach was to change in the late 1970s, when economic ideas of neo-liberalist political ideologies took hold. The precise details of such political changes should not worry us too much here but, suffice to say, politicians and some academics were starting to argue that there was 'no such thing as society' and that individuals should take more responsibility for themselves in terms of providing for their welfare (instead of relying on the state). In terms of crime and its control, the commitment to rehabilitation declined as prison populations started to increase (you will read more about all of this in **Chapters 24** and **25**).

It has also been argued that the world is becoming increasingly globalised (basically more interconnected) and that this, in turn, poses new risks and dangers for us all. Living has always posed risks to human beings—but perhaps these risks have changed in recent times and we are possibly more aware of them. If we think of something as seemingly uncontrollable as a 'natural' disaster, for instance, we learn about it within minutes of it happening and we watch it unfold on our screens; we know more about the threat because we've seen the tidal wave or the lava flow and we see the faces of those who suffer the impact, and hear them speak about the dreadful thing that has happened to them. We get a sense of our own fragility and vulnerability, and probably think how lucky we are to live in a country where on the whole we can be sure we won't be crushed or burned or washed away. But earthquakes and tornadoes have always happened—the difference today is that we find out sooner and can (sometimes) send help faster. Imagine a world in which thousands could die and suffer, but nobody in the outside world knew a thing about it until it was too late … Now take that idea and instead of famine, think of murders and riots; how much more secure did people feel when they only learned of crimes long after the event?

Regardless of the label we choose to pin on all this talk of social change (whether this be late modernity, postmodernity, an information society, a post-industrial society, a neo-liberal one, etc.), the basic point to make here is that the very nature of crime and its control has been changing too. For instance, there are new forms of crime developing, such as cybercrimes, environmental crimes, people trafficking, the 'war on drugs', and the 'war on terror', etc. Not only has there been this shift in types of crime, but new forms of control are emerging too, like increasing prison sentences and sending more people to prison for more offences. We are also using new technologies of surveillance like CCTV, number plate recognition cameras (see **Figure 16.1**), forms of bio-recognition at airports, and Internet 'dataveillance'.

Figure 16.1 West Midlands Police stopping vehicles using the automated number plate recognition technology, which allows them to stop vehicles flagged as wanted or uninsured

Source: West Midlands Police/CC BY-SA 2.0

As you can imagine, critical criminology has taken a lot of notice of such changes, and this chapter will briefly consider some of the ways in which it has responded. In particular, we will look at the ways in which the critical ideas which were first developed by Becker and his colleagues at the University of Chicago in the 1960s, and Jock Young and others at the University of York in the 1970s, have been developed and adapted by today's critical criminologists who are trying to understand and change the world in the 21st century. Against the backdrop of the rise of realist criminologies (see **Chapter 17** for a discussion of these) and the rise of *crime science*, changing global crime problems and increasing global inequalities, it could indeed be argued that the need for a critical criminology is as important today as it was 50 years ago, if not more so. So, how has the new generation of critical criminologists responded to all of this change?

In this chapter we will concentrate on four main recent developments in critical criminology. These are;

- Zemiology—the study of social harm.
- Cultural criminology—which re-focuses the critical criminological imagination on the emotional and carnivalesque aspects of crime and control.
- Green criminology—which focuses on environmental crime as a growing crime problem committed by powerful groups.
- Convict criminology—which develops ideas of how knowledge is produced and how the marginalised voices of prisoners are silenced and muted in both criminological and policy debates.

But first, let us return to the idea which was highlighted in **Chapter 15**; that all forms of critical criminology are part of a broader political project which seeks to engage with real issues and real people to challenge forms of injustice and to bring about social change.

Critical criminology as a political project

As we saw in **Chapter 15**, critical criminology has always claimed to be a political project; that is, one which is fully engaged with existing inequalities, which seeks to work with 'marginalised' groups to challenge dominant discourses and ideas, and aims to bring about social changes which would lead to greater social justice. Indeed, critical criminologists have worked with organisations such as Inquest (which studies deaths in police and prisons custody) and Radical Alternatives to Prison (RAP) which does precisely what it claims to do in terms of challenging the very existence of prisons and the infliction of pain through forms of punishment (see **Chapter 27** for further discussions on critical perspectives on punishment).

In **Conversations 16.1** we hear from Professor Phil Scraton who, perhaps more than any other European critical criminologist, has carried out research *with* marginalised and silenced groups, challenging state legitimated 'official accounts' and mainstream discourses. Through his work he seeks to bring powerful groups to account, and to achieve recognition and redress for relatively powerless groups.

On 15 April 1989, following catastrophic failures in policing and ground safety at an FA Cup semi-final soccer match in Sheffield, England, 96 men, women, and children died and over 400 were physically injured (see **Figure 16.2**). Many who survived suffered lasting psychological and

---

CONVERSATIONS 16.1

The Hillsborough tragedy and the view from below: speak truth to power—with Professor Phil Scraton

A football fan all my life, I knew what it was like to be crushed on terraces. It never seemed threatening, just thrilling and literally breath-taking. As Liverpool's great soccer team played yet another memorable match at Anfield, we experienced the intrinsic excitement of the Kop's ebb and flow. Compression only lasted seconds, followed by release. Then everyone would shake themselves down, fill lungs, sing loudly, and anticipate the next crowd surge. Occasionally someone would faint and be passed over our heads to the waiting St John's Ambulance volunteers, then along the perimeter track to be wheeled away on a stretcher-cum-trolley. After tragedies at Maine

Road, Manchester and Ibrox Park, Glasgow, we shared the assumption that however uncomfortable, the wide and high standing terraces would be populated within agreed capacity limits, and that regular safety inspections would be carried out by the local authority whose certification established compliance with legislation. Of course, accidents would happen, people would sprain ankles, suffer heart attacks and so on, but it was taken for granted that crowd safety would never be compromised.

Then, on a spring day in April 1989, the warm sun encouraging a carnival atmosphere for the FA Cup

Figure 16.2 Liverpool Memorial to fans who died at Hillsborough, Liverpool Football Ground Anfield Liverpool
Source: Edmund Gall (Flickr)/CC BY-SA 2.0

Semi-Final between Liverpool and Nottingham Forest hosted at Sheffield's neutral Hillsborough stadium, disaster struck. Unlike Anfield, the decrepit terracing at the Leppings Lane end of the stadium, allocated to Liverpool fans, comprised a series of pens, a wall at the rear, high fences to the sides and an overhanging fence at the front to prevent access to the pitch. The two central pens, immediately behind the goal, were fed by a 1 in 6 gradient tunnel beneath a high grandstand. Once in the pens it was virtually impossible to retreat as fans, having entered an inner concourse from the turnstiles, walked down the tunnel directly opposite. For those unfamiliar with the stadium and with an absence of crowd stewards, the tunnel offered the obvious access to the terraces.

As kick-off approached, the crowd became dense and tightly confined outside the 23 turnstiles expected to admit 26,000 people. In the Police Control Box high above the terrace, witnessing on monitors the build-up outside the turnstiles and hearing pleas from a senior officer attempting to marshal the crowd, the police match commander ordered exit gates to be opened to relieve the crush. Thousands entered the ground via exit Gate C and, without direction, headed down the tunnel into the backs of already full pens. With pens full well beyond official capacity the match began. Compression intensified, offering no possibility of relief in any direction. Under pressure, a safety barrier collapsed. People were trapped, dying in front of the world's media.

On the perimeter track, rescuers tried to gain access to the pile of bodies through a single narrow gate into each pen. As the enormity of the disaster dawned, in the police control box the South Yorkshire Police match commander told the Football Association's president that Liverpool fans had arrived late, forced exit gates and rushed the tunnel. Within hours his lie was discredited but already it had set a hostile agenda. In the immediate aftermath 95 men, women and children had died, over 400 were injured and thousands traumatised. The dominant narrative was that Liverpool fans were responsible. *The Sun*, along with seven other newspapers, under a banner headline 'THE TRUTH' published allegations that fans had arrived late, many drunk and without tickets, stolen from the dead, sexually abused a dying young woman, and urinated on police officers. These unsubstantiated allegations became the bedrock on which was built a sustained campaign to place responsibility for the disaster on fans. Provoked by journalists, politicians, and some academics, the obsessive popular discourse on 'hooliganism' diverted attention from the institutional deficiencies in ground safety and complacent policing.

Four months later, Lord Justice Taylor, appointed by the Home Secretary to hold a judicial inquiry, published an interim report specifically addressing 'urgent questions of safety, especially at football grounds'. He found overcrowding in the central pens to be the 'main cause' of the deaths and injuries, the 'main reason' being a profound failure in police control. Alongside egregious deficiencies in police leadership and decision making, particularly singling out the match commander CS David Duckenfield, Taylor criticised Sheffield Wednesday Football Club (the stadium owners), their safety engineers, and the local authority. Without explanation, his final report made little mention of Hillsborough, diverting focus towards the spectre of soccer-related violence. A year later the Director of Public Prosecutions concluded there was no evidence to justify criminal proceedings against the stadium owners, the safety engineers, the local authority, or the South Yorkshire Police. There was 'insufficient evidence' to pursue individuals, including senior police officers.

Following these decisions, the longest inquests in legal history became an adversarial battleground as police officers and other witnesses vilified fans, reviving graphic allegations of drunkenness, violence, late arrival, and ticketlessness. The strategy worked and the jury's majority verdict of accidental death was received and reported as vindication of the police and all other organisations involved. The bereaved and survivors were devastated. In 1997, under pressure from Hillsborough families, the newly-elected Labour government's Home Secretary, Jack Straw, appointed former MI6 Commissioner LJ Stuart-Smith to review 'new evidence' that might lead to prosecutions or disciplinary proceedings. Having consulted the Hillsborough archive, visited key organisations, and taken my evidence and that of 34 families, that he concluded that no new evidence of substance had emerged and he rejected claims that evidence had been suppressed or falsified. Assessing the conduct of the inquests as exemplary, his 1998 report found no basis for further public inquiry. He dismissed my proposal for the quashing of the inquest verdicts and my call for new hearings. Two years later, after a seven week private prosecution of the match commander and his assistant for manslaughter, the jury found the latter not guilty and were unable to reach a verdict on the former.

Over 30,000 people attended the 20th anniversary gathering at Anfield, Liverpool's stadium. Andy Burnham, the government's Minister for Health praised the families and survivors for their 'remarkable courage' in the face of what was a 'major injustice'. He committed to full disclosure of all documents generated by the previous inquiries and inquests, thus abandoning the 30 years' restriction on disclosure. Against the odds, and requiring a modification in legislation, it happened. In early 2010 the Hillsborough Independent Panel was appointed. I headed its research team. Responding to the guiding principle of 'maximum public disclosure', over 80 organisations submitted documents. On 12 September 2012, in closed session, the Panel presented the 395 page report to the bereaved families. Its 12 chapters detailed 153 findings. The conclusions were unambiguous: crowd safety had been compromised by institutional complacency and neglectful custom and practice; the Leppings Lane access and egress, outside and inside the stadium, were inherently unsafe; the stadium failed comprehensively to meet minimum safety requirements; the prevailing mind-set shared by the South Yorkshire Police and the Club prioritised crowd regulation over crowd safety; there was a failure by the Ambulance Service to recognise the crisis in the pens; the pathologies had been rushed and insubstantial; in conception, process, and outcome the inquests and their verdicts were profoundly

flawed; senior police officers had orchestrated negative media coverage in the immediate aftermath; the review and alteration of statements, first revealed in my 1999 book, had corrupted police evidence; and no evidence existed 'to verify the serious allegations of exceptional levels of drunkenness, ticketlessness or violence among Liverpool fans'.

Within an hour of my two-hour presentation of the Panel's report to the families, the Prime Minister, David Cameron, addressed a packed House of Commons. On behalf of the coalition government, he delivered an emotional 'double apology' to families, 'for all they have suffered over the past 23 years'. First, the 'injustice of the appalling events—the failure of the state to protect their loved ones and the indefensible wait to get to the truth'. Second, 'the injustice of the denigration of the deceased—that somehow they were at fault for their own deaths'. Echoing her leader's comments, Home Secretary Theresa May stated her intention to act on the Panel's 'comprehensive ... shocking and disturbing' findings to ensure progress 'from truth to justice'. Consequently, the Crown Prosecution Service established a major criminal investigation led by a retired Chief Constable and staffed by 100-plus police officers. In response to the Panel's revelations of 'extremely serious and troubling issues for the police' the Independent Police Complaints Commission embarked on an investigation into police misconduct unprecedented in size and scope. A full review of all disaster emergency response procedures was ordered by the Secretary of State for Health, focusing on ambulance services, hospital preparedness, and medical pathology. Finally, and most significantly for the bereaved families, the High Court quashed the accidental death verdicts. It concluded that 'the interests of justice' could be served only through an 'order for a new inquest' that would shine a 'light' on the 'truth'. Through this process 'the families of those who died in the disaster will be vindicated and the memory of each victim will be properly respected'.

Between April 2013 and February 2014 the coroner, a High Court judge, held preliminary hearings, receiving submissions from the legal teams representing organisations and individuals designated 'interested parties': the bereaved; South Yorkshire's police chief constable; Police Federation; three sets of retired senior police officers; Sheffield Wednesday Football Club; Sheffield City Council; Yorkshire Ambulance Service; St John Ambulance; Yorkshire Fire and Rescue Service; Sheffield Teaching Hospitals Trust; Football Association; West Midlands police; and the Independent Police Complaints Commission. On 31 March 2014 the new inquests opened before an 11 person jury. The ground-floor of an office block, located on a modern industrial estate near Warrington, was transformed into a coroner's court. At the preliminary hearings several counsel representing police interests were clear that, although the behaviour of the 96 who died was beyond reproach, they would resurrect the allegations discredited by the Panel: that fans arrived ticketless and late, drank excessively, their behaviour uncontrollable. While the Coroner stated that the inquests should not degenerate into an 'adversarial battle', the battle-lines had been drawn. The most significant focuses of the inquests were stadium safety, pre-match planning, policing and police response to the disaster, emergency response, and the pathologies of the 96.

On 5 January 2016, Day 279 of the longest inquests in legal history, the evidence was completed. Twenty days later the Coroner began his summing-up. He told the jury that only one short-form verdict was appropriate—unlawfully killed. Whether or not they delivered that verdict, he instructed them to provide a narrative statement covering ten key issues. Controversially, the issue of fans' behaviour was back on the agenda. The bereaved and survivors were shocked. Police officers

who, unbeknown to the jury, were facing potential criminal prosecution, had given evidence criticising fans' behaviour. Before the inquests began I had stated my reservations about progressing inquests ahead of criminal prosecutions and police disciplinary proceedings. It is why inquests always are held after all other legal proceedings have been pursued: known as the 'exhaustion of domestic remedies'. Yet, on 26 April 2016, the jury returned a majority verdict that all who died had been unlawfully killed. Its unanimous narrative levelled 25 serious criticisms against those in authority; primarily the South Yorkshire Police and its commanding officers, but also the Ambulance Service, the stadium owners, the safety engineers and Sheffield City Council. The jury exonerated the fans from all culpability and responsibility for the disaster. Twenty-five years on from the initial inquests, verdicts of accidental death were expunged and the families' and survivors' campaigns vindicated.

Professor Phil Scraton, Professor of Criminology in the Institute of Criminology and Criminal Justice, Queen's University, Belfast

emotional harm. Twenty-five years on, as a member of the Independent Panel, Phil Scraton headed its research and was principal author of its in-depth report into the context, circumstances, and aftermath of the disaster. This research led to new inquests, a full criminal investigation, and disciplinary review of policing by the Independent

Police Complaints Authority. Here he talks about his long-term commitment to uncovering the 'truth' about the Hillsborough disaster and working with the bereaved and survivors to ensure legitimacy for the 'view from below'; reflecting his commitment to revelatory social research and critical analysis in 'speaking truth to power'.

A new era and a new 'ology': Enter the zemiologists

At the turn of this century a group of critical criminologists got together to discuss and re-assess where critical criminology was at and where it was going (you can read more about this in Hillyard et al. 2004). In revisiting some of the familiar themes which we have already talked about in **Chapter 15**—such as the social and ideological construction of crime, the ability of the powerful to avoid criminalisation whilst criminalising the behaviour of the relatively powerless and so on—they offered what could be called a radical critique of critical criminology. The rise of right and left realist criminologists in the 1980s (as you will see in **Chapter 17**) had side-lined much critical thought, and in a sense, the return to the main guiding issues of the critical criminology project was, in many ways, for them, a return to confront unfinished business.

At the centre of this critical group's arguments was the fundamental one that criminology itself needed to move beyond narrow and partial conceptions of 'crime' and to consider things which can cause great *social harm*. In other words, they were interested in the behaviours of groups and individuals, whether active or passive, which can kill and maim people. They pointed out that such actions and inactions are not ordinarily thought of as being 'crime' and in fact are rarely covered by the criminal law at all. Such issues would include things such as pollution, poverty, disease, miscarriages of justice, and the hundreds of deaths every year which are a direct result of the violation of health and safety legislation in the workplace. This is not an exhaustive list but, as you can see, this approach can cover a very broad range of issues. Such events and happenings are often defined as being 'accidents' or 'disasters' through the media and these come to inform the public imagination and political and legal responses to them. As such, these forms of harming behaviours are not thought of as being 'crime' at all.

This approach was given the rather confusing name of zemiology. The term is derived from the Greek word Zemia, which means harm. So zemiology is basically the study of harms (rather than 'crime').

In their important contribution to this debate, Hillyard and Tombs (2004: 10–18) list nine critical themes which they argue need to be re-addressed by critical scholars in our changing worlds. Let us quickly look at these before we discuss them further. They are that:

1. 'Crime' has no ontological reality.
2. Criminology perpetuates the myth of 'crime'.
3. 'Crime' consists of many petty events.
4. 'Crime' excludes many serious harms.
5. Constructing crimes through the criminal law is myopic (that is, short-sighted).
6. Criminalisation and punishment inflict pain.
7. 'Crime' control is ineffective.
8. 'Crime' gives legitimacy to the expansion of crime control.
9. 'Crime' serves to maintain power relations.

Many of these ideas were covered in **Chapter 15**, even if they were expressed in slightly different ways. To briefly re-cap and bring these nine critical themes together, the first thing to note is that these authors place the word 'crime' in inverted commas; this suggests that they regard the very concept of 'crime' itself as being problematic and one which should be replaced because it has no objective 'reality'. As we have seen, the 'problem of crime' is perhaps as much one of definition rather than one of behaviour per se (see **Chapter 3**). For instance, at the beginning of **Chapter 15** when we discussed labelling perspectives we noted that there is a sense in which 'crime' as a concept is socially constructed through various social processes; that certain behaviours, in certain periods of time, can be criminalised and de-criminalised and so on. Crime is not therefore a self-evident and unchanging concept. By failing to recognise the contested nature of 'crime', much criminology accepts how the state defines it and so effectively also accepts the relations of power involved in defining it. In doing so it is argued that much (mainstream) criminology perpetuates the idea that we all know and agree on what crime actually is. This in turn leads to focusing more on everyday 'crime' where the perpetrators are, more likely than not, drawn from those less powerful groups in society.

The next point which Hillyard and Tombs (2004) make is that much 'crime' is often not of a serious nature. How we define 'seriousness' is far from being straightforward, but the point being made here is that much of the volume crime (that is the majority of everyday crimes such as theft and damage to property, as recorded by the police), which daily passes through the criminal courts, is of a relatively petty nature when compared with the harms caused by large corporations to millions of victims through, for instance, promoting tobacco and formula baby milk to people in the developing world.

In case you are wondering why selling baby milk can be considered criminal, you might want to look at the history of companies who promote it in poor and developing countries. Corporations have a history of aggressive marketing to people with little or no education, using tactics like dressing sales representatives as nurses to give the impression that sophisticated western medicine recommended the powdered formula over breast milk. This was despite the fact that mothers in these countries could not afford the formula, and were unlikely to have clean water with which to make the milk or sterilise bottles. In 2007, the charity Save the Children estimated that in Bangladesh, one of the poorest countries in the world, the baby milk and baby food import market was worth a staggering £16 million. The situation became so grave that in 1981 an international code of practice for the marketing of formula milk was ratified by the World Health Organisation (WHO); in 2010, WHO published research stating that if all babies were breastfed for their first six months, 1.5 million lives would be saved. If you look at a website for any brand of formula milk you'll see pictures of happy (and usually white) babies contentedly breast feeding … but how is that message getting across to women and families in the poorest parts of the world? Indeed, is it? If 1.5 million babies could be saved, does that mean that by promoting bottle milk, corporations are in fact contributing to 1.5 million infant deaths? Should this be regarded as being criminal and should these companies be punished for their actions and inactions?

In terms of the criminal justice system, zemiologists argue that overall it is ineffective (you will get a chance later in the book to consider the so-called functions of the police and prisons, so you can make up your own minds on these issues then). The effects of labelling, the expansion of prison populations, growing police powers, and all the other ideas which we looked at earlier, are relevant here too. The last point is also a very important one, as it reiterates the fundamental issue for critical criminologists concerning the exercise of power and its impact on the powerless. In other words, 'crime' is a concept which is constructed by powerful groups to maintain their positions of power and privilege.

As we all know by now, none of these themes are particularly new to critical criminologists. By bringing them together when they did, however, Hillyard and Tombs (2004) certainly helped to reinvigorate the debate amongst critical criminologists who were grappling to understand new and emerging crimes and crime control problems, and to raise these with the generation of critical criminologists who had inspired them in the previous decades. It has been said that the very concept of harm is a broad one which lacks precision, and this will indeed be an ongoing debate for critical criminologists. One thing that zemiology has certainly done has been to help us refocus on these issues, especially when studying the wide range of crimes (or harms) which are committed by powerful groups.

Let us put some flesh on these dry theoretical bones. In **Conversations 16.2** Professor Steve Tombs discusses the zemiological agenda and his own research on the harms caused by 'safety crimes'.

We usually think of 'health and safety' as boring, a world full of pedantic people banning playground games—it's a rare day when a tabloid newspaper doesn't have a story

---

CONVERSATIONS 16.2

The Bhopal 'disaster'—with Professor Steve Tombs on studying safety crime

On the night of Sunday, 2 December 1984, in Bhopal, India, a chemical plant operated by the US multinational Union Carbide Corporation (UCC) spewed out a cocktail of poisonous gases, vapours, and liquids [see **Figure 16.3**]. This toxic cloud included up to 40 tonnes of the deadly chemical methyl isocyanate, and it spread rapidly across the city. Quickly termed 'the world's worst industrial disaster', tens of thousands of people died, and are still dying, as a result of the gas leak. Many more have had their lives ruined by chronic ill-health effects, and the deadly legacy of environmental damage remains—the site, now owned by Dow Chemical, has yet to be cleaned up.

Figure 16.3 5 December 1984, two men carry to hospital children blinded by the Union Carbide chemical pesticide leak in Bhopal, India

Source: AP Photo/Sondeep Shankar

At that time, in 1984, I was a postgraduate student of Marxist political theory—indeed, I confess that I had not then, and have not to this day, ever been taught or studied criminology. Also at the time of the Bhopal gas leak, I was politically active in Wolverhampton, a town where the Indian Workers' Association was an important organisation in the local labour movement, which meant that the mass killings at Bhopal had a peculiar local resonance. Two images in particular affected me: the rows upon rows of dead bodies, and the Chief Executive Officer of Union Carbide, Warren Anderson, being whisked out of Bhopal and back to Florida on a private jet, never to return, regardless of there being a warrant out for his arrest (which stood until his death in 2014). These two sights stirred my political and then academic interest, to say the least. And as the facts of the explosion and gas leak began to be revealed—the plant was being deliberately run down as it had ceased to be profitable, with all its safety systems in disrepair and basic maintenance virtually non-existent—it did not make sense to me that this was being termed an 'accident' or 'disaster'. It was instead, it seemed to me, many things—a reflection that Indian lives did not matter as much as western ones; an effect of power and privilege; and a manifestation of the socially harmful effects of multinational capital. But it was also a crime, literally, in the sense that basic health, safety, and environmental protection laws had been violated.

Five years later, whilst I was working on a PhD researching the regulation of the multinational chemical industry, an out-of-court settlement was reached between UCC and the Indian Government, which included a bar on any subsequent legal action. The compensation—$470million—would not reach most victims, and where it did, it would fail for most even to pay for medicines for one year, even for people who would never work again and who would need medication until their premature death. Clearly this settlement, too, was an effect of power, and not a matter of justice. So it was that I began to research and write around issues which are now more commonly termed as 'safety crimes'—violations of law by employers which cause death, injury, or illness as a result of work related activities. These are, I have consistently argued, commonplace, and have devastating physical, psychological, and economic consequences (Tombs and Whyte 2007). Despite this, such crimes remain relatively invisible at the level of political and popular consciousness. Indeed, where events that *may* be represented as safety crimes do emerge in such contexts, they tend not to be represented as such—as with Bhopal, they are likely to be viewed as accidents, disasters, tragedies, and so on. Even less forgivably, safety crime as an area of focus is also obscured by the overwhelming focus of criminological teaching, research, and writing.

More than proposing that occupational death, injury, and illness need to be considered as potential crimes, I have also argued that these are forms of *violence*. Once these phenomena are viewed not as 'accidents' but as incidents which are not only largely preventable, but which the law requires to be prevented, they fall within the ambit of criminology. Then, if we consider these illegalities in terms of their potential or actual consequences—debilitating illness, injury, or death—we realise that they look remarkably similar to the results of those events that most men and women, as well as policy makers, politicians, and academics, deem to be 'proper' violence. However, to reach this conclusion, we have to shed some of the assumptions which still pervade criminology—not least, that violence requires intent, and has an interpersonal quality. More crudely, we need to challenge our common sense understanding of what crime *is*, and who the criminals *are*.

That said, safety crimes, like corporate crimes in general, now have a presence within what counts for academic criminology. Certainly most textbooks, undergraduate courses, and conferences on criminological issues include references to corporate crimes, and this has been, in my view, a positive development *in* the discipline. But it is my belief that research on safety crime, and indeed on corporate crime in general, has an important role to play *for* the discipline of criminology. A focus upon safety and corporate crime requires us to question definitions of crime in law, and to scrutinise critically the activities and priorities of criminal justice systems. *We need to ask why particular laws are enforced and others are not, to question sentencing patterns, and to challenge our understanding of how crime occurs.* In other words, thinking beyond the 'usual suspects' is an exercise in criminological reflexivity.

Professor Steve Tombs, Head of Department (SP&C), Faculty of Arts & Social Sciences, The Open University

---

about 'Health and Safety Gone Mad'. But if we look behind this we can see that Steve raises some very important points in **Conversations 16.2**. For instance, if we take a moment to put the following terms into a search engine and read the results, we will see some clear links to Steve's points:

- Camelford Water Pollution incident, 1988;
- Radium girls;
- Ministry of Defence asbestos;
- Three Mile Island;
- Challenger O Ring.

If we remember that the study of power and power relations is at the heart of criminology, we can start to see how a critical review of the power relations in these situations reveals underlying causes for the violence and harm that resulted in each case. Furthermore, if we take the story that we find the most shocking and surprising, and note down the basic points of what happened—for instance, failure to pass on an important safety warning—we can start to compare the corporate and private environments. We can ask ourselves whether things would happen in the same way in each—for instance, whilst someone in business could be too fearful of their boss or their targets to fill in a report, in the home harm might arise when someone is too drunk or careless to put out a cigarette properly or to take a chip pan off the heat. This then leads to an analysis of our reactions. Are we more shocked by someone who lets their baby drink methadone than we are when a chemical tank is left open? What does this tell us about power relations within systems that allow 'accidents' to happen (and in terms of systems we should include relationships and power relations between people)?

Next time—and sadly, there will undoubtedly be a next time—there is a similar news story, make sure you read or watch the reports with a questioning mind. Remember Steve's point about violence. 'Explosion Disaster at Petrol Station Kills 18' may be the starting point, but as a critical criminologist, start to look below and behind the story to see exactly why this is not just a tragedy for the victims but a crime as well.

The critical study of safety crimes and crimes of the powerful moves us on to consider another developing area of critical criminology; critical green criminology.

The greening of critical criminology?

The natural/physical world and the human/social world are often seen as being discrete and separate from each other. This separation will probably be reflected by your university. You will have distinct academic departments and faculties which teach and research the natural sciences (chemistry, physics, biology, and so on) and the social sciences (criminology, sociology, and so forth). After all, in the western world we are taught from an early age that people are somehow above the animal kingdom; in the Christian tradition, for example, only human beings have souls. Are we however correct to think in terms of such clear distinctions and to think in these ways?

Such ideas have certainly been challenged in recent decades. For instance, the Gaia hypothesis suggests that life-forms interact with, and affect, their environment; old and new religious traditions such as Buddhism and Neo-Paganism highlight the importance of reverence and responsibility towards the natural world. On a more obviously practical level, there is a growing scientific interest in human interactions with nature, an immediate example being the widespread concern and debate about climate change (also referred to as global warming). The idea that the natural and social worlds interact with each other in complex ways, which can impact with disastrous consequences on both, is becoming part of public discourse and argument.

Whilst it is important to bear in mind the various ways in which people affect the natural world (and are affected by it in their turn), this section of the chapter looks at the ways in which society—in the form of human beings—interacts with the so-called natural world through the production and consumption of goods and services. We will be looking at the negative and harmful consequences this can have. This will be our way to examine a critical strand of the new and developing perspective of 'green criminology', which is beginning to have a presence in the contemporary criminology imagination. It is a broad and diverse perspective which is truly interdisciplinary—in other words, it interests people who specialise in a great many subject areas, such as environmental scientists, marine biologists, and some criminologists. In fact, it is so broad that many people prefer to use terms like 'environmental criminology' or 'eco-crime' to demonstrate the range and depth of this aspect of criminological study.

It's tempting, when we start to look at green crimes, to think of them as only concerning the obvious areas of crimes against the environment, like animal cruelty, the disposal of toxic waste, using products which deplete the ozone layer, the destruction of the rain forest, and so on. These are important, as are more modern forms of eco-crime like bio-piracy; this is where traditional knowledge (and flora) from indigenous peoples is taken without their knowledge and/or without payment, perhaps for medical use or for food production. There is profit to be made in this work, because as Time Magazine reported in a 1998 article:

Around a quarter of all prescription drugs sold in the United States are believed to be based on chemicals derived from only 40 plant species. So far, fewer than 1% of the world's 265,000 flowering plants have been tested for their curative powers. And so the bio-sleuths are everywhere.

http://content.time.com/time/world/article/0,8599,2054278,00.html

Not all of what passes as green criminology fits neatly within a critical paradigm, and indeed many criminologists who study ecological issues would not consider themselves as being on what we could call the critical spectrum. However, as this is a chapter on critical criminology, this section will focus on one eco-element which clearly does fall into the critical remit. We will follow on from Steve Tombs's discussion of safety crimes which you read in the last section, to look at how such environmental harms relate to crimes of the powerful. To put it another way, our approach in this chapter to a *critical green criminology* will be to think about how the acts and omissions of *economically powerful* groups can cause misery to both human beings and other animals, as well as to the environments in which we all live. We will also be considering how societies respond to such issues through legislation, and the enforcement of such laws in terms of prosecution and sentencing practices, and we will consider whether these are effective. By the end, you will also be thinking about whether there are viable alternatives to all of this.

The environmental price of living in a market society?

To start with, let us think about where our things come from. Make a list of everything on your desk. Include things like your half-eaten sandwich, the pen you are using, the glass of water, the calculator you're using to work out how many more words you need to write for your next essay, the cardigan you've hung over the back of your chair.

None of these things is likely to be terribly unusual or even terribly expensive. However, it's a fair bet that you didn't actually make any of them from scratch; even if you did put together the sandwich or knit the cardigan, it is highly likely you didn't bake your own bread, churn your own butter, or shear your own sheep. In this respect, our lives in the developed world are unrecognisable compared to those of our ancestors. Only a few generations ago, people either made what they used, or else knew the person (the blacksmith, the weaver, the farmer) who did. But since the industrial revolution in the 18th and 19th centuries, our relationship with how we get the things we need or want has changed immensely.

Nowadays, most of us in the west live in market societies. This means we buy most of the goods and services we use rather than making them ourselves. As an alternative, websites like Freegle and Trash Nothing offer a form of barter, where people get items for free in return for taking them off the hands of owners who don't want them any more. But have you ever wondered how markets actually work? Why do you pay a price for a particular good or service? Why do these prices fluctuate and change and why do different (but essentially the same) goods vary in price? For example, why do we pay more for a particular brand of baked beans than a supermarket's own?

Some of this reflects the ideas we talked about in **Chapter 15** where we touched on the ideas of labels and how they influence our spending. However, from an ecological point of view, we need to think about the impact of markets on the world around us. For a start, before something can be sold, it needs to be made; it needs to be transported, advertised, packaged, its batteries charged, its owner convinced that actually what's really needed is the upgraded version … none of which happens out of thin air. The production, marketing, and distribution chains for these products may well involve waste or pollution and the use of rare and scarce resources. Transport needs the burning of fossil fuels. Supermarkets leave their lights on all night so anyone who wants to can do their weekly shop at three in the morning. Thrown-away food waste produces the greenhouse gas methane. Much packaging is in the form of non-biodegradable plastics. Someone in Australia generates 16.5 metric tonnes of carbon dioxide per year, compared to 0.4 metric tonnes for someone in Bangladesh (http://data.worldbank.org/indicator/EN.ATM.CO2E.PC). And so it goes on.

This can seem to be an overwhelming problem. So let us take a moment to break the issues down by studying one particular case study. We shall think about something we take for granted; the availability of electricity. It can seem like it is an inexhaustible commodity—after all, it comes out of the wall and we just have to flick a switch to boil a kettle or fire up a laptop. However, before we can consider this in depth, we will first have to think about the science of economics and what it can bring to our criminological table.

Adam Smith's 'invisible hand' and the price mechanism

At its most basic, the social science of economics is all about how increasingly scarce resources are distributed. We have already talked about how most of us today live in market societies in which goods and services are traded by what can be called 'economic agents'—which may be companies, governments, organisations, or individual people. To some extent, we are all 'free' economic agents, although there may be restrictions according to the laws under which we live (you can't buy a gun in a supermarket in the UK but you can in the US, the sale of things like unpasteurised milk is controlled, and so on). For most other things, there is competition for customers, and the price is, in theory, determined by competitive market forces.

At this point, most economic writers will quote the economist Adam Smith (1723–90), who spoke of what he called the 'invisible hand':

> Every individual necessarily labours to render the annual revenue of the society as great as he can. He generally neither intends to promote the public interest, nor knows how much he is promoting it … He intends only his own gain, and he is in this, as in many other cases, led by an invisible hand to promote an end which was no part of his intention. Nor is it always the worse for society that it was no part of his intention. By pursuing his own interest he frequently promotes that of the society more effectually than when he really intends to promote it. I have never known much good done by those who affected to trade for the public good.
>
> *An Inquiry into the Nature and Causes of the Wealth of Nations*, 1776.

Figure 16.4 Royd Moore wind farm
Source: Barry Hurst/CC BY-SA 2.0

What Smith is suggesting here is that both producers and consumers act in the market place to get their best competitive advantage. Therefore producers will aim to get the most profit, and buyers will want to buy at the cheapest possible price. However, Smith felt that there was no need for intervention if things went wrong, as the 'invisible hand' of the market would sort out any problems; as you can imagine, historians and economists have been arguing about the accuracy of this pretty much since Smith put down his quill pen, but for our purposes we need to think about it in the context of power relations.

One such argument goes that without regulation of the relationship between producers and buyers, problems may well start. Private and social costs increase and environmental damage is more often than not the consequence. Economists would call this a '*negative externality*'; meaning that neither producers nor consumers shoulder the full social costs of their decision making. A good example is waste (either from production or consumption) which is dumped elsewhere; one form of this is acid rain, produced through the industrial production processes of a particular industry, but which spreads globally.

The search for cleaner energy?

Keep all this in mind when we look in detail at the production of electricity. We will all have seen the advertisements that tell us to switch off appliances—the Energy Saving Trust estimates that an ordinary household will spend around £86 a year just to leave things on standby—and we have a guilty knowledge that to generate power means the burning of 'dirty' fossil fuels, when we are not using the even more unnerving nuclear option. So we are relieved to think that we can instead get our power from the wind (**Figure 16.4**), which can seem clean, sustainable and innocent (although some of the groups campaigning against wind turbines in areas of natural beauty may think otherwise).

So where is the controversy? Wind, after all, is natural and there's no smoke or smell or fear of contamination. Some unfortunate birds might get hurt by the blades and a relatively small number of countryside-dwellers might have their view spoilt, but really, do we care? Does the sense that we have found a renewable and safe source of energy which means we can use our gadgets with a clean conscience absolve us from concern? If we don't look any deeper then yes, we can sit back with a contented sigh. We are exercising our right to *negative externalisation*. We don't care enough about our choice.

But now let's look at what goes on behind the blades of that elegant turbine.

Rare earth elements have impressive names like cerium and ytterbium. There are 17 of them (they are called 'earths' simply because they can be dissolved in acid) and they are used in all sorts of technology, like televisions and the catalytic converters in cars. Two rare earths—neodymium and dysprosium are especially useful in that they help solve a key problem with wind turbines. Turbines contain complicated gear systems, because the blades turn much more slowly than the generators inside. Needless to say, the more complex a piece of machinery, the more expensive it is to repair, especially when the turbine is out at sea or in the middle of a moor. Anything which helps reduce the reliance on gears is going to be snapped up by turbine manufacturers. The two rare earths are used to create magnets which can replace gear systems.

So far, so good. Better turbines means more wind power means less pollution. Or does it? This being a critical issue, you can probably guess the answer. The rare earths have mainly been mined in China, where regulation on environmental issues has not always been upheld. The earths are often found with radioactive substances such as uranium; separating them all involves toxic chemicals which can wash into the water supply and affect the health of the miners; in some places, animals have developed genetic problems, like two sets of teeth. When China said it would restrict supplies—ostensibly so it could clean up its mining industry, but arguably to give an advantage to internal manufacturers—the price of rare earths spiked and mines were opened in other countries, such as the US and Australia, where at least it is reported that environmental conditions are better and where recycling is being developed (*The Guardian,* 20 March 2014, 'Rare Earth Mining in China; the bleak social and environmental costs'). In the meantime, the toxic water remains, the Chinese miners are out of work, and the long-term health effects are uncertain. In short, environmental victimisation is diffused.

The problems are also economic. In 2013, smugglers managed to get 40,000 tonnes of the earths out of China (compared to official exports of 28,000 tonnes), which has driven down prices but put mining companies and jobs at risk in America and Australia (Reuters, 7 July 2015, 'Fate of global rare earth miners rests on China smuggling crackdown'). If official supplies remain restricted, it is probable that illegal and unregulated mines will be dug, with unknown consequences for people and the environment.

All of which makes our wind turbine suddenly seem a lot less attractive and much less 'green'. We see how the market—both for cheap power and for the earths—has affected the exploitation of the natural world, as well as the exploitation of people involved in mining the elements that make it all possible. It is unlikely that the smugglers carry out their trade without committing or encouraging other, related crimes. As China takes steps to keep its grip on the supply, prices are going up again; our demand for technology and our ability to close our eyes to the background story means that few of us give a moment's thought to the power—in every sense of the word—involved.

Responding to green crime

Given that green criminology is such a diverse field containing so many perspectives, it won't surprise you to learn that there are many arguments and debates about the best and most effective ways in which societies can (and should) respond to forms of green criminality. Indeed, as we saw when we looked at zemiology earlier in the chapter, there are disputes about the use of the word 'crime' rather than 'harm', on the grounds that by referring to 'crime' we are narrowing our view to only consider actions which are actually governed by national

and international criminal law. Some criminologists also argue that by staying strictly within legal frameworks, we are being 'anthropocentric'—that is being concerned only with human beings—rather than being more 'bio-centric' and taking the entire natural and physical world into account. Many critical green criminologists would highlight that forms of regulation do not seem to work, pointing out that the levels of fines or sentences imposed on offending corporations and their senior employees are wholly inadequate. Indeed, some would go further and call for the greater criminalisation of the corporations themselves—with suitable punishment being in terms of heavier fines in relation to a corporation's profit margin, and even imprisonment for the senior executives involved.

As you saw in **Chapter 4**, the very concept of 'justice' is in itself a contested one. Green criminology perhaps pushes such debates on 'justice' that bit further by developing different aspects of this debate: *environmental justice* is the focus on the human population, with a concern for everyone having equal access to safe, healthy environments—for example, clean water and sanitation; *ecological justice*, concerned with the natural world and where the preservation of ecosystems is seen as worthwhile in itself; and *species justice*, ensuring the well-being of particular animals or plants, such as through habitat preservation or prevention of cruelty. Critical green criminologists would still however accent the fact that many green crimes exacerbate criminal and social (in)justices.

Taking on the points discussed so far you may now want to consider **What do you think? 16.1**.

So, we are faced with a situation where nobody quite knows what the boundaries of green/eco/environmental crime/harm may be; it's no wonder then that there are similar uncertainties and debates about the best way to respond to the undoubted consequences of environmental damage. Equally unsurprisingly, the arguments for and against the various types of reaction will be influenced by the emphasis each gives to the bio-centric or anthropocentric approach. Let's continue with our electricity example to think about the challenges of acting upon this thorny question.

We noted that one of the problems with the mining of rare earths was the less than stringent regulation of the industry within China. This led to poor working conditions for miners and the pollution of water sources from the processes used to wash out the toxic elements often found with the rare earths. Other countries mining for these elements claim to uphold stricter standards, but what if they don't? What should be done if, say, a company in Germany was found to be washing uranium into the sea and failing to protect its miners?

The obvious answer is that our fictional company should be held accountable to the laws both of Germany

WHAT DO YOU THINK? 16.1

Figure 16.5 Woman portraying a piece of meat—demonstration in the support of animal rights, Milan, Italy

Source: Eugenio Marongiu/Shutterstock.com

- There are many groups worldwide who have been labelled as being 'extremist' in their approach to animal rights, using tactics such as arson, violence and intimidation in their campaigns (see the example of one demonstration in **Figure 16.5**). In one especially gruesome case, a British guinea-pig farm breeding animals for experimentation was targeted by the Animal Liberation Front in a campaign which lasted for years; when the owner's mother-in-law died, her body was dug up from the cemetery and stolen, with activists from a group called the Animal Rights Militia claiming responsibility.

- How do you react to this type of conflict? Are your sympathies with the farmer or the guinea-pigs? If you firmly believe that animal experimentation is wrong, would you refuse medication that has been tested on animals even if you were sure to die without it?

- Go back to the list you made of all the things in your room. Be honest. How much do you actually care about where they came from, who made them, and what harm was caused by their production? Would these questions alter your choices next time you need a phone, a laptop, or a pair of jeans? And what do you think should happen to the people who are responsible for the production of your stuff when they don't answer questions of responsibility, ethics, and harm?

- In other words, just how just is your desk?

and any wider legal system such as the European Union. There are, after all, plentiful laws imposing standards for environmental care, health and safety, worker well-being, and so forth. But who exactly should be punished? The owner of the company, the manager of the mine, the shift leader who didn't order enough safety helmets? The sharp-eyed amongst you will have recalled that in Steve Tomb's **Conversations 16.2** on the Bhopal tragedy, the leader of the company that owned the chemical plant escaped arrest (literally, on a private jet) and was never held to account.

The use of legal processes as a response to green crime (or harm) has been criticised for just this sort of reason. Very often, the people who are actually responsible for the harm (or crime!) are too powerful to be punished. Remember what we said at the beginning of **Chapter 15** on powerful groups' abilities not only to define what 'crime problems' are but also their power to evade the criminalisation of their own criminal and harmful behaviours, whereas the powerless may not be able to escape victimisation. For example, would someone who lost their job when an unsafe mine was closed down be considered a 'victim'? If the shift leader had been trying for months to get safety helmets but been ordered by his manager to send miners down the shaft regardless, is he culpable for any harm that arises, or is he a victim in his own right? Modern transnational corporations have complex bureaucratic structures; from the inter-locking shareholder interests whose aim is to achieve a return (in the form of a dividend) on their investment, to layers upon layers of directors, senior managers, middle managers, and finally lower level employees. Can we draw clear lines of culpability between them, and how can we do so legally? Can we hold the corporations themselves to account for acting with malign intent or as having a 'guilty mind'? Such things are very complex, and any attempt to sort them out inevitably involves long and expensive court cases, appeals, and counter-appeals.

This is before we consider the fact that laws usually only protect people, so the sheep with the extra sets of teeth won't be taken into account, although we may think that they should be. We may also argue that we should offer legal protection to the animals and plants whose habitat is destroyed by mining, and that we should consider those actions which are harmful but not covered by any legal framework. For example, think back to **Chapter 15** and the example of women washing clothes that had been contaminated by asbestos but who were not protected by any laws and for whom the harm suffered was thus actually legal. All of which raises very complicated questions—which is why the notion of 'green compliance', the adherence to rules and laws designed to address environmental concerns, can be seen as problematic in itself.

Power is a common thread to this debate about legal justice. Why do you think that other countries have never challenged China for its poor management of its mines? For a start, having access to the technology made possible by the rare earths is the sort of thing that is very popular with voters. In their 2015 election manifestos, for example, both Labour and the Conservatives made pledges to improve access to high speed broadband which uses another rare earth, erbium. This desire for shiny new technology perhaps overrides our scruples about the consequences. However, the point could also be made that the cost of improving our mine would be deemed too high. Governments are usually unwilling to pass this sort of expense on to businesses; corporations don't want to pay out because that will reduce profit; whilst passing the cost on to the consumer means higher prices and lower sales. (In some cases—and this is where forms of economic and

political power can become blurred—businesses are significant sources of income to political parties and can be seen to have influence in the party's stance on legislation). So the easiest, if not the cleanest, answer is to carry on as before and let the mine stay dangerous and the lakes remain full of toxins.

A second approach is the use of regulation as a means of reducing environmental impact. Such regulations may well be influenced by the use of informal social mechanisms that seek to improve the production and consumption processes, although this again has many of the same problems as the more formal use of laws for the same purpose. Examples of such an approach include using public opinion to encourage corporations to change their actions. If enough people want to buy a deodorant that doesn't deplete the ozone layer, companies will see the profit in switching their product to a less damaging one. Campaigns to highlight the cruelty of battery hen farming meant that more people bought free-range eggs, with the result that in 2012 battery farms were banned in Europe. So perhaps this form of 'naming and shaming' offending corporations can, in turn, impact on consumers' choices, and their actions may sometimes lead to positive outcomes.

This less formal, market-led approach is similar to the use of legislation in that it relies on society to agree that a particular issue (such as a hen's suffering) is harmful or a crime; in other words, both regulation and law see green crime as a social and ideological construct. However, as we saw when we looked at the ways in which the definition of crime have changed, social constructs are pretty fluid, and those relating to green issues are no exception. Using the regulatory approach means that any attempts to reduce the impact on people, plants, and animals are at risk from shifting political, social, and economic values. For example, in 2015 the Conservative government in the UK removed subsidies for renewable energy sources, whereas such subsidies had been promoted by the previous government.

The third, and perhaps most visible, way of responding to green crime and harm is the reaction of individuals and informal groups of people. These are often seen on television news reports and are notable in that they may not always conform to public stereotypes; the so-called eco-warrior of the 1980s with his dreadlocks and tattoos is now as often as not replaced by nicely dressed middle-aged and middle-class people protesting against fracking. This type of 'citizen action' can be more radical than the traditional protest march. The Occupy movement, for example, used encampments outside corporate offices to make its point about unfairness and inequality, whilst other protestors have stormed the shops of companies which they accused of failing to pay enough tax. It is not surprising that the powerful corporations targeted in this way have used legal and financial systems to prevent such protests and to punish the protestors, with police, for example, being given powers to confiscate sleeping equipment from anyone taking part in an Occupy camp.

Where does all this leave us? Firstly, we need to remember that as theoretical perspectives go, (critical) green criminology is relatively new and is still developing. This, coupled with the rapidly changing world in which it operates, means that as yet there are few clear-cut answers to the questions it raises.

This relatively new area of criminological study will continue to challenge and stimulate academic and public interest over the coming years. It might also ignite your critical green criminological imagination and lead you to taking an active interest in learning more. (See South and Brisman (2014) for a good, diverse collection of papers relating to green criminology.)

Cultural criminology: Deviant subcultures, emotions, and the carnival of crime

It could be said that the word *culture* is one of the most difficult words in the English language to define and understand, as it carries with it so many different complicated ideas and meanings. For instance, it can mean being able to cultivate something like a plant, it can refer to friendly germs in a yoghurt, or it can mean a bundle of concepts relating to tradition, norms, values, ideas, beliefs, style, images, and so on. In this section of the chapter, though, we will use it in a more precise but limited sense to simply refer to how *webs of meaning* in society are created, maintained and how they can change. This last point is important, as it is clear that *culture,* in terms of our understandings of the world (including our understandings of, and the meanings we give to, crime and its control) is not something which is static and on which everyone agrees. In other words, it is something which is dynamic and, perhaps more importantly, it is something which is contested vigorously and is in a constant state of flux.

One of the important emerging strands of critical criminology since the 1990s is something which has been called *cultural criminology.* As with the very concept of culture, cultural criminology is hard to define in any straightforward or precise manner, as the idea of culture is at its very core. At first sight, cultural criminology appears to many to be a rather strange and many-tentacled beast which seeks to simultaneously embrace and juggle everything under the sun. In doing so, it draws on and reworks many of the insights from the original variants of critical criminology which we considered in **Chapter 15** (that is interactionism, labelling, neo-Marxist, and feminist perspectives) and adds a few more (such as cultural studies, anarchism, and postmodernism). It is however regarded as being a new form of critical criminology because, as with these previous theories, it engages with issues of how the meanings of crime and control are socially and culturally constructed, and it also engages with the broader concepts of power and social injustice. It does however raise some new and emerging issues which reflect the changing times in which we are living.

Indeed, since the 1950s onwards, some criminologists have been writing about the existence of subordinate (or sub) cultures which have their own distinct 'styles,' shared symbols and so on. These studies focused mainly on subcultures amongst the young working class, and which were seen to challenge and resist mainstream cultures by giving alternative meanings and understandings to their social worlds (see **Chapter 14**). More recently, as we move into the 21st century, others have written about emerging cultures of fear and control. So, as we can see, cultural criminology offers an ever-shifting menu of ideas and concepts for us to consider.

As Muncie (2015: 215) notes, the aims and scope of cultural criminology are indeed many and varied but they can, he argues, be summarised by the following eight key features:

1. Explorations of the convergence of cultural and criminal processes and dynamics in everyday life.

2. A fusion of aspects of cultural studies, *postmodernism*, critical criminology, interactionism, *anarchism*, and media/textual/discourse analysis.

3. The use of *ethnographic methodologies* to reveal issues of meaning and representation.

4. Investigations into *deviant subcultures as sites of criminalisation.*

5. Explorations of the role of the emotions of excitement, fun and pleasure in *processes of transgression.*

6. Journeys into the spectacle and carnival of crime.

7. The linkages (and disconnections) between *marginality*, illegality, media representations, and the criminalisation of popular culture.

8. Crime control as a cultural enterprise.

This is all looking a bit complicated, isn't it? Take a look at **What do you think? 16.2** to help you get your thoughts in order.

Holly's reflection in **Telling it like it is 16.1** gives you some excellent pointers which we hope you will take on board as you progress through your studies. For now, however, let us return to discussing cultural criminology. In the next section of the chapter we will be looking at investigations into deviant subcultures as sites of criminalisation, and the role played by emotions (such as excitement, fun, and pleasure) in the way we give meaning to our actions. We will then end by bringing so-called *culturalist* and *structuralist* cultural criminological accounts together, and reflecting on what cultural criminology can bring to the table in terms of understanding crime and its control today.

WHAT DO YOU THINK? 16.2

Becoming independent, active learners and taking responsibility for your learning

- Read Muncie's list again carefully and make a note of anything which you do not immediately understand.

- Think hard about these and try to further research what they actually mean, *making notes as you do so.*

You may be pleasantly surprised to discover that some of the items listed by Muncie (2015) have already been considered in this book (without explicitly saying that what we were talking about was a form of cultural criminology). For instance, look again at points 2 and 7 and flick back to **Chapter 7** where we considered the relationships between the media and crime, the criminalisation of popular culture, and in particular, the criminalisation of popular musical forms. We also, in that chapter, considered how crime and violence have become commodities which are carefully marketed and sold to us to play with; for instance in computer games such as Grand Theft Auto. See if you can link point 3 on ethnographic methodologies and the discussion in **Chapter 6** on 'How criminologists learn about crime'. Finally, have a look forward to **Chapters 23** and **24** on penology and control and penology and punishment. Make a note of this and when you come to read the chapters try to make these connections for yourselves with point 8 on forms of crime control being cultural enterprises. It is really important that you get in to the habit of doing this; *it is excellent student practice.*

We all read things which, on first reading, we do not fully understand. There is always the temptation to gloss over them. As alluring as this may seem, key ideas and concepts will not go away and your lecturers will easily tell if you are writing about something or presenting on a topic which you do not fully grasp. So, in the long run, this will not do any of us any good at all.

It is really important that throughout your journey into criminology, you become active learners—in other words, that you critically engage with what you are reading. Looking up a concept which you do not fully understand in the index of a book, applying an idea to something which you are interested in (and not just what the textbook is using for illustration), referring to suggested further reading, and consulting more specialist dictionaries on a subject will all mean that you are taking responsibility for your learning and that you are developing strategies through which you can effectively fill in gaps in your knowledge and understanding. Ultimately, this will mean that you are becoming an independent and critical learner.

TELLING IT LIKE IT IS 16.1

A student's view—with Holly Jackson

Holly recently graduated with a first class honours degree in Sociology and Criminology from the University of Westminster. Here she reflects on her three year journey into criminology and how, in the first year of her studies, she developed strategies to become an independent, critical learner; winning several prizes on the way.

You probably realised very early on that university is nothing like school. One thing that I struggled with in my early

days was accepting the fact that there was no longer a teacher there to spoon-feed me and to constantly tell me exactly what I needed to do and when I needed to do it! Lovely as your lecturers are, they will have very different expectations, and although this can be a bit of a culture shock it is your chance to take control over your own development and maturity. If you take a proactive approach to your work rather than a reactive one you'll really see the benefits. Easier said than done? Well, not really, if you follow some simple ideas and work practices.

First things first, do not simply copy lecture slides. Why? One, because it drives lecturers crazy and two, it's not an effective or efficient way to learn. Instead, listen to what your lecturer is saying, absorb it and write your own personal notes, using your own examples to really own the material. Do not be fazed or discouraged by what, or how fast, other students seem to be scribbling down. In other words, trust your own judgement! My first year at university taught me that learning is a personal process, one which has the ability to unlock bundles of potential and originality if you stay true to yourself and your own learning development. This can be scary; to branch out on your own, intellectually and practically, is a huge leap for most of us, and to come up with new ideas in an environment where you feel everyone else is an expert can be a truly brave thing to do. But you really should give it a try. It is, of course, important to adhere to academic frameworks that are put in place to aid your essay writing and to listen to your tutor's views and ideas—they do actually know what they are talking about, but they are more than anything interested in you developing opinions and arguments.

Try not to feel too constrained by things you read in books. Many criminologists, especially those coming from the deconstructivist/cultural criminology perspective, would argue that criminology is a discipline without limits and you can be part of that exciting sort of world. John Lea, a prolific critical criminologist, once wrote that 'the act of defining is an act of excluding' (Lea, 1998). And to this end, I would encourage all students to be as original and creative with their writing as humanly possible; because what is criminology as a discipline without innovative thinkers? You are now a criminologist in the making—so do yourself proud! Take a chance, have an idea, write it down, and see what happens.

It is also another common mistake to listen to postgraduate fossils who will tell you 'yeah, all you need to do is pass the first year, don't worry about it'. This, in my experience, is possibly the worst advice one can give—your first year of university is crucial! It is crucial in the sense that it lays the theoretical and philosophical groundwork for you to go on to develop and produce truly engaged

and well-founded work. Howard S. Becker, the founder of the labelling perspective, raised a timeless and extremely important point for all social scientists when he wrote 'Nothing stays the same. Nothing is the same as anything else ... we can never ignore a topic just because someone has already studied it' (Becker 1998). In other words, just because someone else has written argument A, there is no reason whatsoever for you not to write argument B.

I agree with Becker, who goes on to say that interpretation is everything. Therefore engaging in your first year is vital, because that's when you'll be equipping yourself with a solid understanding of criminology as a discipline. You'll need this because it will give you the tools to produce original interpretations, as opposed to regurgitating the interpretations of others. Achieving the goal of becoming an independent thinker is impossible without understanding the basics, so ensure that you do not become lax and let standards slip under the impression that your first year will be a breeze. This makes me sound like a bit of a bore—I'm not, I promise—but you really do need to build good study habits. Otherwise your course will become a struggle and a hassle, something you try to fit in with your job/relationship/hobbies rather than the life-enhancing experience it should be.

One way that I was able to combat the temptation to neglect my work and go for a 'cheeky Nandos' instead, was to set myself personal targets and make 'to do' lists. This really aided me with my time management, and gave me an invaluable sense of organisation and satisfaction when I could cross things off when they were done. This approach helped me to work consistently, rather than caving in under built-up and unachievable work-loads. I found that going to the library regularly, even when I did not really need to, helped me to juggle my reading and my assignment deadlines. Getting my reading done early in the week also freed up more time so I was able to work on essay plans as well as fitting in my social life. Oh, and while I'm on the subject, if you stumble across something interesting—or even that may seem unrelated but you think it's taking you off in a new direction—then use it! Reading lists are not sacred; they are there to give you a steer and an indication, but you can and should go beyond them. Don't forget to follow up references, and take time to check if an author you like (or one with whom you violently disagree) has published anything new. Criminology is a multi-stranded discipline so you might find yourself being inspired by history, art, film, music, fashion ...

The single biggest tip I can pass on to any aspiring independent learners is that planning is also critical; it was, I believe, the key to my success at university. Planning gave my writing structure and clarity, and enabled me to effectively communicate my points thematically, whilst at the same time managing to respond critically to essay questions. Lack of structure will lure you into going off on a tangent, so please take my advice when I say 'plan, plan, plan'! Your tutor will be delighted to have a student who thinks, plans and challenges; they want to see you develop, and grow as a thinker.

Anyway, I hope my words of wisdom have been useful—keep going, persevere, and stay true to yourself. Good luck and enjoy the rest of your studies and this book!

Deviant subcultures as sites of criminalisation

For some people there can be few more wholesome and picturesque sights than that of quaintly dressed Morris dancers performing their songs, dances, and rituals on a English village green. The locals will stand and watch, children will copy the moves, and some will murmur about how lovely it is to see the old traditions and celebrations, such as 'traditional' Mayday and Sweeps festivals, some of which date back to the 17th century, are maintained in this day and age.

Now change the focus slightly. Instead of some white-clad dancers waving hankies in the sunshine (or black-clad dancers clashing sticks) let's imagine that the dance is taking place at night, that the people there are all in their 20s or younger, and that instead of a village fete we are at a rave. Many of the villagers will be calling the police and will be fearful and shocked that such a thing can happen on their doorstep or in 'their backyard'.

Yet really, what's the difference? Two cultural forms and groups are simply doing 'their thing'—in this case, performing certain steps to a certain style of music (and enjoying themselves or protesting in a peaceful way against injustice and exclusion). The interesting thing is that one is seen as deviant and frightening whereas the other is fun and exciting; although which is which you can decide for yourselves. Which description you give to which scenario will tell you a lot about yourself and your views, and it is this kind of question which forms the basis for what cultural criminologists have to say about illicit and deviant subcultures and their criminalisation.

Cultural criminology is, as we said, related to *culture* in a broader, more personal sense; that of groups, belonging, and identity or, as we said at the beginning of this section, how *webs of meaning* are created and maintained and how they can change. Or, perhaps more importantly for us here, how these webs can be used to inform regulation and control by powerful groups who find things that are popular amongst 'dangerous people' to be threatening and frightening. As we have already seen in the section on labelling in the previous chapter, we all belong to various groups—racial, religious, and so on—and which have their own styles, symbols, and meanings. These of course may vary within the groups themselves, sometimes causing dissent and even violence—the clashes between different sects within Christianity, for example, having been the cause of wars, massacres, and division for hundreds of years. Some groups are seen as acceptable; some, however, are causes of fear and hatred which often lead to demands for public and political action. These 'unacceptable groups' will have their own interpretations of their actions, beliefs, and so on—in a word, they may well form their own subculture—which can often be viewed as illicit and deviant by the wider society in which they are operating.

As we saw with the example of religious conflict, these illicit subcultures are perhaps nothing new; if you want to read about others try looking up the Luddites, Teddy Boys, or the 19th-century New Woman. However, other than as a source of social anxiety or mockery (the humorous, satirical magazine *Punch* in the early 20th century published cartoons of Victorian 'New Women' smoking, drinking and making men wear dresses and do the housework) these groups were not studied sociologically in any systematic way until the mid-20th century. It was at this point that the collective meanings, symbols, and styles of subcultures were really examined for the first time, with a particular focus on their relationship—often being one of conflict and resistance—to the more dominant social environment or dominant culture. Subcultures, especially youth subcultures, were seen as a form of resistance to a social order in which working-class, poorly-educated, and excluded and marginalised people—generally men—could form their own identity and rules, creating a space where they could literally make their own rules and meet their own emotional and interpersonal needs in order to resist and resolve the sense of dislocation and marginalisation they felt. This emotional element is an important feature of any subculture and one which we will return to later.

This idea of a subculture as a way for marginalised people to form an identity and solve their problems (whether at a real or 'imaginary' level) was not really studied in Britain until the development of the Birmingham School, or to give it its full title, the Birmingham Centre for Contemporary Cultural Studies (CCCS), in the 1970s (see Hall and Jefferson 2006 [1976]). This was one of the first mainstream academic attempts to examine what its founder, Richard Hoggart, called 'mass culture'—meaning culture in its widest forms, such as popular music, television programmes, and advertising, rather than the previously accepted idea that culture was opera, ballet, and theatre; in other words, those forms which could be called 'high culture'. This new approach—which in itself could perhaps be described as an illicit academic subculture—allowed people from different academic disciplines and backgrounds to work together, and produced some of the first work to show the political and social significance of day-to-day, mainstream activities and behaviours. Most importantly, it considered the political and social structures of subcultures and the way in which they relate to the wider world, and looked at groups which were otherwise invisible, such as young women, and their roles and meanings within subcultures. As Angela McRobbie, one of the academics working at the CCCS wrote in her book *Feminism and Youth Culture*:

> the objective and popular image of a subculture is likely to be one which emphasises male membership, male focal concerns and masculine values. When women appear within the broad framework of a moral panic it is usually in more innocuous roles. The fears of rampant [female] promiscuity which emerged from the hippy culture … was widely condemned and taken as a sign of declining moral values as well as personal degradation [but] the entertainment value … balanced out and even blunted the hard edge of the cries of horror of the moral guardians.
>
> 2000, 15

Such work at the CCCS began to shift the understandings of how we contextualise our understanding of crime and its control. It could be said that the CCCS was *structuralist* in its orientation, as it focused on how the formation of various subcultures was, in part, a reaction to forms of disadvantage and exclusion. It also looked at how subcultures were an attempt by the participants to gain some form of control over their lives. As McRobbie (and others working within the Centre) points out, the media inevitably concentrates on the sensationalist aspects of subcultures, a trend which is as true today as it was when she was writing in the 1970s; an Internet search for 'US Biker Group' (not the pejorative term 'gang') will bring up pages of stories about violence, guns, and danger, whereas the group 'Bikers Against Child Abuse', which works with the police and social care agencies, does not appear until the fourth page of results. Why do you think this is the case?

Likewise, the majority of subcultures which receive social or media attention are those which can be seen as questioning or challenging the powerful, dominant groups (and their definitions of social 'reality') with much less attention being paid to subcultures amongst the rich and elite. Indeed, the CCCS mainly concentrated their

research on the subcultures of the excluded and marginalised in order to try to understand their behaviour and understand and appreciate their lifestyles and choices. Let's, for a moment, however think about what could be called subcultures within dominant groups. Why do you think little research has been carried out on such groups? One such subculture we could examine in this way is the Bullingdon Club. This is a dining club for students at Oxford University, open only to men and where the club uniform costs over £3,000; several senior British politicians have been members, and it has been alleged that the club causes expensive damage to restaurants and dining halls. One report states that the club's initiation ritual (we are back to symbols, meanings, and identity again) involves burning a £50 note in front of a beggar (*Daily Mirror*, 23 February 2013). Yet the club receives much less coverage and causes much less concern than groups of other, less privileged young people who cause less damage and offence. Similarly, little work has been carried out on occupational subcultures of the 'games changers' in the criminal justice system, such as the police or judges.

So how do illicit subcultures respond to the dominant interpretations of their actions, rituals and identity? The behaviour of such subcultures—the riding of a motorbike, the wearing of torn clothing and 'bondage' clothing, the preference for listening to jazz in a dark basement—can be viewed through a structural lens. Essentially, this means seeing social structures as being at least partially at the root of the group's behaviour, and making a judgement as to whether this behaviour is deviant or acceptable.

Foreground factors: the role of emotions in the carnival of crime

Many of today's cultural criminologists, however, have come to think more about a person's individual 'agency'—their choices, the meanings they give to their actions, and their views of the world. The rationale for this is that people simply try to understand their world as they perceive it. The cultural criminologist will not make a judgement one way or the other as to whether or not the exercise of this agency is good or bad; it will be seen as a personal decision that is guided by emotional and physical factors. In other words, their approach is more *culturalist* than *structuralist*. In his controversial book *The Seduction of Crime; The Moral and Sensual Attractions of Doing Evil* (1990) Jack Katz focused on what he called the 'foreground' factors. He argued that criminology had for too long focused on the 'background' factors of crime; on such as things as social class, together with forms of social exclusion through poor education, inadequate housing, and a general blocking of opportunities. For him, this neglects an important element in crime; that of emotions. Things

A. Stuff.

Q. Such as?

A. An HDTV, an iPod dock, massive speakers.

Q. Let's suppose that you have worked hard at your studies, and achieve the degree that you want but that you don't immediately find your dream job, or that your starting salary is less than you expect, that you cannot immediately buy your home and put your stuff in it... How would that make you feel?

Some of more polite responses to this final question will include anger, the feeling of being cheated, let down, upset, depressed, deeply frustrated, and so on. The graduate labour market fluctuates and after all, none of us really knows what the demand for graduates will be when you graduate. However, as you will see in **Chapter 30**, a good, well designed degree in criminology will hopefully give you a start several rungs up the ladder, as you will graduate equipped with what we know are the kinds of skills and attributes employers are looking for. So persevere and good luck. But this can't disguise the fact that you may end up being disappointed, at least at first.

This scenario in some ways illustrates what Jock Young has to say about late modern societies and how people's expectations and the economic realities have changed. He argues that there was a so-called 'golden age' of post war affluence, which was characterised by a political commitment to full employment, where welfare was funded, and there was not talk about swingeing cuts and austerity. People felt more secure and communities were more cohesive and inclusive. As a result of economic changes since the 1970s, however, today's workers are in a very different place; there is no longer a political commitment to full employment, and a state based on welfare provision is slowly being replaced by one of personal responsibility and privatised prudentialism (where people look after themselves, for example through pensions savings schemes or by paying for private health care). People feel less secure and more fearful about their own futures and those of other people. Young argues that societies have thus become more exclusive (shutting others out). This is despite the fact that we are all, to some extent, 'culturally included'—for instance, we are all bombarded with advertisements for consumer goods in a society which has distinct lifestyle options. But can everyone achieve the glittering prizes, baubles, and trinkets which are on offer in our winner/ loser society? For Young (and many other commentators) the clear answer is a resounding no. So, let's ask ourselves why is this? Well, we think that, as you have seen from our discussion thus far, society 'structurally

Figure 16.7 Olympics stadium
Source: Jiano74/CC BY-SA 2.0

excludes' groups of people from the dominant group and the late modern dream of prosperity, security and, for many today, celebrity. However we measure it, the gap in income and wealth distribution is getting larger, people are more anxious and fearful and so on.

What has all of this got to do with crime and crime control? Let's think about it in another way.

Look at **Figure 16.7**.

This is an athletics stadium. The oval area around the green square in the middle is the race track which by Olympic standards should be 400 metres long. Now, if we lived in a meritocracy (a world where people had equal opportunities and achieved success through merit, by hard work and learned skills rather than an accident of birth) we would expect everyone taking part in the race to start at the bottom hand right corner of the track. Everyone would start at the beginning and have 400 metres to run. Young however argues that in today's society not everyone starts at the same place. Some will start with only 300 metres to run, others only 200 metres, some with only 100 metres and some only having a few steps to complete the race. In other words, the race is not a fair one. This should not surprise us—it is nothing new, because capitalist market societies have always been based on fundamental inequalities.

Now, this is where things get a little more interesting for us. What sits outside the actual race track? Rows and rows of spectators. These want to be given the opportunity to join in the race, but are not allowed to do so; instead they can only sit and watch. Then we could ask the question—what lies outside the arena? We could say that there are many people who are excluded altogether and are not even allowed to watch the race at all. Everyone inside and outside the stadium is culturally included—they all aspire to winning the same prizes (be this a medal or a view of the race)—but for some there are structural barriers that prevent them from joining the race in the first place; for others, there are structures which mean they start from an unequal position.

Let's pause for a minute and try to relate this metaphor of 'cultural inclusion' and 'structural exclusion' to people's possible emotions and reactions. Suppose you were allowed to participate in the race. How would feel about those watching you from the sidelines (and wanting to join in)? Do you feel differently about those who want to spectate and join the race but are not allowed into the arena? Would you feel pity, or fear that you could become one of them; a fear of being relegated to the role of spectator? Could you maintain your position in the race by asking the race organisers to erect fences, barriers, walls, surveillance cameras? Would you want those excluded from the race to be somewhere else where they would not bother or threaten you—in prison perhaps? Similarly, if you were a spectator or one of the excluded would you then feel anger, resentment, or any other emotions? Would you just give in and stop trying, or would you like to set up your own similar race where you could get similar rewards (perhaps by committing crime)?

This is perhaps a rather simplistic image but it is one which nicely illustrates what Young means by processes of cultural inclusion and structural exclusion and how this can lead to anger, crime, fear, and control. What do YOU think?

who are 'critical' of it, it offers us nothing radically new, or it is simply regarded as being 'new wine in old bottles'; in other words, its claim to re-work older foundational ideas from critical criminology is said to be unfounded. For others, it is too broad a project and is simply not coherent enough to call itself a fully worked out theory. Furthermore, some might be critical of its methodological individualism, that is its call for ethnographical research into the real and many layers of meaning which people ascribe to their behaviour, plus the wider meanings and understandings of crime and its control. Finally, some would argue that it neglects victims of crime and romanticises those who break the criminal law and cause suffering. Whatever you make of all this (so do think hard and critically about these issues) it certainly has helped to reinvigorate debates within critical criminology and amongst critical scholars. It has redirected attention to emerging social conditions and new media forms. The same can be said of the last new frontier in critical criminology which we will consider in this chapter; that is, convict criminology.

Convict criminology

There are many different ways that people who have been imprisoned are represented and portrayed through art, film, and television programmes. And yet, despite the growing prison population (see **Chapter 24** for a further discussion of this), it's probable that most of us don't actually have any strong relationship with someone who is a prisoner or ex-prisoner. Most of us have not set foot within prison walls. So as we saw in the media chapter (**Chapter 7**), it's far more likely that we form our views about prisons and their inhabitants from sources other than direct personal experience. We might read about prisoners living in the lap of luxury, able to access drugs and Facebook with ease, or we might hear stories about miscarriages of justice that have resulted in false incarceration. We develop clear ideas about what is 'deviant' or 'acceptable' and we are given a view of prisons as places that have two distinct roles: to inflict punishment on those who are deserving of it, and to keep the rest of us safe from the 'dangerous' people who are locked away for our protection.

Yet how much do we hear about the way prisoners see themselves and their lives? For instance, many use art, education, and therapy to change and heal their lives. Others use their knowledge and experiences to mentor and educate, such as ex-prisoners who visit schools to give a first-hand account of the reality of incarceration in an attempt to deter young people from committing crime. There may be an occasional news story about an inspection report criticising a particular prison, but there is little public debate about overcrowding, poor health care, lack of access to mental health services, and the impact of an ageing prison population needing ramps, hand rails, and disabled toilets that are not often found within our secure estate.

The emerging critical perspective that has become known as convict criminology tries to address these, and other, questions. As a movement, it started in America in 1997 and was founded by two former prisoners (Steven C. Richards and Jeffery Ian Ross), both of whom had become academics, and who knew at first-hand how much wisdom was being left out of the conventional literature and research that dealt with prisons, including much criminological research. The perspective has only recently spread across the Atlantic and has been described by Ross et al.

as: 'a collection of PhD-trained former prisoners, prison workers, and others who share a belief that in order to be a fully rounded discipline, mainstream criminology needs to be informed by input from those with personal experience of life in correctional institutions' (2014: 2).

This idea—that criminology needs to be informed by multiple sources—reinforces the point that we hope you have, by this point in the book, come to have as a key concept in your criminological thinking: that there is no such thing as a single 'truth'. When we consider prisons and prisoners, we can see this as a triangle: the criminal justice system (the police, courts, prisons and so on) and sometimes—although less frequently—the victims of crime. But it is rare for the third side of this triangle to be heard, even though, without it, we are missing a crucial strand of knowledge and wisdom: the voice of the prisoner. Look at **What do you think? 16.5** to consider your own viewpoint on this.

At this point you may be asking yourself what is so radical and critical about involving prisoners in criminological research—after all, it seems to be a blindingly obvious thing to do when considering issues of crime and punishment. Historically, however, the main way in which prisoners have been involved in this type of work has been as passive, sometimes unwitting, subjects of studies and tests. This meant that criminology, despite seeing itself as a dynamic and challenging discipline, actually helped to maintain the accepted view of prisoners, which in turn went on to feed and shape public opinion. The 'radical' change came when a new generation of academics started to question the accuracy and indeed the ethics (moral issues) of research that did not take into account the knowledge, opinions, and experiences of the very people

it was supposed to be studying. Thus 'convict criminology' aims to focus on the views and ideas of prisoners, and to ensure that their 'dark' and potentially 'dangerous' knowledge—the knowledge of the outcast and deviant—is given as much status as that of professors, doctors, and lecturers. The notion here of 'knowledge' is important and takes us back to thoughts about power, so we need to pause for a moment and think about what we mean by it. We all have forms of knowledge, some of which is common to us all—don't put your hand into the fire for instance—and some of which is hidden and almost unconscious. This might be that there is a certain dark road that people 'know' not to walk down, or that despite its inclusion policy, black people 'know' they will be turned away from a particular club. Yet like the voice of the prisoner, this knowledge (real or imaginary) is not shared or spoken, unless in ways that reinforces it—when someone is attacked or sues for discrimination. Power relations, such as the power of a white bouncer to turn away a black clubber, reinforce the knowledge and rub it in deeper. Yet by not being voiced, this hidden knowledge is not shared with those who can make a difference. Street lighting will not be improved if the council don't know that people avoid a particular lane because it is dark and scary. Prison policy will not change if the Home Secretary is only told safe, voter-pleasing things by criminologists.

Like with other considerations of power, this can end up as a vicious circle whereby people with an interest in crime control (often those who make money out of it) influence criminological research—rather like when a fizzy drink firm sponsors research into whether sugar really is bad for our teeth, and finds that it is not. This sort of research is often based on statistics and other highly technical material, which as we all know can be manipulated to prove pretty much anything we like (you may wish to go back and have another look at **Chapter 5** where we confronted the issue of facts and statistics).

This is all very well, and of course quantitative data (that is, data based on figures) have an important part to play. However, critical convict criminologists have two arguments to make here: that without the more qualitative information (data based on ideas, opinions, and lived experiences) we are not going to be able to make fully informed judgements that take everything into account; and—which is probably the most radical point to bear in mind—if we fail to use all the information we can get our hands on, some knowledge will be given more status than the rest of it, and this is where we risk silencing those ideas and people which we value less. Many of us would be shocked at the idea that there is modern-day censorship of ideas and opinion, but could it be argued that this is in fact what is going on with criminological research?

WHAT DO YOU THINK? 16.5

- Do you have the instinctive reaction that someone who is being punished for breaking the law doesn't deserve to be heard?

- Do you think that by carrying out a crime they have given up their right to be taken seriously? If so, does that cover all prisoners equally? Should we treat a teenage burglar in the same way as a mature murderer?

Hopefully your reading of the section on 'labelling' perspectives will already have made you broaden your thinking on this sort of issue but it's an important point to bear in mind when we talk about how we engage with, and portray, those people who have been judged by society to need the punishment of prison.

Convict criminology would certainly agree that this is exactly what is happening, although very subtly, especially when you factor in changes to the ways in which universities and criminological research is funded and organised.

Today, research is probably even more crucial to a university's financial situation than the teaching of students, and if you speak to academic staff you will learn about the way that research drives the institution and its policy, together with the way that it is complicated by issues of ethics, safety, and the need to employ what are considered to be 'acceptable' research methods. Of course we can't just barge around, demanding information from anywhere we choose—but we do need to think about the ways in which research is shaped by factors other than the academic learning it aims to promote. If we are only 'allowed' to research in certain ways, does it follow that we are only 'allowed' to research certain things with certain people? Who decides? And what happens to the people we don't listen to because we cannot access them?

These complications can be vividly illustrated when we think about research involving law-breaking, dangerous people (or at least, people who have been labelled as such). Academics may be personally nervous about working with murderers, rapists, and conmen. Universities may not want to be associated with people who have committed offences, and funding organisations may believe that someone who has been in prison is going to be naturally dishonest and therefore will skew the findings. Not least of these anxieties is the fear of being sued, or of being ridiculed or criticised.

Convict criminologists and others would call this a 'market led' research environment and are concerned that it silences (or censors) any kind of movement towards a wider, riskier debate in which the voices of prisoners and their families are heard, taken note of, and given an equal footing. It is one of the aims of convict criminology to challenge and, where possible, to reverse this process, and one of the ways it seeks to do so is by actively involving prisoners in the research programme; not by treating them as research subjects (laboratory rats) but instead giving them a figurative white coat and actually treating them as though they have something worthwhile and valuable to say. Prisoners are not only interviewed and surveyed, but are involved in designing and carrying out research themselves, often whilst they are still serving their sentences.

So, one of the main aims of convict criminology is to produce a different sort of prison research, that is firmly rooted in the experiences and knowledge of those people at the sharp end—prisoners themselves. As well as increasing its relevance, this approach means that information is less likely to be tainted or skewed by the beliefs or prejudices of the researcher. After all, many of them (like the rest of us) are likely to have formed their ideas about

prisons from the media or other research which has focused on those socially and politically acceptable notions which convict criminology wishes to challenge. It sees the prisoner as having knowledge which is equal to, if not greater than, that of the privileged 'expert' who is usually considered to be the only person worth listening to (see Aresti et al., 2015 for a fuller discussion of these and other issues which convict criminologists are interested in).

The experience of the American lawyer Bryan Stevenson is a good way to think about this. Speaking on Radio 4's Desert Island Discs in March 2015, he described how 'not too long ago' he arrived early in a court he had not previously visited. The judge took one look at this black man in a suit and told him to wait outside until his lawyer had arrived; when Stevenson said 'I AM the lawyer' the judge and other lawyers simply laughed. A black man was someone whose voice could only be heard through that of an acceptable person—his (probably white) lawyer. How much could the judge have learned if he had been able to see past his prejudices to listen and take note?

The acceptance that prisoners have something valid to say leads to the second aim of convict criminology: to ensure that prisoners' voices are heard in the public arena as well as just by academics. In other words, it seeks to make sure that they are reported accurately and respectfully in the *Daily Mail* as well as in the *British Journal of Criminology*. This means that we need to allow an honest portrayal of prisons and prison life, even if this goes against the grain of those readers (and voters) who believe that most prisons would earn Michelin stars for their cuisine and that anyone slopping out should have to pay for their own bucket. It follows that this open, well-informed, and frank debate would be a platform for prison reform, yet to do so would mean challenging what the public and therefore the electorate 'knows' about prisons.

Ironically, the one thing this section has yet to do is to think about the impact of all of this on prisoners. So let us be convict criminologists for a moment and bring them to the foreground.

Anyone in prison is highly vulnerable in a number of ways, but for our purposes we need to think about the huge amount of trust that must be built up between prisoner and researcher even before a project can begin. The prisoner has to believe that the academic is someone worth listening to, who will treat them with respect, and that the research has a purpose; that their voice will be given equal weight to that of the 'normal' person and that overall they will be taken seriously. The research needs to be designed with the prisoners, and not just be done to them; and solutions and findings should be arrived at by researcher and prisoners working together. This can seem a tall order to a researcher who will have his or her own anxieties and preferred ways of working, which makes this kind of active research less attractive for some criminologists.

However, if done well, the work of a convict criminologist is a powerful way to challenge and shape public perceptions (and misconceptions) about prisons and prisoners. It essentially humanises and makes real the otherwise faceless and frightening idea of the hidden deviant, who is behind bars for our protection. Additionally, it means that organisations and agencies whose work affects prisoners can gain a wider, more accurate view of the arena in which they are operating. After all, if you are a probation officer or a social worker, surely you would want to have the best possible basis on which to make your professional decisions? We would hope this is the case, but it may be unclear that this is how these groups operate. Alternatively, we could ask whether they go along with the general ideas about prisoners and prisons, following those 'realities' that do not include the voice of the very people they are supposed to be helping. Does the fact that very few of these agencies have ex-prisoners on their staff contribute to the censorship of the prisoner voice and the reinforcement of accepted ideas and power relations? Could we argue that the current situation in fact contributes to the labelling of prisoners as dangerous people who should be silenced?

Take for example the problems faced by ex-prisoners seeking work. How would you feel if you were filling in an application form and were asked to declare any previous convictions? Perhaps you were simply relieved that you did not have to disclose your parking fines, but you may have been discouraged, knowing that you had something in your past which meant you knew you would not get the job. One the one hand, this can seem obvious; no school, for instance, is likely to employ a teacher with a record of dishonesty and violence and it might seem right and proper that this has to be declared. But what if your illegal parking meant a fire engine couldn't get past and three children died as a result? Why is it acceptable to keep quiet about one sort of crime and not another? Taking the views of ex-prisoners into account could, instead, actually help to develop better ways to help them find employment opportunities—yet there is a strong legal framework which blocks access to work, regardless of how useful and creative a prisoner's knowledge might be to that field. For example, if you have been to prison you will have to forego any plans to become a clinical psychologist even if you achieve a PhD in psychology—but how valuable would your experience as a former prisoner be if you wanted to work within the criminal justice system as part of a rehabilitation programme?

Convict criminology aims, amongst many other things, to 'bridge gaps,' with perhaps the biggest one being that between the public and the prison population. What it does not do is argue that only prisoners should be involved in research or policy direction. Instead it looks to promote the balanced generation of knowledge through the equal participation of prisoners, academics, and policy makers, to arrive at a broader and more accurate understanding of (and from) people who have experience of being convicted and locked up. It seeks to use this knowledge to challenge complacency, to shape opinion, and to improve the ways in which we use prison as a form of crime control. It is a relatively new perspective, and one which is still finding its feet amongst the better known, more established criminologies; but as a movement it is one which perhaps presents the greatest degree of challenge and debate to the current political and social views on prisoners and their lives.

In **Telling it like it is 16.2** we hear from Dr Andreas Aresti. Andy is one of the founders of British Convict Criminology (BCC) and is a senior lecturer in criminology at the University of Westminster. He is also a former prisoner. As you read the account of his journey see if you can make any connections with what we said about labelling perspectives and the concept of stigma in **Chapter 15**. Also, make some notes of your responses on what he has to say about the need for a 'convict criminology'; do you agree with him? Why, or why not?

TELLING IT LIKE IT IS 16.2

A journey into criminology ... via prison—with Dr Andreas Aresti

I wouldn't say crime was my profession as such. I was a tradesman, and had been working as a roofer since leaving school at the age of 15. Even then, however, my mates and I were always involved in some form of 'illegal activity'. Typically, these activities were usually motivated by the desire for financial gain, but of course, they were also inextricably linked to other complex factors, such as status, identity, and masculinity.

In August 1998, I walked out of the prison gates, having served three years in mainly category B prisons, and straight into university. At that moment in time, I had little awareness of what lay ahead and how my life would turn out. I remember my first day at university vividly. I was consumed with anxiety and fear, questioning myself as I looked around the grounds and at the other students waiting to enrol.

I thought to myself 'what the hell am I doing here?'—or words to that effect! These were not my kind of people and this was not an environment that I was familiar with. At this point, my old life appeared quite attractive despite my strong urge to change and find fulfilment in other ways.

Needless to say I stuck with my course, and gained my momentum. I walked out of university with a very good first degree in psychology, and full of confidence and self-belief. I had worked my backside off. It wasn't easy, it was definitely a struggle, and there were times I wanted to give it up. But I did it. I had proved something to myself, and that something was that 'I can do this. I can change my life'. Education was pivotal in this process. For me, desistance from crime could only be achieved through my education and by developing a career on the back of that. You may be surprised, but this is the case for a number of people like me who are former prisoners (or as they may also be known, ex-convicts).

When I left prison I thought I was the only ex-con(vict) who had gone on to go to university. Other ex-cons have said the same. Look around you ... one of your peers may be one of us! One of us, an ex-con: someone who is morally contaminated in the eyes of the wider society. This 'spoiled identity' that I have inherited from my days in prison never really impinged on my life in the early days of my transition to conventional life, and it was never really a source of great tension either. I didn't really give my ex-con identity much thought until it slapped me in the face, at the moment when I was considering my career options after doing my Masters' degree. Up until this point, life was looking good. I had goals and I was achieving them. I was determined to achieve them. The past was becoming a distant memory, I was moving forward.

I had a first class, first degree (BA, Hons) in Psychology and an MSc in Cognitive Neuropsychology, and my goal was to be a clinical psychologist. I started looking into the clinical psychologist training programme and quickly discovered that my past criminal convictions were an issue. I realised that because of my criminal record, I would never be able to work as a clinical psychologist. This is also the case for a number of other positions that are exempt from the Rehabilitation of Offenders Act (ROA) 1974. Entry in to certain jobs and professions are literally barred to those who have been behind bars.

As you might imagine I was devastated. I simply couldn't believe it. I had invested so much effort into changing my life, experienced struggles and difficulties, and yet had overcome these only to be confronted by these structural constraints. It made me question the system.

Once again, as on my first day at university, my old life on 'the wrong side of the law' seemed a lot more attractive. My ex-offender status would never be an issue there—in fact in many instances it would be respected. What an injustice! All this talk about 'rehabilitation' and helping people to desist from crime was bullshit. And this is still the case now. In my view nothing has changed. If anything, things have got a lot worse! It is almost as if my past follows me around like a shadow. Frequently, I have to negotiate this 'spoiled identity' in social situations; do I disclose my past? If I do, what are the implications? In other instances, I am forced to disclose my status on forms that require you to advise if you have a criminal record—for instance on job applications, insurance forms, visas applications if I want to go abroad, and so on. So like many others, despite the dramatic changes I have made in my life, I still have to live with the damaging effects of the label, 'ex-offender'.

Anyway, feeling quite deflated I ended up contacting UNLOCK (this is an independent award-winning charity which provides information, advice, training, and advocacy, dealing with the ongoing effects of criminal convictions) and had a lengthy conversation with someone who empathised with my situation. They helped me to put things into perspective; I needed to take 'the bull by the horns'.

In the end I decided to study for a PhD, the focus of which was on former prisoners' experiences of self-change and identity negotiation. Specifically, my work considered what it is like to live with the stigmatised status of ex-prisoner, exploring how these 'forced' identities are negotiated in everyday life; this undoubtedly being a means of making sense of my own situation as well as a career choice.

It was whilst doing my PhD that I came across convict criminology (CC). In short, CC is a theoretical perspective and an academic network that takes a critical approach to criminal justice issues and challenges the traditional understandings of crime, criminal justice issues, prisoners, and ex-convicts. Many of the convict criminologists have had direct experience of prison and use this as a basis for their work. They use their personal experience to generate knowledge on the lived realities of prisons, prisoners and life after prison.

To date, little of the knowledge or policy work on prisons, prisoners, and the criminal justice system comes directly from people that have had first-hand experience of prison. In many respects, the voice of prisoners (including former prisoners) is muted and often silenced all together. We need to question why this happens, and consider whether work that fails to hear that voice can truly capture the lived realities of prisoners and ex-convicts.

On developing a relationship with the convict criminologists in the USA, I, along with two colleagues, decided to push CC forward in the UK. Like convict criminologists in America, we believed that much of the knowledge on prisons and prisoners did not resonate with our personal experiences. In terms of our lived realities, the dominant discourses on such matters were, and still are, predominantly negative, and the existing policies that directed our lives were constraining and typically ineffective. Having had such experiences, and subsequently having made that transition into 'conventional life', I believe that like many others before me, I can utilise this personal experience to provide an alternative lens through which to view an authentic understanding of the lived realities of prisons, prisoners, and the criminal justice system, from an 'insider perspective'.

And whilst my aim is not to discredit some of the very good and valuable good work being generated by other academics, especially those of a critical orientation, I also believe there is no substitute for personal experience. So, having had such experiences, and achieving the academic credentials, I believe that I can utilise this personal experience to, as many a convict criminologist has commented, really '*tell it like it is*'.

Dr Andreas Aresti, Senior lecturer in criminology,
University of Westminster

Conclusion

In this chapter we have explored how critical criminologists have responded to the demands of living in a rapidly changing world in the early decades of the 21st century, and to the changing, challenging criminological conundrums that result. As we have seen, there are new, emerging forms of criminality as well as developing strategies and methods for its prevention and control. Many of these issues are developed further elsewhere in this book (see for instance the chapters in Part 4).

We have however only had the space in this chapter to discuss four, important emerging strands of contemporary critical criminology: zemiology, critical green criminology, cultural criminology, and convict criminology. As we have seen, what connects these four strands is a commitment to challenging the dominant discourses which circulate about crime, criminality, and its control. They also all share a commitment to highlighting social injustice and working towards social change for a fairer and more equal world. It should be very clear to you by now (having read both this chapter and **Chapter 15**), that at the very core of critical criminology is the analysis of power and power relations and a speaking of truth to power.

This is however a long way from being a final word on all of this. Critical criminology will continue to adapt to the rapidly changing juggernaut that is the social world in which we all live. New forms of inequality and abuses of power will rise, adapt to continuous changes, and will be re-imagined. It is in this way that it could be said that critical criminology is in a constant process of 'becoming'. There will undoubtedly be new economic, social, and political crises. For instance, recently in the UK we have seen swingeing cuts to public services, increasing un- and under-employment, increasing levels of poverty, and so on. All of these things will have implications for crime and its control at both local and global levels—not least, increasing levels of (legal and illegal) migration and a clampdown on migration in certain countries, increasing anger, discontent and changing levels of tolerance, more criminalisation and incarceration … who knows?

As you progress through your studies and develop your criminological imaginations, you may well develop into becoming more critically engaged, active citizens. I certainly hope so. Try to view the changing world around you through the lens of the critical criminologist and avoid settling for simplistic answers to what are often, after all, very complex issues. Critical criminologists will no doubt continue to throw Young's (1998) 'metaphorical bricks' both at, and through, establishment and mainstream criminological windows. To badly paraphrase a well-known political economist (see if you can guess which one); most criminologists have only interpreted the world, in various ways; the point for the critical criminologist is to change it.

SUMMARY

- Discuss some of the recent social, political, and economic changes that have occurred as we move into the 21st century, and appreciate how critical criminology has responded to these

We have clearly witnessed profound social, political, and economic changes in the last 40 years or so. Such changes have led to new and developing forms of crime and crime control. Social theorists have attempted to capture the scale and scope of such changes in various ways; for instance, by characterising society as being late modern, post-industrial, information, globalised, or some other descriptor. This has led to critical criminologists re-imagining their foundational concepts (of power, ideology, and so on) in ways to meet such changes and to highlight developing forms of inequality across the world. Closer to home, Young has argued that there has been a general shift to an atmosphere of uncertainty and insecurity, and from a society that was more inclusive to one which is seen as being exclusive and exclusionary. He argues that between 1945 and the 1960s there was a sense that inequality could be addressed through political and economic action, and that fairness and welfare were important political and social goals. In terms of crime (and its control), this meant that there was an emphasis on rehabilitation and improving the life chances of offenders; the point was to meet their needs rather than to punish their deeds. However, from the 1970s onwards, the focus shifted to be on individuals, who had to take responsibility for their actions, rather than on society as whole; this led to an increase in the use of prison as a response to crime. Critical criminology seeks to analyse and understand such changes in ways which highlight inequalities.

- Show an understanding of the four key strands of critical criminology today (zemiology, green criminology, cultural criminology, and convict criminology) and explain what their common features are

Although the four stands of contemporary critical criminology covered in this chapter are diverse in that they focus on differing aspects of crime and its control, as with aspects of critical criminology, underpinning all of these critical variations is the notion of power and the way it is used to define and control behaviour. The idea of knowledge is also important, both in terms of how it is produced, and how it is used to promote or silence dissenting voices. By analysing the use and possession of knowledge in each of these areas, critical criminology seeks to reassess the meanings and ideas they bring to the discussion of crime and harm.

- Develop an awareness of what it means to say that critical criminology is a 'political project'

Critical criminology challenges the mainstream discourses in order to bring the concerns and struggles of powerless groups to the fore, in order to seek greater social equality and justice. In some cases, this means challenging public conceptions of what constitutes 'crime'. One example is the way in which breaches of health and safety law are generally described as accidents or disasters instead of as crimes. As we saw in Phil Scraton's **Conversations 16.1** on his work on the Hillsborough tragedy, critical criminologists try to redress the powerlessness of people who suffer as a result either of the incident itself and/or the ways in which powerful groups (such as employers or the police) may seek to avoid punishment.

- Critically assess the argument put forward by zemiologists that the main weakness and limitation of traditional criminology is that is focuses too much on notions of 'crime' rather than 'social harm'

Zemiology focuses on the causes and impact of social harm, which may not actually be illegal or even considered to be a crime in the first place. Criminologists, however, have traditionally looked at the idea of crime as illegal acts, generally committed by individuals and defined as crime by the state. Harm, on the other hand, could be caused by businesses, organisations, political parties, or in the case of war, entire political ideologies, and does not need a legal definition. This, it is argued, narrows the horizons of much criminology and perpetuates various myths of crime which, in turn, allows powerful groups to harm and victimise the relatively powerless groups in society.

- Develop an understanding of basic economic concepts and ideas and how these fit into the world of critical green criminology when studying crimes of the (economically) powerful

Critical criminology challenges the ideology that most people in the western, neo-liberal world act as free economic agents in a market society—one in which they are able to trade at will with people or organisations offering goods or services. The drive to get the best value or the greatest profit is affected by the power (or lack thereof) possessed by buyers or sellers, and the need to either make or save money affects the choices made by each group. For critical green criminologists, the impact of living in a market society leads to discussions about the environmental aspects of production and distribution, as well as the ways in which further crimes or harms can be encouraged by market forces together with political and power-related pressures.

- Discuss how and why the features of subcultures and emotions are important to cultural criminologists

Subcultures may appear to be deviant, frightening, and challenging to the dominantly powerful part of a society. In these cases they may lead to calls for political or public action to be taken in order to 'control' the behaviour of the subculture. Subcultures often develop their own interpretations of this behaviour, with internal meanings, symbols, and styles which can be seen as a reaction to the dominant social order. Cultural criminologists will examine these interpretations and their relationship to all forms of wider society, including those aspects which are not generally considered to be 'culture'—for instance, television programmes and advertising. In particular, cultural criminology considers the experiences of groups whose views and ideas are either challenging to the accepted order, or are not generally heard or valued due to the powerlessness of their members.

Some cultural criminologists see people's behaviour as a result of (constrained) choices. This choice can be affected by many things, including their view of the world, their experiences of it, and the meaning they give their actions. Some of these factors may be connected to social elements such as poverty but others will be sparked by emotions such as lust, anger, or fear. The desire for excitement is seen as particularly important, being seen by some writers as a reaction to the control, economic pressures, and boredom experienced by most people in their day-to-day lives. Understanding such emotional impact means that some cultural criminologists may give less importance to structural issues (such as poverty) than they do to the personal and psychological.

- Evaluate the claim made by convict criminologists that the prisoner's voice should be a central one when considering prison reform and penal change

Convict criminology is a developing, critical social movement. One of its main challenges to mainstream forms of criminology is that it questions how knowledge is produced in prison studies. It calls for participatory forms of research, which involve prisoners and former prisoners on an equal footing. The idea that prisoners' and ex-prisoners' experiences and knowledge are crucial when challenging perceptions and prisons policy has proved controversial, not least as it challenges those powerful groups who make such policy. Many also question the idea the such groups should be involved as researchers.

REVIEW QUESTIONS

1. List and evaluate why, in the 21st century, there is need for a critical criminology.

2. What does it mean to 'speak truth to power'? Give two examples of this.

3. What are safety crimes? Are they really crimes?

4. Give three examples of issues which are of concern to critical green criminologists. Why should we care about environmental protection?

5. What you do understand by the terms 'cultural inclusion' and 'structural exclusion'? What do they contribute to our understandings of present day crime and its control?

6. By focusing on the so-called foreground factors of crime (such as the emotions of anger, excitement, and boredom) some cultural criminologists have nothing practical to say or offer to criminal justice policy makers. Do you agree or disagree?

7. List three reasons why convict criminologists argue that prisoners and former prisoners be involved in prisons research as more than participants.

FURTHER READING

As with the previous chapter, the following two books on critical criminology are recommended.

Ugwudike, P. (2015) *An Introduction to Critical Criminology*. Bristol: Policy Press.
This book offers a clearly written introductory account of both the foundations of and contemporary theoretical positions within critical criminology.

DeKeseredy, W.S. and Dragiewicz, M. (eds) (2011) *The Routledge Handbook of Critical Criminology*. London: Routledge.
A good, although more advanced, collection of original essays which cover a range of critical perspectives and contemporary issues at both national and international levels.

Beyond that:

Scraton, P. (2016) *Hillsborough; The Truth*. Edinburgh: Mainstream Publishing.
This is a very powerful and moving account of the Hillsborough tragedy and its aftermath, written by an eminent British critical criminologist. It is an excellent example of what critical criminology is all about and what it can achieve.

Hillyard, P., Pantazis, C., Tombs, S., and Gordon, D. (eds) (2004) *Beyond Criminology; Taking Harm Seriously*. London: Pluto Press.
This is good starting point for those of you wishing to take forward your study of the notion of social harm. It contains many interesting essays on a wide range of areas (from state and workplace harms to poverty and disease) to which the harm perspective can be applied.

South, N. and Brisman, A. (eds) (2014) *Routledge International Handbook of Green Criminology*. London: Routledge.
For those of you wanting to take your study of green criminology to that next level this is a good (albeit more advanced) wide-ranging collection of original essays and case studies; from the impact on the environment from forms of corporate criminality to environmental justice and wildlife trafficking.

Ferrell, J., Hayward, K., and Young, J. (2015) *Cultural Criminology; An Invitation*. London: Sage.
An important book in the developing area of cultural criminology written by three of its leading scholars. It covers many issues in entertaining and innovative ways (from war and terrorism to the politics of gender). It also lists many good films and documentaries from which to develop your understanding of this perspective. Well worth persevering with.

Earle, R. (2016) *Convict Criminology: Inside and Out*. Bristol: Policy Press.
A crisply-written and lively book which covers the development of convict criminology in both the US and in Europe.

 Access the **online resources** to view selected further reading and web links relevant to the material covered in this chapter.
www.oup.com/uk/case/

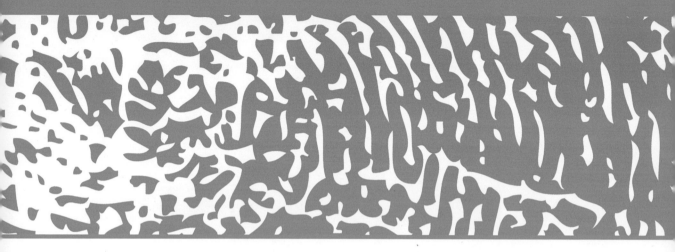

CHAPTER OUTLINE

Introduction: The emergence of realist perspectives   480

Right realism: Key ideas   482

Right realism: Policy implications   483

Evaluating right realism   488

Left realism: Key ideas   489

Left realism: Policy implications   492

Evaluating left realism   495

Conclusion   497

Right and left realism

KEY ISSUES

After studying this chapter, you should be able to:

- appreciate the links between criminological theorising, and broader law and order politics;

- understand the political context surrounding the emergence of realist criminologies;

- identify and critically analyse the key ideas of both right and left realism;

- relate realist theorising to criminal justice policy initiatives and critically evaluate these.

Introduction: The emergence of realist perspectives

Realist criminologies were, in the most basic terms, theoretical reactions to both sociological positivism (right realism) and critical criminologies (left realism). Two main strands of realist criminologies which emerged in the late 1970s and early 1980s were right realism, and left realism; so called because of the political leanings that influenced them. Before delving into the key ideas and concepts associated with these two strands, it is firstly important to better understand the political and theoretical context in which they emerged.

In **Chapters 15** and **16** we described and analysed the foundational ideas and subsequent development of critical criminologies. Although there are clear differences in focus between them (especially in the later variants of zemiology, green, cultural, and convict criminologies) these perspectives have many things in common. For example, all critical criminologists have an interest in researching and highlighting crimes and social harms committed by powerful groups in society, and use a focus on structural inequalities to analyse such crime and the official responses to it. They are also committed to revelatory social research and critical analysis that 'speaks truth to power' through working with marginalised and silenced social groups (the powerless); and they advocate for radical reforms in social, economic, and penal policies to achieve greater social justice and a fairer, more equal society.

Critical criminologies retain a real and important presence in our current thinking about crime and its control. However, they have never been the dominant paradigm in criminology, and given their critical and radical focus on issues of power and processes of criminalisation, it is perhaps not surprising that policy gains resulting from such critical research have been minimal.

By the late 1970s the foundational ideas of critical criminology (especially the more Marxist inspired variants) were under a sustained attack of intellectual critique from disparate groups of so-called 'realist' criminologists, who came from both the political right and left wings. The basic thrust of these critiques was quite simply that critical criminology was utopian and idealistic in both its analysis of crime and the prescriptions recommended for its control. For instance, it was forcibly argued by left realists that some of the early critical criminologists tended to see the rule of law as being little more than a simplistic reflection of capitalist class relations, but this viewpoint failed to recognise the fact that the law, however ideological it might seem, can also protect relatively powerless groups against the misuse of power by other people.

Left realist authors such as Lea and Young (1984) criticised what they regarded as the romantic portrayal of working class offenders who were characterised as victims of structural inequalities and oppression. It was also argued by left realists that a reluctance to critically engage with the 'real world' of law and order politics of the late 1970s and early 1980s was failing working class (and especially female) victims of crime and not recognising their very real suffering; to simply say that much crime was an expression of class conflict and media-inspired moral panic was unsympathetic to those who experienced it and who had to live with the practical and emotional consequences.

It was also argued that this allowed for right-leaning criminological theorising to gain the ascendency and influence policy in reactionary and repressive ways, in terms of increasing police powers, reducing police accountability, and relying too heavily on prison sentences. Furthermore, for those on the right, criminal justice policies which were informed by positivist theorising, highlighting individual needs and rehabilitation, were regarded as simply being wrong, and were often caricatured as offering criminals a culture of excuses for their behaviour.

In short, there was a growing sense amongst a range of commentators that the foundational critical criminologies had nothing practical to offer policy debates apart from a rather detached call for revolution. Critics argued that if a theoretical perspective claims to take crime seriously it must engage with policy initiatives on a practical level, so that it can address all forms of crime—not just those committed by the relatively rich and powerful. This willingness to take action is at the core of theoretical claims to being 'realist'; that is, getting real about the crime problem(s) which exist and being realistic about what can be done about them.

One of the central themes of this current part of the book on 'Explaining Crime' is that whilst criminological theorising can, at first, appear to be abstract and complicated, most theories do contain (whether implicitly or explicitly) certain assumptions. These assumptions can, for instance, be about the human actor—such as whether our behaviour is best characterised as being rational or driven—or about the nature of society, which can be described as sitting on a continuum that runs from being consensual to being conflictual. You may well notice others as you broaden your reading and continue your studies. The most important assumption we are examining in this chapter is that there are links between criminological theory and policy. For instance, in this section of the book we have already seen how classicism links with policies based around the idea of deterrence (**Chapter 13**) and how the logic of forms of positivism(s) leads us to consider crime control and prevention based on the idea and concept of rehabilitation (**Chapters 12** and **14**). In short, broader contexts are important when studying and understanding criminological theories, and perhaps of even greater importance when considering the rise of so-called 'realist' criminologies. This next section will outline such broader contexts (in both the US and UK) in the late 1970s and early 1980s when these perspectives were being developed.

The political context to the rise of realism

Perhaps a useful concept for us to draw on here is that of a 'critical election'. This idea has a long pedigree in American political science but Evans and Norris (1999) have developed it to broaden our understanding of British politics. For them, one of the main conditions which mark a critical election is a radical realignment of, and ruptures in, the ideological basis of competition between the various political parties. As they note, such ideological changes often have important and long-lasting consequences for public policy agendas, which of course include criminal justice policy. The elections which saw Margaret Thatcher becoming the Conservative Prime Minister in the UK in 1979 and Ronald Reagan being elected as the Republican US president in 1981 (see **Figure 17.1**) are perhaps good examples of such critical elections, as they heralded significant shifts in the ways in which both of the main parties presented themselves and decided on their priorities for action and legislation.

It was against a backdrop of increasing crime rates and a related public fear of crime in this period that

Figure 17.1 Portraits of Margaret Thatcher (1925–2013), former Conservative Prime Minister in the UK, and Ronald Reagan (1911–2004), former President of the United States of America

Source (Thatcher): Nationaal Archief/CC BY-SA

Source (Reagan): Public domain

new forms of right wing, populist, and public criminological theorising were developed. In these critical elections law and order, perhaps for the first time, became a fundamental issue; crime and its control were becoming politicised. The shift in political ideology away from the *social democracy* which characterised much of the post-war period in the UK (with its stress on equality of opportunity, fairness, social citizenship, and social justice) to *economic liberalism* (with its prime social values being individual responsibility, freedom, and social order) was to have profound consequences across a range of social policy domains—see for instance Hughes and Lewis (1988) for an analysis of how the welfare state was being reconstituted at this time in the UK along these lines.

Perhaps as a consequence of this shift, new discourses on criminal justice were also emerging; these in some ways developed existing theories but were given various new labels, such as neo-conservative authoritarianism, neo-liberal responsibilisation, and neo-conservative re-moralisation. This led to significant shifts in the ways in which those who transgressed the criminal law were being conceptualised; they went from being seen as vulnerable people whose individual needs and multiple forms of deprivation needed to be recognised and addressed, to simply being regarded as being irresponsible or immoral individuals who needed to take responsibility and be held to account for their behaviours, usually through forms of punishment; ranging from having their welfare benefits curtailed or through more formal criminal justice sanctions. Taken together it could be argued that such approaches coalesced to form what became known as right realism.

What all of these perspectives share is a shift away from the social democratic consensus on crime control. This, in the main, recognised multiple forms of disadvantage as being a cause of crime, and prioritised welfare and rehabilitative policy responses (see the discussion in the introduction of **Chapter 16** on Young's (1999, 2007) account of the rise and consolidation of the *exclusive society* and the implications of this for criminal justice policy and the criminalisation of welfare. See also **Chapter 25** for a detailed discussion of the decline of the rehabilitative ideal). In time, of course, right realism developed its own critics who began to oppose these discourses, and this, unsurprisingly, became known as left realism. As we will see later in this chapter, the key ideas of left realism developed as a direct response to the influence right realist ideas had on policy, especially in the UK under the Thatcher government. We will also see that as left realist ideas developed, they too had a real impact on the policies of the first New Labour government (1997–2001), especially in terms of its espoused policy focus on issues of social exclusion; summed up by the mantra of being 'tough on crime, tough on the *causes of crime*', which they adopted as a response to Conservative penal repression when in opposition.

This chapter will set out the key ideas of both right and left realism and encourage you to critically engage with the very real impacts which they have had on criminal justice policy formation in both the US and the UK. We will begin our discussion by considering right realism, and then move on to look at the response to this by some of those criminologists on the political left.

Right realism: Key ideas

Right realism is often regarded as being an inconsistent and rather contradictory criminological perspective. This is because it is influenced by, and situated within, political philosophies of the 'new right'—which concentrate on issues of social order and criminal justice on one hand, and individual responsibility and freedom on the other. The main contradiction lies between a belief in so-called *free market (neo-liberal) economics* which champions individual freedom of choice, and *neo-conservative politics*, with its emphasis on the need for a strong government to create a disciplined society around a very particular version of 'social order'. This is all reflected in right leaning realist criminologies. For instance, in the most influential right realist work discussed in this chapter we can discern a re-imagining of certain theoretical ideas and concepts which you will already have encountered in this book (see in particular **Chapters 12 and 13**). These include:

• a re-imagining of classicist themes with a focus on the offender as a rational actor and a call for crime control policies based on deterrence, greater social controls (both formal and informal), and on an increased use of punishment and imprisonment (Wilson 1975);

• a re-imagining of certain ideas associated with individual positivism, which focus on offending having a genetic basis (as opposed to a social one). In particular, the controversial argument that there is somehow a link between social behaviour and intelligence (as measured by the intelligence quotient—IQ) and that offenders suffer from a form of 'cognitive disadvantage' (Wilson and Herrnstein 1985; Herrnstein and Murray 1994); and

• a re-focusing on the idea that crime is linked to (im)morality and that most crime is committed by a growing 'underclass' who lack a moral conscience—in short, the idea that it is 'moral poverty' rather than economic poverty which is linked with criminal behaviour (Murray 1990).

Despite these clear tensions, contradictions, and the varying levels of analytical sophistication within right realist theorising, Platt and Takagi (1977) have identified three common themes which unite it and give it a form of coherence. These are:

1.   **A focus on 'street crime'**—In the work of James Q. Wilson, 'crime' is simply defined as being 'predatory crime for gain, the most common forms of which are robbery, burglary, larceny, and auto theft … (as) … it is a far more serious matter than consumer fraud, antitrust violations, prostitution, or gambling, because predatory crime … makes difficult or impossible the maintenance of meaningful human communities' (1975: xx). In short, right realists are united in focusing entirely on legal definitions of crime and in particular on 'street crime'. It could be argued that these forms of crime are almost exclusively specific to, or are located within, the working classes. You will find very little—if any—focus on crimes committed by powerful groups (such as corporate or state criminality) in right realist texts.

2.   **Anti-intellectualism**—This common thread relates to the right realists' outright rejection of any deep analysis of the 'causes of crime', especially the idea that crime might have social and economic causes (sociological variants of positivism). Such a line of thought, especially the idea of there being any causal links between crime rates and rates of poverty, is dismissed as simply being misplaced. The basis of this dismissal is the rather simplistic and crude argument that crime in the post-war period has risen, despite there being very real increases in the distribution of wealth and income (we will re-visit this argument later in the chapter when we consider left realist arguments about the concept of relative deprivation).

3.   **A focus on punishing criminals**—As we saw in point 1, right realists regard what they call 'predatory street crime' as being the most urgent and damaging threat to a particular 'way of life'. As a result, they call for tough responses to it. These proposals focus on policies based on deterrence which, at the soft end, would include different and more aggressive styles of policing and forms of situational crime prevention (see **Chapter 22**) and, at the hard end, indeterminate prison sentences and even, in some cases, capital punishment. In short, issues of order and control are prioritised over those relating to the broader issues of social justice and welfare.

The next section of the chapter will begin to set out and analyse the policy implications of right realist theorising.

We will begin by considering the work of James Q. Wilson (who was a policy advisor to President Reagan in the 1980s) and, in particular, his very influential (and controversial) work *Thinking About Crime* (1975). We will then move on to discuss and analyse Charles Murray's (1984; 1990; 1994) arguments that much criminality is located within a violent and feckless underclass. The important and very controversial right realist biosocial theory of Herrnstein and Wilson (1985), which posits the provocative and hotly contested idea that low intelligence is related to criminality, is covered elsewhere in the book (see **Chapter 18**).

Right realism: Policy implications

James Q. Wilson: *Thinking About Crime*

As just noted, the origins of right realism in criminology could arguably be linked to the sense of disillusionment and retrenchment associated with the 1970s and the decline of the welfare ideal. Crime became increasingly seen as a fact of life, and as something which could not be treated or planned out of existence. The seeds of this change of mood were sown in the USA, but its influence rapidly spread across the developed world. James Q. Wilson, in particular, is associated with the articulation of the underpinning arguments on which much subsequent realist criminological thinking and policy making has been based. The arguments he set out effectively provided a rationale for making '*crime control*' the central feature of criminal justice practices (see **Chapter 23** for more detail on this). Wilson consciously and deliberately bridged the domains of academia, policy making, and public debate in order to popularise his position and to actively counter what he saw as an unhelpful consensus of opinion which tended both to minimise the effects of crime on victims and communities, and to misrepresent the true nature of criminality.

In his most influential book, *Thinking About Crime*, Wilson effectively set out a five-point critique of what was at the time (1975) an established liberal consensus within criminology (Delisi 2010: 194). These five points can be summarised as follows:

1. The individual is the source of crime, and social causes are of no significance.

2. Previous criminological thinking was dominated by ideology and conjecture rather than empirical evidence; the facts of crime were being ignored.

3. Crime which occurs on the streets and in geographical neighbourhoods is more significant and more harmful than white collar crime, and thus needs to be taken more seriously.

4. Crime should be treated as a moral issue. Blame and responsibility are important constituents in any system which accounts for and responds to offending.

5. Some people are criminal by nature—their disposition to do bad things is innate.

Although these ideas were articulated forcefully and systematically by Wilson, it is likely that they gained credence and became influential at least partly because they were not new, but actually picked up on and amplified long held beliefs about the origins and reality of crime. Indeed, for him, the 'problem of crime' and his perceived solution to it, was simply (and rather simplistic): 'Wicked people exist. Nothing avails except to set them apart from innocent people' (Wilson 1975: 235).

Such ideas could be traced back to the 17th century British political philosopher Thomas Hobbes, who argued that there is a need for state structures and systems of law in order to regulate and control the behaviour of those who are naturally inclined towards unlawful behaviour. The vagaries of self-interest and human nature ensure that we cannot predict which individuals in particular will be inclined towards such behaviour, although we know that this is an inherent possibility within all of us. Hobbes felt that a strong and comprehensive system of controls needs to be put in place in anticipation of law-breaking:

> annexed to the sovereignty [is] the right of judicature; that is to say, of hearing and deciding all controversies which may arise concerning law, either civil or natural, or concerning fact. For without the decision of controversies, there is no protection of one subject against the injuries of another; the laws concerning meum and tuum are in vain, and to every man remaineth, from the natural and necessary appetite of his own conservation, the right of protecting himself by his private strength, which is the condition of war, and contrary to the end for which every Commonwealth is instituted.
>
> Hobbes' Leviathan, Ch 18

Such assumptions of course underpin much of the subsequent development of judicial structures and modern forms of policing, with the implicit assumption that coercive control will be a necessary and central part of their remit.

In a sense, the work of Wilson, and others such as Kelling, served to reawaken and reinforce persistent concerns about public order and the threat to security represented by the predispositions of certain elements of the population. Indeed, their argument was for a return to an idealised past where police-community relations relied on a common sense of purpose and cooperation.

For centuries, the role of the police as watchmen was judged primarily not in terms of its compliance with appropriate procedures but rather in terms of its attaining a desired objective. The objective was order, an inherently ambiguous term but a condition that people in a given community recognised when they saw it (Kelling and Wilson 1982: 13).

As we can also now acknowledge, these threats are often associated with difference and the perceived threat from outside, of people who are 'not like us', and who do not naturally share the same cultural assumptions or behavioural norms. 'Othering' of this kind is also a powerful driver of right realist sentiments (we will develop this further later in the chapter when we will consider and evaluate Murray's (1990) use of the term 'underclass').

The emerging tide of concern about lawlessness and loss of control was perhaps crystallised on both sides of the Atlantic by the respective and coincidental periods of office of Ronald Reagan (the US President between 1981–89) and Margaret Thatcher (UK Prime Minister 1979–90), both of whom arguably came to power at least partly because of their appeal to populist fears about endemic threats to the social order. Much was made of a renewed concern for the interests of victims and the need to shift the balance away from a misplaced interest in offender welfare.

Taken in combination, these ideological shifts produced a number of outcomes in terms of the organisation and focus of criminal justice, results which arguably had a degree of coherence. At least in rhetorical terms, prominence was given to the interests of victims and the importance of promoting community safety, following the 'Broken Windows' thesis. Associated with this was an explicit commitment to a more proactive approach to policing which would target those areas and situations where the likelihood of a crime being committed was greatest. Thus policing strategies associated with the principle of 'zero tolerance' (see **Chapter 23** on this) became more prominent, and some key individuals, like the New York police commissioner, Bill Bratton, became closely associated with this idea; and, in turn, its implementation was claimed to be a significant factor in reducing levels of violent crime, particularly in that city during the 1990s.

Exploring the notion of pre-emptive control of this kind further, we can identify a number of other key features of this model. Firstly, it seems that the idea of unspecified 'danger' is significant, in that there is a pressing need to develop better means of identifying the risk of crime and responding accordingly. Concepts of targeting and *risk management* become important, both in shaping

intelligence gathering and designing intervention strategies. There is an apparent need for much better information in order to anticipate and choke off crime, wherever it is most likely to occur. And, where it does occur, a swift and certain response is required, with the objective of preventing a recurrence of the problem.

From this derives a number of further features of the right realist strategy. These include the use of physical security measures to enhance security for businesses and communities; a robust and focused police presence in those areas most vulnerable to crime; speed and certainty of enforcement action where infringements occur; definitive action to control offenders and restrict their future opportunities to commit crime; and prison sentences which aim to reduce the likelihood of further criminality.

Many substantial claims have been made for the effectiveness of crime control strategies deriving from 'right realist' arguments. There was a substantial drop in crime in New York, for example, following Commissioner Bratton's adoption of a proactive approach to policing; and similar claims have been made elsewhere for their effectiveness, although as we shall see, these have been challenged.

Another form of 'othering'—focusing blame for crime on a specific group of people—which we find in right realism is to be found in Charles Murray's thoughts on the existence of a criminal 'underclass'. We shall turn to this now.

Charles Murray on the (criminal) 'underclass'

Imagine that you are an unskilled worker who decides to move in order to find a job. You leave home, make your lengthy journey, arrive at your destination … only to be locked up until you can get someone to lend you the cash to go home again. Your crime? Not carrying a reference from the local justice of the peace, confirming that you had an acceptable reason for leaving, and that you are not actually a beggar.

This might sound like a story from modern times, with its hints of economic migration and fears of benefits scroungers; in fact, it describes the 'Cambridge Statute' from 1388, a piece of legislation that illustrates the lengthy history of attempts to control those who do not fit into wider social ideas of how people should behave. These controls are not always formal and legislative; they may be informal, unspoken, almost secretive ways of regulating behaviour, keeping people 'in their place', and reinforcing the boundaries between the social classes. For instance, do you see anything wrong in the following paragraph?

> Lucy finished her letter and put down the sheet of notepaper. She got up from the settee and went over the mirror, putting on some perfume before going in to the lounge at noon for dinner.

According to some social rules, this immediately marks Lucy as someone who is lower class. Had she been upper class, she would have used writing paper, sat on a sofa in the drawing room, admired herself in a looking glass and worn scent; her midday meal would have been luncheon (Mitford 1959). Yet these 'rules' are not formally set out anywhere. They have accumulated over time, and become a way whereby we can place other people in the hierarchy of the class system, so we know whether they are someone to whom we should look up or whether instead they can be looked down upon and even perhaps feared.

If we acknowledge that there is a class structure in the UK—however flexible and shifting it may be—it follows that there has to be a lowest class, a group which is at the bottom of the social heap. It is this lowest group which was targeted by laws such as the Cambridge Statute, and which has been characterised in art and drama for centuries as reckless, immoral, and lazy. In 1747 the artist William Hogarth published a set of engravings called 'Industry and Idleness' which compare the consequences of hard work to those of drinking and idleness, in which the idle apprentice ends up being hanged whilst his industrious friend becomes Lord Mayor of London (see **Figure 17.2**).

This disdain and hostility towards the non-productive continued. By the time Henry Mayhew was writing in the 1840s, he could categorise non-workers as those who need not, could not, or would not get jobs (Mayhew 1861: 601); in 1926, volunteers drove buses and ran canteens to counter the impact of the General Strike which had been called to improve the conditions and wages of coal miners; and in 2008, when Karen Matthews was convicted of staging the kidnap of her daughter to claim a reward, her role as a member of the 'underclass' was given prominent media attention (see the following extract from the *Telegraph*). These examples serve to show that hostility towards those who rely on state benefits and support is neither new, nor has it subsided in recent years.

Karen Matthews and the underclass thrive on labour's welfare state

The case of Karen Matthews, convicted of kidnapping her own daughter in order to claim a reward, has again pulled back the curtain to allow us a glimpse of this netherworld of taxpayer-funded fecklessness.

Telegraph, 6 December 2008

The term 'underclass' was, by the time the *Telegraph* article was published, in common use to describe a particular group of people—those who were unemployed, who subsisted on state welfare benefits, were generally poorly educated, and who were unwilling to live up to societal expectations of hard work and industry. In criminological terms, the word was first given prominence by Charles Murray in his 1990 work 'The Emerging Underclass'. For Murray, being in the underclass was not simply about being financially poor, but rather living in a specific type of social and *moral poverty*. He critiqued the idea that 'there was no such thing as the ne'er do well poor person—he (sic) was the figment of the prejudices of a parochial middle class, (Murray, in McLaughlin and Muncie 2013: 128) and instead argued that there are three key elements which identify and categorise the underclass. We shall examine these in the next section, but before we do so, take a moment to think about what the key elements may be by reading **What do you think? 17.1** on 'Who are the underclass?'.

For Murray, there are three main indicators of an underclass. These are: illegitimacy rates, violent crime, and non-participation in the labour force. Murray's principal concern was that of illegitimacy—children born to parents who are not married to each other. As well as any possible religious implications, Murray saw the decline in traditional two-parent families as meaning many children grow up without suitable male role models, due to the absence of fathers from family life and the preponderance of single mothers. Whilst this may not be a problem in individual households, he argues, it becomes significant in communities where the majority of families lack a father.

Moving on from the notion of illegitimacy, Murray then identified engagement with violent crime as the second feature of the underclass. For him, crime—especially violent crime—amongst the underclass is normal behaviour and is often based on the way young boys and men choose role models from older male members of the community. Murray predicted that England would become a 'more dangerous place in which to live: that this unhappy process is not occurring everywhere, but disproportionately in particular types of neighbourhoods; and that those neighbourhoods turn out to be the ones in which

Figure 17.2 A scene from Hogarth's *Industry and Idleness* series of engravings
Source: William Hogarth/Public domain

WHAT DO YOU THINK? 17.1

Who are the underclass?

Imagine that you are producing a new television soap opera. In the document pitching the ideas and storyline, one of the characters is described as being 'someone from the underclass'. You need to give instructions to the scriptwriters, wardrobe department, and casting agents about this character. How do you visualise him (or her)? Use the headings below to write down your ideas about them:

Age:	Name:
Gender:	Education:
Housing:	Habits (e.g. smoking, gambling):
Clothing:	Race:
Marital status and children:	Job:
Probable storylines:	

Keep your list in mind as we look to see what Murray's views were. Did this task make you feel uneasy in any way?

---

the underclass is taking over. Reality will once again force theory to its knees.' (Murray, ibid: 136). We can see this association of violence and threat with one particular sector of society if we look at the reaction to the London riots of 2011; some prominent politicians were quick to identify social dissatisfaction and exclusion as a cause. For others, rioters were described as feral, or alternatively as organised looters planning their activities through social media. Noticeably less attention was given to the shooting of a young black man by the police, which one local community saw as the trigger for the disorder.

Such social anger was, in some cases, linked to the difficulty young people have in finding suitable employment. One person who was arrested after the riots told the *New York Times*:

'No one has ever given me a chance; I am just angry at how the whole system works,' Mr James said. He would like to get a job at a retail store, but admits that he spends most days watching television and just trying to get by. 'That is the way they want it,' he said, without specifying exactly who 'they' were. 'They give me just enough money so that I can eat and watch TV all day. I don't even pay my bills anymore.'

New York Times, 9 August 2011

Murray would have seen Mr James as one of the 'economically inactive—someone who would like to take a job, but who has lost the will to seek work; in Murray's words they have 'given up'. (Murray, ibid: 136) He sees this as something associated with young men, living in economically deprived areas and who lack the sense of shame that older men feel when unemployed and claiming benefits. These young people have not been 'socialised into the world of work' (Murray, ibid: 139). For Murray, the problem is not so much that these young men are supported by the tax payer; rather that they are not helped to develop a sense of pride or to make important social connections that benefit their entire communities.

Murray reached a bleak conclusion: that there was a growing underclass and that it would only be improved if it were given the tools to help itself; in other words, to take some form of individual responsibility for the plight of its members. He argued that neighbourhoods did not want to experience high rates of crime, youth unemployment, or illegitimacy, and that they would self-regulate to reduce these problems. In later work, he advocated reducing benefits for single mothers in order to discourage them from having illegitimate babies; instead, there should be social and financial incentives that encourage moral and social responsibility. Although this approach received strong criticism (for example, see MacDonald's (1997) collection of critical papers on the existence of a youth underclass in the UK) we can see its legacy in more recent policy discussions, such as the adoption of 'workfare' schemes which require claimants to carry out unpaid work in order to be eligible for benefits. Take a moment to look at **What do you think? 17.2** and consider Murray's theories further.

As we can see, simple descriptions of—rather than detailed, empirically-informed explanations for—the existence of an impoverished underclass are controversial. One of the main critical responses to the underclass thesis it that such a description individualises (and pathologises) people who suffer from what are perhaps deeply entrenched issues relating to socio-economic forms of disadvantage, which can limit the real choices they have. In doing so, it also brackets off and dismisses the possibility that forms of disadvantage can be addressed through various policy domains. We will take a short break from right realist theorising here to consider how the concept of an underclass has been developed to have a particular resonance in popular culture today.

Beyond the underclass: the making of the 'chav'

Although, as we have seen, we can still encounter the word 'underclass', other ideas and descriptions have risen to take its place. Some have become replacement

WHAT DO YOU THINK? 17.2

Murray's research and writing was carried out in the 1990s. Since then, there have been many social shifts that may affect our interpretation of, and reaction to, his work. Take a moment to jot down some of these as they occur to you.

Your list will probably be a personal one, influenced by your own background and attitudes. However, some important things to bear in mind when thinking about the concept of an underclass and Murray's key elements are as follows:

- He was writing before the idea of single-sex families became acceptable; we might like to consider how his views would accommodate this important social shift. Would illegitimacy in a single-sex partnership, where a male role model remained, cause him such anxiety?

- The British Conservative Government shares Murray's views that illegitimacy is undesirable, introducing tax rules that benefit married couples

(although take-up of these has been relatively low) but according to the Office of National Statistics, the rate of marriage continues to decline.

- Murray quoted statistics that illustrated a rising illegitimacy rate—from 14.1 per cent in 1982 to 25.6 per cent in 1988. In 2012 the Office of National Statistics reported that 47.5 per cent of children were born 'out of wedlock'—a rate of increase that suggests that by 2016 children born to married parents will be in the minority. How does this compare to current crime rate statistics?

- Murray thinks of crime and the underclass as being largely concerned with male identities and role models. How would his work have been affected by the studies of female offenders? Does he consider bearing illegitimate children to be a form of female deviance, and how should we analyse his work in the light of feminist criminologies?

---

language for what can be seen as an outdated and almost offensive term; perhaps the most common of these is the (equally offensive) word 'chav'. Hayward and Yar (2006) suggest that 'chav' has in fact become what they call 'a popular reconfiguration of the underclass idea' and, as such, it is worth briefly considering further here.

The origin of the word chav is disputed, but it is generally thought to have originated as a word meaning child or youth. However, by the early 21st century it had become a slang term for someone wearing particular styles of clothing; baseball caps on backwards, heavy 'gold' jewellery and counterfeit designer shoes (see **Figure 17.3**). Chavs were generally young and, more importantly for this discussion, likely to exhibit antisocial or offending behaviour.

Hayward and Yar (2006) suggest that most writers consider the underclass in relation to its failure to be part of a productive industry, which in turn causes various undesirable 'side effects' such as crime. In contrast, the discourse around chavs is connected to consumption. This is not in itself a new phenomenon; indeed, in another course of paintings titled 'Marriage a la Mode,' Hogarth illustrates the risks of marrying for wealth and prestige by depicting the story of the young woman who is effectively sold to a rich husband: the series ends with a hanging, a suicide, and a syphilitic child (see **Figure 17.4**). Hayward and Yar argue that this desire for money and status can

be traced into the modern era, with the development of youth subcultures which value differing styles of clothes, shoes, cars, and so on.

As opportunities for work become increasingly insecure—a recent example would be the rise in 'zero hours'

Figure 17.3 Young adults, such as this young male, have been branded 'chavs' because of the way they choose to dress.

Source: The Arches (Flickr)/CC BY 2.0

Figure 17.4 *The Marriage Settlement* by William Hogarth
Source: The National Gallery/Public domain

Current popular discussion of the 'chav' focuses not on the inability to consume, but on the excessive participation in forms of market-oriented consumption which are deemed aesthetically impoverished. The perceived 'problem' with this 'new underclass' is that they consume in ways deemed 'vulgar' and hence lacking in 'distinction' by superordinate classes. ... 'chavs' and 'chavishness' are identified on the grounds of the taste and style that inform their consumer choices.

Hayward and Yar 2006: 7

Not only is the chav despised for his or her choices, Hayward and Yar go on to argue that these choices and the associated culture are irresponsible and pathologised. If the consumption of goods is a means of self-expression, then what does it say about someone who chooses to consume things that are seen as unrefined and unattractive? The authors argue that the 'new British underclass' is increasingly understood as 'flawed consumers', unable or unwilling to make the 'right' type of consumer choice'. (Hayward and Yar 2006: 11). Such criticism is not confined to those who are financially poor; for instance, in 2012 the singer Cheryl (Cheryl Fernandez-Versini, formerly Cheryl Cole) was 'branded' a chav by the fashion designer Julien MacDonald. And if wider society mocks and despises a group for its aesthetic choices, it is hardly surprising when that group becomes marginalised, excluded, and labelled as dangerous, different, and to be feared. Hayward and Yar conclude by pointing out that there is a fundamental clash at the heart of society's disdain for the 'chav'. On the one hand, there are economic factors—recession, the decline in manufacturing industries—which limit the employment opportunities available to the less well-educated or aspirational. Whether they want to be productive or not, there are fewer chances for them to participate in the creative life of the economy. And yet, they also suffer from 'the relentless dissemination of messages that link social worth and well-being to one's ability to consume at all costs' (Hayward and Yar 2006: 25). Small wonder perhaps that they struggle for an acceptable identity that does not consign them to the role of threat, danger, and mistrust that they seem fated to fill. We will return to the idea of the growing culture of consumption in late modern societies and its potential links with criminality later in the chapter when we consider left realism.

contracts—so its intrinsic value is lessened; the authors argue that self-expression and self-respect are now rooted in the ownership and display of goods, rather than in participation in productive labour. And it is the inability to consume, rather than the inability to create, that is now commonly identified as a cause of social exclusion. Many young people now talk about 'FOMO'—Fear of Missing Out—as a cause of anxiety and strain, and a driver for social behaviour, to the extent that a popular BBC television series, 'I've Never Seen Star Wars' could be based on the notion that not having taken part in a common social activity was so unusual as to be worthy of exploration and discussion.

Yet Hayward and Yar (2006) take a slightly different stance. For them, the chav is marked out by levels of consumerism that are viewed as excessive and vulgar rather than refined and tasteful. As an example, they highlight the chav's association with lager as opposed to good wine, or their fondness for obvious, rather than subtle, makeup and hairstyles. Rather like Lucy having dinner in her lounge, the chav is marked out by his or her visible breaches of social rules of taste, decorum, and sophistication; it is their perceived tastelessness which marks them out as a group which can be looked down upon and stigmatised:

Evaluating right realism

Right realism has been criticised on a number of grounds. Firstly, questions have been raised about claims made for the effectiveness of zero tolerance or other aggressive crime reduction measures. For instance, it is suggested that area-wide initiatives to tackle specific types of crime, such as burglary or drug dealing may just displace these to other areas which are less intensively policed (Bottoms 2012). More generally, it is suggested that some of the grand claims made for crime control strategies may simply overstate the case, or fail to take account of other contributory factors, such as demographic trends which reduce the likelihood of certain types of behaviour.

In addition, approaches which are based on targeting certain communities or particular offences are questioned because of their likelihood of incorporating discriminatory practices at the heart of law enforcement. This has for a long time been a criticism of the use of 'stop and search' powers by police in London and other metropolitan areas, where black young people have been disproportionately targeted (see **Chapter 10** for a more detailed discussion of this). More broadly, an emphasis on anticipatory policing may afford implicit acceptance of misuse of police powers, in the wider public interest.

Similarly, too, the emphasis of right realists on certain types of visible and interpersonal offences is believed to distract attention from equally and potentially more harmful 'white collar' crimes which are not prioritised.

We also need to bear in mind that the emphasis on certain types of interpersonal crime and the identification of individuals and groups (such as a welfare dependent, 'barbarian', 'underclass') as the cause of the problem does, as right realism at least partly intended, shift attention away from more distant and perhaps less readily demonstrable factors underlying criminal activity, which are located in structural inequality, systemic disadvantage, and discrimination. These neglected structural issues relating to the possible social causation of crime became a central part of left realism's critique of right realism. We will now set out the key ideas of what became known as left realism, before identifying, analysing, and critically engaging with their policy proposals.

Left realism: Key ideas

As we noted at the beginning of this chapter, 'realist' perspectives in criminology were developed in the late 1970s and early 1980s (mainly in the US and UK) against a backdrop of profound social, economic, and political change. With crime rates on a seemingly never-ending upward trajectory and similar increases in forms of urban disorder, there was a perceived growing public fear of crime, and its control became a key political issue in the 'critical elections' of 1979 (UK) and 1981 (US). The results of these saw a distinct shift to the right in politics and in economic and social policies whilst, as we have seen, criminal justice policies became centred around a module of strict crime control and orientated towards punishment; you can read more about this in Downes' and Morgan's (1994, 1997, 2002, 2006, and 2012) detailed discussions of the changing politics of law and order in British politics since 1945.

Criminological theorising, especially more Marxist informed forms of critical criminology, was scrutinised by many criminologists who found it wanting and not attuned to these 'new times'. Criminologists on the left of the political spectrum initially focused their ire on some of the fundamental Marxist-inspired arguments—for instance, that those who broke the law should be regarded as being the victims of an oppressive and exploitative capitalist system. Here the tacit argument was that much offending behaviour, amongst working class and marginalised groups, should be seen as being a form of primitive rebellion or an act of resistance, whereas for left realists this both idealises and romanticises the offender.

It was also argued that these writers were both utopian and idealistic in their calls for radical non-intervention, abolitionism (see **Chapter 26**) and the kind of wholescale revolution which would somehow herald a crime-free society. Another argument posited that it was a mistake to

solely concentrate on an analysis of how the state criminalises some forms of behaviour, and the harms that directly resulted from the actions of powerful groups. It was however equally mistaken to neglect the equally harmful behaviour of the relatively powerless; such an approach meant that the public's greatest fears, which were identified as being street crime and the fear of falling victim to it, were largely ignored.

As a result, the previous Marxist-inspired critical criminologies were characterised by the left realists with the rather pejorative label of 'left idealism' and a fierce theoretical debate between the two radical orientations ensued (see Gilroy and Sim 1987 for the 'left idealist' response). Jock Young, one of the key thinkers behind left realism, had after all been one of the co-authors of the seminal neo-Marxist text, *The New Criminology* (1973). As well as this, left realism can also be seen as being a reaction to the right realist perspectives which we considered in the previous sections of this chapter, and which were starting to have real impacts on criminal justice and the crime control policies which were at that time gaining public support. Authors such as Jock Young, John Lea, and Roger Matthews, all then working at Middlesex University, argued that in order to counter the growing influence of right-wing criminologies, there needed to be a response from those criminologists on the left (and social democratic) of the political spectrum. Such a response had to be seen as taking crime 'seriously' and to see it as a real problem; to be credible, it also needed to be pragmatic in its approach to both crime causation and in how it proposed to develop realistic prevention policies and strategies. As Jock Young makes clear:

> The central tenet of left realism is to reflect *the reality of crime, that is in its origins, its nature and its impact.* This

involves a rejection of tendencies to romanticise crime or to pathologise it, to analyse solely from the point of view of the administration of crime or the criminal actor, to underestimate crime or exaggerate it … *most importantly it is realism which informs our notion of practice; in answering what can be done about the problems of crime and social control.*

(1986: 21, emphasis added)

There were however clear points of convergence and divergence between both right and left realist approaches. Both argued that 'crime' (as defined by the state, with its focus on forms of street crime) was a genuine and growing problem. Both also accepted that the public's fear of becoming a crime victim was also a very real issue, and one which needed to be addressed in a measured and practical way. Where they differ markedly is in what they had to say about the causes of crime and what should be done about it. Whereas, to a large extent, right realists neglected issues of causation, we can discern in their work an implicit, and often contradictory, re-imagining of classist and individual positivist stances which focused on the individual—and their potential to exhibit pathological and immoral behaviours. By contrast, left realism drew on and developed work which is situated within more sociological forms of positivism. These include drawing on and developing insights derived from subcultural theories and concepts such as anomie, as well as broader issues like social exclusion and marginalisation—see **Chapter 12** and Young's (2003) article which re-works Merton's notion of anomie in a more culturally attuned way. As such, it could be said that this form of realism is an integrated theory (see **Chapter 18**) which seeks to capture the real complexities of crime and its control and not to reduce and over-simplify it, as it was argued previous (including right realism) theories had done.

So, left realism firmly locates its analysis of crime causation within broader social structural factors, together with questions of class, gender, and racial inequality. Although left realists still claimed to recognise that crimes committed by powerful groups did impact on the relatively powerless, their main focus was on day-to-day volume crime. Here it was argued that these acts perhaps had a greater impact on the working classes and marginalised communities and that, a result, their fear of it was a rational one which demanded to be taken seriously. In other words, it was argued that the types of crime that people feared most, and which had the greatest impact on their lives, were those committed by people within their own communities; crime should therefore not be seen exclusively as taking place between (inter) social classes but that much is also committed within (intra) communities.

In seeking to develop left realism as a theoretically grounded empirical project, its claims were based mainly on local crime and victimisation surveys (see **Chapter 6**) which asked people about both their problems with crime as well as their perceptions of the effectiveness of the police. For instance, there were local crime surveys carried out by Jones et al. (1986) and Crawford et al. (1990)—both in Islington, North London—which gave some empirical support for the idea that the experiences of being, and fear of becoming, a victim of burglary and street crime were very real ones for residents of these London boroughs. The surveys also identified that there were high levels of dissatisfaction with how this was dealt with at a local level by, for instance, the police.

Whereas for right realists the 'solution' to street crime is the use of crime control strategies which maintain a particular vision of social order through deterrence, left realism, by contrast, sees economic and social policies as having a central part to play in tackling marginalisation and forms of social exclusion. Perhaps the most important concept they draw on and develop in relation to exploring the possible social causes of criminality is that of *relative deprivation*. Relative deprivation is a phrase used to refer to the perception or experience of being deprived of something which an individual believes they are entitled to. It encapsulates the idea that people look both downward (on those who have fewer possessions and opportunities) as well as upwards (to those who have more of these) as well as considering their emotional reactions to this.

Our personal, subjective perceptions of, and reactions to, perceived injustices are important when thinking about the idea of relative deprivation. These are explored further in **What do you think? 17.3**, 'What does it mean to be relatively deprived?'.

Left realists (Lea and Young 1984; Young 2007) pick up and develop the idea of relative deprivation and relate it to crime by arguing that late modern societies are increasingly characterised by an *ethos of individualism* and a *culture of consumerism*, and that it is this which perhaps sets our age apart from previous epochs. You might want to revisit the discussion of Young's development of the ideas of *cultural inclusion* and *structural exclusion* in **Chapter 15**, as it is highly relevant here; both in terms of what he has to say about the anger and frustration which may be felt by those who are culturally included yet structurally excluded, as well as the feelings of anxiety, fear, and lack of empathy towards these marginalised groups which may be felt by those who are structurally included, and who can consume more and who have greater resources and opportunities.

The desire to consume and possess things can provide individuals with a sense of identity, and possessions can also provide them with a sense of recognition, status, and fulfilment. The ethos of individualism and culture of consumption can, according to Lea and Young (1984), lead to

WHAT DO YOU THINK? 17.3

What does it mean to be relatively deprived?

You may have heard the term 'first world problem'—a phrase meaning something which is portrayed as being important and difficult (although sometimes amusing) but which is really reflective of privilege and abundance: 'I cut myself halving an avocado' and 'I can only use two devices on this Wi-Fi router' are examples. But does seeing this sort of thing as a 'problem' distract us from real issues of deprivation, such as the 2.4 billion people in the world who do not have access to a toilet? Do we develop a false sense of priority, seeing things as important when in fact they are perhaps not? Let us think about this idea of need and deprivation by considering a basic part of our existence—our need for nutrition—in the light of some seemingly unconnected facts.

- The British supermarket Waitrose offers an 'essential' range of groceries that includes Essential Raw Prawns, Essential Coconut Milk, and Essential Gnocchi; the budget supermarket Aldi also runs an 'essential' range which features cheddar cheese, lemonade, and frozen Yorkshire puddings.

- Essential foods were rationed during the Second World War; by 1945 an adult's weekly entitlement included 57 grams of cheese, 113 grams of bacon or ham, and one egg. Many people turned their gardens or public spaces into smallholdings where they grew vegetables and kept chickens, and communities would club together to buy and raise a pig for meat.

- The charity Love Food, Hate Waste estimates that 15 million tonnes of food are thrown away in the UK each year, and yet in the UK the Trussell Trust operates over 400 food banks which in 2015 gave out over a million packs of emergency supplies to people who otherwise were unable to buy essential food items.

Think about the people associated with these statements; the supermarket shoppers, the wartime housewife, the cook throwing away unwanted food, and the foodbank user.

Then consider how you think the person in each of these groups feels about their access to food—do you imagine the 1940s shopper was resentful about rationing, or welcomed it as doing their bit for the war effort? Do food bank users feel anger about food waste? You might want to reflect on how your personal circumstances or experiences have affected your decisions.

Next, take a look around the space where you are reading this book. Jot down a list of the things around you, such as the furniture, your possessions, the equipment you are using, and again, give them a ranking; 1 being essential, 3 being nice but not completely necessary, and 5 a luxury.

As a last activity, take a (discreet) look at the people around you. Note their clothes, jewellery, what they are carrying. Write down the things they have that you envy—perhaps they have a better laptop than you, or more fashionable shoes. Then the things that you prefer from amongst your own possessions—is your jacket newer, your coffee from a trendier shop, or your mobile phone the latest upgrade? Finally, write down how this has made you feel—such as angry, resentful, smug, and grateful, or any other emotional reaction you may have experienced.

The point is, of course, that such things are *relative* to circumstance. If we have plenty of money, and are accustomed to eating well, then perhaps items such as coconut milk are something we learn to take for granted. If, on the other hand, we struggle to buy basic ingredients, the sight of someone spending several pounds on a large cup of coffee may cause us to feel aggrieved and bitter about the difference between their circumstances and our own.

What does it mean to feel deprived for people living in the developed world today? In what ways do you feel deprived or excluded and marginalised? As standards of living increase, our expectations and sense of entitlement develops. For instance, briefly consider your own expectations, wants, and desires and how you might feel if these are not met. Compare your expectations with those of your parents and grandparents. What do you have (in terms of both material goods and opportunities) which they did not at your age? Overall, economic growth in developed countries over the last 60 years has been exponential. Many of us now own and have 'things' (and have opportunities) which would have been simply unthinkable and unobtainable for our forebears.

Ultimately, you should think about this question: how would a right or left realist view us if we then stole something we desire or believed we deserved?

crime mainly, although not exclusively, within excluded groups. Such a cultural atmosphere can also lead to calls for greater controls from within included groups; who, in their efforts to maintain their relatively privileged positions and their fear of falling out of this group, may also transgress the law. For Young (2007), the relationship between relative deprivation and crime is not a simplistic, unilinear one. He does however argue that relative deprivation can:

> in *certain conditions* … (be seen) … as being a major cause of crime. That is, when people experience levels of unfairness in their allocation of resources and utilise individualistic means to attempt to right this condition. It is a reaction to the experience of injustice. Experienced injustice, coupled with individualistic 'solutions', can occur at different parts of society; like crime itself, it is certainly not a monopoly of the poor.
>
> Young 2007: 488

In other words, feeling relatively deprived can contribute to crime. As he and Lea put it:

> The equation is simple; relative deprivation equals discontent; discontent plus lack of political solution equals crime.
>
> Lea and Young 1984: 88

We will now turn our attention to what these political solutions might be and consider to what extent these ideas can be translated into realistic policies and political 'solutions' to the 'problem of crime'.

Left realism: Policy implications

Given its prime focus on the issues of relative deprivation and marginalisation, it is perhaps not surprising that left realism translates into policy proposals and objectives which focus primarily on the socio-economic causes of crime. Therefore, in terms of policy, it emphasises forms of social crime prevention, although it argues that situational and deterrent measures also have a minor role to play. In other words, left realism favours policies which seek to de-marginalise the marginalised and include the excluded; and seeks to find policy interventions which would bring about more cohesion and less crime within otherwise fractured communities. As we have seen, left realists are also concerned with addressing the public's fear of crime as well as acknowledging the needs of the victim, and so they argue also for a fairer and more accountable criminal justice system.

Whilst Young (1997: 42) argues that issues of social causation should be accorded the 'highest priority' he also contends that crime control policy should involve interventions 'on all levels'. In developing this idea he identified what he believed to be the four most important fundamental components which explain crime. These are: the victim; the offender; state agencies (such as the police and local multi-agency crime prevention partnerships); and the wider public and community. These are brought together in what is referred to as the 'square of crime'.

The argument developed here (as can be seen from the diagrammatic representation of the square of crime in **Figure 17.5**) is that it is essential for criminologists to explore the various interactions and interrelationships which exist between these four components. As I hope you can see, this conceptualisation attempts to capture the complexities involved, both in terms of action and reaction but also in terms of the constantly changing relationships between both informal and formal systems of control. It is often noted that this conceptualisation of crime and crime control heavily influenced the first New Labour government (1997–2001) in directing their policies on crime; for instance, in legislation such as the Crime and Disorder Act 1998 which set up various multi-agency crime prevention partnerships at the local level (see **Chapter 12** for a further discussion of this).

Social inclusion, exclusion, and policy

As we have seen, left realists base much of their analysis of crime on the concept of relative deprivation. In his later work, Jock Young (1999, 2007) developed this further in terms of the concepts of *inclusion* and *exclusion*. His main argument was that late modern societies had shifted away from being inclusive and had instead become more exclusive (see **Chapter 16**).

Figure 17.5 The 'square of crime'

When elected in 1997, the New Labour government's Prime Minister, Tony Blair, set up the Social Exclusion Unit (SEU); this was abolished in 2006 and replaced with a Social Exclusion Task Force, which, in turn, was abolished in 2010 when the Coalition government was elected. This perhaps shows a declining political commitment to addressing issues of social exclusion.

But what do the terms *social inclusion* and *social exclusion* actually mean—and how, as social scientists, can we meaningfully operationalise them in our research and policy evaluations? For some commentators, issues of exclusion are tightly linked to broader issues of poverty and welfare, seeing the spheres of education, employment, health, and housing as key areas. The issues of addressing exclusion and the inter-related and problematic issues it involves through policy is considered further in **What do you think? 17.4** 'Implementing inclusivity through policy'.

WHAT DO YOU THINK? 17.4

Implementing inclusivity through policy

A new housing estate is being built on the outskirts of the town where you live. The developers and local council have asked for volunteers to sit on a multi-agency committee responsible for improving the area and addressing some fears which have been raised about crime and antisocial behaviour. You put your name forward and have been selected to take part.

The committee's task is to spend a grant of £500,000 which has to be divided up between its 'stakeholder' members. These are:

- the police, who have an annual target of reducing youth crime by 30 per cent and who want to fund two beat officers for the area;

- the local Children's Centre, which aims to offer education and health care to 70 per cent of the children under the age of 5 on the estate;

- a Housing Association, which will be offering half of the new homes as affordable housing;

- the local branch of Age Concern, which already has a small social centre for the elderly in the area;

- the new school being built on the estate, which will cater for children who have been excluded from other schools;

- you, representing the young people on the estate who will not have access to any recreational or social facilities such as a youth centre.

You can also nominate up to three new stakeholders—think about who you think could also be involved, e.g. social workers, local transport providers, etc.

Use the grid below to write down the arguments you think each member will put forward to get the biggest share of the money, and why they might disagree with their fellow stakeholders. As you do so, look ahead to the list of Levitas' discourse models. Which do you think best fits the aims of each of the committee members? Do you think that the various stakeholders' interests differ in terms of the potential for fostering inclusivity or exclusivity?

When you have done this, take some time to consider the things that influence members' attitudes to these issues in terms of the aims of their organisations.

Police	
Health	
Housing	
Education	
Youth	

Lastly, imagine that you are given the casting vote to decide who gets the biggest grant. Who do you choose, and why? What do your reasons tell you about your response to inclusion and exclusion? Do your personal experiences and political position have any influence on your choice?

One of the key factors that will affect such stakeholder groups is the power—real and perceived—of the members. Looking at this example, rank the five members in order of their probable power within the housing estate committee. Which member did you think was the most powerful, and which the least? Write down the reasons for your decision. Then take a moment to think about how the power relations within the group will affect the final decision and therefore the policy adopted by the committee. You will probably decide that there is no clear boundary between inclusive and exclusive outcomes, and that the adoption of any one approach is complex and emotive.

The 1997 New Labour government offered the following definition of social exclusion:

> Social exclusion is what can happen when people or areas suffer from a combination of linked problems, such as unemployment, poor skills, low incomes, poor housing, high crime, poor health and family breakdown.
>
> Social Exclusion Unit 1997

It is clear that the issues of social inclusion and exclusion are inherently contentious and contested—not only in terms of definition, but also in terms of how they should be dealt with through practical and workable policy measures.

You may argue that all of the issues outlined by the New Labour government can be addressed through macro policy interventions, like increasing welfare spending to narrow the gap between the rich and the poor. You may also argue that more social housing should be funded and managed by local authorities. Alternatively, you might regard these issues as being connected to problems experienced by individual people who are responsible for dealing with them. Ultimately you would consider these to be individual problems which require individual solutions, rather than being social and structural problems which can only be dealt with by national and local policy interventions. Perhaps you think that individuals should take responsibility for improving their skill levels, their education, and their health and so on—or you might think that the state has a duty to address them instead.

The first New Labour government initially argued that the best way to address these problems—unemployment, housing, and so on—was not by looking at them in isolation but through multiagency partnerships. As they claimed:

> Our remit is to help improve government action to reduce social exclusion by producing 'joined-up solutions to joined-up problems'. We work mainly on specific projects, chosen following consultation with other government departments and suggestions from interested groups.
>
> Social Exclusion Unit 2004

The Social Exclusion Unit was responsible for publishing many reports on what it identified as being five key issues. These were neighbourhood renewal; rough sleepers; teenage pregnancy; young people not in education, training, or employment (so-called NEETS); and truancy and school exclusion. The overall findings of these reports focused on how deprived groups and areas had been let down by both central and local government responses to these issues, and called for more to be done to alleviate them.

The social policy scholar, Professor Ruth Levitas in her analysis of New Labour policy (2005) argued that there are three main ways of thinking (or discourses) about social exclusion. These are:

- **RED**—this is a Redistributive Discourse (rooted in a critical social policy tradition) which emphasises poverty as being a key cause of social exclusion. In other words, it suggests that economic and social policies should aim to redistribute wealth and income; for example through taxation and welfare policies.

- **SID**—this is a Social Integrationist Discourse, which focuses on paid work as being the key to greater social integration (but it does not focus on poorly paid employment or unpaid work).

- **MUD**—this relates to the Moral Underclass Discourse, which we considered earlier in the chapter when we looked at the work of the right realist Charles Murray.

Clearly these analytical devices take different positions as to what kind of inclusion is being offered. It is also noted that there can be shifts between these three discourses in terms of policy initiatives and implementation. Levitas' (2005) main conclusion is that under New Labour there was a discernible move away from the more socially democratic RED model (which argues for macro solutions to what are seen as being essentially macro problems) to more economically liberal SID and MUD ones (which argues for individual solutions to what are seen as being essentially individual problems).

Similarly, Rodger (2008) has argued that during its time in office, New Labour's policies shifted away from issues of social inclusion to embrace a discourse around a so-called moral underclass. As he argues, elements of social policies aimed at *including* vulnerable and marginalised groups also contained within them aspects of criminalisation and hence exclusion. In other words, to paraphrase their well-used soundbite, New Labour came to be rather tougher on *crime* rather than on *the causes of crime*.

It would be fair to say that there have been very few, if any, real policy initiatives which effectively bring together all four of the dimensions outlined in the 'square of crime', (**Figure 17.5**), if this is indeed even possible. As criminologists, we need to be aware of the very real difficulties and complexities which are involved in translating theoretical perspectives and their policy prescriptions into practice. Part of the problem here, in relation to left realism, is related to the constantly shifting power relations between the components of the 'square of crime'. This can result in there being a real gap between what, at first sight, appears to be progressive and potentially ameliorative policy, and the ways in which it is subsequently implemented. For instance, the same policy can be applied differently (and result in very different outcomes—which are sometimes beyond the intended ones) at different local levels.

Despite this, even if gains resulting from a particular policy that benefit some people in some conditions are small, they are gains (and important) nevertheless.

For argument's sake, imagine that you are evaluating a programme which brings victims, offenders, and the wider community together to resolve their disputes (the notion of restorative justice as an alternative to punishment is considered in more detail in **Chapter 26**). Having been clear and meticulous in terms of what a positive outcome looks like, your findings are that in 48 per cent of the cases evaluated, the process was 'successful'. In other words, in these cases the process was fully restorative and, as the result of genuine dialogue and participation, plans were made which led to higher levels of victim satisfaction or community reparation being made. There were also real, supportive opportunities for offenders to address broader issues of their exclusion, and so on. Yet 'only' 48 per cent of the cases met these standards. Is this therefore a 'bad', ineffective, and failed policy which should be abandoned? You may wish to further investigate why the programme had less 'positive outcomes' and was 'less successful' in the other 52 per cent of cases. It is worth considering how your findings might influence the development of the programme. In short, policy gains are often incremental, growing over time, which may make initial results seem less impressive than the final outcome of a project may eventually turn out to be.

If a policy can reach even a relatively small percentage of the people it was intended to reach through good, constructive means (and help to change their lives in positive, inclusive and demarginalising ways) then is it a good thing? After all, no policy will have a 100 per cent success rate, despite what some governments claim. Evaluating policy is an incredibly difficult thing to do with precision; we live in a highly complex world and, as social scientists, in conducting our applied research, we need to recognise that all such research has limitations (see **Chapter 6**). For left realists, purely theoretical work, whilst both interesting and intellectually rewarding, needs to be related to developing realistic policy interventions which can make a real difference. If nothing else, left realism offers a challenge to responses to crime which are based solely on (punitive) crime control policies and which regard offenders as primarily pathological individuals. In doing so, it opens up possibilities in both dialogue and practice which mean that it might be possible to do 'criminal justice' in more progressive and democratic ways which foreground notions of social justice.

Evaluating left realism

It could be rather crudely stated that criminological perspectives aimed at explaining crime develop through a critical dialogue with each other. For instance, forms of positivism challenged and critically questioned the central tenets of classicism; critical theories challenged and critically questioned the central tenets of positivism; realism challenged and critically questioned critical theories ... and so on. Whilst this is over-schematic it is perhaps a useful way for you, as students at the start of your criminological journeys, to think about how such theories interlink.

Over your studies you will be tasked with evaluating a particular theoretical position, and an effective way of doing this is through comparison with other theoreticians' work. Such a task may be in relation to considering a particular dimension of a theory. The dimension of realist criminologies that we have considered most in this chapter is the logic they present in terms of policy development. This is important because some theoreticians would argue that it is not their place to get directly involved in the world of policy formation and implementation at all—their role is instead simply to concentrate on constructing their theories and arguments, and they leave it up to others to decide if the work has any policy relevance. On the other hand, as this chapter has shown, realist perspectives are directly engaged with policy solutions to crime; in other words, as well as being of a pure theoretical nature, they also claim to have a clear applied element.

One of the problems with such theoretical debate and critique is that often one thinker might criticise another for omitting an analysis of something which his or her theory was never intended to address in the first place. Sometimes this may be more connected with what the critic feels or believes, rather than the content of the theory itself. After all, as is mentioned in **Chapter 18**, criminologists are human beings who have their own political opinions, strong personal beliefs, and ideas about what a 'good society' should look like (see also **Chapter 6**).

It is therefore vital to consider both sides of every argument and to offer as balanced a viewpoint as possible (based on the available evidence), regardless of the strength of your personal or professional beliefs. We will therefore illustrate this in **Table 17.1** by simply stating the main critical points which have been raised against left realism, and what the left realist response to these might be. You might also want to think about what the critics' response to the initial reply would be.

Criticism of left realism	Response from left realists
It totally abandons the gains of critical criminology by uncritically accepting state defined notions of crime. It is therefore regressive	Left realists would argue that this is not so; they may adopt a 'softer' social constructionist conception of crime, but their first aim was to develop a policy-relevant, radical criminology which challenged the punitive thrust and exclusionary nature of right wing government policies. Unlike the right realist perspectives, it does not accept crime figures as measured by police recorded crime statistics as being an accurate measure. Its use of local crime surveys seeks to uncover rates of victimisation from within marginalised groups, as well as obtaining their perceptions about policing in the areas where they live. To challenge right wing discourses on crime, left realism needed to be seen to be challenging those ideas on a similar terrain; an acceptance of a 'harder' sociological/ ideological reconstruction of the concept of crime would simply not make this possible. Its overall aim was to be 'realistic' about crime and its causes, and to advocate for reforms in the shape of 'realistic' policies which address these. In this sense left realists were moving debate and analysis forwards in practical and applied ways and not backwards
It totally abandons the gains of critical criminology by neglecting to focus on crimes committed by powerful groups (which are more harmful)	Left realists would refute this by saying that they note the very real social harms which are caused by the actions and inactions of powerful groups. Left realists initially felt, however, that the need to challenge right wing arguments was the most pressing, as these were impacting on the lived realities of excluded groups of people. For instance, Left realists focused their analysis on increasing police powers, a decline of police accountability, and increasingly harsh prison sentences. This, along with the political abandonment of the social causes of crime, had to be vigorously contested As left realism has developed, it is now seeing some work from left realist thinkers which is analysing crimes committed by powerful groups
It has a weak empirical base and it over-relies on local crime surveys and victimisation within poor, marginalised communities	Left realists would describe themselves as being realistic about crime, and argue that what can be done about it requires an empirical base. Left realists note the limitations of local victim surveys, but feel that they are a 'democratic' research tool. Such surveys clearly reveal (unlike official police recorded crime statistics) 'real' hidden crime problems in communities which require both attention and 'realistic' solutions
It over-predicts crime, especially crime committed by BME (black and minority ethnic) groups. It is therefore racist	Left realists posit that their arguments do not in any way perpetuate the myth of black criminality or subscribe to the meaningless and potentially dangerous idea of 'black-on-black' crime. They argue that local surveys have shown that some crime is intra-ethnic (that is, carried out between people of the same race or minority ethnic group). This should not be a surprise if that survey has been carried out in an area with a higher than average population of BME residents. Left realism has thus highlighted an issue which requires further investigation within a broader framework in terms of relative deprivation, especially if readers see the term 'race' as a proxy for 'class'. Left realists' empirical work has also highlighted perceptions of disproportionate policing against certain ethnic communities. It cannot therefore be said to be racist
That it neglects feminist issues in terms of the social inequalities which affect women	Not so; left realism is informed by socialist feminism, and so focuses on gender inequalities. However, like all theoretical perspectives, it is a developing one. Early work did not perhaps have a firm enough focus on issues relating to the patriarchal nature of society, and critics were right to point this out. Later work (for instance Mooney 2000) addressed these issues more thoroughly, and the developing work within our perspective is clearly in dialogue with contemporary feminist theory. More work on this, and other areas, clearly still needs to be done
It integrates diverse theories (i.e. labelling, strain, radical, control) which are theoretically contradictory	Whilst left realists are clearly seeking to develop an integrated theory, they would argue that they are not in the business of trying to reconcile what can be regarded as theoretical niceties and elegant theoretical debates By drawing on and developing insights and concepts from a variety of theoretical positions, left realists are aiming to develop a theory which helps to further our understandings of crime, the processes of criminalisation, and crime control in our rapidly changing times. They aim to be able to offer radical, social democratic policy alternatives which will achieve greater social justice. To this end the left realist project is not at an end and, as such, it will always be in the process of 'becoming'
Not all of those who are relatively deprived commit crime	Quite true; however, left realists have never claimed this to be the case. As they argue, relative deprivation can in certain conditions be seen as being a major cause of crime. Also, they clearly say that crime (and experiences of relative deprivation) are certainly not a monopoly of poor, marginalised groups. Left realists feel that they have made a start on this work in ways that effectively challenge both older critical theories and right wing criminologies. There is still much to be done in challenging the current neo-liberal hegemony which characterises the economic, political, social, and cultural landscapes of late modern societies

Table 17.1 Critiques of left realism

Conclusion

The aim of this chapter has been to set out and evaluate the key ideas of both right and left realism. Both make claims of 'taking crime seriously' and being 'real' about 'crime problems'. They also both put forward their own views on practical solutions, and we have deliberately focused on the policy proposals associated with them as theoretical approaches. We will end this chapter by encouraging you to think further about their relationship to policy making by critically applying both 're-alisms' in terms of what they might each have to say about a real issue: urban disorder (see **Controversy and debate 17.1**).

CONTROVERSY AND DEBATE 17.1

Realism and the 'Riots'

Drawing on the work of Jock Young (1990), John Muncie (2015: 147) has succinctly summarised the key points of similarity and difference between right and left realist approaches. These are set out in **Table 17.2**.

If we work through these carefully, we can focus on how the two perspectives differ; this is particularly noticeable in terms of which criminological theories they re-work, what they have to say about crime causation, and what they both prioritise in terms of policy proposals. Let us now think further about these, and apply them to a very visible example—that of urban disorder.

In August 2011, thousands of people 'rioted' across several London boroughs and in towns and cities across England. Television news programmes showed acts of arson and looting, as well as the mass deployment of police officers (see **Figure 17.6**).

To be sure, the causes of these disturbances were many and complex but in the aftermath many articles

Figure 17.6 Image from the 2011 London riots
Source: © 1000 Words/Shutterstock

were published whose commentary on both the causes and remedies chimed with both right and left realist arguments. For instance, some commentators argued that the disorder was a clear example of the moral decay

Right Realism	Left Realism
Rejection of utopianism in favour of neo-conservatism	Rejection of utopianism in favour of democratic socialism
Acceptance of legal definitions of 'crime'	Acceptance of legal definitions of 'crime'
Primary focus on 'crime' as represented by official statistics	Primary focus on 'crime' as perceived by victims
Fear of crime as a rational response	Fear of crime as a rational response
Reworking of genetic and individualistic theories	Reworking of subcultural, anomie (lacking usual moral or social standards), and structural conflict theories
Crime caused by a lack of self-control	Crime caused by relative deprivation, social injustice, and marginalisation
Prioritising order (rather than justice) via deterrent and retributive means of crime control	Prioritising social justice via programmes of crime prevention

Table 17.2 Summary of the differences between left and right realism

of British society and the resultant increasing levels of criminality and thuggery; these authors felt that the lengthy prison sentences given to some of the 'rioters' were justified. Furthermore, it was argued that 'order' could only be restored to the streets of Britain by increasing police powers and the sentencing powers of the courts (right realism).

Other writers saw the key contributory factors as being forms of social exclusion, high levels of unemployment, and poverty. For these more liberal commentators, such issues can and should be addressed through social policies, such as urban regeneration programmes. They also argued that it was necessary to reverse government 'austerity' measures such as the spending cuts which have created and exacerbated social divisions, leading to feelings of anger, frustration, and discontent that many young people now experience—a strongly left realist response.

Clearly, the disorder aroused strong feelings amongst theorists and commentators on both sides of the political divide. The then Government instituted a Riots Communities and Victims Panel, which concluded that improving education, parenting, and employment opportunities would prevent further riots—echoing the work of Murray and promoting a right realist approach. Indeed, the final report's cover features a photograph showing one of the volunteer groups that cleaned up broken glass and debris as an alternative image of local people (see **Figure 17.7**).

A further report was produced by a group of academics from the London School of Economics and Political Science in partnership with the *Guardian* newspaper (*Reading the Riots*, 2011). This involved not only interviews but an analysis of Tweets made about the events; whilst another perspective was offered by Fully Focussed, a youth organisation which produced the award winning documentary 'Riot from Wrong' (2012). The film-makers attempted to ascertain the 'truth' behind

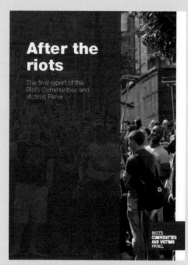

Figure 17.7 Cover of the final report of the Riots Communities and Victims Panel

Source: National Archives, content available under the Open Government Licence v3.0

the disorder and its causes; whilst they acknowledge the impact of the violence they also discuss how cuts such as the removal of the Education Maintenance Allowance were equally significant. Both the report and the film emphasise that poor relationships between communities and the police were seen by those involved as a primary cause—something which the Communities and Victims report places much lower in its list of factors.

From this we can see how both right and left realist perspectives can be used to analyse and rationalise incidents such as the riots, as well as informing the proposals for measures that aim to prevent them. Given the emotive nature of the riots—and the heavy impact they had on local communities—it is crucial that we maintain our critical approach when we consider both left and right realist perspectives and their use in formulating both national and personal responses.

SUMMARY

- Appreciate the links between criminological theorising, and broader law and order politics

Throughout this part of the book on 'Explaining Crime' we have been suggesting various ways in which you, the student, can critically engage with what can at first appear to be abstract theoretical arguments. As we have also seen, an important point for us to recognise and develop is that criminological theory does not exist in a vacuum. In this chapter we have deliberately focused on relating theoretical perspectives to the broader economic, political, social, and cultural times in which they were being developed; in other words, the broader law and order politics of an era. For instance, in **Chapter 15** we argued that our understanding of labelling perspectives is enhanced if we know and understand something about what was happening in the US in the 1960s when its main proponents, such as Matza and Becker, were writing.

- Understand the political context surrounding the emergence of realist criminologies

The point that broader political contexts are important when studying and understanding criminological theories is perhaps of greater importance and significance when considering the rise of so-called 'realist' criminologies. In this chapter we noted that the late 1970s and early 1980s, in both the UK and US, were witnessing a turn to the right in their national politics. Successful right wing governments were espousing neo-liberal economic arguments and socially conservative views and policies. By drawing on material which otherwise might be best thought of as belonging to the study of political science, economics, social policy, history, and so on, we hope to have underscored the truly interdisciplinary nature of criminology and illustrated why it is such a dynamic, interesting, and challenging subject area. In terms of crime and its control in this period we noted that it was (amongst other things) a perception of increasing crime rates, instances of urban unrest, and a developing fear of crime which informed the development of right realist perspectives (and all that this entails in terms of calls for tougher crime control strategies and a strengthening of 'social order' and so on). Similarly, we documented how, in part, the left wing variants of realism emerged as a challenge to right wing governments' policies, with their calls for crime prevention policies which prioritised social justice. With both perspectives claiming to 'take crime seriously' and to be 'realistic' about its causes and what can be done about these at a practical level, we have also highlighted how criminological theorising can engage with 'real world' issues and impact on policy formation and implementation; for instance, the influence which left realist ideas initially had on New Labour government's policy initiatives on social inclusion.

- Identify and critically analyse the key ideas of both right and left realism

In working through the main tenets of both right and left realism we noted the main concepts which they draw on to develop their arguments. At the end of the chapter in the controversy and debate box, which focused on urban unrest, we brought these ideas (such as the existence of an underclass, the concept of relative deprivation) together, suggesting ways in which you can critically engage with these by way of comparison. For instance, this chapter has set up a series of debates with which you can critically engage. For instance:

- Crime is individualistic in its origin *versus* social in its origin.
- Crime is caused by a lack of self-control *versus* social deficits.
- Political priorities are to restore order *versus* to implement policies which address social disadvantage.
- The main policies to deal with the 'crime problem' are deterrence and retribution *versus* social crime prevention.
- Relate realist theorising to criminal justice policy initiatives and critically evaluate these.

Following on from the above list, this chapter has also focused on the links between theory and the development and implementation of policy, highlighting some of the very real difficulties and tensions which exist when we attempt to bring the theoretical and the practical together. Having worked through the **What do you think?** boxes (especially the one on 'Implementing inclusivity through policy') you will have had the opportunity to further develop your critical evaluation skills. Policy responses to crime and the development of your critical responses to these are further developed in **Part 4: Responding to Crime**.

REVIEW QUESTIONS

1. What is meant by the term 'critical election' and why is that important in this instance to the rise of realist criminologies?

2. What, according to Platt and Takagi (1977) are three common themes which unite right realism and give it a form of coherence? Are there any inconsistencies here?

3. What are the problems of identifying a (criminal) underclass who suffer from 'moral' poverty?

4. Why, and in what ways, did Lea and Young (1984) portray previous critical theories as being 'left idealist'? Were they correct to do so?

5. How can the ideas of individualism, consumerism and relative deprivation be linked to criminal behaviour? Are these explanations convincing?

6. What are the four points of Young's 'square of crime'? Apply and analyse this conceptual device with regard to one particular form of criminal behaviour.

FURTHER READING

Rather than over-relying on the secondary discussions on those issues in the many good theoretical criminology textbooks which have been published, you should try to read the original authors wherever possible. In terms of theory textbooks both of the following are useful starting points.

Hopkins-Burke, R. (2013) *An Introduction to Criminological Theory*. London: Routledge.
Tierney, J. and O'Neill, M. (2016) *Criminology; Theory and Context*. London: Routledge.

As we have said in the further reading sections throughout this book, there is no real substitute for you reading and engaging with the 'classic' texts themselves.

For right realism these are:
Herrnstein, R.J. and Murray, C. (1994) *The Bell Curve*. New York: Basic Books.
Murray, C. (1990) *The Emerging Underclass*. London: Institute of Economic Affairs.
Wilson, J.Q. (1975) *Thinking About Crime*. New York: Vintage.

On left realism see:
Lea, J. and Young, J. (1984) *What Is To Be Done About Law And Order?* Harmondsworth: Penguin.
Currie, E. (1985) *Confronting Crime*. New York: Pantheon.

Shorter, edited extracts of the work of Wilson, Murray, Lea and Young, Young and Currie can be found in the reader:
McLaughlin, J. and Muncie, J. (2013) *Criminological Perspectives; Essential Readings* (3rd edn). London: Sage.

 Access the **online resources** to view selected further reading and web links relevant to the material covered in this chapter.
www.oup.com/uk/case/

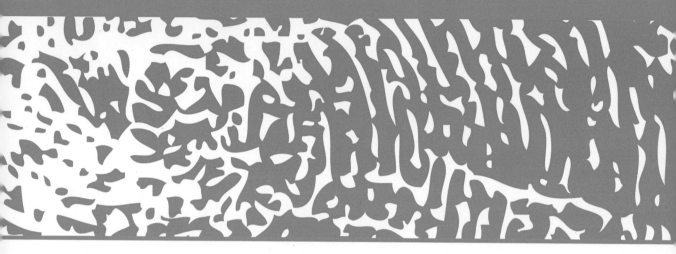

CHAPTER OUTLINE

Introduction	504
Integrated explanations of crime	505
Evolving integrated explanations of crime	505
Integrated risk factor theories: Predicting, not explaining crime	511
The two sides of the integrated coin	520

Integrated theories of crime

KEY ISSUES

After reading this chapter, you should be able to:

- place integrated theories of crime in the context of the historical development of criminological theories;

- analyse and evaluate integrated positivist theories of crime in explanatory and practical terms;

- analyse and evaluate integrated risk factor theories of crime in explanatory and practical terms.

Introduction

This chapter is about explaining crime in ways that integrate the ideas from more than one theory. The integrated explanatory theories that have evolved in criminology represent an evolution from the criminological theories discussed in previous chapters. These theories have integrated the main concepts and arguments from existing theories and challenged their position as the hegemonic (dominant) theoretical explanations of crime. Welcome to the integrated theories chapter.

There are four main groups, or schools, of explanatory theories in criminology, each of which has been discussed at length throughout the 'Explaining Crime' part of our book: classicism, positivism, critical criminology, and realism. We do not intend to duplicate what has already been discussed in previous chapters, so skimming back over the details of these theories in previous chapters will provide a clear context for the following discussion and evaluation of the integrated theories of crime. Integrated theories have merged ideas, explanations, and arguments from more than one theory within a school of theories and even across different schools, thus they may also be called *multi-factor* or *hybrid* theories. Now may be a good time to look at **What do you think? 18.1** in order to focus your thoughts as you continue with this chapter.

We will start by placing integrated theories in their historical context in terms of theory development in criminology—the first key issue for this chapter. The foundation for theoretical development in criminology has been the single theory (or school of explanation) that explains crime in a specific way—often replacing a previous theory that has either been rejected or has fallen out of favour. For example, biological positivism replaced the classical theories that it had originally challenged as the hegemonic explanatory theory in criminology, then fell out of favour itself and was replaced by psychological and later sociological forms of positivism (Williams 2012). As discussed, each criminological theory and school of theory has specific (and shared) strengths and weaknesses. Often, however, weaknesses or criticisms are terms used in criminology to better describe limitations—what the theory will not, does not, or cannot, do due to its focus, objectives, methods, and biases.

A common limitation of explanatory theories of crime has been their exclusivity—their single-minded focus on a specific way of explaining crime, whilst ignoring other theories as either potential contributions to their own explanation or potential alternative explanations of crime in their own right (Akers and Sellers 2013; Agnew 2011). Of course, it can be a strength to be single-minded in developing a line of argument (it demonstrates commitment, faith, confidence, clarity of thought), but this can run the risk of narrow-mindedness and artificially restricting *explanatory utility* if criminologists are too exclusive to develop or reject their own ideas in the face of compelling evidence and argument (see also **Chapter 6**: 'How does criminology 'know' about crime?'). Exclusivity in explanatory theories can be demonstrated between-schools, for example classicists rejecting positivist explanations or positivists ignoring critical arguments. It is also demonstrated within-schools; biological positivists excluding psychological or sociological explanations, critical Marxists rejecting the ideas of critical feminists, right realists ignoring left realists, and so on. As the **What do you think? 18.1** activity should have indicated, this exclusivity can result in certain types of crime being easier to explain for certain people using one theory but not another. What is far less common in criminology is an explanatory theory that can explain all crimes at all times by all kinds of people. However, such a *universal* theory may not be feasible, nor even desirable in our complex, multi-faceted, and nuanced area of study.

Identifying theoretical/explanatory limitations does not mean that a theory's basic explanation of crime is wrong—it may be valid for a particular person committing a particular crime at a particular point in time, or you could say for some crimes at some times. But it is not valid to claim that a theory is universally-applicable

WHAT DO YOU THINK? 18.1

How should we explain crime?

From what you have read thus far in this book, what do you think is the most convincing explanation of why people commit crime? Is it easy to answer such a general question? Should the answer be contingent on what form of crime we are trying to explain? For example, how would you explain:

- violent crimes such as murder and assault?

- property crimes such as vandalism and burglary?

- sexual crimes such as rape and child abuse?

- corporate crimes such as fraud and environmental pollution?

Is it possible for explanations to be different for different people at different times and even for the same people at different times? What do you think and why do you think this?

(i.e. generalisable)—that it can explain all crimes at all times by all people. Therefore, there are criticisms of explanatory theories, pointing out parts that are arguably inaccurate or misleading (e.g. ignoring/excluding an explanation because it doesn't fit the theory or policy), but there are also limitations, parts that are missing and areas that cannot be explained using that theory alone. This is where an understanding of integrated theories becomes essential.

The summary just given is a necessary over-simplification regarding the nature and evolution of explanatory theories in criminology. Issues are often far more complicated than politicians, media, and even criminologists would have us believe. Most explanatory theories have developed with a degree of acknowledgement and even integration of concepts and arguments from other competitor theories. Two notable examples of theoretical evolution through the integration of additional explanations are Lombroso's eventual acceptance that social factors are far more influential on crime than biological factors and the linking of labelling theory to structural influences on crime by critical criminologists (Hopkins Burke 2013). Ostensibly, the neo-classical compromise and right realism are also good examples of early theoretical integration through their acknowledgement that a person's capacity to make fully rational choices is influenced by biological, psychological, and sociological factors (cf. Agnew 2011).

Integrated explanations of crime

We will begin the discussion of integrated theories with an exploration of *integrated positivist theories*, which will be divided into two main groups:

- **Socio-biological theories**—an integration of biological factors and sociological and environmental influences (positivist in focus).
- **Social control theories**—an integration of psychological, sociological, and structural factors (a blend of positivist theories).

Integrated positivist theories will be evaluated in terms of their strengths, weaknesses, limitations, and utility, including a focus on their subjective, supposition, and study elements. There follows an exploration of *integrated risk factor theories*, which will also be divided into two main groups:

- Artefactual risk factor theories—explanatory frameworks that identify quantifiable psychological and sociological risk factors and presents these as predictors of crime.

- **Enhanced pathways risk factor theories**—an evolution of artefactual theories through the integration of socio-structural factors and personal constructions and meanings in order to understand individual pathways into and out of crime.

Integrated risk factor theories have a particular way of conceptualising the causes of and influences on crime—essentially through the simplistic quantification and measurement in early life of factors that are assumed to predict future offending. This chapter goes into significant depth when evaluating these theories—not least because they are (arguably) the hegemonic explanatory theories within criminology today, certainly for explaining crime by young males. The chapter will trace the evolution of integrated risk factor theories to their present day, cutting-edge, integrated forms that merge arguments from classicism (rational choice) with positivism (mainly psychological and sociological influences) and with critical criminology (e.g. qualitative understandings of how young people make meaning of their lives). As with the previous discussion of integrated theories, this section will evaluate the strengths, weaknesses, limitations, and utility of integrated risk factor theories, with a detailed consideration of the role of subjectivity, supposition, and study (the 3 Ss) (see **Chapter 6**). The chapter will end by revisiting the role, context and influence of integrated theories in the evolution of explanatory theories in criminology. Arguments reiterate the role of the 3 Ss in the construction, development, and evolution of these explanatory theories and conclude that integrated forms of explanatory theory remain inconclusive regarding the *causes* of crime—the focus of the following chapter.

Evolving integrated explanations of crime

When asked in 2015 how they see the study of crime evolving over the next 10 years, the cultural criminologists Jeff Ferrell and Keith Hayward responded:

We suspect that criminology will continue to bifurcate. On the one hand the logic of positivism and positivist methodologies operates as an intellectual self-fulfilling prophecy, creating methodological residues that masquerade as objective research findings. ... On the other hand, and largely in opposition, alternative criminological paradigms continue to percolate and build momentum.

Ferrell and Hayward 2015—Promotional quote for SAGE 'Voyages of Critical Discovery' retrospective

In many ways, the following discussions illustrate this **bifurcation** of criminology along two distinct integrated explanatory pathways. The evolution of explanatory theories in criminology has been evidenced by integrated theories—explanations of crime that mix, merge, and fuse together concepts, arguments, research methods, evidence, and explanations from more than one criminological theory. Integrated theories can operate in one of three ways:

1. **Within-theory**—a theory may integrate arguments from a similar theory/theories within its own strand of explanation. For example, an integrated biological positivist theory may consider explanations of crime that incorporate substance use, hormonal imbalance, and biochemical dysfunction in the brain.

2. **Within-school**—a theory may integrate arguments from other strands of explanation within its own school, yet outside its own specific theoretical framework. For example, an integrated biological positivist theory may consider the influence of social/sociological factors on offending behaviour and on the very biological factors that were originally thought to be the only influences on offending (e.g. the refinement of Lombroso's original theory to include social, cultural, and economic factors—Akers and Sellers 2013). Such theories would be known as socio-biological theories—our first illustration of integrated theories in this chapter.

3. **Between-schools**—a theory may integrate arguments from different schools of explanation. For example, the neo-classical compromise position is a tentative attempt to fuse traditional rational choice explanations with select positivist influences. Several theories thought of as critical criminology are actually integrated theories that bring in arguments from outside of traditional critical criminology (e.g. from sociological positivism). *The New Criminology* is a good example here (Taylor, Walton, and Young 1973; Walton and Young 1998), as are the new forms of social control theories that will be discussed in this chapter as the second illustration of integrated theories.

As stated earlier in this chapter, it is possible and helpful to divide integrated theories into two distinct bifurcated groups or pathways: integrated positivist theories and integrated risk factor theories. Let us start where much research-based criminological explanation starts: positivist theory.

Integrated positivist theories

Integrated positivist theories have addressed the explanatory and practical weaknesses and limitations of traditional single factor theories by combining their individual strengths (thus compensating for their individual weaknesses and limitations) in order to offer more holistic, universal/generalisable, and valid explanations of crime. By integrating different explanations, epistemologies, and research methods, integrated positivist theories have the potential at least to offer a more open-minded and less subjective/biased way of knowing about how to explain crime. But we must *Always Be Critical* (ABC) as you know (cf. the first Part of this book), so let us analyse and evaluate examples of integrated positivist theories in more detail (the second key issue for this chapter), specifically *socio-biological theories* and *social control theories*.

Socio-biological theories: nature and nurture?

Where once the ideas and methods of biological positivism were considered ground-breaking and even revolutionary in criminology, they soon became viewed by some as controversial and unethical as psychological and sociological explanations gained in popularity. Certain arguments of biological positivism began to be considered to be overly-deterministic, even veering towards racist, sexist, ageist, and classist. Their recommended responses to offending behaviour such as chemical castration, electroconvulsive therapy, and genetic engineering, were excessive, even barbaric (Vold, Bernard, and Snipes 2002). The dominance of biological factors when explaining crime was superseded by a more palatable body of psychological factors, albeit a focus that still tended to view the causes of crime as illnesses or flaws or problems in the person, otherwise known as *pathological* explanations (Bernard, Snipes, Gerould, and Vold 2015). The popularity of these explanations was challenged by a more socially-acceptable (less blaming and pathological) focus on sociological factors (Winters, Globoklar, and Roberson 2014). However, in recent years, exploring biological factors as potential explanations for crime has undergone a resurgence in popularity in criminology, particularly in the USA, which has always favoured a more bio-psychological form of criminology over the more sociological and critical forms privileged in the UK. This rebirth has been driven by the emergence of socio-biological theories offering explanations of crime that combine biological influences with sociological and environmental (socio-environmental) influences as part of multi-factor integrated approaches (see Vold et al. 2002; Bernard et al. 2015). The development of socio-biological explanations is best illustrated by its two most prolific strands of theory: the *biosocial theory* of the late 1970s–1980s and 21st century *socio-biological risk factor theories*.

Biosocial theory

The possibility of explaining crime as the result of interactions between biological and socio-environmental factors was introduced by a criminologist called Sarnoff Mednick (1977), who argued that: 'the value of biological factors is more limited in predicted antisocial behaviour in individuals who have experienced *criminogenic* social conditions in their rearing' (Mednick et al. 1987: 68). Mednick's main argument was that we all have natural, biological instincts and urges to commit crime, but that most people can control these urges. Those who do commit crime are more likely to experience a combination of socio-environmental problems, for example inadequate learning of appropriate behaviour in the family, interactions with criminal and antisocial peer groups; and biological problems, for example, an autonomic nervous system that responds slowly to external stimuli such as punishment (cf. Rafter 2008). Mednick's biosocial theory is, therefore, an integration of and interaction between nature (biological factors) and nurture (socio-environmental factors). Another criminologist called C. Ray Jeffery (1977) added psychological factors into the mix to produce what could be more accurately described as a *biopsychosocial theory* of crime. Jeffery offered a two-pronged theory suggesting that the biological and psychological characteristics that people are born with (i.e. nature) could cause offending behaviour in their own right or interact with socio-environmental processes such as socialisation (upbringing, being taught social norms) in the family and school (i.e. nurture) to cause offending. For example, according to this theory biochemical imbalances in the brain, acting alone could cause offending behaviour, but they could also interact with and be exacerbated by socio-environmental factors such as poverty and its associated problems (e.g. poor diet, increased exposure to pollution), which could then lead to behavioural problems and offending (cf. Rafter 2008).

Right realist biosocial theory

The biosocial interactions proposed by Mednick and Jeffery in the late 1970s were built upon in explanatory terms in the mid-1980s by the forefather of right realism,

James Q. Wilson and his colleague Richard Hernnstein. Wilson and Hernnstein (1985) concluded that most crime is committed by young men and so this group should be the focus of explanatory theories of crime. Arguably, there are validity issues associated with making this claim, but there is also much available evidence from official statistics and criminological research data to support such androcentricism (see **Controversy and debate 18.1**).

For the purposes of their right realist biosocial theory, Wilson and Hernnstein (1985: 69) viewed crime by young men as the product of an interaction between biological and sociological factors, asserting that:

> It is likely that the effect of maleness and youthfulness on the tendency to commit crime has both constitutional and social origins: that is, it has something to do with the biological status of being a young male and with how the young man has been treated by family, friends and society.

In other words, being male (as in your biological sex and your sociological and cultural gender) means that you may receive different treatment and experience different interactions in society compared to if you are female. The theory argues that we carry certain constitutional/biological characteristics into the social world (e.g. gender, age, intelligence, personality) that positively or negatively affect our ability to learn or internalise the norms of behaviour and to learn from any reinforcement or punishment of behaviour. It can also be that some people are less likely to receive reinforcement for positive behaviour, but may be more likely to be rewarded for negative behaviour, so they are more likely to choose to become criminal (in a given situation) and to persist with criminal behaviours. Consequently, right realist biosocial theory can be viewed as an integration of rational choice and biopsychosocial factors. Its arguments recommend the prevention, treatment and punishment of crime that focus on influencing people's (young males') rational choices to commit crime and to comply with social norms (i.e. their self-control).

Biosocial risk factor theories

Since the late 1990s, an updated form of biosocial theory has become popular (especially in the USA), with three notable tweaks in its focus compared to traditional biosocial theory:

(a) an emphasis on risk factors (predictors) rather than causes as the way to explain crime;

(b) a desire to explain and predict future behaviour rather than past behaviour;

(c) a focus on antisocial behaviour rather than crime per se.

! CONTROVERSY AND DEBATE 18.1

Androcentric bias or justified focus?

- Do we prioritise explanations of crime that apply to males because they commit the majority of crimes? This would be a **realist** view in both theoretical and epistemological terms.

- Is our androcentric focus the product of a **self-fulfilling prophecy**—we assume that males commit the most crime so we target our empirical research, our academic explanations, and our criminal justice practices (e.g. police activities) on this group to the exclusion of other populations?

- Is it possible that the androcentric nature of biosocial explanations of crime is (in part) a product of academic theorising by an exclusive group of white, middle-class, male researchers? (For example **Figures 18.1**, **18.2**, **18.3**.)

- To what extent have we socially-constructed the extent and nature of crime committed by males and the need to respond to this crime?

Figure 18.1 Sarnoff Mednick (biosocial theory)
Source: Photo by Terrie E. Moffitt

Figure 18.2 C. Ray Jeffery (biopsychosocial theory)
Source: American Society of Criminology/Public domain

Figure 18.3 James Q. Wilson (right realism theory)
Source: Photo by Ron Hall, Pepperdine University

This strand of theories links neatly into the risk factor theories section that follows the integrated theories, but it is relevant and appropriate to introduce and discuss it here to give you a better idea of the types of explanation offered. The premise of risk factor theories of crime is that it is possible to identify certain biopsychosocial factors in early life (pre-birth, childhood, adolescence, young adulthood) that place a person at an increased risk of committing crime/antisocial behaviour in the future and so can be seen as predictors of these behaviours and ideal targets for pre-emptive preventative intervention (see Case and Haines 2009). For example, several theorists explain crime as the result of a baby experiencing complications during pregnancy, which has a knock-on effect on other areas of life. These effects could include the creation of problems with central nervous system functioning and subsequent wellbeing (Moffitt 1993), which could interact with the mother's rejection to lead to violent behaviour (Raine, Brennan, and Mednick 1997), and mix with poverty (e.g. living in a deprived environment) to predict physical aggression (Arsenault, Tremblay, Boulerice, and Saucier 2002). There have also been a group of biosocial risk factor theories linking poor parenting with later antisocial behaviour, with poor parenting defined variously as unresponsiveness and rejection (e.g. Shaw, Ingoldsby, Gilliam, and Nagin 2003) or harsh, controlling behaviour

and lack of acceptance of the child (e.g. Younge, Oetting and Deffenbacher 1996).

Sociobiological theories of crime: so what do we think?

Advocates argue that the emerging synthesis of perspectives demonstrated by sociobiological theories has benefitted criminological theory by providing broader and more versatile explanations of crime (e.g. Vold et al. 2002). The explanatory utility of biological (positivist) theories in isolation has been characterised as narrow and *reductionist*—reducing the causes and explanations of crime to their most (over) simplified and basic forms at the expense of a broader focus on other potential influences (Mitchell Miller 2009). Consequently, integrating psychological and sociological explanations (to a lesser extent, rational choice theories) into broader integrated theories can moderate the determinism of biological theories (the extent to which they claim that biological factors inevitably cause/predict/affect crime) and offers more holistic, comprehensive explanations that fit more crimes at more times for more people (Akers and Sellers 2013). Contrary to the broad focus of sociobiological theories, however, it is possible that subjectivity may encourage theorists to privilege particular factors and to reject or neglect other potential sources of explanation from other schools of thought. For example, integrated biosocial theories appear to privilege positivist explanations at the expense of giving more detailed consideration to free will/rational choice (with the exception of right realist biosocial theory) or giving full consideration to the role of criminalisation in identifying, targeting, and dealing with individuals in the criminal justice system. Therefore, biosocial theories remain reductionist to a degree, in the sense that they are limited in scope and over-simplified in explanation.

The androcentric focus on males within integrated biosocial theories is also worthy of discussion, especially as androcentricism is a critical issue for criminology. As discussed, this androcentricism is in part justified by the dominance of males in crime statistics and research evidence. However, it is also in part a product (social construction) of the excessive prioritisation of young males in law-making, law enforcement, and in criminological research—somewhat of a chicken and egg situation. A by-product of androcentricism is that it can weaken theoretical explanations by making them less representative of, and valid for, all people who commit crime or who are criminalised. Integrated positivist (sociobiological) theories, therefore, can exacerbate the androcentric positivist/criminological tendency to develop explanations of crime with male populations and then uncritically apply these explanations to females who offend (relying on *supposition* that they are applicable—see also **Chapter 6**), rather than studying the particular lives, contexts, experiences, and behaviours of those females in developing a theory from there (Hagen 2013). As we know, similar criticisms can be made of the extent to which explanatory theories in criminology are *ethnocentric*—dominated by explanations of crime generated in the industrialised western world and then uncritically applied to non-western populations. Explanatory theories can also be accused of being class-centric—dominated by explanations of working-class crime and criminals, whilst ignoring the middle classes.

Notwithstanding any identified limitations, the central argument here is that sociobiological forms of integrated positivist explanatory theory have built on and evolved traditional single factor positivist explanations of crime, whilst retaining a degree of their narrow focus and explanatory preferences. All of which begs the question of what else is there? Enter, social control theories.

Social control theories

A second strand of integrated positivist theories, *social control theories*, is concerned with why people *do not* commit crime. It offers a more promising set of integrated

explanations of crime compared to sociobiological theories for at least three reasons:

1. **Longevity**—having been around since the 1950s, so have had more time to develop and to be refined (Hagen 2013).

2. **Empirical research**—more evidence to support their explanations, perhaps more than any other explanatory theory in criminology (Winters et al. 2014).

3. **Between-schools**—more of an attempt to integrate explanations between-schools, such as integrating rational choice and positivist explanations and more recently by incorporating elements inspired by critical criminological theories and the Victimised Actor Model (Hopkins Burke 2013).

Social control theories are unique as criminological explanations of crime because they subvert the question of 'why do some people commit crime?' into 'why don't some people commit crime?' and 'why do people obey the law?' Building on mid-20th century control theories that focused on the psychological influences (e.g. personality) that control people's behaviour and stop them from offending (e.g. Reiss 1951; Nye 1958), social control theories introduced a greater focus on the social factors that bond people to the norms of a given society—factors such as socialisation processes in the family, school, and peer group.

For the purposes of clarity and relevance, this discussion will be divided into two groups of social control theory: traditional and 21st century. Traditional social control theories will cover the original social control theory (Hirschi 1969), integrated social control theory (Elliott, Ageton and Canter 1979), and the general theory of crime (Gottfredson and Hirschi 1990). The 21st century social control theories will include power control theory (Bates, Bader and Mencken 2003), control balance theory (Tittle 2000), and differential coercion theory (Colvin 2000).

Traditional control theories

The forefather of all other social control theories is Travis Hirschi's (1969) *social control theory*, which explains why some people obey the law and, by extension, why others don't. Hirschi (1969: 16) explained that 'delinquent acts result when an individual's bond to society is weaker or broken'. Therefore, obeying the law is the result of a strong social bond to the rules and norms of your society. Social control theory divides this bond into four social elements:

(a) attachment to significant and important people, organisations and institutions (e.g. relationships);

(b) commitment to conventional, traditional, normal behaviours and actions (e.g. a rational choice to conform);

(c) involvement in conventional behaviours and activities (i.e. being too busy to commit crime); and,

(d) beliefs in the importance of normal behaviour and in each of the other elements of the social bond.

Social control theory is supported by large amounts of data from a wealth of empirical studies. It is integrated because it utilises arguments from rational choice theory and positivism (mainly sociological forms such as strain theory, with some consideration of psychological controls). There are also close links to later risk factor theories (see the next section) in claims that strong social bonds protect against offending, whilst weak social bonds are essentially risk factors for offending, especially for young people. As with other explanatory theories, critics tend to focus on what the theory does not consider, such as the extent of the influence of delinquent friends or the influence of historical and structural contexts on social bonds and on offending behaviour. Critics also focus on what the theory cannot explain, such as the extent and nature of offending behaviour that may result from weak social bonds (see Agnew 2011).

Just as Hirschi had done ten years previously, Elliott et al. (1979) argued that crime is the result of weak social bonds that are themselves the product of poor, negative socialisation in early life. Therefore, strong social bonds are the result of effective socialisation. These social bonds are further weakened or strengthened by later socialisation experiences in the home, school and community and especially exposure to delinquent peer groups. In structural terms, Elliott et al. (1979) believed that social bonds can be further weakened by a person experiencing blocked opportunities, social disorganisation, unemployment and economic recession. Therefore, the *integrated social control theory* explains crime by integrating arguments and concepts from social control, anomie, and social learning theories.

Twenty-one years after his social control theory, Travis Hirschi collaborated with Michael Gottfredson to produce the *general theory of crime* (Gottfredson and Hirschi 1990), also known as 'self-control theory'—an attempt to offer a universal explanation all of 'all crimes, at all times' (Gottfredson and Hirschi 1990: 117) in all places by all people. As the title suggests, the common explanation of all crimes is low self-control. People with low self-control, it is argued, are much more likely to make rational choices to commit crime, as well as to smoke, drink, and have lots of sex. This situation is made worse by ineffective parenting during childhood, which means that self-control is likely to stay at lower levels throughout the person's life. The general theory of crime attempted to address a key criticism of social control theory in that it is able to explain and account for specific types of crime using the same explanation—low self-control. However, it is not strictly a social form of control theory because it rejects the influence of social factors on crime, preferring to talk about the more psychological motivation to commit crime, as opposed to the causes of crime, and explaining all crime as a personalised, immediate rational choice linked to low self-control. This being the case, the general theory of crime has much more difficulty explaining white collar and corporate crimes, which are typically the product of long-term, detailed, patient, and considered planning and all of which seem incompatible with the immediate rational choices implied by the low self-control hypothesis.

21st century social control theories

A series of modified social control theories have been developed since the end of the 20th century. *Power control theory* integrates control and social class theories to argue that patriarchal attitudes in the home can explain gender differences in offending. Put simply, girls are controlled far more than boys in the family setting (usually by their mothers who were themselves controlled as girls) and so are less likely to take risks and commit crime. However, if the balance of power in controlling the child is shared more equally between parents then girls will not be subjected to excessive control and will be as likely to offend or not offend as boys (Bates et al. 2003).

Control balance theory is the brainchild of Charles Tittle (2000), who asserts that crime results from an imbalance in the amount a person's behaviour is controlled compared to others in society. If a person is subjected to excessive amounts of control (i.e. they have a control deficit) then this leads to resentment, anger, weak social bonds, and ultimately to offending. Where a person has an excess of control over others and over their environment (i.e. they have a control surplus) then they get greedy, corrupt, and obsessed with dominance, which leads into offending. This is a need versus greed situation—the need to alleviate a control deficit versus the need to extend a control surplus.

The final 21st century social control theory, known as *differential coercion theory* (Colvin 2000), focuses as you might expect on the criminogenic role of exposure to coercion—the pressure to behave in a certain way. Colvin asserts that high levels of consistent coercion (actual or threatened) in the family, school peer group, or neighbourhood can be criminogenic. For example, coercion in the family or school could manifest in the form of the removal of social supports or the use of physical force. Peer group coercion could be evidenced by gang violence, whilst neighbourhood coercion may take the form of poverty or unemployment. According to the theory, coercion can produce a series of social-psychological deficits (flaws, failings, missing parts) that encourage criminal behaviour. These deficits include anger, low self-control (see also Gottfredson and Hirschi 1990), weak social bonds (see also Hirschi 1969) and an increased commitment to using coercion to achieve personal goals, which is known as 'coercive ideation'.

Social control theory has been dubbed 'the most tested theory of crime causation' (Hopkins Burke 2013: 218), although this claim could now be challenged by the rise to prominence of artefactual risk factor theories (see 'Integrated risk factor theories' section). Such a high level of empirical/evidential support is a major strength of social control theories—indicative of a reliable/replicable set of explanations that are appropriate and applicable (valid) to a range of populations. This may in part be due to the broader range of influences on crime considered by social control theories when compared to single factor and single school theories, including their focus on the socio-structural factors that have been traditionally under-researched by positivist explanatory theories. However, despite the 'grand theory' claims of certain theorists (most notably, Gottfredson and Hirschi 1990), social control theories remain unable to explain all crimes at all times. An associated limitation when compared to other aetiological (causation) theories appears to be an inability to identify what types of crime would result from the specific explanations of social control theories. The complex concept of crime is, therefore, ill-defined and oversimplified by social control theorists (see also Downes and Rock 1998). Hopkins Burke (2013) goes as far as to claim that crime (or deviance in most social control theories) is reduced to the gratification of basic appetites—acquisitive (to obtain goals, property), aggressive (e.g. violent), or sexual. This over-simplification and reductionism in social control explanations is compounded further by overlooking/neglecting a key avenue of explanation—the influence of *criminalisation* processes on the social construction of crime.

Integrated positivist theories

Taking sociobiological theories and social control theories together, let us evaluate what they can tell us about how crime can be explained. The intention has been to provide criminology with hybrid theories of how a range of different factors may interact and interrelate to cause and influence crime. In this respect, they are an improvement over potentially more limited, narrow, subjective, and reductionist single factor theories. However, integrated positivist theories remain subjective and reductionist in their own right to some extent. They may privilege certain explanations over others, for example, fusing two single factor theories such as biological and sociological positivism or merging rational choice with a form of social control theory (see Agnew 2011). Indeed, integrated positivist theories could be accused of ignoring certain explanations altogether, such as the critical criminological concept of criminalisation and the left realist interactions within the 'Square of Crime' (see **Chapter 17**; see also Ugwudike 2015). They still privilege explaining the behaviour of certain groups (e.g. males, populations in the western world) and ignore or relatively neglect other groups (e.g. females, non-western populations). Integrated positivist theories can also be reductionist in their uncritical view that crime is an accepted, agreed, and uncontested concept that simply needs explaining, rather than a dynamic and contingent phenomena specific to historical, socio-structural, cultural, and temporal context (MacDonald and Marsh 2005). In conclusion, a major limitation of integrated positivist theories, as with all explanatory theories in criminology, is their inability to be universal—to explain all crimes at all times by all people. In fact, certain integrated theories (social control theories in particular) may attempt to overgeneralise to such an extent that they cannot identify the specific forms of offending that result from their explanations. In trying to explain too much, they can end up explaining too little. There is a sense, therefore, that integrated theories may occasionally over-reach and over-claim when trying to outperform single factor theories. In doing so, they risk compounding the weaknesses and limitations of the single factor theories they are integrating, without compensating for them by merging their strengths and dramatically improving their explanatory power. So what else is there?

Integrated risk factor theories: Predicting, not explaining crime

In the 1990s, a socio-political risk perspective began to gain popularity within criminology in the industrialised western world. Two central tenets of this perspective were:

(a) that we live in a 'risk society' characterised by rapid social and economic changes brought on by globalisation (Beck 1992), which results in populations feeling unsafe and uncertain and thus needing to control their environments;

(b) that in this risk society, crime is rapidly increasing, especially crime committed by young males, which indicates that official criminal justice system responses to crime (e.g. deterrence, incapacitation, treatment, prevention) are not working.

This notion that crime is increasing strongly implies that the understandings and explanations of crime offered by criminological theories—consolidated by official statistics, political rhetoric, media representations, and public opinion—have not been fit for purpose—the purpose being to identify the most appropriate factors and influences to target through criminal justice systems and interventions. Throughout the 1990s, governments in the western world, especially the post-1997 UK government under Tony Blair, challenged key stakeholders to produce an explanatory theory of crime that was straightforward, politically acceptable (e.g. that did not necessarily focus on the contribution of governments to creating and exacerbating crime), and most of all, practical. In other words, governments needed an apolitical explanation that focused on micro- and meso-level dynamic factors (Andrews and Bonta 2010) that could be easily targeted and changed, whilst macro-level factors such as unemployment, poverty, social disorganisation, and economic recession were largely overlooked. Enter integrated risk factor theories.

This section will analyse and evaluate integrated risk factor theories (key issue three for this chapter)—a range of explanations, each with a slightly different take on the same basic explanatory framework—that it is possible to identify and measure certain factors in the lives of children and young people that increase the risk of them committing crime in the future. (See **Figure 18.4** for a poster for *Minority Report*—this 2002 futuristic action-thriller depicted a mid-21st century 'Pre-Crime' police department that is able to predict crime and so intervene and sentence offenders before any crime actually takes place.) These so-called 'risk factors', typically psychological and sociological (psychosocial) in focus, therefore can be seen to predict crime (or an increased likelihood of crime) and should be targeted by preventative interventions before they occur or by early intervention once they occur, but before they get worse (Farrington 2000). This practical model of identification and targeting (i.e. assessment and intervention) is known as the Risk Factor Prevention Paradigm (RFPP) (Hawkins and Catalano 1992). Risk-based explanations of crime actually emerged in the 1930s in the USA (Glueck and Glueck 1930). By the 1990s, their time had truly come and since then the political and academic popularity of risk-based theories has grown to such an extent that integrated risk factor theories are now arguably the hegemonic set of explanatory theories in criminology (Case and Haines 2009).

For clarity and simplicity, risk-based explanations of crime can be divided into two groups: artefactual risk factor theories and *enhanced pathways risk factor theories*. Artefactual theories focus on the conversion of risk to a quantity/number (a risk factor), whereas enhanced pathways theories complement this positivist quantification of risk with interpretivist qualitative measures of how risk is personally constructed and experienced. Consequently, artefactual theories tend to be within-school integrations of positivist theories, whilst enhanced pathways theories are more concerned with integration between-schools, such as fusing positivist, rational choice and critical theories. Discussion begins with artefactual risk factor theories because these make up the vast majority of integrated risk factor theories and are the form of theory that is dominant within criminology. Conversely, enhanced pathways risk factor theories have been marginalised as minority and militant theories within the risk factor research movement (Case and Haines 2009).

Artefactual risk factor theories

The vast majority of integrated risk factor theories have conceived of risk as an objective fact that can be measured/assessed, quantified, and turned into a numerical factor, or artefact. This 'factorisation' (Kemshall 2008) is typically for the purposes of statistical analysis—to identify statistical relationships between quantified risk factors and quantified measures of offending. Statistical relationships or correlations are interpreted as demonstrating how risk factors predict (an increased risk of) offending behaviour in the future. The conflation of correlation with

Figure 18.4 *Minority Report* (2002, Dir. Spielberg), film poster
Source: AF archive/Alamy Stock Photo

prediction is a key supposition of artefactual risk factor theories (see Kemshall 2008; France 2008) and one that will be challenged later.

The other basic supposition of artefactual risk factor theories is both developmental and deterministic—that risk factors tend to occur in childhood and adolescence and then develop to the point that they determine offending behaviour in later life (see also McAra and McVie's developmental criminology chapter in *The Oxford Handbook of Criminology*—Liebling, Maruna, and McAra 2017). These risk factors can be biological (e.g. related to physique or hormones), but they tend to be psychosocial, that is micro-level psychological (e.g. related to cognition, impulsivity, hyperactivity, attitude, emotion, mental health) and meso-level sociological (e.g. in immediate social domains—family, education, lifestyle, neighbourhood). But first we need to develop a clear understanding of the types of artefactual risk factor theory that have evolved over the years. They share very similar arguments, strengths and weaknesses/limitations, so it is unnecessary to discuss each one in great detail (if you are interested in a more detailed discussion, read Case and Haines 2009), but a broad

overview will help us to understand the nature of these theories. Better understanding of a theory should make it easier to evaluate its value and utility. As you will see from **Table 18.1**, despite a clearly evolving focus over time, each artefactual risk factor theory is essentially a within-school integration of various positivist theories.

The table demonstrates the clear evolution of artefactual risk factor explanations of crime—starting with integrated biopsychosocial explanations of officially-recorded crime in adolescence (in the first half of the 20th century), moving into psychosocial explanations of both official and self-reported crime in adolescence and adulthood (1970s and 1980s theories) and finally more holistic theories integrating psychosocial factors with socio-structural influences (1990s).

An important consideration when evaluating explanatory theories is to assess their *validity*—to separate their actual strengths from any potentially invalid claims made by their supporters about their supposed strengths. To this end, let us examine the common claims made by advocates as they relate to the validity, reliability, and practicality of artefactual risk factor theories.

When?	What, Who and How?
1930s	**Multi-factor developmental theory (Glueck and Glueck 1930, 1934)**
	Biological, psychological, and sociological (biopsychosocial) characteristics measured in childhood correlate with officially-recorded offending in adolescence
1940s–1950s	**Developmental crime prevention theory (Cabot 1940; McCord and McCord 1959)**
	Biopsychosocial factors measured in childhood correlate with officially-recorded offending in adolescence and can be prevented and reduced through official interventions
1970s	**The criminal careers model (West and Farrington 1973)**
	Psychosocial risk factors experienced in childhood exert a developmental influence on (i.e. correlate positively with) the extent and nature of official and self-reported offending in adolescence and adulthood
1980s	**Social development model (Hawkins and Weis 1985)**
	Psychosocial risk factors (e.g. opportunity for and involvement in conventional activities, positive interactions, skills to participate and reinforcement for behaviour) interact with cognitive ability, socio-structural status (e.g. gender, age, race) and external constraints (e.g. in/formal reactions to behaviour) to cause offending at different developmental stages of a child's life. This is the first self-proclaimed 'integrated' risk factor theory
Early 1990s	**Age-graded theory of informal social control (Sampson and Laub 1993)**
	Informal social controls in the family and school interact with structural factors (e.g. poverty, unemployment) to cause offending in childhood and adolescence. Social bonds, significant transitions, and critical life events in adulthood can encourage desistance from offending
Late 1990s	**Ecological theory (Wikstrom and Loeber 1998; Sampson et al. 1997)**
	Psychosocial risk factors interact with socio-structural context (e.g. community characteristics, immediate situational factors) in childhood and adolescence to influence offending at different times in different places

Table 18.1 The evolution of artefactual risk factor theories (adapted from Case and Haines 2009: 102–103)

Artefactual risk factor theorists assert that their explanations have validity—that they are common sense, simplistic, acceptable, practical explanations of crime (see, for example, Farrington 2007). This validity is increased by the integration of a range of explanatory influences, from the biological to the psychological to the sociological to rational choice and situational influences (see **Table 18.1**). An excellent example of the faith put in the validity of artefactual risk factor explanations is their application in the *Asset* risk assessment process conducted with all young people who enter the youth justice system (YJS) of England and Wales (see **What do you think? 18.2**). In other words, the ways that youth justice practitioners are expected to understand (assess) and explain offending of young people who enter the YJS is significantly shaped by artefactual risk factor theory (see Stephenson, Giller, and Brown 2011).

In contrast to claims that artefactual risk factor theories provide valid, holistic understandings of offending, a number of methodological criticisms have been aimed at these theories; criticisms that could diminish the validity of their explanations and conclusions. For example, there have been psychosocial, deterministic, and reductionist biases to artefactual explanations of crime (see Haines and Case 2015). Theories have privileged psychological and sociological factors (i.e. psychosocial bias—see **Table 18.1**) over socio-structural issues such as poverty, unemployment, social/neighbourhood disorganisation, and economic instability (see Muncie 2009). There has also been an overriding supposition that risk factors inevitably determine crime in the future (i.e. deterministic bias—see **Table 18.1**) at the expense of examining the processes of criminalisation such as the criminogenic influence of contact with the formal YJS (McAra and McVie 2007). There is the further issue regarding the common sense, simplified understandings of crime that typify artefactual risk factor theories and whether they have been *reductionist* by *over*-simplifying risk into a quantified factor, thus dumbing down explanations of crime and washing away the complexity of how risk may be experienced and negotiated by young people (i.e. reductionist bias). Of course, similar criticisms of psychosocial, deterministic, and reductionist biases could be levelled at the biological, psychological, and sociological theories promoted by positivism, but that does not make these criticisms of artefactual theories any less valid.

WHAT DO YOU THINK? 18.2

Risk-based assessment and intervention in the youth justice system

The artefactual RFPP is the driver for understanding and responding to the behaviour of all young people who offend and enter the YJS of England and Wales. Since 2000, all young offenders (aged 10–17 years old) who have contact with the formal YJS (i.e. they are not diverted from it or given pre-court interventions) have been subject to a risk assessment called *Asset* which is completed by adult youth justice practitioners following interview with the young person (see also **Chapter 9**).

Asset rates/measures the likelihood (risk) that factors in different psychosocial areas of a young person's recent and current life (attitudes, emotions, thoughts, motivations to change, family, education, neighbourhood, lifestyle) will encourage reoffending in the future. *Asset* is a clear animation and application of artefactual risk factor theories, in particular, the criminal careers model (West and Farrington 1973; see **Table 18.1**) because it measures a set of psychosocial risk factors and uses these measures to predict and prevent future offending. Youth justice practitioners use *Asset* to assign to a young person a risk score, which leads to them being rated as at high, medium, or low risk of future reoffending. This

rating can influence their sentence and definitely determines the amount, frequency, and duration of intervention that they then receive from youth justice agencies. This process is known as the 'scaled approach' to assessment and intervention (see Stephenson et al. 2011) because the intervention that results from the assessment is scaled to the assessed level of risk. This artefactual risk focus dominates how we explain and respond to the behaviour of young people who commit crime in England and Wales; it is also popular in other wstern countries such as the USA, Canada, Australia, and parts of western Europe. So what do you think of it? Specifically:

- Is a risk-based approach the best, most valid, and most practical way to explain the criminal behaviour of young people in our society?

- What are the advantages and disadvantages of this approach theoretically and practically?

- Could artefactual risk factor understandings of youth crime be enhanced by the inclusion of any elements of other explanatory theories? If not, should they be replaced entirely by other explanatory theories? If so, what and why?

A major strength of artefactual risk factor theories, one very attractive to politicians and practitioners, has been their *reliability*—the ability of thousands of different studies to replicate findings and conclusions and thus confirm the central explanatory assumptions that risk factors predict later offending. Study after study over different times and places and populations has identified that exposure to psychosocial risk factors during childhood and adolescence increases the likelihood/probability/risk of offending behaviour at some point in later life (see Farrington 2007). These reliable/replicable psychosocial risk factors are located within the risk domains of individual/psychological (e.g. hyperactivity, impulsivity, lack of empathy), family (e.g. lack of parental supervision, parents arguing, criminal siblings), school (e.g. academic underachievement, disliking school, truancy), neighbourhood (e.g. criminal friends, lack of community resources, easy availability of drugs), and lifestyle (e.g. drug use, lack of positive activities). For sheer weight of numbers/replications, artefactual risk factor theories would seem to be the most reliable explanatory of crime, replacing social control theories as having produced the largest body of supportive research evidence (Case and Haines 2009).

However, remember your ABC. Closer examination could lead us to question exactly how reliable this body of studies has been in terms of content, design, and methods. Varying measures of risk factors have been employed (within or between studies), such as ratings scales of different sizes and dichotomous yes/no measures; all taken over varying measurement periods, such as in the past month, past year, over the lifetime, etc. Furthermore, these varying definitions and measures of risk factors have been linked to varying measures of offending (e.g. non-offenders, self-reported offenders, young people identified as antisocial, convicted offenders, re-offenders). They have also been linked to different types of offending (e.g. property crime, violent crime, lifetime offending, recent offending) and different definitions of offending, some of which are not actually offending at all, but broader categories such as deviance, delinquency, and antisocial behaviour. Artefactual research studies have used differing understandings of the risk factor-offending relationship—variously understanding risk factors as correlates, predictors, indicators, causes, and even symptoms of offending (see later in this chapter). **Table 18.1** illustrates how theories have evolved by prioritising different sets of risk factors over others—indicated by the evolution from biopsychosocial factors, to psychosocial factors, to psychosocial plus socio-structural factors. Therefore, artefactual risk factor theories have presented themselves as a unified, reliable explanatory movement (cf. Agnew 2011), in broad agreement on the nature of what a risk factor is and how it relates to offending, but the research has been less reliable than claimed in terms of its working definitions and measures of its central concepts,

the methods used to collect evidence and the explanations of the risk-factor-offending relationship that result.

The findings and conclusions from artefactual risk factor theories offer a degree of *practicality* beyond the other explanatory theories that have gone before them, particularly when they are targeted in practice through the RFPP, thus linking explanation with responses. Professor David Farrington has robustly championed the practicality of the RFPP since it was imported to the UK from the USA in the 1990s, asserting that:

> The basic idea … is very simple: Identify the key risk factors for offending and implement prevention methods designed to counteract them. There is often a related attempt to identify key protective factors against offending and to implement prevention methods designed to enhance them.
>
> Farrington 2007: 606

A key argument for the practicality of artefactual risk factor theories is that they identify the predictors of future re-offending, so they can be used to guide youth justice staff in how best to target their time, resources, and money (e.g. on high-risk individuals, neighbourhoods, and crimes—see Baker et al. 2005). Consequently, the RFPP has gained popularity as a practical model for official (YJS) responses to youth offending across the western world, for example, the use of the *Asset* risk assessment tool in England and Wales (see **What do you think? 18.2**; see also **Chapter 9**). Put simply, the explanations of crime clearly guide the responses to crime. However, there are certain problems with this claim to practicality. Firstly, risk assessment tools are not necessarily very good predictors of crime. The *Asset* instrument, for example, accurately predicts whether or not a young person will reoffend in 67–69 per cent of cases (Baker et al. 2005), which is a higher predictive accuracy than similar tools in the adult criminal justice system. But what about the one third of young people whose offending future is incorrectly predicted by *Asset*? They may be subject to excessive intervention that they do not necessarily need because they have been incorrectly judged as likely to reoffend, but they do not (i.e. false positives). Conversely, they may not receive sufficient levels of intervention because there have been incorrectly judged as *unlikely* to reoffend, but they do (i.e. false negatives). Such disproportionate levels of intervention could be viewed as ineffective, inefficient, unethical, and inappropriate responses to crime due to a flawed explanatory model (Bateman 2011; Paylor 2011).

In explanatory terms, artefactual risk factor theorists may have been over-confident in their claims and conclusions. That these theories have become the dominant explanations of why crime is committed by young people and have guided policies and practices to tackle youth crime globally, indicates that this confidence is shared by a growing number of politicians and policy makers

(Stephenson et al. 2011). Is this explanatory confidence misplaced based on the methods employed to reach these deterministic conclusions? The explanatory basis (validity) of artefactual risk factor theories is that risk factors identified in childhood and adolescence predict crime in later life. A typical research design for artefactual risk factor studies is to measure a person's exposure to risk factors and the occurrence of offending behaviour over the same time period (e.g. the past year), with little (if any) consideration of which occurred first in the person's life (i.e. which has temporal precedence). If we do not measure which comes first, then how can we support conclusions about the direction or nature of the relationship between risk factors and offending. Let us tease out the difficulties in establishing the risk factor-offending relationship with an example from a hypothetical cross-sectional study that measures risk factors and offending over the past year:

- **Predictive relationship**—the central claim of artefactual theories is that risk factors predict crime. To illustrate this relationship, assume that during the measurement period, a young person experienced a series of risk factors at a particular time (e.g. from January to March), after which they offended (e.g. in July). In this case, it looks as if the risk factors predicted the offending, because they have temporal precedence. However, even if they predated offending, we cannot be definite (from statistical analysis alone) that the identified risk factors influenced the offending in any real, qualitative, explainable way or that they were the only influences on offending. At best, we can conclude that risk factors came first in a young person's life; at worst, that they were identified/measured first.

- **Interactive relationship**—a young person could experience certain risk factors (e.g. experience family breakdown, temporary school exclusion) at a particular time (e.g. January–March), then they offend (e.g. in July). They may then experience exacerbated versions of the original risk factors or different risk factors (e.g. going into care, permanent school exclusion) at a later point (e.g. December), then offend again. In this case, risk factors and offending seem to interact in a kind of vicious circle. But again, how this relationship works in reality, beyond being identified via a statistical test, is less clear.

- **Symptomatic relationship**—offending could predate and/or exacerbate the effects of exposure to risk. In our example, a young person could have offended in the period immediately prior to the measurement period, which could have created the risk factors (e.g. led to family breakdown or school exclusion)—so the risk factors may actually be symptoms of offending, not predictors of it. But … if offending comes first,

the resultant symptoms/experiences (e.g. family breakdown) are not really risk factors in any predictive sense, as what they predict has already happened. They may, however, be risk factors for further offending at a later date.

- **No relationship**—it could be that risk factors and offending are totally unrelated. This is unlikely, but certainly possible. In our example, exposure to risk factors and offending behaviour may have occurred almost simultaneously or at least so close together that they did not affect one another. Maybe family breakdown, school exclusion and offending were all the products of other, unmeasured risk factors or problems? We shouldn't assume a real-life, directional relationship (e.g. predictive, causal) between risk factors and offending based on their co-occurrence in the life of a young person or even when temporal precedence can be established, especially when our evidence is based entirely on statistical relationships between quantitative factors. Longer-term, qualitative measures are required for these theories to move beyond what risk factors and levels of offending are present and into the how and why of the risk factor-offending relationship.

Figure 18.5 illustrates the potential for these different relationships between risk factors and offending outcomes.

It is arguably most valid to conclude that the risk factors identified by artefactual risk factor theories are correlates with offending—factors that have a statistical relationship with offending and have been present in the life of a person who has also offended at some point. However, correlates are not causes, neither are they predictors.

Bear in mind the points raised in this section when looking at **What do you think? 18.3**.

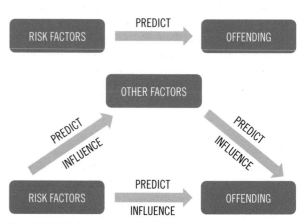

Figure 18.5 Different relationships between risk factors and offending outcomes

WHAT DO YOU THINK? 18.3

Explaining crime using quantified risk factors

Based on the previous discussions of the contested validity, reliability, and practicality of artefactual explanations, how would you assess the utility of this group of theories? Specifically:

- What do you think are the theoretical and practical advantages of understanding crime in terms of identifying risk factors?

- Does converting the potentially complex concept of risk into a numerical factor inevitably over-simplify it and/or is this a helpful process that enables us to target the key indicators of future crime?

- Does the emphasis on risk factors as predictors rather than causes give criminologists more flexibility in their explanations as they do not need to be as precise and definite about how these factors influence crime?

In other words, does the common sense, practical nature of artefactual risk factor explanations allow us to forgive an element of overstatement about their rigorous methods and over-confidence about their conclusions?

Enhanced pathways risk factor theories: broadening risk perspectives

Although artefactual risk factor theories dominate contemporary explanations of (youth) crime, this chapter would be oversimplifying the discussion of risk factor theories if it were to end here. Theories of crime continually evolve through challenge, fresh research, new ideas and refinements, processes reflected in the risk factor research movement. A new movement of what can be seen as enhanced pathways risk factor theories has gained momentum since the late 1990s and into the 21st century. This group of explanations has attempted to address the alleged explanatory and methodological weaknesses/limitations of artefactual risk factor theories, particularly their oversimplification of risk by converting it to a number ('factorisation'—Kemshall 2008) and neglecting to elicit the qualitative understandings of those who experience risk (Case 2006). The enhanced element, therefore, refers to viewing the traditional weaknesses of risk

factor theories more as limitations of an otherwise valid explanatory framework (i.e. understanding offending as the product of exposure to risk factors) that should be enhanced and improved rather than rejected. The pathways element derives from the explanatory emphasis on exploring and explaining (typically young people's) pathways into and out of crime. These pathways explanations tend to focus on between-school interactions between exposure to risk factors (measured in a positivist way) and personal constructions and understandings of these experiences (measured in an interpretivist way). Two progressive sets of enhanced pathways theories have emerged: the *Edinburgh integrated pathways theory* and *constructivist pathways risk factor theories*.

Edinburgh integrated pathways theory

The research team behind the 'Edinburgh study of youth transitions and crime' (D.J. Smith, Lesley McAra, and Susan McVie) have conducted several sweeps of data collection as part of their longitudinal study of over 4,000 young people—starting with a cohort of 12–17 year olds and most recently when that cohort was aged 24–25 years old. The commonly-abbreviated 'Edinburgh study' set out to produce a contemporary, integrated theory of youth crime that was 'not concerned with early childhood influences, but with transitions and personal transformations during adolescence and adulthood' (Smith and McVie 2003: 169–70). By utilising a range of data collection methods (e.g. questionnaire, interview, official statistics) from a range of participants (e.g. young people, parents/carers, teachers), the study produced an holistic explanation of youth crime—the *Edinburgh integrated pathways theory*. For clarity of discussion, the theory has been given a label, because the researchers so far have not. This theory explains young people's pathways into and out of crime as the result of interactions between psychosocial risk factors and socio-structural factors such as social controls in the community and physical environment, interactions with agencies of informal and formal such control such as the family, school, police, and the YJS. These interactions influence young people's pathways into/out of crime and their self-rated ability to navigate and negotiate these pathways. Therefore, the theory integrates positivist understandings of risk (factors) with interpretations of risk (experiences) and contextualises these by examining macro-level socio-structural influences. The relationship between risk and offending is framed as a complex, qualitative process rather than an over-simplified, quantitative/statistical artefact (France 2008).

The synthesised, integrated pathways explanation enabled the Edinburgh researchers to 'understand the causes of youth crime and how offending emerges in the process of development from childhood to adulthood' (Smith and McAra 2004: 14). The most important 'explanatory variables' (essentially risk factors, but the Edinburgh team appear to reject the term) for offending were:

- family-based—poor parental supervision, parent-child conflict;
- school-based—negative attitudes to school, poor relationships with teachers, misbehaviour;
- neighbourhood-based—social deprivation, unemployment, social disorganisation;
- peer- and lifestyle-based—gang membership, contact with the YJS in Scotland;
- individual-based—impulsivity;
- 'critical moments' in teenage years—especially school exclusion.

A particularly notable finding was that 'repeated and more intensive forms of contact with agencies of youth justice may be damaging to young people in the long-term' (McAra and McVie 2007: 333) due to their labelling effects and exacerbation of existing explanatory variables. The identification of system contact as a key, explanatory variable contradicts the central premise of the RFPP—that risk factors should be identified and then targeted by official intervention. The Edinburgh study discovered that such risk-focused targeting is, in itself, criminogenic. In other words, official intervention can make offending worse.

The Edinburgh integrated pathways theory enhances the explanatory utility of risk factor theories by adopting a broader theoretical perspective and by measuring more areas of risk through the use of multiple research methods (Tashakkori and Teddlie 1998). The psychosocial bias of artefactual theories is addressed through a focus on socio-structural factors and system effects. In addition, the longitudinal design and complex statistical analysis employed help to identify the temporal precedence of certain risk factors over offending, complemented by interpretivist, qualitative research to fill the explanatory gap (the 'black box'—see **Chapter 19**) between exposure to risk factors and offending behaviour (Pawson and Tilley 2004). As such, traditional risk factor theories are enhanced in terms of their ability to explain the nature of risk factor-offending relationships at different stages of life.

Constructivist pathways risk factor theories

Two groups of integrated studies have enhanced risk-based explanations of (largely youth) crime by considering in detail how young people 'construct' (build, understand, create) their experiences of risk. These constructions influence how they experience, navigate, and negotiate risk and their pathways into and out of crime (see also Sampson and Laub 1993 in **Table 18.1**). These two main constructivist risk factor studies are: *Pathways into and out of crime* (see France and Homel 2007; Hine 2005) and the *Teesside studies* (see MacDonald and Marsh 2005; Webster et al. 2004).

'Pathways into and out of crime: Risk, resilience and diversity' (Hine 2005) is a partnership of five longitudinal studies in the UK. The studies explored how young people construct, negotiate, and understand their experiences of risk factors and their pathways into/out of crime, with a particular focus on the social processes that mediate (influence, intervene, interfere with) these pathways. The five studies focused on: young people in youth offending teams and pupil referral units (Hine et al. 2007); black and Asian young people (Haw 2007); young people with a parent in prison (Walker and McCarthy 2005); young people's social capital or social and material resources (Boeck et al. 2006); and, the role of risk in substance misuse by young offenders (Hammersley et al. 2003). The Pathways' studies identified 'substantial differences between the reality of their [young people's] everyday experiences and the theory presented within the dominant current policy framework for interventions' (Hine 2006, in Case and Haines 2009: 144). The dominant current policy framework in this case was heavily influenced by artefactual risk factor theories/the RFPP and prioritised risk-focused interventions in the YJS of England and Wales.

The explanatory theory that emerged from the Pathways studies is risk-based, but views risk as a complex and dynamic *process* that is actively experienced, constructed, resisted, and negotiated by young people. This contrasts with artefactual explanations of risk (factors) as experienced helplessly by young people. The artefactual notion of exposure to risk as harmful to passive young people is illustrated on the contentious front cover of author member Steve Case's book, *Understanding Youth Offending: Risk factor research, policy and practice* (Case and Haines 2009). The cover portrays young people as 'crash test dummies' hurtling uncontrollably towards offending outcomes once exposed to risk factors—but such a deterministic explanation overlooks young people's ability to interpret and shape their own lives.

The constructivist pathways theory enhances risk factor explanations by examining the standard psychosocial risk factors that populate artefactual theories, but giving equal significance to social factors and influences (e.g. interactions, socio-structural, cultural, and historical factors) and to the qualitative voices of the young people whose behaviour is being explained. Like the Edinburgh study, the range of research methods used (e.g. interviews, questionnaires, official statistics), the range of participants/data sources accessed (e.g. young people, parents, teachers, youth justice staff), and the range of factors examined has produced a more holistic version of a risk factor theory (France and Homel 2007). The resultant theory seems to offer a more holistic, valid, and up-to-date explanation of crime due to its broader focus on qualitative measures of risk processes over longer periods (not single measurement periods) and the detailed integration of young people's views, perspectives, and experiences of these risks as a vehicle to explaining the risk factor-offending relationship.

The Teesside studies conducted in north-east England focused on how young people construct risk and their experience of risk factors in particular socio-cultural contexts such as living in a socially deprived neighbourhood, being from an ethnic minority, and being a member of a lower social class. Three biographical, interview-based studies make up the Teesside trilogy: *Snakes and ladders: Young people, transitions and social exclusion* (Johnston et al. 2000); *Disconnected Youth: Growing up in Britain's poorest neighbourhoods* (MacDonald and Marsh 2005); and *Poor transitions: Young adults and social exclusion* (Webster et al. 2004—published second but conducted last). *Snakes and Ladders* examined the lives of 98 young people aged 15 to 25 years old and focused on their social class and ethnic background; *Disconnected Youth* studied 88 young people aged 15 to 25 and focused on neighbourhood; *Poor Transitions* followed 34 original members of the other study samples into adulthood (aged 23–29). The theory that resulted from the Teesside studies explained crime as a result of interactions between 'rough approximations' of psychosocial risk factors (e.g. dislike of school, truancy, single-parent family, no educational qualifications, traumatic life, domestic violence, parent in prison, difficult parental divorce, living in care) and socio-structural barriers to success (e.g. socio-economic dependence, lack of employment opportunities, low wages, positive poverty). The most influential socio-structural barrier in the Teesside context was the influx of cheap heroin into the neighbourhood. The researchers also identified 'unpredictable critical moments' in young people's lives (e.g. experiencing rape, suffering a road accident) that could influence their future vulnerability or resistance to risk factors. The Teesside studies concluded that the extent and nature of the socio-structural risks identified:

> could not have been predicted by artefact-based approaches that neglect historical, socio-economic and geographical context … [and] that the relationship between risk factors and offending is complex and multifaceted rather than unproblematically causal and predictive, as depicted in traditional risk factor research.
>
> Webster et al. 2004, in Case and Haines 2009: 149

The explanatory utility of the Teesside studies is inevitably limited by their narrow focus on explaining crime amongst one specific sample in one specific neighbourhood in the UK at a specific time. However, the theory that emerges moves beyond the psychosocial, deterministic, and reductionist biases of artefactual risk factor theories by incorporating socio-structural foci, examination of critical life moments, qualitative interpretations of risk and, perhaps most importantly, the importance of context in shaping how young people experience and construct (understand, negotiate, respond to) risk. Perhaps this enhanced form of risk factor theory emerged precisely because of the self-imposed limitations of the Teesside studies, in the sense that the researchers limited their ambitions to an intensive focus on explaining in detail the behaviour of a small group of people in a specific context. The Teesside studies have conducted research and produced a theory that was never intended to be reliable, generalisable, universal, or deterministic in quantitative terms—it was deliberately limited in focus. The result is an holistic, dynamic, multifaceted, and sensitive explanation of crime based on how risk is constructed by context and by young people's active experiences and responses to it.

Enhanced pathways risk factor theories as explanations of crime

The pathways-focused theories from Edinburgh and Teesside have offered broad, wide-ranging explanations of (youth) crime, enhancing the risk-based explanations of their artefactual counterparts. Enhanced pathways theories have integrated measures of psychosocial risk factors with socio-structural factors and consideration of young people's personal understandings and constructions of how risk factors interact with one another, how they are shaped by context, and how they are experienced by young people. It could be argued, therefore, that these enhanced forms of integrated risk theories are more valid than artefactual alternatives because they incorporate more factors/influences into their explanations and are the products of more personalised, meaningful research with the very people whose behaviour they are trying to explain (France and Homel 2007). This approach could be viewed as a more appropriate, open-minded, and ethical way of researching and developing explanatory theories—asking the focus group for their own interpretations (whilst always maintaining *reflexivity*—see **Chapter 6**) and considering multiple influences on their lives at the micro-, meso-, and macro-levels.

These enhanced risk factor theories do, however, remain committed to the notion of risk as their central explanatory concept (Case and Haines 2009). Whilst this risk focus moves explanations away from potentially more invalid discussions of *causes* (see **Chapter 19**) and onto understandings based on predictors, the concept of risk is also problematic on theoretical, methodological, and ethical grounds (Case and Haines 2015; see also Muncie 2009). Explaining young people's lives as collections of risks, however these may be resisted and negotiated, dictates that we as criminologists understand young people's lives as risky and dangerous; as bundles of deficits, flaws, and weaknesses. Whether adults intervene/interfere through applying the RFPP or whether young people are capable of intervening themselves (as indicated by enhanced pathways risk factor theories), we are still compelled to understand and explain crime largely as the result of a personal failure to resist risk. This of course illustrates the reductionist self-fulfilling prophecy of many explanatory theories—we only look in certain ways at certain factors and inevitably generate only particular explanations, but not others.

The two sides of the integrated coin

Taking a broad overview of the integrated theories that have been covered in this chapter, it is possible to (over-) simplify them into two dichotomous groups of positivist theories and enhanced pathways risk factor theories (see **Figure 18.6**).

Group one (positivist) has tended to quantify the causes and predictors of crime in order to identify static relationships between psychosocial factors offending at one point in time. Group two (pathways) has used more qualitative research methods to identify personal understanding, dynamic processes, and interactions between psychosocial factors and a broad range of socio-structural factors, along with cultural, historical, and economic factors. Group one has produced purportedly generalisable, universal explanations of crime through research with large groups; group two has preferred detailed, nuanced (non-generalisable) explanations of crime committed by smaller, specific groups in specific places. Both groups have attempted to explain crime by integrating a range of theories from within-schools (e.g. different positivist theories) and between-schools (e.g. blending positivism with constructivism).

This chapter has analysed and evaluated the explanatory and practical utility of integrated theories of crime. It has demonstrated that explaining crime by exploring a broader range of possible factors, influences, and interactions has increased the potential of integrated theories to be valid (in the sense of appropriate, relevant, comprehensive, and up-to-date) compared to outdated and narrower single factor theories. However, integrated theories suffer similar problems of *androcentricism*, *ethnocentrism*, *reductionism*, and *supposition*. These issues all raise questions as to exactly what and how much we can realistically expect explanatory theories to be able to explain? Just how feasible is it to pinpoint the factors, influences, and processes that explain all crimes at all times by all kinds of people? Exactly what can we expect from criminologists and criminology in terms of explaining crime? Which brings us to **Chapter 19** (Searching for the causes of crime).

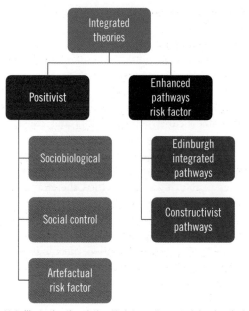

Figure 18.6 Illustrating the relationship between integrated theories of crime

SUMMARY

- To place integrated theories of crime in the context of the historical development of criminological theories

This chapter argued that the foundation for theoretical development in criminology has been the single theory explaining crime in a specific way. A common limitation of these single explanatory theories of crime has been their exclusivity—a single-minded focus on a specific way of explaining crime, to the exclusion of others as potential contributors to their explanations, or as potential alternative explanations of crime. However, many explanatory theories have developed by acknowledging and integrating concepts and arguments from other theories. These integrated explanations have been within-theory, within-school, and between-schools.

- To analyse and evaluate integrated positivist theories of crime in explanatory and practical terms

Integrated positivist theories were divided into two main groups: socio-biological and social control. Socio-biological theories integrate biological factors with sociological and environmental influences, whilst social control theories integrate psychological, sociological, and structural factors. It was argued that these hybrid theories of how different factors interact and interrelate to create crime are more holistic and less subjective and reductionist than single factor theories, thus they may have more explanatory utility and validity. However, integrated positivist theories retain elements of subjectivity and reductionism, privileging certain explanations over others, tending to focus on male and westernised groups (so demonstrating androcentrism and ethnocentrism), and being unable to provide a universal explanation of crime.

- To analyse and evaluate integrated risk factor theories of crime in explanatory and practical terms

Integrated risk factor theories were divided into two main groups: artefactual and enhanced pathways. Artefactual theories identify quantifiable psychological and sociological risk factors that purportedly predict crime in the future, whilst enhanced pathways theories integrate socio-structural factors and personal constructions with these risk factors in order to understand individual pathways into and out of crime. The advantages of risk factor theories were explored, notably their superior practicality, validity, reliability, evidence-base, and explanatory utility when compared to traditional single theory explanations. However, several explanatory and methodological limitations were identified, particularly in terms of a degree of psychosocial bias, reductionism, and determinism (mainly within artefactual theories).

REVIEW QUESTIONS

1. Which single-factor explanations of crime have dominated the evolution of criminological theory?

2. Can you identify two main groups of integrated positivist theories of crime?

3. Can you identify two main groups of integrated risk factor theories of crime?

4. What explanatory advantages do integrated theories have relative to single-factor theories?

5. Could integrated theories be limited in explanatory utility in similar ways to single-factor theories?

FURTHER READING

Case, S.P. and Haines, K.R. (2009) *Understanding Youth Offending: Risk Factor Research Policy and Practice*. Abingdon: Routledge.
The only text available that is entirely dedicated to a detailed explanation and critique of all forms of (integrated) risk factor theories and their links to policy and practice.

Hirschi, T. (1969) *Causes of Delinquency*. Berkeley: University of California Press.
Quite simply, one of the seminal, must-read criminological texts. Hirschi provides a detailed and accessible, yet challenging, overview of his ground-breaking social control theory.

Hopkins Burke, R. (2013) *An Introduction to Criminological Theory* (4th edn). Abingdon: Routledge.
This is a very well-known and popular criminological theory text that offers an ideal supplement to the theory chapters in this book. It is comprehensive, clearly-written, informed, and research-based.

Access the **online resources** to view selected further reading and web links relevant to the material covered in this chapter.
www.oup.com/uk/case/

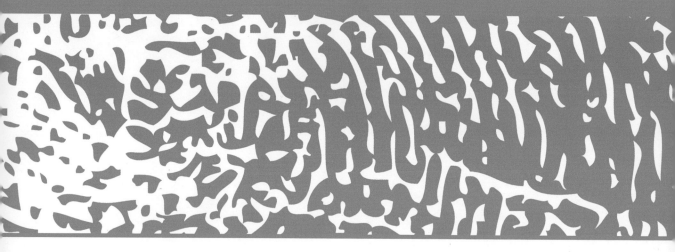

CHAPTER OUTLINE

Introduction   526

Epistemology and the causes of crime   526

Operationalising the causes of crime   529

Exploring the causes of crime through
scientific experiment   530

The rebirth of experimental criminology in
the 21st century   536

Responding to crime   539

Chaos theory   542

Conclusion: Do we really search for the causes of crime?   545

Searching for the causes of crime

KEY ISSUES

After reading this chapter, you should be able to:

- explore the reasons why we search for the causes of crime in criminology, with particular focus on positivism;

- discuss the definitional issues relating to the concepts of crime and causes that influence the valid and reliable identification of the causes of crime;

- assess the implications of these definitional and explanatory issues for producing valid and reliable responses to crime;

- evaluate the feasibility and necessity of identifying the causes of crime.

Introduction

Exploring causality has been a high priority within criminology as a central means of informing explanations of and responses to crime. This apparent causal obsession will be the focus of the current chapter.

The explanatory theories discussed throughout this 'Exploring Crime' part of this book have focused mainly on the **aetiology** of crime—the origins of crime explained in terms of its causes. Classical and right realist theories assert free will and rational choice as the causes of crime. Positivists identify biological, psychological, and sociological causes of crime, as do multi-factor and risk factor integrated theories. More recently, critical criminology and left realism, along with some integrated theories such as enhanced pathways risk factor theories, have explored qualitative processes and interactions (e.g. criminalisation, the Square of Crime), rather than the influence of single factors. However, these processes and interactions are still viewed as being in some way causal of crime. Whether different criminological theories and theorists choose to badge or spin the factors and processes that underpin their aetiological explanations, as predictors, indicators, influences, risk factors, criminogenic interactions, and so on, the primary goal of these theories is to identify the causes of crime or the causal mechanisms leading to crime. Consequently, many explanatory theories in criminology have been developed and utilised as if they have unequivocally been able to identify the causes of crime.

From the very start of this book, criminology has been characterised as a three-part process consisting of definitions, explanations, and responses to crime. Once the earliest criminologists had defined crime and different types of crime (see **Chapter 3**), there followed a pressing need to explain such crime(s). In this chapter, the term crime(s) indicates both crime in general and specific, individual types of crime. The pressure to explain crime has come largely from politicians, policy makers, practitioners, the media, the general public, and academics themselves. It has never gone away; if anything, it is increased as the concept of crime has become more diverse and problematic in the political sphere and public eye.

Take a look at **What do you think? 19.1** for some questions which encourage you to think about the context of this chapter.

Arguably the most important reason for wanting to explain crime(s) (beyond simple academic and human curiosity) is so that we as criminologists can understand it better and thus respond to it appropriately through prevention activity, sentencing, punishment, deterrence, rehabilitation, treatment, intervention, policy and practice, further academic research and scholarship. If we are able to better understand crime, we are able to respond to it in more valid, appropriate, and effective ways. But in the spirit of *Always Be Critical* (ABC—see **Chapter 1**), it is important to firstly ask some key questions:

- Why do criminologists privilege the identification and exploration of causes, and to a lesser extent, causal mechanisms, as their explanatory gold standard or Holy Grail?

- Why are causes rated more highly and assigned a greater explanatory power than other potential modes and mechanisms of explanation?

The answer to both questions is arguably science, or more accurately, pseudo-science. Criminological research, methodology, knowledge generation, and explanation has been dominated by positivism—positivist epistemology and positivist methodology.

WHAT DO YOU THINK? 19.1

Why search for the causes of crime?

- Why do you think that so many criminologists over so many years have prioritised the identification of the causes of crime over other potential ways of explaining crime?

- Do you think that the concept of causes has any explanatory or practical advantages over other forms of explanation, such as talking in terms of the predictors, indicators, drivers, and influences related to crime?

Epistemology and the causes of crime

The evolution of explanatory theories in criminology been dominated by positivism, which pursues an **epistemology** (theory of knowledge generation) based on gathering data in the social world to form the basis of universal laws of behaviour (see also **Chapter 6**). Positivism also supports on objectivist **ontology** (theory of how to understand reality) that the real world is external to the person measuring it and consists of unequivocal facts that can be objectively measured. Positivist epistemology, with its accompanying objectivist ontology and the methodologies that follow from these have dominated criminological research and knowledge generation since the heyday of Lombroso. In this respect, the hybrid discipline of criminology betrays its favouritism towards its older brother, psychology, over its eldest brother, sociology.

Traditionally, sociologists have given equal consideration in their research methods and theory generation to *interpretivism*, the opponent of positivism. Interpretivist epistemology asserts that knowledge is generated internally within the person (in the mind and consciousness), so relies on how people experience their worlds and make them meaningful. Therefore, there are no universal facts or truths, but rather subjective, dynamic, and personalised constructions of phenomena in the social world. The accompanying ontology is *constructionism*—arguing that reality is created by the individual through their social interactions, personal experiences, and cognitive understandings of these interactions and experiences. For interpretivists, perception is reality. Accordingly, social research should be qualitative in order to explore behaviour from these epistemological and ontological bases. **Figure 19.1** sets out the central characteristics of interpretivism when compared to positivism.

Methodologically, positivists claim to be able to apply the empirical research methods of the natural sciences, particularly experiment and controlled observation, to the study of human behaviour in the real, social world. Consequently, positivism privileges quantitative forms of criminological research that generate numerical data (e.g. statistics, ratings), that quantify social phenomena (e.g. crime, personal experiences) and that search for statistical relationships between these phenomena (see Bryman 2015). Through the hegemony of positivism, criminology has pursued its claim to being a social science. Much like its older brother, psychology, criminology (especially positivist forms of criminology) has exploited the status of social science as if this makes the subject of criminology and the knowledge it produces somehow more valid—in the sense of more legitimate, credible, evolved, disciplined, and trustworthy (see **Chapter 6** for more discussion of positivist method). Criminology has utilised positivist research and theory as the main vehicle to maintain and enhance this status.

Searching for and ultimately identifying the causes of crime gives criminology an ostensibly scientific and academic credibility to many criminologists, not to mention politicians, practitioners, and the general public. The concept of causes is definitive, confident, and practical—especially in the minds of the biased, the uncritical, and the novice. Causality has a superficial and specious attraction to the academic searching for explanations, to

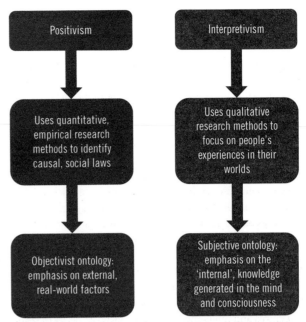

Figure 19.1 An illustration of the different characteristics of positivism and interpretivism

the key stakeholder searching for the best targets for their responses to crime and to the general public searching for straightforward and unequivocal answers to a huge social problem. However, the overriding issue here is that this certainty and confidence in causes, their validity, reliability, generalisability, or practicality, has taken the attention of criminologists away from their possible flaws and limitations as an explanatory tool.

Privileging causes as vehicles for explanation in criminology can be viewed as the product of a self-fulfilling prophecy, itself caused by the 3 Ss: subjectivity that social scientific methods should be the priority for criminology, supposition that causes are the preferable and most valid tool to explain crime, and study, notably the dominance of positivist methods and conclusions—possibly at the expense of detailed reflection and critique (see **Chapter 6**).

Explaining crime as a dynamic social construction

A major problem with identifying the causes of crime is that criminologists cannot seem to agree on what they understand or mean by either causes or crime—the two concepts central to this entire exercise. Both of these criminological concepts are typically understood from a positivist perspective as objective facts, yet both are arguably interpretivist social constructions. This argument implies that positivism may be an invalid or less valid tool (at least when used on its own) for exploring and explaining crime and its causes, especially if searching for universal causes that apply to all crimes at all times by all kinds of people.

We have already discussed the definitional issues relating to what counts as crime and the extent to which this notion is socially constructed (see **Chapter 2** for a detailed discussion of this issue). The concept of crime, which is the foundation and centrepiece of the study of criminology, should be permanently consigned to inverted commas—indicating that it is dynamic, contested, ambiguous, and contingent on the historical period, culture, country, or demographic characteristics of those people socially-constructing the concept of crime. The implication here is that searching for and pinning down the causes of this free-floating, shape shifting and highly subjective behaviour/s that sits within these inverted commas is like herding cats or nailing jelly to a wall. It is somewhere from extremely difficult to practically impossible to pin down the causes of a behaviour(s) that at any given point in any given place may change in definition, may be the subject of disagreement, or may not even exist! (See **What do you think? 19.2**.)

You may agree with the suggestion that we seek to explain some crimes that are committed sometimes by some kinds of people in order to justify moving forward following the **What do you think? 19.2** exercise. You may think that there is still plenty of explanatory mileage in searching for the causes of crime—albeit a contingent, dynamic and yet, more restricted definition of crime that may not be applicable to everyone, everywhere, every time. The alternative is to become so staunchly interpretivist and constructionist that we abandon the idea of any form of measurable reality existing external to the human mind and we give up entirely on trying to explain, respond to, or change any aspect of the social world. Surely there is hope—enough potential similarity and overlap between individual experiences, perceptions, and meanings to make the search for explanations (though not necessarily causes) worthwhile?

Criminologists could, perhaps, limit themselves to a more valid search for the causes of crime(s) committed at specific times in specific places—a temporally-specific, time-limited, transient notion of causality that is also sensitive to the type of crime being explained and to the cultural and country context. That is not to say that the identified causes of crime(s) at a specific time in a specific place could not and should not be applied to crimes at other times (e.g. new crimes that emerge later in time, such as Internet crime) in other places (e.g. in different cultures and contexts). The over-riding argument is that we should guard against the unhelpful supposition that certain causal explanations need to be generalisable and universal and guard against the invalid over-confidence that they actually *are* generalisable and universal.

Instead, we as criminologists should conduct open-minded and reflective research to test and develop more valid explanations of crime. By acknowledging the constraints placed on our explanatory conclusions by the difficulties in defining and measuring crime, the result should be a series of (more) sensitive, flexible, fit the purpose, valid, and practical explanations of crime. If the nature of crime can be dynamic and contingent, then perhaps we should produce explanatory theories that are similarly dynamic and contingent. In this way, we can use our ABC mindset in the pursuit of both theoretical advancements in criminology and the practical application of criminological knowledge. But regardless of what we understand by crime, should the foundation stone of these theories and practical applications be the search for and identification of the causes of crime?

WHAT DO YOU THINK? 19.2

Identifying the causes of a chameleon concept

Given the reservations just given in the main text, we could consider shutting up shop on this chapter right now. However, that is not in the spirit of ABC. Criticality is really important, but it should be as much a tool for progressing arguments, theories, debates and the practical utility of criminology as it is a tool used for undermining and rejecting them. We should always try to be progressive and forward thinking in our critique, not simply reactionary against the past. With that in mind, what do you think about the issue that the effect (crime) in the cause and effect relationship we are trying to identify here is so changeable and volatile and difficult to define? Specifically:

- Should we abandon our search for the causes of crime on the basis that we can never agree or be certain about what crime actually is? If so, what is our alternative? (Maybe have a quick peek at **Chapter 20** for some ideas).

- If we accept that crime is difficult, but not impossible to define, what are the benefits of searching for its causes?

- What type of constraints and restrictions should be placed on the interpretation of any results that claims to have identified the causes of crime? For example, think about the validity, reliability, generalisability of practical utility. Also, consider the role of the 3 Ss: subjectivity, supposition, and study.

Operationalising the causes of crime

In a previous section, we focused on the dynamic and socially constructed nature of crime when exploring the search for the causes of crime. Here, we move on to addressing the causes element of this crucial question. We must start with a crucial definitional and operational issue—what exactly do we mean when we talk about and *operationalise* a cause of crime? Does cause assume a static, objective, quantifiable factor or variable or mechanism that causes crime to occur at a fixed point in time and/or does causes relate to a dynamic, subjective, qualitative interaction or process that causes crime at multiple points in time in multiple different ways? Do we understand cause in the sense of a factor, variable, or mechanism making crime happen for the first time in a person's life? Conversely, does this cause bring about *re*-offending and somehow change existing criminal behaviour, such as increasing its frequency (known as escalation), changing its nature (diversification, specialisation), encouraging its continuance (maintenance), or even promoting its cessation (desistance)?

Does a cause make something new happen or does it change/affect an existing behaviour? Criminologists have neither decided nor agreed. Much like the definitional ambiguity around how we understand the concept of crime, if we cannot agree on what we understand by the concept of cause or causation then it is difficult, if not impossible, to produce universal, valid, and reliable causal/aetiological explanations of crime. This is just the start of the difficulties for criminology—an academic subject committed to explaining crime through causes, yet where much of the underpinning knowledge has been based on conjecture or research that has merely identified correlations.

The culture of causality in explanatory theory

It is possible to argue that the majority of explanatory theories in criminology have laid claim to identifying the causes of crime. They may make these claims directly and explicitly, particularly if they are positivist. They may imply that their central explanatory factors, variables, predictors, influences, or mechanisms are somehow causal (e.g. as do classical theorists, some integrated theorists)—implying causality through the degree of influence assigned to their explanations and by the definitiveness of the conclusions that targeting these explanatory areas can reduce and prevent crime. Indeed, one of the motivations to identify causes could be to give a greater air of validity to those factors identified for targeting through criminological responses such as sentencing, crime reduction/prevention activity, and policy. Theorists may even slip into referencing causality under the radar as a way of solidifying their explanatory claims—artefactual risk factor theories are particularly prone to this possibly inadvertent confusion and elision (see Case and Haines 2009). But ABC—are the claims of experimental, positivist, and otherwise cause-obsessed criminology valid? Classical theories have never been empirical, research-based explanations and have never claimed to be, let alone are they based on any experimentation. The conclusions about the explanatory utility of free will and rational choice are based on subjectivity and supposition, not study. Free will and rational choice are therefore not

---

TELLING IT LIKE IT IS 19.1

The hegemony of positivist criminology—with author Steve Case

> positivism has long ceased to be a viable option, but the message has still not got through to some researchers.
>
> Robson 2015: 163

Positivism's domination of explanation in criminology is at its peak due in large part to the popularity of the experimental method, consistent support from high profile criminologists (e.g. Lawrence Sherman, David Farrington) and continued endorsement by large official funding bodies in the UK (e.g. Home Office, Ministry of Justice, Economic and Social Research Council) and the USA (e.g. Office of

Juvenile Justice and Delinquency Prevention) (see **Figure 19.2**). Consequently, positivist theory and research has a far greater influence on crime prevention and reduction policy than any other criminological theory and form of research. Positivist research privileges empiricism—validating knowledge by using scientific method, particularly experiment, but also survey (Williams 2006) as the main routes to acquiring criminological knowledge. Positivist method is seen as the gold standard for developing the evidence-base in criminology and has been animated by experimental criminology, the randomised controlled trial, survey research and statistical testing of relationships between variables and measures of offending. The reductionism and simplicity of experimental and quasi-experimental (e.g. survey) methods has enabled positivism to identify deterministic (causal), stable, predictable, replicable relationships between variables and offending. However, these conclusions have been highly dependent upon the researcher's ability to control complex behaviours, systems and situations (Hope 2009). The explanations of crime that have emerged from positivist research been underpinned by two central principles or suppositions:

1) **Linearity**—that there is a direct, straight line, deterministic, causal relationship between variables and offending behaviour—basic cause and effect.

2) **Proportionality**—that increases of a given size in these (causal) variables produce increasing in offending behaviour of the same size/proportion.

Critics have attacked positivist theory and research for being pseudo-science characterised by reductionism, narrow and unambitious methodology, and dubious representations of reality (e.g. Young 2011; Goldson and Hughes 2010). Positivist researchers have been accused of over-stating the validity and utility of the research findings that inform their explanations (see France and Homel 2007) and for assuming an invalid level of control over the real world variables that they study (see Bateman 2011; Case 2007). More recently, advocates of *chaos theory* have challenged the validity of positivism's claims to be able to identify linear and proportional relationships between causes and offending behaviour (see the chaos theory section later in this chapter). However, in general, positivists have brushed off such criticisms in favour of reasserting their dominance through rhetoric (often about how their work is scientific) and the consistent application and replication of their existing (arguably flawed and invalid) methods, findings, and conclusions.

Figure 19.2 Logos of the Economic and Social Research Council, the Ministry of Justice, and the Office of Juvenile Justice and Delinquency Prevention
Source: Public domain

causes in any experimental or empirical sense; they are the (possibly expert) guesses and conjecture of armchair theorists. These arguments may be convincing, but they are not causal. Similarly, much critical and realist theory is the result of polemic—argument, debate and compelling scholarship, not research. A well-known critical (youth) criminologist once said 'Why should I do any research? I know the answers already!'. Such a lack of empirical basis (or even the perceived need for it) may be one reason why some theorists shy away from presenting their findings as explicitly causal and instead rely on implication and supposition that their explanations have a causal basis.

In the spirit of this book's objective to make criminology more accessible and less complex, here is a short section of a complex piece of criminological writing produced as a chapter called 'Youth justice—From linear risk paradigm to complexity' for an edited text entitled *Applying Complexity Theory* (Case and Haines; in Pycroft and Bartollas 2014). The arguments are highly relevant to our discussions up to this point in our chapter. Essentially, this is an attack on positivism, specifically what Goldson and Hughes (2010: 222) call the 'positivistic hubris of experimental criminology'—hubris being an unjustified and unmerited arrogance. **Telling it like it is 19.1** is a flavour of the arguments in normal speak; see what you think.

Exploring the causes of crime through scientific experiment

As discussed in **Chapter 6**, the foundation of empirical research and the generation of positivist scientific knowledge is the experiment. The objective of any scientific experiment in the natural and social sciences is to identify universally applicable cause and effect relationships between variables—aspects of behaviour that change and

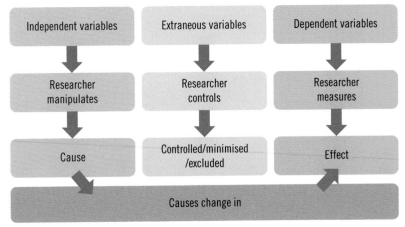

Figure 19.3 Experimental cause and effect relationships

that can be changed through manipulation. Scientists conduct experiments by attempting to manipulate some part(s) of the natural environment or behaviour of a living organism in order to measure the impact of this manipulation, such as any changes in the environment or behaviour. What is manipulated is known as the independent variable (IV) and what is measured is known as the dependent variable (DV).

The typical experimental hypothesis or research prediction is that manipulating the IV will either cause a new DV or cause a change in an existing DV—classic cause and effect. But how can scientists be so confident that their manipulating the IV was the only cause of any change (effect) in the DV and not other potentially unmeasured variables having an influence? Well, scientists claim to be able to control for and protect against any additional unmeasured influences (known as an extraneous variable or EV) and thus to isolate the influence of the IV by using comparison groups, rigorous procedures, controlled conditions, standardised instructions, statistical manipulation and the like. Therefore, control is the bedrock of any experiment. **Figure 19.3** illustrates the classic experimental design, where the researcher manipulates the IV and controls the EV(s) in order to cause a measurable change/effect in the DV.

High levels of control may very well be possible and achievable in the natural sciences in the laboratory or other artificial environment. For example, if we want to observe and measure the effect when two chemicals are combined, we can mix them together in a test tube and stand well back. Provided that we can control for other extraneous influences on the resultant chemical reaction, such as any chemicals already in the test tube, contamination from the experimenter or from pollutants in the air, we can be confident that mixing these two chemicals (IVs) causes the measured chemical reaction (effect on the DV). That is a valid conclusion—as far as we can tell

it is true, accurate, and comprehensive. If we repeat the experiment in an identical manner with identical equipment several times, we should get the same results. That is a reliable conclusion—as far as we can tell it is consistent, replicable, and repeatable.

Experiments in criminological research

Alcohol as a trigger for youth crime

Now let us move our ABC discussion forwards with a hypothetical example of a criminological experiment. Say we wanted to test the criminogenic effects on excessive alcohol intake on young people. We could start with the idea that giving our sample group eight pints of lager each (the IV) is likely to encourage certain criminal acts (e.g. violence, criminal damage, public disorder) compared to the behaviour of an equivalent group of young people who are not given alcohol. For a start, it is highly unlikely that we could get ethical approval for this study, even if we sampled young people above the legal drinking age—we certainly would not get permission to break the law by using young people under the permitted age for alcohol consumption. However, if by some miracle we were granted permission, we could identify two groups of young people of equivalent gender, age, and physical size (we would say that they were matched samples in experimental terms). We could then administer the eight pints of lager to the experimental group and give the control group no lager. We then measure the change in the behaviour of the experimental group compared to the (lack of change in the) behaviour of the control group. This comparison should allow us to conclude, provided that we have controlled for any extraneous variables, that any differences in the experimental group's behaviour (effects) were caused by our

Figure 19.4 The difficulty of trying to map social interaction networks
Source: © Grasko/Shutterstock

manipulation (i.e. giving them lager—the IV). But ABC—not just because of the grossly unethical nature of this experiment and its potential to cause harm and suffering to the participants and to innocent outsiders (i.e. we are essentially attempting to cause crime). As criminologists, we should ABC about the possibility of fully controlling for all potential extraneous variables that could affect the outcome of this experiment, even assuming that we have taken steps to thoroughly match the groups on key criteria (which does not always happen and/or is not always possible). For example, what if certain individuals within the comparison groups had not eaten for days (e.g. were more vulnerable to the effects of alcohol) or were ill or injured or pregnant, thus introducing extraneous physiological variables? What if young people in the experimental group were highly traumatised or overexcited by the experimental conditions, thus introducing extraneous physiological and psychological variables? What if any of the subjects in either group had done the experiment before, thus introducing practical variables? They may have more capacity for lager as a result (practice effects) or less capacity if they did the experiment recently (fatigue effects). Therefore, can we ever control for the influence of extraneous variables in the natural world? Even if we could, how can we ever be certain that any changes/effects measured in experiments are the products/outcomes of our manipulation as a researcher and not the result of chance, fluke, measurement error, or experimenter bias? What do you think?

The issue of control takes on even more significance when we explore the transfer and application of the experimental method from the natural sciences to the human world of the social sciences (see discussion of the experimental method in **Chapter 6**). In fact, the experimental need for control over variables in order to identify universal cause and effect relationships raises the most serious validity issues when pursued in the social, human world, such as:

1. Is it even less possible or impossible to control for extraneous variables when studying human behaviour, which we could assume to be more complex and psychologically driven than that of chemicals, plants, and animals in the natural world?

2. Conversely, is it possible to control human behaviour to such an extent that it becomes artificial and no longer represents the real life, natural behaviour that we are trying to measure (**Figure 19.4**)? This latter issue, the extent to which measured human behaviour in an experimental environment reflects real-world, everyday behaviour, is known as ecological validity.

Ecological validity is a serious issue for the social sciences in general and for criminology in particular (see **Chapter 6**)—a problem to which we will return. But let us start with the first control problem. Is it feasible to fully control for all of the influences on human behaviour, even in an experimental situation? Human beings are complex organisms with complex systems of physiology and, interacting with other complex human organisms in complex human systems—societies, networks, cities, communities, families, media, workplace, universities, schools, teams, clubs, relationships, and so on. In other words, if you take the problems associated with controlling for the influences on the behaviour of other organisms (e.g. plants and animals) and multiply them by a few million, you get somewhere close to the problems associated with controlling for all of the influences on human behaviour!

Every one of these problems has a potential effect on the validity of the measures, methods, findings, and conclusions relating to experimental research with humans. Let us take an example from the complex area of psychology, before we even get into the hyper-complexity of criminology! Professor Case studied for a MPhil (research-based postgraduate Masters degree) in applied cognitive psychology, which essentially means doing real world (applied) research into how people's thought processes influence their behaviour. His research looked at the effectiveness of the 'Cognitive Interview' with primary schoolchildren—a popular police interview technique with eyewitnesses of crimes that was invented by Ronald Fisher and Ronald Geiselman in the USA (e.g. Fisher and Geiselman 1992). The technique involves stimulating the eyewitness's memory using four mnemonic strategies: 1. Context reinstatement—encouraging the eyewitness to recall the environmental and personal contexts around the event they witnessed, such as where they were and how they felt; 2. Report everything—report every detail that they can, no matter how trivial they may think it is; 3. Different perspectives—recall events from the perspectives of other people, such as other eyewitnesses, the victim, and the offender; 4. Different orders—recall events from different starting points, such as forwards (start to finish), backwards (finish to start) and from the middle to the start in the middle to the end. The findings are discussed in **Telling it like it is 19.2**.

TELLING IT LIKE IT IS 19.2

The experimental effectiveness of the Cognitive Interview—with author Steve Case

I conducted an experiment with two groups of primary schoolchildren aged 7 years and 11 years drawn from a number of schools across England and Wales. I showed each child a three minute clip from the film 'Bugsy Malone'—a gangster film where the entire cast are children pretending to be adults. I then interviewed each child individually to assess how much detail about the clip they could recall. There were four study groups: 7 and 11-year-olds who received a basic interview (the two control groups) and 7 and 11-year-olds who received the Cognitive Interview (the two experimental groups). My hypothesis was that the Cognitive Interview (the IV) would significantly increase the number of items recalled from the clip (the DV) by the experimental groups compared to control groups. In other words, I predicted that the Cognitive Interview technique would cause an increase in eyewitness recall—which is exactly what I found. My conclusion as a devout (highly uncritical and unreflective) experimental psychologist was that the Cognitive Interview causes an improvement in eyewitness recall; a conclusion that was pleasingly in line with much similar research coming from the USA and the UK. This approach, I believed, proved to me that my experiment had worked, which was good because the last thing that inexperienced researchers want is to have to explore and explain results that contradict the hypothesis, their colleagues, their preferred theory, or their expectations and preconceptions. But, what about ABC? Was I able to control for all potential extraneous variables that could have influenced eyewitness recall beyond the IV? For example:

- Did I check whether any child had already seen the film clip? No.

- Had any of the children done this or a similar experiment before? I do not know, I did not ask.

- Had any child used any of these recall strategies before? Who knows?

- Had any subject been in an interview situation before? No idea.

- Were there any other pre-existing differences between the control and experimental groups, such as intelligence/academic ability, language issues, gender, emotional and physical state on experiment day, fatigue, vision or hearing problems? I do not know.

- Did I introduce any experimenter bias into the study, such as giving some subjects longer to recall than others, prompting or helping in any verbal or non-verbal ways, accepting answers at different levels of detail and accuracy? Probably, but I certainly did not control for this.

- Did I account for any recall strategies and other influences within the basic interviews I employed with the control groups? You know the answer.

- Did I conduct every interview in a similar way, so the study method had reliability? Ask me another.

- Could I explain exactly how the Cognitive Interview enhanced memory in the experimental groups? No, but I am not convinced that experiments actually can enable explanation (see later).

What a minefield! I was not a terrible researcher, nor was I necessarily even a terrible experimenter. What I was in this particular study was uncritical, unreflective, and over-confident in my conclusions about my ability to control for extraneous variables, the causal influence and effects of cognitive interview (IV), and the explanatory utility of the experiment as a research method. All of this affected the reliability of my methods and the validity of my findings and conclusions. But I have only realised this later in my career.

Steve's personal experience conducting applied psychological research demonstrates that even in a fairly controlled situation, there is a massive difference between the level of control over your ability to manipulate people's behaviour that you think you have compared to the level of control that you actually have. When we start looking outside of the artificial bubble that is the laboratory and into the real world where crime is committed, defined, explained, and responded to, this control problem is magnified and amplified.

Exploring the causes of crime through survey research

There is a large contradiction at the heart of explanatory theory in criminology. For a subject dominated and shaped by positivist method and the search for causes, the explanatory theories that have emerged from empirical research (not from the armchair or based purely on subjectivity, supposition, experience, and anecdote), have been largely the product of survey methodology (questionnaire, interview, focus group), and to a lesser extent observation, rather than experimental method.

Positivist and *artefactual risk factor* theories, for example, have relied heavily on data obtained using the survey method, typically the identification of statistical relationships between quantified factors reported in questionnaires and interviews and quantified measures of offending behaviour (see **Chapter 6**). The statistical relationships identified between different factors and offending behaviour/crime are correlational, not causal. Let us take an example from artefactual risk factor research (see **Chapter 18**), the dominant explanatory theory in the field of (youth) criminology. John Pitts (2003) asserts that this body of research has been unable to establish the 'causal primacy' of risk factors—whether they precede offending behaviour or whether they are symptoms of effects of offending behaviour. Even the most influential artefactual risk factor theorist, David Farrington, has confessed that 'it is difficult to decide if any given risk factor is an indicator (symptom) or a possible cause of offending' (Farrington 2007: 605).

In analysis terms, the statistical tests used (e.g. ANOVA, t-test, Person's regression, etc., if you are interested) are able to indicate that two factors/variables (supposed criminogenic influences and offending/problematic behaviour) are correlated/associated/related in statistical terms (not necessarily in reality). However, these tests cannot conclude that one variable (criminogenic influence) specifically causes or causes a change in the other (offending behaviour) in a linear and proportional way. This analytical restriction holds true, despite the dominance of these so-called linear statistical tests

in positivist criminology and across the social sciences (see, for example, Gendreau and Smith 2007; Salsburg 2002). Such invalid utilisation and representation of statistical testing in the social sciences has led Freedman et al. (2010: 16) in the book *Statistical Models and Causal Inference*, to assert that 'an enormous amount of fiction has been produced, masquerading as rigorous science'. Of course, survey questionnaires, interviews, and focus groups are also able to measure variables and collect data in qualitative, meaningful, personalised formats through the use of open-ended questions. Even then, however, there has been a preference for the quantification or 'factorisation' (Kemshall 2008) of qualitative data through criminological survey research (see Farrington 2003)—turning it into handy, usable numerical form (e.g. counting the number of incidences of a particular phrase, opinion, or behaviour) for easier manipulation and analysis through statistical tests. This quantification represents yet another example of the over-simplification and reductionism in criminological research methodology that can wash away the complexity and (ecological) validity of the original measured data. Therefore, the criminological research underpinning many explanatory theories has strongly privileged quantitative forms of data collection and analysis, (in part) under the misguided assumption/supposition that collecting and analysing rafts of quantitative data from very large samples assigns some scientific credibility and legitimacy to the research that qualitative methods lack. But quantitative surveys and statistical analyses are restricted to identifying correlations. As asserted repeatedly during the critique of artefactual risk factor theories in **Chapter 18**, correlation is not cause! See also, **Controversy and debate 19.1**.

Many studies in criminology have measured the occurrence of criminogenic (crime-causing) factors and offending behaviour over the same time period, but few studies have been willing or able to tease out the temporal precedence of criminogenic factors over offending behaviour—in other words, establishing that they come first in a person's life and that the direction of any relationship with offending is therefore one way (uni-directional).

Even studies that have attempted to tease out the temporal precedence of criminogenic factors have not conclusively proved, demonstrated, or even discussed the nature of the influence that these preceding (also known as antecedent) factors may have on the offending behaviour they are alleged to have caused or changed. So these factors may be experienced first in someone's life, but precisely how do they influence offending? We cannot conclude causation just because certain factors occur first. In fact, we should not conclude that someone has actually experienced a factor in any personal, meaningful

CONTROVERSY AND DEBATE 19.1

Correlation is not causality

Having reviewed the use of experiments and surveys to identify the causes of crime, it is useful at this stage to revisit some of the most influential (and controversial) explanatory theories in the history of criminology. In doing so, we are able to take a closer look at the nature of the relationships between criminogenic variables and offending that underpin their explanations.

Biological positivism

Lombroso's atavistic stigmata; Ferri's interactions between physical, individual, and social factors; Goring's genetic inheritance; and Sheldon's mesomorph physiques were all correlates with crime identified through observation (see **Chapter 13**; see also Hopkins Burke 2013). Later experiments have correlated (not manipulated and caused) physical measures such as sexual hormones, adrenal sensitivity, and brain injury with offending behaviour (see Jones 2013). But correlation is not causality.

Psychological positivism

Freud's psychodynamic theory (interview); Eysenck's extraversion-introversion scale (questionnaire); and Bandura's social learning theory (observation, quasi-experiment), for example, correlated personality, extraversion, and imitation (respectively) with criminal behaviour or criminogenic attitudes (see **Chapter 13**). But correlates are not causes.

Sociological positivism

Merton's Strain Theory (observation, focus group); the Chicago School thesis (see **Chapter 14**, secondary analysis of official statistics, geographical mapping and analysis, case studies); Cloward and Ohlin's subcultural theory (observation, case study); and Hirschi's social control theory (questionnaire) identified correlations between deviant, non-conforming attitudes, social disorganisation, and crime (see **Chapter 14**; see also **Chapter 18**). But correlation is not causality.

Artefactual risk factor theories

Every theory discussed in **Chapter 18** has employed questionnaires, observation, and secondary data analysis of official statistics to identify the psychosocial risk factors in childhood and adolescence that are correlated with (predictive of) some form of offending behaviour in later life (see **Chapter 18**; see also Case and Haines 2009). But correlates are not causes.

The most influential, seminal studies in terms of the development of positivist and quasi-positivist (artefactual risk factor) theories have been largely survey-based and to a lesser extent based on observations (but less often experimental) and have tended to identify the correlates of crime. Arguably, any subsequent claims that these studies have identified the causes of crime, often the claims of other criminologists, politicians, policy makers, and journalists (not necessarily the original authors) have been invalid—based on misunderstanding, overstatement, or misrepresentation of the original research.

qualitative way simply because it has been measured as present in their life through official records, statistics, or the reports of others. Nor have survey studies attempted to or ever been able to control for the influence of extraneous variables (e.g. the unmeasured socio-structural risk factors missing from so many psychosocial artefactual risk factor theories), because these studies were not experimental.

These survey studies arguably possess more ecological validity than experiments due to their relative lack of control or attempted control over people's behaviour and responses (although survey questions can be highly leading and biased, as we know from **Chapter 6**). However, this same lack of control has introduced more subjectivity and supposition into the interpretation of survey results and has deprived studies of the capacity to draw

valid conclusions about the nature of the relationships between their so-called explanatory factors and offending behaviour. The most valid conclusion possible from the majority of the studies that underpin explanatory theories in criminology should be that they have been able to identify correlates with crime/offending behaviour, not the causes of it, but this does not stop criminologists (mainly positivists) from laying claim to causal explanations. But, being able to conclude that certain factors are more likely than others to be measured in the lives of people who offend is a long way from identifying them as causes and being able to explain exactly how they are causal. Do you see the invalidity here? The majority of explanatory studies claiming to have identified the causes of crime have relied on a research method that is unable to identify causality.

The rebirth of experimental criminology in the 21st century

The dominance of positivist experimentation within criminology and the associated search for causes has been re-animated in the 21st century by the growing popularity of experimental criminology, particularly in the USA (see Sherman 2009; Farrington 2003). This popularity has been influenced and animated by the 'what works' experimental method of evaluating crime prevention programmes and responding effectively to crime based on empirical evidence. In 1996, the US Congress requested a comprehensive evaluation of the effectiveness of crime prevention programmes across the USA that used 'rigorous and scientifically recognized standards and methodologies' and that emphasised 'factors that relate to juvenile crime ... including 'risk factors' in the community, schools, and family'. The resulting report, *Preventing Crime: What Works, What Doesn't, What's Promising* (Sherman, Gottfredson, MacKenzie, Eck, Reuter, and Bushway 1998) has become extremely influential globally in the field of criminology and policy and programme evaluation due to its application of (alleged) 'high standards' of robust evaluation as a measure of what works in crime prevention.

The Scientific Methods Scale

Sherman et al. (1998) used the 'Scientific Methods Scale' (invented by Cook and Campbell 1979) to assess the methodological quality of individual crime prevention evaluations according to three methodological criteria: measurement error (the accuracy of measurement of variables), statistical power (the validity of the results of statistical tests) and most importantly, control over extraneous variables that might influence relationship between intervention and outcome, to detect the effects of a crime prevention programme (see Hope 2005). The Scientific Methods Scale (SMS) consists of five levels of analysis, escalating in detail and alleged rigour:

1. Correlation between the programme and level of crime measured at one point in time.
2. Comparing levels of crime measured before and after the programme, but with no control condition.
3. Comparing levels of crime measured before and after the programme in experimental (programme) and control (no programme) conditions.
4. Comparing levels of crime measured before and after the programme in multiple experimental and control groups, controlling for extraneous variables.

5. As level 4, but with random assignment to experimental and control groups—the randomised controlled trial gold standard of evaluation methodology.

For a programme to be considered 'what works' as crime prevention by the SMS, we must be 'reasonably certain' that it prevents crime or reduces risk factors (i.e. illustrating the dominance of the RFPP—see **Chapter 16**) in the social context in which it is evaluated. The intervention must have findings that are generalisable to similar settings in other places and times, in addition to at least two successful evaluations at level three on the SMS or above. The strong implication here, of course, is that these 'what works' programmes cause reductions in crime levels and risk factors by tackling the causes of crime. Programmes were categorised by Sherman et al. as 'what's promising' if the level of certainty regarding reduction of crime or risk factors was considered too low to support generalisable conclusions, but there was some empirical basis for predicting that they could attain this, plus they had at least one successful evaluation at level three of the SMS. Sherman et al. classified 'what doesn't work' as programmes they were reasonably certain failed or couldn't be demonstrated to prevent crime or reduce risk factors.

The SMS has been commended for promoting the utility of experimental research for evaluating the effectiveness of prevention and intervention programmes and for creating evidence to underpin responses to crime. Supporters also allege that the method can enable the identification of cause and effect relationships between programme measures and outcomes (see Sherman and Strang 2004; Farrington 2000), thus linking explanations with responses. The SMS and the concept of 'what works' has become extremely popular amongst policy makers and researchers/evaluators keen to underpin crime reduction and prevention programmes with a scientific, empirical evidence-base and to ensure that programmes demonstrate cost effectiveness (see Applied Research in Community Safety 2008). Without getting into yet more definitional ambiguities, regarding what we understand by prevention and reduction, or critiquing the rampant conflation of these subtly different objectives (e.g. preventing a behaviour from starting versus reducing an existing behaviour), let us put the explanatory utility of what works under the microscope in **Controversy and debate 19.2**.

> ## ⚠ CONTROVERSY AND DEBATE 19.2
>
> ### The problem of the 'what works' explanation: What is in the black box?—with author Steve Case
>
> Despite the huge popularity of the 'what works' model of evaluating crime prevention programmes, it has been subject to several strident methodological and ethical criticisms. The 'what works' approach employs a positivist experimental methodology in order to physically and statistically manipulate (control) aspects of the environment in order to identify constant and predictable causal relationships between interventions (alleged causes) and outcomes (alleged effects). The most common criticism of the positivist 'what works' approach has been that the focus upon interventions (inputs/causes) and reductions in offending (outputs/effects) has neglected to examine mechanisms and processes of change that intervene between the two, and has neglected the potential influence of context upon programme implementation and outcomes (see Pawson and Tilley 1998; Hughes and Edwards 2005). Instead, what works makes assumptions as to what is going on in the black box (Pawson and Tilley 1998) between inputs and outputs (e.g. a person's individualised interpretations, meanings, perception, constructions, decisions). It also bleaches out the complexities of context by treating these complexities as variables to be controlled (Applied Research in Community Safety 2008). As a result, it is almost impossible to understand *how* a particular intervention generate positive impacts or, as Pawson and Tilley (1998) put it, 'what works for whom and in what circumstances?' In other words, we could be either deliberately damaging or deliberately de-
>
> priving some people in order to benefit others and to measure this benefit as change/cause and effect.
>
> The experimental emphasis upon control over subjects creates other issues unrelated to explanation. For example, the need for control creates *practical* difficulties—such as the feasibility of accounting for all possible extraneous influences upon everyday behaviour and the confounding and invalidating effects of controlling and measuring social behaviour (see Robson 2015). There are also contemporaneous ethical issues relating to randomised controlled trials (level 5 of the SMS), where subjects are randomly allocated to control and experimental groups for the purposes of measuring the impact of an intervention on recipients compared to non-recipients. Exerting a high degree of control over individuals in a social situation is an ethically questionable practice if the underlying objective is to deprive some participants of potentially vital services and information in order to measure any resultant damaging/negative effects.
>
> The evidence-based, experimental, 'what works' evaluation model is unable to evidence (as opposed to assume) the relationship between programme implementation (causes) and programme outcomes (effects) because any explanation of this relationship is located within the black box of unmeasured and unexplored influence. Consequently, the 'what works' approach fills this 'dark figure' of unexplored, imprecise, and indefinite explanation with supposition about how programmes cause changes in crime levels, or simply ignores the need for explanation altogether.

The dark figure of explanation in criminology

The critical issues of supposition and lack of criticality run wild throughout explanatory theories in criminology, especially those populated by causes and the proxy indicators of causes. The term proxy indicators (or proxy causes) refers to concepts and labels that are used as a substitute for causes as if they make the claims and conclusions more tentative, sensitive and valid, yet still somehow causal. These proxy indicators are actually used in such a way as to strongly imply some form of causal influence—we know such proxies as indicators, influences, predictors, drivers, motivators, risk factors, criminogenic factors, and so on. To allow us to move forward with an

exploration of causes, let us assume that there is a relationship, beyond chance or luck, between these alleged causes/proxy causes and offending behaviour and that we are somehow able to discern the direction of this relationship by identifying the temporal precedence of causes/proxy causes. Of course, these assumptions/suppositions go against the critical spirit of this book and the previous criticisms in this chapter, but it is always useful to contextualise, understand, and explore counter-arguments to yours in order to provide a fully informed perspective. However, despite the focus on causes, what the experimental method cannot tell us is anything about the nature of this influential relationship—*how* and *why* different factors influence crime. In other words, experiments can identify and measure potential causes and influences in a quantified way, but they cannot explain (they can only suppose and conjecture) how a cause works qualitatively and thus, whether it is actually a cause at all. Extending the 'what works' critique of Pawson and Tilley (1998), experiments leave us with an empty, unexplored black box between input (manipulating the IV) and output (the effect on the DV)—as illustrated in **Figure 19.5**.

The foregoing critique asserts that experiments are limited as an explanatory tool in criminology; that they simply identify and measure rather than explain the mechanisms and processes of influence upon crime. Never mind, therefore, the dark figure of unreported and unreported crime, what about the dark figure of unmeasured and unaccounted for explanation? On the other hand, surveys (particularly interviews and focus groups) can obtain qualitative, personalised data, can enable us to explore the how and why that we can then use to populate our explanations of crime. What surveys do not allow us to do, however, is to identify causes (in an explanatory sense) or to necessarily validate the explanatory information we obtain, because surveys lack sufficient control over people's subjective responses and behaviours, including the subjectivity of the researcher when designing and implementing the method and interpreting the findings. So we are left with a choice between identifying causes with no explanation of how they operate or providing explanations that cannot claim to be causal—neither of which option constitutes a causal explanation.

At this point in the chapter, it is time for a reality check. It would be invalid and misleading to suggest that the factors, variables, mechanisms, and processes identified through experimental and survey research in criminology (not to mention identified by using observations and other qualitative methods) do not or cannot exert some form of influence on the occurrence and reoccurrence of offending behaviour. Of course they do. It is very likely that the different areas of people's lives identified and explored by empirical research and explanatory theories (e.g. free will/rational choice, biological, psychological, sociological and socio-structural factors, criminalisation processes, interactions between the state-public-victim-offender) have an influence on some crimes at some times for some kinds of people. To claim otherwise would be delusional and narrow-minded.

The argument pursued in this chapter is that to represent and label these influences as causal or even proxy causal and to be so definitive and lacking in doubt about the nature of their influence on offending behaviour based on the type of criminological research that has been conducted is invalid—misleading, incomplete, subjective, suppositional, over-confident, and uncritical. The recommendation is not to reject established explanations of crime and look elsewhere, even though more study of socio-structural issues, situational influences, personal constructs, and identity formation would be helpful in

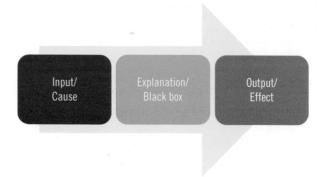

Figure 19.5 The 'black box'

order to move causal research past its psychosocial biases. There is also an argument for much more exploration of the potential for offending behaviour itself to be the cause of further crime through its influence on exacerbating existing causes—criminogenic factors and offending behaviour could have a relationship of reciprocal influence where they each affect the other and so-called causes could actually be symptoms of crime.

Criminologists, including students of criminology, should resist the compulsion to overstate our explanations in definitive, causal terms when our current dominant positivist criminological methods and results do not support such conclusions. Criminologists should acknowledge and address the complexities involved in defining crime, establishing causes, and controlling and measuring human behaviour in the real world. One argument would be to advocate for more tentative and flexible explanations than we have now, prioritising realism and pragmatism, not the relentless pursuit of definitive and unequivocal causes resulting from pseudo-scientific study. Only then can we produce explanations of crime that are valid in the sense of being meaningful, relevant, applicable, sensitive, appropriate, and practical to the populations whose behaviour we are trying to explain and then respond to.

Explaining crime by identifying causes

It is useful to summarise where we are so far and what we (think we) know from this chapter. Defining crime is problematic because as already noted it is a contested, ambiguous, and socially constructed concept. Defining cause is equally problematic for exactly the same reasons. Explaining crime through the identification of its causes, therefore, is highly problematic because of uncertainty over these two central concepts.

Further complicating the search for the causes of crime is the lack of reliability of the empirical research that claims to have identified these causes. Criminological research within and between schools has been inconsistent in terms of:

- the empirical research methods and designs used—for example, the degree of control researchers have exerted or have tried to exert over the potential influences on crime;

- the types of relationships (causal, predictive, indicative, symptomatic, etc.) identified between potential influences and offending—for example, surveys tend to identify correlations, not causes;

- the areas of potential influence investigated—for example, the common psychosocial bias in measured experimental and survey variables;

- the types of offending measured—for example, self-reported, official, general and specific forms of offending;

- the demographic characteristics of the populations sampled—for example, the typical, but not universal, bias towards investigating and explaining the behaviour of young males (*androcentricism*);

- the country/legal system in which the research was conducted—for example, the typical, but not universal, focus on exploring offending in the industrialised western world;

- the historical period during which the research was conducted—for example, the application of outdated research findings to explanations of crime in modern contexts.

We are ultimately left with a body of so-called explanatory research that is arguably invalid and unreliable due to its epistemological and ontological bias, inconsistent operationalisation of its central research concepts (crime and causes), its variable research methods, and its dubious interpretation of research findings. This causes major problems when we get to stage three of the triad of criminology (see **Chapter 2**): responding to crime. In other words, how can we promote desistance from crime by people who have offended (i.e. crime reduction) and prevent the occurrence of crime if we cannot identify the antecedents and predictors of crime?

Responding to crime

Searching inside the black box

How can we respond appropriately and effectively to a behaviour or social construction if we cannot be sure what it is or how to explain it (causally) for a particular person or group in a particular place at a particular point in time? Before reading the rest of this section try focusing your own thoughts by looking at the questions in **What do you think? 19.3**.

How does the dark figure of explanation affect our ability to respond to crime in terms of reduction and prevention interventions that are meant to target its causes? Traditionally, explanations of and responses to crime have been stuck on supposition—enthusiastically assuming and conjecturing (or just ignoring) what is happening in the black box between inputs (factors, variables, sentencing responses, programmes, interventions) and outputs (outcomes, the nature of influence on offending behaviour). This rampant supposition, jumping from A to C without considering B (black box) has encouraged over-confident and invalid conclusions regarding the universal causes of crime and what works when intervening to reduce and prevent crime.

The polemic across this chapter strongly implies that what is needed in order to turn these suppositions into actual meaningful explanations that can inform targeted responses is a much better understanding of the mechanisms, processes, and interactions that could be occurring within the black box and that ultimately influence offending behaviour. Whether these explanations will be necessarily focused on causes and causality is debatable, but the bigger issues involve searching for explanations that are more sensitive, valid, and therefore more useful in practical terms.

An alternative perspective for exploring the influence of causes is to adopt a focus on desistance—the cessation of crime. Similar to how social control theory asked why people *do not* commit crime (see **Chapter 18**), it is useful

WHAT DO YOU THINK? 19.3

How should we respond to crime?

Consider the arguments in this chapter regarding the supposition that runs throughout causal explanations of crime and the knock on effects of this supposition on their validity, reliability, and generalisability:

- How can we measure whether our responses work?

- How do you think we should respond to crime?

- Can we ever really identify the cause of crime that we can then target?

CONVERSATIONS 19.1

The causality-desistance relationship—with Shadd Maruna

SC (Steve Case, one of the authors of this book): What are the main ways in which the criminological literature has defined desistance?

SM (Shadd Maruna): Good question. Desistance is a tricky variable for criminologists because it is an absence of something rather than a tangible event or occurrence in itself. Specifically, desistance refers to the absence of repeat offending for individuals who have previously engaged in a pattern of offending and would be predicted to re-offend. Colloquially, desistance used to be described with now anachronistic phrases like 'going straight' or 'going legit'. The key here is the 'going'. Desistance is not a moment or an event, although some individuals may experience a sort of epiphany where they decide to stop offending, what is important is the process of actually staying stopped once that decision is made. Other words associated with desistance include things like 'rehabilitation' or 'reform', but the difference is that those words typically connote structured interventions or so-called 'correctional treatment'. Desistance refers to the overall process of change whether people 'rehabilitate themselves' or make this change with the support of a structured program. At one point, in fact, the term 'desistance' was seen as something of the opposite of rehabilitation. Either one was rehabilitated by others or else one 'desisted on one's own'. Today, few believe that state programs can rehabilitate someone who does not want to change or make efforts to change; likewise, it is hard to imagine individuals desisting 'on their own' without the help of others, inside or outside of structured programmes. Both rehabilitation and desistance, then, are socially constructed and negotiated. One of the real difficulties, in fact, for those seeking to desist from crime is to convince others that their change is genuine and not an act put on to avoid criminal detection. After all, desistance is not something that can be easily proven. We tend to 'know it when we see it', but this is a subjective judgement that is notoriously difficult to research or measure.

SC: Based on these definitions, what are the main theories employed to understand desistance?

SM: Traditionally, only a limited number of theories existed to explain desistance, but today the theoretical explanations are growing rapidly in both number and in their sophistication. Some of the earliest theories, based on the strong correlation between age and crime (street crimes, in particular, appear to be a 'young person's game') posited that desistance was a largely biological process akin to puberty. Individuals were said to 'grow out of crime' as they matured out of the exuberance of youth. Later theories challenged this biosocial explanation by pointing out that although the age-crime relationship is strong, it is anything but perfect. Many individuals desist from crime around the age of 17, but others persist well into their 20s or 30s, and some persist even longer. A new body of theories posited that normative changes in the social sphere, such as employment and marriage, and not biological ageing itself, were the primary causes of desistance from crime. This was the idea that desistance required 'a steady job and the love of a good woman' (or man, presumably, although the evidence is less strong regarding the latter). The difficulty here was that things like marriage and employment are not random occurrences; typically, they are the outcome of agentic efforts on the part of individuals. Therefore, newer theories argue that desistance is the product of an interplay between changes in motivation, cognition and identity, as well as biology and social structure. It is a complicated enough business and should keep criminologists busy for numerous decades in the same way that the field has struggled to explain and understand crime itself.

You can read more on desistance in *The Oxford Handbook of Criminology* (Shapland and Bottoms, in Liebling et al. 2017).

Dr Shadd Maruna, Dean of the School of Criminal Justice, Rutgers University, Newark

to explore what might cause people to stop offending once they have started? Steve Case spoke to Shadd Maruna, co-editor of *The Oxford Handbook of Criminology* (Liebling, Maruna, and McAra 2017) and leading criminological expert on desistance, about his views on the relationship between causality and desistance (see **Conversations 19.1**).

In this discussion, Shadd Maruna appears to be claiming that explaining desistance from crime is as complex and uncertain as explaining crime itself. Like crime, the explanatory difficulties begin with pinning down a clear definition for such a contested and dynamic concept, not least because desistance presents as a process of change, rather than a static, easily measurable DV. Desistance theories have evolved from identifying correlates into focusing on what Shadd calls 'the primary causes of desistance from crime'. However, more contemporary multi-factor, integrated theories of crime (see **Chapter 18**) acknowledge the complex interplay between biopsychosocial factors, socio-structural influences, agency, motivation, and identity, thus spanning positivism and interpretivism. Therefore, bearing in mind previous arguments regarding the (in)ability of certain explanatory theories and their associated research methods, is it valid to conclude that desistance theories have been able to identify the causes of desistance from crime, rather than simply the correlates of this behaviour? What do you think?

Innovative evaluation methods

In addition to the theoretical and explanatory alternative models gaining prominence in criminology (see the sections on chaos theory and the butterfly effect—later in this chapter; see also enhanced pathways risk factor theories—MacDonald and Marsh 2005, Smith and McVie 2003), alternative models of implementing, explaining, and evaluating crime prevention programmes are emerging. These models are far less obsessed and constrained by causation and the ambitious search for universal, generalisable, definitive recipes for curing crime encouraged by positivist method and the 'what works' approach. In other words, these models acknowledge the necessary complexity and practical realities of explaining and responding to crime; complexities and realities that may preclude the identification of causes to target. Two particularly useful models are worth considering here: realistic evaluation (Pawson and Tilley 2009, 1998) and the theory of change model (Blamey and MacKenzie 2007; Weiss 1995).

The realistic evaluation approach

What works for whom in what circumstances?

Ray Pawson and Nick Tilley (1998, 2009) have created a realist method of exploring and evaluating crime prevention programmes that addresses the black box issues ignored by the 'what works' methodology. In their book, *Realistic Evaluation*, Pawson and Tilley argue that positivist 'what works' evaluation is insensitive to what is going on inside the black box between programme inputs (causes) and changes in crime/behaviour (effects). They advocate for a more sensitive, realistic, and pragmatic evaluation approach that focuses on 'what works for whom in what circumstances'.

Pawson and Tilley's realistic evaluation model is made up of the following three parts:

1. **Context**—where and when is the programme/intervention taking place and with whom? This is the 'with whom and in what circumstances?' part of their evaluation question.

2. **Mechanisms**—what does the programme/intervention do and what does it intend to do? What processes and mechanisms does it activate? How can any changes be explained in theoretical and practical terms?

3. **Outcomes**—what are the consequences and effects of the mechanisms activated by the programme/intervention?

The Context-Mechanisms-Outcomes (CMO) model of realist evaluation, therefore, actually does more than examine its original (1998) descriptive question of 'what works for whom in what circumstances?' and moves into examining the more explanatory questions of 'in what respects, and how?' (Pawson and Tilley 2004: 2). Realistic evaluation offers a more sensitive, pragmatic, and (obviously) realistic approach of explaining and responding to crime—one that is neither wedded to nor constrained by the search for quantifiable causes or the pursuit of single factor theories and explanations (see **Chapter 18**). Instead, realistic evaluation incorporates qualitative considerations of individualised and contextualised mechanisms and influences into its more holistic explanations of crime and how crime prevention/reduction programmes may work.

The theory of change model

Explaining how multiple interventions work

Theory-based evaluation is a method for addressing the limitations of the experiment-based 'what works' model and for enabling more context-sensitive evaluation of crime prevention programmes (e.g. interventions in the community) that looks inside the neglected black box of explanation. The theory of change model (Connell, Kubisch, Schorr, and Weiss 1995; Kubisch, Fulbright-Anderson, and Connell 1998) starts from the premise that methods-driven evaluation is insufficient to discover and explore the explanatory causal pathways, processes, and contexts through which (community) interventions have an effect. The conclusion is that crime prevention programmes should make explicit their theory of *how* interventions are intended to achieve certain outcomes, that this theory should inform their methods, and that this theory should be the basis by which their effectiveness is evaluated.

The theory of change model focuses on programme implementation (Weiss 1995)—hypothesising links between the 'nuts and bolts' of programme activities and the linkages between them and their outcomes. The theory/ rationale for a crime prevention intervention is evaluated in terms of how it has informed the programme's design (Blamey and MacKenzie 2007). The 'nuts and bolts' of specific interventions and the linkages between them are examined as potentially 'causal triggers that fire appropriate mechanisms in certain circumstances' (Blamey and MacKenzie 2007: 446), but this causal aspect is secondary to the main focus on searching for qualitative explanations of how programmes operate and are intended to operate as the basis for evaluating whether or not they work. Whereas the realistic evaluation approach of Pawson and Tilley has been predominantly focused upon individualised interventions and policies (e.g. prison education programmes), the theory of change model has been applied far more frequently to the evaluation of community-wide, multiple intervention programmes, which realistic evaluation has proven far less suited to (Blamey and MacKenzie 2007).

A realistic theory of change?

Both approaches to evaluation make a clear break from positivist epistemology and methodology by offering a post-positivist, enhanced version of positivist explanation (e.g. Blamey and MacKenzie's 'causal triggers') that is more sensitive to context and underpinning theory. However, neither realistic evaluation nor the theory of change model offers any qualitative investigation of the individualised interpretations, experiences, perceptions, and thought processes that may explain how a crime prevention programme operates or may work.

Despite their more sensitive exploration of context and theories of change, there remains little exploration within the black box, only the confident identification of the pre-formed theories that should populate this box. That said, both approaches consciously distance themselves from positivist 'what works' methodology and its associated limitations, most notably the quantified over-simplification of complex issues and relationships (*reductionism*). Both approaches remain under-developed, under-researched, under-exposed, and under-supported in criminology. However, both approaches offer viable, feasible, and open-minded alternatives to established positivist 'what works' methods, understandings and explanations of supposed cause and effect relationships and what works in the social world of crime prevention programmes.

Thus far in our discussion, the overriding argument has been that positivist methodology is obsessed with identifying the causes of crime and then responding to these through 'what works' interventions that are evaluated using an experimental model. Alternative models have emerged for implementing and evaluating crime prevention programmes; models based on post-positivist, realistic, and 'theory of change' based methodologies and understandings. However, even these models remain committed, to some degree, to explaining causality.

So is criminological explanation and response so wedded to the relentless pursuit of causality that it is unable to evolve towards more up to date fit for purpose and contextually-sensitive explanations of crime? Perhaps not. We will now consider *chaos theory*.

Chaos theory

Non-linear, unpredictable, anti-causal theory

The inherent nonlinearity of many social phenomena … must explain, in part, the challenges social scientists face when attempting to understand the complexity of social dynamics … a simple deterministic equation can generate seemingly random or chaotic behaviour over time.

Elliott and Kiel 2000: 4

Critics of positivism have caricatured its methods and analyses techniques as narrow, pseudo-scientific, reductionist, and offering only partial representations of reality

(cf. Wright Mills 1959; Goldson and Hughes 2010; Young 2011). These critics have often maintained that positivist method and analysis has a place within criminology, but that it is not the only route to knowledge and that proponents have overstated its general validity and utility (see Walgrave 2008). Others have criticised positivism's erroneous presumption of control over a range of dynamic experimental variables (e.g. risk factors), which, they argue, simply cannot be readily or validly reduced to static, quantitative form (e.g. Bateman 2011; O'Mahony 2009; Case 2007).

An effective challenge to the positivist hegemony in criminology can be found in complex systems science, also known as chaos theory (see Lorenz 1963; Gleick

1997; Young 1991; Elliott and Kiel 2000). Although a full exposition of the development and principles of complex systems science is beyond the scope of this chapter (but see Gleick 1997; Young 1991), two of its essential components will be used to underpin a critique of positivist criminology and the explanations of crime it produces: fractal measurement and sensitive dependence on initial conditions (the butterfly effect).

Fractal measurement

The complexity critique

> Smooth shapes are very rare in the wild but extremely important in the ivory tower and the factory ...

> A cloud is made of billows upon billows upon billows that look like clouds. As you come closer to a cloud, you don't get something smooth, but irregularities at a smaller scale [see **Figure 19.6**].

> Mandelbrot 2004
> (in interview with www.edge.org)

Chaos theory challenges the validity and reductionism of positivist method in criminology through the concept of fractal measurement. In 1967, mathematician Benoit Mandelbrot attempted to accurately measure the length of the British coastline. He discovered that the smaller the instrument/unit of measurement (e.g. when using a six-inch ruler compared to a yardstick), the longer the measured length became, because the measure is laid along a more curved route. From this, he drew two conclusions (Mandelbrot 1967, 1982):

1. That objects in the real world could be conceived of as fractals—reduced size copies of a larger whole.

2. That an object's dimensions are relative to the observer and can be fractional—sensitive to the scale of measurement employed.

The concept of fractals, therefore, provides a realistic and useful model for understanding the measurement of rough (i.e. complex) and non-linear phenomena. The significance of fractal measurement for criminological research lies in what it tells us about the importance of method and scale of measurement for the reliability and validity of the measures employed to identify causes and influences on crime (e.g. the quantitative ratings scales used in questionnaires) and the confidence we can have in these understandings/assessments. Ratings scales and risk assessments for example, are rife with rudimentary and unsophisticated measurement and analysis that readily

Figure 19.6 The chaos of clouds
Source: Fir0002/CC BY-SA 3.0

pursues understandings of causes, risk factors, and correlates as 'smooth shapes' rather than rough phenomena better understood as fractals. Questions around the nature and validity of the measurement of criminogenic variables/factors are, therefore, of central importance to any pursuit of a suitably complex and valid explanatory theory in criminology.

An excellent example of the invalidating reductionism of positivist criminology (challenged by chaos theory) is artefactual risk factor theories (see **Chapter 18**) and their associated research—the current hegemonic model for explaining crime and shaping interventions designed to reduce and prevent crime. These theories have operationalised potentially multi-faceted, context-specific, and dynamic processes (e.g. family conflict, commitment to school) as simplistic, static, decontextualised factors based on overgeneralisation and crude ratings scales (e.g. over-simplified dichotomous yes/no scales). The invalidation of risk by converting it to a quantified factor has been exacerbated by unreliability—a lack of consensus between and within studies regarding how to operationalise risk (e.g. the extent and nature of the statements to use, type of measurement scale to use). As Mandelbrot (1982: 1) states:

> On a map an island may appear smooth, but zooming in will reveal jagged edges that add up to a longer coastline.

However, positivist and artefactual risk factor research determined to identify the causes and predictors of crimes does not offer researchers enough scope for 'zooming in' to reveal the fractal qualities and 'jagged edges' of these causes and predictors. Instead, the research privileges superficial understandings of smooth, generic influences on crime.

Lorenz and the butterfly effect

Sensitive dependence on initial conditions

> Clouds are not spheres, mountains are not cones, coastlines are not circles and bark is not smooth, nor does lightening travel in a straight line.
>
> Mandelbrot 1982: 1

Whilst conducting meteorological research in the 1950s, American mathematician Edward Lorenz contradicted one of the fundamental assumptions of modern statistical analysis, that small measurement errors are irrelevant. Instead, Lorenz found that minute differences in the measurement of initial conditions (IVs) caused points of instability throughout complex systems that could result in unpredictable and fundamentally non-linear, unpredicted outcomes (DVs)—implying complexity and chaos. Lorenz also discovered that the introduction of intervening variables (EVs) could exacerbate the unpredictable (non-linear), complex, and chaotic nature of a system's outcomes. He concluded that the accurate analysis of any behaviours required 'sensitive dependence on initial conditions'; a phenomenon he dubbed the butterfly effect. **Figure 19.7** illustrates the

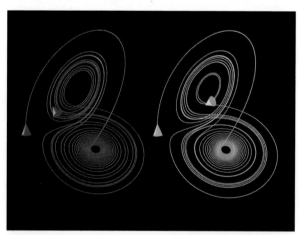

Figure 19.7 The butterfly effect—Equivalent starting points yet different trajectories

Source: Hellisp/CC BY 2.5

butterfly effect that can occur when two equivalent variables have minutely different starting points (initial conditions) on a journey, thus leading to markedly different trajectories and outcomes.

The possibility of chaos or instability in complex systems indicates that small changes in (the measurement of) initial variables can lead to large differences in outcomes or conclusions. Consequently, analysing the relationships between criminogenic variables/factors and offending in a manner that is sensitive to chaos theory could enable an exploration of criminal behaviour 'in ways not possible in … [Positivist methods] … and the linear causality they presume' (Young 1991: 447). Nevertheless, the linearity, stability, and proportionality of relationships between variables is an assumption at the core of positive, experimental analysis (Ziliak and McCloskey 2007; McGrayne 2011).

The chaos and complexity critique

Unfractal measurement and insensitive analysis

Taken together, the concepts of fractal measurement (method) and sensitive dependence on initial conditions (analysis) pose major problems for positivist criminology and the explanatory, causal-based theories that have emerged from it. Plugging crudely measured variables/factors into ill-conceived statistical models produces insensitive analysis. The outcome can be invalidity and unreliability. Positivism has paid very limited attention to initial conditions—both in terms of when these initial conditions are measured (in time) and how they are measured (in terms of sensitivity). Nor have positivists acknowledged sufficiently that iterative interactions between measured (and unmeasured) variables produce the unpredictable. Consequently, the crude and imprecise measurement of criminogenic, causal and risk variables and factors has fed into insensitive analyses and produced invalid conclusions that these variables and factors exert a linear, proportionate, deterministic, causal influence on offending behaviour.

With everything you have learnt in this chapter now read **Controversy and debate 19.3** for a discussion on the possible promise of mixed methods.

CONTROVERSY AND DEBATE 19.3

The promise of mixed methods

A major issue evident from the discussion of positivism thus far is that its explanatory utility is limited when the method is used in isolation. It has been argued throughout this chapter that positivist methods such as quantitative experiments and surveys, along with 'what works' evaluation, can identify and measure areas that are statistically associated with crime, but cannot easily explain how these areas may operate. Conversely, qualitative, interpretivist research methods (e.g. open-ended questions used in questionnaires and interviews) can identify possible explanations, but cannot conclude that these are causal in any positivist sense. Thinking critically, let us consider the following question: what if we were to combine positivist/quantitative and interpretivist/qualitative methods in order to explore and explain crime? What if we were to pursue a mixed methods approach of combining different research methods in the same study in order to address specific questions regarding what causes crime? This raises a series of crucial, mutually-dependent questions such as: Are these supposedly competing epistemologies and research methods fundamentally incompatible?

Conversely, could they actually complement one another and compensate for each other's weaknesses to provide more realistic, pragmatic, and realistic explanations of crime?

If so, could we claim that these explanations were casual? For example, could criminologists employ quantitative methods to identify/indicate the potential influences on crime and then follow up with qualitative research to examine whether these influences are causal and if so

(or even if not), how they operate?

Could we therefore combine methods and epistemologies in order to produce causal explanations?

Prominent social research methods scholars (e.g. Bryman 2015; Robson 2015) have argued that mixed methods approaches offer significant benefits to the development of explanatory theory in the social sciences due to enhancing triangulation (the ability to check validity using multiple sources), completeness (gaining a broader picture of an issue, identifying new issues and questions), and mutual facilitation (each method complements and enhances the other).

Whilst it is difficult to disagree with these assertions, one concern is that mixed methods designs remain unable to identify causes in any conclusive, unequivocal, and experimental sense due to the respective causal limitations of quantitative and qualitative methods discussed throughout this chapter. Mixed methods designs in criminology appear very well placed, however, to identify in a valid and reliable way the influences, mechanisms, and processes associated with crime, which can then serve as useful targets for further research and for the targeting of our responses to crime. However, the continued causal obsession sets up criminological research to fail, even such innovative mixed methodologies.

Conclusion: Do we really search for the causes of crime?

So, where does all of this leave us in terms of our criminological knowledge? The central argument of this chapter has been that the hegemonic explanatory theories in criminology (positivism, artefactual risk factor theories) and to a lesser extent the more contemporary theories (critical criminology, realist criminology) have attempted to understand, explain, and respond to crime by identifying its causes and what works to prevent, reduce, and eradicate these causes. The central critique that follows from this argument is that the claims of these theorists who have identified causes, causal mechanisms, and proxy causes are lacking in validity and reliability. Why? Because the integral concepts of crime and cause have been defined, operationalised, understood, applied, and analysed in inconsistent, ambiguous, and uncritical ways across criminological research—an assumption that they are objective facts and with little exploration of their dynamic, contingent, contested, and constructed nature.

Therefore, how can criminology identify the causes of crime and what works to tackle it when it cannot agree on how to define crime or how to examine and understand the meaning of causes?

The subsequent critique in this chapter has been that the experimental, positivist research has been over-confident in its claims to be able to control extraneous variables in people's lives to such an extent that the real causes of crime can be unequivocally tested, identified, and targeted in valid and reliable ways. Positivism has been similarly over-confident and uncritical that controlling human behaviour in experiments can produce ecologically valid results that are somehow applicable to the real world. More damningly, many explanatory theories in criminology have based their conclusions on the inadvertent or deliberate conflation of causes with correlations identified using survey methodology—an invalid supposition. Finally, much explanatory theory has been based on empirical research that identifies and measures (sometimes in crude ways), rather than actually explains. Consequently, we remain unclear as to how and why different factors, variables, mechanisms, and processes relate to and produce crime, if indeed they actually do at all.

To answer the title question, searching for the cause of crime *is* an impossible goal in the strict experimental, positivist sense, because there are simply too many unknowns and unmeasured dark figures of crime and explanation to enable us to draw valid and reliable conclusions from research. But the search for the unequivocal, universal, reliable causes of crime is also arguably unnecessary. What is needed in order to enhance our understanding of crime is more sensitive, specific, contingent, dynamic, and reflective explanations of different crimes at different times by different kinds of people. The types of explanations facilitated by innovative, contemporary explanatory models such as chaos theory and evaluation models like realistic evaluation and theory of change. This more nuanced and sensitive, less deterministic and definitive approach to understanding requires:

- more sensitivity to and critical reflection on the constraints set by our research methods and what they can and cannot tell us about crime, including more consideration of mixed methods designs;

- more sensitivity to and critical reflection on the roles of subjectivity, supposition, and study on the production of explanatory knowledge of the causes and explanations of crime;

- more sensitivity to and critical reflection on the nature of the explanations we produce—with particular focus on exactly what they explain how they explain it.

The result of this constructive application of our critical mindsets should be a set of necessarily limited, yet more valid, explanations of crime that move away from the unhelpful obsession with causes and begin to explore and explain crime inside the black box in more mixed (epistemologically and methodologically), qualitative, and meaningful ways. This would lead us into identifying and exploring influences and processes of change (not causes) that relate to specific crimes at specific times by specific kinds of people. Subjectivity and supposition are inevitable and integral components of criminological study (research and scholarship), so we should be transparent, acknowledge them and explore their influences on our explanations of crime. Ultimately, our goal should be to offer understandings of crime that are practical and realistic—underpinned by logical, reflective, meaningful, and valid relationships between criminological definitions, explanations, and responses.

SUMMARY

- To explore the reasons why we search for the causes of crime in criminology, with particular focus on positivism

In this chapter, it was argued that the most important reason for wanting to explain crime (beyond simple academic and human curiosity) is so that we as criminologists can understand it better and thus respond to it appropriately through prevention activity, sentencing, punishment, deterrence, rehabilitation, treatment, intervention, policy and practice, further academic research, and scholarship. If we are able to better understand crime, we are able to respond to it in more valid, appropriate, and effective ways. The evolution of explanatory theories in criminology has been dominated by positivism, which pursues an *epistemology* (theory of knowledge generation) based on gathering data in the social world to form the basis of universal laws of behaviour and an objectivist *ontology* (theory of how to understand reality) that the real world is external to the person measuring it and consists of unequivocal facts that can be objectively measured. Privileging causes as vehicles for explanation in criminology was viewed as the product of a self-fulfilling prophecy resulting from subjectivity that social scientific methods should be the priority for criminology, supposition that causes are the preferable and most valid tool to explain crime, and study through positivist methods and conclusions—possibly at the expense of detailed reflection and critique.

- To discuss the definitional issues relating to the concepts of crime and causes that influence the valid and reliable identification of the causes of crime

A major problem with identifying the causes of crime is that criminologists cannot seem to agree on what they understand or mean by either causes or crime. Both of these criminological concepts are typically understood from a positivist perspective as objective facts, yet both are arguably social constructions born from *interpretivism*. Throughout the chapter, the reflective argument was made that criminologists could limit themselves to a more valid search for the causes of crime(s) committed at specific times in specific places—a temporally-specific, time-limited, transient notion of causality that is also sensitive to the type of crime being explained and to the cultural and country context. In other words, we should guard against the unhelpful supposition that certain causal explanations need to be generalisable and universal and instead prioritise more sensitive, flexible, fit the purpose, valid, and practical explanations of crime.

- To assess the implications of these definitional and explanatory issues for producing valid and reliable responses to crime

Several theories in criminology claim or imply that their central explanatory factors, variables, predictors, influences, or mechanisms are somehow causal—providing their explanations with a degree of definitiveness that implies validity and practical utility. It was discussed that a central motivation for identifying causes is to offer a greater air of validity to the factors then targeted through criminological responses such as sentencing, crime reduction/prevention activity, and policy. This causal definitiveness was contested by arguments that the key positivist and quasi-positivist (artefactual risk factor) theories have been largely survey-based and to a lesser extent based on observations (but less often experimental) and have tended to identify the correlates of crime, not the causes. However, the dominance of positivist experimentation within criminology and the associated search for causes has been re-animated in the 21st century by the growing popularity of experimental criminology in the USA, most notably the 'what works' experimental method of evaluating crime prevention programmes. Further discussion was provided of contemporary challenges to the experimental, 'what works' approach, namely realistic evaluation, the theory of change model, and chaos theory.

It was concluded that experiments are limited as an explanatory tool in criminology; that they tend to identify and measure rather than explain the mechanisms and processes of influence upon crime—leaving us with a 'dark figure' of explanation. Conversely, surveys obtain qualitative, personalised data to enable an exploration of the how and why that we can then use to populate explanations of crime. What surveys do not allow us to do, however, is to identify causes (in an explanatory sense). Consequently, we are left with a choice between identifying causes with no explanation of how they operate or providing explanations that cannot claim to be causal—neither of which option constitutes a causal explanation.

- To evaluate the feasibility and necessity of identifying the causes of crime

The chapter concluded that searching for the cause of crime is an impossible goal in the strict positivist, experimental sense, because there are simply too many unknowns and unmeasured dark figures of crime and explanation to enable us to draw valid and reliable conclusions from research. It was asserted that we should pursue more sensitive, specific, contingent, dynamic, and reflective explanations of different crimes at different times by different kinds of people. In particular, criminologists should have more sensitivity to and critical reflection on the roles of subjectivity, supposition, and study on the production of explanatory knowledge of the causes and explanations of crime.

REVIEW QUESTIONS

1. What are the main differences between positivism and interpretivism in terms of how they seek to explain crime?

2. What are some of the main issues we must address in order to identify the causes of crime?

3. What is the main difference in focus between the realistic evaluation approach of Pawson and Tilley, and the theory of change approach by Connell and others?

4. Explain what fractal measurement is and why it is important to chaos theory.

FURTHER READING

Bryman, A. (2015) *Social Research Methods* (5th edn). Oxford: Oxford University Press.
A comprehensive guide to social research methods, including detailed and accessible discussions of quantitative and qualitative research methods and their related causal assumptions.

Case, S.P. and Haines, K.R. (2014) 'Youth justice: From linear risk paradigm to complexity' in A. Pycroft and C. Bartollas (eds) *Applying Complexity Theory: Whole Systems Approaches to Criminal Justice and Social Work*. Bristol: Policy Press.
Using youth justice as its illustration, this critical chapter offers an innovative exploration of the central causal claims of positivism in criminology, followed by a detailed exposition of an alternative theoretical and methodological perspective—chaos theory.

Sherman, L. (2009) 'Evidence and liberty: The promise of experimental criminology' *Criminology and Criminal Justice*, 9 (1): 5–28.
A critical discussion of the role of experimental criminology in the creation of evidence to inform our explanations of crime and appropriate responses to it. Why not read Hope's (2009) response to Sherman's arguments too?

 Access the **online resources** to view selected further reading and web links relevant to the material covered in this chapter.
www.oup.com/uk/case/

PART OUTLINE

20. Criminal justice principles

21. Criminal justice—policy, practice, and people

22. Crime prevention: Ideas and practices

23. Crime control, policing, and community safety

24. Punishment and the idea of 'just deserts'

25. Rehabilitation of offenders

26. Alternatives to punishment: Diversion and restorative justice

27. Critical perspectives on crime and punishment

This Part of the book, *Responding to crime*, shifts our focus to the practical and theoretical challenges associated with the question of what to do about crime and its impact on individuals and societies.

Chapters are organised in logical order, starting with a discussion of the underlying principles which inform the decisions and actions of key players in the criminal justice system (**Chapter 20**). The next chapter (**Chapter 21**) goes on to discuss the implications of these principles for the delivery of criminal justice, in the shape of its policies, practice, and people, and offers an overview of contemporary trends and developments.

The subsequent chapters focus on different perspectives on responding to crime, starting with a discussion of crime prevention strategies and the ideas that inform them (**Chapter 22**).

The following chapter (**Chapter 23**) evaluates approaches to intervention which are informed by the goals of minimising opportunities to offend and taking swift action to stop it where the limits of acceptable behaviour are breached—the 'crime control' perspective.

The following chapters then critically consider the ways in which criminals are dealt with by the justice system, including the justifications and implications of a punitive approach (**Chapter 24**); and the issues associated with delivering both socially acceptable and effective rehabilitative programmes (**Chapter 25**).

Chapter 26 discusses recent developments in ideas and practice which concentrate on problem-solving and resolving the harms caused by crime (diversion and restorative justice), based on the argument that forward-looking responses to offending produce sustained social benefits.

Finally, **Chapter 27** reviews critical perspectives on crime and punishment, inviting you to reflect on whether conventional assumptions and approaches actually obscure fundamental questions of how crime is defined and whose interests are served. In light of this, alternative models for constructing and delivering socially just forms of criminal justice are considered.

PART 4
RESPONDING TO CRIME

CHAPTER OUTLINE

Introduction: The criminal justice game changers   554

The rule of law   555

Adversarial justice   565

Restorative justice   566

The police, the courts, and the CPS   568

Criminal justice principles

KEY ISSUES

After reading this chapter, you should be able to:

- recognise the source and changing nature of essential criminal justice principles;

- outline the importance of the rule of law doctrine;

- discuss the essential features of an adversarial justice system;

- assess the force of the restorative justice principle;

- critically evaluate the ways the different courts of justice can be brought into action.

Introduction: The criminal justice game changers

Criminal justice can be generally defined as the system of law enforcement for potential crimes. It is a complex and dynamic field and as explained in **Chapter 4** ('What is justice?') is inextricably linked to the discipline of criminology. These next two chapters (**Chapters 20 and 21**) build on that content by considering a process of change for criminal justice featuring four factors labelled as 'game changers': principles, policies, practices, and people. The idea of game change, or practical modifications, is a key focus for this part of the book and the chapters are structured to reflect the importance of these four concepts. It is hoped that using the lens of 'the 4Ps' will enable you to see the array of influences when 'changing the game' for something as intricate as criminal justice. This chapter will consider the first of the four terms: principles.

We will be considering the '4Ps' in light of the 'responses, responders, and receivers' of the criminal justice system, as considered throughout the next two chapters. The *responses* from the criminal justice system (through its policy and practice) seek to support its *responders* to change the 'game' for the *receivers* (the people who experience the impact of the criminal justice system). The 'game changer' label is used specifically for the responders of the police, courts, Crown Prosecution Service, prisons, and politicians. In preparation for this, a wide-range of issues have to be featured to demonstrate examples of the changing nature of criminal justice. This will include the influence of the constitution, so frequent use is made of relevant legal sources across the framework of the '4Ps' in relation to the responses, responders, and receivers.

The present chapter deals with fundamental principles for the criminal justice system as these tenets seek to shape the operation of the justice system. More time is spent on this part as these principles underpin the entire system; despite this integral importance, they are fluid concepts and can be subject to change.

In countries that have a written constitution, or a written penal code, there can be definitive statements of the essential principles that guide the policies, practices, and people in their criminal justice systems. The Code of Ur-Nammu (**Figure 20.1**) was written over 4,000 years ago and performed this function for a place known as Mesopotamia (recognised today as covering parts of Iraq, Kuwait, Syria, Turkey, and Iran). It is the earliest known legal code and surprisingly perhaps, financial compensation to a victim or family member was its most common type of response. It contained few examples of the principle of *lex talionis* (*laws* based on *retaliation*) subsequently made famous in *'eye for an eye'* conceptions of justice.

In the UK there is neither a written constitution nor a penal code (or even stone tablets!) but this lack of a 'rulebook' does not prevent authoritative principles guiding its processes of justice. They cannot be located in one document but instead these principles exist in a variety of sources such as: Acts of Parliament, decisions of the higher courts (judicial precedents), and international treaties and obligations. Whilst overarching principles guide criminal justice, their clear identification can be problematic because of the vague nature of 'tenets such as equality before the law, prospectivity of legislation, judicial impartiality and a reasonable degree of legal certainty' (Lacey 2013: 350). These beliefs are all addressed in this chapter and you are encouraged to note the times in this chapter when you believe such 'rules' have been modified, replaced, or improved. The source of these principles for a criminal justice system also hinders their identification as they emanate from 'rules, values, policies, doctrines,

Figure 20.1 The first known version of the Ur-Nammu code in its current location, the Istanbul Archaeology Museum

Source: Istanbul Archaeology Museum/ CC 0

interests, and various other things' (Gardner 2012: 4). The key principles giving force to the abstract aims of criminal justice selected for this chapter are:

(a) the rule of law (including due process and human rights);

(b) adversarial justice; and

(c) restorative justice.

The final part of the chapter considers the roles of the police, the courts, and the CPS in the administration of justice.

The rule of law

The rule of law is the first key criminal justice principle to be covered by this chapter. This concept has been of the highest order in the UK since it displaced the will of the monarch as supreme power in the so-called 'Glorious Revolution' of the 17th century. This followed the English Civil War (1642–51) where the Parliamentarians triumphed over the Royalists and subsequently the law and not the monarchy became the highest form of authority. It can be explained as meaning:

> That all persons and authorities within the state, whether public or private, should be bound by and entitled to the benefit of laws publicly made, taking effect (generally) in the future and publicly administered in the courts.
>
> Bingham 2010: 8

So the rule of law means everybody and everything is subject to the law in open court proceedings. This law is prospective (i.e. it applies in the future) and not retrospective where people would be punished for crimes which at their time of commission were not actually recognised as such. Parliamentary sovereignty is one of the key features of the rule of law and means Parliament is the supreme authority when it comes to the making of law. Nothing can be done to restrict this power and nor can any court question the validity of its statutes (legislation or Acts of Parliament). Parliament, based in the Palace of Westminster in London (**Figure 20.2**) also has the power to delegate its legislative

powers to other individuals and organisations. Debate on whether this means it can pass anything it likes has been qualified by the UK's membership of the European Union and the requirement that its laws are compatible with these legal obligations (although following the outcome of the referendum in the UK in June 2016, Parliament will no longer be required to ensure compatibility with EU laws once the UK officially breaks away from the EU).

The constitutional doctrine of the separation of powers is also vital to the rule of law and this contends that the power of a state should be divided into three separate and distinct branches (De Montesquieu 1748). Each branch should therefore act as a 'check' and a 'balance' on the others to ensure power is effectively shared between:

- the executive (the Government and associated agencies);
- the legislature (Parliament, i.e. the House of Commons, the House of Lords and the monarch); and
- the judiciary (the courts).

This doctrine is not strictly followed in the UK (see **Figure 20.3**) as many members of the Government (e.g. the Prime Minister and other members of the Cabinet) can also be Members of Parliament. There have been other examples of the blurred lines of separation and it was not until the Constitutional Reform Act 2005 that the major contradiction to De Montesquieu's theory, the role of Lord Chancellor, was rectified. This position held power in all three arms of the state as the Lord Chancellor was a Cabinet Minister, a member of the House of Lords and also the head of the Judiciary (so until 2005, the position of Lord Chancellor sat firmly in the very middle segment of the diagram at **Figure 20.3**). This statute also reformed the judicial appointment process and ended the existence of 'two Houses of Lords'. Previously this name could refer to either the second chamber in Parliament or to the country's highest ranking court ('a court of appeal' from the Court of Appeal). However, this dual identity was ended by the legislation that made the UK's highest court known as the Supreme Court.

The lack of separation of powers means concerns are often expressed and whilst the language used in these

Figure 20.2 The UK Parliament resides in the Palace of Westminster, London
Source: jeffwarder/CC BY-SA 3.0

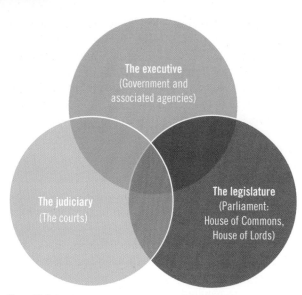

Figure 20.3 Interlinking nature of the different branches of criminal justice

disagreements may seem timid, disputes and clashes between politicians (members of the executive) and members of the judiciary can have much deeper constitutional ramifications. Power struggles of this kind have a long history (e.g. 'the monarchy vs the church' in the Middle Ages and 'the monarchy vs Parliament' as above). The modern day tension between the executive and the judiciary is generally traced to the precedent of *Entick* v *Carrington* (1765) EWHC KB J98 where it became accepted that the executive could be held accountable by the judiciary under the rule of law's mandate that no-one is above the law. A high profile example occurred in 2002 when Princess Anne was the defendant at Slough Magistrates' Court; she was convicted and fined £500 after one of her dogs had bitten two children in Windsor Great Park. Although this punishment clearly does not compare with the trial at the Palace of Westminster in 1649 where King Charles I was the defendant and was convicted of treason and subsequently lawfully executed!

Independent judiciary

The rule of law principle requires a judiciary that is separate and independent from the other branches of a state. It holds impartial court hearings to be essential for the valid delivery of law and so an independent judiciary (including magistrates) is needed to run them. The concept of judicial independence is given considerable weight by the rule of law but, in reality, how can it be delivered? Absolute independence is arguably impossible as apart from people who have lived hidden away from society, life experience inevitably influences opinions and values.

But even if people with this detachment could be found would they have the attributes for being a good judge? Absolute independence is neither attainable nor desirable, but its importance as a criminal justice principle means many safeguards are in place to promote it. The most well-known is the requirement for judges to be apolitical and so they have to be seen as completely removed from politics and cannot be seen supporting a particular party or set of beliefs. This alleged apolitical identity could be criticised as until the Constitutional Reform Act 2005 the monarch, acting on recommendations (the constitutional way of saying 'choices') from the Prime Minister or the Lord Chancellor, was responsible for appointing the members of the judiciary. This situation led many observers to claim there was clear political influence on a purportedly separate branch of the state. Both Margaret Thatcher and Tony Blair were criticised when Prime Minister for 'recommending' appointments of judges who were suspected of lacking this impartiality. The radical reforms of 2005 therefore upgraded the role of the Judicial Appointments Commission to allow it to nominate candidates or make appointments itself. Since 2009 all new judicial members of the Supreme Court have been appointed through this system. The reforms also made the Lord Chief Justice the head of the judiciary and ended the situation where a politician and Cabinet Minister (the Lord Chancellor) was the highest ranking judge.

The need for independence means judges are prohibited from being directors of private companies and are encouraged to maintain a low profile in society. This is something they seem to do extremely well because if you were asked to name three current UK judges, could you even name one? More senior members such as the Lord Chief Justice may do occasional interviews with a serious part of the media, but they are highly unlikely to be on chat shows or in giving interviews in newspapers or magazines, etc. This desire for anonymity is partly why the judiciary wear formal wigs and gowns when hearing a trial.

Judging the judges

The impact of judicial independence means that once appointed a judge has security of tenure so their position is secure until they retire, as they can only be removed from office following a resolution from both Houses of Parliament. There has been just one High Court judge (in effect the 150 or so senior judges who sit in appellate courts) to have gone through this procedure, Sir Jonah Barrington in 1830. This considerable security provides immunity from political pressure through the executive and also from democratic pressure through the legislature. However, this lack of accountability makes it very difficult for their 'performance' to be evaluated. The principle of

WHAT DO YOU THINK? 20.1

The ultimate legal power

- The appropriate boundaries for law making powers between governments and the courts have long been contested. The flexibility in the rule of law doctrine makes it very difficult to be definitive about the ultimate source of legal power. So where do you stand on this important principle?

- Is this a simple question easily answered by the fact that as a democracy with Parliament being chosen by society (to an extent), then it is *always* right they have the ultimate power?

- Why might an unaccountable judiciary be better than an elected Parliament for protecting the rights and freedoms of citizens?

whether an unelected judiciary should be able to stop the wishes of a democratically elected government? Take a look at **What do you think? 20.1** and consider the questions posed there in relation to this quandary.

In order to appreciate the complexities in the judges' role it is essential to identify the differences in the courts in which they sit. Familiarity with the basic court structure of appellate courts and courts of first instance is important as only the former can set precedents that are binding in the future for all those lower in the hierarchy (and generally those at the level that set the precedent). **Figure 20.4** outlines the structure dividing the courts into appellate and first instance courts, showing where the five different types of court sit within this hierarchy.

Judging offences

The simple representation in **Figure 20.4** could be criticised for omitting the European Court of Human Rights (ECtHR) at the top (the Brexit referendum of 2016 applies to the European Union which is separate from the ECtHR); but it seeks to emphasise the importance of distinguishing between courts of first instance and appellate courts. In the former, the judiciary (including magistrates) are required to act as either a trial court or a sentencing court if the defendant has pleaded guilty. The Crown

the rule of law counterbalances this freedom by holding the judiciary accountable to the law itself rather than a particular body. This freedom may look like it should be undoubtedly welcomed but it poses the question of

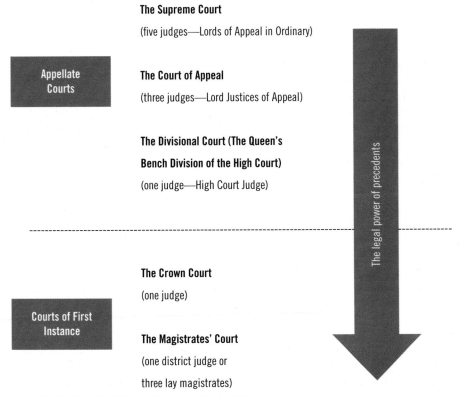

The Supreme Court

(five judges—Lords of Appeal in Ordinary)

Appellate Courts

The Court of Appeal

(three judges—Lord Justices of Appeal)

The Divisional Court (The Queen's Bench Division of the High Court)

(one judge—High Court Judge)

The legal power of precedents

The Crown Court

(one judge)

Courts of First Instance

The Magistrates' Court

(one district judge or

three lay magistrates)

Figure 20.4 The hierarchy of Criminal Courts in England and Wales

Court setting is generally what people have in mind when they use the term 'court' although due to the way criminal offences are classified, they are very much the exception and generally represent a mere tenth of the number heard in the Magistrates' Court (Ministry of Justice 2015). The classification system has three categories of indictable offences that can only be tried in the Crown Court, summary offences that can only be tried in the Magistrates' Court, and either way offences that can be tried in either court of first instance.

It may only be in a relatively small number of cases but when one does proceed to trial in the Crown Court, the responsibilities of the judiciary can be more easily highlighted. In these trials the judge acts as *the tribunal of law* with responsibility for deciding all matters of law (such as admissibility of evidence). The jury is *the tribunal of fact* and has to decide all factual questions such as the defendant's possible guilt. This clear separation of roles in a criminal trial is rare as magistrates simultaneously acting as both the tribunal of law and the tribunal of fact are far more common. These are known as summary trials and whilst they have the potential for increasing subjective bias, they are generally considered acceptable for less serious incidents such as some motoring or regulatory offences. The right to a jury trial appears more important for more serious cases such as 'either way' offences that the Labour Government (1997–2010) tried twice to restrict. The fact the executive was checked by the legislature on both occasions illustrated the separation of powers principle at work.

In the appellate courts the role of a judge can become quite different to those lower in the hierarchy. When a court is hearing an appeal, traditionally against a conviction (although following the 'double jeopardy reform' considered later it can now also be against an acquittal), there are more issues for it to address. In addition to retrying the facts of an individual case, in an appeal there are also questions of law to consider. Their answers can involve the setting of precedents that become binding in the future. This is particularly true of precedents from the Supreme Court, although arguably the Human Rights Act 1998 means the ECtHR produces the most authoritative precedents. However, there have been times such as *Boyd v The Army Prosecuting Authority* [2002] UKHL 31 when the Supreme Court did not feel bound by decisions from the ECtHR. The complexity of the relationships between these two courts is considered in the second part of this chapter.

Due process

The provision of a fair procedure is the principle of the highest importance in the due process model of a justice system. It is distinct from the crime control model where the provision of an efficient procedure is arguably the comparable principle. These models are famously associated with the writings of Herbert Packer and the crime control model is expanded upon in **Chapter 23**. The two models do not represent actual systems but instead illustrate the ideals and values they tend to enforce. Due process is a principle that seeks to assure justice is done by treating people fairly and in accordance with the law. It prioritises safeguarding individual freedom and so can be contrasted with approaches that give the same importance to controlling crime. These models have clear differences (for example, see **Table 4.1** in **Chapter 4**) but also share similarities. They both seek to reduce crime but differ in the ways they believe it could be done. Packer (1964) himself pointed out these resemblances and also cautioned against exaggerating the accuracy of their representations—their purpose was to explain general themes and approaches to justice, rather than describe an over-riding principle for a jurisdiction's system (which he was also keen to stress, was not in existence anywhere). A justice process which has a 'fair procedure' will develop with time as meanings of both of these words seem to change. For example, it was not until the Criminal Evidence Act 1898 that it was 'fair' to allow a defendant to testify at his/her own trial and less than a century later (the Criminal Justice and Public Order Act 1994) it became fair to see it a sign of guilt should a defendant not testify at their trial. In addition, changes in what is recognised as 'procedure' also occur and these consequences are explored in the 'adversarial justice' section later in this chapter.

Due process shares the rule of law's commitment to equality and the benefits from this kind of treatment are also found in the concept of procedural justice. This notion is supported by at least 40 years' of respected research and has developed 'a robust empirically grounded understanding of the relationship between individuals and authorities that revolves around process fairness' (Bradford 2014: 23). It is an approach to justice that seeks to encourage positive standards, as where people respect and feel fairly treated in their experiences with state authorities, beneficial effects such as increased willingness to comply with the police are produced (Antrobus et al. 2015). These benefits demonstrate instrumental advantages from having a fair procedure, but arguably these are of secondary importance to the due process model which prioritises the significance of the overall integrity of the criminal process. This key value means it takes precedence over all other considerations (including questions of fact) with guilty verdicts only acceptable if their cases have been dealt with in a 'procedurally regular fashion… [by] rules designed to safeguard the integrity of the process' (Packer 1964: 16).

A due process can be recognised when sufficient safeguards are in place and the law is intentionally structured formally to 'check and balance' the power of the criminal process. The 'brakes' can be applied through the different stages of the process that are designed to filter out cases that should go no further. Due process systems take the possibility of errors and mistakes extremely seriously; so to reduce this possibility, they are 'designed to present *formidable impediments* to carrying the accused any further along in the process' (Packer 1964: 13, emphasis added). These features mean the 'obstacle course' image for due process can be appropriate, although arguably there are fewer negative connotations with its association of 'a factory that has to devote a substantial part of its input to *quality control*' (Packer 1964: 15, emphasis added). It means protecting the legal rights of people charged with an offence is given a higher priority than any efficiency principle. Their slower process though has financial implications and these costs can be seen as one of their major disadvantages. (Please see **Chapter 23**, 'Crime control and due process models', for a fuller discussion of crime control, the common ground these principles share, and, importantly, how they are different.)

The Blackstone ratio

The priority given by due process to the rights of innocent people has an extremely famous representation in the Blackstone ratio which asserts it is 'better that ten guilty persons escape, than that one innocent suffer' (Blackstone, 1769, Vol. 4: 27). This statement is from the *Commentaries on the Laws of England* by Sir William Blackstone that was published between 1765 and 1769. It is one of the first-known systematic studies of a common law system of justice and the Blackstone ratio has long been regarded as a key principle of justice. It is a clear statement of intent as to where the balance should lie between protecting the innocent and convicting the guilty:

> The trade-off is inevitable because decision making about guilt is decision making which invariably involves a degree of uncertainty. Errors made by judges or juries who decide on the issue of guilt or innocence are either *false positive* (i.e. convicting an innocent person) or *false negative* (i.e. acquitting a guilty person).
>
> De Keijser et al. 2014: 34, emphasis added

The willingness to accept that errors could be made by the justice system is a relatively recent phenomenon as, for example, the Court of Appeal only began in 1907. The idea of miscarriages of justice had received little mainstream interest until the end of the 19th century when newspapers, periodicals and people such as the creator of Sherlock Holmes, Sir Arthur Conan Doyle, began to campaign for the introduction of an appellate safeguard (Thomas 1998). Due process values are clearly apparent in the ratio which hold a *false negative*—i.e. falsely

deciding the defendant *did not* do it, is a far less fundamental mistake than a *false positive*,—i.e. falsely deciding the defendant *did* do it. This may not be a view shared by the general public as evidence has been found suggesting their crime control preferences have false negatives as their main concern (Roberts and Hough 2005). However, the thoughtful study from De Keijser et al. (2014) found the public's views on the Blackstone ratio vary with the seriousness of the alleged offence. Its methods are considered in **Chapter 28** but it found in progressively more serious cases (shoplifting, burglary, and rape) the public were less willing to accept the error of acquitting a guilty person. This illustrates the dynamic nature of the ratio and the public's safety concerns in not convicting a guilty person of rape and burglary. This could have major implications for the rule of law and its insistence on equal treatment for all possible offences. It could mean suspects in very serious cases, who arguably need the most protection against a mistake, may not actually benefit from the ratio's safeguard.

Refashioning fundamental principles

The overlap between due process and the rule of law can also be seen in their emphasis on lawful procedures and safeguards such as the presumption of innocence. This principle is often referred to as the golden thread of criminal law:

> Throughout the web of the English criminal law one golden thread is always to be seen that it is the duty of the prosecution to prove the prisoner's guilt.
>
> Viscount Sankey LC in *Woolmington* v *DPP* [1935] AC 462 at page 481

It has become a well-accepted principle of justice that the state has the burden of proof for imposing criminal liability on an individual to a required standard of proof ('beyond reasonable doubt'). The prosecution's burden applies to proving the occurrence of each element of the crime in question and this can require evidence of mental elements (*mens rea*) as well as prohibited actions or conduct (*actus reus*). The need to prove *mens rea* does not apply in strict liability offences but for the rest it is an example of the *fault principle* which prevents criminal liability being imposed on people who cannot reasonably be deemed responsible. The traditional examples of where such fault is considered lacking are children and persons not of sound mind; reading critiques on these exemptions will enhance your understanding of the attitudes in the rule of law (see the further reading section).

Despite the rule of law's 'golden thread' there are many situations when presumption of innocence does not apply and instead the legal burden of proof is on the defence. This reversal is authorised by the common law when the defence of insanity is pleaded (the McNaghten Rules (1843) 10 C & F 200). It can also be transferred by an *express* statutory provision, such as s.139 of the Criminal Justice Act 1988 where unless the defence can show 'good reason or lawful authority' for possessing a knife in a public place, an accused will be convicted. Similarly, the partial defence of diminished responsibility, which is only available to charges of murder by s.2 of the Homicide Act 1957 (if successful it reduces it to manslaughter), also expressly states the accused as having the legal burden. Statute can also *imply* that the burden has been transferred and according to s.101 of the Magistrates' Court Act 1980 this occurs whenever a defence relies on 'any exception, exemption, proviso, excuse or qualification'. This switch applies to indictable offences as well as summary offences (*R* v *Hunt* [1987] AC 352). An effect of this kind of policy in English criminal law has led to estimates several years ago in the influential journal *Criminal Law Review*, that around 40 per cent of all indictable statutory offences contain this reverse burden (Ashworth and Blake 1996). It would therefore seem the rule of law, via both statute and common law, has revalued its 'golden thread' to a much lower level than 80 years ago.

Other fundamental due process principles demand a court to have the jurisdiction to deal with the accused (the legal power), who must be legally competent to stand trial (possess criminal responsibility) and did not commit the offence too long ago or have been previously acquitted or convicted of it (double jeopardy). These pillars of criminal justice integrity have seen significant changes in recent years as both criminal responsibility and double jeopardy have taken a new appearance. The *doli incapax* principle used to mean children were deemed to lack the sense of criminal responsibility needed to establish a criminal case. It was a *rebuttable presumption* which meant it could be defeated by appropriate evidence, but it strongly inferred a child would not have the level of understanding needed for a prosecution. It was abolished for children aged ten or over by s.34 of the Crime and Disorder Act 1998 and in the case of *R* v *JTB* [2009] UKHL 20, where a 12 year old boy was convicted of a dozen counts of causing or inciting a child under 13 to engage in sexual activity, the abolition of the entire defence was confirmed. You should read s.34 as it is a good example of ambiguous wording in statutes and shows why clarification from the common law can be needed.

The undermining of another previously esteemed principle occurred through the changes to the **double jeopardy** rule in the Criminal Justice Act (CJA) 2003. This rule prevented individuals being tried again, for an offence identical in law, after they had been acquitted or convicted. So successive prosecutions, firstly under the Health and Safety at Work Act 1974 and then for manslaughter after

a victim had died, could be allowed (*R* v *Beedie* [1998] QB 356). However, until relatively recently prosecutions for the same offence, after a verdict of not guilty, were not allowed at all. The first adaptation was introduced by the tainted acquittal procedure from ss.54–57 of the Criminal Procedure and Investigations Act 1996. This means a process can be invoked where there has been an acquittal and somebody has been convicted of an administration of justice offence that involved interference with, or intimidation of, a juror or a witness. If a court decides that but for the administration of justice offence, the acquittal would not have occurred, then a retrial can be ordered.

The beliefs against exposing people to double jeopardy have stronger foundations and are found in the common law doctrine known as the *autrefois* ('another time') rule. It goes back to the Middle Ages at least, where the dual system of courts (those under the jurisdiction of the monarch and those under the church) clearly increased the chances of 'double prosecutions'. This was deemed both unfair to an accused and encouraged diligence and efficiency in criminal investigations and prosecutions (Law Commission 2001). However, thanks to the provisions in ss.75–91 of the CJA 2003, this absolute protection is no longer guaranteed and in principle, it can be possible to have more than one go at a defendant. It has been modified rather than abolished as a prosecution following a not guilty verdict is only possible for 'qualifying offences' where there is 'new and compelling evidence' and the Court of Appeal believes it 'in the interests of justice' to prosecute again. The qualifying offences are listed in Schedule 5 to the Act (they currently total 30 different offences) and go far beyond the recommendation from the Law Commission that cases of murder should be the only *autrefois* exception.

These changes have significantly altered the importance of the principle of finality of criminal proceedings which has been noted for providing trust and confidence in the criminal process through the acceptance of its definitive judgments (Roberts 2002). So far under this process there have been 13 applications to the Court of Appeal; out of the nine cases that passed the test for a retrial, the defendant was convicted in eight (Dennis 2014). The fact this reform can be used retrospectively has meant that even though the *autrefois* rule may have been in force at the time of the offence or acquittal, a defendant can still be retried. Whether a retrial is 'in the interests of justice' is decided by the Court of Appeal's answers to the three questions contained within s.79:

- Is a subsequent retrial likely to be fair?
- How long ago was the qualifying offence allegedly committed?
- Was due diligence conducted by the police and prosecution in the original trial?

WHAT DO YOU THINK? 20.2

Do 'technicalities' prevent the wheels of justice from turning?

Man who filmed 100 women's feet escapes charges on a technicality.

The Times, 30 June 2007

In this case a man had taken photographs of the legs and feet of more than 100 unsuspecting women after claiming that his car had broken down in supermarket car parks across Devon between 2003 and 2006. He had asked the women to sit in the driver's seat and rev the engine whilst he pretended to repair it under the bonnet. The women were unaware that a camera was concealed in the car's footwell.

The man could not be charged with the criminal offence of voyeurism because according to s.67 of the Sexual Offences Act 2003 this can only be committed if the victim is 'is in a place which, in the circumstances, would reasonably be expected to provide privacy'. The local police decided that a car in a car park was not one of those places. In his interview with the police the accused was reported as saying 'I'm doing something totally innocent.'

A criminal prosecution was not brought because what the accused had said was 'technically' correct—but *do you think* this was 'actually' the right decision? What would have been gained (and lost) if the rule of law had been applied 'less technically' in this case?

In the case itself, the police used their civil powers to successfully apply for an ASBO that prohibited the man from approaching or taking photographs of women without their consent for the next 10 years. Does this change your view?

Such questions are not in themselves new to the criminal process as the *autrefois* rule is enforced by the common law and its *abuse of process* principle. This stops prosecutions (in legal terms, a 'stay') deemed unfair and the House of Lords' decision in *Bennett v Horseferry Road Magistrates' Court and Another* [1993] 3 All ER 138 is the leading authority. The principle holds a stay should be granted when either it would be impossible to give the accused a fair trial or the circumstances of the prosecution amount to a misuse of process that disregards justice and propriety. It is a discretionary power possessed by the judiciary that emphasises values such as fairness, the circumstances of the case, and contravening senses of justice and decency. Their

vague nature means production of specific or even consistent guidelines is not possible. An unreasonable amount of time between an offence and subsequent prosecution can be an abuse of process if it is considered unfair to the defendant. This is supported by the '*justice delayed is justice denied*' maxim that protects individuals against long drawn out (and now, repeated) prosecutions.

Despite the view that 'double jeopardy reform involves renegotiating, or reneging on the criminal justice deal' between consenting individuals and the state; its refashioning contained very little theoretical justification (Roberts 2002: 405). However, a frequently quoted view from the Law Commission (cited by both senior judiciary and academics) might reveal how such dilemmas can be resolved:

> There is, further, the spectre of public disquiet, even revulsion, when someone is acquitted of the most serious of crimes and new material (such as that person's own admission) points strongly or conclusively to guilt. Such cases may undermine public confidence in the criminal justice system as much as manifestly wrong convictions. The erosion of that confidence, caused by the demonstrable failure of the system *to deliver accurate outcomes* in very serious cases, is at least as important as the failure itself.
>
> 2001: para. 4.5, emphasis added

Acknowledgment that illegitimate acquittals inflict as much damage to the credibility of the criminal justice system as convictions that are clearly wrong, suggests a weakening of the importance of the Blackstone ratio in favour of a priority for accuracy of outcomes. In the *autrefois* debates much was made of it being in the interests of justice to use scientific advances in acquiring fresh evidence; yet in the influential paragraph quoted from the Law Commission, the chosen example of 'compelling new material' was actually a person's confession.

Have a look at **What do you think? 20.2** and try to apply some of the issues discussed so far in this chapter.

Open justice for 'real' reality TV?

The principle of open justice has long been established as a revered principle of criminal justice and its recent endorsement by the Court of Appeal suggests its importance has been maintained:

> The rule of law is a priceless asset of our country and a foundation of our Constitution. One aspect of the rule of law—a hallmark and a safeguard—is open justice, which includes criminal trials being held in public and the publication of the names of defendants. Open justice is both a fundamental principle of the common law and a means of ensuring public confidence in our legal system.
>
> as per Lord Goff in *Guardian News and Media Ltd* v *AB CD* (2014) EWCA Crim 1861 at para. 2

Despite these professed benefits an exception was al-lowed in the appeal which came from the largely secret trial of *Guardian News and Media Ltd* v *Incedal* (2014) EWCA Crim 1861. Lord Goff went on to say excep-tions to the open justice principle are rare and have to be justified on the facts of a case, with only minimum deviations that are necessary and proportionate. When permitted, these trials are hidden from public view and result in situations like Incedal who was convicted of collecting information useful for terrorism, under s.58 of the Terrorism Act 2006, but acquitted on the far more serious charge of preparing a terrorist act as contrary to s.5. A significant part of these trials took place be-hind locked doors 'in camera' (the legal term for 'secret', which to modern eyes is surely ironic?); exclusion of the public and media has resulted in no public knowledge as to why the prosecution was brought, nor of the evidence that acquitted him. This happened twice as a retrial was ordered following the first jury being unable to reach a verdict on the s.5 charge.

However, as well as permitting some closed trials, open justice has also been recently extended as both the Court of Appeal and the Supreme Court (**Figure 20.5**) now allow live broadcasts of their hearings (with a delay of around one minute). Increasing public confidence through these opportunities is also an aim for the Crime and Courts Act 2013, which gave the Lord Chancellor and the Lord Chief Justice the power to create policy that permitted the filming and broadcasting of more court proceedings. Some official parts of the justice sys-tem, such as HM Courts and Tribunals Service, can also have a presence on social networking sites; although the need to preserve their independence means this does not extend to contributions from serving judges! These methods for improving confidence by increasing the

Figure 20.5 The interior of Court 1, the largest of the three courtrooms of the Supreme Court of the United Kingdom in Middlesex Guildhall, London, England
Source: David Iliff/CC BY-SA 3.0

transparency of the court process reflect the importance given to the well-known saying:

> It is not merely of some importance but is of fundamental importance that justice should not only be done, but should manifestly and undoubtedly be seen to be done.

> as per Lord Chief Justice Hewart in *R* v *Sussex Justices,* ex parte *McCarthy* (1924) 1 KB 256, KBD at p. 259

The emphasis on justice being 'manifestly and undoubt-edly' seen to be done is often used to promote due pro-cess values, although such priorities do not seem as forceful in the current test for bias in a court hearing, which instead emphasises whether a fair-minded ob-server would have a reasonable possibility the tribunal was biased (*Porter* v *Magill* [2001] UKHL 67). Assessing whether the standards have been met of 'a fair-minded observer' (or more frequently a 'reasonable person') can be an important part of a judge's role. These supposedly objective decisions are in reality the subjective views of a judge, but their independence, training and experi-ence is designed to reduce the possibilities of bias. There is considerable authority over the years to recommend open justice as the most important safeguard against such prospects:

> Publicity is the very soul of Justice. It is the keenest spur to exertion, and the surest of all guards against improbity. It keeps the judge himself, while trying, under trial. …It is through publicity alone that justice becomes the mother of security.

> Bentham, 1843: 115

Human rights

The impetus for human rights to become a major crimi-nal justice principle was the European Convention on Human Rights (ECHR) which was a treaty drafted in 1950 by the organisation, the Council of Europe. This body was established by the UK and nine other European countries in order to protect human rights, democracy, and the rule of law in Europe with the hope of avoiding repetition of the horrors from the 20th century's two World Wars. The Council of Europe is a separate organisation to the European Union and the ECHR was not directly incorpo-rated into UK law until the passing of the Human Rights Act 1998 (HRA). See Schedule 1 of this statute for the list of rights (known as Articles) that are now protected; it means UK citizens can take their cases about the alleged infringement of their human rights, to a UK court rather than the ECtHR in Strasbourg, France. It also imposed an obligation on all public authorities in the UK to respect the Convention rights. A public authority includes courts and tribunals plus people with public functions, such as police officers; prison staff; probation staff; local authorities; and government departments.

Arguably it has also changed the game dramatically for the judiciary as the influence of human rights on the rule of law means they must, as far as possible, interpret legislation in a way that is compatible with the Convention rights. They now have the power to declare legislation incompatible and whilst this does not affect the validity of the law (unlike the obligations that existed from the European Union); Parliament then has to decide whether to amend its law under a process known as the Remedial Order. This has increased the opportunities for the judiciary and legislature to work together through a 'dialogue model' where the courts can be asked by Parliament to specify when legislation is incompatible. Although the supremacy of deciding whether and how to respond remains with Parliament.

If an individual's human rights have been found to have been breached by a public authority the court has the discretionary power to grant relief in the form of a 'judicial review'. This is a court hearing that reviews of the lawfulness of a decision by a public authority; if the court adjudges it to be unlawful, then among other things, the court can make this declaration, cancel the decision or prevent the authority from acting in a particular way. Generally when a decision is found unlawful at judicial review, the public authority will make the decision again; or according to s.8 of the HRA, a court can award compensation to the claimant if it is necessary, just, and appropriate.

The topic of human rights often receives negative and inaccurate commentary from some sections of the UK media. These concerns can be fostered by politicians such as the establishment of a commission by the coalition government of 2010–15, under Prime Minister David Cameron, for investigating the replacement of the HRA with a 'British Bill of Rights'. It is uncertain whether the result of the 'Brexit' referendum of 2016 is going to affect the question of human rights. This uncertainty has led to claims that Parliament should strengthen its safeguarding role for human rights (Hunt et al. 2015). These assertions are beyond the scope of this chapter which instead concentrates on the types of protection available from the principle. It is therefore important to distinguish between absolute rights, strong rights, and qualified rights.

Absolute rights

The clearest example of an absolute right is arguably Art. 3, as this forbids the use of torture and inhuman or degrading treatment or punishment on a person. Public authorities cannot depart from their obligations under an absolute right, even in times of war or other national emergencies. Nor can an absolute right be 'balanced' against the needs of other individuals or the public interest, except in rare circumstances where two absolute rights are balanced against each other. Under this heading are rights guaranteed by Articles 2, 3, 4(1), and 7.

The retroactive criminalisation of acts and omissions is prohibited by Art. 7 but your reading in this chapter so far should have given you some scepticism for the strength of this claim—e.g. the 'double jeopardy' reforms and the general common law tradition in the UK.

Strong rights ('special' or 'limited' rights)

These are similar to absolute rights in that they cannot be 'balanced' against the rights of other individuals or the public interest. But governments are entitled under the Convention to *derogate* (deviate) from their application in times of war or national emergency (Art. 15). The right to liberty (Art. 5) and the right to a fair trial (Art. 6) are examples of limited rights for these purposes. Under sections 14 and 16 of the HRA, derogation can only be made by the Secretary of State for Justice and these last for five years, unless they are renewed.

The right to liberty may be provided, but arrest or imprisonment in fulfilment of the law is permitted as the right does not apply to 'lawful detention' following 'conviction by a competent court'. The right to a fair trial includes the right to be presumed innocent until proved guilty according to law—the force of this right has also been questioned in this chapter.

Qualified rights

These are rights which can be restricted not only in times of war or emergency but also in order to protect the rights of another or the wider public interest. In general, qualified rights are structured so that the first part of the Article sets out the right, while the second part establishes the grounds on which a public authority can legitimately interfere with that right in order to protect the wider public interest. This category of rights includes those guaranteed by Articles 8, 9, 10, and 11.

Getting it wrong by using 'rights'?

The influence of human rights has seen it grow to become one of the rule of law's fundamental ideals with comparable significance to the protection of democracy (Bingham 2010). Despite these assertions it can still be common for some politicians and parts of the media to vociferously criticise the principle of human rights. These objections can be confused over whether the real source of the anger is the EU or ECHR but such details appear not to trouble the UK tabloid press. This kind of outrage appears less vocal in countries such as Germany—who, like most European countries have also had their extremely 'hard' human rights' cases.

In *Gäfgen* v *Germany* (2010) Application No. 22978/05 a successful claim for 3,000 euros was granted in compensation to the applicant for breach of his human rights during his arrest and detention in a police station. He was arrested after collecting a ransom of one million euros he had demanded from the parents of a missing 12 year old boy (see **Controversy and debate 4.1** in **Chapter 4**). Initially Gäfgen refused to say anything

to the police (he had already suffocated the boy and disposed of the body near a lake) and believing the boy to be in serious danger, the police responded with extremely sinister threats of torture in order to make him say where the boy was. On receiving the threats Gäfgen immediately broke down, confessed to the crime, and disclosed the location of the body. It was unanimously held by the ECtHR judges that this was a breach of Art. 3 as Gäfgen had received degrading treatment for which no derogation was possible. This right's absolute nature re-categorised Gäfgen as a victim and his entitlement to compensation is a stark example of the force of absolute human rights. However, see **Controversy and debate 21.1** for another highly contentious issue from this notorious case.

CONTROVERSY AND DEBATE 20.1

Cross-examination is 'the greatest legal engine ever invented for telling the truth' [but even if this is true, do we know how it runs or for how long it will last?]

The claim that cross-examination is the 'greatest legal engine ever invented' for finding the truth is from the highly distinguished American legal scholar John Henry Wigmore (**Figure 20.6**), who in 1904, published his *Treatise on the Anglo-American System of Evidence in Trials at Common Law*. Its authority for evaluating processes in criminal trials is such that it is often abbreviated to 'Wigmore on Evidence' or even just 'Wigmore'.

Cross-examination was given its honour thanks to the nature of English and American adversarial trials demanding live oral evidence and bestowing credibility on those perceived as a 'good witness'. It is generally agreed by both jurists (legal scholars) and practitioners that this applies to a person who is articulate, confident, and emotionally balanced. If true, these suppositions clearly demonstrate potential for unfairness as such characteristics are highly subjective and disregard individual differences.

The courtroom is one of the most important stages in a criminal process and yet due to restrictions on research, there is considerable secrecy with enhanced guesswork responsible for much of its generated knowledge. Any mystery over the adversarial criminal trial process can be dispelled by simply seeing it as 'a game of two halves'. Each half is always the same, in that each side produce their witnesses for firstly, examination in chief (questioned by their own side) and then cross-examination (by the opposition). The prosecution always starts first and if by 'half-time' (the end of the prosecution case),

Figure 20.6 Major John Henry Wigmore

Source: Library of Congress Prints and Photographs Division/Public domain

a case to answer has not been established; the tribunal of law must stop the proceedings. This simple sketch misses out a few less important stages but in essence a trial can be conceived as a procession of witnesses who deliver their testimony via examination in chief, cross-examination, and re-examination (where questions can be asked from the witnesses' own side as a result of what came out of cross-examination).

This outline demonstrates the vital importance of in-court oral evidence from witnesses in adversarial proceedings. When this testimony is cross-examined, it is believed the 'best' witnesses react well to their versions of events being forcibly tested. Such witnesses provide the tribunal of fact with highly cogent (influential) evidence. Supporters of the 'greatest invention ever' believe it 'beats and bolts out the Truth much better' than when a witness is not cross-examined (according to Sir Matthew Hale's (1736) influential *History and Analysis of the Common Law of England*). The perceived ban on jury research means there is an information vacuum when it comes to knowing whether 'twelve randomly selected UK citizens' see truth as the outcome from cross-examination. The 'engine' has been recalibrated recently in recognition of some of its toxic effects, such as the experiences of witnesses in sexual offences trials who have compared it to 'like a second rape'. These modifications have resulted in the presumption that a complainant's previous sexual history is now inadmissible; plus the range of special measures (such as live video links, video recorded evidence and protective screens in court) available in the Youth Justice and Criminal Evidence Act 1999.

The adversarial tradition has also been altered in many other ways such as the legal requirement for the defence to now take part in a full disclosure of evidence process. This effectively means a 'script' for the trial has to be agreed in advance and so only in film and television courtroom dramas will the crucial bit of evidence arrive just in time! The requirement for trials to have this structure is another example of the fluctuating nature of the rule of law. For example, until the mid-1990s its presumption of innocence was deemed to include the suspect's right of silence at arrest, in the police station and at court, but this was removed by ss. 34–35 of the Criminal Justice and Public Order Act 1994. Such silences can now be treated as a sign of guilt as can non-compliance with the rules for disclosure of a defence statement. The defence now have to provide the prosecution with a statement that sets out: the nature of the proposed defence, the defences which will be relied on, the facts that are disputed with the prosecution (including reasons), plus indications of any points of law likely to be raised.

The Criminal Procedure Rules 2014 and decisions such as *R v Gleeson* [2004] EWCA Crim LR 579 have sharpened this focus still further. According to the former, which has the force of delegated legislation, the 'overriding objective is that criminal cases be dealt with justly … [and] dealing with the case *efficiently and expeditiously*' (rule 1, emphasis added). The common law in *Gleeson* clearly supports these new responsibilities as at 'half-time' in that case, the defence made a plea of no case to answer because the charge on the indictment was technically (that word again) impossible for their client's circumstances. The judge agreed this view was legally correct but was still prepared to let the trial proceed into the second half as long as the prosecution redrafted the indictment for a different charge. The defence subsequently appealed against the judge's actions but also lost at the Court of Appeal where it was stated that it was no longer acceptable for a defence to seek an advantage from delaying the identification of any issues of either law or fact in a case—i.e. a 'technical' or 'legal' mistake in the prosecution. Arguably this further refashions the presumption of innocence and means a defence lawyer can be expected to help with their client's downfall!

These changes have deeply altered the game of adversarialism and more are discussed below in the chapter's other parts and have resulted in the UK's criminal justice being described as 'Adversarialism lite' (Cape 2010). So as with other 'lite' products, it looks just like the real thing but completely lacks authenticity and taste!

Adversarial justice

This is the second key criminal justice principle for this chapter and as with the rule of law; it is a standard with many different values. Criminal justice in the UK, particularly England and Wales, is renowned for operating under a system of adversarial justice. It is a system that conceives the criminal process as a battle between an individual and the state which ultimately results in a showpiece trial where the parties can win and lose their cases. The trial is such an important part of the process but it does not set out to establish the truth about a crime in a neutral sense—hence the 'winning' and 'losing' of cases—instead it emphasises the importance of the burden of proof and the need for sufficient evidence for a conviction. It means the police and prosecution cannot proceed with a case, regardless of their views of guilt, until they have sufficient proof the crime was committed by the suspect. There is no burden on a suspect to establish or prove their innocence because, as with the rule of law, the presumption of innocence is rated highly (apart from the numerous 'golden thread' exceptions!) So it is up to the prosecutor to demonstrate through the evidence that the defendant is guilty beyond reasonable doubt.

The evolution of the adversarial system of trial in England was based on procedures instigated by the Ancient Romans and can be described as a *gladiatorial contest*. This can lead to the belief that s/he with the most effective gladiator (lawyer) and the 'best' witnesses will win. The credibility of witnesses on their 'day in court' is hugely important and is something assessed by the tribunal of fact (the jury or magistrates). Whilst the adversarial contest is usually weighted in favour of the prosecution (compare the resources at the state's disposal to those of a local solicitor); this is not always the case. It was clearly reversed in the News International (owned by the billionaire Rupert Murdoch) phone hacking trial of 2014 when Rebekah Brooks and Andy Coulson, former editors of the News of the World were prosecuted:

> Lawyers and court reporters who spend their working lives at the Old Bailey agreed they had never seen anything like it, this multimillion-pound Rolls-Royce engine purring through the proceedings. Soon we found ourselves watching the power of the private purse knocking six bells out of the underfunded public sector.
>
> In the background, for sure, there was a huge publicly funded police inquiry, forced by the stench of past failure to investigate thoroughly the crime which had been ignored and concealed for so long. But when it came to handling the police evidence in court, Brooks and Coulson had squads of senior partners, junior solicitors and paralegals, as well as a highly efficient team monitoring all news and social media.

The cost to Murdoch ran into millions. Against that, the Crown Prosecution Service had only one full-time solicitor attached to the trial and one admin assistant.

Defence barristers would pause, turn and find a solicitor to feed them information while crown counsel often found an empty seat. The defence produced neatly laminated bundles of evidence, while the Crown hastily photocopied material into files which sometimes proved to be incomplete.

The Guardian, 25 June 2014

It is possible that lack of organisation can influence the credibility of a case but largely due to statutory restrictions on criminological research in this area (see **Chapter 29**); little is known on how such essential decisions are approached. In inquisitorial systems the emphasis is on an inquiry into an alleged offence rather than a contest between two parties. An official investigator independently discovers as many facts as possible rather than in an adversarial system where the parties produce all of the evidence, which naturally has the strong possibility of being biased. Instead of a showpiece trial where the parties ultimately confront each other with their witnesses, an inquisitorial process emphasises the importance of preliminary stages, where meetings and written communications between the appointed judge and the parties' representatives, produce the evidence for the case. The 'inquisitorial' term means a judge is responsible for questioning the witnesses and this active role correspondingly diminishes the power and functions of lawyers ('gladiators'). An 'English style cross-examination' is not possible for testing the reliability of a witness's evidence. See **Controversy and debate 20.1** for how such cross-examinations can be expected to work.

Restorative justice

This is the final principle for this part of the chapter and whilst restorative justice (RJ) is a vast topic with many different features, it has a widely accepted general definition as:

> a process whereby parties with a stake in a specific offence collectively resolve how to deal with the aftermath of the offence and its implications for the future.
>
> Marshall 1999: 5

It is an approach to justice that emphasises collective action for dealing with an offence that seeks to repair the harm it has caused. It differs considerably to the standard method of the state having full responsibility in the response to a crime. It is expected that repairing the harm is achieved by providing reparation to the injured parties who are restored, as much as possible, to their pre-offence positions. RJ has become much more extensive in recent

decades but it is not a principle unique to contemporary times, as illustrated by the compensatory function of the Code of Ur-Nammu. However, interest in this potentially game changing criminal justice principle has grown considerably since around the time the Advisory Council on the Penal System (1970) published their 'reparation and community service ideas [that] were the apotheosis of the post-war attitude to offenders' (Hood 1974: 380). This apotheosis (ideal example) had optimism that contrasted starkly with the evolving beliefs in 'nothing works' when it came to the rehabilitation of offenders (Martinson 1974). The response from the 'community service ideal' is one of the main focuses of the chapter as in addition to being the most visible and frequently implemented RJ response, it has also been referred to as 'the paradigm of community restoration' (Ashworth 2003: 170). RJ is a very wide term that includes a diverse range of practices, so in addition to the 'community service ideal', it commonly offers the responses of:

- victim-offender mediation schemes (where the two parties are brought together in the presence of a mediator);
- other types of meetings (often called conferences) where families or other representatives of an offender and victim are present;
- written communications between these parties.

It is a principle that has also been adapted over time and as well as lacking an agreed standard definition that deals with its different features, there is also disagreement on the criteria for deciding how much 'restorativeness' is needed for the response (Sharpe 2004). It has become such a disparate set of practices that it is difficult to talk confidently about its theoretical background because although its practitioners and supporters usually agree on what practices constitute restorative justice, 'they tend to disagree about how to characterize those practices' (Garvey 2011: 510). But despite these uncertainties, RJ responses have some commonalities; such as the involvement of the victim of an offence in the criminal process. This requirement means the process is not limited to the participation of an individual offender and the state. It is a principle that helped 'the return of the victim' in being identified as one of the clearest measures of change in late 20th century criminal justice (Garland 2001: 11).

Reparation for victims can be provided either indirectly where the harm is repaired to the community as a whole (as in 'community service'), or more directly through victim–offender mediation schemes (as illustrated in **Figure 20.7**). Direct arrangements can include face-to-face meetings between a victim and an offender under the direction of an official mediator; initially such practices led the enthusiasm in North America for restorative justice through claims it could offer an alternative to imprisonment (Umbreit and Zehr, 1982). However, these hopes do not appear to have been realised as the countries that have widely implemented it (e.g. the United States, New Zealand, Australia and the UK) are also those who have experienced some of the largest recent increases in rates of imprisonment (Wood 2015). Nonetheless, interest in the UK for offenders making *reparation* to people affected by their crimes has seen it become one of the five statutory purposes of sentencing; with *punishment*, *reduction of crime* (including its reduction by deterrence), *reform and rehabilitation* of offenders, and the *protection of the public* being the others (s.142 of the CJA 2003).

Branding RJ through community payback

The 'community service paradigm' cited in the previous section is a reference to its perceived exemplar status as the response for harm restoration through criminal justice. The next chapter will consider the influences of policy and practice respectively on this response; but for now it is important to be clear on what we are discussing. Despite sentences of 'community service' being widely understood, this is a very out dated term as it was officially ended by the Criminal Justice and Court Services Act 2000 (CJCSA). However, it is still frequently used by the media and in general discourse but to be written about accurately it should be *the unpaid work requirement of a community order*. This name is itself a replacement as CJCSA replaced 'CS' (its common abbreviation which is also still used today!) with the label of community punishment orders.

This statute also ended the existence of probation orders as they were renamed community rehabilitation orders. These labels from CJCSA may have been short lived as they were soon replaced by the generic *community order* in the CJA 2003; but their intentions to distinguish these responses seemed clear. They meant probation was accorded 'rehabilitation' whereas the restorative approach of community service became 'punishment'. This direction facilitated the introduction two years later of yet another new name, 'Community Payback' as the brand name for this form of sentencing. This change was introduced through a publicity campaign that sought to acquire 'a consistent brand and image' for the sanction and requested probation areas to use 'professional PR input' and 'to buy in PR consultancy' (Home Office 2005: Annex 2, paras. 4–6).

As a principle RJ offers hope for changing the game of criminal justice, but 'in the context of wide-spread

Figure 20.7 Prisoners at High Down Prison in Sutton, Surrey, taking part in the forgiveness project, a restorative justice scheme

Source: Richard Saker/Guardian News & Media

social exclusion, even restorative, deliberately reintegrative penalties have little hope of making a serious impact on rates of offending' (Lacey 2003: 101). This social marginalisation results in disadvantages in terms of social welfare, mental health, employment, and education; they are factors that seriously question the abilities of purely criminal justice responses to have a clear effect on reoffending. Despite these barriers, there are RJ practices that in principle can limit the disintegrative effects of traditional punishment methods and have social reintegration as an aim. However, despite this aim the remaining parts of the 4Ps have to be considered because the first step of a principle may not be sufficient for clearing these hurdles.

The police, the courts, and the CPS

The term 'criminal justice system' is misleading if used to mean there is one agreed system of justice where organisations and people work towards common priorities and purposes. If this did happen, it would be an authentic system where its different components link together in a consistent and coherent process. The creation of such a unified justice system is frequently called for but has many imposing obstacles to overcome; some agreement for the fundamental 'what is justice' questions that you considered in **Chapter 4** of this book would be a start.

The myriad of central government agencies involved in contemporary criminal justice reveals some of its diversity and these include: HM Courts Service and the Ministry of Justice which oversees the work of the National Offender Management Service (NOMS) which in turn is accountable for HM Prison Service, the National Probation Service, and Community Rehabilitation Companies. At the local level this variety increases to include different members of Local Criminal Justice Partnerships such as youth offending services and many other voluntary and community sector agencies. The development of a unified justice system may be desirable from both academic and political standpoints, but is very difficult to achieve when all of these agencies have their own measurements and interpretations of the system's success.

The police

The first formal system of policing is usually considered to be the one implemented for London by the Metropolitan Police Act 1829. It was though an extension of practices already in place, as 80 years earlier the Bow Street Runners, established by Henry Fielding, were being paid by central government to detect and prosecute crimes such as robberies on the streets and highways, pickpocketing, shoplifting; as well as visibly patrolling the streets and investigating serious offences (Beattie 2012). The professional approach evolved from growing dissatisfaction with the corruption of 'thief-takers', the people who solved crimes for a fee and claimed rewards for bringing suspects to court. The efforts of Sir Robert Peel, the Home Secretary at the time, were instrumental in the creation of the Metropolitan Police Act which over the next couple of decades was rolled out to the rest of the country. The police's nickname 'Bobby' is testimony to the influence of Robert ('Bob') Peel in this establishment of organised policing with local and central accountability.

The governance structure for the police reflects these different interests and this is provided by the tripartite framework from the Police Act 1964; which apart from one major modification is still in force today. It requires power and responsibility to be divided in three ways:

1. The Chief Constable of each of the 43 regional police forces in England and Wales or for the Metropolitan Police, the Commissioner (see **Chapter 30** for a breakdown of different police ranks and roles), has the power to establish the policing priorities and policies in their areas. This role is independent when it comes to operational matters and the directing and controlling of their police forces; this independence is designed to guard against political or other forms of influence. They used to work collectively through the Association of Chief Police Officers (ACPO) but since 2015 the National Police Chief's Council has been the body with expectations for police leadership and sharing expertise.

2. The Home Office is the government department with responsibility for the police and provides much of the funding to its individual forces (with the Department for Communities and Local Government or the Welsh Assembly Government, plus local council tax revenue known as the police precept, being the other sources). The provision of funding is contingent on targets and other performance indicators set by the Home Office being met; this gives it substantial influence in the delivery of local policing services (Rowe 2013).

3. The final part of the tripartite system used to be the police authorities which were local bodies comprising councillors and magistrates with responsibility for maintaining an adequate and efficient police force in their area. However, they were replaced in the Police Reform and Social Responsibility Act 2011 by the role of a Police and Crime Commissioner (PCC) and now every police area in England and Wales must hold a local election every four

years where the public can vote for their preferred PCC. The main powers of a PCC are the hiring and firing of chief constables; setting the force's budget and establishing the Police and Crime plan to include the strategies and priorities for their term in office.

The PCCs are advised and scrutinised by a Police and Crime Panel who can veto proposals to increase the budget precept or for a new appointee as chief constable. It is unclear whether this amendment will ensure adequate separation of powers, particularly when a PCC and Police and Crime Panel are both dominated by the same political party. There have been two PCC elections so far and both have witnessed very low levels of voter turnouts; both have also seen consistent successes for the candidates from the Conservative and Labour parties. This dramatic change to police governance is in its infancy but you should still be considering what threats this new system may pose to its independence.

The role of the police

There were widespread concerns about 'police soldiers' appearing on the streets of England so the intention of Peel's original 'boys-in-blue' (a colour intentionally chosen to differ from the army's traditional red; and from the 20th century included 'girls-in-blue') was to take a more consensual style of policing by a 'citizen-in-uniform' (Emsley 2009). This approach is said to be enabled by the police mandate which is the name given to the authority for the police to do their role. The mandate mirrors other parts to the English constitution in that it is unwritten, ill-defined, and vague. It is said to represent the authority of the people but its elusive nature leads to significant disagreements over the importance of 'catching crooks', preventing crime, and helping people in emergencies, to name just three of the possible sides to the policing role. The independence of the police is equivalent to the independent judiciary principle in that they are ultimately answerable to the rule of law and not a particular organisation or body of people. But as with any principle you encounter on your course into criminology, the concept of police independence requires your 'ABC approach'.

Ethnographic research from the 1960s and 1970s led to police scholarship and research becoming a major topic of interest for criminology. This kind of research is advocated many times in this book (see **Chapter 21** for a specific example) and with regard to the police, these methods for an insider's perspective opened up new territory such as the vital importance to the policing role of police culture, discretion, and attitudes to the criminal law (Ellison 2013). The role of the police is a huge topic and therefore you are advised to co-ordinate your studies of this area with carefully reading the 'Policing' chapter

by Trevor Jones, Tim Newburn, and Robert Reiner in the latest edition of *The Oxford Handbook of Criminology*.

Challenges for the police

It may have been difficult to acquire initially but for around 100 years between the mid-19th and 20th centuries, the police experienced a 'Golden Age' of high levels of public support; which are unlikely to return given the deep changes since then in law, culture, and society (Jones et al. 2017). Even so, your consideration of the latest public opinion research findings for the workings of the criminal justice system, illustrate levels of backing and confidence in the police that other criminal justice agencies could only dream about (Hough and Roberts 2017). It will clearly be a major challenge to maintain these views in a system that is likely to consist of fewer police numbers and consequently, less visibility.

The police's position as the sole provider of policing services is being challenged by the array of bodies now operating in a pluralisation of policing (Jones et al. 2017). The increasing use of private security and other forms of privatisation risks further fragmenting the policing system; one where the Metropolitan Police Commissioner does not discourage schemes such as that used by the residents of the London Borough of Hampstead, that privately raised £160,000 towards a target of £600,000 to pay for a police sergeant and two constables for three years (*The Telegraph*, 10 November 2015). A similar strategy was attempted in Bedfordshire where the plan from the PCC to increase council tax to fund an additional 100 police officers was subject to a local referendum; but it was defeated by almost 70 per cent of voters (BBC 2015).

Despite such difficulties the police are still the central organisation in the criminal justice system. Their mandate for policing might be contentious but it enables them to turn the first cog in the wheels of justice and their influence pervades much of the system. This was apparent in Operation Elveden (see **Figure 20.8**) which was a five-year investigation into the making of inappropriate payments to police officers and other public officials; its impact on the Crown Prosecution Service is discussed later in this chapter.

The courts

It is essential to be able to distinguish between matters of public law and those of private law as these classifications determine which court will hear the case and which party has the responsibility for bringing legal action. Cases deemed to be public law are reasoned to affect the whole community and are classed as an offence against the state; the trials for these possible crimes would be the result of

Figure 20.8 A summary of the work of Operation Elveden (2011–16)
Source: The Metropolitan Police/Public domain

the state bringing cases to either the Magistrates' Court or the Crown Court (see **Figure 20.4**). If a case is deemed to be private law (also known as civil law) then the individuals affected have the responsibility for bringing the case to court; with the likely venues being the County Court or the High Court. Appreciating the ways these cases can be cited will help you understand the divisions between these types of courts:

• In criminal cases the citation takes the form of: *R v The Defendant's Surname* and the year it was reported—several examples have already been provided by this chapter and these citations may also include a reference to the Law Reports, as these sources are official statements of the common law. Thanks to electronic databases they are now far more accessible so particularly whilst you have enhanced access, take advantage of your institution's resources and search for some cases; you will soon see just how different these case reports are to those reported in the press!

• In civil law citations there will not be an 'R' (standing for either Rex or Regina depending on whether a King or Queen is in existence at the time) as instead it will comprise the surnames of the individuals or the names of the organisations involved. The party bringing the action is known as the claimant and the one with potential liability ('guilt' is not a term used in civil law) for it is the defendant. It is usually the claimant whose name comes first although this can be reversed if the citation is for an appeal. When being spoken out loud, the convention for civil cases is to express the 'v' between the parties' names as 'and'—this is not the case in criminal trials which are always referred to as 'versus'.

The civil case of *Halford* v *Brookes* (1991) illustrates these citation methods, as does its subsequent criminal case of *R v Brookes* (1996). These examples of cases (also known as litigation) demonstrate the clear dividing lines between

criminal and civil law; but also in how they can overlap. In the initial civil case, Halford sued Brookes for the assault that had killed her daughter and it was held by the trial court (i.e. it was decided by Justice Rougier) that Brookes was liable for the assault (in civil law known as trespass to the person) and therefore had to pay compensation to the deceased's estate.

A more well-known example of this distinction is the litigation involving the American celebrity O.J. Simpson in 1995–97. First a criminal court in Los Angeles found him not guilty of the murder of his ex-wife and a friend, but then a civil trial at Los Angeles County Superior Court held him to be liable for the killings. Both cases clearly show the separation in the different parts of the court system and following the civil litigation the sanctions imposed were orders to pay financial compensation. They are stark examples of the nature and purpose of civil law; in effect, officially pronounced murderers could literally dump a wad of cash on the court bench and walk free (although it has been reported that neither Brookes nor Simpson actually paid any compensation). This may seem like an affront to justice but possibly not when the context and guiding purpose of civil law is recognised—it does not exist to punish, it is there to compensate injured parties who have suffered a loss. This includes financial punishment so compensation is awarded in line with the principle of *restitutio in integrum*. This aims to restore the injured party, as much as it is possible to do so through an award of money, to the situation they would have been in had the injury not been sustained. A claimant should not be in a 'windfall position' as any award is supposed to be making good for what has been lost. There can be some rare situations when compensation is awarded that exceeds a claimant's loss (known as punitive damages) but these are seldom imposed as restitution is the purpose behind the civil courts' judgments. In some cases money may not be an issue at all, as the civil litigation involving Brookes was the family's way of keeping the case alive in the hope of pressurising the criminal justice system into bringing a prosecution (*Independent*, 3 August 1996).

The Crown Prosecution Service (CPS)

The public law status given to suspected criminal offences means they are tried and dealt with by a state implemented system. This difference with the justice provided by the civil courts means there is a risk potential victims feel excluded, as the CPS is an independent prosecuting authority and not 'the victim's lawyer'. It became operational in 1986 when the Prosecution of Offences Act 1985 came into force and until then it had been the responsibility of individuals themselves and then the police to decide whether suspected criminal cases should be prosecuted. The involvement of the police had been criticised for many years from voices such as the law reform pressure group JUSTICE in 1970 and by the Royal Commission on Criminal Procedure in 1981. The lack of separation in the police's role for both investigating and prosecuting suspected offences was proving a concern for the growing numbers of miscarriages of justice. Further disapproval was also expressed for the way this dual policing role led to regional differences in the practice of prosecutions. An independent prosecuting body that was clearly distinct from the police's investigatory functions was therefore created.

The CPS is the principal prosecuting body in England and Wales but it is not the only one, as such powers are also held by numerous agencies such as: the Health and Safety Executive, Civil Aviation Authority, Maritime and Coastguard Agency, Financial Conduct Authority, Office of Fair Trading, and the Department for Environment, Food and Rural Affairs. It has been estimated these bodies may be responsible for one in four prosecutions and this is very different to Scotland where the only authority with prosecuting powers is the Crown Office and Procurator Fiscal Service (House of Commons Justice Committee, 2009: paras. 118–19). The common law rule in England and Wales for allowing private prosecutions can also be used; a right that was preserved in the legislation that established the CPS and is available to organisations as well as individuals.

The head of the CPS holds the title of Director of Public Prosecutions (DPP) and reports to the Attorney General who is accountable to Parliament for the service. The Attorney General is a member of the government who provides legal advice to its different departments. The fact this high level appointment is a political one demonstrates how the principle of separation of powers is again a live issue. Supporters of the current Attorney General's role point to its relatively limited role in the justice process but this can be questioned as the so-called narrow role has included decisions on highly contentious matters such as the legality of

the war in Iraq in 2003; the dropping of corruption charges in 2006 following the dealings between BAE Systems and Saudi Arabia for the sale of Eurofighter jets; and in 2007 acquiring a court order preventing the BBC from broadcasting an item about the 'cash-for-honours' investigation where links had been discovered between donations or loans of money to political parties and people receiving a peerage and a parliamentary place in the House of Lords.

The role of the CPS

The CPS is organised into geographical areas for England and Wales and each one is led by a Chief Crown Prosecutor; their general responsibilities are as follows:

- Advising the police on cases for possible prosecution; this includes deciding on the appropriate charge in serious and/or complex cases. These powers to decide the charge were introduced by the Criminal Justice Act 2003 as it used to be the case that the responsibility of the CPS began after the police had decided the charge. The involvement of the CPS in the charging stage of the system now accounts for around one third of the total number of cases (Crown Prosecution Service 2016). These services are provided by CPS Direct which makes charging decisions for all police forces across England and Wales. This national network of telephone and online advice is available 24 hours a day and has replaced previous policies of having a CPS office in every police station.

- Taking cases from the police once a defendant has been charged or summonsed (ordered to attend court). The CPS has the responsibility for reviewing all of this evidence and assigns cases to teams in the local area. This team is then responsible for preparing the case for court and its progress throughout the prosecution process.

- Presenting cases at court by lawyers known as Crown Prosecutors. This is an essential role for adversarial criminal trials that can be seen as a gladiatorial contest, an image that signifies the fierce competition that could occur and the key influence of lawyers (gladiators) in the outcome. The CPS is not always the strongest party in these battles (see the extract earlier in the chapter with regard to the News International 'phone hacking' trial); reports of low quality advocacy from the CPS that were cited in the Fuller Review made clear the influence of recently reduced budgets (HM CPS Inspectorate 2015).

This work is fulfilled by people in the three main CPS roles:

- **Crown Prosecutors**—the barristers and Higher Court Advocates who are responsible for presenting the cases in court on behalf of the Crown. They are not always exclusively employed by the CPS so may also work in private practice as defence lawyers.

- **Paralegals**—this role used to be known as case-workers and involves the work needed to help a case's preparation for court.

- **Administrators**—the broad category of workers who assist the CPS with financial, managerial, and information technology issues.

The Code for Crown Prosecutors is issued by the Director of Public Prosecutions and contains the key guidelines for prosecutors when making their decisions on whether to prosecute. It also provides guidance on charging decisions, out-of-court disposals, the acceptance of guilty pleas, and mode of trial applications (the hearings in Magistrates' Courts that decide which criminal court of first instance will hear an alleged either way offence). The decision to prosecute a case in court is based firstly on an evidential test and whether the case has a realistic prospect of conviction. This is answered by a prosecutor deciding whether a court is more likely than not to convict the defendant of the alleged charge. The term 'more likely than not' is often called 'on the balance of probabilities' and it is this level of proof that is needed in the civil courts of justice, as opposed to the 'beyond all reasonable doubt' that is eventually required by a criminal court. If very crude numbers are your thing this means 51 per cent sure in a civil court and 95 per cent sure in a criminal court.

If the first stage is passed then the case will be subject to the public interest test; the prosecutor must believe it is in the public interest to prosecute the case. This is obviously a difficult decision that sounds like a grand power but this discretion is guided by the factors that encourage prosecution such as the perceived seriousness of the offence and the suspect's level of involvement. An offence could be deemed serious if it was premeditated or it is deemed there is a need to safeguard the public. If there is hostility against the victim's ethnic or national origin, gender, disability, age, religion or belief, sexual orientation or gender identity; or if there is a position of trust or authority between the suspect and victim or the victim was at the time someone serving the public then these will be factors recommending it is in the public interest to prosecute. The other factors in this decision are the age of the suspect, national security considerations, the impact of the offence on the community, and whether a prosecution is a proportionate response.

Challenges for the CPS

The criticism that follows not guilty verdicts, particularly in high profile cases such as the 'unsuccessful' trials involving celebrities during Operation Yew Tree, can suggest the CPS is desperately underperforming. Similarly negative views can also be based on the numbers of cases that for many reasons do not actually proceed to trial. However, just how revealing is the number of discontinuances or

the current acquittal rate? Does it mean in all the cases where there wasn't a conviction, the defendant should have never been prosecuted?

The outcome of a case can be incredibly difficult to predict, particularly if the prosecution have little knowledge of the defence case. The system for the disclosure of evidence is intended to improve this as it requires both sides to disclose the evidence they are going to use at trial; plus, if relevant, to disclose evidence they are not going to use. This, it is hoped, overcomes the bias in traditional adversarial trials where evidence risked being suppressed as each side would only present evidence favourable to their case. The first statutory system of disclosure began in the Criminal Procedure and Criminal Investigations Act 1996 and imposed these obligations on both sides. It is now common practice for the defence to provide a statement of their defence before their trial; this quickens up the court hearings and emulates the approach used in the civil courts.

The CPS is required to provide value for money and many measures such as the average number of court hearings required by cases are taken to monitor its efficiency. It is a principle of the Code that the CPS should not make decisions on matters of justice purely on financial reasons; this does not prevent stringent criticism given to it when large amounts of money are spent and the right kind of results are not achieved. An example could be Operation Elveden which cost £14.7m and resulted in 34 convictions, nine of which were police officers with 21 being other public officials (Guardian, 26 February 2016).

The Court of Appeal's decision in *R v Chapman and others* [2015] EWCA Crim 539 clearly demonstrated the difficulties in the CPS's role in the criminal justice system. It was a result of Operation Elveden and its trials for the common law offence of misconduct in public office; a crime committed when a public officer wilfully takes part in misconduct or wilfully neglects to perform their duty. It is deemed to be wilful misconduct when the actions (or inactions) have no reasonable excuse or justification and are believed to abuse the public's trust in the office holder. In this case it was a trial of a former prisoner officer who had made more than £40,000 from selling stories about one of the prisoners at his institution to the newspapers from 2003–11. The CPS initially secured a conviction but lost at the appeal on the grounds the judge's directions to the jury were unsatisfactory; the Court of Appeal judgment included guidance for further prosecutions and the CPS changed their policy accordingly. This meant the proceedings against nine journalists, all of whom had been charged with the criminal offence of conspiracy to commit misconduct in public office, were discontinued. Bearing the contents of this section in mind you may now want to consider **What do you think? 20.3.**

WHAT DO YOU THINK? 20.3

How would you judge the success of the CPS?

If the rates of discontinuances or the current acquittal/conviction rates do not provide the evidence you feel you need for evaluating the work of the CPS, then consider alternative sources such as research into victim and witness satisfaction levels. For example, the CPS regularly carry out thematic reviews into this topic which can produce revealing findings; presumably they are hoping they improve on the latest figures where one in five respondents identifying as victims and one in ten witnesses, reported they were dissatisfied with the service they received (Crown Prosecution Service 2016: 5–6).

The annual reports for the CPS and other potential game changers in the criminal justice system are freely available and their content can provide large amounts of numerical evidence for grounding your reflections. However, they need to be read in their context which is a review of that service's performance that year; so in isolation their value can be limited.

The information in these annual reports, such as 'A Year in Numbers' CPS (2016: 3, see **Figure 20.9**), give

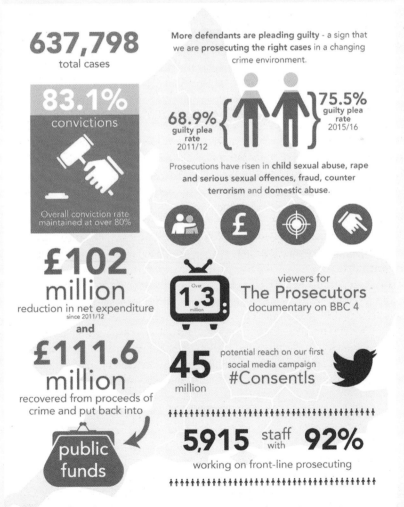

Figure 20.9 A Year in Numbers infographic from p.3 of Crown Prosecution Service (2016)
Source: National Archives, content available under the Open Government Licence v3.0

you an ideal opportunity to deploy your 'ABC'. These bold statements are the kind of things we can all question—for example does the increasing number of defendants now pleading guilty really mean the right cases are being prosecuted? Is there not a danger this ignores other reasons people may have for pleading guilty? They may lack the financial resources to contest the charge or seek to take advantage of the sentencing discount available to people who plead guilty at the first reasonable opportunity. If they feel such a discount could be the difference between going to prison and receiving a non-custodial sentence, then regardless of actual guilt a defendant may feel compelled to admit their legal guilt.

SUMMARY

After reading this chapter and working your way through the different features of this chapter you should now be able to:

• Recognise the source and changing nature of essential criminal justice principles

In the initial sections it was demonstrated how despite their fundamental importance, the criminal justice principles of: the rule of law, adversarial justice, and restorative justice are dynamic rather than static concepts. The extent of their evolving nature means previously deeply accepted values can be changed. Awareness of some of the conflicts arising from these modifications will enable you to explain how priorities in the justice system can change.

• Outline the importance of the rule of law doctrine

The rule of law doctrine was stressed to illustrate its status as the ultimate authority for democratic systems of justice. However, reflections on three of its supplementary concepts: an independent judiciary, due process, and human rights, enabled you to question this source of power. Your assessment of the difficulties in creating a judiciary with full independence, or for providing a system of justice that is based on either the Blackstone ratio or on guaranteed human rights, will support analysis of the impact of the doctrine.

• Discuss the essential features of an adversarial justice system

The key features of adversarialism were discussed to encourage your thoughts on its belief in gladiatorial courtroom processes as the most effective way for discovering truth. The traditional adversarial contest between two opposing sides means such hearings can lack impartiality as the role of the judge is limited to ensuring the rules are followed. This was shown to differ in inquisitorial systems where the judiciary have a more active role and undertake 'lawyer-like' functions such as examining witnesses and discovering new evidence.

• Assess the force of the restorative justice principle

It was recognised how in recent decades, this principle has become a much discussed alternative to the traditional criminal justice processes of state inflicted punishment on convicted wrong doers. The restorative justice principle was shown to offer a different dimension; one that prioritises the repairing of the harms suffered by injured parties. The limits to the principle's status as a key function of justice were seen in the recent popularity of a much tougher approach to community sentencing.

• Critically evaluate the ways the different courts of justice can be brought into action

The work of the police and the Crown Prosecution Service drive the criminal justice system in bringing its cases to court. The roles each organisation is expected to fulfil in their guiding concepts of the police mandate and the public interest test illustrate the complexity in their work. Awareness of the different branches of the court system enabled you to distinguish their different powers and to explain how their conceptions of justice can vary.

REVIEW QUESTIONS

1. How does the rule of law principle seek to ensure an independent judiciary?

2. What would be emphasised by a due process model of justice?

3. What is the Blackstone ratio of justice and is it a concept with general support?

4. In recent decades, what examples have there been of the weakening of the principle of adversarial justice?

5. How has the restorative justice principle been used in the work of the criminal justice system?

6. In what ways do civil and criminal courts differ in their approaches to the provision of justice?

FURTHER READING

It is worth bearing in mind that many primary sources, including Blackstone's *Commentaries on the Laws of England 1765-9* are available for free online at Project Gutenberg: www.gutenberg.org

Ashworth, A. (2015) *Sentencing and Criminal Justice.* Cambridge: Cambridge University Press.
This text addresses the place of sentencing within the constitution and provides up-to-date analysis of current principles and policies. It includes comparative sentencing research to investigate how the approach in England and Wales relates to the models of justice followed by other countries.

Dockley, A. and Loader, I. (eds) (2014) *The Penal Landscape: The Howard League Guide to Criminal Justice in England and Wales.* London: Routledge.
This is a comprehensive guide to the criminal justice system and covers a range of controversial issues affecting the police, probation, prisons, and youth justice. Issues affecting different minority groups are also investigated.

Hucklesby, A. and Wahidin, A. (eds) (2013) *Criminal Justice.* Oxford: Oxford University Press.
This text thoroughly investigates the issues, institutions, and agencies involved in the work of the criminal justice system. It provides in-depth political and historical context in its critical analysis of all stages of the criminal justice system.

Sanders, A., Young, R., and Burton, M. (2010) *Criminal Justice.* Oxford: Oxford University Press.
This is a comprehensive analysis of the different stages in the criminal justice system. It builds an argument for the work of the system to be based on the 'Freedom model' in order to prioritise its conflicting principles and rights.

 Access the **online resources** to view selected further reading and web links relevant to the material covered in this chapter.
www.oup.com/uk/case/

CHAPTER OUTLINE

Introduction   578

Criminal justice policies   578

Criminal justice practices   584

People in criminal justice   593

Criminal justice—policy, practice, and people

KEY ISSUES

After reading this chapter you should be able to:

- identify the changing influence of criminal justice policy, including penal populism;

- assess the effects of policy on selected criminal justice practices, such as community payback;

- examine the influence of criminal justice professionals in the delivery of criminal justice;

- engage with the 4Ps process (principles, policies, practices, and people) for changing the game in criminal justice.

Introduction

This chapter is divided into three parts of criminal justice policies, criminal justice practices, and people in criminal justice to complete your consideration of the 4Ps criminal justice process (principles were covered in **Chapter 20**) This process is represented in **Figure 21.1** through the interlocking features of the different elements, in this case cogs. The cogs and wheels signify the movement and change within criminal justice as well as the interconnected nature of these four central parts. It is shown as a cycle of change where each component can have an influence on the direction of criminal justice. From **Chapter 20** you are aware the 'principles cog' can frequently be turned, so now you should be thinking whether this pressure affects the other links in the chain and makes them travel in the same direction. This chapter aims to explore this question.

The oil can in **Figure 21.1** is a reminder that to keep running smoothly, any system of gears will need appropriate loosening. This chapter will explore the effects on the other three cogs in the figure: policies, practices, and people. We will be considering penal populism as a policy, as well as the concept of 'adversarial-lite' in respect of the

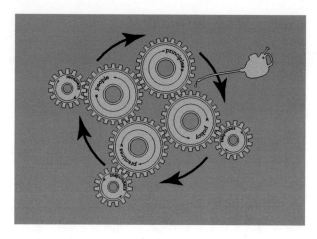

Figure 21.1 Turning the 'wheels of justice' through the 4Ps of criminal justice

UK. Moving onto practices, the chapter will take a closer look at community payback and will consider the due process model in practice. Finally, the chapter will consider the effects of merging principles and policies on the people who work in the criminal justice system.

Criminal justice policies

Policy is the catchall term for strategies and proposed courses of action, in this case in responding to crime. Criminal justice policies predominantly come from the government but other organisations and individuals such as the media, academics, corporations, and lobbyists can have an influence. They are approaches that seek to result in implementation, and to effectively make this transition they need to appeal to shared values in society. Acquiring agreement on what these values might be is a highly complex task, particularly in contemporary diverse societies, but arguably such principled quests are not attempted. Instead the constitutional power of the executive enables it to put forward its proposals for validation from the legislature, which as a result of the lack of separation of powers in the UK is generally given.

The government is the main policy maker for criminal justice and responsibility for contributing to it is shared across many of its different parts. The policy area for law and the justice system is shaped by about 20 different government departments such as the Ministry of Justice and the Home Office; plus, other public bodies such as the Crown Prosecution Service, HM Prison Service, National Probation Service, and the Parole Board. The

imperatives facing these policy makers have been succinctly summarised as: 'We must be *tough*; we must be *modern*; we must get *value for money*; we must get *re-elected*' (Cavadino and Dignan 2006: 75, emphasis added).

Penal populism

Until the last decades of the 20th century, acting on what the public's views on criminal justice were deemed to be was not something policy makers seriously considered. Instead, policy makers such as politicians, senior administrators, penal reformers, and academic criminologists saw themselves as 'platonic guardians' and believed the role of the government was 'to respond to crime (and public anger and anxiety about crime) in ways that, above all, seek to preserve 'civilized values' (Loader 2006: 563). This detached position changed in the 1990s with the increased relevance of what was initially known as **populist punitiveness** and the creation of policies that suited politicians' own purposes to meet the assumed punitive stance of the public (Bottoms 1995: 40). This view did not expressly use the term 'penal populism' but nonetheless it is recognised as its original conception. It refers to the implementation of *'penal policies to win votes rather than to reduce crime rates or to promote justice'* (Roberts et al. 2003: 3, emphasis added). Policies believed to have popular appeal with the public rather than maintaining standards of civility became the preferred directions for criminal justice. Whilst this seems a victory for democracy, particularly as policy was renowned for being a closed and elitist process (Ryan 2005), it is dependent on having accurate readings of public opinion for guiding the way.

Criminal justice policy that lacks consensus with public opinion risks losing its authority under the rule of law as this support legitimises the system's use of its power. This backing could be threatened by clear gaps between the public's expectations and the reality of the responses actually invoked. Such gaps seem to be present in the Crime Survey of England and Wales which has often found around three-quarters of respondents believing court sentences to be too lenient (Roberts and Hough 2013: 240). But the reliability of these views is affected by the lack of knowledge the public have of the justice system, as with regard to sentencing practices most people underestimate the severity of what is usually imposed (Hough et al. 2012). In addition, question order, wording and general information can all have an influence (see **Chapter 30**). The combination of these issues has provided evidence to suggest public opinion is a far more varied and complex matter than what is generally assumed (Roberts and Hough 2013). Despite these known uncertainties, influential policy documents such as the Casey Review have still felt able to state:

> policy makers, professionals, lobby groups and law makers [should] take note of one thing—the public are not daft. They know what's wrong, they know what's right, and they know what they want on crime and justice. And it's time action was taken on their terms.
>
> Cabinet Office 2008: 3

Such calls for action 'on their terms' have increased public involvement in penal affairs through the policy of 'dealing the public in' (Indermaur 2008). The national changes to New Zealand's sentencing policy in 2002, following a campaign instigated by one person, exemplifies the penal populist situation where 'the opinion of the shop-keeper petition organizer can be at least as good as that of the senior civil servant' (Pratt 2007: 45–6). The practices these policies can lead to are very different to those guided by modern justice sensibilities which required punishment to be hidden away from general view. An example was provided by John Pratt (2000), in *The Return*

of the Wheelbarrow Men; Or, The Arrival of Postmodern Penality? who cited Louis Masur's (1989) book *The Rites of Execution*, to compare this situation with that from two centuries ago and to:

> describe how 'those criminals sentenced to public labour … became known as the [W]heelbarrow [M]en. Ironed and chained, with shaved heads and coarse uniforms lettered to indicate the crime committed, they cleaned and repaired the streets of Philadelphia and the surrounding towns' … [this] seemed able to speak not just of the distant past but of present trends as well.
>
> Pratt 2000: 128

The 'Wheelbarrow Men' system was brought into law in 1786 and was based on beliefs that offenders' reformation could be achieved through public humiliation, hard work, and sobriety. It was distinct from the general developments of this time which were progressing towards the more modern conceptions of criminal justice with the values of *productivity*, *restraint*, and *rationality* (Pratt et al., 2005). Such priorities contrasted sharply with those for the 'Wheelbarrow Men' and also the carnage at the public execution in 1757 so powerfully described by Foucault (1977) in the opening pages of *Discipline and Punish: The Birth of the Prison*.

These examples stand out because modern practices did not seek to involve the public as witnesses; and rather than inflicting physical pain on the body of an offender they preferred to work *productively* on that person. The growing recognition that criminal sanctions can produce disproportionate amounts of harm has led to many calls for limits on their use. However, the thousands of new criminal offences each five-year Parliament now seems to create, record adult prison populations, extending the use of community sentences, and harsher disposals for first time offenders illustrates the lack of support the principle of *restraint* currently has (even though it would be significantly cheaper). Arguably a *rational* justice system would take such possibilities seriously and have official policy agendas rooted in research. This is not the case in the new millennium where the reported gap between policy makers and the academic research community has been said to be wider than at any time in the last four decades at least (Morgan 2008: 25). Despite the general agreement that policies based on penal populism are leading the justice system in a completely new punitive direction, this can be disputed as some scholars point to the earlier existence of such attitudes in penal policy (Matthews 2005; Moore 2015).

In offences that are believed to be extremely serious, a prison sentence of a *whole life order* of imprisonment (s.269 of the CJA 2003) is the starting point for a court's decision on punishment. The cases intended for this policy are (Schedule 21, para. 4 of the CJA 2003):

(a) the murder of two or more persons, where each murder involves a substantial degree of premeditation or planning; the abduction of the victim, or sexual or sadistic conduct;

(b) the murder of a child if involving the abduction of the child or sexual or sadistic motivation;

(c) the murder of a police officer or prison officer in the course of his or her duty;

(d) a murder done for the purpose of advancing a political, religious, racial, or ideological cause;

(e) a murder by an offender previously convicted of murder.

There has been some doubt on whether whole life orders and whether they are compatible with the ECHR and this was primarily due to the ECtHR decision in *Vinter and Others* v *UK* (2013) Application Nos. 66069/09, 130/10 and 3896/10. It produced front page headlines such as 'Triple killer escapes whole life tariff because of European ruling' and incorrect reports that it diluted the sentencing powers of UK judges and meant life punishment was no longer available (*The Telegraph*, 21 October 2013). But the ruling contained no such prohibition and instead, a clearer exposition of the policy was required for the decision making on the possible release of whole life prisoners. The policy is contained in s.30 of the Crime (Sentences) Act 1997 and the Ministry of Justice's 'Lifer Manual' which only permits such releases if they comply with an 'exceptional circumstances' requirement. This requirement can also apply to a prisoner serving an *indeterminate sentence* (no release date has been set); it will be satisfied when (para. 12.2.1 of the PSO 4700 indeterminate sentence manual):

• s/he is suffering from a terminal illness and death is likely to occur (three months is the general guide) or s/he is bedridden or paralysed;

Then all of the following four issues have to be met:

• the risk of re-offending (particularly of a sexual or violent nature) is minimal;

• further imprisonment would reduce the prisoner's life expectancy;

• there are adequate arrangements for the prisoner's care and treatment outside prison;

• early release will bring some significant benefit to the prisoner or his/her family.

This detail contrasts clearly with the very broad wording of s.30 which merely states a Secretary of State can release a life prisoner on licence at any time, if there are exceptional circumstances justifying release on compassionate

grounds. The UK government argued in the *Vinter* case that this sentencing did not result in an irreducible life sentence (where there is no hope, possibility, or prospect of release) which has been found incompatible with Art. 3 by the ECtHR in 2008. This argument was not accepted and the case meant alterations to the policy were required. The government declined to amend the 'Lifer Manual' and instead the required changes emerged from the Court of Appeal's decision in the conjoined appeals of *R* v *Newell* and *R* v *McLoughlin* [2014] EWCA Crim 188. This confirmed the executive's duty to consider every application where a whole life order could be breaching Art. 3. The policy for 'exceptional circumstances' also had to recognise the principle of possible change in an individual in order to comply with the ECHR and avoid the imposition of *irreducible* sentences (see **What do you think? 21.1**).

This policy was subsequently accepted by the ECtHR in *Hutchinson* v *United Kingdom* (2015) Application No. 57592/08 where the application under Art. 3 failed against the imposition of a whole life order for a conviction for a triple murder, rape, and aggravated burglary. The horrific manner in which these crimes were committed plus the lack of exceptional factors in the case meant release could lawfully be denied. It confirmed that Art. 3 is not automatically breached when a person is required to spend the rest of their life in prison as a consequence of their offence.

A commitment to criminal justice responses that aimed to produce rehabilitation in offenders was the 'organizing principle' for government policy for most of the 20th century (Garland 2001: 35). But this priority was displaced in favour of the tougher attitudes that began to emerge in its latter decades—exemplified by the famous 'tough on crime, tough on the causes of crime' sound bite in the Labour Party's landslide election success in 1997. It is one of the most frequent criticisms of recent government policy that the second half of this sound bite, tough on the causes of crime, received minimal toughness compared with the first. This desire to be tough on crime has meant tenets of sentencing policy have been overridden—such as their imposition from an independent judge and punishments with a specified end point. These principles have been reduced by increases in the practices of *mandatory* and *indeterminate* sentencing. A mandatory sentence is one set by law and therefore not decided by a judge. Murder used to be the only offence that had to receive a mandatory life sentence but judicial discretion has now been restricted in a range of statutes over the last 20 years. According to the Power of Criminal Courts (Sentencing) Act 2000, a third class A drug trafficking offence has to result in at least seven years custody and for a third domestic burglary, a sentence of at least three years has to be imposed. The amended Firearms Act 1968 also has a statutory minimum sentence of five years' imprisonment for the

WHAT DO YOU THINK? 21.1

Should everybody be allowed the 'prospect of change'?

Despite the tension between the UK and the ECtHR over this sentencing practice, the use of whole life orders could have actually been strengthened by these claims, as now the courts have clarified the steps that need to be in place. But do you think it is inhumane to deny a person the right to a prospect of change? Or do you agree with the views that some crimes are so serious they are a just form of punishment?

How relevant are the views of people currently serving these orders? Consider for example, the opinion of Douglas Vinter from an investigation into an offence he was suspected of committing whilst he was in prison:

I can breach any laws I want, no matter how serious, and the law can't touch me. I'm above the law. I said to the governor, don't waste any money on investigations, just give me another life sentence for my collection. They don't mean anything any more.

Guardian, 5 December 2012

If you think whole life orders are a justifiable criminal justice practice, do you agree with the claim from Van Zyl Smit et al. (2014), that due process principles require everybody on whole life orders (51 people in September 2013) to receive some opportunities for rehabilitation as a part of their sentence?

Do you agree with the views from the perfectly-named Lord Chief Justice Judge that in 100 years' time (as we do with the past), society will be shocked at the levels of punishment handed out by the courts in the 21st century? (*Guardian*, 5 December 2012).

possession, purchase, acquisition, manufacture, transfer, or sale of certain prohibited weapons.

Indeterminate sentences, known as imprisonment for public protection (IPP) recently became increasingly common. These had no fixed term for the sentence but the practice was abolished by the Legal Aid, Sentencing and Punishment of Offenders Act 2012. However, this was not before around 6,000 people had been sentenced to an IPP, the terms of which still continue. They were replaced by extended determinate sentences which are aimed at violent or sexual offences and have a recommended period of time (a tariff) that must be served; after which there has to be an assessment, and if the person is still judged to be a danger, they can be kept in prison for a further eight years. The concept of a 'dangerous offender' was brought in by the CJA 2003 and the UK criminal process now has a range of provisions for prescribed minimum sentences for violent and sexual offences (for details on how these measures work, see Sprack 2014).

The disregard of modern principles through mandatory and indeterminate sentencing would have been disliked by the 'platonic guardians'; such measures would be a sign of weakness in the justice system. But in populist times instead of embarrassment these steps are deemed to be signs of strength that serve as 'emblems of political virility' (Pratt 2000: 131). Assumed popularity with the public is a key policy driver and the repeated claims for being on 'the public's side' invariably invoke tougher responses. In addition to the divisive effects from using 'sides' in policy, such methods seem self-defeating because if the public believe crime is increasing (despite the evidence suggesting otherwise) the harsher strategies will be seen as another failure in government policy.

There are other potential limits to the populist advance as seen in the countries that have not taken this route. These different examples can show this policy *not* to be an inevitable part of a society's development. In these jurisdictions it has been possible to maintain the authority of their judiciaries and their stronger political arrangements have resisted the seemingly unstoppable force of penal populism. There are other individual reasons why it has not taken route in countries such as Canada, Finland, and Germany (Pratt 2007), and China (Li 2015). The economic consequences of populism may be another limit in these legal systems and there is some irony in the strongest objectors to the financial costs coming from those who most strongly supported introduction of the harsher approaches two decades earlier. A sense of restraint, albeit one from economic coercion, could be returning to penal policy as even in 'hang 'em high' Texas it has been reported that prisons are being closed to not waste taxpayers' money (*The Observer*, 30 September 2012).

Strategies to reduce the use of imprisonment have to overcome the press and public's apparent deep support for this method of punishment. It may not be possible to defeat these feelings of attraction purely through rational arguments of economic costs and reoffending rates; in a populist age, to be a real game changer the responders 'must deal with the affective as well as the effective, with both the instrumental and sentimental aspects of penal policy' (Freiberg 2001: 266).

'Adversarial-lite' justice policy

Chapter 20 described some of the dilution of the strength of the UK's traditional leanings towards adversarial justice. Once again financial implications have been a dominant concern as seen in the *Review of Efficiency in Criminal Proceedings* (2015). This did not have the force of a Royal Commission like the Runciman Commission in 1993 or the type of review conducted by Lord Justice Auld in 2001; nonetheless its formation showed how seriously the matter is taken. The review of the efficiency and speed of the criminal justice system were its terms of reference and at its conclusion did not call for drastic changes; instead it recommended greater use of the courts' video and other conferencing technology. Its other recommendations concerned more flexible opening hours for the magistrates' courts and stricter controls of the courts' timetables and the responsibilities for avoiding delays to the system when transporting suspects.

The changes to the adversarial system were far more substantial in the policy for *Delivering Simple, Speedy, Summary Justice* launched in 2006 by the Home Office, the Department for Constitutional Affairs (now known as the Ministry of Justice), and the Attorney General's Office. The 'triple S agenda' had three separate parts but together demonstrated the policy imperative for a faster justice system. Therefore *simple* justice expects straightforward cases such as guilty pleas, to only require one court hearing. The abolition of the stage in the criminal process known as committal proceedings is an example of the desire for *speedy* justice. Committal hearings were required because whatever an offence's classification, they all begin at the Magistrates' Court; so for indictable and either way offences going to the Crown Court these cases had to be committed for trial at the higher court by the magistracy. These were opportunities to contest the evidence in the prosecution's case which could be dismissed if the court agreed there was no case to answer. These hearings could have the form of a 'mock trial' where witnesses would testify in the normal way. They were abolished in 2001 for indictable offences and were similarly ended for either way offences in 2013. It now means as soon as a case is deemed serious enough, it is sent straight to the Crown Court without the need for a committal hearing. The ability to contest a prosecution at this pre-trial stage represented a clear due process value (one of Packer's 'formidable impediments' to stop people unnecessarily taken through the process); but in recent times this one statutory right became restricted and so gradually decreased in importance.

Reducing the need for a court?

The summary element of 'triple S' policy should not be confused with a summary trial as this can also be the name for trials that take place in the Magistrates' Courts. Instead it refers to the range of options now available for dealing completely with a case *without* requiring the use of the courts at all. The police and Crown Prosecution Service (CPS) now have powers that have become more diverse as this kind of policy has progressed (see **Table 21.1**).

There are concerns that these powers amount to 'sentencing' but contravene the principles of open justice and due process as they are out of public view, made by relatively low level representatives of the police and the CPS with no independent judicial scrutiny. There is also the strong possibility that these out-of-court disposals are driven by the interests of economy not justice. The fact a conditional caution can result in 'punishing the offender' increases these fears (s.17(2) of the Police and Justice Act 2006). These extra options may also have net-widening effects as offenders who would otherwise have been dealt with informally ('a telling off') may now receive a formal disposal and be moved into the criminal justice system. The fact that cautions count as criminal convictions and can be cited in future court proceedings demonstrates their potential for harm, particularly if they have been awarded inappropriately.

Whilst the graph in **Figure 21.2** suggests a significant decline since the peak of issuing out of court disposals in 2007–08; the exclusion of the disposal for community resolutions (which in 2014–15 numbered almost 120,000) means little difference exists with the numbers from over a decade ago. There are plans to reform the options for the out of court powers listed in **Table 21.1** by the introduction of a two-tier system. Firstly, community resolutions will have a statutory footing and these disposals can be used by the police for minor offences if the victim and offender agree. It gives victims a say in how the offender should be dealt with and can result in an apology to the victim, the provision of reparation or paying financial compensation. It is proposed there will be a higher tier of response for more serious offences with the use of suspended prosecutions. These will allow the police to attach one or more conditions to the disposal for the purposes of reparation, rehabilitation, or punishment. If they are not complied with the individual may be prosecuted for the original offence.

Policy overview

This section has demonstrated the importance of policy on the work of the criminal justice system. These strategies can transform its key principles by endorsing other

Type of Power	Functions
1. Simple cautions	A simple caution is a formal warning given to an individual as a result of their offence. The police have the power to decide whether it is a suitable response (they can consult with the CPS) but they have to follow the guidelines from the Ministry of Justice. If it is an indictable offence then only the CPS can decide if is appropriate. It is possible to appeal to a court against the award of a caution and if successful the offence should be re-investigated There are three preconditions for the issue of a caution: • there must be sufficient evidence to prosecute; • the offender must admit his/her guilt; and • the offender must consent to the caution being given
2. Conditional cautions	These were introduced by the Criminal Justice Act 2003 and require the same three pre-conditions for use as simple cautions. They can be issued when the prosecutor believes reparation to the victim or rehabilitation of the offender will be best achieved by action from the offender (e.g. giving compensation to a victim or participating in treatment for substance misuse, etc.) Failure to comply with the agreed action in the conditional caution can lead to it being cancelled and the offender being prosecuted for the offence
3. Penalty Notices for Disorder (PNDs)	These are notices to an individual to pay an immediate fine (within 21 days) and were introduced in 2001. They were originally intended for cases of disorderly behaviour but can be used in minor cases of theft and criminal damage, wasting police time, or selling alcohol to a minor If the PND is paid then no further action is taken—if not, the fine can be increased and/or referred to the courts
4. Deferred PNDs	The payment of the PND is deferred (postponed) for a period of time where the offender agrees to comply with a set of conditions that aim to deal with the offending behaviour. If the agreement is kept then no payment will be required—if not, the offence can be referred to the courts
5. Fixed Penalty Notices (FPNs)	An FPN is a notice to pay a fine for both traffic and other offences. A recipient usually has 28 days to challenge it. A failure to pay can result in the fine being increased and/or a prosecution for the original offence. They can be issued by police officers, PCSOs, local authority authorised officers, parish councils, waste collection authorities, and the Environment Agency
6. Cannabis and Khat Warnings	These warnings have been available since 2004 and 2014 respectively. They can be issued to adults for possession of small quantities of these substances for personal use

Table 21.1 A summary of the out of court powers from 'the triple S' policy for adult offenders

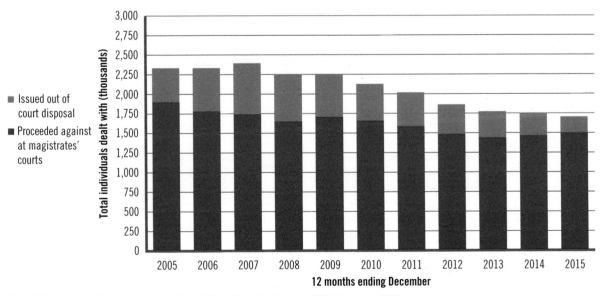

Figure 21.2 Out of court disposals issued, by disposal, 12 months ending December 2005 to December 2015

Source: Ministry of Justice, content available under the Open Government Licence v3.0

requirements such as the perceived political and economic advantages in responding to crime. The pressure for policies that reflect highly punitive values assumed to be popular with the general public does not have a convincing evidence base as there is much doubt on the accuracy of these assumptions. However, this has not prevented approaches of penal populism taking root and changing the game for policy by seeking to involve the public in matters which previously were the responsibility of experts in the field. Its creation of tough, 'common sense' approaches has a further contradiction in that their financial costs make them unsustainable. These conflicting policy imperatives demonstrate the unfeasibility of smooth progression through the '4Ps' of change in criminal justice. It is not only each successive 'P' (the 'cogs-in-the-wheel' of **Figure 21.1**) that offers resistance; as this criminal justice policies' section has shown, it can also come from within the cogs themselves.

Criminal justice practices

The criminal justice practices in this part of the chapter demonstrate the relevance of the earlier '4Ps' as they can be the product of the principles and policy discussed earlier. In this section, the use of general responses is considered first before two specific practices—unpaid work ('community service') and the procedure for admitting disputed confession evidence into court—are highlighted. These have been chosen because of their ability to demonstrate the effects of the earlier 4Ps and also because they are emblematic practices that demonstrate key values and intentions for the justice system.

The most dominant practice of recent years has been the increased use of imprisonment as record numbers of prisoners have been maintained despite formal criminal justice responses against individuals (including companies) standing at a record low. The 12 months of March 2014–15 saw the lowest total figure of criminal justice receivers in the period 1970 to 2015 with 1.72 million individuals proceeded against (Ministry of Justice 2015: 6). This would fit the similar record lows also being found by the Crime Survey for England and Wales (CSEW), although these measurements differ as MoJ totals are based on numbers of defendants with the CSEW providing totals of offences.

It is claimed the high levels of imprisonment are being maintained by increasing numbers of indictable offences coming before the courts and also the increasing numbers of offenders with more serious records. In 2015 it was calculated that 40 per cent such of adults who were convicted of an indictable offence had a long criminal record (classed as 15 or more convictions and cautions) compared to the quarter from ten years ago. (Ministry of Justice 2015: 19). However, the punitive direction of policy has meant the courts have been sentencing more offenders to prison each year and for longer average times—e.g. from 2012 to 2015 the average time served in prison by people serving determinate sentences increased from 14.5 to 16.3 months (see **Figure 21.3**, Ministry of Justice 2015: 1). This tougher drive has also included a decline in the parole release rate which has meant offenders serve longer periods in custody before they are released on licence. An increase in recalling people to prison has also contributed to the growth in the imprisonment response and this has followed the changes to the law that made recalls easier and the Criminal Justice Act 2003 which extended the licence period for most offenders.

See **Conversation 21.1** for a more in depth discussion of the issues surrounding these changes in the statistics and the possible impact.

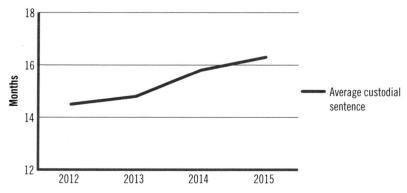

Figure 21.3 Gradual increase in the average custodial sentences from 2012–15

Source: Ministry of Justice (2015) Criminal Justice Statistics, content available under the Open Government Licence v3.0

CONVERSATIONS 21.1

Prisons and their potential as a criminal justice game changer—with Dr Peter Joyce

Are you are aware of the following facts?
In 2014, it was estimated that:

- 46 per cent of adults who were imprisoned were re-convicted within one year of release;
- the total cost of reoffending exceeded £10 billion a year.

Thus tackling reoffending (otherwise known as **recidivism**) is a key issue for the present government's criminal justice agenda.

But why do prisons find it hard to reform the habits of offenders?

One answer to this is that prisons are not the ideal environment to change any person's habits. You have probably read stories that idealise the conditions in prisons—three square meals a day, television, recreation facilities, and gymnasiums. You might think it is almost worthwhile breaking the law to get a stint in what amounts to a hotel. And at the end of your stay you don't have to pay the £36,000 per year bill that it has cost to keep you there!

However, the realities are somewhat different.

When put in prison, an individual loses the ability to make basic decisions which relate to the conduct of their lives and which you and I take for granted—when you can eat, when you can enjoy leisure time, who you can and cannot mix with, when you can go to the toilet, and when you can go to sleep. Persons in this position (especially those sentenced to lengthy terms of imprisonment) often find that this experience leaves them psychologically damaged—mentally a worse person on release than when they were first imprisoned. And possibly a brutalised and more violent person than they were formerly.

'But' you might say 'prisons provide all sorts of opportunities for prisoners to acquire skills that will enable them to get employment upon release'.

In theory, this is true and opportunities do exist. However, since the early 1990s (you may have read about Michael Howard's 'prison works' speech in 1993), the prison population increased. This led to overcrowding in which security assumes paramount importance over and above purposeful activities that might provide inmates with skills to enable them to find lawful employment upon release.

You may have read accounts of prisoners walking through the prison gates when released, expressing a genuine desire never to go back. Initially the experience of prison does deter many criminals from wishing to reoffend. However, their best intentions to 'turn straight' are often thwarted by the social problems that they experience which may include poor education, a history of alcohol and/or drug dependency, and homelessness.

They are also likely to find it hard to obtain work. The experience of being an 'ex con' is not a prized attribute that employers look for on a job applicant's cv. Finding legitimate employment is difficult—you may be aware that it's not that easy when you have a degree nowadays! With little money and no realistic job prospects a former prisoner may return to his or her life of crime, possibly making use of contacts made whilst serving a prison sentence (hence leading to the assertion that prisons constitute 'Universities of Crime').

So what should be done to transform prisoners into law-abiding citizens?

Charles Clarke (who was Home Secretary between 2004 and 2006) clearly saw the importance of tackling reoffending. His key reform to achieve this objective was the creation of the National Offenders Management Service in 2004 which placed the Probation and Prison Services under one organisational umbrella. It was designed to secure 'end-to-end offender management' which meant that rehabilitative work started in prison would continue in the community when an inmate had been released.

Tackling reoffending remained a key issue for the 2010–15 Coalition Government which introduced the Offender Rehabilitation Act 2014. Virtually all offenders receive at least 12-month's supervision in the community on release from custody.

A system of payment by results was also introduced. This was initially piloted in a small number of prisons and later extended to community rehabilitation companies that took over much of probation work in England and Wales. This meant that the money paid to the companies delivering correctional services would reflect the extent to which those who were subject to their supervision went on to reoffend.

The issues raised here can all affect the game changing potential of prisons but what kind of approach would you choose for tackling recidivism?

Dr Peter Joyce, Principal Lecturer in Criminology,
Manchester Metropolitan University

Community service: 'currying favour'?

Further conflict between the 4Ps in the development of criminal justice is the example of the practice of sentencing offenders to complete unpaid work as a condition of a community order. This response is a good vehicle for appreciating the effects of 'game changing through the 4Ps' because it has changed so much in the last half-century. However, despite being almost unrecognisable to the initial proposal from the Advisory Council on the Penal System (1970) it has maintained its place as the most 'popular' (numbers of orders made) community sentencing practice and also the most visible and supposedly understood. The original idea catered to different sentencing philosophies through a cautious approach subsequently described by Baroness Wootton (the chair of the Advisory Council's sub-committee) (see **Figure 21.4**) as 'an undisguised attempt to curry favour with everybody' (1978: 128).

Community service can be a criminal justice response with appeal to both the effective and affective dimensions discussed earlier; its consistent 'lower than prison' reoffending rates demonstrate its ability for the first. It has also been recognised for dealing with the second need but it will be considered later whether the 'wrong' emotions have been used (Maruna and King 2008). Originally the sentiment for the new restorative practice seemed positive and welcoming, despite it being almost unheralded as a standard practice for criminal justice. An example would be the report in the *Daily Mirror* of 16 January 1973 on the first person to be sentenced to community service, which described the offender as 'gentle and inoffensive' (Pease 1980: 32). It is unlikely that contemporary tabloids would use such a style but the original idea of community service attracted wide support for its game changing method of sentencing practice. Apart from occasional schemes in Germany and the USA it was a sentence unique to the UK and soon became the probation service's 'market-leader'

and grew rapidly into a recognised global practice (Harris and Lo 2002). This has led to public recognition where 'community service was for most thought to be the same as community sentencing' (Scottish Executive Social Research 2007: 13).

The practice has such flexibility that it has adapted to changes in policy attitudes (illustrated by the repeated changes in its official name) and still been able to maintain its position as one of the most frequent methods of disposal. The response of requiring offenders to perform compulsory work can mould to whatever penal environment is currently in favour; for example, if you subscribe to one of the three views below (and there is a good chance you will) then it is not hard to see why it has such appeal:

1. Rehabilitation should be an important principle of sentencing and this can be achieved from requiring unpaid work that seeks to provide benefits to an offender such as improved job prospects.

2. Reparation should be an important principle of sentencing and this can be achieved from requiring unpaid work that seeks to restore the harm caused by the offending behaviour such as work that benefits the community.

3. Retribution should be an important principle of sentencing and this can be achieved from requiring unpaid work that seeks to be deliberately unpleasant as a form of punishment such as work requiring hard physical labour.

This flexibility means that the same practice can simultaneously be very different things. This flexibility was emphasised as the key strength of the original proposal which allowed it to be supported by all of the three sentencing philosophies in (1)–(3) above (Advisory Council on the Penal System 1970: para. 33). In the evaluation of its original trials, it was noted for being 'a chameleon, which is able to merge into any penal philosophic background' (Pease et al. 1976: 1). However, is the characterisation of a 'chameleon' an adequate explanation for a sanction that can change so much? The variety of experiences that could flow from the three philosophies mentioned, suggest levels of variety and change in the sanction that run much deeper than superficial variations in skin colour. These changes can transform the sanction into a very different 'animal' and it is this adaptability which explains some of its success in becoming an accepted criminal justice response. A more satisfactory term for this extreme changeability would therefore be protean. This is a word with classical origins in the philosophy from the Ancient Greeks where to be protean was perceived as being a highly successful quality (Philostratus, 1.4 trans. Conybeare, 1960: 14).

Figure 21.4 Barbara Wootton, Baroness Wootton of Abinger
Source: © Illustrated London News Ltd/Mary Evans Picture Library

Community service: levels of sentencing

The Sentencing Council guidelines have some conditions for the use of the unpaid work requirement in order to reflect three levels of offence seriousness. Where it is considered low then 40–80 hours should be imposed; in medium cases the range is 80–150 hours; and, in cases of high seriousness the tariff is 150–300 hours. Apart from these general limits the practice can have many variations in the way it operates. It can differ radically according to things such as the types of work required, whether it has to be done in an individual or group placement; attitudes of supervisors and work organisers can also vary as may the possible relationships offenders have with the beneficiaries of their work. Despite these vagaries the current approach for the sanction is expected to provide:

> hard work for public benefit at the places and times the public can see it … Offenders will wear a uniform and undertake hard community work for several hours a day, with communities themselves directly identifying local projects.
>
> HM Government 2008: 3–4

The introduction of 'community payback' in 2005 required the delivery of unpaid work to focus on its visibility. This was originally deemed to be met by signs and plaques at the sites of the work projects that noted the offenders. but policy demands have extended this to include the wearing of high visibility jackets and the performance of the work at the times when the most number of people will be able to see it taking place (see **Figure 21.5**). The second aspect of community payback is an attempt to engage with the community by giving the public the right to vote for the type of work offenders should perform. Policy seeks to ensure wrong choices are not made as their options can be severely restricted. The nation 'got their say' on this matter in the 'Justice Seen, Justice Done' campaign of 2009 but out of the 270 short listed projects advertised on the government web site Directgov 238 of them required work involving one or more of the following: the clearance of dense overgrowth of trees and shrubs, a 'deep clean' of the project area, the removal of fly tipping, and the clearance of litter or graffiti. It was reported that 18,000 votes were cast and out of the 54 'winners' (one for each local probation area) only seven did not require this type of work.

Figure 21.5 Image taken from the Ministry of Justice UK's flickr account

Source: Ministry of Justice (Flickr)/CC BY-ND 2.0

The importance of visual images to community payback is further confirmed by 160 of the Directgov projects being accompanied by photographs. This type of initiative complemented community payback's presence on other popular and visual web sites such as Facebook, YouTube and flickr. Whilst the use of the Internet may make unpaid work appear to be a forward looking sanction, there is evidence to suggest that its effects on increasing community engagement are very small indeed (Johnson 2010).

The term 'payback' has always featured in the sanction's rationale, as the notion of offenders paying back the harm they had been deemed to cause was an integral part of the sanction's original principles. Whether this was directly to a victim or more broadly to general society to compensate for the financial costs of the crime, these reparative features were perceived as giving a new dimension to sentencing at a time when pessimism with the existing options was very common. The positive perception of what payback could involve was partly the reason why the proposal was so quickly enacted (in the Criminal Justice Act 1972) and then so frequently used by the courts. In these early stages it was hoped that offender-only work groups would be the exception and, wherever possible, offenders would work alongside non-offenders. Despite this hope not being realised, the importance of 'payback' persisted as demonstrated in the collection of community service's good practice from academics and criminal justice professionals entitled *Paying Back: Twenty Years of Community Service*. This publication also contained photographs of projects but these included offenders and the recipients of their work which was construed positively, and took place in a variety of community spaces such as nature reserves and adventure playgrounds. The work also involved close relationships with beneficiaries through tasks such as decorating or gardening for those in need; driving for, or attending to, people in need of care; general assistance in geriatric and psychiatric hospitals; supervising adventure playground activities; and running football teams (Whitfield 1993).

These tasks provided opportunities for offenders to attain new skills, to develop empathy with vulnerable members of society, or for acquiring a sense of responsibility; issues that were being simultaneously established as being beneficial in terms of recidivism (McIvor 1992). The extent of the good practice that was being revealed by research throughout the 1990s resulted in official policy requiring the sanction to be imposed through a method known as enhanced community punishment (ECP). This meant benefit for the offenders was prioritised as much as a punitive outlook (it used to be conceived as 'a fine on a person's time') and work projects were supposed to focus on issues such as offenders' skills

development, their relationships with the beneficiaries of their work, and the potential impact of the staff supervising the work. It was hoped that ECP would see an end to the routine nature of the required work, so neatly described in 1999 by the Howard League's *Do Women Paint Fences Too?* study of female offenders on community service.

The practice of ECP was a sign of the 'what works' policy for criminal justice but this was soon countered by the decisions to first exclude low risk offenders from its approach and then to replace it completely with community payback. An official inspection programme was critical of both ECP's financial costs and its practical experiences as 'some of the chosen tasks were poor in terms of capacity to engage offenders, e.g. litter picking and some graffiti removal schemes' (Home Office 2006: para. 3.39)—in other words, poor in relation to the community payback standard introduced 12 months earlier! In the last decade the term 'grot spot' has been used to explain some of the work that offenders will be expected to do. The public are therefore informed that the work is so unpleasant that no right thinking person would contemplate doing it. The 'painting fences' standard for renovating and gardening work seems replaced by a more physical type of experience that emphasises removing dense overgrowth and performing deep cleans. It is possible for large groups of offenders to perform this work as they can be in placed in groups of 10 offenders per supervisor as opposed to the maximum under ECP of six.

Paying back as retribution

Since the Criminal Justice Act 1991 there have been persistent policy calls for community sentences to become more rigorous and demanding. The manner in which community service practice has been changed from the ideals espoused by Baroness Wootton and the Advisory Council on the Penal System (1970) epitomises this approach. The emphasis of the original schemes on promoting reintegration by concentrating on reparation and rehabilitation has been displaced in favour of the new punitive outlooks. The retributive element to this response was initially deemed to be satisfied by the 'fine on a person's time' concept; however, developments such as the Casey Review have extended this punitive aspect by demanding a 'chain gang' approach where uniformed offenders undertake deliberately unpleasant work at 'grot spots'. Its recommendations for this retributive approach were in preference to reviewing the research findings on when the sanction might reduce reoffending from its receivers. The claim to be on the public's side was not supported with reliable evidence; instead over 30 angry complaints from individual members of the public were presented. The decision to cite one of these in particular illustrated the preferred policy direction for this sentencing practice:

> can we please stop saying 'unpaid work'? Every Tom, Dick and Harry in this room does unpaid work [fellow volunteers]. We are not criminals and I think we ought to get away from that flaming scenario.
>
> Cabinet Office 2008: 55

Due process in practice

The importance given to the principle of due process in the justice system is often said to shine brightest when confession evidence is presented at a criminal trial. This has meant a defendant's admission of guilt has long been seen as the 'gold standard' of evidence and has major probative value against a defendant particularly in the many cases where it is the only piece of evidence in the prosecution case. This can be obviously problematic if the confession is not true. This risk was recognised in the Fisher Inquiry (1977) which addressed the wrongful convictions of three teenage boys for the murder of Maxwell Confait in 1972. The boys had all made confessions in their police interviews but denied their truth at their trials where they were all convicted. The Court of Appeal found their trials unsafe and quashed the convictions. The changed position of the Birmingham Six as illustrated in **Figures 21.6** and **21.7** clearly demonstrates the changes in attitudes from the 1970s. They were sentenced to life imprisonment for the Birmingham bombings in 1974. Their convictions were later overturned by the Court of Appeal.

The Fisher Inquiry influenced criminal justice practices not just in relation to confessions but to treatment in a police station more generally. It pointed out flaws in the adversarial process as a contest between two equal parties and highlighted the need for more safeguards in the system. Its main recommendations were strengthening the right to consult with a solicitor, the recording of interviews (to stop the practice of 'verballing' where police officers could inaccurately attribute statements from a suspect), and special protections for vulnerable people held in police custody. The inquiry was followed by the appointment of the Royal Commission on Criminal Procedure (known as the Philips Commission) and the subsequent enactment of the Police and Criminal Evidence Act 1984 (PACE) and the Prosecution of Offences Act 1985. The latter of these statutes established

Figure 21.6 The battered faces of the Birmingham Six photographed three days after going into prison for the 1974 pub bombings that killed 21 people

Source: PA/PA Archive/Press Association Images

Figure 21.7 The Birmingham Six upon their release in 1991
Source: Sean Dempsey/PA Wire/Press Association Images

the Crown Prosecution Service to act as an independent prosecuting body; it took this responsibility from the police to introduce a check and balance into the adversarial system.

The importance of due process safeguards in PACE could be seen in its creation of statutory rights for everyone in police custody to have the right to have someone informed (s.56) and the right to access legal advice (s.58). However, the strength of these guarantees was diminished by provisions allowing the delay of both rights. This can lawfully happen if there are reasonable grounds to believe they could lead to interference with, or harm to, witnesses or other people; the alerting of other suspects; or they would hinder the recovery of the proceeds of crime. This giving, but then denying, of rights in PACE (and its official codes of practice) questions the influence of the due process principle in this main policing legislative framework.

In addition to the successful appeals for the Birmingham Six, the adversarial justice principle took more criticism in the late 20th century's other infamous miscarriages of justice cases such as the Guildford Four and the Cardiff Three. The numbers of people involved in the names of these cases is a simple but clear indication of the problem's extent which included the adversarial justice system's inability to manage the readiness of both the police and the CPS to secure a conviction. The allegations of evidence being tampered with and fabricated led to critiques of the whole adversarial system. These wider issues are beyond the scope of this part of the chapter which is focusing on the practices involved in using confession evidence at a criminal trial. Such practices have to recognise the problems such evidence can have; these can include whether they actually were made at all (the 'verballing' problem in unrecorded confessions), their legitimacy (they were made as a result of some kind of pressure), and their reliability (people can make false confessions for many reasons). As a result of these issues a detailed process has evolved which will allow the use of confession evidence if it complies with the 'OUTSEX formula' (see **Table 21.2**).

This process for regulating the problematic area of disputed confessions demonstrates the veneer at least of the principle of due process. However, despite these required steps there are many gaps in the

O	**Oppression**—s.76(2)(a) of PACE	Partially defined in s.76 and is said to occur if there has been a breach of authority or disregard of rules which *causes* the suspect to feel more oppressed than is inevitable from time spent in police detention *and* the investigators know they are acting improperly
U	**Unreliability**—s.76(2)(b) of PACE	Answered if anything said and done by the investigators could have the consequence of making the confession unreliable. The criminal justice system adopts the correct question as *not* whether the confession is true, but whether it was obtained as a result of anything likely to make it unreliable
T	**Trial-in-a-trial**	The Crown Court setting is the clearest for this process (often called a *voir dire*). It is a mini-trial but on a matter of law (e.g. admissibility) so the jury leave the court whilst it takes place. In a *voir dire* for a disputed confession the burden of proof is on the prosecution to establish it was not obtained in breach of s.76. They can take place in summary trials but as magistrates have the functions of both 'judge and jury' the process is not as clear as they can be required to disregard evidence they had just heard in deciding on its admissibility!
S	**s.78** of PACE	This is a general power of the judiciary to exclude any evidence which they deem would have an 'adverse effect on the fairness of proceedings'. It is a discretionary power and so there are few specific criteria as to when it can be used. But the power has to be used reasonably to comply with the rule of law (the common law principle of 'Wednesbury unreasonableness' and the 'proportionality' principle derived from the ECtHR). The potential circumstances for an adverse effect on proceedings' fairness can vary infinitely so s.78 applications tend to be dealt with on a case-by-case basis—e.g. cases where trickery produced a confession will generally be inadmissible
E	**Examination in chief**	The adversarial skills of a lawyer are important when dealing with confessions because even if they are ruled to be admissible by the trial-in-a-trial, their credibility can still be challenged before the jury
X	**Cross examination**	If the confession is presented in a credible way, will this part of the criminal process be its 'greatest legal engine ever invented' for discovering whether it was true?

Table 21.2 A breakdown of the due process principles in a criminal trial's use of confession evidence

protection—such as the partial definition of oppression and the very wide discretion in s.78 in deciding whether it would adversely affect the fairness of proceedings. The 'OUTSEX' prompt for remembering this example of due process has a bit of cheat with cross-examination as its last link—hopefully though it is an easy reminder of the depth and different stages, at a practical level, of the due process principle at work in the UK's adversarial justice system. Other examples of safeguards and similar staged approaches limiting police and prosecuting powers can be found across the system. The practice of using disputed confessions conflicts with the priority for accuracy of outcomes as in the double jeopardy changes because in this context their truth is immaterial. If a court believes that what was said and done contravenes the first three parts of 'OUTSEX', there is no discretion and it has to be excluded (*R v Kenny* [1994] Crim LR 284).

Having read this section you may find it interesting to read **Controversy and debate 21.1** on some specific cases where confession evidence was in dispute.

Practices overview

This part of the chapter has considered how criminal justice practices can be shaped in favour of the policy agendas held by the political and legal establishments. Change can occur quickly and so recognised practices, once supported by principles and policies, become very different entities. The two practices that formed the majority of this section were high profile criminal justice examples to illuminate their parts of the criminal justice field. The response of unpaid work ('CS' in its enduring name) illustrates how adaptability (being protean) can ensure a practice with some success. The controversy over the process for admitting confession evidence, demonstrates the conflict and uncertainty in criminal justice practices meeting the competing demands of the preceding parts of the '4Ps'. This doubt and ambiguity gives criminal justice practices a force of their own that can be another countervailing influence in a process of change.

CONTROVERSY AND DEBATE 21.1

The 'ticking bombs' and 'poisoned trees' of confession evidence

The *Gäfgen* case had similarities to the 'ticking bomb' ethical dilemma where the acceptability of using torture on an individual to prevent a bomb exploding that would otherwise kill thousands is the quandary. At the time they threatened *Gäfgen* with torture the police believed the boy was still alive, but surely his confession would be inadmissible under contemporary criminal justice principles? Even if it was possible to know that it would definitely work (which is probably impossible to know) it is still wrong to subject a human being to that kind of thing. To sanction torture would be an extremely worrying precedent. However what about the evidence it produces, should the 'fruits of its poisoned tree' be accepted?

In addition to moral reasons the law would surely have to exclude G's confession if it was in the UK's jurisdiction as under s.76 of PACE it would have been deemed acquired from oppression (the other parts of 'OUTSEX' would also have meant it was inadmissible). But this could mean that if G then stayed silent there would be no means of establishing the murder case against him. It surely would be unfair to allow evidence like this to be used against a defendant? What would it say about the values of criminal justice to allow this type of practice, especially if it produces the only evidence? The American legal doctrine 'the fruits of the poisoned tree' forbids the use of evidence where its source (the tree) is infected; as is the evidence it produces (the fruits).

In the UK there has not really been a problem in eating from rotten trees as there has been an accepted view that, 'It matters not how you get it; if you steal it even, it would be admissible' (as per Crompton J in *R v Leatham* (1861) 8 Cox CC 498 at p. 501). This 'by any means necessary' belief can have ominous consequences if the experiences of undercover policing in the Special Demonstration Squad (1968–2008) are recalled. This was the motto of this investigatory unit and led to undercover police officers stealing the personal details of deceased children to construct fake identities, forming sexual relationships, and fathering children with those under suspicion, trying to discredit the family of Stephen Lawrence, and being an author of the 'McLibel leaflet' which led to the longest civil trial in British history (10 years!) that cost millions of pounds to McDonald's and the two members of London Greenpeace who they were suing for libel (Evans and Lewis 2013). Obtaining truth at-all-costs is not meant to apply to confessions as according to their statutory and common law principles, their admissibility is supposed to depend on the way things are done, *not* whether they are true or false.

The German court did not allow Gäfgen's confession to be admitted but did allow the evidence it obtained (the boy's body and the tyre tracks from the defendant's car at the lake where the body was found). At his trial, for reasons unknown, Gäfgen decided to fully confess again despite being aware of his right to silence and the inadmissibility of his previous confession.

At the ECtHR it was accepted that Art. 3 had been breached, although it was classed as degrading treatment and not torture. If it had been deemed torture it would have been automatically unfair and contrary to Art. 6 to allow it (and the evidence it produced) to be used at trial. However, as it was deemed degrading treatment then the law was deemed to be more flexible and its use would not be a breach of the right to a fair trial under Art. 6. The Grand Chamber (the highest part of the ECtHR) comprised 17 judges and they unanimously agreed that Gäfgen's rights under Art. 3 had been breached; but in his claim under Art. 6, 11 judges considered it not to have been infringed with six dissenting. The majority held the potential breach did not have a bearing on the outcome of the proceedings as Gäfgen's conviction could be based on the confession he subsequently made at his trial. Although the fact this second confession may have been made as a result of the court allowing the physical evidence of the body and the tyre marks was not considered.

According to the view of the majority, the use of any evidence acquired from breaching Art. 3 is not automatically a violation of Art. 6. It therefore suggests the 'fruits of the poisoned tree' taste very differently according to which side of the Atlantic they are grown.

People in criminal justice

This part of the chapter is by far the shortest as the influence of people (the responders and receivers) in criminal justice has been discussed throughout the three preceding aspects of the '4Ps'. The combined might of principles, policies, and practices could suggest little possibility exists for people having an impact, but this is far from being always the case. In the example of community service and the early days of the restorative justice principle, it was the efforts of individual people such as Barbara Wootton and the people in the six probation areas of the country where it was first piloted, that created this now established criminal justice response (Pease et al. 1976).

It is the people, as criminal justice professionals, that have the power to provide the link in the chain between principled approaches and actual practice. People involved with the justice system have the ability to complete the '4Ps' process as the last cog-in-the-wheel. It can offer some ultimate power as a criminal justice game changer but the support of the criminal justice responders is a must for policies aiming for effective practices as individually and collectively, consciously and unconsciously, they can resist the pressure to work in the desired new direction. An example of this kind of resistance was provided by a police detective in research investigating new methods for overseeing policing:

> We have a saying, which I probably shouldn't say ... but it's FIDO, and I don't know if you know what *FIDO* means? Well, '*Fuck It, Drive Off*'. Yeah, and that's exactly what happens.
>
> Campeau 2015: 681, emphasis added

You are presumably already familiar with this type of influence the police can have in relation to crime from the preceding chapters in this book. The making of FIDO-type decisions to overlook conduct and incidents can clearly affect the work of the justice system and if its different parts each have their own 'pet FIDO', the power of the people could be significant.

Despite this influence there are many times when the force of principles, policies, and practices demolish professional interests and inherently change the nature of the criminal justice response. For example, if you had graduated in the 1980s, joined the probation service straight from university and then worked in that role for 30-plus years, your type of criminal justice work might be similar, but many changes in the way it is done will have been required. At the start of your career was the traditional probation aim for 'reaching not breaching' offenders (Bale 2000). This meant the common professional standard was not to take swift formal action (a breach) against an offender for not complying with their community sentence. However, the reluctance to make this kind of response seems to have been overcome by a barrage of policies and practices

typified in the Criminal Justice Act 2003 that creates a presumption for custody following a second unacceptable breach of a community sentence. It means 'breaching not reaching' could be the new mode of working as in the penal populist era and higher enforcement rates have been clearly apparent. It has been so significant that it has had a major effect on the increased prison population from the levels of the 1990s (Ministry of Justice, 2013). It has been estimated that between 1995–2009, 16 per cent of the increase in the prison population was down to changes in enforcement measures from probation officers (Fox et al. 2013: 18).

Merging criminal justice principles and policy practice on people

An effect of the refashioning of accepted principles and the policies for responding to crime, as discussed in the first two parts of this chapter has been the evolution of many new ways of working for criminal justice practitioners. These have included 'polibation officers' where fusion of police and probation roles signifies the tougher policy for probation work (Nash 1999). This is another example of the importance of adaptability for criminal justice professionals. It also highlights the importance of being able to work in partnerships. These arrangements illustrate the desire for a united system of justice that joins up its different parts and creates better methods of response. It may now be a common criminal justice practice but problems can arise if partnerships are coerced or unequal; this could mean contributions from distinctive players in the 'justice game' are lost. The dynamic nature of criminal justice has meant the 'polibation' fears for the loss of the probation service's voice, have been reduced with the newer role of 'Integrated Offender Management police officers', where policing appears the much less dominant partner (Annison et al. 2015).

These subtle changes to criminal justice polices, practices, and people make for some fascinating research opportunities for you as an undergraduate. **Chapter 20** raised the benefits of ethnographic research and the increased understanding it brought for the role of the police. **Conversation 21.2** with Dr David Scott illustrates the benefits of going out into the world and talking to people. The research project he discusses was ethnographic in its approach and explains the insight you can get from this type of activity. It is also included to show we are all initially novices but by having a go and doing things, we develop the attributes to be able to do them in

CONVERSATIONS 21.2

Researching community policing and critical criminology—with Dr David Scott

The best way to engage with critical analysis is to actually undertake a piece of ethnographic research. This is the method of qualitative research that seeks to study diverse social groups or cultures from the perspective of the research subjects. I'm going to briefly discuss here my first research project, now more than 20 years ago, on community policing in Lancashire and how it helped me develop my ideas as a critical criminologist.

Doing an in-depth research project is helpful because it gives you a chance to learn new things and to see the world from a completely different perspective. Through questioning and listening to another person (research participant) you can start to see the world through their eyes. The criminal process is a largely hidden world and the working practices and cultures of magistrates, police officers, prison officers, probation officers, and other occupational groupings are largely closed to those on the outside. The same is true for the lived experiences and culture of prisoners and some groups of lawbreakers. Doing a piece of ethnographic research can provide a detailed understanding of a given role in the criminal process and how people adapt (or fail to adapt) to its specific demands and requirements.

The first piece of ethnographic fieldwork I undertook was on community policing in Lancashire whilst I was an undergraduate student on a BA (Hons) Applied Social Sciences and History degree. I had read widely on the history of policing and was well aware of critical theories that questioned the idea that 'the police are the public and the public are the police'. I wanted to uncover whether community policing was about consensus policing, or if it was the 'velvet glove' covering the state's 'iron fist'.

Studies of policing had historically found that people who had the most contact with police officers—largely people from socially excluded backgrounds—held the lowest opinions of the police. There were also many concerns expressed at the time that 'community police officers' were being used as means of gleaning surveillance: community bobbies were the wolves in sheep's clothing. In addition, the academic literature indicated that many police officers were hostile to the 'social work' emphasis on community policing and that many were reluctant to undertake such duties. These three themes formed the basis of the studies research questions. Methodologically, I undertook surveys with 300 people in three different areas of South Lancashire—Ormskirk, Burscough, and Skelmersdale—with each of the areas chosen because of their different socio-economic contexts. Alongside this I undertook observations, including joining the police officers on their community beats in the three police districts, and held structured interviews with numerous community police officers.

The findings were revealing. In line with previous research, perceptions of the police in the district with the highest social exclusion produced the lowest pro-police scores. The community police officers interviewed were open about their real role: the policing practices in Skelmersdale were 'worlds apart' from the rest of the region and this area was the 'thorn in the bum of the county'. In the most deprived area community police officers 'were laughed off the estate' and some members of the community 'would sooner stab a community officer in the back than talk to him [sic]'. As such, I was told how school liaison trips by community officers could turn into covert surveillance operations where the officers asked questions about the recent movements of the children's parents in the area. Community police officers recognised that they were 'bottom of the pile' and that most police officers 'don't want to walk around' on the beat. The police service in Lancashire demonstrated its commitment to community policing by moving designated officers off their beats to fill in mobile patrols as and when required. Furthermore, it was clear that certain groups of people—those who were from Liverpool—were considered by the police as a problem. Officers talked about 'the scouse problem'; that 'all scousers are thieves'; and that 'Liverpudlians come here to commit crime'.

The long term value of undertaking the ethnographic study on policing was immeasurable. I was given the opportunity to hear and see things first hand. The literature came alive and I was able to experience what I had previously only read about. I was able to connect the critical literature to actual practice and as a result this considerably deepened my understanding of existing critical scholarship.

This research became a pilot study for the 1997 West Lancashire District Council 'Crime and Fear Survey' and though much of my subsequent fieldwork has been on prisons, this experience of ethnography gave me the skills and confidence to pursue the critical analysis of other state institutions and those who work for them.

Dr David Scott, Senior Lecturer in Criminology,
Liverpool John Moores University

other situations. Further guidance for creating your own research journey is provided in **Chapter 28**.

Contemporary criminal justice professionals now have a much greater chance of coming from the private sector as, in addition to the increasing levels of privatisation in the prison system and the ending of the state's monopoly of probation services, it has been reported the police have been recently outsourcing to the private sector 'on an unprecedented scale' for many of its key services areas (White 2015: 284). This practice may help with the financial costs of the 'big 3' criminal justice game changers that create concerns for their poorer quality of services and lower staffing levels. Although conversely it is argued this could result in a smaller and cheaper criminal justice system with reductions in crime as well (Howard League for Penal Reform 2015).

The criminal courts clearly merit a place as a potential game changer as their decisions are the pinnacle of the process. The strength of the independent judiciary principle (the first part of the chapter) was shown to mean that policies alone cannot force them to act in a certain way; their support is therefore essential for criminal justice change. Their constitutional position and need to be impartial traditionally restricts judges from airing their views; this could be changing thanks to the ground breaking work of the 2014 Judicial Attitude Survey. This was the first survey ever conducted with all serving salaried judges in the United Kingdom and its extremely high response rates (100 per cent in some areas) would suggest it is a credible measure of judicial views. As appears now customary for potential game changers, this research demonstrated considerable fears for declining working conditions, but to the extent that an overwhelming number are considering leaving the judiciary early (Thomas 2015).

If judges and magistrates do not have confidence in criminal justice practices that seek to reduce the number of prison sentences they will continue to imprison those found guilty of an offence in their courts.

As you know there have been many attempts to encourage the judiciary to make less use of imprisonment but the figures in **Figure 21.8** demonstrate it is still used in similar proportions. The declining use of community sentences corresponds with the increasing use of the tougher suspended sentence orders. Despite the many attempts to create change, the lack of movement over this 10 year period seems clear. They show that an immediate custodial sentence for an indictable offence was given in almost three out of four convictions and this figure has also stayed pretty constant. Out of those sentenced to immediate custody, around one in three received a sentence of three months or less. This is despite the years of complaints about the futility of such short term sentences (their reoffending rates) and the damage they can do in terms of a prisoner's employment, family, and housing situations. It is in these cases where different practices need to be accepted if reductions in the prison population are to be achieved and not for those lower down the pecking order of crimes.

Whilst there are problems with people still receiving short-term sentences (less than 12 months) there are also problems at the other end of the spectrum as there are more people serving life and indeterminate sentences in England and Wales than in all of the other 46 countries in the Council of Europe combined. The delays in the parole system and a lack of access to work, education, and courses to show readiness for release means large numbers of people are serving more time in custody than intended (Howard League for Penal Reform 2015).

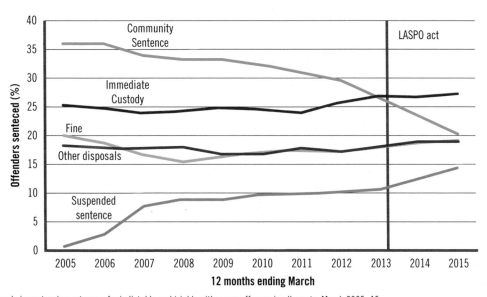

Figure 21.8 Trends in sentencing outcomes for indictable and triable-either-way offences in all courts, March 2005–15

Source: Ministry of Justice, content available under the Open Government Licence v3.0

SUMMARY

After working your way through the different features of this chapter you should now be able to:

• Identify the changing influence of criminal justice policy including penal populism

The chapter opened with an invitation for you to consider the 'wheels of justice' image in **Figure 21.1**, this depicted the flowing process of criminal justice change from the '4Ps'. This had all four central cogs (principles, policies, practices, and people) travelling in the same direction. This chapter sought to help you question whether such widespread agreement exists in such a large and complex field as criminal justice. The influence of penal populism has meant policy responses can be predominantly guided by their perceived public popularity. The influence of policy was also shown to have reshaped the adversarial justice principle into a diluted version where justice has been increasingly delivered without the need for a formal court hearing.

• Assess the effects of policy on selected criminal justice practices, such as community payback

These punitive intentions have had a substantial impact on the attitudes behind community sentencing practices. This was seen by the changed nature of 'payback' in community sentencing, where their reparative features have been displaced by a rationale for providing far more retributive experiences. The interconnectedness of the '4Ps' was shown to affect other criminal justice practices such as the process required when the prosecution seek to use a disputed confession at court; this showed how principles such as human rights and due process can be converted into approaches that seemingly contravene the very ethos of the original concept.

• Examine the influence of criminal justice professionals in the delivery of criminal justice

This potential influence was noted by ethnographic research which is capable of shining light on how people involved in criminal justice practices perceive their work. The fusion from the competing principles, policy, and practices was seen to result in new roles for criminal justice professionals and increasing numbers of different service providers. The influence of the sentencers in the Crown Courts and Magistrates' Courts was shown to be capable of thwarting the hopes of criminal justice policies and practices.

• Engage with the 4Ps process (principles, policies, practices, and people) for changing the game in criminal justice

In any system of gears (interconnected factors) things cannot move forward when one cog-in-the-wheel works against another. This problem was considered for the restorative

Figure 21.9 Obstructing the 'wheels of justice' through the 4Ps?

justice principle; as despite the considerable support being peddled for it, this 'cog' has been unable to generate sufficient momentum to overcome the forces of the other Ps in changing criminal justice. The image in **Figure 21.9** is arguably a more accurate representation of the 'wheels of justice' as this illustrates the lack of possible change when conflicts arise between criminal justice principles, policies, practices, and people. As a critical thinker about the criminal justice system you are now aware of the extensive force required from a genuine criminal justice game changer.

REVIEW QUESTIONS

1. Why is it claimed that penal populism has changed the role of the public in the making of criminal justice policy?

2. How have the policies for out-of-court disposals affected the principle of adversarial justice?

3. Why can the sanction of unpaid work (formerly known as community service) be said to have protean qualities? Do you know of other punishments that share this characteristic?

4. What does due process require for admitting disputed confession evidence in a criminal trial?

5. What is the role of a polibation officer?

6. How successful were the strategies in 2005–15 for reducing the numbers of short-term prison sentences? Why do you think this was the case?

FURTHER READING

Ashworth, A. and Redmayne, M. (2010) *The Criminal Process*. Oxford: Oxford University Press.
This is a detailed account of the different elements in the criminal process and is supported by critical analysis of relevant legislation and case law. It makes the case for the criminal justice system to base its work on a framework of human rights to overcome the limitations in the other models.

Johnstone, G. (ed.) (2013) *A Restorative Justice Reader*. Abingdon: Routledge.
This is a selection of authoritative sources on restorative justice's practices, philosophies, evaluations, and critical issues. The Reader format means introductions from the editor plus key journal articles or extracts from books are provided for each of these four themes.

Pratt, J. (2007) *Penal Populism*. Abingdon: Routledge.
This book contains numerous national and international examples of populist criminal justice responses. It investigates the possible causes of penal populism and analyses why countries such as Germany, Finland, and Canada have avoided this approach to criminal justice.

Scott, D. (2016) *Emancipatory Politics and Praxis*. Bristol: EG Press.
This is an anthology of essays from members of the European Group for the Study of Deviance and Social Control. This group was founded in 1973 and has since grown across six different continents to become the largest critical criminology forum in the world. This new collection of essays, particularly its second and third parts, builds directly on the critical issues raised in this chapter.

 Access the **online resources** to view selected further reading and web links relevant to the material covered in this chapter.
www.oup.com/uk/case/

CHAPTER OUTLINE

Introduction   600

What is crime prevention?   600

Alternative perspectives on crime prevention   608

Politics, interest groups, and crime prevention   613

Models of practice in crime prevention   616

What does prevention achieve?   619

Consequences of crime prevention   621

Limitations of crime prevention   624

Crime prevention

Ideas and practices

KEY ISSUES

After reading this chapter you should be able to:

- discuss the arguments in favour of taking a preventive approach to criminal justice;

- appreciate the implications of crime prevention for different stakeholders, including potential victims, potential offenders, communities, politicians, interest groups, and others;

- recognise the implications and effects of different approaches to preventing crime;

- consider and assess the evidence base in support of preventive measures;

- evaluate the theoretical dimensions of perspectives on prevention;

- examine the critical arguments questioning the aims and effectiveness of crime prevention strategies, including a consideration of escalation, adaptation, and displacement.

Introduction

Although this chapter sits inside the 'Responding to crime' part of the book, crime prevention occupies a very different position to other perspectives, which focus exclusively on the consequences of offending. A preventive approach is proactive, rather than reactive, and is based on the assumption that crime is to a great extent predictable, and can therefore be avoided by taking precautionary steps in advance. Preventive strategies therefore represent an approach concerned less with dispensing justice, but rather with minimising the risk of crime being committed in the first place. Preventing a crime being committed in the first instance could save emotional or physical distress for victims, sanctions for offenders, and time and resources for the criminal justice system.

Crime prevention strategies incorporate a number of beliefs about the predictability, origins, and motivations of human behaviour; and at the same time, judgements are made about which interests should be prioritised in pre-empting criminal actions. Crime prevention strategies draw on assumptions about predictability and human motivation to develop evidence-based interventions. However, critical analysis suggests that these can also have diverse and sometimes problematic consequences. Because of this, crime prevention may be seen as less obviously straightforward and desirable than at first sight, and more complex and uncertain in both its aims and effects; and therefore similarly more open to criticism, as this chapter concludes.

The first section of this chapter will explore the notion and definitions of crime prevention strategies. We will be looking at the factors which may influence decision making concerning which crimes to try and prevent, and we will also be considering the objectives of crime prevention in relation to three main areas: potential victims, potential offenders, and 'risky' places or criminogenic situations. The complexity of decision making in this area will be considered as you will be asked to put yourself in the position of a local politician making difficult tough choices. The section will end with a brief overview of the emergence of crime prevention strategies and an exploration of the framework proposed by Brantingham and Faust.

The second section will move on to consider alternative perspectives on crime prevention covering social crime prevention and situational crime prevention, potential offenders (in light of deterrence and diversionary approaches), potential victims, and the concept of community safety and well-being. The implications of crime prevention strategies and approaches will be explored in relation to other key stakeholders including politicians and interest groups.

The chapter will then outline some major models of practice in crime prevention, including the rational choice perspective, and routine activity theory before considering crime prevention in action in the shape of the influential Kirkholt project. Ultimately the chapter will conclude with a critical analysis around what preventative methods actually achieve in practice, and the consequences and limitations of crime prevention.

What is crime prevention?

The Crime and Disorder Act 1998 (s.37(1)) incorporated as one of its key elements the stipulation that:

> It shall be the principal aim of the youth justice system to prevent offending by children and young persons.

Although this requirement related specifically to youth crime, it captured the sense of how important prevention had become as a feature of the criminal justice agenda in the late 1990s. There had been a growing conviction that, with the right technology effectively used, with relevant expertise and with sufficient resources, crime could largely be anticipated and thus prevented. For Tilley (2002: 15), this was essentially the height of a movement to place crime prevention 'centre-stage', as it became increasingly clear that other strategies to tackle persistently high levels of crime were failing to address public concerns: 'Punishment did not appear to deter; confidence in treatment had disappeared. In relation to criminology, "Nothing works" … had become the dominant orthodoxy'. As Tilley pointed out,

there were other developments which fuelled a belief in the potential value of crime prevention as the core strategy for tackling crime. These included the increasing availability of knowledge and expertise to help understand the drivers of crime, as well as a growing recognition of the threat to social cohesion associated with 'fear of crime' (Lee 2007). There was also desire on the part of government to cut the costs of a very expensive justice system.

In addition to these influences on beliefs and policy in the public domain, crime prevention—to many—simply makes sense as an idea. For virtually everyone, the thought of being able to live safely without coming to harm or losing property through criminal actions is a powerful aspiration. As a consequence, we might also all agree on the desirability of measures which offer a greater degree of certainty of achieving this goal. And, even if crime itself cannot be eradicated, a reduction of popular fears about its incidence and impact appears to be an almost equally desirable objective for many.

Crime prevention strategies

Crime prevention strategies are organised around the belief that crime and its causes can be understood and that, in turn, appropriate measures can be taken to eradicate crime (or certainly substantially reduce its frequency) based on this knowledge. Of course, behind this belief are the further assumptions that we can identify those at risk, that the causes of crime are capable of being quantified; and that we can then identify effective measures to be put in place based on this knowledge. Clearly, if it is possible to anticipate the occurrence of crime with any degree of certainty, then it seems to make sense to use what means we can to ensure that it is prevented.

In everyday terms, we can equate this to the actions we might take to avoid children running into a busy road. In this instance, we would probably expect to combine: education about the potential dangers; risk mitigation by keeping young children away from the road; risk management in the sense of controlling their movements; and direct action by restraining them at the point of crossing the road (see **Figure 22.1**). Even in this context, there are a number of factors to consider and a number of different strategies which could be deployed. But of course most situations in which crime might occur are not as easy to identify or 'read' as this example. Likewise, our knowledge of what constitutes a practical or effective preventive measure may also be limited.

Despite this, the idea of being able to prevent crime 'at source' is highly attractive, and so considerable emphasis has been placed on this as a desirable objective, and similarly a great deal of time and money has been invested in discovering what is effective in reducing the likelihood of crimes being committed. Tilley (2002: 14), for example, has identified 37 separate 'key developments' in crime prevention policy and practice in the UK from 1976–2001. Prominent amongst these were the initiation of the British Crime Survey in 1983, the Safer Cities programme in 1988, the Morgan Report on 'Safer Communities' in 1991, and the Crime and Disorder Act 1998 with the prevention of crime explicitly becoming the cornerstone of criminal justice policy at this point.

Crime prevention then, appears to be inherently desirable as an objective. But this leads us to acknowledge the need to unpack the concept itself, since it is certainly not as simple as it might appear. Firstly, there arises the question of just what it is that we might wish to prevent. 'Crime', might well be the obvious answer, but even this inevitably leads to further questions. Which crimes should be targeted? All of them? Or should we prioritise certain crimes, and if so, how? Crimes of violence? Racist crimes? Only the most serious crimes, however they are defined? Should we direct our energies towards

Figure 22.1 Actions we may take in order to prevent crime

stopping offenders committing crimes or ensuring potential victims are better protected against the risk of harm and therefore less fearful as they live their everyday lives? Should we rely on official definitions of crime or the perceptions and experiences of crime held by communities?

As we know, the extent of crime goes well beyond what is officially recorded, and also merges with other types of problematic behaviour, such as bullying in schools and the workplace, antisocial behaviour, harassment, and even violence in sport. A global prevention strategy would thus need to be very extensive, and very expensive, and it would probably still be unable to cover all the areas which a broad definition of crime would comprise (Tilley 2002: 17):

> Crime in general is complex, with many features, causes, motivations and conditions … it will not be possible for any agency on its own successfully to address all aspects of all crime prevention problems.

Importantly, this observation suggests that crime prevention is not just a matter for criminal justice agencies, but needs to incorporate a much wider range of organisations and interests if it is to be properly targeted and have any chance of being implemented successfully. Stopping crime is a matter for everyone, it seems.

When making choices about how to approach prevention, though, we are still faced with a number of dilemmas when it comes to determining its practical 'face', and deciding which crimes should be prevented. One option would be to base our decisions on certain thresholds or qualifying criteria, so that only certain types of crime or harms are to be prioritised. Firstly, of course, we would need to establish a basis for making this kind of judgement. Should we concentrate on individual crimes of violence, for example, that is those acts having the most significant effect on the people affected? Or should we base our decisions on the principle of minimising wider disruptions to community life, which may be less harmful in individual cases, but cause more misery overall such as acts of damage to communal property? Or maybe we should concentrate our efforts on minimising the harm and losses caused to business and commercial interests in order to avoid the risk of damaging the local economy, with the consequences that might involve? In effect, the underlying question here is which potential victims' interests should be given preference? It quickly becomes apparent, then, that the outcome of this kind of moral and ethical choice will have a significant impact in terms of the form and content of preventive strategies and practices. Try the exercise in **What do you think? 22.1** to better understand the sort of decision that a local politician might be faced with.

Linked to these considerations is a further series of questions to do with the targets of prevention; that is to

WHAT DO YOU THINK? 22.1

If you were a local politician and member of a community safety partnership, you might find yourself having to make this sort of choice concerning the allocation of limited financial resources.

Imagine, for example, that you had to make a choice between committing police officers and other resources in response to one of the following scenarios:

- Anti-social behaviour in your town or city centre on a Saturday night which has resulted in damage to buildings and other public property, with individuals involved in an affray.

- A sexual attack on an individual in a park that has taken place in a usually quiet and safe neighbourhood.

Which of these situations would you prioritise? What are the implications of this? How do you think other interested parties might respond to your decision?

say where preventive work should be concentrated to achieve the most effective results. There are at least three potential focal points where such efforts might be concentrated (see **Figure 22.2**):

(a) criminogenic ('risky' situations);

(b) potential offenders ('risky people'); and,

(c) vulnerable groups or communities ('at risk' people).

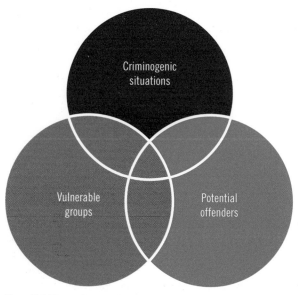

Figure 22.2 Three main areas where crime prevention strategies could be focused

These three classifications will be revisited in the course of this chapter. Examples falling within each category come to mind quite readily, such as:

(a) late night drinking zones in city centres;

(b) drug users with expensive addictions;

(c) children from care at risk of sexual exploitation.

Whilst there may also be significant interplay between contexts and populations at risk from crime, these are just examples of a very wide range of possibilities when it comes to the potential for crime to take place. This breadth of possibilities, in turn, helps to highlight considerable variations in the way we might understand the issue of crime prevention, depending on the stance taken towards the problem. **Figure 22.2** illustrates three main areas where crime prevention strategies could be focused, yet as you can see these are not distinct from one another, they also overlap. Can you list some additional examples for each of these areas not provided in the list earlier?

The objectives of crime prevention

The idea of 'crime prevention' has already become more problematic than it might have appeared at first; and this is further complicated when we think more deeply about how we might put the concept into practice. From the start, there are differences of opinion as to whether crime prevention activities should concentrate their attention on victims, offenders, or the combinations of circumstances which create the conditions for crime to occur. The growing emphasis on the needs and rights of victims of crime (and potential victims) might, for instance, lead to the conclusion that we should prioritise high risk groups and introduce measures to protect them in the first instance. Even here, there is a distinction to be made between those most 'at risk' of being victimised (typically, young men, for example), and those who are most worried and potentially most adversely affected in the event of becoming victims. We will now look at each of the three areas in **Figure 22.2** in more detail.

Fear of crime: vulnerable groups

Fear of crime amongst older people is one well-recognised area of concern. Concerns have been quite widely expressed about the self-limiting responses of some sectors of the population to the possibility of being affected by crime. Older people, for instance, may decide not to go out at night, and this may have an effect in terms of reducing the risk of victimisation somewhat, but at the expense of restricting their freedoms and diminishing

the quality of life they are able to enjoy (Chakraborti et al. 2011: 34).

As this study goes on to observe, though, concentrating on the needs and wishes of victims (or potential victims) is not straightforward:

> When you're talking about someone who is elderly or with a disability, trying to get them to understand that they are being targeted and it is a hate crime is difficult. It's getting people to understand that they shouldn't suffer.
>
> Local Authority representative quoted in
> Chakraborti et al. 2011: 34

And there is also the risk that concentrating efforts on those most fearful of crime may exacerbate their fears rather than allaying them.

'Nipping crime in the bud': potential offenders

Alternatively, it might make sense to target those believed to be most likely to commit crime—although, as with 'victim' groups, there are clearly a considerable number of sub-categories of this population as well. Thus, 'within group' targeting and prioritisation is likely to be required. So, for example, whilst young people in general may be seen as liable to get involved in crime and antisocial behaviour, anticipatory interventions might be geared toward selective means of prevention (Prior and Paris 2005: 8):

> of the onset of criminal and anti-social behaviour amongst children who have not previously exhibited such behaviour and the prevention of the escalation of anti-social behaviour from minor to more serious levels.

The corresponding problem here is the basis on which such categorisations are decided and whether or not this effectively builds discriminatory assumptions and practices into the crime prevention agenda.

Risky places: criminogenic situations

Finally, preventive measures could seek to prioritise those situations and circumstances where crime is believed to be more likely, apparently irrespective of the identity of either perpetrators or victims. This approach is normally based on the application of prior knowledge of patterns of crime and the use of a variety of predictive tools to identify 'real world' risks associated with known features of the lived environment. The aim is to reduce the potential for crime to take place in contexts which are known to be criminogenic. So, an approach which focuses on the geography of crime rather than crime-prone populations, such as the strand of work associated with *'situational' crime prevention* (see also **Chapter 23**):

> departs radically from most criminology in its orientation…. Proceeding from an analysis of the circumstances giving rise to specific kinds of crime, it introduces discrete managerial and environmental change to reduce the opportunities for those crimes to occur.
>
> Clarke 1997: 2

In each case, though—looking at potential victim, potential offender, and potential situation—there are common challenges en route to achieving the goal of effective crime prevention. These are linked to developing the tools and techniques necessary to do the job. 'Risk' has to be specified and quantified; 'what works' has to be developed, evaluated, and implemented systematically; and desired outcomes must be clearly identified and achieved. Considered in this way, crime prevention can be seen as a technical task, concerned with problem identification and resolution. The only challenges to effective interventions are those of limited knowledge, imperfect information-gathering, insufficient resources, and inefficient programme delivery—substantial issues, but all capable of being resolved with the right combination of will and skill.

On the other hand, it might be argued that these are potentially limiting alternatives, since their shared assumptions incline us to take a particular kind of problem-solving and pragmatic approach. There is arguably a form of 'preventive logic' at play which depends on, and at the same time helps to reinforce, the way we think about crime as a particular kind of social problem. Embedded in this logic are a set of underlying (and socially constructed) assumptions about what constitutes a 'typical' crime, where it is likely to take place and who will perpetrate it. However, 'crime' and its effects are not necessarily quantifiable in this way, nor are instances of harm, conflict, exploitation, and loss and their effects reducible to an exchange between stereotypical offenders and victims. It may be extremely difficult to disentangle and apportion criminal intent and blame; and as a result it may be restrictive to rely on conventional assumptions about 'normal' crimes and their causes when approaching the question of crime prevention. This is underlined for us when we broaden the notion of prevention to incorporate wider questions of how to tackle social harms and their origins. Much recent work has been undertaken, for example, to place the issue of 'hate crime' on the agenda, and to shift the preventive 'gaze' accordingly (see **Telling it like it is 22.1**).

> The reality faced by many people across Britain is one of being targeted on a daily basis because of who they are.
>
> Chakraborti et al. 2011: p. v

Tilley (2002: 19) suggests that initial notions of crime prevention by policy makers were quite narrow and technical:

[T]here was no political dimension to the conception of crime prevention…. Several matters which could, in other circumstances, have played a large part in crime prevention were not considered. For example, questions of large-scale social structural change affecting the class, 'race' and gender distributions of power, the decriminalization of some behaviour, and much crime committed by the powerful, did not find a place on the crime prevention agenda, in part because this is set by the political and bureaucratic context.

So, in reflecting on just what 'crime prevention' is, we must also pay attention to how it comes to be constituted in specific social and political contexts, and how this might lead to a rather partial view of both its objects and the manner in which it is delivered (see **What do you think? 22.2** for an exercise in prioritising different factors to help in such decision making).

The emergence and development of crime prevention

The historical development of crime prevention has been rather uneven, with a particular focus on systematic and scientific approaches to the subject only emerging relatively recently. Crawford (1998: 30) locates the origins of contemporary approaches to crime prevention in the establishment of the modern police force under the Metropolitan Police Act 1829. Here, prevention was identified as a primary objective of policing. Subsequently, though, policing priorities shifted towards responding to crime and the preventive function of the police became marginalised (Crawford 1998: 32).

Gilling (1997: 76) suggests that it was the gradual recognition of opportunist crime as a particular problem, and the work of the Cornish Committee on crime prevention and detection (Home Office 1965), that eventually changed the emphasis of criminal justice policy in favour of preventive strategies. This, in turn, led to the establishment of an infrastructure for implementing this approach, and with the support of the Home Office, 58 crime prevention panels had been established by 1969, rising progressively to over 400 by the 1990s (Gilling 1997: 78).

It seems to be broadly agreed that there has been a growing interest in developing new approaches to preventing

WHAT DO YOU THINK? 22.2

If you had to make a decision about what type of crime to prevent, what would it be, and why?

Would your choice be influenced by any of the following factors:

- the severity of the effect of the crime;

- the vulnerability of those affected;

- the extent to which victims may or may not contribute to their own problems;

- your thoughts about your own or family members' safety and security;

- the common good;

- the economic and social well-being of the community;

- the need to challenge oppression and promote human rights;

- the threat of exploitation or environmental damage represented by corporate interests?

Is there any other consideration you would take into account? There are eight factors listed above; try ranking these in order of importance to your decision by assigning each a number from 1–8 (where 1 = most important). Was this an easy task? It's complicated, isn't it?

crime over recent years. The recognition of preventive activity as a legitimate and potentially fruitful area of intervention is associated with recent social changes and the emergence of a particular view of the role of the state in relation to crime. For some, the starting point of modern crime prevention practices dates back to the period following the Second World War and the emergence of a more active role for the state in creating the conditions for communal well-being (Hughes and Edwards 2011: 16). As the state gained a more prominent role in social life there was also a growing sense of confidence in the capacity of science and rational planning to understand the conditions giving rise to crime; and thus also to devise effective forms of intervention to tackle these: 'There was a widespread belief that the political will and scientific means now existed to remould and improve virtually all aspects of society' (2011: 17).

Much of the responsibility for achieving these changes was vested in the 'new professions of the welfare state', such as those working in children's departments, for instance. It was believed that these workers, with a clear understanding of family dynamics and therapeutic need, would be able to forestall outbreaks of juvenile delinquency originating in 'problem families'. As West (1967: 240) pointed out, 'the

children's departments of each local authority watch over the whole', providing necessary additional support 'for children whose parents are prevented' from giving adequate care. There was a mood of optimism, buoyed by the idea that 'problem families' could be readily identified, and their difficulties resolved through judicious use of expert guidance and firm behaviour management.

In this spirit, the Children and Young Persons Act 1963 incorporated requirements for local agencies 'to seek out and advise parents of children who appear to be at risk of becoming delinquent' (West 1967: 241). However, West (1967: 254) also noted the absence of any evidence to justify such interventions. At the same time, the American experience of similar programmes was not encouraging, with significant examples of failure becoming apparent, notably the Cambridge-Somerville project (McCord 1992) and other substantial prevention schemes in Washington and New York.

These reported failures subsequently contributed to a growing mood of despondency (amongst the probation service and other welfare professionals) and the sense that 'nothing works' in the field of social interventions to discourage crime. However, this did not lead to the conclusion that crime prevention was an unrealistic objective. Rather, there was a 'shift' of focus (Crawford 2007: 867), incorporating a wider range of agencies and a broader understanding of the risk of crime as a generalised threat, rather than depending on the delinquent tendencies of identifiable individuals. The Morgan Report (1991) commissioned by the Home Office, was seen as particularly influential in de-emphasising the role of statutory agencies and formalised interventions, and instead establishing the principle that crime prevention was the responsibility of the whole community.

By 2000, the emphasis in crime prevention work had been transformed (Garland 2001: 16):

> Over the past two decades, while national crime debates in Britain and America have focused upon punishment, prisons and criminal justice, a whole new infrastructure has been assembled at the local level that addresses crime and disorder in a quite different manner... this network is designed to foster crime prevention and to enhance community safety, primarily through the cultivation of community involvement and the dissemination of crime prevention ideas and practices.

The loss of faith in the idea of welfare-led interventions and rehabilitation (see **Chapter 25**) was associated with a growing interest in broader technologies of risk identification and risk management. Originating with the Safer Cities programme of the late 1980s (Tilley, 2002) an array of community-based partnerships and programmes were established to reduce crime; although evidence of their efficacy appears somewhat limited (Berry et al. 2011). Underpinning these developments there had emerged new theoretical constructs of prevention, too.

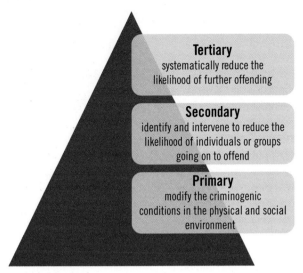

Figure 22.3 Brantingham and Faust's model of a policy and practice framework for crime prevention

A framework for policy and practice

Brantingham and Faust (1976) proposed a framework for policy and practice based on ideas of 'primary', 'secondary', and 'tertiary' prevention. Primary prevention would focus on managing and modifying the 'criminogenic conditions in the physical and social environment' (1976: 284); secondary prevention would aim to identify and then intervene to reduce the likelihood of individuals or groups going on to offend; and tertiary prevention would be concerned with reducing the likelihood of reoffending (see **Figure 22.3**).

Having articulated the model, the first question the authors posed for themselves was whether it was helpful to establish such a broad framework that it would cover almost any intervention within (and sometimes beyond) the remit of the criminal justice system. Their considered response was that it enabled a proper analysis to be made of the state of knowledge and practice associated with each level; which would, in turn, facilitate a more nuanced understanding of what kind of approach would be most effective in each case. Thus, in their view, the state of knowledge at the time did not indicate that tertiary prevention was very effective, consisting as it did of 'treatment' measures with little knowledge of their likely effectiveness (Brantingham and Faust 1976: 293). Similarly, they argued that in the case of secondary prevention, 'the inadequate state of knowledge precludes' effective 'diagnosis and intervention', partly because of the 'premature and inappropriate assignment of the "potential offender" label (see also Lösel and Bender 2012)'. Their conclusion, then, was that primary prevention offered the most promising

prospects, and this therefore prompted a significant shift in effort towards wider-ranging environmental and social programmes (see **What do you think? 22.3**).

The coincidence of a loss of confidence in targeted programmes aimed at known or potential offenders, and the parallel growth of concern about personal security generated a shift towards a wider-ranging more diverse preventive philosophy. Drivers identified by Hughes and Edwards (2011: 17) included: a persistent increase in recorded crime and criminality (until the early 1990s, at least); identifiable weaknesses in the justice system, such as poor clear-up rates; increasing emphasis on the 'costs of crime'; and a recognition of the limited impact of formal criminal justice interventions. As the system itself became associated with failure and inadequacy, so the focus shifted and crime prevention objectives began to infuse other aspects of social policy: 'The inflated cultural, social and political salience accorded to crime and insecurity since the 1970s has resulted in policies and strategies previously defined in terms of other outcomes increasingly redefined in terms of their possible crime preventive effects' (Crawford 2007: 871). In contemporary terms, we might recognise the same tendencies at work in the context of welfare and educational interventions with those believed to be at risk of being 'radicalised' (Shain 2011).

A number of authors, including Crawford (1997) and Rodger (2008), have described these trends as a form of 'criminalisation of social policy', whereby a whole range of measures come to be seen not simply in terms of their primary objectives, such as 'the quality of education, nutrition, health' or housing (Crawford 2007: 871), but also as crime prevention projects.

Another way of thinking about this, as Crawford (1998) has observed, is in terms of a shift away from the offender as the target of intervention, towards the 'offence'. Thus, because we cannot be even reasonably sure who will offend, where and when, but we are able roughly to estimate that a certain number of offences will be committed against some people from vulnerable groups in certain areas then this knowledge should shape intervention. However, because we still cannot be precise about either victims or sites of crime, there need to be broad and generalised strategies of crime-proofing and protection across communities.

This does not mean that efforts have been abandoned to improve attempts to anticipate and prevent offending at either secondary or tertiary levels (as is evident from the range of criminogenic assessments that continue to be carried out with identified offenders—OASys, *Asset* (subsequently *AssetPlus*) and the like, and the continuing research into the developmental causes of youth crime in particular; Welsh and Farrington 2012), but it does illustrate the logic behind the substantial growth in what we have previously identified as 'situational crime prevention'.

The driving force behind this shift in emphasis is often seen as the Home Office in the UK (Crawford 2007: 872),

WHAT DO YOU THINK? 22.3

Establishing a police presence in schools has been a policy inspired by a range of motives. It is designed, naturally, as a means of enhancing the relationship between the police and young people, in light of an acknowledged degree of historic hostility and mutual distrust. Additional benefits of police coming into schools are also believed to include a greater level of availability and thus readiness on the part of school students to share their concerns and alert police to potential crimes. Police presence in schools was formalised through the Safer Schools Partnerships (SSP) initiative which were launched across the UK in 2002 (see **Figure 22.4**). The main objectives behind such partnerships was to keep young people safe, reduce crime (and the fear of crime), and improve behaviour in schools and their communities.

In 2006 the Cambridge Constabulary introduced their own partnerships and following that secured a presence in ten secondary schools across the county. The presence of officers is hoped to provide a focus on early intervention and preventions of crime, ultimately resulting in students who respect police officers, and their wider communities. According to the Cambridgeshire Constabulary website, SSPs aim to ensure:

- the safety of pupils, staff, and the school site and surrounding area;

- help for young people to deal with situations that may put them at risk of becoming victims of crime, bullying or intimidation, and to provide support to those who do;

- focused enforcement to demonstrate that those who do offend cannot do so without facing consequences;

Figure 22.4 PCSO Nicky Smith standing outside Smithdon High School, Norfolk, working with the Norfolk Constabulary's Safer Schools Partnership
Source: Norfolk Constabulary

- early identification, support and where necessary challenge of pupils involved in or at risk of offending;

- improved standards of pupil behaviour and attendance, and less need for exclusions;

- more positive relations between young people and the police and between young people and the wider community; and

- effective approaches to issues beyond the school site that negatively impact on pupil safety and behaviour.

(Cambridgeshire Constabulary, 2015; https://www.cambs.police.uk/crimeprevention/safer_schools/)

Do you think it is helpful to have police officers routinely present in schools?

Should education and schools be used as a vehicle for promoting crime prevention messages?

---

although Crawford believes that this was also associated with a growing number of local and relatively modest initiatives, grounded in pragmatic attempts to reduce or eradicate identified problems of crime in specific communities. Hughes and Edwards (2011: 19), too, identify a significant level of government interest in developing crime prevention strategies culminating with the enshrinement of prevention in law in the Crime and Disorder Act 1998, as the principal objective of the youth justice system, as we noted earlier; interestingly, this section of the act includes a further subsection (s.37(2)) requiring all relevant agencies to 'have regard' to this aim, including some such as the health service for whom crime prevention is by no means the principal focus of their activities.

Associated with this particular legislative change has been a heightened requirement for local authorities to coordinate action to address problems associated with crime, and the establishment of local crime reduction and community safety partnerships (Gilling 1997), again intended to involve all relevant agencies and other community interests in managing the threat of crime and victimisation in the locality.

The extensive scope of this overarching goal of reducing levels of crime has also meant that crime prevention has come to be characterised by multiple stakeholders, diverse objectives, and a wide range of interventions falling under its umbrella. It is not simply a matter of 'target hardening', as Crawford (2007: 873) observes. Instead, it may be a matter of invoking strategies to reduce temptation and 'opportunity', for example by (adapted from Crawford 2007: 873):

- increasing the required effort to commit the crime (e.g. erecting better fencing, or creating 'gated' communities);
- increasing the risks of being obstructed or found out in the commission of the crime (e.g. better street lighting);
- reducing the rewards of the crime (e.g. security marking of valuable goods or animals);
- reducing 'provocation' (e.g. hiding presents on the back seat of the car);
- removing excuses (e.g. sending reminders to pay taxes or renew TV licences).

The example of gated communities and secure compounds is interesting, since it raises the question as to whether this is actually a measure designed to prevent crime, or rather to act as a form of social control. Instead of situational prevention, Rose (2000: 329) refers to this type of initiative as a form of 'situational crime control', whereby those who are able to establish secure communities which do not so much act to prevent crime in general but rather just to guarantee their own safety and 'eliminate or expel those who have no legitimate … reason to be there', as Rose (2000: 330) puts it. Paradoxically, though, while this may be an effective strategy for some affluent neighbourhoods, it is suggested that in poorer areas of public housing, the use of gates and barriers might actually make it more difficult to respond effectively to crime and disorder (Morgan 2013: 33).

As Crawford also goes on to point out, the change of emphasis noted does not mean that crime prevention simply shifted its focus from changing people and their behaviour to changing the physical world, in order to improve the security of potential victims and make transgression more difficult. He cites the example of speed bumps, for instance, where the change in the physical environment supplements speed awareness initiatives and encourages adaptive behaviour on the part of the motorist, promoting a greater sensitivity to speed limits in general.

This kind of reasoning process has recently been elaborated upon in the form of *nudge theory* (Thaler and Sunstein 2008), which it is argued can exploit unconscious as well as conscious thought patterns to discourage opportunistic criminal behaviour, such as shoplifting (Sharma and Scott 2015). So, for example, publicly displayed video footage of criminal activities such as shop thefts in progress might increase 'natural surveillance' by the general public whilst also prompting second thoughts amongst those inclined towards shoplifting. Indeed, this is consistent with a wider trend associated with the effects of austerity which is about devolving responsibility from government to local communities and initiatives such as Neighbourhood Watch, supported by electronic media, whilst practical support is effectively withdrawn (Home Office 2011).

You should now have a good understanding of the basic elements of crime prevention strategies, their objectives, origins, and emergence, and an insight into the framework put forward by Brantingham and Faust. This next section will move on to consider alternative perspectives on crime prevention.

Alternative perspectives on crime prevention

As we have seen, the idea of crime prevention—in terms of what it is—is actually rather more complex and nuanced than it might appear. Not all crimes are the same, victims' interests vary, some crimes are 'victimless', and prevention involves making choices about policy and resource priorities. Inevitably, then, when we start to think beyond the definition of prevention, and move on to its aims and implementation, we find that these are similarly variable, and the implications of different approaches are quite diverse. It is possible to provide a lengthy list of alternative goals towards which preventive measures may be directed. Some of these can be seen to overlap, whilst others involve potentially conflicting choices, such as when criminal activities are 'displaced' from one target to another. The objectives of prevention may include:

- diverting potential offenders from crime;
- avoiding 'bad lives';

- safeguarding potential victims;
- providing reassurance to the general public;
- promoting community safety;
- protecting commercial interests;
- building social capital; and
- defending the moral order.

Building on the framework suggested by Brantingham and Faust (1976), Crawford (1998) developed a more elaborate classification of an 'audience/target' typology of crime prevention, distinguishing not just between the different groups involved, but also the level at which intervention might be targeted (see **Table 22.1**).

As we have already recognised, the object of intervention might be the potential offender, the potential victim, or the community in general.

	Primary	*Secondary*	*Tertiary*
Potential victim	Target hardening Campaigns Secure technology	Risk assessment and protection of 'at risk' groups	Repeat victim support, 'hot spot' interventions
Community safety	Neighbourhood watch (see **Figure 22.5**) Surveillance technology Planning strategies Building social capital	Identifying and modifying risk potential in specific community settings	Regeneration 'High crime' area strategies
Potential offender	Citizenship education Early intervention social programmes (see **Figure 22.6**) Reducing incentives to offend	Work with 'at risk' groups, constructive leisure activities, alternative opportunities	Aftercare, monitoring of ex-offenders, resocialisation

Table 22.1 Levels at which intervention might be targeted

Source: Adapted from Crime Prevention and Community Safety: Politics, Policies and Practices 1e, Adam Crawford, Pearson Education Limited, Addison Wesley Longman Limited 1998

Figure 22.5 You may recognise this neighbourhood watch logo

Source: Neighbourhood Watch Association: www.ourwatch.org.uk

Figure 22.6 The 'Values Versus Violence' programmes in the West Midlands integrate the police into schools in the Birmingham area

Source: The Dot Com Children's Foundation (www.dotcomcf.org)

Next, we will consider another analytical framework for making sense of crime prevention.

Individual, social, and community crime prevention

Another way of considering the distinctions between approaches to crime prevention is to make a distinction between addressing the social factors associated with offending on the one hand; and controlling the situations which are criminogenic, on the other. Crawford recognises that these are based on different assumptions about the causes of crime. The idea of social crime prevention is based on the assumption that criminality is the product of a range of interacting influences which impact on individuals and shape their predispositions towards offending

behaviour; whilst situational crime prevention relies on the assumption that offending is essentially rational and contextual, and can thus be curtailed by limiting the opportunities for crime (Crawford 1998: 18).

The kind of early intervention and educational programmes outlined in **Table 22.1**, for example, are designed to address personal and social factors which have been linked with crime (see Farrington et al. 2012, for example). Social crime prevention:

is most commonly directed at trying to influence the underlying social and economic causes of crime, as well as offender motivation. This approach tends to include crime prevention measures that take some time to produce the intended results. This may include action to improve housing, health and educational achievement, as well as improved community cohesion through community development measures.

Morgan et al. 2015:15

Situational measures, by contrast, are based on the more pessimistic assumption that criminality is endemic and is, indeed, a natural form of self-interested behaviour. The underlying belief here is that we would all be willing to commit crimes if they offered risk-free potential gains. In this context, crime prevention can only be expected to be effective if it restricts opportunities or increases the potential risk—the use of physical security measures to protect homes and businesses being an obvious example of this kind of strategy, for example.

Situational crime prevention is based upon the premise that crime is often opportunistic and aims to modify contextual factors to limit the opportunities for offenders to engage in criminal behaviour. Situational prevention comprises a range of measures that highlight the importance of targeting very specific forms of crime in certain circumstances. This involves identifying, manipulating, and controlling the situational or environmental factors associated with certain types of crime (Morgan et al. 2015: 13).

Potential offenders

Drawing on Crawford's typology and starting with those who are seen as potential future offenders, preventive approaches aim to ensure that the incentives and attractions of offending are minimised; or that alternative opportunities are provided for this group to undertake 'constructive' activities and to live productive lives, free from crime. Here, though, we are already confronted by the possibility of adopting very different strategies to reduce the likelihood of someone going on to offend. Essentially, it is a matter of 'the carrot or the stick'. That is to say, prevention programmes targeting those at risk of offending may opt for either a *deterrent* or a *diversionary* approach; or, perhaps a combination of the two.

Deterrence

Conventional deterrent measures include various forms of confinement or community punishment (dealt with in detail in **Chapter 24**), but of course deterrence can only have any prospect of being effective if potential offenders understand the consequences of their actions.

So, for example, the UK government developed an anti-fraud strategy which devoted considerable attention to getting across the message to potential fraudsters that they would be found out and punished (see **Figure 22.7**).

> From September 2001, the campaign [to prevent benefit fraud] focused on dishonest claimants. Messages of

Figure 22.7 An advert commissioned by the Department for Work and Pensions aimed at curbing benefit fraud
Source: Department for Work and Pensions, content available under the Open Government Licence v3.0

> deterrence and detection aimed to raise the fear of getting caught and portray the likely consequences. Scenarios used in television advertisements showed benefit fraudsters being caught or punished, or both. In addition, the campaign used radio and regional press advertisements, the latter featuring real newspaper headlines from fraud prosecutions.
>
> In June 2003, the next phase used the slogan 'We're on to you'. It featured a spotlight that followed fraudsters in realistic scenarios, such as at work, to show them that they would be found out if they were continuing to claim benefits to which they were no longer entitled, and to warn potential cheats that benefit fraud is a serious crime.
>
> HM Treasury and National Audit Office 2008: 22

Another rather eye-catching example of the deterrent approach which has gained some interest is the 'Scared Straight' program which was established in the US in the 1970s. Under this program, groups of young people 'at risk' of offending are taken to custodial institutions to give them a flavour of just how tough and unpleasant it is to be incarcerated—a version of 'aversion therapy'. The programmes usually involve a tour of the institution and the 'at risk' juvenile is made to live the life of a prisoner for a full day. The visit could include aggressive 'in-your-face' presentations by inmates as well as one-on-one counselling (*Office of Juvenile Justice and Delinquency Prevention News*, March/April 2011).

The intention in this case is effectively to enhance the deterrent effect of custody for those young people who are believed to be at risk of committing crime at some point, and are open to persuasion of this kind. Interestingly, though, the available evidence suggests that this is a particularly ineffective strategy, which may even have the effect of increasing the likelihood of offending by those in receipt of the programme. Petrosino et al. (2004) carried out a 'meta-analysis' of programme evaluations of 'Scared Straight' initiatives, and concluded that 'programs like "Scared Straight" are likely to have a harmful effect and increase delinquency relative to doing nothing at all to the same youths'. These findings were based on a 'systematic review' of nine studies carried out over a 25 year period (1967–92) in the USA. Overall, the review found that those young people required to take part in institutional visits with the aim of deterring them from future crime were actually more likely to offend subsequently. Although they were unwilling to speculate on the reasons for this outcome, the reviewers concluded that in light of their observations 'we cannot recommend this program as a crime prevention strategy' (Petrosino et al. 2004: 8). Ironically, as the authors noted on completing their review, despite the evidence such programmes remained in demand, regardless of their apparent ineffectiveness.

Diversion from crime

By contrast, a significant body of work has been developed over the years which seeks to promote a 'diversionary' strategy—that is, interventions geared towards encouraging those children or young people identified as potential offenders to find more constructive uses for their time, particularly leisure time, when it is believed they may be at risk of 'drifting' into unlawful activities (see Matza 1964). Informed by such insights, there has been a long tradition in the UK of developing and delivering just such programmes, originating with Intermediate Treatment in the 1970s, and continuing in the same vein subsequently, with variations on the theme; such as Intensive Intermediate Treatment, then Supervised Activity Orders, and subsequently activity requirements for those subject to court orders, and an array of activity-based programmes for those merely 'at risk' of offending. **What do you think? 22.4** invites you to consider the value of this kind of programme in light of reported public criticisms of them.

WHAT DO YOU THINK? 22.4

* In the 1980s, in response to a series of outbreaks of unrest, the French government introduced a programme called *Étés Jeunes*, to provide a programme of cultural and sporting activities for young people during the summer months. In 1983, in its second year, the programme involved 100,000 young people and by 1986 it was estimated by the police that there had been a 10 per cent fall in youth crime during the period when the programme was active (Pitts 1988: 168)

* This programme seems to have had much in common with the Summer Splash programme introduced in the UK in 2000 with a similar crime prevention focus.

* Some people criticise the idea of spending money on 'treats' for those at risk of offending. How would you go about justifying this?

Other approaches

The deterrent approach and diversionary approaches are not the only ways in which this subject can be considered. Other approaches have seen crime prevention differently, based on alternative views of the nature of the 'processes which a crime prevention measure seeks to affect' (Crawford 1998: 17), as well as the effectiveness of different types of intervention.

Crawford contrasts 'developmental' and 'community' models of crime prevention. Developmental models aim to address those aspects of the individual's characteristics and behaviour which are believed to predispose her/him to commit crime. On the other hand, the modification of individuals' criminality is held to be dependent on influencing aspects of the social life of the community to reduce those features which might be criminogenic. Strengthening schools, for instance, is a recent example of one such community approach which has been adopted tentatively in some areas. Improving the 'whole school' ethos is believed to have a generally beneficial effect on student discipline and behaviour, including reductions in criminal activity in and beyond the school itself. Targeting schools in this way may also be seen as sharing assumptions with a 'situational' prevention strategy, especially if they are also connected with or located within what are believed to be high-crime neighbourhoods.

In the case of school based prevention, though, there has been limited research and thus little evidence as to the impact of such approaches (see Luiselli et al. 2005; and Gottfriedson et al. 2014, for example).

Overall then, a strategy which targets individual propensities to offend has to take account of the limited capacity we have to predict exactly who will commit what sort of crime, where and when. Any predictions are based either on those imperfect tools such as *Asset* and *Onset* (see **Chapter 9** on youth justice for an explanation of these terms) used by criminal justice practitioners, or on academic investigations which have generated a substantial body of work identifying broad associations between individual characteristics and circumstances and likelihood of offending (for example, Sutherland et al. 2005; see also Case and Haines 2009: 116). Given that the ability to predict offending at the individual level remains crude, it might appear to make sense also to address the wider needs of the public to feel and to be 'safe'.

Potential victims

While 'social' measures are more likely to be directed at potential offenders, this is not exclusively the case, and they may be directed at enhancing the capacity of victims and communities to enhance their own protection or exercise 'informal social control'. We can distinguish, therefore, between securitising approaches which are purely 'situational' and concentrate on making crimes harder to commit, and personal safety measures which place an emphasis on potential victims' own responsibility for

self-protection. Understandably, perhaps, this latter approach has potentially controversial consequences, in turn, with the risk of 'victim-blaming', and the sense that people are being asked to forego their own natural rights, to freedom of movement, for example, which they are entitled to expect the state to guarantee. This point has been powerfully illustrated for us by women's groups who have deliberately set out to 'reclaim the night' in the face of advice to avoid certain places at certain times in their own interests (see **Figure 22.8**).

> In every sphere of life we negotiate the threat or reality of rape, sexual assault and sexual harassment. We cannot claim equal citizenship while this threat restricts our lives as it does. We demand the right to use public space without fear. We demand this right as a civil liberty, we demand this as a human right.
>
> The Reclaim The Night march gives women a voice and a chance to reclaim the streets at night on a safe and empowering event. We aim to put the issue of our safety on the agenda for this night and every day.
>
> Reclaim the Night, www.reclaimthenight.co.uk/why.html

Community safety and well-being

Following on from this, the third strand of prevention identified by Crawford prioritises changing communities, rather than targeting individuals. The objective here is to generate a greater sense of well-being and communal security in general. This strategy can perhaps be associated

Figure 22.8 Marchers from the 2016 Reclaim the Night event in Manchester
Source: Barbara Cook/Alamy Stock Photo

with the notion of building or enhancing the supply of 'social capital'; the collective resources available to enhance the quality of life enjoyed by community members. Some support for this perspective is offered by the findings of Sampson and colleagues (1997), whose research seemed to demonstrate the protective value of 'collective efficacy' in the form of strong established informal networks of support operating within defined communities. The aim of preventive initiatives based on these findings would be to find ways of building and maintaining stronger interpersonal bonds which will both create greater security through building effective connections between people and generate a sense of mutual obligation and regard. Of course, in causal terms, it is debatable as to whether building social capital could be expected to lead to a lower crime rate; or whether effective crime prevention strategies might themselves generate enhanced social capital. The answer to this question could lead to very different priorities for community intervention.

One variation on this kind of argument might distinguish between different community interests, and perhaps make the case for prioritisation of commercial and business interests. Specific objectives might be advocated, such as reductions in theft and vandalism, in the interests of retaining key contributors to the local economy, such as shops and other small businesses. Of course, this in turn takes us back to an earlier question about whose interests should be prioritised in a context of finite resources and diverse needs. If instead we were to accept the principle of diverting our efforts and funds to those most 'at risk' according to the available evidence (Reza and Magill 2006), then black and minority ethnic groups and people living in poorer neighbourhoods would be the first to benefit from crime prevention measures. Indeed, this perspective might lead us to reconceptualise the idea of crime prevention entirely, if we are to take account of the kind of analysis advanced by commentators such as Wacquant (2008). In his view, community decline and marginalisation are the consequence of social and economic changes at the macro-level which combine to produce homogeneous and racialised neighbourhoods ('the American hyperghetto') in which crime and disorder become institutionalised.

Alternatively, prevention of crime might be thought of in broader and more symbolic terms, as a means of maintaining the moral order and promoting the common good by reaffirming general principles of 'right and wrong'. Considered in these terms, this might mean making strategic and practical choices about establishing priority areas for action, relating to those crimes which are believed to represent the most substantial and persistent threat to our combined sense of moral integrity as a society—we might think of 'extreme' crimes such as child abuse or disability hate crime in such purely preventive terms, for instance.

What does crime prevention achieve?

As we have seen, the question of 'what is crime prevention for?' is a deceptively simple one. In fact, it generates many further questions about the underlying assumptions and moral judgements we make about what crime is, and which crimes are the most serious, and who we should be protecting from its effects. Prevention strategies and interventions, however, have to be based on just such value judgements, as well as more pragmatic considerations of effectiveness and what constitutes a successful intervention. It may therefore be helpful, then, to focus more closely on these questions before going on to consider preventive practices in more detail.

Politics, interest groups, and crime prevention

Crime prevention, like many other areas of public interest and policy-making, is subject to negotiation and debate depending on the interests of different stakeholders. It is therefore important to try and understand these and how they inform the different sets of assumptions put forward on the subject. Hughes (1998: 18) has pointed out that: 'crime prevention strategies may be geared towards addressing quite distinct dimensions to the phenomenon of crime'. Depending on the viewpoint brought to bear on the subject, prevention initiatives may be directed towards modifying 'the context of the crime act, the criminal motive, problems in the environment or the unprotected "at risk" victim'. In Hughes' view this means that 'all correctional ideologies', that is to say, every competing view about the best way to respond to criminal acts, can also claim to be consistent with the goal of preventing crime, even though these will be associated with widely differing approaches in practice. So, strategies of crime control, deterrence, and retribution can all be viewed as preventive in their own way; just as ideas of diversion or restoration might also be viewed as contributing to future reductions in levels of crime. The aim of this section is to introduce the agendas lying behind crime prevention initiatives and how these may be viewed as representing differing and potentially conflicting interests.

Making choices and setting priorities

Tilley (2011: 3) similarly reflects on the contradictory nature of prevention, which he describes as 'both disarmingly simple and bewilderingly complex'. While on the one hand, as already observed, it is straightforwardly attractive to think in terms of developing effective mechanisms for anticipating crime and thereby stopping the incidence of unacceptable behaviour; on the other hand, this glosses over problems of defining crime, prioritising interventions, the ethical challenges of different preventive activities, political contexts, the costs and choices involved, and the trade-off between intended outcomes and what are often described as unintended consequences (Tilley 2011: 5).

For some, the challenge is more or less technical; depending on developing the best technical knowledge and skills in order to be able to find the most effective means of pre-empting the commission of acts which are clearly defined as criminal. However, this is not readily accepted by others who see both defining and preventing crime as reflecting processes of social and moral judgement: 'Crime is socially defined, socially committed and elicits social responses' (Tilley 2011: 5).

Furthermore, the ability to define something as a crime and thus worthy of attention and preventive action is not equitably distributed; it depends on the relationship between different, and sometimes competing, interests within society. Many forms of suspect and possibly unlawful activity rarely or never seem to fall under the scope of crime prevention activity, such as breaches of professional codes of practice, corporate or environmental crime, tax offences or, indeed, most crimes without an obvious victim. Tilley seems to suggest that the very notion of crime prevention conjures up a particular image for most of us of the type of activity which should be the focus of our anxieties, as well as the elements of the broader population who will be the objects of concern (young males, or certain ethnic groups, for example). And even the term itself may be seen as potentially problematic, with the distinction being made between *crime prevention* which is seen as police terminology, and *community safety* which 'is preferred in local authorities … to signify a broader set of interests in crime consequences' (Tilley 2011: 7).

The local politics of crime prevention: a case study

The different origins and implications of varying underlying assumptions certainly raise significant questions about the ways in which preventive initiatives are organised and how they impact, not just on 'crime', but on wider communities, as well as those directly involved in the justice system. Coleman and his colleagues (2002), for example, have drawn on the experience of crime prevention in Merseyside, North West England, to analyse the complex politics of that area. In their view, whilst crime prevention has assumed the position of a 'taken for granted' (Coleman et al. 2002: 86) element of community intervention by local agencies, there are particular assumptions and dynamics underlying this development, which must, in turn, be subject to critical evaluation.

Noting the coincidence between the origins of community safety initiatives in Merseyside with its economic regeneration programme from the late 1990s, they suggest that this implied a merging of a particular group of interests. As a result, this helps to shape what is described as the local agenda.

Developing the case study approach, the authors also observe that the key data used to establish priorities for intervention were those which proved to be most easily countable, namely, police crime statistics and their geographical distribution. The evidence generated in this way lent itself to 'situational' rather than 'social' prevention measures, which were also geared towards protecting business interests and commercial activities, nominally in the interests of promoting a vibrant local economy. And so, a partial definition of the problem lends itself to an apparently obvious solution (Coleman et al. 2002: 91):

> CCTV was to be the centrepiece of this strategy. SMP [Safer Merseyside Partnership] supported this development politically and also funded schemes to enhance training and codes of practice for CCTV operatives in the city centre.

The eventual aim of this project was to set up an integrated system of 'up to 240 cameras' in the city and in some 'hot spot' residential areas. Coleman and colleagues, however, continued to express scepticism about the underlying priorities of the scheme. Although, as they put it, it was 'trumpeted on the back of promoting the safety of women and children' (2002: 92), its core rationale was to demonstrate that Merseyside was a 'safe place to do business' and thus to encourage investment.

Implied in these developments, of course, is the prioritisation of resources, with funding assigned to one form of highly technical intervention at the expense of other projects less reliant on technology and grounded instead on principles of fostering good community relations. The authors note the coincidence of the finalisation of plans to place CCTV cameras in the Dingle area of Liverpool with the loss of public funding to 'the only local youth centre' in the area (2002: 94). Developing the contextual argument further, the authors also pointed out that

Dingle itself at the time was located within sight of an array of chemical plants which had been responsible for a range of environmental breaches; whilst, at the time Liverpool also 'had the highest levels of traffic pollution for any city outside of London' (2002: 95). The conclusion drawn by the authors is that a particular definition of 'crime prevention' came to dominate in Merseyside in this period, with the 'priorities of crime prevention partnerships [sweeping] aside the priorities identified by local communities' (2002: 102); suggesting at the same time that this reordering of priorities also helped to shift attention towards a convenient (and conventional) definition of the crime problem.

On the other hand, as Coleman and colleagues acknowledge, there are powerful reasons for taking crime as it is commonly understood and experienced seriously: 'we are not denying the impact of conventional crimes such as burglary on the socially and economically powerless'; and they also note government attempts 'to introduce crimes such as racist violence, domestic violence and rape onto the political and social policy agenda' (Coleman et al. 2002: 104). So, it seems, crime prevention cannot simply be accounted for as a process of misdirection and mystification of the relationships between powerful interests and exploited communities. It must also be seen as representing a core of legitimate concern about risk, vulnerability, and harm to particular sectors of the population.

Now may be a good time to consider the issues raised in **Controversy and debate 22.1**.

! CONTROVERSY AND DEBATE 22.1

During the 1980s, an influential group of writers came together under the banner 'Left Realism' to argue that the effects of crime on communities could not be ignored by theorists whose analyses had previously attributed all such social problems to the consequences of capitalism and the inequalities it generates (e.g., Quinney, 1970).

Whatever the relative merits of these arguments, authors such as John Lea and Jock Young (1984) for example began to make the case for a better and closer understanding of the destabilising and harmful effects of crime at the community level; and for the initiation of linked research studies and practical, community-led initiatives to alleviate the harms caused. For a more detailed discussion of left realists please see **Chapter 17**.

Community interests and crime prevention

In this sense, then, the proper focus of 'crime prevention thinking' might be viewed as the development of practical strategies for assessing vulnerability and introducing concrete measures to prevent harm for those most at risk. Crime is not necessarily taken as a given, or as a homogeneous category, but as an indicator of a wide range of potential 'harms', which themselves must be subject to detailed understanding, and prioritisation, based on the consensual view of the community as a whole.

Edwards (2002), writing in the same volume as Coleman, has suggested that there is scope within community partnerships for a distinctive approach to problem definition which is not restricted in its focus and helps to create a more grounded approach to dealing with the threat of crime. Moves towards greater local control mean that the capacity for differential approaches to emerge becomes greater, with increased potential, too, for specific local and communal interests to influence strategic decision making. In Edwards' view, it is important to understand actual practices in community crime prevention and their potential consequences in order to generate a clearer insight into what is possible and achievable, rather than imposing prior assumptions.

Based on detailed investigation of local crime prevention and community safety partnerships, Edwards (2002: 146) seeks to exemplify several key challenges which may be expected to arise, but which are capable of being resolved in very different ways. *Competition* over priorities and resource allocation is to be expected, for example, and can exacerbate 'tensions between different communities'; but it can also stimulate new thinking and creativity in problem-solving. *Innovation*, though, also depends on being open to the ideas and aspirations of a range 'of interest groups' (2002: 147), rather than reflecting narrow and entrenched interests. New thinking, in turn, needs to be guaranteed by a degree of '*flexibility*' to adapt within partnerships, rather than finding themselves fettered by 'nationally set performance criteria' (2002: 149). This, though, raises yet further dilemmas of the nature of *accountability*, and the limits to be set to it, where local communities may set priorities which are themselves punitive and exclusionary towards certain, often already marginalised groups (2002: 150).

These potential conflicts of interest have been exemplified in Edwards' study in the form of misalignments between agency and community expectations of crime prevention strategies in Leicester, East Midlands, UK. Whilst 'a coalition of local residents' wanted to act against sex workers by way of 'zero tolerance' policing and anti-social behaviour orders, the police and welfare agencies were more inclined to see this as connected with a need for enhanced welfare services such as 'employment, housing and drug advice' (Edwards 2002: 154).

Edwards, concludes, though, that partnership arrangements on balance offer genuine opportunities to develop effective crime prevention strategies. That is, partnership models offer inherent advantages such as the inbuilt potential for ongoing dialogue. This, in turn, establishes the basis for engagement and education of community members, so as to generate more sophisticated understandings of shared social problems than might be gleaned from relatively crude and exploitative media portrayals (Edwards 2002: 154).

The delivery model for crime prevention, as well as its principled underpinnings, should therefore be grounded in what Edwards describes as 'critical pluralism'. This does not anticipate the debate over what constitutes the necessary terrain and objectives of preventive work; instead, it creates space and the proper conditions for discussion and the development of common understanding and measures of what constitutes community benefit. This is not just a practical compromise, but it also 'provides a core set of normative principles around which advocates of community empowerment can coalesce' (2002: 161). In

practice, then, crime prevention initiatives could be focused at any or all of the potential targets of potential offenders, vulnerable members of the community, or risky situations; but whichever of these is prioritised, the suggestion is that it must be based on an equitable and inclusive form of 'participative democracy' (2002: 162).

Tilley (2011: 9) agrees that a partnership approach is essential. No organisation 'on its own has the capacity to address the full range of conditions giving rise to local crime problems', so working together is a fundamental requirement. At the same time, however, he observes that the actual conditions under which partnerships are expected to operate, including structural constraints and political differences, still present major challenges to the realisation of these aspirations.

Although community itself is a relatively ill-defined term, the gist of these arguments is that strong community relationships and effective collaborative mechanisms will provide a greater sense of security as well as practical safeguards against crime and antisocial behaviour. This, in turn, depends on practical measures to establish effective dialogue and to guard against the dominance of particular interests, neither of which is straightforwardly achieved as a number of the preceding examples make clear.

Models of practice in crime prevention

As understandings of crime prevention have shifted, and arguably become more elaborate and sophisticated, we have also seen the range of strategies put in place expand. It is still the case that preventive initiatives can be categorised according to three domains of 'developmental', 'community', and 'situational' measures (Welsh and Farrington: 2012); but equally, these may not always be quite as discrete and self-contained as each broad term might suggest. Community crime prevention, for example, is sometimes thought of as a 'combination of developmental and situational prevention' (Welsh and Farrington 2012: 9).

The objectives of crime prevention initiatives

It is perhaps the very complexity and multi-level nature of community crime prevention initiatives that makes it difficult to draw precise conclusions about their effectiveness or the methods by which beneficial outcomes are achieved. Developmental and situational crime prevention approaches might, on the face of it, offer more readily understandable means of intervention (and impacts) than measures designed to promote community cohesion.

Developmental crime prevention, for example, is based on the assumption that: 'Traits or propensities conducive to antisocial conduct and crime develop in the womb and early in childhood. The roots of crime thus extend over the life course.' (Cullen et al. 2012: 25). In line with this assumption, desistance from crime requires the development of interventions which both alleviate these predisposing characteristics and provide alternative 'social opportunities for change' (2012: 26). With the application of the right evidence-based interventions it should therefore be possible to provide effective routes out of crime for many individuals, both in the early years and at later stages in their lives.

Changing lives: social crime prevention

It has been suggested that there is now ample evidence available of the risk factors for offending, which can be characterised as 'individual', 'familial', or 'social' (Farrington et al. 2012); and, as these are now well understood, it becomes possible to specify those which should be seen as priorities for intervention. These factors are specified as: 'impulsiveness, school achievement, child-rearing methods, young mothers, child abuse, parental conflict and disrupted families, poverty, delinquent peers, and deprived neighbourhoods' (Farrington et al. 2012: 62). At first glance, this appears a daunting and hugely resource-intensive list of areas of social welfare needing to be addressed. However, there are a considerable number of initiatives of this kind which are claimed to demonstrate some positive effect (Sherman et al. 1998). So, for example, it has been possible to identify beneficial outcomes of what is described as 'poverty deconcentration' (Ludwig and Burdick-Will: 2012), that is rehousing people on low incomes in wealthier areas.

One example of this is the Moving to Opportunity (MTO) experiment in which 4,000 families in public housing in America were randomly awarded housing vouchers to enable them to move from 'high-poverty, dangerous neighbourhoods' to more affluent areas with less obvious signs of social stress. Following family moves, the evaluation reported a reduction in violent crime 'for all youth in the sample' (2012: 190), although at the same time, rates of property crime committed by young males appeared to increase. Despite this inconsistent outcome, the conclusion drawn is that the scheme did 'appear to reduce the social cost of offending for youth living in high concentrations of poverty' (Ludwig and Burdick-Will 2012: 190).

Alongside such generalised ('primary') interventions, more specific and focused initiatives are also believed to be effective in changing developmental trajectories and reducing the likelihood of young people being drawn into criminality. Social skills training, involving parent training, pro-social modelling and coaching for children, is reported to be consistently beneficial in terms of children's propensity to offend (Lösel and Bender 2012). Such programmes are argued to be at their most effective when they incorporate a number of elements: 'Structured, multimodal, cognitive-behavioural approaches revealed the most robust and largest effects ... research supports basic principles of addressing cognitive, emotional, and behavioural facets of social competence in an integrated manner' (Lösel and Bender 2012: 119). The authors of this review of social skills based interventions do not suggest, however, that programmes should necessarily be selective or concentrated only on those most 'at risk' of becoming offenders, because universal programmes can be shown to benefit 'high-risk participants' and because they avoid the risk of 'stigmatisation' or labelling (2012: 120).

Developmental approaches to crime prevention typically focus on early years interventions (this was one of the goals of the national Sure Start programme, for example), parent training, and behavioural programmes, and they are in fact relatively rarely focused on changing the material circumstances of potential offenders. So, the emphasis is on aspects of children's upbringing or socialisation through changing parenting behaviour, or managing challenging behaviour as a means of anticipating and discouraging future manifestations of antisocial tendencies.

More recently, too, government has established and then expanded the Troubled Families programme, targeting those families most at risk of experiencing a range of problems, including the involvement in crime or antisocial behaviour of one or more family members (Department for Communities and Local Government 2012). The Troubled Families initiative has been explicitly geared towards achieving demonstrable behavioural change, associated by some critics with a strategy of 'responsibilisation' without offering additional resources to help families achieve change (Smith 2015).

Criminogenic contexts and situational crime prevention

Although programmes targeted at promoting life course changes are reported to have beneficial effects, these are not easily predictable or consistent: 'Unfortunately mixed success is the current state of the field' (Homel 2011: 97).

It is perhaps unsurprising that there is in parallel a comparably high level of interest in controlling the 'situations' in which crime is likely to occur. Situational crime prevention is based on a range of theories about the processes leading to the commission of crime described as 'opportunity theories' (Clarke 2011: 41), consisting of 'the rational choice perspective (RCP), the routine activity approach (RAA), and crime pattern theory (CPT)' (Smith and Clarke 2012: 292). Taken together, these capture a sense of the 'contingent' nature of much behaviour that is defined as criminal, and how it depends on particular combinations of factors acting together to act as catalysts for anti-social behaviour or delinquency.

Rational choice perspective

This perspective assumes that decisions about whether (or not) to offend are based on a more or less deliberate calculation on the potential offender's part of the 'risks, rewards and efforts of alternative courses of action' (Smith and Clarke 2012: 294). Whilst this does not assume that all such choices are fully rational given constraints of 'time, ability, and knowledge about the circumstances', it does suggest that offenders are, in effect, constantly ready to take advantage of crime opportunities (see, for example **Figure 22.9**) when they are confronted with them if rational calculation suggests this will be to their advantage.

Figure 22.9 An opportunity to commit crime?
Source: Darryl Brooks/Shutterstock.com

Figure 22.11 A woman walks down a dimly lit street, a site of particular risk
Source: Horia Varlan/CC BY 2.0

Routine activity approach

This approach locates the potential for crime in the coincidence of three factors: a 'likely (motivated) offender, a suitable target for the offense, and the absence of a capable guardian to prevent the crime from occurring' (Smith and Clarke 2012: 296). Such coincidences might be more likely to occur if the 'routine activities' of the various parties to the offence converge 'at a particular time and place', thus making the occurrence of crime more feasible—see **Figure 22.10** for one such possible occurrence.

Crime pattern theory

This theory is based on the idea that human behaviours in general, and crime in particular, 'show regularities when viewed across time and space' (Smith and Clarke 2012:

Figure 22.10 A tourist, with an easily accessible bag, is pickpocketed in a busy inner city area
Source: © Jacob Lund/Shutterstock

297), and these can be identified in the pattern of rules governing behavioural decisions, movements related to particular locations and the ways in which crimes are concentrated. From this develops the idea of crime 'hot spots', associated with large scale regular and predictable configurations of 'activity' and 'place'—which might paradoxically include the relative absence of people from suburban housing estates during school time. More predictably, perhaps, dimly lit streets late at night are also thought to be sites of particular risk (**Figure 22.11**).

Situational crime prevention therefore applies these modes of understanding crime to develop systems of classification and prediction, such as those just discussed. These then enable a methodical approach to reducing opportunity; creating inhibitors; and creating greater uncertainty as to the outcomes of crime (greater risk/lower rewards). This, in turn, underpins a variety of practical strategies to influence these different 'enablers' of crime—for instance, in the design of laptop bags to be more secure; in the use of advisory stickers on bike stands; and in creating uncertainty of gainful outcomes for offenders, for instance through the use of passwords for electronic equipment (Ekblom 2012). **Figure 22.12** shows the potentially complementary relationship of these alternative theories of crime prevention.

Crime prevention in action: the Kirkholt Project

The Kirkholt Project, implemented in the North West of England in the 1980s, achieved 'iconic status in worldwide contemporary thinking on crime prevention' (Hope 2002: 44). The aim of the project was to activate a policy goal established by the Home Office in 1984 of promoting a collaborative inter-agency approach to reducing burglaries in a specific geographical area (Forrester et al. 1988: 1).

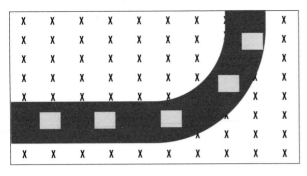

X = High crime area: CRIME PATTERN

■ = Common tourist route: ROUTINE ACTIVITY

□ = Likely targets (e.g. signs of wealth): RATIONAL CHOICE

Figure 22.12 The interrelationship of crime prevention theories

It took the form of an action research project which involved a wide variety of activities coordinated by the project team, including target hardening measures such as improved household security and property marking; behavioural interventions directed at known offenders in the area; social capital initiatives such as the establishment of a credit union and school-based activity programmes; and improved surveillance for and by local residents. Thus, in effect, the project incorporated elements of all three crime prevention approaches outlined; and, according to Hope (2002: 45), it was also supplemented by a range of other initiatives to improve living standards in the local area.

Over the course of the project, some quite dramatic changes were reported by the research team, including a 75 per cent reduction in the household burglary rate from 1986–87 to 1989–90 (Forrester et al. 1990: 42). The successes achieved were not uniform, though, and for some groups and some types of dwellings (short-term tenants, and maisonettes), burglary rates had actually increased

over this period. However, the researchers still concluded that the overall achievements of the project demonstrated its success. It was not possible, according to the evaluation, to be able to identify which specific measures had been associated with which beneficial outcomes reported, although it was asserted that 'the adoption of a series of measures is likely to have much greater impact than simply taking one or two steps' (Forrester et al. 1988: 11). The suggestion was made though that community-oriented prevention initiatives of this kind are likely to depend on continuing maintenance of a 'flow of information' and 'established inter-agency links' as well as building new ones (Forrester et al. 1990: 43) in order to retain its capacity to respond to changing patterns of crime and victimisation—providing heightened surveillance of their homes for 'holidaying older people in September', for example.

Although not disputing the effectiveness of the Kirkholt Project, Hope (2002) does sound a note of criminological caution, suggesting that the mechanisms by which crime reductions are achieved are not always as clear cut as might sometimes be suggested (2002: 51):

> If we asserted that Kirkholt was commendable simply because it brought about huge reductions in burglary – similarly large reductions in incidence, concentration and prevalence can be found to have occurred in other places – sometimes not even as a result of purposive prevention efforts.

Other burglary reduction initiatives have also been shown to be effective, not because they specifically targeted repeat victimisation, as in the case of Kirkholt; but because they also represented 'intensive, efficient and sustainable multiple interventions to bring about' the desired objective of a significantly lower burglary rate in the locality (Ekblom et al. 1996). 'Alley-gating', for example, has been subject to intensive review and is reported to be an effective means of reducing burglary by restricting access to vulnerable properties (Sidebottom et al. 2015).

What does prevention achieve?

In the same way that the 'targets' of prevention differ, we can reasonably expect the success criteria to vary according to the model adopted. Early interventions geared towards achieving behavioural change amongst potential offenders will be measured in a very different way to those approaches which are concerned with reducing the likelihood of crime associated with a particular location or social occasion. Other questions arise when we try to determine what criteria to apply to the question of whether a particular prevention initiative 'works'; is the aim just to reduce or to eradicate a certain type of unacceptable behaviour, to make people feel safer irrespective of changing

crime patterns, to reduce levels of crime in general or target particular offences, to protect 'the public' in general or particular vulnerable groups, to promote social or economic benefits, or even to try to balance these disparate objectives in some way?

And, indeed, measurement of success becomes more complex still when we factor in the costs (human and financial) associated with achieving specified outcomes—achieving crime reduction goals in absolute terms might begin to feel like less of a bargain if this means that other desirable outcomes have to be foregone, or that there are substantial hidden costs involved. (So, for example, the

Daily Mirror reported in January 2015 that it could cost as much as £250 to replace a set of car keys designed, in part, with improved car security in mind.)

Claiming success: working with those at risk of offending

Despite our concerns about defining success, significant claims have been made over the years for the achievements of crime prevention projects, some of which have achieved almost iconic status. For instance, the Head Start programme, originating in the United States in the 1960s has long been associated with a range of socially desirable outcomes, including a reduction in participants' propensity to commit crime as they grow up. A linked initiative, the High/Scope Perry Preschool study was established in the early 1960s to track the progress and outcomes of children identified in their early years as being at risk of school failure, and then randomly allocated to an intensive pre-school intervention programme. These children, and the associated control group, were followed up regularly to the age of 40, with consistently more positive outcomes for the programme group (Schweinhart et al. 2005). At this point, educationally, they were more likely to have graduated from high school (77 per cent vs 60 per cent); they were more likely to be employed (76 per cent vs 62 per cent) and more likely to own their own homes and cars; they were less likely to have used social services at any point in their lives (71 per cent vs 86 per cent); and they were significantly less likely to have been arrested or imprisoned (7 per cent vs 29 per cent with five or more arrests, for example).

Similarly, a number of larger scale reviews of the evidence relating to early prevention programmes ('meta-analyses') have also suggested that these programmes generate a range of socially desirable benefits, including both reduced involvement with the criminal justice system and self-reported delinquency (Manning et al. 2010). Some reservations have been expressed, however, about the quality of the evidence available, the scale of the beneficial outcomes achieved, and the mechanisms by which positive change is brought about: 'there is a need to identify the particular ingredients that make the specific early parent programs successful at inhibiting antisocial and delinquent behaviours ...' (Piquero et al. 2008: 87).

Claiming success: targeting risky behaviours

As the focus shifts from stopping 'at risk' individuals getting into trouble to concentrating on problematic and potentially criminogenic patterns of behaviour, then naturally, approaches to establishing and evaluating the achievement of success criteria are somewhat different, too. Thus, for instance, a particular community action project in Sweden adopted a 'multicomponent strategy' to reduce alcohol-related problems, assessment of which required an evaluation of the extent to which positive changes were 'institutionalised' (Wallin et al. 2004). Therefore, different aspects of the programme were considered independently, in order to identify if and how these had a discernible impact on the target behaviours; namely, 'adoption, sustainability, key leader support, structural change, and compliance' (Wallin et al. 2004: 411).

In this particular case, a range of strategies was initiated, including awareness training of staff in the night-time economy, a mutually-agreed protocol between statutory agencies and purveyors of alcohol, and stricter enforcement. As a result, the programme evaluators were able to claim that: 'the effects of the project are promising. Alcohol service to underage patrons, alcohol service to markedly drunk patrons, and violence have all decreased significantly' (Wallin et al. 2004: 398). Extrapolating from this experience, we might assume that community-based crime prevention initiatives in general will depend for their success on consistent and comprehensive 'buy-in' from those concerned with implementation and programme delivery.

Similarly, a systematic international review of anti-bullying programmes in schools (Farrington and Ttofi 2009) has indicated that such programmes could be effective in reducing bullying (by 20–23 per cent) and victimisation (by 17–20 per cent), and that specific programme elements were particularly closely associated with successful outcome; whilst one, 'work with peers' was in fact associated with an increase in bullying: 'it seems from our results that work with peers should not be used' (Farrington and Ttofi 2009: 69). The conclusion of this review was that a range of programme elements were associated with a reduction in the levels of bullying, including: 'parent training/meetings, improved playground supervision, disciplinary methods, classroom management, teacher training, classroom rules, whole-school bullying policy, school conferences, information for parents, and cooperative group work' (Farrington and Ttofi 2009: 66). However, once victimisation was also taken into account, the programme elements associated with a decline in both were: 'parent training/meetings, disciplinary methods and the length and duration of the programme'. Nonetheless, this appears to offer further illustration of the preventive potential of systematic programmes of intervention which are broadly community-based, target particular types of crime or antisocial behaviour, have widespread commitment from participants, and are implemented rigorously.

Claiming success: making places safer

When it comes to 'situational' prevention, the first thing that becomes clear is that the nature and variety of 'places' where crime may occur demand very different preventive strategies depending on the characteristics of specific locations. Eck (2002: 245), for example, has suggested four 'categories and nine subcategories of places' where crime prevention activities might be carried out at some point:

(a) money spending places (shops, banks/money handling premises, bars);

(b) residential places;

(c) transportation places (airports, car parks, public transport); and

(d) other public places (open spaces, coin operated machines).

This categorisation has since been revised to suggest five rather than four 'place types' (Eck and Guerette 2012: 360): residential, public places, retail, transport, and recreational, with differing and overlapping interventions applied under each heading. CCTV, for example, is a commonly applied preventive strategy across the range of 'place types'.

For each of these, a range of strategies of securitisation or control of activities have been attempted, and Eck (2002) suggests that in a number of cases, substantial changes have been claimed, for example in the case of the 'Clawson Point' housing development, where a 54 per cent reduction in crime was reported, as a result of changes to accessibility and appearance of the estate; in another instance, a substantial majority of residents in public housing complexes in Chicago also reported reductions in 'shootings and fighting' following a number of physical security measures and closer scrutiny of the use of buildings (Eck 2002: 248). However, Eck concludes that the robustness of such findings is not sufficient to be able to suggest that such measures 'work'.

Other 'situational' measures are thought to be more demonstrably effective, however. Both Eck (2002) and Welsh and Farrington (2010) are persuaded that CCTV has been shown to reduce crime, particularly 'in car parks' (Welsh and Farrington 2010: 27). Here, too, though, it is acknowledged that the 'exact optimal circumstances for effective use of CCTV schemes are not entirely clear at present' (2010: 27). Similarly, improved street lighting has been found to be effective, to a robust standard of certainty. According to Welsh and Farrington (2010: 25), 'improved street lighting is effective in city and town centers, residential areas, and public housing communities, and is more effective in reducing property crimes than in reducing violent crimes. In pooling the effects of… 13 [high-quality evaluations], it was found that improved street lighting lead to a 21 per cent reduction in crime'.

Distinguishing between what is 'known' to work and what is 'promising', Eck (2002: 276) also found a range of evidence that street closures may be effective in preventing a range of different types of criminal activity, including kerb crawling, 'drive-by shootings', violent crime, burglaries, and car thefts.

The limits of preventative measures

Despite these apparently encouraging examples, a note of caution has been sounded about taking such evidence strictly at face value. As Eck (2002: 281) points out, even though we can find evidence that targeted place-based interventions are associated with reductions in levels of crime, 'we know little about the place- and crime-specific effects of these tactics'; and, which changes exactly can be seen as causal: 'Even when the effects of a single tactic were identified, other changes were [often] reported that could have confounded the evaluation results. Thus we might learn that crime was prevented, but we do not know what caused the prevention' (2002: 282). There has therefore been a clear and influential move towards developing a consistent 'evidence-based approach to crime policy' (Welsh and Farrington 2012: 510); whilst at the same time, it is acknowledged that the quality of much of the evidence available is 'very thin' (Eck and Guerette 2012: 367).

Over the years, though, proponents of an 'evidence-based' approach to situational (and other forms of) crime prevention have made increasingly confident claims, both for the effectiveness of specific interventions and for the overall value of an evidence-informed strategy (Sherman et al. 1998: 1):

> Many crime prevention programs work. Others don't. Most programs have not yet been evaluated with enough scientific evidence to draw conclusions. Enough evidence is available, however, to create provisional lists of what works, what doesn't and what's promising.

Consequences of crime prevention

Despite the evidence of increasing confidence in the value and success of well-planned, systematic, and evidence-led crime prevention strategies, there have been some concerns raised about the implications of such approaches, and their unintended consequences, alongside the more fundamental political objections mentioned earlier (Coleman et al. 2002).

Escalation

Grabosky (1996), for example, has identified a number of possible outcomes of prevention measures which might be counterproductive. These include what he describes as: 'crime escalation, displacement, overdeterrence and perverse incentives' (1996: 25). In the first of these categories, he refers to the Cambridge-Somerville Youth Study (McCord 1978) which involved an evaluation of an intensive programme targeting 'at-risk' young people, including educational support, leisure activities, family counselling, and additional health services. Despite the array of services provided, when compared with a control group, those targeted for intervention compared unfavourably not only in terms of their likelihood of offending, but also on a number of other criteria, including 'mortality, stress-related disease, and evidence of mental illness and alcoholism' (Grabosky 1996: 27).

Kelly's (2012) more recent qualitative study has identified similar dynamics and suggests a number of possible factors at play in this process of 'escalation'. In this case, a programme was implemented based on targeting the 50 most 'at risk' young people in the 'most deprived' neighbourhoods and undertaking intensive programmes of intervention with them, in this instance with a sporting theme. Notwithstanding a number of individual 'success stories', Kelly also concluded that programmes were associated with a number of adverse effects, including 'accelerating' formal interventions—that is drawing young people into the very system the programme was meant to keep them out of; 'defining deviance up'—heightening concerns and sensitivities to what might otherwise be seen as normal adolescent behaviour; and contributing to processes of exclusion, whereby young people undergoing the intervention programme, or in some cases rejecting it, would be persistently marked out as different from the mainstream population ('othered': Garland 2001). At the same time, the concentration of service provision in this one area would necessarily divert resources from generic and universally accessible services.

As Grabosky (1996: 27) also observes: 'Other forms of escalation are less subtle and more immediately apparent. The construction of physical barriers may invite their defacing or destruction'. He also suggests that suppressed criminal intent may find its expression in more intensified and potentially harmful activities, such as 'expressive violence'. In other words, the preventive measures put in place may actually be perceived as 'provocative', and produce 'defiance not deterrence' (1996: 27); excessive police action can prompt rather than prevent violence in the course of demonstrations, for instance. Similarly, stark warning messages ('don't press the red button') can produce 'perverse effects' (1996: 28), firstly by bringing what

is deemed unacceptable behaviour to people's attention; and then by associating it with a desirable expression of rebellion. In this context, Grabosky refers to the potentially counterproductive effects of stern 'warnings from law enforcement authorities about the perils of various illicit drugs' (1996: 28).

Adaptation

Other examples of misdirected preventive measures might also include those which actually facilitate the act of certain types of crime, such as improved lighting making certain targets more, rather than less accessible. In some cases, well-intended information about the potential vulnerability of certain products or locations might act as an alert to potential offenders; and it may well also be the case that prevention leads to complacency on the part of enforcement agencies, with the effect of reducing rather than enhancing their capacity to anticipate crime.

Preventive measures can be unhelpful in other ways, too. Grabosky (1996: 33) also draws attention to the effects of 'overdeterrence' in restricting everyday legitimate activities, or creating additional inconvenience for people going about their normal routines (over-enthusiastic Internet security software is one such minor irritation, for example). It is also quite likely that social consequences might follow as a result of a general over-sensitisation to the risks of crime; levels of fear might be unnecessarily escalated, and community cohesion and mutual trust might be put at risk.

Preventive measures might also be no more than the precursor of what Grabosky (1996: 32) refers to as 'creative adaptation', that is a process of refining criminal activity to avoid detection, and of borrowing from preventive techniques to facilitate the inventiveness of criminals themselves (Marx 2007).

Displacement

Of continuing concern to those at the forefront of preventive intervention is the problem of displacement, whereby either the criminal activity or its effects are merely shifted from one area, one point in time, or one population to another in the face of specific targeted prevention initiatives. In fact, as Grabosky acknowledges (1996: 31): 'The risk that undesirable activity, rather than prevented absolutely, will be shifted into other areas within or beyond one's jurisdiction or policy domain has become part of conventional criminological wisdom'. So, we might anticipate that strengthening particular targets for crime might just lead to the substitution of other available targets which offer less

CONTROVERSY AND DEBATE 22.2

Crime prevention, crime displacement, or crime promotion?

Periodically, it appears, 'respectable' communities' fears about the impact of sex work on the locality lead to the introduction of 'zero tolerance' policies. Sex workers are effectively criminalised and excluded from certain areas of towns and cities, and dispersed to other locations. But the effect of this may be to expose the sex workers themselves to greater risk of victimisation through theft and violence. Consider the following extracts from letters to *The Observer*, 26 January 2014:

> The article 'Mariana Popa was killed working as a prostitute. Are the police to blame?' … is a turning point in getting senior officers … to admit that criminalisation puts women at risk: 'It would be good to allow a small group of women to work together, otherwise … they are working away from other human support.' It has taken 40 years of campaigning to get this truth out. From the trial of Peter Sutcliffe, who murdered 13 women, many of them sex workers, to the Ipswich murders in 2006, we have complained that the police hound rather than protect sex workers.
>
> *Niki Adams*
> *English Collective of Prostitutes*
> *London NW5*

My report, 'Shadow City', found that police received £500m to tackle trafficking prior to the Olympics. They found no more trafficking cases than the year before—four—but did raid a huge number of brothels. This meant sex workers were displaced and became more vulnerable to violence. The laws on prostitution need to change. Until they do, we need to change dramatically how we police sex workers.

Andrew Boff
Conservative Londonwide Assembly member, leader of
GLA Conservatives
London SE1

- How do you think different groups' rights to protection from the effects of crime and antisocial behaviour could be assured in this context?

- Who should we see as the potential victims in this example?

---

of a challenge. In the not too distant past, certain older makes and models of car were known to be less well protected by security devices than others, so became more attractive options for car thieves as newer models became increasingly difficult to steal, Interestingly, Grabosky also cites the example of tax legislation as 'an ongoing drama' (1996: 32), involving the continuing efforts by tax authorities to close loopholes and the equally diligent efforts of 'a small industry' of accountants and financial interests working to create new 'avenues of avoidance and evasion'. See further discussion on 'displacement' and its consequences for a specific sub-group of the population in **Controversy and debate 22.2**.

The problem of displacement is of particular concern to those wishing to develop the science of prevention because, if it is demonstrated to be widespread and perpetually unavoidable, then it seriously undermines any project of improving or perfecting preventive measures. This 'worst case scenario' is mapped out by Johnson et al. (2012), who describe a 'hydraulic' perspective on criminality, such that: 'people who would have committed crime in the absence of intervention will continue to do so at the same rate. All that would change is how, when or where they commit those offenses; crime would be displaced' (Johnson et al. 2012: 337). Building on Repetto's

(1976) initial formulation, five forms of displacement are identified as potentially problematic:

- how offences are committed;
- when they are committed;
- the types of target selected;
- where crimes are carried out; and
- the type of offence committed.

The possibility of a further form of displacement, in terms of 'who' commits offences is also acknowledged, as might occur in the case of organised crime or gangs, for example.

The notion of a 'steady state' of criminal activity with perfect displacement of one crime for another does depend on a number of assumptions, though. Where an opportunity is blocked, there must be a more or less direct alternative available, offenders must know about such alternatives, and have the means and ability to exploit them, and they must be indifferent to the further consequences of making such choices, such as the implications of offending nearer to/further from where they live, for instance (Johnson et al. 2012: 338). Not only must offenders be 'sufficiently adaptable and capable of committing a variety of crimes in a variety of places or at different times'; but they must also be 'driven by irresistible pressures' to offend, even to the extent that they are prepared to make extra efforts to overcome 'the initial thwarting of intention' achieved by an active crime prevention strategy (Crawford 1998: 81).

Choice and 'deflection'

Doubt has been cast on the presumption of a steady state by those who support a 'rational choice' theory of crime (see 'Rational choice perspective' section earlier), as articulated originally by Clarke and Cornish (1985). According to this perspective, offenders will not automatically look elsewhere for the opportunity to commit crime if it is blocked at their preferred time and place. They will, instead, be guided, and possibly constrained, by a calculative decision making process which may or may not lead to the commission of an alternative offence: 'The everyday constrains on perfect rationality can include limitations of time, ability and knowledge about the circumstances in which decisions are made' (Smith and Clarke 2012: 294); but the 'irrational' influences on potential offenders do not completely override the 'rational elements' involved.

We should think perhaps in terms of actors' 'bounded rationality', when trying to understand the potential for displacement of particular criminal activities to other settings, or towards the use of alternative methods. It is likely, then, that for certain types of crime that involve a deliberative process, effective preventive measures will not necessarily lead to straightforward displacement; and, this is supported by the conclusions of Johnson et al. (2012: 349), who conclude that for certain types of place-based intervention 'crime appears just as likely (or perhaps slightly more so) to decrease in the areas that surround a treatment area following intervention'. It is argued in this respect that some 'displacement' effects may be viewed as positive in the sense that the 'benefits' of the preventive intervention are also dispersed beyond the specific site of intervention—in other words, a sort of 'halo' effect is achieved as crime rates go down in the surrounding area, as well as in the target location (Johnson et al. 2012: 349).

Johnson and colleagues point out, however, that this conclusion is 'based on a relatively small number of studies', focusing particularly on measures designed to improve 'surveillance', such as CCTV (2012: 350). It seems plausible that preventive measures are less likely to result in spatial displacement for certain types of criminal activity (unplanned property crimes, for example); but that this conclusion cannot be generalised.

Barr and Pease (1992) have additionally raised questions about the adequacy or efficacy of displacement as a concept. They appear to be concerned about the risks of taking a one-dimensional view of crime, recognising that it is the interaction between the potential offender and the 'situation' which is crucial (Barr and Pease 1992: 277):

> Crime patterns take the form they do because of a combination of circumstances: offender motivation, the absence of legitimate routes to personal satisfaction, the availability of vulnerable targets, the degree of preparation and investment required to commit different crimes, and the perceived consequences of crime commission.

Thus, they suggest, it may be better to think in terms of 'deflection' when a particular criminal opportunity is 'blocked', which may involve legal or illegal alternatives. It may also be better to think in terms of whether these alternatives are 'optimal'. Displacement can thus be viewed as 'benign' or 'malign', depending on the impact of the alternative activity—less serious offending might therefore be viewed as an acceptable consequence of preventive activity even though the overall crime rate has not seen a decline: 'displacement is not necessarily an undesirable consequence of social intervention' (Crawford 1998: 83). However, displacement may have problematic consequences, even when it is regarded as unproblematic from a 'majority' point of view, as Crawford notes in the case of 'the displacement of prostitutes from residential areas into industrial estates' (1998: 83), referred to above; and therefore to locations where they themselves might be at greater risk of criminal victimisation, whatever the perceived benefits to the community in general, as we have observed (Hubbard 2004).

In sum, therefore, crime prevention has consequences which are not always (or often) straightforwardly measurable—to return to our starting point, what seems like a simple and common sense aspiration may not be without its complications.

Limitations of crime prevention

Despite its inherent attractiveness, the idea of 'crime prevention' has been the subject of criticism. Such criticisms can effectively be categorised in two ways: firstly, that crime prevention initiatives are impractical, ineffective, or even counterproductive; and, secondly, that their inherent assumptions reflect ideological perspectives and trends in criminological thought that are open to question. Of course, these two problems may be linked, in the sense that initiatives which appear to be politically attractive or to offer a ready-made 'quick fix' may also be precisely those measures which are associated with poor or undesirable outcomes.

The 'quick fix' problem 'dispersal orders' were introduced by government under the Anti-Social Behaviour Act 2003 as an apparently popular and practical solution to the problems of 'gangs' of young people responsible for 'low-level but persistent group-related anti-social activity and intimidatory behaviour' (Crawford and Lister 2007: 4). As a community-based preventive measure, the police were given powers to 'disperse groups of two or more people from areas where' such behaviour was believed or perceived to be taking place (2007: 5). In order to obtain the authority to administer these powers within a 'designated zone', the police had to gain the approval of the relevant local authority and specify the area covered and the duration for which such permission was sought. If agreed, the police would be authorised to require people in a group to 'disperse', to require anyone not living locally to leave the area, and to require them to stay away from the area for up to 24 hours. Crawford and Lister (2007: 9) have reported a rather patchy use of the powers provided, and a number of practical challenges associated with implementation, such as the limited capacity of police to sustain the level of engagement required to ensure compliance, and an increase rather than a reduction in the number of 'confrontational situations' (2007: 22).

Additionally, evaluation of the use of dispersal powers in certain police areas suggested that there was strong evidence of 'displacement', not only for the specific problem of young people 'hanging around', but also for certain types of crime, including burglary and criminal damage, with indications of 'a considerable displacement effect' (2007: 49). In this instance, it seems that not only did the intervention have little effect other than moving crime and anti-social behaviour around (a 'domino' effect, 2007: 52), but at the same time diffused rather than defused residents' feelings of insecurity:

> People were concerned that while the area around the shops had become safer during the dispersal order period, the back streets and some of the green spaces had become less safe: 'The groups of young people who were dispersed simply moved to an area just beyond the boundaries of the order and regrouped' (Resident).

Interestingly, there also seems to be some evidence from this study that a superficial concern with dealing with the outward manifestations of community conflict might generate some initial interest and support, but does little to address underlying and arguably more important problems of (lack of) social cohesion:

> It doesn't actually resolve anything. ... Six months later we've still got groups of young people that won't engage with adults and vice versa. Very little has happened as a direct result of the dispersal order.
>
> Housing officer, quoted in Crawford and Lister 2007: 61

Indeed, these authors concluded that none of the benefits associated with the introduction of dispersal powers, such as 'galvanising community capacity and dialogue about the appropriate use of public space', actually depended on their use, and these positive outcomes could have been achieved in other ways (Crawford and Lister 2007: 74).

This is, of course, only one case example, and proponents of systematic crime prevention strategies might well argue that the problems identified in this case were to do with faulty implementation rather than any fundamental problem with the principles of targeted, evidence-based approaches. So, it has been argued that a considerable number of preventive measures do work, and a similarly extensive number have been found to be 'promising', in the sense that concrete but less comprehensive evidence points towards their efficacy (Sherman et al. 1998). But even in the context of encouraging claims, significant caveats are expressed: 'The most important limitation of science is that the knowledge it produces is always becoming more refined, and therefore no conclusion is permanent' (Sherman et al. 1998: 3). That is to say, even in the most convincing examples of the effectiveness of preventive initiatives, we have to accept that our findings remain 'provisional'. This does not, of itself, render the search for better interventions and better evidence pointless. As Popper (2002) has made clear, no causal explanation can ever be proved to be true; all 'theories can be disproved or, more likely, revised by new findings' (Sherman et al. 1998: 3).

Replication and transferability: the 'context' problem

Similarly, it is pointed out that we need to be careful about making unjustifiable generalisations: what 'works' in one set of circumstances with a specific community may well not be transferable to another very different setting, since these external influences may alter the very basis on which an intervention is established—such as cultural perspectives on the use of drugs, for instance. This, in turn, highlights a further problem for the 'science of prevention', and this is the matter of replicability. That is to say, if a particular measure can be demonstrated to be effective, then it ought to be capable of being implemented elsewhere, at least in similar settings, with a similar degree of success, but as Sherman and colleagues (1998: 3) have noted: 'Until replications become far more common in crime prevention evaluations, the field will continue to suffer' from uncertainty about the implications of previous findings, both positive and negative.

Replication, though, does appear to present a very substantial challenge. Cherney (2006: 3), for example, acknowledges the persistent problem of external influences. Failure to think through the impact of contextual factors 'is a key reason that program replication in the crime prevention field has such a dismal record', he observes, citing Tilley's (1993) earlier reflections on this problem. In this instance, Tilley was reporting on the attempts to replicate the Kirkholt Burglary Prevention Project (see earlier), at least one of which deliberately used Kirkholt as a prototype (Tilley 1993: 6). He concluded that the outcomes of these replications demonstrated variable levels of success, but that the project most closely modelled on Kirkholt was notably the least successful of these. However, this prompted the further reflection that: 'Contextual variation is crucial' (1993: 20), and that even where attempts were made to follow the template offered by its predecessor, it was not possible to do so with a sufficient degree of fidelity (1993: 11); it was a different type of area; the crime profile of the area was different; and the resources put into the scheme were also not comparable. In practical terms, then, faithful replication of previous initiatives is hard, if not impossible, to achieve, as Ekblom (2002: 144) concurs.

For those still committed to the 'science of prevention', the challenge remains one of developing better mechanisms for understanding the contexts and processes involved in implementing preventive schemes. Work should be written up so that 'conjectures concerning measures, mechanisms, context and outcome pattern are made explicit' (Tilley 1993: 19), for example. Or, perhaps we should 'assemble generic principles of intervention then apply them alone or in combination as appropriate to specific circumstances [his emphasis]—fitting theories and/or abstract distillations of preventive mechanisms to particular problems and contexts' (Ekblom 2002: 148).

Whose task is prevention? The responsibility problem

The lack of certainty associated with preventive strategies and their outcomes means that initiatives are likely to remain open to external influences and interests which could well determine priorities, and thus shape practice:

> We need to place evaluations within a broader political framework. Debates about 'what works?' only reveal that the politics of success and failure are often struggles about the status of criteria which can rarely be reduced to 'any universally accepted scale of efficiency'.
>
> O'Malley 1992: 263, quoted in Crawford, 1998: 214

Indeed, it seems to be fairly widely accepted that crime prevention is peculiarly susceptible to 'political challenges' (Welsh and Farrington 2012: 511). Advocates of preventive measures may have to deal with the fears of politicians, for example, that they may be perceived as soft on crime by supporting prevention instead of "law-and-order measures"' (Welsh and Farrington 2012: 512). But it is not just the delivery mechanisms and strategic frameworks that are subject to political or ideological influence, according to some. It is rather the way in which the whole conceptual basis and scientific logic of 'crime prevention' is constructed which is subject to this kind of influence. So, for instance, Garland (1996) has argued that it is important to understand the growth of interest in prevention as part of a 'responsibilisation' project, whereby government and the state relinquishes its primary role in preventing and controlling crime, and transfers responsibility (and potential blame) to constituent community interests (Garland 1996: 453):

> Property owners, residents, retailers, manufacturers, town planners, school authorities, transport managers, employers, parents and individual citizens – all of these must be made to recognise that they too have a responsibility in this regard, and must be persuaded to change their practices in order to reduce criminal opportunities and increase informal controls.

Who sets the agenda? The political problem

Linked with this, and of equal importance is the question of just which of the many potential targets for intervention thus provided are identified as most important, and how this helps to construct a preconceived idea of particular groups and particular forms of behaviour as the most problematic to society as a whole. Young people, for instance, are routinely brought under the spotlight when the potential for anti-social behaviour and crime is put on the public policy agenda. As Goddard (2012) has observed, it is 'at-risk' youth who are considered to be particularly prone to committing serious offences or joining gangs, and he notes, at the same time, the spotlight is also most likely to fall on those from minority ethnic groups, with radicalisation, notably, featuring as a particular contemporary concern. The idealised notion of 'crime prevention' itself can perhaps be used as a strategic tool, a powerful and effective one, by which some interests can shape public concern and institutional behaviour in directions favourable to them and direct concerns about criminality, moral disorder, and unacceptable behaviour (such as tax avoidance, for example) away from themselves.

Linked to these possibilities is the potential for popular images of criminality to fuel a somewhat unbalanced 'fear of crime' (Lee 2007), which does not map accurately or directly onto the wider realities of crime and irresponsible and dangerous behaviour.

So, in conclusion, crime prevention in the sense of stopping bad behaviour before it happens seems like a 'no-brainer'; a self-evidently desirable aspiration. But, lying behind this apparently obvious and consensual objective, are the political interests, influences, and dynamics that construct particular groups, particular neighbourhoods, or particular kinds of activities as the targets of intervention; and it is these factors which transfer the mundanely good and desirable into something which needs to be closely examined and evaluated before we can invest our belief, energies, or commitment in it.

SUMMARY

This chapter has been intended to help you:

- Discuss the arguments in favour of a preventive approach to criminal justice

Supporters of crime prevention believe that it is possible to identify risky situations or risky people and on this basis to predict and forestall the incidence of crime, notably supported by ideas such as rational choice theory.

- Appreciate the implications of crime prevention for different stakeholders including potential victims, potential offenders, communities, politicians, interest groups, and others

Deciding which crimes are most problematic to the community in general or particular interests involves making a number of choices about whose needs to prioritise, what level of intrusion into everyday activities is acceptable, and how we can judge what counts as a successful outcome. The implications and success criteria are variable.

- Recognise the implications and effects of different approaches to preventing crime

Crime prevention can be distinguished according to whether it is 'situational', 'community-based', or 'developmental'. Each of these points towards different intervention strategies, and is associated with alternative practices and technologies. Policy and practice decisions can also be differentiated according to the 'level' of intervention, identified as 'primary', 'secondary', and 'tertiary' by Crawford (1998).

- Consider and assess the evidence base in support of preventive measures

A considerable body of work has developed, building up a detailed evidence base which in turn has sought to make claims about 'what works', what's 'promising', and what 'doesn't work'. As well as reflecting on this evidence, the chapter has reflected on the question of how such approaches have shaped our understanding of the prevention agenda.

- Evaluate the theoretical dimensions of perspectives on prevention

The idea of prevention has been shown to incorporate some contestable assumptions about what types of behaviour are unacceptable and who it is that presents the most risk to the community. These assumptions are in turn grounded in theoretical traditions in which notions of criminality, responsibility, and control are rooted.

- Examine the critical arguments questioning the aims and effectiveness of crime prevention strategies including a consideration of escalation, adaptation, and displacement

For some, it has been shown, the idea of prevention is itself a political concept which invites us to prejudge and problematise certain populations (young people, minority groups) or communities and neighbourhoods in a way which supports a divisive and exclusionary approach to targeted interventions and oppressive forms of control and boundary maintenance. We have examined some unintended consequences of crime prevention through a consideration of three issues: escalation, where crime prevention strategies have in fact worsened crime rates; adaptation, where preventive measures have actually facilitated the act of certain types of crime; and, finally, displacement where criminal activity or its effects are merely shifted from one area, one point in time, or one population to another as a consequence of specific targeted prevention initiatives.

REVIEW QUESTIONS

1. What do you understand by the term 'crime prevention'?

2. Who are the principal targets of crime prevention: offenders, potential victims, or communities?

3. In line with Brantingham and Faust's framework for crime prevention, give an example of 'primary', 'secondary', and 'tertiary' prevention tactics.

4. Outline the main differences between deterrence and diversion measures in relation to potential offenders.

5. What are the main features of 'situational' crime prevention?

6. What is the main assumption underlining the rational choice perspective?

7. What do you think of the idea of 'scaring straight' potential offenders?

8. To what extent do you think that displacement of criminal activity is a problem for crime prevention initiatives?

FURTHER READING

Forrester, D., Chatterton, M., and Pease, K. (1998) *The Kirkholt Burglary Prevention Project.* London: Home Office.
An important and influential case study of an extensive and thoroughly evaluated crime prevention initiative in one particular location.

Lea, J. and Young, J. (1984) *What is to be Done about Law and Order?* Harmondsworth: Penguin.
An influential re-evaluation of the effects of crime on working class communities, and critique of the argument that the criminal justice system is simply a tool of the dominant class.

Schweinhart, L. et al. (2005) *Lifetime Effects: The High/Scope Perry Preschool Study Through Age 40.* Ypsilanti, MI: High/Scope Press.
A longitudinal review of one of the earliest and most comprehensive (and extensively evaluated) early prevention schemes and its long-term effects.

Welsh, B. and Farrington, D. (eds) (2012) *The Oxford Handbook of Crime Prevention.* Oxford: Oxford University Press.
An authoritative and comprehensive sourcebook covering a wide range of theoretical perspectives and research evidence on crime prevention strategies and their impact.

 Access the **online resources** to view selected further reading and web links relevant to the material covered in this chapter.
www.oup.com/uk/case/

CHAPTER OUTLINE

What is crime control?	632
Crime control and due process models	633
Objectives of crime control	635
The role of the police in crime control	638
Beyond policing: The place of other agencies and interests in controlling crime	642
Place, property, and people: The objects and technologies of crime control	645
What does crime control achieve?	647
What are the consequences of crime control? Does it work?	651
The limitations of crime control	654

Crime control, policing, and community safety

KEY ISSUES

After reading this chapter you should be able to:

- explain what constitutes 'crime control';

- analyse the different methods of delivering 'crime control', including: deterrence, target hardening, offender surveillance, and incapacitation and associated intervention programmes;

- recognise the role played by the police in crime control;

- interpret the crime control model and the due process model, understanding the implications of each;

- critique the effectiveness of different crime control methods, including the use of deterrent measures and zero tolerance initiatives;

- evaluate the practical and moral limitations of crime control

What is crime control?

The different perspectives on dealing with crime under consideration in **Part 4** of this book are distinguished at their core by the very different assumptions each brings to the question of what to do about behaviour that is deemed unacceptable, antisocial, or unlawful. Approaches grounded in crime prevention start from the position that crime and criminal impulses can be anticipated and understood; and therefore the risks of offending can be minimised or eradicated. On the other hand, as we will see (**Chapter 24**) punitive approaches effectively accept that crime is inevitable, but concentrate on the penalties to be imposed and the suffering extracted in recompense. Lying between these perspectives, those concerned with 'controlling' crime do accept the inevitability of crime; but they also devote considerable attention to minimising its impact, either by restricting opportunities to offend, or by imposing immediate and impactful sanctions where crimes do occur. Whilst accepting that crime, or at least criminal impulses, is/are inevitable, a crime control perspective is also associated with a strategy of 'managing' crime in the sense of minimising its incidence and its consequences.

Crime control and retributive interventions may well coincide, despite their differing motivations, as in the case of imprisonment, for example. But crime control also extends well beyond deterrent sanctions, to include other measures geared towards the assessment and management of potential risks, target hardening, proactive policing, offender surveillance and restrictions—measures such as curfews and antisocial behaviour orders, for instance. In this respect, it is clear that crime control perspectives align quite closely with the crime prevention agenda. Where the two differ, though, is in their principal motivations. Whereas crime prevention approaches are concerned with understanding the causes of crime and intervening to address these, crime control strategies are much more narrowly focused on enhancing security and managing risk in order simply to stop crime.

For those who take a crime control approach, at the heart of the strategy is a belief in the idea that criminality is essentially rational and predictable, and that offenders are responsible for their behaviour; and so that offenders can be persuaded by the force of logic to desist from illegal activities. In effect, they can be led to believe that a crime 'just isn't worth it', if, say, the security system on a particular make of car is enhanced to such a level that it becomes too risky or difficult to break into. And if the force of logic fails, then simple force should achieve a similar outcome—a police blockade, for example. Underpinning this line of reasoning are a number of additional assumptions which we will examine further, in due course.

Firstly, the crime control perspective relies on a non-problematic view of crime; that is, that there is a clear common understanding of what constitutes illegal (rather than simply unacceptable or unpleasant) behaviour, and that there is similarly, a clear, uncontroversial and readily identifiable common interest in taking action to manage, control, or eradicate this behaviour. (Interestingly, at this point a similar issue of 'proportionality' arises as is the case in relation to retributive forms of punishment, but this time complicated by calculations of risk and the likelihood of possible criminal actions being carried out). The further assumption is made that the measures taken in this way are themselves relatively unproblematic, and will result in the achievement of the desired outcome, that is, the prevention or minimisation of the likelihood of crime being committed, and the reduction of harm associated with it.

The crime control perspective takes the position that the principal aim of the justice system is to stop crime, by whatever lawful means are required. The 'rule of law' remains a central feature of this model, since this is essential to its underlying legitimacy. This in turn distinguishes crime control from the naked exercise of coercive force in the interests of those in dominant positions. That is to say, the structures of law and justice constitute the vehicle by which crime is defined and crime control measures are justified. Otherwise, there is nothing to distinguish such interventions from the arbitrary use of power by one group or individual over others.

'Broken windows'

In essence, then, the task of the justice system (starting with those whose role is associated with the detection and prosecution of crime) is to maintain order and to regulate the life of the community, so that ordinary 'law-abiding' citizens are able to feel safe and go about their business without being exposed to undue risk of harm of one kind or another. This thesis is famously associated with the position adopted by Wilson and Kelling (1982) in their article entitled 'Broken Windows' (see **Figure 23.1**). Thus, the principal aim of the police should be seen as being one of controlling or driving away 'someone challenging community standards':

> the most important requirement is to think that to maintain order in precarious situations is a vital job. The police know this is one of their functions ... the police – and the rest of us – ought to recognize the importance of maintaining, intact, communities without broken windows.
>
> Wilson and Kelling 1982: 38

Figure 23.1 Broken windows—a symptom of a bigger problem?
Source: Tomas Castelazo, CC BY-SA 3.0

the justice system) should be judged according to their outcomes, rather than the immediate effects of their actions. We should put aside our utilitarian concerns and commitment to treating people 'fairly' in favour of preserving the integrity of the community and serving the interests of the majority in maintaining public order:

> Arresting a single drunk or a single vagrant who has harmed no identifiable person seems unjust, and in a sense it is. But failing to do anything about a score of drunks or a hundred vagrants may destroy an entire community.
>
> Wilson and Kelling 1982: 35

Whilst this line of argument was originally developed to address the perceived problems experienced in neglected or rundown neighbourhoods, its logic may also seem attractive when applied to the wider challenges associated with the problems of managing and controlling crime.

And so it is understood, for example, that the actions of police (and by implication other practitioners within

Crime control and due process models

Crime control strategies claim to represent a simple, impartial approach to stopping criminal activity. Crime control can be distinguished from crime prevention in that it is essentially *reactive*, being geared to responding to the commission of crime and dealing with its consequences, although there is certainly some common ground between the two, as in the case of physical security (and there are some obvious areas of overlaps with **Chapter 22** on Crime Prevention). Herbert Packer (1964) analysed two distinct types of models related to the delivery of criminal justice: the due process model, and the crime control model. Before considering how these two models differ, we will first consider their similarities.

A crime control perspective does share features with the 'due process model' (Packer 1964; and see **Chapter 20**). Common ground between the two includes the presumption that the legislative methods and procedures for defining behaviour as criminal can be kept separate from the process of detection and dealing with those who infringe the law. Equally, the delivery of justice should be carried out impartially and simply as determined by the requirements of the law. Otherwise, of course, the enforcement process would rely entirely on contingent ad hoc decisions by those in positions of power who would thus be able to define what should be treated as criminal (or not), without reference to key principles such as that of fair and equitable treatment of all citizens under a common legal framework.

In line with this, though, a crime control approach further assumes that it is possible to articulate a single overarching aim for the justice system which takes precedence over all other considerations, as Packer notes:

> The value system that underlies the Crime Control Model is based on the proposition that *the repression of criminal conduct is by far the most important function to be performed by the criminal process*. The failure of law enforcement to bring criminal conduct under tight control is viewed as leading to the breakdown of public order and thence to the disappearance of an important condition of human freedom.
>
> Packer 1964: 9 (emphasis added)

Expressed in these terms, this represents a powerful imperative. Based on the presumption that there is indeed 'common ground' in terms of shared definitions of unacceptable behaviour and the legal sanctions to be applied to it, it also provides legitimacy to a wide range of enforcement activities which are solely to be judged in terms of whether or not they preserve or re-establish public order on behalf of the wider community. So, in effect, the achievement of a 'just' outcome may be seen to justify the means adopted to achieve this.

Setting out the crime control model in this idealised form helps us to understand its aspirations and working principles, but we should also acknowledge that, as with other theoretical models, it is unlikely that we will find it operating in its pure form in any particular real world setting. Nonetheless, it is helpful to use this as a starting point, in order for us to be able to tease out the implications and to consider how the different, pure positions could, and do, interact in the administration of criminal justice as it is realised in practice.

Efficiency, or fairness?

Packer suggests that the crime control model, given its underlying aspiration to protect fundamental freedoms (for the law-abiding), is in the first instance to be judged according to the 'efficiency' with which it operates to identify suspects, achieve findings of guilt, and ensure appropriate disposals are imposed—still consistent with the objective of managing and minimising the effects of crime. As he observes, 'efficiency' often significantly determines actual practices, to the extent that it, necessarily, shapes the operation and establishes the capacity of enforcement agencies. In this respect, routinisation of procedures, and speed and informality of operation might all be beneficial attributes of the justice system, in that they increase efficiency. As Packer famously noted, the 'image that comes to mind is an assembly line or conveyor belt

Figure 23.2i Crime control model (the factory line)
Source: Hamick/Shutterstock.com

Figure 23.2ii Due process model (the obstacle course)
Source: CA Eccles/Shutterstock.com

down which moves an endless stream of cases', on which a predictable series of operations is performed to produce 'a finished product, or, to exchange the metaphor for the reality, a closed file' (Packer 1964: 11).

In this respect, then, a crime control approach is in clear contrast to what Packer describes as the 'Due Process Model', which places much more emphasis on the fair administration of justice and equitable treatment for those believed to be responsible for the commission of crime. According to this position, if the judicial system is to claim the authority to administer punishment, then it must be able to justify this in the quality, fairness, and legitimacy of the fact-finding and adjudication processes which support this: 'If the Crime Control Model resembles an assembly line, the Due Process Model looks very much like an obstacle course' (see **Figures 23.2i** and **23.2ii**) (Packer 1964: 13). **Figures 23.2i** and **23.2ii** provide a visual metaphor to help you remember the fundamental principles behind the crime control model (the factory line) and the due process model (the obstacle course).

Underlying these two perspectives are quite different understandings of society's best interests and the central purposes of the criminal justice system. Under the crime control model, the principal objective is to maintain security, conformity, and public order (see **Figure 23.3**); whilst, the due process model pays greater attention to the rights of the individual in relation to the state and other people (Roach 1999) (see **Figure 23.4**). As Roach observes, the operational emphasis of the crime control model is quite distinctive, in that very substantial weight is placed on the establishment and maintenance of an efficient and effective police force able to act quickly and decisively to investigate and respond to instances of law-breaking or disorder, and to do so decisively without undue constraints. Thus, for example, the police should be able to require citizens to produce evidence of their identity or lawful activities to the extent that this will enable them to identify potential wrongdoers—we should expect our civil liberties to be circumscribed in this manner in the interest of social stability and personal safety:

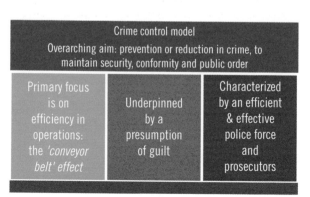

Crime control model
Overarching aim: prevention or reduction in crime, to maintain security, conformity and public order

Primary focus is on efficiency in operations: the *'conveyor belt'* effect	Underpinned by a presumption of guilt	Characterized by an efficient & effective police force and prosecutors

Figure 23.3 An overview of the crime control model

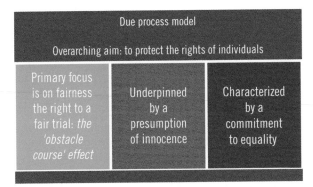

Figure 23.4 An overview of the due process model

The police should have wide powers to conduct searches because only the factually guilty have something to hide. Illegally seized evidence should be admissible at trial. Unlike coerced confessions, guns, drugs and stolen property reveal the truth no matter how the police obtained them.

Roach 1999: 678

Roach does caution us against concluding that this represents a 'thuggish model that is unconcerned with police abuse' (1999: 678)—rather, this is viewed almost as a separate issue from the central concern of whether the guilty are properly identified and held to account for their behaviour. Like the police, the prosecutor should be trusted to act consistently and effectively in the evaluation of evidence and the determination of guilt, and the role of the judiciary and the jury system are relatively less important, because we can expect that this preparatory work will be sufficient in the vast majority of cases, without the need to go to trial.

In this idealised version of the criminal process, there is relatively little merit in establishing elaborate mechanisms for allowing criminal charges to be contested or findings of guilt challenged on appeal. Of course, extending the logic of this perspective would point towards the rather more controversial conclusion that the occasional mistake might be acceptable if it means that in the great majority of cases crimes are being prevented, criminals apprehended, and effective measures are put in place to ensure that further offending is minimised.

WHAT DO YOU THINK? 23.1

UK vs USA

- Conventionally, in the UK, courts have been willing to accept credible evidence even if it has been obtained illegally (see Jackson 2013, for example). On the other hand, in the USA, if evidence is obtained unlawfully it cannot be submitted in court.

- This suggests a clear distinction between the two jurisdictions with the UK favouring a 'crime control' perspective in this instance, and the USA reflecting 'due process' principles in the administration of justice.

- How do you think the courts should deal with evidence which may be significant but may also have been obtained by unacceptable means?

- What are the arguments for and against permitting use of such evidence in criminal trials?

Take a look at **What do you think? 23.1** to consider the issues in relation to the use of evidence.

The principal focus of an approach driven by a crime control agenda is, therefore, the establishment of a criminal justice system which is best placed to identify criminals and potential criminals, to assess and take action to respond to potential threats to community safety or public order, and to intervene to ensure that the potential for infractions to take place in the future is kept to a minimum. In delivery terms, the emphasis is therefore on well-organised, well-resourced, proactive policing, effective identification of risk, comprehensive measures to ensure public safety, rapid and effective responses to crime and disorder, and efficient mechanisms of containment and control for those identified as perpetrators of crime (or representing a future risk of offending). Swift and certain justice is perhaps the watchword of this philosophy of criminal justice.

Objectives of crime control

The operating principles of crime control models

Having articulated a model of criminal justice practice which arises from an underlying logic of 'crime control',

the next step will be to consider the operating principles of such a model, that is to say, what it is intended or expected to achieve. In one sense, this may seem self-evident, in that its aim is to minimise or eradicate crime in all its forms; its purpose is to realise the aspirations on which 'zero tolerance' is based, and suppress any manifestation of antisocial behaviour. By implication, this means that the model also supports anticipatory action to prevent or minimise harm, as well as direct intervention to reduce its immediate effect and measures taken in the light of harm caused to prevent its reoccurrence (target hardening and deterrent sentences being examples of this). The challenge of implementation does become somewhat more complicated, though, when we start considering aspects of the model as alternatives; such as the choices the police might have to make between targeting 'known' offenders or trouble spots and being ready to respond rapidly to instances of crime and disorder in progress.

Crime control is expected to achieve its goals in a number of different ways and, in so doing, to serve several distinct objectives, including:

- reassurance of the public;
- the prevention of crime;
- the direct control of disorder in progress;
- the minimisation of harm caused;
- the detection and apprehension of offenders;
- the incapacitation of offenders; and
- corrections and deterrence.

In this way, it can be seen that the logic of crime control as an operating principle might be expected to run throughout the cycle of intervention from the pre-crime phase to the continuing effects of interventions intended to reduce the possibility of the repetition of crime and further harm.

Target hardening and defensible space

Considered in this way, we might also conjecture that crime control strategies are likely to be varied and ambitious. Its focus includes, but extends beyond, the individual offender, to include the context and consequences of crime. Its starting point, therefore, might be seen as the denial of opportunity, and the work that often goes under the heading of 'target-hardening'. Target hardening is a form of situational crime prevention (for a fuller account of situational crime prevention, see **Chapter 22**) which is also linked to the idea of 'defensible space'. Target hardening, as the phrase suggests, aims to make the physical act of committing crime increasingly difficult, if not impossible. Most of us probably employ a form of 'target hardening' a number of times every day—secure passwords for phones or Internet access, padlocks on our bikes, front door locks, car security devices and so on.

Similarly, the notion of defensible space assumes that crime can effectively be designed out of the living environment, particularly in urban areas:

One of the more widely known and enthusiastically received theories in the field of man-environment relations is the idea of defensible space: the notion that crime can be controlled through environmental design.

Merry 1981: 397

According to this line of argument, it is possible to build into the physical design of communal areas, 'spaces which are easily observed, clearly demarcated as public or private' (1981: 397), and which can become identified by and for community members as their own 'territory' which, supplemented by human security personnel, can be defended effectively from the impact of crime.

Moving beyond ideas associated with the establishment of orderly and safe environments, and partly because of the unpredictability of human behaviour, we can also identify 'crime control' as being about the management of people and their actions, not least to ensure that the space for regular and conventional social interaction remains secure. Business, for example, relies on the certainty of people being able to access commercial premises, or park safely in the vicinity. So, crime control is also concerned with regulating the actions and movement of people in space.

We may observe interesting parallels here with a quite different criminological concept, that of Bentham's Panopticon, the penitentiary design drawn up by Jeremy Bentham in 1787 which was intended to provide an effective vehicle for monitoring and controlling all aspects of the convict's behaviour (see **Figure 23.5**), which also depended on high visibility and surveillance of communal

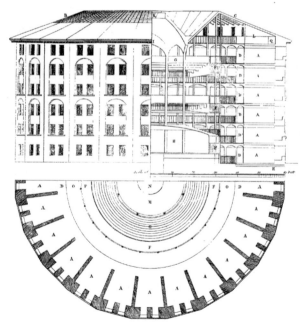

Figure 23.5 An illustration of Bentham's Panopticon
Source: Jeremy Bentham/Public domain

areas as a way of maintaining order, albeit *within* the penal institution rather than outside:

> Defensible space is a design concept consisting of four features: the definition of a space which demarcates areas of influence of the inhabitants and creates territorial attitudes, the positioning of windows to allow natural surveillance of public areas, the adoption of building forms and idioms which avoid the stigma of peculiarity and the suggestion of vulnerability, and the location of developments away from areas that provide continued threat.
>
> Merry 1981: 398

Physical design, then, is one means by which the possibility of criminal or antisocial behaviour can be anticipated and pre-empted, and quickly identified when it does occur, in the interests of maintaining harmony and security in the everyday lives of community members. Of course, as with any such preventive measures, there is another side to this; by defining effective 'ownership' of space which is ostensibly communal, and by simultaneously effectively prescribing what (and who) is acceptable, the creation of defensible space also creates a notion of what (and who) is to be defined as unacceptable and defended against. The presence of 'kids hanging round', and infringing on the sense of orderliness, just by being there, may indeed contribute to a sense of fearfulness and threat, simply in the way that it is conceptualised, and because it does not comply with an idealised design.

Control through incapacitation

Although the preceding example is controversial, it does help to move the focus on to the next logical function of a 'crime control' approach, which is indeed the incapacitation of offenders, or potential offenders. This can be achieved straightforwardly by imposing direct limits on identified offenders' freedom—by means of imprisonment, or less reliable alternatives such as tags and curfews; or it can be achieved in more generalised fashion through the use of broader prohibitions, such as dispersal measures, or the creation of 'no go' areas. See **Figure 23.6** depicting the practice of 'kettling' demonstrators by police, which has become a controversial issue in recent years. Is this crime control or a more oppressive form of state coercion?

In this sense, then, we can see crime control as a means of identifying and containing or minimising specific recognisable threats, whereby the logic and practices of 'risk management' come to the fore, and become key drivers of thinking and practice. Such measures of control cannot 'work' unless they are applied according to the underpinning logic of risk identification, quantification, and proportionate response—linked in turn to judgements

Figure 23.6 Police kettling
Source: Colin Chalmers

about the most efficient and effective use of resources, as well as the mediating influences deriving from political expediency and policy priorities. O'Malley (2010) argues that the emergence of 'risk' as a driver of criminal justice practices was noted by criminologists in the 1980s; and this reflected a shift in the priorities of those concerned with the administration of the penal system away from understanding and attempting to modify or reform the behaviour of offenders towards a more pragmatic interest in dealing with their behaviour in its own terms. That is to say, the priority became one of making actuarial judgements about the likelihood and impact of crime and taking action to minimise the harm potentially caused (Smith 2006).

In the same vein, the final objective of crime control as an operating principle of criminal justice is to eradicate, or at least cut down the level of risk by reducing the possibility of further offending. In this respect, interventions are driven by the threefold aims of 'corrections', that is, changing offenders' behaviour so that it becomes socially desirable and conforming; containment, in the sense of incapacitation; or, deterrence, in which case, irrespective of their motivations, current offenders (or potential future offenders) will be dissuaded from reoffending in light of the potential costs to them.

We might summarise the purposes of crime control as revolving around the notion of 'risk' or 'threat', and how these are averted, managed, minimised, or removed. Following on from this, we might also want to consider the consequential questions such as who or what might be the objects of any such risks or threat, and how judgements are made as to whose interests should take priority in making calculations about how to organise and deliver effective crime control strategies. Is there a trade-off, for example, in terms of dedicating police resources to crowd control at premiership football games, or preventing shoplifting, or responding to calls about racist attacks or domestic violence? And, on what basis could such judgements be made? These questions, in turn, prompt a wider consideration, and this demonstrates the extent to which an apparently neutral term such as crime control represents a range of judgements and choices at different points in the social and political structure which themselves are necessarily selective. That is to say, apparently unproblematic calculations about what constitutes the most significant risk to community safety and public order are themselves based on prior assumptions about common community interests and whose safety and security should be prioritised, as well as who represents the most significant threat. Particular understandings of risk, and of the need to control it, become normalised, and in turn, certain types of troubling behaviour become priority targets, whereas other, perhaps equally concerning, forms of unacceptable activity do not come under the spotlight. So, as well as asking 'what' is crime control for, we also need to think about 'whose' interests it serves.

The role of the police in crime control

'The concept of policing is closely related to that of social control' (Newburn and Reiner 2007: 913). When we start to think about tackling crime and the responsibility for doing so, the police are probably the first body to come to mind. Certainly until relatively recently developed societies have tended to see the police as the exclusive authority for maintaining order and controlling crime, although as has been pointed out, historically many societies have functioned without an equivalent role (Newburn and Reiner 2007: 912).

Despite the growing role of private provision and an increasing emphasis on self-help, for most people, most of the time, the routine responsibility for preventing and responding to crime and antisocial behaviour still rests with the police, whose legitimacy derives from their status as a public body, acting under the authority of the state. Their duties in this respect are generalised, and involve a number of distinct functions, from that of anticipatory action; through immediate response; to monitoring and surveillance. Approaches to the discharge of their broad crime control function will therefore differ, depending on the specific task in hand, and the priorities set for them by way of organisational and policy demands. A recent overview suggests, indeed, that the approach to dealing with crime adopted by the police is not fixed, but varies according to both the expectations placed on them ('politicians and the public still expect and demand a police service that focuses on fighting crime' Karn 2013: 3), and the emerging evidence as to what is 'effective' in practice.

Conventionally, it is suggested, the police adopted an approach to crime control which principally derived from theories of deterrence. By being visible and catching criminals they have been assumed to achieve the dual function of solving crimes that are committed and discouraging further offending. In order to achieve these aims, the police have mainly relied on: 'random patrols, emergency response, stop and search, investigation and detection and intensive enforcement. ... Evidence from research,

however, suggests that these strategies are relatively ineffectual in reducing crime and detecting offenders' (Karn 2013: 3). See **What do you think? 23.2** for a more detailed consideration of stop and search.

Instead, approaches to policing have become more diverse, according to competing ideas about how best to balance a range of responsibilities and expectations. Karn (2013) suggests, for example, that policing strategies have more recently been influenced by principles of 'risk' identification and management; in effect, by shifting the focus of attention towards 'specific individuals (prolific offenders and repeat victims) and places (high crime areas)'. That is to say, the police concentrate their efforts on those people and contexts which are particularly likely to be the focal point of criminal activity. Intelligence-led and problem-based models of policing have thus been developed consistent with these priorities. Although a range of strategies has been adopted as a result, such as 'hot spot' policing, and 'focused deterrence' of potential offenders, the common assumption remains that it is the primary role of the police to reduce the incidence and impact of crime.

This kind of 'targeted' approach was at least partly inspired by prior evidence of the 'limited impact of random patrol, reactive and intensive enforcement on crime rates' (Karn 2013: 14), which prompted the emergence of 'hotspot' initiatives, such as the Minneapolis Hot Spots Experiment. In this case, 'focusing interventions' on the 'micro-locations' responsible for the greatest concentration of police calls delivered 'clear, if modest, general deterrent effects' (Karn 2013: 14). In such instances, the efficacy of police intervention is further enhanced, it seems, where a problem-focused approach is taken, drawing on those concerns and fears expressed directly by the community (2013: 19).

A range of policing strategies have thus become prominent in recent years, with what seem like a number of shared features, and with a common aim of achieving approach is borne out by research evidence (of the deterrent effects of heightening offenders' belief in the likelihood of being caught; Karn 2013: 19)

WHAT DO YOU THINK? 23.2

Stop and search: police powers

A police officer has powers to stop and search you if they have 'reasonable grounds' to suspect you're carrying (see **Figure 23.7**):

- illegal drugs;

- a weapon;

- stolen property;

- something which could be used to commit a crime, e.g. a crowbar.

See www.gov.uk/police-powers-to-stop-and-search-your-rights.

The allegedly arbitrary use of police powers of 'stop and search' has caused considerable controversy over the years, leading to accusations of oppressive and discriminatory practice.

On the other hand, these powers are claimed to be of great value to the police in enabling them to anticipate the possible commission of crime, from the minor to the extremely serious, and this justifies their use of this power.

Do you think that the use of 'stop and search' can be justified, even if it means that innocent people will inevitably be subjected to this experience?

Figure 23.7 A stop and search underway
Source: © Alex Lentati for The Mail Online

a more effective approach to controlling and reducing crime, beyond simply responding to it when it occurs.

A further feature of the targeted policing methods outlined here is that of 'focused deterrence' (Karn 2013: 17), whereby police concentrate their efforts on known or repeat offenders, with the aim of increasing the level of 'certainty' in their minds that further offending will come to the attention of the police and will be dealt with swiftly and severely. Once again, it seems, the value of this

Zero tolerance policing and its influence

The term 'zero tolerance' has become firmly established in our understanding of a particular stance taken in relation to evidence of wrong-doing, not necessarily criminality, but rule-breaking of one kind or another. The rationale behind this position is that prompt and certain action achieves the objectives of both containing and limiting any harm caused, and symbolising the broader societal rejection of unacceptable behaviour. As Newburn and Jones (2007) demonstrate, the term itself has come to be applied in a range of contexts, such as the US president, George W. Bush's arguably ill-advised comments warning against law-breaking in the aftermath of Hurricane Katrina in 2005; and subsequently, the then Home Secretary Theresa May was reported to be taking a zero tolerance approach to illegal immigration *(Daily Telegraph*, 25 May 2012). Others, too, have adopted the term enthusiastically, including Superintendent Ray Mallon in the North-East of England. Zero tolerance seems to have gained widespread use as a form of shorthand for firm and decisive action by enforcement agencies to forestall criminal or antisocial behaviour (Newburn and Jones 2007: 222).

According to Newburn and Jones, the origins of the term lie in the 1980s and the Reagan Administration's war on drugs in the USA, subsequently being picked up and applied in a number of policy domains by George Bush Snr, on becoming president. The direct application of the term in the law enforcement arena is attributed to the New York Police Department under William Bratton, from 1994 onwards.

The argument behind this use of the term was that communities in New York and other major cities had become too tolerant and accepting of routine infractions of public order, which then translated into a broader normalisation of crime. It was believed to be something which was just an undesirable fact of life, like bad weather. To redress the balance, it was argued by advocates of zero tolerance that any manifestation of antisocial behaviour should be stopped at source to provide both practical and symbolic reinforcement of the idea that unlawful behaviour at any level was not acceptable. The strategy adopted involved taking immediate action to put a stop to any infringement of the law, however trivial, reinstate any harm or damage caused, and take strong measures to prevent any repetition. At the same time, a robust and reliable body of statistical knowledge would be built up to inform targeted interventions by the police, based on a 'management information and control system for regulating and directing policing at precinct level—Compstat' (Newburn and Jones 2007: 226). Of course, one of the consequences of this 'aggressive' policing strategy was inevitably a change in the relationship between the police and the community, and this may have been why this approach did not find many converts in the UK.

It seems that this approach gained limited support amongst the wider ranks of the police, with some being openly critical of its likely impact on police-community relations. Alongside this, though, the notion of zero tolerance did prove attractive in political circles, offering a ready-made slogan to the main UK parties seeking to maintain or establish their credentials as being 'tough on crime'.

This period of political grandstanding was 'ushered in' by senior figures in the Labour Party (Newburn and Jones 2007: 228), who went on to play a leading part in the government that took power in 1997. It is wryly observed that: 'Continued sightings of the term are testimony to its enduring power and resonance' (Newburn and Jones 2007: 229). And these characteristics in turn can be attributed to certain attractive features of the idea of zero tolerance: 'it is an apparently simple notion; … it is flexible—it has no fixed meaning; … it has strong symbolic potential; … in policy terms it became associated with a clear "meta-narrative; and … it resonates with contemporary concerns"' (2007: 234). In practical terms, it is also argued that it is an approach that works, with zero tolerance policies and practices being widely credited for achieving substantial reductions in crime and greater public confidence, especially in New York itself, during the 1990s; although such claims have also been the subject of detailed criticism (see Bowling 1999, for example).

Whilst the term 'zero tolerance' itself has been less prominent in policing, as well as policy domains, more recently, it is argued that the methodologies that it foreshadowed and underpinned have continued to exert a considerable influence on policing practices (Braga et al. 2011). The management accountability system known as Compstat, and the idea of focusing police energies on countering criminality though the use of systematic tools for measuring trends and changing patterns of crime has remained influential in New York, it seems. However, there has been a substantial degree of criticism of the pervasive impact of this philosophy in the education system, in particular. Zero tolerance strategies are blamed for creating an undue focus on criminality in the school environment and as a result institutionalising a form of school-based racism (Ofer 2011).

As the idea of an expanded crime management role for the police has taken hold, police forces in the UK have acknowledged a parallel need to move away from a pre-occupation with detecting crimes to one which incorporates a much wider crime control function, it is reported (Braga et al. 2011: 29). Notwithstanding the apparent emergence of a more sophisticated approach, simplistic terminology still plays a part, offering a kind of political comfort blanket at times of crisis: 'We haven't talked the language of zero tolerance enough but the message is getting through', said the then UK Prime Minister following the 'riots' in English cities in 2011 (*Daily Telegraph*, 3 August 2011), as he recruited William Bratton to advise him on how to deal with the problem.

Intelligence-led policing

Intelligence-led policing (Ratcliffe 2016), is distinguished as the term might suggest by the apparent need to develop a more systematic and evidence-based approach to dealing with crime. This includes a perception that historic methods were simply inadequate to deal with rising crime and public expectations; wider expectations of a more professional approach to management across the public services; the availability of methods and technology which should facilitate greater efficiency; and a feeling that criminals were becoming more sophisticated and better organised, necessitating an equivalent response from justice agencies. So it is that intelligence-led policing has come to be recognised as a distinct approach to law enforcement relying on a 'targeted' approach with very specific crime reduction objectives (Ratcliffe 2016: 271). Systematic analysis of available information, offender targeting (based on known characteristics), and strategic use of resources to anticipate or respond to identified crime problems would thus underpin police activities within an intelligence-led framework. This approach is largely proactive, and by anticipating crime and disorder it might be seen as problematic from a civil liberties perspective; but, of course, this is nevertheless consistent with an overarching concern to prioritise crime reduction (Farmer 1984).

Community policing

The idea of community policing appears to take a very different starting point to understanding the role of the police and their relationship with the citizens they serve. It is associated with an underlying belief in the importance of establishing good relations between the police and the public. The central function of the police may, indeed, be less about crime-fighting and the maintenance of order, and more about providing a sense of security and reassurance to ordinary people, allaying their fears about crime rather than prioritising its actual incidence. Nonetheless a community policing philosophy can also be seen as contributing to various aspects of a 'crime control' approach, through actively discouraging wrongdoing by being highly visible in the neighbourhood. Community policing is described as a customer led approach, directed towards establishing partnerships with community interests to assist the community to both prevent and detect crime, as well as decreasing levels of fear and improving the quality of life (Longstaff et al. 2015: 9).

Close knowledge of the locality and its inhabitants also provides a potential source of intelligence for the police, in terms of being able to identify potentially risky situations and early signs of problematic behaviour. In this respect, being visible and 'present' in the community seems to afford a greater degree of awareness and preparation to police at the point where they might need to respond to the incidence of crime or antisocial behaviour. There is also a potential 'payoff' to the extent that the community subjectively feels better protected, almost irrespective of the impact of this policing strategy on crime. Studies have been conducted which support the argument that visible police presence can boost public confidence and satisfaction with the level of police effectiveness (Mackenzie and Henry 2009: 5).

Problem oriented policing

Problem oriented policing also adopts a clear focus on the concerns of the community about crime and disorder. Its principles were initially set out and later expanded upon by Herman Goldstein (1979; 1990). The intention was to achieve a move away from what were perceived inefficiencies in trying to apply a standardised and labour-intensive model of policing across a diverse and increasingly challenging range of demands.

> The public calls upon the police to respond to an astounding range of problems and to perform an extraordinary diversity of tasks, all the while assuming that police have the expertise and resources to do so. Many of these problems and tasks fall to the police through the default of others: from gaps in government services, to the abandonment of responsibility by private citizens, corporations, and other organizations. This has always been a concern. In recent years, through a more methodical approach to policing, police are increasingly pressing for a more rational distribution of responsibilities based upon a detailed examination of the differing facets of police business.
>
> Scott and Goldstein 2005

The idea of using available knowledge about risks and vulnerabilities, communities and their residents, and observable patterns of behaviour to focus their efforts on providing efficient and effective responses to persistent problems is clearly highly attractive (Tilley 2010: 183). In a context of increasing demand and stretched resources, it seems quite reasonable to target effort on the most acute problems and to use tried-and-tested methods to tackle them.

Tilley notes the expansion of interest in problem-oriented policing in the UK as well as the USA, and also observes that as ideas about responsibility for crime control have shifted, the police have become seen as 'partners' in the task of achieving crime reduction, rather than taking sole responsibility for this.

One systematic review of problem-oriented policing has found that studies consistently identified a positive effect associated with policing strategies based on these principles (Weisburd et al. 2010: 140), although the researchers also noted that these benefits were fairly modest on average (2010: 162).

Neighbourhood policing

Neighbourhood policing is described as a further development of the principles of community policing (Longstaff et al. 2015: 10), The aim of those in government and the police force was to enhance the level of police engagement with the community further, but also to incorporate elements of other policing approaches which could contribute to improved performance and better outcomes. So, the 'foot patrol' stands at the heart of neighbourhood policing not least because of its capacity to conjure up an image of a friendly and available public servant always on hand to offer protection and reassurance.

Alongside this though, neighbourhood policing offers a number of other elements which are more directly geared towards dealing with crime, including 'hotspots policing' which focuses on 'micro-locations' where particular problems of offending or antisocial behaviour are concentrated (Longstaff et al. 2015: 22). These sites could be subject to intensified police activity, heightened surveillance (in the form of CCTV) and environmental measures to provide a coherent and integrated strategy.

This approach is also based on principles of problem oriented policing, in that it tries to make explicit links between the most acute problems of law and order affecting communities and causal explanations, in order to target interventions more effectively:

> The model requires a thorough analysis of the causes of crime and disorder, identifying strategies for intervention (beyond law enforcement) and involving other agencies and the community in delivering them It also requires checking whether the intended benefits have accrued.
>
> Longstaff et al. 2015: 26

Here, in effect, we can see intelligence based approaches being tailored to local contexts and very specific problems, where connected patterns of offending can be identified; although sometimes the implementation process has been found to be somewhat flawed, especially in terms of the quality of analysis applied (Tilley 2010).

One study of neighbourhood policing has identified significant benefits in terms of community perceptions and a sense of empowerment (Turley et al. 2012), although there is some evidence that others have found police to be relatively unresponsive to community members when engaging with them (Longstaff et al. 2015).

The police as moral guardians

Beyond the symbolic presence of the police as a visible reminder of social expectations and the consequences of infringement, there are other ways in which the police, as the manifestation of these expectations, are capable of exerting a direct impact on behaviour. Of course, they are mandated with the task of investigating crimes and bringing offenders to justice; but their crime control functions also extend beyond this, in the sense of exerting a more generalised coercive hold over particular populations, communities, or events. They cannot be everywhere at once though, so they are engaged in an active process of prioritising their work, and deciding where to commit time and resources. In this sense, policing becomes directly implicated in determining the nature, content, and purposes of crime control. And this can, in turn, become controversial, since it may lead to observable outcomes which will be open to challenge, such as the disproportionate use of police powers in relation to particular ethnic groups (see **Chapter 10**), or decisions about how to maintain public order which might involve restrictions on freedom of movement of freedom or expression. For instance, Stephen Gough, the 'naked rambler', has been arrested 'dozens of times' according to BBC News (October 2014), resulting in a cumulative total of over eight years in prison at substantial cost to the public purse—this is 'crime control' in action.

Beyond policing: The place of other agencies and interests in controlling crime

As the preceding sections perhaps imply, ideas of crime control are often infused by a number of technical-rational assumptions. Essentially, this perspective on the criminal process is underpinned by a belief in the potential to develop structures, systems, and mechanisms which are capable of maintaining or restoring an ordered universe within which it becomes possible to live daily lives free from unexpected transgressions or unanticipated harm. In Philip K. Dick's *Minority Report*, this is taken to its extreme, with every crime being anticipated by a group of 'precogs' who can see into the future, with punishments being imposed in anticipation of the offence. As in real life though, as the story unfolds things turn out to be a bit more complicated.

Nonetheless, the belief that it is possible to take pre-emptive action to anticipate and avert crime is well established; and this in turn has resulted in the development of a range of interventions consistent with this assumption, some geared towards making crime more difficult to commit and others directed at controlling the behaviour of actual (and potential) offenders. Thus, crime control has often been framed in terms of securitising the physical environment, on the one hand; or constraining the behaviour of likely miscreants on the other. 'Target hardening' is understood as the process of making property and places more difficult to offend against, and we can think of obvious examples of this sort of strategy, such as car alarms, or padlocks on the garden shed.

Planning out crime

Whilst people have probably always taken action of various sorts to safeguard their property, the origins of contemporary thinking about physical security and safe places are attributed to the architect Oscar Newman (1972), and the idea of 'defensible space'. The underlying assumption informing his work was that the way in which buildings and neigbourhoods were (or were not) designed could have a major effect on the safety and stability of community life. Thus:

> Crime control can be achieved by creating a situation in which it is possible for the potential victim to recognize in advance the potential criminal. ... Design can facilitate the process of recognition. Rather than the device of uniformity of population, such a design enables a varied and mixed population to know and control its own territory, to distinguish who (in an apparently complex and anonymous urban space) is neighbour and who intruder.
>
> Newman 1972: 18

Newman therefore argued that appropriately designed and secure housing provision ought to be available to all sectors of the population, and not simply remain the privilege of those few who could afford it. Specific features of such defensible residential areas would include the capacity to 'observe the public areas' of housing developments (1972: 78), and clearly marked out territorial boundaries, so that residents would feel a sense of belonging and responsibility for their own areas.

The assumptions behind this kind of approach made their way across the Atlantic, and the concept of 'situational crime prevention' became popular with the Home Office (Tilley 2002: 68), which launched the Safer Cities programme in 1988, involving the implementation of a range of 'target hardening' measures in a number of selected locations believed to be particularly prone to crime. Thus, for example, residents in certain 'disadvantaged areas' were offered the opportunity to increase the security of their homes to promote burglary prevention through replacing doors, or fitting locks and bolts (Tilley and Webb 1994: 8). The evaluation of the scheme determined that such forms of target hardening, especially when focused on those most at risk (previous victims) did have some effect in reducing burglary levels (Tilley and Webb 1994: 26; and see **Chapter 22**).

The contribution of 'environmental criminology' to debates on community safety and 'designing out crime' has become increasingly substantial over recent years, and linked to arguments about what makes a community 'sustainable' and healthy:

> As a potential tool for delivering such outcomes, crime prevention through environmental design (CPTED) strategies, guidance and policies have become increasingly adopted throughout countries in the developed world and in many developing countries.
>
> Cozens 2011: 482

However at the same time, concern is expressed about the strength of the evidence available to support the idea that crime can be 'planned out' of communities (2011: 499).

This observation in turn shifts our attention away from the built environment, and the physical and technological apparatus available for minimising or eradicating crime, since the question here is not just about the efficacy of such measures, but also about the types of crime and human behaviour towards which they are targeted. Essentially, security and design measures are concerned with crimes against property, whereas an overarching concern to control crime in general must also take account of the many and diverse types of criminal behaviour, the huge range of human activities these represent, and thus the need to adopt a much greater variety of strategies to deal with these than simply manipulation of the physical environment. People are, of course, able to adopt their own forms of personal protection measures, such as weapons (in those jurisdictions such as the US where it is legal to do so), mobile devices which enable them to stay 'connected', or panic alarms (Westmarland et al. 2013). Thus, in effect, part of the responsibility for controlling crime is transferred to the individual citizen, whether or not this is informed by a prior assessment as to whether the individual concerned is deemed to be at particular risk for any reason (such as age, gender, or disability).

Crime control thus becomes a personal as well as a community matter, and this is reflected in the ways that the state devolves such responsibility, for instance through neighbourhood watch initiatives, public information briefings about Internet security, or the promotion of personal safety measures.

The role of the community in crime control

Noting that the responsibility for crime control has historically rested with the community, Bullock (2014) argues that recent trends have seen the 'rediscovery of the citizen' and, in particular, the re-emergence of an expectation that people will take responsibility for responding to crime in their own right without recourse to the established machinery of justice. This, Bullock (2014: 7) believes, is a historically specific development, which increasingly represents 'a challenge to the view that crime control *should* be a state monopoly driven by expert fiat', consistent with a dominant strand of neo-liberal thinking. Earlier models of crime control, such as those outlined by Packer (1964), tended to assume that responsibility for carrying out this function would rest exclusively with the police. Subsequent developments, though, have taken the wider view that citizens and communities both can and should take responsibility for managing and dealing with their own crime problems. This might be achieved partly through taking individual steps to avoid the risk of victimisation, but also partly through taking on a more proactive role as someone who 'discourages' crime (Felson 1995); or who acts as a kind of 'guardian' of order (Reynald 2010). Of course, the risks involved in taking on such a role must be acknowledged, both in terms of the potential harm a self-appointed 'guardian' might suffer, but also the possibility that such forms of intervention will lead to vigilantism and harm to 'innocent parties' (Roehl 1998: 254). Importantly here, the rule of law is not seen as being diluted or compromised by the devolution of responsibility for maintaining order from the state to communities.

Private security providers

Even though we might still more readily think of the police as the appropriate resource when it comes to exercising active crime control measures, it is worth noting that this function may also be provided by a variety of private operations with a security-providing role. Zedner (2006: 268), for example, has argued that the undoubted shift of emphasis from the 'solid state' of the established criminal justice system to the more flexible and 'dispersed' activities of the 'private security sector' are a reflection of wider social changes as markets come to dominate, even in what has historically been seen as the public sphere:

> Put another way, successive governments have created a black hole that the private security industry is only too happy to plug and the state to see filled.
>
> Zedner 2006: 269

Private security itself is a fragmented form of activity, featuring 'bouncers' whose role is to maintain public order (and protect the owners' property) in places of entertainment, security guards whose task is to protect physical property, and others whose expertise is utilised to patrol and securitise the hidden worlds of the financial sector and information technology. Whilst in most of these cases, the rights of those concerned to enforce the law are no greater than those of ordinary members of the public, they do maintain the authority to exercise control and dispense justice in the spaces and places for which they have assumed responsibility, such as gated housing developments, for example. Zedner's view is that the role of private security is increasingly problematic, as 'previously public functions are contracted out to private providers', and this is 'a cause of grave concern when private providers fail to accord with the standards expected of public servants' (Zedner 2006: 272). Exemplifying these concerns is the example elaborated on in **Controversy and Debate 23.1**; in 2016, staff employed by the private security provider G4S were accused of abuse in a young offenders' centre in Kent.

Others, too, have expressed fears about the blurring of the distinction between privately and publicly provided forms of security and crime control—so 'elites' begin to organise and pay for their own 'forms of protection' in place of public provision (Loader et al. 2014: 480).

CONTROVERSY AND DEBATE 23.1

G4S and private security

A BBC *Panorama* documentary, aired in 2016, accused private security provider G4S of abuse at a young offender's centre in Kent. Staff at the Medway Secure Training Centre are alleged to have:

- slapped a teenager several times on the head;

- pressed heavily on the necks of young people;

- used restraint techniques unnecessarily—and that included squeezing a teenager's windpipe so he had problems breathing;

- used foul language to frighten and intimidate—and boasted of mistreating young people, including using a fork to stab one on the leg and making another cry uncontrollably;

- tried to conceal their behaviour by ensuring they were beneath CCTV cameras or in areas not covered by them.

Four of the men were arrested on suspicion of child neglect. A fifth person was held on suspicion of assault, a police spokeswoman said.

Zedner's concerns around private providers and a drop in expected standards of security and treatment seem particularly pertinent in light of this example.

The role of the judiciary in crime control

Extended into the judicial sphere, the crime control philosophy dictates a similar preoccupation with minimising the potential for criminal activity, by utilising a range of interventions to constrain, incapacitate, or deter known or likely future offenders. Once identified, those who pose the greatest risk are subject to a range of strategies designed to limit their opportunities to offend. They can expect to be subject to curtailment of their freedom, by way of imprisonment, electronic surveillance, prohibitions of movement, or curfews, for example; and they will also be subject to sentencing regimes which aim to achieve the maximum deterrent effect. Consistent with this perspective, there is little concern for offenders' welfare, or their rights, since both are subordinated to the more central question of whether or not the crime control measure implemented is, indeed, going to achieve the underlying aim of reducing the likelihood of commission of further offences. In this sense the logic of the crime control perspective readily infuses the judicial process—such as in the bald prescription of the Crime and Disorder Act 1998 that the 'principal aim' of the justice system is the prevention of offending.

Conditional sentences and periods on post-custodial licence might be viewed as a good example of the application of the logic of crime control to the judicial decision-making process. They offer the combined merits of exercising some measure of control (constraint if not incapacitation) over the offender's current behaviour, whilst also acting as a form of deterrent, and the promise of future incapacitation in the event of failure to comply with their inbuilt requirements. As retribution is not a significant consideration for those occupied principally with controlling crime, the prospect of being seen to 'let someone off' by releasing her/him conditionally should not be a major consideration; and financial considerations may also play a part:

> Conditional sentence orders could provide for such dispositions as home detention, electronic monitoring in the community and banishment to remote areas, at a much lower monetary cost to the community and personal cost to the accused than the ... cost of our current reliance on imprisonment.
>
> Gemmell 1996: 340

For some the availability of conditional disposals is welcomed, principally because the consequences of reoffending during the operational period are both 'known and certain' (Armstrong et al. 2013: 16).

So, we can see from this brief overview that the principles behind a 'crime control' approach to crime prevention and criminal justice permeate the whole continuum of policy and practice, from the starting point of 'crime proofing' the lived environment, through security provision and surveillance, to the specific targeted interventions of agents of the justice system and judiciary, with a common objective of minimising or eradicating offending behaviour. There is a strong spirit of rationalism and pragmatism about this orientation, in that the principal concern is to identify the most effective forms of intervention and apply them single-mindedly to securing the overarching objectives of containment and control. If followed through to its conclusion, though, this line of reasoning might lead to significant concerns about the nature, the practicality, and indeed the legitimacy of the 'justice' being administered, though.

Place, property, and people: The objects and technologies of crime control

It seems from the preceding discussion that we can identify a distinctive strand of thought running through the various components of a 'crime control' approach to the organisation and delivery of criminal justice, which might be seen as being underpinned by the 'instrumental [aim] of reducing or containing rates of criminal behaviour' (Garland 1990: 18). As Garland (1990: 126) makes clear, there is a distinctiveness and coherence to this perspective on criminality, which means that 'penal institutions and crime control policies have their own internal dynamics which cannot be regarded as expressions or reflections of events occurring elsewhere'. Implicated in these though are said to be a series of key assumptions, which are nonetheless related to wider strands of social and political thought and underpin specific mechanisms for identifying and responding to criminal activities. Thus, there is an embedded conceptualisation of the offender which stresses the 'freedom, equality and responsibility of the legal subject' (1990: 127), and a belief in the achievability of a 'scientific criminology' (1990: 127), which would enable both the probabilities of crime and effective interventions to be identified and calibrated to achieve maximum effectiveness. This, in turn, points towards and draws upon more generalised assumptions informing policy and practice in modern society, supported by an underlying belief in being able to quantify and address identifiable threats to well-being or social order, whether these be in the form of disease, disaster, or crime; encapsulated effectively in Beck's (1992) characterisation of the *Risk Society*. According to this portrayal, a form of conventional wisdom developed, organised around notions

of 'risk', expertise, and effective management, that dealing with any such threat is essentially a technical matter. Therefore, the potential for any particular adverse event of this kind 'could be redefined as the probability of a negative outcome that was experienced equally by everyone in a defined group', to which it was thus possible 'to forge a complete solution' (Beck and Willms 2004: 110).

Informed by these assumptions, then, those responsible for anticipating, preventing, managing, or eradicating crime might be expected to share a common belief in the capacity to calculate the probability of antisocial acts of one kind or another. Based on this, they would also assume the capability of devising and applying interventions with predictable effects and desirable outcomes. In other words, crime could be predicted and controlled scientifically. It would be possible, for example, to identify and quantify the contextual triggers for crime, and thereby target these for specific practical responses: 'Consideration of situational precipitators expands the range of techniques available for situational prevention and encourages crime prevention practitioners to think in a more focused way about the antecedents of behaviour' (Wortley 2011: 63).

Predictive tools and techniques

Acceptance of the logic of this argument has prompted an increasing interest in developing the tools necessary to be able to make reliable predictions about criminogenic environments, social milieus and events, or situations of conflict; to assess offenders' level of criminality and the future threat they might pose; to design, construct, test, and improve interventions to manage or reduce the risks identified in the preceding phases; and to organise and modify effective systems for administering and delivering these interventions.

It therefore becomes plausible to argue that we can start by identifying, accounting for, and addressing geographical 'patterns' in criminal activity: 'Pattern theory sees crime as a complex phenomenon, but even assuming high degrees of complexity, finds discernible patterns both in criminal events and for criminals that are scale interdependent. That is, the rules behind the patterns can be found at both detailed and general levels of analysis' (Brantingham and Brantingham 2011: 79). Based on this line of argument, attention has turned to the development of techniques for 'mapping' crime and thereby identifying 'hot spots', which can be shown to have certain consistently identifiable criminogenic characteristics. As we know, it is becoming increasingly easy to 'locate' ourselves by use of electronic technology and so it has also become relatively easy to develop geographic information systems (GIS) which can locate and analyse the incidence of crimes with a considerable degree of precision—although of course this does only apply to crimes which can be 'placed' in this way, unlike fraud, say. Although it is acknowledged that there are competing theoretical explanations for the geographical concentration of criminal activity, such knowledge itself is clearly likely to influence both policing policy and practice, and wider discussions about creating sustainable and safer communities.

As Anselin et al. (2011: 98) acknowledge, there are two types of theories offering explanations for the variable distribution of crimes by location: those which attribute this outcome to the 'routine' coincidence of 'suitable targets and motivated offenders' in time and space; and those which offer more structural and contextual explanations, based on the social and economic conditions which might contribute to the emergence of patterns of crime and disorder in particular neighbourhoods (Anselin et al. 2011: 99). Nonetheless, it seems that the identification of patterns of criminal behaviour does suggest a discernible logic at work, an argument further developed in consideration of repeat victimisation; in drawing out the associated implications for policing and other protective interventions (Farrell and Pease 2011); and in articulating the importance of 'designing out' crime when developing new products (Ekblom 2011).

In the same way as 'place' and 'property' can be the foci of strategies grounded in principles of risk analysis and management, so can people. Indeed, there seems to be a continuous thread of logic at play here, whereby the vulnerabilities associated with location may well be bound up with the risks of victimisation, for example because people from particular ethnic backgrounds live in or travel through certain areas, or because there are particular places where people with disabilities are exposed to the risk of being victimised (Sin et al. 2009: 87). It is well known that particular sectors of the population are disproportionately likely to be the victims of crime (see, e.g. Sin et al. 2009; Ministry of Justice 2010), and it therefore might seem that this might justify a 'problem oriented' (Scott et al. 2011) approach to policing crimes experienced by minority groups.

Minimising the risk of reoffending

From the preceding discussion we can see the logic of developing better techniques for assessing and dealing with offenders, once identified. In essence, the question is a simple one: how do we ensure that the risk of reoffending is minimised? The aim may be to prevent crime but the intended means to achieve this are very much about exerting direct control over potential offenders. The risk averse answer would thus be simply to incapacitate the perpetrator of the crime, but this does run into significant challenges in terms of capacity and resource allocation, and (albeit of less concern to crime control purists) due process and natural justice. Whilst preventive detention and indeterminate sentences have been afforded a place in the range of disposals available to the courts, there are clearly still limits to their use (see **What do you think? 23.3**).

Additionally, the growing belief in the capacity of various risk assessment tools to predict future behaviour accurately has encouraged a more pragmatic approach to offender management and punishment; with a balance struck between incapacitation, deterrence, and correctional interventions to secure the most cost-effective possible guarantee against further offending. As Merrington (2004) has pointed out, the notion of managing risk to the public has become a much more central feature of the justice system in recent years, especially in relation to the task of managing offenders who are perceived to represent a potential threat in the community. Thus research and development of assessment tools have also increasingly been concentrated on understanding and enhancing the methods for carrying out precise quantifications of risk and determinations of appropriate interventions. So, for example, probation has experienced three distinct phases in the development of such 'tools': those relying essentially on subjective and 'professional judgement' but with no explicit criteria on which to base such judgements; 'actuarial models' based on what are called 'static' characteristics, such as 'age' and criminal record, including the Offender Group

WHAT DO YOU THINK? 23.3

Indeterminate sentences

[Imprisonment for Public Protection (IPP) was] introduced by the ... Labour Government from 2005. [IPPs] were designed to ensure that dangerous violent and sexual offenders stayed in custody for as long as they presented a risk to society. Under the system, a person who had committed a specified violent or sexual offence would be given an IPP if the offence was not so serious as to merit a life sentence. Once they had served their 'tariff' they would have to satisfy the Parole Board that they no longer posed a risk before they could be released.

The ... Government abolished sentences of imprisonment for public protection (IPPs) for offenders convicted on or after 3 December 2012, and replaced them with different sentences for dangerous offenders. However the change was not made retrospective. It didn't apply to existing prisoners serving those sentences at the time. At the end of March 2015 there were still around 4,600 prisoners serving IPPs.

Strickland 2015: 3

What do you think about the idea of keeping someone in custody because they might pose a future risk of harm, even beyond the release date they would normally expect?

Reconviction Scale (OGRS); and the more recent refinement of this approach to include both static and 'dynamic' factors (such as changing living circumstances, or patterns of drug use), also described as 'criminogenic needs' (Merrington 2004: 48).

There has been particular interest, for example, in the *Asset* tool, developed for the purposes of predicting the likelihood of reoffending by young people (Baker et al. 2005; and see **Chapter 9**). A progressively refined version of the tool resulted in a claim that it was capable of achieving 69.4 per cent accuracy in this respect. It was also suggested that *Asset* was sensitive to changing circumstances and so could incorporate a dynamic element into the process. Subsequent further work and evaluation of the tool led to a slight increase in this figure, supporting a claim that 'Asset is still a good predictor of proven re-offending among young people' (Wilson and Hinks 2011: 29), despite a number of acknowledged criticisms. The sheer amount of work undertaken and the range of tools and measures developed certainly suggest that there is a deep-seated belief in the value and efficacy of such measures in government and policy making circles. This, in turn, has led to observations that other approaches to understanding and quantifying risk have been overlooked in face of 'the unquestioning confidence that has been placed in actuarial-based risk assessments' (Lewis 2014: 122; see also, Smith 2006). The suggestion here is that the emphasis on 'risk' and the technological processes involved in developing increasingly fine-tuned mechanisms for measuring it 'merely [mask] the intended purpose of assessment technologies as a politically fuelled mechanism of governance and regulation' (Lewis 2014: 132). Thus, it is suggested that risk and risk management are attractive in part because they provide a rationale as well as a set of validated tools for taking a particular (politicised) approach to the identification and control of the threat of crime. And, indeed, this argument is perhaps given further credence by the observation that despite all efforts to refine and refocus it, the best available tool (*Asset*), applied in the most rigorous fashion, is still expected to be wrong in about a third of cases in which it is applied, leading to a very large number of 'Type 1' errors (a Type 1 error occurs when the 'null hypothesis', in this case that the offender will not re-offend, is wrongly rejected); that is to say, future-oriented restrictive crime control measures would be applied to a considerable number of young people who would not have reoffended anyway. So, if such tools are relatively inefficient and could in effect result in a considerable degree of injustice in the form of sanctions applied inappropriately, it is perhaps surprising that they have not come under more critical scrutiny. As Case and Haines (2009: 322) conclude: 'Despite over half a century of research, we still lack a clear understanding of risk and its relationship to the behaviour of young people. Furthermore, the evidence that certain risks cause offending and that these risks can be targeted to reduce offending has simply not been provided'.

What does crime control achieve?

As we have seen so far, the 'crime control' perspective on criminality and the proper function of the justice system appears to lead us towards a technocratic approach. This is informed by a number of factors:

- underlying assumptions about the rationality of offenders;
- the possibility of calculating the costs and benefits of crime (and crime prevention);

- the potential for developing effective predictive tools to identify known and potential offenders;
- the ability to tailor interventions to identified offender 'types'; and
- the capacity to impose effective and efficient measures to reduce or eradicate the possibility of criminal behaviour in the future.

Behind this array of assumptions lies a further series of predisposing factors: the belief that it is (a) feasible, and (b) desirable to develop this kind of technological arsenal of crime control measures; and the belief that there is also an underlying consensus (a) as to what constitutes 'crime', and (b) as to the priorities to be pursued in dealing with it.

Given that this represents quite a substantial body of presuppositions on which to base an overarching strategy to address the problems that crime poses to communities and societies, it is certainly worth giving closer consideration to the contexts in which such strategies have been adopted and what results these may have generated. What, for example, have been the achievements of 'zero tolerance' initiatives; how has electronic surveillance been incorporated into criminal and judicial processes; what have been the consequences of applying risk measurement/management techniques?

The use of technology

The influence and capabilities of emerging technologies have also played a part in shaping ideas about crime control, as the capacity has clearly developed to be able to maintain extensive information systems and widely dispersed surveillance and monitoring operations. Although there is something of a contemporary preoccupation with 'new' technologies and their seemingly inexorable expansion, it has been acknowledged that the idea of applying scientific methods in the service of criminal justice has been around for quite some time (Grabosky 1998). Although they are mundane features of the criminal process now, fingerprints, wireless communication, and even the car are all technological developments which were at some point incorporated into policing practice. The argument for innovation has often been informed by the suggestion that continuous improvement in methods is necessary simply in order to be able to match the creativity and advances made by criminals. Grabosky (1998: 1) suggests that the contemporary wave of developments can be viewed as a combination of: 'mechanisms for surveillance and detection, ... blocking devices, and ... technologies of restraint and incapacitation'.

In the first of these categories we find specific technologies, such as the array of detection devices now located in airports, drug detection equipment, and more generalised technologies such as CCTV, evidence from which is now relied on extensively in court and is accepted as persuasive. On the other hand, the normalisation of such technology does have consequences which might be viewed as disturbing: estimates suggest that Britons are caught on CCTV '70 times a day on average' (*BBC News*, 3 March 2011).

Blocking devices are those which inhibit the accessibility of the intended object of a criminal act, such as audio systems in cars which will not operate once removed; but even quite simple measures can be used to achieve the same sort of end, such as tamper proof seals on new consumer products, to guarantee authenticity and avoid the risk of counterfeiting.

Technologies which incapacitate or inhibit, now include weapons of restraint, such as tasers and acoustic devices used for crowd control; various electronic tagging devices to limit the movements of suspects or convicted offenders; and even chemical substances which have been developed to modify the behaviour of convicted criminals (see **Controversy and Debate 23.2**).

It is also likely that technology will play a central part in crime control to the extent that information technologies are becoming increasingly powerful tools; and, perhaps unsurprisingly, in parallel with this, crime itself is increasingly moving into the realm of computing and its associated activities—since a wider range of opportunities are thereby opened up for illegitimate behaviour, including fraud, harassment, sex offences, and various forms of coercion and oppression. There is then almost an inexorable logic about the parallel development of new technologies and ways of utilising them on the one hand; and, on the other, the increasingly inventive and sophisticated application of methods intended to limit their unlawful use, especially but not exclusively in the realm of information and communications technologies. Bowling, Marks, and Murphy (2008: 55) set out a typology of technological applications in crime control, and their associated purposes:

- **Communicative**—the collection and sharing of information.
- **Defensive**—the creation of design features and barriers to inhibit crime.
- **Surveillant**—observation to provide security and prevent crime.
- **Investigative**—collection and analysis of information to prevent, detect or solve crimes.
- **Probative**—gathering of evidence to support conviction of guilty parties.
- **Coercive**—use of force to maintain order and restrain suspects.
- **Punitive**—use of facilities to incapacitate or achieve other purposes of punishment.

! CONTROVERSY AND DEBATE 23.2

Chemical castration

Chemical castration has been used in the UK, and according to the *Daily Telegraph* (3 March 2012):

> The treatment is being piloted by psychiatrists at HMP Whatton, Nottingham, a specialist category C prison which holds male sex offenders.

> The drug, leuprorelin, which is marketed as Prostap, inhibits the production of testosterone, which is linked to the high sex drives in paedophiles.

This form of 'treatment' has been viewed as contentious, though, as the *Daily Telegraph* went on to report:

> Psychologist Dr Ludwig Lowenstein told the *Daily Mirror*: 'Apart from lengthy jail sentences, the only other way to deal with most of these people is through chemical castration.'

> 'The idea of giving sexual offenders a pill to destroy their ability to have intercourse always provokes fierce objections on the grounds of civil liberties. But a child's right to protection is far more morally important than the freedoms of paedophiles.'

> But Frances Cook, of the Howard League for Penal Reform, said: 'Sex offending is often not about sex at all, but about violence and domination. The drugs used will not affect those attitudes.'

As technology becomes more pervasive, of course, there are also likely to be related concerns, about its improper use or misuse. Some have expressed fears of this kind, even whilst acknowledging the apparent advantages it offers:

> But do we really want technology to lead society? Where will it lead? Who will be in control? Will we have time to know that before it is too late?

And so, the:

> warning about the danger of self-amplifying technical means silently coming to determine the ends or even becoming ends in themselves, separated from a vision of, and the continual search for, the good society needs to be continually repeated.

> Byrne and Marx 2011: 34

The fears expressed here summarise increasingly widespread anxieties about the capacity of technologies of crime control to become so pervasive and sophisticated that they impinge upon freedoms enjoyed by the general population.

Whose interests does crime control serve: the victim, the community, or the 'system'?

The note of caution sounded here helps to remind us of the questions we need to ask about the underlying objectives of a strategic approach grounded in principles of crime control, and in particular, whose interests it best serves. As noted previously, the predictive merits of various tools for assessing the risk of offending are not beyond dispute; and in various other ways, the kind of certainty offered aspirationally by this sort of ideology can only come at a price; literally, in the sense of the economic costs of, say, failsafe security, and equally significantly in terms of potential social costs and consequences. It might be the case, for instance, that we all have to accept a certain degree of inconvenience, and perhaps worse, as the legitimate quid pro quo for the exercise of vigilance, as in the experience of the extensive security regime operated by airports. And in turn, it might be felt that this is a price worth paying if we can be (fairly) certain that the justice system will work well most of the time to protect victims' interests. The underlying assumption is that a crime control approach can be established to operate reliably and effectively to achieve this objective. Victims will be served because risks will be identified and reduced, offences prevented, and offenders managed, incapacitated, and deterred; in this sense, the crime control model is held to reflect victims' priorities in that it will provide reassurance and promote public safety, albeit at the expense of accepting higher levels of security.

Similarly, it might be argued that crime control offers guarantees of greater levels of community safety, so that the public lives of people in their neighbourhoods can be conducted safely and free from fear of crime. Once again, it may be the case that the community in general has to accept minor inconveniences (such as the fencing off of a popular short cut, perhaps), but that these are outweighed by the increased security that these provide. **What do you think? 23.4** asks some questions which should help to clarify your thoughts on these issues.

The problem, though, for both victim- or community-led understandings of crime control is that they rely on a number of assumptions which may or may not coincide with direct experience. As Roach (1999) has pointed out, for example, crime control was developed before victimisation studies had revealed some of the critical realities of the victim experience. Notably, as he points out, many victims are not well-served by a system which focuses on and indeed prioritises only a relatively small subset of those crimes committed. Victimisation studies, in fact, have demonstrated 'that the crime control activities of police and prosecutors only affected a minority of crimes'

WHAT DO YOU THINK? 23.4

What sort of minor inconvenience might you be willing to put up with in the interests of reducing levels of crime:

• in your neighbourhood?

• when you're out at night?

• at the airport?

• at sport or musical events?

• in a shopping centre?

Why do you think your tolerances change depending on the situation?

(Roach 1999: 695). And, as a result, in 'many cases victims were aware that contacting police about crimes was useless'; with some fearing that they would be re-victimised by the justice process itself. As Roach goes on to observe, the high level of unreported or undetected crime revealed by research into victims' experiences can be interpreted in several different ways. It may, for example, be the result simply of inefficiencies in the administration of criminal justice, or a lack of resources, which can be resolved by essentially technical means, such as increased spending or better policies and procedures. In other words, for some, the emerging evidence of victims' poor experiences of criminal justice provides a strong argument in itself for greater investment in law and order:

> Victims of crime are being let down. The police are failing to record a large proportion of the crimes reported to them. Over 800,000 crimes reported to the police have gone unrecorded each year.
>
> HMIC 2014

It could also be argued perhaps, that the justice system is overly-concerned with generic procedures at the expense of the victim's needs, and that its work needs to be refocused:

> Too often victims found themselves a 'sideshow' as police, prisons, lawyers and the courts focused on the offender, Louise Casey [Commissioner for Victims] said. She said too much time was spent trying to help all crime victims, rather than focusing on those in genuine need.
>
> BBC News, 20 July 2010

It is certainly plausible to suggest that the inbuilt logic and capabilities of crime control help to focus attention on crimes which are relatively easy to define and target, and which involve measurable losses. This may not reflect very accurately the nature and extent of victimisation and the lived rather than material consequences of being affected by crime. It is also argued by many that the criminal justice system in general, and crime control strategies in particular, have demonstrably failed to meet the interests of certain classes of victims, notably those exposed to what might be termed 'private' crimes, of assault, abuse, and domestic violence (Roach 1999: 696). Similarly, it seems that social inequality is also mirrored in a greater susceptibility of disadvantaged groups to suffering the effects of crime; and, as Roach observes, there may also be a racial dimension to this.

In terms of the wider community, again, there may well be a tendency for crime management efforts and resources to focus on those outcomes which are more easily and visibly achieved.

As Tilley (2002: 71) points out, in its application a crime control initiative incorporates a much greater level of complexity and uncertainty than might be anticipated. Even in the relatively straightforward example of CCTV, both technical and policy aspects of implementation have distinct implications:

> Lighting levels, local offending and offence patterns, lines of sight, patterns of usage, nature and levels of publicity, relationships to supplementary policing and security services and so on will ... vary widely. Even within the apparently simple and mechanical there is huge variation.
>
> Tilley 2002: 71

Some have gone as far as to suggest that the technological and risk driven frame within which such measures are understood, actually steers crime prevention strategies in a particular direction. Thus, for example, in Liverpool, CCTV programmes encapsulated a particular way of conceptualising crime and those affected by it. A new CCTV network was developed in the city to protect essentially commercial and retail areas, at considerable cost (Coleman et al. 2002: 91); and when this approach was extended to other areas of the city, it was noted that it represented an effective choice between investing in technological measures or in alternatives such as improved youth provision. The argument being advanced here is that the initiation and expansion of apparently neutral programmes of 'crime control' organised around specific (unproven) technologies also cement in place a range of underlying assumptions about which crimes are most harmful, and which 'communities' should be prioritised. Such processes:

> not only construct very precise definitions of what is (and is not) a responsible strategy for crime prevention, but they are also based on a very precise definition of what is harmful to the communities subjected to these strategies.
>
> Coleman et al. 2002: 96

Similarly, Stenson (2002) has also argued that public and democratic debates about how to enhance crime control are underpinned by arguments between competing interests about what the terms stands for, and whose interests should be prioritised when determining strategies and the allocation of limited resources; often this results in over-simplified caricatures of what is involved in promoting a greater sense of safety and security amongst a disparate population, where communities are not homogeneous, but overlap and have both common and different interests. Perhaps this accounts in part for the apparent emergence of a 'lowest common denominator', such that: 'As one community safety officer remarked … for a lot of councillors responsible … for community safety, it means little more than CCTV and more bobbies on the beat' (Stenson 2002: 134).

Tackling antisocial behaviour

Similar tendencies are perhaps evident in the recent trend towards developing an array of measures to deal with antisocial behaviour, which have depended very much on an assumed consensus about what constitutes problematic behaviour, what its effects are, and the importance of using tough measures to control it. In a way, these measures have represented an extension of the earlier logic of zero tolerance into the realms of pre-criminal behaviour, and indeed into the remit of non-police public agencies, such as housing providers. As Brown (2004) has observed, this extension of the scope of crime control encompasses wider social control objectives, with marginalised populations being targeted in particular. Drawing on Cohen's (1985) work, she identifies a process, whereby the term 'antisocial behaviour' whilst being symbolically powerful also appears to offer a kind of definitional precision to a wide range of activities which are a potential source of unease and distress in the community, such as 'violence, vandalism, dog fouling, litter and young people "hanging around"' (Brown 2004: 204). It becomes relatively straightforward then to parcel up such eclectic and undefined concerns, and provide apparently neat and precise solutions in the form of sanctions and prohibitions, including civil penalties such as eviction, or behavioural requirements linked to the threat of further punishment (and criminalisation) if breached. It is notable that the legislative measures put in place to tackle antisocial behaviour did not concern themselves with whether or not the criminal law had been broken. Instead, they were constituted in terms of civil law breaches, with correspondingly lower standards of proof (Brown 2004: 205).

Thus, requirements in terms of the quality of evidence and standards of proof to justify the making of an order also fall substantially below those necessary to make a case in criminal proceedings. In the context of antisocial behaviour, crime control strategies are deployed not merely on behalf of the community, but by the community: 'Neighbours are the catalyst for investigation and the primary source of evidence' (2004: 206). The community is supported in its endeavours by what both Brown (2004: 207) and Garland have identified as a newly emerging professional grouping 'a series of new specialists who staff this still rather inchoate and ill-defined set of arrangements' (2001: 171). Under this umbrella, where these emerging specialisms also perform the function of affording legitimacy to formal interventions of one kind or another, the machinery of antisocial behaviour orders 'and associated "civil" means of control are now an intrinsic part of … crime and disorder policy' (Brown 2004: 210), performing a function as an intensified vehicle of both 'responsibilisation' and social exclusion. The elision of crime control and social control, according to this kind of analysis, raises very substantial question about whose interests are being served, and what the underlying effects and consequences might be. Webster (2015: 41) has criticised the very wide terms in which legislation is drawn, as in the case of the Antisocial Behaviour, Crime and Policing Act which allows action to be taken against anyone over the age of 10 who 'has engaged or threatens to engage in conduct capable of causing nuisance or annoyance to any person'.

What are the consequences of crime control? Does it work?

As we have seen, an approach to criminal justice grounded in the philosophy of 'crime control' has an attractive and coherent logic to it, which is able to inform policies and practices that span the justice system from one end to the other. As we have also observed, there have been a considerable number of examples of attempts to put these principles into practice, and to enhance our capacity to predict the likelihood of crime (and antisocial behaviour), to identify the perpetrators of crime, and to take appropriate action to prevent its occurrence, minimise its impact, and discourage its repetition. It follows from this that much of the impetus for intervention in these terms is geared towards establishing and then implementing 'what works' in reducing the level of crime and preventing reoffending (Burnett and Roberts 2004, for example). This is reflected in a clear preoccupation with outcomes as measured by crime levels, harm, and victimisation and reoffending rates. Associated with this has been a growing interest in the development of increasingly sophisticated mechanisms for assessing levels and types of risk, and techniques and technologies to support effective intervention.

'Designing out' crime

Firstly, then, we can consider approaches which have been based on the principle of reducing the 'opportunity' to commit offences, in the same vein as the idea of 'designing out' crime discussed previously in this chapter. Here, the lines are somewhat blurred between crime prevention and crime control, even if they are based on somewhat different assumptions. It has been claimed by some (Clarke 2012, for example) that criminology in both its academic and applied senses has been preoccupied with offenders' prior histories and motivations, at the expense of considering those contextual factors which create the opportunity for crime. It is argued that it is erroneous to assume 'that the earliest and most remote causes are most significant. Instead, the more immediate causes are often more powerful in generating crime' (Felson and Clarke 1998: 3).

Put simply, irrespective of the offender's background, characteristics, or motivation, if it is made harder to commit an offence then it seems plausible, at least, that crime rates will fall. So, rather than seeking to address the potential criminality of individuals, the aim is instead to limit opportunities to offend. This has been the focus of the work of one emerging body of criminologists, who believe that a large proportion of crime is purely opportunist. See **Telling it like it is 23.1** for one personal experience of this.

Support for this argument is provided by a range of evidence, demonstrating that changes in patterns of crime can clearly be documented as a consequence of preceding initiatives or policy change. Thus, for example, it has been suggested that the introduction of motorcycle helmet laws in Germany had an impact on criminal behaviour, as 'opportunistic thieves would be immediately noticed when riding past without a helmet' (Clarke 2012: 4). As a result, it seems, thefts of motorcycles declined by about two-thirds in that country between 1980 and 1986, with little apparent displacement to car or bicycle thefts. Similarly, Clarke (2012: 5) reports that the practice of 'alleygating' has identifiable and sustainable impacts on crime rates, saving '£1.86 in costs of residential burglary for every £1 spent' in the first year after installation in one such scheme in Liverpool.

Again, it has been suggested that correlations between improved car security measures and reductions in car theft also seem to point in the direction of support for the proposition that crime can be designed out, at least in some instances. Thus, as the 'proportion of cars in England and Wales *without* immobilisers fell from 77 per cent to 22 per cent between 1991 and 2006', so the 'number of stolen cars fell around two-thirds from half a million to 175,000 per year and theft from vehicles from 2.4 million to 1.1 million' (Farrell et al. 2008: 18). The extension of such work into a wider range of studies, focusing on different types of crime, situated opportunities, and intervention strategies has led to the suggestion that 'situational crime prevention is applicable not just to "opportunistic" street crimes, but potentially to every form of crime, however complex, and however determined the offenders' (Clarke 2012: 5). This is a strong claim, extended even as far as 'complex crimes such as internet child pornography' (Clarke 2012: 5), which might initially be viewed as less susceptible to 'situational' influences. There are potential criticisms of this approach to analysing and managing opportunities to commit crime, of course, not least that it assumes a common level of rationality and calculation that may simply not be held by all members of a community or wider society (Hayward 2007). With what you have read in mind see **What do you think? 23.5**.

This leads us on to the linked question of whether crime control measures applied to known or suspected offenders are likely to have any kind of effect in terms of reducing

TELLING IT LIKE IT IS 23.1

The price of crime?—with author Roger Smith

Certainly some credence is afforded to this in the experience of one of this book's authors. My son worked in a Woolworth's shop where the constant challenge was to intercept children helping themselves to the large, attractive, and easily accessible pick 'n' mix selection placed a few paces inside the main door to the shop.

Perhaps unsurprisingly, the poorly paid shop assistants did not think that security and crime control was part of their job.

Here, perhaps, the question that might well occur is whether shops could possibly be prepared actually to accept a low level of crime as an acceptable price to pay for attracting customers?

WHAT DO YOU THINK? 23.5

'Designing out' crime

- Can you think of any initiatives similar to the 'alleygates' in Liverpool or East Sheen in the areas or buildings you are familiar with?

- If you have travelled abroad recently, did you notice anything different about the environment there that was clearly aimed at reducing criminal activity?

crime levels over time. As we have already seen in this chapter, considerable amounts of time and effort have been put into developing predictive risk assessment tools, as the basis for determining disposals for offenders. However, as we have also seen these tools, however sophisticated they have now become, are not in themselves especially reliable as predictors of future criminality (Case and Haines 2009). Despite this, it is reported that in a number of areas, interventions have been based on targeting techniques, drawing on calculations of the assessed risk of reoffending and the potential for serious harm to be caused by the offender (Merrington 2004: 59). On the other hand, it is also reported that sentencing plans are often misaligned with assessments of risk and 'criminogenic need' (Cattell et al. 2013: 50). However, as is usually the case, the solution offered is an improvement in the techniques employed, rather than questioning the entire rationale on which such approaches are based (Case and Haines 2009).

Crime control and deterrence

Effectiveness of crime control interventions must also be judged in its own terms, of course, in the sense of if and how sanctions imposed actually affect offenders' future behaviour. That is, does punishment have a deterrent effect? The evidence on this question has been presented in a number of different ways, notably distinguishing between individual level (that is, in terms of known offenders' further offending) and population level (that is, in terms of a general level of use of a particular sanction) outcomes.

Population level deterrence

Population level estimates of deterrent effects have been viewed as important in the USA, in particular, given its extremely high rates of imprisonment. The analytical

methods applied have necessarily been speculative, because this is not the kind of territory in which controlled experiments are possible. Instead, large numbers of studies have applied a range of modelling techniques to try and assess what *would* have happened if sentencers and penal policy makers had behaved differently. A further challenge for those trying to establish meaningful estimates of the global effects of imprisonment is to distinguish effectively between the different ways in which it might have an impact on offending rates. As Tarling observes, it could have deterrent (for both actual and potential offenders), incapacitating, or rehabilitative effects, all of which individually and in combination could potentially have an impact on current and future offending rates. In light of this, and the difficulties in unpicking this complex pattern, Tarling (1994: 175) acknowledges that to achieve any degree of certainty would be 'professionally challenging'.

Despite these methodological issues, a considerable number of attempts to resolve this question have been undertaken. Some claim to have identified substantial effects on offending rates, attributable to the use of custody. Levitt (1996: 348), for example, related crime rates to enforced reductions in prison populations in a number of American states, and noted that locking up: 'one additional prisoner reduces the number of crimes by approximately fifteen per year', effectively claiming a fairly straightforward incapacitation effect. In the UK context, however, Bandyopadhyay (2012: 4) claims to have identified a complex set of effects, whereby shorter sentences appear to be 'counterproductive', whilst longer sentences might still act to reduce levels of crime.

However, when reviewed more systematically, such studies are found to produce inconsistent results:

> One could use available research to argue that a 10 per cent increase in incarceration is associated with no difference in crime rates, a 22 per cent lower index crime rate, or a decrease only in the rate of property crime.
>
> Stemen 2007: 3

Individual level deterrence

When viewed in terms of individual outcomes, which at least has the advantage of relying on identifiable events rather than complex modelling exercises, the signs are rather different, at least in the UK. In this case, the evidence seems to demonstrate that custodial sentences are associated with relatively high reoffending rates—46 per cent of those released in 2000 had reoffended after one year, rising to 78 per cent after nine years (Grimwood and Berman 2012: 24), and 71 per cent of juvenile offenders released from custody in 2010 reoffended within a year. Whether or not it is criminogenic, custody certainly appears to be highly ineffective in terms of discouraging further criminal activity, especially in the case of short-term sentences. As the Ministry of Justice (2013: 4) has found, for 2010, offenders:

sentenced to less than 12 months in custody had a higher one year re-offending rate than similar, matched offenders receiving:

- a community order, of 6.4 percentage points ...
- a suspended sentence order, of 8.6 percentage points ...
- a 'court order' (either a community order or a suspended order), of 6.8 percentage points

For proponents of a crime control model of criminal justice, then, the implications are challenging. It seems that, for certain sectors of the offending population at least, a less 'incapacitating' court disposal might actually be less likely to result in further offences. Of course, this does not necessarily invalidate this approach under all conditions. It is still possible to draw the conclusion that what is needed is a better understanding of risks, risk management, 'what works' and with whom, and a more sensitive, flexible, and better coordinated approach to management and delivery of effective, tailored interventions.

The limitations of crime control

Is crime control simply a matter of developing increasingly sophisticated methods and analytical tools for understanding crime and criminals, and applying these systematically to obtain 'best knowledge' and enhance 'best practice'? Or are there other, more substantial considerations to be taken into account when we weigh up the merits and disbenefits of an approach solely geared to the management and reduction of crime? In effect, there are two types of question to be considered here; those that relate to the practical challenges of implementing a pure crime control approach; and those which address the moral and political dimension of this perspective. Some of the issues are interlinked, of course—such as judging an 'acceptable' rate of miscarriages of justice, or of police overreaction.

Practical limitations of crime control

Firstly, it is helpful to consider the practical issues related to crime control—what does work in terms of reducing levels of crime and criminality, and how easy is it to implement effective solutions? For instance, it seems that there is some evidence that some forms of incarceration achieve a reduction in reoffending rates; risk assessment tools achieve a reasonable level of accuracy in predicting reoffending rates; targeted policing appears to have some degree of deterrent effect; and target hardening and environmental planning also seem to deliver benefits in terms of reducing opportunities to offend.

The issues which have occupied policy makers, strategists, and operational agencies have been to do with continual refinement and enhancement of the methods and delivery mechanisms required to improve system efficiency and effectiveness. In this spirit, for example, the Carter Report commissioned by the UK government in 2003 was rife with criticisms of the operation of

the justice system, and with concerns about the use of ineffective disposals such as imprisonment increasing, as crime rates actually fell. Analysis of systemic problems and proposed solutions were all couched in terms of better management and operation of the correctional machinery available. In line with this, recommendations were made for an extension of the use of electronic monitoring, and use of short-term prison sentences to be curtailed (Carter 2004: 30). The report concluded that (2004: 43):

a new approach is needed to focus on the management of offenders ... Services need to be focused on the management of the offender throughout sentence, driven by information on what works to reduce re-offending.

By 2015, similar language is evident in the articulation of the government's approach to 'integrated offender management':

Local partners ensure that there is a coherent framework in place so that no offender of concern falls through the gaps between existing programmes and approaches. The intensity of management [is] related directly to the severity of risk posed by the individual.

Home Office and Ministry of Justice 2015: 7

It may be, however, that this emerging concentration at a national policy level on the technical challenges of developing and delivering effective means of managing offenders and controlling crime has led to a rather skewed view of the desired aims and objectives of the criminal justice system. In fact what has emerged is a particular configuration of issues, interests, and ways of thinking which are historically and culturally quite specific, as Garland (2001: 72), for example, observes: 'new institutional arrangements originated as problem-solving devices growing out of the practical experience of government agencies and their constituencies ... The crime control field is an institutionalized response to a particular problem of order, growing out [of] a particular collective experience'. Stenson, too, has argued that what might be viewed as an emergent and relatively narrow preoccupation with 'managing' crime has been linked with the wider trends towards a form of social organisation characterised by fear and anxiety and a desire to minimise threats to the natural and social environment. Thus, for him, in 'the sphere of crime control … there is a widely shared criminological view that the new lexicon of risk has downplayed older … concerns with justice as retribution or just desserts and also the welfarist concern with rehabilitation through criminal justice dispositions' (Stenson 2009: 25).

He suggests that the technocratic language and logic associated with this perspective lends itself to a depoliticised understanding of the task of dealing with manifestations of unacceptable behaviour:

> The principal goal of professional practice, consequently, is to keep the lid on problems through pragmatic risk assessment and management policies and practices geared to individuals and social collectivities and 'problem' areas.
>
> Stenson 2009: 25

This ethos has some problematic consequences, however. For an approach which is grounded in generalised calculations of risk and harm, the inexorable logic leads to the development of broad, probability driven intervention strategies and practices. In other words, crime control measures are likely to be driven by a set of calculations that problematise particular subsets of the general population, which may demonstrate what might be described as 'criminal tendencies'. Thus, for example, the identification of a particular neighbourhood as a high crime area might be sufficient to justify a 'crackdown' by the police, or the adoption of particular methods for dealing with potential offenders. This, in turn, has led to a series of controversial outcomes, particularly concerning discrimination against black and minority ethnic groups.

The moral challenges of crime control

Crime control and discrimination

Over a considerable period of time it has been noted that black and other minority groups are disproportionately likely to be the subject of 'stop and search' by the police. In 2011–12, for example, whilst representing 3.1 per cent of the general population aged 10 or over, black people made up 14.2 per cent of those subject to 'stop and search', and subsequently 8.3 per cent of those arrested (Ministry of Justice 2013). Taken on their own, these figures seem to suggest that there is an inbuilt bias towards stopping black people simply on suspicion of unlawful behaviour; and, then, as a relatively smaller proportion of the black population is actually arrested, the implication is that much of the initial action in stopping them is simply speculative, driven in part by crime control logic, which itself is circular. The greater concentration of resources on black populations is of itself likely to generate a higher rate of arrests and convictions (as it would with any group), which in turn provides the logical justification for the initial 'targeting' of those who are believed to represent a particular risk of offending. Thus, it need not be a prior policy decision, or manifestation of direct racism, which leads to this outcome; it is simply a consequence of the impersonal rationality of the machinery in place to control crime.

Apart from being implicated in institutional racism, a crime control perspective also has to deal with the challenge that it legitimises miscarriages of justice. Once again, if practice is led by an overarching goal of reducing crime, then the problem of unintended consequences becomes of lesser importance. In broad terms, this means that the objective of ensuring community safety and reducing the risk of crime overrides concerns for due process and the rights of those suspected of crime, as Stenson (2009) implicitly acknowledges. Whilst it might be argued in some quarters that the occasional over-zealous police action or unsound finding of guilt is a 'price worth paying' for the safety and certainty afforded by a consistent and effective system of justice, this is not a position that can be held comfortably, especially in those jurisdictions where the death penalty, or other forms of extreme punishment, are meted out.

Identification issues in crime control

Associated with these substantive concerns is the underlying problem of legitimacy for crime management strategies grounded in mechanistic forms of problem identification and risk reduction. Decisions about which crimes to prioritise, and which potential offenders are to be the subject of targeted intervention depend on prior moral and political judgements about how harms are to be defined and which of them should be viewed as justifying a response. In other words, despite their claims to impartiality and balance, crime control strategies are underpinned by specific choices about whose interests should take precedence and how they should be safeguarded. Behind a presumed consensus lie social and cultural differences which limit the capacity of any given system of justice to ensure equitable treatment. In a context of wider social inequalities, there is clearly a risk that an apparently 'neutral' approach to dealing with crime will simply serve to reinforce those inequalities. As Garland reminds us, the justice system itself is grounded in shifting social and political terrain:

> The new politics of crime-control are socially and culturally conditioned; and ... the content, timing, and popular appeal of these policies cannot be understood except by reference to shifts in social practice and cultural sensibility.
>
> Garland 2001: 139

Outcomes from the USA appear to give additional weight to such concerns, as the extreme consequences of a crime control approach seem to highlight:

> There is abundant evidence that zero tolerance policies disproportionately affect youth of color. Nationally black and Latino students are suspended and expelled at much higher rates than white students ... nearly a third (31 per cent) of black boys in middle school were suspended at least once during the 2009–10 school year.
>
> Kang-Brown et al. 2013: 3

And:

> Racial minorities are more likely than white Americans to be arrested; once arrested, they are more likely to be convicted; and once convicted, they are more likely to face stiff sentences. African-American males are six times more likely to be incarcerated than white males and 2.5 times more likely than Hispanic males. If current trends continue, one of every three black American males born today can expect to go to prison in his lifetime, as can one of every six Latino males—compared to one of every seventeen white males.
>
> The Sentencing Project 2013: 1

These outcomes cannot be attributed simply to the application of a particular policy framework and machinery for administering criminal justice, but it is undoubtedly the case that the USA is a striking example of a regime where the logic and practices associated with crime control have been highly influential, and where the consequences have been a markedly unequal distribution of what we might term 'substantive justice'.

SUMMARY

Over the course of this chapter we have addressed a number of key themes, and the following provides a brief overview of the way these have been tackled.

- Understand what constitutes 'crime control'

We have built up a picture of the crime control perspective based on its assumption of a morally neutral orientation to dealing with crime, based on the principle of finding the most effective legitimate means of maintaining public safety and reducing the impact of crime.

- Analyse the different methods of delivering 'crime control', including: deterrence, target hardening, offender surveillance, and incapacitation and associated intervention programmes

Crime control is essentially pragmatic in approach, adopting the most reliable and fruitful strategies for addressing the core problem of maintaining security and providing reassurance. As a result it draws on a wide range of methods and approaches, targeting offenders, communities, and potential victims in order to reduce risk. We have reviewed a number of these strategies and their likely effects when applied in practice.

- Recognise the role played by the police in crime control

The chapter has discussed a range of policing strategies designed to extend their role beyond simply catching criminals to develop approaches to policing geared towards crime reduction and providing a sense of security and reassurance to communities.

- Interpret the crime control model and the due process model understanding the implications of each

Whereas a due process approach to the administration of justice demands adherence to principles of good practice and ethical behaviour throughout, crime control strategies are more concerned with 'just' outcomes, and less so with how results are obtained. This might mean, for instance, less of a concern to protect the rights of alleged offenders.

- Critique the effectiveness of different crime control methods, including deterrent measures and zero tolerance initiatives

The reported benefits of crime control strategies are considered, as are some of the problematic issues associated with them, such as the infringement of civil liberties, discriminatory impacts of some community-based interventions, and counterproductive nature of some core methods, notably the use of custody as a supposed deterrent measure.

- Appreciate the practical and moral limitations of crime control

As noted, crime control involves a difficult trade-off between effectiveness and certainty of outcomes on one hand; and ethically sound practice on the other.

REVIEW QUESTIONS

1. Outline the main differences between the crime control model and due process model.

2. How does situational crime prevention differ from exclusionary forms of crime control?

3. What do you understand by the term 'designing out' crime?

4. What are the issues surrounding the use of technology in crime control?

5. What are the challenges and implications of prioritising some interests over others in crime prevention?

FURTHER READING

Coleman, R., Sim, J., and Whyte, D. (2002) 'Power, politics and partnerships: the state of crime prevention on Merseyside', in Hughes, G. and Edwards, A. (eds) *Crime Control and Community*. Cullompton: Willan.
An interesting study of the local politics of crime control, and the outcomes of contested arguments about how best to reduce levels of crime in particular locations. Issues of power and vested interests are explored from a critical perspective.

Clarke, R. (2012) 'Opportunity Makes the Thief. Really? And So What?', *Crime Science* 1 (3) pp. 1–9.
Reflections on the idea that crime is really a matter of rational choice and opportunity, and that the principal focus of criminologists should be to understand and resolve the essentially practical problems associated with reducing opportunities for crime and creating disincentives for potential offenders.

Newburn, T. and Jones, T. (2007) 'Symbolizing Crime Control: Reflections on Zero Tolerance', *Theoretical Criminology* 11 (2), pp. 221–43.
A careful analysis of the emergence of zero tolerance policing, its contribution to the crime control movement, its reported benefits, and some of the challenges that might be associated with a determined attempt to implement a comprehensive strategy of this kind.

Packer, H. (1964) 'Two Models of the Criminal Process', *University of Pennsylvania Law Review* 113 (1), pp. 1–68.
A thorough account of the crime control and due process models of criminal justice, incorporating a consideration of their relative merits and limitations.

Stenson, K. (2009) 'The New Politics of Crime Control' in Stenson, K. and Sullivan, R. (eds) *Crime, Risk and Justice*. Cullompton: Willan.
A critical review of the emergence of crime control in the context of new forms of governance, and the associated technologies of risk management, setting out some of the limitations associated with this approach.

 Access the **online resources** to view selected further reading and web links relevant to the material covered in this chapter.
www.oup.com/uk/case/

CHAPTER OUTLINE

Introduction 662

What is punishment? 662

What is punishment intended to achieve? 664

The delivery of punishment 668

Mind, body, soul: The objects of punishment 673

The organisation and impact of punishment 675

What are the consequences of punishment?
Does punishment 'work'? 677

Objective or subjective considerations: Punishment,
justice, and the public 680

What is wrong with the idea of punishment? 681

Punishment and the idea of 'just deserts'

KEY ISSUES

After reading this chapter, you should be able to:

- appreciate the rationale for retributive approaches to dealing with crime;
- discuss the aims and objectives of retributive approaches to punishment;
- recognise the development of different forms of punishment;
- reflect on the use and impact of penal sanctions;
- evaluate the potential limitations of punitive penal practices.

Introduction

The purpose of this chapter is to consider the place that punishment occupies as a response to crime. It introduces the key arguments advanced in support of the idea of punishment generally, and specific punitive practices, in particular. The chapter will explore aspects of the historical development of punishment, and its changing role in society. Particular forms of penal sanction will be discussed, notably the death penalty, the use of imprisonment, and community-based alternatives to the deprivation of liberty.

The chapter will go on to consider the role of the judiciary in administering punishments, before exploring its impacts and outcomes. The consequences of imposing punitive measures will be considered, including its effects on offenders and reoffending rates. This will lead on to a discussion of the potential criticisms of the use of punishment, including miscarriages of justice, its apparent failure to affect the likelihood of reoffending, and its potentially destructive effect on offenders and those around them, such as their families.

What is punishment?

Punishment requires justification because it is morally problematic. It is morally problematic because it involves doing things to people that (when not described as 'punishment' [and thereby legitimised]) seem morally wrong.

Duff and Garland 1994: 2

Retributive approaches to punishment are based on the assumption that harms caused as a result of criminal acts can and should be redressed by the imposition of an equivalent level of hurt on the perpetrator. This is seen not just as an understandable response to crime, but as morally justified. It has certainly been the case that this vengeful view of crime and punishment has often become seen as a default position, reflecting what might be termed a 'natural' orientation towards the process of dispensing justice. This embedded assumption is reflected, quite clearly, in widely recognised and influential belief systems, such as the biblical endorsement of the principle of 'an eye for an eye, a tooth for a tooth. The one who has inflicted the injury must suffer the same injury' (Leviticus 24: 20). Of course, this position is not shared by other religions, or even in later Christian teachings.

The philosopher Thomas Aquinas articulated the case for seeing retributive punishment as 'natural' in great detail, arguing that this is not just a matter of instinct, but that 'anger' and the urge to punish has a rational basis (Koritansky 2012: 118). More recently, the title of Ignatieff's book, *A Just Measure of Pain* describing punitive practices in the 18th and 19th centuries draws attention to the abiding presumption that the infliction of pain as a form of punishment could be considered fair and equitable as long as it complied with certain rules of equivalence.

Embedded in such well-established arguments is a set of supporting assumptions, of course. They imply, for example:

- that responsibility for an action can be clearly and accurately defined;
- that the consequences of such actions are equally clearly and accurately identifiable;
- that these consequences are predictable and understood;
- that the choice to initiate any such action (or not to prevent something happening) is made freely and rationally;
- that there is a commonly agreed framework within which the extent and nature of any transgressive action can be identified (i.e. what constitutes 'harm' and how it is quantified);
- that an equivalent amount of punishment can be specified for any harm caused; and
- that any such punishment can be administered in such a way as to constitute an equivalent level of suffering from the subjective point of view of the perpetrator.

Of course, translating such statements into the real world of lived experience leaves most of these assumptions open to question, as we shall explore subsequently. Importantly, though, the underlying principles set out here can clearly be identified in persistent and often prevailing notions of 'fault', 'just deserts', 'proportionality', 'equal treatment', and determinacy (in the sense that once the agreed price is paid for a crime, then the offence is dealt with and the matter is closed).

As we can see from this outline, a purely retributive approach to dealing with crime does, by implication, exclude from consideration a number of well-established features of the judicial decision making process; such as the sentencing tariff, mitigation, individualised sentencing, and, indeed, any role of the offence victim, in determining the outcome of the offence (apart from contributing to an assessment of the 'harm' caused). In fact, most of these modifications represent attempts to establish a basis for applying punitive principles in the real world, that is, in the specific and unique circumstances of every individual offence. Punishment therefore has to tread the fine line between apparently objective measures of harm and blame, on the one hand, and the subjective and contextual aspects of human experience and characteristics, on the other. So, in order to represent retributivist principles effectively and precisely, a number of procedures and criteria need to be invoked. If they are not, it then becomes impossible to distinguish punitive measures from other extrajudicial modes of response to perceived hurt, such as revenge-taking or what might be termed 'rough justice'.

The Icelandic sagas, for example, present a picture of a culture infused with a strong sense of justice, but in which punishments could be determined and inflicted by the wronged party, almost without reference to any shared code, thus taking a form which may bear no apparent relationship to the harm caused (Thorsson 2001).

Punishment and its claims to legitimacy

If we are to distinguish retributive forms of punishment from other ways of holding offenders to account or responding to crime, we must try to define them according to their claims to legitimacy, which in turn appear to depend on a clear set of working rules, consistently and fairly applied. These can perhaps be set out as a series of steps, designed to reach a fixed outcome which is 'just' in the sense of being fair and justifiable (both to all parties to the specific offence, and with reference to other punishments administered in other cases).

Considered in these terms, then, the steps to be followed are:

- Establish the nature of the offence (what was the alleged infraction, and what is the evidence for it?).
- Establish the extent of the harm caused (what was the injury and how were those involved affected?).
- Establish responsibility (who did it?).
- Establish intent (was the alleged perpetrator aware of the consequences, did they mean this to happen, and were they influenced in any way?).
- Determine an equitable balance between harm caused and harm intended.
- Decide an equivalent penalty based on this calculation, the facts of the offence, and 'normal' (culturally defined) expectations of punishment.

As a consequence of adopting such a formalised approach to determining the level and nature of punishment to be administered, we have of course moved some way from the position of simply specifying an exact equivalent forfeit to be made by the offender.

These considerations lead to a further series of qualifications to the set of principles underpinning the idea of retributive punishment. Firstly, it seems that the notion of 'simple' retribution in the form of an exactly equivalent harm is open to question, in that it does not lead to a consistently fair outcome in all cases. This might be because of subjective variations in the nature of harm experienced by the victim, the extent of blame to be accorded to the perpetrator, the capacity to apply an exactly equivalent penalty, or the subjective experience of harm from the perpetrator's point of view. In some instances, for example, the effects of *institutionalisation* may well modify the directly punitive impact of being incarcerated—prisoners may become habituated to custody, and so become less likely to experience the kind of deprivation that is intended by the application of a punitive measure. For some, it's harder to live in the world outside the prison walls:

> It's true what they say – your sentence begins the day you get out.
>
> Adult ex-prisoner, quoted in Social Exclusion Unit 2002: 86

> I walked into the supermarket ... and found eleven different types of bread. Eleven. In prison there was one, and you ate it or didn't. I spent ten minutes trying to make a choice, then stressed out and left without buying anything.
>
> Adult prisoner, quoted in Social Exclusion Unit 2002: 86

For those adopting a pure retributivist position, this represents a significant challenge—what *is* punishment in this sort of case? And how can retributivists take account of the subjective element in determining how to administer the appropriate penalty?

Intent and accountability

Similar considerations also apply when we move on to think about the question of 'intent', and whether punishment should be expected to take account of perpetrators' motivations and understanding of their own moral obligations. This may be the case in situations where neglect may be a factor, rather than a proactive decision to infringe the formal rule of law. For example, in the context of *corporate crime*, it seems that judgements of blame are mediated by the difficulty of attributing 'pure' responsibility to specific individuals:

The ambiguous moral character of work-related fatality cases, and of health and safety law, has long been seen as a barrier to the imposition of orthodox criminal liability, and has led to these offences being commonly categorized as 'regulatory'.

Almond 2009: 160

So, if it is difficult to attribute blame in cases of joint responsibility and neglect, what of those cases where there is no doubt about intent to cause harm, but no harm is done—as in the case where player one jumps out of the way of a bad tackle before player two makes contact? This kind of consideration leads necessarily to an important distinction between the conceptual framework, and logic of justification behind a retributivist approach to dealing with crime and the practical and empirical questions which must be addressed, and which are likely to modify a 'pure' and idealised punitive position.

Whilst there may be an absolute and clearly specified basis for imposing a specific and measurable penalty equivalent to the harm caused by an offence, this will inevitably be modified by the human dimension of the crime itself. That is to say, in every case there are specific factors which come into play which will modify this kind of calculation. How, for example, do we estimate the precise extent of blame in cases where carelessness, rather than intent, has led to the offence—as in the case of dangerous driving, perhaps? What account should we take of the personal circumstances which may have contributed towards the offender's actions—such as stealing food to provide for a hungry family? (See **What do you think? 4.1** in **Chapter 4** for more on this example.) We must accept that even the simple administration of punishment according to fixed and apparently definitive principles implies the taking of positions about fairness and justice; as opposed to simply implementing a neutral operational model for applying universal standards underpinning the delivery of 'just' penalties.

What is punishment intended to achieve?

As we have seen, retributive ideas of punishment are quite firmly established, and grounded in what seem to be fairly attractive and straightforward ideas to do with ensuring that offenders pay for their crimes. These ideas, in turn, provide a clear framework for establishing mechanisms of judgement and sentencing in accordance with principles of 'just deserts'; that is, the assumption that each and every offence will have a consistent, fair, and calculable penalty associated with it. Whilst there are problems of equivalence and a common basis for determining guilt, it is believed to be possible to develop rational guidelines for resolving these, in line with the overarching principles of fair and equitable treatment. Beyond determining the basis for imposing a particular form of punishment, though, we might also reasonably have concerns about what it is intended to achieve, and what it should achieve. Is it simply a matter of trying to find a balance by righting a wrong, and responding to one harm with another, for example? Or, might retributive punishment be seen as fulfilling a wider function, in terms of establishing and sustaining wider forms of equivalence, based on consensual social norms? And in doing, so, is punishment also designed to maintain a common sense of accountability and responsibility (usually individualised)?

The question arises as to whether retributive punishment is intended to have simply a practical function, in the sense of responding to a crime on a like for like basis. If this is the case, is it merely concerned with imposing an equivalent degree of harm to that caused by the offence? Is it intended to achieve some kind of effect on the offender, in the sense of removing the 'unfair advantage' accruing to him/her as a result of committing the offence? Does it provide restitution, in the sense that its aim is to achieve some form of direct compensation, and if so, to whom is restitution owed, the direct victim, or the wider community? Is it demonstrative, in the sense that it stands as affirmation of the rule of law and justice to society in general? Or, is it intended to achieve a kind of moral balance, whereby the principles of a fair and equitable rights-based society are maintained and reinforced?

In this context a distinction is being made between the different interests at play; the question might turn to whether it is victims whose interests and perspective should take precedence, or those of the wider community, or even the perpetrator, whose moral integrity might be held to depend on accepting a particular form of punishment. If it is the former, and retribution is to be administered on behalf of the victim (by a legitimate and properly constituted body), then there is clearly an associated argument for the direct involvement of victims in determining the level and nature of the punishment to be administered. Indeed, identifiable trends in the organisation of the criminal justice process suggest that this kind of argument is increasingly being recognised as having some degree of legitimacy.

Strengthening the role of the victim

Recent legal developments appear to have strengthened victims of crime in two respects: in that they have become more clearly entitled to direct compensation for harm caused; and that they have also been more centrally involved in the justice process, in the sense of having their voices heard and their views as to what should happen taken into account. Thus, for example, the Antisocial Behaviour, Crime and Policing Act 2014 made provision in England and Wales for a Community Trigger and a Community Remedy, whereby:

> Victims will be able to use the Community Trigger to demand action, starting with a review of their case. Agencies including councils, the police, local health teams and registered providers of social housing will have a duty to undertake a case review when someone requests one and the case meets a locally defined threshold.
>
> Home Office 2014: 3

And:

> The Community Remedy gives victims a say in the out-of-court punishment of perpetrators for low-level crime and anti-social behaviour. The Act places a duty on the Police and Crime Commissioner to consult with members of the public and community representatives on what punitive, reparative or rehabilitative actions they would consider appropriate to be on the Community Remedy Document.
>
> Home Office 2014: 11

At the other end of the scale of punishments, though, there has also been much debate about the place of victims in determining more severe penalties, and perhaps an emerging consensus about their entitlement to have a say in this regard. Whilst some have strenuously rejected the right of victims to take part in the sentencing process for severe crimes (see Moore 1999: 89, for instance: 'doing justice is the essence of retributive punishment and … victims have neither any moral right nor expertise to say how our legal institutions should achieve that justice'), others view it as a matter of principle that those most closely and deeply affected should have a role in determining the scale and nature of the punishment to be administered. Fletcher (1999), for example argues that victims should be given a role in the sentencing process as a form of empowerment, and as a way or 're-establishing equality between' (1999: 63) them and the perpetrators of crime who have exerted a form of 'dominance' over them. In addition, it is suggested that the administration of a suitable form of punishment is a way of achieving 'closure' for victims and allow them to move on. Bandes (2000: 1599) quotes a victim advocate in the USA who identified the impending execution of a murderer as an opportunity for the victim's family, in that it would 'open the door to being able to go on with the rest of their lives'.

It is also worth noting at this point that different jurisdictions, particularly those differentiated on cultural and religious grounds may also vary in their prevailing views of the place of victims in determining the punishment to be invoked. Thus, Islamic law provides in some circumstances for victims to have a direct say in the sentencing decision. Esmaili and Gans (1999) discuss the implications of this in some detail, in the process helping to dispel over-simplistic understandings of the operation of Sharia (traditional Islamic law). Whilst all parties to an offence are entitled to representation in the criminal justice process, the capacity for victims to exercise a determining voice in deciding sentencing outcomes varies, depending on whether the offence in question is subject to a mandatory or discretionary punishment; as well as the rules of proof applicable in specific cases (Esmaili and Gans 1999: 153). Where it is decided that victims have a part to play in determining the sentence to be imposed, even in extreme cases such as murder, they are entitled to ask for an equivalent retributive sanction (such as the death penalty), an alternative retributive measure (monetary compensation), or 'they can ask for forgiveness' (that is, a non-retributive outcome; 1999: 164).

If, as in the example of Islamic criminal justice, the victim has a central role in determining outcomes in some cases, but not on every occasion, this suggests a degree of ambiguity in relation to the question of whose interests are being served in the administration of punishment, on the one hand; and on the other hand, to the extent that victims may choose not to exercise their right to retributive sanctions, it appears to call into question arguments of principle which suggest that just deserts should be the prime determinant of sentencing decisions. As Edwards has noted, there appears to have been a recent move towards 'victims being encouraged, permitted, required or entitled to have input into criminal justice decision-making processes' (2004: 968), which implies that the state has begun to resign its claims to authority and legitimacy in this area to those directly affected and harmed by the commission of an offence. This, of course, not only reflects a shifting balance of power, but it also means that the consistency or coherence of punishment discourses is likely to be diluted in the process.

Victim personal statements

In the UK, government has increasingly sought to provide victims a voice in the criminal justice process, and particularly in court, as the following extract illustrates:

Victim Personal Statement (VPS)

Making a Victim Personal Statement (VPS) gives you a voice in the criminal justice process. The VPS lets you explain in your own words how a crime has affected you physically, emotionally, financially or in any other way.

Making a VPS is your choice. You do not have to make one if you do not want to. If you choose to make a VPS, it can be written or recorded if recording facilities are available.

If you choose not to make a statement when first offered the chance, you may do so later providing it is before the case comes to court. However, you should be aware that some cases are brought to court very quickly.

Once you have completed and signed your VPS, it cannot be changed or withdrawn if you change your mind about what it says. However you can provide another one to the police to add more information. If your case reaches court, your VPS will be shown to the defence and you may be questioned on it in open court. If you are questioned on it, details could be reported in the media.

The police will ask you whether you would like all or part of your VPS to be read out or played (if recorded) in court if the case goes to trial and the suspect is found guilty. The court will make the final decision on whether the VPS is read out. If read out, this will be done after the verdict is given but before the court decides on the sentence.

You can ask to read out the VPS yourself or ask somebody else to read it out for you. If you do not want your VPS to be read out in court, you do not have to choose this option. The court will still consider your VPS before deciding on the sentence.

Extract from Ministry of Justice (2014) *Victims of Crime: Understanding the support you can expect*

This illustration quite neatly encapsulates some of the key considerations and tensions involved in the practical application of retributive principles. Victims may be afforded a say in the decision making process, but this remains at the discretion of the court, as does the extent to which their views may have an influence on judicial thinking. The extent to which victims' views are influential, though, adds a layer of complication to the idea of equitable treatment of offenders.

Limitations with victim involvement

Whereas the state can adopt a united and principled framework for sentencing, this is less likely to apply consistently where influence over or even control of the process is given to victims. In this case, the victims of crime would then be free to apply their own individual moral judgements and ethical codes to the matter of determining the appropriate outcome in relation to the harm caused, and their subjective perception of it. Although, as Edwards notes (2004: 968) much of the rhetoric concerning a more prominent role for victims has to do with 'balancing' their interests against those of alleged offenders, in practice, the shift of emphasis also appears to modify the role of the state as a third party

to the justice process. This might of course partly be a reflection of a growing recognition of the relatively limited and marginal role of the state in preventing and controlling 'crime' more generally; but it might also be a consequence of an idealised assumption on the part of politicians that 'placing the victim centre-stage' (2004: 969) will necessarily lead to a more punitive approach to offending, in line with parallel assumptions about 'public sentiment':

> In the United States and elsewhere, there has been a considerable overlap between those calling for improvements in the position of victims and those demanding curbs on defendant's rights and protections. Several writers have argued that victim reforms in the 1980s and 1990s have been essentially punitive measures, serving to counter or restrict the protections and rights afforded to defendants.
>
> Edwards 2004: 970

Acknowledging that such moves may at least partly be driven by rather cynical political calculations rather than any underlying concern for the interests of victims (including those who are not 'matched' with an offender, for example, as is usually the case), Edwards goes on to suggest that the victim's role and the nature of her/his 'participation' in the process must be viewed as rather more nuanced; in practice the victim role is usually restricted to that of an 'expressor', one who is enabled and encouraged to express their feelings about the offence, but does not have control either in procedural or decision making terms. In essence, the unresolved 'problem lies in defining the relationship between the public interest and the victim's interest' and in the difficult task of achieving 'procedural and substantive justice for victims *and* offenders: can victims be given particular participatory roles whilst upholding principles of rationality, consistency and objectivity?' (Edwards 2004: 980 (emphasis in original)).

Both in principled and practical terms, then, it is hard to make a case for the argument that punishment in general, or retribution in particular, can remain entirely at the discretion of the victim(s) of an offence. It may rather be viewed as preferable for the state as an independent and rational authority to take responsibility for the determination and imposition of retributive forms of punishment. In this sense, the state can be seen to be acting both on behalf of specific victims but also the wider community and the 'polity', that is, the set of communal interests which are subsumed under the notion of the state. Assuming that the state is capable of acting more rationally and consistently than atomised victims and assuming that it is also able to represent a consensual view about the aims and conditions of punishment, this appears to offer a basis for a more equitable approach to the imposition of penal sanctions, based on a set of guaranteed rights held by all parties to the offence, and thus able to ensure fair treatment in the decision making process and proportionality of disposal at the point of determining the sentence to be applied.

Maintaining moral and social order

Retributive punishment could in this way be said to operate 'on behalf of' the state in that it acts to achieve and maintain a general balance between citizens in terms of harms caused and redress obtained, as opposed to specific instances of victim-determined sanctions which might be inconsistent and relatively more or less 'just'. Retribution therefore could be said to act to maintain a moral and material balance, whilst also asserting and sustaining a particular model of social order, which itself is dependent on the consensual form of communal obligations and responsibilities that this particular way of ordering the criminal justice system implies:

> Once society has decided upon a set of legal rules, the retributivist sees those rules as representing and reflecting the moral order. Society's acceptance of legal rules means that the retributivist accepts the rules, whatever they may be: accepts that the rule makers are justified in their rule making; and claims that those who make the rules provide the moral climate under which others must live.
>
> Banks 2004: 109

The harm caused by an offence is therefore generalised, and the specific hurt experienced by identifiable victims may therefore be subsumed under a wider category of damage to the moral fabric of society and the ethic of mutual responsibility, arguably alongside crimes without readily identifiable victims. Society is authorised by its legal rules to impose punishment in the form of 'censure' and 'penalty' which represent an imposition on the offender and restore either the moral and/or material balance. In this way, punishment may involve the imposition of substantive harms or the symbolic expression of disapproval or condemnation. Although coming close to a statement of principles of deterrence, this view of punishment is distinguished by its emphasis on repairing breaches in the integrity of the social fabric, so that 'punishment serves to teach offenders a moral lesson so that in the process of being punished ... they will come to see what is good' (Banks 2004: 111); whilst at the same time, the rest of the community will be reassured that the moral order has been restored. Banks is concerned, however, that this 'approach does not account for the punishment of those who are already repentant' (2004: 111), for whom punishment in this sense would not be necessary.

On the other hand, however, as some have argued, retributive punishment could well be viewed as justified by those offenders who accept that any harm they have caused merits an equivalent punishment—and in some instances are prepared to accept this risk as a rational calculation of the benefits of committing an offence. William Tenn's 1956 science fiction story, *Time in Advance* is an account of an offender who chooses to serve his punishment before committing the crime to which it relates, and the slogan 'don't do the crime if you can't do the time' also suggests a predisposition to accept the legitimacy of sanctions imposed on the part of the offender population.

And indeed, reports of offenders' views also appear to support the view that they may well accept the underlying rationale for penal sanctions:

> [What do you think is the purpose of a sentence like yours?] Well, safe-guarding shopkeepers. I'm nae entitled to walk oot to shops and jist help myself. I realise that I've got to be punished for daein it. ... 55 year old woman, 120 days imprisonment
>
> Quoted in Armstrong and Weaver 2010: 11

Paradoxically, the same respondent also felt that this punishment was having no effect on her and that it had made her 'worse'.

See **Controversy and debate 24.1** for a discussion about the purpose of sentencing in a specific scenario.

❗ CONTROVERSY AND DEBATE 24.1

On 15 July 2016, a coup d'état was attempted in Turkey against the government. The attempted coup was carried out by the Turkish Armed Forces, but after attempting to gain control of key areas in Turkey, the coup was quashed by supporters of President Erdoğan.

In the wake of this severe threat to his position, government, and safety, President Erdoğan told a rally of more than one million people that he would approve the death penalty if approved by parliament. Erdogan said:

> As the sovereignty unconditionally belongs to the nation and as you request the death penalty [for the coup lead-

ers], the authority which is going to decide on this issue is Turkey's National Assembly. If our parliament takes such a decision, the necessary step will be taken. I am expressing in advance, I will approve such a decision coming from the parliament.

Independent, Accessed 8th August 2016, *http://www.independent.co.uk/news/world/europe/turkey-death-penalty-erdogan-coup-president-backs-capital-punishment-a7178371.html*

In light of the theories discussed in this chapter, what purpose (according to President Erdoğan and the Turkish National Assembly) do you believe the death penalty would be serving in this situation?

So, in considering the question of what punishment is 'for', and whose needs and expectations it is intended to meet, we can perhaps conclude that it might be seen as a legitimate and reasonable imposition by any of those with a direct or indirect investment in the commission of an offence. Its justification in terms of being 'the price to pay'

metaphorically and sometimes literally for breaching the commonly held formal rules of society is widely accepted; but this still leaves open a series of questions about the 'practice' of punishment, its effects and consequences, and whether or not it is justifiable, either in its own terms or more generally—questions to which we shall now turn.

The delivery of punishment

The nature of the punishment inflicted is dependent on two things. Firstly, the way in which crimes are defined, and secondly, on the value system which determines the appropriate sentence. In one sense, perhaps, it may be that the very idea of 'crime' implies an equivalent form of penalty; but as we have already acknowledged, there are debates to be had between the different aims and objectives of the justice system. Adopting a retributive model of punishment is therefore a matter of choice and, in taking this position, it seems that certain forms of penal sanction can be seen to be consistent with this preference; especially those which involve some form of deprivation, suffering, or physical harm. As we have seen, there are clear variations even within the retributive perspective over the meaning of harm and victimisation and therefore just what punishment can and should achieve, and for whom. And it is therefore understandable that the kind of penalties to be imposed should vary, from those relying on the infliction of physical harm, or even death, to those involving deprivations—of freedom, residence, dignity (in the form of the 'stocks', or high visibility unpaid labour, perhaps), or time—and those involving some form of recompense—fines or unpaid labour, for instance. At different times, this has posed specific challenges.

A historical perspective

While it has to be acknowledged that all societies seem to have grappled with the idea of crime and punishment, and how to deal with those who offend, it also seems that their approaches have varied over the course of history. In Victorian times, the problem of who and how to punish was 'exacerbated' (Tomlinson 1981: 126) by the problem that three of its preferred punishment options were called into question at the same time—that is, hanging, transportation, and imprisonment on the 'prison hulks' (as shown in **Figure 24.1**—Britain started converting old merchant ships and naval vessels into floating prisons known as hulks. Many of these were on the River Thames. Convicts spent time on the hulks before being transported to Australia, the new destination for Britain's criminals). Similarly, there are acknowledged problems

over proportionality, and what type and degree of punishment equates to the harm caused and the intentions of the offender. To explore this, it is worth considering the history of punishment.

As we have just observed, the history of punishment provides a striking insight into social norms, and the ideas people have held over time about what is acceptable in terms of the way offenders are treated. What we understand—or what has been understood in the past—by the idea of just and fair punishment is shown to be subject to wide variation. Cultural differences are sometimes stark. Certainly, when we consider historical and geographical variations, it becomes clear that there are considerable variations in prevailing ideas as to what is deemed reasonable and appropriate. Thus, it is suggested: 'Back in the day, retribution tended to be exacted through cruel and violent forms of punishment' (Materni 2013: 267). Materni goes on to cite Foucault's (1979) work, *Discipline and Punishment*, which is recognised as a major contribution to our understanding both of the historical development of punishment and of its wider role in maintaining social order and the rule of law.

Foucault's graphic description of the punishment administered to 'Damiens the regicide', in 1757 is striking and shocking, as was intended, no doubt (see **Figure 24.2** for a visual representation). Damiens had attempted to

Figure 24.1 A depiction of Victorian prison hulks
Source: Public domain

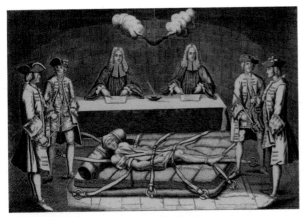

Figure 24.2 Robert-François Damiens lying before his executioners
Source: Bibliothèque nationale de France/Public domain

assassinate the French king, Louis XV, who had in fact survived the attack with only a minor knife wound. This case represented only the extreme form of an established tradition. Although it was an extreme example of execution involving drawing and quartering in France, it was:

> not the exception; in the eighteenth century, the administration of criminal law in continental Europe was barbaric. Gallows, torture, branding, mutilation, and the wheel were commonplace in the administration of 'justice; the death penalty was implemented even for the most trivial of crimes, such as, for example, stealing a handkerchief.
>
> Materni 2013: 268

In Elizabethan England, similarly, the nature of the punishments described seems extreme from the present day perspective. Being 'hung, drawn, and quartered', for example, was to experience a brutal and ritualistic process of dismemberment:

> The greatest and most grievous punishment used in England for such as offend against the State is drawing from the prison to the place of execution upon an hurdle or sled, where they are hanged till they be half dead, and then taken down, and quartered alive; after that, their members and bowels are cut from their bodies, and thrown into a fire, provided near hand and within their own sight, even for the same purpose.
>
> Harrison 1577

And for lesser offences 'rogues and vagabonds' might be 'stocked and whipped', while thieves would be 'hanged', except in Halifax, Yorkshire, where they could expect to be 'beheaded after a strange manner', by way of a form of guillotine (Webb 2011: 40).

The latter example highlights the issue of proportionality of punishment, which poses a particular challenge to retributivists. That is to say, the punishment that 'fits' the crime can be seen to vary enormously in different historical periods; and this suggests that there is likely always to be a chance element to any fixed tariff of criminal sanctions, however reasonable this may appear at the point where it is established. The era of the 'Bloody Code' in England, for example, saw the number of offences subject to the death penalty increase from around 50 to 220 between 1688–1815. It seems clear that the use of such punishments was both fairly common, and a cause of growing concern: 'Executions were enormously popular events, a fact that deeply frightened reformers' (Wiener 1990: 95). See the account in **Telling it like it is 24.1** for a specific example.

On the other hand, it may well have been the very extensiveness of the Bloody Code that progressively enhanced general feelings of unease about the scope and scale of punishments administered: 'Juries appear to have been increasingly unwilling to convict on an array of minor capital charges' note Godfrey and Lawrence (2005: 70). As King and Ward (2015) also show, there was considerable regional variation in jury behaviour in the 18th century, with those in some areas, including Wales, seeking to convict on lesser charges to avoid the imposition of the death penalty.

Prisons

As Wiener notes, it was not so much the retributive nature of such dramatic punishments, and others including the 'convict ship' and transportation, that prompted their decline and eventual abolition, but their 'arbitrariness and their tendency to incite dangerous passions' (1990: 100), at least partly because of their visibility. Instead, retribution came to be substantially catered for in the form of the prison, with the denial of freedom taking over from the infliction of pain as the medium of punishment. Foucault (1979) has written graphically of this transition, suggesting that the prison itself represented almost perfectly the translation of an emerging spirit of rationality into its penal form. The idea of imprisonment mirrored and was 'bound up ... with the very functioning of society', such that it was able to '[banish] into oblivion' other forms of punishment, real and imagined (Foucault 1984: 215). Its characteristics and its relatively straightforward calculability render the use of custody inherently convincing to those concerned with penal policy:

> This 'self-evident' character of the prison, which we find so difficult to abandon, is based first of all on the simple form of 'deprivation of liberty'. How could the prison not be the penalty *par excellence* in a society in which liberty is a good that belongs to all in the same way and to which each individual is attached ... by a 'universal and constant' feeling? Its loss has therefore the same value for all; unlike the fine, it is an 'egalitarian' punishment ... By levying on the time of the

TELLING IT LIKE IT IS 24.1

The spectacle of the gallows—with author Roger Smith

This is written in a building in Durham, in North East England, fronted by a balcony on which paying crowds used to assemble to watch public hangings (see **Figure 24.3**)!

From August 1816, a 'New Drop' style gallows was erected on the steps outside the new courthouse for each hanging. The condemned person came out through a window onto the platform of the gallows set over the main door. This was not an unusual arrangement as it was simpler and more secure than bringing the person out of the prison gates and then making them climb steps up to the gallows platform. It was thus quite convenient and was an easy location to guard. Across the street is the house depicted in **Figure 24.3** with an iron balcony that was rented out to wealthy spectators to watch the hanging from.

(From: http://www.capitalpunishmentuk.org/durham.html)

Figure 24.3 Balcony at 30, Old Elvet, Durham, from which wealthy spectators would watch hangings on the 'new drop' style gallows outside the courthouse in the 19th century

Source: Roger Smith

prisoner, the prison seems to express in concrete terms the idea that the offense has injured, beyond the victim, society as a whole.

Foucault 1984: 215

Of course, for retributivists prison also carries the added advantage that it is possible also to promote it as meeting deterrent or correctional aims, and it need not therefore be the focus of ideological disputes about its true purpose. In Foucault's terms, the prison has a 'double foundation—juridico-economic on the one hand, technico-disciplinary on the other' which made it appear to be 'the most immediate and civilized form of all penalties' (Foucault 1984: 216).

The change in techniques of punishment in Western societies from the early 19th century appears to be quite dramatic, although other forms of 'bodily punishment' continued well into the 20th century, with the abolition of capital punishment in the UK occurring only in 1965. Nonetheless, it is from the early 19th century that the prison was developed as the central element of the machinery of punishment. Its specific features of containment, routinised and uniform treatment, and loss of time were more consistent with the spirit of the age. As a result, there was a 'swathe of prison building during this period' (Godfrey and Lawrence 2005: 75), with a number of what could be described as 'state of the art' institutions being developed during this period. As a result, custodial sentencing became the norm very rapidly, so that in the '1860s, over 90 per cent of those convicted of indictable offences went to prison' (Godfrey and Lawrence 2005: 75).

In fact, at this point debates about the proper purpose of punishment were not focused around the point of sentence or the proper sanction to be imposed, but were found instead to occur within the prison establishment itself. It was not simply the imposition of a custodial sentence which constituted the punishment to be administered, but in many cases the parallel operation of a harsh and intensive regime of 'hard labour'. Measures to intensify the prison experience were passed by parliament and the 'task of enforcing the new-style penal servitude' was given to Sir Edmund Frederick Du Cane in 1863, who declared it his hope that it would become 'the last and most dreaded result of a heinous crime against life and property short of capital punishment', and did his utmost to ensure that it would be (Tomlinson 1981: 141).

Comparing regimes in the mid-19th century to prison conditions 100 years later Godfrey and Lawrence certainly suggest that the role and nature of imprisonment 'was by no means unchanging' (2005: 81), citing an example of a petty offender required to 'turn a hand crank weighted at thirty pounds pressure ten thousand times every ten hours'. This was not untypical of this kind of prison regime in the Victorian era; and, in its pointless repressiveness, this intensification of prisoners' suffering can only really be seen as conforming to the logic of retribution in the form of atonement, taken to its extreme.

Despite the apparent enthusiasm for this kind of meaningless penance in some quarters, others such as Henry Mayhew became concerned at the simplistic association of 'hard labour' with punishment (Wiener 1990: 118).

Pointless activities involving nothing but suffering would make 'regular labour' less attractive, rather than more so, to the criminal, it was argued. This was not to suggest that demanding work should not form a key element of the overall sanction, but that it should incorporate some sort of meaningful productive purpose. The consequences of this kind of logic can be seen in subsequent developments such as the chain gangs of the USA, or labour camps in Russia, but also in the incorporation of mandatory and unpaid labour into a range of punishments administered in the UK.

Punishment in modern times

Indeed, so attractive has the idea of unpaid work as a punitive sanction become that it has gained increasing prominence in penal policy-making over the course of time. Unpaid work in the community by convicted offenders has become a popular option for policy makers. Thus, the former Secretary of State for Justice, Chris Grayling (serving between 2012–15—see **Figure 24.4**), stated: 'I share public concern that offenders given community sentences often feel they are getting away with it, slapped on the wrist rather than properly punished' and

that the government would ensure that: 'Courts will be required to make sure there is punishment in every community order—whether community payback, a curfew that curtails an offender's freedom, or fines' (Grayling 2012: 3–4). And further to this, 'community payback' would 'in future involve a full five day week of hard work and job seeking'. The aim would be to ensure that, irrespective of any other aims, offenders' unpaid labour would be a demanding and uncomfortable experience, 'properly punitive' in the Minister's words; and this in turn would be effectively complemented by the requirement for those engaged in community payback activities to wear high visibility vests so that justice could be 'seen to be done'— perhaps ironically reminiscent of the kind of 'spectacle' associated with historic forms of punishment such as the stocks and pillory.

There are other possible motivations for and applications of the principle of community service, as a form of judicial disposal. As with the prison, the scope for ambiguity may well contribute to its apparent popularity as a sentence of the courts—indeed, it is capable of being construed as at the same time retributive, correctional, deterrent, rehabilitative, and restorative. However, the manner of its administration and, indeed, its outcomes might be taken to indicate a bias in practice towards one or other of these very diverse sentencing objectives.

Fines

Having covered capital punishment, imprisonment, and community punishments, the final example of a retributive measure to be considered here is the fine, which has rather less of a sense of ambiguity about it. On the face of it, it seems to represent a fairly straightforward manifestation of the retributive principle of 'paying the price' for an offence committed. In medieval Iceland, for example, fines were central to the administration of justice, and in some instances could be seen as a legitimate sanction in the case of serious crimes, including murder (Friedman 1979).

The significance and universality of money makes it an ideal vehicle for translating the abstract notion of a 'just and fair punishment' into a form which appears to represent a precise and easily measurable level of hardship to those on which it is imposed. As a consequence perhaps, fines are an extremely commonly used disposal, representing over two-thirds of all sentences administered in England and Wales (Ministry of Justice 2014). Interestingly, of course, fines take the form of a debt to be paid to the state, rather than to the victim of a crime, suggesting implicitly that this form of retributive punishment at least is seen as a forfeit owed for breach of one's obligations as a citizen in general, rather than between

Figure 24.4 Rt Hon Chris Grayling MP, Secretary of State for Justice (2012–15)
Source: Policy Exchange (Flickr)/CC BY 2.0

individuals. It might be argued that compensation orders fulfil that sort of function instead—but they are used very much less often than fines, and are not identified as a 'principal disposal' but rather as a supplementary measure (Lee 2013). Fines, too, offer some of the same attractions to sentencing theorists as imprisonment, in the sense that they can be viewed as simultaneously retributive and deterrent in effect (whilst incidentally helping to defray some of the costs of administering the criminal justice system); although unlike other sanctions they cannot be seen as rehabilitative and by imposing financial hardship may actually have the opposite effect.

Despite the obvious significance of monetary penalties as a feature of the punishment repertoire, it seems that they have been little considered in research and academic literature. There has been some work undertaken by economists, seeking to evaluate the 'utility' of the fine, particularly in terms of its influence on calculative decision making by offenders (or putative offenders; see, Becker 1968, for example); but little discussion of the symbolic or material function of the fine as an element of the justice system, at least according to O'Malley (2009). He argues though that there has been a persistent tendency to overlook its significance in penal thinking, identifying Jeremy Bentham, for example, as someone whose interest in financial penalties has been overlooked in relation to his acknowledged interest in 'the disciplinary prison', and the Panopticon (see also **Chapter 23**):

> Yet he saw money sanctions as the ideally liberal form of punishment for they delivered no physical coercion. Rather than giving pain, they took away pleasure. They were, in the event of injustice, completely reversible.
>
> O'Malley 2009: 67

Bentham also suggested that the level of fines could be calculated so as to deliver equitable punishments to rich and poor alike by calculating monetary penalties as a proportion of the convicted person's wealth, and not simply as a fixed sum—thus prefiguring the 'day-fine', a form of which was briefly brought into law in the early 1990s. Fines were thus precisely calculable, providing for fine-grained proportionality between the offence and the penalty imposed, and at the same time, they were both cheap to administer and promised a degree of future income to the public purses in England and Wales. O'Malley notes that the fine represents 'more than 70 per cent of sentences in all criminal courts' in Australia: and yet, he complains, 'the fine is virtually ignored theoretically' (2009: 68). This may be because the fine's monetary characteristics reflect the wider 'taken-for-grantedness' of money, which means that the 'price of crime' remains self-evident.

This kind of calculative logic has, however, been far less evident in the USA, O'Malley suggests, where fines represent a much smaller proportion of the overall number of sentences administered than in other jurisdictions, amounting to only 29 per cent of disposals in relation to 'misdemeanours' and virtually unused in the case of more serious offences ('felonies' in the terminology of the US justice system). He suggests that it is because fines cannot be viewed as 'reformative' that they have been accorded a very restricted place in sentencing practice in the USA (2009: 72). In England and Wales, on the other hand, where their punitive aspects are more clearly acknowledged, the interplay between the use of fines and imprisonment seems to offer confirmation of their retributive function. Thus, the relative decline in the use of fines during the 1990s is consistent with an intensification in the level of punishment accorded to particular crimes, reflecting what has come to be known in retrospect as 'the punitive turn'.

The emerging trend towards a more populist and repressive agenda in criminal justice was mirrored by a fairly dramatic displacement of monetary penalties by other more severe sanctions, such as imprisonment, notably for offence categories which might be expected to engender strong reactions in the public arena; so, between 1990 and 2000, 'for sexual offences the use of the fine dropped from 29 per cent to only 3 per cent [and] for burglary from 14 per cent to 3 per cent' (O'Malley 2009: 79), reflecting, in turn, a wider upward trend in sentencing tariffs. And, of course, the 'back up', in the form of the sanction in place for non-payment of fines, is usually a term of imprisonment, calculated as a daily monetary equivalent. As O'Malley acknowledges, this consequence implicitly draws attention to another potential feature of the justice system, and this is its unequal impact, because 'many of the high risk offenders are members of the "underclass" who in any case could not afford to pay fines. Prison is their fate once again' (O'Malley 2009: 79).

As we have observed, then, retributive punishments can take a number of forms, involving both direct physical effects of one sort or another (corporal and capital punishment, for example), restrictions of freedom and incapacitation, material forfeits (money, work or time), and even loss of dignity and ridicule (the stocks or high visibility vests). Collectively, this mode of punishment appears to share the common features of the imposition of some sort of loss or harm, determined to be equivalent to the hurt caused by the offender's actions. Interestingly, though, we have also noted how different forms of punishment can be specific to certain cultures, or historical periods and how these become more less fashionable over time. We will now move on to consider the relationship between our belief systems and ideological assumptions and the changing practices in the administration of penal sanctions which are apparent.

Mind, body, soul: The objects of punishment

Key thinkers

The natural starting point for this discussion is the work of Michel Foucault, and particularly his seminal 1979 work *Discipline and Punish* which offers a distinctive vision of the emergence of modern forms of punishment, and their underlying rationale and implications. Starting with an account of the execution of 'Damiens the regicide', mentioned earlier in the discussion of the history of punishment, Foucault develops the argument that the mode and purposes of punishment have shifted, as its concern has become less about inflicting direct and dramatic public harm on the offender, and more diversified and subtle in its attempts to mete out the appropriate response to the crime committed:

> And yet the fact remains that a few decades saw the disappearance of the tortured, dismembered, amputated body, symbolically branded on face or shoulder, exposed alive or dead to public view. The body as the major target of penal repression disappeared.

To be replaced by punishment:

> Of a less immediately physical kind, a certain discretion in the art of inflicting pain, a combination of more subtle, more subdued sufferings, deprived of their visible display.
>
> Foucault 1979: 8

As Foucault points out, the public shaming, humiliation, and harming of offenders was both widespread and appeared to serve a particular kind of social function, in very demonstrably setting them apart and in a sense providing implicit legitimacy for the sanctions applied; but at the same time their very brutality and visibility tended also to implicate spectators in acts as brutal and repressive as those attributed to the criminal. Writing at the time in the mid-18th century, Cesare Beccaria (1738–94) (see **Figure 24.5**)—who is often thought of as the founder of the modern system of law and punishment—set out his essay: 'On Crimes and Punishment' and was one of the eloquent supporters of this sort of sentiment:

> The death penalty is not useful because of the example of savagery it gives to men. If our passions or the necessity of war have taught us how to spill human blood, laws, which exercise a moderating influence on human conduct, ought not to add to that cruel example, which is all the more grievous the more a legal killing is carried out with care and pomp.
>
> Beccaria 1995: 70

As the state became a more central player in the criminal justice system, so logically, and perhaps more comfortably for the community in general, it took closer control over the calculation and administration of sanctions, which would now 'tend to become the most hidden part of the penal process … It is ugly to be punishable, but there is no glory in punishing' (Foucault 1979: 9). In addition, Foucault argues, this transition foreshadowed the emergence of a more civilised rationale for the administration of punishment, as it shifted the balance from retribution towards correction, reclamation or even 'cure'.

Although punishment continued to be administered bodily even after the abolition of the most dramatic forms of harm as public spectacle, it came to take different forms—'imprisonment, confinement, forced labour, penal servitude, prohibition from entering certain areas, [and] deportation' (Foucault 1979: 11). In this way, the effect of punishment changed significantly, so that: 'the pain of the body itself, is no longer the constituent element of the penalty. From being an art of unbearable sensations punishment has become an economy of suspended rights' (Foucault 1979: 11). So, to the extent that the law still found it to be necessary to impose direct constraints on the offender, this would be done 'at a distance', and properly regulated and monitored.

Foucault draws attention to the incorporation of 'caring' professionals into the administration of physical punishments; and the role of the doctor, for example, in alleviating the pain of those subject to the death penalty. Wider processes of social and structural change, it might be argued, necessitated the development of a different form of punitive logic, underpinned by changing patterns of

Figure 24.5 Italian criminologist, Cesare Beccaria
Source: Public domain

social belief and political ideology. Thus, the emergence of rationality and a belief in scientific calculability associated with 'modernism' came to be applied to the field of criminal justice as in all other spheres of human activity:

> Shift the object and change the scale. Define new tactics in order to reach a target that is now more subtle but also more widely spread in the social body. Find new techniques for adjusting punishment to it and for adapting its effects.
>
> Foucault 1979: 89

As the new rationality became dominant, so too did the logic of proportionality, and the belief in the capacity to match the punishment both to the crime and to the offender, since both could be subjected to appropriate forms of measurement and then aligned depending on the specific characteristics of each recorded crime and its perpetrator. It was at this point, too, that the potential alignment of retributive and correctional purposes was recognised, and in this way, too, the nature of punishment was transformed, with the emphasis now on its impact on the offender's mind, rather than simply on the body. Hence, in Foucault's view, the emergence of the prison as an apparently logical and almost 'natural' form of punishment, acting on the shared sensibilities of the offender and society, as much as it exercises a regime of physical constraint that represents a clearly quantifiable form of deprivation in the shape of time forfeited:

> By levying on the time of the prisoner, the prison seems to express in concrete terms the idea that the offence has injured, beyond the victim, society as a whole. There is an economico-moral self-evidence of a penality that metes out punishments in days, months and years and draws up quantitative equivalences between offences and durations.
>
> Foucault 1979: 232

David Garland agrees that 'modern state punishment no longer addresses itself to the body of the criminal offender' (2011: 767), suggesting that this is partly a result of the 'civilisation' process of modern societies which have become sensitive to barbaric forms of human suffering, and less willing to be associated with the administration of punitive measures which inflict direct pain. On the other hand, as he also acknowledges, it is difficult to avoid imposing some form of physical restraint in the course of applying penal sanctions. Although couched in terms which might be seen as less offensive, defining imprisonment as 'deprivation of liberty' does not dispense with the physical act of containment which is implied by this terminology. These 'bourgeois' sensibilities, Garland believes, ensured that forms of punishment 'involving bodily exposure of suffering—the stocks, the pillory, flogging, birchimg, and branding—were mostly abandoned' (Garland 2011: 776), and the death penalty, too, became less frequently used, and abolished in some countries, including the UK (in 1965). Garland also refers to the process of 'refinement'

of the death penalty in the USA, and the 'transformation of execution techniques', both to reduce suffering and to effect a sense of distance between the state and the community and the act of killing in the name of the law.

Thus, a series of anomalies has emerged in the development of punishment and penality in modern societies. Firstly, as the direct infliction of pain and suffering has become seen as excessive and uncivilised, new forms of punishment have emerged, which are represented in forfeits of time, money and other forms of currency (work, or dignity, for example), especially as these have taken on increased symbolic value in contemporary societies. But, secondly, these have not resulted in the complete abolition of punishments which involve the body in some way. This, though, has led to a tendency to underplay the direct bodily effect of punishment, in Garland's view, whether by utilising generic notions which deflect attention from the physical conditions of imprisonment, or by developing techniques which give the effect of 'sanitising' the punishment inflicted. Far from leading to a more civilised system of justice, Garland concludes that this perpetuates the legitimisation of repressive treatment:

> The fiction of imprisonment as 'deprivation of liberty' occludes millions of suffering bodies and the regimes of discipline and neglect that produce them. Similarly, the fiction of a disembodied death penalty and an execution that 'ends life without touching the body' help ensure the 'dignity' and acceptability of capital punishment … in this country [the USA] long after it has been abolished elsewhere in the West.
>
> Garland 2011: 790

In acknowledging our tendency perhaps to think of 'the west' as a homogenised set of state forms and social practices, it is perhaps useful to pause for a moment to reflect on the substantial and significant differences between (neo-liberal) societies which might otherwise be viewed as very similar in many other respects, when we come to consider the organisation and administration of their systems of punishment.

What we have observed in this section is the complex array of understandings and beliefs held about the purposes that punitive interventions serve. They can be both symbolic, in the sense of representing fundamental ideas about the value of life and freedom and how these should be preserved; and at the same time, highly practical, in the sense simply of righting a wrong, or redressing an imbalance caused by an illegal act. Punishment can, therefore, have a number of objects, including the body, mind, and even soul of the offender, whose reputedly rightly-earned suffering may therefore be imposed in a number of different ways. What all such retributive sanctions share in common though is the principle that the offender must make amends for her/his crime through some form of atonement. The price must be paid.

The organisation and impact of punishment

In moving on from a consideration of its aims, its forms, and its ideological and cultural trappings, we need perhaps to consider punishment now in terms of its practices and consequences. How is it used and how is it experienced? Whilst we must acknowledge, as we have, that in most cases it is impossible to define punishments in terms of distinct objectives (as solely retributive, deterrent, restorative, or rehabilitative, for example), it is perhaps possible to distinguish between them at least in terms of the principal or significant effects; thus, we will focus at this point on those which may be viewed substantially in retributive terms, at least.

It is clear from policy pronouncements, judicial rulings, and the sentencing practices of the courts that retribution and 'just deserts' are never far from the thinking of those principally concerned with the organisation and delivery of 'justice' in our contemporary society. See **Telling it like it is 24.2** for a great example of this in relation to Chris Grayling.

As far back as 1988, the Home Office issued a Green Paper setting out its objectives for the future of the justice system, entitled *Punishment in the Community*, and subsequent measures demonstrated considerable continuity in this respect, illustrating two key points: that retributive

punishment remained the benchmark against which court disposals should be judged; and that political expediency required sentences to incorporate elements of 'punishment', even when this was not their principal objective ostensibly—usually for fear of appearing 'soft on crime'. It has frequently been observed that the New Labour government (1998–2010) continually sought to present itself as 'tough on crime' because of its perceived historical weakness in this respect. The soundbite 'tough on crime and tough on the causes of crime' was crucial to both the ideological rebirth of the Labour Party as 'New Labour' and its landslide victory in the 1997 General Election (McLoughlin et al. 2001: 301). According to McLoughlin, one of New Labour's most notable achievements, during its first term of office, was the creation of a 'Third Way' law and order position that has successfully challenged the idea that social democratic political parties are by definition 'soft on crime' (McLoughlin et al. 2001: 301).

Giving further substance to that sense of continuity and rigour in dealing with crime at all levels, the proposals for community sentences published by the Ministry of Justice in 2012 under the subsequent Conservative/Liberal Democrat coalition government were titled *Punishment and Reform: Effective Community Sentences*:

TELLING IT LIKE IT IS 24.2

The political power of punishment rhetoric—with author Roger Smith

As this chapter was in preparation, a radio interview was broadcast with Chris Grayling then Secretary of State for Justice (1 February 2015), describing his continuing belief in the appropriateness of short prison sentences (in a context of significant overcrowding and discomfort), because of the supposed desire of the public to see criminals pay the price for their crimes, irrespective of the very limited evidence of the value of such sentences. This was one in a series of similar pronouncements by the Justice Secretary following his appointment in 2012. In October of that year:

Mr Grayling said he was 'putting punishment back into community sentencing'.

'This is about sending a clear message to offenders and the public that you if commit a crime, you can expect to be punished properly,' he said. 'Community sentences are not a soft option any more.'

More offenders are expected to be forced to clean up graffiti, clear litter or perform other community projects.

Offenders' movements will also be tracked using GPS – global positioning system – technology in a move intended to help protect the public.

The £5,000 cap on fines that magistrates can set will be removed 'to provide proper compensation to victims', Mr Grayling said. Courts will also be able to take criminals' belongings into account, as well as their incomes, taxes and benefits, when deciding on financial penalties.

The reforms are intended to strengthen the punitive elements of criminal justice.

Daily Telegraph, 16 October 2012

Although Grayling was seen as taking a more strongly punitive line than some of his predecessors, and indeed his immediate successor, Michael Gove, there is nonetheless a continuous strand in the rhetoric of senior politicians and those directly responsible for criminal justice which emphasises the punitive and retributive aspects of sentencing.

we will: ensure that there is a clear punitive element in every community order handed down by the courts. As a matter of principle, it is right that those who commit crime should expect to face a real sanction.

Clarke 2012: 1

These sentiments are found to be mirrored in the utterances and sentencing practices of those in the judiciary, too. The 'default position' in respect of punishment is helpfully illustrated by the debate about the usage and character of 'alternatives to custody' which has taken shape over recent years.

As Brownlee (1998: 9) has observed, there is a kind of 'beauty-contest' at play, in which those who wish to promote non-custodial sentencing options seek to present them 'in a light which will make them attractive' to courts who are predisposed towards conventional assumptions about the use and purposes of punishment. He describes the process of adding extra conditions to probation orders (as in the Criminal Justice Act 1972), as a means of enhancing the 'punitive bite' of the probation order itself (1998: 12), by incorporating restrictions on offenders' liberty within the terms of the order. This was intended to act as an incentive to sentencers who might not be persuaded of the order's merits solely by its rehabilitative objectives. That this is a persistent trend in strategic approaches to influencing sentencing is confirmed by Allen's (2008) subsequent account of much later attempts by government to shore up support for non-custodial measures again by enhancing their retributive characteristics, by encouraging greater use of fines and 'increasing the use of *robust* community sentences' (Allen 2008: 389 (emphasis added)).

In keeping with this aspiration, Allen notes, the Community Order, introduced under the Criminal Justice Act 2003, explicitly attempted to provide a graded, tariff-based sentence which would enable courts to attach requirements to the order in keeping with the seriousness of the offence: 'Twelve requirements are available to be used with the Community Order including unpaid work [and] a curfew backed by a tag' (Allen 2008: 390). On the other hand, as Allen observes, there were those who took the view that such measures did not convince sentencers that non-custodial sentences could be 'effective', including senior members of the judiciary (Phillips 2007, quoted in Allen 2008: 390). A subsequent analysis of alternatives to custody also found that 'confidence was a key theme' (Taylor et al. 2014: 45), and that courts needed to be persuaded that particular non-custodial options (in this instance, the pilot Intensive Alternative to Custody (IAC) scheme) would represent 'a sufficiently punitive alternative' to custody.

The IAC itself represented a further variation on the 'Order +' model of the two previous measures described, in that it enabled courts to build upon the requirements of the Community Order by 'combining' sentencing components in new ways. In the evaluation undertaken by Taylor et al., it was indeed noted that the IAC orders incorporated on average 3.4 requirements, as compared to 1.7 requirements per offender given the 'standard community order' (2014: 46), and of these, it was the more punitive elements such as 'community payback' and 'curfew' which seemed to be more attractive to the courts.

Interestingly, one of the findings of this study was that sentencers were not readily persuaded by the introduction of yet another innovation in what seemed to be an endless stream of new sentencing options, viewing the IAC as 'just another fad', according to one criminal justice professional interviewed (Taylor et al. 2014: 48). And, indeed, there 'was a prevalent perception amongst sentencers that the IAC was simply an attempt to "dress up" community orders' (Taylor et al. 2014: 48). In fact, the new sentencing option represented by the IAC seemed to fall foul of the same kind of response as many of its predecessors had done, going back to the Community Service Order and enhanced Probation Order of the early 1970s, captured in the terse response of a district judge interviewed for the study: 'there's no alternative to custody; custody has to be used' (quoted in Taylor et al. 2014: 49). Custody is the benchmark against which sentencers appear to judge the severity of a sentence, and it seems that amongst them there is a consistent view that alternatives are just not equivalent to it in terms of their punitive impact.

This observation is further borne out by the recurrent finding that 'alternatives to custody' do not often function very effectively as a genuine alternative to incarceration. Brownlee notes, for example that following the introduction of new community sentencing options such as the Community Service Order, the proportion of convicted adult offenders receiving immediate custodial sentences actually increased, from 16 per cent in 1975 to 21 per cent in 1985 (Brownlee 1998: 11); and in the 1990s when the proportion of community sentences given for more serious (indictable) offences was increasing, *so also* was the absolute number of custodial sentences, as a feature of whole system expansion (Brownlee 1998: 135). Similarly, Allen (2008: 390) noted that the Community Order did not have the desired effect in terms of making significant inroads into the number of shorter prison sentences administered; and Taylor et al. (2014: 55) found that recommendations for the IAC made in court reports were not consistently responded to positively by sentencers. Indeed, as these authors observe, the tendency for policy makers (and practitioners, it should be noted) to continually seek out ever more intensive 'alternatives' both plays into the underlying punitive ideology, and at the same time, conveys the implicit message that existing (and potential) non-custodial measures are simply not tough enough:

An ever increasing demand for punishment is clearly set out in the current government consultation on community sentences and the sentiment is one of 'harsher' and 'tougher' community sanctions ... In this context alternatives to custody will need to be effective in articulating how they will punish and inconvenience offenders.

Taylor et al. 2014: 55

In a further note of irony, other researchers have found a quite widespread view amongst sentencers that they only use custody as a genuine 'last resort', with some clearly expressing 'difficulty and distaste' when feeling compelled to impose custodial sentences (Hough et al. 2003: 35). Given that they already seemed to believe that they were only using imprisonment where

absolutely necessary and where no other option could apply, the authors of this study observed that 'it is no surprise that many ... sentencers were resistant to the idea that they should reduce their use of custody in order to reverse the rise in the prison population' (Hough et al. 2003: 39). Despite significant observable shifts in sentencing trends and the custodial population over a period of time, it seems that there is an irresistible internal logic at play in the judicial process, with retributive punishment as the default sentencing consideration, and custody, in particular, as the epitome of the punitive disposal. Specific sentencing calculations and their underpinning rationales all seem bound to this dominant discourse at the heart of the criminal justice process.

What are the consequences of punishment? Does punishment 'work'?

As we have discovered, punishment has an embedded and largely irresistible logic at its heart, grounded in retributivist principles, and against which all other interventions and outcomes are to be judged. So, in the face of this, it makes sense to ask the question: how does punishment do? What are the impacts and achievements of retributive disposals? Of course, in one sense, a punitive measure can be said to be 'successful' purely in that it has been administered. This is self-evidently the case in those historical and, indeed, contemporary measures which are simply about causing physical harm or pain. Execution 'works' if it results in the death of the offender on whom this sentence is passed. Imprisonment 'works' if the specified period in custody is served. A fine 'works' if it is paid in full. However, once we pause for a moment to reflect on the apparently neat symmetry of intention and outcome, we do find room for doubt. Although the principle of balance can be effectively articulated, it may be harder to achieve as Bentham illustrates:

> The perfection of frugality, in a mode of punishment, is where not only no superfluous pain is produced on the part of the person punished, but even that same operation, by which he is subjected to pain, is made to answer the purpose of producing pleasure on the part of some other person.
>
> Bentham 2003/1859: 93

How do we know, and on what basis can we calculate that punishments administered are 'just', equitable, and fair? What is an appropriate period of imprisonment for a specific crime, for example, and how do we weigh mitigating and aggravating factors? What consideration should we give to indications of repentance and remorse? And

what of sentences that are irreversible—death, chemical castration, amputation, for example—what if there is a miscarriage of justice in such cases? Can such sentences be justified in general terms notwithstanding the heavy probability that they will be administered to innocent people in some cases? We will go on here to consider two areas which are both central to considerations of the effectiveness of retributive justice and which may prove to be particularly challenging for this as a sentencing rationale: proportionality and miscarriages of justice.

Proportionality

As recognised by Bentham in the preceding quote, the question of the 'commensurability' of a punishment to the crime committed is of considerable importance when setting the criteria by which sentences should be determined. It is, of course, possible to develop a framework for grading punishments in relation to each other when they are of the same kind—for example in terms of the duration in days, months, or years of a custodial sentence; but as Bentham acknowledges, this becomes problematic when punishments are of 'different kinds' which 'are in few instances uniformly commensurable' (Bentham 2003/1859: 92). His recommended solution to this problem is to apply a scale of penalties within which a 'greater punishment' always incorporates the 'lesser punishment' which precedes it in the scale. Whilst this may prove to be an effective basis for determining the relationship between different forms and quantities of penal sanction, however, it does not address the more fundamental question of the relationship between a punishment of any kind and the crime to which it applies.

The umbrella term 'crime' of course covers a wide range of problematic behaviours (see **Chapter 3**) with and without victims, individual or corporate, against property or person, reckless or intentional, and simply expressed in these terms, establishing parity in terms of sanctions can be seen as highly problematic. In the UK, definitional distinctions between 'summary' and 'indictable' offences are intended to provide some guidance as to the seriousness of the alleged offence and therefore the scale of penalties to be imposed. Similarly in France, the distinction is made between 'délits' (less serious) and 'crimes' (more serious), and in both countries the level of court proceedings and scale of punishments available reflects this distinction. In addition, the sentencing framework is geared to enable courts to make individualised assessments of the seriousness of the offence in each case proved, in light of specified mitigating or aggravating factors, and to pass sentence accordingly.

There is clearly a mismatch here between the apparently rational and objective basis for standard sentencing decisions on the one hand: and, on the other the very wide variation in the pattern of sentencing decisions across jurisdictional boundaries, and in some cases even within the same jurisdiction. In the field of youth justice in England and Wales, for example, the arbitrary outcomes of 'justice by geography' have been recognised for many years (see Morris and Giller 1987, for example); and this is a phenomenon which has again been acknowledged quite recently. As Bateman (2011: 10) comments, there is a very wide disparity between the use of custody between youth offending areas in England and Wales, with as many as one in five young people appearing in court in Merthyr Tydfil being incarcerated, as compared with less than one per cent in Dorset. Whilst he recognises that 'demographic factors and the local prevalence and nature of youth crime account for some of the divergence between areas' (2011: 10), the disparity seems too great to be explained by these variables alone. In this respect, then, it seems that in practice, the principle of proportionality is compromised by 'real world' factors which distort the judicial process and lead to inconsistent outcomes. Concern on this point is further heightened, when we observe, too, that geography is not the only variable at play; and, in particular, that ethnicity can be a significant factor in relation to inconsistent use of custody. A study commissioned by *The Guardian* newspaper found in 2011 that 'black offenders were 44 per cent more likely than white offenders to be sentenced to prison for driving offences, 38 per cent more likely to be imprisoned for public disorder or possession of a weapon and 27 per cent more likely for drugs possession' and a similar pattern applied in the case of Asian offenders (*The Guardian*, 26 November 2011).

Inconsistencies of this kind are also to be found in international comparisons, with France, for example, being much more likely to impose prison sentences than England and Wales, but for much shorter periods, with the result that it has a much smaller prison population per 100,000 of the overall national population (National Audit Office 2012). Figures produced by the Institute for Criminal Policy Research in 2016 show a very wide variation in the rate of imprisonment globally, and even within a fairly homogeneous region of the world such as Europe (see **Table 24.1**).

Sentencing patterns are thus widely disparate and raise significant questions about the notion of 'proportionality' as a guiding principle in sentencing policy and practice, since the application of such rules seems to be highly situated and specific.

Miscarriages of justice

'People think that miscarriages of justice are rare and exceptional,' says Dr Michael Naughton, founder of the UK Innocence Project. 'But every single day, people are overturning convictions for criminal offences. Miscarriages of justice are routine, even mundane features of the criminal justice system. They are systemic.'

Daily Telegraph, 4 September 2014

The retributive basis for punishment rests, as we have seen previously, on a series of assumptions, crucial amongst which is that it is possible to be sure of the guilt of the convicted offender on whom the punishment is imposed. Of course, it is impossible in a human context to guarantee total certainty on this sort of issue, especially where the question of intent is at issue, so it might be reasonable to argue that we can accept that penalties will be erroneously imposed in a very small number of cases—this, it could be argued, is a legitimate price to pay (in terms of the risk thereby incurred by law-abiding people who just happen to be in the wrong place at the wrong time). That is to say, if society determines that punitive sanctions should have a place at the heart of the criminal justice system, then society must equally accept that there will be occasional innocent victims of miscarriages of justice. This may be so, but it would nonetheless leave open the question of what is a reasonable ceiling on the number or proportion of cases in which punishment is wrongfully administered.

Naughton, for example, suggests that there are in fact many more miscarriages of justice than is popularly thought to be the case, and that there are 'many thousands of victims of wrongful criminal conviction who are able to overturn their convictions in the appeal courts each year' (2005: 166). He appears to suggest that discussions of

1	Russian Federation	445		29	Bulgaria	125
2	Belarus	306		30	Luxembourg	112
3	Lithuania	268		31	Belgium	105
4	Georgia	262		32	Kosovo/Kosova	100
5	Latvia	239		33	France	99
6	Turkey	238		34	Austria	95
7	Azerbaijan	236		35	Isle of Man (United Kingdom)	92
8	Moldova (Republic of)	227		36	Greece	90
9	Estonia	215		37	Italy	88
10	Czech Republic	205		38	Switzerland	84
11	Poland	189		39	Ireland, Republic of	81
12	Slovakia	186		39	Croatia	81
13	Albania	184		41	Cyprus (Republic of)	80
14	Hungary	183		42	United Kingdom: Northern Ireland	78
15	Ukraine	177		43	Germany	76
16	Montenegro	174		44	Monaco	74
17	Gibraltar (United Kingdom)	158		45	Slovenia	73
18	Jersey (United Kingdom)	152		45	Bosnia and Herzegovina: Federation	73
19	Serbia	148		47	Andorra	72
20	United Kingdom: England & Wales	147		48	Norway	71
20	Macedonia (former Yugoslav Republic of)	147		49	Netherlands	69
22	Romania	144		50	Bosnia and Herzegovina: Republika Srpska	67
23	United Kingdom: Scotland	143		51	Denmark	61
24	Portugal	139		52	Finland	57
25	Spain	133		53	Sweden	55
26	Malta	131		54	Iceland	45
27	Armenia	130		55	Faeroe Islands (Denmark)	23
28	Guernsey (United Kingdom)	127		56	Liechtenstein	21

Table 24.1 Prison population rates in Europe per 100,000 of the national population (May 2016)

Source: (http://www.prisonstudies.org/highest-to-lowest/prison_population_rate?field_region_taxonomy_tid=14)

World Prison Brief, Institute for Criminal Policy Research

notable cases where convictions are reversed tend to understate the extent to which the initial decisions of courts are reversed; thus 'all criminal cases in magistrates' courts', 'all those cases … that did not incur a custodial sentence', and 'all those criminal convictions that incur a custodial sentence of less than four years' are typically excluded from consideration (Naughton 2005: 169). Similarly, he observes, the conventional notion of a miscarriage of justice does not easily allow for all those instances where the judicial process fails to operate fairly and consistently and an injustice follows, whether in the form of an unsafe conviction or an inappropriate sentence. He concludes that the 'main consequence' of this line of argument is that it changes the focus of the debate:

> The impossible pursuit of innocence can be discarded and a more appropriate debate about 'justice in error' can proceed. This … can feed into attempts to promote confidence in the criminal justice system by provoking a more adequate discussion on miscarriages of justice.
>
> Naughton 2005: 179

This might lead us to conclude, for example, that if we cannot be sure of the justice of the outcome in a great number of cases going through the justice system then the use of irreversible or very harsh or stigmatising forms of punishment should be avoided. Otherwise, the legitimacy of any form of punitive sanction must fall into question, it could be argued.

Objective or subjective considerations: Punishment, justice, and the public

Notwithstanding the very real concerns associated with the risk of punishment becoming unfair though its administration and impact on those who are punished, the fallback position for those who uphold its use, and its undoubted position as the central rationale for sentencing, can largely be explained by its continuing and deeply-rooted popularity. It is commonplace in political discourse to hear of justifications framed in terms of public expectations and the need for justice to be 'seen to be done'.

To a considerable extent, this perception seems to be borne out by the evidence from research. For example, in the context of very low levels of public confidence in the delivery of youth justice, Roberts and Hough (2005: 214) report that, 'they [the public] also think that the system is too lenient', a finding mirrored, they observe, in similar investigations in other countries such as Canada and the USA. When considering, the British public's optimal 'purposes' for sentencing, the authors found that in relation to adult offenders, 'there was more support for proportionality [just deserts] … : 46 per cent of the sample endorsed proportionality for adults' (2005: 216), compared to 31 per cent favouring deterrence, for example. At the same time, it is of interest to note that there was less support for the principle of just deserts in relation to young offenders, and relatively more (although not as much) backing for rehabilitative goals. Other studies, too, indicate a readiness on the part of the public to distinguish between young and adult offenders, so that whilst there is evidence of generalised concern about the behaviour of young people, punitive sentiments are tempered by other considerations such as the 'potentially damaging long-term impact of a criminal record on a young person's prospects' (Jacobson and Kirby 2012: 3). On the other hand, when it comes to sentencing in general, it is reported that there is a well-established pattern of public concern that 'sentences are much too lenient' (Hough et al. 2013: 23).

It has also been demonstrated that 'public opinion', at least as it is perceived, has direct and indirect effects on courts and sentencing decisions. This is at least partly responsible for creating the sense of a punitive culture. In one study, for example: 'All the sentencers interviewed … were acutely aware that their sentencing decisions are not made in a vacuum, but in a highly pressured political and social context' (Hough et al. 2003: 53). Sentencers described a feeling of 'there being too much political interference', for example, and of government tendencies to 'make 'knee-jerk reactions' (2003: 53). But they also experienced a sense of direct pressure from the public: several of the sentencers, particularly district judges and magistrates, talked of being criticised by the media or the public for not being tough enough with the offenders who come before them' (2003: 53). Thus, it seems, there is a particular concern amongst sentencers about the credibility of community disposals which they feared would be viewed as a 'soft option' or 'cop out' (2003: 54). Thus:

> A senior judge commented that his 'biggest regret' was over a six-month sentence he once imposed for death by dangerous driving. He felt in hindsight that he should have used a non-custodial penalty; however he opted for custody because 'I was scared of what the world would say'.
>
> Hough et al. 2003: 57

Although it was clear from this study that not all the judiciary felt beholden to public opinion in the same way—for one crown court judge, media criticism would be 'water off a duck's back', for example (2003: 56), the strong overall message is that an anticipated punitive response from the media and/or the public would necessarily be one of the parameters to take into account when sentencers make their decisions on disposals.

This, in turn, poses additional dilemmas for both fairness and equity in sentencing. First, an assumed consensus around sentencing practices does not necessarily reflect the views or expectations of individual victims in specific cases—should we therefore seek to rely on some kind of objective construct of public expectations of the appropriate level of harm to be inflicted on the offender, or should we rely on the specific views of the 'real life' victim in a specific case? Secondly, however this raises concerns about equity from the point of view of the offender, and perhaps implies that a more 'objective' set of criteria would be fairer in general terms.

This, though, brings us to our second dilemma—concerning the subjective effect of punishment and whether there should be incorporated an assessment of the specific impact of a particular sanction on a particular offender—this might be one of the arguments in favour of applying mitigation to sentences, not just in the sense of minimising culpability, but also in terms of equalising the effect on the offender:

> Suppose two people commit the same crime and are sentenced to equal terms in the same prison facility. I argue that they have identical punishments in name only. One may experience incarceration as challenging but tolerable while the other is thoroughly tormented by it. Even though people vary substantially in their experiences of punishment, our sentencing laws pay little attention to such differences.
>
> Kolber 2009: 182

Bronsteen et al. (2008) make the important point that the impact of punishment is inevitably modified by the capacity of humans to 'adapt' to their circumstances and to the privations to which they are subject. Thus, for example, they argue that a bigger fine will not 'ultimately diminish an offender's happiness much more than will a small one, nor will a long prison sentence impose much more suffering than a short one' (Bronsteen et al. 2008: 43).

In practice then, it seems that establishing an entirely fair and equitable system of punishments which meets collective expectations as well as the wishes of individual victims; and at the same time, exacts reasonable and equitable forms of retribution on the offender, is unachievable. Punishment of this type must then be viewed as much in terms of its symbolic function as its actual effects—because of its apparent reflection of the 'natural' and consensual view that harm must be effected in return for harm caused.

What is wrong with the idea of punishment?

We might finally conclude by reflecting on the argument that if punishment does, indeed, perform an effective symbolic and cohesive function, then this is good enough. We might accept the qualification that certain forms of punishment should be ruled out because of the unnecessary or irreversible harm they cause, but otherwise retribution might be viewed as a perfectly legitimate aim and driver of sentencing. If it satisfies such popular aspirations, isn't that sufficient to justify its position as the cornerstone of sentencing practice?

Perhaps so, but this must mean modifying the purist view that public opinion should always determine the sentence to be imposed—as in the case of capital punishment, where opinion surveys consistently demonstrate a majority in favour of it amongst the general population, although this support may be declining (*The Guardian*, 12 August 2014).

Taking this approach would also necessitate accepting that there is (and must be) a continuing debate about if and how the punishment can be made to 'fit the crime'—what length of prison term should apply to what offence, for example; a question which appears to lead to very different answers in France or Norway and the UK, for example.

More significantly, however, persistent questions arise over what exactly punitive penal sanctions achieve, especially in the case of imprisonment. These are recognised as being disruptive not just to those sentenced but to others around them, especially if they have family or caring responsibilities (some might, indeed, prefer to take a short prison sentence rather than incur a debilitating fine); it is

similarly acknowledged as being associated with high reoffending rates (47 per cent of adults, 58 per cent of young adults, and 73 per cent of children reconvicted within a year of release; Prison Reform Trust 2013); it carries very substantial associated costs, directly attributable to the sentence itself (£34,766 annual cost per prisoner in 2012–13; Ministry of Justice 2013) and to its consequences (see Anderson 2011, on the social care needs of short-sentence prisoners); and it is also socially divisive—custodial sentences, for instance, are disproportionately likely to be imposed on offenders from black and minority ethnic groups:

> Out of the British national prison population, 11% are black and 6% are Asian. For black Britons this is significantly higher than the 2.8% of the general population they represent.
>
> Prison Reform Trust (www.prisonreformtrust.org.uk),
> 12 February 2015

This observation of course acts as a direct reminder of the social context of punishment, as opposed to its abstract legal basis. The consequences of punishment are socially distributed, and as the Prison Reform Trust has reminded us, this is manifested in the form of institutional (and direct) racism (Edgar 2010).

On the one hand we are thus faced with what appears to be a 'natural' desire for crimes to be punished and justice to be done in the form of a penalty imposed in direct proportion to the harm caused by the offence—although this may be mediated by assessments of culpability and mitigating factors, such as mental health needs; whilst, on the other, we have to take account of the meaning and consequences of taking a purely punitive approach to dealing with crime. Whatever modifications are made to sentencing frameworks and practices, punishment cannot be made perfectly equitable and fair. And, at the same time, there are a number of associated consequences which are attributable to the social context in which punishment is administered. Punishment practices themselves are socially determined and, as we have seen, different cultures and periods of history have shown a readiness to use forms of retribution which might be viewed as brutal and unacceptable in the extreme. Sentencing regimes vary and seem only to be based on a very tenuous link between the harm caused and the penalty imposed—an equation which itself is subject to cultural and historical variation.

This tension in turn poses a constant challenge to policy makers, practitioners of criminal justice, philosophers and even criminologists, both in terms of questioning the moral basis of a retributive approach to punishment and in terms of the organisation, administration, and delivery of punishments that might meet certain commonly agreed minimum standards of consistency, fairness, and decency. We might then seek to review retributive philosophies and practice in light of the following questions:

- Is retributive punishment justifiable in its own terms?
- What are its principal features and effects? What are its limits?
- Can it be made fair and equitable? How can effective safeguards be put in place?
- What are the social costs of retributive sanctions? Who is affected?
- What are the implications for other forms of criminal justice disposal of the use of penal sanctions?

SUMMARY

On completing this chapter, you will have covered a number of central debates about the nature and purposes of punishment, focusing on the key themes introduced at the start of the chapter. Revisiting the themes, the following areas have been considered:

• Appreciate the rationale for retributive approaches to dealing with crime

The chapter has reviewed the main arguments advanced by proponents of retributive punishment, namely that it offers a fair and equitable means of redress for those harmed by offences; and it represents a commonly agreed form of sanction given legitimacy by the authority of the state.

• Discuss the aims and objectives of retributive approaches to punishment

The distinctive features of retributive, as opposed to other, approaches to punishment such as deterrence or maintenance of social control, have been highlighted.

• Recognise the development of different forms of punishment

We have considered historical changes in the form and uses of punishment, notably the shift from dramatic, public, and brutal measures to the use of restrictive sanctions such as containment and loss of time.

• Reflect on the use and impact of penal sanctions

The extent of the use of punishment and its impact on offenders have been considered, including issues of proportionality, subjective vs. objective assessments of fairness, and the implications of miscarriages of justice.

- Evaluate the potential limitations of punitive penal practices

Evidence of the relatively high reoffending rates associated with imprisonment, and the discriminatory effects of punishment on black and minority ethnic groups has been introduced, along with a series of challenges to be taken into account by those seeking to develop effective frameworks for the administration of penal sanctions.

REVIEW QUESTIONS

1. What are the distinguishing features of a retributive theory of punishment?

2. Why do you think the idea of 'making the punishment fit the crime' appears to be popular?

3. What have been the most significant historical changes in the administration of punishments?

4. Why is it difficult to establish a basis for judging the fairness and consistency of specific punitive measures?

5. What are some of the problematic consequences of the use of sanctions such as imprisonment?

FURTHER READING

Beccaria, C. (1986) *On Crimes and Punishment*. Indianapolis, IA: Hackett.
A highly significant publication as it represents one of the earliest attempts to systematise the administration of law and punishment and to introduce a rational basis for the calculation of the penalty commensurate with the offence.

Foucault, M. (1979) *Discipline and Punish*. New York: Vintage Books.
An influential account of the emergence of modern penality, and in particular the replacement of dramatic and highly visible forms of punishment with imprisonment, although his account of contemporary forms of control is not necessarily consistent with retributive principles.

Hough, M., Bradford, B., Jackson, J., and Roberts, J. (2013) *Attitudes to Sentencing and Trust in Justice*. Ministry of Justice: London.
A research review of public attitudes to sentencing which attempts to understand the prevalence of punitive attitudes amongst the general population, and the widespread preference for harsher rather than more lenient sentences.

Kolber, A. (2009) 'The Subjective Experience of Punishment', *Columbia Law Review*, 109, pp. 182–236.
An important reminder of the relevance of the subjective dimension of punishment and the problems this causes for calculations of equivalence in the sentencing process.

Prison Reform Trust (2013) *Prison: The Facts*. London: Prison Reform Trust.
An occasional publication (which may be periodically updated) from a prominent lobbying organisation, setting out in considerable detail the realities of imprisonment in contemporary Britain.

 Access the **online resources** to view selected further reading and web links relevant to the material covered in this chapter.
www.oup.com/uk/case/

CHAPTER OUTLINE

Introduction   686

What is rehabilitation?   686

What is rehabilitation for?   689

How is rehabilitation organised and administered?   693

Mind, body, soul: The objects of rehabilitation   695

Models and practices in the delivery of rehabilitative
services   698

What are the outcomes of rehabilitation: How do
we judge success?   701

What is the impact of rehabilitation? What does it achieve?   704

The limitations of rehabilitation   707

25

Rehabilitation of offenders

KEY ISSUES

After reading this chapter you should be able to:

- explain the concept of rehabilitation as applied in criminal justice;
- recognise different objectives to which rehabilitation aspires;
- identify and describe alternative models of rehabilitative practice;
- evaluate the achievements and outcomes of rehabilitative interventions;
- understand critical perspectives on rehabilitation and its aims.

Introduction

As we have seen, much discussion of crime and criminality focuses on the culpability of the offender, the management and control of crime, and the nature and legitimacy of punishments. However, there is another strand of criminological inquiry (and practice) which is more concerned with understanding offenders, appreciating 'what makes them tick', and seeking out tools and methods for reintegrating them into society, as conventional law-abiding citizens. In effect, such approaches are concerned with identifying causes and consequences, and developing interventions which will enable those concerned to adapt and reform through processes of capacity-building and creation of legitimate opportunities to live decent lives. In this chapter, we will explore some of the beliefs and assumptions which underlie this kind of orientation to crime and criminality. We will consider some of the implications in terms of criminal justice practices and we will evaluate the outcomes of rehabilitative approaches. Finally, this chapter will also reflect on some of the limitations of this perspective on crime, both empirically and theoretically.

What is rehabilitation?

Unlike other perspectives on crime and criminality, rehabilitative ideas and practices are principally concerned with making sense of and addressing the origins and causes of offending at the individual level. That is to say, the focus of attention is not on general patterns of behaviour, or on the nature of crime in the abstract, but on the drivers and influences which lead to particular people committing particular crimes at particular points in time. What, in effect, are the causal factors which underpin manifestations of criminality? And, from the point of view of the criminal justice system, what sort of interventions can help to address these influences and return offenders to conventional law-abiding lives? The distinction is made here between rehabilitation in the sense of being able to regain the status of a law-abiding citizen, a more substantive process of achieving behavioural change, and a return to relatively conventional and acceptable forms of daily activity:

> If asked to describe a 'rehabilitated offender', it is likely that the majority of lay people would indicate a person with some history of offending behaviour which has now ceased. We might think of this as a return to 'normal', law-abiding behaviour … it is about a change in the way a person behaves. So the action of rehabilitation might involve the provision of interventions to remove the propensity, desire or necessity to offend.
>
> But the notion of rehabilitation also has a symbolic dimension, such that it implies a return to a former status that of a law-abiding citizen.
>
> Robinson and Crow 2009: 2

The Rehabilitation of Offenders Act 1974 enshrined this principle in law in England and Wales. Subject to certain caveats, concerning the type and severity of the offence, offenders could therefore 'spend' their convictions and reclaim full citizenship status and rights after a certain period of time following conviction.

In both the formal and substantive senses, rehabilitation can be equated to processes which restore a former and more desirable way of being for those convicted of offences. It is the case, however, that the idea of 'restoration' actually incorporates a problematic assumption; restoration assumes that the previous state of existence of the offender was adequate or socially acceptable. This, however, may not have been the case especially for those whose offending may have been triggered by their adverse circumstances in the first place. With this in mind, it might not be enough simply to 'restore' the offender to her/his previous living conditions; but it might be necessary to go further and achieve concrete improvements—'this would suggest a definition of offender rehabilitation as "change *for the* better"' (Robinson and Crow 2009: 3). Underlying these ideas about what rehabilitation looks like are a number of other implicit assumptions. We will now move on to explore some of these.

Rehabilitative assumptions

There are five main assumptions underlying the principle of rehabilitation, and these are as follows.

A change in an offender's circumstance is likely have future positive effects

The first of these assumptions is that the achievement of changes in the offender's circumstances is likely to have a positive effect on future offending; in other words, the removal of harmful features of the individual's life is also likely to remove the triggers to offending—say, in the form of a craving for drugs or alcohol which might be viewed as inherently criminogenic.

Offenders do not choose to commit crime

Secondly, the rehabilitation perspective views an offender as more or less constrained to act in the way that s/he does, due to biological, psychological, or social influences which have behavioural consequences. Offenders are assumed not to have free will or full responsibility for their behaviour, or to be able to respond rationally to the known risks of being caught or made subject to deterrent sentences. Rehabilitation is therefore not concerned with addressing the superficial manifestations of offenders' behaviour but engaging with them to understand and resolve underlying causes, of which offenders themselves may be unaware and which they are certainly unable to control.

Offenders are not fully culpable for their crimes

Thirdly, associated with the second assumption, is the belief that offenders are neither fully responsible for their behaviour nor therefore fully liable for it, in terms of the blame accorded to them or the punishment to be imposed. Punishment is not justifiable in retributive terms as the price to be paid for wilfully errant actions, simply because offenders are not in full control of what they do; but nor is it likely to be effective as a deterrent because the underlying 'drivers' of the offender's actions are not being addressed by a punitive response.

Change will help address the offender's needs and serve a community purpose

Fourthly, it is assumed that effective rehabilitative measures will meet both the offender's needs and serve wider social purposes, in terms of improving the quality of life of those around the offender; and, of course, in ensuring that the effectively reintegrated individual will no longer be subject to those influences which lead her/him to commit crime.

Ultimately, rehabilitation 'works'

Finally, implicit in the concept of rehabilitation is the belief that it is actually possible to return offenders to conventional, socially acceptable ways of life, by virtue of the interventions provided with this end in mind. That is, most, if not all, offenders are believed to be capable of responding to positive help, guidance, or correctional treatment. Underlying the notion of rehabilitative practice is the presumption that it can be developed and delivered in a manner that will 'work'. Any difficulties in obtaining persuasive evidence of the efficacy of particular intervention strategies can thus be attributed to design or implementation problems rather than any underlying shortcomings of the rehabilitative ideal itself.

Reform, resettlement, reintegration

As we shall see, the concept of rehabilitation remains keenly contested, and in setting out its apparent scope and intent, we must be careful to avoid conveying the impression that it can be straightforwardly understood, or implemented in practice. Rehabilitation is 'surprisingly difficult to pin down' in the words of Robinson and Crow (2009: 2). They observe that this is partly because the idea of rehabilitation can be complicated by its association with several other closely-related terms, such as 'reform', 'resettlement', or 'reintegration', which all share the same prefix, and all therefore promise some form of normalisation of the deviant individual. Here, the common goal is to enable the (ex-)offender to take up or resume his/her place as a conforming and productive citizen. At the same time, however, these aims do differ in emphasis, and therefore perhaps also in the kind of processes and practices with which they might be associated. Where 'reform', for example, can very easily be construed in terms of changing someone's behaviour, and (hopefully) making it more acceptable, 'resettlement' is more suggestive of effective service provision to enable the (ex-)offender to have access to the material requirements of everyday life, with the same entitlements and access to facilities as anyone else. Further to this, 'reintegration' might be seen as taking this process a step further, so that the (ex-)offender would now become able to play a full part in community life in exactly the same way as, and indistinguishably from, any other citizen. As we shall see, these differing understandings of rehabilitation are likely to be reflected in a varying range of responses from the criminal justice system and other agencies responsible for meeting welfare needs, or safeguarding individual rights.

McNeill (2012: 1) also suggests that we must approach rehabilitation cautiously, and with a readiness to accept that it is riven with what he describes as 'paradigm conflicts'. These conflicts are associated with a number of unresolved issues in the way the concept is implicitly defined; for instance, its 'underlying *crime theories ...* have to engage somehow with the problem that crime is (at least in part) a social construct' (McNeill 2012: 6). Therefore interventions geared towards 'reform' and normalisation of offenders are based partly on a selective understanding of what kinds of behaviour are to be criminalised, and how. Rehabilitation for drug offenders, for example, could be viewed in terms of promoting desistance from crime, on the one hand: or, on the other, it could be undertaken with a view to ensuring that the identified offender is able to pursue a drug-free life, thus establishing the individual's well-being as the priority, over and above a concern to prevent reoffending.

Models of rehabilitation

In an attempt to map out a route towards resolving this kind of conceptual (and operational) challenge, McNeill argues that we should adopt a multi-dimensional view of rehabilitation:

- **Psychological rehabilitation** 'is principally concerned with promoting positive individual-level change in the offender' (McNeill 2012: 14).

- **Legal or judicial rehabilitation** relates to the formal 'decriminalisation' of the offender, by means of setting aside a criminal record, or ensuring that one is not incurred in the first place.

- **Moral rehabilitation** effectively requires the offender to demonstrate acceptance of the reciprocal mutual obligations that citizens hold in common; and this could be demonstrated practically by some form of reparation, or visible atonement for the offence and harm associated with it.

- **Social rehabilitation** 'entails both the restoration of the citizen's formal social status and the availability of the personal and social means to do so' (McNeill 2012: 15).

As a result of this apparent uncertainty about how we should conceptualise the term itself, there is a similar degree of uncertainty as to how it should be operationalised. What does rehabilitation look like in practice? Where and how is it delivered by the justice system? Thus, for Robinson and Crow (2009: 5), the problem arises of how it relates to the punitive aspects of responses to offending. Is rehabilitation to be associated with a particular form of punishment, or is it perhaps incompatible with the idea of punishment? Perhaps it should be viewed as an alternative to punishment, maybe as a feature of diversionary programmes which seek to address welfare needs. Or, in the event that the offender is subject to a form of punishment, does it follow on from this as a means of reinstating the offender

in the community, and perhaps minimising the harm caused by the experience of punishment itself.

As Robinson and Crow acknowledge, these different approaches may lead to distinctive forms of intervention. For instance, where offending is seen to be linked to other needs, such as mental health issues, the case may be made for diverting reported offenders away from the justice system so that they can obtain treatment for the underlying problem. Weak and strong versions of this argument can be put forward, too, with one simply emphasising the underlying health need, and the other stressing the positively harmful consequences of drawing someone into the justice system who may already be suffering difficulties in their lives and thus be particularly vulnerable as a result.

Where rehabilitation is viewed as an integral element of a punitive measure, it is also concerned with making changes in the offender (Robinson and Crow 2009: 7), but these are directed mainly towards reducing the likelihood of reoffending. So, in this respect, rehabilitation could be seen to share some of the characteristics of a 'crime control' approach, and may be viewed as principally interested in reforming the offender, and producing a law-abiding and productive citizen; that is to say, producing behavioural change which will be beneficial both for her/him and for the wider community in reducing levels of crime.

Where rehabilitation follows punishment, it is likely to be viewed as a necessary form of intervention to enable the offender to return to a 'normal' life; that is, to take her/his place as a respectable member of the community again, with no adverse effects as a consequence of experiencing punishment (such as homelessness, say). Or, indeed, rehabilitative measures might be required in order to address problems which may have led to offending in the first place (which could also have included homelessness, potentially). This view of rehabilitation of course stands in contrast to the notion of rehabilitative punishment, since it reflects an underlying belief that punishment is often more likely to be a source of continuing hardship than a vehicle for reintegration. Punitive sanctions, such as the imposition of fines or prison sentences, can themselves compound the difficulties experienced by offenders, and possibly their families as well. As a result, reintegration into the community may become more problematic, necessitating additional rehabilitative provision merely to offset the disruptive effects of the initial punishment.

Despite the obvious differences in understandings of and approaches to the subject of rehabilitation, it is clearly distinguishable from other philosophies of intervention in the justice system, notably because of its concern for the outcomes for the offender, its assumptions about the 'causes' of crime, its belief in reintegration, and its relative de-emphasis of punitive sentiments.

What is rehabilitation for?

Given the range of 'models' of rehabilitation we have identified, it will not be surprising that this also means that the ends and means adopted by their proponents also differ in emphasis and content. In essence, rehabilitative aims can be viewed as having a number of potential outcomes in mind, from the formal reinstatement of the offender as a competent and well-adjusted citizen, through the achievement of positive change in the individual, to the amelioration or removal of the external or internal conditions which are likely to inhibit social reintegration. Whilst they might share what could be described as 'normalising' goals, achievement of these (or steps on the way to them) is not assessed in the same way.

Formal rehabilitation

Thus, for example, 'formal' rehabilitation has both a procedural and symbolic dimension, in that it is concerned with reinstating the conventional and expected social and moral order. Thus, in the criminal sphere and related territory, we might think of rehabilitation as the achievement of some form of formal recognition or the termination of some form of prohibition. So, someone who commits driving offences might be seen as rehabilitated on the return of their licence, or the expiry of penalty points. Similarly, the end of bans on movement or participation in certain events might also be viewed in this way. The end of a period on licence following a prison sentence can also be viewed as significant in signalling that the offender concerned is no longer a recognised target for intervention.

The underlying objective of this kind of measure is exemplified by the Rehabilitation of Offenders Act 1974 (as amended in 2012), which 'aims to give those with convictions or cautions the chance—in certain circumstances—to wipe the slate clean and start afresh' (Lipscombe and Beard 2014: 2). Significantly, the opportunity to make a fresh start is not afforded to all offenders in all circumstances, and there are certain types of offence and certain contexts which are expected to set limits to this principle. Under the Act, in general, convictions or cautions would become 'spent' after a specified period of time—the 'rehabilitation period', which itself varies according to the age of the offender and the nature of the caution or conviction. There are exceptions; as it stood following the 2012 amendments, any conviction resulting in a prison sentence of more than four years could never become 'spent'. Rehabilitation periods could be subsequently affected by the commission of a further offence before their completion, but on completion a conviction would be 'spent', and remain so, irrespective of any further offences. When a person's conviction or caution becomes spent s/he will become a 'rehabilitated person', although the actual length of time that needs to elapse varies greatly depending on sentence length and the age of the offender on conviction. Indeed, calculating the exact circumstances and which precise rehabilitation period applies might seem an unnecessarily complex procedure for those seeking to follow the guidance on the subject offered by the Ministry of Justice (see https://www.gov.uk/government/uploads/system/uploads/attachment_data/file/216089/rehabilitation-offenders.pdf).

The central objective of this legislation is to ensure that ex-offenders need not disclose previous 'spent' convictions when applying for employment, except in relation to 'excepted positions', which might involve working with children or vulnerable adults, or in other positions of trust. On the other hand, spent convictions still remain a matter of record and would be likely to be taken into account at any subsequent court appearance.

The original 1974 Act had been introduced to remove what had been seen as a significant barrier to rehabilitation, with former offenders being excluded from employment simply on the basis of having committed a crime of any kind at some point in their lives, potentially many years previously. However, this legislation in turn came in for criticism because it was believed to impose undue limits on rehabilitation periods (too long) and qualifying prison sentences (too short). With the arrival of a new government in 2010, with an explicit commitment to rehabilitation (Ministry of Justice, 2010), changes were introduced (effective from 2012), because the 1974 Act was felt to 'fail in its aim to help reformed offenders resettle into society … rehabilitation periods are too long and do not reflect the point at which reoffending tails off following a conviction' (Ministry of Justice 2010: 34).

Further legislation was introduced in the form of the Offender Rehabilitation Act 2014, which has sought to provide a more comprehensive system of support on release for offenders receiving relatively short custodial sentences who pose relatively low levels of risk to the community, but are believed to suffer as a result of limited continuing support on release.

The legislation on this issue does indicate a broader government commitment to removing barriers to rehabilitation, particularly in the employment context. Such measures only offer what might be termed a negative form of recognition, however, rather than constituting positive provisions to support resettlement, say, or tackle continuing personal problems. In this sense, rehabilitation is seen as a formal process whose objectives are to create a level playing field and provide the same or similar

Figure 25.1 Community payback projects for young offenders–preparation for the Royal Wedding
Source: Photo by: Jeff Moore/Jeff Moore/PA Images

opportunities to former offenders as any other member of society would enjoy, especially in terms of access to work. The overarching aim of the government's rehabilitation proposals in 2010 was to 'put more offenders on the right path' and to enable them to 'become law-abiding citizens and contribute to society' (Ministry of Justice 2010: 32). In this sense, then, we might think of rehabilitation in terms of removing the stigma that might be attached to offenders and therefore inhibit their ability to resume normal everyday lives. Such objectives can thus be clearly contrasted to those which might work in a very different way to mark out those convicted as different or as potential threats. Thus, visible and potentially stigmatising signs of criminality, such as electronic monitoring devices or high visibility tabards might be seen as running counter to rehabilitative aims, even when supporting objectives such as learning about the discipline and routines of work. Nonetheless, such measures may still be associated with practical reintegrative objectives, such as the provision of work opportunities (paid or unpaid, see **Figure 25.1**) and the chance to acquire skills to enhance employability.

Rehabilitation as a social and moral project

The association of reform and reintegration with work has been identified as a particular feature of the 19th century, when concerns arose about the brutal treatment of convicted criminals in prison, at the same time as wider developments in the industrial world brought demands for new and disciplined forms of labour to the fore. Michael

Ignatieff (1978) has offered an account of the transformation of punishment in the age of the industrial revolution, linking this explicitly to wider currents of social change, citing the example of Elizabeth Fry, and her proactive attempts to change the nature and function of the prison. The introduction of 'order' into the penal establishment lay at the heart of her work to change the lives of women who had been imprisoned, inspired by the goal of promoting their subsequent rehabilitation into the community as law-abiding and productive citizens (see **Figure 25.2**). In order to achieve this, she initiated a systematic approach to identifying and then working with women who could be helped:

First, the tried and the untried, the young and the old, the first offender and the 'hardened, drunken prostitute' were

MRS. FRY READING TO THE PRISONERS IN NEWGATE.

Figure 25.2 Elizabeth Fry's attempts to rehabilitate women serving a prison sentence in Newgate prison by reading to them
Source: Jerry Barrett/ CC BY 4.0

divided and placed in separate wards. The women's children were placed in a school within the prison, run by one of the prisoners.

Ignatieff 1978: 143

In an attempt, almost, to cleanse them of their previous criminal tendencies, and remake them as productive and conformist members of the community, steps were taken to impose a more ordered and sober appearance amongst the inmates, and so attention was paid to their outer appearance as well as their inner feelings and attitudes. The women's hair was cut short and they were required to wear white uniforms. Soon, too, they were put to work, sewing (Ignatieff 1978: 144).

In an instructive twist to the notion of self-discipline, Elizabeth Fry also appointed 'monitors' from within the ranks of the women prisoners to watch over them. She wanted to show that even those most difficult to reform could be 'turned round'.

Many of those who visited were inspired to the same conclusion. They had seen Elizabeth Fry working with those she has identified as 'the very lowest order of the people ... the scum of the city and country' and she appeared to be demonstrating that their lives could be changed and they could show penitence and become respectable members of society (Ignatieff 1978: 145).

In the early 19th century, then, rehabilitation had very much the flavour of discipline and instruction, whereby old unsavoury habits and problem behaviour could effectively be overridden by clear and consistent practices designed to mould and direct wrongdoers into more acceptable ways of ordering their lives. Rehabilitation thus had a strong correctional flavour, with its punitive aspects being viewed as an essential element of the reform process. Attention in this era was focused very much on controlling the behavioural manifestation of criminal impulses rather than remedying their underlying causes.

Changing internal mechanisms: rehabilitation as a psychological project

Subsequently, however, from the late Victorian period onwards, the principal focus of rehabilitation could be said to have shifted, with a growing interest in psychoanalysis and those internal influences on thought and emotions which might in turn be associated with wrongdoing and harmful behaviour. Freudian notions of the 'id', 'ego', and 'superego' suggested a set of complex internal interactions affecting individuals' propensities to behave in a particular way. In those instances where the 'id' was not subject to sufficiently rigorous controls

by the other elements of the psyche, uncontrolled and thus sometimes criminal behaviour could be anticipated. In this way, the unconscious could be viewed as the determinant of manifest behaviour. This, in turn, suggested that interventions based on the idea of changing behaviour alone would run the risk of leaving underlying causal mechanisms untouched. 'Treatment' therefore would necessitate an approach designed to understand and resolve those internal syndromes or characteristics which operate as the underlying causes of criminal behaviour. In Mary Gordon's (2010) terms, simply applying force or correctional interventions of the kind associated with Elizabeth Fry would be pointless where offenders were 'insusceptible of being managed by force'. Writing in 1922, Gordon argued that:

The time is ripe for us to convince ourselves of this. We should turn a fresh leaf in our treatment of the offender, fortified not by precedent, or by age-long prejudice, but by the findings of science which is, at last, in the act of discovering the mechanism of the whole man. We know enough already about how he 'works' to be able to consider when, under stress, he falls, what to be at in the matter of restoring him.

Gordon 2010: 57

Arguing that most recognised forms of 'penal discipline' could only be viewed as unproductive, failing to 'impress, punish or deter the vast majority of petty offenders', she proposed the substitution of one principle of intervention with another, which would be geared to the application of 'scientific' methods of understanding and treating the offender. Advocating the 'deferred sentence', which would act as a reminder to the offender of the importance of compliance, she argued that he (sic) should then be handed over to 'the doctor' or 'the educator', and reap the benefits of an effective casework relationship. This view of the key purposes of intervention and its potential value became increasingly influential throughout the first half of the 20th century, and certainly played a significant part in shaping the development of the probation service, and the emerging belief in the capacity of skilled professionals to achieve positive behavioural change.

These ideas are clearly represented in contemporary approaches to changing offender attitudes and motivations, as epitomised by cognitive behavioural therapy, for example (see **What do you think? 25.1**).

Rehabilitation: meeting offenders' needs

As this perspective on rehabilitation, focused around behavioural issues, became increasingly well-established in the early part of the 20th century under the influence of Freud and others, methods and mechanisms of

WHAT DO YOU THINK? 25.1

Methods such as cognitive behavioural therapy can be used in rehabilitation:

> Cognitive behavioural therapy (CBT) is a talking therapy that can help you manage your problems by changing the way you think and behave …
>
> CBT cannot remove your problems, but it can help you deal with them in a more positive way. It is based on the concept that your thoughts, feelings, physical sensations and actions are interconnected, and that negative thoughts and feelings can trap you in a vicious cycle.

> CBT aims to help you crack this cycle by breaking down overwhelming problems into smaller parts and showing you how to change these negative patterns to improve the way you feel.

> http://www.nhs.uk/Conditions/Cognitive-behavioural-therapy/Pages/Introduction.aspx

- Do you think the objectives of rehabilitation can be achieved simply by changing the offender's patterns of thought?
- Why do you think so?

intervention proliferated, offering a wide and varied array of individual and sometimes group-based programmes, drawing on diverse practice models. All, however, shared an orientation towards enabling offenders to gain insight into their own actions and to develop the resources and capacity to exercise self-control and to change that behaviour. However, an alternative view of rehabilitation would see it not simply as a matter of remaking the offender to fit and feel comfortable with the expectation of conforming with social norms; but that it should also take account of the needs of the offender. In fact, from this point of view, it might be argued that interventions of any kind would be unlikely to succeed if the material needs of the offender could not be met. Thus, for example, returning a former prisoner to a jobless and homeless existence would not only fail to meet her/his material needs but would also leave her/him more exposed to the risks and temptations of reoffending. Rehabilitation, then, should be about meeting offenders' needs and ensuring that they are effectively resettled into the community, not simply in their own interests but also as a way of preventing reoffending, a point of view extensively argued by the incoming coalition government in 2010, for example (Grimwood and Berman, 2012). Indeed, this presumption lay at the heart of the 'Breaking the Cycle' reforms set out by that government (Ministry of Justice, 2010). Interventions which prioritise offenders' needs can be controversial, though (see **Controversy and debate 25.1**).

CONTROVERSY AND DEBATE 25.1

Sometimes rehabilitative interventions have come in for criticism, either because they do not work, or because they seem to be rewarding offenders for their crimes, as in the following example:

> A serial burglar dubbed 'Safari Boy', after being sent on a trip of a lifetime to Africa in a failed bid to stop his offending as a boy, was jailed today for his latest offence—breaking into an elderly widower's home.
>
> Mark Hook, now 38, was taken on an 88-day safari to Egypt and Kenya at public expense when he was just 17—sparking a national outcry which included condemnation in the House of Commons by the then prime minister John Major.
>
> But it proved to be a waste of taxpayers' money as Hook has continued to offend ever since.

> Today Gloucester crown court heard that in April this year, he smashed his way into 86-year-old Frederick Talbot's remote home near Dorsey, ransacked it and stole property and cash, including photographs of sentimental value.

> *Daily Mail*, 4 December 2014 (http://www.dailymail.co.uk/news/article-2861147/Safari-Boy-career-criminal-38-jailed-burglary.html#ixzz3ydyOcdMZ)

In contrast, some evaluated positive activity programmes are reported to contribute to a reduction in crime levels.

> Kickz is a national programme, funded by the Premier League and Metropolitan Police, that uses football to work with young people at risk of offending in deprived areas. In the evaluation data crime rates on the days of the project were compared with general trends in the

same area from official statistics. This method allowed the programme providers to argue that on the days that Kickz sessions were running, the overall results for crimes often associated with young people reduced by 23 per cent for robbery, 13 per cent for criminal damage, 8 per cent for anti-social behaviour and 4 per cent for violence. Such a method shows a correlation between youth crime and the Kickz interventions.

http://project-oracle.com/uploads/files/Project_Oracle_Synthesis_Study_02-2013_Sport_interventions.pdf, p. 12

How is rehabilitation organised and administered?

It seems clear that there was a historical process of change, emerging from the wider restructurings and social transformations of the 19th century, which led to the emergence of a new understanding of crime and criminality. According to this analysis, the notion of crime as a deliberate act of transgression, based on free will, came to be extensively modified or even rejected, to the extent that crime was viewed as pathological and pre-determined, driven by individual characteristics of the offender. The consequence of this line of reasoning was a call to develop an individualised approach to sentencing and intervention:

> We thus reach an individualization of punishment, which, once and for all, replaces the entire punitive procedure prescribed by the law according to the outer character of the crime – an individualization adjusted not to the crime but to the organic, latent or manifest criminality of the individual. This point alone persists; the conception of responsibility disappears.
>
> Saleilles 2010: 46

This argument also therefore gave rise to critical observations about the unsuitability of purely penal regimes for dealing with offenders, with calls from some, for instance, for the criminal to be handed over 'to the doctor' or 'to the educator' (Gordon 2010: 58), thereby effectively articulating the need for a new type of professional role in criminal justice.

Probation

Originating in the UK in liberalising penal reforms of the late 19th century, the probation service progressively took on this function, carrying out a central role in offender rehabilitation (until its effective abolition in England and Wales in 2015). For younger and petty offenders, imprisonment seemed increasingly inappropriate to Victorian legislators, and in 1887 the Probation of First Offenders Act became law, creating space for rehabilitative interventions, even if it did not actually create the means to deliver these (May 1991: 5). To occupy this space, it was firstly police court missionaries, linked to the Church of England, who took on the role of providing advice and support to those placed 'on probation'. In 1907 the Probation of Offenders Act made provision for the appointment of paid probation officers to 'advise, assist and befriend' those for whom they were made responsible. Using their influence and guidance skills to promote reform became the expected approach of those taking on this role:

> This era in the formation of the service took its impetus from a convergence between the inappropriateness of existing penal sanctions to a particular class of offenders – habitual, drunken and petty – and a reforming zeal motivated by religious belief.
>
> May 1991: 9

Over the course of time, the role of the probation officer and the probation service became increasingly formalised and institutionalised. In 1912 the National Association of Probation Officers was established, which gave an organised professional focus to the development of this form of work with offenders; and by 1914, the service was sufficiently well developed to form the subject matter of a book setting out its form and functions (Leeson 1914). The aims and scope of the emergent service were by this point fairly clearly articulated; and it should perhaps be noted that they incorporated certain assumptions about the limits of its operation. That is, it was believed to be of particular value as a means of dissuading and reforming offenders who were, as yet, uncommitted to a life of crime, or affected by particular adverse personal circumstances or influences. By implication, 'hardened' or experienced criminals would be less eligible for this kind of intervention, and could, perhaps, expect more straightforwardly penal sanctions for their behaviour:

> Probation is a system by which reclaimable offenders are given an opportunity to reform. It is applied to those in whom wrong-doing is not habitual, and whose youth, previous good character, or other circumstances, give reasonable hope of reformation.
>
> Leeson 1914: 3

In expanding on this in relation to the probation officer's role, Leeson also gives a flavour of the nature of the intended relationship between probation officer and probationer. This would be essentially paternalistic, but at the same time it would be underpinned by the threat of court imposed further sanctions in the case of non-compliance. The approach of the probation officer to the offender on probation is that of a reliable friend, bringing insight and common sense to bear. It would not be expected that the probation officer would either idealise the relationship and be too forgiving of the probationer; or that s/he would be too directive, and thus undermine the value placed on the relationship by the probationer. The aim is to use the relationship productively as a vehicle of persuasion and to provide a good example; but the availability of stronger sanctions will also form part of the ongoing dialogue. Although the probation officer 'will not threaten without just cause, he will, when the occasion demands it, not hesitate to remind offenders refusing his suggestions of the court which is behind him' (Leeson 1914: 114).

The emergence of probation, then, in the early part of the 20th century, is associated in one sense with a growing recognition that offending could be associated with factors outside the offender's control and susceptible to non-punitive intervention; but, at the same time, such reforming or rehabilitative interventions would not be carried out on an entirely voluntary basis, free from any threat of further sanctions. This sense of ambiguity and compromise with the punitive underpinnings of the justice system has persisted in the subsequent growth and development of rehabilitation in criminal justice.

The casework approach

Further changes saw the probation service becoming increasingly clearly established as a statutory service; the Criminal Justice Act 1925 required all criminal courts to have probation officers attached to them (May 1991: 11), with probation areas created and the work administered by local Probation Committees. As the number of offenders placed on probation increased, so too did the rationale for probation practice become more clearly oriented towards problem diagnosis and 'treatment'. As May (1991: 15) observes, the probation service had by now become clearly wedded to a social casework approach to intervention:

> Officers no longer engaged in special pleading on behalf of individuals in the courts, but provided a scientific assessment of their predicament. With the casework method the offender became the subject of professional diagnostic appraisal, all of which drew upon a phase in criminological thought which provided for the treatment of the offender who was in some way maladjusted.

As the 'casework' ethos of the service became increasingly well established, probation practice became more and more closely aligned with the broader domain of welfare-oriented social work, and this influenced the work of subsequent policy reviews and legislation such as the Criminal Justice Act 1948, which extended the role of probation officers to provide after-care for prisoners, in keeping with broader rehabilitative aspirations and a view of probation as essentially a helping profession.

The Scottish approach

Scotland went even further than England at this point, following the publication of the Kilbrandon Report in 1964 on child care and juvenile offending. This report set the scene for the effective removal of children in trouble from the remit of the criminal justice system, paving the way for the establishment of the Children's Hearings system in place of the criminal courts. This philosophy was extended to the adult criminal sphere, too, with the probation service being integrated with generic social work departments, and the associated dominance of a welfare approach to the provision of community support or offenders. Ironically, as it happens, in parallel with these 'welfarist' developments, it has been acknowledged that from '1905 to 2004 most informed observers have recognized that the Scottish courts sent disproportionate and unacceptable numbers of the population to jail' (McNeill 2005: 34).

As McNeill also acknowledges, the period from the 1990s onwards saw a change of emphasis in criminal justice policy in Scotland with significant implications for agencies with primary responsibility for working with offenders in the community. He identifies this change of direction as being inspired by 'a growing emphasis on public protection' (McNeill 2005: 34). This was reflected in a growing use of measures of compulsion and conditions attached to community-based court disposals such as supervision and probation orders. Reflecting on these trends further, he goes on to speculate about the apparent contemporary threat to both the organisational forms and the underlying aims and objectives of probation and social work in criminal justice: 'Perhaps the most pressing question … is whether the objectives that probation was established in Scotland to pursue—improving justice and helping offenders to change—can survive' (McNeill 2005: 35).

From care to correction

These trends towards a more correctional and controlling orientation for probation are mirrored in England and Wales, as both organisational change and the framing and delivery of practice seemed geared towards reducing the role of rehabilitation in service provision. The separation of probation and social work training in 1997 and the subsequent changes in structural arrangements for service delivery clearly signalled a down-playing of rehabilitation, since this function was being marginalised in the one organisation best equipped to deliver it. Emerging trends towards more restrictive and coercive community sentences in the early 2000s led Robinson and Crow (2009: 162) to conclude that in light of 'penalties with more conditions and restrictions than at any time in the past ... it is difficult to see rehabilitation as a priority for policymakers or sentencers'. In parallel with this concern, the fear is expressed that rehabilitation has come to be seen in purely utilitarian terms, with offenders no longer being seen as its 'main beneficiaries'. So, the value of rehabilitation would be judged according to whether it contributes to a reduction in reoffending or meets victims' needs, rather than merely whether it helps offenders get back on their feet.

Despite the apparent resurgence of rehabilitation as a central objective of criminal justice policies and practice with the publication of *Breaking the Cycle* by the incoming coalition government in 2010, the continuing structural changes in respect of community punishments and supervision of offenders continued to create doubt as to the role and place of probation in the framework for service delivery. 2015 saw the culmination of a process of sub-division and partial privatisation of community-based offender management services, including aspects of the probation function, creating considerable uncertainty about how the new service arrangements would operate, and how welfare and rehabilitative functions could be retained within the restructured delivery arrangements. At the point of transition, certainly, many experienced practitioners were highly concerned about the potential threat to their ability to continue to provide an effective welfare-led service, even though much of the workload had been nominally transferred to 'community rehabilitation companies':

> I've been in this job for 25 years and I've never known morale so bad and so low ... You just don't want to go to work on Monday mornings. We've just had enough.
>
> Probation Officer, quoted in *The Guardian*, 9 April 2015

Although rehabilitation has clearly retained a place in the delivery of criminal justice, changing patterns of organisation and intervention suggest a considerable degree of historical volatility, and a distinct susceptibility to change: in the way in which it is conceptualised; in its place and standing in the wider justice system; and in its practices.

Mind, body, soul: The objects of rehabilitation

As the history of rehabilitative provision reveals, the objectives and practices which it encompasses are both variable and subject to change and refinement over time. What was originally defined essentially in terms of moral lassitude and reform has gone through a process of transformation and development, becoming increasingly associated with closely-defined and thoroughly evaluated 'scientific' solutions to the problem of deviance and offenders' 'inadequacies'. Lying behind this diversity of thinking and practice, are a number of significant differences in the understanding of need and the intended targets for change. This can essentially be summed up in the form of the distinction between material needs and their resolution by practical means of support and reintegration, on the one hand; and moral and psychological needs and interventions focusing on changing thoughts, attitudes, or behaviours, on the other. McNeill's (2012) typology, as mentioned previously, clearly suggests a range of different approaches to the task of delivering 'rehabilitation', depending on the starting point we adopt.

Faith and redemption

In its early days rehabilitation was characterised by a strong spiritual element, even where this was associated with programmes of practical reform. Holmes (2010: 47), for example, argued for fair rents, better schooling, and controls on the strength and sales of alcohol, at the same time as he sought moral redemption for those involved in acts of 'hooliganism':

> From apathetic content may God deliver the poor! From such possibilities may wise laws protect them! 'Righteousness – right doing – "exalteth a nation"', and a nation whose poor are content because they can live in cleanliness, decency and virtue ... is a nation that will dwell long ... and among whom the doings of hooligans will no longer be remembered.
>
> Holmes 2010: 47

Similarly, Poulton (2010: 60) argued for close attention to be given to offenders' 'spiritual' as well as material needs 'perhaps above ... all'. As has been recognised, the notion of rehabilitation itself has long been associated with religious ideals of forgiveness and redemption; these aspirations would, in turn, be reciprocated in the form of penitence and reform on the part of offenders themselves. It is observed that prior to the 20th century 'nearly all reform efforts were justified as religiously informed, if not inspired, undertakings' (Cullen and Gendreau 2000: 114). The underlying assumption is that the inherent goodness of all, even those who had strayed into wrongdoing, could be unlocked by enabling offenders to transform themselves spiritually. This was clearly reflected in the strong sense of 'missionary zeal' in many of the forms of practice associated with rehabilitation in the 19th century and beyond; and this has been associated by some with a notion of pre-scientific ignorance. Early proponents of prison reform are therefore attributed with 'only a rudimentary understanding of human behaviour', associating offending purely with a lack of moral fibre, in turn linked with the absence of a proper understanding of religion (Cullen and Gendreau 2000: 116). It would be a mistake, though, to conclude either that these early proponents of rehabilitation had no understanding of the material factors, such as poverty, which were associated with crime; or, that the association of religion and redemption was entirely superseded by the more scientific approaches to 'treatment' which emerged in the 20th century.

The rehabilitative ideal

In the US, 'Faith-based correctional' programmes (see **Figure 25.3**) are to be found quite widely operational (Duwe and Johnson 2013), as are 'faith-based prisons', and there is reported to be some evidence that taking up religion is associated with reductions in criminal activity (Johnson and Jang 2010: 119). On the other hand, Volokh (2011) has found no evidence that faith-based prisons 'work', in the sense of reducing reoffending. Explanations for any claimed positive effects of religion-based intervention programmes are sometimes framed in terms of the material as well as affectual connections afforded by a sense of spiritual belonging. It is noteworthy that the potential value of 'religious groups' is still recognised in contemporary policy documents in the UK (Ministry of Justice 2013: 8).

Figure 25.3 Group of inmates in a US prison join hands in prayer as part of a faith-based programme
Source: Inside CCA (Flickr)/CC BY-ND 2.0

As more 'scientific' approaches to understanding crime and criminality have taken the place of accounts grounded on the moral disposition of offenders, so the focal point for intervention has also shifted, from the soul to the mind. The emergence of the social sciences and their growing position of authority in the late 19th century was associated with an increasing belief in the capacity to identify the causes of individual's criminality, and accordingly to devise means of influencing their attitudes and thinking, and thereby changing their behaviour. Indeed, reform and rehabilitation were seen as going hand in hand. Thus emerged the 'rehabilitative ideal', which has to a great extent continued to underpin efforts to understand the causes of crime and design effective interventions ever since, notwithstanding a period of ontological crisis and doubt in the 1970s. As Cullen and Gendreau have observed, this 'paradigm' was characterised by several linked assumptions:

> First, it embraced the belief that crime was caused by an array of psychological and social factors that ... intersected to push a person to the other side of the law. Second, and relatedly, the way to prevent future crime was to change the unique set of factors that drove each individual into crime. Third, the process of corrections should be organized to identify these crime-causing factors and to eliminate them. That is, the goal of the correctional system should be rehabilitation. Fourth, since each offender's path into crime was different, the rehabilitation that was delivered had to be ... *individualized* [their emphasis]. Fifth, to provide individualized treatment, the state, through its agents in the correctional process, was to be invested with virtually unfettered *discretion*.
>
> Cullen and Gendreau 2000: 117

The actual nature of the crime committed, and indeed the harm associated with it, would be almost irrelevant to the process of analysing the root causes of individual behaviour and the development of non-punitive and non-criminalising forms of intervention to ensure that offenders were effectively reintegrated into society. This meant, in addition, investing a great deal of 'faith' and trust in those experts whose task it was to assess and understand the criminality of those identified as offenders and put individualised programmes together to promote their reform. The concepts of 'treatment' and 'cure' became central to the process, and sat sharply at odds with the idea that the punishment should 'fit' the crime, or that the interests of victims demanded to be taken into account in the sentencing process.

The language of welfare and treatment became much more integral to the criminal justice process, and informed the kind of diagnostic practices evident in the production of reports for the courts, assessing the offender and his/her needs in relation to the offence committed. Similarly, of course, a range of interventions was developed, collectively designed to provide insight into the offender's behaviour and to build within him/her the capacity to act responsibly and play a full and legitimate part in society as a reintegrated citizen. In this sense, although ostensibly quite similar to correctional measures, rehabilitative interventions could be seen as more ambitious and more inclusive than those aimed mainly at curbing criminal tendencies or controlling behaviour. Although compliance with interventions might be mandatory, as ordered by the court, this would be for the offender's 'own good', rather than simply as a means of exerting authority and control. Indeed, in many instances, offenders would be invited to recognise this, by 'voluntarily' agreeing to comply with the terms of a probation order, for example, until they were made compulsory in 1997 (in England and Wales), and then replaced by the community order in 2005. It should perhaps be noted that the persistence of the probation order in Scotland is another indicator of the rather distinctive philosophy of criminal justice practice applying there.

The emergence of alcohol and drug treatment as an adjunct to criminal justice disposals is perhaps a good example of the strand of rehabilitation which was about changing the harmful ways of thinking and associated behaviours of those whose criminal activities were believed to be linked to problems of substance abuse. Increasingly, interventions of this kind have been formalised and incorporated into the mandatory requirements of court disposals. For example, drug testing (see **Figure 25.4**) and treatment began to be incorporated as conditions of community orders in the 1990s, and the Drug Testing and Treatment Order itself was introduced in England and Wales by the Crime and Disorder Act 1998. Here, though, an element of compulsion had crept back into the process (see **What do you think? 25.2**), perhaps associated with the loss of self-control attributed to addictions.

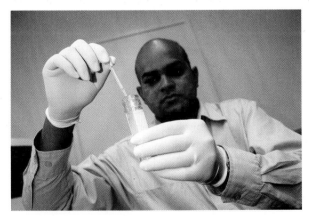

Figure 25.4 Drug counsellor testing urine for traces of drugs
Source: Janine Wiedel Photolibrary/Alamy Stock Photo

WHAT DO YOU THINK? 25.2

Some rehabilitative interventions are compulsory, and attendance or participation in the prescribed programme is mandatory.

- How far, and in what circumstances, do you believe that it is acceptable to impose mandatory forms of treatment, reputedly for the offender's own good?
- What safeguards would you apply, if any?

Resettlement of offenders

In addition to forms of rehabilitation which focus on the purported 'problems' of the offender, and their impact on her/his behaviour, there has also been a consistent strand of rehabilitation practice which has focused on the practical needs and entitlements of those who are to be reintegrated into the community, particularly on release from custodial establishments. Although, this form of intervention, too, has tended to vary in its popularity over time, it can also be seen as well-established and well-supported by principled arguments, based on the recognition that resettlement and a 'fresh start' depend to a great extent on the material conditions of those who are attempting to begin new lives as 'ex-offenders'. From Victorian times, discharged prisoners' aid societies were established, whose aim was to organise charitable support for ex-offenders so as to promote their resettlement and enable them to meet their immediate material needs. By 1884, every prison except one had established an aid society, and their work was coordinated by a national Central Committee of Discharged Prisoners' Aid Societies (established in 1877). Over the course of time, this body developed and became established as a central feature of the criminal justice system, in respect of prisoner rehabilitation in particular, acquiring its contemporary name of the National Association for the Care and Resettlement of Offenders (Nacro) in 1966. Nacro (see **Figure 25.5**) has become one of the biggest providers of rehabilitation services in criminal justice, and has also become an influential body in terms of providing policy advice and information to government and statutory bodies.

Nacro's activities are designed to reduce crime, the fear of crime and reoffending. Our services give offenders and those at risk of offending skills, support and motivation to change their lives and move away from crime. We support the work of our services by working with policy makers and commissioners to improve reoffending outcomes and develop cost effect criminal justice services.

From Nacro's Charity Commission entry, 2015

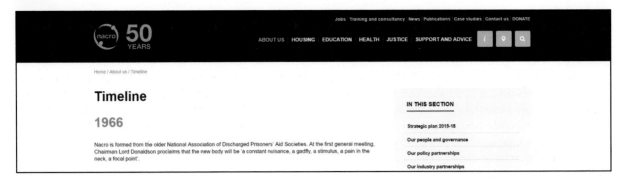

Figure 25.5 Screenshot showing the timeline page of the Nacro website
Source: Nacro: www.nacro.org.uk

Importantly, the idea of resettlement offers a rather different view of the aims and objectives of rehabilitation to those approaches which focus on changing the beliefs, morality, thoughts, characteristics, or behaviour of offenders. In essence, the focus is shifted from engendering change in the individual to make her/him fit the expectations of society to promoting change in her/his material circumstances so that s/he is better supported to resume life as a ('normal') member of society.

Models and practices in the delivery of rehabilitative services

As we have already seen, the idea of 'rehabilitation' is open to a variety of interpretations; and, inevitably, this means that there are an equal (or greater) number of approaches to practice which claim to be rehabilitative. It might be helpful to think in terms of a spectrum, with interventions which are solely focused on individual change at one end, to those which are principally concerned with creating the right social conditions for effective reintegration at the other. At one end of the spectrum, where the emphasis is very much on achieving individual change, rehabilitative and correctional interventions come closely into alignment, with the only clear distinction being that the correctional approach seeks only to put a halt to criminal behaviour; whilst rehabilitative measures are also interested in improving quality of life. At the other end of the spectrum, rehabilitation shares much in common with radical perspectives whose approach is geared towards limiting harm caused by the criminal justice system itself. In what follows, the aim will be to identify and explore different practice models which can be located at different points on this spectrum, according to their underlying assumptions and value bases.

Some approaches to rehabilitation, for example, are based on assumptions about the relationship between the offender's 'needs' and the 'risk' of reoffending. Where these two are closely aligned, interventions which target either of these are also presumed likely to have a beneficial effect as far as the other is concerned:

The assumption is that risk is a rough indicator of clinical need and, therefore, according to this principle, high-risk individuals should receive the most treatment ... while those designated as low-risk warrant little, if any, intervention.

Ward and Maruna 2007: 71

Cognitive behavioural therapy (CBT)

Cognitive behavioural therapy (CBT) has gained considerable popularity as an evidence-based intervention which, according to extensive evaluation, is capable of reducing levels of recidivism when implemented rigorously (Lipsey et al. 2007).

CBT programmes have been developed to address the problems associated with faulty reasoning which predisposes criminals to offend. That is to say, offenders are able to persuade themselves by a variety of modes of thinking that their actions are justifiable, even if illegal. It may be that the offender feels him/herself to have been victimised previously, and thus the offence is no more than a means of redressing the balance; the offender may rationalise property theft on the basis that it does no real harm, or by assuming that the victim is insured against loss; or it may be the case that the offender perceives antisocial behaviour as broadly accepted or even encouraged, as may be the case if s/he is part of a wider group engaged in antisocial activity.

CBT thus attempts to unpick the thinking processes which lead to such forms of distorted thinking, and thereby strip away the underlying justifications for the offending behaviour. Typically, the focus will be on trying to develop pro-social forms of reasoning and problem-solving; and developing techniques for dealing with problematic and stressful situations without resorting to unacceptable responses (anger management, for example).

A considerable number of bespoke CBT programmes have been developed to address different aspects of offending and targeting identified offender 'types'.

CBT has been widely endorsed by government and other agencies, such as the Youth Justice Board (Wikstrom and Treiber 2008) because of its wide scope and the substantial evidence base in support of its effectiveness (Lipsey et al. 2007):

> Cognitive behavioural interventions can affect many different areas of cognition and behaviour, as they may target, for example, emotional characteristics of behaviour, decision-making processes or the application of cognitive activity to behaviour.
>
> Wikstrom and Treiber 2008: 27

Despite its popularity and reports of its effectiveness, some doubts are raised about CBT, particularly in relation to precisely what its effects are and the mechanisms by which it impacts on offending rates. There is some concern about the 'black box' issue—that is, exactly what goes on in the course of programme delivery, and precisely what aspects of the intervention might be having an impact. At the same time, questions are raised about the almost exclusive focus on offending rates as a measure of success and the limited attention given to making improvements in other aspects of offenders' lives—that is to say, the social dimensions of rehabilitation. In general, though, CBT remains popular in criminal justice.

Risk, need, responsivity (RNR)

For those who do seek to focus interventions more precisely, it is seen as important to distinguish between 'static' and 'dynamic' risk factors; that is, those which are unchangeable, and those where appropriate forms of treatment might indeed achieve beneficial outcomes. Such dynamic risk factors might include such attributes as 'impulsivity or deviant sexual preferences' (Ward and Maruna 2007: 71). According to what Ward and Maruna describe as the 'Risk-Need-Responsivity Model', the next stage of the intervention process is to target 'treatment' programmes on 'changing criminogenic needs', such as impulsiveness or poor problem-solving capabilities, but not to prioritise other possible needs which are not associated with offending. The individual's well-being is therefore subordinated to the primary objective of reducing the chances of further offending. The third element of this model, 'responsivity', establishes the principle that interventions should be adapted to the 'relevant characteristics' of the offender, such as their 'cognitive ability' and 'preferred learning styles' (Ward and Maruna 2007:

71). Responsivity itself can be further sub-divided into its 'internal' aspects, such as individual circumstances and characteristics, and its external features, such as culture, peer influences, and opportunities. Although this suggests that programmes need to be carefully tailored to account for variations between offenders in these respects, it is also suggested on this basis that, in order to be successful, programmes will share certain common elements. They are expected to be (Ward and Maruna 2007: 73):

(1) cognitive-behavioural in orientation;

(2) highly-structured, specifying the aims and tasks to be covered in each session;

(3) implemented by trained, qualified and appropriately supervised staff;

(4) delivered in the intended manner ... to ensure treatment integrity;

(5) manual based; and

(6) housed within institutions with personnel committed to the ideals of rehabilitation ...

Programmes incorporating these components have been implemented widely, especially in Canada. Typically, they will seek to offer a range of options, so that interventions can be tailored to meet individual requirements. In British Columbia, for example, it is reported that interventions based on the RNR framework have been delivered for a considerable period of time; and they include core programmes incorporating: cognitive-behavioural techniques, violence prevention, respectful relationships modules, substance abuse management, and specific interventions designed for female offenders (Government of British Columbia 2012). Considerable success in reducing reoffending is claimed for the RNR model (for example, Bonta et al. 2011).

The Good Lives Model (GLM)

Some, however, have been critical of the tendency for the RNR model to under-recognise or mis-recognise 'need' (Hannah-Moffat 2005), effectively locating this approach at the correctional end of the rehabilitation spectrum outlined earlier. Ward and Maruna (2007: 107) have proposed an alternative formulation, described as the 'Good Lives Model' (GLM), stating that it was originally developed 'as an alternative approach to correctional treatment that has the conceptual resources to integrate aspects of treatment not well dealt with by the RNR perspective'. Essentially, the GLM looks more towards promoting beneficial outcomes for offenders and less towards managing risk through behaviour change:

> RNR is associated with a risk management approach and as such tends to regard offender welfare as of secondary

interest, as a 'means' to the 'end' of increased community safety. By way of contrast, the GLM proposes that advancing offenders' needs will also reduce risk.

Ward and Maruna 2007: 172

The claim being advanced here is that while one approach focuses on 'deficits' in offenders' capacity to achieve positive change, the other is concerned with actually creating the conditions to facilitate this. This approach is based on the argument that there are a number of common 'primary goods' which overall contribute to our well-being, but which may be sought or met in inappropriate ways by those who become involved in offending behaviour. The ten 'primary goods' are:

> life (including healthy living and functioning), knowledge, excellence in work and play (including mastery experiences), excellence in agency (i.e., autonomy and self-directedness), inner peace (i.e., freedom from emotional turmoil and stress), friendship (including intimate, romantic, and family relationships), community, spirituality (in the broad sense of finding meaning and purpose in life), happiness, and creativity. Instrumental or secondary goods provide concrete ways (or the means) of securing these goods, for example, certain types of work (i.e., good of mastery), relationships (i.e., good of intimacy), or leisure activities (i.e., good of play).

Ward and Gannon 2006

The goals of the GLM approach are to understand and address the reasons and motivations for adaptive but unacceptable behaviour. As such, the GLM adopts an orientation towards achievement and making improvements in offenders' lives which in turn reduce the incentives to reoffend, but without necessarily addressing offending behaviour directly. Ward and Maruna (2007: 170) cite the 'Make it Work' programme in Victoria, Australia as an example of a GLM initiative to 'support positive lifestyle change … and to reduce recidivism through a combination of vocational training and a mentoring system'. There have been a number of studies which appear to have demonstrated successful outcomes of interventions based on the GLM (see Purvis et al. 2011), in the sense of generating an improved quality of life for ex-offenders and thus potentially increasing the likelihood of sustained desistance from offending.

In the Northwest of England, the G-map project has applied the GLM to its work as a specialist service for young people who have exhibited sexually harmful behaviour (Wylie and Griffin 2013). Although distinguishing itself from the initial articulation of the GLM, G-map seeks to follow the objectives of enabling young people to pursue a number of 'primary goods' or 'needs', which will enable them to achieve outcomes which are both beneficial to them and pro-social. The

five 'primary needs' identified are (Wylie and Griffin 2013: 347):

- having people in my life;
- being healthy;
- having fun and achieving;
- being my own person; and
- having a purpose and making a difference.

The project aims to work with young people who have been responsible for sexually harmful behaviour, from initial meetings which attempt to understand what primary needs the harmful behaviour might have been designed to satisfy, and to develop an action plan to identify alternative ways of meeting these. Over the course of time, typically 18–24 months (2013: 353), therapeutic work is undertaken with the young person to focus on those specific needs which have been met by way of sexual offending. Accordingly, very explicitly and directly, the rehabilitative intervention works to identify a causal connection between the young person's needs and the risk they might pose to others arising from these. Thus, the notion of 'criminogenic need' is operationalised and underpins the rationale for this approach to service delivery and reintegration of young people who offend. The argument is further developed to suggest that it is very often the traumatic nature of young people's background that underlies the adoption of 'maladaptive strategies' to cope with stressful aspects of their own lives. So: 'Trauma-informed practice can be directly relevant to addressing the Good Lives need of being healthy, addressing indirectly other needs such as belonging and being my own person … and potentially mitigating risk' (Wylie and Griffin 2013: 354). Based on the practice experience of G-map, the argument is also advanced that the model adopted for this specific sub-group of offenders could equally easily be applicable to 'other populations'.

Desistance and social capital

Although it is noted that there is a 'dearth of outcome research' to provide any evidence of its 'efficacy' (Wylie and Griffin 2013: 354), the rationale for this kind of approach, addressing and linking offenders' needs and motivations seems well-established. In turn, this is linked with wider arguments in support of a 'desistance' based approach to offender management, on the basis of the claim that sustainable change is only likely to be achievable from within. Again, importantly, the link is made between addressing and working with the needs, interests, and distinctive characteristics of the offender and achieving pro-social change which is likely to reduce levels of offending behaviour. As McNeill (2009: 17) puts it: 'Put simply, the argument is that criminal justice social work services need to think of themselves less as providers of correctional treatment (that belongs to professional experts) and more as supporters of desistance processes (that belong to desisters)'. In acknowledging the potential contribution of the RNR and GLM models, McNeill and colleagues have also argued in favour of a broader approach, which avoids the risk of over-individualising rehabilitation, and recognises that there is a social dimension to the process as well. Observing that 'social capital' may also be as important as changes at the individual level. McNeill and Weaver (2010) make the case for including work with families and wider networks in the repertoire of rehabilitative interventions. 'Such work may involve helping offenders, ex-offenders and their families, where appropriate, to repair the bonding social capital represented in family ties ...' (McNeill and Weaver 2010: 21).

Further than this, the social capital available to ex-offenders can also be developed through the forms of intervention which actually promote positive ties in the wider community, and which thereby provide those concerned with additional resources and support in making changes in their lives. This can be exemplified, again in the case of sex offenders, by the Circles of Support Model, developed particularly in Canada. In this example, offenders are directly engaged with community members whose role is to provide mentoring and encouragement, and also to hold them to account should their thoughts or behaviour appear to show signs of reverting to previous unacceptable patterns. More generally, it is suggested, identifying pro-social roles in the community for offenders, perhaps by way of volunteering, may be another mechanism by which their 'civic reintegration' may be encouraged, and they (and others) may become able to see themselves as 'positive contributors to communities rather than risks or threats to them' (McNeill and Weaver 2010: 21).

Social rehabilitation

A more wide-ranging and welfare-oriented approach to rehabilitation would take as its starting point the well-being and reintegration of the ex-offender, rather than retaining a primary or exclusive focus on reoffending. Thus, the principal aim is to ensure that those who have been involved in crime, and especially former prisoners, are resettled effectively, and enabled to take up opportunities to enhance their lives and claim or reclaim a valued place in society. The emphasis here is on providing practical access to accommodation, work and training, health services, and other welfare provision; and at the same time, supporting or encouraging social reintegration within the community and through establishing a positive network of relationships. In some ways, this may be seen as an extension of the desistance model, but by reversing the priorities for intervention it argues more explicitly for a reassertion of the everyday rights of ex-offenders as the basis for resuming full and equal citizenship. This may in turn reduce the likelihood of further offending, but in this instance this would be seen as a beneficial by-product of intervention rather than its principal goal.

What are the outcomes of rehabilitation: How do we judge success?

When turning to the question of how rehabilitation efforts are evaluated, it is immediately apparent that success criteria can be many and varied, depending on whether or not these are limited to assessments of reoffending rates, or extended to consider other outcomes which can also be seen as positive, such as stable housing, successful drug treatment or employment. Typically, though, the key criterion of success is seen to be whether or not rehabilitative measures act directly or indirectly to reduce levels of reoffending. On this basis, there has been a recurrent controversy as to whether any form of intervention actually 'works', in the sense of positively influencing the future behaviour of offenders undergoing such programmes. This kind of gloomy prognosis came to prominence with a number of widely-reported studies, particularly in the USA. The Cambridge-Somerville study, for instance reviewed the outcomes of an intervention programme with a cohort of young offenders based on individual counselling, as against the results for a comparison group offered no such support, matched on a number of criteria, including age, personal characteristics, and family background. The study found that no improvement could be detected for those subject to the intervention programme in terms of a series of 'undesirable outcomes', including reoffending, early death, or diagnosis of alcoholism or mental health problems; and indeed, rather more of the 'treatment' group experienced these adverse outcomes than those from the control group (McCord 1992: 202). Ironically, the more likely the family receiving the 'treatment' was to be cooperative, the less likely was the outcome to be beneficial: 'These findings strongly suggest that the treatment itself had been harmful' (McCord 1992: 202).

Explanations for the failure of the programme tended to imply that there are inherent weaknesses in rehabilitative approaches which cannot easily be resolved (for example, the creation of dependency, 'value conflict' between service providers and recipients, the effects of labelling, the consequences of raised, or unmet, expectations, or 'contagion'; see Zane et al. 2015).

Nothing works?

Of course, this was only one study and it only evaluated one intervention method, so it might be reasonable to argue that either the method used, or the study itself were deficient in some way. However, it did not stand alone, and in fact contributed to a growing mood of doubt and despair, as a consensus emerged by the 1970s that there was very little evidence to support the value of rehabilitative interventions in general, encapsulated most forcefully by Martinson (1974), who concluded that 'nothing' or at least 'not much' works in rehabilitative terms and particularly in reducing recidivism. Martinson evaluated over 200 studies spanning a wide range of intervention programmes and methods, institutional and non-institutional, and found: 'very little reason to hope that we have in fact found a sure way of reducing recidivism through rehabilitation' (Martinson 1974: 49). In concluding this, Martinson did acknowledge that there could be several reasons for this outcome, including the models of treatment then in use themselves being insufficiently well-developed. If that were the case, all that would be required was a redoubling of efforts to eradicate the flaws in existing programmes of supervision, education, or personal development, for example. But:

> It may be, on the other hand, that there is a more radical flaw in our present strategies – that education at its best, or that psychotherapy at its best, cannot overcome, or even appreciably reduce, the powerful tendency for offenders to continue in criminal behavior.
>
> Martinson 1974: 49

The effect of this seminal article was to cast a shadow of gloom over rehabilitative practices for a considerable period of time. Instead, currents of opinion favouring deterrent or retributive measures of punishment, or indeed approaches grounded in principles of crime control and risk management became increasingly dominant. Only after a considerable period of time had elapsed—in the early 2000s—did rehabilitation make a significant comeback, at least in policy terms. Even though Martinson's claims came under critical scrutiny (Hollin 1999), the belief that 'nothing works' became cemented in place, as a form of orthodoxy in criminal justice: 'Against this academic and political backdrop,

the policy and practice generated by acceptance of the futility of treatment were implemented on an increasing scale' (Hollin 1999: 362).

Despite this, and having been confronted with this challenge, practitioners and researchers went on to make extensive efforts to develop effective treatment-based interventions, and to show 'what works, for whom, and under what conditions?' (Hollin 1999: 362). Lipsey (1995), for example, carried out a further review of 400 studies of delinquency treatment and claimed to have identified a number of factors associated with positive outcomes. These did not necessarily reflect highly sophisticated treatment programmes or techniques, but did demonstrate associations with particular 'treatment types'. Lipsey (1995: 75) found that consistently certain types of intervention were associated with 'positive outcomes', especially but not exclusively defined in terms of reduced levels of recidivism. Thus, for example, employment-based programmes, those described as 'multimodal', and those geared towards behaviour change and skills development were the most successful, although all except 'vocational counselling' and 'deterrence' were adjudged to have some kind of positive effect. In addition, Lipsey observed that successful outcomes were associated with more extensive and intensive programmes (longer-term with higher levels of weekly contact), which appeared to be more beneficial (1995: 76); and that close attention to effective programme delivery by supervisors was also important. In other words, it was not so much 'rehabilitation' per se that was problematic, but the nature and integrity of programmes being delivered. It seems, then, that over time, rehabilitation itself was being rehabilitated.

Rehabilitation revived

McGuire and Priestley (1995) built on this renewed spirit of optimism, arguing that it was possible to describe and construct the kind of cognitive-behavioural and 'multimodal' programmes which could achieve success by addressing different aspects of offenders' needs and behaviour and thereby addressing the complexities of their lives and the factors associated with offending behaviour. The focus of intervention should be on 'risk' (assessed on the basis of prior offending history) and 'criminogenic need' rather than needs which are 'more distantly related, or unrelated' to offending (McGuire and Priestley 1995: 15). So, the shift in approach was encapsulated in the movement in the underlying predisposition to rehabilitation, from 'nothing works' to 'what works?' (sometimes without a question mark). This process culminated in the series of announcements by the UK government which represented a positive endorsement of rehabilitation (see earlier; Ministry of Justice 2010), and which proclaimed that government had launched a 'Rehabilitation Revolution' in 2012.

Underlying this new spirit of optimism about rehabilitation, there has undoubtedly been some very detailed analysis, both of the available evidence and of the assumptions on which our understandings of and criteria for 'success' are based. Given that there are a very wide range of factors in offenders' lives which are in one way or another, criminogenic, this does suggest that the targets for intervention in rehabilitation work in criminal justice can, in fact, be very widely drawn, especially if the embedded assumption is that we can only hope to reduce reoffending rates by addressing linked 'needs' of those who offend. This, indeed, is the conclusion drawn by at least one review of the evidence:

> **Holistic interventions that address multiple criminogenic needs are more likely to be effective in reducing offending.** The evidence suggests that offenders often experience multiple problems, many of which are considered 'criminogenic' in the sense that they contribute directly towards offending. [Emphasis in original text]
>
> Sapouna et al. 2011: 12

Success might therefore be assessed according to certain interim measures such as the level or extent of offenders' 'habilitation' or 'integration' (2011: 14), especially in light of findings that offenders in custody 'have a greater number of needs' than the general population (2011: 13). This, for example, points towards a need for a comprehensive and sustained approach to aftercare provision.

Harper and Chitty (2005: ix) have produced an overview which suggests that offenders on average are assessed as experiencing four criminogenic needs, and that this rate is higher for those in custody. This again provides support for 'multimodal' approaches to intervention, and the establishment of a range of intermediate success criteria, aside from that based on rates of reoffending: 'multi-modal interventions offer the prospect that work on several fronts could be tackled simultaneously, with the potential to achieve more than the traditional "linear" approach' (Harper and Chitty 2005: 59).

Key areas identified for intervention by Harper and Chitty in this review were: employment, education, accommodation, drug misuse, and mental health. Thus, for example, a number of possible approaches to supporting offenders into employment or training are identified, although in this respect a number of challenges also arise for those concerned with effective delivery—where programmes are targeted at those in custody, for instance, they are unable to provide direct experience of work in a conventional setting, so are limited to providing skills training or work preparation. Success in these terms might be viewed in terms of programme attendance, certificated skills attainment, or jobs arranged for prisoners on release. In practice, one study of the circumstances of prisoners nearing release found that limited help of this kind was available, and even when it was, it did not lead directly to employment for two-thirds of those receiving vocational preparation (Niven and Olagundoye 2002).

Similarly, it is suggested that community-based employment support initiatives might be beneficial for offenders. Indeed, throughout its history, the probation service in the UK has viewed work and training as priority areas for intervention, with a particular focus on 'employability', although as is acknowledged, the evidence as to what sort of skills to develop, and how to do so, is limited. In determining which of 'key skills', that is generic preparation for the work environment, or 'vocational skills', meaning specific job training, is of greater benefit it is reported that: 'We have as yet no information on employment or offending outcomes from such schemes, on which to make a soundly-based choice between the options' (Johnson and Rex 2002: 198).

See **What do you think? 25.3** for more detail on an organisation providing rehabilitative services for prisoners, and then consider the questions raised.

In other areas, too, whilst it may seem fairly straightforward in theory to base intervention programmes on general aims such as improving offender education or providing secure accommodation, this becomes rather more problematic and evidence becomes less conclusive when practice examples are considered in detail (Harper and Chitty 2005: 62). Grimshaw (2002) found, for example, that accommodation support needs vary over the life course, so we could expect that different interventions would be required at different points in time for ex-offenders; that housing needs were connected with and interacted with other needs; that specific groups, such as sex offenders and mentally disordered offenders would have quite distinctive needs; and that continuing support might be necessary, beyond the initial provision of somewhere to stay for offenders.

As one survey of recently sentenced prisoners has found, there has been a relatively recent acknowledgement of:

> the complex and interlocking problems facing prisoners ... The majority of offenders enter prison with a range of health and social problems, including poor mental health, drug and alcohol misuse and low levels of literacy and numeracy ... These problems are known to be associated with offending behaviour.
>
> Stewart 2008: 1

In response to this, government undertook to put in place a range of 'delivery plans' to address these varied

WHAT DO YOU THINK? 25.3

The North East Prison After Care Service (NEPACS, see **Figure 25.6**) has been established as a rehabilitative resource for ex-offenders since the 19th century.

NEPACS and its forerunners have been working in the north east of England to support a positive future for prisoners and their families for over 130 years. During this time, the structure of the organisation and the activities we undertake have changed, but our commitment to helping people affected by imprisonment remains constant.

- NEPACS works in prisons across the north east of England and we welcome over 140,000 visitors through our centres each year.
- Nearly 20,000 children use NEPACS' play facilities at prisons in the north east each year.
- NEPACS provides tea bars and staffs play areas within the prison visits rooms and organise special visits for children so they can spend quality time with their parent, learning through organised play activities.
- NEPACS helps about 500 offenders and/or their families each year with a small grant to help them through financial difficulties and get their lives straight.
- NEPACS provides free caravan holiday breaks for up to 40 families with a relative in prison each year.

- NEPACS promotes good practice in resettlement through our Annual Awards and raises awareness through public lectures and events.

(www.nepacs.co.uk)

Do you think rehabilitation services such as this should primarily be a state responsibility, or is it more appropriate for them to be provided independently, by voluntary or other organisations? Why?

Figure 25.6 The NEPACS home page
Source: www.nepacs.co.uk

needs, along with 'a commitment to commission research to monitor ... success ... in delivering effective interventions'.

Despite this commitment, it still seems clear that if we agree that offenders are likely to have complex and inter-linked needs, which are in turn likely to contribute to a predisposition to offend; and if we agree that because of this, these needs should be addressed as part of a wider goal of achieving effective rehabilitation; then establishing and delivering suitable interventions and appropriate measures of success will almost certainly remain highly problematic. The diverse nature of offenders' needs and circumstances make it extremely difficult to identify exactly what we would agree to be a desirable outcome, although initiatives such as the GLM and other desistance-based approaches attempt to provide a means towards this goal. Undoubtedly, though, the changing dynamics of offenders' lives provide very substantial challenges in identifying when 'successful' results have been achieved.

What is the impact of rehabilitation? What does it achieve?

From the preceding discussion we have understood that there is considerable support for the principle of rehabilitation of offenders, and that the evidence to justify this assumption is relatively limited, and often contested. So, at this point we should consider what kind of evidence we do have available to us, and what it tells us about the wider objective of promoting offender reintegration.

One study of employment-based programmes for prisoners starts on a very pessimistic note:

The scarcity and generally poor quality of previous research means that it is difficult to come up with firm advice about 'what works' which goes beyond the usual principles of programme integrity, targeting offenders and matching teaching and learning styles.

Webster et al. 2001: iii

This study goes on to establish in no uncertain terms what does not work: 'prison workshop experience emerges as unhelpful in securing future work' and the 'most common complaint from inmates is that the tasks they do in workshops are boring and repetitive' (2001: 65). A number of factors seem to be associated with the observed limitations in prison-based employment programmes, including the lack of suitable aftercare services, organisational constraints associated with the prison as an institution, and the associated impact on programme integrity, which is seen as being so central to ' "what works" principles'. On the other hand, the same study also incorporates a detailed review of other studies which appear to identify potential characteristics of employment-based programmes that do claim to generate sustained benefits, suggesting that a combination of individualised planning and advice, practical help, post-release support and incentives for employers may be associated with greater success in obtaining and keeping work and reduced recidivism (Webster et al. 2001: 73).

Searching for the evidence base

A comparable inquiry into the effectiveness of systematic 'Pathfinder' resettlement strategies suggested that programme integrity and consistency of support were associated with 'meaningful work' and acknowledgement by over 70 per cent of prisoners that 'they had gained benefits from the project' (Lewis et al. 2003: v), and that 'participants showed significant positive change in crime-prone attitudes and self-reported problems' (Raynor 2004: 313). The study concluded, like many others, that the resettlement needs of prisoners arise 'typically' from 'a combination of difficulties which have their roots in the prisoner's attitudes, beliefs and habitual responses to problems', suggesting the need for 'holistic' and continuing support (Lewis et al. 2003: vii). However, this study did not provide any evidence on reconviction rates, even though the authors at the same time considered that 'the reduction of offending is [likely] to assume a central role in resettlement work' (2003: 4).

Reflecting on the findings from this and other 'Pathfinder' projects, Raynor (2004) noted a sense of disappointment amongst policy makers that evaluations had been unable to provide more conclusive evidence of their achievements (or, indeed, failings): 'we had not so much an end product as a variety of interesting interim products, with a mixture of positive and negative findings and few clear answers' (Raynor 2004: 314). This, in his view, demonstrated the importance of reading research carefully and critically, rather than being seduced by 'headline results' (2004: 316). On the other hand, Raynor was careful at this point not to throw the whole body of 'what works' research into question, as some allegedly did, such as the probation officers' union NAPO. The union's concerns with evidence-based approaches such as 'what works', included: 'the belief that programmes are inherently conservative, pathologizing individual offenders and ignoring social causes of crime … NAPO refers to "a simplistic model of offending that isolates individual behaviour from its social, economic and political context" ' (Raynor 2003: 336).

Programmes might prove difficult to evaluate positively for other reasons, too, such as flawed implementation. Raynor was writing at a time of particularly feverish and uncritical policy innovation, and he also drew attention to the important distinction between 'demonstration' and 'practical' project developments:

The former are the special pilot projects, which are often the source of the research covered in systematic reviews, and the latter are the routine implementations which follow organizational decisions to adopt new methods, as in the rapid roll-out of the Probation Service's new programmes. Better results are more commonly found in the 'demonstration projects'.

Raynor 2004: 318

Despite such reservations, Lipsey and Cullen (2007) have argued that 'practical projects' are able to demonstrate consistently positive effects if, and when, properly implemented. Similarly, Sherman et al. (1998) have provided an encyclopaedic overview of interventions in criminal justice and concluded that a range of rehabilitative interventions can be shown to be effective. Included in this list are: therapeutic drug treatments in prison; rehabilitation programmes tailored to identified 'risk' factors; ex-offender job training for older males. At the same time, this review identified a number of other 'promising' interventions, where the evidence was not yet robust enough to support unqualified claims of effectiveness. These included: community-based mentoring; prison-based vocational programmes; and intensive supervision and after-care for juvenile offenders (Sherman et al. 1998: 12).

Increasing certainty

Over the course of time, the body of available evidence relating to rehabilitative interventions has increased, and by 2013 the Ministry of Justice was able to publish an updated report, based on a further review. This time, the distinction was made between 'static' and 'dynamic' risk factors, with the suggestion that intervention programmes should be targeted towards specific changes to the latter: 'Dynamic factors, such as education, employment and drug use, are amenable to change' (Ministry of Justice 2013: 3). In addition, the emerging interest in 'desistance' has helped in identifying aspects of change in offenders' lives which are particularly associated with a reduction in re-offending, and which rehabilitative interventions might therefore be expected to promote or reinforce; such as, for instance 'hope and motivation' to change (2013: 8). This line of argument is consistent with the case made by McNeill and others (see earlier) which argues that interventions to support dynamic processes of change in this way are likely to be more effective than simply focusing on offending behaviour, particularly by way of punitive sanctions which are consistently shown not to work well in terms of reducing recidivism (Lipsey and Cullen: 2007).

According to the Ministry of Justice (2013: 16), there is now 'good evidence' of the effectiveness of 'a wide range of drug interventions' in 'reducing reoffending', and that custodial treatments are 'most effective' if they are consolidated with effective after-care provision. There is 'mixed/promising evidence' of the effectiveness of targeted housing support for offenders with mental health issues; of the effectiveness of employment/education programmes; and of the potential benefits of disposals which 'require offenders to engage with mental health treatment' (Ministry of Justice 2013: 20).

Although there is thus a range of evidence to support particular approaches to rehabilitation, there also remain unresolved questions, not so much about 'what works', but about 'how' and 'why' it works. On the one hand, there is an understandable tendency for programme evaluations to tend to frame their conclusions in terms of the achievement of the programme itself, as a discrete intervention model. This, in turn, encourages the assumption that all that is needed is to replicate successful approaches through a top-down process of rolling them out. On the other hand, as Lipsey (1999) shows, there is considerably less evidence of success when interventions are not carried out in experimental conditions—which might be favourable in a number of ways, such as funding, practitioner commitment, institutional support, researcher bias and so on. Indeed, it may be the case that successful interventions do not depend so much on the design, imposition, and delivery of standardised programmes, but on the ways in which practice is geared towards the needs and circumstances of individual offenders, given their widely differing life trajectories.

Desistance and effective practice

The need for responsive and individually tailored interventions is central to the arguments put forward by those who promote a 'desistance' model of practice. According to this 'paradigm' (Durnescu 2011), positive change for offenders can be attributed to a combination of features of their experience and personal characteristics, to which successful interventions are attuned. That is to say, effective practice achieves its objectives by adopting a strategic but focused approach to intervention, geared to the specific features of the offender's life and circumstances, rather than relying on uniform programme-based models which by definition are less able to be responsive to the individual. To maximise the chances of successful outcomes, intervention must therefore adopt a series of principles, rather than a list of pre-defined programme components:

1. Agency is as important as … structure in promoting or inhibiting desistance from crime.

2. Individuals differ in their readiness to contemplate and begin the process of change.

3. Generating and sustaining motivation is vital to the maintenance of processes of change.

4. Desistance is a difficult and often lengthy process, not an 'event', and relapses are common.

5. While overcoming social problems is often insufficient on its own to promote desistance, it may be a necessary condition for further progress.

6. As people change they need new skills and capacities appropriate to their new lifestyle, and access to opportunities to use them

Maguire 2007: 408

Farrall's (2002) research, for example, offers insights into a rather different perspective on effectiveness in criminal justice interventions, by suggesting that 'successful desistance was the product of individual motivation, social and personal contexts, probation supervision and the meanings which people hold about their lives and their behaviours' (Farrall and McNeill 2011: 211). This, in turn, implies the prioritisation of relationships and sustainable engagement with offenders as the basis of effective intervention, rather than highly-structured and rigorously enforced change programmes. Criticising attempts to put such programmes into operation systematically in England and Wales, Farrall and McNeill (2011: 212), argue that instead 'personal motivation', the 'social context', the 'organisational context', and practitioner relationships and skills are crucial in supporting the 'change process'. Nor do such desistance-based arguments fall into the trap of relying entirely on the intervention to facilitate change in people's lives:

> The way in which we think about interventions and case management needs to be embedded within an understanding of the change process that it exists to support – and even

desistance itself is not the ultimate concern. People do not simply desist, they desist *into* something … Ultimately, desistance is perhaps best understood as part of the individual's ongoing journey towards successful integration within the community.
>
> Farrall and McNeill 2011: 213

The limitations of rehabilitation

On the face of it, rehabilitation seems to offer a 'win-win' option in criminal justice. Beneficial and usually less punitive interventions are provided for the offender, which are in turn likely to facilitate reintegration into the community and at the same time reduce the likelihood of recidivism. It is difficult on the face of it to find grounds for objecting to it as a central element of the justice system. But, as we have seen, it has not always been popular, or viewed as particularly desirable by those determining policy. As we have seen, for example, the suggestion associated with Martinson (1974) in particular that 'nothing works' did appear to exert some influence in legitimising, if not prompting, a move away from treatment-based interventions to more punitive, correctional, or risk-based models of practice. It is unlikely that Martinson's contribution on its own generated what has been described as an 'era of "nothing works pessimism" and "lock 'em up" punitiveness' (Ward and Maruna 2007: 8), but it certainly seemed to capture the spirit of the times and give added legitimacy to arguments against constructive measures aimed at improving the lives of those in trouble with the law. It must be acknowledged, too, that the goal of achieving absolute certainty about what interventions are effective (as well as why and how) remains challenging (Harper and Chitty 2005).

It is significant, however, that Martinson's subsequent (1979) retraction of his original claim was far less influential, although based on an equally considered re-evaluation of his previous conclusions, and where he argued forcefully for the effectiveness of some forms of intervention as against others. It is perhaps likely that the suggestion that rehabilitative programmes made no difference suited the influential claims of those who viewed any kind of measure which offered help or self-improvement to offenders as being insufficiently punitive, and in some cases akin to 'letting them off'. Notably, in 2012, in setting out detailed reform plans and under the guise of promoting rehabilitation, the Ministry of Justice also committed itself to incorporating more demanding elements in community disposals to allay fears that rehabilitative measures might be viewed as insufficiently punitive, whilst ironically at the same time recognising that this might have an adverse effect on reoffending rates.

The question of proportionality

Similarly, it may be argued that paying undue attention to offenders' needs and well-being is to discount the wishes and interests of victims in seeing the offence dealt with by way of an appropriate punitive sanction (see **Chapter 24**). So, as Raynor and Robinson (2009: 11) argue, rehabilitative principles are vulnerable to moral arguments based on principles of proportionality of sentencing and the pure administration of justice, rather than any form of compromise with competing principles, such as taking account of the needs and circumstances of the offender, or even the wider public interest.

On the other hand, there are also those who argue that rehabilitative interventions imposed without taking account of the need for proportionality in sentencing may be excessively punitive rather than unduly lenient. Once beneficial effects are claimed for interventions, it becomes easier to advance justifications for a wide range of practices, many of which may be viewed as unacceptable:

> faith in rehabilitation has manifested itself in a wide variety of practices for which 'rehabilitative effects' have been claimed, from the treadmill and the crank through extended periods of solitary confinement, to psychosurgical and medical interventions. … The history of rehabilitation includes the use of drugs to 'chemically castrate' sexual offenders; to tranquilise 'dangerous' offenders; and to arouse pain and fear in the context of 'aversion therapy'.
>
> Robinson and Crow 2009: 11

This raises the further question of whether incorporating coercion in the administration of measures of treatment or reintegration can be justified, especially where it involves the imposition of sanctions such as confinement of physical restraint which go beyond what would be legitimate as a purely punitive measure. Rehabilitative interventions could thus breach the principle of 'just deserts'. Irrespective of this argument, current practice is widely characterised by the use of mandatory additional conditions and requirements to supplement the treatment element of community orders, as in the case of the Drug Treatment and Testing Order introduced under the Crime and Disorder Act 1998, and replaced in 2003 by the Drug Rehabilitation Requirement, for example.

The problem of compulsion

As Raynor and Robinson (2009: 9) also argue, the problem of compulsion in the delivery of treatment programmes is also bound up with a particular view of the coherence and relevance of the intervention that is being provided. This suggests a greater degree of both programme integrity and certainty about its effectiveness than much of what we know entitles us to assume. Indeed, the notion of 'treatment' that is sometimes incorporated into rehabilitation programmes is suggestive of a 'medical model' of intervention which McNeill (2014: 6) links with the influence of 'dubious expertise'. The offender is the focus of what might be deemed 'coerced correction', according to a predetermined set of desired outcomes; and in pursuit of which it is assumed the appropriate treatment dosage or behavioural tool will be administered unproblematically. The distinctive characteristics and capacity for independent thought and action of the offender become subsumed under this model, and her/his sense of 'agency' and capacity for 'self-determination' (Farrall and McNeill 2011: 212) are disregarded.

Robinson's (2008) view is that the recent and continuing re-making of rehabilitation has represented a process of re-alignment, bringing intervention into line with a number of other influential strands of thought in criminal justice. It may be seen as: 'utilitarian rehabilitation'; 'managerial rehabilitation'; or 'expressive rehabilitation', in each case developing a rationale for the association, but equally in each case becoming significantly modified in the process.

'Utilitarian rehabilitation' relegates other potential objectives, such as reintegration or resettlement in favour of reducing levels of offending behaviour. Cognitive-behavioural programmes are identified as appropriate vehicles for delivering this strategy, promoting pro-social attitudes and behaviour, purportedly in the interests of offender and community alike. Rehabilitation becomes principally a means of ensuring the protection of the public and potential future victims, rather than promoting the welfare of offenders themselves. 'Managerial rehabilitation' provides a framework for the preservation of rehabilitative practice in an environment principally dominated by discourses of risk assessment and risk management; so: 'contemporary rehabilitation has evolved by learning to speak the language of risk' (Robinson 2008: 434). Associated with this trend, we can perhaps see particular types of intervention becoming more prominent, given their particular focus on risk reduction; these might include drug rehabilitation programmes or therapeutic interventions with sexual offenders. 'Expressive rehabilitation' associates reintegrative interventions with

explicitly punitive objectives: 'rehabilitative sanctions and interventions have entered a new discursive alliance with punitiveness, which has been essential to their continuing legitimacy' (Robinson 2008: 435). In this way, the inclusion of punitive requirements into notionally rehabilitative interventions is only to be expected. Tracing this trend back to the late 1980s, Robinson (2008: 436) suggests that the emerging policy goal of delivering 'punishment in the community' and the alternatives to custody movement of that era helped to usher in rehabilitative programmes, such as intensive supervision, which integrated punishment and treatment within the same disposal. It is not a coincidence, in her view, that the Probation Service and probation training were effectively decoupled from their social work origins in 1995 (in England and Wales), highlighting the relegation of concerns with offenders' welfare to the margins: 'Indeed, it is arguably now the case that the "pure" rehabilitative sanction is extinct' (Robinson 2008: 437). As Cohen (1985) anticipated some time earlier, rehabilitation becomes closely associated with 'control' as a consequence of these developments.

Rehabilitation: putting the offender first?

Common to all these tactical realignments of rehabilitation has been the relative absence of concern with the well-being of the offender. This is seen and acted upon as ancillary to the central objective of reducing levels of crime and promoting public safety. This, as Robinson (2008: 431) and others note, completely obscures 'a vision of rehabilitation *as a right of the offender*' (her emphasis), and as something for which the state has a responsibility because of the disadvantages associated with being an offender (both historic and in the future). So, questions of 'stigma' and 'social exclusion' which might legitimately be seen as consequences (if not causes) of being processed as an offender are, in turn, de-emphasised as reasonable objectives for rehabilitative interventions. As a consequence, those aspects of reintegration which might address the challenges facing ex-offenders also become de-emphasised, and this is reflected in the relatively poor provision of services and opportunities for those leaving custody in particular.

By contrast, the case made increasingly strongly by desistance theorists is that effective reintegration of offenders into society and the associated cessation of offending careers is dependent on life changes to a much greater extent than specific programmes targeted at certain features of their behaviour or mental functioning. So it is that the evidence generated by research into desistance suggests that there are 'a range of factors associated with the ending of active involvement in offending' and that these factors are associated with changes such as gaining 'employment, a life partner or a family' (Farrall 2002: 11). In addition, it is suggested, it is the subjective meaning of such changes which matters, depending on the kind of 'narrative' that offenders build around them; how do they value such changes and what do they imply for their understandings of their own identities (McNeill 2009: 18).

Interestingly, it seems that the insights expressed in **Conversation 25.1** with Nicole Westmarland are also increasingly acknowledged in policy development, with the Prison Reform Trust (Edgar et al. 2012), for example, explicitly accepting the importance of desistance theory as a guide to good practice.

CONVERSATIONS 25.1

Arguments for rehabilitation: the case of community interventions and domestic violence—with Professor Nicole Westmarland

RS (Roger Smith): Fundamentally the question for the purposes of this conversation is 'What do you think we should do about gender-based or gendered violence?' and particularly 'How should we exercise control over it?' or is that the right way to think about it?

NW (Nicole Westmarland): People say that the place for domestic violence perpetrators is in prison, we should stamp it out, we should never accept it, domestic violence is wrong. So we have all of these messages on the one hand at a very kind of high level policy level, which are all obviously correct, but then I think once that starts filtering down into practice we get a much more complicated and nuanced picture about the problems that are linked with this crime, happening within families, which has ripple effects not only to the children living within that family but huge ripple effects in families and friends. And I think that we can often be accused of over simplifying the problem of domestic violence and falling into a trap of stereotyping victims and perpetrators and the impacts on them.

RS: I know that you're interested in perhaps challenging some of the conventional criminal justice responses and I wonder if you could say a bit more about some of the work that you're doing that questions the sort of routinely tough perspective?

NW: I think the problem is that we have a tough perspective in policy but not actually in practice. Recently I've spent a lot of time with individual police officers and also I've spent a lot of time in court observing judges and magistrates and sentencing around domestic violence related crimes. And what we see in a *lot* of those cases is actually much more of a therapeutic based approach to dealing with men's violence than a punitive approach. So we see things like alcohol, mental health … bereavement etc., being used as more the rationale, actually, for men's use of violence than things we see in policy, in academic life, around it being about gender inequality, power and control. So I think on the one hand we think of a court

as somewhere where kind of quite tough sentences are given potentially, for domestic violence, and in fact I find that to be a myth in a lot of the cases.

RS: It is almost supported by the media a bit though isn't it? Because the impression I would get from the media, as just a disinterested reader, is the courts just do dispense tough sentences.

NW: It is and I think it's also a myth, even among some parts of researchers and activists as well, there is this idea that there is a 'tough on crime' stance. Once, when talking to some Home Office ministers, the idea was raised of a hostel for perpetrators of domestic abuse to be taken to, rather than removing women and children into refuges and, the statement was given 'Well we already have hostels for domestic violence perpetrators, they're called prison'. But, but in reality men who commit domestic violence offences, in the large, aren't going to prison. They're given fairly low-level community sentences and rarely even domestic violence perpetrator programmes, actually. I suppose that brings me onto kind of one of the topics that I've been looking at a lot recently, which is the issue of domestic violence perpetrator programmes. The ones which we've looked at are those which are outside of the criminal justice system, so they're not ones which men have been mandated to attend by a court but they're not really truly voluntary either. These aren't men who are waking up one day and thinking 'Next thing on my to-do list is to tackle my use and misuse of power and control within the relationship'. It's men who are at risk of losing their children, it's men who want to regain contact with their children, it's men who are told 'This is the end of the line, the relationship is over unless you get professional help to change your behaviour'. And these types of programmes have often been kind of dismissed as, the soft edge of responses. They're sometimes seen as, tackling the middle-class men who are willing to be educated on topics, rather than, the majority of perpetrators. And that's really not what we found in our interviews with men, we found that men had been very open, actually, about their use of violence, some of the men had tried to kill their partners. And these were on community programmes and many of these had never had any contact at all with the criminal justice system, at any point. So, this isn't really a diversionary sentence, this isn't really an alternative to a tough sentence, this is men who, for whatever reason, have never been in touch with the criminal justice system, possibly because their partners are so fearful of the criminal justice response, of what might happen, that they're never going to make a report. So, to me, one of the advantages of domestic violence perpetrator programmes is you are at least doing *something* rather than in many of these cases, which it would be, doing nothing, it's not an alternative to; it's not a diversion to. We can't change the fact that some people do want to remain with that partner and we can't change the fact that even if they separate, the chances are that that man will have more relationships in the future and it's what we do about those future relationships as well.

RS: So do you think those types of programmes demonstrate their value? I wouldn't say that they were successful or not successful but do they change things in some way?

NW: I think they do change things and I think our research has shown that they change things in a number of ways. Sometimes that was that they were giving the women power to change, so sometimes that was that they were emboldening women to be able to make decisions to leave.

RS: Like the Freedom Programme? I know that is victim oriented but is it similar?

NW: No, it's more that when a man goes on a programme the woman gets an independent safety worker to support her and she knows that there is a weekly check-in where somebody is looking at what the behaviour of that man is.

So I think, for some women, they feel this kind of safety net of somebody else knows what is happening in this relationship, somebody else is there, there is a weekly contact point. Somebody else is holding him accountable, it's not just them all the time. So that can embolden women, it can empower them to leave, it can enable them to say to themselves, to their families, to the perpetrator's family, 'Look, I've done everything I can, I've even gone to the extent of engaging with this programme and he's got professional support and he still hasn't changed'. So it can give them the confidence to leave or to change their behaviour. It can make men change their behaviour, we found particularly in relation to physical and sexual violence that there was dramatic reductions, over time, in their use of physical and sexual violence in terms of things like respectful communication, their use of coercive and controlling behaviours. They all did reduce but not to the same extent as physical and sexual violence did.

Ultimately, we found there's a bit of a myth around perpetrator programmes that they will make men *worse*, that they'll learn new tactics, that they'll somehow skew the programme to make them better abusers. And we found very little evidence of that and that's why we called our ... report 'Steps Towards Change' because we're not saying that these programmes are entirely successful, we're not saying that they make all of these men into, perfect, model men. But we are saying that for most of the lives of the women, children and men who were in our study, their lives were better to some extent. And maybe, at this moment in time that's all we can ask for because I don't know of any other interventions that we're doing, which can do anything more than that and I guess that's the next big question, if not these then what?

Professor Nicole Westmarland is the Director of the Durham Centre for Research into Violence and Abuse (CRiVA), and Professor of Criminology, at Durham University

---

Equally strikingly, though, the available evidence suggests that welfare provision, within and beyond the justice system, is not systematically available to provide continuing support to facilitate desistance. Suitable accommodation is often not provided for ex-offenders on release from custody, for example, especially those with mental health problems (Edgar et al. 2012: 21); and the employment rates for prisoners on release has remained consistently low (2012: 54). Further to this, in September 2014 a thematic review of resettlement provision was published jointly by the inspectorates responsible for oversight of criminal justice services, which found consistent failings in the quality of services available for those released from custody. The study observed, for example, that despite its importance in helping to rehabilitate ex-offenders, there was 'no evidence' of prisoners' families being involved in the resettlement process (HM Inspectorate of Prisons et al. 2014: 5), a finding which seems directly at odds with the conclusions of the desistance literature.

Might we conclude then, that there is a significant mismatch between approaches to rehabilitation which focus on the offender alone, perhaps applying a 'deficit model' to the individual taken out of context, and the sort of intervention strategy suggested by both desistance theory and current evidence which would work with the ex-offender *in situ*, developing individualised programmes which reflect specific circumstances and social needs? Once again, the key question seems to be 'what works, for whom, and in what circumstances'?

SUMMARY

During this chapter we have covered the following key issues:

- Explain the concept of rehabilitation as applied in criminal justice

We have introduced the argument that the principal consideration in dealing with offenders is their effective reintegration into society, by means of interventions which promote their well-being and address their needs and personal problems.

- Recognise different objectives to which rehabilitation might aspire

We have acknowledged various approaches to rehabilitation, from those which focus on changing aspects of the offender's lifestyle or habits to those which are concerned with ameliorating her/his circumstances and improving life chances.

- Identify and describe alternative models of rehabilitative practice

The chapter has provided an account of a range of interventions, which are designed to deliver the stated outcomes of rehabilitation, including resettlement initiatives and treatment programmes.

- Evaluate the achievements and outcomes of rehabilitative interventions

We have reviewed the claimed and actual outcomes of rehabilitation programmes, including those which appear to have negative consequences in terms of reoffending, and the explanatory accounts which seek to make sense of these apparently anomalous effects.

- Assess the critical perspectives on rehabilitation and its aims

The chapter concluded with a discussion of the possible shortcomings of arguments for rehabilitation, in terms of its uncertain benefits, possible failures to reflect the interests of all stakeholders, and its potential to act as form of disguised punishment.

REVIEW QUESTIONS

1. What do you understand by the term 'rehabilitation'?

2. What are the five main assumptions underlying the principle of rehabilitation?

3. What are the arguments for and against compulsory treatment of offenders for rehabilitative purposes?

4. What are some of the key methods used in rehabilitation?

5. How can rehabilitative interventions avoid the accusation that they represent an easy option for offenders?

6. How do you think the effectiveness of rehabilitation is best measured?

FURTHER READING

Hannah-Moffat, K. (2005) 'Criminogenic needs and the transformative risk subject', *Punishment and Society*, 7 (1), pp. 29–51.
An interesting analysis of the relationship between 'risk' and 'need' and how tensions are managed between these apparently competing perspectives on understanding offenders and accounting for their crimes.

McNeill, F. (2009) *Towards Effective Practice in Offender Supervision.* Glasgow: Scottish Centre for Crime & Justice Research.
Provides a detailed overview of the arguments in favour of 'desistance' based approaches to offender management.

Ministry of Justice (2013) *Transforming Rehabilitation: A summary of evidence on reducing reoffending.* London: Ministry of Justice.
A government-commissioned overview of the available evidence on the contribution of rehabilitative practice to the reduction of further offending.

Ward, T. and Maruna, S. (2007) *Rehabilitation.* Abingdon: Routledge.
A full and helpful overview of the principles and practices central to rehabilitation in criminal justice.

 Access the **online resources** to view selected further reading and web links relevant to the material covered in this chapter.
www.oup.com/uk/case/

CHAPTER OUTLINE

Introduction	716
Alternatives to punishment and offence resolution	716
The purpose of alternatives to punishment and offence resolution	720
Transformational goals	723
Alternatives to punishment: Structure, organisation, and operation	725
Delivering alternatives to punishment: Practices and challenges	728
The achievements of alternatives to punishment: Considering the evidence	732
Alternatives to punishment: The implications	734
The limitations of alternatives to punishment	737

Alternatives to punishment

Diversion and restorative justice

KEY ISSUES

After reading this chapter, you should be able to:

- describe the approaches to the delivery of criminal justice which challenge conventional assumptions about crime and punishment;

- explain the origins and development of restorative ideas and practices;

- understand the emergence and impact of diversion as an intervention strategy;

- consider examples of the implementation of 'alternatives to punishment' and their impact;

- critique the arguments in favour of alternative forms of intervention, appreciating the potential criticisms of alternative forms of intervention;

- develop your own arguments for and against these more informal methods of dealing with offences.

Introduction

Relatively recent developments in criminal justice have seen the emergence of a number of distinctive arguments in favour of 'alternative' means of responding to offenders and their crimes. Those who favour such innovations have tended to reject conventional assumptions and approaches. They believe that it is not enough just to problematise the offender, who should be seen instead as an active participant in the justice process, who is able to play a significant part in offence resolution alongside others affected, including victims.

This viewpoint has informed the development of a strand of thinking and practice based on restorative principles. Definitions of restorative justice can be seen to differ substantially from established assumptions about the objectives of criminal justice processes, at least as they have operated in modern western societies:

> Restorative justice is a process to involve, to the extent possible, those who have a stake in a specific offense to collectively identify and address harms, needs and obligations in order to heal and put things as right as possible.
>
> Zehr 2003: 40

Over a similar timeframe, proponents of *diversionary interventions* have also initiated a concerted effort to promote the use of informal means of dealing with criminal behaviour. Thus, Zimring (2000) among others has suggested that, especially for young offenders, diversion from formal judicial processes has now become a central objective of criminal justice practice. Diversionary interventions provide an opportunity for the offender to avoid criminal charges or formal judicial processes by completing various other forms of requirements. These can include community service, restitution, and education.

This chapter will introduce some of the reasoning behind the contemporary development of both these models of intervention, going on to feature a range of associated practice initiatives. The chapter will conclude by discussing their impact and reviewing potential criticisms, such as their reliance on administrative rather than judicial procedures for dealing with offences, their apparent failure to hold offenders properly to account, and their reputed lack of concern with conventional criteria of success, such as reoffending rates.

Alternatives to punishment and offence resolution

Relatively recent developments in criminal justice thinking and practice have shifted attention from the offender to the offence in relation to decisions about sentencing and desired outcomes. Where conventional perspectives on crime and punishment have focused on the behaviour and characteristics of the offender, this has to some extent been challenged by arguments for a sharper consideration of the offence, its context and its consequences. So, considerations such as intent, guilt, responsibility, and mitigating factors, whilst seen as relevant, are not seen as ultimately determinant of the eventual disposal.

The purposes of sentencing, and indeed the criminal justice process as a whole, are no longer construed in terms of individualised measures for dealing with the offender, but in terms of the need to 'resolve' the problems associated with the commission of an offence, and compensating for any harm that might have arisen from it. Not only does this suggest a realignment of the central purposes of the criminal justice system, but also a reconfiguration of the relationships between key interests ('stakeholders') in determining what is to be done in response to an offence. The victim, for example, becomes a much more central and active figure in deliberations and the decision making process, whilst, if anything, the state becomes a somewhat less influential player. Other interests, too, such as families and the 'community' come to acquire a more significant place in the problem-solving process, whilst the offender is expected to take on a much more active form of 'responsibility' for putting things right than simply accepting a pre-determined penalty (see **What do you think? 26.1**).

In this sense, the state's role might be seen as shifting from one of arbitrator and agent of justice, towards acting more as guarantor and facilitator of decisions arrived at by

WHAT DO YOU THINK? 26.1

Approaches which prioritise offence resolution may be seen as distinguishing between being 'held responsible' for your actions and 'taking responsibility' for them.

• Do you think this is a justifiable distinction?

• If so, do you think it is right then to claim that a 'taking responsibility' approach requires us to think differently about the ways in which the justice system operates?

others (principally, offender and victim). Importantly, too, these relatively new models of justice can be seen as concrete and targeted, being tailored to the specific offence, the specific context, and the specific dynamics of the interactions between stakeholders. These new models appear in sharp contrast to those principles of conventional justice models which rely on generalisable and fixed measures of guilt, proportionality, and desert. Indeed, notions of equivalence between offence and punishment are of no relevance in this context—two identical acts of criminality could thus legitimately result in quite contrasting outcomes, depending on the wishes and decisions of the key players in each case.

Challenging conventional assumptions

The distinctive models of criminal justice which have gained increasing prominence also differ from other perspectives because of what we might term their temporal frame—that is, they are very much about dealing with the immediate issues generated by the offence, and achieving a solution in the here and now. This can be contrasted with strategies of deterrence, treatment, or prevention which are effectively future-oriented; and those which are essentially backward-looking, being concerned principally with antecedents and historic factors in determining the proper nature and scale of any disposal. Taken together, the key features of an 'offence resolution' approach represent something of a challenge to most other philosophies of justice and punishment, particularly if implemented in its purest form.

Formal determinations of guilt, assessment of offender culpability and need, mitigating circumstances, and standardised calculations of penal sanctions (whether deterrent, rehabilitative, or retributive) all become irrelevant. In other words, an offence resolution perspective not only advances a distinctive set of objectives for the criminal justice system, but it calls into question existing approaches to evaluating the offence itself, which measure guilt and administer a 'just' response. The proper considerations, it seems, are rather the determination of whose interests are to be taken into account, how these can be determined in light of negotiated understandings of the offence itself, and how any outstanding needs or expectations can be met in light of this. It is thus a situated contextual 'problem-solving' approach rather than a standardised and calculative model of decision making. The administration of justice therefore becomes a discrete process, adapted to the precise circumstances of the offence, rather than being based on generalised principles and replicable forms of disposal.

Offence resolution

Within the overall framework of offence resolution there are differences of emphasis, particularly concerning whose interests should be prioritised and what, therefore, represents a successful resolution of the offence. For those for whom 'diversion' is the principal aim, the central concerns are to minimise the consequences of the offence for the offender. In particular, the adverse consequences of 'labelling' (Lemert 1967) and criminogenic interventions are regarded as potentially harmful, both to the offender and possibly more widely. Diversion is thus seen as both economically and socially useful. Minimum intervention is therefore a desirable objective. It is both a relatively cheap option, avoiding the mobilisation of further effort on the part of criminal justice agencies; and at the same time, it reduces the likelihood of the offender being further criminalised.

On the other hand, for those who identify other interests as paramount, such as those of the victim or the community, then the primary purpose of offence resolution is to find ways to make amends or put right the harms and disruption associated with the offence. Restorative justice has come to be viewed as the most effective means by which these aims can be achieved.

The implications of taking a 'resolution' approach to solving the problems associated with an offence go beyond its distinctive aims and objectives; they can also be observed in the ways in which the justice process itself is reconstituted to enable these to be achieved. Clearly, the conventional machinery of state sponsored prosecution, formal court hearings, attributions of guilt and responsibility, and the imposition of penal sanctions do not sit well with the goals of achieving less clear cut and more consensually-based outcomes. As a consequence, there has been a considerable growth in the number of alternative procedures and structural arrangements put in place to offer informal means of addressing the problems associated with an offence.

At their most straightforward, these might involve the formal recognition of police discretion and encouragement of its use, particularly in relation to minor offences which can be dealt with on the spot, by way of the (now, but not always) metaphorical 'clip round the ear' (Smyth 2011); a term associated with Victorian and early 20th century policing practices. Despite the term's original association with physical mistreatment, this is now understood in terms of an informal telling off, and an expression of leniency. Smyth observes that the use of police cautions can be traced to very shortly after the establishment of the modern police force in the 1830s, even though various forms of physical chastisement seem to have been associated with this:

The Metropolitan Police Act of 1839 ... left the [police] officer considerable discretion ... broad enough to encompass the administration of a caution as an alternative to arrest. Moreover, the occasional police officer would also act outside this discretion from time to time by resorting to the technically unlawful 'clip round the ear'.

Smyth 2011: 154

Restorative justice

As is the case with diversionary interventions, the emergence of restorative justice has seen the development of parallel mechanisms for considering the offence and reaching an agreed conclusion as to how to put things right, whether by way of reparation, apology, or some other compensatory mechanism. Restorative justice gives the victim a chance to meet their offenders in person, often within a controlled environment as shown in **Figure 26.1**. In such an environment, the victim can explain the real impact of the crime committed. It can empower the victim, and help them to better understand why the crime may have been committed in the first place.

Restorative principles have underpinned the aim of constructing a decision making forum which would carry the authority of the community and therefore gain respect and legitimacy from all concerned, without necessarily drawing on the coercive or symbolic resources of a more formalised and remote state institutional framework.

The origins of this kind of mechanism have been traced to indigenous populations who have often constructed distinctive deliberative mechanisms for resolving community disputes and allegations of wrongdoing. Howard Zehr is often credited with developing a 'new paradigm of criminal justice' (Johnstone 2002: 87), drawing on ideas from these traditional practices in opposition to the retributive model on which western systems of justice are based.

Barnes (2013) locates the origins of much contemporary restorative practice within the problem-solving traditions of a number of indigenous communities, including the Maoris, Canadian First Nations peoples, and Australian Aboriginals. Family Group Conferencing, for example, has emerged from Maori problem-solving traditions to become recognised as a highly promising model for practice in both criminal justice and child welfare contexts. These developments, Barnes argues, have not only introduced new forms of justice into conventional western criminal procedures, but have also gone some way to redress discriminatory treatment of minority groups in the alienating setting of the formal courtroom. Citing a number of Canadian initiatives, including 'circle courts', based on First Nations traditions, he argues that these 'were designed to impact positively the justice system's unequal treatment of first nations people' (Barnes 2013: 105).

Importantly, restorative justice has consistently been seen as an international movement, connecting and providing mutual reinforcement for a range of indigenous and culturally varied practices, all of which are believed to share common features, grounded in concepts of healing and reconciliation. Thus, for example, attempts to develop effective responses to serious crimes in the aftermath of genocide in Rwanda relied on the reassertion of traditional modes of dispensing justice, in the form of the gacaca courts (see **Figure 26.2**) (Brehm et al. 2014). Although it is acknowledged that the outcome was by no means a perfect solution, nor a pure form of restorative justice, it is suggested that this did provide a distinctive avenue for the emergence of viable responses to many of the harms caused:

In short, the gacaca courts represented a powerful response to mass crime and an important element in the struggle to address society-wide tragedy and move forward. While these courts represent a 'home-grown' Rwandan solution in many ways, their blending of punitive and restorative aims and traditional and contemporary elements holds important

Figure 26.1 A group of people sitting together in a scene typical in restorative justice

Source: The Centre for Justice & Reconciliation: (www.restorativejustice.org)

Figure 26.2 A gacaca court in action

Source: STR/AP/Press Association Images

insights for justice pursuits around the world. To the extent that a hybrid model such as gacaca can address the 'crime of crimes', it should encourage other innovative approaches to lesser offenses in wide-ranging social contexts.

Brehm et al. 2014: 346

It is perhaps also helpful here to recognise that alternative structures for dealing with offences and resolving the problems associated with them do not necessarily lead to outcomes which might be seen as radically different from those achieved under conventional justice processes. The distinctiveness of approaches based on principles of offence resolution is perhaps as much to do with the legitimacy afforded to the process as it is to the range and flexibility of outcomes that are achievable. As Barnes (2013: 107) notes, in one case involving traditional methods of 'healing' and restorative practices used by the Heiltsuk First Nations people of Bella Bella in British Columbia, the outcome for an offender responsible for offences of assault was 'banishment' for seven months to a nearby uninhabited island, in accordance with Heiltsuk tradition. So, in this case, the eventual 'punishment' determined for the offender was probably no less punitive than would have been determined in the conventional criminal courts, although undoubtedly different in character and meaning.

This again perhaps points to an area of uncertainty about the underlying principles and aims of criminal justice practices which are framed as 'alternatives'. Are they designed, for example, to stand as authentic means of resolving problems of criminality in their own right; or are they intended to operate as a counterbalance to the established machinery of justice, to modify its acknowledged flaws and limitations? And, if the latter, are alternatives to punishment intended to represent an entirely different and better way of doing justice; or are they intended merely to mitigate some of the unfairnesses and excesses of the established criminal justice system?

Alternatives to custody?

This debate, then, raises a further question about the nature and context of these deviations from conventional understandings of procedures in criminal justice. This question concerns the extent to which the newer processes are expected either to supplant or to supplement existing practices and decision making frameworks. This tension can perhaps readily be highlighted by the 'alternative to custody' concept which has, according to Mills (2011: 34) 'been a mainstay in thinking about criminal justice since at least the 1970s'. When it was introduced, the idea was particularly associated with the 'decarceration movement',

which aimed to supplant custody as the default sentence for many offences. Mills argues, though, that this strong version of the idea is not its only potential interpretation, and that its practical application is 'ambiguous'. She suggests that the term can actually be understood in one of three ways:

- As a means of extending prison constraints and conditions into the community by imposing additional requirements on community sentences

- As a means of diverting 'some people' from custody, particularly more minor, short-term offenders

- In its original, strong version, as a principled means of challenging 'the use of custody'

Mills 2011: 34

As Mills goes on to observe, this confusion can have practical as well as theoretical consequences, and reforms have often failed to produce the desired effect when 'alternatives to custody' have been introduced or modified with the aim of reducing the prison population; the Criminal Justice Act 2003, for example, failed to influence the proportional use of custody (24 per cent in 2004, 25 per cent in 2009), despite the 'key stated intention of these reforms ... to provide credible community alternatives to custodial sentences of less than 12 months' (Mills 2011: 35). So, irrespective of the underlying purposes of such measures, designed to offer alternatives to custody, their limited impact in practice seems fairly clear:

Those concerned with identifying credible long-term strategies for addressing the use of prison ... will not find answers working only within the limited confines of the 'alternatives to custody' debate.

Mills 2011: 36

Historic and deeply-entrenched conceptualisations of law and justice are not easily discarded; and this underlines the extent to which alternatives have consistently encountered pressure to modify their aims and make practical compromises.

We can conclude at this point that the terrain of 'alternatives to punishment' and 'offence resolution' is not simply constituted independently of the prevailing criminal justice system. There may be common ground in terms of acceptance of processes of determining guilt and responsibility for instance; and there may also be similarities in terms of the punitive nature of decision making processes, even though these may be conducted very differently from the formal procedures associated with contemporary westernised judicial structures. It will now be helpful to explore in a bit more depth just what 'alternatives' aim to achieve, and how.

The purpose of alternatives to punishment and offence resolution

As we have seen previously, approaches to criminal justice decision making which emphasise problem solving rather than attribution of guilt and blame seem to imply a distinctive view of crime, what it represents, and how offenders should be understood. There are strong currents of healing, redemption, and reintegration here, which seem to prevail over a concern to impose sanctions, extract compensation, or compel penitence on the part of the offender. Whilst, as we have acknowledged already, the precise rationale for offence resolution strategies may vary, they do share a commitment to putting things right, by way of mutually determined and mutually legitimised solutions.

These approaches may perhaps be summarised under the following headings: mutuality, inclusion, legitimacy, restoration, and trust. This clearly sets offence resolution apart from conventional criminal justice decision making forums, which could only really lay claim to share the quality of legitimacy from this list. But even on this ground, many of the arguments for the institution of new approaches to dispute resolution and problem solving in the context of alleged crimes depend on supplanting the legitimacy of state-sponsored and state-controlled judicial processes with new forms of justification. Nils Christie (1977) has famously advanced the argument that court procedures need to be fundamentally rethought to ensure effective participation of those most affected by the supposed offence (see **Figure 26.3**).

Figure 26.3 Nils Christie, Norwegian sociologist and criminologist
Source: Don LaVange/CC BY-SA 2.0

Recognising the impersonality of courtroom settings and their processes, he has drawn attention to the way in which those most centrally concerned with the case and its outcomes appear only intermittently in proceedings, and at 'the periphery' (Christie 1977: 3): 'The parties are represented, and it is these representatives and the judge or judges who express the little activity that is activated within these rooms'. Although he acknowledges the interests of the state in resolving conflict and protecting the victim's interests, Christie believes that other interests intercede. Lawyers, he suggests: 'are particularly good at stealing conflicts' (Christie 1977: 4). By this, Christie means that the formalities of the legal process often appear to exclude the voices of those most directly affected by the offence.

He also argues that those who adopt therapeutic roles in the justice system are adept at defining problems in ways which justify their position. Notably, this involves redefining the conflict between offender and victim as the consequence of 'the criminal's ... defects', and so effectively the actual lived realities of the conflict are 'defined away' (1977: 5). Cohen also describes the emergence of sophisticated systems of classification which are preoccupied solely with defining more and more offenders as belonging to 'special populations meriting specialised treatment' (1985: 195), at the expense of any concern for what actually happened when the offence was committed. The precise nature of the offence and its consequences for both victim and offender are thus deemed of lesser importance. The victim is thus effectively disenfranchised in the way in which criminal processes and decision making authority are constituted.

Writing as he was in 1977, Christie was one of the early proponents of the reinsertion of the victim into the judicial process, so that attention could be shifted to 'the victim's losses', which, in due course 'leads into a discussion of restitution' (Christie 1977: 9), and the offender 'gets a possibility to change his [sic] position from being a listener to a discussion ... of how much pain he ought to receive, into a participant in a discussion of how he could make it good again'. At the same time, Christie stresses that his principal interest is in producing a more authentic means of responding to crime, and his argument is not based on 'a belief that a more personalised meeting between offender and victim would lead to reduced recidivism' (1977: 9). That is very much a secondary consideration.

Christie's central point is that there is a need to restore 'ownership' of the crime and its consequences to those who are closest to it, and are most likely to be strongly affected.

By implication, he is suggesting that what has happened is of no real concern to most people, and therefore there is no need for them to be involved in resolving the matter, even by proxy in the form of the state. Indeed, the withdrawal of the state (at least to an extent) is an important precondition for the creation of a forum for victims and offenders alike to regain control of the process of sharing experiences and feelings and agree a means of resolving the harm done and restoring social harmony. Perhaps idealistically, the opportunity is created for a negotiated outcome with responsibility acknowledged and accepted (and not necessarily all on one side), and the determination of a sustainable and mutually acceptable outcome.

Approached in this way, offence resolution is thus about asserting a distinctive rationale for the criminal justice process. Not only does the victim come first, but also formal attributions of guilt and abstract calculations of the punishment to be administered are replaced by highly specific and situated negotiations based on the circumstances of the particular offence in question. From the point of view of the offender, the most important aspect of the process is the acceptance of responsibility, both for the original offence and for making amends for it. Rather than simply being 'held responsible', the expectation is that perpetrators will genuinely recognise the harm caused and its direct impact on the victim; and this, in turn, is anticipated to lead to a genuine sense of remorse and commitment to putting things right (see **What do you think? 26.2** for a powerful and thought-provoking example). Although it is not the primary aim, the argument also holds that the insight gained by the offender will have some continuing effect in reducing the likelihood of reoffending.

The aims of diversion

Whilst restorative models of offence resolution are often grounded in a vision of bridge-building and reconciliation, with a significant tone of redemption and emotional healing, diversionary approaches are geared perhaps rather more towards minimising harm and moderating the impact of the formal justice system on the offender. Grounded in principles of minimum intervention, and evidence of the unhelpful consequences of formal criminalisation, diversion seeks to promote normalisation and social inclusion of the offender and to avoid the damaging consequences of 'labelling'.

Diversion is distinguished from restorative approaches in the sense that it is forward- rather than backward-looking. It is concerned primarily with future outcomes for the offender rather than resolving the harms caused by the offence. So far, diversion has also been viewed principally as a vehicle for dealing with young offenders, and

WHAT DO YOU THINK? 26.2

Szmania and Mangis (2005: 352) describe a restorative meeting, taking place outside any formal criminal justice setting. It involves the offender and the mother of the victim, who died in a car accident caused by the offender:

> The victim then begins to show the offender pictures of her daughter who was killed in the crash, and she reads several personal letters sent to her family after the car wreck. The victim's opening dialogue shows no hostility or anger towards the offender; she even explicitly forgives him. The offender responds to these gestures with his apology: I get so mad sometimes at the choices I made. I know in my heart that I'd never would [sic] have hurt anyone on purpose. God, I'd give anything to change what I did. I'm just sorry. God has brought me through too. But when I look at y'all, I see so much goodness, and so much (offender pauses), she had so much potential. And I know that no matter how much I play 'what-if' I can't change what I did. And I know there's been a lot of good has come out of it. I'm just sorry, [victim's name]. Part of me just wishes that you would just get mad and beat on me and uh. It's just so hard, you know.

This account is very powerful, and clearly demonstrates the offender's remorse, but how would it change your views about the punishment to be administered in this case, if at all?

decriminalising their behaviour, on the basis that they are capable of growing out of crime. For this reason, diversionary initiatives have been much less in evidence in the adult domain.

Support for diversionary objectives has been provided by McAra and McVie (2007), who have measured the effect of 'system contact' on young people in Scotland. The Scottish approach is quite distinct in its reliance on a children's hearing system which is fundamentally based on welfare principles and seeks to avoid criminalising young people who offend.

Where children are reported for offences in Scotland, they may well be asked to attend a children's hearing, which is a meeting to consider the offence in light of the child's circumstances and identified needs. The principal aim of the hearing is to reach an outcome with the agreement of all participants which will promote the child's future well-being. The basic assumption of the children's hearings system is that children and young people who commit offences, and children and young people who need care and protection, should be dealt with in the same way—as they are often the same children and young people (see http://www.chscotland.gov.uk/the-childrens-hearings-system/).

In this sense, the hearings system appears closely aligned to diversionary principles. However, despite the predominantly rehabilitative aims of the hearings system, McAra and McVie (2007: 333) have found that those 'who were brought to children's hearings' at a particular point in time 'were significantly more likely to report involvement in serious offending one year later than were their comparable counterparts'. As they put it, 'desistance' from offending is actually more likely amongst those who have minimal or no contact with the system than those who receive interventions which are precisely directed towards reducing their levels of problem behaviour. They conclude that this evidence goes a long way towards validating the theoretical arguments about the effects of 'labelling' on offenders, and on young people in particular:

> The findings have shown a complex filtering process ... in terms of gate-keeping practices, which means that certain groups of youngsters ...—'the usual suspects'—become the principal focus of agency attention ... recycled into the hearing system again and again.

McAra and McVie 2007: 337

They argue that early intervention strategies which target those believed to be at risk of offending are themselves likely to draw young people into the system and, if anything, intensify the likelihood of further criminal involvement on their part. By contrast, McAra and McVie point out that diversionary mechanisms which rely on police warnings rather than formal referrals into the hearings system are associated with lower rates of serious subsequent offending. They therefore conclude, based on their own and other evidence, that the underlying principles of work with young offenders should be grounded in 'maximum diversion and minimum intervention' (2007: 340). The starting point for the justice system, then, especially as it applies to young offenders, is to avoid interventions which are damaging to them, but also increase the potential for their subsequent behaviour to lead to further harm to the community.

'Minimum intervention', then, seems to be one fairly distinctive starting point for thinking about diversion in principle and practice. Here, the central objective is to achieve *diversion from* the harmful impacts and consequences of the criminal justice process; and this principle is quite explicitly underpinned by a series of international agreements on the treatment of children and young people in the criminal justice system. The United Nations, for example, has consistently expressed its commitment to 'diversion' and the avoidance of formal processes of criminalisation wherever possible, as set out in the 'Beijing Rules' (1985), the 'Tokyo Rules' (1985), and the 'Riyadh Guidelines' (1990) on juvenile justice (see Smith 2010 and Hamilton 2011, for example):

The need for and importance of progressive delinquency prevention policies and the systematic study and the elaboration of measures should be recognized. These should avoid criminalizing and penalizing a child for behaviour that does not cause serious damage to the development of the child or harm to others.

Extract from the United Nations Guidelines for the Prevention of Juvenile Delinquency (the Riyadh Guidelines), UN General Assembly, 1990 (http://www.un.org/documents/ga/res/45/a45r112.htm)

Although diversion is often thought of principally in these terms, that is, the avoidance of involvement with, and possibly contamination by, the criminal justice system, it can also be understood in other ways (Smith 2014b). In particular, associated with the idea of minimising potentially harmful contact with the system as far as the offender is concerned, it is also held to be important to divert young people from further criminal behaviour; and, thirdly, and also a matter of concern to McAra and McVie (2007), is the question of diversion *towards* services and opportunities which will address the needs of those whose behaviour has given initial cause for concern. In these two senses, then, diversion is not simply about doing nothing, since it can also be geared towards proactive forms of intervention and positive outcomes in the eyes of its proponents. For example, The Diversion Project provided by Halton & Warrington Youth Offending Team was developed in 2008. The project was established with two Diversion Workers, one with a social care background and the other a seconded mental health nurse from the child and adolescent mental health service (CAMHS). The CAMHS worker was identified as a major feature of the scheme, who could assess young people for mental health or communication needs and link them directly into appropriate health services. The key aim of the project is to divert children and young people with particular needs away from the youth justice system, and to make suitable welfare interventions available to them (see https://www.justice.gov.uk/youth-justice/effective-practice-library/the-diversion-project-youth-justice-liaison-and-diversion-scheme).

Despite the degree of ambiguity which these alternative understandings of diversion generate, there remains considerable common ground with restorative strategies (Smith 2011a). Both are concerned to set limits to the role and reach of formal state institutions; both are predisposed towards informal means of resolving problems associated with offending; and both seek to devolve control and decision making to those most closely involved with and affected by the offence. Procedures are simplified and those directly involved are empowered, it is argued, since the offence can be effectively 'processed' without ceding control to distant, complex, and only partially informed administrative and judicial mechanisms: 'The true story [of restorative justice] offers some hope, not only for a better way to do justice, but also for strengthening mechanisms of informal social control, and consequently, to minimize reliance on formal social control, the machinery and institutions of criminal justice' (Daly 2002: 72). As an ancillary benefit, of perennial interest to those responsible for public finances, these alternative offence resolution processes are believed to be much less costly to operate than courts and prosecuting bodies (Centre for Mental Health et al. 2010, for example)—although arguably a secondary consideration, this is no doubt a persuasive element of the argument in favour of informal forms of justice.

Transformational goals

As we have observed, emerging models of criminal justice—which rely on informal and negotiated processes to achieve consensual outcomes—offer certain purported benefits to offenders, victims, and wider agency and community interests. These direct gains, though, are also associated with wider and more fundamental aspirations for a transformation in the way we 'do' justice. In a sense, there may be an underlying belief that achieving change of this kind in an important symbolic sphere such as the administration of criminal justice can also prefigure and indeed energise wider shifts in the configuration of social relations (Boyes-Watson 2000). The justice system is the material and practical realisation of our combined conceptualisation of morality and fairness; and there is undoubtedly an aspiration embedded in models of restorative and integrative practice to replace what may be termed the 'blame culture' with a more conciliatory and mutually respectful approach to human relations, especially in dealing with conflict:

> The social movement for restorative justice does practical work to weld an amalgam that is relevant to the creation of contemporary urban multicultural republics.
>
> Braithwaite 2004a: 46

As such, of course, proponents of consultative or mediated offence resolution mechanisms have also argued that these are transferable to any such context where disputes or conflicts of interest arise (neighbour disputes, bullying in schools, consumer complaints or employee conflicts, for example)—see **New Frontiers 26.1**.

However, reintegrative aspirations do not necessarily depend on a readiness to take crime less seriously, or to diminish commitment to victims' interests, which is sometimes a criticism levelled at extra-legal crime resolution initiatives. Braithwaite's pioneering work, for instance, seems to be strongly grounded in a commitment to promoting concern for the victim, encouraging the offender to accept responsibility and make amends, and

---

NEW FRONTIERS 26.1

Restorative practice in the community

Source: The Centre for Justice & Reconciliation: www.restorativejustice.org

The Restorative Justice Council has sought to establish key goals and values to underpin effective restorative practice. Here the aim is to articulate guiding principles which will inform practice, and to prioritise the needs of communities' and their members' interests, without reference to the justice system or any other statutory adjudicatory forum. The focus of intervention is very much on promoting and rebuilding strong ties and community relationships, echoing Christie's (1977) plea for conflicts to be reclaimed by those most directly affected and resolved within their community settings.

> Restorative practice in communities resolves conflicts and disputes before they escalate into crime and is an effective approach to dealing with antisocial behaviour and neighbour disputes.
>
> It enables people to understand the impact of their behaviour on others. It delivers effective outcomes owned by the local community and creates stable, positive community environments …
>
> Restorative practice can be used to build strong communities and to ensure that disputes and disagreements are dealt with positively and constructively.
>
> Restorative Justice Council (https://www.restorative-justice.org.uk/restorative-practice-community) 15 October 2015

to reduce the risk of future harm. The offender should be placed very squarely in the spotlight, and the basis for reintegration and reconciliation lies in what he terms 'shaming ... Societies with low crime rates are those that shame potently and judiciously' (Braithwaite 1989: 1).

In these terms, restorative justice, whilst aspiring to reintegration, focuses very strongly on ensuring that the offender takes responsibility. Braithwaite outlines a model of restorative 'conferencing' which draws out the experiences of those who have been harmed and uses these to focus the collective disapproval of the community on the offender. Because the process of engagement at this level involves the direct evidence of victims' experiences and it may also be mediated by those closest to the offender, the product of the restorative meeting is expected to be one of genuine recognition of the human consequences of the offence, and genuine feelings of remorse and commitments to put things right where possible. Achieving this, then, creates the basis for 'efforts to reintegrate the offender back into the community of law-abiding or respectable citizens through words or gestures of forgiveness' or even 'ceremonies to decertify the offender as deviant' (Braithwaite 1989: 100).

The idea of 'reintegrative shaming' has clearly made some uncomfortable, with the recognition that the idea is 'not uncontroversial within the restorative justice community' (Harris and Maruna 2006: 456). Whilst it is recognised that Braithwaite has advocated an approach to 'shaming' which maintains a sense of respect for the individual, avoids condemnation, and seeks to promote forgiveness, its consequences are less easy to predict, and may not be positive. For example, there is a risk of piling guilt and blame onto someone who is already feeling remorse: 'shaming in contexts that are already highly shaming is unnecessary and may even be interpreted as stigmatizing' (Harris and Maruna 2007: 457). The potential threat to the offender's fragile sense of self-worth may well be problematic. In such cases, it is possible to imagine the use of shame as counterproductive and unlikely to lead to the sort of reconciliation to which restorative justice aspires, especially if the offender feels 'unfairly treated' in the process (2007: 459).

Of course, a parallel question arises as to whether it is possible to predetermine an essentially unscripted encounter such as a restorative meeting between offender and victim, so that feelings of shame can be generated and then used constructively, irrespective of the feelings participants will already bring to the table. Indeed, as Harris and Maruna acknowledge (2007: 460), there appears to have been a shift in Braithwaite's thinking, too, from an emphasis on 'shaming' to a concern with 'shame management', within a reintegrative framework; since it is this more conciliatory approach which is likely to generate a more constructive response from the offender. The process is likely to lead to more positive responses if all concerned in the restorative encounter are able to 'tell their stories' (2007: 460) and share (and hopefully resolve) their feelings, rather than experience a one-sided moralistic 'holding to account'.

This more open-ended approach is also likely to be more attuned to the ambiguous and confused feelings and understandings that participants may bring to a restorative encounter. Guilt and victimisation may not be neatly apportioned to one party or the other, and neither is it easy to quantify the expectations of those coming to an encounter with which none are likely to be familiar (see **What do you think? 26.3** for a description of one such encounter).

WHAT DO YOU THINK? 26.3

One study of restorative justice reports that:

> One case sent for a conference involved two teenage boys—one English speaking and the other Spanish speaking. The English speaking boy had been harassing the other boy and eventually started a fight with him ... The victim's mother was very worried that this conference may result in more bullying, so working closely with each family was very important ... The day of the conference the tension in the room was very high. ... As the offender began talking it became clear that there was no personal reason for the bullying and fight that took place. ... After ... some prompting, the offender revealed that many of the boys at school bullied the victim because he was from Mexico. He had simply joined in the group and quickly became their ringleader. At first it did not appear that he

> would show any remorse ... but he surprisingly revealed that he too had been bullied a few years before. He discovered that becoming a bully himself was an easy way to divert the bullying. ... onto someone else. The discussion that followed seemed astonishingly honest and heartfelt. While the boys did not become friends after this incident ... the kindness and forgiving nature of the victim's family stood out to the offender's family'.

> *Mongold and Edwards 2014: 209*

- What are the advantages of this form of conflict resolution in your opinion?

- And, what might be some of its limitations? Does it help to resolve wider, systemic problems, for example?

In **What do you think? 26.3**, we can see that the offender, whilst acknowledging his wrongdoing, saw it in a context of adaptation to his own prior victimisation and the need to adopt a particular social role from his perspective. On the other hand, as often appears to be the case with restorative encounters, the opportunity to personalise the offence and to acknowledge the impact on the victim was important to the offender and enabled him to recognise and take responsibility. The participants were now able to gain a shared sense of having a common experience.

Restorative justice and diversion: rationales for intervention

In distinguishing between the objectives of restorative and diversionary approaches, it is perhaps helpful to acknowledge their different orientations towards intervention. On the one hand, restorative justice is based on a belief in the importance of the process itself as a vehicle for reconciliation, acceptance of responsibility, making good, and the rebuilding of social bonds. On the other hand, however, diversion seems more strongly grounded in the notion of avoiding harm by minimising the effects of intervention, and only taking action where necessary in the specific circumstances which apply. This could, of course, lead to a restorative intervention, but only where this was justified and desirable. Clearly, here, there is less emphasis on meeting the needs of the victim, but this is consistent with the underlying rationale of minimising the damage associated with formal intervention, and providing the opportunity for a 'normalising' outcome. In this respect, though, the aims of diversion and restorative justice come back into alignment, since both are committed to the principle of reintegration of the offender.

In its purest sense, diversion might simply aim to minimise intervention on the part of formal systems, based on the assumption that avoiding system 'contamination' is both the most effective and the least resource intensive course of action (or inaction). On the other hand, at the risk of seeming paradoxical, there are arguments for a more proactive approach to diversion which seeks actively to promote the reintegration of the (usually) young offender. In this case, an intervention programme may well be offered, and this is sometimes conditional, with the objective of addressing the problems associated with the offending behaviour; such as achieving re-inclusion in mainstream schooling, for example. The Halton and Warrington project referred to previously was part of a national pilot programme geared towards testing alternative forms of intervention to address identified welfare needs outside of the justice system, principally those concerned with mental health issues; with a specialist practitioner recruited for this purpose (Haines et al. 2012).

More comprehensive models of diversion, such as those established in Northamptonshire in the 1980s (Smith, 2011a) and Swansea more recently (Haines et al., 2013), would incorporate a range of objectives, including both restorative and welfare outcomes, depending on the issues identified on notification of an offence.

Alternatives to punishment: Structure, organisation, and operation

By definition, alternatives aim to set themselves apart from conventional approaches to criminal justice; although portrayed in these terms, they are always defined in relation to the norm from which they seek to distinguish themselves. The relationship between 'alternatives' and established understandings of individualised rights and responsibilities, 'due process', adversarial justice, notions of guilt and mitigation, and the sentencing tariff is inherently problematic. Neither a diversionary nor a restorative perspective sits easily with these ideas and processes, all of which are central to the operation of the machinery of law and justice as they have been historically organised. Of course, in practice, there are different degrees to which diversion and restorative justice make compromises with this established and ideologically powerful model. The Referral Order, introduced as a youth justice disposal in 1999 (see **What do you think? 26.4**), is a particularly good example of an attempt to insert restorative processes into the existing framework of disposals available to the courts, but without disturbing underlying principles of guilt and the sentencing tariff.

In essence though, the progressive emergence of alternatives to punishment may be seen as a process of engagement with a well-established body of ideas and formal structures, most of which are antithetical to ideas of informal, negotiated justice, where ideas of responsibility are diffuse, and tailored outcomes do not sit well with the idea of a single progressive sentencing tariff. This has meant that diversionary or restorative initiatives have often had to present themselves as small scale and experimental, so as not to disturb or threaten the prevailing consensus; and at the same time they have been subject to continuing

WHAT DO YOU THINK? 26.4

Youth offender panels should operate on restorative justice principles, enabling young offenders, by taking responsibility and making reparation, to achieve reintegration into the law-abiding community. Victims must be given the opportunity to participate actively in the resolution of the offence and its consequences, subject to their wishes and informed consent. The youth offender panel process is an opportunity to address the victim's needs for information, answers to questions and reparation for harm done. Victims who attend restorative justice processes such as a youth offender panel can derive considerable benefit and they generally report high levels of satisfaction with the process. The presence of victims also can substantially enhance the beneficial impact of the panel on both young offenders and parents.

Para 6.1, *Referral Order Guidance*, Ministry of Justice, 2015

- Is the recurrent emphasis on victims at all problematic here? Why do you think that might be the case?

- Is there a risk that outcomes might be contrived at the expense of being meaningful and effective for all concerned? What are the incentives for those involved to achieve neat but unsatisfactory solutions?

challenges to the extent that they do not comply with conventional wisdom. Thus, for instance, the idea of repeat cautioning, or indeed, the reversal of the sentencing tariff has seen a number of 'false starts' and setbacks prior to its explicit adoption under the Legal Aid, Sentencing and Punishment of Offenders (LASPO) Act 2012. As **Controversy and debate 26.1** illustrates, there has remained a groundswell of unease about the principle of repeat cautioning amongst influential interested groups, such as the Magistrates' Association.

The credibility of alternatives to punishment

In the context of restorative justice, judicial concern focuses on the problems of sentencing consistency and guaranteeing outcomes that meet both public expectations and the specific needs of the victim:

> Moreover, judges often emphasize that 'it is not merely of some importance but is of fundamental importance that justice should not only be done, but should manifestly and undoubtedly be seen to be done.'
>
> Gabbay 2005: 355

Gaining a foothold, and achieving credibility have thus been a continuing challenge for approaches to the administration of justice which are innovative, and offer potential challenges to deep-seated beliefs (and vested interests, such as the judiciary). One tactical solution to this has been to build alliances and to seek to generate

! CONTROVERSY AND DEBATE 26.1

Repeat cautioning—with Professor Roger Smith

One of the criticisms encountered by practitioners in youth diversion is that offenders were 'getting away with it', and taking advantage of the leniency afforded to them. This was unfair on victims, it was claimed, and would only encourage reoffending.

Thousands of violent criminals, sex offenders, and burglars were let off with a caution amid concerns from magistrates that police were infringing upon sentencing powers which should be left to the courts.

John Fassenfelt, chairman of the Magistrates' Association, has written to Chris Grayling, the Justice Secretary, to call for an inquiry into police use of cautions, which can help stretched forces cut down on paperwork.

'It seems to have got out of hand, to be honest,' he said.

Cautions were 'constantly being used for violent and sexual offences', he added, robbing victims of their chance for compensation and to see the offender in court.

Mr Fassenfelt went on: 'When you see continuous cautions being given out you do begin to think the police are using them for some other reason'.

Daily Telegraph, 27 Jan 2013

- Do you think repeat offenders should be 'let off' with a caution? Does it matter if it's the same type of offence? Does it matter if it's a violent offence?

- To what extent should the victim's views be taken into account when deciding on whether or not to administer a caution?

- Are there any offences which should not be eligible for a caution? Why?

support for these forms of practice amongst those who might be reluctant to do so. Thus, an early juvenile liaison initiative was established in Liverpool, under the auspices of the police authority, and the direct supervision of the Chief Constable, partly to accord legitimacy to the scheme, reportedly (Mays 1965). The Juvenile Liaison Officer scheme in Liverpool 'began in a small exploratory way', as Mays notes (1965: 186), with a stress on intervening early with young people 'on the verge of delinquency'. Cautioning was presented as one of the options available to the scheme to try and discourage further offending where children had perhaps 'got away with things' (1965: 188) previously. A caution, however, would only be administered in place of prosecution for minor offences (burglary being specifically excluded, notably), and the decision to do so could only be taken at a very senior level in the police force.

Acknowledging potential criticisms that the police could be seen to be usurping the 'authority of the courts' (Mays 1965: 195), the limits of the scheme were stressed repeatedly, and its function as an adjunct to the existing justice process was clearly signalled as 'filling a gap in existing services' (1965: 187). So, in this case at least, the potentially radical message of diversion from the judicial process was significantly modified in order to create a legitimate (and non-threatening) space for the scheme. In the case of diversion and cautioning, the persistence of this form of defensive rationale can be identified in the recurrent stress on the limits of such schemes—targeted only at minor offences, first or early career offenders, and remaining under the aegis of the police.

Institutionalising diversion

Such limitations were later effectively institutionalised under the New Labour government's Crime and Disorder Act 1998 with the institution of the framework for 'Reprimands' and 'Final Warnings', strictly tariff-bound disposals to be administered progressively on the occasion of a young person's first and second offences. In addition, the clear expectation was expressed in government guidance that the final warning would be accompanied by a programme of intervention designed to discourage further offending behaviour, thus effectively instituting a pre-court tariff.

Making the case for restorative justice

Like diversion, restorative justice has its origins in relatively small scale and experimental schemes, which actually predate the widespread adoption of the term itself.

A number of 'mediation' and 'reparation' schemes were funded by the Home Office in England in the 1980s, with the aim of promoting new ways of resolving the harms associated with crime. The forerunner of these schemes was a victim/offender mediation project established by the highly innovative South Yorkshire Probation Service in 1983. This initial project, in turn, prompted ministerial interest and the Home Office established a programme of four reparation projects in Cumbria, Leeds, Wolverhampton, and Coventry for two years from 1985 (Graef 2000: 24). A further adult reparation project was established in Northamptonshire in 1987, building on the initial success of the county's Juvenile Liaison Bureaux. All of these developments, though, were restricted in scope—they were clearly seen as experimental, and their funding was time limited. In such circumstances, demonstrating a track record of achievement is problematic, and none survived in their original form. Arguably, at this point, the underlying rationale and sustained commitment to what became known as 'restorative' practice had not been established, and as Graef observes, their timing was unfortunate as political attitudes on crime 'hardened' during the early 1990s.

Indeed, it seems likely that subsequent renewed interest in restorative interventions was grounded as much as anything in a strengthening recognition of the place of the victim in the justice process; restorative justice offered a vehicle for giving substance to this, whilst at the same time retaining a vision of a more inclusive approach to offence resolution in general. In advancing his argument in favour of restorative justice, Graef (2000: 30) placed great reliance on the benefits to victims, noting that in 'the Leeds Victim-Offender Unit in 1996–7, 58.3 per cent of victims said they were very satisfied with the service, 33.3 per cent fairly satisfied and 8.3 per cent satisfied—there was no dissatisfaction'. Similar results were reported in North Wales and Aberdeen. So, just as diversionary initiatives appear to have been careful to avoid directly challenging conventional assumptions to do with the sentencing tariff, so early restorative practices were celebrated largely because of the enhanced benefits they appeared to offer to victims rather than offenders (Umbreit 1989, for example).

The referral order

As with diversion, subsequent attempts to formalise restorative justice, such as the referral order, have relied on extensive compromise with existing structural arrangements, as noted previously. In addition, though, it has been recognised that aspects of practice under the referral order have also reflected conventional assumptions with offenders experiencing the intervention as essentially routinised, coercive, and punitive rather than inviting or encouraging the kind of reflective and deliberative approach outlined by many proponents of restorative justice. An extensive evaluation of referral order projects found that, at least in the early stages, implementation was highly problematic:

> The referral order represents both a particular and a rather peculiar hybrid attempt to integrate restorative justice ideas and values into youth justice practice. It does so in a clearly coercive, penal context that offends cherished restorative ideals of voluntariness.
>
> Crawford and Newburn 2003: 239

The 'context' to which the authors refer is one of a strict alignment of the order with the tariff—administered only once, and on the young person's first court appearance—and a set of requirements incorporated into its delivery which heightened the sense of compulsion and conditionality as far as the young offender was concerned. In this sense, the order represented no real challenge to conventional penological assumptions.

On the other hand, as Crawford and Newburn (2003) also acknowledge, the mandatory nature of the referral order as a disposal meant that 'a steady supply' of young people to the youth offender panels set up to administer the order would be guaranteed. In principle, this would offer the potential to cement restorative practices into the justice process: 'Coercion provided the capacity to move certain restorative values to the very heart of the youth justice system, and the loss of voluntariness was the price

paid' (Crawford and Newburn 2003: 239). This, in turn, did create the opportunity for the panels to engage young people and parents in a 'very different, and more positive' process of discussing and attempting to resolve the problems and harms associated with the commission of the offence. The question for this, and other restorative initiatives, is thus whether the price paid in terms of loss of fidelity to the restorative ideal is 'worth it' in that it affords restorative practice and outcomes a degree of legitimacy as an alternative and more restitutive means of delivering justice (see **What do you think? 26.5**).

WHAT DO YOU THINK? 26.5

The issue of compulsion in restorative justice has been a matter of continuing debate amongst its proponents.

- Is it better to require offenders to participate in order to ensure that victims' interests are protected and there is a greater degree of certainty that the benefits of restorative intervention will be delivered?

- Or, on the other hand, does compulsion undermine the potential for genuine engagement of offenders and a sense of ownership and commitment to agreed outcomes?

Delivering alternatives to punishment: Practices and challenges

Having reflected on the somewhat anomalous observation that 'alternatives to punishment' very often find themselves in a position of having to make structural and operational compromises with existing and conventional forms of practice in the justice system, we will move on and explore aspects of implementation. In the space available, it is not feasible to try and cover the very extensive range of projects and initiatives which might fall under the umbrella term of 'alternatives', so it will be helpful to consider examples of particular interest; from these it may be possible to draw out more general observations.

Diversion and youth justice

As we have already observed, it has proved easier to develop models of diversionary or restorative practice in the field of youth justice than in the adult sphere. This may well

be because of the inherent assumptions that young people are less responsible, less culpable, and more open to developmental change. They are perhaps assumed not to understand the full implications of their antisocial or criminal behaviour and therefore to be open to the kind of deliberative process represented by restorative justice. At the same time, their commitment to criminal behaviour is assumed to be less well established, and so, the argument goes, diversion may well be sufficient to direct them towards a more law-abiding future. Practice may thus be directed towards facilitating change through a kind of moral educative process, which encourages offenders to reflect on the harm caused by their behaviour, what they could do to put it right or make amends in other ways, the effects of offending on their social identity and life chances, and how they can avoid the longer term hazards of further criminalisation.

Sometimes also incorporated into practice is the belief that young people are not necessarily committed to change and that, therefore, an element of coercion is needed to reinforce the socialisation and educative work to be undertaken. The coercive element of programmes also helps to reassure potential critics that what is offered by 'alternative' programmes is not a 'soft option'. Indeed, much is also made of the challenging aspects of facing up to your own wrongdoing and acknowledging responsibility for harm caused; as is represented by Braithwaite's (1989) concept of 'reintegrative shaming'. In sum, there is a strong moral message of repentance and redemption underlying much practice in diversion and restorative justice. For a fuller discussion on youth justice, please see **Chapter 9**.

Restorative practice in its idealised form will typically be organised around a 'conference' of some kind, where the offender, family members, victim, supporters and other key individuals will meet to share understandings of the offence, and gain insight into each other's experience.

> Our definition of an RJC [Restorative Justice Conference] is this: a planned and scheduled face-to-face conference in which a trained facilitator 'brings together offenders, their victims, and their respective kin and communities, in order to decide what the offender should do to repair the harm that a crime has caused'.
>
> Strang et al. 2013: 8

The opportunity will be created for the offender to express regret or apologise, and to commit to doing something to put right any harm caused; and, similarly, the victim will have a chance to acknowledge the offender's contrition and express forgiveness if s/he wishes to do so (see **Telling it like it is 26.1**).

According to Strang et al. (2013), and based on their systematic review of restorative justice conferences, they typically follow a prescribed format, lasting from 1 to 3 hours, encompassing (Strang et al. 2013: 8):

- Preparatory work with victim and offender, to explain the process and identify whether they agree to participate in the conference.

- Planning the meeting on the victim's terms.
- Establishing a democratic forum for the event (seating on the same level, privacy, neutral setting, for example).
- Inviting participants to share their experience of the crime and the harm caused.
- Encouraging a restorative discussion of how things could be put right.
- Agreeing 'next steps' and registering these with a formal body, in order to encourage compliance.

Strang et al. (2013) also acknowledge, however, that the umbrella term 'restorative justice' covers a 'wide range' of practices which might share common aspirations but operate in very different ways. So, there is a significant difference between the formalised processes associated with set-piece restorative conferences, and more informal ad hoc measures.

Specifically mentioned by these authors is the recent development in the UK where police have been trained and then encouraged 'to undertake "restorative disposals" or "community resolutions" that may involve negotiations on the street immediately after a crime has occurred, in which an apology is made, no further action is taken and that is the end of the matter' (Strang et al. 2013: 7).

Instant justice?

The Youth Restorative Disposal (YRD) was introduced as a pilot scheme in eight police forces in 2008, and subsequently extended nationally as one of the options available under the umbrella term 'Community Resolutions' in 2011. The YRD has operated in a rather different way, concentrating on rapid and proportionate resolution of crimes and misdemeanours as near as possible to the point at which they occur. It may perhaps be argued

TELLING IT LIKE IT IS 26.1

Restorative justice in Darlington

Darlington Youth Offending Service offers restorative interventions to victims and offenders in order to seek mutually agreed informal resolutions to the offence.

> Restorative facilitators visit and carefully prepare each party, whether it is a victim and an offender, or a pair of warring neighbours—before giving them the opportunity to meet in a safe environment to agree a way forward. Victims are given the right to confront their offender, to explain the impact of their actions and sug-

gest how amends might be made in the presence of a facilitator.

Volunteer Stephen Twist has viewed how the process looks to open offenders' eyes to the impact of their behaviour and often leads to a genuine commitment to change their ways.

> He said: 'Letting go of a damaging conflict can be really empowering for the parties, freeing them to get on with their lives.'

The Advertiser, Darlington, Aycliffe and Sedgefield,
21 July 2014

here that the benefits of immediacy and making a direct connection between the offending behaviour and the response is as beneficial as a lengthy process of preparation and a highly formalised conference.

The YRD was 'intended to be a quick and effective means for dealing with low-level, anti-social and nuisance offending, offering an alternative to arrest and formal … processing' (Rix et al. 2011: 2). Typically, (in 75 per cent of cases, according to one study) the YRD would be carried out 'instantly', 'on the street' (Rix et al. 2011: 4), and consists of an immediate verbal or subsequent written apology made to the victim of an offence by the offender. Importantly, it is reported, the administration of a YRD was usually dependent on the wishes of the victim; in fact: 'many victims did not want the offender to be criminalised … , and simply wanted an apology, or an assurance' that the offence would not be repeated (Rix et al. 2011: 4). In its early days, the YRD was reported to meet with considerable approval, both from police officers who appreciated the opportunity to exercise professional discretion; and from both victims and offenders, not just in the latter case because it represented a 'second chance'. Young people also reported the impact of being made aware of the effects of their actions on others. Parents, too, were reported to be satisfied with the outcome and the positive effects of the experience on young people's behaviour.

Diversion in practice

Unlike restorative interventions, but consistent with the approach outlined previously, diversion initiatives have focused more explicitly on the offender (and in most cases the young offender) with the aim of promoting an out-of-court resolution of the offence. One of the best known models of diversion was established in Northamptonshire during the 1980s, in the form of three Juvenile Liaison Bureaux (JLB), in Wellingborough, Corby, and Northampton. A subsequent, and rather less successful, attempt was made to establish an adult equivalent, although with a rather more 'restorative' flavour— the Kettering Adult Reparation Bureau (Dignan 1990). The JLBs were developed as a response to the very low use of out-of-court disposals in the area, and had a strong underlying commitment to avoiding formal intervention, whether by way of prosecution or child care measures. They were set up on a multi-agency basis, bringing together police, probation, youth and social services, and education (and in one case, health and the voluntary sector as well); and their remit was to consider the cases of young people referred for offending by the police and to make recommendations about the appropriate disposal. However, recommendations would be informed by the principle that the least intrusive intervention possible would limit the risks of escalation into the justice system and the consequences of 'labelling'.

This approach has been compared to the philosophy associated with Schur (1973), of 'radical non-intervention', by Davis and his colleagues (1989). Although the Northampton JLB was apparently committed to a purist diversionary position, based on 'the Bureau's distrust of intervention of *any kind*' (Davis et al. 1989: 231), this was not the case elsewhere in the county, with Corby, for example, offering a more active approach to offence resolution and problem-solving. Reparation, for example, became a prominent element in that particular JLB's repertoire (Blagg 1985). Despite these internal differences, the Northamptonshire 'model' became highly influential, based on its dramatic success in reducing levels of prosecution in the county (without any evidence of 'net-widening'; see Austin and Krisberg 2002, for a detailed discussion of this phenomenon). At the same time, those interventions which were undertaken by the more pro-active bureaux were associated with high levels of victim and offender satisfaction (Blagg et al., 1986; Smith, 2014a).

Although diversion appeared to fall into disfavour in the 1990s and early 2000s, it re-emerged as a prominent feature of the youth justice landscape from 2007 onwards, encouraged by a shift in government policy and rhetoric, and a desire to rationalise policing practice (Flanagan 2007); and as time went on and 'austerity' struck, to save money. New initiatives emerging from that point included the Youth Restorative Disposal (see earlier); the 'Triage' model of initial decision-making (Haines et al. 2013); and the Youth Justice Liaison and Diversion (YJLD) scheme (Haines et al. 2012). Several of these appeared to be infused by a 'welfarist' assumption that, in certain cases and under certain conditions, young people should be referred out of the justice system into more appropriate forms of service provision, as in the second-tier outcomes provided for by the Triage model and the mental health provisions linked to the YJLD services. Interestingly, similar models of welfare-oriented diversion also seem to have shown a recent growth elsewhere, as with the Ohio Behavioral Health Juvenile Justice Initiative (Kretschmar et al. 2016).

A further development, associated with 'an emergent difference between … policy in Wales and England' (Haines et al. 2013: 170) has been the Swansea Bureau, whose principal aim is to 'divert young people out of the formal processes of the Youth Justice System' (2013: 168). Described as a 'new approach in diversion', although acknowledging a debt to the Northamptonshire model, the Swansea Bureau also adopted a partnership frame for its development, and sought explicitly to treat young people referred for offences as 'children first'. The underlying aim would be to work with parents and children to focus on positive outcomes, and avoid the negative consequences

CONVERSATIONS 26.1

The Swansea Bureau diversion initiative (Haines et al., 2013)—with Professor Kevin Haines

RS (Roger Smith): Please could you briefly summarise what the Swansea Bureau Initiative is, and what that stands for?

KH (Kevin Haines): The Swansea Bureau is designed as a non-criminal justice based response to offending by young people. It's based partly on the view that any significant involvement with the formal criminal justice system has negative implications for young people, in terms of their immediate behaviour, but also long term consequences for employment and such things. It's also based on the view that it's better to engage with young people with a positive agenda rather than a negative agenda. And placing the family at the core of responding to what is, for most young people, fairly normal adolescent behaviour.

RS: You mentioned 'children first, offenders second' in your discussion of the project, is that a good way of summing it up?

KH: Well, it is about responding to what is, for the vast majority of young people, a fairly normal adolescent behaviour. And it's about not overreacting to that with a punitive criminal justice system, whether it intends to be punitive or not, it's about responding to them as children and the fact that children need guidance and support and help. But it's best to do that in a constructive manner rather than in a negative manner.

RS: What does that mean in practice, in terms of the way something like the Bureau operates?

KH: For most young people, what [the agencies] found when they started to run the Bureau, was that in most cases the arrest of the child was the first time that the parents got to find out that their youngster was doing things that we wouldn't really want youngsters to get involved in. And in most instances, parents put in place boundaries, some cases sanctions, but broadly, a variety of responses that reinforced their role as parents and were broadly constructive. There was no particular need for the youth justice system to do any more than parents were already doing.

RS: It's supported by all the relevant agencies; do you have a sense that there's a collective will to succeed behind this?

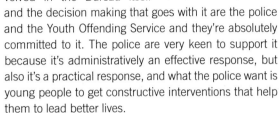

KH: The main agencies involved in the Bureau itself and the decision making that goes with it are the police and the Youth Offending Service and they're absolutely committed to it. The police are very keen to support it because it's administratively an effective response, but also it's a practical response, and what the police want is young people to get constructive interventions that help them to lead better lives.

RS: Were the success criteria broader than just preventing reoffending; would 'that they lead better lives' be a better way of summarising the success criteria?

KH: If you're trying to engage a young person, either parents are trying to or professionals are trying to, you're not going to engage a young person on the prevention of offending. You could engage a young person on improving positive outcomes. So that's what makes it 'children first', it's about something that children will engage with.

RS: Can you summarise the achievements of the Bureau?

KH: Yes, the evaluation that we've done so far was on the first twelve months, and what that showed was that the reconviction or re-arrest rates for young people was below ten per cent.

RS: Does that refer to everybody who's eligible go through the Bureau—all young people, first offenders or repeat offenders?

KH: Originally the police went with first time offenders, first time arrestees, with a gravity score of one to three on the police gravity score scale, but the experience of the police in the Bureau was so positive that they opened it up to a broader range of offence gravity scores and to reoffenders.

Professor Kevin Haines, Professor of Criminology and Youth Justice, Swansea University, Director of the Centre for Criminal Justice and Criminology

of formal criminal processes (see **Conversations 26.1** with Professor Kevin Haines).

Interestingly, this model explicitly sought to 'de-couple' the issues associated with young people involved in crime from the needs or wishes of the victim. Thus, restorative interventions would not be pursued as a specific element

of bureau work; although they would be facilitated if an opportunity to make amends did arise, for example. Nor would the Swansea model adopt an overly 'rehabilitative' approach; instead it would focus on ensuring children would be able to enjoy the normal entitlements and opportunities to which they should have access. The emphasis on informal problem-solving and inclusionary approaches underlying the Bureau's approach can be seen to generate a range of substantive benefits, it is suggested:

> Early indications are that the Swansea Bureau has been able to employ proactive, yet informal, non-criminalising and prosocial measures, to divert young people from the formal YJS [Youth Justice System] and to reduce levels of reconviction. In this way, practitioners have begun to address some of the negative unintended consequences of contact with the

YJS through sensitive and principled intervention, rather than a non-intervention ethos.

(Haines et al. 2013: 185)

Diversion, then, has primarily developed as an informal mechanism for substituting negotiated and considered interventions, tailored to children's specific circumstances and needs, rather than standardised formal measures which have no demonstrated effectiveness either in this respect or in reducing levels of offending.

The achievements of alternatives to punishment: Considering the evidence

As we have seen, in the case of desistance (**Chapter 25**) there is an element of controversy about the criteria to be applied when judging the outcomes of interventions in the criminal justice system. For some, the test of effectiveness is relatively straightforward, being based simply on reoffending rates. But, in the case of 'alternatives' to punishment, it is less clear that this should be the only, or even a principal consideration. After all, the main aims of restorative intervention, or diversionary non-intervention, are not framed in terms of the criminality of the reported offender, but rather in relation to wider potential benefits, such as victim satisfaction and harm reduction in a wider sense. Nonetheless, reoffending rates are often cited in support of claims for the overall effectiveness of these models of practice.

So, for example, analysis of the impact of the Swansea Bureau—whose principal aims are diversionary—pays close attention to the impact of the project's encouragement of 'non-criminal disposals' (NCDs), arguing that 'a general trend can be tentatively discerned that reconviction rates for NCDs are lower than those for all other disposals ... '(Haines et al. 2013: 178). Thus, it is argued 'the combination of engagement, participation, informal action, appropriate intervention and the adoption of a pro-social approach appear to be critical ingredients in the ability of the Bureau to reduce FTEs [first time entrants to the justice system] and reconviction' (2013: 185).

On a wider scale, a 'meta-analytic review' undertaken in America found 'strong support for the efficacy of diversion programs, whether these involved cautioning or direct interventions. ... In nearly all cases, these programs led to lower levels of reoffending than traditional processing through the juvenile justice system' (Wilson and Hoge 2013: 514); thus, leading to the conclusion that there is 'little reason to abstain from adopting a strategy that is more effective than traditional processing and considerably cheaper'.

In the same vein, the Restorative Justice Consortium (2006), perhaps not an entirely disinterested contributor to the debate, published an overview of more than 45 studies, offering clear support for the claim that restorative interventions are associated with a reduction in reoffending rates. The important point here is not the validity and strength, or otherwise, of these claims, but that one of the leading proponents of restorative justice should consider it so important to produce this kind of affirmative material with its specific emphasis on reoffending. If anything, this suggests something of a lack of confidence in the inherent value (or effectiveness) of other purported benefits of restorative practice.

Indeed, as Robinson and Shapland (2008) have observed, there is perhaps a degree of ambiguity in the position adopted by advocates of restorative justice on the relative importance of reoffending as a measure of success. Noting Schiff's (2003) claim that restorative justice is distinctive precisely because it does not focus simply on what happens to offenders, they acknowledge that it is not principally presented as 'an offender-centred approach' (Robinson and Shapland 2008: 337). At the same time, however, the concern with reoffending rates is recognised as a continuing matter of significant interest for policy makers. It has, therefore, been viewed as something of a 'tactical' adjustment for proponents of restorative justice to promote offender rehabilitation and prevention of reoffending as legitimate goals. On the other hand, critics of this kind of pragmatic accommodation with political realities have suggested that 'reducing recidivism is a somewhat unrealistic goal for restorative justice' (Robinson and Shapland 2008: 340); and that taking this approach also runs the risk of diminishing the 'importance or salience of other goals, particularly victim-centred ones'. In practice, as Robinson and Shapland (2008: 341) observe, there appears to be a considerable degree of enthusiasm for the idea that restorative practices might be effective in reducing reoffending. Indeed, 'victims, in common with other participants, actively wished to focus on addressing the offender's problems and so minimising the chance of reoffending' (Robinson and Shapland 2008: 341). Therefore, offenders' expressed intentions to 'do something' about their behaviour actually constituted a form of reparation from the point of view of some victims. Restorative justice, then, might be viewed as capable of encompassing rehabilitation as a subsidiary aim, without compromising its underlying principles:

> There is a case to be made for a subtle shift in ways of thinking about the recidivism reduction potential of restorative justice. Instead of thinking about restorative justice as a new-style 'intervention' – something which is 'done to' offenders – we might be better advised to re-frame restorative justice as an opportunity to facilitate a desire, or consolidate a decision, to desist.
>
> Robinson and Shapland 2008: 352

Diversion, too, reflects a degree of ambiguity when it comes to its potential contribution to desistance. In the case of the Northamptonshire Juvenile Liaison Bureaux in the 1980s, diversion from crime featured as one of the four principal aims of the initiative, but only as a subsidiary objective to enabling 'agencies' to respond effectively, based on the operational logic suggested by labelling theory (see earlier). In other words, if labelling theory actually 'works' in practice, then non-intervention should help to reduce the level of further offending ('secondary deviance'; Lemert 1967), more or less automatically. However, it is clear from accounts of both early schemes such as that in Northamptonshire and subsequent developments, as in Swansea, that the success criteria of these projects extend much more widely than that, and imply a much more substantial form of social reintegration of young people.

In Northamptonshire, then, diversion also encompassed the promotion of 'informal networks of control, support and care', and encouragement of 'the normal institutions of society to respond constructively to adolescent behaviour' (Bell et al. 1999: 96). So, too, the Swansea Bureau describes its first aim as being to 'divert' young people away from the justice system, and then to offer programmes to promote positive behaviour (Haines et al. 2013: 171). In both cases, then, the achievement of a lower rate of formal processing of young people through the justice system was the primary criterion on which they sought to be judged. And, indeed, in both cases, substantial reductions were recorded in this respect. By 1992, over 90 per cent of those referred for offences to the Northampton JLB were not prosecuted (Bell et al. 1999: 98); and in Swansea, the introduction of the Bureau was associated with a 70 per cent reduction in the number of 'first time entrants' to the justice system from 2008–09 to 2011–12.

Ironically, though, it is perhaps more straightforward for alternatives to punishment such as these to demonstrate (or at least claim) success in quite conventional criminal justice terms, than it is to show similarly positive outcomes in relation to their more ambitious aspirations to achieve a radically different way of 'doing justice'. Robinson and Shapland (2008), for example, are dubious about the capacity for restorative conferences to build 'social capital', or to provide systematic opportunities for engagement between the offender and the 'community'. On the other hand, a number of sources have identified benefits for victims and offenders arising from restorative processes which do appear to distinguish them from other disposals. Larsen's (2014) review of restorative justice in the Australian context suggests that not only was there evidence of lower reoffending rates in at least some practice settings, but that 'both victims and offenders reported that [restorative] conferences were fairer than court proceedings and that there were greater benefits for victims who attended conferences (including feeling less fearful and having their sense of security restored)' (Larsen 2014: 25). The effects of 'humanising' the offender are thus believed to offer significant benefits to victims who take part in restorative processes, and gain a sense of the person behind the offence; at the same time, active engagement of victims seems to provide an effective counterbalance to the sense of alienation and uninvolvement they typically experience under conventional criminal justice processes. Shapland et al. (2007) have also reported very high levels of victim (and offender) satisfaction, particularly associated with restorative conferencing: 'Around three-quarters of both victims and offenders thought the process was useful for them and were satisfied with the outcome'; and interestingly: 'Conferencing was perceived as significantly more useful by groups with more serious offences' (Shapland et al. 2007: 36).

Larsen's review also draws attention to the potential benefits for offenders of a closer sense of engagement through restorative processes, with some evidence of higher levels of 'compliance' with agreed responses to offences than in the case of court ordered outcomes; and a greater degree of 'satisfaction' with the restorative justice experience itself (Larsen 2014: 27).

Some work has been undertaken, too, to determine the relative cost-effectiveness of both restorative and diversionary interventions. As Larsen (2014: 28) acknowledges, this is often a significant political consideration; and at least in some cases, research has suggested that there is a substantial cost saving associated with restorative practices. The additional argument is made that reductions in reconviction rates associated with restorative justice also

WHAT DO YOU THINK? 26.6

'Justice reinvestment' has become an increasingly fashionable term to describe an emerging strand of policy development which emphasises the financial gains to be made from pursuing less intrusive and intensive forms of punishment, especially custody.

> The six Justice Reinvestment Pilots (Greater Manchester, Croydon, Hackney, Lambeth, Lewisham, and Southwark) aim to incentivise local statutory partners to reduce demand on courts, legal aid, prisons and probation and, consequently, reduce the costs on the justice system. This was based on the premise that there are significant potential reductions in crime and offending to be made by partners working more effectively together at the local level. The pilots commenced on the 1st July 2011 and are due to run for two years. The model differs from the other reoffending payment by results pilots in that:

> * The local area is rewarded if demand on the criminal justice system, rather than reoffending, falls; and
>
> * The estimated savings that this demand reduction creates for the Ministry of Justice are shared between the local partners involved to reinvest in reducing reoffending and crime locally.
>
> Ministry of Justice, 2012

* Is cost-effectiveness a good basis for judging whether or not to deal with offences in one way rather than another?

* Do you think it is possible to devise a way of relating human and economic costs in order to enable us to make this kind of judgement?

represent a future saving in terms of the expected costs of further crimes (which will have been avoided).

Studies have been undertaken to try to estimate the actual and potential savings achievable through the implementation of diversion and restorative justice (e.g. Matrix Evidence 2009), although these are inevitably hampered by the need to estimate what *would* have happened if a different course of action had been pursued. Nonetheless, it has been claimed that diversion of young adults (18–24) from formal court disposals to restorative pre-court interventions in England could have led to 'lifetime' savings of around £275 million at 2009 prices (Matrix Evidence 2009: 3). That is to say, the combined effects of lower processing costs and reduced offending would produce a significant net saving over the lifetime of the offender. Similarly, the Centre for Mental Health et al. (2010) has estimated that the costs of diversion to appropriate alternative provision for offenders with mental health problems would be offset by savings in direct provision of criminal justice services and an

estimated 30 per cent reduction in reoffending (Centre for Mental Health et al. 2010: 2). This evidence is supported by reports from specific schemes, with the local authority reporting annual savings to the public purse of over £2.8 million following the introduction of 'robust pre-court disposals' in Swansea (Haines et al. 2013: 185).

It is interesting in this context to reflect on the apparent necessity for 'alternatives to punishment' to justify themselves in terms of their cost-effectiveness, whereas this does not seem to be the case for conventional forms of criminal justice, whether in the shape of the judicial mechanisms for processing offences, the community and custodial disposals in use, or the consequential costs of further offences and reconviction. It is only relatively recently, with the emergence of arguments for 'justice reinvestment' that these default assumptions have come into question in public policy debates to any great extent (House of Commons Justice Committee 2009)—see **What do you think? 26.6**.

Alternatives to punishment: The implications

In one sense, it might seem that the justifications for alternatives to punishment are self-evident. They are, apparently, cheaper than conventional approaches; they are, apparently, capable of reducing reoffending rates; they offer additional benefits to both victims and offenders; and, they represent a rebalancing of the relationship between the state and the community, at least in respect

of criminal justice. As a result, alternatives might be seen as offering a powerful challenge to established assumptions about the underlying objectives and operation of the justice system. They seem to call into question widely held beliefs about 'just deserts', deterrence, the sentencing tariff, legal authority and expertise, and the relationships between victims, offenders and the formal agencies of criminal justice. As such, they might be viewed as prefiguring a radical shift in the way in which criminal justice is organised, as well as its underlying purposes.

To some extent, though, this perception hinges on whether or not the arguments in support of alternatives to punishment are articulated in their 'weak' or 'strong' forms (Smith 2011b: 171); that is whether, they are presented as representing a direct challenge to conventional justice models, or whether they are viewed as a form of 'modification', perhaps acting as a kind of brake on the most harmful or wasteful aspects of established practice.

Restorative justice, for instance, is viewed as a 'critique of traditional forms of justice ... and many of its proponents depict it as an oppositional paradigm to retributive justice. ... The benefits of restorative justice are typically set out with reference to the failings of the traditional criminal justice system. Advocates of restorative justice argue that it resolves many of these criticisms by addressing the needs of the victim, offender and wider community' (Campbell et al. 2006: 5). Crawford and Newburn (2003: 19) have equally suggested that restorative justice is 'one of the most significant developments in criminal justice' in recent times, because it offers a different perspective on conflict resolution and the repair of harm to that of the traditional fault-finding ideology and machinery of the justice system. Although they express some doubts about the realisation of restorative ideals in practice, in summary Crawford and Newburn (2003: 20) suggest that these principles act as a direct challenge to:

- the ineffectiveness of conventional models of justice;
- the limited capacity of the justice system to respond effectively to crime;
- the 'theft' of conflicts from those most affected by the offence (following Christie 1977);
- the failure to engage effectively with offenders in resolving the issues associated with their crimes;
- the reliance on 'punishment', such that 'one harm is met by another harm', to no beneficial effect;
- the lack of capacity of conventional processes to acknowledge or incorporate cultural differences and diversity;
- the distance in space and time of formal processes from the actuality and context of the offence.

Essentially, then, restorative justice appears to be based on a claim to assert a different set of values, which are to do with resolving problems and making good the effects of harm rather than formal processes of fault finding, blame, and penalisation.

This view of the justice process points towards a rather different formulation of its core principles. The idea of a 'tariff' of disposals, for example, clearly comes into question, since this does not allow for the specific circumstances of the offence or the expressed interests of the victim (and others affected) to take precedence in determining the outcome.

Diversion, too, represents a challenge to the principle of a graduated sentencing tariff, whereby disposals are progressively more punitive, depending on the gravity of the offence, and the persistence of the offending. Firstly, the concept of 'minimum intervention' underpinning diversion suggests that any form of statutory proceedings need to be justified in every case, rather than simply following from the number of prior offences committed by the individual concerned. Secondly, the arguments associated with the idea of 'labelling' would support the principle that no record should be kept of any prior involvement with the justice system—so, each subsequent offence would be treated as the first. And thirdly, even where an offender had a history of prior formal involvement in criminal proceedings, this should not preclude a diversionary outcome in relation to any subsequent offence. For proponents of both diversion and restorative justice, the point here is that the response to the reported crime can be much better 'tailored' to its specific characteristics if there is no requirement to follow a standardised and formulaic procedure which is incapable by definition of taking these into account.

Wider benefits

Not only are alternatives presented as more effective and better tailored responses to crime, but they are also believed to support broader objectives, such as enhanced social cohesion and reintegration of those at risk of being marginalised. The active involvement of the community is seen as an important objective for criminal justice, offering the opportunity to return control to those most directly affected, as Christie (1977) advocated. This aspiration was undoubtedly at the forefront of the ambitious restorative justice initiative in Northern Ireland, where 'community justice' was also believed to be an important element of the wider post-conflict reconciliation strategy. The highly positive evaluation of the youth conferencing service introduced in Northern Ireland in 2003 recognised that the service had quickly 'become established as a mainstream approach to young people who come in contact with the criminal justice system'; and that the high rates of satisfaction recorded, for both offenders and victims suggested that 'the process itself may be seen to have inherent value' (Campbell et al. 2006: 144).

Indeed, it has been further argued that restorative justice may have an important role to play in enhancing peace-building initiatives in societies which have experienced longstanding conflict, such as Northern Ireland and South Africa:

The extent to which the language and concept of restorative justice has permeated transitional justice in recent years has been nothing short of remarkable. Overall, this advance is to be welcomed: restorative justice approaches evidently contain a capacity to bolster peace-building in offering a flexible and pluralistic means of resolving conflict at macro and micro levels.

Clamp and Doak 2012: 359

However, the same authors are sceptical as to the extent and substance of change achieved as a result of the introduction of restorative practices, questioning whether the adoption of 'singular components' of restorative justice, such as mediation, apologies, or reparation is sufficient to achieve a genuinely different kind of outcome than those associated with conventional justice systems.

Although some advocates of alternatives to punishment certainly aspire to radical objectives, others take a more moderate view of their scope and realistic goals. Thus, in effect, the aim is to achieve better 'balance' in the justice process, rather than to see it transformed. Alternatives are seen as a useful way of moderating the justice process to avoid the risk of disproportionate or unfair outcomes, but clearly within rather than in opposition to the accepted framework of judicial decision-making. Diversion, then, could be viewed reasonably and realistically as a means of extending the sentencing tariff rather than as an alternative model for dealing with crime. It would therefore be available at the lower end of the scale, for early and minor offences, and where offenders accept responsibility and demonstrate remorse. Similarly, restorative justice could be seen as offering a useful adjunct to conventional processes and disposals, offering a stronger voice for victims and an opportunity for offenders to make amends, but within the context of mandated punishments and the attribution of culpability for criminal behaviour.

Pragmatic compromises

In practical terms, it does seem that both diversionary and restorative interventions occupy this sort of position and role within the justice system; being allocated a specific operational 'space', where they come into play, but only at the invitation and on the terms of the existing judicial authorities (the courts or prosecutors). As we have observed previously, the referral order represented a particularly clear cut example of just this sort of accommodation between the apparently radical aspirations of restorative justice and the reluctance of the judicial system to cede any ground, either symbolic or substantive, to other perspectives. The initial location of the referral order at a very specific point in the tariff of disposals made this point

very clearly. Despite subsequent reforms, the underlying logic of the tariff remains essentially unaltered.

Similarly, diversionary measures are very often presented as only being justified in relation to minor or early offences, and certainly not appropriate in more serious circumstances, especially in cases where the offence involves violence:

> We are particularly encouraged that many youth offending teams and police forces are using a restorative approach to resolving minor offending.

House of Commons Justice Committee 2013: 8

Alongside this implied limit to the remit of diversionary intervention, government policy also consistently makes clear the notional limits to diversion, specifying:

> circumstances in which even a low level offence would not be appropriate to be dealt with in this way. Examples included where it was part of a pattern of repeat offending or was associated with racial or domestic violence.

Northern Ireland Office 2008: 20

The influence of established thinking about guilt, responsibility, deterrence, and retribution is also evident in the administration and delivery of alternatives. Some proponents of restorative justice, for example, believe that it can incorporate mandatory requirements to engage in consultative processes, and subsequently to make amends without compromising its essential qualities of negotiation, recognition, and reconciliation. There is understandable support for the idea that reparation should be made conditional, in the interests of victims, and that alternative sanctions should be available in the event of failure to comply. This principle has been extended, too, to other diversionary measures such as the conditional caution, introduced under the Legal Aid Sentencing and Punishment of Offenders Act 2012.

Walgrave has argued that, even though voluntarism is the preferred option for restorative practice, to be pursued wherever possible, there must be provision (and safeguards) at some point for the introduction of 'coercion', where it 'finally appears to be the only possible way of doing justice' (Walgrave 2003: 62). He goes on to argue that 'restorative justice proponents are increasingly aware that due process and some kind of proportionality are important constraints to safeguard rights and justice in general' (2003: 76). On the other hand, though, he does assert that such limitations should be integrated with the logic of restorative practice, rather than dominating or marginalising it.

In various ways then, conventional assumptions rooted in the ethos of blame, individual responsibility and holding offenders to account have become embedded in a range of disposals which still claim that they introduce radically different principles and operational logic into the justice system.

The limitations of alternatives to punishment

As we have just observed, one of the central questions to be addressed by proponents of alternative approaches to punishment in criminal justice is just what they understand their aspirations to mean. The only real area of agreement in relation to restorative justice, for instance, is that it is a complex and disputed concept. Fundamental disagreements are to be observed, as to whether compulsion has any part to play in the process of bringing offenders into the process of offence resolution and reparation, albeit in the cause of achieving beneficial outcomes for other stakeholders (including victims). The underlying threat of alternative sanctions for non-compliance is believed by some to fatally undermine the key objectives of securing mutually and freely agreed outcomes which are viewed as fair and beneficial by all concerned. Others, though, would argue that the role of the state and the law as 'guarantor' of satisfactory procedures and appropriate outcomes logically extends to securing compliance, as would be the case with any form of contractual agreement.

In practice, much of what takes place under the broad umbrella of alternative mechanisms for resolving crime does incorporate conventional assumptions about holding offenders to account, reinforcing a sense of responsibility, and making good; so, questions perhaps need to be asked about the limits beyond which this sort of compromise actually subverts the underlying principles of restorative or diversionary practice. This consideration assumes a greater degree of significance when we acknowledge the evidence that offenders themselves do often experience 'alternative' interventions as no more than another form of punishment and humiliation.

Thus, Maruna et al. (2007) identify limitations associated with youth conferencing, which are to do with its apparent similarities to other aspects of young people's experience, such as being continually blamed and berated:

> It was all: 'How you'd feel if this happened to you?' And I was like, 'Yes I know. I get the point'. For an hour maybe every week. It was just talk crap in me ear. ... You know. It took an hour of my week. I think I had to go on a Friday. You know I love my Friday!'
>
> Young person quoted in Maruna et al. 2007: 52

As Maruna et al. go on to explain, the experience of being vilified in this way, and being unable to get across their own accounts of what had happened could be very negative for some offenders. Their attempts to rationalise and contextualise their offences seemed to be dismissed as mere 'excuses' and this left them feeling angry that they had not been taken seriously in the restorative conference.

Lacey (2012) also expresses concern about the potential variability in the way in which 'restoration' is achieved, identifying contrasting experiences in different settings. Discussing the reparation element of referral orders, she notes that:

> At YOT [Youth offending Team] B 'restoration' was achieved in that young people did work that they tended to feel made a tangible contribution and that they were therefore 'better off' as a result. In contrast, young people at YOT A viewed their reparation work as a punishment and did not feel that they were 'restoring' the harm that had been caused by their crime.
>
> Lacey 2012: 161

Alternatives *as* punishment

The implication of such findings is that alternatives to punishment may not, in fact, be experienced by those on the receiving end as any less of a punishment, whilst at the same time they may not be assured of the safeguards available to those going through conventional adjudication and sentencing processes. In other words, 'alternatives' may actually be less fair than conventional criminal justice mechanisms. Conventional understandings of appropriate and proportionate punishment may, in fact, be breached, purely because of the absence of proper legal safeguards. Pratt (1989), in particular, was one of the early and quite trenchant critics of the idea of 'administrative justice', describing the Northamptonshire diversion scheme as 'corporatist', and concerned principally with achieving agencies' internal policy goals rather than ensuring that participants' rights were protected: 'instead of a shift from the inhumanities and injustices of the institution, we find these features of the carceral system now being reproduced in the community—in those projects that are supposed to be alternatives to the institution' (Pratt 1989: 252). Whilst these conclusions were disputed by others, based on empirical observations of diversion schemes in operation (Hughes et al. 1998), there remains a degree of support for the idea that alternative forms of justice are not necessarily just, in their administration or effects. It is argued that where alternative interventions do not act as genuine alternatives but as an adjunct to conventional processes, they effectively expose offenders to more intrusive and less effectively regulated forms of punitive sanction than they would otherwise have experienced. Thus, pursuing the apparently laudable objective of 'making amends' may achieve what is expected of it in a formal sense; whilst actually involving excessive and demeaning impositions on the offender (Menkel-Meadow 2007).

In a similar vein, concerns are raised about the extent to which purported 'alternatives' to formal interventions simply run alongside them, contributing to a general 'system' expansion, rather than limiting intervention, as intended. 'Net-widening' of this kind has been identified as a significant potential risk associated with attempts to develop informal and extra-legal disposals, outside the remit of conventional adjudicating forums. Austin and Krisberg (2002) offer a detailed analysis of the phenomenon, depicting the criminal justice system as a series of 'nets' which are able to develop their own criteria for sifting and 'catching' those for whom intervention of one kind of another are deemed suitable. Their argument is that each new theoretical model and reform movement in criminal justice either adds another 'net' to the array of options available, or strengthens or expands existing nets. Alongside other reform initiatives (in the domains of decarceration, due process, decriminalisation, deterrence, and just deserts), diversion is viewed as a contested area of practice, where a range of agency interests come into play. In similar vein to Pratt (1989), Austin and Krisberg (2002: 259) view this as territory ripe for exploitation by 'corporate' interests:

> Diversion has been implemented through the addition, by criminal justice agencies, of new programs and new resources to the existing system ... The pre-trial criminal justice process is ... an 'open' system, in which agencies compete and conflict with one another and in which various and diverse decision makers exert considerable discretionary powers.

At the time of their original study of the subject (1981), Austin and Krisberg were able to identify a number of examples of diversion programmes 'expanding' and 'strengthening' nets as well as creating new ones. That is to say, schemes were extending their terms of reference to deal with new forms of apparently problematic behaviour, 'formalizing previously informal organizational practices' (Austin and Krisberg 2002: 260), and establishing new procedures to ensure engagement. In the process, they note, questions of guilt and responsibility appear to have been subordinated to the procedure, and requirements imposed conditionally on those 'diverted', at the expense of 'due process'.

In this context, too, there is a concern that the lack of effective safeguards regarding out-of-court decision making may also lead to inequalities and discriminatory outcomes on ethnic grounds. The risk of minority ethnic groups being drawn arbitrarily into the justice system has clearly been recognised (Bowling and Phillips 2003); and even a 'diversionary' outcome in such cases can result in a criminal record, with longer term consequences.

In fact, there has been evidence of system expansion at various points in time. The use of juvenile cautions increased dramatically in the UK from the 1950s onwards, following the implementation of the pioneering Juvenile Liaison Scheme in Liverpool, but with little actual effect on prosecution rates. It was this cumulative trend associated with other developments in the use of care orders which prompted the expressions of concern of Thorpe et al. (1980) and others about the substantial parallel growth in the criminalisation of children and their institutionalisation on welfare grounds.

Similarly, following the Crime and Disorder Act 1998, the prescriptive framework of reprimands and final warnings, the development of an array of targeted 'early prevention' programmes, and the introduction of the antisocial behaviour order were also associated with a period of system expansion and increasingly punitive treatment of an increasing number of young people across the range of interventions (Bateman 2015).

At other times, however, it is clear that 'net-widening' is not a necessary consequence of the introduction of diversionary initiatives. Indeed, Thorpe et al. (1980: 130) made an important distinction between 'process' and 'practice' intervention, arguing that diversion could be effective if its goal was to change system behaviour, rather than simply to develop yet more ways of working with young people. This kind of 'systemic' approach was indeed a feature of the diversionary initiatives of the 1980s, and is arguably once again a feature of the reduction in formal processing of young offenders in England and Wales from 2007 onwards.

However, when diversion does appear to be successful in these terms, and offenders are subject to less obviously punitive interventions, whether in the form of diversionary or restorative outcomes, they are exposed to another form of criticism, namely that offenders are 'getting away with it'. Not only is justice not being served, but victims in particular are believed to lose out in the context of an approach which is designed to meet the interests of offenders. Within a wide context in which victims feel poorly served by the justice system, sharper concerns about diversion and restorative practices are perhaps to be expected. As Victim Support (the national victims' organisation) puts it:

> Confidence in the criminal justice system among victims remains far too low. The rule of law rightly demands that victims do not dictate justice or sentencing, but the engagement and confidence of victims in it is nevertheless vital. Victims and witnesses have been historically marginalised in the field of sentencing. While this has begun to change and the need to consider victims' perspectives is acknowledged more widely, the views of victims continue to be misrepresented and misunderstood.
>
> Victim Support 2012: 5

A survey of views on community sentences carried out by Victim Support suggested a considerable degree of wariness about restorative justice, and comments to the effect that it should not be used as a means for reducing the level of punishment for the offender. It seems that concerns about the marginalisation of victims' interests are persistent; as is the fear that alternative measures will be associated with undue leniency (Jacobson and Kirby 2012). Such fears are endemic, undoubtedly, and coincide with a broader mood of public (and political) opinion in favour of punitive sentences for most types of crime (Hough et al. 2013).

In some respects, though, criticisms seem somewhat misplaced. For example, alternative interventions with known offenders are not well placed to address victims' interests because of their structural location in the justice system. In most cases, offenders are not matched with victims because crimes are not solved, and thus restorative interventions are not best placed to consider the interests of victims in general. In light of this, then, we might find the justice system's preoccupation with the offender less surprising; although at the same time, this might also lend weight to the suspicion that victims' involvement in restorative interventions is a secondary consideration. At the same time, of course, in the interests of fairness, it would seem unreasonable to afford victims who are matched with offenders and play an active part in resolving offences a greater role in determining sentencing disposals than in other cases.

So, it is plausible to conclude that alternatives to conventional forms of punishment may struggle to reflect public expectations, or meet victims' interests, even though they may sometimes make ambitious claims to this effect.

Finally, though, for those arguing from a critical perspective (see **Chapters 15** and **16**), the complaint is that 'alternatives' do not go far enough. This derives from the inherent ambiguities associated with an approach to dealing with crime and offenders which operates predominantly within the confines of a justice framework but with which its underlying principles (such as challenging the sentencing tariff or decriminalising young offenders) appear to be in conflict. Thus, for example, diversionary and restorative alternatives retain a primary focus on the individualised offender, and implicitly accept the structures and procedures according to which decisions are made, and through which they obtain their 'clientele'. Established assumptions about who offenders are, what causes crime, and how to address it are not fundamentally challenged by the way in which alternatives operate, albeit they may be subject to some modification and relaxation. As Wood (2015: 11) observes, restorative justice 'cannot readily fix ... structural problems'; going on to cite Braithwaite's acknowledgement of its 'modest' approach to changing the shape of criminal justice. Restorative justice, it is argued: 'cannot resolve the deep structural injustice[s] that cause problems' (Braithwaite 1998: 329).

SUMMARY

Based on the key themes set out at the start of the chapter, this chapter has considered the development of alternatives to punishment and emerging approaches based on the idea of 'offence resolution'. Revisiting our initial objectives, we have covered the following ground:

- Be aware of approaches to the delivery of criminal justice which challenge conventional assumptions about crime and punishment

The chapter has introduced a number of perspectives on responding to crime which do not depend on conventional theories of blame, or individual failings but instead focus on addressing the specific implications and consequences of the offence.

- Know about the origins and development of restorative ideas and practices

The relatively recent development of offence resolution techniques has been explored, with reference to their origins in diverse cultural practices, based around notions of healing, reconciliation, and forgiveness.

- Understand the emergence and impact of diversion as an intervention strategy

The emergence of diversion as an informal and then increasingly formalised mechanism for dealing with minor and less problematic offences has been outlined; and the chapter has also discussed recent patterns and trends in the use of 'out of court' disposals.

- Be familiar with examples of the implementation of 'alternatives to punishment' and their impact

Restorative and diversionary practices have been considered in detail, noting the complex and problematic relationship between these forms of intervention and traditional ways of organising and delivering criminal justice.

- Critique the arguments in favour of alternative forms of intervention, appreciating the potential criticisms of alternative forms of intervention

Critical arguments directed at alternatives to punishment have been aired, especially in relation to their limited capacity to address stakeholders' concerns and their sometimes counterproductive impact on the justice system as a whole.

- Develop your own arguments for and against these more informal methods of dealing with offences

This chapter has provided you with the persuasive arguments put forward by others, but you should apply this knowledge to develop your own viewpoints. Use the answers to the questions in the **What do you think?** boxes as a starting point. Creating your own arguments is good practice for essays and examinations.

REVIEW QUESTIONS

1. What do we mean by the term 'alternatives to punishment'?

2. What are the distinctive features of offence resolution strategies?

3. Why do you think these approaches have gained more ground when working with young offenders rather than adults?

4. What are the advantages and disadvantages of informal attempts to deal with offences?

5. What do you think of the suggestion that employing 'alternative' means of dealing with offences is just letting criminals off lightly?

FURTHER READING

Braithwaite, J. (2009) *Crime, Shame and Reintegration*. Cambridge: Cambridge University Press).
This book has been seen as highly influential in setting out a clear rationale for restorative justice, and seeking to bring together diverse interests (victim, offender, and community) in a way which provides an effective justification for this form of offence resolution.

Christie, N. (1977) 'Conflicts as Property', *British Journal of Criminology*, 17 (1), pp. 1–15.
Nils Christie's seminal article made a strong case for communities reclaiming offence resolution from the conventional justice system, which was believed to be impersonal and sometimes unresponsive to the interests of those most directly involved, particularly victims.

Haines, K. et al. (2013) 'The Swansea Bureau: A Model of diversion from the Youth Justice System', *International Journal of Law, Crime and Justice*, pp. 1–21.
This article provides a detailed account of one model of diversionary practice in youth justice which has been thoroughly evaluated and makes credible claims for the effectiveness of dealing with many offences 'out of court'.

Wood, W. (2015) 'Why Restorative Justice Will Not Reduce Incarceration', *British Journal of Criminology*, 55 (5), pp. 883–900.
This article makes the argument that restorative justice will have only a marginal effect on the operation of the wider criminal justice system and whatever its merits it cannot compete for centre stage with conventional approaches to dealing with crime.

 Access the **online resources** to view selected further reading and web links relevant to the material covered in this chapter.
www.oup.com/uk/case/

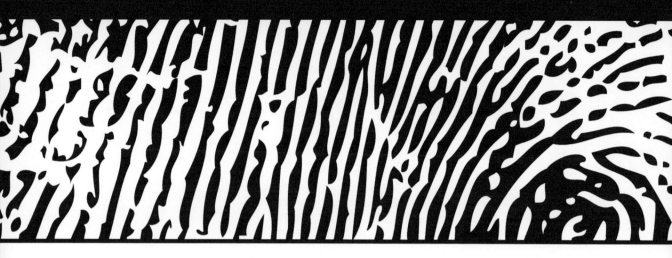

CHAPTER OUTLINE

What are critical perspectives on punishment?   744

Unjust punishment   746

Punishment and hegemony: Justifications and legitimacy   749

Crimes of the privileged   751

What is to be done about crime?   755

Limitations of critical perspectives on punishment   763

Conclusion   765

Critical perspectives on crime and punishment

KEY ISSUES

After reading this chapter, you should be able to:

- explain what is meant by the idea of critical perspectives on punishment;

- consider a range of critical perspectives on the justice system including the abolitionist position, social control theories, and transformative justice;

- identify the disparities in treatment between white, BME, and other sectors of the population in the criminal justice system;

- explore how 'crimes of the powerful' and state crimes can remain unseen or unpunished;

- evaluate radical responses to the problems associated with crime, such as: truth and reconciliation, community justice, and abolitionism;

- analyse the limitations of critical analyses of crime and punishment.

What are critical perspectives on punishment?

In this final chapter on the justice system and its outcomes, the aim will be to summarise a range of perspectives which effectively question the underlying assumptions behind the concept of 'punishment'. This represents a shift in emphasis from the system 'as it is' to a critical evaluation of its social foundations, and some reflections on how it might be different if we follow through the implications of some of these critical arguments. In light of this, inevitably, questions will also arise (and answers be offered) as to the relationship between criminal and social justice, and, indeed, whether or not these are compatible concepts.

Critical perspectives on punishment and its uses are derived from a number of sources. There are those, for example, who are predominantly concerned with evidence of systemic injustices, such as those associated with the persistent evidence of discrimination against minority ethnic groups in the administration of justice (see **Telling it like it is 27.1**). Criticisms of this kind may be associated with a 'rights' perspective, which argues in effect for a recalibration of the justice system to eradicate the potential for systemic oppression of particular groups.

As will become clear, the scale of disproportionate treatment of offenders in terms their ethnic background is striking, and this is illustrated even more graphically by the experience of the USA. In a country with what is acknowledged to be an extremely high prison population, it is reported that there are proportionally six times as many black men as white men in custody: 'Almost 3 per cent of black male U.S. residents of all ages were imprisoned on December 31, 2013, compared to 0.5 per cent of white males' (Carson 2014: 1).

For some, this kind of pattern of unfair treatment is evidence that the criminal justice system as it is currently constituted does not, and cannot, serve the common interest and is always likely to favour those who are in positions of power and privilege, both within and outside the system itself.

Other critiques might well concur with this kind of sentiment, but would also make links with the underlying symbolic role of the justice system in maintaining belief in the legitimacy of a particular social order (see **Chapter 14** on sociological positivism). That is to say, the organisation and delivery of criminal sanctions according to an established set of rules and assumptions is self-serving, in that it helps to perpetuate an inevitable sense of order and logic about the way it operates. Critics would argue that the way that the institutions of law and justice are invested with status and the trappings of authority (as in courtroom dress, for example) is a direct exemplification of this attempt to establish and maintain a sense of legitimacy, and effectively to institutionalise unfairness—the very opposite of the underlying qualities claimed for the justice system, of course.

Again, associated with such criticisms are arguments about what the justice system does not do. Its existing form and practices also serve the function of diverting attention from the 'crimes of the powerful' (Pearce 1976). Such crimes, of corporate entities and covert but powerful networks, may have extensive and dramatic consequences, but somehow do not readily result in determinations of guilt or punishment of those responsible, it is suggested.

The massive gas leak at Bhopal in India in 1984, for which the American corporation Union Carbide was responsible, and which resulted in an estimated 16,000 deaths (see **Figure 27.1**):

> was first a criminal justice issue. Crime No. 1104/84 was registered, *suo moto*, by Hanumanganj Police Station House Officer Surinder Singh Thakur on December 3, 1984, 1 less than 24 hours after the onset of the disaster, while hundreds of corpses still lay scattered across the roads, parks, and gullies of the old city.
>
> On the day that Crime No. 1104/84 was registered, five local junior officers of Union Carbide India Limited (UCIL) were the first company officials to see the inside of a jail. They were also the last: their release on bail after 12 days marked the final day in custody for any Union Carbide representative before or since. Though convictions were secured for seven UCIL officials over 25 years later, each of the convicted were granted immediate bail and remain at liberty at time of writing, with vigorous appeals still pending.
>
> Edwards 2015: 53

Similarly, it might be argued that the criminal justice system does not even hold accountable those responsible for a wide range of unacceptable, or quasi-unlawful activities,

Figure 27.1 Protesters during a rally on the 29th anniversary of the Union Carbide gas leak
Source: Photo by Gagan Nayar/Hindustan Times via Getty Images

such as tax avoidance, environmental harm, and exploitation of labour in developing countries. Green criminology, for example, lays claim to examine 'complex issues in criminological enquiry that extend beyond the narrow confines of individualistic crime which dominate criminological discourse and are the main focus of criminal justice policy. Simply put, green criminology thinks bigger' (Nurse 2014: 3).

It is, of course, easier to formulate criticisms of the existing framework for delivering criminal justice than it is to articulate alternative approaches to determining responsibility for wrongdoing and conflict resolution which might be seen as progressive ways of 'doing justice', and achieving socially desirable as well as legally valid outcomes. Nonetheless, this chapter will also move on to consider a number of arguments and proposals which, at least in the eyes of their proponents, do pre-figure more acceptable ways of resolving the problems of unacceptable behaviour and harm arising at both individual and wider societal levels.

Abolitionism

Here, too, there are a range of critical perspectives to consider. Firstly, and perhaps most unsurprisingly, there is the abolitionist position (Mathiesen 1974), which shuns any notion of punishment and blame entirely. Abolitionism derives from the view that any justice system that relies on individualised notions of guilt and responsibility, and is supported by institutional forms of punishment and restraint, is unacceptable and unjustifiable. All aspects of conventional systems of fault-finding and imposition of penal sanctions are therefore to be opposed. Abolitionism is unashamedly concerned with the principle of rejecting conventional punitive practices; and, according to its leading proponent, does not seek

to engage in a process of compromise with alternative views: 'When something is said to be "necessary", you should beware. ... The abolitionist stance goes beyond (some of) the parameters [of the system]. For example, it is possible to say "sorry, but public opinion is not my concern", or perhaps better "public opinion can be changed ... "' (Mathiesen 2008: 59).

So, rather than seeking to improve unacceptable prison conditions in the short term, abolitionists simply adopt a position of outright opposition to the use of imprisonment in any form. To concede legitimacy to custody in any form is to accept and effectively condone oppressive institutional treatment and the inequitable social system that it represents. By contrast, radical attempts to change custody for the better are said to have been subverted and incorporated into arguments in support of supposedly reformed institutions (Sim 2009: 133).

Although abolitionism does provide an effective basis for questioning some of our implicit assumptions about crime and punishment, it appears less obviously capable of providing a practical and achievable basis for resolving problems of 'transgression'. Pure opposition may serve a purpose, but it is unhelpful as a basis for articulating alternative frameworks for dealing with crime and the problems associated with it. Both morally and practically, there are clearly questions to be answered as to whether we wish to dispense with notions of blame and accountability entirely; and, relatedly whether this is even possible in the face of wider societal wishes and expectations. How, for example, can we provide protection for vulnerable and less powerful groups if we dispense with notions of individual responsibility and justice entirely? Nor, indeed, is it likely to be possible to wish away deeply held differences and grievances without offering some form of resolution.

Transformative justice

On the other hand, ideas of transformative justice do take a more proactive view of the question of how to understand and resolve the 'harms' which are the result of human actions of one kind or another. Lea (2002), for example, has argued for a return of the power to resolve conflicts to 'communities': 'Communities could take the law into their own hands again ... But these systems will function *only* if substantive equality exists between groups and individuals such that disputants have equal power and some willingness to sort out conflicts. This requires fundamental social and political change' (Lea 2002: 189 (emphasis in original)).

What this approach would help us to do, seemingly, is to set out common, agreed, and exhaustive frameworks for collectively identifying wrongdoing and acting to remedy this, irrespective of its origins and impacts. We might, here, turn to some of the known examples of indigenous justice mechanisms which depend on communal negotiation and consensus—somewhat akin to some of the aspirations for restorative justice set out previously, and often seen as the inspiration for restorative initiatives. Despite this, once again, limitations may be identified in the 'transformative' argument when it comes to the task of implementation and realisation, especially in complex industrial societies. Of course, if 'fundamental change' of the kind Lea aspires to is a prerequisite, then this only illustrates the scale of the task—it is not simply a matter of internal reform of the justice system or improving its effectiveness.

Community justice

In order to gain a better sense of what may be practically achievable in this respect, we will turn finally to consideration of a number of attempts to insert critical principles of human rights and social justice into the workings of the criminal justice system. In this respect, we will give further consideration to attempts to develop models of 'community justice', particularly in post-conflict situations; and we will also consider a number of specific projects and initiatives which have sought to articulate critical challenges 'from within'.

In a sense, this also reflects Lea's argument that transformation can be achieved locally and in piecemeal fashion, although clearly this does depend on achieving at least sufficient independence from the prevailing system to establish separate frameworks and processes for resolving conflict. Whether this is ultimately feasible is perhaps open to question, as some recent experiences of 'community justice' appear to have confirmed. The community

justice initiatives in the north-west of England established in 2005, for example, were closely tied in to existing court structures, and were unable to establish a distinctive identity outside the conventional sentencing framework. The introduction of a 'problem-solving' ethos and the promotion of community engagement through these schemes did not seem to have a notable effect on changing the ways in which justice was delivered, or in its outcomes:

> It is very clear from our interviews that there was some agreement and frustration that only a minority of local residents were being 'engaged'. Respondents spoke about scratching the surface, about community apathy, about people only taking an interest in the [Community Justice] Centre when they had a problem – and, of course, this is exactly how support services are used by the general public.
>
> Mair and Millings 2011: 100

Such initiatives may not have the capacity to achieve whole system change, but in favourable circumstances and free from undue constraints they may be seen as pre-figurative, or at least of sufficient influence to open the way for radical developments in policy and practice: 'Community justice in general, and the North Liverpool Community Justice Centre in particular, could have a potentially transformative effect on criminal justice' (Mair and Millings 2011: 101).

In the following sections, we will explore further both the critical analyses of the existing criminal justice system, and the alternative models of justice outlined here. Unlike previous chapters in this section these will be organised sequentially rather than thematically. This will enable us to explore each of the varied arguments coherently in detail, before ending with some concluding reflections on the overall strengths and limitations of critical approaches to punishment.

Unjust punishment

Problems for criminal justice of discrimination and inequality

The sustainability of the criminal justice system depends on it being able to demonstrate that it operates according to its own rules of fairness and procedural justice. It is, of course, open to criticism over the extent to which these principles are breached. It would naturally be unreasonable to expect any system, and especially one so dependent on human interaction and judgement, to operate perfectly. But, at the same time, we would probably also expect to see this kind of system at least meet minimum

standards of fairness, or to be called seriously into question. The available evidence of inconsistency and discriminatory outcomes is therefore of considerable interest.

It is fair to say that there have been persistent concerns in this respect, over a considerable period of time, especially in regard to discrimination on ethnic grounds, although other groups, too (such as young people in the care system) have problematic experiences of criminal justice interventions. In fact, as reported by Bowling and Phillips (2007) in their detailed analysis, the justice system appears to operate in a way which progressively intensifies discriminatory impacts at each stage of the process.

Discriminatory practice and BME communities

Stop and search

Disparities in treatment are apparent throughout the justice system, right from the very point of entry onwards. As Bowling and Phillips (2007: 434) observe, it is the practice of 'stop and search' which is the most problematic of all aspects of the relationship between police and minority ethnic groups. They observed that black people were over six times more likely, and Asians twice as likely, to be stopped and searched as white people. As *The Independent* reported on 6 August 2015 ('Stop and search: Can transparency end this abuse of police powers?'), this is a persistent problem. Despite considerable regional variations, the article reported that in all parts of the country police were continuing to subject black people to 'stop and search' unnecessarily and disproportionately. Such practices are not justified by the number of arrests resulting from the use of police powers in this way—with only 13 per cent of 'stops' involving black people resulting in subsequent arrests, according to Bowling and Phillips (2007: 435). Similar disparities, specifically in relation to young black people were documented by May et al. (2010), who also found evidence of the possibility of discrimination at other stages in the criminal process, including decisions about custodial remands, for example.

As Bowling and Phillips observe, too, the cumulative effects of what is perceived as unfair treatment at the entry point may be felt in a number of ways, with black suspects less likely to 'co-operate' with the police, in the sense of exercising the right to silence, or seeking legal assistance, with the result that they are less likely to be offered a caution in the absence of an admission. So: 'Whilst these decision points can be regarded as racially neutral … historical tensions and a present day mistrust of the police may often operate to deny minority ethnic offenders the benefits of cooperation' (Bowling and Phillips 2007: 440). As they observe, this could be viewed as amounting to 'indirect racial discrimination'.

Attempts to understand the progressive effect of discriminatory practices at the point of sentencing have been undertaken, too. There is no doubt that ethnic minorities are substantially over-represented at the conclusion of the justice process, when sentencing decisions are made; and as the official statistics consistently show, this trend seems to be intensified at each stage of the process (Ministry of Justice 2013). Thus, in 2011, the Ministry of Justice reports that 87.1 per cent of the population of England and Wales aged over 10 was white, and 3.1 per cent black; and yet in 2012, 70.6 per cent of those sentenced to immediate custody were known to be white, and 8.9 per cent of this group were black. More recent analysis has confirmed that there is a greater risk of being sentenced to custody for minority ethnic defendants (see, Hopkins 2015).

Whilst there are risks in drawing simplistic conclusions from population-wide figures of this kind, the implication is clearly that the justice system either compounds or at least fails to modify the discriminatory effects of disproportionate initial contact.

As Bowling and Phillips (2007: 450) argue, there appear to be a number of discriminatory mechanisms at play. At the onset of the involvement of black people in the justice system, they argue that police stereotyping has a part to play, and that this is compounded by the interaction between policing practices and the 'availability' of certain groups—such as young people from ethnic minorities—in the sense that they are more likely to be in public places, for example, where they may come to the attention of the police. In some cases, it seems, they are more likely to be stopped by the police simply because what they are doing appears unexpected or 'untypical' in some way, such as driving an expensive car (see **Telling it like it is 27.2**).

Moreover, what Bowling and Phillips describe as 'supposedly neutral' decision making criteria actually compound systemic disadvantages. For example, decisions on whether or not to grant bail may be based on housing status, and thus implicitly work against those defendants from minority groups which are known to experience less secure accommodation. Indeed, from their point of view there is a clear link between socioeconomic disadvantage, the 'visibility' of certain types of behaviour and discrimination, resulting in the progressive 'criminalisation' of minority ethnic, and particularly African and Caribbean groups. Noting that outcomes for different ethnic groups

---

TELLING IT LIKE IT IS 27.2

Black and minority ethnic celebrities report being apprehended by the police, seemingly just for being in a wealthy area, or driving an expensive-looking car.

Chris Rock took a selfie after being pulled over by police while driving Tuesday, marking the third time in seven weeks he's posted while being stopped by a police officer.

Rock posted the photo to his social media accounts early Tuesday, writing: 'Stopped by the cops again wish me luck.' In the shot, the comedian can be seen behind the wheel of a car with blue police lights shining through his rear window.

Huffington Post, 4 April 2015

vary, the role of distinctive stereotypes and their differential effects is stressed:

> '[R]ace', class and ethnicity are not *ahistorical* essences, but socially constructed categories upon which iniquitous social structures are based. Racism interacts with class disadvantage to produce patterns of social inequality experienced differently by minority ethnic groups ... [their] experiences of crime and criminal justice do not result *solely* from their socioeconomic position, as shown by research on criminal justice decision-making.
>
> Bowling and Phillips 2007: 451

The effect of difference has been conceptualised as a form of 'ethnic penalty', which systematically disadvantages members of particular groups as compared to majority (white) people with the same backgrounds and characteristics (Roberts 2015: 19).

Additionally, a more recent development has been the progressive problematisation of followers of Islam and young Muslims in particular. By the mid-2000s, the Muslim Council of Great Britain was expressing the fear that institutional racism was becoming evident in the way that young Muslims were treated (Smith 2009: 42). In its 2014 report, the Young Review on young black and/or Muslim men in the justice system concluded that Muslim prisoners comprise 13.4 per cent of the prison population compared to 4.2 per cent of the general population; and that Muslim prisoners felt that they were being 'stigmatised as extremists' (Young 2014: 11). The review reiterated the evidence of a range of 'drivers' for the disproportionate representation of black and minority ethnic young people in the justice system, including stop and search practices, use of powers of arrest, and embedded assumptions about gangs (2014: 31). In addition, Young (2014: 31) reports that black and Muslim prisoners feel that they experience 'differential treatment as a result of their race, ethnicity or faith'. One of the current authors, recalls interviewing a Muslim young person who recounted the difficulties being created for him in carrying out his religious observances in one prison establishment (Smith and Fleming 2011), and this experience is echoed by the evidence gathered for the Young Review. Internal prison practices and disciplinary decision-making processes ('adjudications', in prison terminology) appear to compound the effects of prior discrimination: 'the continued presence of discrimination within our prisons has a significant effect' (Young 2014: 31).

It is also important to note here that the Young Review was only the latest in a consistent line of high profile inquiries into racism in the justice system which have come to similar conclusions, including the Scarman Report (1982), the Stephen Lawrence Inquiry (Macpherson 1999), and the inquiry into the death of Zahid Mubarek whilst in custody (Keith 2006). As these inquiries have often graphically illustrated too, the sense of injustice associated with unequal and unfair treatment is worsened by the experiences of ethnic minority communities as victims of unlawful acts, and the perception that they do not receive a respectful or active enough response when they suffer the effects of crime (Yarrow 2005).

Notwithstanding the justifiable concern about unequal treatment on grounds of ethnicity, critics of the justice system would also suggest that other groups are likely to be singled out for particular attention, and this may be for similar reasons in some respects, such as the perceived threat offered, or the visibility of certain forms of behaviour which is problematised. Pettit and Western (2004), for instance, have suggested that in America, class and ethnic factors interact to influence the likelihood of experiencing imprisonment over the life course: 'class bias in criminal sentencing is suggested by findings that more educated federal defendants receive relatively short sentences in general ... Imprisonment may be more common among low-education men because they are the focus of the social control efforts of criminal justice authorities' (Pettit and Western 2004: 153).

In the UK context, it has been consistently shown that certain sectors of the population are much more likely to be sentenced to custody, and these characteristics are interlinked. The Prison Reform Trust produces a regular overview of the pattern of sentencing (Bromley Briefings), which showed in 2014 (Prison Reform Trust 2014: 1–6):

- Fewer than 1 per cent of all children in England are in care, but looked after children make up 33 per cent of boys and 61 per cent of girls in custody.
- 25 per cent of children in the youth justice system have identified special educational needs, 46 per cent are rated as underachieving at school and 29 per cent have difficulties with literacy and numeracy.
- 53 per cent of women in prison reported having experienced emotional, physical or sexual abuse as a child, compared to 27 per cent of men.
- 20–30 per cent of all offenders have learning disabilities or difficulties that interfere with their ability to cope with the criminal justice system.
- 26 per cent of women and 16 per cent of men in prison said they had received treatment for a mental health problem in the year before custody.

These findings are confirmed by Williams et al. (2012), who note that many of those in custody have complex and problematic personal histories, which are representative of a cumulative experience of 'social exclusion', which features poverty and other difficult circumstances.

This combination of factors, and the persistently uneven impact of imprisonment on specific elements of the general population have led theorists to conclude that the underlying function of punishment in general and custody, in particular, has been to exert a form of social control over them; in contrast to its more conventional portrayal as a fair and equitable mechanism for maintaining social order and safeguarding communal interests, especially amongst the most vulnerable. Rothman has concluded, for example, that with the historic emergence and institutionalisation:

> [O]f prisons, mental hospitals, [and] reformatories … it is now apparent that no simple links connect these places to a spirit of humanitarianism. That all of their wards were filled

with the lower classes … that within a few decades of their founding, they were invariably places of last resort (overcrowded, brutal and corrupt) … these considerations remain beyond the explanatory powers of a concept of 'reform'.
>
> Rothman 1985: 113

Criminalisation and control, then, are associated with a process of 'bifurcation' (Rock 2007: 23), whereby the justice system operates effectively to target those from particular backgrounds as problematic, and in doing so, predictably finds evidence to justify its expectations and support its punitive interventions.

Punishment and hegemony: Justifications and legitimacy

Critics have extended the argument that punishment is selective and oppressive to suggest that this not only serves a practical function of exercising targeted social control, but it also serves as a form of implicit self-justification. In other words, the fact that the punitive arm of the justice system operates in the way it does is sufficient also to grant it a sense of legitimacy (see also **Chapter 6**, where the topic of legitimacy and consent is discussed in more detail). The formalisation and ceremonial aspects of its procedures and decision making act to establish the basis of belief in the fairness and authority of the judicial process. This viewpoint was associated with an emerging radical strand in criminological thought, associated with authors such as Quinney (1970), Chambliss (1976), and Taylor et al. (1973): 'Crime control was said to be an oppressive and mystifying process that worked through legislation, law-enforcement, and ideological stereotyping to preserve unequal class relations' (Rock 2007: 23).

The machinery of justice, then, could be seen to have a logic of its own, which need not reflect its expressed values of equality before the law and preservation of rights; but rather should be seen as serving particular interests, disguised by this rhetoric. Indeed, by treating unequal populations equally, the system does not compensate for pre-existing effects of disadvantage or discrimination, and so compounds wider social inequalities.

Social control theorists: Foucault, Cohen, and Gramsci

Foucault and the shift of punishment from the 'body' to the 'soul'

The symbolic value of punishment and its effects is a theme of the writings of Michel Foucault. In his view this symbolism and its mechanisms have changed over time,

in tune with wider historical developments; and, indeed, its very longevity indicates its powerfully effective role in sustaining the wider social order. He suggests that in pre-modern times, punishment was often exercised in a graphically visual fashion, so as to demonstrate the force of the law in action, often in quite brutal terms. Legitimacy in this case was associated with the power to exert control, and with a belief in the value of representing that power directly through its imposition. In this way, punishment was not simply a matter of applying the appropriate penalty, but was also about asserting the *right* to do so, and thus needed to be seen to be delivered. As we have seen (**Chapter 24**), Foucault (1977) offers several graphic accounts of punishment as spectacle, supporting the idea that highly visible and dramatic displays of justice being done had a degree of historic importance.

By contrast, Foucault argues, over the course of the next century the idea of 'punishment as a spectacle' (1977: 8) died out, or certainly became less prominent (notwithstanding community punishments and prison clothing perhaps—see **Figure 27.2**).

Associated with this apparent shift of emphasis, Foucault observes: 'The body as the major target of penal repression disappeared' (1977: 8). Instead, punishment became 'the most hidden part of the penal process' (1977: 9) reflected in the close ordering and severe discipline to be applied to the custodial regime. Foucault gives as an example of this the very tightly specified timetable for a day's activities at the 'House of young prisoners in Paris'. The rationale for the imposition of punishment shifts as well. The form of discipline to be imposed through the institutional regime closely matches the organisation of work in modern (capitalist) society:

> If the penalty in its most severe forms no longer addresses itself to the body, on what does it lay hold? The answer … seems to be contained in the question itself: since it is no

Figure 27.2 Modern day version of a chain gang—offenders forced to wear striking clothing to visually distinguish them

Source: Patrick Denker/CC BY 2.0

longer the body, it must be the soul. The expiation that once rained down upon the body must be replaced by a punishment that acts in depth on the heart, the thoughts, the will, the inclinations.

Foucault 1977: 16

As the age of modernity became established and new forms of social organisation took shape, so, Foucault argues, the mechanisms of social control and punishment also adapted. In particular, they became infused with assumptions about technologies of power and the capacity to shape and correct human behaviour, in the same way as the material world could be managed and transformed. Thus, the emphasis shifted from highly visual demonstrations of the legitimate power to punish towards the use of more technical forms of assessment, discipline, correction, and behavioural adjustment.

This has most recently been a trend identifiable in the technologies of risk and risk management, for example (see Beck 1992, on the 'risk society'). Further than this, Foucault suggests, the relationship between the logic and machinery of control and wider social relations became mutually reinforcing. The same forms of discipline and incentivisation for good behaviour were extended into other institutional settings ('orphanages', 'establishments for apprentices', 'factory-convents'). As a result:

the carceral archipelago transported this [penitentiary] technique from the penal institution to the entire social body ... This vast mechanism established a slow, continuous, imperceptible gradation that made it possible to pass naturally from disorder to offence and back from a transgression of the law to a slight departure from a rule, an average, a demand, a norm.

Foucault 1977: 298

Associated with these developments, what we observe is a modification of the function of the law, so that it has a more 'educative' role, and the rapid development of 'disciplinary networks', comprising a range of professional experts, who all have the capacity to assess and determine the nature of the delinquent's problem, and the proper correctional intervention to be applied.

Stanley Cohen (1985) developed this line of argument further (in *Visions of Social Control: Crime, Punishment and Classification*) suggesting that the machinery for administering and delivering criminal justice has a particular 'bifurcatory' function; that is, it serves to act as a pivotal point, distinguishing between, and determining, the treatment of the (socially) included and excluded. The assumption of this role by the state has been the outcome of the kind of historical process earlier outlined by Foucault, whereby the 'centralised, rationalized' bureaucracy (Cohen 1985: 12) would preside over processes of assessing and classifying deviant individuals into specific intervention categories. Each of these would be the domain of a particular 'body of "scientific" knowledge and its own recognised and accredited experts' (Cohen 1985: 12). Such precise and apparently well-informed judgements would then inform provision of specific forms of institutional care, treatment, or correction, depending on the classification achieved.

Significantly, such a framework for adjudication and disposals achieves the contradictory outcome of strengthening its underlying justifications by allowing room for disagreement, sometimes quite vehement, between competing 'expert' assessments, or principles of intervention. Thus, for example, the recurrent conflict between 'welfare' and 'justice' positions in relation to young offenders can readily be accommodated within a wider and cohesive rationale for the organisation and delivery of youth justice. So, as Cohen (1985: 37) was able to point out, critical voices arguing for a reformed justice system emerging in the 1960s and 1970s were not able to dislodge the established system: 'Instead of any destructuring ... the original structures have become stronger'. And, indeed, consistent with Beck's (1992) arguments, Cohen views these trends as symptomatic of a wider shift towards a risk-sensitive and risk-driven social ethos, in the face of 'rapid economic, demographic and technological change' (Blomberg and Hay 2007: 178).

This analysis coincides with other social control theorists, too. Antonio Gramsci (1971), for example, is seen as making an important contribution in the shape of the concept of 'hegemony' (as you will know from earlier chapters, the term hegemony refers to ideological domination or control). This, in effect, represents the mechanism by which the state and other powerful interests maintain a sense of both the inevitability and the legitimacy of the way the social order is constructed and maintained. 'Hegemony' is of particular value because it provides a vehicle for the maintenance of conformity and domination without the routine alternative to measures of coercion; although, the legitimate use of force is also available where 'consent' breaks down (Gramsci 1971: 12).

The criminal justice system is an important element in the networks of control, in that it unites both the legitimacy derived from the implicit authority of the judicial machinery; and, at the same time is able to call on the directly coercive power of law enforcement agencies and punitive institutions. The effective exercise of coercion, in this sense, depends on broader popular consent to the claims to legitimacy made by the institutions of criminal justice; at the same time, of course, in the absence of effective challenge, coercive action helps to reinforce these claims, too.

The English riots

Interestingly, the English riots of 2011 (also discussed in **Chapter 17**) have sometimes been depicted in Gramscian terms, whereby the outbreak of rioting in the aftermath of the shooting of Mark Duggan represented a 'crisis of authority' (Jefferson 2015: 21), to which the immediate response was the use of coercive force by the police. On the second day of the riots: 'The policing strategy entailed flooding the streets with riot-clad officers … From midnight, Scotland Yard introduced an additional weapon, namely, the power to stop and search without reasonable suspicion … in Lambeth, Haringey, Enfield and Waltham Forest' (Jefferson 2015: 7). By day four, 'London was relatively calm. The police presence increased from 6,000 to 16,000 and [then Prime Minister] David Cameron returned from holiday, offering police the option of using plastic bullets for the first time in the UK, outside Northern Ireland' (Jefferson 2015: 8).

Direct confrontation of this kind represents both a physical and a symbolic challenge to the legitimacy of the state's role in maintaining order; and, in turn, the immediate response involved the state effectively ascribing new powers to itself to act outside the previously constructed (and legitimated) framework for doing so. Again, in Gramscian language, the task for those in positions of power was not just to take appropriate and effective coercive measures, but to account for their actions in a way which reasserted or restored their rightful authority to act in these ways.

In strategic terms, this is argued to have taken the form of a sustained campaign to de-politicise and instead 'criminalise' the actions of those involved in the riots;

and, in turn, to bring the might of the established justice framework to bear on them. And so, the construction of the rioters as greedy and materialistic thieves rather than politically motivated protesters (who might have a point) was a critical element of the response, from the then Prime Minister outwards and downwards. Cameron is reported to have said in his initial response to the outbreak of disorder: 'I have this very clear message to those people who are responsible for this wrongdoing and criminality: you will feel the full force of the law' and subsequently stated that 'anyone convicted should expect to go to jail' (quoted in Lamble 2013: 578–79).

Following the riots, over 3,000 people were charged on related criminal matters over the next year. These were typically conventional criminal charges, but the response of the judiciary was one 'of quite stunning harshness' (Jefferson 2015: 15), with 70 per cent of those appearing before magistrates being remanded to custody and a similar figure being imprisoned and for periods of time often considerably longer than 'normal'. The 'spectacular show of criminal justice might' evidenced by the police and legitimised by the courts' actions, supported by agencies such as the Crown Prosecution Service represented both a reassertion of coercive power and a parallel attempt to coordinate a legitimisation of its use. Although Sim (2012) has argued that excessively severe sentencing of the kind seen in this instance might actually undermine the legitimacy of the justice system, it could also be argued that it was actually operating to reinforce the narrative that the riots represented an extreme form of criminality and thus needed to be dealt with accordingly:

> these punitive responses were consistently framed as rational and appropriate responses to the 'mindless criminality' that had emerged on the streets. In doing so, the government was able to cloak its own class anxieties … These [responses] were the hallmarks of a civilized outrage … This was the riotous behaviour of the elite classes, who mete out legally sanctioned modes of violence while naming it otherwise.
>
> Lamble 2013: 583

Therefore, from a critical perspective, the process of criminalising those who represent a specific threat to the social order, serves to support the exercise of a particular form of legitimised authority; against a sub-group of the population largely comprising young, black, and poor people (Jefferson 2015).

Crimes of the privileged

One of the additional consequences of the hegemonic enterprise, according to the critical perspective on punishment, is that it deflects attention from the crimes of

those in positions of power and dominance, whether these be influential individuals, corporations, or even states themselves. The scope of such wrongful behaviours is enormously wide, but what they have in common is that they are rarely treated as criminal actions, and equally rarely is any attempt made to bring perpetrators to some form of justice. Here, one apparent exception might be war crimes where there is well-developed machinery in place to hold those responsible to account.

In this context, it is worth noting that the estimates of the level of harm caused in the course of conflict suggest that extraordinarily high numbers of people are victimised as a result of 'armed conflict and state-sponsored aggression … Approximately 191 million people lost their lives to collective violence in the twentieth century, more than half of whom were civilians' (Hoyle and Zedner 2007: 469). It is also noted here that an estimated 70 per cent of those who have been casualties in recent wars have been non-combatants, mostly women and children (2007: 467).

In some instances, the crimes associated with these shocking figures are acknowledged and action taken, although the international methods for dealing with war crimes have also been subject to criticism.

The Lieber Code and war crime tribunals

The Lieber Code ('Lieber Instructions') was introduced during the American Civil War by Francis Lieber of Columbia College in New York (see **Figure 27.3**). The code was established to set limits to the behaviour of troops in the course of combat and to prevent the commission of atrocities in the pursuit of military action. The code was subsequently highly influential in setting the standard for further international development of binding rules of conduct for those engaged in formalised conflict. The Lieber Instructions led to the establishment of an international convention on the legal framework for the conduct of war, presented to an international conference in Brussels in 1874 and eventually leading to the agreement of the Hague Conventions on land warfare of 1899 and subsequently 1907 (see https://www.icrc.org/ihl/INTRO/110).

Thus, the history of the idea of war crimes and the attempt to codify legal frameworks for dealing with them stretches back around 150 years, and is associated with attempts to criminalise excessive behaviour on whichever side amongst those engaged in armed conflict. Since the formulation of the original Lieber Code, there has also been developed a substantial machinery for the administration of justice in relation to war crimes. Most notably, perhaps, the war crimes tribunals established at the end of the Second World War at Nuremberg (see **Figure 27.4**) and Tokyo have been widely recognised as a successful attempt to use formal penal mechanisms to punish those most centrally involved in war-related offences,

Figure 27.3 Francis Lieber
Source: Library of Congress Prints and Photographs Division, Brady-Handy Photograph Collection/Public domain

Figure 27.4 Nuremberg war crimes tribunal
Source: The Truman Library/Public domain

whilst at the same time enabling the countries involved (principally Germany and Japan) to re-establish peaceful democratic societies. Importantly, this was seen as a mechanism for bringing culpable *individuals* to account, rather than imposing drastic punishments on entire societies, with the negative consequences that were experienced, for example, following the First World War: 'Nuremberg initiated a process whereby individuals, as opposed to nation-states, were subject to criminal prosecution for the atrocities of war and violations of the laws of war' (Penrose 1999: 330).

It has been suggested that war crime tribunals have brought a sense of order and legitimate and impartial international authority to the process of holding perpetrators to account for extreme actions committed in the course of conflict, such as systematic mistreatment of the inhabitants of occupied territories and brutalities committed against prisoners of war. It has been concluded, for example, that: 'the experience of the two ad hoc International Criminal Tribunals for the former Yugoslavia and for Rwanda has proved constructive in many respects, despite the difficulties encountered and the weaknesses and flaws inherent in the two structures' (Tavernier 1997: 661). Although they are recognised as imperfect, war crimes tribunals are seen as a relatively recent development, whose flaws can be gradually addressed and eliminated over time as they gain more widespread endorsement and respect.

On the other hand, sceptics argue that these tribunals have proved inadequate to the task of delivering effective and consensual forms of justice in the aftermath of conflict, for a number of reasons. Firstly, it appears that the problem of 'enforcement' has not been effectively resolved; and as a result, any 'deterrent' potential of the tribunals has been diluted to the point of ineffectuality (Penrose 1999: 326). Although war crimes tribunals have certainly presided over the imposition of highly retributive punishments, it is said to be clear from the level of continuing conflict in the world that they have had no deterrent effect, and perhaps could not be expected to do so, given the nature of the hostilities and hatred which tend to fuel armed conflicts. Nor, though, are tribunals believed to do much to tackle the underlying causes of conflict, at least in part because their conventional, individualising approach to the administration of justice does nothing to address the deep-seated sources of antagonisms based on ethnic and religious differences, for example. Tribunals offer no implicit basis for healing wider social divisions and achieving reconciliation (as alternative approaches seek to do, as we shall see). And, further, it is suggested, unjustified faith in a relatively untested institution such as international tribunals might actually weaken the potential for other forms of conflict resolution to be initiated; thus leading to the question:

> Should the international community completely abandon ICTs [International Criminal Tribunals] in favour of purely political or local approaches to combating humanitarian atrocities? We do not presume to answer that question. What we do know is that it is dangerously naïve to ignore

the possibility that ICTs might not only lack any significant deterrence benefits, but might actually exacerbate conflicts in weak states.

> Ku and Nzelibe 2006: 833

And, of course, the additional problem for international tribunals, specifically those to do with conflict, is determining an agreed basis on which to operate, that is, finding a common definition for what constitutes a 'war crime', and determining the framework for taking legal action across state boundaries. This has been exemplified recently by the calls to hold Tony Blair and George Bush responsible for war crimes allegedly committed in their joint commitment to military action (and all that entailed) in Iraq (see **Controversy and debate 27.1**).

State crimes

In a similar vein, but outside the specific context of international military action, there are a range of other activities which are increasingly understood as constituting state crimes. This is usually seen in terms of unjustified use of surveillance, force, or restraint against its own (or foreign) citizens by agents of the state. As such, the recent imprisonment without trial of suspected terrorists in the detention camp at Guantanamo Bay by the US has been as a particularly high profile example.

For those who are critical of the excessive use of state powers, though, this can only be seen as part of a recurrent pattern of activity, more or less prevalent across regimes and political systems, where checks and balances against improper use of state power do not exist or fail to operate effectively.

Although this kind of misuse of power may well be more or less constant, concerns about the harms caused and the failure to hold those in authority to account tend to crystallise around key events which seem to typify state-sanctioned illegalities. The brutal suppression of demonstrations against the Vietnam War in Chicago in 1968 by the police is one such example which has remained a point of reference ever since (see **Figure 27.6**).

Similarly, in the UK, the apparent use of excessive force by police brought in from around the country in the course of the 1984–85 miners' strike also has powerful historical connotations.

> During the first few days of the strike, on 14 March 1984, ministers pressed Home Secretary Leon Brittan to get chief constables to adopt a 'more vigorous interpretation of their duties'. A clampdown followed that prevented pickets reaching the working coalfields of Nottinghamshire and Leicestershire in large numbers.

> *Channel 4 News*, 3 January 2014

CONTROVERSY AND DEBATE 27.1

'I will be with you, whatever'

A bombshell White House memo has revealed for the first time details of the 'deal in blood' forged by Tony Blair and George Bush over the Iraq War [see **Figure 27.5**].

The sensational leak shows that Blair had given an unqualified pledge to sign up to the conflict a year before the invasion started. Tony Blair wrote to George W Bush eight months before the invasion into Iraq, saying 'I will be with you, whatever'. This flies in the face of the Prime Minister's public claims at the time that he was seeking a diplomatic solution to the crisis. He told voters: 'We're not proposing military action'— in direct contrast to what the secret email now reveals.

Daily Mail, 17 October 2015

Based on what you know of the circumstances of the Iraq War, do you think that Blair and Bush could reasonably be prosecuted for 'war crimes'?

Figure 27.5 Blair and Bush meet in Washington
Source: Photo by Mark Wilson, Getty Images

Figure 27.6 Chicago policemen surround a crowd of anti-war protestors that were aggressively sent to the ground
Source: Ed Molinari/NY Daily News Archive via Getty Images

the use of coercive measures to maintain control. Althusser (1971) has described this distinction in terms of the twin elements of Ideological and Repressive State Apparatuses, which carry out complementary and mutually reinforcing functions—each one acting as justification and reinforcement for the other.

Importantly for the critical perspective, those who are victimised by these means have neither the physical capability nor the basis in legitimate authority to hold the alleged perpetrators of state crimes to account. It is only the diligence and persistence of determined investigators which are able to shed light on these events.

Crime and power

Viewing crime through a critical lens also leads us to consider the 'crimes of the powerful' (Pearce 1977) more broadly, both as a feature of the unfettered expansion of commercial interests, and as a reflection of efforts to distort systems of reward and resource distribution, as in the case of tax evasion (which is illegal) or avoidance (which is legal, but morally dubious).

In a sense, critical arguments see the 'crimes' of the powerful as the end point of a series of processes of the kind outlined above: that is, by defining, enforcing, and reporting 'crime' in a particular way, popular conceptions of what constitutes an offence and who are the offenders are constructed. This, in turn, creates space for a range of unacceptable and possibly criminal activity to be normalised, and taken for granted as routine and perhaps inevitable features of contemporary society (such as

The critical perspective would argue that this simply provides evidence of the alliance between the state and other powerful vested interests to reinforce the dominance of private and business interests over those of working people and their communities. Their position of control is maintained not principally by simple force, but through the process of constructing a logical and authoritative rationale for the preservation of the established social and institutional order. This, in turn, is generally sufficient to secure the consent of the general population and agreement to shared principles of law and order (see earlier). However, when the basis for consent fractures, the state and its allies resort to more basic means, and in particular attempts to avoid paying tax). And, further, by diverting attention onto a specific group of potential deviants, the 'hegemonic' (see Gramsci 1971) project of the powerful has also contrived to hide from view its own reputedly much greater crimes. This is captured, for example, in the point often made by critical commentators that much greater interest is taken in the relatively small amount of benefit fraud than in the comparably much larger sums involved in fraudulent business activity or questionable schemes to reduce tax liabilities. In both cases, it would seem, the public purse has been denied resources to which it is entitled, but the collective anger of the community and state enforcement activity seem only to be targeted in one direction—at the crimes of the poor (Cullis et al. 2015).

Once again, such evidence as has been assembled by critical commentators suggests that crimes of the powerful do have a similarly drastic impact, and yet lead to uncertain and at best only partial attempts at enforcement action. The implausibility of lone culprits being responsible for major stock market frauds seems obvious (Bruce 2007), but this is typically the way in which the activities of Nick Leeson and others are portrayed (see Greener 2006, for example).

What is to be done about crime?

Critical solutions (1): truth and reconciliation

In light of the wide-ranging critical analyses of what is wrong with the ways in which the justice system conceptualises and responds to crime, it will be helpful to move on to consider the kind of solutions advocated by the critics. In this context, we will look at both radical alternatives to the organisation of responses to crime, and at those arguments which simply reject the notion of punishment and argue for a different way of thinking about and acting upon the social problems which 'crime' represents. Firstly, it may be helpful to reflect upon society-wide models for resolving conflicts which are conceived as 'collective' rather than individualised problems. This, in a sense, represents an extension of restorative justice principles into the wider arena; and it is largely represented in a range of models for delivering 'truth and reconciliation' in the aftermath of conflict.

Nations including South Africa, Northern Ireland, and Bosnia and Herzegovina are amongst those associated with country-wide, state-led attempts to resolve internal conflict and 'crimes' committed by one section of the population against another. These are often associated with the historic legacy of colonisation or invasion, resulting in the overwhelming dominance of one section of the community by another, possibly on grounds of religion, ethnicity, or nationality (or a combination of these). Such dominance has often also been associated with routinised exploitation, oppression, everyday violence, and brutality. There is therefore a very substantial legacy of blame, guilt, and culpability to be addressed when the period of domination ends. It is for this reason that states and communities have sought to find a coherent and negotiated process for resolving the strong feelings and hostilities associated with this history, without resort to acts of counterviolence or revenge. As such, this offers an alternative mode of conflict resolution to those based on conventional processes of fault-finding, the attribution of guilt, and imposition of punitive sanctions.

The Truth and Reconciliation Commission (TRC) for South Africa (see **Figure 27.7**), for example, sat for seven years from 1995–2002, hearing testimony from victims of conflict during the apartheid regime, and considering requests for amnesty from those responsible for harm in the same period. As well as determining levels of compensation and recommending further political and social reforms: 'The TRC encouraged victims, offenders, and the community to be directly involved in resolving conflict. In its quest to make peace with the past, the TRC looked at the restorative dimension of both traditions in South Africa: the Judeo-Christian tradition and African traditional values of *Ubuntu …*' (Vora and Vora 2004: 306). The commission effectively acted as an umbrella for a painstaking and highly detailed exercise in allowing those affected by the previous regime to express themselves and,

Figure 27.7 The Truth and Reconciliation Commission press conference
Source: Eye Ubiquitous/Alamy Stock Photo

where they wished for it, to seek redress (or absolution). Many of the mechanisms for encouraging dialogue and achieving change remained in place following the completion of the commission's work, and it could therefore be argued that this approach to conflict resolution had a lasting impact.

On the other hand, as a number of commentators have observed, the process itself was significantly flawed in a number of respects and its outcomes represented only a partial achievement of the goals to which it aspired (Vora and Vora 2004; Gibson 2005). The sheer scale of an initiative such as a commission to achieve reconciliation across an entire nation might be expected to involve constraints and limitations:

> All truth commissions might be considered compromises and deals worked out within the framework of political negotiations surrounding the transitions. South Africa was faced not only with a transition but also with an immense transformation from an oppressive minority-ruled racist regime to a democratic government.
>
> Vora and Vora 2004: 304

So, for instance, choices had to be made about whether or not to guarantee amnesty to those responsible for acts of oppression or barbarity during the apartheid era, which other reconciliation initiatives had done. In South Africa's case amnesty was not offered automatically but determined on the basis of representations made to the TRC, so perhaps reinserting conventional principles of individual responsibility and blame into the process.

Interestingly, the rationale for making amnesty conditional seemed to be that this offered a greater incentive for those concerned to tell the truth about their own unlawful actions. In the event, what seemed like a pragmatic compromise emerged, whereby many of those applying for amnesty were denied it, but were not subsequently prosecuted either (Wilson 2001: 562). At the very least, the introduction of a mechanism designed to align the discovery of uncomfortable truths and at the same time to achieve reconciliation appears to represent a challenge to prior understandings of the place of prosecution and due process in the search for justice: 'On the one hand the revelation of the truth in sufficient details may lead to calls for, and may even be designed with a view to, prosecution. On the other hand, the cathartic, or liberating, effect of revealing the truth and the pursuit of reconciliation may lead to arguments against prosecution' (O'Shea 2008: para. 24).

The South African TRC is seen as an exemplar because of its sheer scale, and as a result, considerable effort has gone into assessing both its character and its achievements. Did it in reality represent a genuinely different way of 'doing justice'? And, if it did, to what extent can it be seen as having achieved its fundamental objectives

in retrospect? Both are, of course, highly significant questions in relation to any attempt to replicate this model of resolving crime elsewhere. As Gibson (2009: 124) notes, there is certainly a considerable degree of belief in the capacity of truth commissions to 'contribute to the development of a rule-of-law culture that respects human rights' and 'advance political tolerance'; and this perhaps accounts for their increasingly widespread international use: 'The world has clearly registered its opinion about the desirability and effectiveness of truth commissions. From South Korea to Peru, truth commissions (and functionally equivalent institutions) have been established as a means of addressing historical injustices' (Gibson 2009: 123).

As Gibson (2005: 356) concludes elsewhere, the evidence does suggest that there is potential value in attempts such as this to achieve truth and reconciliation, because it creates a forum for dialogue and mutual understanding which does not involve a struggle for dominance in terms of either ideas or material power. Gibson's extensive survey of public opinion in South Africa led him to the conclusion that: 'Perhaps the most important achievement of the truth and reconciliation process … is that all racial groups have come to see the past in equivocal terms, not as a struggle between absolute good and infinite evil' (Gibson 2005: 355).

Although the structures and processes which characterise the 'peace process' in Northern Ireland are rather different, it is also widely recognised as a 'model' for post-conflict reconciliation between hostile communities (Hughes 2015). It is noted that the process of continuing dialogue and essentially piecemeal negotiation gained widespread international approval, including from US Presidents. In criminal justice terms, the process crucially involved initially setting aside any previous acts of wrongdoing, and 'talking to terrorists. … It was a case of building peace from the extremes rather than from the moderate centre ground' (Hughes 2015: 247). Important, too, was the role of external interested parties in establishing the basis for dialogue and acting in a mediating role where necessary. The role of George Mitchell as the US mediator in the initial stages of peace-building is viewed as pivotal. The promotion of mediated dialogue also, of course, is central to the principles and practices of restorative justice. Hughes notes, too, that as in the case of South Africa, lessons from Northern Ireland were subsequently applied elsewhere, in attempts to resolve ethnic and religious confrontations in Sri Lanka and Iraq, for example (Hughes 2015: 248). As well as the promotion of dialogue, Northern Ireland saw the initiation of 'a de facto amnesty for perpetrators', and the establishment of a well-funded mechanism for the support of victims' groups and the promotion of their distinctive interests (Hughes 2015: 266). But for Hughes and others, there are concerns about the extent to which high-level claims about the effectiveness of new models of peace-building and reconciliation accurately reflect a more complex and uncertain reality. McGrattan (2012), for example, argues that in both Northern Ireland and Bosnia and Herzegovina, there is less evidence of open dialogue and mutual engagement between opposing interests than of a kind of institutionalised co-existence, with little significant exchange. In consequence, reordered institutional structures whilst giving the appearance of integrated and collaborative models of governance, instead merely cement in place existing divisions:

> the consociational structures of governance in each case reflect and, arguably, reproduce the segregation that characterizes everyday life.
>
> McGrattan 2012: 103

Consociational democracy can be found in countries that are deeply divided into distinct religious, ethnic, racial, or regional segments— which may create conflicts unfavourable for achieving stable government. Others, too, have recognised the complex and shifting nature of debates and experiences of 'transitional justice' (Nagy 2013; Skaar 2013) and the consequent challenges of making sense of partially-achieved aspirations. Skaar (2013: 10) acknowledges that academic understandings of what is involved in pursuing justice in post-conflict situations is continually evolving, and that an initial 'focus on retributive justice has' been extended 'to include other elements such as forgiveness, healing and reconciliation'. This, however, has meant that evaluating practical achievements against these criteria has remained an uncertain task.

At the same time, the sheer diversity of lived experiences and localised variations in implementation have made it very difficult to establish common core elements of reconciliation processes and transitional justice. As Skaar (2013: 47) comments, even the term 'justice' itself has generated a range of interpretations in this context: 'forward-looking justice, backward-looking justice, retributive justice, restorative justice, retroactive justice, reparatory justice, administrative justice, local justice, traditional justice, historical justice, and more'.

Nagy (2013) comments, too, on the complexities of translating uncertain understandings of a novel process into an established institutional framework, in the Canadian context. The Canadian Truth and Reconciliation Commission was established in 2006 to address the unresolved issues of oppression and harm associated with the Indian residential school system imposed on the country's indigenous people from the 19th century until 1996. In reflecting on the impacts of this aspect of colonial activity, Nagy acknowledges the potential value of the commission in enabling evidence to be heard and victims' accounts and claims to be validated; but at the same time,

she identifies significant limitations to the process, where it is limited in scope to resolving 'legal-political' issues, rather than promoting 'social justice': 'The most strenuous objection is that the pacifying' language of reconciliation helps to allay white guilt while deflecting responsibility for the 'broader harms perpetrated against Indigenous Peoples' (Nagy 2013: 53).

We might conclude, therefore, that the notion of 'truth and reconciliation' as establishing a distinctive framework for the delivery of justice on a society-wide and collective level is obviously both attractive and has prompted innovative structures and processes for resolving deeply-felt historic harms. At the same time, however, both supporters and critics have identified a range of understandably deep-rooted challenges to the effective implementation of programmes designed to achieve 'transitional justice'. Not least, as Nagy (2013: 52) observes, implementation necessarily occurs within a pre-existing institutional context, where embedded interests may wish to set limits to what is known and what is done about past injustices.

Critical solutions (2): community justice

Often grounded in similar historical experiences and traditions, forms of 'community justice' share significant characteristics with transitional justice. Underlying the notion of community justice is the belief that it is better to allow solutions to harm and disorder to emerge from the collective wisdom and wishes of those most directly affected, rather than hiving off responsibility to some distant and potentially disinterested administrative arm of the state. Northern Ireland is again an interesting starting point for a discussion of community-based offence resolution processes, because of its acknowledgement of these as a component of the wider peace-building project; but, also, because its experience is similarly viewed as a potential model for adoption elsewhere.

McEvoy and Mika (2002) have charted the emergence of community-based restorative justice in Northern Ireland, identifying its emergence as an alternative way of practising justice in direct contrast to the similarly 'community-based' legacy of 'beatings, shootings and exclusions by paramilitary organisations as a response to local crime and anti-social behaviour' (Mika 2006: i). Thus, the notion of 'community' was not idealised, but seen as a site of active engagement for projects designed to promote a more cohesive and integrative approach to dealing with the problems associated with unacceptable behaviour in localities.

The work of dedicated projects in Northern Ireland, philanthropically funded and promoting an 'alternative' justice model (Chapman 2012), is seen as crucial to the reported successes of community justice (Mika 2006). In this case, the model depended on establishing a credible local forum for engaging all parties to the reported offence, including paramilitary organisations which still held a degree of authority in the area, and negotiating an appropriate response. Importantly, the emphasis on voluntarism and agreed solutions was central to the process and, in this sense, it represented a more radical form of restorative practice than is sometimes achieved under the auspices of conventional justice systems:

> In conducting its work, Northern Ireland Alternatives subscribes to published principles of good practice, including an inclusive approach, non-violence, confidentiality, responsiveness to community needs, child protection, voluntary participation, accountability and transparency, a holistic approach, rights of the individual, value of the individual, a person-centred approach, human rights, working within the rule of law, and evaluation.
>
> Mika 2006: 9

The importance of genuine community ownership of the process is emphasised, and although these were project-based initiatives, so did not emerge spontaneously from the local context, it became clear that they had provided a catalyst for a broader re-shaping of the life of the community. The evaluation of the Northern Ireland projects' work concluded that they quickly became recognised as 'essential community assets' (Mika 2006: 28). Despite these initial achievements, concerns have subsequently been raised about the 'co-option' of community justice in Northern Ireland, and the consequent risks of actually undermining 'its capacity for maintaining social cohesion and for socialising young people' (Chapman 2012: 587).

Nonetheless, certainly at their inception, the community justice initiatives in Northern Ireland exemplified some of the key attributes associated with community justice which are taken to set it apart from more conventional, top down and adversarial models. In particular, this form of justice needs to be grounded in the networks, relationships, and shared beliefs of those in the locality concerned; its processes need to be participatory, consensual, and open; all those with an interest need to be able to contribute to the process and have their voices heard; doubts or uncertainties must be aired; support is to be provided for anyone who needs help in stating their views; outcomes need to be agreed, fair, and reasonable; and the resolution decided upon needs to be seen as the end of the matter.

Contemporary models of community justice are often seen as deriving from traditional or indigenous forms of social practice, which commonly assume some element of negotiated and collectively-sanctioned resolution of conflict or harm. These include the 'family group conference' derived from Maori dispute resolution traditions in New Zealand/Aotearoa, which were then incorporated into law in that country in 1989; and 'sentencing circles' which originate in the 'traditional sanctioning and healing practices of Canadian Aboriginal peoples and indigenous peoples in the Southwestern United States', according to Bazemore (1997: 26; and see **Chapter 26** on restorative justice). Circle sentencing, too, received a modern-day revitalisation in Canada in the 1990s. Sentencing circles are described as a supportive vehicle for the expression of strong feelings about the offence and harms caused; for achieving a degree of 'healing of the offender, victim, and community'; but also as a means of reasserting 'social control through help and support' (Wilson et al. 2002)—a form of 'tough love', it would seem.

Bazemore, though, makes a clear distinction between a 'one-dimensional definition of community justice' (1997: 28), which simply consisted of changing the location of justice services, introducing greater informality or increasing the flexibility of arrangements; and forms of practice which would substantively 'change the role of neighbourhood residents from service recipients to decision makers with a stake in, or feeling of ownership in' the process of determining outcomes and engaging with criminal justice intervention (Bazemore 1997: 28). Similar views are aired by Weaver (2011) who also stresses the importance of active community engagement in justice processes if they are to have substantive meaning and offer a real sense of involvement for people affected by localised experiences of conflict and harm. For Weaver, the principle of 'co-production' of just outcomes is of central importance. Recognising that communities are not only harmed by crimes, but also may be the focal point of the 'ills that provoke it' (Weaver 2011: 1052), she argues that community justice should be a vehicle for promoting genuine dialogue about the offence and its origins; and at the same time a vehicle for all parties to consider what they might contribute to 'the process of change' (2011: 1052).

Karp and Clear (2000) sought to develop a 'conceptual framework' for community justice, recognising its emergence as a distinctive strand of ideas and practice in the criminal justice arena. The integrative goals and achievements of justice delivered for and by communities are seen as the most important feature of the 'community justice ideal', as they put it. They note the potential for communities to be able to act autonomously to address the problems associated with crime; and they stress the rejection 'of punishment as a sanctioning philosophy' (Karp and Clear 2000: 325). Community justice is believed to offer a vehicle for unifying different ideological perspectives in linking their shared concerns to promote public safety and the quality of communal life. Key elements of the community justice model are: its neighbourhood focus; its problem-solving ethos; the diffusion and decentralisation of authority; prioritisation of the quality of community life as an outcome; and the direct involvement of citizens themselves in the justice process.

These aspects of the model are in turn underpinned by a series of operating principles which are 'democratic' and 'egalitarian'. Community justice is thus seen as participatory and equalising in the sense that it factors differences between participants into the frameworks and processes for achieving just and agreed outcomes. Importantly, then, the background characteristics of offenders are recognised; and at the same time, justice interventions seek to promote inclusion:

> A community justice approach favours public safety but rejects the simplistic claim that removal of the 'bad guys' is the core strategy for solving community safety problems. Residents existing on the margins of community life are potential resources for community development. The challenge is not to isolate as many dubious residents as possible but to find ways to include as many community members as possible in efforts to improve … quality of life.
>
> Karp and Clear 2000: 335

The principle of inclusion implies that offenders should also be actively engaged in the process of resolving the problems associated with crimes, including 'having a say' (Weaver 2011: 152) in how the offence should be dealt with and what forms of response—rehabilitation, reparation, or punishment—are most appropriate. By implication, too, this also modifies conventional assumptions about guilt and responsibility, which become understood more in collective terms, with the focus on building community cohesion and creating opportunities for mutual benefit, rather than fault-finding and exacting punitive sanctions.

Indeed, some would take the argument even further to suggest that 'crime' is not the starting point for thinking about community justice. In other words, it is the creation of effective relationships and working models for problem solving which establishes the basis for dealing with problematic behaviour or harm when it occurs. Community justice, then, is not just a mechanism or a technique, but depends on a form of social organisation that is embedded in a wider network of positive relationships and underlying trust (Blagg 2009). Criticising the limitations of 'traditional' justice systems, Gilbert and Settles (2007: 5) also advocate a community justice approach because 'crime is a deeply embedded social problem', involving complex and conflicting needs. In this context, it is very much local knowledge and locally-based relationships which can underpin effective responses to any breakdown of the social order, in their view.

Chantrill's (1998) depiction of the establishment of a community justice programme in Kowanyama, Queensland nicely captures the idea of the community wresting space for its own distinctive approach from government, partly because the community already felt detached and of little interest to the centralised state authorities. As a result, aboriginal traditions of mediation, offence resolution, and prevention were incorporated into, and often usurped, conventional adversarial and hostile criminal justice practices. Chantrill (1998: 55) concluded that this was not simply a matter of 'returning' to traditional ways, but setting out a new model for the administration of justice in a changing social context, which was crucially informed by those traditions and in which local community members and interests retained leading roles. In other words, community justice was here, as elsewhere, very much about establishing legitimacy and authority for the measures adopted to deal with and resolve harms associated with unacceptable behaviour; and the benefits associated with more appropriate justice outcomes also extended into 'broader community development processes that are making Kowanyama a safer and better place to live' (Chantrill 1998: 55). This particular form of community justice initiative has subsequently been recognised as offering substantial benefits, and has become more or less institutionalised within the wider governance framework (Ryan et al. 2006).

Critical solutions (3): abolitionism

The final strategy we shall consider here that is associated with a radical or critical perspective is essentially captured by the term 'abolitionism'. The abolitionists' aim is to seek an end to the use of penal sanctions in the administration of criminal justice and the decommissioning of the mechanisms and institutions by which what they see as a partial form of justice is imposed. Prisons, for example, should simply be shut down (Sim 2009: 153).

As this implies, abolitionists argue that any attempt to respond to crime by way of a punitive intervention is unacceptable. Instead, we should be concerned first and foremost with the conditions under which the alleged offence takes place, the means by which it comes to be defined as a crime, and the organisation and delivery of mechanisms of control. It is not enough just to think in terms of a neutral system for identifying and dealing with crime; rather, we should see a judicial framework built on principles of individual accountability and guilt as a political vehicle for the regulation and maintenance of the social order. It is the system itself which should be problematised, both in general terms and in respect of the practices it puts in place. Any criminal justice intervention initiated under these conditions is therefore considered to be inherently biased in some way, resulting in inappropriate or disproportionate outcomes for those adjudged to be offenders. This is to disregard the socially constructed nature of the justice system and the collective responsibility of the members of society for the offence.

Abolitionism therefore fundamentally rejects the rationale on which conventional forms of intervention and adjudication of the offender take place. It takes this position irrespective of the rationale on which intervention is based, whether this be punitive, rehabilitative, deterrent, or restorative. Whichever of these applies, they share a common concern with determining individual responsibility and putting measures in place which are directed at influencing, changing, or controlling offender behaviour. Instead, the efforts of those concerned with rights and social justice should be directed towards opposing the imposition of sanctions based on this narrow framing of criminality. Both the response of the system and the underlying rationale of the justice system should come into question. There is no scope for negotiating or modifying the impacts of the justice process; instead, the only valid position, it is argued, is to oppose those sanctions for which it is responsible, especially those which involve the denial of liberty. There is thus no scope for compromise positions, such as those adopted by proponents of 'alternatives' to punishment, simply because these offer implicit justifications for the underlying penal logic. Mathiesen (1974) has thus argued that it is important not to enter into negotiations with the existing system of justice over making improvements to penal facilities. To take this sort of position would simply be to collude with the discourse of individualised blame and punishment. Abolitionists are unapologetic about taking this kind of apparently 'extreme' position. The grounds for taking an abolitionist position may vary. It is possible, for instance, to oppose the imposition of punishment of certain kinds, or in general, primarily on the grounds that it is ineffective, and even counter-productive; that is, it is opposed on practical grounds and on the basis that it does not 'work'. On the other hand, the use of penal sanctions may be opposed on more principled grounds, in the sense that the aims and ethos of punishment are essentially inhumane and therefore unacceptable.

Consistent with the former line of argument, attention could be drawn to the absence of any real evidence to support the effectiveness of any particular form of punishment, including custody, despite the well-known claim by a former Home Secretary, Michael Howard, that 'prison works' (this phrase featured prominently in a speech made by Michael Howard to the Conservative party conference in 1993). Bianchi (1994: 337), for example, takes

an abolitionist position, at least partly on the grounds of the inherent problems associated with the imposition of compulsory measures of punishment. 'Even the docile convict', he argues, is unable to make any meaningful contribution to (her or) 'his own social salvation', because s/he has no say in the administration of the punishment imposed and must simply accept the harmful 'stigma' associated with it. So, the recipient of punishment is denied any role in putting things right, and instead must accept a permanent stain on her/his character.

Not only is punishment harmful in this respect, but Bianchi also argues that it has demonstrably failed to achieve any of the other positive outcomes claimed for it, such as therapeutic healing or rehabilitation. In effect, because of their misleading claims to do good: 'Adaptation and therapy programmes have even strengthened the destructive power of the criminal law system' (Bianchi 1994: 338). Penal measures are thus called into question to the extent that they fail to meet many of the positive claims advanced for them; there is little or no evidence to suggest that they have any rehabilitative effect; they do not offer an effective deterrent; and they provide no opportunity to make amends. Indeed, in many ways, it could be suggested that punishment is more likely to escalate than reduce offending. As a consequence, it might seem simply a rational economic argument to suggest that the very substantial investment of money and human resources into prisons and other penal facilities might be better directed elsewhere, into social prevention measures, for example. Although cautious about the risks of co-option into the system and thereby reinforcing it, Bianchi (1994: 345) does offer some possible indicators of alternatives which might be supportive of the abolitionist principle, such as 'neighbourhood centres' to resolve minor local disputes and harms. It is likely, though, that others such as Mathiesen (1974: 211) would take issue with this, on the grounds that most such changes would run the risk of being 'absorbed by ... the main system', consolidating support for it. So, for example, the alternatives to custody movement in the UK led to practitioners being 'held responsible' (Mathiesen 1974: 20) for the administration of the new arrangements, and thus by extension maintaining the justifications underpinning the existing and continuing punishment regime.

A stronger version of the argument against punishment is that based in the principle that deliberate imposition of harm, on whatever grounds, is wrong. It is not sufficient to establish a system for arbitration and determination of just deserts, no matter how fair in principle, because it is simply not the role of the state to allow or authorise the infliction of hurt on any of its citizens, even where they have themselves already caused harm.

According to this line of reasoning, the imposition of any form of punishment is viewed as morally unjustifiable, and an unacceptable expression of primal instincts of revenge and vindictiveness. In other words, those responsible for seeking and imposing punishments are in effect no different from the perpetrators of an offence, especially if we are to accept that offences are socially contextualised and socially constructed. The principle of 'an eye for an eye' is rejected by the abolitionists, who argue instead for a spirit of tolerance and forgiveness in the administration of criminal justice. So, both the avoidance of negative outcomes such as the infliction of pain, and the promotion of more harmonious human relationships through the expression of forgiveness and reconciliation are associated with the aim of ending the use of state-sanctioned punishments. The abolitionist, therefore, rejects the retributivist position on the basis that it is morally unacceptable. There is no place for the imposition of harm for its own sake.

Wider justifications are also sought for the abolitionist position in the acknowledgement of the inherent injustices embedded in the justice system, to the extent that it reflects and reproduces wider social inequalities, through institutional discrimination, for example. The justification for abolitionism is thus not simply humanist, grounded in moral arguments, but also material, in that it actually supports wider political aspirations, such as social justice. If fairness is viewed as a fundamental requirement of legal systems and criminal processes, then institutional practices which operate unfairly should be brought to an end, according to this logic.

For proponents of abolitionism, however, there has been relatively limited scope to make progress in practical terms, given its limited popular appeal. However, one example of an attempt to bring the use of custody to an end has been initiated in relatively recent times, and this was the 'Massachusetts experiment' whereby the recently appointed head of the Department of Youth Services, Jerome Miller, shut down all penal establishments for young people in the state in 1971 and 1972. Instead, a range of genuine alternatives was put in place of custody, under a global policy of 'deinstitutionalisation'. Importantly for the success of this policy, Miller did not enter into a process of negotiation with the existing penal structures, but simply used his authority to close them down, despite resistance; and without having instituted a process of establishing a range of 'alternatives' first. In this sense, his actions complied with the expectations of abolitionists. Interestingly, too, the deinstitutionalisation policy has remained largely in place in Massachusetts over the intervening period. Of course, it could be argued that the success of the scheme itself was limited. Much of the machinery of justice was unaffected by the reform, and an array of alternative forms of penal sanction remained in place; the policy only applied to young offenders and not adults; and the Massachusetts experience has not gained support more widely.

On the other hand, it has been possible to claim that the initiative has not led to an increase in crime levels; it did result in the establishment of new ways of dealing with youth crime, some of which were influential in the UK; and it did generate improved outcomes for those young people no longer subject to punitive regimes (Krisberg and Austin 1993; Jones 2012).

Aside from this example, the abolitionist case has typically been advanced more in the pursuit of policy change and targeted campaigns of opposition, focusing on the adverse and harmful effects of penal regimes on many of those who experience them—prison, essentially, has been the principal target. Sim (2009) has argued that abolitionism need not simply be about expressing 'opposition' (Mathiesen 1974: 14), but has also been associated with a series of positive developments in theory and practice with demonstrable concrete outcomes. The abolitionist campaigning group established in 1970, Radical Alternatives to Prison (RAP), is highlighted as being very active in pursuing targeted short-term reforms, such as the ending of the use of drugs as tools to control behaviour, and an end to the use of solitary confinement. In this case, and more widely, Sim appears to endorse a movement from a purist position of simply rejecting the idea of penal sanctions, especially prison, to one which takes an activist approach to make the prison 'more effective, responsive and accountable' (Sim 2009: 11).

This is somewhat at odds with the position taken by Mathiesen in 1974 on the publication of his highly influential book *The Politics of Abolition*. Here he argued that abolitionism must necessarily pursue a path of pure opposition, setting out its principles in their own right, and not simply as a counter-argument to the established justice system. Abolitionism, therefore should be thought of in terms of the 'unfinished'; that is, as a continuous questioning of conventional penal assumptions and practices, rather than seeking to find an accommodation with these at any point: 'The alternative is "alternative" in so far as it is not based on the premises of the old system, but on its own premises, which at one or more points *contradict* those of the old system' (Mathiesen 1974: 13). Being unpopular and being dismissed as idealist is suggested as a necessary price to pay in order to sustain the integrity of those arguments which, in the end, are likely to be particularly influential and actually secure important changes in penal policy. See **Conversation 27.1** with Thomas Mathiesen for a view from one of the principal architects of 'abolitionism'.

CONVERSATIONS 27.1

Abolition—with Thomas Mathiesen

'Abolition', and 'to abolish', means 'to erase', 'get rid of'. 'Abolitionism' is a word covering the movements dedicated to the abolition of an institution or a sentiment which is considered immoral or politically wrong. It is opposed to but also akin to 'reform', which means to change and make a situation better without really getting rid of it.

Reforms at times develop into abolitions—one moves from attempts to make a situation better to getting rid of it. An example would be slavery, which in several places started out as attempts to improve the conditions of slaves, but later moved to an abolitionist stance to slavery. But the opposite development, where an abolitionist stance moves to a reformist stance, also takes place.

Historically, five examples may be mentioned: the death penalty; slavery; segregation of populations based on race; torture; and imprisonment have been goals of abolitionism.

The death penalty, slavery, and racist segregations

In many parts of the world, *the death penalty* has increasingly been met by an abolitionist stance, whereby it has receded in importance. An example would be the USA. *Slavery* is also an example, again in the USA, where it today is forbidden. *Racist segregation of the population for example in schools* is a third example. In the USA, the abolition of segregation in schools was prompted by a long political and moral debate, and finally took place in the 1960s. US president John F. Kennedy was among the politically active politicians. These abolitions are regularly met and strengthened by new legal standards of human rights and equality before the law. But the movement against racist segregation has also in part been reversed by popular political opinion/resistance groups. The conditions creating such popular political opinions are complex.

Torture

Torture, for example during interrogation, is now forbidden under most conditions in countries where the rule of law has a strong standing. But a long abolitionist struggle took place before we reached this stage. Unfortunately, torture is still widespread in some parts of the world and among some population groups, but at times secretly and in hiding.

Imprisonment

Imprisonment is our final example. Here I will go into some detail. Popular groups exist in western countries

Source: Photo by Astrid Renland

such as Norway, England, and the USA, which have abolition of imprisonment as a goal. In connection with abolition of imprisonment, several questions are regularly raised.

A point of departure is that in the Western world, some prisons (in some places many prisons) have very detrimental conditions for the prisoners. Is all imprisonment, then, to be abolished? Some people for various reasons answer 'yes' to this question, but there are also several other answers to it. The answers are often that some of the poor prisons, with bad conditions, should be abolished, but not all of them, and—more radically—while imprisonment has to be used for some very dangerous and repetitive criminals, it may be abolished for large groups of the prison population.

The latter question in turn raises the issue of prediction, which is hotly debated among psychiatrists, psychologists, and criminologists. It also raises the question of alternatives to prison, such as *conflict resolution boards* and *new technological inventions* such as electronic fetters.

Conflict resolution boards is an entirely different type of reaction than prison, where the point is that the lawbreaker and the victim meet with a third party—a moderator—to discuss the issue and find the best reaction. Discussions may be long. But they often lead to fruitful results. To be sure, it perhaps does not fit all offenders, and some offences do not have clear cut victims. But it may be used much more widely than today, and reduce prison populations very sizeably.

Modern electronic fetters may be used while the law breaker stays at home instead of in prison. There are also several other attempts at finding alternatives to prison, which exist or are being tried out.

And in fact, changes are taking place in connection with the use of prison in countries such as Sweden and the Netherlands, and even in the USA, which has the largest prison population in the western world. Sweden in fact now has some empty prisons, and prison populations are at least receding a little in some parts of the USA.

Of course, such developments may be caused by a decreasing crime rate in the countries concerned. But the development is much more likely to be caused by the political situation and climate in the outside society. Norway has recently had a more or less constant crime rate or a crime rate which is increasing only for some crimes. Yet Norway has in recent years had a sizeable increase in the number of prisoners (from 44 per 100,000 population in 1980 to 73 per 100,000 population in 2010 (Scott 2013)), partly due to longer sentences and the political climate in the community. Norway in fact exports a sizeable proportion of its prisoners to the Netherlands, which has vacant prison facilities! Some of the Norwegian increase could have been solved by a minor reduction of prison sentences.

Further questions along the same line are at times raised, such as: are new technological inventions, such as electronic fetters or surveillance of various kinds, any better than prisons? Some of the movements which started out as abolitionist movements have for reasons of such questions ended as critical reformist movements, emphasising vital reforms—improvements of various kinds in living conditions—for prisoners.

A further question is that of the effectiveness of prisons. In many places and under many conditions, recidivism—a relapse to prison after release—is high, and has been a very important argument for abolitions or critical reform.

Social change

Finally, I briefly wish to mention *social change* (or perhaps better, societal change), which may be caused by a more or less abolitionist stance, or by more or less reformist opinions. This is an important historical question.

The Chinese revolution, which ended in a victory in 1949 and the escape of Chang Kai Chek and his forces to Formosa (now Taiwan), is an example of the former.

Another, different example is Norway, which in the first part of the 1900s had quite a radical labour party, but then quickly entered a long reformist stage before and after World War II, with a social democratic welfare state and welfare law as the main goal.

But the further questions concerning broad social change belong to a different order and are not discussed further here.

Suggested further reading

Thomas Mathiesen (2015): *The Politics of Abolition Revisited*, Routledge.
Thomas Mathiesen (2005): *Prison on Trial*, 3rd edn, Waterside.
David Scott (2015): *Why Prison?*, Cambridge University Press.

Thomas Mathiesen, Norwegian sociologist

Limitations of critical perspectives on punishment

Of course, it is in the nature of criminological argument that the positions we take prompt criticism; but the critics themselves must be prepared for yet further counter-arguments. For those adopting critical perspectives on punishment, and what might be termed 'mainstream' criminological thought, the challenges they encounter are essentially of two kinds: that they go too far, on the one hand; and that they do not go far enough, on the other.

Absence of practical solutions

Much doubt is cast on critical commentators for the absence of practical answers they offer. Critical criminology is often viewed as idealistic and unrealistic in its aspirations. Lea (1999) suggests, for example, that there is a strand in critical criminological thinking which is influenced by radical historians' acknowledgement of 'social crime' as a form of political resistance to oppression, as in the 'Robin Hood legend' (Lea 1999: 309). Indeed, radical criminology has been called to account for its political leanings; and for allowing these to compromise its objectivity and integrity, with Walker (1974: 47), for example, describing supposedly critical criminologists as

being 'glamorous partisans'. As such, it seems the radicals were believed to be unconcerned with the practical implications and applications of academic analyses, and they were seen to be 'refusing to engage practically with the real public and private circumstances of criminal activity' (O'Brien and Penna 2007: 248). Some might respond that there is no such thing as a 'neutral' position in criminology, or any other academic discipline, and that the key question, following Becker (1967) is merely 'whose side are we on?', a position subsequently endorsed by Scraton (2002), among others.

Sykes (1974) would also have concurred with the suggestion that critical criminology did not have an obvious material or empirical basis, but was rather a matter of choice, originating from an existing perspective: 'In this sense, the viewpoint of critical criminology as it stands today probably cannot be said to be true or false. Rather, it is a bet on what empirical research and theoretical development in the field will reveal in the future' (Sykes 1974: 212). However, even though he thought this bet might be 'not a bad one', Sykes was also clear about some of his reservations. Critical criminology, he believed, was too ready to look for the worst and oversimplify complex patterns of social interaction in order to convey an impression of a deliberately stratified social system, with the criminal law and its processes acting simply as a vehicle for maintaining control on behalf of vested interests. That, in turn, led to a number of other problematic misreadings of the reality of crime and criminality, and a failure to recognise that there was a demonstrable relationship between official (state) accounts of crime and its impact, and the ways in which it was actually experienced in the daily lives of those affected: 'Persistent criminals or criminals considered serious may be singled out for the law's attention without reducing a criminal conviction to a mere label that has no connection with an objective reality' (Sykes 1974: 213).

Romanticising crime

This was the point recognised by the 'left realist' school of criminologists, emerging in the 1980s (see **Chapter 17**), some of whom such as Jock Young were effectively revising their own previous assumptions about the meaning and impact of 'crime'. Formulations of the origins of crime as some sort of product of an undeveloped and emerging radical consciousness were called into question. Doubt was cast on sympathetic interpretations of deviant activity, such as those associated with Quinney and others influenced by Marxist theory:

> Crime is ... an incomplete but not altogether mistaken response to a bad situation ... coming into active existence only by overcoming the resistance of inherited values and internalized sanctions.
>
> Quinney 1977: 99

Instead, a process of adjustment took place, whereby a 'romanticised' view of 'criminal as revolutionary' was progressively rethought, and supplanted by a recognition that 'crime' should be understood as a form of 'social harm' that 'negatively affects working class people's lives' (Pavlich, 1999, p. 33). Whilst still claiming to be 'of the left' and committed to progressive change, those associated with the left realist position were clearly prepared to accept crime at face value; so that 'the major task of radical criminology is to seek a solution to the problem of crime and that of a socialist policy is to substantially reduce the crime rate' (Young 1986: 28). In this way, the focus of attention for critical criminology shifted, towards what were described as the harms done to 'the most vulnerable members of capitalist societies' (Young 1986: 29).

Reifying crime—taking it at face value

This, though, leads to another form of criticism of critical and radical approaches; that they are unduly prepared to compromise with established criminological conventions, such as taking conventional definitions of 'crime' at face value: 'One need not deny the value of contesting neo-conservative "law and order" programs to see left realism's engagement with administrative criminology as variously compromising a commitment to critical practice' (Pavlich 1999: 34). By taking this approach, it is argued, critical criminologists have become virtually indistinguishable from the mainstream in their concern to find technical solutions to the (undoubtedly real and damaging) harms experienced by particular communities. And so, what might well be a perfectly legitimate concern with community safety and protecting those at risk has the effect of diverting attention from questions to do with the prior definition of what counts as crime and which offenders should be targeted for intervention. Feminists, for example, challenged the readiness of left realists to accept conventional definitions of crime because it risked failing to address the distinctive concerns of women and the gendered nature of crime and 'fear of crime' (Walklate 2004). So, too, criticisms could be levelled at radical perspectives which simply take crime for granted to the extent that the preoccupation with its effects on communities deflects attention from punishments and their consequences. In fact, conventional assumptions about the need to be 'tough on crime' become implicit elements of a 'left realist' position, at least to the extent that it was incorporated into Labour's criminal justice policy in the early 1990s (Blair 1993).

Thus, for many critical criminologists the concern is with what is not addressed as much as it is with deliberations over the legitimacy or otherwise of conventional understandings of crime. For example, the relative lack of attention paid to antisocial activities and corporate crime which do not routinely engender interest is a critical point for some commentators. In their discussion of corporate crime, Slapper and Tombs observe that there are many obstacles in the way of criminologists who wish to investigate this area of human activity, concluding that 'most of what constitutes criminological theorising has signally failed even to attempt to account for corporate offending' (1999: 110). They suggest that this may partly be related to criminology's concern to identify the 'pathological' and to seek explanations for behavioural abnormalities; whereas, in fact 'corporate crime is widespread and routine' (Slapper and Tombs 1999: 129). Corporate crime is a feature of normal organisational behaviour, and so cannot really be accounted for by theories of deviance, even those which have critical leanings, such as labelling theory. In this sense, then, criminology, no matter how critical or radical, does not have the 'explanatory power' (1999: 130) to account for the routine immoralities of corporate interests. As Tombs and Whyte (2009) have argued, this realisation prompts a re-evaluation of the relationships between distinctive interests, and the dynamics of power, both to organise things in their own favour, and to define other interests and activities as of less validity or of questionable legitimacy. In other words, it is this kind of analysis, in their view, which must precede any kind of discussion of crime and its effects, even as these are played out at the micro level in communities, which themselves are organised and lived according to the interests and wishes of those in dominant positions.

Reaching the limits of critical criminology

Tombs and Whyte's (2009) analysis of the interplay of state and corporate interests in the context of regulatory regimes and their enforcements conveys a sense of how these relationships operate in the construction and implementation of 'criminal justice' in one sphere of activity. In their view, there is a necessary relationship between the state and its institutions under capitalism, and the corporate sector, whose continuing legitimacy depends at least in part on the authority of the state itself. Theories which are essentially critical of the state on the grounds of its inadequate functioning, or even its co-option effectively overlook this symbiotic relationship between the two. Critical arguments which are concerned with inadequacies in the ways in which the state functions, or is misdirected, are still culpable of failing to understand its underlying rationale, which is to preserve the basis for capitalist accumulation and all the potential injustices which follow from that. In a complex formulation, Tombs and Whyte describe the process involved as creating a sense of 'externality—the positioning of the state in direct opposition to capital' in order to create an 'imaginary legal order' in which the state acts 'in the public interest' while actually still serving the purposes of capital (2009: 109). It could, indeed, be argued that the machinery of justice is conceptualised and constructed in ways which enable corporate interests to avoid being held culpable for their wrongdoing rather than facilitating this possibility.

In a way, this brings us full circle, back to the case of Bhopal, and the failure of conventional systems of national and international justice to hold those responsible to account over many years. Criticisms and campaigns which have focused principally on the failure of these mechanisms to work properly are held to fall short by this kind of argument from some radical criminologists. That is to say, they believe that the systems of justice available are themselves inherently geared to serving business interests and concealing or misrepresenting the inevitable consequences of capitalism in terms of human distress and harm: 'our analysis has attempted to indicate that in thinking about corporate crime and its regulation, what is really at issue is not "crime"—rather, it is an issue of state, corporate and class power' (Tombs and Whyte 2009: 115).

Barton and colleagues (2007: 199) conclude starkly that it is, in fact, an endemic problem for criminology that its 'structural relationship to the capitalist state ... can only be described as parasitical'. In this sense, criminology is constrained only to consider problems of order and disorder from within the confines of what they describe as a 'liberal conceptual framework'; no matter how progressive some of its insights and observations may appear, they seem to be bound by conventional concepts of individualised responsibility, guilt, and redemption. Thus, criminology must at all times, according to them, incorporate understandings of 'structurally embedded harm' into its 'consciousness' and incorporate these into its evidence-gathering and explanatory frameworks (Barton et al. 2007: 206). And so, they conclude:

> If the development of the critical criminological imagination is to play a part in escaping the straitjacket that criminology has created, then we have once again to think in terms of *social* justice rather than *criminal* [their emphasis] justice, to enhance, rather than undermine democratic and legal accountability, and to develop research agendas that provide the potential to challenge, rather than consolidate, the interests of the powerful.
>
> Barton et al. 2007: 211

Conclusion

This chapter has introduced a range of critical criminological perspectives which have illustrated a number of problematic aspects of conventional approaches to the study of criminal justice and offending behaviour. In various ways, these critical arguments have pointed towards the supposed need for radical overhaul, or even in some cases, the abolition of existing systems for delivering and maintaining law and order. However, critical perspectives, too, can be criticised; for being unrealistic, for underestimating the impact of crime on ordinary lives, and for failing to provide credible solutions to the problems they claim to identify.

SUMMARY

The chapter has addressed the following objectives as set out in the introduction:

- Explain what is meant by the idea of critical perspectives on punishment

We have considered a number of the problems identified with contemporary forms of punishment, such as their role in maintaining social control, and their unequal impact on different sectors of the population.

- Consider a range of critical perspectives on the justice system including the abolitionist position, social control theories, and transformative justice

The chapter has discussed the contribution of several key theorists of punishment and social control; it has provided a detailed account of the abolitionist position on punishment; and it has introduced several international examples of attempts to develop a form of post-conflict justice based on principles of dialogue and reconciliation.

- Identify the disparities in treatment between white, BME, and other sectors of the population in the criminal justice system

We have reviewed evidence on the disproportionate impact of policing and punishment on specific groups, including minority ethnic communities in particular.

- Explore how 'crimes of the powerful' and state crimes can remain unseen and unpunished

The chapter has explored some of the arguments suggesting that privileged and powerful interests are able to divert attention from their own crimes, and that this sometimes is also associated with the co-option and misuse of the apparently legitimate authority of the state.

- Evaluate radical responses to the problems associated with crime, such as truth and reconciliation, community justice, and abolitionism

A number of alternative perspectives on the definitions of crime and the organisation and delivery of criminal justice have been considered and critically analysed in light of their achievements and possible shortcomings.

- Analyse the limitations of critical analyses of crime and punishment

The chapter concludes by discussing a number of criticisms of critical perspectives themselves, such as the tendency of some to romanticise criminal behaviour, or their failure to offer practical solutions to the problems they identify.

REVIEW QUESTIONS

1. What are the distinguishing features of a critical perspective in criminology?

2. Can you identify some of the key theorists of social control and their contributions to criminological thinking?

3. Why might it be important to try and understand the 'crimes of the powerful'?

4. What do you think has been achieved by international efforts to promote truth and reconciliation?

5. Outline the benefits and limitations of the abolitionist perspective.

FURTHER READING

Bowling, B. and Phillips, C. (2007) 'Ethnicities, Racism, Crime and Criminal Justice' in Maguire, M., Morgan, R., and Reiner, R. (eds) *The Oxford Handbook of Criminology* (4th edn). Oxford: Oxford University Press.
This chapter provides a thorough analysis of the problems of racism in criminal justice.

Chapman, T. (2012) 'The Problem of Community in a Justice System in Transition: The Case of Community Restorative Justice in Northern Ireland', *International Criminal Law Review* 12(3): 573–87.
A useful discussion of the possibilities and challenges of putting alternative community-based mechanisms in place for resolving crimes.

Nurse, A. (2014) 'Critical Perspectives on Green Criminology: An Introduction' Nurse, A. (ed) *Critical Perspectives on Green Criminology*, Internet Journal of Criminology (available at: http://www.internet-journalofcriminology.com/Critical_Perspectives_On_Green_Criminology_June_2014.pdf).
An introductory collection on environmental crime and the criminological response.

Pearce, F. (1997) *The Crimes of the Powerful.* London: Pluto Press.
A hugely influential book, which was one of the earliest attempts to provide a comprehensive account of the ways in which those in positions of power are engaged in criminal activity, as well as the ways in which they evade accountability

Sim, J. (2009) *Punishment and Prisons: Power and the Carceral State.* London: Sage.
A critical account of the symbolic and material impacts of the machinery of punishment and its role in maintaining the authority and control of the contemporary state

 Access the **online resources** to view selected further reading and web links relevant to the material covered in this chapter.
www.oup.com/uk/case/

PART OUTLINE

28. Becoming a researcher and knowledge producer

29. Applying your skills to employability or future study

30. Journeying into employability and careers: From university to the workplace

This Part is all about making the best use of the detailed body of knowledge and high levels of critical understanding that you will acquire from this book. It offers a range of guidance intended to put you in charge of your undergraduate journey, the reward being the stimulating and original experiences promised in **Chapter 1**.

Chapter 28, on researching and producing knowledge, looks at your current role and identity: it seeks to enhance your undergraduate studies by encouraging you to think and act as an independent researcher. The chapter provides an array of practical and creative tips for developing your role as a knowledge producer and becoming a person who contributes to what is, and what is not, known about crime and the criminal justice system.

Chapter 29 focuses on reflective learning, and how you should use this to make the most of your degree by applying it either to future study, or employability. It will equip you with a disciplined system for establishing how you learn, as it is this kind of ability that enables you to transfer the knowledge and skills acquired from your undergraduate experience to the new and different situations you will face in the future.

Finally, **Chapter 30** helps you think about what comes next, guiding you through some of the career options you are likely to have after completing your degree. It also contains a strategy for achieving the skills and attributes employers expect to see in contemporary undergraduates. This method will help ensure that your employability is continually refined as you progress through the next stages of your life and future career.

PART 5

BECOMING A RESEARCHER OF CRIMINOLOGY

CHAPTER OUTLINE

Introduction	772
Why research?	772
Where to begin?	775
Planning your research	780
The importance of ethical standards ('The Only Way Is Ethics')	786
Barriers for research	789
Writing up your research	793
Disseminating your findings	796
Where to next?	799

Becoming a researcher and knowledge producer

KEY ISSUES

After reading this chapter you should be able to:

- appreciate the breadth of opportunities offered by being an undergraduate researcher in criminology;

- identify effective ways of choosing your research topic;

- plan the core features of a dissertation or research project;

- engage with ethical standards for researchers in criminology;

- consider unconventional methods of dissemination for your research.

Introduction

The high levels of work you have put in whilst reading the first four parts of this book; plus the establishment of your system for advancing your own ways of learning in **Chapter 27**, means you are a different person to the one who started your course into criminology. You now have the tools for being an effective undergraduate but you need to decide what to do with them. This chapter (and the whole book) is encouraging you take the role of a 'knowledge producer' as your next step. This is probably a concept most easily associated with a dissertation module but the chapter provides different practical guidance to show it is much broader than that. The awareness you now have for the influences and limitations on how knowledge has been produced for criminology means you are equipped for producing it yourself.

The idea of undergraduates being knowledge producers has been the most exciting concept in undergraduate teaching and learning for many years. It means that students are fully recognised for their potential to contribute to the fundamental rationale for their university's existence—the pursuit of knowledge. Adopting the role of an independent thinker for how knowledge is produced should not be limited to the occasional module but should instead influence all of your undergraduate work. It will mean you avoid being a mere consumer of knowledge where you simply absorb unquestioningly the things you have been taught. As you now know from this entire book's preceding chapters, passive acceptance of facts when studying criminology is not going to get you very far. Becoming a knowledge producer may sound a grand term but if you want to do it, the advice in this chapter plus the help available from your formal course of study will get you there.

Much of this chapter will focus on the work required for doing a dissertation, as this can provide more tools for knowledge production but you will find that its content and features are just as applicable to smaller research projects. Across the chapter you will find six 'conversations' features with colleagues working in criminology at universities across the country. These examples have been selected to illustrate how we learn from others whilst doing our research; the benefits of such dialogues can help you overcome problems and maximise opportunities from your research.

Figure 28.1 Research is key to gaining to attaining the degree classification you are aiming for
Source: © Nisakorn Neera/Shutterstock

The chapter begins with advice for choosing a dissertation topic followed by considering how your project can be effectively planned and organised. We will then look at the fundamental ethical principles for conducting research, encouraging engagement with ethical thinking that far exceeds a tick on a box of a dissertation proposal. In order to help you use this knowledge, issues of visual criminology and peoples' online practices and customs will be considered. Advice on the writing up of your research and how to demonstrate your critical thinking is then provided before we end the chapter by considering how you can use your research experience and skills for your 'next step' and the continuation of your higher education or progression into employment.

Why research?

You have read the book's previous chapters and so, amongst other things, have acquired detailed knowledge of the extent, nature, and distribution of crime. In doing so you considered the usefulness of the best known criminological theories for helping you with your inquiries into these developments. If you think back to each of these theories (you might want to consider (neo)classicism, positivism, critical criminologies, and realist theories), which of these do you feel has most to offer?

Contemplating your 'preferred' of these theoretical backgrounds for advancing the knowledge base in criminology may seem a very basic thing to do, but as will be shown later in this chapter, when you are developing skills in critical evaluation through your academic writing, many other equally simple questions need to be asked.

The grounding you have in the essential questions in criminology and criminal justice will enable you to feel confident in applying some approaches. The critical approach we have been championing throughout this text should be firmly established in your skill toolkit, and applying it should help to move you beyond simple acceptance of supposed criminological knowledge to a critical analysis. This chapter seeks to help you with your next stage, where everything you have learnt to date comes together in your research work and you become a producer of criminological knowledge in your own right. It is where you are in charge and where you will be rewarded well for simply using your imagination; confirmation of your creativity can come from asking basic questions that have been neglected in the thing you are studying.

The word 'research' can be intimidating if it is perceived as something only undertaken by people who are somehow superior and exclusive. However, research is an integral part of all criminology undergraduates' experiences and underpins everything you are studying; it is not restricted to methods' modules. A first part in demystifying research is to think about the word itself—research; the second syllable shows that it as an act of searching.

So as long as you are looking, and can write about it (in the manner recommended in this chapter), then you are researching.

Popular culture abounds with research; it is not just the remit of elite researchers or university life. We see it in television shows such as *Eight out of Ten Cats* (a popular channel 4 show whose title pokes fun at the unreliability of some claims some researchers make) and the many similar *'Family Fortunes/Pointless'* types of programmes. The title of *Eight out of Ten Cats*, which may seem a little bit bizarre, was actually derived from a well-known television advert of the 1980s which claimed '8 out of 10 cats prefer Whiskas to any other cat food'. If true this was an astounding claim as it implied that their researchers must have found ways to communicate with cats like no human had ever done before, in order to ask cats their opinions! Famously the advert then adapted its claim to '8 out of 10 cat owners' as well as including 'who expressed a preference'. These additions made little difference as it could have been the case that only ten owners were actually asked! Before you dismiss this possibility as too far-fetched, check the small print in television adverts for the latest hair and beauty wonder products, as they regularly show reliance on samples only in the double figures. The term 'like "8 out of 10 cats"' has deeply insulting connotations at universities everywhere; we want to use this chapter (and the whole book) to help you to avoid such traps, and conduct much more thorough research.

Now would be a good time to read the contents of **Conversations 28.1**.

In addition to this potential for impact on the criminal justice system, the practice of students acting as producers

---

CONVERSATIONS 28.1

Students as knowledge producers—with Professor Stuart Kirby

Are you an engaged student of criminology? If so, let me ask you a question. Do you perceive yourself as a knowledge consumer and a passive recipient of previously generated research? Or, do you see yourself, as a knowledge producer, a person who is proactive in the field of research?

One of the benefits of studying criminology is its relevance to contemporary society. A change of emphasis in the late 1990s saw the UK government spending more of its resources in research, in an attempt to understand and apply 'what works' in tackling crime. This started to nudge the organisational cultures of academia and criminal justice closer together, a theme that has continued ever since. More recently the austerity measures affecting public agencies have pushed these organisations ever closer in their ambition to embrace evidence-based approaches. Running in parallel to this have been changes to the academic funding regime, with the term 'impact' entering the academic lexicon. Now, those who distribute research money want to know the level of academic and societal impact the funded research will create. With this zeitgeist, the opportunity for collaboration with criminal justice agencies is emerging earlier for academics. Although for many students, knowledge production remains at postgraduate level (with a Masters or Doctoral research thesis), for some this opportunity can emerge at undergraduate level.

This move has been recognised by one of our national newspapers who highlighted a number of initiatives taking place to facilitate the process of students as knowledge producers (*The Independent*, 27 March 2015). In one university, a number of final year Criminology undergraduates were placed with local police forces to research a particular topic. Over the years the students had researched subjects including: the night time economy, open drug markets, organised crime, antisocial behaviour, homicide, domestic violence, and the responses to victims of crime. The benefits of these partnerships were diverse. To the police force it provided quality research, at little or no cost, generating evidence to assist with policy decisions and improve operational tactics. One of the cited examples involved a student asked to examine the escalating trend for domestic cannabis cultivation. The student was able to provide an objective overview of cultivated cannabis seizures, a profile of those arrested, and an interview summary as to the opinion of operational officers dealing with the problem. Setting this alongside wider UK and international findings the student was able to point out the ramifications for the police and wider policy makers.

Further, for the students involved, the benefits are much wider. Being able to use anonymous operational data provides the thrill of being involved in real world research. In this particular case the student, commented, 'This encouraged and inspired me to join the police and has given me a wealth of knowledge and experience which benefited me during interviews and assessments'. Another student, who took employment in the commercial business sector following graduation commented, 'The module definitely helped me, I now work in predictive crime analysis software … and the work I did has really given me a good knowledge base. I also use the experience to build a rapport with those in police forces, who make up a predominant part of my client base'. The experience of engaging with police officers and other criminal justice agencies (with some even presenting their findings to Chief Constables and representatives of the Home Office), allowed the development of personal skills. Also, the research has often been of sufficient quality to be published in international peer-reviewed journals.

This process is increasingly occurring across different universities, encompassing an increasing number of agencies. Forensics is one of the areas encouraged by this increased collaboration. One university has been pioneering new fingerprinting techniques, while another uses a mock crime scene house to examine new methods of training sniffer dogs and expose their students to more realistic scenarios. Further, higher education institutions are increasingly collaborating with criminal justice agencies; offering visits, work experience, and other research opportunities. As well as the police these agencies encompass the Crown Prosecution Service, youth offender teams, and the Prison Service. These approaches are increasing the confidence, knowledge, and skills of the students involved, who are in turn sharpening their research into peer-reviewed publications that are ultimately inspiring other knowledge producers.

Professor Stuart Kirby, Policing and Criminal Investigation, University of Central Lancashire

---

of knowledge, rather than just consumers, offers many opportunities for enhanced standards of learning (Faust 2009):

> Universities are meant to be producers not just of knowledge but also of (often inconvenient) doubt. They are creative and unruly places, homes to a polyphony of voices.

This demand for universities to house productivity and different voices came from an article written by the President of Harvard University, Drew Faust, the first woman to have attained this position. This level of support 'from the top' emphasises the expectation for all undergraduates to use independent thinking, not only those at elite institutions. The prospect of becoming a creative and disruptive producer of knowledge can seem unlikely and daunting but this chapter seeks to offer you some perspective on this. Every undergraduate is currently in this position so the breakdown of sections in this chapter is a realistic plan for overcoming this challenge. The 'student as producer' role has been advocated for over a decade as the leading pedagogical approach in higher education; it can provide deeper and more meaningful learning experiences (Lambert, Parker, and Neary 2007; Neary 2013) than the idea of student as recipient.

We hope that this chapter, indeed the whole book, will furnish you with the grounding knowledge you need to begin, and the critical mindset you need to excel in the exciting prospect of becoming your own producer of criminological research. Let us now move on to the practical matters concerned with research.

Where to begin?

When faced with the need to complete a dissertation or other similar research project, you may feel overwhelmed by the seeming size of the task before you. However, these fears can be reduced by recognising the many similarities between a dissertation and the other forms of course work you have already done to reach this stage. It might help to see the dissertation as an extended essay; it may be three or four times longer than those you normally produce but it is still just another piece of academic work. So, whatever it is you choose to do and whether you need to collect primary data or analyse secondary data, or a combination of the two; the academic principles are the same as for your usual work. These standards will be met when you are capable of managing the different forms of information you acquire and creating a logical and coherent argument for the question or hypothesis you have chosen to investigate.

Dissertations offer a showcase for your academic abilities and can often be referred to as capstone modules. This means they are modules that bring together all the knowledge and skills learnt from each preceding one. They are your opportunity to display your knowledge, abilities, and skills and so require critical use of sources and construction of coherent arguments. In some ways they can be easier than a conventional essay as in a dissertation some of the expected use of sources will include data you have collected yourself; the greater the effort you make in your data collection, the more issues you will have to critically evaluate, and the better the opportunity to display your criminological skill.

Choosing your research topic

When beginning your research, one of the hardest issues can be choosing your topic area. The freedom you have in this part of your course can be unsettling, as it may be the first time in your education where you are completely in charge. Whilst this may sound great, having this power can be unnerving if you normally rely on being directed on what you study. Many parts of this book seek to help you take direction of your studies and examples such as the 'triad of criminology' (**Chapter 2**) can provide this support.

The triad approach is based on defining, explaining, and responding. This means your research could be based on a topic that is relevant to *defining* the extent and nature of crime; are you aware of new things being criminalised or decriminalised? You could base your project on *explaining* the influences on crime; are there new research findings out there which interest you? Or is the

final part of the triad, *responding* to crime through the criminal justice system and crime prevention strategies, of more interest and you wish to research new initiatives being implemented? Whilst this book likes to see these three aspects as part of a continuum of 'crime' rather than separate entities, appreciating these three broad features of criminology can still guide you in your choice of research area.

Researching new frontiers of crime?

The structure is a way of tackling any criminological issue you encounter; so as suggested in **Chapter 29**, you could take the example of cybercrime and apply these elements. If 'exploring' is your preference then it is important to ask fundamental questions about the nature of cybercrime, what it actually is, what it includes and excludes, how it is measured, and the reliability of these measurements. Whereas if the second element is of more interest, then 'explaining' cybercrime would mean you take assistance from any of 'the usual suspects'; do any branches of the classical or positivist schools provide you with help? Or maybe it is the critical or realist approaches with the most to offer your inquiries. Alternatively, if 'responding' to crime is where you feel your passion rests then you could investigate how cybercrime is being responded to. Your research could then assess the work of the police, the courts, and CPS in relation to these offences; or possibly the services provided by organisations like Victim Support as these new forms of victimhood may need different kinds of work to the traditional.

Whilst we know more cybercrime offences are these days being referred to the National Fraud Intelligence Bureau via bodies such as Action Fraud, Credit Industry Fraud Avoidance System (Cifas), and Financial Fraud Action UK, there is still plenty we need to know. Refer back to **Chapter 7** for consideration of the difficulties in trying to get young people to appreciate dangers in this new frontier. It is not only children where it is difficult to convey this message; see the short film *Data to Go* that was released in 2016 by researchers working for Cifas. This illustrated considerable ignorance and shock from customers in a coffee shop with regard to the ease their personal information could be accessed through social networking sites.

Despite their many similarities with writing essays, a dissertation usually clearly differs in the longer length of time available for its submission. This will mean more detail is required, so it is obviously important to choose a topic you are interested in. This extra time reflects the control you have over what is studied but despite the opportunity for independence, acting on the guidance and support from your supervising tutor is integral to a successful project. It can be disconcerting not to be told what you are studying and this freedom of choice can seem paralysing. If you feel you are in this position and have no idea at all what you are going to do, one strategy you might like to use is setting yourself a time limit of 10 minutes and compile a list on a blank piece of paper (or even on your phone) of the five things that have interested you the most in what you have studied so far. These could be large or small topics, specific readings or small parts of lectures and seminars that really connected with you; in other words, things that represent the 'best bits' of your studies so far.

Whilst thinking quickly for such an important decision as your dissertation topic is not always recommended, if you are at a complete loss the setting of a short time limit can stimulate your memories and thoughts. If the process works, or you already have a topic in mind, you need to think carefully think about the available literature and potential support from your institution. A dissertation can be considered a hallmark for an undergraduate so to prove your high-level abilities for independent learning, your proposed topic should be able to contribute to the existing literature and not just replicate it. Having a realistic view of what counts as original research will help considerably; it is possible to conduct original research even investigating what someone else has already found, as long as your new research is from a different place or perspective. If you are still struggling to come up with a topic then think of the things you could do that may interest next years' undergraduates or search the *Internet Journal of Criminology* for examples of dissertations previously done by your peers.

Consider a locally inspired topic

A research topic could be something that produces knowledge which might be in the interests of your community. There are likely to be many organisations capable of providing a topic area, such as social enterprises, charities, hospices, foodbanks, etc. Alternatively, in keeping with the 'responding to crime' part of criminology's triad, there are likely to be initiatives in your local area that come under this general theme. It surely must have been a good time to have been a criminology undergraduate a few years ago in Bolton, Lancashire when a scheme aimed at reducing crime and antisocial behaviour saw late night revellers on the streets being given bubble-blowers in an attempt to stop them causing trouble (*Daily Mail*, 1 December 2008, see **Figure 28.2**). Or

Figure 28.2 Policeman handing out bubble-blowers to late night revellers in Bolton, Lancashire, UK
Source: Newsteam/www.swns.com

equally to have been in Torquay, Devon when police officers carried flipflops to prevent similar revellers injuring themselves from falling over or carrying their shoes and walking barefoot at the end of the night (*Daily Express*, 28 November 2008). These kinds of initiatives normally make headlines when they are announced and are often accompanied by hostile reactions against the 'nanny state'. Similar coverage is rarely given to any results of these schemes and so their use and the type of reporting make fascinating research subjects (see **Telling it like it is 28.1**). Being aware of what is going on in your local community with regard to its policing priorities or community safety measures will really help you find a topic; cultivating this awareness can start at the beginning of your undergraduate studies.

Consider a personally inspired topic

One of the joys of studying as a criminologist is the chance to research things that are personally meaningful. It is very common to find undergraduate study difficult but with patience and persistence, moments of discovery can occur and powerful moments of understanding can arise where you make clear connections to use your learning (see **Conversations 28.2**).

Consider an employability inspired topic

If the suggestions in the prior sections do not provide anything suitable, then motivation for a topic could come from choosing something with potential to help your future career. Your research has the potential to strengthen your

TELLING IT LIKE IT IS 28.1

Building on the work of others in your research—with author Phil Johnson

Inspired by the Bolton bubble blowers a research project was created for students to look into supervised football sessions known as 'street soccer'; these were being provided free of charge on Friday and Saturday nights for young people aged 11–17, in seven areas of the local community that had been designated as 'hot spots' for antisocial behaviour. The crime figures available at the police.uk website enabled the students to compare the numbers of reported instances of antisocial behaviour when street soccer was being provided, to those in the times when it was not. The project was designed to emulate methods used in the then British Crime Survey (now the Crime Survey for England and Wales) in these areas.

The survey the students produced (see **Table 28.1**) provided a means for identifying whether respondents had high perception levels of antisocial behaviour in their areas (defined as places within a 15-minute walk from their home) by asking seven sub-questions. The accepted measure for high perception levels was formed by a points system where if a respondent answered that the specific instance was 'a very big problem' in their area it was given three points; with 'a fairly big problem' counting for two; 'not a very big problem' awarded one and nothing given where it was considered 'not a

problem at all'. A maximum of 21 points was possible and if a respondent scored 11 or more they could be considered to have high perception levels of ASB for their area.

This system of classification can be applied to other inquiries where some quantitative data are going to be beneficial. Their findings could be expanded through doing some follow-up qualitative research with interviews on some of the sample. The advantages of working with multiple and mixed research methods were considered in **Chapter 6** and so using them in a local area means the results from your project could be compared to the national position. If you have a term time address that differs to your home one then you have double the opportunities for doing something similar!

Whilst you know from **Chapter 5** (Crime statistics) that recorded rates are only partial stories when it comes to measuring crime, they nonetheless give you a starting point and provide opportunities that until the growth of the Internet were beyond most researchers. These days you do not necessarily need special access agreements or inside contacts in a justice organisation as much of the work of the system is publicly available online. Use of others' methods and work will not prevent your work being deemed original; if the right balance is provided it will probably strengthen it.

	Not a problem at all	Not a very big problem	A fairly big problem	A very big problem
Teenagers hanging around on the streets				
Vandalism, graffiti and other deliberate damage to property or vehicles				
People using or dealing drugs				
People being drunk or rowdy in public places				
Rubbish or litter lying around				
Noisy neighbours or loud parties				
Abandoned or burnt-out cars				

Table 28.1 Breaking down perceptions of antisocial behaviour (Parfrement-Hopkins and Hall 2009)

employability, as the completion of research is going to clearly evidence your project management abilities, as well as your skill as a criminologist. It is another situation where working towards your degree and seeking employability

can be effectively combined. Your research could therefore increase your business and customer awareness for the particular type of employment or role you are interested in. This is in addition to the more general employability skills

CONVERSATIONS 28.2

Becoming a researcher in criminology—with Dr Marian Duggan

I began my criminology degree largely, I suspect, for the same reasons as many other criminology students: because I was curious about crime.

I had expected to learn about different types of crime and perhaps why people committed it, as well as the differences in crime trends over time, but what I received was much more than that thanks to some truly inspiring lecturers. They discussed issues about crime, harm, and victimisation which were not only fascinating but also hugely relevant to real-world contexts. Lecturers spoke anecdotally about topics, drawing on their own research while demonstrating the vested interest they had in seeking to effect positive change. They brought in criminal justice experts to share their experiences and field all manner of (often quite personal!) questions from us inquisitive students.

My undergraduate degree inspired me to explore criminology in a way which felt more engaged and invested. However, it was my exposure to feminist theory and research during specific gender-based modules which really sparked my desire to contribute to this body of knowledge. I recall sitting in class discussing feminist readings which theorised gendered experiences of sexism, victimisation, fear, and harm. Without initially realising it, we gradually migrated from discussing 'them' (the women in the research) to 'us' (the women in the seminar). Suddenly, we were engaging with the research to theorise our *own* experiences in a way we hadn't been able to do so before; our exposure to this literature furnished us with the language, evidence, and critiques we needed to better articulate our perspectives. The importance of research, and the powerful impact it could have, became abundantly clear to me in those discussions and from that point onwards I felt I had found my passion, both personally and professionally.

Soon after, I was lucky enough to be given the opportunity to do an independent, desk-based research project on the harms of 'Battered Women's Syndrome' prior to my final year dissertation project on 'Rape Victims and Legal Discourse'. The autonomy I was given to undertake these in-depth investigations harmonised various components of my degree whilst allowing me the freedom to shape my own developing area of academic interest.

The level of engagement I felt from doing those projects gave me the confidence I needed to progress onto postgraduate study, where I honed my feminist researcher skills under the mentorship of several other inspiring tutors. I broadened my Master's research to address sexuality-based victimisation in light of legislative changes concerning homophobic hate crime, which was a prominent issue at the time. This led on to my PhD research which was one of the first academic studies to highlight the socio-legal complexities of addressing lived experiences of homophobia in Northern Ireland.

I've been actively engaged in researching victimisation on the basis of gender and/or sexuality for over a decade now and am still hugely passionate about this topic. My engagement with a range of people working in the community voluntary and charitable sectors regularly reminds me of this power differential and demonstrates the importance of pursuing truly purposeful research activity. For me, this has included: writing articles for relevant community publications on the issues I'm researching to disseminate this information to a wider audience; speaking at a range of community events with a view to exploring a combined academic-practitioner approach to effecting positive change; and liaising closely with the police with regards to effective community interaction and sensitive approaches to awareness-raising which acknowledges and avoids 'victim-blaming'.

I can only hope that my research inspires students in the same way as the scholars who I studied for my degree inspired me. They—and the fantastic tutors I had—taught me that pursuing research is important in order to effect positive change; moreover, *somebody* has to do it, so why not you?

Dr Marian Duggan, Criminology Lecturer, University of Kent

---

such as communication, problem solving and enterprise. It could—for example—be a topic that provides an insider's view of working in the justice sector and this would be an extra opportunity to learn about the type of work you might like to do in the future from professional people.

So if the brain-storming exercise for the 'best bits' of your criminology course failed to give you any inspiration, do a similar one for your five preferred types of employment following your degree. If you are doing (or have done) volunteering or work experience in a criminological or criminal justice setting then this might supply your topic. Bear in mind that projects of this nature need to be planned and a series of small steps can get you there—although you might find that your direction changes along the way. See **Conversations 28.3** for one example.

As an independent undergraduate, people may freely want to talk to and assist you—so take advantage of this! Once you have a provisional title in mind for a dissertation, your supervising tutor will be able to let you know whether it is a manageable project in terms of the resources available to you.

CONVERSATIONS 28.3

My journey of engaging students in applied research—with Dr Liz Frondigoun

Having been a social scientist—teacher and researcher—for almost 20 years, I am aware that sometimes students struggle to appreciate the value of their critical academic skills and to recognise how their academic knowledge can support and be applied to employment opportunities in social and criminal justice.

My first foray into the research world was in relation to lone parenting, which was challenging and interesting but also brought a new perspective to my understanding of the issues single parents faced. Until this opportunity, my studies had focused mostly on women and social policy, as men were almost absent from the literature. This was clearly not the case in the real world and as an undergraduate I was fortunate enough to have the opportunity, in the first instance as part of my studies, to undertake a small piece of research for an external organisation, a third sector lone parents support organisation.

My role in the project was to identify the key policy papers and academic studies that would support their clients in accessing the correct information in relation to a number of issues. My first task was to interview the staff to find out what they did and didn't know or have access to and then interview some of their clients—lone parent men and women—to identify their main concerns and the issues they most needed help/guidance on. It was interesting discovering that lone parent men contextualised problems and defined themselves in a different way from many of the women in the study. The men—although there were only a few who took part in the study—had very different perceptions of women who were lone parents than they had of themselves. The experience helped me to recognise that academic work—teaching and researching—gave me an outlet for my passion for working for and with people in order to inform social and criminal justice policy and practice.

The initial project then enabled me to acquire part-time (hourly paid) employment with the Scottish Poverty Information Unit, whose main focus was on issues in relation to child and family poverty and more generally socially excluded and marginalised groups. Joining this research team meant I was able to observe and really begin to understand how knowledge is applied to examining and extending knowledge and understanding of social and criminal justice issues. Undertaking this research reaffirmed that knowledge was not—as so many undergraduate students sometimes perceive it—high order, or remote from lived experiences but in fact essential for undertaking a critical examination of a social and or criminal justice issue in order to support the development of policy or initiatives.

Scotland has seen significant changes in the last two decades in relation to its governance and policy and practice for youth justice. While there are many similarities in the culture of the nations in the UK, Scotland has its own justice system. While criminology has been an established discipline for some considerable time, its development as a stand-alone degree programme has come more slowly than elsewhere in the UK. Within the Scottish context, criminology and criminal justice tended to be taught within the broader framework of the social sciences or law. Therefore, there has been a need to develop new and innovative ways to engage criminology students in learning and in particular in engaging them in applied criminal justice programmes. Since I became a lecturer, like many of my peers across the country, I have drawn from my existing networks in the criminal justice field, to provide opportunities for students to undertake research for statutory, community, or voluntary organisations.

If you can get involved with an organisation like this it can be meaningful to both your course and also for the organisation. The students at my university who have done this have applied their research skills in developing questionnaires, conducting interviews, and holding focus groups. Such a project also provides experience in documentary analysis, critical analysis, and the writing up of reports in various formats to meet the needs of their host organisation. Through this research process the key skills learned in methods' modules and abilities for using substantive academic material come to life in the applied setting.

If you take the opportunity to focus your undergraduate research on a community-based topic then it could be a win-win situation. It provides organisations with a research output they almost certainly wouldn't have and at the same time it offers a unique opportunity: an insight into the world of academic practice and research. Your work, however small, could feed in to policy development or policies for service and practice with the exciting opportunity to be part of social change, however slow it may be.

The impact I have seen from my involvement in this kind of teaching and learning includes stronger links between academia and the community; but also enhanced employment opportunities for the students upon graduating and the exchange of knowledge between the student researcher and the organisation. These community settings offer an ideal base for dissertation topics. The value of what these organisations offer in relation to grounding academic knowledge in the lived experiences of citizens will benefit your studies of criminology considerably.

Dr Liz Frondigoun, Criminal Justice Lecturer, University of the West of Scotland

Planning your research

It is common for undergraduates to be unsure of the correct structure to use when producing a dissertation, so awareness of the essential sections which make up any such piece of work is needed. This should be addressed at the planning stage where you compile a scheme of work for meeting these requirements. It does not matter if you do not yet know much about their detail, but it is important to have a clear break down of what you need to do. You should therefore closely refer to any dissertation template your institution provides you with, which usually consists of the elements laid out in **Table 28.2**. Once you begin your research project or dissertation you might find it useful to pencil in some dates to help you plan ahead.

Literature reviews

A dissertation must contain a detailed review of the relevant literature on the issue being investigated and the variables in your study (see **Chapter 6** for the discussion of the different types of variables in research). In your review you should be able to explain how this influenced the direction of your research and your awareness of the key readings and recent publications is also expected. Find other literature reviews in your topic area and read them to get an idea of the ways in which it could be organised. You can do a database search to find examples so put the words 'literature review' along with your keywords to retrieve them. You need to have a well-defined literature review question or a statement of purpose that allows you to claim specialist knowledge and understanding for the published material in the issue you are investigating. Your review question needs to specify the key words for your study and does not have to argue for a particular position or opinion. If your review is too broad it will be overwhelming so focus your search of the literature by adding particular places or professions to your topic as recommended above. Your review needs to work in partnership with your methodology section so the philosophy underpinning your research and choice of methods need to be reflected here. Other helpful parameters for shaping your review can come from its scope and whether it includes journals, books, official documents, and other sources.

Your organisational skills will be vital as you need to keep careful records of what you have read. This is absolutely invaluable if your original question gets modified somewhat as a result of what you have learnt from your review. To meet this requirement your quick reading skills are needed to record your thoughts on:

- an author's academic reputation in your topic area (prominent authors can help you justify the relevance of your research);
- does the author seem to have a particular bias?
- are opposing positions discussed or ignored?
- do these views contradict your ideas (authors like this can strengthen your work)?

The checklist in **Table 28.2** should usually be tackled in order but there could be times when slight adjustments are needed in order to meet the needs of your research. The third column in that table highlights the importance of time management; such dates are likely to change but clearly planning them all at the start will direct your work and remind you how the key parts to a dissertation are interconnected. It is an outline of the different parts of the research process and further guidance on the detail for each should be provided by your institution; if it is not, ask for it.

Historical methods

Aspects of the exploring, explaining, and responding framework can be applied to any example of criminality, this includes whether it is a contemporary issue or something more historical. If you are interested in using a

Key Part	Description	Proposed Date for Completion
Cover Page	Dissertation/project title, researcher's name, degree programme, and university details	
Table of Contents	The page numbers for the different chapters, these will frequently change so do this last	
Acknowledgements	Recognition to the people who have helped you in your research	
Abstract	A summary of your whole project, usually between 150–300 words. This should clearly state the aim and scope of your project and be written in a way that anyone can easily understand	
Introduction	This part needs to capture the reader's attention immediately so do not leave your best points until the end (we have often seen students make this same mistake in essays as well). Your supervising tutor is likely to have marked many projects before so yours will stand out with a clear introduction that explains: • the motivation for your research; • a statement of the problem you are investigating; • your research question and objectives	
Literature Review	See the section titled 'Literature reviews' for detailed information	
Methodology	Along with a literature review, this part is likely to be one of the longest chapters in a dissertation. It is where you present the general philosophical framework for your chosen research methods. This will include the justifications for your choice of quantitative or qualitative methods, or a combination of both In addition to the theoretical underpinning for your research, this part will also explain: • the variables in your study; • the population and research samples; • methods of data collection and data analysis; • the limitations of your chosen methods Remember the view that good research is shaped by astute questions not highly sophisticated methods	
Ethical Considerations	See the discussion under 'The importance of ethical standards' heading later in this chapter for incorporating ethical principles into your research	
Results and Findings	Guidance from your institution will tell you whether the results and the findings from your research need to be in two separate chapters. In either situation it is essential to remember you need to do both. When writing about the results you simply need to describe what they were for each of your inquiries. All of your results need to be expressed and these descriptions should have clear connections to your methodology chapter It is the findings section where deeper levels of thought are required and this part could be expected in a separate 'analysis' chapter. It can be a daunting section as it can only be done by your individual thought—but hopefully your five-stage learning journey explained **Chapter 1** of this book, demonstrates your experience in developing this skill. It is essential you put your analysis skills to good use; ensure you apply the same level of evaluation to your own research	
Conclusions	It may be that some of this has been done in the results/findings or analysis chapter but a final section is needed that summarises: • your key findings and how they relate to what you expected to find; • the relevancy of your work to researchers and practitioners; • if possible, your recommendations for future researchers and practitioners; • the conclusions you have drawn from this research	

Table 28.2 Unlocking the key parts of a dissertation *(continued)*

Bibliography	As with all academic writing the 'house style' (in this case your institution's expectations) needs to be followed as regards the required manner of referencing for the sources used in your research. If you are unsure of your institutions 'house style' then get in touch with your tutor. Not following this could have a detrimental impact on your mark	
Appendices	Again, the conventions followed by your institution will determine what needs to go in this section. Often appendices are not marked so if you feel the information is important, include it in one of the earlier sections. The standard things for inclusion in an appendix are: • blank copies of questionnaires (NB. analysis of their results must not be left to this point); • observation sheets; • interview transcripts; • supplementary data that adds value to your work but is not essential to it	

Table 28.2 *(continued)*

historical perspective for your research then this will give you the space to deeply explore the development of your topic. If it is something that involves a response to crime then this historical awareness will help you identify what is recognised as good practice in this area. Your ability to make comparisons with these different periods of time will be integral to your success—so comparative analysis where you investigate both the similarities and the differences in your topic can get you there. To do this you will need to collect, review, and analyse 'secondary' data; this is work already done by someone else and if it is valid and reliable it provides many opportunities as discussed in **Chapter 6**.

Documentary data are also going to be relevant so your critical frame of mind is essential for verifying a document's credibility, reliability, representativeness, and ethical position. These are questions you need to ask of every 'document' you use in your research; for research in the social sciences 'document' is a very broad term that as well as the obvious text-based sources also includes visual data, virtual data, works of art, and other artefacts (Caulfield and Hill 2014). Whichever formats they are in, you must be asking yourself to what extent these documents present a complete view of the reality they depict.

Even though you will not be doing empirical research there is still much to be gained by being aware of the importance of its methods. So just as empirical researchers have to clearly defend their choices for the people and places in their research, similar justifications are needed for the documents you include in your research—again a clearly defined strategy for acquiring these sources is needed. A thoughtful plan for the keywords in your online searches is absolutely essential and it is at this stage that help from your tutors and library staff will be very useful. This strategy is fundamental to your success and a critical questioning approach is vital. The reflexive learning abilities you will gain from **Chapter 29** mean you should be able to apply critical thinking to all the work that you produce, as well as to that of others. You could apply the

'ABC questions for writing critically' from **Figure 28.5**; so with any document, first ask the basic, initial questions of 'what', 'when', and 'where' then progress to deeper questions of 'why' and 'how' before concluding with evaluative questions like 'so what' and 'what if'.

As criminology students we have the advantage of knowing about the truth seeking methods of the adversarial justice system. Think about the traditional view in **Chapter 20** for adversarial cross-examination as the vehicle for taking us to the truth. If you apply that critical questioning approach to the documents you read, as well as to those you produce yourself, then your work will be defensible and robust. Think about the evidence they present; how convincing does it seem? If it is a scholarly piece have they recognised and overcome the other sides to the debate?

Whilst this kind of research can be very different to empirical methods, there are many forms of overlap. A similar plan is needed for your analysis and again a clearly justified strategy is required. Is qualitative content analysis appropriate thanks to its ability to answer 'why' questions or quantitative content analysis and its generation of answers to the 'what' questions? Or is discourse analysis needed with its focus on analysing the power of language in structuring the ways problems are conceived (or ignored). Your research might need narrative analysis as your method so you can understand the lives of individuals and their social context by qualitatively analysing biographical accounts, oral histories, and other personal stories. A similar approach could be thematic analysis such as grounded theory analysis where, rather than testing things with a pre-existing theory in mind, your questions such as 'what is/was happening' and 'why', emerge from the data you collect. Remember all of these different methods of analysis have their own principles (and limitations) so whilst you are at the design stage, plan ahead and consider which of them are appropriate for your research. Each of these methods could merit a full chapter on their own but the priority of this present one is to get you to the point of being a knowledge producer; the analytical methods represent some of the ways you can get there. Help and guidance on these different approaches will be provided in your research methods' modules and by specialist texts such as Chamberlain (2013).

Creative methodologies for extracting data

Whilst working out your chosen methodology can feel daunting, it can be actually broken down into three clear parts: the theoretical background to your research design; your methods of data collection; and then your chosen methods of analysis. Again, you need to be self-critical on your plans, so question the clarity of your research design and its potential validity and reliability.

Creative methods are adopted by researchers who believe traditional research methods should not have the monopoly for generating knowledge and understanding. They are ways of researching that open up new spaces for research and can involve processes where everybody involved can learn from each other. So when you are studying a social situation or phenomenon you could collect and analyse the texts and artefacts produced by the people in these situations. If you believe your topic needs this type of research then many creative participatory methods are available for your use. These could include things produced by your research participants such as: film-making, digital story creation, photographs, paintings, murals, theatre performances, and written narratives. These methods can have an authenticity about them that produce evidence which interviewing and observing may never reach. However, if you do choose an alternative method like this it is still essential to deal with all the standard elements of academic research like its validity, reliability, and ethical position. The checklist in **Table 28.2** might need minor adjustments when you take a purely qualitative approach, such as a chapter where you interpret your research material as opposed to labelling it 'results and findings'. But whichever approach you take, your research needs to be broken down into a similar general structure that clearly addresses the separate stages of your activity.

An interesting example of the conflicting interpretations that can arise from different sources of data concerned the photography that followed the execution by electric chair of Allen 'Tiny' Davis in 1999. These images showed his graphically distorted face and considerable spattering of blood over his chest and neck after the device had been used; the images were leaked by a judge in the case's appeal as a protest against the state of Florida using this form of execution (it has since been replaced by lethal injection). His protest was though not seen this way as the public discussions of these photographs in their numerous online comments were very approving of what had happened; they were read in a very different way to that intended by the judge who initially circulated them (Lynch 2015).

There are vast amounts of different types of texts and artefacts used by creative researchers in their search for data; see the work of Cunneen (2010) and Young (2012) to name just two examples. The first of these used production of works of art for explaining peoples' attitudes to justice, with the second using graffiti as its documentary evidence in investigating the ways its illicit writer or artist is constructed.

Planning effective methods of communication

The abundance of conversational examples provided by different academics in this chapter demonstrates the research advantages in finding people 'with a story to tell'. They reaffirm this book's belief in the benefits of 'travel partners' for your journey into criminology—people who can help you get where you want to go (see **Telling it like it is 28.2**). Such individuals can be those who share your research interests and so are motivated to help and give you some time; their experiences can help you discover answers for deep questions in criminology and criminal justice. You will increase your chances of finding such people if you extend your networks whilst you are an undergraduate by joining different committees, initiatives, and groups at your institution; there are people out there who can help you, and you them.

The imaginative study cited in **Chapter 20** from De Keijser et al. (2014) is another example of the benefits from getting out into the world and talking to people. This research sought to acquire public perceptions of the Blackstone ratio of justice ('better that ten guilty persons escape, than that one innocent suffer'). They measured views on three ranks of offence seriousness (shoplifting, burglary, and rape) on four different levels: where the researchers provided information about the consequences of false positives (wrongly deciding someone is guilty); where information was provided about the consequences of false negatives (wrongly deciding someone is not guilty); where balanced information was provided about false positives and false negatives; and where no information was provided at all. This combination meant there were 12 issues under investigation and the researchers found in the progressively more serious cases of shoplifting, burglary and rape, the public were less willing to accept the error of acquitting a guilty person.

The practical aspect to this research was as impressive as academic content; the questionnaires took 10 minutes to complete so train timetables were researched to

TELLING IT LIKE IT IS 28.2

The value of travel partners for your research—with author Phil Johnson

In my early days as an academic I too was fortunate in finding someone employed in the criminal justice system that was very keen to talk about the challenges they faced in their career. It came about through my involvement in a teaching and learning group that was being formed at my institution to foster closer working relationships with local employers. It was in the mid-1990s and the drive for producing employability in higher education was nothing like it is today. The prospect of combining applied research with conventional undergraduate study seemed remote in those days but, thanks to the regular contact I was able to have with a representative from the probation service, my professional practices changed completely. The open nature of these talks included the sharing of problems and issues with a desire to improve our respective services. It resulted in a series of collaborative research projects whereby my students helped the probation service acquire data from samples of offenders and the general public (Johnson and Ingram 2007). The mutual nature of these projects meant the students acquired academic and professional knowledge and they also led to my PhD. The importance of choosing the right travel partners was rightfully emphasised in **Chapter 1** and my own experiences (and for many of the academics in this entire book) would support the significant benefits they can have on your education and career.

identify journeys of at least 15 minutes without a stop. It was an extremely successful strategy as they acquired participation from around three-quarters of the people they approached (over 500 in total). It confirms the value in planning your research and data acquisition in situations where people are more likely to have that rare commodity of spare time.

Before going on to the next section of this chapter you may find it useful to consider the experience of Deborah Drake in **Conversations 28.4**.

CONVERSATIONS 28.4

Researching life in men's maximum-security prisons—with Deborah Drake

For me, the process of becoming a researcher in criminology has been an ongoing one. It has been relational in the sense that, as a researcher in the field, I have learned the most about the topics I have studied when I have viewed them through the eyes and actions of those I encountered and in my observation of and interactions with them. I will briefly discuss one illustrative example of an incident that occurred whilst I was conducting research in maximum-security prisons, which demonstrates the way in which relational moments in research can be extremely telling.

Maximum-security prisons are daunting places. Their environments are harsh, austere, heavily controlled and, more often than not, severely deprived of warmth, compassion, and other essences of what it means to be human (see **Figure 28.3**). As a researcher, I entered these prisons with an aim to understand the experiences of prisoners and staff both in isolation from and in relation to one another. As separate groups and as individuals they were equally complex, their experiences equally valid, their individual perspectives equally worthy of respect and understanding. However, the relational elements between staff and prisoners were complicated and often obscured by the power held by staff. The very nature of the concept of imprisonment subjugates the position of prisoners and elevates the position of staff. Moreover, the dominance of staff perceptions, knowledges, and discourses in shaping the prison environment as a whole meant that it was difficult to study the prison environment, prisoner perspectives, and staff perspectives as equally weighted influences. They are not—and they are designed not to be so.

It goes without saying, perhaps, that within prisons and in mainstream society more generally prisoners are the obvious 'villains' whilst prison staff members are the ascribed 'heroes'. However, from the perspective of a researcher interested in experiences of imprisonment, such categorisations are, at best, a crude distraction and, at worst, an invitation to unhelpful and sometimes

Figure 28.3 Maximum security prisons can be daunting, intimidating places
Source: Michael Sheehan/Shutterstock

misleading pre-judgements. Moreover, they assume an acceptance of an infallible criminal justice system and limit one's openness to hearing how research informants describe their own lives, situations, and perspectives.

One of the biggest challenges in undertaking experiential research on prisoners and staff in maximum-security prisons was avoiding being drawn in to the way the prison institution constructed prisoners—as 'other', as 'undeserving', as 'risky', as 'dangerous', and—sometimes—as less than human.

I recall one incident, in particular, that illustrates how pervasive the view of prisoners as 'other' in maximum-security prisons was. I had been in the prison for about two months (coming in five days a week for between 8 and 12 hours a day). Over that period of time I had built up good relations with both staff and prisoners and was relatively 'trusted' (as much as an outsider can be in a maximum-security prison) by both groups. One day, I was standing on a landing with a couple of officers and a prisoner passed by us who I knew well. I had interviewed him formally a month before and we had had many conversations over the course of the time I'd been in the prison. He stopped to pass a few words with me because we hadn't seen each other for several days. As he was leaving he touched my elbow lightly as he said 'good to see you, pop by later on and we'll have a chat'. When one of the officers who I had been standing with saw this, he was visibly angered and firmly grabbed my other arm and pulled me away from the light touch of the prisoner and said: 'she is observing us today, clear off back to work.' His grip was unnecessarily firm and later on I noticed it left bruising. The prisoner gave me a knowing look and stalked off without another word.

The above incident illustrates how a researcher's perceptions might be both implicitly and explicitly shaped by the 'rightful' authority of the prison staff. The action of the officer, the look on his face, the violence with which he yanked me away from the touch of a prisoner gave very clear messages about power, status, safety, and entitlement. He, as prison officer, was entitled to touch, grab, and even (unintentionally) hurt me—because he was on the side of 'good', protecting (from his own perspective) my young, naïve self from having to spend time with or be touched by this villainous creature. This interaction captured a moment that was loaded with telling complexity and both subtle and overt power dynamics on many levels—too many to discuss in this brief space. But this incident illuminates just how easily a researcher might be drawn in to the dominant (staff) view. The actions of the officer could have frightened me, it may have biased me against further conversations with this particular prisoner (or with others), it could have, in fact, traumatised me about even entering a prison wing on my own such was the violence of the response.

In the event, however, I felt none of these things. The prisoner in question was an informant I knew well. He was not someone I deemed likely to pose a danger to me. I based this judgement on his offence history, the demonstrable care he regularly showed to other prisoners, and our numerous conversations over a couple of months. The response of this officer to this prisoner on this occasion was—on the basis of objective evidence—disproportionate. As a result, it gave me an insight into the brute force of staff, the vulnerability of prisoners, and the lack of opportunity that staff members have to gain a detailed, interpersonal understanding of individual prisoners. It demonstrated a one-size-fits-all approach to the risk and danger that people in prison may pose. It also added to my understanding of why prisons, ultimately, fail so spectacularly in helping people to overcome their past difficulties and transgressions in order to find ways of living their lives more safely. The lack of opportunity given to people in prison to move beyond the label of 'criminal' was startlingly evident through this one anecdotal moment.

The enduring lessons learned through this story, for me, are couched in feminist, stand-point epistemology and particularly the work of Dorothy Smith. Smith's ideas about socially-situated knowledge have had a profound effect on my thinking. Her work helped me to recognise that people in socially marginalised positions could often have a very different—and sometimes fuller—view of the social world than those in more powerful positions or those who occupy the 'mainstream'. Moreover, the simple—and somewhat obvious—idea that individuals are always 'the experts' in their own lives has perhaps been the single most important influence over my research life. Holding to this maxim has continually reminded me to enter the field with humility, with respect and with openness to understanding the world from the perspectives of those I meet. This approach continues to shape my 'becoming' as a researcher—guarding against over-claiming my own expertise or over-privileging the expertise of those in dominant positions.

Deborah Drake, Senior Lecturer in Criminology,
The Open University

The importance of ethical standards ('The Only Way Is Ethics')

We are indebted to the Student Union at the London School of Economics for the second part of this heading as in 2011 they began their own wonderfully named TOWIE programme. But rather than being another reality TV show, this was an initiative seeking to emphasise the importance of ethical standards in all aspects of undergraduate life. Such embracing approaches can contrast sharply with dissertations and other projects where consideration of ethics is relegated to merely proving compliance with an institution's regulations. Naturally, the standards required by your course have to be met but engaging with ethics can be far more rewarding than that; hopefully they will influence the lifetime of your project (and beyond). The broad nature of what criminology involves means such a commitment can be demonstrated in your research in many ways; this part of the chapter will highlight two examples of such dilemmas: visual criminology and the ethical use of online resources. Thoughtful engagement with these two issues can put you at the heart of these debates in ways that traditional essays and documentary research cannot.

The Statement of Ethics from the British Society of Criminology in 2015 is a document freely available on the society's website. It clearly breaks down the research responsibilities of criminologists. This statement outlines the range of responsibilities on researchers and promotes thought and debate for ethical dilemmas in criminological research; the guidance in its several case studies and frequently asked questions is well worth reading. This resource is also extremely helpful for its links to the statutory provisions in the Data Protection Act that can affect researchers and also for explaining the permissible limits of confidentiality in research; namely, where suspected offences of terrorism, money laundering, and the neglect or abuse of children are excluded.

Ethical considerations in visual criminology

Ethical concerns in the development of visual criminology can be traced to the work of Walter Benjamin and his lecture, 'Author as Producer', given to the Society of Anti-Fascists in Paris in 1934. Its content is still highly pertinent, particularly its fears for how photography 'has even succeeded in making misery itself an object of pleasure' (Benjamin 1934: 5). Its call for authors to become producers of visual images was held up by Benjamin as the approach most likely to resolve this ethical challenge. It would lead to the production of images that accurately document social life and are inspired by desire for social change not financial gain. This is something that your undergraduate studies of criminology could easily contribute towards. Once you have dealt with the few legal constraints on public photography that are discussed in **Chapter 29**, effective use of your camera phone, as opposed to a keyboard or pen and paper, can result in you 'doing criminology' in many situations. Being a criminologist whilst doing routine things can make your course part of your everyday life and the use of your phone allows these experiences to be recorded.

The widespread ownership and use of camera phones has meant the act of taking photographs in public places is not as unusual as it used to be, so why not take advantage of this new freedom for documenting public life? Try using the antisocial behaviour research methods cited in **Telling it like it is 28.1** earlier in this chapter and select places within a 15-minute walk of your home, for taking snapshots whenever you see anything that reminds you of things you have studied. Using your imagination in this way will help you to see the similarities between taking photographs and writing essays; they are both creative tasks that illustrate your productivity. The complexity of thought in a photograph's rationale can be comparable to that when you are writing, so it is an excellent way of demonstrating your adaptability.

Ethical principles for research

It is generally recognised there are four main areas in which contentious issues could arise with your research:

(a) informed consent;

(b) misrepresentation;

(c) accuracy of data;

(d) no harm to research subjects, and protection of their privacy.

The first of these requires you to take appropriate steps to ensure there was informed consent on the part of your research subjects. They have the right to be fully informed about the nature and consequences of your research, its methods, potential risks, and its general purpose. The principle of informed consent means physical or psychological coercion cannot be used in acquiring the voluntary participation from your research subjects. In order to attain this level of informed consent, the use of deception in research is not permissible. This is the second key ethical principle and therefore means deliberate misrepresentations from researchers are forbidden. However, it is not always easy to identify deception, for example is not telling a person something as morally unacceptable as telling them something that is false? In these situations, deception could arise respectively through omission and commission of representations to a research subject. Absolute prohibitions on all kinds of deceptions do not exist, as in some areas of life information could not be attained without it; so if there is knowledge with a clear value to society, minor deviations to the ethical principle (such as deception by omission) might be tolerable (Christians 2011: 72):

> The standard resolution for this dilemma is to permit a modicum of deception when there are explicit utilitarian reasons for doing so.

The third guideline concerns the accuracy of the data produced in your research as this must truthfully represent what you found and any lies or manipulations will invalidate your work. The fourth general rule is sometimes divided into two and means your research must not cause harm to your research subjects, and their privacy has to be protected. Harm is a broad concept and so the potential for it needs to be appreciated in your choice of methods—for example the use of interviews would inconvenience your research subjects by simply impinging on their time. In this context the amount of harm could be negligible but this may not be the case if individuals are identified or identifiable from your research. If the need for anonymity is high, then this could affect your methodology as quantitative research and its more limited nature of permissible responses makes it less likely that individuals could be subsequently identified. This general principle of ethics means the identity of research subjects (people and locations) has to be protected and assurances of anonymity need to be given to safeguard against the disclosure of personal data. The potential for harm in matters such as a research subject's professional or social reputation includes the duty on a researcher to ensure any records are secured safely with only access from the researcher allowed. See **Telling it like it is 28.3** for real life application of the principles just discussed.

Visual research methods

The use of visual methods such as photography could breach the anonymity safeguard and it could be harmful for a person to be identified in a particular place and time (e.g. were they absent from work?). This can mean that some visual research methods risk being rejected as unethical so extra care might need to be taken; this enhanced sensitivity for the interests of others will enable display of high-level ethical engagement. An insistence on absolute anonymity may negate the whole research and could prejudice research subjects who want to be identified in order to further their interests; so the circumstances of each case should be the deciding factor. The use of photographs will facilitate your critical analysis as their alleged objectivity is reduced by the discussion in **Chapter 29**; the influence of a photographer is comparable at least to that of the language, structure, and tone taken by a writer, which imposes a certain framing around an event or set of circumstances.

Despite these risks, visual research methods have considerable strength and allow individual thought that the written word may not be able to reach. This can include photographic elicitation whereby images stimulate responses from participants; this could come from increased recall in memory from using images shown to research subjects or using them to promote original opinions. It could also come through subjects creating their own images in a research style known as photovoice

TELLING IT LIKE IT IS 28.3

Different situations but the same ethical principles—with author Phil Johnson

In my research with the probation service there were three projects where people were needed to provide the data. The offenders at unpaid work project sites was the first, 'sentencers' (judiciary and magistracy) provided the second, with the third being members of the public that included the first respondents to the Community Payback offer of public involvement in suggested unpaid work projects. The principle of informed consent meant all of these research subjects were entitled to know the full information about the research as listed above. But it also meant different treatment was required to comply with its insistence of participation in research being voluntary. The coercive environment of unpaid work project sites clearly threatened this ethical standard so extra care was needed to ensure involvement was indeed voluntary. So at the commencement of every interview the point was made that although the support of the Probation Service had been invaluable to the research, there was no question of it being conducted 'for' them. The interviews were conducted by a small group of my undergraduates acting as research assistants to reinforce the impression that the research was not being undertaken for an official organisation.

This project was mainly quantitative in nature as it sought to measure specific parts of the offenders' experiences, such as their contact with beneficiaries and skills development. So apart from finding out how many hours had been served on the current order, there was no need for other identifiers like names and criminal histories. Nonetheless the offenders were assured they would not be identifiable and were told the findings would be written up for academic publication where the unpaid work sites would only be referred to as being from the western, central, and eastern areas of the county. Further reassurance was also given by framing the interview questions in non-contentious terms that merely asked whether beneficiary contact or certain types of new skills had been experienced.

The potential for your research to harm your participants has to be a constant concern so applying ethical thinking through a TOWIE approach is the only way. Whoever you are fortunate enough to involve in your research, you inconvenience them by simply imping-ing on their time. This could be interpreted as 'harm' so starting from this fundamental position will remind you of its persistent potential. In terms of the offenders at the unpaid work projects this kind of harm was not a problem at all as the researchers acquired participation from everybody they approached; it produced a sample of 120 offenders who seemed to welcome this interruption in their time as an opportunity to 'lay down tools' for a while!

whereby photographic narratives and video diaries reveal different things to conventional interviews.

In order to attain ethical approval, visual researchers need to demonstrate their care and compassion for the research subjects and act in ways likely to benefit the individuals or groups being researched. There are many ways they could be incorporated into your research and their increased use is taking place across all of the disciplines in the social sciences. It has now reached a point where some believe it to be inevitable that visual methods will be one of the most significant qualitative research methodologies in the 21st century (Prosser 2011). If people in our discipline get involved with photography, both individually and collectively, it is possible to produce work that illustrates how a visual criminology can help with the shaping of attitudes towards crimes. It is something that Phil Johnson, one of this book's authors, regularly used with his students, who through their research have been able to show in public exhibitions of their work, statistically significant changes in viewers' opinions on matters of crime, harm, and injustice (Johnson 2011). Phil sees being involved in assessments that require photographs of so-called hidden crime as a highly satisfying part of his job—as it allows him to see students appreciate how a task for 'photographing the invisible' is no longer as daft as it might have sounded at the start of a module.

Ethical alternatives to copyright?

One of the most difficult parts of the undergraduate experience can be learning the difference between plagiarism and effective use of sources in your work. Getting the right balance is what is required and so it is understandable that this can sometimes cause confusion for students. It is likely that information for overcoming concerns over plagiarism will have been provided by your institution, as it is an essential feature of any induction into higher education; if it hasn't been you might want to ask if the library or your department can provide any guidance. The amount of sources you will be expected to use in your project will be guided by the marking criteria and with regard to academic sources, any plagiarism fears can be dispelled by appropriate referencing. However, if your work uses other sources such as photographs, videos, and interview recordings then copyright issues may also affect the ethical nature of your work. The creators or purchasers of the works are likely to have the 'all rights reserved' protection of copyright and so have rights in law enforceable against you if you use them in your work without permission—being in higher education does not exclude your liability. However, the commonly accepted practice of 'fair use' allows limited use of copyrighted materials so small amounts of text can be used without asking permission. It is where the full work is being used, such as a photograph or a table of data, that permission should be sought from the copyright holder.

In addition to potential liability, the ownership of the intellectual property in undergraduate dissertations is rarely considered and it used to be the norm for institutions to claim the intellectual property rights in their students' work. This position has become difficult to defend considering the application of current consumer laws on unfair contract terms to the legal relationship between a university and a student. It means that a term risks being deemed unfair and therefore not legally enforceable, if in all cases it assigns all intellectual property (IP) rights to the university for any of your work (Competition and Markets Authority 2015: para. 3.6). It is therefore a contractual matter between you and your institution and currently the practice varies amongst higher education providers.

It can be argued that traditional copyright laws are out of step with the digital age as everything on the worldwide web is a copy of something. The amount of enforcement that should take place for potential breaches of IP is much contested and there are numerous ethical issues in using and producing online resources in your research. However, it is still your responsibility to be a responsible researcher and be aware of what does sit under copyright and what doesn't. The recent development of the so-called sharing economy has included the introduction of the Creative Commons licensing system. This alternative to copyright uses a 'some rights reserved' approach and its broadest form of permission is a Free Culture Licence which allows and encourages the use and reuse of its content. The licences invariably require attribution to the creator (a citation) and often forbid commercial gain from them. They aim to inspire the reuse, repurposing, revision, and redistribution of the resources that can come under the umbrella term of Open Educational Resources (OERs). They are aimed at inviting people to build on these resources and derive further value from them.

The term Open Educational Resources (OERs) has been used since the turn of the century to promote free access to educational resources on a global scale. The first higher education institution to actively produce such resources was the Massachusetts Institute of Technology (MIT) in the USA. This institution, which routinely comes very near the top of the different university world rankings, started a project in 2001 called OpenCourseWare to put all of the educational materials from its undergraduate courses freely available online. These initiatives are part of the free and open-source software movement that has been responsible for much of the developments on the Internet. Other well-known examples include the Internet browser Mozilla Firefox and the virtual learning environment Moodle.

Work that displays Creative Commons licences can be bought and sold in the standard commercial way but such rewards are not a driving factor in their use. Instead, their main purpose is to contribute to the spirit of openness that some parts of the online world are very keen to promote. This can range from governments across the world requiring their publicly funded works of research to be freely available to the public, to individual artists of all types (e.g. authors, musicians, DJs, professors, photographers) opening up their work for input from others. It was created by a charitable foundation through the work of Lawrence Lessig, a law professor at Harvard University, and subsequent global support has resulted in the availability of over a billion freely licensed works (Creative Commons 2015). This means diverse work supported by a Creative Commons licence can now be ethically used from extremely popular websites for: audio (soundcloud), photographs (flickr), presentation slides (slideshare), and video (YouTube).

Barriers for research
The need for independence

An ethical issue that is fundamental to all academic research is the need to ensure that the research is independent. This can be problematic if finances dictate research agendas so the Haldane Principle, which evolved in the early 20th century, aims to reduce these influences and ensure the independence of research in UK universities. This principle requires decisions about funding to be taken by independent research councils and not government departments. Research Councils UK is the nondepartmental public body made up of seven individual research councils that organise and fund research for the different disciplines in the arts, humanities, science, and engineering. The Arts and Humanities (AHRC) and the Economic and Social Research (ESRC) councils are the two most relevant for criminology and they both fund individual projects and postgraduate degrees.

Legal issues

The law may be an impediment for your research, as you may find that it will prohibit your proposed study altogether. An example of this might be researching how jurors come to their verdicts. Knowledge of what factors determined these outcomes would clearly be useful but, despite the fundamental importance of jury decisions, little is known about this important stage of the criminal process. Much of what is known about juries emanates from research conducted in the US but the different methods of practice reduce their application to England and Wales. A major reason for the gap in knowledge is the law governing such research, as there are both common law and statutory provisions that enshrine secrecy for all deliberations by a jury. The importance given to this secrecy stretches back at least 200 years and includes cases where jurors may have tossed a coin to come to their decision, and used a ouija board to contact the spirit of a potential victim of murder (see *Vaise* v *Delaval* (1785) 99 Eng. Rep. 944 (K.B.) and *R* v *Young* (1995) QB 324 respectively). The significance of secrecy for the events in a jury room is that criminal liability can be imposed even if a juror believes they are exposing the prejudice and misconduct of other jurors (*Attorney General* v *Scotcher* (2005)

UKHL 36). There have been statutory rules in place for over 40 years, which were recently amended in 2015, primarily to deal with misconduct on behalf of individual jurors and their use of the Internet to research details about an offence and/or an offender. But for researchers interested in this part of the criminal justice process, the criminal offence of contempt of court is committed when a person discloses, obtains, or asks about 'statements made, opinions expressed, arguments advanced or votes cast by members of a jury in the course of their deliberations' (s. 20D of the Juries Act 1974), which means that little research is possible.

This legislation, although intended for the press and individual jurors, is believed to have deterred academic research and contributed to 'an information vacuum about juries in this country' (Thomas 2010: 1). This is not the case in the US where far more research has been done but the substantial differences between the two legal systems considerably hinder potential application to the UK. The contrasts include having alternate jurors (a 13th member for cases of illness etc. in any of the 12 selected jurors) and significantly different relationships with the media. This can mean all jurors potentially giving interviews that explain their decisions or as in 2011, following their acquittal of Casey Anthony for murdering her 2-year-old daughter, all of the jury refusing to do such interviews (see **Figure 28.4**). The lack of provided explanations and subsequent knowledge for jury decisions may be controversial for all offences, but it is often deemed particularly so when it comes to serious sexual offences such as rape. The vacuum of knowledge is unlikely to be easily filled as, in

Figure 28.4 An alternative member of the jury?

Source: AP Photo/Joe Burbank, Pool

WHAT DO YOU THINK? 28.1

An inaccessible 'black hole' for criminological knowledge?

The UK's statutory prohibition on acquiring any statements, opinions, arguments, or votes cast by jurors in the course of their deliberations means very little is known about this crucial part of its justice system. But should such research always be a step too far for your discipline?

Consideration of its ethical implications should enable you to see the potential for harm in this kind of research. It would include the lack of voluntariness on behalf of jurors as their service is coerced by a court summons supported by the threat of imprisonment should it not

be done. Anonymity is a key principle of jury service and harm from any research would considerably increase if raising the veil of secrecy was found to have influenced any decision making. This would have serious implications for both the defendants and victims in these trials plus others in the future. It could also damage wider society through a loss of trust in the jury system; a level of faith often explained by Lord Devlin's famous description of a jury as 'the lamp that shows freedom lives'.

So do you agree that these matters should be completely off limits to academic researchers? What could the consequences be if this black hole in criminological knowledge began to be filled?

the lead-up to the amended contempt of court offence, the Parliamentary Under-Secretary for the Ministry of Justice clearly stated, 'academics may not at present research the substance of jury deliberations' (Criminal Justice and Courts Bill Deb 25 March 2014, col. 412). See **What do you think? 28.1** for more on this issue.

The data in **Table 28.3** shows little change for either the county of Lancashire or England & Wales in that half-decade period in the numbers of prosecutions brought for charges of rape. This was also the case for the 'headline figure' and the percentage resulting in a conviction. The prosecutions that do not end in a conviction can be mapped against six potential reasons: jury acquittals; victim retraction; victim evidence did not support the case; victim non-attendance; conflict of prosecution evidence and other. Jury acquittal has been the most common of these, as for England & Wales in 2013–14, it accounted for 61 per cent (941 cases) of the total reasons for non-conviction; it has risen annually from the 45 per cent (693 cases) in 2009–10 (HMIC, 2014: 43–44). The reasons why

juries may be less inclined to deliver guilty verdicts in sexual offences can be a source of much conjecture although it must be remembered that they still convict more often than they acquit in these trials and at higher rates than for other serious offences such as attempted murder, manslaughter, and grievous bodily harm (Thomas 2010).

Bear in mind what you have read so far in this section when you look at **New Frontiers 28.1**.

Reviewing your ethical approach

'The Only Way is Ethics' statement may be grammatically dubious (and have obvious connections to the famous reality TV show) but it is a memorable way for appreciating the absolute importance of ethical principles in your research. The fact it is in the present tense illustrates the constant need to take these matters into account. The different examples in this section have all shared a commitment to research activity that takes the interests of its participants

Financial year	Prosecutions (E & W)	Convictions (E & W)	%(to 1 dp)	Prosecutions (Lancashire)	Convictions (Lancashire)	%(to 1 dp)
2009-10	3,819	2,270	59.4	123	90	73.1
2010-11	4,208	2,465	58.6	135	79	58.5
2011-12	3,864	2,414	62.5	136	92	67.6
2012-13	3,692	2,333	63.2	136	85	62.5
2013-14	3,891	2,348	60.3	158	106	67.1

Table 28.3 An example from the work of the Rape Monitoring Group, HMIC (adapted from HMIC, 2014: Figs. 5.3–5.4)

NEW FRONTIERS 28.1

Having criminology students as a 13th member of the jury—with Belinda Child

I was invited to start a research project into the criminal trial process for sexual offences. I was asked to be involved by two people, Nazir Afzal, then Chief Crown Prosecutor for the Crown Prosecution Service's North West Area and Saima Afzal MBE, a former student of mine and local Human Rights activist. It was originally called 'Juror 13' and set about independently observing sexual offence trials at two local Crown Courts. Over three months, ending February 2015, a hypothetical 13th member of the jury was placed in every such trial that was estimated to last one week or less at both courts. They were all undergraduate criminology students and observed everything witnessed in court by the 12 members of the jury proper. This meant they left the court whenever the real jurors did and followed any other instructions from the judge. The ushers and judiciary were essential to the success of this data acquisition and the hypothetical jurors completed various documents to record their experiences.

The project provided a unique form of evidence through original, low-cost, and innovative methods. At every stage there have been major ethical issues with regard to potential for harm for everyone involved in the court processes. These took considerable time to overcome but this planning was well worth it as it facilitated meaningful research journeys for both me and my students; ones that hopefully can be repeated in the future.

Belinda Child, Criminology Lecturer, University Centre at Blackburn College

into account. They have shown how the principle of informed consent is much deeper than a tick-box response on a questionnaire. They also showed how the potential for research to cause harm requires similar appreciation; perspectives that can often be neglected in undergraduate dissertations. The principles have been shown to overlap but they merge into standards that underpin research in higher education. Specific application of the Statement of Ethics from the British Society of Criminology to your project will assure its sound ethical nature.

Evaluating your work (and that of others)

The role of evaluation within criminological research can be criticised if it takes the discipline away from its quest in seeking to understand the causes of crime. But as the official criminal justice policy responses involve big decisions, sometimes costing millions of pounds, you would think careful evaluations are an important feature of the official system. However, this is not necessarily true as criminal justice practices, if they are evaluated at all, will take the form of either impact evaluations which measure the outcomes of a response; process evaluations which measure their practical aspects and feasibility or cost-benefit evaluations which seek to investigate the efficiency of a response (Lab 2016). The use of impact evaluations are the most popular of these measures and for criminal

justice practices it is the rate of reoffending that forms the basis for the impact evaluation.

If you are interested in researching these types of measures for current criminal justice responses then consider using the Justice Data Lab which was set up in 2013 by the Ministry of Justice. The intention behind this resource is to provide voluntary and community sector organisations that work with offenders, the aggregate reoffending data for the people they have been working with. They are also given comparable data for a matched control group with very similar characteristics to these offenders. This data are then analysed to see whether any differences in reoffending rates are statistically significant. Previously such organisations would have not have known these outcomes unless they were able to use professional researchers with access to the data on the Police National Computer. But now this data are publicly available it could be an excellent resource if you are interested in evaluating the use of community sentences. However, such measures of success can be strongly criticised as there are many other variables that may have influenced possible re-offending. But that said the Justice Data Lab offers plenty of data that could be useful for your research. It could also be very beneficial for your career development as it provides numerous examples of current criminal justice practices; this will make you aware of the different organisations involved in these types of contemporary work.

A process evaluation is one that measures the practicalities of a response and they are a limited form of research that measures its feasibility rather than effectiveness. It has been claimed for several years that the popularity of these kinds of studies illustrate the downgrading of the influence in criminal justice research (Garland 2001). However, there are views from even further back that question whether research has ever had a significant influence on any innovations in the criminal justice system (Radzinowicz 1961).

A cost-benefit evaluation seeks to measure the costs and benefits of an initiative and in a world where financial resources are so scarce you would think something like this is regularly used in criminal justice. However, this is rarely the case as the financial costs of criminal justice interventions are often secondary to other interests. A stark example is provided by the 'war on drugs' policies of recent decades; see the podcast from Harvard Professor Jeffrey Miron in 2014 that claims tens of billions of dollars would be saved every year if a less punitive approach was taken. Miron advises people to disregard their moral compass in order to be a good researcher. This does not mean being unethical as the ethical standards needed for your research will guard against such possibilities. Arguably it is this level of detachment that can allow researchers to discover such surprising findings such as the known association between tougher police enforcement against drug dealers and higher rates of homicide (Miron 2001).

So more than anything else, good evaluation is about asking good questions and not necessarily having advanced research skills. In the case of criminal justice these questions would need to address how credible information needs to be given to influential but sceptical people (particularly government departments such as the Ministry of Justice and HM's Courts and Tribunals Service). In addition, an effective researcher may also want their work to reach the audiences that are least informed. This is relevant to the public's knowledge and attitudes for criminal justice which as you know are likely to be shaped by the superficial information they have received from the media. Public awareness evaluations are therefore another potential method of appraisal and these are considered essential for evaluating public educational campaigns (Pickett et al. 2014). Any communication strategy seeking to inform members of the public about the

deeper workings of the criminal justice system needs to be engaging and influence instinctual views. To achieve both, factual types of information such as the sentencing guidelines plus personal stories from people affected by the sentence such as an offender's parents, spouse, or child are needed (Pickett et al. 2014). If you had the relevant information for this type of activity, would it be something that you could produce?

The limited role evaluative research plays in criminal justice results in a lack of interest in its theory and its concepts. It means attention is not usually given to why a particular response works (or not) and whether it could be transferred to somewhere else. A theoretical void will produce limited research. This has often been the case with crime prevention initiatives which tend to concentrate on the hot-spot status of areas with high rates of recorded crime; this focus ignores the dimensions to this offending and the other influences on the commission of crime. The research referred to earlier in this chapter that Phil conducted into antisocial behaviour recognised some of this depth as the initiative combined hot-times (Friday and Saturday nights) with hot-spots (geographical areas) in its provision of street soccer. In comparison with the recorded figures from 12 months earlier when the service was not available, there had been a drop in the numbers of recorded offences in six of the seven areas where it was provided; this reduction resulted in 131 fewer recorded incidents over the research period of three months. This suggested there may have been substantial financial savings as it could have prevented the need for a response from the criminal justice system; but also in the significant costs had the incidents resulted in a court order which had been breached with a custodial sentence imposed as a result. However, the limited nature of the research meant such benefits could not be claimed to have derived from the street soccer initiative; the quantitative evidence for the numbers of recorded instances told us absolutely nothing about why this might have happened. This limited research unfortunately meant 'it just did' was probably one of its most accurate findings! (This was not quite true as there was a second stage of qualitative research with the local residents and providers of the service that provided more depth.)

Writing up your research

Any writing up of your work will be influenced by the approach you have taken to your research, by the type of reading you have done and the type of evidence you have acquired. Your style of writing will need to be different if your research has a quantitative bias, as you will have

to incorporate statistical information into your work. Observing how other studies have presented their evidence in relevant academic journals is the best way to appreciate this; so your efforts in doing effective literature reviews will rewarded here.

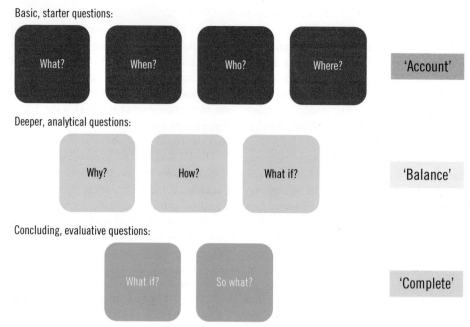

Basic, starter questions:

What? When? Who? Where? 'Account'

Deeper, analytical questions:

Why? How? What if? 'Balance'

Concluding, evaluative questions:

What if? So what? 'Complete'

Figure 28.5 ABC questions for writing critically

The clarity of your writing will be helped by breaking down your research down into parts or phases (see **Figure 28.5**). Such a structure will help immensely when your final piece seems unimaginable. The proverb from the Chinese philosopher Laozi is always worth remembering— 'a journey of a thousand miles begins with a single step'— every researcher has to start somewhere and we all begin with a small step. Each subsequent step in your research journey will probably be equally small and together they will generate momentum in the process of knowledge creation.

The thoughts in **Figure 28.5** should be applied to everything in your research. Your own findings require this process just as much as the information in journals, books, media, etc. so apply these steps to everything you write in your project. It might mean considerable redrafting so you need to be organised in the file names you use to save your work. The first row contains straightforward questions; answering these will give clear descriptions and 'account' for what is already known in your research area and what could be known from your study. The second step requires questions that enable you to analyse your work and these deeper thoughts will 'balance' your writing. The final row is where you 'complete' your work by evaluating what you have found; to do this your opinions on your study's value as well as the value of other studies are required. The 'so what' question is arguably the single most important question when evaluating something as it makes you think about the knowledge's worth, its implications and its different levels of importance. The question is fundamental to the justifications you give for your work which—as you know—is at the heart of the academic exercise.

Working on your writing style

The writing up of your work should hopefully be an enjoyable part of your studies as it is here where you can showcase your abilities. Your style of writing will be in the spotlight so it is important to practice it as much as you can. You have probably heard the saying, 'practice makes perfect', but arguably it should be 'perfect practice makes perfect'. This means you take every opportunity you can to practice your academic writing; such as the work expected for seminars or other parts of your course. If possible it also includes getting your writing checked by someone at your institution, preferably before your work is formally marked. Once you start receiving your marked work back, this feedback is central to your development as an undergraduate writer. The temptation just to look at your grade and then forget all about it, is understandable given the importance of grades and the difficulties in taking criticism when you have worked so hard. But the ability to act on constructive feedback is a significant feature of a successful undergraduate.

The style of your written work can influence subsequent grades so neat presentation is essential. This means following guidance from your course about issues such as font sizes, line spacing, etc., and also the fundamental importance of doing spelling and grammar checks on everything you write. We all know these tools may not be perfect but nonetheless they can identify issues in the way you construct your sentences. If further improvements to your building of sentences and paragraphs are needed, then this kind of development will be possible by working your way through sources such as Chapter 7 of Finch and Fafinski (2016).

Your writing should be aiming to avoid the faults you are now accustomed to detecting in many forms of criminological knowledge; so to reduce perceptions of bias you should generally avoid the use of the first person in your work. Instead a more formal style needs to be provided by writing in the third person. The first person could be acceptable in a reflective piece or a research report where it could be appropriate to write 'I interviewed…' or 'I analysed…' but the crucial point is whether such a choice adds value to your work. It could threaten your objectivity and detract from the overall quality of your writing so it and other personal terms are generally best avoided. It is similarly inadvisable to refer to yourself as 'the author' as this is also too personal and can sound pretentious; so using the third person through statements such as 'it can be argued that…' or 'it was found that…' will provide the detached, objective impression you need to convey. The use of the formal third person may feel unnatural at first but it will help you avoid the use of informal language and slang. Such terms usually have no place in academic writing where use of appropriate language is essential. Think about it: as a budding criminologist you have doubtless spent a considerable amount of time criticising the language used by the media in reporting on crime or in the choices of words taken by Parliament and the courts in creating the criminal law—so you should be as critical on your own writing.

In the same way that good research involves breaking the task down into stages through manageable steps, effective academic writing requires a similar approach. There is no need to overcomplicate it as credit will be given for doing the simple things well; remember all good writing has the same basic structure of a beginning, a middle, and an end. It can be easy to neglect introductions or conclusions when word limits are tight, as the middle part of your answer is likely to contain the majority of your critical thinking. This can be a serious mistake as it means you will miss the relatively easier marks for introducing and summarising your work.

Referencing your work

To develop an effective style of writing you have to be able to reference academic literature in the expected ways. This can cause new undergraduates much concern but it is not that difficult if you first write the required entry for the list of references that has to be provided at the end of academic writing. Incorporating the reference into the main body of your writing then becomes much easier and precisely what is needed will depend on whether you are including a direct quote from this source.

Direct quotes should follow the pattern used throughout this book; as seen in the example provided earlier in this chapter for how photography 'has even succeeded in making misery itself an object of pleasure' (Benjamin 1934: 5). The author's surname, year of publication, and page number are required for direct quotes—in the Benjamin source the quote was taken from page 5 of his book that was published in 1934. This can be an excellent way of proving your wider reading but direct quotes should be used sparingly as otherwise it damages your claims that your work is original and produced by yourself. In addition to getting the right balance right for both the number and length of direct quotes, problems can also arise when they are not naturally incorporated into your writing. When they do not flow with the previous sentence this can raise questions in a marker's mind as to whether they are only being included for the sake of it. However, they can add real value if they support (or contradict) the point you are trying to make in your writing.

In situations where you are not taking a direct quote and are using your own words, the conventional way is to just put the author's surname and year of publication at the end of the sentence. So in the example from the previous paragraph it could be something like: … there have been ethical concerns over the exploitative potential of photography (Benjamin 1934).

As you can see from this text book and in academic sources generally, the indirect use of references is the most common way of incorporating academic literature. If you wish, it is possible to put the surname (or name of an organisation) and year of publication earlier in a sentence, but this is rare so if you are doing it, re-read your work carefully to check it does not disjoint your writing.

At the end of your work you will need to provide a list of references, which if done correctly will prove that your writing complies with the standard referencing conventions. Initially this can be intimidating but such fears can be overcome by simply following the different patterns for the different kinds of sources you have used in your writing. There is not the space in this chapter to list them all but the most common forms of patterns for your list of references are:

1. For published books you need to provide the:
   - author surnames, commas, initials, full stops;
   - date of publication in brackets;
   - full title;
   - edition number (if it is after the first);
   - place the book was published and the publisher's name (if you remember 'place' then 'publisher' is in alphabetical order, you will get this convention right).

An example used in this chapter was:

Caulfield, L. and Hill, J. (2014) *Criminological Research for Beginners*. Abingdon: Routledge.

2. For articles published in academic journals you need to provide the:
   - author surnames, commas, initials, full stops;
   - date of publication in brackets;
   - the title of the article in inverted commas;
   - the title of the journal in italics;
   - the volume number, and if there is one the issue number of that volume;
   - the start and end page numbers for the article.

An example used in this chapter was:

Pantazis, C. and Pemberton, S. (2012) 'Harm audit: the collateral damage of economic crisis and the Coalition's austerity programme', *Criminal Justice Matters*, 89, 42–45.

3. For something from an edited book, these two patterns are effectively merged and each chapter is treated in a similar way to a journal article.

An example used in this chapter was:

Prosser, J. (2011) 'Visual Methodology: Toward a More Seeing Research' in N. K. Denzin and Y. S. Lincoln (eds) *The Sage Handbook of Qualitative Research* (4th edn). London: Sage, pp. 479–96.

4. If you are seeking to use a secondary source then you need to provide both the primary and secondary citations in your text, but only include the secondary source in your list of references. Suppose you want to refer to work published in 2011 by Taylor-Gooby and Stoker which you read about in the 2012 study by Pantazis and Pemberton; your writing should include something like:

Taylor-Gooby and Stoker (as cited in Pantazis and Pemberton, 2012) found public sector spending cuts in the UK would result in there being a smaller role for state provided public services than that in the USA.

Or:

The public sector spending cuts led to studies that found there would be a smaller role for state provided public services in the UK than that in the USA (Taylor-Gooby and Stoker, as cited in Pantazis and Pemberton, 2012).

It is far from ideal to use this kind of referencing as you are completely relying on the source you have read for this second-hand information. You will not be able to check its accuracy and its use is therefore not generally welcomed; but as ever, exceptions can sometimes be allowed so carefully read the referencing guidelines from your institution. If it is permitted, then in your list of references you should only cite the source you have actually read.

It is essential that your list of references is presented in alphabetical order of the surnames or organisations responsible for your sources. These days many automated ways exist for generating references but surely as with a calculator for doing your maths, it's advisable to understand the principles of what you are doing!

Disseminating your findings

The standard readership of a dissertation is usually the producing student and their supervising tutor. This can be extended to include tutors who are involved in the second marking processes but clearly this is still a very limited audience. Is this a missed opportunity? Considering the amount of effort you have put in should there not be a wider circulation of your work? An increase could occur if your research involved a community group or organisation as they may be interested in parts of your dissertation. In several European countries the research findings of a student's PhD have this extra dissemination as their *viva voce* stage (the oral examination of the research) is conducted in public. This requirement to defend your research in a public arena is desired by some academics in the UK (*Times Higher Education*, 22 October 2015). Undergraduate research may be more of a closed affair but the recent expansion of open education means there are new options for acquiring interest in your work. Whether this is through blogs, open access journals, or presentation sites, there are now more opportunities than ever for cascading your research and publicising your work.

If you have photographs from your research they can easily be transferred to various websites, particularly if they are saved as jpeg files; if a professional standard is required then tiff files are generally used. Your images can then be converted into other formats such as PowerPoint and video. Similarly a PowerPoint can be effortlessly converted into jpeg (or other formats) and then through either free movie making software (paid-for versions are also available) or free screen recording services (ditto), your work can soon be uploaded to an online video sharing site of your choice. YouTube is normally the preferred destination due to its potential for huge audiences and some of criminology students' productions have been known to attract over 1,000 views. The image in **Figure 28.6** began its 'life' as an image in an undergraduate PowerPoint

Figure 28.6 'The Shocking Potential of Hidden Crime', by Andrea Green and Michelle Green, BA Criminology students as part of a video resource for a 'What is Crime?' research project

Source: Creative Commons Licence

For every **one** homicide in the UK there are...

"**three times** as many deaths from road traffic accidents...

four times as many deaths from hospital infections...

five deaths caused by individuals intentionally killing themselves...

forty-five people [who] die from deaths related to excess pollution in the atmosphere"

(Pantazis and Pemberton, 2012: 43).

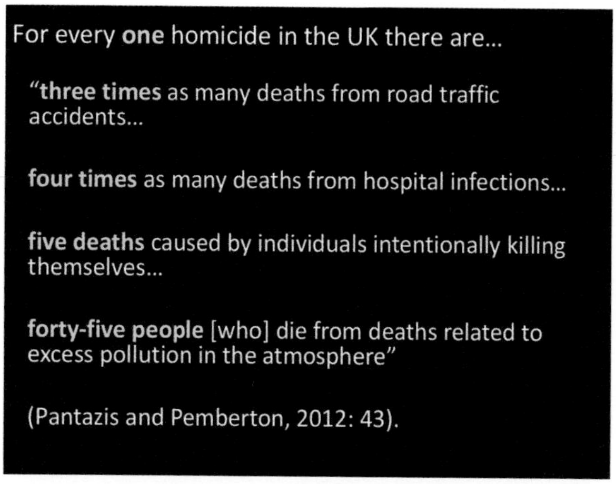

Figure 28.7 Using the harm audit from Pantazis and Pemberton (2012) as part of a video resource for a 'What is Zemiology?' research project

Source: Phil Johnson/Creative Commons Licence

presentation and has since been repurposed in these different formats of a video on YouTube and different screen recordings. This image is a good example of the benefits visual learning strategies can bring as it enabled the students to illustrate a different take on matters of community safety. Instead of low level crime and antisocial behaviour being the perpetual focus, this image of neglected electricity equipment in the community illustrated other dangers (potentially more harmful) that are rarely considered. This student-produced resource was distributed under a Creative Commons licence and is something author Phil Johnson regularly uses in his teaching. The value of the numbers these online resources attract and whether they can be manipulated to produce quantitative [in]significance could be something you are interested in testing.

This kind of dissemination could be your contribution to the disciplinary debates for how criminology knows about crime considered in **Chapter 6**. In addition to communicating important issues in accessible ways to wider audiences, such as those in **Figure 28.7**; your production of online resources can bring personal benefits. This kind of activity will demonstrate high levels of engagement with your studies and verify your possession of a range of different skills. You do not have to wait until the end of your project; you could incorporate it into your research. Dissemination of your interim findings opens up many possibilities for experimentation in your research, as suggested in **Chapter 6**; the measurement of peoples' views before and after they have seen your work would be one way of doing this.

Now would be a good time to look at **Conversations 28.5**.

Dissemination dilemmas

The importance of impact to contemporary research means transparency and openness for its results are now

integral to the whole process. It is usually a condition for acquiring funding in the first place that dissemination activities are proposed. In addition, bodies such as the AHRC and the ESRC offer 'follow-on' funding opportunities for conducting this kind of work. These awards tend to be reserved for large projects so your potential dissemination activities such as blogs, websites, videos, posters, workshops, community meetings, etc. will probably need to be self-funded. But inquiries should always be made from your higher education provider with regard to any available help for this kind of action. This range of distribution options for your work sits alongside the more conventional methods such as writing an article for a professional magazine or a scholarly publication at your institution. In all cases they can demonstrate your high level communication skills for presenting work in different formats for different audiences.

Ethical thinking has to be a priority for any dissemination practices so safeguards need to be taken against the possibility of harming any of your research participants. This could arise in a number of ways—for example if assurances for anonymity were essential to informed consent, would these steps mean they become identifiable? It could also lead to harm if your findings were critical of individuals and organisations in your research; this can be a common problem so the ability to use language sensitively is an essential part of an ethical researcher's toolkit. Alternatively your participants might stand to benefit from your research so could be keen to help you with its dissemination. This is where effective planning for your topic will pay off as research concerning community groups, campaigns and professionals can lead you to people with an interest in publicising your findings.

CONVERSATIONS 28.5

The personal value in researching new topics—with Barry Smith

Phil Johnson (one of the authors of this book) discusses with a student how they found the experience of choosing, researching and completing their dissertation.

PJ (Phil Johnson): How did you choose your dissertation topic?

BS (Barry Smith): My original topic was going to be the doctrine of joint enterprise as I was interested in miscarriages of justice and abuses of human rights. I had done some reading over the summer but it all changed at the start of term when I saw my institution promoting research opportunities for undergraduates interested in studying local issues. One of these was a request for research into antisocial behaviours that were supposedly happening in the grounds of the local cathedral. I really liked this sense of purpose so this became my research subject even though I had not previously considered it at all.

PJ: Did this change cause you any problems?

BS: I liked it at first because it was a completely new topic for me and so I felt I had fewer preconceptions. But it in other ways it was very problematic as I had to do plenty of thinking fast! The research request was not specific at all so I had the freedom to devise the strategy of my choice.

PJ: How did you choose your methodology?

BS: I limited the scope of my literature review to antisocial behaviour in a religious environment so this made it more manageable. I felt this lack of specific evidence enabled me to try a methodology based on grounded theory as this had always seemed to me to be the least biased of all the conventional research methods. I knew it was ambitious in the time I had available but I thought my background and the context of this research made it possible for me to give it a go.

PJ: So what did you do then?

BS: I believed an empirical study was the right way forward because the only evidence I had for the alleged problem was the evidence of the one community stakeholder. So I interviewed a range of people that included a variety of stakeholders; one from the cathedral, seven adjacent businesses, and eight of the people who regularly associated in the grounds. This data acquisition gave me common themes for my research objectives and my research question came from that.

PJ: What was the most interesting thing you learnt whilst doing your research?

BS: I was shocked at the lack of knowledge being shared by the different official groups with responsibility for looking after the cathedral grounds. This was very different to the people who associated there as they all seemed to share information and know what was going on.

PJ: How did you feel when it was completed?

BS: A mixture of relief and joy! It was really hard work but I am glad I did it because my project gave me a sense of achievement that a library based study might not have done. I think this is down to my feeling that I had created 'new' knowledge for this problem rather than interpreting that of others.

Barry Smith, BA Criminology student, University Centre at Blackburn College

When seeking publicity of any kind, it is also your duty as an ethical researcher, to ensure your work is reported accurately. This can pose major challenges for academics if the mass media is used in their dissemination and fears often exist of being misquoted and having their research distorted to fit in with other agendas (see **Telling it like it is 28.4**).

TELLING IT LIKE IT IS 28.4

The power of television on a researcher—with author Phil Johnson

Dissertation dilemmas certainly existed for me following my involvement with a popular television programme which a few years ago broadcast an episode related to community service (the unpaid work element of the community order to give its correct title). Twelve months earlier I had completed my PhD, which had been a study of these orders. I was asked for my expert views to be included in the programme. A number of my colleagues were also asked and declined. For me the invitation really was a dilemma. If I accepted the offer, would it damage my professional reputation for being associated with such television? If I turned it down then surely I would regret missing the opportunity to talk to a national broadcaster about some of the findings in my PhD? The predicament was intensified as I did not have long to think about it. In the end I decided that I would do it and was very pleased that my colleagues in that group understood my reasons.

I exchanged a couple of emails and had a 30 minute telephone conversation with the producer followed by an interview at the Television Studios. I was told the programme had been commissioned following 'a chance conversation with a guy who said his friend had done community service' and he had 'whiled away his time playing snooker and computer games'. This 'friend' was not prepared to go on television so the television company had provided cameras to offenders who were, and subsequently they acquired almost 50 hours of secret footage from unpaid work sites across the Midlands and North West. A couple of days before I was due to go for the interview, I was surprised to receive an email saying that as a result of this communication, a script had been prepared for me.

I did not believe this was an accurate representation at all for what I had been telling the producers (all of the potentially positive aspects to this sentencing practice had been edited out as had all the critique of the Ministry of Justice's confused approach) but I still decided to go for the interview. I added what I thought were only a couple of amendments and it seemed to go well. But on the morning of the day the programme was broadcast, I received an apologetic phone call from the producer, explaining that my interview had been edited out in favour of a 'last minute contribution' from the former Conservative Home Secretary! This blow was cushioned by the fact I was aware this could happen so had only told a couple of people about my brush with fame! The phone call made me realise that I was in a good company of 'rejects' as the same thing had happened to the Chief Inspector of HM Inspectorate of Probation.

Where to next?

Once your dissertation has been submitted and you are at the end of your undergraduate course you will probably have two decisions, whether to progress into employment or to carry on in higher education. Planning your future progression can still pay off even though you may be like many undergraduates and feel completely unsure about which direction you would like to take.

Stepping further into higher education for your research

The drives towards open education have included access to resources and courses in higher education. Their advocates frequently claim that new and affordable homes for higher education are being built online with universities of the future constructed from 'clicks' not bricks. These could be places such as the Peer to Peer University and the Open Education Resources university, both of which claim to have tens of thousands of registered students. The acronym MOOC (massive open online course) can be the umbrella term for these educational opportunities and in recent years, among many others, the University of Strathclyde has provided a six week course in forensic science and the University of Sheffield offered a course on the role of the state and criminal justice interventions. The FutureLearn initiative from the Open University has many other similar opportunities.

In answering the 'so what' question that you are hopefully now asking regularly, there is evidence to indicate the open approach of MOOCs positively impacts on the motivation of students and tutors and facilitates social learning experiences (Scanlon et al. 2015). These courses offer opportunities for extending your networks and joining what are pedagogically referred to as a 'community of practice'. This name is given to the groups of people who share a keen interest in something they do and learn how to do it better by interacting with each other (Lave and Wenger 1991).

This rich potential from online opportunities is leading to interest in (some would argue acceptance of) a new learning theory, connectivism. This believes in the learning provided from participation in a network which then develops and enhances existing levels of knowledge. It has been put forward by George Siemens who in 2008, with Stephen Downes, was responsible for the first recognised MOOC. The connections between people in the networks are the driving force of this theory that believes:

> The pipe is more important than the content within the pipe. Our ability to learn what we need for tomorrow is more important than what we know today.
>
> (Siemens 2005)

In addition to these courses, the conventional 'offline' world also provides routes for your future learning (see **Conversations 28.6**).

CONVERSATIONS 28.6

Post graduate options for criminology graduates—with Dr Kathryn Chadwick

Further study may be something you are considering. Many criminology graduates are often captivated by the subject matter and wish to immerse themselves in and learn more about the discipline. Post-graduate study at Masters' level provides the opportunity to expand your criminological knowledge further and to develop advanced analytical, critical thinking, and other transferable skills which should enhance career opportunities and professional practice within criminal justice and related agencies or in non-related career settings. Currently there are 31 masters' courses in UK universities each offering their own distinct criminology programmes. So how do you choose the right course for you? Perhaps a starting point is to establish exactly what you want:

- Do you want to study full or part time? (Typically the duration is one year full-time or two years part-time.)

- Are you looking for a course that combines theoretical debates in criminology with aspects of criminal justice policy and practice, or are you interested in one of these elements?

- Are you looking for a course that is more vocationally orientated and offers a placement?

- Do you want a taught course or do you have a specific topic that you would like to pursue via a programme of research?

- Do you want to attend a university or are you looking for a distance learning package?

Once you have established the answers to these questions you can then consider which university might be best for you. It is also worth considering the different types of masters' courses available. Taught masters' programmes are always popular as students like the structure of the classroom experience. However, many universities also offer research based masters—for example 'Masters by Research'. On this kind of course you will devise your own research project and direct your own studies under the supervision of academic staff rather than attending a set timetable of lessons. Alternatively, some courses are delivered via a distance learning package.

Here at my institution the MA in Criminology caters for students whose aims and interests are purely academic alongside those who want to develop a more practice-related focus. Our student cohorts are drawn from a diverse range of backgrounds and experiences, both academic and professional. We attract recent criminology graduates, criminal justice practitioners, students from other social science and humanities disciplines, and those who just love the idea of studying criminology. Many of our students have progressed into jobs and opportunities across a range of crime and criminal justice related fields including youth justice, the police and prison system, probation service, victim support, child protection, crime prevention, and other statutory, private and voluntary sector agencies. Others have gone into research related jobs or have progressed onto PhD research programmes. These quotes from Masters criminology graduates illustrate the value of post graduate study not only for future careers but also for individual learning and development:

Criminology is a wonderful discipline to study. Its ability to bring to life the atrocities and injustices of the world, whilst in the process instilling core values to protect, be respectful, empower and support people is special. It's all in my day-to-day working practice.

The staff are well respected within the wider criminological and academic fields and renowned for their critical approach. Because of this, the course attracts a diverse range of students armed with significant life and professional experience enabling interesting perspectives to be voiced via challenging debate, which ultimately enhances the student experience.

Dr Kathryn Chadwick, Principal Lecturer in Criminology, Manchester Metropolitan University

SUMMARY

After working your way through the different features of this chapter you should now be able to:

- Appreciate the breadth of opportunities offered by being an undergraduate researcher in criminology

The chapter explained how thanks to your knowledge and skills acquired from the first four parts of this book, you are now in a position where you can produce things of value to yourself, the discipline of criminology and others. It is now where, as promised in **Chapter 1**, your studies can genuinely become fascinating, dynamic, and stimulating. This chapter considered how you can take a variety of approaches in your criminological research, such as quantitative or qualitative; contemporary or historical; conventional or unconventional.

- Identify effective ways of choosing your research topic

The second part of the chapter explained how thinking carefully about your research topics will enable you to get the most out of your research and maximise its impact on you. This included considering things you personally care about, such as community issues and campaigns as well as your own professional reasons for conducting research. Hopefully this is something you will talk about to the people around you as the different 'Conversations' in the chapter illustrated how common it is for researchers to be helped whilst doing their criminological research.

- Plan the core features of a dissertation or research project

The core features of a dissertation were considered in the middle of the chapter and a general structure was put forward that could be adapted according to the size of your project. The checklist served a clear reminder of these essential elements and showed the absolute importance of recognising the different stages in the research process. It also illustrated how effective research projects will make clear efforts to link these different parts together.

- Engage with ethical standards for researchers in criminology

The fourth key issue conveyed by the chapter was the importance of engaging with the ethical standards for researchers in criminology. These duties such as informed consent and avoiding harm to research participants were shown as being integral to academic research; following these principles proves you are capable of showing appropriate sensitivity for others. Both ethical thinking and action were shown as things you can routinely do, such as in your use of technology like camera phones and the Internet.

- Consider unconventional methods of dissemination for your research

The chapter's final issue considered the rich potential in openly disseminating your research. A variety of methods was recommended to take advantage of the communicative power in technology; a form of openness that means undergraduate research findings no longer have to be limited to you and your supervisors. Plus, if you get involved in these kinds of steps you will be immersed in the ongoing nature of research, as the effectiveness of your dissemination could be your next topic and the cycle of research could start again.

REVIEW QUESTIONS

On completing this chapter please spend time considering:

1. What kind of research do you now want to do? Why?

2. What do you want to produce? Why?

3. What would be the essential stages in this research?

FURTHER READING

Bachman, R.D. and Schutt, R.K. (2017) 'The Practice of Research' in *Criminology and Criminal Justice*. London: Sage.

This text supports its comprehensive discussion of quantitative and qualitative research methods with numerous case studies based on research findings from a range of controversial issues such as gun crime, sexual offences, and police misconduct.

Chamberlain, M. (2013) *Understanding Criminological Research: A Guide to Data Analysis*. London: Sage.

This text provides a thorough and stimulating guide for appropriate research methods in different stages of your research. The author uses many examples of his own experiences to help you understand the content and apply it to your own research work.

Chakraborti, N. and Garland, J. (eds) (2014) *Responding to Hate Crime: The Case for Connecting Policy and Research*. Bristol: The Policy Press.

Through the subject of hate crime, this collection of chapters from academia, policy making, and activism demonstrates the difficulties faced when trying to connect separate worlds of research and policy making.

Drake, D. H., Earle, R., and Sloan, J. (2015) *International Handbook on Prison Ethnography*. Basingstoke: Palgrave.

This authoritative text details challenges and experiences in ethnography from over ten different countries. It is of significant value to anyone interested in this research method and its contemporary use in the closed world of prisons.

Hayward, K. and Presdee, M. (eds) (2010) *Framing Crime: Cultural Criminology and the Image*. Abingdon: Routledge.

This collection of a dozen papers analyses things such as Hollywood films and television advertisements to help you understand the numerous ways visual images are used in the construction and dissemination of the contemporary 'story of crime'.

Kirby, S. and Peal, K. (2015) 'The Changing Pattern of Domestic Cannabis Cultivation in the United Kingdom and Its Impact on the Cannabis Market', *Journal of Drug Issues*, 45(3), 279–92.

This article will inform you about the innovative ways that criminology undergraduates have been collaboratively working with criminal justice agencies.

Miller, J. and Palacios, W. R. (eds) (2015) 'Qualitative Research in Criminology'. New Brunswick: Transaction Publishers.

This text features 17 essays that investigate the ways qualitative research fosters improved levels of understanding for issues of crime and justice. It will encourage you to think deeply about the acquisition and analysis of qualitative data.

 Access the **online resources** to view selected further reading and web links relevant to the material covered in this chapter.
www.oup.com/uk/case/

CHAPTER OUTLINE

Introduction   806

Climbing the levels of your higher education   811

Future concerns for criminology   817

Future concerns for criminal justice   818

Campaigning in criminology   820

Seeing crime differently   823

Applying your skills to employability or future study

KEY ISSUES

After reading this chapter you should be able to:

- engage with a reflective learning approach for enhancing your higher education;

- identify methods for independent learning in the different levels of higher education;

- apply reflective learning to your employability;

- consider how your personal learning journey could help future directions of study for the discipline of criminology.

Introduction

This is the second of three chapters in **Part 5** which is the section of the book that encourages you to do something with your newly acquired criminological knowledge and understanding. It is where your prowess as a criminology undergraduate can pay off by applying the detailed body of knowledge you now have from the preceding chapters. Amongst other things, you now have specialist knowledge regarding the fluctuating nature of crime, its numerous explanations and the multitude of responses employed to deal with it. For fully exploiting your knowledge and skills, knowing how you acquired them will be more important than what you now know.

This chapter recommends you take a disciplined and reflexive approach to your journey into criminology. It begins with the core elements of reflective learning practice before suggesting how they can be applied to your independent learning and official identity as an undergraduate. The links between reflective learning and enhanced employability are then considered. The chapter then progresses to considering how these learning experiences could assist with future directions of the discipline of criminology.

Where are you (the reflective learner) now?

The general concept of learning is said to arise when there is a partial or permanent change in a person's emotional,

mental, and physiological state; or in two words: knowledge and understanding. The new information you acquired from your degree has to be made sense of. This concept of learning is shared by the three traditional learning theories for systems of education as shown in **Figure 29.1**. (It is worth noting that Connectivism is now considered by some as a fourth general theory. Its supporters attribute this to the power of technology and online learning.)

Whichever theoretical approach you most prefer, this change in your emotional, mental, and physiological state can be summed up as the difference between your current levels of knowledge and skills compared with those at the start of your course. This is what you have learnt from being an undergraduate and to benefit, your ability to self-reflect and make self-improvements is essential. The importance of reflective practice in undergraduate learning has been recognised across the disciplines since the 1990s at least. Its theoretical support is often attributed to David Kolb's *experiential learning theory* which holds learning from life experience to be superior to traditional teaching and learning methods, when real experiences of what is being studied are part of the learning process (Kolb 1984). There is clear proximity between reflective practice and employability and this has been repeated in the latest edition of this influential work:

> it might well be said that learning is an increasing *occupation* for us all; for in every aspect of our life and work, to stay abreast of events and to keep our skills up to the 'state of the art' requires more and more of our time and energy.
>
> Kolb 2015: 2 (original emphasis)

Behaviourism

- the influence of conditioning (such as rewards and punishments) on an individual's behaviour. Can be effective for learning some things, such as when being told what to do is sufficient (e.g. practical and repetitive tasks) but not for things requiring problem solving and individual thought.

Cognitivism

- dissatisfaction with behaviourism led to this change in approach from the 1950s (around the same time that a critical view was being cast on criminology). It held learning to be driven by the psychological processes within an individual's mind rather than the responses to different conditions.

Constructivism

- the dissatisfaction with behaviourism also included acceptance of the learning theory of constructivism. Learning is influenced by people interpreting their own experiences and thoughts, and constructing their own understandings.

Figure 29.1 The three traditional learning theories for systems of education

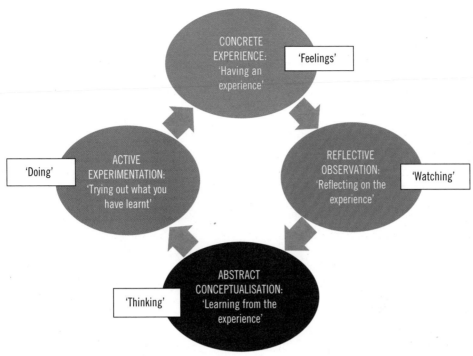

Figure 29.2 The four key stages of Kolb's learning cycle

The well-known Kolb's learning cycle is presented in **Figure 29.2** and your engagement with it can prove profitable. It has the process of reflection beginning with a '*concrete experience*'—an event such as starting a new job or task; recalling your feelings at these times will kick-start your reflective cycle. Then by watching how your peers do their work, the second stage of '*reflective observations*' can occur. This leads to '*abstract conceptualisation*' where your thoughts and judgements on this experience take place. The conclusions you draw are the lessons learnt from the experience and lead to understanding how things are done; if the cycle is done well it will include expected problems and potential sources of help. The final stage in the cycle, '*active experimentation*' puts into practice what you have learnt for doing things effectively. Completing the cycle is evidence of your higher level abilities for developing what you already know; this can be referred to as synthesising knowledge.

Good grades on your course may suggest you have high abilities, but being able to understand and express how you got them will be impressive evidence of your future capabilities. Remembering the cycle can help you cope with the stress in learning new things; so think back to when you did something new on your course (like an essay, formal presentation or piece of seminar work, etc.); simply recollecting your feelings begins your analysis. So recalling what these feelings were and when you got them will get you started. Good research comes from asking good questions, not unnecessarily complex ones; there are many examples in this book where the use of simple questions has proved rewarding. So reflecting back on your feelings is the first small step. If they were negative, such as feeling things were getting out of control, identifying what they were and the issues responsible for them will help you avoid them in the future. Thinking about these basic questions will help you learn from your experiences, so when you put it into action the next time, you will justifiably be a reflective practitioner.

The process should be widely repeated as with each full cycle, your confidence for this type of thinking and action will increase; hopefully such repetition will lead to it becoming engrained into how you practice and learn (like riding a bike ...). It can therefore be used for your academic as well as your work-based learning. Being able to identify your feelings from the concrete experience of writing an essay or delivering a presentation might help you recognise and take the help available from your lecturer, institution, and fellow students. There will be times when it feels you are cycling up an extremely steep hill but such arduous journeys can be broken down into achievable stages. See **Conversations 29.1** for one student's personal experience.

CONVERSATIONS 29.1

Fitting in with Criminology—with Natalie Atkinson

My journey into undergraduate criminology was not the most conventional; I had only returned to education the year before and had been heavily involved in the Youth and Criminal Justice System for the previous nine years. After spending 13 periods in secure units and prisons, I witnessed many young people who had been involved in the care system, like myself and spent a significant amount of time in custody. Many were facing similar complex needs, mental and emotional health needs, substance misuse, isolation, homelessness, self-harm and suicide attempts, and finding it hard to break away from the cycle of offending. I decided that I could use my own experiences to help other young people involved in offending, by being in a position one day to challenge and influence policy and practices. In order to do this I needed academic knowledge to sit alongside my 'lived experience' and this is when I decided to study a BSc Policing, Investigation and Criminology degree. My first year as an undergraduate was spent building my foundation knowledge of the core theoretical concepts in criminology, studying introductory courses in crime and deviance, the criminal justice system, and criminal investigation. During this time I was working for the YMCA and volunteered with young people and the homeless within my local community.

Within my second year I decided to choose my optional modules on the basis of my future career, as it was important for me to be able to draw from my academic knowledge within a professional environment. This became more apparent when I began employment within the homeless sector early into my second year, supporting many service users who were involved in the youth and criminal justice system. Two of my modules were penology and policing vulnerable populations. Penology, which enabled me to consider the larger role of the penal regimes, focusing on the imprisonment of children and young people and policing vulnerable populations, where I was able to use theoretical knowledge to explore and analyse the policing of children and young people. Both of these modules interlinked and enabled me to develop a more critical understanding of the challenges surrounding children and young people involved in the 'system'. This in turn helped me to understand some of my own past experiences and challenges, relating to my relationship with the police and time spent in custody.

The final year of my undergraduate degree was by far the best. I had developed my own academic writing style, demonstrating critical analysis and felt confident in my developing academic knowledge. For years I had self-doubted myself and always felt different to other young people; however I was now in a position where I knew I could achieve academically. During my final year I was approached by a BBC Researcher who had been following my progress on twitter and read a couple of my blogs about being a looked after child and an ex-offender. Reluctant at first, I eventually agreed to present the BBC Three documentary, 'Banged Up and Left To Fail?' focusing on the key areas that contribute to the successful rehabilitation of young adults following their release from prison including; support, housing, education, training and employment, and mental health.

Again, as in my second year I used my modules to benefit my future career, the investigating professions in the social sciences module allowed me to focus directly on my future professional employment and make a plan, which included postgraduate study.

For me my dissertation module was the most important module of my whole undergraduate degree, as I was able to draw from all of my previous undergraduate modules as well as my lived experience and this for me was key; finally able to use my personal life experiences within my current educational journey. I conducted my own research into the importance of consistent support in the rehabilitation for young adult offenders, with a view to be able to develop this research in future years. My findings included that young adult offenders perceived the terminology of 'consistency' to be different to professionals, they did not directly identify 'consistency', however what they did highlight, that they needed to be successfully rehabilitated, did fall into the concept of consistency. For this research I was awarded a 95 per cent grade, graduated with a first class honours degree and was selected to receive the NUS Endsleigh Student of the Year Award 2014 for my academic achievement, overcoming many barriers to return to education and empowering others to make changes. Winning this award was a huge shock for me and was the 'icing on the cake', I finally felt proud of myself and proud of the University of Cumbria's lecturers on my BSc Policing, Investigations and Criminology course, who had offered me consistent support throughout somewhat challenging times.

Not only did my undergraduate degree help me develop academically, it helped me develop as a person. I was able to understand some of my own life experiences, using my gained academic knowledge, my confidence in my own ability and motivation to succeed, to accept my past and was finally able to move on. I no longer saw myself as 'not fitting in' and was now Natalie Atkinson, a graduate with a future ahead of her. After graduating in 2014, I relocated to London to study an MSc Criminal Justice Policy at the LSE and commenced employment within the criminal justice system delivering the Post Sentence Supervision under Transforming Rehabilitation. Within my role I supervise individuals who have received an adult custody sentence of 12 months or under, focusing on their resettlement within the community; housing, education, training and employment, substance misuse, health needs, and so on. Post Sentence Supervision is brand new and has been implemented to try to reduce the high rate of reoffending following short custodial sentences.

My 'criminological journey' contributes massively to my current employment, I continue to use both my academic knowledge and lived experience to develop professionally and fulfill my role to the best of my ability. Studying my undergraduate degree has been the foundation for the rest of my life and I would go further to say that it has contributed to saving my life. It has given me the confidence to believe that I can continue to achieve both in an academic and professional setting.

Natalie Atkinson, BSc Policing, Investigations and Criminology, University of Cumbria

Now you can be a criminologist anywhere

The detailed knowledge and understanding you now have for the ways criminology can be researched (the four usual suspects) should mean you have at the very least, a partially open mind for what it may achieve in the future. Thanks to their 'neo' versions they are all persistent suspects and so it is likely that all of them will help us with our future inquiries at some point. Focusing on the issue under investigation rather than slavishly following a suspect's specific methods and approaches (such as positivism or 'anti-positivism') could be the most productive way forward for advancing what is known in your discipline.

So whilst it can be tempting to completely dismiss certain approaches:

> Think of the impact that epidemiological research has had on demonstrating the connection between smoking and lung cancer. That could not have been achieved through an 'appreciative account' of how smokers felt about their habit or viewed the effect of it on their health!
>
> Hood 2002: 165–66

The body of knowledge you now have for criminology and criminal justice is hopefully enabling you to appreciate the wide-ranging relevance of what you have studied. See **Conversations 29.2** and **29.3** for a specific example.

The enormous number of situations when your studies of criminology could have relevance was shown in

---

CONVERSATIONS 29.2

Imaginatively linking justice and sustainability— with Dr Katja Hallenberg and Dr Maryse Tennant

What does criminology and criminal justice have to do with sustainability? Why should criminologists and criminal justice practitioners care about climate change, destruction of ecosystems, decreasing resources, or the diminishing capacity of our planet to sustain its inhabitants? Criminology is about crime, right? Not tree-hugging!

These are the questions and assumptions we aim to address and challenge in our School, both in the curriculum (in modules we teach) and outside it. Because criminology/criminal justice *is* a discipline with clear links to the sustainable development agenda. This is apparent in various theoretical approaches (e.g. critical criminology, zemiology, green criminology, and public criminology) but in particular via the broader framework of justice. Agyeman and colleagues (2003: 3) note how 'justice and sustainability are intimately linked and mutually interdependent, certainly at the problem level and increasingly at the solution level'. Issues of inequality and injustice (and crucially, ways of addressing them) can thus be linked to the four areas of environmental, social, economic, and cultural sustainability (UNESCO, 2005). So sustainability is not about tree-hugging, and criminology/criminal justice has a vested interest in it. Global warming will lead to various changes at micro-social level that will strengthen the criminal environment while at the same time weakening nation states' ability to maintain effective criminal justice processes and systems (see e.g. Crank and Jacoby 2015 for a recent overview of the research). Things like increased resource scarcity will exacerbate both conflicts and migration, flourishing illegal markets and resulting in even larger numbers of people in vulnerable situations and thus at increased risk of exploitation.

So yes, sustainability matters to criminology and criminologists!

[An] extracurricular project was centred on the Whole Earth? exhibition (http://www.hardrainproject.com) hosted by several universities internationally, including ours. It comprises over 60 meters of images and text, relating to the major problems facing humankind and the planet we inhabit. However, the focus is on encouraging people to find ways to address those problems, to seek solutions, and enact positive change. The exhibition issues several 'university challenges' to encourage disciplines to think about how they can contribute to such solutions. And we felt criminology needed to pick up the gauntlet!

The project is student-centred, seeking to gather and facilitate students' cognitive and affective responses to the Whole Earth? exhibition as well as any concrete actions and behaviours it may invoke. This is done via two principal approaches. The first involves a number of directed reflective activities and experiential learning sessions, using the exhibition as a key stimulus to thinking about links between sustainability and criminology/criminal justice and what the discipline as a whole, including its students, both as a group and individually, can and should do. The second approach invites the students to engage with a 'photo blogging' activity by photographing, posting and reflecting on pictures of anything that they consider relevant to the exhibition themes and sustainability/justice in general. While the exhibition images and text focus mostly on the developing world, the photo blogging allows students to draw the connections to their local context and encourages them to develop a 'critical lens' through which to view the issues of (in)justice and (in)sustainability in their own communities.

The Sustainability Walk the students talk about [see **Conversations 29.3**] was one such opportunity to consider both local issues and the connections between us and the developing world within our daily lives [see **Figure 29.3**]. Throughout the project we have all learned a lot about how crime, justice and sustainability connect together and to our everyday actions and locations. We look forward to embedding the walk and other experiential learning activities within the formal curriculum.

Dr Katja Hallenberg and Dr Maryse Tennant,
School of Law, Criminal Justice and Computing,
Canterbury Christ Church University

Figure 29.3 Staff and students at Canterbury Christ Church University out on the town exploring justice
Source: Dr Katja Hallenberg and Dr Maryse Tennant

CONVERSATIONS 29.3

Perspectives on 'imaginatively linking justice and sustainability'—with Canterbury Christ Church University students

We got involved with the Justice and Sustainability project for various reasons, such as increasing our awareness of the way criminology links to sustainability and to apply the theories taught in our degree, to our surroundings. We used a reflection blog to interact between our group and post relevant information regarding sustainability to change and challenge our knowledge and habits.

The Whole Earth exhibition was a starting point for this project. It enabled us to gain an understanding of sustainability around the world. Migration and environmental crimes were the key aspects in connecting criminology and sustainability, for example, we reflected upon issues such as hate crime and social injustice. The next part of our project was to explore sustainability within our local community. As a group we visited community areas within Canterbury, such as Abbotts Mill. This project aims to develop sustainability and they hope to offer volunteering opportunities to marginalised groups such as offenders. Next, we visited our high street shops, where we discussed ethical consumerism. We made another link to criminology through issues such as worker rights and human rights in general. We discovered how shops make their produce through outsourcing to countries where there are fewer workers' rights compared to the UK. Next, we went to visit a local food bank donation point, advertised within our community, however upon arriving there, we were advised that the food bank wasn't positioned in a place for the public to easily access. We challenged this idea, through discussing that this is purposely hiding poverty. This was a way for us to gain an increased awareness of injustice and how criminology applies to our everyday lives.

Overall, this project has made us reflect upon why our studies matter and that sustainability is the answer to make this world a better place!

Students Georgia Cole (Applied Criminology/Psychology),
Margit Guenther (Crime and Policing),
Fleur-Elise Williams (Applied Criminology),
Canterbury Christ Church University

Chapter 4 with its wonderfully engaging 'who gets the flute?' example. This demonstrated the pervasive nature of justice and how its conflicting ideals underpin crucial decisions in society such as the allocation of resources. The problem also demonstrated how utilitarians, egalitarians, and libertarians would differently solve the problem by respectively ensuring it is given to the child who can play it, the one with no toys, or the child who made it. Supporters of the sharing economy would claim a new redistribution was possible, that of common ownership shared through an online platform! This is very different to the vengeful interpretations of justice in popular Hollywood films such as *Justice* in 2011 and *Law Abiding Citizen* in 2009.

Climbing the levels of your higher education

Whilst the 'cap and gown' and graduation ceremony is a standard symbol of completed undergraduate journeys, it is possible to claim success before then. The Framework for Higher Education Qualifications in England, Wales and Northern Ireland and the Framework for Qualifications of Higher Education Institutions in Scotland was first published in 2001 (see **Table 29.1**). There have been several updated versions since and they have all continued the desire to recognise the different levels of higher education. The standard undergraduate journey under this framework takes in levels 4–6 which generally correspond to years 1–3 of a full time undergraduate degree course.

As you progress through your course, you will be expected to reach the different levels under its two general requirements of a knowledge descriptor and a skills descriptor. They are fairly abstract statements as they

Level 4: Certificate of higher education

Level 5: Foundation degree; HND/C; Diploma of higher education

Level 6: Bachelor's degree with honours

Level 7: Master's degree

Level 8: Doctoral degree

Table 29.1 The Different Levels of the Framework for Higher Education Qualifications

represent the expected levels of knowledge and skills for the entire undergraduate population. But they offer value in their representation of an 'undergraduate skeleton'; so if you can express them naturally they offer extremely useful terms for your CV and job applications. The expected developments in your knowledge and skills are presented in **Tables 29.2** and **29.3**.

The first row of **Table 29.2** illustrates the importance of practical, theoretical and technical knowledge as it is required to complete each level. Practical knowledge will be possessed when you know how to apply things you have learnt to real-world situations. To name just one example, the academic knowledge you now have for the subject of crime prevention (**Chapter 22**) means you are capable of producing something of value for relevant organisations and initiatives. Technical knowledge is usually more associated with engineering-type disciplines but can have relevance for criminology when understanding the use of technology itself is needed. The achievement of each year of your course should give you confidence in your increasing levels of theoretical and practical criminological knowledge.

The second row should be another constant in your progress and this clearly emphasises the problem solving abilities expected from undergraduates; who will complete the Knowledge Table (**Table 29.2**) when they can do so in complex situations with many interrelated issues. This is exactly what you have been doing throughout this book by working on interconnected issues such as the triad of criminology. The mental dexterity you have performed by sticking with the criminological detail in this book is

clear testimony to your ability to cope with the processing of complex information. You now have rare abilities; a criminology undergraduate often has to question their own prior understandings and being able to do this successfully, is another admirable quality. Who else but us have to deal with the dynamics of the punishment dilemmas considered in **Chapter 24**? Our friends and family think it's easy—just punish people to stop them doing it again! But being able to suggest more effective solutions to these problems, or at least being able to challenge conventional wisdom means you have probably had to overcome thoughts that have been drummed into you from an early age. Your time as a criminologist should mean when you are faced with a problem of this kind you will avoid simplistic responses and instead follow six lines of inquiry: the nature of the offence, the extent of the harm caused, responsibility, intent, the balance between harm caused and harm intended and then, the actual penalty to be imposed (see the 'What is punishment?' section in **Chapter 24**).

The third row of **Table 29.2** represents the traditional knowledge levels associated with undergraduates and explains 'how' you can establish them. Only at level 6 is a fourth requirement needed for the knowledge descriptor; a level of critical thinking inherent in the ABC approach to studying criminology. The highlighted words in the Knowledge Table represent what new things you will be able to claim from each level and their relative infrequency illustrates how gradual development is expected in your learning journey.

Your undergraduate status does not only depend on your levels of academic knowledge as the Skills Table (**Table 29.3**) broadens the expected products from your degree. The different verbs in the first row of this table illustrate the active nature of higher study and the anticipated small steps in levels. The second row indicates how these abilities can be achieved through appropriate cognitive (understanding and comprehension) and practical skills. At level 5 this expectation extends to skills in criminological techniques (e.g. statistical methods, the experimental method, case studies, and surveys). The advanced cognitive skills

	Level 4	Level 5	Level 6
What?	Practical, theoretical, or technical knowledge and understanding of criminological issues	Practical, theoretical, or technical knowledge and understanding of criminological issues	**Advanced** practical, theoretical, or technical knowledge and understanding of criminological issues
Why?	To address **well-defined**, complex problems	To address **broadly defined**, complex problems	To address **very broadly defined** problems with many **interacting factors**
How?	By analysing, interpreting, and evaluating **relevant information and ideas**	By understanding **different perspectives, approaches, or schools of thought** and the reasoning behind them	By understanding different perspectives, approaches or schools of thought and the theories that underpin them. To **critically analyse, interpret, and evaluate** complex information, concepts, and ideas

Table 29.2 The Knowledge Table for undergraduates (adapted from Ofqual 2015: 7–8).

	Level 4	Level 5	Level 6
What?	**Identify, adapt, and use**	Identify, adapt, use, and **determine**	Identify, adapt, use, determine, and **refine** criminological things
How?	Through **cognitive and practical skills**	Through cognitive and practical skills and **appropriate criminological techniques**	Through **advanced** cognitive and practical skills and criminological techniques
Why?	To address **fairly well-defined**, sometimes complex, problems	To address **broadly defined, complex** problems	To address **very broadly defined** problems with many **interacting factors**
When?	**Reviewing** the effectiveness and appropriateness of using the three level 4 skills	**Using research** to evaluate the effectiveness and appropriateness of the use of the three level 5 skills	**Designing research** to evaluate the effectiveness and **implications** of using the above three level 6 skills

Table 29.3 The Skills Descriptors for undergraduates (adapted from Ofqual 2015: 7–8)

you will acquire at level 6 refer to talents in analysis and evaluation; it also includes, as said above, synthesis of knowledge where you do things with existing knowledge. These words may seem unfamiliar but you should claim these skills, and through your productive reflective practice they will be transferrable to other situations.

The third row in the undergraduate skills' table echoes the importance of developing problem solving abilities. But the importance of reflective practice for successfully climbing the different levels in your higher education is clearly shown by the final row in **Table 29.3**. This demonstrates the integral importance for undergraduates to be reflective thinkers; your success is expected when you can reliably judge how effectively you have addressed the first three parts of the skills' descriptor (their what, how, and why questions).

Bearing all this mind, now might be a good time to read **Conversations 29.4**.

CONVERSATIONS 29.4

Where am I now: a student's perspective—with Emily Barnes

It was the criminology module options available to sociology students at my university that really got me into the subject. I thought studying at St Mary's would give me the best of both worlds, studying a little criminology whilst still focusing mainly on sociology.

I discovered my love for criminology early on, during the first criminology module I undertook, 'Criminology: a Sociological introduction'. I realised that, like sociology, criminology is so current, it is everywhere, and its many focuses are ever changing. I find it easy to engage with, and keep myself interested in all that it has to offer. There are so many different sides to criminology that I think studying it can appeal to anyone. This in itself can make studying criminology challenging. Personally I think you have to be constantly up to date with the news (which is no bad thing!) but when you're a little busy one week and you're not so hot on what is going on in the world then it is more challenging to fully engage with your work. Nevertheless, a solution to this is not getting bogged down with the stuff that doesn't interest you. Criminology is a vast discipline; there really is something

out there to capture everyone's interests, especially with there being new material shared by anyone and everyone on a daily basis. I found it didn't take long for my love of reading anything criminological to flourish, especially stuff related to the criminal justice system. I frequently find myself scanning news websites on my breaks at work these days! It is never a chore.

With so much on offer, I am motivated to venture further into the field of criminology. At St Mary's, my first and second year criminology modules mostly revolved around crime and the media, but here I am in my third year having chosen to do my dissertation on restorative justice. These are two topics in criminology that are pretty different, but nevertheless they're still linked. Such is the nature of criminology; you are never restricted to a certain area. Whilst completing a single honours sociology degree I feel I've had a well-rounded experience of criminology too, quite unintentionally, and I have thoroughly enjoyed it.

Emily Barnes, BA Sociology undergraduate, St Mary's University, Twickenham

Can people HEAR your successes?

Whether your formal course at your institution offers the chance to compile a Higher Education Achievement Report (HEAR), a portfolio of your development and achievements, or any other format, it is important for reflective learning to take advantage of such opportunities. Documenting the things you have done whilst being an undergraduate can mark you out as an engaged learner; it will also save considerable time when applying for different jobs. In addition to the work required by your course, this evidence can come from being involved with your institution's quality assurance system, such as being a student representative on the staff/student meetings during your course. The recent moves for students to be more involved in their higher education means there will be many occasions when student views are needed by your institution. Getting involved with these and other initiatives such as the Students' Union or student groups and societies will also illustrate your engagement with undergraduate life.

Until fairly recently students in the social sciences did not generally produce portfolios from their courses as they were more associated with other disciplines. However, they are now important weapons in the armoury of all undergraduates, as they are vital for exploring, examining, and developing your skills, knowledge, and attributes. They demonstrate commitment to continuing personal development and your active involvement with reflective learning; it will also sharpen your abilities in the production of supporting evidence. A document of this type needs to include the following sections:

- personal information (up to date CV; employment history);
- educational history (summary of educational achievements to date; evidence of training/staff development);
- skills audit (see **Chapter 30**);
- critical incidents' reflection (select at least five memorable incidents that have affected your learning at either university, work, or in general life and apply the reflective learning cycle);
- contributions by third parties (references are normally sent between employers but any testimonials about you and your work are important assets in a portfolio).

An eportfolio is the most common way of producing these type of records so please access this chapter's **online resources** for some suggested formats **www.oup.com/uk/case/**. See now **Conversations 29.5**.

CONVERSATIONS 29.5

Different stages in my learning journey—with Hayley Bury

The knowledge I gained through studying criminology synthesised brilliantly with the varied volunteer work I undertook as part of a work-based learning module in my first year. This gave me practical experience of the subjects we were covering in lectures and enhanced my understanding by bringing criminological topics, issues, and theories to life.

In my second year, austerity measures were biting hard and the cuts to the public sector, including my local YOT, made me question whether my initial desire to work in youth offending was a realistic employment option on graduation. Halfway through this year I knew I had to approach things differently. An opportunity arose following something I had written for an e-magazine, created by a fellow criminology undergraduate, 'Poverty Pawn: are our streets being regenerated or degenerated?' My article considered the potential for increased harm following the increasing number of pawn shops in my local town; where a major regeneration project was currently under way.

My piece was seen by a member of the town's Business Improvement District (BID) board and subsequently I was commissioned by the BID to carry out some research on perceptions of safety and security in this part of the town. I was responsible for everything, including finances so it was a daunting and pressurised task! I combined this work with the research methods' module in my second year and together they matured the skills I needed to produce valid and reliable criminological research. My report for the BID was used to inform strategies for improving crime and safety in my own home town with some of its recommendations for more family centred events and a social space for families in the town centre, actually being implemented.

In the first two years of my course, I acquired voluntary work experience at a young person's substance and alcohol misuse charity, the local YOT, and a young person's homeless charity. A part time paid position then came up at the homeless charity and I applied, treating the application as an assignment, ticking off the criteria as I filled out each section. At the interview I was able to use an assignment answer from my course to show my understanding of some of the issues concerning the young people I was hopefully going to be working with. I have since been told my research for the BID along with my volunteering experience got me the job, and the chief executive commented that my application and interview were exceptional.

Combining my work at the charity with studying for my final year is where everything I have learnt on my course has become a reality, lived out in front of me by the young people I try to support, mentor, and nurture potential in. Criminology's vast range of issues along with the analytical and evaluative skills I feel it has taught me,

have changed my outlook immeasurably. It has enabled me to understand on a deeper plane, to empathise and make progress with young people often dealing with the very issues I am studying.

I feel my experiences so far will prepare me to work in so many different environments in which crime is associated, just as I had hoped when I first embarked on the degree.

Hayley Bury, BA Criminology undergraduate, University Centre at Blackburn College

Reflecting on the USP of HE

To use a term like unique selling point (USP) for higher education would be distasteful to those who see it with a higher purpose than that of a standard commercial transaction. But arguably it is not out of place in today's context of rising tuition fees, decreasing public funding, and increasing consumer rights. However, purely commercial undertones do not apply to all of higher education's practices, such as its collaborative peer review system which contravenes usual business behaviour for outright competition between rival entities. Peer review is integral for ensuring the standards of what is presented in undergraduate courses and academic books, journals, and conferences; it has been significant in the production of this book where the peers included current students of criminology. Collaboration between peers is the essence of an academic community that prides itself on advancements in knowledge and progression of teaching and learning rather than 'win-at-all-costs' business. This spirit of co-operation should encourage you to ask questions of relevant people; most scholars welcome any opportunity to talk about their work!

Another influential example of the system's collaborative ethos is the Higher Education Academy (HEA), the registered charity founded in 2003 as the national body for promoting excellence in higher education. It is not an organisation with regulatory powers and instead offers support to higher education lecturers, accreditation and professional recognition and a variety of funding opportunities for initiatives that seek to enhance teaching and learning. A glimpse at the 'events calendar' on the HEA website will quickly show you what is currently going on in different institutions and their collaborative and diverse nature.

Awareness of what others are doing in higher education is needed for appreciating your 'student experience'. Being an undergraduate is a unique time for everybody so the support and resources produced by the National Union of Students (NUS) can help you feel part of this academic community. The NUS is responsible for the National Student Survey (NSS) which is completed by

final year students to measure their opinions of their overall course in relation to: teaching; assessment and feedback; academic support; organisation and management; learning resources; and personal development. A complete set of all the NSS data are openly available online (it began in 2005) and positive views have been consistently acquired for all six areas. The personal development section has consistently recorded views from the vast majority of social sciences' respondents (containing the views of criminology students) that validate their overall course as having positive effects on their employability.

The unqualified importance of employability

It may not be a formal part of your course but for more people than ever it is the defining rationale for becoming an undergraduate. In the last few decades a range of employability models have been produced by universities and the HEA; work that included arguably the nearest thing to an agreed general definition for it:

a set of achievements—skills, understandings and personal attributes—that make graduates more likely to gain employment and be successful in their chosen occupations, which benefits *themselves, the workforce, the community and the economy.*

Yorke 2004/2006: 8, emphasis added

This definition is useful because the interests of the three external stakeholders can focus your employability work. It is a reminder of the challenging nature of a course to 'employability' and the length of time such journeys can take. Approaches have therefore emerged to break it down into smaller stages (tiers) in employability teaching and learning. For example, the scaffolding system at Sheffield Hallam University which was given the 2014 National Award for Excellence in Teaching Criminology by the British Society of Criminology's Teaching and Learning Network. This award is supported by both the British Society of Criminology and the HEA to recognise best practice and innovative teaching in criminology across UK higher education providers. Take a look at **Conversations 29.6** to hear more from one of the lecturers at Sheffield Hallam.

The support from these tiers has played an important role in students' stepping up into becoming employable and attaining employment (see **Conversations 29.7**).

Looking for the 'cutting edge'?

All providers of UK higher education have to follow the relevant Subject Benchmark Statement for the courses they offer. These build on the general framework for higher education by its subject specific detail and the knowledge and skills expected from an undergraduate in criminology. The development of both is fundamental to your degree as there are 11 general requirements for the knowledge descriptor and 16 for the skills descriptor (QAA 2014: paras. 7.3–7.5). These numbers clearly indicate the expected active nature of a criminology undergraduate; this does not mean you have to be doing complex or highly sophisticated things but actively involved in a reflective process of simple questions for reviewing your actions. The benchmark statements also cite new directions for their disciplines which for criminology were expressed as cultural criminology, cybercrime, and zemiology (QAA 2014: para. 1.5); so is there a way you could do something in these areas to show your prowess as a 'cutting edge' undergraduate?

CONVERSATIONS 29.6

Employability for criminology: work-related learning, skills, and guidance—with Dr Vicky Heap

When students cram their UCAS forms with criminology courses their minds are likely filled with ambitions of studying high profile serial homicide cases and exploring the more unconventional (gruesome) explanations as to why people commit crime. Let's face it, employability skills don't quite possess the same wow-factor, which is why our criminology subject group at Sheffield Hallam embed employability skills throughout our degree programmes using a combination of simulation and experiential learning, skills, and guidance.

The structure of our provision is key, with a tiered approach utilised throughout the three years of study. The development of employability and transferable study skills really does start from day one, with core Graduate Research and Development modules focusing on introducing concepts such as reflection, action planning, and CV building. However, these topics are not covered in isolation (as they could be a bit boring!). We use criminological content as the vehicle to explore the skills in a practice-focused way. For example, our students consider the themes of ethics, equality and diversity within the context of research methods and a research project, which every student puts into practice on a short placement. These skills are then developed and enhanced through our research methods and dissertation modules in the second and third years.

Employability-wise, students build on their foundational knowledge in the second year, where the next tier of provision includes work-related learning through simulation (imitating real-world processes within a safe

classroom environment). Students on our Criminal Justice Realities module simulate a fictional case from the commission of the crime through the investigation process, with different criminal justice system practitioners leading the sessions each week. This includes: the police investigation with a retired Chief Superintendent, forensic evidence recovery with crime scene investigators and a prosecution solicitor detailing what evidence the Crown requires. For the assessment, students have to reflect on how and why research and policy dictates practice. We also provide a range of placement opportunities for our students (experiential learning), which they can use to gain academic credit in both their second and third years. This culminates in the third year with a module that credits a one day per week placement, with staff helping students in taught sessions to relate their experiences to the discipline of criminology and theoretical developments through a reflective approach.

Surrounding these developmental tiers our criminology modules reflect theory, research, practice and values to contextualise the simulated and real-life experiences. Outside of the curriculum we arrange placements, encourage students to meet agencies, and identify volunteering opportunities through our Volunteer Fair and provide careers mentors. All of these elements combine to ensure our students have the necessary graduate attributes to successfully gain employment.

Dr Vicky Heap, Criminology Lecturer, Sheffield Hallam University

CONVERSATIONS 29.7

A student's perspective on employability for criminology—with Charlotte Beevor

The employability-related modules that I have studied have been really beneficial. During my first year the guest lectures and basic study skills modules enabled me to develop a good foundation with regards to knowing what careers are out there; what skills I hold that are essential to them; and how to acknowledge and present the skills I hold in a CV. In second year I chose the module 'Criminal Justice Realities', this module was really interesting, as it allowed me to gain a deeper understanding of the existing jobs within the criminal justice system, as well as providing access to practitioners, this allowed me to build up rapport and ask questions regarding their careers. More specifically, I feel that the placement module in my third year has enhanced my employability; this module required my involvement in a weekly placement alongside my academic modules. This opportunity was extremely beneficial; I was required to communicate with the university and prison staff in a professional manner and was expected to carry out duties that contributed to the charity's work. This placement developed my skills base no end, and I learnt how to talk about my developed skill in an interview environment, as a result I was successful during the interview process for a job within operational support at a local prison.

Charlotte Beevor, BA Criminology and Sociology undergraduate, Sheffield Hallam University

Future concerns for criminology

To set this section in context see **New frontiers 29.1**.

In the summer of 2016 it was reported that cybercrime is now the most common type of crime in England and Wales thanks to its inclusion for the first time in the Crime Survey for England and Wales. The media reports tended not to go into the details of these offences, where, despite online fraud attracting the majority of attention, it was estimated that around a third of these offences came from being the victim of a computer virus or an email or social media account being hacked. The offences were said to have a wide distribution and were not influenced by a victim's age, social background, or geographical place; some reports were predictably fearful and contained views so beloved by newspapers that now, 'no-one who uses a computer regularly can feel safe' (*The Telegraph*, 21 July 2016). But how extensive are these fears? What kinds of problems can do these figures suggest? Are they just 'the tip of the iceberg' where the majority of offences are not seen or reported? How could you use the knowledge and skills from your degree in criminology to help? These questions were taken up in **Chapter 28** where you were encouraged to apply your research methods' abilities for the production of needed knowledge.

NEW FRONTIERS 29.1

Cyberspace: a realm of opportunity for criminal behaviour— with Dr Lella Nouri-Bennett

Since the mid-1990s the world has seen an explosion of crimes and criminality related to information technology and the Internet. This explosion coincides with the ever-expanding growth of the Internet into our daily lives transforming communication, trade, leisure, and politics. With this profound change and the promise of further opportunity, has emerged a darker usage of cyberspace for criminality and criminal behaviour. A phenomenon that Criminologists refer to as 'cybercrime': an all-encompassing term referring to crimes in which computers are the tool or computers are the target. The first category, those crimes which use computers, tend to refer to crimes which predate the invention of the Internet but are now also being conducted online. This includes crimes such as: intellectual property offences, stalking, hate speech, various types of fraud including identity theft, child pornography, unauthorised copyright of content such as films and music, and the buying and selling of illegal substances and other restricted or prohibited materials such as guns and knives. These crimes are not unique to cyberspace rather they have diversified as a result of the opportunities that information technology presents. In some cases, indeed for those crimes related to the selling of illegal or restricted items—the Internet has arguably made these crimes easier to enact. For example, using online forums, similar to Amazon and Ebay, buyers and sellers are able to exchange goods and services using digital encryption that conceals their identities—referred to by some Criminologists as **cryptomarkets** on the **dark web**. The dark web is a hidden Internet only accessible through the use of specific software authorised to access it. As a result of these transactions (which also use **cryptocurrency**), illegal products can then be mailed out to buyers using the normal postal services—more often than not without detection. The second category, cybercrimes in which computers are the target is by contrast a newer problem for the criminal justice system to deal with. These types of offences take as its target electronic infrastructure. Examples of this include: viruses, worms, and Trojans that can corrupt files and hard drives, denial of service attacks which can crash websites, and the defacement of web content to change its meaning, and or delete/grant access to content without authorisation.

Beyond the distinction between different types of cybercrimes, crimes in cyberspace have also been categorised based on the perpetrator. In Criminology texts, it is not unusual to see references to different types of criminal actors' use of the Internet such as: 'cyberterrorists', 'hacktivists', or for actions of the state, 'cyberwarfare'. These actor-based distinctions are based on motivation rather than the type of crime involved. For example, terrorists are understood to use the Internet to carry out a variety of different functions, most prominently: spreading their propaganda, financing operations, recruiting new members or radicalisation, and providing training. These activities are nothing new to terrorism, rather what

is different is that they take place in the online environment. An example of terrorist use of the Internet for propaganda purposes is highlighted in the case of Younis Tsouli (known as 'Irhabi 007'). Amongst other activities, Tsouli posted extremist videos and propaganda online and was an administrator of al Ansar, a password protected web forum for the sharing of extremist content and communication. In December 2005, Tsouli was the first offender to be sentenced for incitement to commit an act of terrorism *through the Internet*.

Further to the cybercrimes highlighted in this section, we can expect to see a growth over the coming years. One of the key challenges for the criminal justice system is keeping up with the evolving nature of information technology. For example, whilst the Internet is continually monitored for extremist content and websites, videos and so forth and are repeatedly taken down by enforcement officials: the rate in which new ones appear are rapid making it in some ways counter-productive. As such, it is becoming increasingly more and more difficult for the police to remain vigilant online. Further, the anonymity that the Internet provides for criminals presents further barriers to arrest and prosecution in relation to all of the cybercrimes illustrated above. In addition, the borderless nature of the Internet presents difficulties in terms of jurisdiction of policing and the enforcement of legislation. These issues emphasise the need for research in criminology to further understand the myriad of different actors using cyberspace for criminal activity and how the criminal justice system can better deal with this phenomenon.

Questions from this new frontier

- To what extent has the Internet excelled the possibilities for criminals such as terrorists and drug dealers?
- How has the Internet facilitated the global networking of organised criminals?
- How can the criminal justice system better deal with the explosion of criminality across new forms of media?

Dr Lella Nouri-Bennett, Criminology Lecturer, Swansea University

Future concerns for criminal justice

See **New frontiers 29.2** for a discussion on politicians and their role in criminal justice.

NEW FRONTIERS 29.2

Politicians and their role in criminal justice—with Dr Peter Joyce

Crime is a major political issue. If crime is seen to be rising, the public are likely to turn to a party that promises a firmer approach towards law and order. So ensuring that the public feel safe and can sleep easily in their beds at night is a key challenge for the new Conservative government that was elected in 2015.

The main concern of the previous (2010–2015) coalition government was to reduce the budget deficit and the solution it put forward was to reduce public spending. We thus embarked on an era of financial austerity which entailed less money being spent on all public services, including those in the criminal justice system.

The new government will continue on this path and the budgets of key criminal justice agencies will be cut still further. So how can the new government spend less money on criminal justice whilst satisfying the public demand for an effective response to crime and disorder?

One solution is that the public will be encouraged to devote more of its energies into taking responsibility for combating crime. Neighbourhood Watch and the Special Constabulary will be further pushed as important methods to prevent crime within our communities and in terms of involvement in sentencing, we should expect to see restorative justice being put forward as an important response to low level crime.

There are pros and cons of this approach that the government calls 'empowerment' but which others may see it as a cynical way to get services delivered on the cheap.

One advantage is that a greater level of public involvement in the delivery of criminal justice services will enable agencies such as the police to focus on issues that are newly emerging onto the crime agenda—cybercrime (in all its forms) will be certainly a major challenge in the future. It will be far easier to meet these new challenges if the public are themselves dealing with low level crime.

But there are problems—does the public want (or have the time) to be routinely involved in criminal justice matters?

A further concern is that it may encourage the adoption of vigilante justice and result in mob rule directed against those whose actions are unpopular to 'respectable opinion' within a community—whether illegal or not. The tar, feathers, and the neck tie parties we associate with the American Wild West could be the future response to crime and deviance delivered within communities by empowered and active citizens.

What other developments are we likely to see affecting the nature of criminal justice policy over the next five years?

Partnership work will be further developed. The essence of a partnership approach is a recognition that no one body has total responsibility for combating crime and disorder but this responsibility should instead be shared between a range of agencies who pool their efforts (including their staff and their budgets) to produce a joint solution to a crime problem. In future years we can expect to see a wider spread of bodies (including voluntary agencies and charities) becoming partners to prevent crime and disorder.

We can also expect to see privatisation pursued more vigorously. This means that the work previously performed by established criminal justice agencies will instead be carried out by companies that operate in the private sector and whose prime purpose is to make a profit from the services that they deliver. An important reform to promote privatisation has been the creation of community rehabilitation companies who took over much of the work previously carried out by the National Probation Service in 2015. This approach was adopted as private sector companies deliver services more cheaply than had previously been the case.

One of the key challenges faced by politicians in pursuing their post 2015 reform agenda is the attitude that criminal justice practitioners will adopt towards them. Criminal justice practitioners have power and their support is important to the success of a reform agenda.

As an illustration of this, the 2015 government will promote non-custodial (or community) sentences in favour of terms of imprisonment—the former are far cheaper. However, if judges and magistrates have no confidence in the effectiveness of these sentences, they will continue to imprison those found guilty of an offence in their courts.

This emphasises the need for governments to actively court the support not just of the general public but also of criminal justice practitioners when embarking on their criminal justice reform agenda.

Questions from this new frontier

- What are the main priorities from politicians for the criminal justice system?
- How can criminal justice professionals impede political desires for criminal justice?

Dr Peter Joyce, Principal Lecturer in Criminology, Manchester Metropolitan University

Campaigning in criminology

The knowledge you now have for the extent of the many problems facing criminology and criminal justice might make it easy to despair that things cannot improve. But applying your graduate-level knowledge and skills for trying to improve an issue you feel strongly about, will be a rewarding way of spending your criminological interest and expertise. There is a long history of activism within criminology as illustrated by campaigns such as that led by the National Council for the Abolition of the Death Penalty. This may have achieved it aims in 1965 but similar campaigning for reforms of punishment practices have continued through groups such as the Howard League, the Centre for Crime and Justice Studies, and the European Group for the Study of Deviance and Social Control. These organisations are often working on several different projects and welcome assistance from anybody in the academic community. There are many other organisations and people currently campaigning in criminology and so this chapter's section in the **online resources** puts forward many links **www.oup.com/uk/case/**. In order to show how people get involved in campaigning work and to illustrate some of its diversity, this chapter now includes three different **Conversations** (**29.8**, **29.9**, and **29.10**). One of these is from an academic with the other two being from people working in different environments.

The problems for these new frontiers for both criminology and criminal justice from the digital world were pertinently illustrated in the dispute between Apple and the FBI in 2015–16. This arose following the shooting of 14 people and serious injuries to 22 others, in San Bernardino, California in December 2015. The killings were carried out by a married couple who were themselves shot dead by the police four hours later. The dispute concerned the husband's iPhone which due to a lack of communication between his employers who owned the phone, and the FBI, had its password reset. This meant there was a period of time before the massacre when activity on the phone had not been synced to the Internet cloud in the standard way. Normally the FBI would put such phones through their automated systems that try every possible passcode combination until access is granted, but with this model after ten incorrect guesses all of the data stored on it is automatically destroyed. The FBI believed the phone was important evidence in the killings and requested Apple to build a crack into the phone's software to enable access. Apple refused and claimed the request was unconstitutional as it would be an unlawful form of forced labour and also contravened the right to free speech. In addition there were concerns that once a precedent had been set that legitimised such actions, the security of the billion plus Apple

---

CONVERSATIONS 29.8

Going from 'car boot criminology' to 'speaking truth to power'—with Dr Lisa White

My journey into criminology began with a Sunday morning trip to a 'car-boot' sale. Criminology was becoming increasingly popular around this time and knowing little about the subject, I picked up an old copy of an introductory criminological text for about 50 pence. Expecting to find out about the 'mind of the serial killer'—a media obsession at this time—I was pleasantly surprised to discover that criminology encompassed much more than this. I had a keen interest in the meaning of 'justice' and the myriad of ways it can be understood, so found exploring the field of criminology a really attractive endeavour. I was (and remain) fascinated that so much of our social, political, cultural, and economic life revolves around

supposedly 'common sense' assumptions about what are, in reality, very unstable concepts like 'deviance', 'crime', and 'justice'.

I suspect that my own personal biography has also played an important role in the kind of criminology that I am most interested in. I grew up in a small town on the edges of Liverpool and vividly remember the harmful ways in which the city and its people were dehumanised, stereotyped, and misrepresented, particularly following the Hillsborough 'disaster' of 1989. An interest in the interactions between powerless and powerful groups was borne out of these experiences and was further cultivated by a growing awareness of state violence and the ways in which this violence and its victims came to be represented. I was (and remain) supportive and interested in research which seeks to 'speak truth to power' and greatly admire the works of critical criminologists, such as Phil Scraton and Bill Rolston.

My most recent research project was based in Northern Ireland and explored the meaning, motivation, and significance of talking about torture for mostly Republican former detainees, whose accounts of state violence experienced in the detention system form part of a contested history of the conflict. My research took place at a time when discussions about the best ways to 'make peace with the past' were becoming increasingly commonplace. I hoped to add to this by finding out why people 'spoke out' about torture and brutality both during and after the conflict. What motivated them? What significance did they (and wider society) attach to their narratives? What were the consequences of 'going public' with accounts of state torture and brutality? The research itself began with the documentary analysis of published narratives detailing torture and brutality. These included former detainees' experiences as featured in newspapers, pamphlets, reports from non-governmental organisations, and prisoner memoirs. These narratives were often harrowing. I wondered what those who had 'gone public' had hoped would happen as a result of their narratives and what value they gave those experiences—both of torture and of 'truth sharing'—in the present. I was also keen to explore the risks of 'making public' such painful and personal experiences of trauma.

Many of those who 'spoke out' about torture found their experiences of state violence being denied by the British state, through mechanisms of denial which closely resembled those described in Cohen's (2001) *States of Denial*. Using a mixture of documentary analysis and semi-structured interviews, I was able to examine not only the content of this official discourse, but also the lived consequences for former detainees. Some of those I spoke to recalled feeling that state denials were inevitable and that they were unsurprised by this approach, yet others recalled feeling angered by it and frustrated by the ease with which state agencies could invoke literal, interpretive, and implicatory denials.

Interviewing former detainees about state violence inevitably brought with it a range of opportunities to reflect on ethical issues around avoiding harm. Although my research was primarily concerned about the motivation, significance, and consequences of speaking out about torture, rather than torture itself, it was inevitable that former detainees might want to talk about their original experiences of this particular form of state violence. I was worried that former detainees might find the process upsetting, despite my best efforts to avoid this. In the end, a minority of detainees did discuss what had happened to them, with one stating 'I want you to know how it was'. Rather than finding the re-living of these experiences as upsetting, a number of detainees suggested that spreading knowledge of what they had experienced was more empowering than traumatising, and this feeling seemed to be reflected in many of the interviews I carried out. Ethical considerations are deeply, deeply important and should not be overlooked and research—particularly alongside survivors of violence—undoubtedly has the capacity to cause real harm. Yet denying survivors the opportunity to 'speak' can also be experienced as harmful, particularly in situations where survivors' voices are rarely heard.

The desire to provoke a greater, more in-depth discussion of the state's capacity for violence is what continues to motivate me. I believe strongly in the academic-as-activist approach of the European Group for the Study of Deviance and Social Control and often leave the group's conferences feeling motivated and inspired. These conferences are a great opportunity to meet people working in the field and are also a great 'sounding-board' for testing out new theories and/or receiving feedback on research findings. Such things are deeply beneficial—not only for so-called 'Early Career Academics' like myself, but for others too. Finally, and perhaps most importantly, working alongside survivors of state violence and those who support them reminds me of the value of criminology in exposing and exploring the problems of harm, agency, and regulation in regards to state violence.

Dr Lisa White, Criminology Lecturer, University of Lincoln

CONVERSATIONS 29.9

Using higher education for personal freedom—with Saima Afzal

I was born in Pakistan in a remote village called Mathana Chak where life adhered to strict gender norms and rules; a set of rules I have questioned throughout my childhood and adult life. Thanks to my mother's persistence I was able to settle in England and I studied criminology as a mature student. In 2003 I found myself removed from my undergraduate studies in order I be taken back to Pakistan for a marriage that I did not consent to. I was able to overcome this challenge and this life experience drew me closer to my studies of criminology. It increased my need to understand and question the selective nature of equality and the indifference from authorities to people suffering this plight.

My time as an undergraduate in criminology heightened my interest in safeguarding the human rights of vulnerable people. The diverse topics I studied have stayed with me and help me in my casework for the National Crime Agency in forced marriage and 'honour' based abuse cases. I feel studying criminology allowed me to contest this unfairness as this experience provided me with the tools, the ability to articulate and present evidence for 'my cause'. These skills were applied in my work on the introduction of the Forced Marriage Civil Protection Act 2007 which largely was responsible for the award of my MBE for services to Policing and Community Relations in June 2010. Before I graduated there were many times where I thought doing this kind of work for the benefit of others was simply impossible.

Saima Afzal MBE, Forced Marriage Expert

CONVERSATIONS 29.10

The value of the undergraduate community—with Gloria Morrison

In 2006 my oldest son's best friend, Ken, was convicted of murder using the doctrine of joint enterprise. Back then if you searched for joint enterprise you would get a joint specialist for hip replacements in Australia! Ken had been training to be a youth offending officer and had tried to stop a fight when someone was tragically stabbed to death. He had not murdered anyone and hardly witnessed the fight as at its outset he had been assaulted himself and was semi-conscious on the ground. Determined to help him with an appeal I went to several lawyers and support groups, only to be told that as it was a 'joint enterprise' case there were no grounds for appeal.

In 2009 I met Janet Cunliffe via a BBC documentary called *Lethal Enterprise* and she told me about her 15 year old son Jordan who was convicted of murder even though he did not touch the victim or indeed see him; Jordan was blind at the time. We decided to start a campaign against the use of the doctrine of joint enterprise and JENGbA was launched in 2010. We have met some fantastic people over the years of campaigning and now support over 600 prisoners, all on a voluntary basis. When we met Paddy Hill one of the Birmingham Six, I asked him whether he was convicted using joint enterprise (since there were multiple defendants) and his response was 'they didn't charge us with anything they tortured us and told us we were murderers'—which actually, is a bit like joint enterprise. Paddy also told us that it wasn't just the lawyers fighting for them that finally got the Birmingham Six justice after three failed appeals, it was *students*. Students from all disciplines, but especially law and criminology, recognised that their case was a miscarriage of justice and fought for their release. JENGbA would ask all budding and current criminologists reading this to recognise the importance of getting behind cases maintaining innocents, you will be surprised just how many there are and how difficult it is for the courts to recognise their plight. JENGbA will continue fighting and welcome your support until we succeed in getting innocent people released from prison (see **Figure 29.4**).

Gloria Morrison, Campaign Co-ordinator, Joint Enterprise Not Guilty by Association (JENGbA)

Figure 29.4 Image of people campaigning on behalf of JENGbA
Source: JENGbA: www.jointenterprise.co/default.html

users could be at risk from hackers and suspect political regimes. The dispute was eventually resolved informally as the FBI subsequently paid over $1.2m to buy a hack from a security company that by-passed the automatic deletion function (*The Guardian*, 21 April 2016). The lack of formal litigation has meant this integral question of whether law enforcement agencies have the right to access every area in cyberspace has not been addressed.

Seeing crime differently

To meet challenges in the new frontiers it may be necessary to consider new methods of study for undergraduate journeys into criminology. It is always an exciting time to be a criminology student as the subject is constantly evolving; the triad of criminology you worked through in **Chapter 2** offers you a structure for recognising and critiquing the explorations, explanations, and responses that constitute your subject. The shifting needs for understanding crime and criminalisation and the nature of the right responses can be seen in the relevance of technology to peoples' everyday lives. The significant increase in use of screens, through mobile phones, tablets, PCs, etc. has led to questions comparing the significance of this development on the human mind with climate change (Greenfield 2014). The growing reports of 'screen-agers'—people (of any age) who spend more than 12 hours a day looking at a screen—justify this concern. This displacement of the real, physical world seems to have important implications for your discipline:

Images of transgression, victimization, and vigilante justice punctuate the Internet, popping up on computer screens and cell phone displays. Criminals videotape their crimes, protestors photograph their protests, police shoot far more images than they do people, security agents scrutinize the image-making of criminals and protestors … How, today, can there be a viable criminology that is not also a visual criminology?

Ferrell et al. 2008: 184

Starting your analysis

Treating images as a form of research data has the potential to add a new dimension (new era?) to criminology which traditionally has relied on words and numbers for its production of knowledge (see **Telling it like it is 29.1**). The cliché 'the camera never lies' is founded on their

TELLING IT LIKE IT IS 29.1

The new originals?

Nigel: Well there was, there was another group, in the east end, called The Originals and we had to rename ourselves.

David: The New Originals.

(This is Spinal Tap, 1984)

This conversation is from the renowned *This is Spinal Tap* film which wonderfully satirised the behaviours and attitudes of people involved in rock music 'super groups'. It was filmed in the 'mockumentary' style (a spoof of the documentary format) so the lack of logic for their choice of name was never questioned. Despite the obvious joke in being a 'new original' the extract emphasises the attractiveness of being involved in something 'new'. Distinctions between the old and the new help us make sense of the world as recognising a new era suggests the earlier one was somehow different and therefore explicable. It might make for a good story but

surely great care is needed when deciding one era has ended and been succeeded by another? If not, there is a danger of believing that the first days of 1789 and 1989 really did witness very different criminal justice systems compared a few days before …

Having said that, potential new eras can be great for scoring good grades in your assessments because if you know the old one as well, you will have plenty to write about! They could occur in small areas of criminal justice practice as well as much grander scales. Possible examples of the latter, from just the last half century alone, reveal an impressive list of *The New Criminology* (Taylor et al. 1973); *The New Penology* (Feeley and Simon 1992), and *The New Punitiveness* (Pratt et al. 2005).

If you could compile your own **Telling it like it is** feature with regard to what was possibly new about these three texts you will have the outline of an impressive map of your discipline's history.

---

perceived ability for providing objective evidence and an accurate record of how things really are. These beliefs underpinned the 'golden age' of the documentary tradition in photography in the 1930s–1950s when the supposed objectivity of images received little critique (Carrabine 2012: 477–480). It is testament to this power that it has persisted despite the common knowledge for today's 'photoshop' world where all kinds of images of people and events are routinely 'airbrushed' (altered in some way). In the lead up to Remembrance Day in 2015, even the government's official Facebook page did this when it superimposed a poppy onto a photograph of the Prime Minister David Cameron that was actually taken two years earlier. A more serious example occurred in 2004 when the *Daily Mirror* published five photographs alleging torture was being committed in Iraq by members of the British Army. The detail from their content analysis revealed major doubts on many aspects of the photographs, such as the uniform and equipment, but particularly the vehicle in which they were taken, as according to the analysts this was a type that had not been used in Iraq (BBC, 2004).

Photographs can be strong evidence of the reality they depict as, like tape-recordings of conversations, they have a connection with the events they document that cannot be found in data such as questionnaire responses and field notes. A scholarly approach to understanding images involves 'reading' them and a conscious effort to appreciate their detail is needed. If the saying is true that 'a picture

is worth a thousand words', then their use requires similar tactics as with written pieces. So firstly spend time scanning the whole image to try and take in what you think is being communicated. It might be necessary to break the image down into different parts (just as you do with writing and its paragraphs and sub-headings, etc.) by starting at the top of the frame and concentrating across and down the whole image until all of it has been observed. However, if you end up focusing on a specific part of an image, take note of why your eye was drawn in that particular direction (see **What do you think? 29.1** for a practice exercise).

The content of a photograph is its information, what it actually shows, and so tends to be an immediate impression; this in itself is useful for analysis but on its own risks superficial and misleading thinking. It can even be problematic to describe what is literally in front of us as evidenced in the Twitter-induced mania of 2015 about a dress (other examples followed) which depending on a person's eyesight characteristics was either blue and black, or white and gold; this was a wonderful example that people can see things differently.

Context

An organised system for reading images will help you analyse and interpret them; it should also help you understand how they can demonstrate doubt and uncertainty.

WHAT DO YOU THINK? 29.1

Reading the content of photographs

In order to extract the full information from these sources you need a disciplined approach that asks routine questions about them:

- What is being shown in the photograph?

- Is it a realistic portrayal or has it been artificially scripted?

- Can a story or concept be deduced?

- How has the photograph been framed—what is in/out of the actual shot?

- How have the people and objects in it been positioned?

- How has the lighting been used in the photograph?

- Was it taken as a close up or a long shot?

To practice seeing crime differently, look at the above image and ask yourself the seven key questions for analysing an image's content. Some can be answered fairly

Figure 29.5 'Their First Murder': early crime scene photography
Source: Photo by Weegee (Arthur Fellig)/International Center of Photography/Getty Images

quickly but others will require more time; a questioning habit will be developed if you apply these questions to other images you see.

When conducting your analysis you must remember that their context is as important as their content so do not restrict your thoughts to just what they literally depict. The context for which they were made and in which they are intended to be seen can reveal much of what is being communicated. This latter context, their intended audience, is vital for interpreting their message; for example, a wedding photograph in a ceremonial album is intended to be seen by a different audience to one taken for posting on a social networking site.

Remember you are trying to analyse both the content and context of photographs—this can be a difficult task as often they are inextricably linked—but remembering they are separate questions will deepen your analysis. Again, the use of simple questions is required. Whilst the disagreements over the content and the colour of 'that dress' were attributable to physical factors, the Kuleshov Effect as detected in the early 20th century is the classic example of how people can see the same thing differently. In that experiment people were shown exactly the same facial expression of an actor but it was interspersed with images of a bowl of soup, a body in a coffin, and a beautiful woman. The viewers responded by attributing different emotions (hunger, sadness, and lust) to exactly the same image of the actor. A memorable contribution to this discussion came from the famous film director Alfred Hitchcock who by positioning

his smiling face next to a shot of a young woman with a child, showed a kind old man, but when exactly the same image of his smiling face was next to a photograph of a young woman sunbathing, it showed a dirty old man!

Having awareness of context is vital for deducing what is being communicated and supports a content analysis by recognising the processes responsible for the creation of the image. According to the subtitle of a famous article by Howard Becker (1995) in the academic journal, *Visual Sociology* (now known as *Visual Studies*), when it comes to reading images, 'It's (Almost) All a Matter of Context'; this far-reaching importance led Becker to claim (1995: 8):

> If we think there is no context, that only means that the maker of the work has cleverly taken advantage of our willingness to provide the context for ourselves.

A visual criminologist needs to use both methods of analysis, as fully understanding the content of what you and others are seeing will only be possible by appreciating their context. This means you should inquire into the reasons they were produced and assess who had the control in their production. The consideration of the arrangements that produced the image (e.g. commercial reasons) and on its intended consumption (who was it for?) can help you understand it as criminological data. Was it the photographer or the viewer who had control, or those represented in the pictures? Are there wider structural forces such as political advantage, social expectations, or commercial factors, in control of the production of the image? These queries are similar to questioning the source of the source that was recommended in **Chapter 6** for developing your criminological research with a critical eye.

When reading images it is essential to consider whose point of view is being shown. The angles of the shots and whether they were taken at eye level could illustrate otherwise invisible power relationships in the scene. A powerful example of the camera person's perspective and influence on the framing of images is provided by the only surviving photographs to have been smuggled out of the Auschwitz prisoner of war camp in 1944. Recognising these hellish circumstances explains why the angles were tilted in some of these four photographs; these conditions meant they had to be taken surreptitiously from the Nazi prison guards by Jewish members of the Sonderkommando, the teams of people who were forced to herd their fellow prisoners to their deaths in the camp's gas chambers (Carrabine 2014).

When conducting an effective context analysis for visual images such as photographs, you need to inquire into the work of the photographer—for example, why and how, were the images actually made? The notorious work of Arthur Fellig, who was far better known by his nickname Weegee, is an example of these benefits. Thanks to his unofficial use of a police scanner he was often able to arrive at crime scenes before any emergency service to capture them on his camera. He took many photographs of such scenes and other night time incidents in New York in the 1930s–1940s and published them in his book, 'The Naked City', in 1945. It contained a chapter simply called 'Murders' with its first page being just a receipt for $35 from Life magazine for the photographs of two murders. Even in this example it is strikingly clear that not all murders were treated equally, one was just worth $10 because it was 'only a cheap murder, with not many bullets' (Weegee 1945: 78). Interest in his work has recently been revived thanks in part to the Hollywood film, *Nightcrawler*, released in 2014 where Jake Gyllenhaal played the part of a cameraman selling footage of violent crimes to a Los Angeles TV station. With these examples in mind it is understandable to think there are no limits in this kind of press reporting but this would ignore examples such as the newspapers' relatively moderate coverage of the murder of the British grandmother who was stabbed to death, then decapitated and paraded in the street by her killer in a busy tourist resort in Tenerife in 2011 (Gekoski et al. 2012).

The visual language in an image may also be supported by written text to reinforce its message. For example, in the Weegee photograph in **Figure 29.5** now known as 'The First Murder', the original shot was accompanied by 30 words of text which included 'A woman relative cried ... but neighbourhood dead-end kids enjoyed the show when a small-time racketeer was shot and killed ...' (Weegee 1945: 86). Now you know its context, look back at the image and see whether this combination of words and image influences you in how you now read the scene?

The blending of visual and written messages can be influentially employed by newspapers when reporting on crime; this was demonstrated in revealing research from Jones and Wardle (2008). This study into the publicity given to Ian Huntley and Maxine Carr during their trials in 2003 followed the extremely serious nature of Huntley's crimes (the murders of two schoolgirls). It meant there was extensive press coverage in the lead-up to the trial as well as the trial itself. The researchers found the reporting by *The Sun*, the *Daily Mail*, and *The Times* newspapers contained photographs of Carr that were both larger than those of Huntley and they also appeared more often—despite the fact she was accused and convicted of a much less serious offence (conspiring to pervert the course of justice). This culpability meant she was released on licence from custody after five months. In addition to the illuminating quantitative evidence for both size and frequency, it was also found that the deliberate arrangement of words and images in the reports could influence a reader. A blatant example of this combination was the 'No emotion, no sympathy' headline in *The Sun* that appeared next to:

> two equally sized black and white images of Carr and Huntley are positioned over a list of the charges against them, making it appear as if both defendants were charged with five separate counts. Visually, their crimes appear to have similar levels of seriousness. The two defendants are on an equal visual level ... [and] due to the lack of context within the headline, the reader must ask, 'who' is being described; who has 'no emotion, no sympathy'? Subconscious association pulls the images of Carr and Huntley across to fill this contextual gap.
>
> Jones and Wardle 2008: 65

But instead of coming from the defendants, the source of the quote was actually the trial judge who asked the jury to ignore their emotional feelings when considering the evidence in the case. Following her conviction repeated threats were made to her life from members of the public, so in 2005 the High Court agreed it was necessary to grant Carr an injunction for lifelong anonymity. This is a court order that means nothing can be published about her identity, residence, or employment; at the time only three other individuals in the UK had ever received such orders (Mary Bell, Robert Thompson, and Jon Venables). The difference in the seriousness of the offences committed by these people is stark as Carr is the only one not to have committed a murder. The Jones and Wardle study is worth reading in full as it contains many other examples of how leading press reporting used images and text to reinforce each other. Its conclusion is particularly memorable as the researchers compare Carr's situation with that

Figure 29.6 'The misleading influence of visual images?'

Source: HoldtheFrontPage: www.holdthefrontpage.co.uk

of Alison Chapman who committed the same offence in 1967 (2008: 68–9). The fact that you have probably never heard of this second woman clearly illustrates their point concerning the very different approach taken by the newspapers in this study (see **Figure 29.6**).

The future for this kind of research is going to involve many interesting questions about the potential impact of online press reporting as its formats are very different to that used in newspapers. The printed versions vary considerably on matters like headlines, font sizes, colours, page arrangements, and combinations of words and images. It may well be the case that publicity from front page coverage is becoming secondary to 'trending' on the Internet, but whilst both forms of reporting co-exist it is important to recognise their essential differences. Using electronic sources for researching newspaper coverage is problematic because 'the natural relationships which occur on the printed pages get lost ... we lose any sense of how newspaper readers experience the content which we study so closely' (Jones and Wardle 2008: 69). If reading a printed newspaper is something you never do, have a look at all the front pages when you are in a queue at the petrol station, supermarket, etc. and if your eyes are drawn to a particular one, think about why that happened.

New visions or 'criminal' photography?

Using these analytical approaches is another opportunity to apply your reflective learning cycle. It could benefit your discipline as it is still very early days in the formation of a visual criminology. This was demonstrated by the fundamental questions asked in the highly respected study *Just Images: Aesthetics, Ethics and Visual Criminology* (Carrabine

2012). This work was given that year's Radzinowicz prize, the annual award for the British Journal of Criminology article which in the editors' opinion most contributes to the knowledge of issues in criminology and criminal justice. It called for 'a more sophisticated understanding of the visual [to] confront the ways in which contemporary societies are saturated with images of crime' (2012: 463). To reach this refined understanding for the ingredients of a 'just image' it is necessary to understand the aesthetics and ethics of a visual criminology. The issue of aesthetics is profoundly important in the art world as they are a means for classifying and adjudging 'good art'; they can be the principles in a particular art movement and their appreciation can signify 'good taste'. Understanding the values behind the aesthetics of a visual criminology will be central to its quest for understanding images in a just and fair manner. Without this guidance the fast-increasing criminological interest in the visual risks exacerbating harm to victims because if images have been taken to intentionally humiliate and degrade, paying attention to them could reward this abusive behaviour. This point illustrates how questions of aesthetics and ethics are intrinsically linked.

Conversely the power of the image can hold the powerful, as well as the powerless, to account and the opportunity to document these realities is now within most peoples' grasp thanks to common ownership of camera phones. It could be something you do either in your course or alongside it as for example photographing an invisible crime or anything else signifying injustice would be a clear sign of an advanced visual criminologist! A snapshot on your phone could effectively demonstrate a sign of control (photographing 'no photography' signs being a personal favourite) and your original thinking on matters of crime, harm, and injustice.

When taking photographs in public you need to be aware of the potential for infringing the law. Such consequences are unlikely as the general rule of 'if you can see it you can photograph it' still applies to images taken in public places as provisions such as Article 8 of the ECHR (the right to privacy) only apply if there are aggravating circumstances (*Wood v Commissioner of the Police for the Metropolis* (2009) EWCA Civ 414). A more obvious source of potential illegality is photography in a 'prohibited place' as defined by the Official Secrets Act 1911 (such as a Ministry of Defence establishment). Despite the presumption in favour of unrestricted public photography it has been reported that many photographers have experienced the police using stop and search powers on them; public disapproval at this form of policing was expressed at a demonstration in Trafalgar Square (see **Figure 29.7**) attended by more than 2,000 photographers (*The Guardian*, 23 January 2010).

A criminal offence contravening s.58 of the Terrorism Act 2000 could be committed if a person 'collects or makes a record of information of a kind likely to be useful

Figure 29.7 Photographers protesting against police intimidation in Trafalgar Square
Source: Andy F/CC BY 3.0

to a person committing or preparing an act of terrorism'. It merely needs to be established that the photograph could be considered 'useful' to somebody for terrorist purposes and there is no reasonable excuse for having it. The specific elements of the offence are vague but it is clear that it is deemed a serious one as the maximum sentence is 10 years' imprisonment. It is committed unless a person has a reasonable excuse for collecting, recording or possessing the information; so, if taking your photograph was connected to your course then hopefully this procedural safeguard of 'reasonable excuse' will apply! Although even if it does, the presumption of innocence has been weakened for this offence so it would be your responsibility to prove it. It is another example of how a major criminal justice principle (see **Chapter 20**) can be affected by policies, practices, and people (see **Chapter 21**).

A second possibility for criminal photography is provided by the offence in s.58A as this occurs when a person elicits, publishes, or communicates information about members of the police, armed forces, or intelligence services. It shares the requirement with the offence in s.58 that the information has to be deemed 'useful' and the same maximum penalty and obligation to provide a reasonable excuse also apply. The experiences of Andrew Carter in August 2008 illustrate the potential for harm from this

provision as a dispute over the legality of photographing a police officer led to his arrest, being taken away in handcuffs, detention for five hours in a police station cell, and having his fingerprints and DNA taken (*The Telegraph*, 19 August 2008). An apology was eventually given and these interpretations of the law had to be censured by Shahid Malik, the Parliamentary Under-Secretary of State for the Department for Communities and Local Government:

> It has been suggested that the new offence could criminalise people taking or publishing photographs of police officers. A photograph of a police officer may fall within the scope of the offence, but would do so in only limited circumstances'.
>
> Hansard, 2009

So rather than being used to discipline members of the public, photography and its instant connections to social networking, seems to have produced a new level of visibility for criminal justice. Mass ownership of camera phones has potentially increased the observing role of the public to such an extent that it justifies the view that facets of the system, such as front line policing, now work under the equivalent of the 'all-seeing-eyes' of Jeremy Bentham's Panopticon. This system would give institutions the power to acquire total compliance from prisoners in the production of the 'docile bodies' desired by modern criminal justice systems (Foucault 1977). Its application to the new visibility for law enforcement means examples of policing misconduct, which previously could be denied and contested, are just a few seconds away from being witnessed by millions of people. Evidence from experienced police officers on the impact of these visionary powers on their working practices is coming to light:

> You used to be able to grab a slice [of pizza], a coffee, have a smoke and relax in the cruiser between calls without anyone fucking with you or recording you. Now, who wants to be that guy? What if some jackass you can't even see, with an iPhone, is zoomed right in on you from half a block away and the next thing you know you are viral on *YouTube*?
>
> Quoted in Brown 2016: 303

This new environment for justice poses many questions which, thanks to the strong body of knowledge and understanding you now have from the first four parts of this book, you are equipped to answer. You could take any of the exploring, explaining, and responding lines of inquiry (the core of this book) for providing a route into learning more about relationships between justice and the visually connected world. You already know that using simple questions underpins successful development as a reflective learner and similar ones are needed for your criminological work and the production of knowledge required by your discipline. This approach could see you overcome the problem faced by all contemporary learners, the challenge of studying in a world where thanks to technology and its untold facts at our finger tips, we are in a situation neatly identified as answer-rich but question-poor (Greenfield 2014).

Effectively using your learning journey into criminology for generating knowledge for either your career development or the overall discipline requires you to build on what you now know. So if for example this new era of visibility for the justice system is motivating you to learn more, think about what you have learnt about the concept of deterrence in **Chapter 23**; how likely is it the all-seeing-eyes of a networked public will deter bad behaviour from law enforcers? Your critical thinking skills, fine-tuned by the variety of perspectives you have encountered in your course, could equally be used in exploring whether perceptions of virtual panopticans, from people working in the justice system, actually exist. Is it ethically right to have such systems or even to undertake such research?

SUMMARY

After working your way through the different features of this chapter you should now be able to:

• Engage with a reflective learning approach for enhancing your higher education

The use of a reflective learning cycle was shown as a means for getting the most out of your higher education. It supports your learning of new things by breaking down the learning process into its sequence of four stages: experiences, observations, reflections, and applications. This system allows you to recognise how far you have already travelled as an undergraduate and your evolving abilities for making sense from the vast criminological knowledge base you now have, with regard to its key concepts, themes, issues, debates, and theories.

• Identify methods for independent learning in the different levels of higher education

The levels of knowledge and skills expected from all undergraduates at each level of higher education were discussed to help you to review the progress of your learning journey so far. Abilities for independent learning were shown to be essential for your intended development as recorded at the outset of this book in **Chapter 1**. Your gradually increasing levels of independence were shown to support the progression in your learning abilities from:

(a) understanding and comprehending (you now know what criminological things mean);

(b) to application (you can now use this knowledge in another way);

(c) to critical analysis (you can now investigate its strengths and weaknesses);

(d) to critical evaluation (you can now appreciate the value of this knowledge);

(e) to knowledge production (you are now equipped to create new and original criminological knowledge).

- Apply reflective learning to your employability

The reflective learning cycle has direct relevance for the development of your work-based learning abilities. Its first two stages of acquiring new experiences and the thoughtful observations of others, naturally lend themselves to the work environment. The chapter emphasised how the process of learning itself can be more important than the content of what you have actually learnt. The importance of being organised in your studies was stressed to acquire the benefits from a disciplined, personal reflective framework. Such a system permits you to transfer your abilities into new areas and is a perquisite for beginning your employability strategies as presented in **Chapter 30**.

- Consider how your personal learning journey could help future directions of study for the discipline of criminology

The use of a reflective learning framework can help you study some of the emerging areas in your discipline. The chapter considered how you can use your time as an undergraduate to investigate issues such as cybercrime, the political demands of the criminal justice system, or visual criminology.

REVIEW QUESTIONS

1. What are the four stages in the reflective learning cycle?

2. Which specific ability will demonstrate your possession of the required skills at each level of higher education?

3. What is meant by 'the dark web' and why is it problematic for law enforcement?

4. Should Apple have been forced to build the crack requested by the FBI during the dispute between these organisations in 2015–16?

5. Why was the plan for the panopticon considered to be the 'perfect' prison? Are there contemporary equivalents of it?

6. What legal restrictions are there to forbid the taking of photographs in public?

FURTHER READING

Carrabine, E. (2012) 'Just Images: Aesthetics, Ethics and Visual Criminology', *British Journal of Criminology*, 52(3): 463–89.
This article has a detailed historical background to enable you to assess the supposed objectivity of film documentaries and other visual resources. It also poses a range of difficult questions in regard to the aesthetics and ethical standards of a visual criminology.

Copley, S. (2011) *Reflective Practice for Policing Students*. London: Sage.
This text investigates the concept of reflective practice and examines it within the specific context of policing. It uses a range of case studies and examples that will reinforce your own development in becoming a reflective practitioner.

Finch, E. and Fafinski, S. (2016) *Criminology Skills* (2nd edn). Oxford: Oxford University Press.
This text has a 'Swiss army pen knife' on its front cover and such an image is befitting for both this book and the discipline of criminology. It meets this expectation by being a multipurpose text that helps your use of criminological resources and acquisition of academic and research skills.

Pawar, M. and Anscombe, B. (2015) *Reflective Social Work Practice: Thinking, Doing and Being.* Port Melbourne: Cambridge University Press.
This is a practical guide to reflective practice and considers a variety of social work settings for its use. It uses a variety of different contexts for professional reflective practice such as when working with individuals, families, groups, and communities.

 Access the **online resources** to view selected further reading and web links relevant to the material covered in this chapter.
www.oup.com/uk/case/

CHAPTER OUTLINE

Introduction   834

Producing your own employability   836

Employers' perceptions of graduate employability skills   837

Producing your 'RARE' employability framework   840

Getting a lift from work-based learning   840

Applying graduate employability to your career   842

People in criminal justice careers   846

Different types of career   859

Self-employability and social enterprise   862

Transferring your employability to your career   864

Journeying into employability and careers

From university to the workplace

KEY ISSUES

By the end of this chapter you should be able to:

- display evidence for all of the required attributes of the E3—effective, engaged, employable student that was put forward in **Chapter 1**;

- produce your graduate employability and refine it through a strategy of reflection, assessment, reaction, evaluation (RARE);

- journey into potential careers opportunities with 'criminal justice game changers' by engaging with career development learning and experiences from people in these careers;

- consider an alternative approach for different careers that require the attributes for self-employability.

Introduction

The final chapter in this book seeks to help you succeed in the next stage of your learning journey. It may feel like an endpoint with it being the last chapter and also the conclusion of your undergraduate days, but you are encouraged to see it as a new departure point. It is now where you are really going to be able to use what you have learnt so far. Progressing from university to the workplace can be a daunting prospect so the chapter contains two parts to support your journey into employability and careers. Employability can be an uncertain and unpredictable area of study so in this respect is akin to much of criminology—therefore the experiences acquired from your degree will help you develop your employability. It is a term that is rarely defined but in the view of this book employability is understood as: the graduate skills and attributes individuals need for successful graduate careers.

These days the concept is such an integral part of undergraduate life (see **Chapter 28** and the discussion of your graduate identity); that your Higher Education (HE) provider will have many people wanting to help you with your travels. So in the same way effective criminological research includes listening to as many voices as possible, you should similarly be open minded in talking to whoever you can about your employability. This chapter and its related section in the online resources will assist throughout your excursions, but engagement with the employability services at your institution has to be your first port of call (see also **Chapter 1**'s discussion of 'travel partners' on your learning journey).

This chapter serves as a travel guide in your progress to employability, including both:

- *being* an employable graduate; and,
- *gaining* graduate employment.

In order to help you reach these challenging positions this chapter has been broken down into two parts:

- Learn how to produce your own graduate employability, in accordance with good practice in this area, and to build a framework for its continual refinement.
- Apply principles of career development learning to make successful transitions from university to the workplace and your future careers.

A good first step is to look at the questions raised in **What do you think? 30.1**.

Employability and careers are two different, but linked, concepts and you are advised to work towards them in this order.

WHAT DO YOU THINK? 30.1

Your vision of employability

Employability can be explained as something that enables people to gain meaningful employment—but what does this mean to you? Consider the following prompts before answering the questions below:

- Does it include all forms of employment? If not, why not?
- Is it something exclusively defined by financial reward? Or by things such as autonomy, professionalism, and the purpose of the employment?
- If money was not an issue (but you still had to work) what kind of employment would you choose to do?

Stepping into employability

Continuing in higher education through a MOOC could be something to do whilst you are trying to get into your preferred type of employment. Such experience can signal your commitment to continuing professional development (CPD), an attribute welcomed by so many employers. These open access resources and courses, supported by their Creative Commons licences, are part of a much broader concept known as 'the sharing economy'. According to people such as Robin Chase, the author of the 2015 book, *Peers Inc: How People and Platforms are Inventing the Collaborative Economy and Reinventing Capitalism*, this is something which is going to substantially change the custom of work in the 21st century. As the co-founder of the extremely successful car-sharing site, Zipcar, it is predictable Chase believes so strongly in this prospect, in fact she has become known for her view:

> My father had one job in his lifetime, I will have six jobs in my lifetime, and my children will have six jobs at the same time.

It may sound unlikely that people in the future could simultaneously have so many different jobs but arguably it may not be that remote if they include: trading on Ebay; driving for Uber; and renting space in your house as a 'hotel' room for Airbnb. Though they can add to your 'portfolio' you probably won't want to rely entirely on these latter kinds of work, so a strategy for producing and refining your graduate employability is put forward in this chapter. It emphasises the amount of time this can take, so again the most important advice is to start working on it as soon as you can—even if you are currently near the beginning of your studies. The unpredictability of the current job market means to increase your chances of success you need to be prepared to be flexible; this can include taking on traditional employment but doing it in untraditional circumstances. See **Conversations 30.1** for one person's rewarding experience.

CONVERSATIONS 30.1

Picture postcard policing?—with Ashley Tiffin

Sun shining over an azure sea. Palm fringed beaches. Colonial style uniform to reflect the tropical sun. Peace and tranquility. While these are all images of policing in the Cayman Islands, the British Overseas Territory lying ten hours flying time from London in the Caribbean Sea (see **Figure 30.1**), what is the reality and how is policing different in Cayman from Cornwall or Cumbria?

My opportunity to discover this question evolved from my 30 years' service in the UK during which I moved, initially, into Police Professional Standards as an investigator. But I always hankered for one last policing challenge and knowing the Royal Cayman Islands Police (RCIPS) were actively recruiting as part of their recovery from the devastation of Hurricane Ivan in 2004, I applied for a post with them. At my interview, it was clear that the very infrastructure of the service was in the process of rebuilding and, with my background as a police trainer, I was offered a post and asked to develop a training strategy for the RCIPS. On my arrival, while some work had been carried out in the interim, it was clear there was much work to do to provide a sustainable training strategy and ensure the service had the skills, knowledge and expertise to deliver this very unique policing function.

In many ways there are few differences between policing either Cumbria or Cayman—uniform patrols deal with the routine crimes and incidents one would expect from their environments. The public face of policing in the Cayman Islands differs little to that of a provincial UK police service—drivers crash, tourists and locals get drunk and the RCIPS are at the forefront of dealing with all manner of human issues, many, as in the UK, not directly linked to law enforcement.

However, a more relaxed pace of life, necessary in such a hot climate, brings its policing problems. The unwary tourist alighting from their cruise ship might step in front of a car on the busy George Town waterfront or on the fringes of the world famous Seven Mile Beach and, if you add to that a lower standard of driving, it is little wonder that deaths and serious injuries from road traffic collisions are higher than one might expect. Another area where subtle differences emerge is with illegal drugs. While the Cayman Islands have robust, some would say draconian, anti-drugs legislation, including penalties for consumption, the level of drug misuse, particularly amongst the resident population, remains stubbornly high. Again, there are cultural and geographic reasons behind this, not least the proximity and historical links to neighbouring Jamaica.

Whilst routine policing provides the bulk of its work, the RCIPS has two additional activities that set it apart from comparable UK services—the securing of territorial integrity and financial crimes. The territory of the Cayman Islands comprises three islands which together make a land mass six times smaller than that of Greater London. Its islands' territories are primarily protected by immigration and customs units with its fishing limits policed by an environmental agency. The RCIPS has a dedicated joint marine unit to work collaboratively with these bodies which is trained and supported by the Royal Navy.

In 2014 it was reported that the Cayman Islands were home to 210 banks with assets in excess of £1.0 trillion as well as the £1.15 trillion held by various investment or hedge funds. The basic reason for these startling numbers is quite simple—taxation. Cayman is 'tax neutral' and does not levy direct taxes on individuals or institutions. Its government raises money through a series of levies on company and fund registrations and on each transaction conducted. This relatively lenient financial control is supported by a highly regarded legal system and an infrastructure capable of servicing the industry. These factors make the islands one of the most

Figure 30.1 Policing activities in the Cayman Islands
Source: Photo by Norma Connolly for The Bahamas Press

important financial centres in the world and a leading Offshore Financial Services Centre (OFC).

This position comes at a cost and policing can be a real challenge in Cayman because of these complicated financial and international relationships. On the one hand the RCIPS has a responsibility to uphold Cayman law, which is designed to allow the OFC to both function and grow, but on the other, it has responsibilities to the international community. These duties include paying sufficient attention to money laundering, financing of terrorism, and tax avoidance. These duties lead to much work for the RCIPS Joint Intelligence Unit in order to service intelligence and share information both regionally and internationally. This clearly shows the importance of partnerships in contemporary policing.

So policing in Cayman brings together and is challenged by a complex structure of local, regional, and pan-national law enforcement that is set against the unique culture of a jewel set in the blue waters of the Caribbean. Its policing strategy has had to recognise two very important factors: firstly, expertise can be bought and this means expatriate staff can be brought in as required. Secondly, and more importantly, there had to be recognition that using expatriate staff did not deliver sustainability that would only come through training permanent staff into the service. The RCIPS is still composed of a 50/50 blend of local and regional permanent staff and expatriates officers and I would like to think that I left the islands in a slightly better place than when I arrived. My sun tan certainly improved!

Ashley Tiffin, Senior Lecturer in Policing, Cumbria University

Producing your own employability

This section and the online resources take you through a method for frequently reflecting on your graduate employability both during and after your undergraduate studies. It is an efficient approach as it seeks to maximise the employability value in the formal, credit-bearing assessments that you are required to take on your undergraduate course. As discussed in **Chapter 1** you will probably have to undertake work such as essays, exams, dissertations, and presentations; fully exploiting these obligations for employability effects should therefore be your aim. The mandatory assessment work in your course is inevitably going to be time-consuming but spending small additional periods can result in the creation of your graduate employability.

This chapter will show you exactly how to map each skill you have developed from formal academic work against the skills that employers are looking for today.

You will be encouraged to take an active role in the monitoring of your employability for which self-assessment is an integral feature. The ability to learn independently is a characteristic you can enhance by assessing graduate-level work and the fact this experience comes from your own work has the potential to deepen your reflections on your learning process.

Working independently in this manner will illustrate your active engagement as an undergraduate and develop your employability because:

looking at the employment 'gains' for diverse groups of students now participating in higher education suggests that the ability to articulate learning and raising confidence, self-esteem and aspirations seem to be more significant in developing graduates than a narrow focus on skills and competences.

Pegg et al. 2012: 9

Recording your progress as an undergraduate and how it has influenced you will be invaluable when recalling your experiences, possibly years later, in future job applications. It is an active approach to 'doing' employability and provides experience of judging it. Familiarity with these principles will enhance your ability to articulate what you have learnt as an undergraduate. This self-recognition should facilitate the desired increases in affective competencies such as self-confidence, self-esteem, and aspirations.

The online resources contain the assessment exercises for this process and they are based on recent research into employers' expectations of graduates. It is predominantly contained in the form of a user-friendly matrix but a simplistic 'tick box' approach must be avoided. You hopefully now know producing employability is a far more dynamic process, one that requires genuine reflective thinking throughout your journey.

Self-assessment for your employability

The forms in the online resources provide a structured means of self-assessment for the production of your employability. Self-assessment means making judgements about your learning, and monitoring your own performance like this will help you grow in confidence and encourage you to take greater responsibility for your learning. Critical self-reflection is also a key attribute which will help you develop your evaluation and analysis skills, whilst at the same time discovering how to become an autonomous learner.

Self-assessment is used in universities for practices known as formative or summative assessment with the latter occurring when it is part of an official grading process (see also discussion of assessment in **Chapter 1**). However, it is more frequently used in formative assessment which does not have the pressure of formal grading and instead seeks to enhance abilities for critique and judgement. Involving yourself in this kind of self-reflection should raise awareness of your strengths and weaknesses and the lack of judgement from either a tutor or peers can reduce the pressure. The ability to make these judgements is an important part of being an autonomous learner—an attribute that all higher education providers seek to instil in their graduate students. Its purpose here is to empower you with

regard to your employability and to capitalise on the additional learning from the shift in power when students make judgments upon their own work (Sadler and Good 2006).

Employability is a self-motivated and intrinsically personal journey; as such, self-assessment is a vital part of this process. Whilst you can seek help and advice from others, it is ultimately you that will need to identify and assess your strengths and weaknesses in an objective way. Effective self-assessment is an invaluable tool to help you enrich your employability.

Employers' perceptions of graduate employability skills

It is now time to consider the exact types of skills that employers look for in recruits. A review of the research into employers' perceptions of graduate employability skills was conducted for the Higher Education Academy (HEA) by Pegg et al. (2012) and they recorded seven specific preferences that are illustrated in **Figure 30.2**.

Reflection and development in all of these seven areas are encouraged by this part of the chapter and the online resources; they combine to provide a framework for recording and evaluating your progress. It can be applied to every piece of assessment you undertake on your course as you merely need to select three or four skills that were

needed for its completion and then self-assess your performance in those areas. The seven elements are expanded into 21 sub-skills in the online resources and this detail will add depth to your employability awareness.

Travelling with the 'Magnificent Seven'

In order to work on the seven highlighted skills it is important to appreciate what distinguishes them but also their presence in your undergraduate programme. Things you have

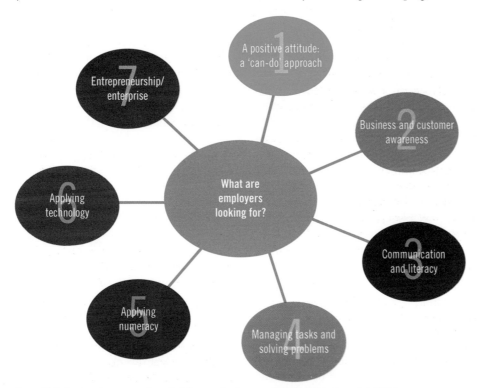

Figure 30.2 Seven preferences employers look for according to research for the HEA by Pegg et al. (2012)

done in your studies may not have been explicitly labelled 'for employability' but many of them may have this consequence.

A positive can-do attitude

The first, a positive can-do attitude, is exemplified by the work and attributes of the E3 student. An effective and engaged undergraduate is one that is employable and by taking on this challenge you will show initiative and a willingness to consider what undergraduates can do whilst they are in HE. Your abilities for understanding knowledge generation in the complex subject of crime and your role as a potential producer within it, will display 'can-do' of a high order.

Business and customer awareness

The second expectation, business and customer awareness, emphasises the importance of commercial acumen, plus knowledge of the work environment, and respecting and interacting with other people. High level employability requires you to explain when you have successfully worked with/for ranges of people and how you related to their involvement with their differing values and opinions. Evidence of this kind is a valuable asset as it demonstrates your flexibility and potential for dealing with different people such as customers and clients. These examples will add substance to bland 'I am a good team player' statements.

Communication and literacy

High level abilities in communication and literacy, in both verbal and non-verbal forms, can also be acquired from your degree; this is particularly so with the latter as production of clear, structured written work will probably have been a requirement of the majority of your assessment work. The variety of complex information you have accessed as a criminology undergraduate which had to be followed by your critical evaluation of it will provide you with extensive experience of using this skill. Communication experience may have come in different ways—in the course of your studies you may have asked people to complete questionnaires, interviewed them, conducted focus groups, held formal and informal meetings, as well as regularly communicating with your fellow students. Giving PowerPoint/Prezi presentations is another great example of communication.

Problem solving

Problem solving abilities can also be developed from your degree because although 'solving' might not be a byword for academia—'problem' certainly could be! Hopefully as

an undergraduate you have found your questioning mind-set where you have realised the 'facts' you have previously been taught, may no longer be what they first seemed. Your experience of analysing ranges of alleged facts from diverse perspectives is an integral part of studying criminology (as discussed in **Chapter 28** and throughout this book). Hopefully you have learnt there can be questionable processes behind 'facts' and their generation so this experience can help employers' need for graduates who can use creative thinking that provides appropriate, possibly alternative, solutions to different problems.

Numeracy

Confidence in your ability for application of numeracy could come from your statistical awareness following use of quantitative methods in your research and other modules. Even if you found this a challenging area of study it does not mean your abilities are low, as the required levels will be determined by the kind of work sought. So unless it is a specialist area, the expected mathematical abilities are for understanding things like averages, probabilities, and evaluating the potential information in numbers. This is another area where a criminology undergraduate has an advantage because all of us at some point will have studied criminal statistics and recognised their partial story in the phenomenon of crime.

Information technology

The application of information technology (IT) criterion will also be a natural result from your undergraduate studies. However, as with the previous expectation, the self-rating of your IT attributes may be influenced by the type of work you are applying for. The general employability expectations for graduates in this area have been reported as abilities in using Internet search engines, file management, and using standard software (Pegg et al. 2012). You will probably have much more experience than this, particularly if your criminological journey has also included the assessment options for blogs, visual images, and PowerPoint/Prezi presentations discussed in **Chapter 1**.

Entrepreneurship/enterprise

The final of the seven graduate expectations, for entrepreneurship/enterprise, may not be as immediately evident from ordinary progress to a criminology degree, but the varied opportunities in your discipline could well mean you have accrued this experience. This element is best considered as two separate issues because *enterprise* is a broad concept and known as 'the process of equipping students (or graduates) with an enhanced capacity to generate ideas and the skills to make them happen' (QAA 2012: 2). It can be demonstrated when creative ideas and innovations are applied to practical situations and also includes collaboration and risk taking. Its label may not have been expressly used but your studies could still provide evidence of your attributes in this area. Involvement in group work for example, will show collaborative experience and so whilst these forms of assessment can be unpopular with some students, they can be valued highly by employers. So being able to cite evidence of how you overcame difficulties in the group, of how you took part in the allocation of roles and its communication methods, plus the successful production of its work, are things likely to be of interest. The chances in your course for this kind of work (both formal and informal) should be fully exploited as traditional teaching and learning in HE has individuals working in isolation; a role far removed from the world of work where listening to others' points of view and participating in teams are such common features.

Evidence of *entrepreneurship* prowess may be relatively harder to acquire as it is recognised as being derived from the 'knowledge, attributes and capabilities required to apply these [enterprise] abilities in the context of setting up a new venture or business' (QAA 2012: 2). Their dependence on creating new undertakings may seem to limit opportunities for developing these talents, but this may not be the case as they also include actions as an intrapreneur (an 'inside entrepreneur') where the same role is taken for new projects and ventures within existing organisations. In part three of this chapter there is further discussion of entrepreneurship possibilities within the context of your career.

The diagram in **Figure 30.3** contains examples of how your reflective thinking for what you have done on your degree can benefit your employability. With some thought, you can apply the full list of these expectations to your own employability as they can all be aspects of the undergraduate experience. By seeing things through the lens of the 'magnificent seven' your progress towards employability should start to appear.

Using your degree for enriching your employability

Figure 30.3 shows how you might directly apply specific skills and attributes you have learnt during your degree to the generic skills we identified in **Figure 30.2**. It is giving these specific examples in interview situations which will set you apart from the crowd.

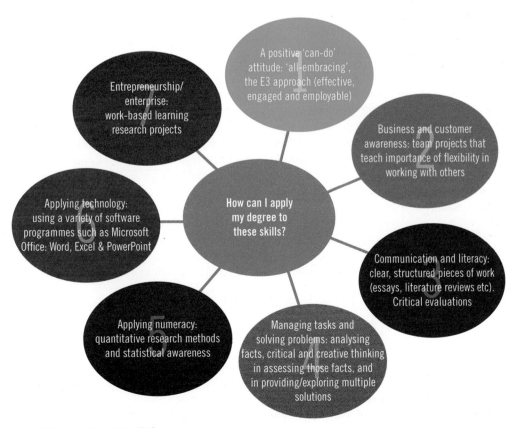

Figure 30.3 How can I apply my skills?

Producing your 'RARE' employability framework

Once you have started the process of producing and systematically recording your relevant undergraduate experiences—preferably via the template documents in the ORC—your next step should be to refine this work by considering your overall progress towards employability. This can be achieved by your creation of an employability framework which is a development system based on the four stages of refining employability (Cole and Tibby 2013). The system puts you in control of the production of your graduate employability via a strategy requiring four steps.

Stage 1: Reflect

Reflect on both your understanding of employability and those from the stakeholders (your university, regulatory and professional bodies, potential employers etc.) in your employability.

Questions to consider:

- What are the graduate employability expectations for where you want to work?
- Who can help you find out what they are?
- Who are the stakeholders (influential people and organisations) that set the expectations?
- Are their perceptions of employability comparable with yours?

NB. You are advised to revisit this first stage for refining your framework after you have read this full chapter.

Stage 2: Assess

Assess and map your current employability features by assessing your own level against those required from the areas of work you are interested in.

Questions to consider:

- What aspects of graduate employability ('*the magnificent seven*') do you currently possess?
- What are needed for the work you seek to acquire?

- Are there any gaps?
- What are the areas you feel most/least confident in?

Stage 3: React

React by filling in gaps you identified at stages 1 and 2.

Questions to consider:

- Who can help you fill in these gaps?
- Can they be addressed by your undergraduate course?
- Could your life/work experience be used?
- What is your action plan for answering these questions?

Stage 4: Evaluate

Evaluate the development plan you created from stages 1–3.

Questions to consider:

- Is your strategy from stages 1–3 defined and organised?
- Is it comprehensive?
- Is it effective?
- Who can help you make this judgement?

The cyclical nature of this strategy means it can be taken more than once; in fact it should be, as the more frequently you work on each stage, the more progress you will make. The first time you use it, you should start with the first stage, and then work through the others in the advised order; a structured framework for expressing your employability will emerge. It has a dynamic nature where each stage influences the others and so repetition is advised as neither your employability nor your potential careers remain static. It is a process that can make you a 'rare' undergraduate with a personal and effective strategy for advancing your employability.

Getting a lift from work-based learning

The rise in the employability's profile has been accompanied by more interest in **work-based learning** (WBL); although evidence of its use in UK universities can be traced back to the 1950s at least (Little and Harvey, 2006). The

Dearing Report expressed the desire for every undergraduate to be given the opportunity to undertake a relevant work placement but despite increases since then—e.g. the third of final year students doing it as reported by NUS/HSBC

(2011)—participation from UK students has still been found to be considerably lower than in many European countries (Brennan et al., 2006). The UK numbers appear to increase with each year of undergraduate study but it is inadvisable to leave it so late and making steps for getting it as soon as you land in HE would be far more valuable.

The term WBL (spoken colloquially as 'wibble'!) refers to the learning activities in a formal course of study that take place in a work setting rather than that of the university or college. It is provided by internships, service learning, and work placements that offer experience in working with different people, meeting diverse tasks in accordance with deadlines, and coping with the general pressures and demands of the job. These opportunities can vary considerably with different sizes and types of providing organisations, complexity of required work, and the length of the placement itself. The benefits from getting experience in the area in which you are interested, even if it was a short and relatively simplistic form of work, will result in your increased awareness of what the work can be like and provide you with detail for constructing your four stage 'RARE' employability framework.

In addition to employability enhancement, participation in work placements has been found to have a significant effect on final-year grades thereby increasing the chances of attaining a good class of degree (Mandilaras 2004; Balta et al. 2012). The potential reasons for these correlations were said to be increased focus on studies and enhanced time management skills. These findings support the view that placements increase the likelihood of attaining full-time paid employment following graduation and a correlation between social sciences' graduates with work experience and their early employability was found almost two decades ago (Bowes and Harvey 2000). If you are still undecided about whether it is worth doing then consider the finding that 40 per cent of new graduate-level vacancies are filled by individuals who have already worked for these organisations (High Fliers 2014).

Placements are a popular way of acquiring WBL experience and the length of these opportunities can range from a matter of days to year-long arrangements. The latter often occur in 'sandwich courses' where a year of full-time work, often paid by the employer, is a mandatory requirement. An internship can be the name for either summer or year-long placements and traditionally these were obtained by students coming towards the end of their studies. Although in recent years it has become more common for first year students to take them as well and 'eternal intern' is an emerging term for describing a person who undertakes more than one of these placements! They have acquired negative publicity recently for potential exploitation from employers, although research has found that payment is provided in two out of three cases (Sutton Trust 2014). Another form of placement can be work shadowing where an interested party directly observes

a specific individual or role in an organisation. These arrangements generally last for short periods of time and are unpaid but as well as providing relevant work awareness they offer excellent networking opportunities.

WBL experience could also be acquired by *volunteering work* which, despite sharing the same financial barrier as unpaid internships, can be far more accessible due to its sheer number of opportunities. The National Council of Voluntary Organisations (NCVO), the UK Civil Society Almanac, and the Charity Commission provide the primary sources for data on the size of this sector and annual estimates of total income have been made at £64 billion (Keen 2014). It has been reported that almost two thirds of undergraduates are involved in this kind of work (Brewis et al. 2010); a level of participation comparable with the reported national figures for society as a whole (Cabinet Office 2014). Political approval for this type of work has been regularly expressed in the 'Big Society' debates that accompanied the flagship policy of the 2010–15 coalition government. However, to ascribe this kind of involvement to such recent initiatives discounts the UK's strong volunteering traditions in criminal justice sector work.

Contemporary criminal justice work now takes place in a mixed economy of voluntary organisations working alongside private and public sector bodies. The organisations work in delivering services, campaigning, giving mutual aid, and providing coordination support to other voluntary sector bodies (Tomczak 2014: 273–74). This means there can be numerous WBL opportunities for you to consider and your involvement in it will enhance your knowledge of this mixed economy. It could provide you with experience that helps you judge the claim that voluntary organisations should be derided as superficial 'bid candy' as opposed to equal partners in the new system of operations (Maguire 2012: 488). That is to say, the presence of voluntary organisations is merely to sweeten concerns over the increased privatisation of the penal economy.

What does this mean for your employability?

There are many volunteering organisations that will provide you with relevant experience and these opportunities are unlikely to diminish as policies such as the 'Big Society' encourage their place in public life. From a criminological perspective you may well agree their presence in competitive bids can be derided as 'candy' where they merely 'sweeten the deal' in the commissioning of former public services—and get 'chewed up and spat out' once the bid has been won. However, even if this position is accepted, from your employability position the work is still going to be there and so these opportunities provide you with an accessible opportunity to start producing and refining the required attributes and experience. The employability and careers advisers at your institution (or the links in this book) will be able to guide you towards its commencement.

Part-time work in combination with your studies is another way of attaining the required work experience. This can enhance your employability as it demonstrates reliability and commitment as well as developing generic transferrable skills such as teamwork. It can also be an impressive way of demonstrating your prowess in time management. Concerns about excessive workloads have led to some universities completely banning their students from doing part-time work during academic terms although most advise a maximum of around 15 hours per week. Part-time jobs may not offer the experience of internships or work shadowing but their successful combination with the demands of a complex programme of undergraduate study could nonetheless enrich your employability. You could seek out part-time work that is related to the skills you identified earlier in the chapter as requiring improvement. For instance, if you need to brush up on IT skills then look for an office job where using a computer is necessary.

The different means of obtaining work experience illustrate the diversity in options and the type of work available and please refer to the chapter's online resources for access to the latest databases that offer this work. Experience in the justice sector (and others) can look extremely impressive on CVs and time spent in this environment will develop job-relevant skills such as clarifying your career choice and opening up networking prospects with individuals that can guide your search for employment. Students applying for work placements in their first or second year at university are these days selected through a similar recruitment process to that used to recruit graduates, so in many ways you can treat it like a mock examination. Going through a process of researching suitable opportunities, completing successful applications, and succeeding at interviews can all be described as career management skills. These experiences should not be left until you are approaching graduation as they can be worked on throughout your time as an undergraduate. There are important arguments that WBL activities can be exploited by employers and hence risk losing the essence of HE (Gibbs and Morris 2001): but if you feel in control and believe it can benefit your career then it simply needs to be done. It will provide you with a different experience beyond your formal course and it can shape undergraduates to become well-rounded team players who understand how to work with a diverse range of people in different environments and within a given timeframe.

Overview of producing graduate employability

Self-assessment forms of judgement have long been done by graduates as they are widely recognised as an integral part in the process of becoming an independent learner. It can be difficult to do—especially when your previous education may not have emphasised it as much—but it is an ability that can be learnt by taking part in the suggested practice recommended.

Effective monitoring of your employability will develop the evidence you will need to possess in order to convince an employer of your graduate potential. 'The magnificent seven' aims to remind you of the *range* of attributes and skills expected as well as their specific features. We have discussed how all have them can be inherent features of the undergraduate experience if you adopt this book's recommendation for an E3 student.

Employability (both yours and the outside world's) is constantly changing but the structured framework in this part of the chapter can support you in this challenging journey. The effects of its cyclical nature can intensify with its repetition and the four discrete stages (reflection, action, review, and evaluation) will ensure that you travel in first-class status.

This part of the chapter also encouraged you to realise the opportunities that exist in both your course and general life in working towards employability. Getting lifts from people who want to help—from your HE institution plus those you meet at work and at leisure—is something we have all done, so why should you be any different?

Applying graduate employability to your career

This section provides you with the necessary support and guidance for the final section of your journey from university to the workplace. This move will be a successful one if you follow the advice for maximising *career development learning opportunities* and participate in enhanced studies of careers. It is important to remember that 'employability' and 'careers' are two separate concepts and therefore each of them require high levels of graduate understanding and awareness.

It is important to know as much about '*careers*' as you do about '*employability*' and so this part of the chapter will encourage you to undertake career development learning and apply its principles to your own life journey. It is obviously impossible to feature every career so emphasis is given for those typically associated with criminology undergraduates. Experiences from people employed in criminal justice 'game changers' (**Chapter 21**) have been added in order to deepen your reflections on the processes behind career acquisition. These perspectives plus the coverage of the required competencies and standards needed for national and international 'criminology careers', aim to prepare you with knowledge for establishing your career. The options for creating your own career through self-employment associated with criminology undergraduates will also be discussed.

Journeying into careers

The careers' phase of the undergraduate journey is generally given little attention by HE providers and this is unsatisfactory considering it can be such a daunting step. It means you are not alone in entering uncharted territory and so feelings of uncertainty can be common. It may be similar to when you are away somewhere new—what tactics do you employ to have a good holiday? Get advice on recommended things to do, places to visit, directions, etc. from people who have already been? Seek the help of the people there when you arrive (some of whom will be there because it's their job)? The extra efforts we may make at communicating when we are away from home can be replicated when working on your career. So find the people who can advise you (your travel partners) at, firstly, your HE provider and then the equivalent people at your place of work. Talking to people with such relevant experience is a fundamental part of learning about careers and this part of the chapter seeks to complement this by equipping you with 'a guidebook and suggested itineraries' for this stage of your travels.

The difficulties in creating a graduate career can be illustrated by the well-known snowclone (a jokey word or expression) of *The Career Is Dead: Long Live the Career* by Douglas T. Hall. Clearly derived from the royal proclamations following the death of a king or queen to show the monarchy's continued existence, Hall and many others have endorsed similar permanence for careers. However, there is a *major caveat with this successor being a protean career* and therefore a starkly different incarnation—it is one where a career became 'a process which the person, not the organization, is managing' (Hall 1976: 201). Remember the *protean* term was used in **Chapter 21** to describe the development of the use of *community service* (officially, the unpaid work condition of the community order) as a criminal sanction. This protean description enabled your understanding of a sentence that somehow stayed constantly popular with sentencers and yet constantly altered its practice in order to meet the different penal expectations for providing *reparation, rehabilitation*, and *retribution*. A similar sense of continual change can be seen in personal careers as individuals are also

expected to play a range of roles and regularly regenerate their identity:

> Pursuing the protean career requires a high level of self-awareness and personal responsibility. Many people cherish the autonomy of the protean career, but many others find this freedom terrifying, experiencing it as a lack of external support.

Hall 1996: 10

The independence and freedom in these career structures can be unsettling so the support of your travel partners will be invaluable for your journey. One of the most important of these will be the advisers at your current HE institution so you are urged to use their services as soon as you can! The more people you talk to, the more opportunities you will discover and these are highly useful options in contemporary times where people are no longer 'pigeon holed' into only one or two careers. Flexibility is your major asset, as individuals who can adapt to the changing demands of the workplace are those with the highest potential for success in their careers. The abilities you recorded in addressing the '*magnificent seven*' clearly demonstrate the multiple expectations and different roles for employability—plus you know your '*RARE*' employability framework will continually evolve. It is your ability to adapt that will show your protean qualities at their highest and *this versatility will enable you to transfer your graduate employability to a number of different careers*. So keep your options open and recognise your potential for simultaneously working towards several possibilities.

Read **Conversations 30.2** and **30.3** for examples on the approach employed at one HE institution.

Career development learning

The high levels of self-awareness and personal responsibility required for today's careers can be acquired by development of metaskills and metacompetencies. These will exist when you have the skills and ability to develop the required skills and competences for enhancing your career. Their importance to contemporary HE arguably means 'learn how' has replaced 'know how' as *the* defining outcome of the undergraduate experience. Your ability to learn how you effectively develop and learn will provide you with the means to apply your graduate knowledge to different career routes. The actual number of different jobs you may have throughout your career is very difficult to predict due to the dearth of longitudinal research in this area. Although there has been some for sections of the US population, where it was found that people born in the years 1957 to 1964 held 11 different jobs during their ages of 18 to 46 (Bureau of Labour Statistics 2012). However, this kind of research is further limited by the difficulty

---

---

in reliably deciding whether changes in jobs amount to changes in career.

Adaptability in your career could also be needed as a result of the potential impact of technology on the labour market; as according to research from Oxford University and Deloitte, in the years 2015–35, it is predicted to cause the losses of ten million jobs in the UK (*The Telegraph*, 10 November 2014). The view that individuals will therefore have to change jobs and careers more regularly in the future, has support from many people such as 'Google's top rated futurist speaker', Thomas Frey from the DaVinci Institute in the USA. For example, in the build-up to his 2011 book, *Communicating with the Future*, he blogged a view that is often repeated: '60 per cent of the best jobs in the next ten years have not been invented yet'. If accurate, this is clearly going to be a challenge to both you and your HE institution, but at the same time could provide some great new opportunities. This level of possible change and much uncertainty should remind you that employability and careers' development should not come to an end after you have left university. The skills and abilities you have acquired as an undergraduate will need to be maintained

in order to protect you in such situations. It is also the time when you can take advantage of having an experienced 'travel partner' (the Careers Service at your institution) for effective guidance on your learning journey (see **Chapter 1**).

Joining the DOTS in your career plans

One of the most respected approaches to career development learning is the DOTS approach which advises four stages of: *Decision learning*; *Opportunity awareness*; *Transition learning*; and *Self-awareness* (Law and Watts, 1977). It is a memorable prompt for the different parts of career planning which requires you to think logically to be effective —i.e. to 'join the dots'. However, it would be a mistake to approach it in that sequence as many careers advisers prefer an order of SODT as illustrated in **Figure 30.4**. This is because it is far more logical to start with '*self*' when beginning your careers' learning as it underpins the other three elements in the model. So your views of your *efficacy*

CONVERSATIONS 30.3

Employability as a multi-agency approach—with Laura Hanson

Perhaps, owing to an increase in student fees, it is clear that now, more than ever, first year students are coming to university with the notion that it will help 'make them more employable'. The strength in this compulsory first year module, as a foundation for the BA Criminology course, is that it immediately provides students with a 'real-world' understanding of criminal justice in-action. Through a variety of workshops, pre-arranged visits, academic and guest lectures, students are provided with an invaluable insight into the realities of working within the criminal justice system. They can begin to develop their personalised action plans and compare their existing skill set to the skills and experience they would need to succeed within the range of job roles they are presented with. Moreover, through the volunteering forum, they are provided with the opportunity to make tangible networks with local volunteering agencies within the area. Through a dedicated timetable slot, we also ensure that students are equipped with the tools needed to apply for such opportunities, hosting a targeted CV and cover letter workshop to prepare the students for engaging employers within their sector.

In addition to providing students with the direct opportunity to gain experience and reliably identify if this is the career path they would like to follow, volunteering also assists them to further their practical understanding of the realities of the criminal justice system and assists them to begin to make meaningful evaluations of the academic theory they are, and will continue to be, presented with throughout their degree.

The strength of this module lies in the multi-agency approach that we have adopted. By establishing a strong partnership between the Careers and Academic departments we readily recognise that students can find added value with their degree when they are provided with the opportunity to test their learning through experience gained in the real world environment.

Laura Hanson, Careers, Employability and Enterprise Centre, Durham University

---

(self-theories) can be the fundamental base for enhancing your employability and acquiring the necessary levels of understanding, skills and metacognition.

Your self-theories are your views about yourself as a person, so your opinions of your abilities, personality, interests, and values are important when planning your career. Reflection (obviously followed by evaluation) on these different personal features, plus on the other things that amount to you as a person, can influence the kinds of jobs and careers you seek. Achieving these levels of personal awareness can be difficult but participation in this chapter's strategic and reflective approach to both

employability and careers, can guide your practice and subsequent work. These strategies can produce the levels of considered self-awareness for helping you with the model's second stage and the taking advantage of '*opportunities*' that come your way.

If you have had the confidence to begin your employability work in your undergraduate course then various chances and openings for learning about the world of work are likely to have materialised. This is where the next part of the model is relevant because you will have to exercise '*decision making*' as not all of the options will be suitable. You will therefore have to be accustomed to making decisions and so it is beneficial to have awareness of how you normally decide on things and the actions you take. For example: Do you assess the costs and benefits in your decisions? How important are things such as intuition, external advice, 'trial and error', or weighing up the 'pros and cons'? Try the exercise in **What do you think? 30.2** to consider some possible decision making scenarios.

It is beneficial to reflect on your approach to these and other decision making as it will help you appreciate how you think about them and whether your approach changes in different circumstances. If it does vary—what are the reasons for this? Decision making with regard to your career will need to start early in your undergraduate days—e.g.

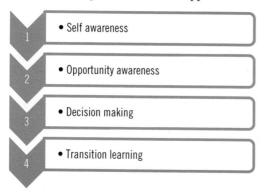

Figure 30.4 Outline of the SODT approach to career development learning

WHAT DO YOU THINK? 30.2

Your decision making at work

- Imagine that you are coming to the end of a period of work experience when you are offered two different positions in the organisation. You have to decide which one to take—How do you choose the right one for you?

- You are involved in a team project for your organisation and when it reaches a successful conclusion, the whole team is praised by the senior managers. However, you know that one of the team did not take their share of the responsibility—How do you decide what to do?

- A rival organisation has offered you a position—should you stay with your present employer or move to the new one?—How do you make the right decision?

These are all realistic and common scenarios you are likely to face in your career.

---

how you will acquire work experience—so your skills will soon be put to the test. In today's world of protean careers you should not worry that these initial decisions will shape your entire future but as contemporary careers are so changeable, frequent decision making will be required.

The final stage in effective career planning for undergraduates is 'transition learning'. This requires you to be aware of how the careers system works in your chosen areas. Learning how to make the move from university into careers involves discovery of opportunities and also of the ingredients of successful applications in these occupations. Many graduates seem able to procure this knowledge of the career system as seen in the 'Players' and 'Purists' typology (Brown and Hesketh 2004). Learning the game is complex—think about the sizeable numbers of positions of various types that are filled without any advertising at all. This practice clearly indicates the importance of networking and the adage, 'It's not what you know—it's who you know'. If you make effective use of the travel partners at your institution (your careers advisors, tutors, and peers) then you will increase this level

of knowledge. Networking is an essential aspect of forming a graduate career and so you need to invest your time in doing it. The current pervasiveness of social networking services makes this easier in some respects and this popularity has resulted in the snowclone for the digital age of, 'it's not what you know or who you know—*but who knows you*'. This kind of claim is supported by research, that even back at the start of this decade, found more than 90 per cent of organisations using sites such as Facebook, Twitter, or LinkedIn to advertise their graduate opportunities (Lowden et al. 2011: 20). It is likely that you will already have an account for one of these services, so creating social networks of relevant people and organisations working in careers of interest, can be an important first step in your undergraduate career development learning.

These sections of the chapter seek to emphasise the importance of adaptability for success in contemporary careers. This flexibility is something that can be worked on during your time as an undergraduate where you will have different opportunities for building a variety of relevant career networks.

People in criminal justice careers

This section will develop your learning of employability and careers by illustrating how the two concepts can be directly used in your own life and career journey. It aims to show how the personal transferrable skills ('the magnificent seven') that are needed for possession of high-level graduate employability are fundamental in acquiring specific jobs in the criminal justice sector. The 'people' highlighted in this section are all employed by a criminal justice 'game changer' (see **Chapter 21**) and these views and experiences should demonstrate the relevance of what you have learnt so far about employability and careers. The criminal justice jobs in this section

are practice-based but a degree in criminology can open doors for other types of employment such as researcher, academic, teacher, and civil servant. This sheer diversity of options makes it impossible for this part of the chapter to deal with them all with the same level of detail, so later on you will be signposted to these careers and also referred to the ORC for further coverage and directions.

To give coherence to this section it has been structured along the lines of a continuum of criminal justice practice—therefore it starts with careers in the police, before moving on to those in the courts, probation, and prisons. These four options tend to be popular choices of careers for criminology graduates and so are given most of the attention. For this reason the majority of the focus is on the 'game changing' criminal justice careers in the UK (and at times England and Wales) as differences in countries' legal systems mandate this kind of specialism. However, the emphasis on transferability in both employability and careers ensures that what you learn in this section can be adapted to a wide range of jobs and professions.

Police

This section has been designed to encourage you to reflect on the skills and attributes needed for procuring a career in policing. This guidance will help when you are applying to join the police as the key elements of successful applications are considered. The advice of a travel partner (a successful serving officer) has also been included to clarify the potential routes into this kind of career (see **Conversations 30.4**).

The police is the largest single employer of game changers within UK criminal justice as, at the time of writing, almost 230,000 people were employed within the 43 police forces across the UK and the British Transport Police (Home Office 2014). The police workforce statistics in **Table 30.1** divide this total into six general roles where

it can be seen that almost half of this total are not employed as police officers. These figures provide a snapshot of the overall composition, but they may change year on year; they are put forward to give you an idea of its overall composition. The fact that police staff, police community support officers (PCSOs), designated officers, and special constables account for nearly half of the workforce illustrates some of the diversity in this type of work. A summary of the main duties in these job categories is provided in the table below and for further analysis of these roles please see **Chapter 21** of this book.

Each force can differ in their recruitment procedures, but a standard procedure for becoming a Police Constable involves completion of the online application form. These are judged on the expected qualities and competencies with successful applicants invited to an Assessment Centre. Here a range of assessments possibly lasting five hours will be conducted. These can include a competency-based interview, numerical and verbal reasoning tests, and communication and group work exercises. If you graduate with a 2:1 or higher (a 2:2 is permitted in exceptional circumstances) then you will be eligible to join the police's Fast Track Programme. This is a scheme designed to take an individual through the ranks of constable, sergeant, and inspector in just three years. Members of the special constabulary and serving police staff can also apply to join the fast track. The application

Role	Numbers	Principal Duties
Police Officers	127,909	Arrest; Detention, Treatment and Questioning; Identification and keeping of criminal records; Search and seizure; Stop and search; and Out-of-court disposals. This total number of officers is more than ten per cent down on the all-time high in September 2009
Police Staff	64,097	Can vary considerably (e.g. the London Metropolitan Police has over two hundred of these roles). These positions include: Administration; Auditing; Business Support; Custody Nurse Practitioners; Human Resources; IT; Laboratory Technicians; and Occupational Psychologists
Police Community Support Officers (PCSOs)	13,066	Introduced in the Police Reform Act 2002 and do not have powers of arrest nor for interviewing and processing prisoners. Duties vary between forces but generally focus on minor offences (with power to issue fixed penalty notices); providing a visible presence in supporting on the street policing; conducting house-to-house enquiries; participating in crime prevention initiatives; and guarding crime scenes
Designated Officers	4,273	This role has also existed since the Police Reform Act 2002 which empowered the Chief Officer of a force to allocate the role of a Police Community Support Officer, Investigation Officer, Detention Officer or Escort Officer to a designated person
Traffic Wardens	16	This very small number reveals how little involvement the Police now have in this area. The Road Traffic Act 1991 gave powers to civil enforcement officers for dealing with parking disputes and after commencing in London, this was rolled out nationwide
Special Constables	17,789	These are unpaid volunteers but have full police powers. There are no contracted hours as such and it is often combined with civilian roles in the police. Their total numbers are half what they were in the early 1970s but it still remains a frequent first step for people pursuing a policing career

Table 30.1 Numbers of Police Officers by role in 2014

process takes account of the managerial responsibilities that come with the planned progression and so additional selection stages and testing of policing abilities take place. Its Assessment Centre lasts for two days and uses job simulation exercises, a competency-based interview, a presentation, and cognitive ability tests.

For examples of the kinds of questions asked at Assessment Centres please see the **online resources** that accompanies this chapter at **www.oup.com/uk/case/**. For a first hand account of what makes a candidate employable to the police see **Conversations 30.4**.

The opinions in **Conversations 30.4** demonstrate the importance of portraying a professional approach and guidance on this theme is provided by the Policing Professional Framework (PPF) as introduced by Skills for Justice in 2013. This framework deals with all of the officer ranks in the UK (i.e. from constable up to Chief Superintendent) and with levels 1–5 for police staff. It is a very useful guide for policing careers as each of these positions are accompanied by statements known as National Occupational Standards and required Policing Personal Qualities. The National Occupational Standards set out the expected abilities from the different roles in relation to five broad

---

CONVERSATIONS 30.4

What makes a candidate employable to the police?—with a police professional (name withheld for security purposes)

I am the Head of Leadership and Professional Development for Lancashire Constabulary and the Professional Lead for recruit training in both Lancashire and Cumbria Constabularies. In considering the question, 'what makes a candidate employable to Lancashire Constabulary?' I feel it is important to give you an insight into where my organisation has come from, before moving on to where we are now.

When I joined the police, over 20 years ago, the selection criteria included such things as the requirement to be at least 5'8" tall and to have a 'good' but undefined level of education. For me being a little over 6'3" tall and at the time having a handful of GCSEs (O levels to be truthful about my age!) meant that I met these two criteria and was part way along the recruitment pathway. The next steps were a series of maths, English, observation, physical, and medical tests and finally an interview in which I was asked a series of questions about what I would do in hypothetical situations.

Things are a little different now. In order to support diversity and inclusion there is no longer a height restriction and a 'good' level of education has been specified as at least a level 3 qualification.

The testing that I have just described is still present but in addition candidates are required to undertake a national assessment centre, during which they are put through a series of role play exercises designed to provide candidates with the opportunity to display the qualities expected of a police officer under the National Policing Professional Framework. In addition, the final interview is now much more focused on what candidates have done, not what you might do in theory.

So what are we looking for in a candidate nowadays? *Strong verbal communication skills* are a must. Police officers have to talk to people on a daily basis and they need to be able to do so at all levels. One minute they might be trying to communicate with a child who has been the subject of abuse, the next presenting evidence in a court room, trying to calm down a potentially violent situation, or chairing a public meeting. Officers need to be able to adapt their communication style to the needs of the audience and at all times present a professional image.

In my operational experience I have found that officers who are strong communicators and can demonstrate a variety of styles of verbal communication are those who tend to consistently achieve more positive results, are less prone to being assaulted on duty, and are more likely to succeed in their probationary period and subsequent career.

Often these people are also those who tend to be good team players and *the ability to work as part of a small team* is another very important attribute that we look for in a candidate. Team work is important in many avenues of employment but unlike most other jobs, in which poor team working might lead to an awkward dynamic in the workplace or perhaps the failure to achieve certain performance targets, in the police it could literally result in someone sustaining serious injury or much worse. The ability to work as part of a close knit team and put others before one's self, in what can be exceptionally demanding circumstances, is imperative. Although it makes good viewing figures for Hollywood movies, there is no place in the constabulary for the 'Dirty Harry' style of maverick cop who goes it alone!

Linked to putting others first—quality of service is a top priority for the constabulary and we want people who understand how to deliver *excellent customer service* and appreciate the benefits that this brings to the organisation and our communities. Unlike in some other retail or service sectors the public do not have a choice over which police force they use; where the incident or crime occurs decides which officers will deal with it. Therefore it is even more important that we deliver a first class service because we want our communities to trust us and have confidence in us. This is not only what our public deserves, but also because the way we police is built on the concept of policing by consent, not by oppression or unreasonable use of force, and to do so we need people to come to us with information and support us in fighting crime.

Excellent written communication skills are also vitally important to our organisation. Despite attempts by successive governments to reduce the police's paperwork, it is still a fact that there is a lot of it. In reality this is inevitable in a criminal justice system in which documentary evidence is vital to a fair and equitable legal process. Therefore written evidence needs to be of a first class standard. I have personally noticed over recent years that the use of 'text speak' has sometimes crept into the statements of young probationary officers. It may be the case that abbreviations such as 'LOL' and 'TBH' have now found their way into the Oxford English dictionary but I can assure you that, in general, barristers and Crown Court judges don't take kindly to such things appearing in the files of evidence placed before them.

IT skills are another area that is of increasing importance to the constabulary. The government's austerity measures over the last four years have led to the police service investing in various IT solutions in order to realise longer term savings in staff hours. Officers now need to be computer and mobile technology literate; using palm pilots, tablets, tough books, and mobile terminals in police vehicles in order to input and access information.

I mentioned earlier that the *level of academic achievement* for entry as a police officer has now been set at a minimum of level 3. However, I do believe that there are advantages for those entering the service who have studied at a higher award level. As I said I entered the service with just O levels but since then I have undertaken a degree programme as a mature student and have seen for myself the benefits that a Higher Education course of study can bring. In particular, the development of the ability to *critically evaluate large amounts of information*, prepare *detailed and balanced arguments* and draw *rational conclusions from the available evidence*; all of which are skills that are directly transferable to the investigative role of a police officer.

All that said, arguably the most important attribute that the constabulary values in candidates is *life experience*, we need candidates to have had experience of actually doing all the things I have mentioned, not just learning about them. Our recruits go through a two year probationary period during which they receive extensive training in

the classroom, and in the operational workplace. But we need people who already possess the social skills that will facilitate them in picking up the role quickly. At interview candidates are tested on their experience of respecting difference, managing volatile situations, and customer care. Therefore it is crucial that candidates have experience of life beyond their college or university classrooms.

We are looking for people who *understand the needs of our various diverse communities*, have experience of interacting with individuals from diverse backgrounds or are themselves from such backgrounds. We need people who understand that it is appropriate to treat people differently in order to meet their individual needs—far too often during interviews I am told by candidates that they understand diversity because they treat everyone the same way.

Special Constables—a possible first step

One way of possibly achieving and being able to demonstrate the level of experience we need is by becoming a Special Constable. For those of you who are not already aware the Special Constabulary is effectively the Police Reserve—volunteers who receive comprehensive training, are issued with the same police equipment as a standard regular officer and have the full range of policing powers at their disposal. They work alongside regular police officers, but do so in their spare time, many having alternative full or part time employment or while undertaking courses of study. The benefit of this is that not only do they obtain invaluable experience of policing, which they can use as evidence should they decide to apply to become a regular officer, but also it gives them the opportunity to see whether they actually want to be a full time police officer. The reality is that being a police officer is a very challenging and demanding role and it is not one that everyone is suited to. Sampling the role, as a Special Constable, allows individuals to make a more informed decision on their potential future career path.

The police are always working to raise young people's awareness of the Special Constabulary, in particular young people from the BAME (black, Asian and minority ethnic) community. To this end we have established partnerships with universities and colleges. Together we have developed things such as Special Constabulary Feeder Courses on which students undertake a number of sessions in the evenings and at weekends and are given an enhanced insight into the training and role of a Special Constable. These can be an excellent way of demonstrating your employability to the police.

Police professional (name withheld for security reasons)
working as Head of Leadership and Professional Development
for Lancashire Constabulary and as the Professional Lead for
recruit training in Lancashire and Cumbria Constabularies

areas of policing—Community Partnership, Intelligence, Investigation, Organisational/Operational Support, and Response. The PPF is easy to use and anyone with online access can use it to discover the expectations of say, a Chief Inspector in Intelligence, or a Sergeant in Community Partnership, etc. National Occupational Standards have not been set for levels of Assistant Chief Constable and above but the PPF does apply to these roles with its five Policing Personal Qualities. These are attributes in decision making, leadership, professionalism, public service, and working with others; and are required from each policing rank with their detail increasing with the seniority of the position.

The senior ranks that are excluded from full coverage in the PPF are those of Chief Constable (the most senior rank for most of the UK) and Commander and Commissioner ranks (the equivalent for London only) and also the deputy and assistant positions for these roles. The status of these positions provides membership to the Association of Chief Police Officers (ACPO) which is an organisation with almost 300 members. According to the Parker Review the two chief outputs of ACPO are deliverance of operational coordination services for national policing and provision of a professional voice for the service (2013: 7).

This section has sought to convey the amount of variety currently available within police work. The advice of your 'police travel partner' has shown how your employability is essential for taking the first step in this career. This is expanded by the PPF which is freely available on the Skills for Justice website and provides virtually a complete breakdown of all of the required skills and attributes. If we summarise the main officer roles as constable, sergeant,

and inspector, awareness of the PPF will inform you of the differences in responsibilities. The National Occupational Standards (NOS) for a constable have 10 different requirements and include abilities in things such as 'arrest', 'interview', and 'search'. Whereas for a sergeant there are some supervisory (i.e. managerial) responsibilities (of constables) and therefore its NOS include terms such as 'prepare', 'supervise', and 'manage'. An inspector has responsibilities for supervising the officer ranks of constable and sergeant and the NOS therefore include terms such as 'develop and implement', 'identify and manage', and 'allocate and monitor'. However, despite the differences in accordance with rank there are many similarities as shown by the Policing Personal Qualities. This is also the same when it comes to international policing careers and this issue is discussed in more detail in **Table 30.3**. The College of Policing which was established in 2012 is the professional body for training and development matters in the English and Welsh police. Their website contains many resources to help you acquire and demonstrate these qualities.

Specialist and international policing careers

This section provides information on policing careers outside the formal UK structure. It is here where you can observe the many similarities in contemporary careers regardless of their location. The advice of an international travel partner is provided and confirms this belief in the parallels of different policing careers (see **Conversations 30.5**).

CONVERSATIONS 30.5

International policing careers—with Dr Jonathan McCombs

The Federal Bureau of Investigation (FBI) is a federal law enforcement agency in the United States under the Department of Justice and overseen by the Attorney General. Their training academy is one of the best and most advanced training academies of its kind in the country. New agents go through 21 weeks of training at this academy in Quantico, Virginia. It is commonly referred to as one of the premier law enforcement agencies in the world.

Specialised skills needed for employment with the agency include analytical skills, critical thinking skills, writing skills, and the ability to learn on the job. The law enforcement community is replete with examples of how lifelong learning is essential to the success of these

individuals. Tactical skills are taught in the academy, but soft skills that allow agents to interview, build relationships with local authorities, and to garner information from all possible sources are very important to their success.

For undergraduates interested in this work as a career the FBI offer an Honors Internship Program and a Volunteer Internship Program. The former offers payment for the internship although this means funding dictates its availability. Both are available in the summer months and involve the opportunity for working closely with FBI employees.

Jonathan McCombs, Ph.D., Criminal Justice Administration Program Chair, Franklin University, USA

The National Crime Agency (NCA) offers an additional option to people interested in policing as a career. This is a specialist UK law enforcement body that was introduced in 2013 to deal with serious and organised crime. The recruitment of 400 trainee cyber-intelligence officers in its first few months of operations, onto a two-year training programme that led to them becoming officers in the NCA, is one example of its focus that also includes various forms of smuggling such as people, firearms, and drugs.

It is an organisation that also recruits people who are interested in being Specials. People are sought who can provide specialist skills that are currently deemed lacking within law enforcement. So if you believe in the societal benefits of this kind of role and have in-depth cultural awareness, language skills, or forensic accountancy skills, then this is something to consider. The chapter's section in the online resources will direct you to the opportunities within the NCA which also includes expertise from people in academia as a form of specialism. The online information will also guide you towards opportunities in governmental organisations such as the UK Ministry of Justice and Home Office.

The Secret Intelligence Service (MI6) in the UK is an organisation that acquires secret foreign intelligence in the national interest. It is a possible career for people who are UK citizens with a minimum of a 2:1 degree and it is the role of an Intelligence Officer which is usually associated with this organisation. However, there are also positions in corporate services (such as human resources, procurement, and finance), for business support officers and language specialists. Due to the nature of its work, abilities in different languages are rated very highly by MI6. Along with the Security Service (MI5)—the organisation that deals with threats to national security—and GCHQ (Government Communications Headquarters)—it offers Higher Apprenticeship programmes, although the Foundation Degree in Communications Systems, Security and Computing and Level 4 Diploma in IT Professional Competence that are awarded at its completion shows their design for students with further education qualifications. However, MI5 offers graduates the opportunity to join either the Intelligence Officer Development Programme or the Intelligence and Data Analyst Development Programme. The first of these is the most common route for graduates and apart from the ability to accurately work with complex data sets for the latter programme, neither of them mandates a particular degree discipline or employment background.

Europol is the law enforcement agency for the European Union and employs almost 1,000 citizens of these countries to work on cross–border policing investigations. The *Europol Review* is published annually and gives more detail on its current work which also includes a variety of internship projects. These can lead to expertise in specific aspects of its work as well as a greater understanding of how the organisation itself operates. INTERPOL is a

further option as this is the world's largest international police organisation comprising 190 member countries to facilitate police forces around the world working together. It also offers internship programmes for people who are fluent in English and are enrolled in, or in the six months prior to the date of the application have graduated from, an accredited academic institution. The kind of work undertaken by these two bodies means that as with MI6 in the UK, linguistic abilities are very highly regarded.

A synopsis for this policing section must surely include the recognition of the clear similarities in the required attributes and skills for these different jobs. However, their similarity to the personal transferrable skills inherent in graduate employability also illustrates their close proximity to other careers (see **Table 30.2**).

 Interested in a career with one of the agencies featured in this section? Then visit the **online resources** and follow the links for **Chapter 30** for more information on pursuing a career in policing, governmental, and security organisations, and international policing **www.oup.com/uk/case/**.

The courts

In **Chapter 20** the work of the courts was explained as a potential game changer for criminal justice although this was not in recognition for the services of just one player. Instead, 'the courts' is a collective term for several organisations that provide work for this essential part of the legal process. In its broadest sense it could be represented by HM Courts and Tribunals Service (HMCTS) as this is an executive agency sponsored by the Ministry of Justice, which employs around 20,000 people to administer the criminal, civil, and family courts and tribunals in England and Wales and the non-devolved tribunals in Scotland and Northern Ireland. This status means that applications to it must be made through the standard civil service jobs website. It is a role that requires people to work closely with the judiciary and other members of the legal profession to fulfil the responsibilities of HMCTS for all aspects of the courts and tribunals' system.

The legal profession

The legal profession contains a variety of possible careers with *barristers* and *solicitors* being the most well-known. The Bar Council is the professional body for barristers in England and Wales with the Law Society performing the same role for solicitors. A qualifying law degree is the first step for either and these can be acquired from a full law degree (LLB) or joint honours degree programmes in law and criminology. A non-law degree can be converted into a qualifying one by taking the Common Professional

'The Magnificent Seven'	MI5	Interpol
1. A positive attitude: a 'can-do' approach	**Planning and organising:** Drive and determination to achieve complete goals	**Dedication to improvement:** Commitment to continuous learning; exhibiting drive, creativity, and energy for achieving goals
2. Business and customer awareness	**Working with others/teamwork:** Relating effectively with others; developing rapport and managing and resolving interpersonal conflict	**Teamwork:** Ability to work cooperatively and effectively in multi-cultural and multi-disciplinary teams
3. Communication and literacy	**Communicating:** Clear and concise verbal expression, use of appropriate language/grammar, listening and responding appropriately, and communicating for different audiences and purposes	**Ability to communicate well:** Ability to speak, write, and interact clearly and persuasively; aptitude for establishing credibility and influence; language abilities; and capability in using technical communication tools
4. Managing tasks and solving problems	**Analysis and problem solving:** Organisational skills; Developing effective work plans; setting appropriate and resourcefully accomplishing all goals	
5. Applying Numeracy		
6. Applying Technology		
7. Entrepreneurship/ enterprise	**Leading and decision-making:** Managing and adapting to changing situations successfully; shifting focus onto new priorities; developing new approaches or methods to accomplish different objectives	
		Integrity: Clear beliefs and practice in objectivity, impartiality, and personal and corporate integrity
		Respect: Commitment and respect for universal human rights and cultural diversity
		Dedication to Police Profession: Commitment and respect for the police profession

Table 30.2 Essential Competencies for Graduate Employability and International Policing Careers

Examination/Graduate Diploma in Law. Barristers and solicitors generally inhabit different courtrooms in their work as barristers have the *right of audience* (the ability to represent people) in the Crown Court with solicitors having it for the Magistrates' Court. Both careers then require a professional qualification from their respective organising body, followed by a period of apprenticeship (known as *pupillages* for barristers and *training contracts* for solicitors) before qualifying status is awarded. The two careers have major differences in employment status as a barrister is generally a self-employed person whereas a solicitor tends to have the status of an employee. This can be an important consideration for someone's career and so later in this chapter the issue of graduate self-employability is considered further.

The legal profession has, like many other professions, recently tried to open up its practices and accommodate more diverse experience and qualifications in its work. So there are now more opportunities for roles such as legal assistants and paralegals (a legal equivalent to a paramedic). There is also a third branch to the legal profession and the work of *legal executives*. Their professional body is the Chartered Institute of Legal Executives (CILEX) which has around 20,000 members. A legal executive tends to be a specialist in a certain area of law, such as criminal or family law, and in recent years their ability to represent people and provide legal advice has been increased. To become fully qualified as a Chartered Legal Executive you must undertake a similar combination of academic and vocational study of law as required by barristers and solicitors. However, there is usually a major difference in that these studies are conducted whilst an individual is working as a paid employee in a solicitor's office or an organisation's legal department.

The Crown Prosecution Service

The Crown Prosecution Service (CPS) is one of the largest employers of 'court-based game changers' as it is a public agency with around 6,000 employees distributed across 13 regions of England and Wales (Crown Prosecution Service 2014). It has the responsibility for prosecuting cases in the criminal courts and its work is considered more fully in **Chapter 20**. However, the careers of its individual workers can be compared with those of barristers and solicitors in private practice. Its *Crown Advocates*, for which there are also Principal and Senior positions, work almost exclusively in the Crown Courts and so this advocacy work makes it very similar to that of a barrister—but without the self-employed status. Barristers in private practice can still be called upon to prosecute cases in the Crown Court (and they may also defend in other cases) but the frequency of this is aimed to be reduced by the positions of Crown Advocates. This was also a factor behind the CPS's launch in 2015 of the Legal Trainee Scheme that offers pupillages or training contracts to successful applicants. The organisation also employs *Crown Prosecutors*, for which there are positions of Senior Crown Prosecutors, to prepare for prosecutions and undertake advocacy at the Magistrates' Courts. The role involves a high volume of casework that needs review, advice, and representation at court. The CPS also offers professional careers in human resources and equality and diversity, plus roles for administrative officers and administrative support assistants. These positions may have the 'administration' tag but they require individuals to sensitively act as the CPS's first point of contact for people external to it. They can therefore be required to deal with highly emotional matters and other enquiries.

Interested in a career in the courts? Then visit the **online resources** and follow the web links for **Chapter 30** for more information on pursuing a career in the courts **www.oup.com/uk/case/**.

Probation

This section on probation work includes careers in social work and youth offending teams (YOTs) as these forms of employment also involve working with vulnerable people. Probation is given more focus because in recent years, this type of work has become an exemplar for the existence of changeable (protean) careers. This can be demonstrated by considering that in the timespan of just one person's career (i.e. from the mid-1970s to now) it has not only altered its entire philosophical rationale (from the rehabilitative ideal to one of public protection and risk); but seen its place as the public service providing this work, significantly undermined by policies of contestability and privatisation. These issues are discussed further in **Chapter 21** where it is noted that despite the constant uncertainty and change, its status as 'a criminal justice game changer' might be deserved. However, this section concentrates more on the career itself, and the threats and opportunities from this persistent political interference that have been posed to the people actually working in it.

Social work

Social work is contained in this section because this career also requires expertise in providing services to vulnerable people. Although in this case there can be a wider reach than offending behaviour as it involves work such as support for drug and alcohol users, homeless people, and people with mental health issues. The sector skills council that establishes the required standards in this career is Skills for Care and their website should therefore be approached in the same way as Skills for Justice (the provider of those for policing). There can be a difference in the terminology for these requirements as in England applicants need to show they meet the Professional Capability Framework (PCF) for social work whereas for the rest of the UK it is the National Occupational Standards for Social Work that set the standards. These conceptions of what employability actually means for careers in social work can be addressed by using the strategic and reflective methods for producing your graduate employability presented earlier in this chapter.

Youth offending teams

Working with vulnerable people is also the reason why youth justice has been put forward in this section of career discussion. These career possibilities increased significantly following the effects of the Crime and Disorder Act 1998 and subsequent policy and legislation. The provision of a youth offending team (YOT) is now a part of every local authority's remit and these can offer employment such as YOT Manager, Senior YOT Worker, and YOT Worker. Skills for Justice set the expectations for these careers that are organised under 'Performance Criteria' and 'Knowledge and Understanding'. The first of these details what counts as satisfactory performance in these positions, such as when specified measures of success are attained. The need for knowledge and understanding clearly indicates the relevance of your undergraduate degree to your employability, as they include awareness of issues such as the contributing factors to problematic behaviour in young people. It is not possible to consider all of these performance criteria and requisite knowledge and understanding in this chapter, but such detail can be easily acquired through the Skills for Justice website. The importance of youth justice to local authorities means there can be many opportunities for exploring this kind of career and it is therefore another situation where the advice of a travel partner can be invaluable.

Probation work

Whilst these kinds of work offer many opportunities, in the context of changeable careers the probation service is an ideal organisation to focus on. Indeed a highly critical view might claim its 21st century redevelopments have brought more changes to the careers of staff than those affected on many of the offenders they have worked with! At the beginning of this century there appeared to be a significant increase in the numbers of probation service employees with the total growing by almost a third. However, it was the lower rank of probation service officers (PSOs) rather than qualified probation officers that accounted for most of this growth; in 1997 there were 1,919 people employed in this role but by 2006 the number of PSOs had increased to 7,247 (Oldfield and Grimshaw 2010: 20, Table 11). Additional numbers of both senior support staff and managers also contributed to the rise, and as it was accompanied by a 27 per cent growth in the number of community sentences in this period, the expansion was not what it appeared to be (Canton 2011: 203).

The recent myriad of changes to probation's practice and structure provide a clear example of the shifting nature of contemporary careers. Incessant oscillation between different penal philosophies is one of its constant pressures but this has been eclipsed by the dramatic transformation to its place as a public service. This has been driven by the decision to divide up probation work and allocate it to either the public sector and new National Probation Service (NPS) or the private sector and Community Rehabilitation Companies (CRCs). The

NPS was created following the abolition of probation trusts in 2014 and is responsible for high risk offenders only which account for 30 per cent of probation services. Just before the split there was a total of 16,110 full time equivalent (FTE) staff employed by the Probation Service and the diversity in their work can be reflected by its break down into 26 types of work with 15 different job groups. A more manageable means for appreciating the variety is the demarcation between *offender management* and *interventions* as these two forms of probation work are by far the most common types; Other Agency/Services and Corporate Services complete the list of expected functions. In terms of specific work, the three most frequent areas in which individuals are employed are supervision, unpaid work, and accredited programmes (Ministry of Justice 2014).

The remaining 70 per cent of probation labour has been given to the private sector, i.e. CRCs, for offenders classified as low to medium risk. A CRC has been created for 21 areas of England and Wales and their ownership is composed of a variety of partnerships between private companies, charities, social enterprises, and community interest companies. The area of Kent, Surrey & Sussex is an exception as it is exclusively owned by the private limited company Seetec Business Technology Centre. The use of private companies has resulted in many problems that were forcefully criticised by the House of Commons Committee of Public Accounts (2014); although this did not prevent two private companies, Sodexo Justice Services and Interserve, being placed in charge of over half of the 21 areas. Durham Tees Valley is the only area not to have involvement from a private company and instead has a joint venture between a Probation Staff CIC, a Registered Social Landlord, a Social Enterprise, a NHS Foundation Trust, two charities, and two Borough Councils.

The workforce figures for CRCs used to be collated by the Ministry of Justice, NOMS (National Offender Management Service), and the NPS (National Probation Service) but following their incorporation in early 2015, the companies themselves took responsibility for producing this data. The final central report as compiled by the three governmental bodies revealed a workforce that amounted to just under 8,300 FTE staff at the end of 2014 (Ministry of Justice 2015).

Anybody interested in pursuing a career with the probation service needs to be aware of the qualifications under Community Justice Learning (CJL). This has introduced the qualification for Probation Officers named the Professional Qualification in Probation (PQiP). The CJL system is also bringing in qualifications from 2017 for different levels across the community justice sector in the hope of encouraging career progression. The PQiP is a level 6 qualification (the same as an honours degree) and according to Skills for Justice this is designed to prepare people for probation work by ensuring they are able to:

- assess the risk, needs, and responsivity of offenders;
- protect the public and manage risk of harm;
- create an enabling environment conducive to change;
- build and sustain effective working relationships;
- reflect on their practice and continuously develop by demonstrating professional ethics and values;
- rehabilitate, resettle offenders, and promote desistance;
- prepare reports including court reports;
- manage their own and others' work.

This section has sought to illustrate the different possibilities for careers in 'probation' which are varied as these days the work is no longer the province of one public sector organisation. It has mentioned a range of organisations for which this work may be available. The growth of the private sector and the recurring political demands may have changed the nature of some of this kind of work but resilience and adaptability in the face of these pressures can lead to rewarding careers. Finding a travel partner who is experienced in overcoming these challenges can therefore be highly beneficial in forming this kind of career as illustrated by Mohammed Farooq in **Conversations 30.6**.

Probation careers in Scotland and Northern Ireland emphasise social work in their training and for these

---

CONVERSATIONS 30.6

Personal reflections on changing careers in the probation service—with Mohammed Farooq

My career with the service began in 1994 when I obtained a job as a Probation Officer in Greater Manchester. I had an offender management caseload and worked in a court team doing Pre-Sentence Reports and other court work. I shared a busy office with five people and at that time money seemed available for new initiatives, and officers had the autonomy to invest in things such as education and training programmes or other services for addressing offenders' cognitive deficits such as a lack of self-control or low levels of critical reasoning and problem solving.

I wanted a management career within the probation service so after four years I took a role as a Practice Development Assessor with the North West Training Consortium on the Diploma in Probation Studies programme. It was delivered in partnership with Lancaster, Liverpool, and Manchester universities and as it brought me into contact with all of the probation areas in the north-west, I saw it as a good way for progressing to Senior Probation Officer (SPO) rank.

After two years I applied for a SPO position and I can still remember my feelings of amazement when I was told I had been successful! At the time parts of the probation service were renowned for relying on internal progression so I really didn't think I would get it. I remember taking the call in my car and nearly driving off the M61 in shock! So for the next five years I was based in a town centre office on another side of the county and spent three of these as an Area Manager with responsibility for implementing the Criminal Justice Act 2003 reforms to community sentences.

I enjoyed the team management role for eight probation officers that went with being a SPO so I was keen

to apply when an opportunity arose for a District Manager in Greater Manchester. This was a position one step up in the organisation and had responsibility for managing ten SPOs with an annual strategic budget of £1.5m. It was a very challenging role as there were many problems in the district such as funding, industrial relations, and negative attitudes towards targets. I had to learn a lot, in a very short space of time, particularly about financial things such as budget management which I mostly did myself through online learning resources. I was proud that my district overcame its earlier difficulties and in three years became the highest performing one in Greater Manchester.

In 2009 as a result of the financial problems affecting the whole public sector, the trust decided to disestablish the District Manager role. At the time there were 15 of us at this rank and we were to be replaced by 10 positions of Assistant Chief Executives with the other five reverting back to the role of SPO. This process was decided at an Assessment Centre before which I had to submit a policy paper then on the day another had to be written followed by a 10-minute presentation to the panel. This paper was 'unseen' and 30 minutes' preparation time was given. I went into the Assessment Centre with a plan to use the European Foundation for Quality Management (EFQM) Excellence Model. I was confident it could be adapted to any topic and the strategy meant I was not daunted by the chosen question on the performance of probation districts with regards to the numbers of people getting custodial sentences of less than 12 months. It proved successful as the panel graded my paper at 'nine out of ten'. There were seven people on the panel and then there was a Q&A session where each member asked one question. We had three minutes to answer each of these and if you went over the time that was it—you were out! After passing this rigorous process and getting the job I was immediately told that I had to relocate to another area in Greater Manchester. I worked there as Assistant Chief Executive for three years and again helped turn a low performing area into one that became recognised for exceptional performance.

In 2014 I took a regional position within the National Probation Service (North West) as Head of Stakeholder Engagement. In this role I have a budget of £5m and a department of 120 people with responsibility for re-settlement policies, regional court strategies, and legal services. It requires a considerable amount of partner-ship work and contract management with bodies such as prisons and CRCs is integral. It is a very demanding role because my career has taught me that things be-come more difficult the further up in an organisation you go—there are more variables when you do this so get-ting outcomes becomes harder. Political skills in keeping people happy are so important and I've gone through a huge amount of learning in developing these. For ex-ample, when I got my first management job I wanted to change the world in 24 hours but these days I'm much more realistic.

I believe the probation service has changed hugely since 1994 as it has become far more business-like. In my early days its social work base didn't really focus on performance and practice but now it has taken on board the efficiency agenda—something that has not always been a byword for the public sector. In this time I have learnt how to market probation work and generate in-come streams such as supporting the legal profession and engaging corporate victims in restorative justice. My career has provided me with a huge amount of learning and has allowed me to do things that I've wanted to do, such as lecturing at universities and writing for the legal publication *Criminal Law & Justice Weekly*. It has been a real journey and I've learnt so much from so many good people—I've picked up things with every step and I've ditched them as well—you have got to learn what works for you.

Mohammed Farooq, Head of Stakeholder Engagement for the National Probation Service (North West)

opportunities reference should be made to the Scottish Social Services Council and the Probation Board for Northern Ireland.

Interested in a career in probation work? Then visit the **online resources** and follow the web links for **Chapter 30** for more information on pursuing a career in probation work **www.oup.com/uk/case/**.

Prisons

Attaining graduate employment with the final game changer in this section requires a similar process of demonstrating competencies and abilities to those cited already. There have also been recent decreases in its work-force as seen in the 41 per cent reduction in the number of officer grade staff in 2010–14 to a total of 14,170; in-cluded in this fall were 1,375 officer posts following the closure of 15 public sector prisons in this period (Howard League 2014). Although officer grade staff is just one part of NOMS employment opportunities, as the overall total that year was three times higher. This included NPS staff as well as for the plethora of other roles within a prison, such as managerial, operational support, and other speci-fied services such as education or catering.

If you are interested in this as a career then it is essen-tial you are familiar with the competency and qualities framework (CQF) for the Prison Service. This consists of 12 behavioural competences that are collated under the three headings of: working professionally, working with others, and working to achieve results. Examples of your successful experience with these values need to be pro-duced and guidance in the chapter's online resources is designed to help you with this purpose. The 12 competen-cies include resilience, team work, problem solving, and developing self—the transferrable nature of the expecta-tions can be seen from only two of them even containing the word 'prison'. Evidence from outside the custodial en-vironment is therefore relevant but it is vital that you can express and apply it to this setting. Awareness of the CQF will also provide you with knowledge of Prison Service staff duties and expectations and this also has to be dis-played in your applications. See **Conversations 30.7** for more detail about what makes a candidate employable from someone who has experienced it first hand.

Interested in a career in the prison service? Then visit the **online resources** and follow the web links for **Chapter 30** for more information on pursuing a career in the prison service **www.oup.com/uk/case/**.

The organisation of the UK's penal estate provides an alternative career option to NOMS as it has 'the most pri-vatised prison system in Europe'; 16 per cent of the total prison population are held in such institutions, a ratio almost double that of the United States (Prison Reform

CONVERSATIONS 30.7

What makes a candidate employable to the Prison Service?—with Ken Seed

A lot of people think they know what life inside a prison is like. They see portrayals on TV and in films, and imagine these are a true reflection of reality. Until you've worked in a prison, built trust, exercised authority without throwing your weight around, and ultimately changed people's lives for the better, you've no real idea what a difference prison life can make to offenders, society, and to you.

Prison Officer ranks involve different bands for Officer, Supervising Officer, and Custodial Manager. This can be followed by progression to governor grade. The NOMS graduate programme offers you the chance to make a difference to society, rather than just the bottom line. In just three years, you'll develop the leadership qualities and operational expertise to manage one of the most complex and challenging environments around a HMPS prison.

From graduate to prison officer starts with six weeks of training at our national training centre in Rugby. As well as learning about prison service values and responsibilities, you'll develop the skills you need for your first role on the programme: Prison Officer. These include using handcuffs, basic control and restraint techniques, and how to carry out searches. Your last week of training will be spent shadowing an officer in the prison where you'll first be posted; then you'll take on the role yourself.

Over the next 12 to 18 months, you'll gain further experience and responsibility, as you progress from Prison Officer to Supervisor Officer level. You will then move to a different prison and take up the role of Custodial Manager, with a group of staff to manage and finally you will move into a middle-management governor-grade role as an Operational Manager. Here you'll head up an entire area of a prison, such as Residence, where you'll take on responsibilities that include preventing suicide and self-harm and managing all the prisoners' living facilities. When you have completed your programme, usually after two to three years, you can apply for a managerial post. You'll then have a number of career paths open to you.

As a prison Governor you could work in establishments ranging from high security prisons holding category A prisoners to open prisons for category D prisoners. Larger prisons can have several governors on different grades. Your duties would vary according to the size and type of prison, but are likely to include: supervising security; making inspections; carrying out disciplinary procedures; writing reports; managing the prison budget and other resources; overseeing the development of the prison to meet government targets on, for example, prisoners welfare; working with other professionals, such as medical staff, and providers of others services such as Substance Misuse Services.

These are demanding roles and so you won't be surprised to find out that the recruitment process for our Graduate Scheme is quite demanding at times, although most of our candidates tell us that they find the experience quite enjoyable and often learn a lot about themselves as they go through.

The process looks like this: short application form with personal details and security questions; online situational judgment tool; online numerical reasoning test; job simulation assessment centre; written assessment and interview; medical and fitness test; security clearance.

We do get a lot of candidates applying each year, and at each stage we do have to reduce our numbers significantly, so you will need to be successful at every stage before we can consider offering you a place on the programme.

Whether you're a recent graduate or an experienced people manager, there are certain personality traits that will set you out as a potential prison leader. These include:

- resilience;
- integrity;
- the ability to get through to people from all walks of life;
- decisiveness, even under intense pressure;
- the ability to stay calm in emotionally charged situations;
- being someone who loves being set, and beating, targets.

On top of all this you'll need to be the sort of person who can bounce back if things go wrong. You'll also need to be adaptable, as you'll be dealing with some pretty unpredictable people day in, day out. And it's important that you believe in the benefits of rehabilitation.

Ken Seed MBE, Head of Industries,
HMP Preston

Professional Standards	Duties	Transferrable Skills
The Policing Professional Framework		
NOS 10 (Constable)	Provide initial support to victims, survivors, and witnesses and assess their need for further support	Effective **communication**—keeping calm and active listening
NOS 4 (Sergeant)	Supervise investigations and investigators	**Business and customer awareness**—awareness of required procedures in the police environment
NOS 5 (Inspector)	Allocate and monitor the progress and quality of work in your area of responsibility	**Entrepreneurship/enterprise**—recognition of efficient working in the police environment
The Probation Qualifications Framework		
Level 3 VQ3 Risk GC1(3) (Probation Services' Officers)	Contribute to the protection of individuals from abuse	**Business and customer awareness**—awareness of required procedures in the probation environment
Level 5 VQ5 Risk GC3(5) (Probation Officers)	Manage abusive and aggressive behaviour	**Managing tasks and solving problems**—developing appropriate plans for achievable targets
The Competency and Qualities Framework for the Prison Service		
1A (All staff)	Achieving a safe and secure environment	**Business and customer awareness**—awareness of required procedures in the custodial environment
1A (First line management)	Ensures the team contributes to the maintenance of physical security	**Business and customer awareness**—establishing rapport and managing interpersonal conflict
1A (Middle management)	Supports and implements strategies, policies, and processes that contribute to the achievement of a safe and secure living and working environment	**Managing tasks and solving problems**—developing appropriate plans for achievable targets
1A (Senior management)	Creates strategies, policies, and processes that contribute to the achievement of a safe and secure living and working environment	**A positive attitude: a 'can-do' approach**—commitment to continuous improvement for achieving targets

Table 30.3 The 3Ps and Different Levels of Game Changers

Trust 2014: 9). There are currently 14 private prisons and at present these are run by Sodexo Justice Services, Serco Custodial Services, or G4S Justice Services; the latter two companies, along with Tascor (Capita) and MITIE Care and Custody, also run seven Immigration Removal Centres in England and Wales. These companies have autonomy over issues such as their workforce recruitment, staff development, and management, so direct approaches to them are required. The database in the online resources will provide you with all their required details. It is frequently remarked that private prisons pay lower salaries to their officers although according to the *Thirteenth Report of the Prison Service Pay Review Body*, the overall pay ranges between the sectors are 'roughly comparable' (2014: para. 2.49). Such judgments can be difficult to make as the roles may not be precisely comparable and there can be differences in the overall reward packages that include pension benefits or leave entitlements.

This section has illustrated how a career in the prison service can be shaped by the standards in the CQF and that mapping your experience against these expectations is essential for successful applications. We have already discussed how this is similar to producing your graduate employability framework so if it is a career you are considering, then acquisition of the 'prison specific' features is essential. You can attain the 'missing links' in this version of your employability from acquiring experience of this work environment where you will also encounter additional travel partners. However, in order to get this kind of opportunity the advice from your course and institution (and this textbook!) needs to be taken.

Interested in a career in prison work? Then visit the **online resources** and follow the web links for **Chapter 30** for more information on pursuing a career in prison work **www.oup.com/uk/case/**.

Applying your career development learning

The experiences from the travel partners in this part of the chapter have all been acquired by people who have progressed in their organisations. In planning your career development it is therefore important to be aware of the different ranks and expectations in your preferred career. This knowledge can be used to make you aware of what is required and also illustrates how your employability will need to continually evolve. An example of this kind of career progression is provided in **Table 30.3** where the standards are considered in the context of the 3Ps (police, probation, prisons).

The Policing Professional Framework that is available at Skills for Justice is an extensive resource that allows for online searches of many permutations of ranks and categories. The presentation of the others is not as impressive although the Competency and Qualities Framework for the prison service does provide the expected requirements for employees at managerial levels. The Community Justice Learning Framework for Probation is what you need to be aware of should this be the kind of career you are interested in acquiring.

Different types of career

This section seeks to help you with careers that have not yet been discussed. It cannot cover all possibilities so, instead, common alternatives are provided to illustrate the width of possibilities from your undergraduate degree. In **Chapter 1** you considered criminology as a hybrid academic discipline, i.e. something that has evolved out of other disciplines such as anthropology, law, geography, economics, politics, sociology, psychology, etc. This mixture of influences has resulted in criminology being inherently interdisciplinary and it is this diversity that is reflected in the many different careers open to you.

Researcher

This kind of career can involve different types of work such as research analysis, data analysis, and market research. The Researcher Development Framework (RDF) put forward at www.vitae.ac.uk is an excellent tool for appreciating the expected knowledge, intellectual abilities, techniques, personal qualities, and professional standards in this line of work. The RDF is broken down into four areas, each with sub-areas, and should be approached in the same way as National Occupational Standards and the 'magnificent seven' of graduate employability. So it will give you direction for what is expected but you must be able to demonstrate how you have experience of successfully meeting all of them. The seven transferrable skills stressed earlier in the chapter as essential for your graduate employability have much relevance as your task is to apply them to the field of research. Your active involvement and experience of the research process, knowledge and understanding of methods, ability to effectively communicate research findings, and experience of collaborative research will therefore be your important assets.

A research assistant is a common first position in this kind of career and it is a role found in many different work environments such as universities, engineering firms, pharmaceutical companies, and other organisations (public, private, and third sector) that require data collection and analysis, the preparation of reports, and accurate record keeping. The role can include clerical work, administration, and general support for the research and subsequent publication of results.

A Graduate Research Assistant is a position available in universities and has the significant advantage of being a job that can pay you to get a PhD! A good class of undergraduate degree and successful experience of the research process will be required as they are highly competitive positions. The providers of HE who class themselves as research universities are likely to offer these roles. whose purpose is to support lecturers and other faculty members in carrying out funded research projects. These duties will usually be on top of the responsibilities involved in studying for a PhD. They can vary according to the nature of the research being assisted but your general research abilities, such as conducting scholarly literature reviews, searching for requisite sources, and all of the others you acquired as an undergraduate, will be relevant.

The role can include work for the publication of the research such as presentations at academic conferences or publication in academic, peer-reviewed journals. The work an assistant does for these important methods of communication can lead to inclusion as a co-author on these presentations or publications.

Academic

This career is commonly sought by people who have completed their PhD and/or research assistant role. It is equally competitive, if not more so, as the roles discussed above—as contemporary jobs in academia invariably require a range of high-level experience in things such as: HE teaching; course administration; publications in peer reviewed journals; research supervision; and participation in successful funding applications. Acquisition of these can take a long time so the sooner they can be combined with your undergraduate or postgraduate work then the quicker your progress will be. It is another area where you should be able to find an experienced travel partner at your HE institution.

The expectations for a strong publication record in academic journals and the acquisition of different sources of funding can vary according to the university that is offering the work. They are likely to be essential for an institution that is 'research led' but for those that identify themselves as 'teaching led' there can be other preferred experiences. In these places and those of other HE providers, the emphasis for their academics is on their teaching abilities. Therefore your awareness of the work of the Higher Education Academy (HEA) will be a major help. The HEA is a publicly funded body that works to enhance the quality and impact of learning and teaching in HE. It is the professional body for this sector of education and the expected attributes of its members are put forward in the UK Professional Standards Framework (UKPSF). This structure consists of four grades of seniority for HE work and each of them are based on three fundamental competencies:

- *Areas of activity* (e.g. the organisation and planning of learning experiences and the provision of assessment and feedback).
- *Core knowledge* (e.g. disciplinary knowledge plus awareness for how students learn both generally and within your discipline).

- *Professional values* (e.g. commitment to equal opportunities in HE and your use of evidence-informed approaches in delivering teaching and learning).

These competencies are further broken down into sub-elements and as with the other examples in this chapter they must be individually addressed and supported with evidence.

Teacher

There are different options for a teaching career such as in primary schools, secondary schools, and further education colleges. These opportunities have different methods of entry although they all require acquisition of an undergraduate degree as a first step. Following this, there are several postgraduate routes into teaching that have the general name of Initial Teacher Education or Training (ITET) programmes.

Apart from those employed in independent schools, academies, and free schools, teachers in the UK need to attain Qualified Teacher Status (QTS) or the Teaching Qualification (TQ). These can be acquired through your choice of ITET where most require one year's full-time study although some can be taken via part-time study over two years. Many of these programmes will include additional qualifications such as the Professional Graduate Certificate in Education (PGCE); the Professional Graduate Diploma in Education (PGDE); the Postgraduate Certificate in Higher Education (PGCHE); the Postgraduate Certificate in Academic Practice (PGCAP) or a Postgraduate Certificate in Teaching and Learning in Higher Education (or something similarly named). You should take advice on which of these courses are appropriate for your career interest and it will be even better if your choice is aligned with the UKPSF and accredited by the HEA.

In order to gain entry onto an ITET, in addition to your undergraduate degree from a UK provider of HE, you will need to have achieved a standard equivalent to a grade C or above in both English and mathematics' GCSEs (grade B or above if applying in Wales). If early years or primary school (ages 3–11) is your intended area of teaching then you also must have achieved a standard equivalent to a grade C or above in a GCSE science subject examination.

You will also have to undergo professional skills tests that assess your numeracy and literacy attributes in the context of professional teaching. As with many of the careers discussed in this chapter, relevant prior experience will be an advantage. This could range from a couple of weeks' classroom experience or other periods of time spent observing other teachers and generally helping them out.

Civil servant

In the UK, the Civil Service is a vast organisation employing hundreds of thousands of people to help the government develop and implement its policies. This can be through either the work of around 20 government departments (e.g. the Ministry of Justice), 350 government agencies (e.g. the Criminal Injuries Compensation Authority) or the 20 or so non-departmental government bodies (e.g. the Youth Justice Board). There are several routes into this career with the Civil Service Fast Stream the recommended approach for graduates, thanks to its accelerated promotion and salary prospects. A range of streams that are appropriate for Criminology graduates are annually advertised such as the Generalist Fast Stream and the Government Social Research Service. They involve a rigorous application process that can involve the following stages:

- *Self-assessed numerical and verbal reasoning tests* that are timed; practice online selection tests are freely available.

- A *situational judgement questionnaire* which is untimed and gives you a range of information from which you have to choose the most effective course of action.

- *Online selection tests* for numerical and verbal reasoning that are timed and an untimed *Fast Stream competency multiple choice questionnaire* that assesses the expected professional competencies in this work.

- *Analytical fast stream assessment* where your possession of the role's required skills is assessed at a half-day event in London.

- *The e-Tray exercise* where your ability to handle a typical workload of tasks in the email inbox of a Fast Streamer is tested. This is taken at your own home and online practice tests are also available.

- A final *Assessment Centre* that lasts a full day and participation in a range of group and individual exercises is assessed, as well as a formal one to one interview.

It is possible for a graduate to join the Civil Service directly as opposed to going through this process because the service can advertise for many professional roles—such as legal services, communicators, finance, social research, and procurement managers. The Civil Service is currently made up of 25 professions and each has their own competency framework. Experience of this work can be acquired through its annual undergraduate placements and internship programmes.

Victim Support

There are many different roles in this organisation that can be highly suitable for a criminology graduate as much of its work values high levels of knowledge for victim and crime related issues. This can be in a *case worker* position with responsibility for dealing with individual cases or *project manager* roles where responsibility is given for specific initiatives or areas of work. The positions can be in specific areas of crime such as domestic violence, restorative justice, and antisocial behaviour.

It is an organisation that encourages voluntary work from all parts of the community so it could be a way of acquiring your work-based learning as discussed earlier. However, take care that you are honest with them about your circumstances (e.g. if you are living temporarily in the area) and have a genuine interest in this type of work—doing it 'to get your WBL hours in' is not a welcomed approach! If it is the right work for you then acquiring this experience early in your undergraduate days will be very advantageous; Victim Support generally expect the applicants to its career roles to have a minimum of one year's experience in doing the work.

Combining it with your course should enhance your criminological studies as the organisation is a key component of the criminal justice system. It offers careers for people with abilities for working in partnership with other agencies to help victims of crime. It can therefore enhance your studies of issues such as the multi-agency framework for criminal justice through your experience of attending things such as a Multi-Agency Risk Assessment Conference (MARAC). These careers will also expect applicants to have a record of advocacy work on behalf of others and getting involved in this type of work early will increase your chances of acquiring it.

Charity advocate

Advocacy roles can also be varied but often involve supporting vulnerable people such as the homeless or otherwise disadvantaged. They can have a focus on environmental, health, and community issues and their level of responsibility can range from that of an *advocate* for a specific person to an *advocate caseworker* with a full caseload of different problems. There can also be *project manager* work with responsibility for specific issues and initiatives.

The role of a *Policy Advisor* can be important to some charities and to do this you will need to have strong research and advocacy skills. It requires proven ability in both understanding policy issues and in communicating them effectively to a range of audiences. Your undergraduate course may provide you with opportunities for gaining this kind of experience in public speaking as the presentations you were asked to do may have involved different audiences. Experience of developing and implementing campaign strategies is also useful for this type of work, so you should consider the NUS services at your institution as an important travel partner in this career.

There can be many employment opportunities within charities and they are not solely for people working on a purely voluntary basis. They can offer careers comparable with other sectors and their 'commercial outlook' can be similarly as intense—for example the 'money making machines' of both FIFA and the National Lottery are charities!

Community development worker

For acquiring this type of career it is important to have a proven interest in community and social issues. It is another area where you can combine your time as a criminology undergraduate where you are formally studying these issues, with actual work on their behalf. Participation in voluntary work for local community projects, youth groups, tenants' associations, or women's groups, can benefit both your career and your community. Advice on the current options for possible community project experience can be acquired at your local volunteer centre, your HE provider or through the do-it.org website.

Work in these types of careers typically includes learning about a community's needs, problems, and barriers. The ability to develop new opportunities for resolving these issues and the monitoring of existing projects may also be required. Helping raise public awareness on these issues can be expected in order to encourage local people to take action, have their say, and settle their differences of opinion. Professional skills for dealing with administration, planning meetings and events, liaising with other groups and agencies, managing budgets, fund raising, and the recruitment and training of staff and volunteers, can also be expected.

If you enjoy building good relationships with people and believe in the advantages of strong communities then you will be well suited to this kind of career. It is another area where prior experience is so important. Competition for these jobs is intense, particularly for the limited number of community development posts with local authorities. This competition is influenced by the political climate and current issues and the groups identified as needing support. Many community development and social inclusion organisations offer short courses, research projects, seminars, and conferences. Your HE provider should have an up to date list of these kinds of opportunities but if not, then access the website for the Federation for Community Development Learning. It can be a major boost to your employability and network of career contacts if you can access these opportunities.

Summary

The professional nature of these careers means they share the expectations for the different facets of graduate employability discussed in part one of this chapter. You will need to display this high level of professionalism in all of your applications regardless of their salary and status. These careers tend to share a focus on working directly with young people or vulnerable adults; so in England and Wales applicants will be required to undergo a Disclosure and Barring Service check, in Scotland membership of the Protecting Vulnerable Groups Scheme will be required, whereas in Northern Ireland, the checks will be made by Access Northern Ireland.

Self-employability and social enterprise

As discussed in the courts section earlier, a career as a barrister offers a traditional option for using the attributes and skills inherent in graduate self-employability. In recent years another choice has materialised thanks to the global interest in a new form of business venture known as *social enterprise*. It is an approach that has being growing considerably since the turn of the century and refers to an organisation 'that innovates or trades for a social purpose' (Ridley-Duff and Bull 2011: 1). These organisations can offer conventional careers with salaries and employee status, etc. but differ radically in their overall purpose. A limited company is required by law to maximise profit for its shareholders whereas in a social enterprise (which can also have investors and shareholders) it is their social purpose that legally takes priority. The popularity of this way of doing business is challenging its orthodoxy as it has been estimated that one quarter of small to medium enterprise (SME) employers class themselves as a social enterprise (BMG Research 2013: 1). So, whilst these organisations offer conventional careers there are increasing numbers of people from across the globe who are turning to this form of business to seek to achieve their own aspirations for social change (Ridley-Duff and Bull 2011: 1).

A social enterprise is not a legal term for a business but instead represents an approach to doing it. One can be established to make a profit or to run on a non-profit basis with the term 'more-than-profit' often used to indicate their different methods to those of conventional businesses.

The work of national bodies such as Social Enterprise UK or international ones like the Social Enterprise Association demonstrate the wide popularity of this kind of employment. So if you wish to consider the opportunities that are local to you then ask your HE provider about relevant initiatives and also search on the website www.do-it.org—at the time of writing this chapter there were over 1.3 million volunteering opportunities being advertised! It can therefore offer the work-based learning experiences that can be so beneficial to your employability. Thoughtful use of the site's search boxes with regard

to what you would like to do and where you would be prepared to do it can narrow this down to a manageable number. All of the vacancies will welcome applications from reliable people who know how much time they can offer and so planning your commitments is an essential first step. The careful investment of your time can be rewarding on many levels from enhancement of your personal employability to the wider beneficiaries from your work itself. Your experience in the third sector may eventually result in your development of *self-employability* and the establishment of your own social enterprise. The online resources detail the available choices for setting up these kinds of operations. The potential benefits to your employability from involvement in this work appear strong as **Figure 30.5** demonstrates. It is not simply your employability that will benefit either—think about the people in your community that will also be helped by work such as this.

In recent years, there has been increasing interest from universities in social enterprises and this can lead to many new directions and experiences for their students and lecturers. Read **New Frontiers 30.1** for information on a social enterprise called Cycle Roots that was started in Blackburn, Lancashire.

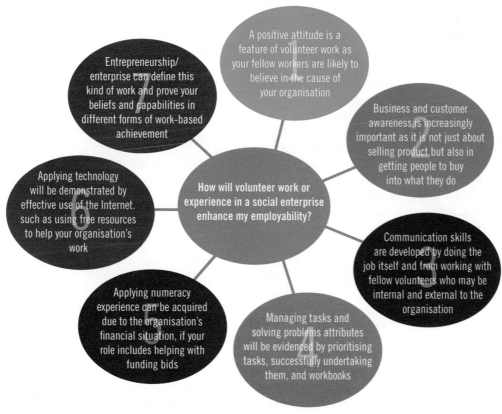

Figure 30.5 Volunteer work and employability

NEW FRONTIERS 30.1

Establishing a Community Interest Company (CIC)—with author Phil Johnson

In my first decade of HE lecturing I rarely encountered interest in social enterprises but in my second and third, the level of interest has risen greatly. It is now something that regularly features in dissertations and funding applications—and student participation in external initiatives such as 'Grad Factor' which is a national HE competition for student social enterprises.

This has resulted in my own venture into the business world as a director of a social enterprise created by two of my former BA Criminology students. They incorporated Cycle Roots CIC (see **Figure 30.6**) as a company limited by guarantee in December 2013 in the hope of increasing the accessibility of cycling by supplying affordable bikes to people who otherwise would not be in a position to purchase one. Their Blackburn-based business therefore 're-cycles bicycles' by restoring unwanted and unused ones back to sellable standards (see **Figure 30.7**). In addition to promoting healthy lifestyles the business also contributes to reductions in carbon emissions and landfill waste.

Its founders had limited prior business experience and only became aware of social enterprises thanks to their undergraduate studies.

In its first year of business, Cycle Roots CIC acquired almost £40,000 from five separate funding bodies and

Figure 30.7 The Cycle Roots CIC workshop, Blackburn, Lancashire
Source: Phil Johnson

has met its initial aim of creating two permanent jobs (that each pay 'living wage' remuneration). The generation of additional sustainable employment via contracts with local organisations plus a range of volunteering opportunities are also imminent for the enterprise that is working towards three bottom lines (people, planet, and profit). In 2015 it won the Best New Project Award from the Lancashire Community Recycling Network.

The creation of this social enterprise was something of a surprise as none of these students had previously displayed much of an interest in the business world and this illustrates the appeal such ventures can have. My role as a company director is equally something I would not have predicted! Obviously it is an unpaid role and my personal liability is limited to the £1 guarantee that was given at its incorporation. It is purely an advisory role that involves attendance at a couple of meetings a year and monthly email updates so it is something I can combine with my 'real' job. In fact, I believe it has deeply benefited my 'real' job as I have been able to share these experiences with other undergraduates interested in social enterprises.

Are you interested in becoming involved in a social enterprise? Visit the online resources to learn more about different social enterprises. The resources also contain links to Cycle Roots CIC where you can read more about this organisation.

Figure 30.6 Logo for Cycle Roots CIC
Source: Phil Johnson

Transferring your employability to your career

Following career development learning principles by engaging with the professional competencies in the environment in which you seek a career is crucial to your success. It is important to appreciate that employability and careers are *different*, but *linked* concepts. In order to get

exposure to the places where these experiences can be acquired you *first* have to ensure your graduate employability itself can demonstrate your possession of the attributes and skills expected of undergraduates from employers. Examples of how transferable your employability can be

The Seven Features of your Graduate Employability	Police	Courts & the Legal Profession	Probation	Prisons
A positive attitude: a 'can-do' approach	Strong beliefs in the values and purposes of policing; supportive of community interests	Abilities for engaging different kinds of people; genuine interest and enthusiasm for the legal system	Motivation and commitment to probation values; resilience and openness to new ideas and initiatives	Commitment to the role of prisons in the criminal justice system and their place in communities
Business and customer awareness	Knowledge of police procedures and methods of work; awareness of influences on criminal behaviour	Academic ability for the discipline of law; appreciation of the commercial environment for legal services	Knowledge and understanding of group and individual work in probation; ability to relate to others	Awareness of social issues; ability to act with authority should prisoners be abusive and/or violent
Communication and literacy	Ability to communicate clearly in all forms; adaptability of styles to meet the needs of the situation	Confidence in dealing with different clients and colleagues; successful experience of persuasive communication	Abilities for case work and report writing; effective oral and non-verbal communication skills	Verbal skills for resolving conflict in tense situations; report writing for a variety of audiences
Managing tasks and solving problems	Using a variety of information and assessing its reliability; risk awareness and decision making	Pro-active ability for using initiative in problem solving; ability to prioritise work and respond quickly	Planning and organising caseloads; making critical decisions and problem-solving whilst working under pressure	Organisational skills and ability to learn from others; calmness and decision making in pressurised situations
Applying numeracy	Using numerical reasoning for interpreting data; identification of trends and drawing correct conclusions	Numerical reasoning; ability to: compile records, understand financial statements and interpret accounts	Ability to interpret information accurately; ability to make correct comparisons to draw conclusions	Using numerical reasoning for interpreting data: addition, subtraction, multiplication, division, percentages, fractions, averages, and ratios
Applying technology	Using latest technological devices in the course of detecting and preventing crime; general IT skills	General IT skills for software such as Word, Outlook and Excel; use of professional and academic databases	General IT skills; use of electronic means of communication and offender management software	General IT skills; use of software used in the management of secure institutions
Entrepreneurship/ enterprise	Abilities for working efficiently in varied contexts; intrapreneurship to improve service provision	Ability to respond positively to academic and commercial challenges; intrapreneurship and finding new clients	Self-management for working with high caseloads; intrapreneurship to improve service provision for vulnerable people	Self-motivation and willingness to take responsibility; leadership potential for acting in volatile situations

Table 30.4 Transferring your employability for careers in criminal justice game changers

in underpinning your career are shown in **Table 30.4**—whilst these have a context of 'criminal justice game changers', this approach can obviously be applied to other types of careers.

NB: Competencies taken from the PPF (police officers), Law Society and Bar Council guidelines, the Community Justice Learning Framework for Probation, and the CQF (prison officers).

SUMMARY

By the end of this chapter you should be able to:

- Display evidence for all of the required attributes of the E3—effective, engaged, employable student that was put forward in **Chapter 1**

This chapter provided you with the necessary equipment for a successful journey into employability and careers. It is here where your status as an effective and engaged learner has to be displayed as peoples' judgements on your employability will be based on the evidence that verifies your skills, knowledge, and personal qualities. International 'career readiness' is the goal of this chapter and its reflective and strategic approaches are the vehicles that can take you there.

- Produce your graduate employability and refine it through a strategy of reflection, assessment, reaction, evaluation (RARE)

The production of your graduate employability will arise from your engagement with the desired attributes and skills employers have for undergraduates ('the Magnificent Seven'). Your engagement will be effective if you can reliably self-assess your progress in these areas and the chapter recommended using the work required by the formal course at your institution for an efficient way of doing this. Once you have started producing your employability in this manner, the 'RARE' framework will be a system for its continual refinement.

- Journey into potential careers' opportunities with 'criminal justice game changers' by engaging with career development learning and experiences from people in these careers

The hiring of graduates can be a brutal process and one where employers use 'weapons of mass rejection' (WMR). I must accredit colleagues at Liverpool John Moores University for this term as it is a powerfully succinct description of what can happen in the shortlisting stage. Understaffed HR departments or, in smaller organisations, the employers themselves, can be swamped with applications that they do not have the resources to deal with. So they use WMR and very crude sifting techniques such as degree classifications and any spelling or grammatical mistakes, are employed to eliminate large swathes of applicants and make the number manageable. Awareness of this highly ruthless practice illustrates the standards you are competing against and the clear need for a high-level approach in producing your graduate employability.

- Consider an alternative approach for different careers that require the attributes for self-employability

The attributes and skills expected from 'the Magnificent Seven' are equally relevant to self-employability and the chapter suggested getting involved with a social enterprise as an alternative form of career. In your course to employability and careers you are advised to adopt a traveller's mind-set and not one of a tourist. A traveller is renowned for trying different things, going to new places, and taking risks whereas the passive tourist only explores (if at all) when, and where, they are told to. Travellers tend to learn about where they are going before they arrive and so mirror effective career learners. A similarity that is enhanced by a traveller's interest in communicating with people they meet on their journeys and taking on board different customs and practices. Their independence is in stark contrast to a tourist where everything they do is arranged to fit in with a predetermined itinerary set by somebody else. The progress of a traveller is at a much slower pace than that of tourist and so this is fundamental to the chapter's learning objectives because hopefully you have realised your graduate employability is not something produced from 'two weeks in July'!

REVIEW QUESTIONS

1. Conduct a self-assessment of the seven core employability expectations ('the Magnificent Seven') expected in undergraduates by employers.

2. Apply the 'RARE' framework (reflect, assess, react, evaluate) to your current levels of employability.

3. Plan how you are going to make improvements to your responses to both of these questions.

FURTHER READING

Brown, P. and Hesketh, A. (2004) *The Mismanagement of Talent: Employability and Jobs in the Knowledge Economy*. Oxford: Oxford University Press.
This book is a critical examination of the way employability is being perceived in the job market. It may be a few years old but it still reveals the competitive nature of employability and the strategies adopted by job applicants such as the 'players' and the 'purists'.

Ragonese, E. R., Rees, A., Ives, J., and Dray, T. (2014) *The Routledge Guide to Working in Criminal Justice: Employability skills and careers in the Criminal Justice sector*. Routledge: London.
This text offers comprehensive help for students seeking a career in the criminal justice system. It details a range of options and provides many tips and techniques for acquiring employment in probation, police, prisons, the courts, and youth justice.

Ridley-Duff, R. and Bull, M. (2011) *Understanding Social Enterprise: Theory & Practice*. London: Sage.
This text considers the theoretical perspectives behind the considerable increase in the numbers of social enterprises in the UK. It also investigates the possible reasons for their enthusiastic embrace from recent governments.

Helyer, R. (2010) *The Work-Based Learning Student Handbook*. Basingstoke: Palgrave Macmillan.
This handbook offers advice and guidance for acquiring a work-based learning opportunity and then maximising their subsequent benefits. It includes help for reflective practice and for taking full advantage of formal assessment opportunities.

Schmalleger, F. and Marcum, C. D. (2017) *A Guide to Study Skills and Careers in Criminal Justice and Public Security*. Thousand Oaks: Sage.
Whilst this text is focused on careers in the American criminal justice system it nonetheless provides many helpful tips for your career development. Its chapters on the skills needed by undergraduates are transferrable to learners anywhere.

 Access the **online resources** to view selected further reading and web links relevant to the material covered in this chapter.
www.oup.com/uk/case/

GLOSSARY

Abolitionism Represents the position taken by some criminologists that all forms of penal sanction are unacceptable and should be eradicated, because they rely on misleading concepts of individualised guilt and responsibility.

Adulterisation Treating children and young people as if they were adults, for example by explaining and responding to their offending as if they had equivalent maturity and responsibility.

Adversarial justice This is the term given to the traditional approach to justice in the UK and other jurisdictions such as the USA. It perceives criminal procedure as a contest between two opposing sides who have the responsibility for producing all the evidence they seek to use. It emphasises the importance of formal court hearings and cross-examination for discovering the truth.

Aetiology The study and identification of causes, for example, the causes of abnormal behaviours or disorders such as crime or illness.

Agenda bias The degree to which a pre-existing subjectivity or preference on the part of a researcher, scholar, or other key stakeholder can influence how they pursue knowledge creation within criminology.

Agentic Having or displaying agency, that is, rational choice and autonomous decision-making ability.

Androcentricism Represents a male-centred view of the world; it involves prioritising the interests of men over the welfare of women, and privileging masculine traits.

Anomie Refers to the breakdown of social standards or controls (a lack of ethical guidance) which leads to a dysfunctional society in which the rules have broken down and people feel free to act in criminal ways.

Anti-essentialism An explanatory theory within race theory that sees group identities as fluid, and categories such as race, gender, and sexual identity as socially constructed and imposed by those with power. Universal claims on deviance and those who commit crime are seen as leading to marginalisation and exclusion.

Apolitical The position required from judges which means they are not allowed to show any allegiance or involvement with politics. The requirement is in place to protect the principle of judicial independence.

Artefactual risk factor theories A set of explanatory, developmental theories of youth offending that identify quantifiable, psychosocial risks in the lives of children and young people and assert that these 'risk factors' are predictive of offending in later life.

Avoidance learning This is where a person learns to behave in a positive way through adopting an automatic response to a stimulus. Treatments based on classical learning are limited because the person who is learning is passive.

BAME community The black, Asian, and minority ethnic groups which, thanks to the power of criminological research, it is known can be discriminated against in the criminal justice system. They are also groups that agencies such as the police aim to improve their relations with and recruit officers from.

Before and after experimental design Taking measures of the independent variable before and after implementation of an intervention in order to compare any differences and explain them as the effect of a cause.

Bentham's Panopticon The panopticon was a penitentiary design drawn up by Jeremy Bentham in 1787 which utilised surveillance to maximise the capability for monitoring and controlling all aspects of inmates' lives and behaviour.

Bifurcation Going in two different directions at once, for example, where criminal justice policy may advocate severe punishments for serious offenders, but more lenient punishment (even diversion) for less serious offenders.

Biological positivism A group of explanatory theories identifying the biological characteristics internal to the individual as the causes of crime.

Blackstone ratio This is the criminal justice concept that holds the protection of innocent people to be a greater priority for the system than conviction of the guilty. Its statement of it being better to release 10 guilty people than convict one innocent person should not be taken too literally as instead it signifies the harm caused when the system mistakenly convicts somebody.

Born criminal Theory that crime arises because of something biological or psychological which is 'wrong' with an individual, usually believed to be inherited.

Capitalism Capitalism or a capitalist system of production is a system in which the means of producing goods and services, and the accruing profits, are privately owned by individuals or companies rather than the state.

Central nervous system (CNS) In humans the central nervous system is made up of the brain and spinal cord and it controls the activities of the body.

Chicago school of sociology and criminology Much of the Chicago school were concerned with explaining the physical distribution of crime and they established links between environmental factors and criminal behaviour.

Classical A school of thought in criminology developed during the 18th century, which argued that individuals commit crime through free will, rational choice, and the desire to maximise benefits and minimise costs (e.g. punishment).

Classical criminology Arose in the 18th century and is based on the idea of rational choice and free will. It portrays offenders as rational, calculating, and as choosing to offend because they calculate that they will gain something. As offenders choose to offend they can and should be punished but that punishment should be proportionate to their wrongdoing.

Cognitive The process of acquiring knowledge and in criminology this places the problem behaviour clearly in the mind of the individual. Crime arises out of processes in the conscious mind which are engaged in choosing how to behave.

Cognitive learning It is based on cognitive psychology and suggests that all aspects of and processes of the conscious mind are engaged in choices about how to behave—learning involves behaviours, skills, attitudes, and morals. It is therefore necessary to interact with many aspects of learning to fully alter behaviour. The idea is that an informed learner is more likely to retain the positive activity because it becomes part of what is important to them.

Communitarianism Turns away from a focus on self-interest and individual's personal rights and interests. Instead it calls on us to accept that social order is best upheld by protecting and nurturing communal bonds. It assumes that humans are social and need controls to live together. Its focus is to ensure that everyone behaves in a law abiding and orderly fashion and calls on individuals to respect each other and the whole community.

Consensus theorists Hold the belief that society is held together or 'works' because the people in that society share a set of key values and beliefs, and agree on the same norms or rules. Consensus theorists emphasise harmony, integration, and stability within a society.

Consociational An arrangement whereby countries with deep divisions—along religious, ethnic, racial or cultural lines—share parallel social and political structures in order to create stability and avoid domination of one group by another, as is observable to some extent in Belgium, for instance.

Contempt of court The name for the criminal offence that is committed when disrespect for the court system has been shown. It is designed to protect the integrity of court proceedings and any conduct interfering with the course of justice can be deemed as a contempt of court. It is a strict liability offence so it can be committed regardless of any fault from an individual or organisation.

Content analysis A technique for systematically describing written, spoken, or visual communication. It typically provides a quantitative (numerical) description of qualitative data. Many content analyses involve media—print (newspapers, magazines), television, video, films, and the Internet.

Convict criminology A branch of critical criminological study and social movement which aims to bring to the foreground the voices of those who have been convicted of criminal offences. Convict criminology places the experiences and opinions of prisoners and ex-prisoners at the centre of criminological research, and encourages the (ex-) prisoners to take an active role in designing and carrying out such studies and to become academic criminologists.

Cost-benefit evaluations This is a type of evaluation that aims to measure whether the costs of an initiative are justified by its possible benefits. It is a method that combines evaluation of impact as well as process. Assessing the costs and benefits in a response to crime is highly important considering the limited resources available to the criminal justice system. However, they can be difficult to achieve as it is extremely difficult to quantify the financial benefits of things such as reductions in crime or improvements in perceptions of safety.

Covert A form of study that is conducted secretly (undercover), without the knowledge of study participants or subjects.

Crime control model The model of criminal justice that advocates efficiency when dealing with criminal cases. It is often characterised as an assembly line and aims to deal with the maximum number of cases with the minimum amount of resources.

Criminalisation The process of transforming behaviours and individuals into crimes and criminals.

Criminogenic Causing or likely to cause criminal behaviour.

Critical and radical theories A group of explanatory theories challenging the assumptions of positivism by asserting that crime is the product of the perceptions of law-making and law enforcement activities of powerful groups (e.g. the ruling classes, whites, adults) to the detriment of less powerful groups (e.g. the working classes, black and ethnic minorities, children).

Critical criminology Emerged in the 1960s and challenges traditional understandings such as the classical, positivist, and interpretivist epistemologies. It claims to uncover false beliefs about crime and criminal justice and often studies the effects of power and context on behaviour.

Critical moments A point in a young person's life when their individual characteristics and the social influences shaping their experiences are exposed to specific influences or forces which may lead to significant changes in their lives, such as the onset of offending or desistance from offending.

Critical race theory A theoretical framework that deconstructs and challenges racial inequality in society by illustrating how such inequality is reproduced through casually accepted structures and assumptions.

Cross-cultural comparisons Theoretical and statistical comparisons made between cultures (typically between countries) in relation to dominant explanations of crime; the extent, nature, and patterns of crime and justice, etc.—in other words, definitions, explanations, and responses to crime.

Cryptocurrency These are currencies used to buy goods and services from vendors who accept this form of payment. They are digital currencies such as bitcoin which is a system of money not supported by any official banking system or government.

Cryptomarkets This is the term for online black markets which are websites that use techniques known as advanced encryption. These methods ensure their users remain anonymous whilst using these sites.

Cultural criminology A criminological perspective that is concerned with the interaction between commonly experienced cultural influences such as media, advertising, and politics, and the acts committed by both criminals and the State. Cultural criminology is particularly concerned with issues of social injustice, the significance of sub-cultures, and the heightened emotions associated with acts of deviancy.

Cybercrime A developing and wide-ranging form of crime that involves the use of technology, particularly the Internet and computer networks, in the planning and commissioning of criminal activity and deviance.

Dark web This is the term given to the websites that are publicly visible but hide the identities of the people and organisations that run them. One of its infamous examples is the Silk Road website which has been used for the buying and selling of recreational drugs. The anonymity of the dark web creates much concern but offers valuable services for people living in oppressive, totalitarian societies.

Deconstruct/deconstruction In social science research, deconstruction involves analysing textual, verbal, visual, and other information to uncover the underlying message the information seeks to convey. Often, the objective of deconstruction is to expose the limitations of dominant beliefs and the agenda that motivates their perpetuation.

Deductive research Research that tests and refines existing hypotheses and understandings.

Defensible space The idea of defensible space is based on the assumption that the living environment can be designed and constructed to minimise or prevent the possibility of crime occurring.

Demand characteristics An artefact of the research process where participants form an interpretation of the study's purpose and (sub)consciously change their behaviour to fit that interpretation.

Dependent variable The variable within an experiment that is measured with the intention of identifying it as an effect of manipulating the independent variable.

Descriptive theory A theory that arises when a researcher gathers data (what the researcher hopes is typical data) and describes what is happening. It uses the data to build categories and predict and explain behaviour.

Desistance Desistance is understood as both the process and the outcome of a former offender achieving a long-term and sustainable cessation of offending.

Determinism The assumption that the causes of crime are predetermined and preceded by identifiable causes, rather than the result of the individual's free will.

Deterrence theory Suggests that rather than punishing after someone offends we should structure our world and our punishments to deter future offending.

Developmental A form of criminological theory that identifies the causes and predictors of crime in early life (childhood and adolescence) and seeks to explain their influence on offending in later life.

Deviancy amplification A media-induced phenomenon where an isolated act of perceived deviance is over-reported or exaggerated, leading to further episodes of deviance and a moral panic regarding the reported behaviour.

Differential association A learning theory which assumes that crime is learned behaviour and that people need knowledge, skills, and recognition of opportunities in order to offend. It claims that all behaviour is learned and crime will only be learned if it is part of an individual's environment. It also discusses the social circumstances in which crime or other behaviour might be learned but does not consider how the learning occurs (that would be a psychological learning theory).

Discourse analysis An approach to analysing written, vocal, or sign language use, or any significant event that is 'semiotic' (the study of signs and symbols and their use or interpretation).

Displacement The concept of displacement suggests that intensive crime prevention activity in one geographical area is likely to lead to a relocation of offending behaviour elsewhere rather than eliminating it altogether.

Distributive justice Assumes that in modern societies there is an acceptance that goods and evils will be fairly distributed through society. So there are often expectations or rules such as 'equal pay (or other benefits) for equal work'. This seemingly simple idea contains many complex facets, one must take account of equality (of opportunity and outcome), proportionality, and fairness.

Diversion In the context of crime, diversion constitutes the informal disposal of offences outside of the official processes for dealing with offences by way of prosecution and court hearings.

Documentary analysis *see* **Content analysis** and **Secondary data analysis**.

Double jeopardy This is the name given to the long established rule that a person who has been found not guilty cannot subsequently be tried again for that offence. The rule experienced major reform in the Criminal Justice Act 2003 which, subject to certain safeguards, allows retrials of selected serious offences even after an original verdict of not guilty.

Due process the idea of a justice system that exercises just and appropriate adjudication of offences whilst ensuring that alleged offenders are treated fairly and equitably, and with suitable safeguards, by the judicial system.

Ecological validity The degree to which a research method, finding, or conclusion provides an accurate representation of real-world behaviour.

Either way offences These are the category of criminal offences that can vary in their deemed seriousness and so can be tried at either the Crown Court or the Magistrates' Court. A person charged with one of these offences has traditionally had the right to ultimately elect for a trial by jury, but the extent of this right has been questioned on several occasions.

Empirical Knowledge generated using sensory experience, particularly through experiment and observation.

Empiricism The theory and practice of generating knowledge 'scientifically' through sensory experience, typically using experiment or observation.

Epistemological reflexivity The critical examination by a researcher of how their belief system has shaped their research design and interpretation of findings.

Epistemology In social science research, a researcher's epistemological stance reflects that researcher's philosophical position on what constitutes valid knowledge of the social world, and how such knowledge should be generated. The concept of epistemology is underpinned by questions such as:

- What constitutes valid knowledge?
- How can we generate valid knowledge of aspects of the social world?

Essentialist/Essentialism Essentialism represents the belief that social categories such as gender or crime have distinct or intrinsic characteristics with which we can identify and define them.

Ethnocentric The dominance of a particular cultural perspective (typically that of the white, westernised world) in the creation of knowledge in criminology.

Ethnographic The systematic study of people and cultures from the point of view of the subject of the study.

Evolutionary psychology Applies Darwinian ideas to the development of the human psyche and so claims that the human mind has evolved various methods or mechanisms to process information in a way which permits us to resolve problems which humans often meet. Evolutionary psychology claims that in order to understand behaviour today one needs to consider the environment in which our ancestors lived.

Fair procedure The elements of what is considered to be a fair criminal procedure can change considerably with time. For example, it was not until 1898 that a defendant was allowed to testify in their defence at trial; conversely in 1994 the law was changed in order to hold it against a person who did not give evidence at their trial. Today a fair procedure is taken to include the protection currently within the Human Rights Act 1998.

Folk Devils Negative stereotyping of groups and individuals who are portrayed as an embodiment and cause of social and crime problems.

Functionalist Sociology This is a sociological approach which sees society as a system of interconnected parts working together to ensure that the balance and equilibrium of a social group is not interfered with.

Globalisation The process by which the world is becoming increasingly interconnected as a result of massively increased trade, cultural exchange, easier international travel, the expansion of media/social media, and other technological advancements.

Grand theory This is generally a fairly abstract theory, based on formal theorising by one person or a group of people rather than growing out of measured phenomenon. In grand theory the organisation of concepts takes priority over understanding or explaining the social world. In criminology, grand theory is often an integrated theory and purports to offer an explanation to a problem which is applicable in most situations. It often draws together other ideas or theories which are based on observed and measured facts and is too broad to be tested.

Green criminology The study of criminal offences that affect the natural world, the reasons why these are committed, and the impact on those who are harmed as a result. Green criminology also examines the national and international responses to such crimes and those who commit them.

Haldane principle This is the principle which states that decisions on the funding of research should be made by researchers rather than politicians. It is a concept that seeks to preserve the independence of research and separate it from political influences. It is interpreted these days by the government providing funding for their general priorities with the research community selecting specific projects based on their merit.

Harm principle This is a principle often used to test whether an activity should be criminalised—conduct should not be criminal unless it is harmful to others.

Hate crime Crimes committed against an individual or group of people because of an actual or perceived difference, such as race, disability, sexual orientation, or religious affiliation.

Hegemonic masculinity The values and characteristics which a particular society or culture deems to be the most desirable aspects of maleness and which therefore become the dominant features associated with masculinity.

Hegemony Hegemony is understood as the set of structures, relationships, and meanings by which a particular form of social order and domination is achieved, maintained, and legitimised.

Impact evaluations This is the name for evaluative research that seeks to measure the outcomes of an intervention or policy strategy. In the criminal justice field it seeks to measure things such as the rate of crime following the introduction of an initiative. They can be often used in crime prevention work but their ability to tell the whole picture should be questioned. The changing rates of crime can be often attributed to a range of factors and consequently it can be very difficult to isolate their occurrence to one specific initiative.

Independent variable The variable within an experiment that is manipulated by the researcher with the intention of identifying it as a cause of behaviour.

Indeterminate sentencing This is the name for the sentences imposed by a court which do not have a fixed length of time. They will be imposed if the court believes the offender to be a danger to the public and mean no date is set for when they will be released. A minimum period of time has to be served in prison, known as a tariff, before an offender can be even considered for release. Once this has been served they will be eligible to appear before the Parole Board who are responsible for deciding whether their release can be ordered.

Indictable offences These are the category of criminal offences which due to their deemed seriousness can only be tried at the Crown Court in front of a judge and jury. They carry maximum penalties of life imprisonment and unlimited fines.

Individualised Tailored to explaining the behaviour of an individual; concerned with explaining behaviour (e.g. crime) as due to individual (biological, psychological, sociological) factors rather than broader socio-structural influences.

Inductive research Research that generates new hypotheses and understandings.

Institutional racism A term introduced into public discourse in the UK by the Stephen Lawrence Inquiry in 1999. Refers to unwitting, as well as overt, practices and stereotypes within organisations that disadvantage groups of people because of colour or ethnic origin. Implies that organisations can collectively be held responsible for unwitting racial discrimination.

Integrated theories Criminological theories that integrate explanations from multiple theories to produce a more holistic, multi-factor, hybrid theory of crime. Such theories include integrated positivist theories, which merge explanations from different positivist theories (e.g. social control theory) and integrated risk factor theories, which fuse explanations from multiple risk factor theories (e.g. artefactual risk factor theories tend to blend psychological and sociological explanations).

Internships These are formal positions, offered for a fixed period of time by organisations that provide a structured introduction to the work it undertakes. They are often available in the summer months and in some situations they can be paid positions. In addition to providing valuable work experience they offer a range of research opportunities and potential topics for your dissertation.

Interpretivism or interpretivist criminology An approach to the study of the social world (typically qualitative) seeking to understand human behaviour by exploring individual experiences, perceptions and meanings. Interpretivist criminology rejects the idea that complex social and human interactions can ever be fully measured. It argues that science cannot measure the subjective thoughts and feelings that give rise to human behaviour and human interactions. It interprets or understands behaviour and situations through the eyes of those participating. It seeks to give meaning to situations and is founded on qualitative research.

Intersectionality The interaction between various factors that impact on a person's experience and identity and the way that the state and society react to that person. Examples of such factors are race, social class, sexuality, and gender.

Just deserts According to the principle of 'just deserts', sentencing theory understands that the form and amount of punishment administered can be made exactly equivalent to the harm and distress caused by a crime.

Justice gap – the discrepancy between the numbers of crimes that are committed and recorded, and the numbers which are actually prosecuted through the criminal justice system.

Legal moralism Prohibiting acts merely because they are offensive to the majority in that society, or because it is believed that if one fails to prohibit them they might destroy the very fabric of a society.

Labelling perspectives These include a number of ideas. Firstly, it considers a consideration of how and why certain behaviours become controlled whilst others do not. It focuses not on the behaviour and the person participating but on the reaction of other people to that behaviour. Secondly, it considers how the way in which people in a society behave towards an individual when he or she transgresses may affect whether or not they commit further 'crimes'. Finally, it considers how groups may be controlled because of the way in which they are treated by others in society and again how that might impact on the way in which people in the group or the group as a whole responds.

Labelling theory An explanatory theory maintaining that behaviours and individuals become criminalised only when society assigns them the label of 'criminal'; a label that they may choose to react to in a self-fulfilling way.

Lex talionis This is the term for the ancient system of laws (*lex*) that were based on retaliation (*talion*). It could result in an offender experiencing physical punishment that is deemed to fit the crime. The system is most famously associated with the 'an eye for an eye' method of justice.

Liberal feminist theory Associated with the view that the sexist socialisation of women into gender roles that are associated with passivity and conformity, underpins the gender inequality which disadvantages women in many social institutions including the criminal justice system.

Macro-level The broadest level of analysis, focusing on nation states, countries, and international and global-level issues.

Mandatory sentencing This form of sentencing exists when the punishment to be imposed for an offence is set by Parliament rather than the judge of the particular case. This applies to all murder convictions which, regardless of the circumstances, by law have to receive a life sentence of imprisonment. Other examples that prevent judicial discretion in sentencing include firearms and knife offences, repeat offending in Class A drugs and burglary offences plus the commission of a second listed offence according to the Criminal Justice Act 2003.

Marxist feminism Identifies the capitalist system of production and the higher socio-economic status men occupy within that system compared to women, as the primary factor that provokes the oppression of women in society.

Masculinities Masculinities theorists believe that there is no singular 'masculinity' that can be ascribed to all men. Instead, multiple 'masculinities' exist and these are structured around a social constructed hierarchy which comprises the highly-valued hegemonic masculinity and other masculinities including subordinated masculinities.

Meso-level A mid-range level of analysis focusing on neighbourhoods, communities, localities, and organisations in particular social contexts.

Metacompetencies This is the term which signifies a person's ability for having the higher-order competencies needed for successful contemporary careers. They include competencies such as being able to learn effectively and the development of attributes such as judgement, instinct, and expertise.

Metaskills Term that signifies a person's ability for using their skills effectively. They are higher-order skills such as critical thinking and reflective learning that are essential for acquiring the skills needed for successful contemporary careers.

Micro-level An individual level of analysis focusing on the individual or small group interactions in particular social contexts.

Moral panics A disproportionate social reaction to a perceived problem or issue. A moral panic serves as a distraction, diverting public attention away from what are perhaps more urgent and pressing problems and issues. Moral panics can be used by the state to manipulate public opinion and thus steer policy decisions.

Neo-liberalism A political and social position which promotes the reduction of state intervention in both public and private affairs, together with the removal of controls on markets and commercial competition.

Neo-positivists Believe that social events and behaviour, including crime, can only truly be studies through measurement. They see similarities, sometimes equivalence, between the natural world and social events and use the laws of the natural world to explain human behaviour and social events. Here behaviour should be considered without reference to concepts such as feelings, motives, values, and will.

Non-participant observation A form of observational study where the researcher/observer does not participate in the activities of the individual or group under observation.

Normative theory Sets out what (in that theorist's thinking) is right and wrong, desirable or undesirable or just and unjust in a society. It sets out ideal standards about the way in which things should, in that theorist's opinion, happen.

Norms or rules The standards by which people in a society are expected to live. Many are just types of behaviour which are expected or frowned upon.

Observer effects Changes that the act of observation make on a phenomenon and individuals being observed. This is often the result of instruments that, by necessity, alter the state of what they measure in some manner.

Official statistics Statistics compiled by public agencies. In the context of criminology, these are the figures collected by the police and courts and which are regularly published by governments to indicate the extent of crime.

Ontology In social science research the term ontology refers to the study of what exists in the social world. It concerns itself with issues to do with whether or not concepts such as gender and crime are realities that exist objectively without prior description, and have unique qualities, or whether they are social constructs.

Operant learning Here behaviour is controlled by an individual learning the consequences of their behaviour—whether they are rewarded or punished for a particular behaviour (or expect rewards or punishments) will decide whether they are likely to participate in the behaviour.

Operationalise To express or define something in terms of the operations and measures used to examine it.

Overt A form of study that is conducted openly and with the knowledge of study participants or subjects.

Parliamentary sovereignty Also known as parliamentary supremacy, meaning the UK Parliament, which consists of the House of Commons, the House of Lords, and the monarch, is the most powerful source of law in the UK. It means the laws it produces must be followed by all of the courts of justice.

Participant observation A form of observational study where the researcher/observer participates in the activities of the individual or group under observation.

Paternalism A policy or criminal law designed to restrict the freedom of an individual in order to protect that person from him- or herself, intended to be for their benefit (to protect their life, health, or safety) when they may not choose to be protected. The interference reduces their liberty or autonomy.

Pathological Showing signs of illness or abnormality.

Pathways The routes or trajectories a young person may take into and away from offending behaviour.

Patriarchy Refers to a system or state of affairs in society that is characterised by unequal gender relations and it manifests as the oppression of women by men.

Pedagogy The method and practice of teaching as an academic subject.

Peripheral Nervous System (PNS) Made up of all the nerves running through the body that carry signals from the senses and permit communication between the central nervous system and the rest of the body. The PNS carries instructions from the brain to other parts of the body and information from the body to the CNS.

Personal transferable skills Skills developed in one situation (e.g. during university study) that can be transported and applied to another situation (e.g. the workplace).

Placements These are positions, usually offered on a short term basis that provide practical work experience in organisations for undergraduates. In addition to providing valuable work experience they offer a range of research opportunities and potential topics for dissertations.

Populist punitiveness This term is more commonly known as penal populism and is an approach to the making of penal policy that has been recognised since the 1990s. It means policy is shaped by its perceived popularity with the general public rather than its actual effectiveness.

Positionality The stance/position that the researcher has chosen to adopt within a specific study and the researcher's evaluation of that position in terms of its influence on the subject matter being studied, the research context, and the research participants, including the influence of their chosen epistemology, disciplinary perspective, and preconceptions.

Positivism An approach to the study of the social world (typically quantitative) using the methods of the natural sciences to generate universal laws and cause and effect understandings of human behaviour.

Positivist criminology Arose in the 19th century and assumes that human behaviour, crime in this case, can be studied scientifically, using the same methods as are used in the natural sciences. By studying past events it aims to explain them and then predict future behaviour. Positivists tend to study the criminal rather than the crime. Their explanations draw on biological, psychological, social, or economic factors outside the control of the individual, suggesting that their behaviour is determined rather than chosen and therefore questioning punishment in favour of rehabilitation.

Practicality The extent to which a method, practice, or policy is useful, usable, and applicable in the real world.

Process evaluations This is the type of evaluation that investigates how well a particular initiative has been implemented. They provide detailed descriptions of the process involved and make recommendations for its future use. They can be criticised for their narrow interpretations of success that are often based on internal aspects of the initiative rather than its wider effectiveness.

Procedural justice This is the term given for ensuring people feel fairly treated in their interactions with the police and other state authorities. It is recognised in many research findings as an important influence on a person's potential for reoffending.

Protean This is a description that can be given to things that are able to markedly change their form. It is used to explain the high levels of adaptability needed by individuals for creating successful careers. The term is exemplified in the criminal sanction of unpaid work (formerly known as community service) where the disposal is capable of being adapted to suit retributive, rehabilitative, or reparative demands.

Psychological positivism A group of explanatory theories identifying the causes of crime as the psychological characteristics internal to the individual.

Punishment Can have many meanings. In this book it generally means that a state has imposed on someone (or a group) an unpleasant outcome (or one intended to be unpleasant) because that person has broken the law (or the state believes that they have broken the law).

Qualitative A branch of research concerned with understanding human behaviour and phenomena in terms of words that depict personalised meanings, experiences, and perceptions.

Quantitative A branch of research concerned with understanding human behaviour and phenomena in quantifiable, numerical, and statistical forms.

Radical communitarianism Justice is better achieved in small communities which choose just outcomes through each member participating in a full discussion of the plurality of values (often multi-cultural).

Radical feminist theory A theoretical tradition that identifies patriarchy as the fundamental factor which drives the gender inequality that pervades society and oppresses women regardless of their ethnicity, social class, or other attributes.

Rational choice Assumes that offenders want to gain by their criminal behaviour. They argue that offenders choose the behaviour which they believe is most likely to be most beneficial to them. They make a rational decision using the information available to them and taking into account the opportunities they enjoy at that time, their risk of being caught and punished and their own ability to decide and to act.

Realism A set of explanatory theories viewing crime as a real, measurable phenomenon with tangible effects on victims and society, thus challenging critical criminology's 'idealist' view of crime as a social construction.

Recidivism This is a general term to describe an individual's relapse into undesirable behaviour which in a criminal justice context means a repeat of their offending behaviour. The most common measure of rates of recidivism is the number of offenders who are reconvicted in the two-year period following their punishment by the criminal justice system. The relatively high levels of recidivism following either custodial sentences or community sentences indicate their lack of effectiveness in reducing the amounts of criminal behaviour.

Reductionism The practice of measuring or analysing a concept or behaviour in simplistic terms, for example, by reducing it to a category or quantity.

Reflection A critical process whereby the researcher evaluates the quality and validity of their research processes, findings, and conclusions.

Reflexivity A process by which researchers consider their position, preconceptions, choices and influence during the study and how these have affected the research process.

Rehabilitation Broadly this means preventing crime by addressing causative factors whether they be economic, social, or individual. However, in this book and in criminal justice terms this often means working with an individual to alter their behaviour and so reduce their offending.

Reintegrative shaming Emphasises the importance of positive shaming in crime prevention. The shaming focuses on the criminal act not the offender as a person—the behaviour is bad, not the person. Ideally the offender apologises and their apology is accepted. The process should include both a rejection of the act as well as a clear acceptance of the offender as well as support to help them not to offend in the future.

Relative deprivation A concept drawn on by left realists to highlight the changing perceptions of injustice and deprivation.

Reliability The repeatability, replicability, or consistency of a research design, method, or finding.

Responsibilisation The phenomenon of placing responsibility and blame on individuals, families, or communities for offending behaviour and the inability of these individuals, families, or communities to resist the criminogenic influences that contribute to it.

Restorative justice Restorative justice is based on the principle that those most closely involved and affected are encouraged and enabled to resolve and make good the harms caused by crime through a process of dialogue and reconciliation.

Routine activity theory Whilst it assumes a choice by the offender to offend it focuses on the action, the crime and particularly the situation in which it occurs. It assumes that for crime to occur three things are necessary: a motivated offender; a suitable target; and, the absence of guardians. It assumes crime is not affected by social problems such as poverty but rather it arises out of opportunities that occur in everyday life situations.

Secondary data analysis The analysis of data collected from other sources for the purposes of the current research.

Security of tenure The name given to the employment position of individuals, particularly judges, that protects them against being dismissed from their position. It is informally known as 'a job for life', although 'until retirement' is more accurate. This security is designed to protect judges from external pressures to preserve their independence when adjudicating cases.

Self-fulfilling prophecy A prediction that directly or indirectly causes itself to become true due to positive feedback between belief and behaviour. For example, if an individual offends and is then labelled a 'criminal', they may come to accept this label and reoffend as a result of their new 'criminal' identity.

Separation of powers This is the constitutional principle for the way power is shared between the government (the executive), Parliament (the legislative) and the courts (the judicial). The doctrine holds that each of these three parts of the state should be kept separate to act as a check and a balance on each other to ensure none has excessive power.

Situational crime prevention Crime prevention strategies or policies which focus on reducing opportunity for criminal behaviour. These often involve redesigning products (e.g.

improving car locks) or altering environments (e.g. removing conductors on buses, introducing street lighting or CCTV) to either reduce the possibility of criminal activity or to increase the likelihood of being caught.

Social conflict theories Claim that individuals and groups interact on the basis of conflict. The idea is often that those in power use the legal system to ensure that they remain in power and that the powerless remain controlled. In essence, social conflict theory is the study of the distribution and use of power in order to control others.

Social construction The notion that crime and associated concepts (e.g. justice) are the dynamic and subjective creations of institutions and individuals in societies at specific points in time.

Social contract This assumes that a person's moral, political, and legal obligations depend upon a contract or agreement among people within their community. The theory assumes that without controls people would do whatever they wanted and that some would become very powerful and violent/abusive whilst others would suffer. To allow people to live safely in communities these theorists argue that people enter into contracts agreeing to social restraints to prevent them harming others (and protecting them from harm by others). They give up part of their freedom to ensure their security.

Social control theory This generally starts with the assumption that conformity needs to be learned. The theory is very broad and considers all ways in which conformity might be learnt – social, psychological, through families, other groups, societal expectations.

Social crime prevention Assumes that the origins of crime lie in potential offenders' social circumstances, and that if these can be improved then their likelihood of offending is correspondingly reduced.

Social desirability bias A demand characteristic relating to the tendency of participants to behave in a manner that will be viewed favourably by others, for example, answering survey questions to exaggerate good behaviour and under-report bad behaviour.

Social disorganisation This is an aspect of the Chicago school which links crime to environmental or ecological aspects of the neighbourhood and to a breakdown in social integration in an area. High crime rates occur in areas which are not socially cohesive, they may be divided on ethical, racial, cultural, religious, inter-generational, or political grounds. These communities are fragmented and dysfunctional.

Social harm An evolution of the traditional criminological focus on the individual harms caused by crime to consider the social harms and injuries that result from the activities of nation states, corporations, and businesses—some of which activities may not be considered criminal.

Social interaction or social process theories Claim that crime and deviance are socially constructed. They also accept that the choices made by each individual impact on those around them and that this constructed environment then impacts on the way in which people behave.

Social learning theory Suggests that humans learn through social interactions and that people tend to mimic other people's behaviour. Here all behaviour is learned, including criminal behaviour.

Social mores These are traditional customs, rules and expectations of proper or acceptable behaviour. Each society sets its own standards and within a society different groups may set different social mores, different standards of behaviour.

Social structural theories Often referred to as structuralism. This studies the way in which a society is structured. The idea is that the way in which a society is shaped affects the way in which people behave. It looks at the way in which the structure of a society has an influence on our daily lives.

Socialisation Refers to the way in which we all learn the norms and rules of our society, learn what is expected of us, and learn how to behave in order to live up to those expectations.

Socialist feminism The theory that the intersection of the patriarchy and the class inequality that disadvantage women in capitalist societies underpin the oppression of women by men in those societies.

Sociological positivism A group of explanatory theories identifying the causes of crime as the sociological characteristics external to the individual.

Somatotyping A classification of people according to their body shape and used to predict future behaviour, including criminal behaviour.

Standardised Ensuring that a research design or method adheres to a common standard or rule.

Stigmata In criminology this is something which visibly marks someone out as being deviant or criminal or as having deviant or criminal tendencies. It may indicate marks or physical types more likely to participate in particular types of behaviour.

Stigmatisation Labelling, marginalisation, exclusion, and other negative treatment that portrays certain individuals or groups as harmful, risky, deficient, and pathological.

Strain theory Argues that when society (or part of a society) puts pressure on individuals to succeed then they will turn to illegitimate means such as crime to achieve their goals if they cannot meet them by legitimate means.

Structuralism Considers that human culture can be best understood in terms of their relationship to an overarching system or structure. The idea is that the structure is more important than the function.

Substantive justice A treatment that is fair, just, and reasonable. What is accepted as substantive justice will vary from person to person but it usually claims to reflect the prevailing moral leaning of a society or community—it is therefore culturally bound and socially constructed. In many modern western cultures it is seen as similar to distributive justice.

Summary offences These are the category of criminal offences that due to their deemed minor nature can only be tried at the Magistrates' Court in front of either a district judge (a professional magistrate) or three lay magistrates (volunteers from the community traditionally known as Justices of the Peace).

Supposition Guesswork, assumption, conjecture.

Target hardening Refers to physical security measures which are designed to increase the difficulty of committing crime against a potential object or victim.

Temporal precedence When one variable or event can be shown to have occurred before another.

Thematic analysis One of the most common forms of analysis in qualitative research. It emphasises pinpointing, examining, and recording patterns (or 'themes') within data. Themes are patterns across data sets that are important to the description of a phenomenon and are associated to a specific research question.

Theory A theory should provide a simple explanation of the observed relations relevant to the phenomenon. It draws together data or general principles to build a supposition or system of ideas that allow us to make sense of the world, to make choices that work for us and enable us to make sense of things outside our own experience.

Trajectory The path of development into and out of crime.

Transformative justice An emerging concept which is based on the principle that the mechanisms and processes for resolving crime should also be grounded in and driven by wider objectives of achieving norms by means of social and structural change.

Transition A significant change or move in a young person's life, such as entering secondary school, leaving school, leaving home, or getting a job. Transitions can be stressful and uncertain and may contribute to criminal behaviour.

Turning points *see* **Critical moments**.

Utilitarianism This assumes that actions are right or just if they maximise utility, usually by benefitting the majority. Basically, one assesses the whole pleasure or benefit which arises out of an action (for the actors and others) and set that against any suffering or negative impact involved. If the pleasure outweighs the suffering the action is beneficial (of use) and should be permitted.

Validity The accuracy, honesty, suitability, and relevance of a research method, result, or conclusion. Whether something measures what it says it measures.

Victimisation Either the process by which a person comes to see him- or herself as a victim (for instance through the way certain groups are represented in the media, which also affects the social reaction to those who have experienced crime) or the factors which lead to groups becoming perceived as victims (such as the targeting of young people by police operations).

Victim surveys These are surveys which aim to address the problem of crimes which the police do not record or the public do not report. They involve asking members of the public to recount their experiences of crime in an attempt to get both a more accurate measure of the crime rate and to assess the impact of crime on victims.

Weberian sociology Max Weber is often said to be one of the three founders of sociology. Amongst his many important contributions was his claim that in order to understand the world it is necessary to study social actions by interpreting the purpose and meanings which individuals attach to their actions. He also analysed power relations breaking them into three distinct strata: class which relates to wealth; status which relates to prestige; and influence which relates to political spheres and power. He saw each of these playing a part in shaping a society and the distribution of control and power within a community.

White-collar crime Offences which are committed by those in a position of responsibility and respectability, those of high social status. They are possible because of the position of the individual in society.

Work-based learning This refers to using practical experiences in the workplace to complement the studies on your degree. It enables you to apply your learning to real world situations and illustrate the value of what you have learned on your formal course. In addition to providing valuable work experience they offer a range of research opportunities and potential topics for your dissertation.

Work shadowing Term for observing and following a person around whilst they are working. They are opportunities to acquire understanding of how the job works in practice. In addition to providing valuable work experience they offer a range of research opportunities and potential topics for dissertations.

Zemiology From the Greek word Zemia, meaning harm, zemiology examines the nature and causes of harm. Such harm can be social, financial or physical; zemiology seeks to examine harm caused by and to individuals as well as that which results from the acts and omissions of the State and its agencies.

BIBLIOGRAPHY

Chapter 1

Case, S. (2017) *Contemporary Youth Justice*. Abingdon: Routledge.

Case, S. and Haines, K. (2015) 'Children First, Offenders Second Positive Promotion: Reframing the Prevention Debate' *Youth Justice Journal* 15(3): 226–39.

Finch, E. and Fafinski, S. (2016) *Criminology Skills* (2nd edn). Oxford: Oxford University Press.

Goleman, D. (1996) *Emotional Intelligence—Why it Can Matter More than IQ*. St Ives: Bloomsbury.

Hopkins-Burke, R. (2009) *An Introduction to Criminological Theory*. Cullompton: Willan.

Liebling, A., Maruna, S., and McAra, L. (eds) (2017) *The Oxford Handbook of Criminology* (6th edn). Oxford: Oxford University Press.

Maslow, A. (1943) 'A Theory of Human Motivation' *Psychological Review* 50(4): 370–96.

Newburn, T. (2008) *Handbook of Policing*. Cullompton: Willan.

Parker, H. (1974) *View from the Boys*. Aldershot: Gregg Revivals.

Sampson, R. and Laub, J. (1993) *Crime in the Making*. Harvard: Harvard University Press.

Smith, R. (2011) *Doing Justice to Young People*. Cullompton: Willan.

Taylor, I., Walton, P., and Young, J. (1973) *The New Criminology: For a Social Theory of Deviance*. London: Routledge.

Taylor, W., Earle, R. and Hester, R. (2010) *Youth Justice Handbook*. Milton Keynes: Open University Press.

Tilley, N. (2005) *Handbook of Community Safety*. Cullompton: Willan.

Tobin, L. (2015) *A Guide to Uni Life: The One Stop Guide to What University is REALLY Like*. Bath: Trotman.

Walton, I. and Young, J. (1998) *The New Criminology Revisited*. London: Macmillan.

Whichlow, C. and Haskins, M. (2011) *How to Survive University*. Chichester: Summersdale.

Williams, K. (2012) *Textbook on Criminology*. Oxford: Oxford University Press.

Young, J. (2011) *The Criminological Imagination*. London: Wiley.

Chapter 2

Arksey, H. and Harris, D. (2007) *How to Succeed in your Social Science Degree*. London: Sage.

Bryman, A. (2015) *Social Research Methods*. Oxford: Oxford University Press.

Finch, E. and Fafinski, S. (2016) *Criminology Skills* (2nd edn). Oxford: Oxford University Press.

Hale, C., Hayward, K., Wahidin, A., and Wincup, E. (2013) *Criminology*. Oxford: Oxford University Press.

Harrison, J., Simpson, M., Harrison, O., and Martin, E. (2012) *Study Skills for Criminology*. London: Sage.

Jones, S. (2013) *Criminology*. Oxford: Oxford University Press.

Laurillard, D. (2011) *Supporting Teacher Development of Competencies in the Use of Learning Technologies*. IoE: London.

Liebling, A., Maruna, S., and McAra, L. (eds) (2017) *The Oxford Handbook of Criminology* (6th edn). Oxford: Oxford University Press.

Redman, P. and Maples, W. (2011) *Good Essay Writing*. London: Sage.

Savage, J. (2001) *England's Dreaming*. London: Faber and Faber.

Williams, K. (2012) *Textbook on Criminology*. Oxford: Oxford University Press.

Chapter 3

Alvesalo, A. and Tombs, S. (2002), 'Working for Criminalisation of Economic Offending: Contradictions for Critical Criminology?' *Critical Criminology: An International Journal* 11(1): 21–40.

Ashworth, A. and Zedner, L. (2008) 'Defending the Criminal Law: Reflections on the Changing Character of Crime' *Criminal Law and Philosophy* 2: 21.

Baker, D. (2007) 'Moral Limits of Criminalizing Remote Harms' *New Criminal Law Review* 10: 370.

Berlin, I. (1958) 'Two Concepts of Liberty' reprinted in Berlin, I. (1969) *Four Essays on Liberty*. Oxford: Oxford University Press.

Boreham, R., Cronberg, A., Dollin, L., and Pudney, S. (2007) *The Arrestee Survey 2003–2006*. London: Home Office Statistical Bulletin, 12(07).

Box, S. (1983) *Power, Crime and Mystification*. London: Tavistock.

Brunstrom, R. (2007) *Drugs Policy: A Radical Look Ahead?* North Wales: North Wales Police Authority (http://www.drugequality.org/files/Drugs_Policy_Paper_2007.pdf).

Cane, P. (2006) 'Taking Law Seriously: Starting Points of the Hart-Devlin Debate' *The Journal of Ethics* 10: 21–51.

Dempsey, M. (2005) 'Rethinking Wolfenden: Prostitute Use, Criminal Law and Remote Harm' *Criminal Law Review* 255.

Devlin, P. (1965) *The Enforcement of Morals*. Oxford: Oxford University Press.

Dorling, D., Gordon, D., Hillyard, P., Pantazis, C., Pemberton, S., and Tombs, S. (2008) *Criminal Obsessions: Why Harm Matters More Than Crime* (2nd edn). London: Centre for Crime and Justice Studies.

Drug Equality Alliance http://www.drugequality.org/reading.htm

Duff, R. (2007) *Answering for Crime: Responsibility and Liability in the Criminal Law*. Oxford: Hart Publishing.

Durkheim, E. (1895) *The Rules of Sociological Method* (Translated by Steven Lukes in 1982). London: Macmillan Press.

Feinberg, J. (1984–88) *The Moral Limits of The Criminal Law*. Oxford: Oxford University Press. Vol. I: *Harm to Others* (1984); Vol. II: *Offense to Others* (1985); Vol. III: *Harm to Self* (1986); Vol. IV: *Harmless Wrongdoing* (1988).

Film Exchange on Alcohol and Drugs http://www.fead.org.uk/

Gardner, J. (1994) 'Rationality and the Rule of Law in Offences against the Person' *Cambridge Law Journal* 53(3): 502–23.

Green, P. and Ward, T. (2004) *State Crime: Governments, Violence and Corruption*. London: Pluto Press.

Henry, S. and Milovanovic, D. (1996) *Postmodernism and Constitutive Theory: Beyond Modernism*. London: Sage.

Hillyard, P. and Tombs, S. (2004), 'Beyond Criminology' in Hillyard, P., Pantazis, C., Tombs, S., and Gordon, D. (eds) *Beyond Criminology: Taking Harm Seriously*. London: Pluto Press.

Hulsman, L. (1986) 'Critical Criminology and the Concept of Crime' *Contemporary Crisis* 10: 63–80.

Husak, D. (2007) *Overcriminalization: The Limits of Criminal Law*. New York: Oxford University Press.

Jones, H. (2004) 'Opportunities and Obstacles: The Rape Crisis Federation in the UK' *The Journal of International Gender Studies* 8: 55–71.

Marshall, S. and Duff, R. (1998) 'Criminalization and Sharing Wrongs' *Canadian Journal of Law and Jurisprudence* 11: 7–22.

Mill, J. (1859) *On Liberty*. London: Longmans, Green and Co.

Nutt, D., King, L., Saulsbury, W., and Blakemore, C. (2007) 'Development of a Rational Scale to Assess the Harm of Drugs of Potential Misuse' *The Lancet*, 369(9566): 1047–53.

Pemberton, S. (2004) 'A Theory of Moral Indifference: Understanding the Production of Harm by Capitalist Society' in Hillyard, P., Pantazis, C., Tombs, S., and Gordon, D. (eds) *Beyond Criminology: Taking Harm Seriously*. London: Pluto Press.

Reiman, J. (2006) 'Book Review: *Beyond Criminology: Taking Harm Seriously*.' *British Journal of Criminology* 46(2): 362–4.

Schwendinger, H. and Schwendinger, J. (1970) 'Defenders of Order or Guardians of Human Rights?' *Issues in Criminology* 5: 123–157.

Tombs, S. and Whyte, D. (2003) *Unmasking the Crimes of the Powerful: Scrutinizing States and Corporations*. New York: Peter Lang Publishing.

Vold, G.B., Bernard, T.J., and Snipes, J.B. (2002) *Theoretical Criminology* (4th edn). New York: Oxford University Press.

von Hirsch, A. (1996) 'Extending the Harm Principle: "Remote" Harms and Fair Imputation' in Simester, A. and Smith, A. (eds) *Harm and Culpability*. Oxford: Oxford University Press.

von Hirsch, A. and Jareborg, N. (1991) 'Gauging Criminal Harm: A Living-Standard Analysis' *Oxford Journal of Legal Studies* 11(1): 1–38.

Chapter 4

Aristotle (384–322 B.C.) *The Politics*. Found at Justice with Michael Sandel of Harvard University http://www.justiceharvard.org/resources/aristotle-the-politics/

Bazelon, D.L. (1976) 'The Morality of Criminal Law' *Southern California Law Review* 49: 385–405 (esp. 389).

Bazelon, D.L. (1981) 'Forward: The Morality of Criminal Law: The Rights of the Accused' *The Journal of Criminal Law and Criminology* 72: 1143–70.

Beccaria, C. (original from 1767) *On Crimes and Punishments*, reprinted in Bellamy, R. (ed.) Davies, R. (translator) (1995) *Of Crimes and Punishments and Other Writings*. Cambridge: Cambridge University Press.

Braithwaite, J. (2002) 'Setting Standards for Restorative Justice' *British Journal of Criminology* 42(3): 563–577.

Cooper, R. (2012) 'Trial by Jury Faces Axe in up to 70,000 Cases Per Year to Cut Costs' *Mail Online* 16 January 2012.

Currie, E. (1997) 'Market, Crime and Community' *Theoretical Criminology* 1(2): 147–72.

Duff, R. (2001) *Punishment, Communication and Community*. Oxford: Oxford University Press.

Durkheim, É. (1982) *Rules of Sociological Method*. New York, NY: The Free Press.

Etzioni, A. (1994) *The Spirit of Community: The Reinvention of American Society*. New York, NY: Touchstone.

Howard League Justice website (http://www.howardleague.org/).

Howard League Justice Conference podcasts can be found at http://www.howardleague.org/conference-podcasts/.

King, M. (1981) *The Framework of Criminal Justice*. London: Croom Helm.

Macpherson 10 years on (2009) *The Macpherson Report – Ten Years on*. House of Commons, Home Affairs Committee Twelfth Report of Session 2008–09. HC427 London: Stationery Office.

Macpherson, W. (1999) *The Stephen Lawrence Inquiry: Report of an Inquiry by Sir William Macpherson of Cluny*. Cm4262–1, London: The Stationery Office.

Packer, H. (1968) *The Limits of the Criminal Sanction*. Stanford: Stanford University Press.

Pakes, F. (2004) *Comparative Criminal Justice*. Cullompton: Willan.

Quinney, R. (1970) *The Social Reality of Crime*. Boston: Little, Brown.

Rawls, J. (1971) *A Theory of Justice*. Cambridge, MA: Harvard University Press.

Sen, A. (2010) *The Idea of Justice*. London: Penguin Books.

Skogan, W. (2006) 'Asymmetry in the Impact of Encounters with Police' *Policing and Society* 16(2): 99–126.

Tulkens, F. (1995) 'Main Comparable Features of the Different European Criminal Justice Systems'. Found in M. Delmas-Marty (ed.) *The Criminal Process and Human Rights: Towards a European Consciousness*. Dordrecht: Martinus Nijhoff.

Weber, M. (1922) 'The Nature, Conditions and Development of Bureaucratic Herrschaft' in Roth G., and Wittich, W. (eds) (1968) *Max Weber Economy and Society*. New York: Bedminster Press.

Zander, M. (1993) in *Royal Commission on Criminal Justice, Runciman Report*, Cm 2263.

Chapter 5

Flately, J., Kershaw, C., Smith, K., Chaplin, R., and Moon, D. (2010) *Crime in England and Wales 2009–2010*. London: Home Office.

Her Majesty's Inspectorate of Constabulary (2014) *Crime-Recording: Making the Victim Count. The final report of an inspection of crime data integrity in police forces in England and Wales*. London: HMIC. (https://www.justiceinspectorates.gov.uk/hmic/wp-content/uploads/crime-recording-making-the-victim-count.pdf).

Hope, T. and Norris, P. (2013) 'Heterogeneity in the Frequency Distribution of Crime Victimization' *Journal of Quantitative Criminology* 29(4): 543–78.

Magnello, M. (2011) 'Vital Statistics; The Measurement of Public Health' in Flood, R., Rice, A., and Wilson, R. (eds) *Mathematics in Victorian Britain*. Oxford: Oxford University Press.

Maguire, M. (2012) 'Criminal statistics and the construction of crime' in Maguire, M., Morgan, R., and Reiner, R. (eds) *The Oxford Handbook of Criminology* (5th edn). Oxford: Oxford University Press.

Maguire, M. (2007) 'Crime Data and Statistics' in Maguire, M., Morgan, R., and Reiner, R. (eds) *The Oxford Handbook of Criminology* (4th edn). Oxford: Oxford University Press.

Maguire, M. (2002) 'Crime Statistics; the "Data Explosion and its Implications"' in Maguire, M., Morgan, R., and Reiner, R. (eds) *The Oxford Handbook of Criminology* (3rd edn). Oxford: Oxford University Press.

Maguire, M. (1997) 'Crime statistics, patterns and trends' in Maguire, M., Morgan, R., and Reiner, R. (eds) *The Oxford Handbook of Criminology* (2nd edn). Oxford: Oxford University Press.

Maguire, M. and McVie, S. (2017) 'Crime data and criminal statistics: a critical reflection' in Liebling, A., Maruna, S., and McAra, L. (eds) *The Oxford Handbook of Criminology* (6th edn). Oxford: Oxford University Press.

Mayhew, H. (1812–1887 [2012]) *London Labour and the London Poor*. Oxford: Oxford University Press.

Office for National Statistics (2015) *User Guide to Crime Statistics in England and Wales'*. London: ONS (www.ons.gov.uk/ons/guide…/crime-statistics…/user-guide-to-crime-statistics.pdf).

Walby, S., Towers, J., and Francis, B. (2015) 'Is Violent Crime Increasing or Decreasing? A new methodology to measure repeat attacks making visible the significance of gender and domestic relations' *British Journal of Criminology*, doi: 10.1093/bjc/azv131

Chapter 6

Aronson, E., Wilson, T. D., and Akert, R. (2010) *Social Psychology* (7th edn). Upper Saddle River: Prentice Hall.

Baker, K. (2005) 'Assessment in Youth Justice: Professional Discretion and the Use of Asset' *Youth Justice* 5: 106–22.

Bryman, A. (2015) *Social Research Methods* (5th edn). Oxford: Oxford University Press.

Case, S. (2015) 'Criminology as a Social Science: How Does Criminology "Know" About Crime?' in Vaidya, K. (ed.) *Criminology and Criminal Justice for the Curious: Why Study Criminology and Criminal Justice?* NY: Curious Academic Publishing.

Case, S. (2007) 'Questioning the "Evidence" of Risk that Underpins Evidence-Led Youth Justice Interventions' *Youth Justice* 7(2): 91–106.

Case, S. (2006) 'Young People "At Risk" of What? Challenging Risk-Focused Early Intervention as Crime Prevention' *Youth Justice* 6(3): 171–79.

Case, S. and Haines, K. (2009) *Understanding Youth Offending: Risk Factor Research Policy and Practice.* Cullompton: Willan.

Caulfield, L. and Hill, J. (2014) *Criminological Research for Beginners.* Abingdon: Routledge.

Chamberlain, J. M. (2015) *Criminological Theory in Context: An Introduction.* London: Sage.

Chamberlain, J. M. (2013) *Understanding Criminological Research: A Guide to Data Analysis.* London: Sage.

Creswell, J. (2013) *Research Design: Qualitative, Quantitative, and Mixed Methods Approaches.* London: Sage.

Crow, I. and Semmens, N. (2008) *Researching Criminology.* Maidenhead: Open University Press.

Crowther-Dowey, C. and Fussey, P. (2013) *Researching Crime: Approaches, Methods and Application.* Basingstoke: Palgrave.

Davies, P., Francis, P., and Jupp, V. (eds) (2011) *Doing Criminological Research* (2nd edn). London: Sage.

Farrington, D. (2007) 'Childhood Risk Factors and Risk-Focused Prevention' in Maguire, M., Morgan, R., and Reiner, R. (eds) *The Oxford Handbook of Criminology* (4th edn). Oxford: Oxford University Press.

Farrington, D., Bowen, S., Buckle, A., Burns-Howell, T., Burrows, J., and Speed, M. (1993) 'An Experiment on the Prevention of Shoplifting' in Clarke, R.V. (ed.) *Crime Prevention Studies*, Vol. 1. Monsey, NY: Willow Tree Press.

Ferraro, K. (1995) *Fear of Crime: Interpreting Victimization Risk.* Albany: State University of New York Press.

Gilbert, N. (2001) *Researching Social Life.* London: Sage.

Gray, D. (2013) *Doing Research in the Real-World.* London: Sage.

Hagan, F. (2013) *Research Methods in Criminal Justice and Criminology.* New York: Prentice-Hill.

Haines, K. and Case, S. (2015) *Positive Youth Justice: Children First, Offenders Second.* Bristol: Policy Press.

Hall, S. (1978) *Policing the Crisis: Mugging, the State, and Law and Order.* London: Macmillan.

Hawkins, J. and Catalano, R. (1992) *Communities That Care.* San Francisco: Jossey-Bass.

Hoefnagels, P. (1973) *The Other Side of Criminology.* New York: Springer.

Hope, T. (2009) 'The Illusion of Control: A Response to Professor Sherman' *Criminology and Criminal Justice* 9(2): 125–34.

Janis, I. (1972) *Victims of Groupthink: A Psychological Study of Foreign-Policy Decisions and Fiascoes.* Boston: Houghton Mifflin.

Kahneman, D., Slovic, P., and Tversky, A. (1982) *Judgment under Uncertainty: Heuristics and Biases.* Cambridge: Cambridge University Press.

Kemshall, H. (2008) 'Risk, Rights and Justice: Understanding and Responding to Youth Risk' *Youth Justice* 8(1): 21–38.

King, R. and Wincup, E. (2008) *Doing Research on Crime and Justice.* Oxford: Oxford University Press.

Lincoln, Y. and Guba, E. (1985) *Naturalistic Inquiry.* London: Sage.

McAra, L. and McVie, S. (2010) 'Youth Crime and Justice: Key Messages from the Edinburgh Study of Youth Transitions and Crime' *Criminology and Criminal Justice* 10(2): 179–209.

Mitchell Miller, J. (2014) *The Encyclopaedia of Theoretical Criminology, Volume One.* Oxford: Wiley.

Nightingale, D. and Cromby, J. (1999) *Social Constructionist Psychology.* Buckingham: Open University Press.

Noaks, L. and Wincup, E. (2004) *Criminological Research: Understanding Qualitative Methods.* London: Sage.

Oakley, A. (1999) 'Paradigm Wars: Some Thoughts on a Personal and Public Trajectory' *International Journal of Social Research Methodology* 2(3): 247–54.

Parker, H. (1974) *A View from the Boys. A Sociology of Downtown Adolescents.* Newton Abbot, Devon: David and Charles.

Pawson, R. and Tilley, N. (2004) *Realistic Evaluation.* London: Sage.

Pollock, J. (2016) *Ethical Dilemmas and Decisions in Criminal Justice.* Boston: CENGAGE Learning.

Reichardt, C. and Rallis, S. (1994) *The Qualitative-Quantitative debate: New Perspectives.* San Francisco: Jossey Bass.

Robson, C. (2015) *Real-World Research* (4th edn). London: Wiley.

Savin, M. and Howell-Major, C. (2013) *Qualitative Research: The essential guide to theory and practice.* London: Routledge.

Stout, B., Yates, J., and Williams, B. (2008) *Applied Criminology.* London: Sage.

Taleb, N. (2001) *Fooled by Randomness: The Hidden Role of Chance in Life and in the Markets.* New York: Random House and Penguin Books.

Tashakkori, A. and Teddlie, T. (1998) *Mixed Methodology: Combining Qualitative and Quantitative Approaches.* Thousand Oaks, California: Sage.

Utting, D. (1999) *Guide to Promising Approaches.* London: Communities that Care.

West, D. and Farrington, D. (1973) *Who Becomes Delinquent?* London: Heinemann.

Westmarland, L. (2011) *Researching Crime and Justice: Tales from the Field.* Abingdon: Routledge.

Williams, K. (2012) *Textbook on Criminology.* Oxford: Oxford University Press.

Willig, C. (2001) *Qualitative Research in Psychology: A Practical Guide to Theory and Method.* Buckingham: Oxford University Press.

Youth Justice Board (2005) *Role of Risk and Protective Factors.* London: YJB.

Chapter 7

Allen, W. and Blinder, S. (2013) *Migration in the News: Portrayals of Immigrants, Migrants, Asylum Seekers and Refugees in National British Newspapers, 2010 to 2012.* Migration Observatory, COMPAS: University of Oxford.

Balch, A. and Balabanova, E. (2014), 'Ethics, Politics and Migration: Public Debates on the Free Movement of Romanians and Bulgarians in the UK, 2006-2013' *Politics* 36(1) (2016): 19–35

Burscher, B., van Spanje, J., and Vreese, C. (2015) 'Owning the Issues of Crime and Immigration; The Relation between Immigration and Crime News and Anti-Immigration Voting in 11 Countries' *Electoral Studies* 38: 59–69.

Chibnall, S. (1977) *Law-and-Order New.* London: Tavistock.

Cohen, S. (2011 [1973]) *Folk Devils and Moral Panics: The Creation of the Mods and the Rockers.* London: Routledge.

Colbran, M. (2015) 'Penal Reform Groups, New Media and Mainstream News: Strategies for Managing the New Media Landscape'. London: The Howard League for Penal Reform.

Ditton, J. and Duffy, J. (1983) 'Bias in the Newspaper Reporting of Crime News' *British Journal of Criminology* 23 (2): 159–65.

Dunaway J., Branton R. P., and Abrajano, M. A. (2010) 'Agenda Setting, Public Opinion, and the Issue of Immigration Reform' *Social Science Quarterly* 91(2): 359–78.

Gabrielatos, C. and Baker, P. (2008). 'Fleeing, Sneaking, Flooding: A Corpus Analysis of Discursive Constructions of Refugees and Asylum Seekers in the UK Press 1996–2005' *Journal of English Linguistics* 36(1): 5–38.

Garrelts, N. (2006) *Meaning and Culture of Grand Theft Auto: Critical Essays*. Jefferson: McFarland & Company.

Greer, C. (ed.) (2010) *Crime and the Media: A Reader*. London: Routledge.

Greer, C. and Reiner. R. (2015) 'Mediated Mayhem: Media, Crime, Criminal Justice' in Maguire, M., Morgan, R., and Reiner, R. (eds) *The Oxford Handbook of Criminology* (5th edn). Oxford: Oxford University Press.

Hall, S., Critchley, C., Jefferson, T., Clarke, J., and Roberts, B. (1978) *Policing the Crisis*. London: Macmillan.

Hancox, D. (2009) *Public enemy no 696*. Available at: https://www.theguardian.com/culture/2009/jan/21/police-form-696-garage-music.

Horsley, L. (2005) *Twentieth Century Crime Fiction*. Oxford: Oxford University Press.

Hough, M. and Roberts, J. V. (2004) *Youth Crime and Youth Justice: Public Opinion in England and Wales*. London: Policy Press.

Howe, A. (ed.) (1998) *Sexed Crime in the News*. Sydney: Federation Press.

Huesmann, L. and Malamuth, N. (1986) 'Media Violence and Anti-Social Behaviour' *Journal of Social Issues* 42(3): 1–6.

Jewkes, Y. (2015) *Media and Crime* (3rd edn). London: Sage.

Jewkes, Y. and Yar, M. (eds) (2009) *The Handbook of Internet Crime*. Cullompton: Willan Publishing.

Jonsson, L., Copper, K., Quayle, E., Sveding, C. G., and Hervy, K. (2015) 'Young people who produce and send images: Context, motivation and consequences' www.spirto.health.ed.ac.uk/download/website_files/SPIRTO_FULL_InterviewAnalysis_FINAL.pdf.

Knight, S. (2010) *Crime Fiction Since 1800: Detection, Death, Diversity* (2nd edn). Basingstoke: Palgrave Macmillan.

KhosraviNik, M. (2009) 'The representation of refugees, asylum seekers and immigrants in British newspapers during the Balkan conflict (1999) and the British general election (2005)' *Discourse & Society* 20(4): 477–498.

Livingstone, S. (1996) 'On the Continuing Problem of Media Effects' in Curran, J. and Gurevitch, M. (eds) *Mass Media and Society*. (3rd edn). London: Arnold.

Livingstone, S., Haddon, L., Görzig, A., and Ólafsson, K. (2011) *EU Kids Online: Final Report*. London: EU Kids Online, London School of Economics & Political Science. Available at: http://www.lse.ac.uk/media%40lse/research/EUKidsOnline/EU%20Kids%20II%20(2009-11)/EUKidsOnlineIIReports/Final%20report.pdf.

Mason, P. (2007) 'Prison Decayed: Cinematic Penal Discourse and Populism 1995-2005' *Social Semiotics* 16(4): 607–26.

Mason, P. (2006) 'Lies, Distortion and What Doesn't Work: Monitoring Prison Stories in the British Media' *Crime Media Culture* 2006 (2): 251.

Mayr, A. and Machin, D. (2012) *The Language of Crime and Deviance; An Introduction to Critical Linguistic Analysis in Media and Popular Culture*. New York: Continuum.

Moore, S. (2014) *Crime and the Media*. Palgrave: Macmillan.

Mullison, K. (2009) 'The Common Folk: The Demolition of Class Boundaries in *The Beggar's Opera*' http://www.jbu.edu/assets/academics/journal/resource/file/2009/kendramullison.pdf.

Muncie, J. (2015) *Youth and Crime* (4th edn). London: Sage.

Nopporn Wong-Anan. (2008) *Thailand halts Grand Theft Auto sales after murder*. Available at: http://uk.reuters.com/article/us-crime-thailand-grandtheftauto-idUKBKK22888820080804.

Pearson, G. (1983) *Hooligan: A History of Respectable Fears*. London: Macmillan.

Picard, R. G. (2014) *Public Opinion, Party Politics, Policy, and Immigration News in the United Kingdom*. Oxford: Reuters Institute for the Study of Journalism.

Priestman, M. (ed.) (2012) *The Cambridge Companion to Crime Fiction*. Cambridge: Cambridge University Press.

Rafter, N. (2006) *Shots in the Mirror: Crime Films and Society*. Oxford: Oxford University Press.

Rafter, N. and Brown, M. (2011) *Criminology Goes to the Movies: Crime Theory and Popular Culture*. New York: NYU Press.

Reilly, J. (1998) *Belsen: Liberation of a Concentration Camp*. London: Routledge.

Reiner, R. (1997) 'Media Made Criminality' in Maguire, M., Morgan, R., and Reiner, R. (eds) *The Oxford Handbook of Criminology* (2nd edn). Oxford: Oxford University Press.

Routledge, P. (2011) 'London riots: Is rap music to blame for encouraging this culture of violence?' *Daily Mirror*. Available at: http://www.mirror.co.uk/news/uk-news/london-riots-is-rap-music-to-blame-146671.

Simons, R., Wu, C.-I., Johnson, C., and Conger, R. (1995) 'A Test of Various Perspectives on the Intergenerational Transmission of Domestic Violence' *Criminology* 33: 141–72.

Schramm, W., Lyle, J., and Parker, E. (1961) *Television in the Lives of Our Children*. Stanford, Cal.: Stanford University Press.

Thompson, K. (1998) *Moral Panics*. London: Routledge.

Wayne, M., Henderson, L., Murray, C., and Petley, J. (2008) 'Television News and the Symbolic Criminalisation of Young People' *Journalism Studies* 9 (1): 75–90.

Wilkins, L. (1964) *Social Deviance*. London: Tavistock.

Williams, P. and Dickinson, J. (1993) 'Fear of Crime: Read All About It? The Relationship Between Newspaper Crime Reporting and Fear of Crime' *British Journal of Criminology* 33 (1): 33–56.

Wilson, D. and O'Sullivan, S. (2004) *Images of Incarceration: Representations of Prison in Film and Television Drama*. Winchester: Waterside.

Yar, M. (2010) 'Screening Crime: Cultural Criminology Goes to the Movies' in Hayward, K. and Presdee, M. (eds) *Framing Crime: Cultural Criminology and the Image*. London: Routledge.

Yar, M. (2013) *Cybercrime and Society* (2nd edn). London: Sage.

Chapter 8

Amir, M. (1971) *Patterns in Forcible Rape*. Chicago: University of Chicago Press.

Baker, D. (2016) *Death after Police Contact: Accountability and Regulation in the 21st Century*. Basingstoke: Palgrave-Macmillan.

Barker, P. (2002) 'The Construction of Gay Identity via Polari in the Julian and Sandy Radio Sketches' *Lesbian and Gay Psychology Review* 3(3): 75–83.

Chakraborti, N. and Garland, J. (2015) *Hate Crime: Impact, Causes and Responses*. London: Sage.

Chakraborti, N. and Garland, J. (eds) (2015) *Responding to Hate Crime: The Case for Connecting Policy and Research*. Bristol: Policy Press.

Christie, N. (1977) 'Conflicts as Property' *British Journal of Criminology* 17: 1–15.

Christie, N. (1986) 'The Ideal Victim' in Fattah E. A. (ed.) *From Crime Policy to Victim Policy*. London: Macmillan.

Gerstenfeld, P. (2013) *Hate Crimes: Causes, Controls, and Controversies*. London: Sage.

Godfrey, B. and Lawrence, P. (2015) *Crime and Justice since 1750* (2nd edn). Abingdon: Routledge.

Hall, N., Corb, A., Giannasi, P., and Grieve, P. (eds) (2014) *The Routledge International Handbook on Hate Crime*. Abingdon: Routledge.

Hastings, S. (1986) *Nancy Mitford*. London: Hamish Hamilton.

Karmen, A. (1990) *Crime Victims: An Introduction to Victimology*. Pacific Grove, CA: Brooks Cole.

Mason-Bish, H. (2014) 'Beyond the Silo: Hate Crime and Intersectionality' in Hall, N., Corb, A., Giannasi, P., and Grieve, J. (eds) *International Handbook of Hate Crime*. Oxford: Routledge.

Mawby, R. and Walklate, S. (1994) *Critical Victimology*. London: Sage.

Mendelsohn, B. (1956) 'Une Nouvelle Branche de la Science Bio-psycho-sociale Victimologie' *Revue Internationale de Criminologie et de Police Technique* 10–31.

Perry, B. (2001). *In the Name of Hate: Understanding Hate Crimes*. New York: Routledge.

Petrosino, C. (2003) 'Connecting the Past to the Future: Hate Crime in America' in Perry, B. (ed.) *Hate and Bias Crime: A Reader*. London: Routledge.

Roberts, S. (2013) *Order and Dispute: An Introduction to Legal Anthropology*. New Orleans: Quid Pro LLC.

Shakespeare, T. (2013) 'The Social Model of Disability' in Leonard, J. (ed.) *The Disability Studies Reader*. London: Routledge.

Simons, R., Wu, C.-I., Johnson, C., and Conger, R. (1995) 'A Test of Various Perspectives on the Intergenerational Transmission of Domestic Violence' *Criminology* 33: 141–72.

Spalek, B. (2006) *Crime Victims: Theory, Policy and Practice*. London: Palgrave Macmillan.

Von Hentig, H. (1948) *The Criminal and His Victim*. CT: Yale University Press.

Wolfgang, M.E. (1958) *Patterns of Criminal Homicide*. Philadelphia: University of Pennsylvania Press.

Chapter 9

Agnew, R. (1992) 'Foundation for a General Strain Theory of Crime and Delinquency' *Criminology* 30(1): 47–87.

Ariès, P. (1962) *Centuries of Childhood*. New York: Vintage Books.

Arnett, J. (1999) 'Adolescent Storm and Stress, Reconsidered' *American Psychologist* 54: 317–26.

Arnull, E. and Eagle, S. (2009) *Girls and Offending—Patterns, Perceptions and Interventions*. London: Youth Justice Board.

Baker, K. (2005) 'Assessment in Youth Justice: Professional Discretion and the Use of Asset' *Youth Justice* 5(2): 106–22.

Bakker, E. (2006) *Jihadi Terrorists in Europe, their Characteristics and the Circumstances in which they Joined the Jihad*. The Hague, Netherlands: Institute of International Relations.

Bateman, T. (2015) *The State of Youth Justice 2015: An Overview of Trends and Developments*. London: National Association for Youth Justice.

Bateman, T. (2012) 'Who Pulled the Plug? Towards an Explanation of the Fall in Child Imprisonment in England and Wales' *Youth Justice* 12(1): 36–52.

Bateman, T. (2011) 'Punishing Poverty. The Scaled Approach and Youth Justice Practice' *Howard Journal* 50(2): 171–83.

Bateman, T., Hazel, N., and Wright, S. (2013) *Resettlement of Young People Leaving Custody: Lessons from the Literature*. London: Beyond Youth Custody.

Becker, H. (1963) *The Outsiders*. New York: Free Press.

Blakemore, S-J. and Frith, U. (2005) *The Learning Brain*. Oxford: Blackwell.

Bourdieu, P. (1977) *Outline of a Theory of Practice*. Cambridge, Cambridge University Press.

Byrne, B. and Brooks, K. (2015) 'Post-YOT Youth Justice', Howard League for Penal Reform at: http://socialwelfare.bl.uk/subject-areas/services-client-groups/young-offenders/howardleagueforpenalreform/174662HLWP_19_2015.pdf.

Case, S. (2017) *Contemporary Youth Justice*. Abingdon: Routledge.

Case, S. and Haines, K. (2015) 'Children First, Offenders Second Positive Promotion: Reframing the Prevention Debate' *Youth Justice Journal* 15(3): 226–39.

Case, S. and Haines, K. (2010) 'Juvenile Delinquency: Manifestations and Causes' in Herzog-Evans, M. (ed.), *Transnational Criminology Manual*. Nijmegen: Wolf Legal Publishers.

Case, S. and Haines, K. (2009) *Understanding Youth Offending: Risk Factor Research Policy and Practice*. Cullompton: Willan.

Children's Commissioner for England (2015) *Unlocking Potential: A Study of the Isolation of Children in Custody in England*. London: Children's Commissioner for England.

Christmann, K. (2012) *Preventing Religious Radicalisation and Violent Extremism*. London: Youth Justice Board.

Cloward, R. and Ohlin, L. (1960) *Delinquency and Opportunity*. New York: The Free Press.

Cohen, A. (1955) *Delinquent Boys*. Chicago: The Free Press.

Cohen, S. (1972) *Folk Devils and Moral Panics*. London: Paladin.

Coleman, J. and Hendry, L. (1999) *The Nature of Adolescence* (3rd edn). London, Routledge.

Creaney, S. and Smith, R. (2014) 'Youth Justice Back at the Crossroads' *Safer Communities* 13(2).

Crofts, T. (2009) 'Catching up with Europe: Taking the Age of Criminal Responsibility Seriously in England' *European Journal of Crime, Criminal Law and Criminal Justice* 17(4): 267–91.

Cunningham, H. (2005) *Children and Childhood in Western Society since 1500* (2nd edn). Harlow: Pearson Longman.

Erikson, E. (1995) *Childhood and Society*. New York: Vintage.

Farrington, D. (2007) 'Childhood Risk Factors and Risk-Focused Prevention', in Maguire, M., Morgan, R., and Reiner, R. (eds) *The Oxford Handbook of Criminology* (4th edn). Oxford: Oxford University Press.

Farrington, D. (2003) 'Key Results from the First Forty Years of the Cambridge Study in Delinquent Development' in Thornberry, T. and Krohn, M. (eds) (2003) *Taking Stock of Delinquency: An Overview of Findings from Contemporary Longitudinal Studies*. New York: Kluwer.

Farrington, D. (1988) 'Studying Changes Within Individuals: The Causes of Offending', in Rutter, M. (ed.) *Studies of Psychosocial Risk: The Power of Longitudinal Data*. Cambridge: Cambridge University Press.

Feilzer, M. and Hood, R. (2004) *Differences of Discrimination?* London: Youth Justice Board.

France, A. and Homel, R. (2007a) 'Societal Access Routes and Developmental Pathways: Putting Social Structure and Young People's Voice into the Analysis of Pathways into and out of Crime' in France, A. and Homel, R. (eds) *Pathways and Crime Prevention*, Cullompton: Willan.

France, A. and Homel, R. (eds) (2007b) *Pathways and Crime Prevention*. Cullompton: Willan.

Freeman, M. (2007) *The best interests of the child*. Leiden: Martinus Nijhoff.

Freud, S. (1977) *On Sexuality*. Harmondsworth: Penguin Books.

Garland, D. (2001) *The Culture of Control*. Oxford, Oxford University Press.

Glueck, S. and Glueck, E. (1930) *500 Criminal Careers*. New York: Alfred Knopf.

Gill, P. (2007) 'A Multi-Dimensional Approach to Suicide Bombing' *International Journal of Conflict and Violence* 1(2): 142–59.

Goldson, B. (2013) '"Unsafe, Unjust and Harmful to Wider Society": Grounds for Raising the Minimum Age of Criminal Responsibility in England and Wales' *Youth Justice* 13(2): 111–30.

Goldson, B. (2005) 'Child Imprisonment: A Case for Abolition' *Youth Justice* 5(2): 77–90.

Goldson, B. (2002) *Vulnerable Inside: Children in Secure and Penal Settings*, London: The Children's Society.

Goldson, B. and Muncie, J. (2015) *Youth Crime and Justice* (2nd edn). London: Sage.

Goodnow, J. (2007) 'Adding Social Contexts to Developmental Analyses of Crime Prevention', in France, A. and Homel, R. (eds) *Pathways and Crime Prevention*. Cullompton, Willan.

Hagell, A. and Hazel, N. (2001) 'Macro and Micro Patterns in the Development of Secure Custodial Institutions for Serious and Persistent Young Offenders in England and Wales' *Youth Justice* 1(1): 3–16.

Haines, K. and Case, S. (2015) *Positive Youth Justice: Children First, Offenders Second*. Bristol: Policy Press.

Haines, K., Case, S.P., Charles, A., and Davies, K. (2013) 'The Swansea Bureau: A Model of Diversion from the Youth Justice System' *International Journal of Law, Crime and Justice*. 41(2): 167–87.

Hall, S., Critcher, C., Jefferson, T., Clarke, J. and Roberts, B. (2013) *Policing the Crisis (35th anniversary edition)*. Basingstoke: Palgrave Macmillan.

Hanson, E. and Holmes, D. (2014) *That Difficult Age: Developing a More Effective Response to Risks in Adolescence*. Totnes: The Dartington Hall Trust. Available at: https://www.rip.org.uk/news-and-views/latest-news/evidence-scope-risks-in-adolescence/

Hawes, M. (2013) *Legitimacy and social order: A young people's perspective*. Unpublished Phd thesis. Swansea: Swansea University.

Hendrick, H. (2015) 'Histories of Youth Crime and Youth Justice' in Goldson, B. and Muncie, J. (eds) *Youth Crime and Justice*. London: Sage.

Her Majesty's Chief Inspector of Prisons and the Youth Justice Board (2013) *Children and Young People in Custody 2012–13*. London: The Stationery Office.

Heywood, C. (2001) *A History of Childhood*. Cambridge: Polity Press.

Hopkins-Burke, R. (2013) *An Introduction to Criminological Theory*. Abingdon: Routledge.

House of Commons Justice Committee (2013) *Youth Justice: Seventh Report of 2012-13*. London: The Stationery Office.

Jacobson, J., Bhardwa, B., Gyateng, T., Hunter, T., and Hough, M. (2010) *Punishing Disadvantage: A Profile of Children in Custody*. London: Prison Reform Trust.

James, A. and James, A. (2004) *Constructing Childhood*. Basingstoke: Palgrave Macmillan.

Jenks, C. (1996) *Childhood*. London: Routledge.

Kelly, L. (2012) 'Representing and Preventing Youth Crime and Disorder: Intended and Unintended Consequences of Targeted Youth Programmes in England' *Youth Justice* 12(2): 101–17.

Kelly, L. and Armitage V. (2015) 'Diverse Diversions: Youth Justice Reform, Localized Practices, and a "New Interventionist Diversion"?' *Youth Justice* 15: 117–33.

Kemshall, H. (2008) 'Risk, Rights and Justice: Understanding and Responding to Youth Risk' *Youth Justice* 8(1): 21–38.

Kitsuse, J. (1962) 'Societal Reaction to Deviant Behaviour: Problems of Theory and Method' *Social Problems*, 9: 247–56.

Laub, J. and Sampson, R. (2003) *Shared Beginnings, Delinquent Lives. Delinquent Boys to Age 70*. London: Harvard University Press.

Lawrence, J. (2007) 'Taking the Developmental Pathways Approach to Understanding and Preventing Antisocial Behaviour' in France, A. and Homel, R. (eds) *Pathways and Crime Prevention*. Cullompton, Willan.

Lemert, E. (1967) *Human Deviance, Social Problems and Social Control*. Englewood Cliffs, NJ: Prentice-Hall.

Matza, D. (1964) *Delinquency and Drift*. New York: John Wiley & Sons.

Matza, D. (1969) *Becoming Deviant*. Englewood Cliffs, NJ: Prentice-Hall.

May, T., Gyateng, T., and Hough, M. (2010) *Differential Treatment in the Youth Justice System*. London: Equality and Human Rights Commission.

McAra, L. and McVie, S. (2007) 'Youth Justice? The Impact of System Contact on Patterns of Desistance from Offending' *European Journal of Criminology* 4(3): 315–45.

McNeill, F. and Barry, M. (2009) 'Conclusions' in Barry, M. and McNeill, F. (eds) *Youth Offending and Youth Justice*. London: Jessica Kingsley Publishers.

Merton, R. (1957) 'Priorities in Scientific Discovery: A Chapter in the Sociology of Science' *American Sociological Review* 22(6): 635–59.

Ministry of Justice/Youth Justice Board (2016) *Youth Justice Statistics 2014/15. England and Wales*. London: Ministry of Justice.

Ministry of Justice and Youth Justice Board (2013) *Youth Out-of-Court Disposals Guide for Police and Youth Offending Services*. London: Ministry of Justice.

Mullen, J. (2014) *Improving Outcomes for Young Black and/or Muslim Men in the Criminal Justice System*. London: Barrow Cadbury Trust.

Muncie, J. (2004) *Youth and Crime*. London: Sage.

Muncie, J. and Goldson, B. (2006) *Comparative Youth Justice*. London: Sage.

Nacro (2003) *A Failure of Justice: Reducing Child Imprisonment*. London: Nacro.

National Association for Youth Justice (2016) *Response to Review of the Youth Justice System: An Interim Report of Emerging Findings*. London: NAYJ.

Piaget, J. (1959) *The Language and Thought of the Child*. London: Routledge.

Pitts, J. (2008) *Reluctant Gangsters*. Cullompton: Willan.

Pollock, A. (1983) *Forgotten Children*. Cambridge: Cambridge University Press.

Prison Reform Trust (2013) *Bromley Briefings Prison Factfile Autumn 2013*. London: Prison Reform Trust.

Redmond, A. (2015) *Children in Custody 2014–15: An Analysis of 12–18-year-olds' Perceptions of their Experience in Secure Training Centres and Young Offender Institutions*. London: HMI Prisons.

Richards, K. (2014) 'Blurred Lines: Reconsidering the Concept of 'Diversion' in Youth Justice Systems in Australia' *Youth Justice* 14(2): 122–39.

Rutter, M., Giller, H., and Hagell, A. (1998) *Antisocial Behaviour by Young People*. Cambridge, Cambridge University Press.

Rutter, M., Graham, P., Chadwick, O., and Yule, W. (1976) 'Adolescent Turmoil: Fact or Fiction?' *Journal of Child Psychology and Psychiatry* 17: 35–56.

Sampson, R. and Laub, J. (1993) *Crime in the Making: Pathways and Turning Points through Life*. Harvard: Harvard University Press.

Sampson, R. and Laub, J. (2005) 'A General Age-Graded Theory of Crime: Lessons Learned and the Future of Life-Course Criminology' in Farrington, D. (ed.) *Integrated Developmental and Life-Course Theories of Offending*. New Brunswick: Transaction.

Sharpe, G. (2011) *Offending Girls. Young Women and Youth Justice*. Abingdon: Routledge.

Sherman, L., Gottfredson D., MacKenzie, D., Eck, J., Reuter, P., and Bushway, S. (1998) *Preventing Crime: What Works, What Doesn't, What's Promising*. Department of Criminology and Criminal Justice, University of Maryland: Baltimore.

Smith, R. (2014) *Youth Justice: Ideas, Policy and Practice*. London: Routledge.

Smith, R. (2014a) 'Reinventing Diversion' *Youth Justice* 14(2): 109–21.

Smith, R. (2011) *Doing Justice to Young People*. Cullompton: Willan.

Smith, R. (2010) *A Universal Child?*, Basingstoke: Palgrave Macmillan.

Stephenson, M., Giller, H., and Brown, S. (2013) *Effective Practice in Youth Justice*. Abingdon: Routledge.

Taylor, J., McGue, M., and Iacono, W. (2000) 'Sex Differences, Assortative Mating and Cultural Transmission Effects on Adolescent Delinquency: A Twin Family Study' *Journal of Child Psychology and Psychiatry* 41: 433–40.

Thomson, R., Bell, R., Holland, J., Henderson, S., McGrellis, S., and Sharpe, S. (2002) 'Critical Moments: Choice, Chance and Opportunity in Young People's Narratives of Transition' *Sociology* 36(2): 335–54.

Thornberry, T., Krohn, M., Lizotte, A., Smith, C., and Tobin, K. (2003) *Gangs and Delinquency in Developmental Perspective*. Cambridge: Cambridge University Press.

Tyler, T. (2007) *Legitimacy and Criminal Justice: International Perspectives*. New York: Russell Sage Foundation.

UN Committee on the Rights of the Child (2016) *Concluding observations on the fifth periodic report of the United Kingdom of Great Britain and Northern Ireland*. UNCRC.

UNICEF (1989) *United Nations Convention on the Rights of the Child 1989*. Geneva: United Nations.

Vygotsky, L. (1986) *Thought and Language*. Cambridge: MA, MIT Press.

West, D. (1982) *Delinquency: Its Roots, Careers and Prospects*. London: Heinemann.

West, D. (1969) *Present Conduct and Future Delinquency*. London: Heinemann.

West, D. and Farrington, D. (1973) *Who Becomes Delinquent?* London: Heinemann.

Wikstrom, P-O. and Loeber, R. (2000) 'Do Disadvantaged Neighborhoods Cause Well-Adjusted Children to Become Adolescent Delinquents? A Study of Male Juvenile Serious Offending, Individual Risk and Protective Factors and Neighborhood Context' *Criminology* 38(4): 1109–42.

Wilkins, L. (1964) *Social Deviance*. London: Tavistock Publications.

Yates J. (2012) 'What Prospects Youth Justice? Children in Trouble in the Age of Austerity' *Social Policy and Administration* 46: 432–47.

Young, T., Fitzgibbon, W., and Silverstone, D. (2013) *The Role of the Family in Facilitating Gang Membership, Criminality and Exit*. London: Catch 22.

Youth Justice Board (2016) *Monthly Youth Custody Report April 2016: England and Wales*. London: Ministry of Justice.

Youth Justice Board (2014) *Deaths of Children in Custody: Action Taken, Lessons Learnt*. London: YJB.

Youth Justice Board (2013) *Assessment and Planning Interventions Framework—AssetPlus. Model Document*. London: YJB.

Youth Justice Board (2007) *ASSET Young Offender Assessment Profile*. Available at http://www.yjb.gov.uk/en-gb/practitioners/Assessment/Asset.htm.

Youth Justice Board (2006) *YIP Management Guidance*. London: YJB.

Youth Justice Board (2004) *National Standards for Youth Justice Services*. London: YJB.

Youth Justice Board (2003) *Assessment, Planning Interventions and Supervision*. London: YJB.

Chapter 10

Alexander, M. (2010) *The New Jim Crow: Mass Incarceration in an Age of Colorblindness*. New York: The New Press.

Allen, R. (2011) *Last Resort? Exploring the reduction in child imprisonment 2008–11*, London: Prison Reform Trust.

Bowling, B. and Phillips, C. (2002) *Racism, Crime and Justice*. Harlow: Pearson Education Limited.

Capers, B. (2014) 'What is Critical Race Theory?' in Dubber, M. and Hornle, T. (eds) *The Oxford Handbook of Criminal Law*. Oxford: Oxford University Press.

Delgado, R. and Stefancic, J. (2012) *Critical Race Theory: An Introduction*. New York: New York University Press.

Delsol, R. and Shiner, M. (eds) (2015) *Stop and Search: The Anatomy of a Police Power*. London: Palgrave Macmillan.

Eastwood, N., Shiner, M., and Bear, D. (2013) *The Numbers in Black and White: Ethnic Disparities in the Policing and Prosecution of Drugs Offences in England and Wales*. London: Release.

Equality and Human Rights Commission (2011) *How Fair is Britain? The First Triennial Review*. London: EHRC.

Equality and Human Rights Commission (2013) *Stop and Think Again: Towards Race Equality in Police PACE Stop and Search*. London: EHRC.

Feilzer, M. and Hood, R. (2004) *Differences or Discrimination - Minority Ethnic Young People in the Youth Justice System*, London: Youth Justice Board.

Gilroy, P. (1987) *There Ain't No Black in the Union Jack*. London: Hutchinson.

Hall, S., Critcher, C., Jefferson, T., Clarke, J., and Roberts, B. (1978) *Policing the Crisis: Mugging, the State and Law and Order*. London: Macmillan.

Hansard, *Brixton Disorders: The Scarman Report*, House of Lords, 4 February 1982, Vol. 426, cc. 1396–474.

HMIC (2013) *Stop and Search Powers: Are the Police Using them Effectively and Fairly?* London: HMIC.

HMIC (2015) *Stop and Search Powers 2: Are the Police Using them Effectively and Fairly?* London: HMIC.

Home Affairs Committee (2007) *Young Black People and the Criminal Justice System, Second Report of Session 2006–07*, Vols 1 and 2. London: The Stationery Office.

Hood, R. (1992) *Race and Sentencing*. Oxford: Clarendon Press.

Hopkins, K. (2015) *Analysis of Ethnicity and Custodial Sentences*. London: Ministry of Justice.

Justice Keith (2006) *The Zahid Mubarek Inquiry*. London: The Stationery Office.

John, G. (2003) *Race for Justice: A Review of Crown Prosecution Service Decision Making for Possible Racial Bias at each Stage of the Prosecution Process*. London: CPS/GJP.

Laming Review (2016) *In Care, Out of Trouble?* London: Prison Reform Trust.

McGhee, D. (2005) *Intolerant Britain? Hate, Citizenship and Difference*. Buckingham: Open University Press.

Ministry of Justice (2015) *Statistics on Race and the Criminal Justice System 2014*. London: Ministry of Justice.

MacPherson, W. (1999) *The Stephen Lawrence Inquiry, Report of an Inquiry by Sir William MacPherson of Cluny*, Cm 4262-1. London: Home Office.

Nacro (2002) *Policing Local Communities: The Tottenham Experiment*. London: Nacro.

Phillips, C. and Bowling, B. (2012) 'Ethnicities, Racism, Crime, and Criminal Justice' in Maguire, M., Morgan, R. and Reiner, R. (eds) *The Oxford Handbook of Criminology*. Oxford: Oxford University Press.

Roberti, A. (2016) *Home Secretary Announces Recording of all Traffic Stops*. London: StopWatch. (available at http://www.stop-watch.org/news-comment/story/home-secretary-announces-recording-of-all-traffic-stops).

Rollock, N. and Gillborn, D. (2011) *Critical Race Theory (CRT)* London: British Educational Research Association (available at http://www.bera.ac.uk/wp-content/uploads/2014/03/Critical-Race-Theory-CRT-.pdf).

StopWatch (2013) *StopWatch Submission to the Consultation on Police Powers to Stop* and Search (available at www.stop-watch.org/uploads/documents/StopWatch_consultation_final.pdf).

Ugwudike, P. (2015) *An Introduction to Critical Criminology*. Bristol: Policy Press.

Williams, P. and Clarke, B. (2016) *Dangerous Associations: Joint Enterprise, Gangs and Racism*. London: Centre for Crime and Justice Studies.

Young Review (2014) *Improving Outcomes for Young Black and/or Muslim Men in the Criminal Justice System*. London: BTEG, Clinks and Barrow Cadbury Trust.

Chapter 11

Acker, J. (1992) 'Gendering Organizational Theory' in Mills, A. and Tancred, P. (eds) *Gendering Organizational Analysis*. Thousand Oaks, CA: Sage.

Acker, J. (1990) 'Hierarchies, Jobs, Bodies: A Theory of Gendered Organizations' *Gender & Society* 4: 139–58.

Adler, F. (1977) 'The Interaction Between Women's Emancipation and Female Criminality: A Cross-Cultural Perspective' *International Journal of Criminologyand Penology* 5: 101–12.

Adler, F. (1975) *Sisters in Crime: The Rise of the New Female Criminal*. New York, NY: McGraw-Hill.

Baca Zinn, M. and Thornton Dill, B. (1996) 'Theorizing Difference from Multiracial Feminism' *Feminist Studies* 22: 321–31.

Balderston, S. (2013) 'Victimized Again? Intersectionality and Injustice in Disabled Women's Lives After Hate Crime and Rape' *Advances in Gender Research* 18: 17–51.

Ball, M. (2016) *Criminology and Queer Theory: Dangerous Bedfellows?* Basingstoke: Palgrave Macmillan.

Batchelor, S. (2009) 'Girls, Gangs and Violence: Assessing the Evidence' *Probation Journal* 56(4): 399–414.

Batchelor, S. (2005) '"Prove Me the Bam!" Victimisation and Agency in the Lives of Young Women Who Commit Violent Offences' *Probation Journal*, 52(4): 358–75.

Belknap, J. (2015) *The Invisible Woman: Gender, Crime, and Justice* (4th edn). Stanford, CT: Cengage Learning.

Belknap, J. (2001). *The Invisible Woman: Gender, Crime, and Justice*. Belmont, CA.: Wadsworth.

Belknap, J. and Holsinger, K. (2006) 'The Gendered Nature of Risk Factors for Delinquency' *Feminist Criminology* 1: 48–71.

Box, S. and Hale. C. (1983) 'Liberation and Female Criminality in England and Wales' *British Journal of Criminology* 23: 35–49.

Brownmiller, S. (1975) *Against Our Will: Men, Women and Rape*. New York: Simon and Schuster.

Burgess-Proctor, A. (2006) 'Intersection of Race, Class, Gender, and Crime: Future Directions for Feminist Criminology' *Feminist Criminology* 1: 27–47.

Burman, M. and Batchelor, S. (2009) 'Between Two Stools? Responding to Young Women Who Offend' *Youth Justice* 9(3): 270–85.

Butler, J. (1999) *Gender Trouble: Feminism and the Subversion of Identity*. New York: Routledge.

Butler, J. (1990) *Gender Trouble: Feminism and the Subversion of Identity*. New York: Routledge.

Cain, M. (1990a) 'Towards Transgression: New Directions in Feminist Criminology' *International Journal of the Sociology of Law* 18: 1–18.

Cain, M. (1990b) 'Realist Philosophy and Standpoint Epistemologies or Feminist Criminology as a Successor Science' in Gelsthorpe, L. and Morris, A. (eds) *Feminist Perspectives in Criminology*. Milton Keynes: Open University Press.

Cain, Maureen (1986) 'Realism, Feminism, Methodology, and Law', International *Journal of the Sociology of Law* 14: 255–67.

Carlen, P. (1988) *Women, Crime and Poverty*. Milton Keynes: Open University Press.

Carlen, P. (1983) *Women's Imprisonment*. London: Routledge and Kegan Paul.

Carrington, K. (2008) 'Critical Reflections in Feminist Criminologies' in Anthony, T. and Cunneen, C. (eds) *The Critical Criminology Companion*. Sydney: Hawkins Press.

Chesney-Lind, M. (1999) 'Media Misogyny: Demonizing 'Violent' Girls and Women' in Ferrel, J. and Websdale, N. (eds) *Making Trouble: Cultural Representations of Crime, Deviance and Control*. Chicago: Aldine Transaction

Chesney-Lind, M. (1988) 'Girls in Jail' *Crime and Delinquency*, 34: 150–68.

Chesney-Lind, M. and Karlene F. (2001) 'What About Feminism? Engendering Theory-Making in Criminology' in Paternoster, R. and Bachman, R. (eds) *Explaining Criminals and Crime*. Los Angeles: Roxbury.

Chesney-Lind, M. and Morash, M. (2013) 'Transformative Feminist Criminology: A Critical Re-thinking of a Discipline' *Critical Criminology* 21: 287–304.

Chesney-Lind, M. and Pasko, L. (2013) *The Female Offender: Girls, Women, and Crime*. Thousand Oaks, CA: Sage.

Chesney-Lind, M. and Pasko, L. (2004) *Girls, Women, and Crime*. Thousand Oaks, CA: Sage.

Chesney-Lind, M. and Shelden, R. G. (2004). *Girls, Delinquency, and Juvenile Justice*. Belmont, CA: West/Wadsworth.

Chigwada-Bailey, R. (1997) *Black Women's Experiences of Criminal Justice*. Winchester: Waterside Press.

Connell, R. (1995) *Masculinities*. Cambridge, UK: Polity.

Connell, R. (2000) *The Men and the Boys*. Cambridge: Polity.

Connell, R. and Messerschmidt, J. (2005) 'Hegemonic Masculinity: Rethinking the Concept' *Gender and Society* 19(2): 829–59.

Coy, M., Kelly, L., and Foord, J. (2008) *Map of Gaps: The Postcode Lottery of Violence against Women Support Services in Britain*. London: End Violence Against Women and EHRC.

Coyle, C. (2007) 'Feminism, Victimology and Domestic Violence', in Walklate, S. *Handbook on Victims and Victimology*. London: Sage.

Comack, E. (1999) 'Producing Feminist Knowledge: Lessons from Women in Trouble' *Theoretical Criminology* 3: 287–306.

Corston Report (2007) *Review of Women with Particular Vulnerabilities in the Criminal Justice System*. London: Home Office.

Crenshaw, K. W. (1994) 'Mapping the Margins: Intersectionality, Identity Politics, and Violence against Women of Colour', in Fineman, M. and Mykitiuk, R. (eds) *The Public Nature of Private Violence: The Discovery of Domestic Abuse*. New York: Routledge.

Crenshaw, K. 1989. 'Demarginalizing the Intersection of Race and Sex: A Black Feminist Critique of Antidiscrimination Doctrine, Feminist Theory and Antiracist Politics' *University of Chicago Legal Forum* 1989: 139–67.

Crew, B. K. (1991) 'Sex Differences in Patriarchy: Chivalry or Patriarchy?' *Justice Quarterly* 8: 59–83.

Curry, T., Lee, G., and Rodriguez, S. (2004) 'Does Victim Gender Increase Sentence Severity? Further Explorations of Gender Dynamics and Sentencing Outcomes' *Crime & Delinquency* 50(3): 319–43.

Dalton, K. (1961) 'Menstruation and Crime' *British Medical Journal* 2: 1743–52.

Daly, K. (2010) 'Feminist Perspectives in Criminology: A Review with Gen Y in Mind' in McLaughlin, E. and Newburn, T. (eds) *The Sage Handbook of Criminological Theory*. London: Sage.

Daly, Kathleen (2006) 'Feminist Thinking About Crime and Justice' in Henry, S. and Lanier, M. (eds) *The Essential Criminology Reader*. Boulder: Westview Press.

Daly, K. (1994) *Gender, Crime and Punishment*. New Haven: Yale University Press.

Daly, K. (1992) 'Women's Pathways to Felony Court: Feminist Theories of Lawbreaking and Problems of Representation' *Southern California Review of Law and Women's Studies*, 2: 11–52.

Daly, K. (1989). 'Rethinking judicial paternalism: Gender, work-family relations, and sentencing' *Gender & Society*, 3, 9–36.

Daly, K. (1987) 'Discrimination in the Criminal Courts: Family, Gender, and the Problem of Equal Treatment' *Social Forces* 66(1): 152–75.

Daly, K. and Chesney-Lind, M. (1988) 'Feminism and Criminology' *Justice Quarterly* 5: 497–538.

Davis, A. (1983) *Women, Race, and Class*. New York: Vintage.

Davis, K. (2008) 'Intersectionality as Buzzword: A Sociology of Science Perspective on What Makes a Feminist Theory Successful' *Feminist Theory* 9: 67–85.

Derrida, J. (1976) *Of Grammatology*. Baltimore, Md.: Johns Hopkins University Press.

Dobash, R. E. and Dobash, R. P. (2004) 'Women's violence to men in intimate relationships: Working on a puzzle' *British Journal of Criminology*, 44(3): 324–49.

Dobash, R.E. and Dobash, R.P. (1998) *Rethinking Violence against Women*. Thousand Oaks, CA: Sage Publications.

Dobash, R. E. and Dobash, R.P. (1992) *Women, Violence and Social Change*. London: Routledge.

Dobash, R. E. and Dobash, R. P. (1983) 'The Context Specific Approach', in Finkelhor, D. et al. (eds) *The Dark Side of Families*. Beverly Hills: Sage.

Dobash, R.E. and Dobash, R.P. (1979) *Violence Against Wives*. New York, Free Press.

Dobash, R. E. and Dobash, R. P. (1978) 'Wives: The "appropriate" victims of marital violence' *Victimology*, 2: 426–42.

Eaton, M. (1986) *Justice for Women? Family, Court and Social Control*. Milton Keynes: Open University Press.

Erez, E. (1992) 'Dangerous Men, Evil Women: Gender and Parole Decision-Making' *Justice Quarterly* 9: 105–26.

Farrington, D. and Morris, A. (1983) 'Sex, Sentencing and Reconviction' *British Journal of Criminology* 23(3): 229–48.

Flavin, J. (2001) 'Feminism for the Mainstream Criminologist' *Journal of Criminal Justice* 29(4), 271–85.

Flavin, J. and Artz, L. (2013) 'Understanding Women, Gender and Crime: Some Historical and International Developments' in Renzetti, C., Miller, S., and Gover, R. (eds) *Routledge International Handbook of Crime and Gender Studies*. London: Routledge.

Franklin, C. and Fearn, N. (2008) 'Gender, Race, and Formal Court Decision-Making Outcomes: Chivalry/Paternalism, Conflict Theory or Gender Conflict?' *Journal of Criminal Justice* 36: 279–90.

Gelsthorpe, L. (2004) 'Female Offending: A Theoretical Overview' in McIvor, G. (ed.) *Women Who Offend*. London: Jessica Kingsley.

Gelsthorpe, L. (2006) 'Women and Criminal Justice: Saying it Again, Again and Again' *Howard Journal of Criminal Justice* 45(4): 421–4.

Gelsthorpe, L. and Morris, A. (1988) 'Feminism and Criminology in Britain' *British Journal of Criminology* 28(2): 93–110.

Gilbert, P. R. (2002) 'Discourses of Female Violence and Societal Gender Stereotypes' *Violence Against Women* 8: 1271–300.

Hanmer, J. (1978). 'Violence and the Social Control of Women', in Littlejohn, G. et al. (eds) *Power and the State*. London: Croom Helm.

Harding, S. (2004) 'Introduction: Standpoint Theory as a Site of Political, Philosophic and Scientific Debate' in Harding, S. (ed.) *The Feminist Standpoint Theory Reader*. Abingdon: Routledge.

Harding, S. (1993) 'Rethinking Standpoint Epistemology: What is "Strong Objectivity"?' in Alcoff, L. and Potter, E. (eds) *Feminist Epistemologies*. London: Routledge.

Harding, S. (1991) '"Strong Objectivity" and Socially Situated Knowledge' in Harding, S. (ed.), *Whose Science? Whose Knowledge? Thinking from Women's Lives*. New York: Cornell University Press.

Harding, S. (1987) *Feminism and Methodology*. Milton Keynes: Open University Press.

Harding, S. (1986) *The Science Question in Feminism*. Milton Keynes: Open University Press.

Hartsock, N. (1987) 'The Feminist Standpoint: Developing the Ground for a Specifically Feminist Hstorical Materialism' in Harding, S. (ed.) *Feminism and Methodology: Social Science Issues*. Bloomington: Indiana University Press.

Hartmann, H. (1981) 'The Unhappy Marriage of Marxism and Feminism: Towards a More Progressive Union' in Lippit, V. (ed.) *Radical Political Economy: Explorations in Alternative Economic Analysis*. New York: M.E. Sharpe.

Heidensohn, F. (2012) 'The Future of Feminist Criminology' *Crime, Media and Culture*. 8: 123–34.

Heidensohn, F. (1996) *Women and Crime* (2nd edn). Basingstoke: Macmillan.

Heidensohn, F. (1968) 'The Deviance of Women: A Critique and an Enquiry' *British Journal of Sociology*. 19: 160–73

Heidensohn, F. M. (1985) *Women and Crime*. London: Macmillan and New York University Press.

Heidensohn, F. and Silvestri, M. (2012) 'Gender and Crime', in Maguire, M., Morgan, R., and Reiner, R. (eds) *The Oxford Handbook of Criminology* (5th edn). Oxford: Oxford University Press.

Her Majesty's Inspectorate of Constabulary (2014) *Everyone's Business: Improving the Police Response to Domestic Abuse*. https://www.justiceinspectorates.gov.uk/hmic/wp-content/uploads/2014/04/improving-the-police-response-to-domestic-abuse.pdf (accessed July 2014).

Hester, M. (2013) *From Report to Court: Rape Cases and the Criminal Justice System in the North East*, Centre for Gender and Violence Research, School for Policy Studies, University of Bristol and Northern Rock Foundation.

Home Office (2014) *Strengthening the Law on Domestic Abuse Consultation: Summary of Responses*. https://www.gov.uk/government/uploads/system/uploads/attachment_data/file/389002/StrengtheningLawDomesticAbuseResponses.pdf.

Hood, R. (1992) *Race and Sentencing: A Study in the Crown Court*. Oxford: Clarendon Press.

hooks, b. (1984) *Feminist theory: From margin to center*. Boston: South End.

hooks, b. (1981) *Ain't I a Woman: Black Women and Feminism*. Cambridge Massachusetts: South End Press.

Houston, C. (2014) 'How Feminist Theory became (Criminal Law): Tracing the Path to Mandatory Criminal Intervention in Domestic Violence Cases' *Michigan Journal of Gender and Law* 21(2): 221–72.

Howe, A. (1994) *Punish and Critique: Towards a Feminist Analysis of Penality*. London: Taylor and Francis.

Hull, G. T., Scott, P. B., and Smith, B. (eds) (1982) *All the Women Are White, All the Blacks Are Men, But Some of Us Are Brave: Black Women's Studies*. Old Westbury: Feminist Press.

Jauk, D. (2013) 'Gender Violence Revisited: Lessons from Violent Victimization of Transgender Identified Individual' *Sexualities* 16(7): 807–25.

Jeffries, S., Fletcher, G. J. O., and Newbold, G. (2003) 'Pathways to Sex-Based Differentiation in Criminal Court Sentencing' *Criminology* 41(2): 329–354.

Klein, D. and Kress, J. (1976) 'Any Woman's Blues: A Critical Overview of Women, Crime and the Criminal Justice System' *Crime and Social Justice* 5: 34.

Knight, C. and Wilson, K. (2016) *Lesbian, Gay, Bisexual and Trans People (LGBT) and the Criminal Justice System*. Basingstoke: Palgrave Macmillan.

Koyama, E. (2003) 'The Transfeminist Manifesto' in Dicker, R. and Piepmeier, A. (eds) *Catching a Wave: Reclaiming Feminism for a 21st Century*. Boston: Northwestern University Press.

Liebling, A., Maruna, S., and McAra, L. (eds) (2017) *The Oxford Handbook of Criminology* (6th edn). Oxford: Oxford University Press.

Lombroso, C. and Ferrero, W. (1895) *The Female Offender*. London: T. Fisher Unwin.

MacKinnon, C. (1989) *Toward a Feminist Theory of the State*. Cambridge, MA: Harvard University Press.

Maidment, M. (2006) 'Feminist Perspectives in Criminology' in DeKeseredey, W. and Perry, B. (eds) *Advancing Critical Criminology: Theory and Application.* Lanham, Maryland: Lexington Books.

Martin, J., Kautt, P., and Gelsthorpe, L. (2009) 'What Works for Women? A Comparison of Community-Based General Offending Programme Completion' *British Journal of Criminology* 49: 879–99.

Matczak, A., Hatzidimitriadou, E., and Lindsay, J. (2011) *Review of Domestic Violence Policies in England and Wales.* London: Kingston University and St George's, University of London.

Mawby, R. (1977) 'Sexual Discrimination and the Law' *Probation Journal* 24(2): 38–43.

Mawby, R. and Walklate, S. (1994) *Critical Victimology.* London: Sage.

Mellor, D. and Deering, R. (2010) 'Professional Response and Attitudes Toward Female-Perpetrated Child Sexual Abuse: A Study of Psychologists, Psychiatrists, Probationary Psychologists and Child Protection Workers' *Psychology, Crime and Law* 16(5): 415–38.

Messerschmidt, J. (1986) *Capitalism, Patriarchy, and Crime.* Totowa, NJ: Rowman and Littlefield.

Messerschmidt, J. (1993) *Masculinities and Crime.* Lanham, MD: Rowman and Littlefield.

Messerschmidt, J. and Tomsen, S. (2012) 'Masculinities' in DeKeseredy, W. and Dragiewicz, M. (eds) *Handbook of Critical Criminology.* Abingdon: Routledge.

Ministry of Justice (2014) *Statistics on Women in the Criminal Justice System 2013, A Ministry of Justice publication under Section 95 of the Criminal Justice Act1991.* Available at: https://www.gov.uk/government/statistics/women-and-the-criminal-justice-system-2

Mirrlees-Black, C. (1999) *Domestic Violence: Findings From a New British Crime Survey Self-Completion Questionnaire.* Home Office Research Study 191. London: Home Office Research, Development and Statistics Directorate.

Myhill, A. and Allen, J. (2002) *Rape and Sexual Assault of Women: Findings from the British Crime Survey.* Home Office Research Study, Findings No. 159. London: Home Office.

Naffine, N. (1997) *Feminism and Criminology.* Cambridge: Polity Press.

Nelson, E. (2014) 'If You Want to Convict a Domestic Violence Batterer, List Multiple Charges in the Police Report', Sage Open. http://sgo.sagepub.com/content/spsgo/4/1/2158244013517246.full.pdf.

Oakley, A. (1972) *Sex, Gender and Society.* London: Maurice Temple Smith.

Office for National Statistics (2014) *Chapter 4 - Intimate Personal Violence and Partner Abuse.* Available at: http://webarchive.nationalarchives.gov.uk/20160105160709/http://www.ons.gov.uk/ons/dcp171776_352362.pdf (accessed January 2017).

Pakso, L. and Chesney-Lind, M. (2004) *The Female Offender: Girls, Women, and Crime.* Thousand Oaks, CA: Sage.

Pearson, R. (1976) 'Women Defendants in Magistrates' Courts' *British Journal of Law and Society* 3: 265–73.

Pollak, O. (1961) *The Criminality of Women.* New York: Barnes.

Pollock, O. (1950) *The Criminality of Women.* Philadelphia: University of Pennsylvania Press.

Potter, H. (2006) 'An Argument for Black Feminist Criminology: Understanding African American Women's Experiences with Intimate Partner Abuse Using an Integrated Approach' *Feminist Criminology* 1: 106–24.

Rafter, N. (1990) *Partial Justice: Women, Prisons, and Social Control.* New Brunswick, NJ: Transaction.

Renzetti, C. (2012) 'Feminist Perspectives in Criminology' in DeKeseredy, W. and Dragiewicz., M. (eds) *The Routledge Handbook of Critical Criminology.* New York: Routledge.

Rodriguez, S., Curry, T., and Lee, G. (2006) 'Gender Differences in Criminal Sentencing: Do Effects Vary Across Violent, Property, and Drug Offenses?' *Social Science Quarterly* 87(2): 318–39.

Romain, D. and Freiburger, T. (2016) 'Chivalry Revisited: Gender, Race/Ethnicity, and Offense Type on Domestic Violence Charge Reduction' *Feminist Criminology* 11(2): 191–222.

Russell, D. (1975) *The Politics of Rape.* New York: Stein & Day.

Schwendinger, J. and Schwendinger, H. (1983) *Rape and Inequality.* Newbury Park, CA: Sage.

Seitz, T. (2005) 'The Wounds of Savagery: Negro Primitivism, Gender Parity, and the Execution of Rosanna Lightner Phillips' *Women and Criminal Justice* 16: 29–64.

Silvestri, M. and Crowther-Dowey, C. (2008) *Gender and Crime.* London: Sage publications.

Simon, R. (1975) *Women and Crime, and Criminology?* Lexington: Lexington Books.

Smart, C. (1976) *Women, Crime and Criminology.* Abingdon: Routledge.

Smart, C. (1997) *Women, Crime and Criminology: A Feminist Critique,* London: Routledge.

Smart, C. (1995) *Law, Crime and Sexuality.* London: Sage Publications.

Smart, C. (1990a) 'Law's Power, the Sexed Body and Feminist Discourse' *Journal of Law and Society* 17: 194–210.

Smart, C. (1990b) 'Feminist Approaches to Criminology, or Postmodern Woman Meets Atavistic Man' in Gelsthorpe, L. and Morris, A. (eds) *Feminist Perspectives in Criminology.* Philadelphia: Open University Press.

Smart, C. (1977) 'Criminological Theory: Its Ideology and Implications Concerning Women' *British Journal of Sociology* 28(1): 89–100.

Smith, D. (1987)*The Everyday World as Problematic: A Feminist Sociology.* Lebanon, New England: Northeastern University Press.

Smith, O. and Skinner, T. (2012) 'Observing Court Responses to Victims of Rape and Sexual Assault' *Feminist Criminology* 7(4): 298–326.

Stanko, E. (1990) *Everyday Violence.* Pandora: London. Steffensmeier, D. (1980) 'Trends in Female Delinquency' *Criminology* 18: 62–85.

Sudbury, J. (2005) 'Feminist Critiques, Transnational Landscapes, Abolitionist Visions' in Subdbury, J. (ed.) *Global Lockdown: Race, Gender, and the Prison-Industrial Complex.* New York: Routledge.

Walby, S. (1990) *Theorizing Patriarchy.* Cambridge: Basil Blackwell.

Walby, S. and Myhill, A. (2001) 'New Survey Methodologies in Researching Violence Against Women' *British Journal of Criminology* 41(3): 502.

Walby, S. and Allen, J. (2004) *Domestic violence, sexual assault and stalking: Findings from the British Crime Survey.* Home Office Research Study 276. London: Home Office Research, Development and Statistics Directorate.

Walklate S. (1991). *Victims, Crime Prevention and Social Control,* in Reiner, R. and Cross, M. (eds), *Beyond Law and Order: Criminal Justice Policy and Politics into the 1990s.* Basingstoke: Macmillan.

Westmarland, N. (2015). *Violence against Women. Criminological Perspectives on Men's Violences.* Abingdon: Routledge.

Wolff, K. and Cokely, C. (2007) '"To Protect and to Serve?": An Exploration of Police Conduct in Relation to the Gay, Lesbian, Bisexual, and Transgender Community' *Sexuality and Culture* 11(2): 1–23.

Worrall, A. (2004) 'Twisted Sisters and the New Penology: The Social Construction of Violent Girls' in Alder, C. and Worrall, A. (eds) *Girls' Violence: Myths and Realities.* Albany: State University of New York Press.

Worrall, A. (1981) 'Out of Place: Female Offenders in Court' *Probation Journal* 28: 90–3.

Young, A. (1996) *Imagining Crime.* London: Sage

Chapter 12

Beccaria, C. (1764) *On Crimes and Punishment (Dei Delitti e Delle Pene)* http://www.thefederalistpapers.org/wp-content/uploads/2013/01/Cesare-Beccaria-On-Crimes-and-Punishment.pdf.

Bentham, J. (1789 reprinted 1907) *An Introduction to the Principles of Morals and Legislation*. Oxford: Clarendon.

Clarke R. (1997) *Situational Crime Prevention: Successful Case Studies* (2nd edn). New York: Harrow and Heston.

Cohen, L. and Felson, M. (1979) 'Social Change and Crime Rate Trends: A Routine Activity Approach' *American Sociological Review* 44(4): 588–608.

Coleman, A. (1990) *Utopia on Trial* (2nd edn). London: Hilary Shipman.

Cornish, D. and Clarke, R. (1986) *The Reasoning Criminal: Rational Choice Perspectives on Offending*. New York: Springer-Verlag.

Cornish, D. and Clarke R. (2006) 'The Rational Choice Perspective' in Henry, S. and Lanier, M. (eds) *The Essential Criminology Reader*. Boulder, CO: Westview Press.

Cornish, D. and Clarke, R. (2014) *The Reasoning Criminal: Rational Choice Perspectives on Offending*. London: Transaction Publishers.

Garland, D. (2000) 'Ideas, Institutions and Situational Crime Prevention' in von Hirsch, A., Garland, D., and Wakefield, A. (eds) *Ethical and Social Perspectives on Situational Crime Prevention*. Oxford: Hart Publishing.

Locke, J. (1690) *Second Treatise of Civil Government*. Found at: https://www.marxists.org/reference/subject/politics/locke/ch08.htm

Newburn, T. (2009) *Key Readings in Criminology*. Abingdon: Willan Publishing.

Newman, O. (1972) *Defensible Space: People and Design in the Violent City* London: Architectural Press.

Pease, K. (1997) 'Crime Prevention' in Maguire, M., Morgan, R. and Reiner, R. (eds) *The Oxford Handbook of Criminology* (2nd edn). Oxford: Oxford University Press.

Popper, K. (1959) *The Logic of Scientific Discovery*. English translation of *Logikder Forschung* (1935). London: Hutchinson.

Radzinowicz, L. (1966) *Ideology and Crime: A Study of Crime in its Social and Historical Context*. London: Heinemann Educational.

Tonry, M. and Morris, N. (1985) *Crime and Justice: A Review of Research*. Chicago: University of Chicago Press.

Chapter 13

Aichhorn, A. (1936) *Wayward Youth*. New York: Viking Press.

Anda, R and Felitti. V. (1997) *Adverse Childhood Experiences*. San Diego: Ace Study.

Bandura, A., Ross, D., and Ross, S. (1961), 'Transmission of Aggression through Imitation of Aggressive Models' *Journal of Abnormal and Social Psychology* 63(3): 575–82.

Baumeister, R. (1982), 'Reducing the Biasing Effect of Perpetrator Attractiveness in Jury Simulation', *Personal and Social Psychology Bulletin* 8(2): 286–92.

Berry, D. (1988) 'Facial Maturity and the Attribution of Legal Responsibility' *Personality and Social Psychology Bulletin* 14(1): 23–33.

Bowling, B. and Phillips, C. (2002) *Racism, Crime and Justice*. London: Longman.

Dabbs, J. and Dabbs M. (2000) *Heroes, Rogues and Lovers: Testosterone and Behaviour*. New York: McGraw-Hill.

Dube, S., Felitti, V., Dong, M., Chapman, D., Giles, W., and Anda, R. (2003) 'Childhood Abuse, Neglect, and Household Dysfunction and the Risk of Illicit Drug Use: The Adverse Childhood Experiences Study' *Pediatrics* 111(3): 564–72.

Dugdale, R. (1877) 'The Jukes: A Study in Crime, Pauperism, Disease and Heredity' *Buck v. Bell Documents* Paper 1. http://readingroom.law.gsu.edu/buckvbell/1

Eberhardt, J., Davies, P., Purdie-Vaughns, V., and Johnson, S. (2006), 'Looking Deathworthy: Perceived Stereotypicality of Black Defendants Predicts Capital-Sentencing Outcomes' *Psychological Science* 17: 383–86.

Ellis, L. and Coontz, P. (1990) 'Androgens, Brain Functioning and Criminality: The Neurohormonal Foundations of Antisociality' in Ellis, L. and Hoffman, H. (eds) *Crime in Biological, Social and Moral Contexts*. New York: Praeger.

Eysenck, H. (1959) *Manual of the Maudsley Personality Inventory*. London: UCL Press.

Eysenck, H. (1977) *Crime and Personality* (3rd edn). London: Routledge & Kegan Paul.

Eysenck, H. (1987) 'The Place of Anxiety and Impulsivity in a Dimensional Framework' *Journal of Research in Personality* 21: 489–92.

Eysenck, H. and Gudjonsson, G. (1989) *The Causes and Cures of Criminality*. New York: Plenum Press.

Farrington, D. (1994) 'Introduction' in Farrington, D. (ed.) *Psychological Explanations of Crime*. Aldershot: Dartmouth.

Fishbein, D. (2001) *Biobehavioural Perspectives in Criminology*. Belmont, CA: Wadsworth Publishing.

Freud, S. transl. by Joan Riviere (1935) *A General Introduction to Psycho-Analysis*. New York: Liveright.

Galton, F. (1883 republished in 1907 and 1973) *Inquiries into Human Faculty and its Development*. AMS Press: New York.

Goddard, H. (1912) *The Kallikak Family: A Study in the Heredity of Feeble-mindedness*. New York: Macmillan.

Goring, C. (1913) *The English Convict: A Statistical Study*. London: HMSO.

Hollin, C. (1995) *Psychology and Crime: An Introduction to Criminological Psychology*. London: Routledge.

Hollin, C. (1992) *Criminal Behaviour: A Psychological Approach to Explanation and Prevention*. London: Falmer Press.

Hollin, C. (2002) 'Criminological Psychology' in M. Maguire, R. Morgan and R. Reiner (eds) *The Oxford Handbook of Criminology* (4th edn). Oxford: Clarendon Press.

Jones, S. (1993) *The Language of Genes*. London: Harper Collins.

Joseph, J. (2000) 'Not in their Genes: A Critical View of the Genetics of Attention-Deficit Hyperactivity Disorder' *Developmental Review* 20: 539–67.

Kline, P. (1984) *Psychology and Freudian Theory*. London: Methuen.

Kolb, B. (2009) 'Brain and Behavioural Plasticity in the Developing Brain: Neuroscience and Public Policy' *Paediatric Child Health* 14(10): 651–52.

Kolla, N. J., Malcolm, C., Attard, S., Arenovich, T., Blackwood, N., and Hodgins, S. (2013) 'Childhood Maltreatment and Aggressive Behaviour in Violent Offenders with Psychopathy' *Canadian Journal of Psychiatry* 58(8): 487–94.

Loehlin, J. (1992) *Genes and Environment in Personality Development*. Thousand Oaks, CA: Sage.

Lombroso, C. first published (1876), 5th and final edn (1897), *L'Uomo Delinquente*, Torino: Bocca.

Lombroso, C. (1906, first published in 1899), *Crime: Causes et Remèdes* (2nd edn). Paris: Alcan.

McAra, L. and McVie, S. (2017) 'Developmental Criminology' in Maguire, M., Morgan, R., and Reiner, R. (eds) *The Oxford Handbook of Criminology* (5th edn). Oxford: Oxford University Press.

McGurk, B. and McDougall, C. (1981), 'A New Approach to Eysenck's Theory of Criminality' *Personality and Individual Differences* 2: 338.

Morrison, W. (2004) 'Lombroso and the Birth of Criminological Positivism: Scientific Mastery or Cultural Artifice?' in Ferrell, J., Hayward, K., Morrison, W., and Presdee, M. (eds) *Cultural Criminology Unleashed*. London: Glasshouse Press.

Olwens, D. (1987) 'Testosterone and Adrenalin: Aggressive and Antisocial Behaviour in Normal Adolescent Males' in Mednick, S., Moffitt, T. and Stack, S. (eds) *The Causes of Crime: New Biological Approaches*. Cambridge: Cambridge University Press.

Palmer E. (2003) *Offending Behaviour: Moral Reasoning, Criminal Conduct and the Rehabilitation of Offenders*. Cullompton: Willan.

Pavlov, I. (1927) *Conditioned Reflexes*. Oxford: Oxford University Press.

Pollak, S., Cicchetti, D., and Klorman, R. (1998) 'Stress, Memory, and Emotion: Developmental Considerations from the Study of Child Maltreatment' *Development and Psychopathology* 10: 811–28.

Pollak, S. and Tolley-Schell, S. (2003) 'Selective Attention to Facial Emotion in Physically Abused Children' *Journal of Abnormal Psychology* 112(3): 323–38.

Raine, A. (1993) *The Psychopathology of Crime*. San Diego, CA: Academic Press.

Reavis, J., Looman, J., Franco, K., and Rojas, B. (2013) 'Adverse Childhood Experiences and Adult Criminality: How Long Must We Live before We Possess Our Own Lives?' *The Permanente Journal* 17(2): 44–8.

Ridley, M. (2004) *Evolution* (3rd edn). Cambridge, MA: Blackwell.

Rock, P. (2007) 'Cesare Lombroso as a Signal Criminologist' *Criminology and Criminal Justice* 7(2): 117–34.

Rowe, D. and Farrington, D. (1997) 'The Familial Transmission of Criminal Convictions' *Criminology* 35: 177.

Sampson, R. and Laub, J. (1991) 'The Sutherland-Glueck Debate: On the Sociology of Criminological Knowledge.' *American Journal of Sociology* 96: 1402–1440.

Sampson, R. and Laub, J. (2005) 'A Life Course View of the Development of Crime', *The Annals* 602: 12–45.

Schalling, D. (1987) 'Personality Correlates of Plasma Testosterone Levels in Young Delinquents: An example of Person-Situation Interaction' in Mednick, A., Moffitt, T., and Stack, S. (eds) *The Causes of Crime: New Biological Approaches*. Cambridge: Cambridge University Press.

Sheldon, W. (1949) *Varieties of Delinquent Youth*. New York and London: Harper.

Skinner, B. (1938) *The Behaviour of Organisms*. New York: Appleton-Century-Crofts.

Toates, F. (2007) *Biological Psychology* (2nd edn). Harlow: Pearson Education Ltd.

Vennard, J. and Hedderman, C. (1998), 'Effective Treatment with Offenders' in Goldblatt, P. and Lewis, C. (eds) *Reducing Offending: An Assessment of Research Evidence on Ways of Dealing with Offending Behaviour*. Home Office Research Study 187, London: Home Office Research and Statistics Directorate.

Chapter 14

Auletta, K. (1982) *The Underclass*. New York, NY: Random House.

Bauman, Z. (1994) *Alone Again: Ethics After Certainty*. London: Demos.

Bauman, Z. (2001) *The Individualised Society*. Cambridge: Polity Press.

BBC News (2009) 'Euthanasia: A Continent Divided' Wednesday 11 February 2009. http://news.bbc.co.uk/1/hi/world/europe/7322520.stm

Box, S. (1981) *Deviance Reality and Society* (2nd edn). London: Holt, Rinehart and Winston.

Box, S. (1983) *Power, Crime and Mystification*. London: Tavistock Publications.

Bradford, V. and Holt, G. (2013) 'Google, Amazon, Starbucks: The Rise of "Tax Shaming"'. BBC News Magazine. 21 May 2013. http://www.bbc.co.uk/news/magazine-20560359

Braithwaite, J. (1988) *Crime, Shame and Reintegration*, Cambridge: Cambridge University Press.

Burney, E. (2009) *Making People Behave: Anti-Social Behaviour, politics and policy*. Cullompton: Willan.

Campbell, P. (2014) 'Anger as Starbucks Boss Says: We may not pay UK tax for up to three years' *Daily Mail*. Mail Online 1 December 2014 http://www.dailymail.co.uk/news/article-2856284/Starbucks-chief-reveals-coffee-giant-not-pay-normal-tax-THREE-YEARS.html

Cohen, A. (1955) *Delinquent Boys: The Culture of the Gang*. New York: Free Press.

Cohen, A. (1966) *Deviance and Control*. Englewood Cliffs, NJ: Prentice-Hall.

Clarke, K. (2011) *Punish the feral rioters, but address our social deficit too*. Available at: https://www.theguardian.com/commentisfree/2011/sep/05/punishment-rioters-help.

Cloward, R. and Ohlin, L. (1960) *Delinquency and Opportunity: A Theory of Delinquent Gangs*. New York: Free Press.

Croall, H. (2001) *Understanding White Collar Crime*. Buckingham: Open University Press.

Cullen, S. and Messner, F. (2007) 'The Making of *Criminology Revisited*: An Oral History of Merton's Anomie Paradigm' *Theoretical Criminology* 11(1): 5–37.

Davis, K. (1971) 'Prostitution' in Merton, R. and Nisbet, R. (eds) *Contemporary Social Problems* (3rd edn). New York: Harcourt Brace Jovanovich.

Durkheim, É. (1895) *The Rules of Sociological Method*. Reprinted and edited in 2014 by S. Lukes (ed.) (translated by W.D. Halls) in an edition entitled *Émile Durkheim: The Rules of Sociological Method and Selected Texts on Sociology and its Method*. New York: Free Press.

Durkheim, É (1897) (reprinted 1970) *Suicide*. London: Routledge and Kegan Paul

Durkheim, É. (1938) *The Rules of Sociological Method (1895)*. Chicago, Ill: University of Chicago Press.

Dutton, K. and McNab, A. (2014) *The Psychopath's Guide to Success: How to Use Your Inner Psychopath to Get the Most Out of Life*. London: Transworld Publishers.

Engels, F. (1844) *Outlines of a Critique of Political Economy*. (English translation in Struik, (1970) 197–226).

Erikson, K. (1966) *Wayward Puritans: A Study in the Sociology of Deviance*. New York: John Wiley and Sons.

Fisse, B. and Braithwaite, J. (1993) *Corporations, Crime and Accountability*. Cambridge: Cambridge University Press.

Foucault, M. (1975) *Discipline and Punish: The Birth of the Prison*. London: Penguin Books.

Galbraith, J. (1983) *The Anatomy of Power*. London: Houghton Mifflin.

Giles, H., Noels, K., Williams, A., Ota, H., Lim, T-S., Ng, S., Ryan, E., and Somera, L. (2003) 'Intergenerational Communication across Cultures: Young People's Perceptions of Conversations with Family Elders, Non-family Elders and Same-age Peers.' *Journal of Cross-Cultural Gerontology* 18: 1–32.

Guardian and LSE (2012) *Reading the Riot: Investigating England's Summer of Disorder*. London: The Guardian and LSE. http://eprints.lse.ac.uk/46297/1/Reading%20the%20riots(published).pdf.

Gunter, A. (2008) 'Growing up Bad: Black Youth, 'Road' Culture and Badness in an East London Neighbourhood' *Crime, Media and Culture* 4(3): 349–66.

Jones, D. (1982) *Crime, Protest, Community and Police in Nineteenth Century Britain*. London: Routledge & Kegan Paul.

McCarthy, B. (1996) 'The Attitudes and Actions of Others: Tutelage and Sutherland's Theory of Differential Association' *British Journal of Criminology* 36(1): 138.

Matza, D. (1961) 'Subterranean Traditions of Youth' *Annals of the American Academy of Political and Social Science* 338.

Matza, D. (1964) *Delinquency and Drift*. London: Wiley.

Matza, D. (1969), *Becoming Deviant*. New Jersey: Prentice Hall.

Matza, D. and Sykes, G. (1961) 'Juvenile Delinquency and Subterranean Values' *American Sociological Review*. 26(5): 712–19.

Mayhew (1850) *London Labour and the London Poor*. London: William Kimber.

Merton, R. (1938) 'Social Structure and Anomie' *American Sociological Review* 3(5): 672–82.

Merton, R. (1949) *Social Theory and Social Structure*. New York: Free Press.

Merton, R. (1957) 'Priorities in Scientific Discovery: A Chapter in the Sociology of Science' *American Sociological Review* 22(6): 635–59.

Murray, C. (1984) *Losing Ground: American Social Policy 1950–1980*. New York: Basic Books.

Murray, C. (1990) *The Emerging British Underclass*. London: IEA Health and Welfare Unit.

Murray, C. (2001) 'Underclass + 10', in CIVITAS *Underclass + 10: Charles Murray and the British Underclass 1990–2000*, London: The Institute for the Study of Civil Society (http://www.civitas.org.uk/pdf/cs10.pdf).

Park, R. (1929) 'The City as a Social Laboratory' in Smith, T. and White, L. (eds) *Chicago: An Experiment in Social Science Research*. Chicago: Chicago University Press.

Phillips, D. (1977) *Crime and Authority in Victorian England*. London: Croom Helm.

Purdy, D. with Paul, G. (2010) *It's Not Because I Want to Die*. London: Harper True.

Runciman, W. (1990) 'How Many Classes are there in Contemporary British Society?' *Sociology* 23(3): 377–96.

Sampson, R. and Groves, W. (1989) 'Community Structure and Crime: Testing Social-Disorganization Theory' *American Journal of Sociology* 94: 774–802.

Schlossman, S., Zellerma, G., and Shavelson, R., with Sedlak, M. and Cobb, J. (1984) *Delinquency Prevention in South Chicago: A Fifty Year Assessment of the Chicago Area Project*. Santa Monica, CA: RAND.

Slapper, G. and Tombs, S. (1999) *Corporate Crime*. Harlow: Longman.

Squires, P. and Stephen, D. (2005) *Rougher Justice: Young People and Anti-Social Behaviour*. Cullompton: Willan.

Squires, P. (2006) 'New Labour and the Politics of Anti-social Behaviour' *Critical Social Policy* 26(1): 144–68.

Sutherland, E. (1939a) *The White Collar Criminal*. Speech to the American Sociological Association.

Sutherland, E. (1939b) *Principles of Criminology* (3rd edn). Philadelphia: Lippincott.

Sutherland, E. (1949) *White Collar Crime*. New York: Holt, Rinehart and Wilson.

Sykes, G. and Matza, D. (1957) 'Techniques of Neutralisation: A Theory of Delinquency' *American Sociological Review* 22(6): 664–70.

Taylor, I. (1999) *Crime in Context: A Critical Criminology of Market Societies*. Cambridge: Polity Press.

Tobias, J. (1972) *Crime and Industrial Society in the Nineteenth Century*. Harmondsworth: Penguin Books.

Wheeler, B. (2012) *The Slow Death of Prohibition*. BBC News Washington. 21 March 2012 (http://www.bbc.co.uk/news/magazine-17291978)

Young, J. (1999) *The Exclusive Society: Social Exclusion, Crime and Difference in Late Modernity*. London: Sage.

Young, J. (2002) 'Crime and Social Exclusion' in Maguire, M., Morgan, R. and Reiner, R. (eds) *The Oxford Handbook of Criminology* (3rd edn). Oxford: Oxford University Press.

Young, J. (2007) *The Vertigo of Late Modernity*. London: Sage.

Chapter 15

Becker, H. (1997 [1963]) *Outsiders: Studies in the Sociology of Deviance*. New York: Simon and Schuster.

Chambliss, W. (1975) 'Towards a Political Economy of Crime' *Theory and Society* (2): 149–70.

Connell, R. (1995) *Masculinities*. Cambridge, Polity Press.

Corston, J. (2007) *The Corston Report: A Review of Women with Particular Vulnerabilities in the Criminal Justice System*. London: Home Office.

DeKeseredy, W. and Dragiewicz, M. (eds) (2011) *The Routledge Handbook of Critical Criminology*. London: Routledge.

Lemert, E. (1951) *Social Pathology*. New York: McGraw-Hill.

Lemert, E. (1967) *Human Deviance, Social Problems and Social Control*. Engelwood Cliffs, NJ: Prentice Hall.

Lewin, K. (1952). *Field Theory in Social Science: Selected Theoretical Papers by Kurt Lewin*. London: Tavistock.

Lombrosso, C. and Ferrero, G. (1895) *The Female Offender*. London: Fisher Unwin.

McDougall, E. (1999) *A Wicked Fist: A True Story of Prison and Freedom*. Glasgow: Wild Goose Publications.

Mead, G. (1934) *Mind, Self and Society*. Chicago: University of Chicago Press.

Muncie, J. (2015) *Youth and Crime* (4th edn). London: Sage.

Quinney, R. (1974) *Critique of Legal Order*. Boston: Little, Brown.

Radzinowicz, L. (1999) *Adventures in Criminology*. London: Routledge.

Schur, E. (1973) *Radical Non-Intervention: Re-thinking the Delinquency Problem*. Engelwood Cliffs, NJ: Prentice Hall.

Smart, C. (2014 [1976]) *Women and Crime: A Feminist Critique*. London: Routledge.

Smart, C. (1995) *Law, Crime and Sexuality. Essays in Feminism*. London: Sage.

Tannenbaum, F. (1938) *Crime and the Community*. New York: Columbia University Press.

Taylor, I. , Walton, P. and Young, J. (2013 [1973]) *The New Criminology; For a Social Theory of Deviance (40th Anniversary Edition)*. London: Routledge.

Tomsen, S. and Messerschmidt, J. (2011) 'Masculinities' in DeKeseredy, W. and Dragiewicz, M. (eds) *The Routledge Handbook of Critical Criminology*, New York & London: Routledge.

Ugwudike, P. (2015) *An Introduction to Critical Criminology*. Bristol: Policy Press.

Viding, E., Blair, R., Moffit, T., and Plomin, R. (2005) 'Evidence for Substantial Genetic Risk for Psychopathy in 7-year olds' *Journal of Child Psychology and Psychiatry* 46: 592–97.

Wollstonecraft, M. (2009 [1792]) A *Vindication of the Rights of Women*. Oxford: Oxford University Press.

Young, J. (2011) *The Criminological Imagination*. Cambridge: Polity Press.

Chapter 16

Aresti, A., Darke. S., and Manlow, D. (2015) 'Bridging the Gap': Giving Public Voice to Prisoners and Former Prisoners through Research Activism' *Prisons Service Journal* 224: 3–14.

Becker, H.S. (1998) *Tricks of the Trade: How to Think about Your Research While You're Doing It*. Chicago: University of Chicago Press.

DeKeseredy, W. and Dragiewicz, M. (eds) (2011) *The Routledge Handbook of Critical Criminology*. London: Routledge.

Earle, R. (2016) *Convict Criminology: Inside and Out*. Bristol: Policy Press.

Ferrell, J., Hayward, K., and Young, J. (2015) *Cultural Criminology: An Invitation* (2nd edn). London: Sage.

Hall, S. and Jefferson, T. (2006 [1976]) *Resistance through Rituals: Youth subcultures in post-war Britain* (2nd edn). London: Routledge.

Hillyard, P., Pantazis, C., Tombs, S., and Gordon, D. (eds) (2004) *Beyond Criminology; Taking Harm Seriously*. London: Pluto Press.

Hillyard, P. and Tombs, S. (2004) *Beyond Criminology: Taking Harm Seriously*. London: Pluto Press.

Katz, J. (1990) *The Seduction of Crime: The Moral and Sensual Attractions of Doing Evil*. New York: Basic Books.

Lea, J. (1998) 'Criminology and Postmodernity' in Walton, P. and Young, J. (eds) *The New Criminology Revisited*. Basingstoke: Palgrave Macmillan.

McRobbie, A. (2010) *Feminism and Youth Culture* (2nd edn). London: Palgrave Macmillan.

Muncie, J. (2015) *Youth and Crime* (4th edn). London: Sage.

Pressdee, M. (2000) *Cultural Criminology and the Carnival of Crime*. London: Routledge.

Ross, I. and Richards, S. (2003) *Convict Criminology*. Belmont, CA: Wadsworth.

Ross, J., Darke, S., Aresti, A., Newbold, G., and Earle, R. (2014) 'Developing Convict Criminology Beyond North America' *International Criminal Justice Review* 24(2): 121–33.

Scraton, P. (2016) *Hillsborough: The Truth*. Edinburgh: Mainstream Publishing.

Smith, A. (2008) *Wealth of Nations: A Selected Edition*. Oxford: Oxford University Press.

South, N. and Brisman, A. (eds) (2014) *Routledge International Handbook of Green Criminology*. London: Routledge.

Tombs, S. and Whyte, D. (2007) *Safety Crimes*. Cullompton: Willan.

Ugwudike, P. (2015) *An Introduction to Critical Criminology*. Bristol: Policy Press.

Young, J. (1999) *The Exclusive Society: Social Exclusion, Crime and Difference in Late Modernity*. Thousand Oaks: Sage Publications.

Young, J. (2003) 'Merton with Energy, Katz with Structure: The Sociology of Vindictiveness and the Criminology of Transgression' *Theoretical Criminology* 7(3): 389–414.

Young, J. (2007) *The Vertigo of Late Modernity*. London: Sage.

Chapter 17

Bottoms, A. (2012) 'Developing Socio-Spatial Criminology' in Maguire, M., Rodney Morgan, R. and Reiner R. (eds) *The Oxford Handbook of Criminology* (5th edn). Oxford: Oxford University Press.

Crawford, A., Jones, T., Woodhouse, T., and Young, J. (1990) *Second Islington Crime Survey*. Middlesex: Middlesex Polytechnic.

Delisi, M. (2010) 'James Q. Wilson' in Hayward, K., Maruna, S., and Mooney, J. (eds) *Fifty Key Thinkers in Criminology*. London: Routledge.

Downes, D. and Morgan, R. (2012) 'No Turning Back: The Politics of Law and Order into the Millennium' in Maguire, M., Morgan, R., and Reiner, R. (eds) *The Oxford Handbook of Criminology* (5th edn). Oxford: Oxford University Press.

Downes, D. and Morgan, R. (2006) 'No Turning Back: The Politics of Law and Order into the Millennium' in Maguire, M., Morgan, R., and Reiner, R. (eds) *The Oxford Handbook of Criminology* (4th edn). Oxford: Oxford University Press.

Downes, D. and Morgan, R. (2002) 'The Skeletons in the Cupboard: The Politics of Law and Order at the Turn of the Millennium' in Maguire, M., Morgan, R., and Reiner, R. (eds) *The Oxford Handbook of Criminology* (3rd edn). Oxford: Oxford University Press.

Downes, D. and Morgan, R. (1997) 'Dumping the Hostages to Fortune: The Politics of Law and Order in Post War Britain' in Maguire, M., Morgan, R., and Reiner, R. (eds) *The Oxford Handbook of Criminology* (2nd edn). Oxford: Oxford University Press.

Downes, D. and Morgan, R. (1994) 'Hostages to Fortune: The Politics of Law and Order in Post War Britain' in Maguire, M., Morgan, R., and Reiner, R. (eds) *The Oxford Handbook of Criminology*. Oxford: Oxford University Press.

Evans, G. and Norris, P. (eds) (1999) *Critical Elections: British Parties and Voters in Long-term Perspective*. London: Sage.

Gilroy, P. and Sim, J. (1987) 'Law, Order and the State of the Left' in Scraton, P. (ed.) *Law, Order and the Authoritarian State*. Buckingham: Open University.

Hayward, K. and Yar, M. (2006) 'The 'Chav' Phenomenon: Consumption, Media and the Construction of a New Underclass' *Crime, Media, Culture* 2(1): 9–28.

Herrnstein, R. and Murray, C. (1994) *The Bell Curve*. New York: Basic Books.

Hughes, G. and Lewis, G. (1988) *Unsettling Welfare: The Reconstruction of Social Policy*. London: Routledge.

Jones, T., Maclean, B., and Young, J. (1986) *The Islington Crime Survey*. Aldershot: Gower.

Kelling, G. and Wilson, J. G. (1982) 'Broken Windows' *The Atlantic Monthly*, 249(3): 29–38

Lea, J. and Young, J. (1984) *What is to Be Done About Law and Order?* Harmondsworth: Penguin Books.

Levitas, R. (2005) *The Inclusive Society? Social Inclusion and New Labour* (2nd edn). London: Macmillan.

MacDonald, R. (ed) (1997) *Youth, The 'Underclass' and Social Exclusion*. London: Routledge.

McLaughlin, J. and Muncie, J. (2013) *Criminological Perspectives: Essential Readings* (3rd edn). London: Sage.

Mayhew, H. (1861) *London Labour and London Poor, Vol.1*. London: Griffin, Bohn.

Mooney, J. (2000) *Gender, Violence and the Social Order*. New York: Palgrave.

Mitford, N. (1959) *Noblesse Oblige: An Enquiry into the Identifiable Characteristics of the English Aristocracy*. London: Penguin Books.

Muncie, J. (2015) *Youth and Crime* (4th edn). London: Sage.

Murray, C. (1984) *Losing Ground*. New York: Basic Books.

Murray, C. (1990) *The Emerging Underclass*. London: Institute of Economic Affairs.

Murray, C. (1994) *Underclass: The Crisis Deepens*. London, Institute of Economic Affairs.

Platt, T. and Takagi, P. (1977) 'Intellectuals for Law and Order: A Critique of New Realists' *Crime and Social Justice* 5(3) 8: 1–16

Rodger, J. (2008) 'The Criminalisation of Social Policy' *Criminal Justice Matters* 74(1): 18–19.

Taylor, I., Walton, I., and Young, J. (1973) *The New Criminology: For a Social Theory of Deviance*. London: Routledge and Kegan Paul.

Wilson, J. (1975) *Thinking About Crime*. New York: Vintage.

Wilson, J. and Herrnstein, R. (1985) *Crime and Human Nature*. New York: Simon and Schuster.

Young, J. (2007) *The Vertigo of Late Modernity*, London: Sage.

Young, J. (2003) 'Merton with Energy, Katz with Structure: The Sociology of Vindictiveness and the Criminology of Transgression' *Theoretical Criminology* 7(3): 389–414.

Young, J. (1999) *The Exclusive Society: Social Exclusion, Crime and Difference in Late Modernity*. London: Sage.

Young, J. (1997) 'Left Realist Criminology; Radical in its analysis, realist in its policy' in Maguire, M., Morgan, R, and Reiner, R. (eds) *The Oxford Handbook of Criminology* (2nd edn). Oxford: Oxford University Press.

Young, J. (1990) 'Asking Questions of Left Realism' *Critical Criminologist* 2(2): 1–2, 10.

Young, J. (1986) 'The Failure of Criminology: The Need for a Radical Realism' in Young, J. and Matthews, R. (eds) *Confronting Crime*. London: Sage.

Chapter 18

Akers, R. and Sellers, C. (2013) *Criminological Theories: Introduction, Evaluation, Application*. Oxford: Oxford University Press.

Agnew, R. (2011) *Towards a Unified Criminology. Integrating Assumptions About Crime*. New York: NYU.

Andrews, J. and Bonta, D. (2010) *The Psychology of Criminal Conduct*. Newark: Matthew Bender.

Arsenault, L., Tremblay, R.E., Boulerice, B., and Saucier, J. (2002) 'Obstetrical Complications and Violent Delinquency: Testing Two Developmental Pathways' *Child Development* 73(2): 496–508.

Baker, K., Jones, S., Roberts, C., and Merrington, S. (2005) *Further Development of Asset*. London: Youth Justice Board.

Bates, K., Bader, C., and Mencken, F. (2003) 'Family Structure, Power-Control Theory, and Deviance: Extending Power-Control Theory to Include Ultimate Family Forms' *Western Criminology Review* 4(3): 170–90.

Bateman, T. (2011) Punishing Poverty: The Scaled Approach and Youth Justice Practice' *The Howard Journal of Criminal Justice* 50(2): 171–83.

Beck, U. (1992) *Risk Society: Towards a New Modernity*. London: Sage.

Bernard, T., Snipes, J., Gerould, A., and Vold, G. (2015) *Theoretical Criminology*. Oxford: Oxford University Press.

Boeck, T., Fleming, J., and Kemshall, H. (2006) 'The Context of Risk Decisions: Does Social Capital Make a Difference?' *Forum: Qualitative Social Research* 7(1): Article 17. (http://www.qualitative-research.net/fqs-texte/1-06/06-1-17-e.htm).

Cabot, R. (1940) 'A Long-Term Study of Children: The Cambridge-Somerville Youth Study' *Child Development* 11(2): 143–51.

Case, S. (2006) 'Young People "At Risk" of What? Challenging Risk-focused Early Intervention as Crime Prevention' *Youth Justice* 6(3): 171–79.

Case, S. and Haines, K. (2015) 'Risk Management and Early Intervention' in Goldson, B. and Muncie, J. (eds) *Youth, Crime and Justice*. London: Sage.

Case, S. P. and Haines, K. R. (2009) *Understanding youth offending: Risk factor research policy and practice*. Cullompton: Willan.

Colvin, M. (2000) *Crime and Coercion: An Integrated Theory of Chronic Criminality*. New York: St. Martin's Press.

Downes, D. and Rock, P. (1998) *Understanding Deviance: A Guide to the Sociology of Crime and Rule-Breaking*. Oxford: Oxford University Press.

Elliott, D., Ageton, S., and Canter, J. (1979) 'An Integrated Theoretical Perspective on Delinquent Behavior' *Journal of Research in Crime and Delinquency* 16: 126–49.

Farrington, D. (2007) 'Childhood Risk Factors and Risk-focused Prevention', in Maguire, M., Morgan, R. and Reiner, R. (eds) *The Oxford Handbook of Criminology* (4th edn). Oxford: Oxford University Press.

Farrington, D. P. (2000) 'Explaining and preventing crime: The globalization of knowledge' *Criminology* 38(1): 1–24.

France, A. (2008) 'Risk Factor Analysis and the Youth Question' *Journal of Youth Studies* 11(1): 1–15.

France, A. and Homel, R. (2007) *Pathways and Crime Prevention. Theory, Policy and Practice*. Cullompton: Willan.

Glueck, S. and Glueck, E. (1934) *One Thousand Juvenile Delinquents*. Cambridge: Cambridge University Press.

Glueck, S. and Glueck, E. (1930) *500 Criminal Careers*. New York: Alfred Knopf.

Gottfredson, M. and Hirschi, T. (1990) *A General Theory of Crime*. Stanford: Stanford University Press.

Hagan, F. (2013) *Introduction to Criminology Theories, Methods and Criminal Behaviour*. Thousand Oaks, Sage.

Haines, K. R. and Case, S. P. (2015) *Positive Youth Justice: Children First, Offenders Second*. Bristol: Policy Press.

Hammersley, R., Marsland, L., and Reid, M. (2003) *Substance Use by Young Offenders: The Impact of the Normalisation of Drug Use in the Early Years of the 21st Century*. Home Office Research Study No. 261 London: Home Office.

Haw, K. (2007) 'Risk Factors and Pathways Into and Out of Crime: Misleading, Misinterpreted or Mythic? From Generative Metaphor to Professional Myth' in Hawkins, J. and Catalano, R. (eds) *Communities that Care*. San Francisco: Jossey Bass.

Hawkins, J. and Catalano, R. (1992) *Communities that Care*. San Francisco: Jossey-Bass.

Hawkins, J. and Weis, J. (1985) 'The Social Development Model: An Integrated Approach to Delinquency Prevention' *Journal of Primary Prevention*, 6: 73–97.

Hine, J. (2006) 'Young people, pathways and crime: context and complexity' *Pathways into and out of Crime: Taking Stock and Moving Forward: International Symposium*. Leicester, April 2006.

Hine, J. (2005) 'Early Intervention: The View from On Track' *Children and Society* 19(2): 117–30.

Hine, J., France, A., Dunkerton, L., and Armstrong, D. (2007) *Risk and Resilience in Children who are Offending, Excluded from School or Who Have Behaviour Problems*.

Hirschi, T. (1969) *Causes of Delinquency*. Berkeley, CA: Univeristy of California Press.

Hopkins Burke, R. (2013) *An Introduction to Criminological Theory* (4th edn). Abingdon: Routledge.

Jeffrey, C. (1977) *Crime Prevention through Environmental Design*. Beverly Hills: Sage.

Johnston, J., MacDonald, R., Mason, P., Ridley, L., and Webster, C. (2000) *Snakes & Ladders: Young People, Transitions and Social Exclusion*. Bristol: Policy Press.

Kemshall, H. (2008) 'Risk, Rights and Justice: Understanding and Responding to Youth Risk' *Youth Justice* 8(1): 21–38.

Liebling, A., Maruna, S., and McAra, L. (eds) (2017) *The Oxford Handbook of Criminology* (6th edn). Oxford: Oxford University Press.

Macdonald, R. and Marsh, J. (2005) *Disconnected Youth? Growing Up in Britain's Poor Neighbourhoods*. Basingstoke: Palgrave.

McAra, L. and McVie, S. (2007) 'Youth Justice? The Impact of System Contact on Patterns of Desistance from Offending' *European Journal of Criminology* 4(3) 315–45.

McCord, J. and McCord, W. (1959) 'A Follow-up Report on the Cambridge-Somerville Youth Stud' *The ANNALS of the American Academy of Political and Social Science* 322(1): 89–96.

Mednick, S. (1977) 'A Biosocial Theory of the Learning of Law-abiding Behavior' in Mednick, S. and Christiansen, K. (eds) *Biosocial Bases of Criminal Behavior*. New York: Gardner.

Mitchell Miller, J. (2009) *Twenty First Century Criminology: A Reference Handbook*. London: Sage.

Moffitt, T. (1993) 'Adolescence-Limited and Life-Course-Persistent Antisocial Behavior: A Developmental Taxonomy' *Psychological Review* 100: 674–701.

Muncie, J. (2009) *Youth and Crime*. London: Sage.

Nye, F. (1958) *Family Relationships and Delinquent Behavior*. New York: Wiley.

Pawson, R. and Tilley, N. (2004) *Realistic Evaluation*. London: Sage.

Paylor, I. (2011) 'Youth Justice in England and Wales: A Risky Business' *Journal of Offender Rehabilitation* 50(4): 221–33.

Rafter, N. (2008) *The Criminal Brain. Understanding Biological Theories of Crime*. New York: NYU Press.

Raine, A., Brennan, P., and Mednick, S. (1997) 'Interaction between Birth Complications and Early Maternal Rejection in Predisposing Individuals to Adult Violence: Specificity to Serious, Early-Onset Violence' *American Journal of Psychiatry* 154(9): 1265–71.

Reiss, A. (1951) Delinquency as the Failure of Personal and Social Control. *American Sociological Review* 16: 213–59.

Sampson, R. and Laub, J. (1993) *Crime in the Making: Pathways and Turning Points through Life* Harvard: Harvard University Press.

Sampson, R., Raudenbush, S., and Earls, F. (1997) 'Neighborhoods and Violent Crime: A Multilevel Study of Collective Efficacy' *Science* 15: 918–24.

Shaw, D., Ingoldsby, E., Gilliom, M., and Nagin, D. (2003) 'Trajectories Leading to School-Age Conduct Problems' *Developmental Psychology* 58: 480–91.

Smith, D. and McAra, L. (2004) *Gender and Youth Offending, Edinburgh Study of Youth Transitions and Crime Research Digest No. 2* Edinburgh: Edinburgh University.

Smith, D. and McVie, S. (2003) 'Theory and Method in the Edinburgh Study of Youth Transitions and Crime' *British Journal of Criminology* 43(1): 169–95.

Stephenson, M., Giller, H., and Brown, S. (2011) *Effective Practice in Youth Justice*. London: Routledge.

Tashakkori, A. and Teddlie, T. (1998) *Mixed Methodology: Combining Qualitative and Quantitative Approaches*. Thousand Oaks, California: Sage.

Taylor, I., Walton, I., and Young, J. (1973) *The New Criminology: For a Social Theory of Deviance*. London: Routledge and Kegan Paul.

Tittle, C. (2000) 'Control Balance' in Paternoster, R. and Bachman, R. (eds) *Explaining Criminals and Crime: Essays in Contemporary Theory*. Los Angeles: Roxbury.

Ugwudike, P. (2015) *An Introduction to Critical Criminology*. Bristol: Policy Press.

Vold, G., Bernard, T., and Snipes, J. (2002) *Theoretical Criminology*. Oxford: Oxford University Press.

Walker, J. and McCarthy, P. (2005) 'Parents in Prison: The Impact on Children' in Preston, G. (ed.) *At Greatest Risk: The Children Most Likely to be Poor*. London: Child Poverty Action Group.

Walton, I. and Young, J. (1998) *The New Criminology Revisited*. London: Macmillan.

Webster, C., Simpson, D., MacDonald, R., Abbas, A., Cieslik, M., Shildrick, T., and Simpson, M. (2004) *Poor Transitions: Social Exclusion and Young Adults*. Bristol: Policy Press.

West, D. and Farrington, D. (1973) *Who Becomes Delinquent?* London: Heinemann.

Wikstrom, T. and Loeber, R. (1998) 'Individual Risk Factors, Neighbourhood SES and Juvenile Offending' in Tonry, M. (ed.) *The Handbook of Crime and Punishment*. New York: Oxford University Press.

Williams, K. (2012) *Textbook on Criminology*. Oxford: Oxford University Press.

Wilson, J. and Herrnstein, R. (1985) *Crime and Human Nature*. New York: Simon and Schuster.

Winters, R., Globokar, J., and Roberson, C. (2014) *An Introduction to Crime Causation*. Boca Raton: CRC Press.

Younge, S., Oetting, E., and Deffenbacher, J. (1996) 'Correlations Among Maternal Rejection, Dropping Out of School, and Drug Use in Adolescents' *Journal of Clinical Psychology* 52(1): 96–102.

Chapter 19

Applied Research in Community Safety (2008) Reviewing the Effectiveness of Community Safety Policy and Practice—An Overview of Current Debates and their Background. Montreal: International Centre for the Prevention of Crime.

Bateman, T. (2011) 'Punishing Poverty: The Scaled Approach and Youth Justice Practice' *The Howard Journal of Criminal Justice* 50(2): 171–83.

Blamey, A. and Mackenzie, M. (2007) 'Theories of Change and Realistic Evaluation. Peas in a Pod or Apples and Oranges?' *Evaluation* 13(4): 439–55.

Bryman, A. (2015) *Social Research Methods* (5th edn). Oxford: Oxford University Press.

Case, S. (2007) Questioning the "Evidence" of Risk that Underpins Evidence-Led Youth Justice Interventions' *Youth Justice* 7(2): 91–106.

Case, S. and Haines, K. (2009) *Understanding Youth Offending: Risk Factor Research, Policy and Practice*. Abingdon: Routledge.

Connell, J., Kubisch, A., Schorr, L., and Weiss, C. (1995) *Approaches to Evaluating Community Initiatives: Concepts, Methods and Contexts*. Washington: Aspen Institute.

Cook, T. and Campbell, D. (1979) *Quasi-Experimentation. Design & Analysis Issue for Field Settings*. New York: Houghton Mifflin.

Elliott, E. and Kiel, D. (2000) *Nonlinear Dynamics, Complexity and Public Policy*. Commack, NY: Nova Science Publishers.

Farrington, D. (2007) 'Childhood Risk Factors and Risk-Focused Prevention' in Maguire, M. Morgan, R., and Reiner, R. (eds) *The Oxford Handbook of Criminology* (4th edn). Oxford: Oxford University Press.

Farrington, D. (2003) 'A Short History of Randomized Experiments in Criminology: A Meagre Feast' *Evaluation Review* 27: 218–27.

Farrington, D. (2000) 'Explaining and Preventing Crime: The Globalization of Knowledge' *Criminology* 38(1): 1–24.

Fisher, R. and Geiselman, R. (1992) *'Memory Enhancing Techniques for Investigative Interviewing: The Cognitive Interview'* Springfield, IL: Charles C. Thomas.

France, A. and Homel, R. (2007) *Pathways and Crime Prevention. Theory, Policy and Practice*. Cullompton: Willan.

Freedman, D. and Collier, D., Sekhon, J., and Stark, P. (eds) (2010) *Statistical Models and Causal Inference: A Dialogue with the Social Sciences*. Cambridge: Cambridge University Press.

Gendreau, P. and Smith, P. (2007) 'Influencing the "People Who Count": Some Perspectives on the Reporting of Meta-Analytic Results for Prediction and Treatment Outcomes With Offenders' *Criminal Justice and Behavior*, 34(12): 1536–59.

Gleick, J. (1997) *Chaos: Making a New Science*. London: Vintage.

Goldson, B. and Hughes, G. (2010) 'Sociological Criminology and Youth Justice: Comparative Policy Analysis and Academic Intervention' *Criminology and Criminal Justice* 10(2): 211–30.

Hope, T. (2005) 'Pretend it Doesn't Work: The 'Anti-Social' Bias in the Maryland Scientific Methods Scale' *European Journal on Criminal Policy and Research* 11(3–4): 275–96.

Hope, T. (2009) 'The Illusion of Control: A Response to Professor Sherman' *Criminology and Criminal Justice* 9(2): 125–34.

Hopkins-Burke, R. (2013) *An Introduction to Criminological Theory*. Abingdon: Routledge.

Hughes, G. and Edwards, A. (2005) 'Comparing the Governance of Safety in Europe: A Geo-Historical Approach' *Theoretical Criminology*, 9(3).

Jones, S. (2013) *Criminology*. Oxford: Oxford University Pres.

Kemshall, H. (2008) 'Rights, Risk and Justice: Understanding and Responding to Youth Risk' *Youth Justice* 8(1): 21–38.

Kubisch, A., Fulbright-Anderson, K., and Connell, J. (1998) *New Approaches to Evaluating Community Initiatives: Theory, Measurement and Analysis*. Washington: Aspen Institute.

Liebling, A., Maruna, S., and McAra, L. (eds) (2017) *The Oxford Handbook of Criminology* (6th edn). Oxford: Oxford University Press.

Lorenz, E. (1963) 'Deterministic Nonperiodic Flow' *Journal of the Atmospheric Sciences* 20: 130–41.

Macdonald, R. and Marsh, J. (2005) *Disconnected Youth? Growing Up in Britain's Poor Neighbourhoods*. Basingstoke: Palgrave.

Mandelbrot, B. (2004) *A Theory of Roughness*. http://www.edge.org (accessed January 2012).

Mandelbrot, B. (1982) *The Fractal Geometry of Nature*. San Francisco: W H Freeman and Co.

Mandelbrot, B. (1967) 'How Long Is the Coast of Britain? Statistical Self-Similarity and Fractional Dimension' *Science* 156, No. 3775: 636–38.

McGrayne, S. (2011) *The Theory that Would Not Die*. New Haven: Yale University Press.

Milovanovic, D. (1997) *Chaos, Criminology and Social Justice*. Westport, CT: Greenwood Publishing Group.

O'Mahony, P. (2009) 'The Risk Factors Prevention Paradigm and the Causes of Youth Crime: A Deceptively Useful Analysis?' *Youth Justice* 9(2): 99–114.

Pawson, R. and Tilley, N. (2009) 'Realist Evaluation' in Otto, H.-U., Polutta, A., and Ziegler, H. (eds) *Evidence-based Practice—Modernising the Knowledge Base of Social Work?* Germany: Barbara Budrich.

Pawson, R. and Tilley, N. (2004) 'Realistic Evaluation' in Matthieson, S. (ed.) *Encyclopaedia of Evaluation*. Newbury Park: Sage.

Pawson, R. and Tilley, N. (1998) *Realistic Evaluation*. London: Sage.

Pitts, J. (2003) *The New Politics of Youth Crime: Discipline or Solidarity?* Lyme Regis: Russell House.

Pycroft, A. and Bartollas, C. (2014) *Applying Complexity Theory. Whole Systems Approaches to Criminal Justice and Social Work*. Bristol: Policy Press.

Robson, C. (2015) *Real World Research: A Resource for Social Scientists and Practitioner-Researchers*. Oxford: Blackwell.

Salsburg, D. (2002) *The Lady Tasting Tea: How Statistics Revolutionized Science in the Twentieth Century*. New York: Holt.

Sherman, L. (2009) 'Evidence and Liberty: The promise of experimental criminology' *Criminology and Criminal Justice* 9(1): 5–28.

Sherman, L., Gottfriedson D., MacKenzie, D., Eck, J., Reuter, P., and Bushway, S. (1998) *Preventing Crime: What Works, What Doesn't, What's Promising*. Department of Criminology and Criminal Justice, University of Maryland: Baltimore.

Sherman, L. and Strang, H. (2004) 'Verdicts or Inventions? Interpreting Results from Randomized Controlled Experiments in Criminology' *American Behavioral Scientist* 47(5): 575–607.

Smith, D. and McVie, S. (2003) 'Theory and Method in the Edinburgh Study of Youth Transitions and Crime' *British Journal of Criminology* 43(1): 169–95.

Walgrave, L. (2008) 'Criminology, as I See It Ideally' *Criminology in Europe*, Newsletter of the European Society of Criminology, November 2008, pp. 3 and 15–17. Paper presented following the receipt of the European Criminology Award

Weiss, C. (1995) 'Nothing as Practical as Good Theory: Exploring Theory-Based Evaluation for Comprehensive Community Initiatives for Children and Families', in Connell, J., Kubisch, A., Schorr, L., and Weiss, C. (eds) *Approaches to Evaluating Community Initiatives: Concepts, Methods and Contexts*. Washington: Aspen Institute.

Williams, M. (2006) 'Empiricism' in V. Jupp (ed.) *The Sage Dictionary of Social Research Methods*. London: Sage.

Wright-Mills, C. (1959) *The Sociological Imagination*. Oxford: Oxford University Press.

Young, J. (2011) *The Criminological Imagination*. London: Polity.

Young, T. (1991) 'Chaos and Social Change: Metaphysics of the Postmodern' *The Social Science Journal* 28(3): 289–305.

Ziliak, S. and McCloskey, D. (2007) *The Cult of Statistical Significance: How the Standard Error Cost Us Jobs, Justice, and Lives* Ann Arbor: The University of Michigan Press.

Chapter 20

Advisory Council on the Penal System (1970) Non-Custodial and Semi-Custodial Penalties. London: HMSO.

Antrobus, E., Bradford, B., Murphy, K., and Sargeant, E. (2015) 'Community Norms, Procedural Justice, and the Public's Perceptions of Police Legitimacy' *Journal of Contemporary Criminal Justice* 31(2): 151–70.

Ashworth, A. (2003) 'Is Restorative Justice the Way Forward for Criminal Justice?' in McLaughlin, E., Ferguson, R. and Westmarland, L. (eds) *Restorative Justice: Critical Issues*. London: Sage.

Ashworth, A. and Blake, M. (1996) 'The Presumption of Innocence in English Criminal Law' Crim LR 306.

Beattie, J. M. (2012) *The First English Detectives: The Bow Street Runners and the Policing of London, 1750–1840*. Oxford: Oxford University Press.

Bentham, J. (1843) *Benthamiana, or Select Extracts from the Works of Jeremy Bentham*. Edinburgh: William Tait.

Bingham, T. (2010) *The Rule of Law*. London: Allen Lane.

Blackstone, W. (1769) *Commentaries on the Laws of England 1765–9*. Available from http://www.gutenberg.org/ebooks/30802.

Bradford, B. (2014) 'Policing and Social Identity: Procedural Justice, Inclusion and Cooperation Between Police and Public' *Policing & Society* 24(1): 22–43.

BBC (2015) *Bedfordshire Police Council Tax Rise Rejected at Referendum*, 11 May 2015. Available from http://www.bbc.co.uk/news/uk-politics-32694166.

Cabinet Office (2008) *Engaging Communities in Fighting Crime*. London: Cabinet Office.

Cape, E. (2010) 'Adversarialism "Lite": Developments in Criminal Procedure and Evidence under New Labour' *Criminal Justice Matters* 79(1): 25–7.

Crown Prosecution Service (2016) *Crown Prosecution Service Annual Report and Accounts 2015–16*. Available from https://www.cps.gov.uk/publications/docs/annual_report_2015_16.pdf.

De Keijser, J., De Lange, E. and Van Wilsem, J. (2014) 'Wrongful Convictions and the Blackstone Ratio: An Empirical Analysis of Public Attitudes' *Punishment & Society* 16(1): 32–49.

De Montesquieu, C. (1748) *The Spirit of the Laws*: (Reprint 1989), English translation. Cambridge: Cambridge University Press.

Dennis, I. (2014) 'Quashing Acquittals: Applying the 'New and Compelling Evidence' Exception to Double Jeopardy' *Criminal Law Review* 4: 247–60.

Ellison, G. (2013) 'Policing: Context and Practice' in Hucklesby, A. and Wahidin, A. (eds) *Criminal Justice*. Oxford: Oxford University Press.

Emsley, C. (2009) *The Great British Bobby: A History of British Policing from the 19th Century to the Present*. London: Quercus.

Gardner, J. (2012) 'Ashworth on Principles' in Zedner, L. and Roberts, J. (eds) *Principles and Values in Criminal Law and Criminal Justice: Essays in Honour of Andrew Ashworth*. Oxford: Oxford University Press.

Garland, D. (2001) *The Culture of Control*. Oxford: Oxford University Press.

Garvey, S. (2011) 'Alternatives to Punishment' in Deigh, J. and Dolinko, D. (eds) *The Oxford Handbook of Philosophy of Criminal Law*. Oxford: Oxford University Press.

HM CPS Inspectorate (2015) Thematic review of the CPS advocacy strategy and progress against the recommendations of the follow-up report of the quality of prosecution advocacy and case presentation. Available from: http://www.justiceinspectorates.gov.uk/hmcpsi/wp-content/uploads/sites/3/2015/03/ADVST_thm_Mar15_rpt.pdf.

Home Office (2005) *Visible Unpaid Work*, Reference 66/2005. London: Home Office.

Hough, M. and Roberts, J. (2017) 'Public Opinion , Crime, and Criminal Justice' in Liebling, A., Maruna, S. and McAra, L. (eds) *The Oxford Handbook of Criminology* (6th edn). Oxford: Oxford University Press.

House of Commons Justice Committee (2009) *The Crown Prosecution Service: Gatekeeper of the Criminal Justice System, Ninth Report of Session 2008–9*, HC 186. Available from: http://www.publications.parliament.uk/pa/cm200809/cmselect/cmjust/186/18602.htm.

Hunt, M., Hooper, H., and Yowell, H. (2015) *Parliaments and Human Rights: Redressing the Democratic Deficit*. Oxford: Bloomsbury.

Hood, R. (1974) 'Criminology and Penal Change: A Case Study of the Nature and Impact of Some Recent Advice to Governments' in Hood, R. (ed.) *Crime, Criminology and Public Policy: Essays in Honour of Sir Leon Radzinowicz*. London: Heinemann.

Jones, T., Newburn, T., and Reiner, R. (2017) 'Policing and the Police' in Liebling, A., Maruna, S., and McAra, L. (eds) *The Oxford Handbook of Criminology* (6th edn). Oxford: Oxford University Press.

Lacey, N. (2003) 'Principles, Politics and Criminal Justice' in Zedner, L. and Ashworth, A. (eds) *The Criminological Foundations of Penal Policy: Essays in Honour of Roger Hood*. Oxford: Oxford University Press.

Lacey, N. (2013) 'The Rule of Law and the Political Economy of Criminalisation: An Agenda for Research' *Punishment & Society* 15(4): 349–66.

Law Commission (2001) *Double Jeopardy and Prosecution Appeals* (Cm 5048). London: TSO.

Martinson, R. (1974) 'What Works? Questions and Answers about Prison Reform' *Public Interest* 35: 22–54.

Marshall, T. (1999) *Restorative Justice: An Overview*. London: Home Office.

Ministry of Justice, (2015) *Criminal court statistics quarterly, England and Wales, January to March 2015*. Available from: https://www.gov.uk/government/uploads/system/uploads/attachment_data/file/437672/ccsq-bulletin-january-march-2015.pdf.

Packer, H. (1964) 'Two Models of the Criminal Process' *University of Pennsylvania Law Review* 113(1): 1–68.

Roberts, P. (2002) 'Double Jeopardy Law Reform: A Criminal Justice Commentary' *Modern Law Review* 65(3): 393–424.

Roberts, J., V. and Hough, M. (2005) *Understanding Public Attitudes to Criminal Justice*. Berkshire: Open University Press.

Rowe, M. (2013) 'The Police' in Hucklesby, A. and Wahidin, A. (eds) *Criminal Justice*. Oxford: Oxford University Press.

Sharpe, S. (2004), 'How Large Should the Restorative Justice "Tent" Be?' in Zehr, H. and Toews, B. (eds) *Critical Issues in Restorative Justice*. New York: Criminal Justice Press.

Thomas, D. (1998) *Victorian Underworld*. London: John Murray.

Umbreit, M. and Zehr, H. (1982) 'Victim Offender Reconciliation: An Incarceration Substitute' *Federal Probation* 46: 63–8.

Wood, W., R. (2015) 'Why Restorative Justice Will Not Reduce Incarceration' *British Journal of Criminology* 55(5): 883–900.

Chapter 21

Advisory Council on the Penal System (1970) *Non-Custodial and Semi-Custodial Penalties*. London: HMSO.

Annison, H., Bradford, B., and Grant, E. (2015) 'Theorizing the Role of "The Brand" in Criminal Justice: The Case of Integrated Offender Management' *Criminology & Criminal Justice* 15(4): 387–406.

Bale, D. (2000) 'Reflections: Pure Fiction: An Infallible Guide to National Standards' *Probation Journal* 47(2): 129–31.

Bottoms, A. (1995) 'The Philosophy and Politics of Punishment and Sentencing' in Clarkson, C. and Morgan, R. (eds) *The Politics of Sentencing Reform*. Oxford: Clarendon Press.

Cabinet Office (2008) *Engaging Communities in Fighting Crime*. London: Cabinet Office.

Campeau, H. (2015) '"Police Culture" at Work: Making Sense of Police Oversight', *British Journal of Criminology* 55(4): 669–87.

Cavadino, M. and Dignan, J. (2006) *Penal Systems: A Comparative Approach*. London: Sage.

Evans, R. and Lewis, P. (2013) *Undercover: The True Story of Britain's Secret Police*. London: Faber and Faber.

Foucault, M. (1977) *Discipline and Punish: The Birth of the Prison* (trans. Sheridan, A.). Oxford: Vintage Books.

Fox, C., Albertson, K., and Wong, K. (2013) *Justice Reinvestment: Can the Criminal Justice System Deliver More for Less?* Abingdon, Routledge.

Freiberg, A. (2001) 'Affective versus Effective Justice' *Punishment & Society* 3(2): 265–78.

Garland, D. (2001) *The Culture of Control*. Oxford: Oxford University Press.

Harris, R. and Lo, T. (2002) 'Community Service: Its Use in Criminal Justice' *International Journal of Offender Therapy and Comparative Criminology* 46: 427–44.

HM Government (2008) *Fair Rules for Strong Communities*. London: HMG.

Home Office, Department for Constitutional Affairs and the Attorney General's Office (2006) *Delivering Simple, Speedy, Summary Justice*. London: Department for Constitutional Affairs.

Home Office (2006) *An Effective Supervision Inspection Programme Thematic Report 'Working to Make Amends': An Inspection of the Delivery of Enhanced Community Punishment and Unpaid Work by the National Probation Service*. London: Home Office.

Howard League for Penal Reform (2015) *Media release: Shrinking the justice system would cut crime and save billions*. Available from: http://www.howardleague.org/news/spendingreview2015/.

Howard League for Penal Reform (1999) *Do Women Paint Fences Too? Women's Experience of Community Service*. London: Howard League for Penal Reform.

Hough, M., Bradford, B., Jackson, J., and Roberts, J. V. (2012) *Attitudes to Sentencing and Trust in Justice: Exploring Trends from the Crime Survey in England and Wales*. Available from: http://www.icpr.org.uk/media/34605/Attitudes%20to%20Sentencing%20and%20Trust%20in%20Justice%20(web).pdf.

Indermaur, D. (2008) 'Dealing the Public In: Challenges for a Transparent and Accountable Sentencing Policy' in Freiberg, A. and Gelb, K. (eds) *Penal Populism, Sentencing Councils and Sentencing Policy*. Annandale: Hawkins Press.

Johnson, P. (2010) 'Paying Back or Moving Forwards: The Use of the Unpaid Work Element of the Community Order' *Criminal Justice Matters* 80(1): 8–9.

Li, E. (2015) 'The cultural idiosyncrasy of penal populism: The case of contemporary China' *British Journal of Criminology* 55(1): 146–63.

Loader, I. (2006) 'Fall of the 'Platonic Guardians': Liberalism, Criminology and Political Responses to Crime in England and Wales' *British Journal of Criminology* 46(4): 561–86.

Matthews, R. (2005) 'The Myth of Punitiveness' *Theoretical Criminology* 9: 175–201.

Moore, J. (2015) 'The "New Punitiveness" in the Context of British Imperial Hstory', *Criminal Justice Matters* 101(1): 10–13.

Maruna, S. and King, A. (2008) 'Selling the Public on Probation: Beyond the Bib' *Probation Journal* 55(4): 337–51.

Masur, L. (1989) *Rites of Execution*. Oxford: Oxford University Press.

McIvor, G. (1992) *Sentenced to Serve: The Operation and Impact of Community Service by Offenders*. Aldershot: Avebury.

Ministry of Justice (2015) *Criminal Justice Statistics Quarterly Update to March 2015*. Available from: https://www.gov.uk/government/uploads/system/uploads/attachment_data/file/453309/criminal-justice-statistics-march-2015.pdf (last accessed 5 August 2016).

Ministry of Justice (2013) *Story of the Prison Population:1993–2012 England and Wales*. Available from: https://www.gov.uk/government/uploads/system/uploads/attachment_data/file/218185/story-prison-population.pdf.

Morgan, R. (2008) 'Engaging with honest politicians' *Criminal Justice Matters*, 72: 24–25.

Nash, Mm (1999) 'Enter the Polibation Officer' *International Journal of Police Science and Management* 1: 252–61.

Pease, K. (1980) 'Community Service and Prison: Are They Alternatives?' in Pease, K. and McWilliams. W. (eds) *Community Service By Order*. Edinburgh: Scottish Academic Press.

Pease, K., Durkin, P., Earnshaw, I., Payne, D., and Thorpe, J. (1976) *Community Service Orders*, Home Office Research Studies No. 29 London: HMSO.

Philostratus (translated by Conybeare, F. (1960)) *Life of Apollonius of Tyana*. London: William Heinemann.

Pratt, J. (2000) 'The Return of the Wheelbarrow Men; Or, The Arrival of Postmodern Penality?' *British Journal of Criminology* 40: 127–45.

Pratt. J. (2007) *Penal Populism*. Abingdon: Routledge.

Pratt, J., Brown, D., Brown, M., Hallsworth, S., and Morrison, W. (2005) 'Introduction' in Pratt, J., Brown, D., Brown, M., Hallsworth, S., and Morrison, W. (eds) *The New Punitiveness: Trends, theories, perspectives*. Cullompton: Willan, xi–xxvi.

Roberts, J. V. and Hough, M. (2013) 'Sentencing riot-related offending: where do the public stand?' *British Journal of Criminology* 53(2): 234–56.

Roberts, J., Stalans, L., Indermaur, D., and Hough, M. (2003) *Penal Populism and Public Opinion: Lessons from Five Countries*. Oxford: Oxford University Press.

Ryan, M. (2005) 'Engaging with Punitive Attitudes Towards Crime and Punishment' in Pratt, J., Brown, D., Brown, M., Hallsworth, S., and Morrison, W. (eds) *The New Punitiveness: Trends, Theories, Perspectives*. Cullompton: Willan.

Scottish Executive Social Research (2007) *Community sentencing: Public Perceptions and Attitudes – Summary Research Report*. Available from: https://www.gov.uk/government/uploads/system/uploads/attachment_data/file/453309/criminal-justice-statistics-march-2015.pdf (last accessed 5 September 2016).

Sprack, J. (2014) *A Practical Approach to Criminal Procedure*. Oxford: Oxford University Press.

Thomas, C. (2015) 2014 UK Judicial Attitude Survey. Available from: https://www.judiciary.gov.uk/wp-content/uploads/2015/02/jac-2014-results.pdf (last accessed 25 July 2015).

Van Zyl Smit, D., Weatherby, P., and Creighton, S. (2014) 'Whole Life Sentences and the Tide of European Human Rights Jurisprudence: What Is to Be Done?' *Human Rights Law Review* 14(1): 59–84.

White, A. (2015) 'The Politics of Police "Privatization": A Multiple Streams Approach' *Criminology & Criminal Justice* 15(3): 283–99.

Whitfield, D. (1993) 'Extending the Boundaries', in Whitfield, D. and Scott, D. (eds) *Paying Back: Twenty Years of Community Service*, Winchester: Waterside Press.

Wootton, B. (1978) *Crime and Penal Policy: Reflections on Fifty Years' Experience*. London: Allen & Unwin.

Chapter 22

Barr, R. and Pease, K. (1992) 'A Place for Every Crime and Every Crime in its Place. An Alternative Perspective on Crime Displacement', in Evans D., Fyfe N., and Herbert D. (eds) *Crime, Policing and Place: Essays in Environmental Criminology*. London: Routledge.

Berry, G., Briggs, P., Erol, R., and van Staden, L. (2011) *The Effectiveness of Partnership Working in a Crime and Disorder Context: A Rapid Evidence Assessment*, Research Report 52, London, Home Office.

Brantingham, P. and Faust, F. (1976) 'A Conceptual Model of Crime Prevention' *Crime & Delinquency*, July: 284–96.

Case, S. and Haines, K. (2009) *Understanding Youth Offending*, Cullompton: Willan.

Chakraborti, N., Gadd, D., Gray, P., Wright, S., and Duggan, M. (2011) *Public Authority Commitment and Action to Eliminate Targeted Harassment and Violence*, London, Equality and Human Rights Commission, Research Report 74.

Cherney, A. (2006) 'Problem Solving for Crime Prevention', *Trends & Issues in Crime and Criminal Justice*, 314.

Clarke, R. (2011) 'Seven Misconceptions of Situational Crime Prevention' in Tilley, N. (ed.) *Handbook of Crime Prevention and Community Safety*. Abingdon: Routledge.

Clarke, R. (1997) *Situational Crime Prevention: Successful Case Studies* (2nd edn). Guilderland, NY: Harrow and Heston.

Clarke, R. and Cornish, D. (1985) 'Modelling Offenders' Decisions: A Framework for Research and Policy' in Tonry, M. (ed.) *Crime and Justice: An Annual review of Research, Vol 6*, Chicago, University of Chicago Press.

Coleman, R., Sim, J., and Whyte, D. (2002) 'Power, Politics and Partnerships: The State of Crime Prevention on Merseyside' in Hughes, G. and Edwards, A. (eds) *Crime Control and Community*. Cullompton, Willan.

Crawford, A. (2007) 'Crime Prevention and Community Safety', in Maguire, M., Morgan, R., and Reiner, R. (eds) *The Oxford Handbook of Criminology* (4th edn). Oxford: Oxford University Press.

Crawford, A. and Lister, S. (2007) *The Use and Impact of Dispersal Orders: Sticking Plasters and Wake Up Calls*. Bristol, Policy Press.

Crawford, A. (1998) *Crime Prevention and Community Safety*. London: Longman.

Crawford, A. (1997) *The Local Governance of Crime*. Oxford: Clarendon Press.

Cullen, F., Benson, M., and Makarios, M. (2012) 'Developmental and Life-Course Theories of Offending' in Welsh, B. and Farrington, D. (eds) *The Oxford Handbook of Crime Prevention*. Oxford: Oxford University Press.

Department for Communities and Local Government (2012) *The Troubled Families Programme*. London: DCLG.

Eck, J. (2002) 'Preventing Crime at Places' in Sherman, L., Farrington, D., Welsh, B., and MacKenzie, D. (eds) *Evidence-Based Crime Prevention*. Abingdon: Routledge.

Eck, J. and Guerette, R. (2012) 'Place-Based Crime Prevention: theory, Evidence and Policy' in Welsh, B. and Farrington, D. (eds) *The Oxford Handbook of Crime Prevention*. Oxford: Oxford University Press.

Edwards, A. (2002) 'Learning from Diversity' in Hughes, G. and Edwards, A. (eds) *Crime Control and Community*. Cullompton: Willan.

Ekblom, P. (2012) 'The Private Sector and Designing Products against Crime' in Welsh, B. and Farrington, D. (eds) *The Oxford Handbook of Crime Prevention*. Oxford: Oxford University Press.

Ekblom, P. (2002) 'From the Source to the Mainstream is Uphill' in Tilley, N. (ed) *Analysis for Crime Prevention, Crime Prevention Studies, 13*. Monsey, NY: Criminal Justice Press.

Ekblom, P., Law, H., and Sutton, M. (1996) *Safer Cities and Domestic Burglary*. London: Home Office.

Farrington, D., Loeber, R., and Ttofi, M. (2012) 'Risk and Protective Factors for Offending' in Welsh, B. and Farrington, D. (eds) *The Oxford Handbook of Crime Prevention*. Oxford: Oxford University Press.

Farrington, D. and Ttofi, M. (2009) 'School-Based Programs to Reduce Bullying and Victimization' *Campbell Systematic Review*, 6.

Forrester, D., Chatterton, M., and Pease, K. (1988) *The Kirkholt Burglary Prevention Project, Rochdale. Crime Prevention Unit: Paper 13*. London: Home Office.

Forrester, D., Frenz, S., O'Connell, M., and Pease, K. (1990) *The Kirkholt Burglary Prevention Project: Phase II. Crime Prevention Unit Paper 23*. London: Home Office.

Garland, D. (2001) *The Culture of Control*. Oxford: Oxford University Press.

Garland, D. (1996) 'The Limits of the Sovereign State' *British Journal of Criminology* 36(4): 445–71.

Gilling, D. (1997) *Crime Prevention: Theory, Policy and Politics*. London: UCL Press.

Goddard, T. (2012) 'Post-Welfarist Risk Managers? Risk, Crime Prevention and the Responsibilisation of Community-Based Organisations' *Theoretical Criminology* 16(3): 347–63.

Gottfriedson, D., Cook, P., and Na, C. (2014) 'Schools and Prevention' in Welsh, B. and Farrington, D. (eds) *The Oxford Handbook of Crime Prevention*. Oxford: Oxford University Press.

Grabosky, P. (1996) 'Unintended Consequences of Crime Prevention' in Homel, R. (ed.) *The Politics and Practice of Situational Crime Prevention*. Monsey, NY: Criminal Justice Press.

HM Treasury and National Audit Office (2008) *Tackling External Fraud: Good Practice Guide*. London: National Audit Office.

Home Office (2011) *A New Approach to Fighting Crime*. London: Home Office.

Home Office (1965) *Report of the Committee on the Prevention and Detection of Crime (Cornish Committee)*. London: Home Office.

Homel, R. (2011) 'Developmental Crime Prevention' in Tilley, N. (ed.) *Handbook of Crime Prevention and Community Safety*. Abingdon: Routledge.

Hope, T. (2002) 'The Road Taken: Evaluation, Replication and Crime Reduction' in Hughes, G., McLaughlin, E., and Muncie, J. (eds) *Crime Prevention and Community Safety: New Directions*. London: Sage.

Hubbard, P. (2004) 'Cleansing the metropolis: sex work and the politics of zero tolerance' *Urban Studies* 41(9): 665–86.

Hughes, G. (1998) *Understanding Crime Prevention*. Buckingham: Open University Press.

Hughes, G. and Edwards, A. (2011) 'Crime Prevention in Context' in Tilley, N. (ed.) *Handbook of Crime Prevention and Community Safety*. Abingdon: Routledge.

Johnson, S., Guerette, R., and Bowers, K. (2012) 'Crime Displacement and Diffusion of Benefits' in Welsh, B. and Farrington, D. (eds) *The Oxford Handbook of Crime Prevention*. Oxford: Oxford University Press.

Kelly, L. (2012) 'Representing and Preventing Youth Crime and Disorder: Intended and Unintended Consequences of Targeted Youth Programmes in England' *Youth Justice* 12(2): 101–17.

Lea, J. and Young, J. (1984) *What is to be Done about Law and Order?* Harmondsworth: Penguin Books.

Lee, M. (2007) *Inventing 'Fear of Crime'*. Cullompton: Willan.

Lösel, F. and Bender, D. (2012) 'Child Social Skills Training in the Prevention of Antisocial Development and Crime' in Welsh, B. and Farrington, D. (eds) *The Oxford Handbook of Crime Prevention*. Oxford: Oxford University Press.

Ludwig, J. and Burdick-Will, J. (2012) 'Poverty Deconcentration and the Prevention of Crime' in Welsh, B. and Farrington, D. (eds) *The Oxford Handbook of Crime Prevention*. Oxford: Oxford University Press.

Luiselli, J., Putnam, R., Handler, M., and Feinberg, A. (2005) 'Whole-School Positive Behaviour Support: Effects on student discipline problems and academic performance' *Educational Psychology* 25(2/3): 183–98.

Manning, M., Homel, R., and Smith, C. (2010) 'A Meta-Analysis of the Effects of Early Developmental Programs in at-risk Populations on Non-Health Outcomes in Adolescence' *Children and Youth Services Review* 32: 506–19.

Marx, G. (2007) 'The Engineering of Social Control: Policing and Technology' *Policing* 1(1): 46–56.

Matza, D. (1964) *Delinquency and Drift*. New York: Wiley.

McCord, J. (1992) 'The Cambridge-Somerville Study: A Pioneering Longitudunal Experimental Study of Delinquency Prevention' in McCord, J. and Tremblay, R. (eds) *Preventing Antisocial Behavior: Interventions from Birth through Adolescence*. New York: Guilford Press.

McCord, J. (1978) 'A Thirty-Year Follow-Up of Treatment Effects' *American Psychologist* March: 284–89.

Morgan, A., Boxall, H., Lindeman, K., and Anderson, J. (2015) *Effective Crime Prevention Interventions for Implementation by Local Government*. Canberra: Australian Institute of Criminology.

Morgan, L. (2013) 'Gated Communities: Institutionalizing Social Stratification' *The Geographical Bulletin*. 54: 24–36.

Morgan, J. (1991) *Safer Communities: The Local Delivery of Crime Prevention Through the Partnership Approach*. London: Home Office.

O'Malley, P. (1992) 'Risk, Power and Crime Prevention' *Economy and Society* 21(3): 252–75.

Petrosino, A., Petrosino, C., and Buehler, J. (2004) '"Scared Straight" and Other Juvenile Awareness Programmes for Preventing Delinquency' *Campbell Systematic Review* 2.

Piquero, A., Farrington, D., Welsh, B., Tremblay, R., and Jennings, W. (2008) 'Effects of Early Family/Parent Training on Antisocial Behavior & Delinquency', *Campbell Systematic Review* 11.

Pitts, J. (1988) *The Politics of Juvenile Crime*. London: Sage.

Popper, K. (2002) *The Logic of Scientific Discovery*. Abingdon: Routledge.

Prior, D. and Paris, A. (2005) *Preventing Children's Involvement in Crime and Anti-Social Behaviour: A Literature Review*. Birmingham: University of Birmingham.

Quinney, R. (1970) *The Social Reality of Crime*. London, Transaction Publishers.

Repetto, T. (1976) 'Crime Prevention and the Displacement Phenomenon', *Crime and Delinquency* 22: 166–77.

Reza, B. and Magill, C. (2006) *Race and the Criminal Justice System: An Overview to the Complete Statistics 2004–2005*. London: Home Office.

Rodger, J. (2008) 'The Criminalisation of Social Policy' *Criminal Justice Matters* 74(1): 18–9.

Rose, N. (2000) 'Government and Control' *British Journal of Criminology* 40: 321–39.

Sampson, R., Raudenbush, S. and Earls, F. (1997) 'Neighborhoods and Violent Crime: A Multilevel Study of Collective Efficacy' *Science*, 277(5328): 918–24.

Schweinhart, L., Montie, J., Xiang, Z., Barnett, W., Belfield, C., and Nores, M. (2005) *Lifetime Effects: The High/Scope Perry Preschool Study Through Age 40*. Ypsilanti, MI: High/Scope Press.

Shain, F. (2011) *The New Folk Devils: Muslim Boys and Education*. Stoke: Trentham.

Sharma, D. and Scott, M. (2015) 'Nudge; Don't Judge: Using Nudge Theory to Deter Shoplifters', 11th European Academy of Design Conference, Paris, 22–4 April.

Sherman, L., Gottfriedson, D., MacKenzie, D., Eck, J., Reuter, P., and Bushway, S. (1998) 'Preventing Crime: What Works, What Doesn't, What's Promising', Research in Brief, Washington DC, National Institute of Justice.

Sidebottom, A., Tompson, L., Thornton, A., Bullock, K. and Tilley, N. (2015) *Gating Alleys to Reduce Crime: A Meta-analysis and Realist Synthesis*. London: University College London. Available at: http://whatworks.college.police.uk/About/Documents/Alley_gating.pdf.

Smith, M. and Clarke, R. (2012) 'Situational Crime Prevention: Classifying Techniques Using "Good Enough" Theory' in Welsh, B. and Farrington, D. (eds) *The Oxford Handbook of Crime Prevention*. Oxford: Oxford University Press.

Smith, R. (2015) 'Troubled, Troubling or Troublesome? Troubled Families and the Changing Shape of Youth Justice' in Wasik, M. and Santatzoglou, S. (eds) *The Management of Change in Criminal Justice*. Basingstoke: Palgrave Macmillan.

Sutherland, A., Merrington, S., Jones, S., and Baker. K. (2005) *Role of Risk and Protective Factors*. London: Youth Justice Board.

Thaler, R. and Sunstein, C. (2008) *Nudge: Improving Decisions about Health, Wealth and Happiness*. New Haven CT: Yale University Press.

Tilley, N. (2011) 'Introduction: Thinking Realistically About Crime Prevention' in Tilley, N. (ed) *Handbook of Crime Prevention and Community Safety*. Abingdon: Routledge.

Tilley, N. (2002) 'Crime Prevention in Britain, 1975–2010: Breaking Out, Breaking In and Breaking Down' in Hughes, G., McLaughlin, E., and Muncie, J. (eds) *Crime Prevention and Community Safety: New Directions*. London: Sage.

Tilley, N. (1993) *After Kirkholt—Theory, Method and Results of Replication Evaluations*, Crime Prevention Unit Series Paper 47. London: Home Office.

Wacquant, L. (2008) *Urban Outcasts: A Comparative Sociology of Advanced Marginality*. Cambridge: Polity Press

Wallin, E., Lindewald, B. and Andréasson, S. (2004) 'Institutionalization of a Community Action Program Targeting Licensed Premises in Stockholm, Sweden' *Evaluation Review* 28(5): 396–419

Welsh, B. and Farrington, D. (2012) 'Crime Prevention and Public Policy' in Welsh, B. and Farrington, D. (eds) *The Oxford Handbook of Crime Prevention*. Oxford: Oxford University Press.

Welsh, B. and Farrington, D. (eds) (2012) *The Oxford Handbook of Crime Prevention*. Oxford: Oxford University Press.

Welsh, B. and Farrington, D. (2010) 'The Future of Crime Prevention: Developmental and Situational Strategies', *Paper to National Institute of Justice*, December 2010. Available at http://www.nij.gov/topics/crime/crime-prevention-working-group/documents/future-of-crime-prevention-research.pdf.

West, D.J. (1967) *The Young Offender*. Harmondsworth: Pelican.

Chapter 23

Anselin, L., Griffiths, E. and Tita, G. (2011) 'Crime Mapping and Hot Spot Analysis' in Wortley, R. and Mazerolle, L. (eds) *Environmental Criminology and Crime Analysis*. Abingdon: Routledge.

Armstrong, S., McIvor, G., McNeill, F., and McGuinness, P. (2013) *International Evidence Review of Conditional (Suspended) Sentences: FINAL REPORT*. Edinburgh,: Scottish Centre for Crime & Justice, Research.

Baker, K., Jones, S., Merrington, S., and Roberts, C. (2005) *Further Development of ASSET*, London: Youth Justice Board.

Bandyopadhyay, S. (2012) *Acquisitive Crime: Imprisonment, Detection and Social Factors*. London: Civitas.

Beccaria, C. (1995) *On Crimes and Punishments and Other Writings*. Cambridge: Cambridge University Press.

Beck, U. (1992) *Risk Society*. Sage: London.

Beck, U. and Willms, J. (2004) *Conversations with Ulrich Beck*. Cambridge: Polity Press.

Bowling, B. (1999) 'The Rise and Fall of New York Murder' *British Journal of Criminology* 39(4): 531–53.

Bowling, B., Marks, A., and Murphy, C. (2008) 'Crime Control Technologies: Towards an Analytical Framework and Research Agenda' in Brownsword, R. and Yeung, K. (eds) *Regulating Technologies: Legal Futures, Regulatory Frames and Technological Fixes*. Oxford: Hart.

Braga, A., Hureau, D. and Papachristos, A. (2011) 'An Ex Post Facto Evaluation Framework for Place-Based Police Interventions' *Evaluation Review* 35(6): 592–626.

Brantingham, P. and Brantingham, P. (2011) 'Crime Pattern Theory' in Wortley, R. and Mazerolle, L. (eds) *Environmental Criminology and Crime Analysis*. Abingdon: Routledge.

Brown, A. (2004) 'Anti-Social Behaviour, Crime Control and Social Control' *Howard Journal* 43(2): 203–11.

Bullock, K. (2014) *Citizens, Community and Crime Control*. London: Palgrave Macmillan.

Burnett, R. and Roberts, C. (eds) (2004) *What Works in Probation and Youth Justice*. Cullompton: Willan.

Byrne, J. and Marx, G. (2011) 'Technological Innovations in Crime Prevention and Policing. A Review of the Research on Implementation and Impact' *Cahiers Politiestudies Jaargang* 2011–3(20): 17–40.

Carter, P. (2004) *Managing Offenders, Reducing Crime*. London: Strategy Unit.

Case, S. and Haines, K. (2009) *Understanding Youth Offending: Risk Factor Research, Policy and Practice*. Cullompton: Willan.

Cattell, J., Mackie, A., Prestage, Y., and Wood, M. (2013) *Results from the Offender Management Community Cohort Study (OMCCS): Assessment and Sentence Planning*. London: Ministry of Justice.

Clarke, R. (2012) 'Opportunity Makes the Thief. Really? And So What?' *Crime Science* 1(3): 1–9.

Cohen, S. (1985) *Visions of Social Control*. Cambridge: Polity Press.

Coleman, R., Sim, J., and Whyte, D. (2002) 'Power, Politics and Partnerships: The State of Crime Prevention on Merseyside' in Hughes, G. and Edwards, A. (eds) *Crime Control and Community*. Cullompton: Willan.

Cozens, P. (2011) 'Urban Planning and Environmental Criminology: Towards a New Perspective for Safer Cities' *Planning Practice and Research* 26(4): 481–508.

Ekblom, P. (2011) 'Designing Products Against Crime Theory' in Wortley, R. and Mazerolle, L. (eds) *Environmental Criminology and Crime Analysis*. Abingdon: Routledge.

Farmer, D. (1984) *Crime Control*. Plenum Press: New York.

Farrell, G. and Pease, K. (2011) 'Repeat Victimisation' in Wortley, R. and Mazerolle, L. (eds) *Environmental Criminology and Crime Analysis*. Abingdon: Routledge.

Farrell, G., Tilley, N., Tseloni, A., and Mailley, J. (2008) 'The Crime Drop and the Security Hypothesis' *British Society of Criminology Newsletter* 62: 17–21.

Felson, M. (1995) 'Those Who Discourage Crime' in Eck, J. and Weiburd, D. (eds) *Crime and Place: Crime Prevention Studies*. New York: Willow Tree Press.

Felson, M. and Clarke, R. (1998) *Opportunity Makes the Thief*, Police Research Series, Paper 98. London: Home Office.

Garland, D. (2001) *The Culture of Control*. Oxford: Oxford University Press.

Garland, D. (1990) *Punishment and Modern Society*. Oxford: Clarendon Press.

Gemmell, J. (1996) 'The New Conditional Sentencing Regime' *Criminal Law Quarterly* 39: 334–61.

Goldstein, H. (1979) 'Improving Policing: A Problem-Oriented Approach' *Crime and Delinquency* 25: 236–58.

Goldstein, H. (1990) *Problem-Oriented Policing*. New York: McGraw-Hill.

Grabosky, P. (1998) *Technology & Crime Control: Trends and Issues in Crime and Criminal Justice 78*. Canberra: Australian Institute of Criminology.

Grimwood, G. and Berman, G. (2012) 'Reducing Reoffending: The "What Works" Debate' *Research Paper 12/71*, London: House of Commons Library.

Hayward, K. (2007) 'Situational Crime Prevention and its Discontents: Rational Choice Theory versus the "Culture of Now"' *Social Policy & Administration* 41(3): 232–50.

HM Inspector of Constabulary (2014) *Crime Recording: Making the Victim Count*. London: HMIC.

Home Office and Ministry of Justice (2015) *Integrated Offender Management: Key Principles*. London: Home Office.

Jackson, A. (2013) 'Admissibility of Fingerprints Taken on an Unauthorised Device' *Journal of Criminal Law* 77: 376–79.

Kang-Brown, J., Trone, J., Fratello, J., and Daftary-Kapur, T. (2013) 'A Generation Later: What We've Learned about Zero Tolerance in Schools' *Issue Brief*. New York: Vera Institute of Justice.

Karn, J. (2013) *Policing and Crime Reduction: The Evidence and its Implications for Practice*. London: The Police Foundation.

Levitt, S. (1996) 'The Effect of Prison Population Size on Crime Rates: Evidence from Prison Overcrowding Litigation' *The Quarterly Journal of Economics*, 111(2): 319–51.

Lewis, D-M. (2014) 'The Risk Factor—(Re-) visiting Adult Offender Risk Assessments within Criminal Justice Practice' *Risk Management* 16(2): 121–36.

Loader, I., Goold, B., and Thumala, A. (2014) 'The Moral Economy of Security' *Theoretical Criminology* 18(4): 469–88.

Longstaff, A., Willer, J., Chapman, J., Czarnomski, S., and Graham, J. (2015) *Neighbourhood Policing: Past, Present and Future*. London: The Police Foundation.

Mackenzie, S. and Henry, A. (2009) *Community Policing: A Review of the Evidence*. Edinburgh: Scottish Government.

Merrington, S. (2004) 'Assessment Tools in Probation: Their Development and Potential' in Burnett, R. and Roberts, C. (eds) *What Works in Probation and Youth Justice*. Cullompton: Willan.

Merry, S. (1981) 'Defensible Space Undefended' *Urban Affairs Quarterly* 16(4): 397–422.

Ministry of Justice (2013) *Statistics on Race and the Criminal Justice System 2012*. London: Ministry of Justice.

Ministry of Justice (2010) *Disabled People's Experiences of Targeted Violence and Hostility*. London: Ministry of Justice.

Newburn, T. and Jones, T. (2007) 'Symbolizing Crime Control: Reflections on Zero Tolerance' *Theoretical Criminology* 11(2): 221–43.

Newburn, T. and Reiner, R. (2007) 'Policing and the Police' in Maguire et al. (eds) *The Oxford Handbook of Criminology* (4th edn). Oxford: Oxford University Press.

Newman, O. (1972) *Defensible Space*. London: Architectural Press.

Ofer, U. (2011) 'Criminalizing the Classroom: The Rise of Aggressive Policing and Zero Tolerance in New York City Public Schools' *New York Law School Law Review* 56: 1373–1411.

O'Malley, P. (2010) *Crime and Risk*. London: Sage.

Packer, H. (1964) 'Two Models of the Criminal Process' *University of Pennsylvania Law Review* 113(1): 1–68.

Ratcliffe, J. (2016) *Intelligence-Led Policing* (2nd edn). London, Routledge.

Reynald, D. (2010) 'Guardians on Guardianship: Factors Affecting the Willingness to Supervise, the Ability to Detect Potential Offenders, and the Willingness to Intervene' *Journal of Research in Crime and Delinquency* 47(3): 356–90.

Roach, K. (1999) 'Four Models of the Criminal Process' *Journal of Criminal Law and Criminology* 89(2): 671–716.

Roehl, J. (1998) 'Civil Remedies for Controlling Crime: The Role of Community Organizations' *Crime Prevention Studies* 9: 241–59.

Scott, M., Eck, J., Knutsson, J., and Goldstein, H. (2011) 'Problem-Oriented Policing and Environmental Criminology' in Wortley, R. and Mazerolle, L. (eds) *Environmental Criminology and Crime Analysis*. Abingdon: Routledge.

Scott, M. and Goldstein, H. (2005) *Shifting and Sharing Responsibility for Public Safety Problems: Response Guide No. 3* New York: Centre for Problem-Oriented Policing.

Sin, C., Hedges, A., Cook, C., Mguni, N., and Comber, N. (2009) *Disabled People's Experiences of Targeted Violence and Hostility*. London: Office of Public Management.

Smith, R. (2006) 'Actuarialism and Early Intervention in Contemporary Youth Justice' in Goldson, B. and Muncie, J. (eds) *Youth Crime and Justice*. London: Sage.

Stemen, D. (2007) *Reconsidering Incarceration: New Directions for Reducing Crime*. New York: Vera Institute.

Stenson, K. (2009) 'The New Politics of Crime Control' in Stenson, K. and Sullivan, R. (eds) *Crime, Risk and Justice*. Cullompton: Willan.

Stenson, K. (2002) 'Community Safety in Middle England' in Hughes, G. and Edwards, A. (eds) *Crime Control and Community*. Cullompton: Willan.

Strickland, P. (2015) 'Sentences of Imprisonment for Public Protection', *Briefing Paper 06086*, House of Commons Library.

Tarling, R. (1994) 'Editorial: The Effect of Imprisonment on Crime', *Journal of the Royal Statistical Society. Series A*. 157(2): 173–76.

The Sentencing Project (2010) *Report of The Sentencing Project to the United Nations Human Rights Committee Regarding Racial Disparities in the United States Criminal Justice System*. Washington: The Sentencing Project.

The Sentencing Project (2013) *Shadow Report to the United Nations on Racial Disparities in the United States Criminal Justice System*. Available at: http://www.sentencingproject.org/publications/shadow-report-to-the-united-nations-human-rights-committee-regarding-racial-disparities-in-the-united-states-criminal-justice-system/.

Tilley, N. (2010) 'Whither Problem-Oriented Policing' *Criminology & Public Policy* 9(1): 183–95.

Tilley, N. (2002) 'The Rediscovery of Learning: Crime Prevention and Scientific Realism' in Hughes, G. and Edwards, A. (eds) *Crime Control and Community*. Cullompton: Willan.

Tilley, N. and Webb, J. (1994) *Burglary Reduction: Findings from Safer Cities Schemes*. London: Home Office.

Turley, C., Ranns, H., Callanan, M., Blackwell, A., and Newburn, T. (2012) *Delivering Neighbourhood Policing in Partnership. Research Report 61*. London: Home Office.

Webster, C. (2015) '"Race", Youth Crime and Youth Justice' in Goldson, B. and Muncie, J. (eds) *Youth Crime & Justice* (2nd edn). London: Sage.

Weisburd, D., Telep, C., Hinkle, J., and Eck, J. (2010) 'Is Problem-Oriented Policing Effective in Reducing Crime and Disorder?' *Criminology & Public Policy* 9(1): 139–72.

Westmarland, N., Hardey, M., Bows, H., Branley, D., Chowdhury, M., Wheatley, K., and Wistow, R. (2013) *Protecting Women's Safety? The Use of Smartphone 'Apps' in Relation to Domestic and Sexual Violence* Research Briefing No. 12. Durham: Durham University School of Applied Social Sciences.

Wilson, E. and Hinks, S. (2011) *Assessing the Predictive Validity of the Asset Youth Risk Assessment Tool using the Juvenile Cohort Study (JCS)*. London: Ministry of Justice.

Wilson, J. and Kelling, G. (1982) 'Broken Windows' *The Atlantic Monthly* 249(3): 29–38.

Wortley, R. (2011) 'Situational Precipitators of Crime' in Wortley, R. and Mazerolle, L. (eds) *Environmental Criminology and Crime Analysis*. Abingdon: Routledge.

Zedner, L. (2006) 'Liquid Security: Managing the Market for Crime Control' *Criminology and Criminal Justice* 6: 267–88.

Chapter 24

Allen, R. (2008) 'Changing Public Attitudes to Crime and Punishment—Building Confidence in Community Penalties' *Probation Journal* 55(4): 389–400.

Almond, P. (2009) 'Understanding the Seriousness of Corporate Crime' *Criminology and Criminal Justice* 9(2): 145–64.

Anderson, S. (2011) *The Social Care Needs of Short-Sentence Prisoners*. London: Revolving Doors Agency.

Armstrong, S. and Weaver, B. (2010) *What Do the Punished Think of Punishment*, Research Report No. 04/2010. Glasgow: The Scottish Centre for Crime & Justice Research.

Bandes, S. (2000) 'When Victims Seek Closure: Forgiveness, Vengeance and the Role of Government' *Fordham Urban Law Journal* XXVII: 1599–606.

Banks, C. (2004) *Criminal Justice Ethics: Theory and Practice*. Thousand Oaks CA: Sage.

Bateman, T. (2011) 'Child Imprisonment: Exploring "Injustice by Geography"' *Prison Journal* 197: 10–14.

Beccaria, C. (1995) *On Crimes and Punishments and Other Writings*. Cambridge, Cambridge University Press.

Beccaria, C. (1986) *On Crimes and Punishment*. Indianapolis, IA: Hackett.

Becker, G. (1968) 'Crime and Punishment: An Economic Approach' *Journal of Political Economy* 76(2): 169–217.

Bentham, J. (2003/1859) *The Works of Jeremy Bentham: Volume 1.1*. Chestnut Hill, MA: Adamant Media Corporation.

Bronsteen, J., Buccafusco, C., and Masur, J. (2008) *Happiness and Punishment*. Chicago: Chicago Law School.

Brownlee, I. (1998) *Community Punishment: A Critical Introduction*. London: Longman.

Clarke, K. (2012) 'Ministerial Foreword' in Ministry of Justice, *Punishment and Reform: Effective Community Sentences*. London: Ministry of Justice.

Duff, R. and Garland, D. (1994) 'Introduction: Thinking about Punishment' in Duff, R. and Garland, D. (eds) *A Reader on Punishment*. Oxford: Oxford University Press.

Edgar, K. (2010) *A Fair Response*. London: Prison Reform Trust.

Edwards, I. (2004) 'An Ambiguous Participant: The Crime Victim and Criminal Justice Decision-Making' *British Journal of Criminology* 44: 967–82.

Esmaili, H. and Gans, J. (1999) 'Islamic Law Across Cultural Borders: The Involvement of Western Nationals in Saudi Murder Trials' *Denver Journal of International Law and Policy* 28(2): 145–74.

Fletcher, G. (1999) 'The Place of Victims in the Theory of Retribution' *Buffalo Criminal Law Review* 3(1): 51–63

Foucault, M. (1979) *Discipline and Punish*. New York: Vintage Books.

Foucault, M. (1984) 'Complete and Austere Institutions' in Rabinow, P. (ed.) *The Foucault Reader*. Harmondsworth: Penguin Books.

Friedman, D. (1979) 'Private Creation and Enforcement of Law: A Historical Case' *Journal of Legal Studies* 8(2): 399–415.

Garland, D. (2011) 'The Problem of the Body in Modern State Punishment' *Social Research* 78(3): 767–98.

Godfrey, B. and Lawrence, P. (2005) *Crime and Justice 1750–1950*. Cullompton: Willan.

Grayling, C. (2012) 'Foreword' in Ministry of Justice, *Punishment and Reform: Effective Community Sentences Government Response*. London: The Stationery Office.

Home Office (2014) *Anti-social Behaviour, Crime and Policing Act 2014: Reform of Anti-social Behaviour Powers: Statutory guidance for Frontline Professionals*. London: Home Office.

Hough, M., Jacobson, J., and Millie, A. (2003) *The Decision to Imprison: Sentencing and the Prison Population*. London: Prison Reform Trust.

Hough, M., Radford, R., Jackson, J. and Roberts, J. (2013) *Attitudes to sentencing and trust in justice: exploring trends from the crime survey for England and Wales*. London: Ministry of Justice.

Jacobson, J. and Kirby, A. (2012) *Public Attitudes to Youth Crime: Report on Focus Group Research*. London: Home Office.

King, R. and Ward, R. (2015) 'Rethinking the Bloody Code in Eighteenth-Century Britain: Capital Punishment at the Centre and on the Periphery' *Past and Present* 228(1): 159–205.

Kolber, A. (2009) 'The Subjective Experience of Punishment' *Columbia Law Review*, 109: 182–236.

Koritansky, P. (2012) *Thomas Aquinas and the Philosophy of Punishment*: Washington DC: Catholic University of America Press.

Lee, A. (2013) 'Public Wrongs and the Criminal Law' *Criminal Law and Philosophy* 9: 155–70.

Materni, M. (2013) 'Criminal Punishment and the Pursuit of Justice' *British Journal of American Legal Studies* 2(1): 263–304.

McLoughlin, E., Muncie, J., and Hughes, G. (2001) 'The Permanent Revolution: New Labour, New Public Management and the Modernization of Criminal Justice' *Criminal Justice* 1(3): 301–18.

Ministry of Justice (2014) *Criminal Justice Statistics Quarterly Update to June 2014 England and Wales*. London: Ministry of Justice.

Ministry of Justice (2013) 'Costs per Place and Costs per Prisoner' *Information Release* 17 October.

Moore, M. (1999) 'Victims and Retribution: A Reply to Professor Fletcher' *Buffalo Criminal Law Review* 3(1): 65–89.

Morris, A. and Giller, H. (1987) *Understanding Juvenile Justice*. London: Croom Helm.

Muncie, J. (2002) 'A New Deal for Youth? Early Intervention and Correctionalism' in Hughes, G., McLaughlin, E., and Muncie, J. (eds) *Crime Prevention and Community Safety: New Directions*. London: Sage.

National Audit Office (2012) *Comparing International Criminal Justice Systems*. London: National Audit Office.

Naughton, M. (2005) 'Redefining Miscarriages of Justice' *British Journal of Criminology* 45(2): 165–82.

O'Malley (2009) 'Theorizing Fines', *Punishment and Society*, 11(1): 67–83.

Phillips, L. (2007) 'How Important is Punishment?', Speech to Howard League, 15 November.

Prison Reform Trust (2013) *Prison: The Facts*. London: Prison Reform Trust.

Roberts, J. and Hough, M. (2005) 'Sentencing Young Offenders: Public Opinion in England and Wales' *Criminal Justice* 5(3): 211–32.

Social Exclusion Unit (2002) *Reducing Re-offending by Ex-Prisoners*. London: The Stationery Office.

Taylor, E., Clarke, R. and McArt, D. (2014) 'The Intensive Alternative to Custody: "Selling" Sentences and Satisfying Judicial Concerns' *Probation Journal* 61(1): 44–59.

Thorsson, O. (2001) *The Sagas of Icelanders*. Harmondsworth: Penguin Books.

Tomlinson, M. (1981) 'Penal Servitude 1846-1865: A System in Evolution' in Bailey, V. (ed.) *Policing and Punishment in Nineteenth Century Britain*. London: Croom Helm.

Webb, S. (2011) *Execution: A History of Capital Punishment in Britain*. Stroud: The History Press.

Wiener, M. (1990) *Reconstructing the Criminal: Culture, Law, and Policy in England 1830–1914*. Cambridge: Cambridge University Press.

Chapter 25

Bonta, J., Bourgon, G., Rugge, T., Scott, T., Yessine, A., Guutierrez, L., and Li, J. (2011) 'An Experimental Demonstration of Training Probation Officers in Evidence-Based Community Supervision' *Criminal Justice and Behavior* 38(11): 1127–47.

Cohen, S. (1985) *Visions of Social Control*. Cambridge: Polity Press.

Cullen, F. and Gendreau, P. (2000) 'Assessing Correctional Rehabilitation: Policy, Practice and Prospects' in Horney, L. (ed.) *Criminal Justice 2000 Vol 3*, Washington DC: National Institute of Justice.

Durnescu, I. (2011) *Resettlement Research and Practices. An International Perspective*. Utrecht: Confederation of European Probation. Available at http://www.cepprobation.org/uploaded_files/Durnescu-CEP-Resettlement-research-and-practice-final.pdf.

Duwe, G. and Johnson, B. (2013) 'Estimating the Benefits of a Faith-Based Correctional Program' *International Journal of Criminology and Sociology* 2: 227–39.

Edgar, K., Aresti, A., and Cornish, N. (2012) *Out for Good: Taking Responsibility for Resettlement*. London: Prison Reform Trust.

Farrall, S. (2002) *Rethinking What Works with Offenders*. Cullompton: Willan.

Farrall, S. and McNeill, F. (2011) *Desistance Research and Criminal Justice Social Work*, Utrecht: Confederation of European Probation. Available at http://cepprobation.org/wp-content/uploads/2015/03/Farrall_McNeill_Transnational_Criminology_Manual.pdf.

Freud, S. (1960) *The Ego and the Id*. New York: W. W. Norton.

Gordon, M. (2010) 'The Failure of Prison and the Value of Treatment' in Priestly, P. and Vanstone, M. (eds) *Offenders or Citizens? Readings in Rehabilitation*. Cullompton: Willan.

Government of British Columbia (2012) *Revealing Research & Evaluation*, Issue 6, Fall.

Grimshaw, R. (2002) 'A Place to Call Your Own: Does Housing Need Make a Difference to Crime?' *Criminal Justice Matters* 50(1): 8–9.

Grimwood, G. and Berman, G. (2012) *Reducing Reoffending: The 'What Works' Debate*, Research Paper 12/71, House of Commons Library.

Hannah-Moffat, K. (2005) 'Criminogenic Needs and the Transformative Risk Subject' *Punishment and Society* 7(1): 29–51.

Harper, G. and Chitty, C. (2005) 'Executive Summary' in Harper, G. and Chitty, C. (eds) *The Impact of Corrections on Re-offending: A Review of 'what works'*, London: Home Office.

HM Inspectorate of Prisons, HM Inspectorate of Probation and Ofsted (2014) *Resettlement Provision for Adult Offenders: Accommodation and Education, Training and Employment*. London: HM Inspectorate of Prisons.

Hollin, C. (1999) 'Treatment Programs for Offenders: Meta-Analysis, 'What Works', and Beyond' *International Journal of Law and Psychiatry* 22(3–4): 361–72.

Holmes, T. (2010) 'Reforming Criminals' in Priestly, P. and Vanstone, M. (eds) *Offenders or Citizens? Readings in Rehabilitation*. Cullompton: Willan.

Ignatieff, M. (1978) *A Just Measure of Pain*. London: Penguin Books.

Johnson, B. and Jang, S. (2010) 'Crime and Religion: Assessing the Role of the Faith Factor' in Rosenfeld, R., Quinet, K., and Garcia, C. (eds) *Contemporary Issues in Criminological Theory and Research: The Role of Social Institutions. Papers from the American Society of Criminology Conference*. Belmont, CA: CENGAGE Learning.

Johnson, C. and Rex, S. (2002) 'Community Service: Rediscovering Reintegration' in Ward, D., Scott, J., and Lacey, M. (eds) *Probation: Working for Justice* (2nd edn). Oxford: Oxford University Press.

Leeson, C. (1914) *The Probation System*. London: P.S. King & Son.

Lewis, S., Vennard, J., Maguire, M., Raynor, P., Vanstone, M., Raybould, S., and Rix, A. (2003) *The Resettlement of Short-term Prisoners: An Evaluation of Seven Pathfinders*. London: Home Office.

Lipscombe, S. and Beard, J. (2014) *The Rehabilitation of Offenders Act 1974*. London: House of Commons Library.

Lipsey, M. (1999) 'Can Intervention Rehabilitate Serious Delinquents?' *Annals of the American Academy of Political and Social Science* 564: 142–66.

Lipsey, M. (1995) 'What do We Learn from 400 Research Studies on the Effectiveness of Treatment with Juvenile Delinquents?' in McGuire, J. (ed.) *What Works: Reducing Offending*. Chichester: Wiley.

Lipsey, M. and Cullen, F. (2007) 'The Effectiveness of Correctional Rehabilitation: A Review of Systematic Reviews' *Annual Review of Law and Social Science* 3: 1–44.

Lipsey, M., Landenberger, N., and Wilson, S. (2007) 'Effects of Cognitive-Behavioural Programs for Criminal Offenders' *Campbell Systematic Reviews*, 6.

Maguire, M. (2007) 'The Resettlement of Ex-prisoners' in Gelsthorpe, L. and Morgan, R. (eds) *Handbook of Probation*. Cullompton: Willan.

Martinson, R. (1974) 'What Works?-Questions and Answers about Prison Reform', *The Public Interest* 35 Spring: 22–54.

Martinson, R. (1979) 'New Findings, New Views: A Note of Caution Regarding Sentencing Reform' *Hofstra Law Review* 7(2): 243–58.

May, T. (1991) *Probation: Policy, Politics and Practice*. Milton Keynes: Open University Press.

McCord, J. (1992) 'The Cambridge-Somerville Study: A Pioneering Longitudinal Experimental Study of Delinquency Prevention' in McCord, J. and Tremblay, R. (eds) *Preventing Antisocial Behavior: Interventions form Birth through Adolescence*. New York: Guilford Press.

McGuire, J. and Priestley, P. (1995) 'Reviewing "What Works": Past, Present and Future' in McGuire, J. (ed.) *What Works: Reducing Offending*. Chichester: Wiley.

McNeill, F. (2014) 'Punishment as Rehabilitation' in Bruinsma, G. and Weisburd, D. (eds) *Encyclopedia of Criminology and Criminal Justice*. New York: Springer.

McNeill, F. (2012) 'Four Forms of "Offender" Rehabilitation: Towards an Interdisciplinary Perspective' *Legal and Criminological Psychology* 2012: 1–19.

McNeill, F. (2009) *Towards Effective Practice in Offender Supervision*. Glasgow: Scottish Centre for Crime & Justice Research.

McNeill, F. (2005) 'Remembering Probation in Scotland' *Probation Journal* 52(1): 23–38.

McNeill, F. and Weaver, B. (2010) *Changing Lives? Desistance Research and Offender Management*. Glasgow: Scottish Centre for Crime & Justice Research.

Ministry of Justice (2013) *Transforming Rehabilitation: A Summary of Evidence on Reducing Reoffending*. London: Ministry of Justice.

Ministry of Justice (2010) *Breaking the Cycle: Effective Punishment, Rehabilitation and Sentencing of Offenders*, Cm 7972. London: Ministry of Justice.

Niven, S. and Olagundoye, J. (2002) *Jobs and Homes: A Survey of Prisoners Nearing Release*, Home Office Research Findings 173. London: Home Office.

Poulton, F. (2010) 'The Spiritual Factor' in Priestly, P. and Vanstone, M. (eds) *Offenders or Citizens? Readings in Rehabilitation*. Cullompton: Willan.

Purvis, M., Ward, T., and Willis, G. (2011) 'The Good Lives Model in Practice: Offence Pathways and Case Management' *European Journal of Probation* 3(2): 4–26.

Raynor, P. (2007) 'Theoretical Perspectives on Resettlement: What it is and How it Might Work' in Hucklesby, A. and Hagley-Dickinson, L. (eds) *Prisoner Resettlement: Policy and Practice*. Cullompton: Willan.

Raynor, P. (2004) 'The Probation Service "Pathfinders"' *Criminal Justice* 4(3): 309–25.

Raynor, P. (2003) 'Evidence-based Probation and its Critics' *Probation Journal* 50(4): 334–45.

Raynor. P. and Robinson, G. (2009) 'Why Help Offenders? Arguments for Rehabilitation as a Penal Strategy' *European Journal of Probation* 1(1): 3–20.

Robinson, G. (2008) 'Late-modern Rehabilitation' *Punishment & Society* 10(4): 429–45.

Robinson, G. and Crow, I. (2009) *Offender Rehabilitation: Theory, Research and Practice*. London: Sage.

Saleilles, R. (2010) 'The Individualization of Punishment' in Priestley, P. and Vanstone, M. (eds) *Offenders or Citizens?* Cullompton: Willan.

Sapouna, M., Bisset, C., and Conlong, A-M. (2011) *What Works to Reduce Reoffending: A Summary of the Evidence*. Edinburgh: Scottish Government.

Sherman, L., Gottfriedson, D., MacKenzie, D., Eck, J., Reuter, P., and Bushway, S. (1998) *Preventing Crime: What Works, What Doesn't, What's Promising*. Washington DC: US Department of Justice.

Stewart, D. (2008) *The problems and needs of newly sentenced prisoners: results from a national survey*, Ministry of Justice Research Series 16/08. London: Ministry of Justice.

Volokh, A. (2011) 'Do Faith-Based Prisons Work?' *Alabama Law Review* 63(1): 43–95.

Ward, T. and Gannon, T. (2006) 'Rehabilitation, Etiology and Self-Regulation: The Comprehensive Good Lives Model of Treatment for Sexual Offenders' *Aggression and Violent Behaviour* 11: 77–94.

Ward, T. and Maruna, S. (2007) *Rehabilitation*. Abingdon: Routledge.

Webster, R., Hedderman, C., Turnbull, P., and May, T. (2001) *Building Bridges to Employment for Prisoners*. London: Home Office.

Wikstrom, P-O. and Treiber, K. (2008) *Offending Behaviour Programmes*. London: Youth Justice Board.

Wylie, L. and Griffin, H. (2013) 'G-map's Application of the Good Lives Model to Adolescent Males Who Sexually Harm: A Case Study' *Journal of Sexual Aggression* 19(3): 345–56.

Zane, S., Welsh, B., and Zimmerman, G. (2015) 'Examining the Iatrogenic Effects of the Cambridge-Somerville Youth Study: Existing Explanations and New Appraisals' *British Journal of Criminology*, Online, doi: 10.1093/bjc/azv033

Chapter 26

Austin, J. and Krisberg, B. (2002) 'Wider, Stronger and Different Nets: The Dialectics of Criminal Justice Reform' in Muncie, J., Hughes, G., and McLaughlin, E. (eds) *Youth Justice: Critical Readings*. London: Sage.

Barnes, B. (2013) 'An Overview of Restorative Justice Programs' *Alaska Journal of Dispute Resolution* 1: 101–20.

Bateman, T. (2015) 'Trends in Detected Youth Crime and Contemporary State Responses' in Goldson, B. and Muncie, J. (eds) *Youth Crime & Justice* (2nd edn). London: Sage.

Bell, A., Hodgson, M., and Pragnell, S. (1999) 'Diverting Children and Young People from Crime and the Criminal Justice System' in Goldson, B. (ed.) *Youth Justice: Contemporary Policy and Practice*. Aldershot: Ashgate.

Blagg, H. (1985) 'Reparation and Justice for Juveniles' *British Journal of Criminology* 25: 267–79.

Blagg, H., Derricourt, N., Finch, J., and Thorpe, D. (1986) *The Final Report on the Juvenile Liaison Bureau Corby*. Lancaster: University of Lancaster.

Bowling, B. and Phillips, C. (2003) 'Policing Ethnic Minority Communities' in Newburn, T. (ed.) *Handbook of Policing*. Cullompton: Willan.

Boyes-Watson C. (2000) 'Reflections on the Purist and Maximalist Models of Restorative Justice' *Contemporary Justice Review* 3(4): 441–50.

Braithwaite, J. (2004a) 'The Evolution of Restorative Justice' in UNAFEI (ed.) *Annual Report for 2003 and Resource Material Series No.63* Tokyo: UNAFEI.

Braithwaite, J. (2004b) 'Restorative Justice: Theories and Worries' in UNAFEI (ed.) *Annual Report for 2003 and Resource Material Series No.63* Tokyo:, UNAFEI.

Braithwaite, J. (1998) 'Restorative Justice' in Tonry, M. (ed.) *Handbook of Crime & Punishment*. Oxford: Oxford University Press.

Braithwaite, J. (1989) *Crime, Shame and Reintegration*. Cambridge: Cambridge University Press.

Brehm, H., Uggen, C., and Gasanabo, J-D. (2014) 'Genocide, Justice, and Rwanda's Gacaca Courts' *Journal of Contemporary Criminal Justice* 30(3): 333–52.

Campbell, C., Devlin, R., O'Mahony, D., Doak, J., Jackson, J., Corrigan, T., and McEvoy, K. (2006) *Evaluation of the Northern Ireland Youth Conference Service*. Belfast: Northern Ireland Office.

Centre for Mental Health, Rethink and the Royal College of Psychiatrists (2010) *Diversion: The Business Case for Action*. London: Centre for Mental Health.

Christie, N. (1977) 'Conflicts as Property' *British Journal of Criminology* 17(1): 1–15.

Clamp, K. and Doak, J. (2012) 'More than Words: Restorative Justice Concepts in Transitional Justice Settings' *International Criminal Law Review* 12: 339–60.

Cohen, S. (1985) *Visions of Social Control*. Cambridge: Polity Press.

Crawford, A. and Newburn, T. (2003) *Youth Offending and Restorative Justice*. Cullompton: Willan.

Daly, K. (2002) 'Restorative Justice: The Real Story' *Punishment & Society* 4(1): 55–79.

Davis, G., Boucherat, J., and Watson, D. (1989) 'Pre-Court Decision-Making in Juvenile Justice' *British Journal of Criminology* 29(3): 219–35.

Dignan, J. (1990) *Repairing the Damage*. Sheffield: University of Sheffield.

Flanagan, R. (2007) *The Review of Policing: Interim Report*. Surbiton: The Police Federation.

Gabbay, Z. (2005) 'Justifying Restorative Justice: A Theoretical Justification for the Use of restorative practices' *Journal of Dispute Resolution* 2005(2): 349–97.

Graef, R. (2000) *Why Restorative Justice?* London: Calouste Gulbenkian Foundation.

Haines, K., Case, S., Davies, K., and Charles, A. (2013) 'The Swansea Bureau: A model of diversion from the Youth Justice System' *International Journal of Law, Crime and Justice* 41(2): 167–87.

Haines, A., Goldson, B., Haycox, A., Houten, R., Lane, S., McGuire, J., Nathan, T., Perkins, E., Richards, S., and Whittington, R. (2012) *Evaluation of the Youth Justice Liaison and Diversion (YJLD) Pilot Scheme*. Liverpool: University of Liverpool.

Hamilton, C. (2011) *Guidance for Legislative Reform on Juvenile Justice*. New York: Unicef.

Harris, N. and Maruna, S. (2006) 'Shame, Shaming and Restorative Justice' in Sullivan, D. and Tifft, L. (eds) *Handbook of Restorative Justice: A Global Perspective*. Abingdon: Routledge.

Hough, M., Bradford, B., Jackson, J., and Roberts, J. (2013) *Attitudes to Sentencing and Trust in Justice: Exploring Trends from the Crime Survey for England and Wales*. London: Ministry of Justice.

House of Commons Justice Committee (2013) *Youth Justice*. London: The Stationery Office.

House of Commons Justice Committee (2009) *Cutting Crime: The Case for Justice Reinvestment*. London: The Stationery Office.

Hughes, G., Pilkington, A., and Leisten, R. (1998) 'Diversion in a Culture of Severity' *Howard Journal* 37(1): 16–33.

Jacobson, J. and Kirby, A. (2012) *Public Attitudes to Youth Crime: Report on Focus Group Research*. London: Home Office.

Johnstone (2002) *Restorative Justice: Ideas, Values, Debates*. Cullompton: Willan.

Kretschmar, J., Butcher, F., Flannery, D., and Singer, M. (2016) 'Diverting Juvenile Justice-Involved Youth with Behavioral Health Issues from Detention: Preliminary Findings From Ohio's Behavioral Health Juvenile Justice (BHJJ) Initiative' *Criminal Justice Policy Review* 27(3): 1–24.

Lacey, L. (2012) *Youth Justice in England and Wales: Exploring Young Offenders' Perceptions of Restorative and Procedural Justice in the Referral Order Process*, Phd thesis. London: London School of Economics.

Larsen, J. (2014) *Restorative Justice in the Australian Criminal Justice System*. Canberra: Australian Institute of Criminology.

Lemert, E. (1967) *Human Deviance, Social Problems, and Social Control*, Englewood Cliffs, NJ: Prentice Hall.

Maruna, S., Wright, S., Brown, J., van Marle, F., Devlin, R., and Liddle, M. (2007) *Youth Conferencing as Shame Management: Results of a Long-term Follow-Up Study*. Belfast: ARCS.

Matrix Evidence (2009) *Economic Analysis of Interventions for Young Adult Offenders*. London: Barrow Cadbury Trust.

Mays, J. (1965) 'The Liverpool Police Juvenile Liaison Officer Scheme' *The Sociological Review* Monograph No. 9: 185–200.

McAra, L. and McVie, S. (2007) 'Youth Justice? The Impact of System Contact on Patterns of Desistance from Offending' *European Journal of Criminology* 4(3): 315–45.

Menkel-Meadow, C. (2007) 'Restorative Justice: What Is It and Does It Work?' *Annual Review of Law and Social Science* 3: 10.1–10.27.

Mills, H. (2011) 'The "Alternative to Custody" Myth' *Criminal Justice Matters* 83(1): 34–6.

Ministry of Justice (2012) *Justice Reinvestment Pilots: First Year Results*. London: Ministry of Justice.

Mongold, J. and Edwards, B. (2014) 'Reintegrative Shaming: Theory into Practice' *Journal of Theoretical & Philosophical Criminology* 6(3): 205–12.

Northern Ireland Office (2008) *Alternatives to Prosecution: A Discussion Paper*. Belfast: Northern Ireland Office.

Pratt, J. (1989) 'Corporatism: The Third Model of Juvenile Justice' *British Journal of Criminology* 29: 236–54.

Restorative Justice Consortium (2006) *The Positive Effect of Restorative Justice on Re-offending*. London: Restorative Justice Consortium.

Rix, A., Skidmore, K., Self, R., Holt, T., and Raybould, S. (2011) *Youth Restorative Disposal Process Evaluation*. London: Youth Justice Board.

Robinson, G. and Shapland, J. (2008) 'Reducing Recidivism: A Task for Restorative Justice?' *British Journal of Criminology* 48(3): 337–58.

Schiff, M. (2003) 'Models, Challenges and the Promise of Restorative Conferencing Strategies' in von Hirsch, A., Roberts, J., Bottoms, A., Roach, K., and Schiff, M. (eds) *Restorative Justice and Criminal Justice: Competing or Reconcilable Paradigms?* Oxford: Hart.

Shapland, J., Atkinson, A., Atkinson, H., Chapman, B., Dignan, J., Howes, M., Johnstone, J., Robinson, G., and Sorsby, A. (2007) *Restorative Justice: The Views of Victims and Offenders*. London: Ministry of Justice.

Smith, R. (2014a) *Youth Justice: Ideas, Policy, Practice*. Abingdon: Routledge.

Smith, R. (2014b) 'Re-inventing Diversion' *Youth Justice* 14(2): 109–21.

Smith, R. (2011a) 'Developing Restorative Practice: Contemporary Lessons from an English Juvenile Diversion Project of the 1980s' *Contemporary Justice Review* 14(4): 425–38.

Smith, R. (2011b) *Doing Justice to Young People*. Cullompton: Willan.

Smith, R. (2010) 'Children's Rights and Youth Justice: 20 Years of No Progress' *Child Care in Practice* 16(1): 3–17.

Smyth, P. (2011) 'Diverting Young Offenders from Crime in Ireland: The Need for More Checks and Balances on the Exercise of Police Discretion' *Crime Law and Social Change* 55: 153–66.

Strang, H., Sherman, L., Mayo-Wilson, E., Woods, D., and Ariel, B. (2013) 'Restorative Justice Conferencing (RJC) Using Face-to-Face Meetings of Offenders and Victims: Effects on Offender Recidivism and Victim Satisfaction. A Systematic Review' *Campbell Systematic Reviews* 2013: 10.

Szmania, S. and Mangis, D. (2005) 'Finding the Right Time and Place: A Case Study Comparison of the Expression of Offender Remorse in Traditional Justice and Restorative Justice Contexts' 89 *Marquette Law Review* 335–58.

Thorpe, D., Smith, D., Green, C., and Paley, J. (1980) *Out of Care: The Community Support of Juvenile Offenders*. London: George Allen & Unwin.

Umbreit, M. (1989) 'Crime Victims Seeking Fairness, Not Revenge: Toward Restorative Justice' *Federal Probation* September: 52–57.

Victim Support (2012) *Out in the Open: What Victims Really Think About Community Sentencing*. London: Victim Support.

Walgrave, L. (2003) 'Imposing Restoration instead of Inflicting Pain' in von Hirsch, A., Roberts, J., Bottoms, A., Roach, L., and Schiff, M. (eds) *Restorative Justice: Competing or Reconcilable Paradigms?*. Oxford: Hart Publishing, Oxford.

Wilson, H. and Hoge, R. (2013) 'The Effect of Youth Diversion Programs on Recidivism' *Criminal Justice and Behaviour* 40(5): 497–518.

Wood, W. (2015) 'Why Restorative Justice Will Not Reduce Incarceration', *British Journal of Criminology*, advance access, doi: 10.1093/bjc/azu/108

Zehr, H. (2003) *The Little Book of Restorative Justice* (2nd edn). Pennsylvania: Good Books.

Zimring, F. (2000) 'The Common Thread: Diversion in Juvenile Justice' *California Law Review* 88(6): 2481–95.

Chapter 27

Althusser, L. (1971) *Lenin and Philosophy and Other Essays*. London: Verso.

Barton, A., Corteen, K., Scott, D., and Whyte, D. (2007) 'Conclusion: Expanding the Criminological Imagination' in Barton, A., Corteen, K., Scott, D., and Whyte, D. (eds) *Expanding the Criminological Imagination*. Cullompton: Willan.

Bazemore, G. (1997) 'Conferences, Circles, Boards, and Mediations: The "New Wave" of Community Justice Decisionmaking' *Federal Probation* 61(2): 25–37.

Beck, U. (1992) *Risk Society* London: Sage.

Becker, H. (1967) 'Whose Side Are We On?' *Social Problems* 14(3): 239–47.

Bianchi, H. (1994) 'Abolition: Assensus and Sanctuary' in Duff, A. and Garland, D. (eds) *A Reader on Punishment*. Oxford: Oxford University Press.

Blagg, H. (2009) *Evaluation of the Red Dust Role Models*. Fitzroy, Victoria: Red Dust Role Models.

Blair, T. (1993) 'Why Crime is a Socialist Issue' *New Statesman* 29 January: 27–8.

Blomberg, T. and Hay, C. (2007) '*Visions of Social Control* revisited' in Downes, D., Rock, P., Chinkin, C., and Gearty, C. (eds) *Crime, Social Control and Human Rights*. Cullompton: Willan.

Bowling, B. and Phillips, C. (2007) 'Ethnicities, Racism, Crime and Criminal Justice' in Maguire, M., Morgan, R., and Reiner, R. (eds) *The Oxford Handbook of Criminology* (4th edn). Oxford: Oxford University Press.

Bruce, J. (2007) *The Role of Structural Factors Underlying Incidences of Extreme Opportunism in Financial Markets*, Phd Thesis, University of South Africa.

Carson, E. (2014) 'Prisoners in 2013', *Bureau of Justice Statistics Bulletin*, September, US Department of Justice.

Chambliss, W. (1976) 'The State and Criminal Law' in Chambliss, W. and Mankoff, M. (eds) *Whose Law, What Order?* New York: Wiley.

Chantrill, P. (1998) 'The Kowanyama Aboriginal Community Justice Group and the Struggle for Legal Pluralism in Australia' *Journal of Legal Pluralism* 40: 23–60.

Chapman, T. (2012) 'The Problem of Community in a Justice System in Transition: The Case of Community Restorative Justice in Northern Ireland' *International Criminal Law Review* 12(3): 573–87.

Cohen, S. (1985) *Visions of Social Control*. Cambridge: Polity Press.

Cullis, J., Jones, P., Lewis, A., Castigkioni, C., and Lozza, E. (2015) 'Do Poachers Make Harsh Gamekeepers? Attitudes to Tax Evasion and to Benefit Fraud' *Journal of Behavioral and Experimental Economics* 58, Oct: 124–31.

Edwards, T. (2015) 'Criminal Failure and "The Chilling Effect": A Short History of the Bhopal Criminal Prosecutions' *Social Justice* 41(1–2): 53–79.

Foucault, M. (1977) *Discipline and Punish: The Birth of the Prison*. Harmondsworth: Penguin Books.

Gibson, J. (2005) 'The Truth about Truth and Reconciliation in South Africa' *International Political Science Review* 26(4): 341–61.

Gibson, J. (2009) 'On Legitimacy Theory and the Effectiveness of Truth Commissions' *Law and Contemporary Problems* Spring: 123–41.

Gilbert, M. and Settles, T. (2007) 'The Next Step: Indigenous Development of Neighbourhood-Restorative Community Justice' *Criminal Justice Review* 32(1): 5–25.

Gramsci (1971) *Selections from Prison Notebooks*. London: Lawrence & Wishart.

Greener, I. (2006) 'Nick Leeson and the Collapse of Barings Bank: Socio-Technical Networks and the "Rogue Trader"' *Organization* 13(3): 421–41.

Hopkins, K. (2015) 'Associations Between Police-Recorded Ethnic Background and Being Sentenced to Prison in England and Wales'. Ministry of Justice Analytical Services, https://www.gov.uk/government/uploads/system/uploads/attachment_data/file/479874/analysis-of-ethnicity-and-custodial-sentences.pdf.

Hoyle, C. and Zedner, L. (2007) 'Victims, Victimization and Criminal Justice' in Maguire, M., Morgan, R., and Reiner, R. (eds) *The Oxford Handbook of Criminology* (4th edn). Oxford: Oxford University Press.

Hughes, J. (2015) 'Reconstruction without Reconciliation: Is Northern Ireland a "Model"?', in Kissane, B. (ed) *After Civil War: Division, Reconstruction, and Reconciliation in Contemporary Europe*. Philadelphia: University of Pennsylvania Press.

Jefferson, T. (2015) 'The 2011 English Riots: A Contextualised, Dynamic, Grounded Explanation' *Contention* 2(2): 5–22.

Jones, D. (2012) *Conditions for Sustainable Decarceration Policies for Young Offenders*, PhD thesis, London School of Economics.

Karp, D. and Clear, T. (2000) 'Community Justice: A Conceptual Framework' in Friel, C. (ed.) *Criminal Justice 2000, Volume 2*. Washington: US Department of Justice.

Keith, B. (2006) *Report of the Zahid Mubarek Inquiry (Vol.1)*. London: The Stationery Office.

Krisberg, B. and Austin, J. (1993) *Reinventing Juvenile Justice*. Newbury Park, CA: Sage.

Ku, J. and Nzelibe, J. (2006) 'Do International Criminal Tribunals Deter or Exacerbate Humanitarian Atrocities?' *Washington University Law Review* 84(4): 777–833.

Lamble, S. (2013) 'The Quiet Dangers of Civilized Rage: Surveying the Punitive Aftermath of England's 2011 Riots' *South Atlantic Quarterly* 112(3): 577–85.

Lea, J. (2002) *Crime and Modernity*. London: Sage.

Lea, J. (1999) 'Social Crime Revisited' *Theoretical Criminology* 3(3): 307–25.

Macpherson, W. (1999) *The Stephen Lawrence Inquiry*, Cm 4262–1. London: The Stationery Office.

Mair, G. and Millings, M. (2011) *Doing Justice Locally: The North Liverpool Community Justice Centre*. London: Centre for Crime and Justice Studies.

Mathiesen, T. (2008) 'The Abolitionist Stance' *Journal of Prisoners on Prisons* 17(2): 58–63.

Mathiesen, T. (1974) *The Politics of Abolition*. London: Martin Robertson.

May, T., Gyateng, T., and Hough, M. (2010) *Differential Treatment in the Youth Justice System, Research Report 50*. London: Equality and Human Rights Commission.

McEvoy, K. and Mika, H. (2002) 'Restorative Justice and the Critique of Informalism in Northern Ireland' *British Journal of Criminology* 42(3): 534–62.

McGrattan, C. (2012) 'Working Through the Past in Bosnia and Northern Ireland: Truth, Reconciliation and the Constraints of Consociationalism' *Journal on Ethnopolitics and Minority Issues in Europe* 11(4): 103–26.

Mika, H. (2006) *Community-based Restorative Justice in Northern Ireland*. Belfast: Institute of Criminology & Criminal Justice, School of Law, Queen's University Belfast.

Ministry of Justice (2013) *Statistics on Race and the Criminal Justice System 2012*. London: Ministry of Justice.

Nagy, R. (2013) 'The Scope and Bounds of Transitional Justice and the Canadian Truth and Reconciliation Commission' *International Journal of Transitional Justice* 7: 52–73.

Nurse, A. (2014) 'Critical Perspectives on Green Criminology: An Introduction' in Nurse, A. (ed.) *Critical Perspectives on Green Criminology*, Internet Journal of Criminology, http://www.internetjournalofcriminology.com/Critical_Perspectives_On_Green_Criminology_June_2014.pdf.

O'Brien, M. and Penna, S. (2007) 'Critical Criminology: Continuity and Change' *Criminal Justice Review* 32(3): 246–55.

O'Shea, A. (2008) 'Truth and Reconciliation Commissions' in *Max Planck Encyclopedia of Public International Law*. Oxford: Oxford Public International Law.

Pavlich, G. (1999) 'Criticism and Criminology: In Search of Legitimacy' *Theoretical Criminology* 3(1): 29–51.

Pearce, F. (1977) *The Crimes of the Powerful*. London: Pluto Press.

Penrose, M. (1999) 'Lest We Fail: The Importance of Enforcement in International Criminal Law' *American University International Law Review* 15(2): 320–94.

Pettit, B. and Western, B. (2004) 'Mass Imprisonment and the Life Course: Race and Class Inequality in U.S. Incarceration' *American Sociological Review* 69: 151–69.

Prison Reform Trust (2014) 'Prison: The Facts', *Bromley Briefings*, Summer.

Quinney, R. (1977) *State, Class, Crime*. New York: McKay.

Quinney, R. (1970) *The Social Reality of Crime*. Boston: Little, Brown.

Roberts, R. (2015) 'Racism and Criminal Justice' *Criminal Justice Matters* 101(1): 18–20.

Rock, P. (2007) 'Sociological Theories of Crime' in Maguire, M., Morgan, R., and Reiner, R. (eds) *The Oxford Handbook of Criminology* (4th edn). Oxford: Oxford University Press.

Rothman, D. (1985) 'Social Control: The Uses and Abuses of the Concept in the History of Incarceration' in Cohen, S. and Scull, A. (eds) *Social Control and the State*. Oxford: Blackwell.

Ryan, N., Head, B., Keast, R., and Brown, K. (2006) 'Engaging Indigenous Communities: Towards a Policy Framework for Indigenous Community Justice Programs' *Social Policy & Administration* 40(3): 304–21.

Scarman, L. (1982) *The Scarman Report*. Harmondsworth: Penguin Books.

Scott, D. (2013) 'Why Prison? Posing the Question', in Scott, D. (ed.) *Why Prison?* Cambridge: Cambridge University Press.

Scraton, P. (2002) 'Defining "Power" and Challenging "Knowledge": Critical Analysis as Resistance in the UK' in Carrington, K. and Hogg, R. (eds) *Critical Criminology: Issues, Debates, Challenges*. Cullompton: Willan.

Sim, J. (2012) "Shock and Awe': judicial responses to the riots' *Criminal Justice Matters*, 89(1): 26–27.

Sim, J. (2009) *Punishment and Prisons: Power and the Carceral State*. Sage: London.

Skaar, E. (2013) 'Reconciliation in a Transitional Justice Perspective' *Transitional Justice Review* 1(10): 1–50.

Slapper, G. and Tombs, S. (1999) *Corporate Crime*. Harlow: Pearson Educational Ltd.

Smith, D. (2009) 'Criminology, Contemporary Society and Race Issues' in Bhui, H. (ed) *Race & Criminal Justice*. London: Sage.

Smith, R. and Fleming, J. (2011) *Welfare + rights: UR Boss Legal Service*. London: Howard League.

Sykes, G. (1974) 'The Rise of Critical Criminology' *Journal of Criminal Law and Criminology* 65(2): 206–13.

Tavernier, P. (1997) 'L'Expérience des Tribunaux Pénaux Internationaux pour l'Ex-Yougoslavie et pour le Rwanda' *Revue International de la Croix-Rouge* 79(828): 647–63.

Taylor, I., Walton, P., and Young, J. (1973) *The New Criminology*. London: Routledge & Kegan Paul.

Tombs, S. and Whyte, D. (2009) 'The State and Corporate Crime' in Coleman, R., Sim, J., Tombs, S., and Whyte, D. (eds) *State Power Crime*. London: Sage.

Vora, J. and Vora, E. (2004) 'The Effectiveness of South Africa's Truth and Reconciliation Commission' *Journal of Black Studies* 34(3): 301–22.

Walker, N. (1974) 'Lost Causes in Criminology' in Hood, R. (ed.) *Crime, Criminology and Public Policy: Essays in Honour of Sir Leon Radzinowicz*. London: Heinemann.

Walklate, S. (2004) *Gender, Crime and Criminal Justice* (2nd edn). Cullompton: Willan.

Weaver, B. (2011) 'Co-Producing Community Justice: The Transformative Potential of Personalisation for Penal Sanctions' *British Journal of Social Work* 41: 1038–57.

Williams, K., Papadopoulou, V., and Booth, N. (2012) *Prisoners' Childhood and Family Backgrounds*, Ministry of Justice Research Series 4/12. London: Ministry of Justice.

Wilson, R., Huculak, B., and McWhinnie, A. (2002) 'Restorative Justice Innovations in Canada' *Behavioral Sciences and the Law* 20: 363–80.

Wilson, S. (2001) 'The Myth of Restorative Justice: Truth, Reconciliation and the Ethics of Amnesty' *South African Journal of Human Rights* 17: 531–62.

Yarrow, S. (2005) *The Experiences of Young Black Men as Victims of Crime*. London: Criminal Justice System Race Unit.

Young, J. (1986) 'The Failure of Criminology: The Need for a Radical Realism' in Matthews, R. and Young, J. (eds) *Confronting Crime*. London: Sage.

Young, L. (2014) *Improving Outcomes for Young Black and/or Muslim Men in the Criminal Justice System (The Young Review)*. London: Barrow Cadbury Trust.

Chapter 28

Benjamin, W. (1934) 'The Author as Producer' (translated by John Heckman) *New Left Review* I/ 62, July/August 1970.

Caulfield, L. and Hill, J. (2014) *Criminological Research for Beginners*. Abingdon: Routledge.

Chamberlain, M. (2013) *Understanding Criminological Research: A Guide to Data Analysis*. London: Sage.

Christians, C. G. (2011) 'Ethics and Politics in Qualitative Research' in Denzin, N. and Lincoln, Y. (eds) *The Sage Handbook of Qualitative Research* (4th edn). London: Sage.

Competition and Markets Authority (2015) 'Undergraduate students: your rights under consumer law' Available at: https://www.gov.uk/government/uploads/system/uploads/attachment_data/file/415732/Undergraduate_students_-_your_rights_under_consumer_law.pdf.

Creative Commons (2015) *State of the Commons Report 2015*. https://stateof.creativecommons.org/2015.

Cunneen, C. (2010) 'Framing the Crimes of Colonialism: Critical Images of Aboriginal Art and Law' in Hayward, K. and Presdee, M. (eds) *Framing Crime: Cultural Criminology and the Image*. Abingdon: Routledge.

De Keijser, J., De Lange, E., and Van Wilsem, J. (2014) 'Wrongful Convictions and the Blackstone Ratio: An Empirical Analysis of Public Attitudes' *Punishment & Society* 16(1): 32–49.

Faust, D. (2009) *The University's Crisis of Purpose*. 1 September 2009. New York: New York Times. Available at: http://www.nytimes.com/2009/09/06/books/review/Faust-t.html?_r=2&pagewanted=2.

Finch, E., and Fafinski, S. (2016) *Criminology Skills* (2nd edn). Oxford: Oxford University Press.

Garland, D. (2001) *The Culture of Control*. Oxford: Oxford University Press.

HMIC (2014) *Rape Monitoring Group: Local Area Data for Lancashire 2013/14*. London: HMIC. Available at: http://www.justiceinspectorates.gov.uk/hmic/wp-content/uploads/lancashire-rmg-digest-2013-14.pdf.

Johnson, P. (2011) 'Reframing Assessments for the University of the Future' *Enhancing Learning in the Social Sciences*, 3(3).

Johnson, P. and Ingram, B. (2007) 'Windows of Opportunity for Unpaid Work?' *Probation Journal* 54(1): 62–69.

Lab, S. K. (2016) *Crime Prevention: Approaches, Practices, and Evaluations* (9th edn). New York: Routledge.

Lambert, C., Parker, A., and Neary, M. (2007) 'Entrepreneurialism and Critical Pedagogy: Reinventing the Higher Education Curriculum' *Teaching in Higher Education* 12(4): 525–37.

Lave, J. and Wenger, E. (1991) *Situated Learning: Legitimate Peripheral Participation*. Cambridge: Cambridge University Press.

Lynch, M. (2015) 'Penal Artifacts: Mining Documents to Advance Punishment and Society Theory' in Miller, J. and Palacios, W. (eds) *Qualitative Research in Criminology*. New Brunswick: Transaction Publishers.

Miron, J. A. (2001) 'Violence, Guns, and Drugs: A Cross-Country Analysis' *The Journal of Law and Economics* 44(S2): 615–33.

Neary, M. (2013) ' Student as Producer: Radicalising the Mainstream in Higher Education' in Dunn, E. and Owen, D. (eds) *The Student Engagement Handbook: Practice in Higher Education*. Bingley: Emerald Books.

Pantazis, C. and Pemberton, S. (2012) 'Harm Audit: The Collateral Damage of Economic Crisis and the Coalition's Austerity Programme' *Criminal Justice Matters* 89: 42–45.

Parfrement-Hopkins, J. and Hall, P. (2009) 'Perceptions of Anti-social Behaviour' in Moon, D. and Walker, A. (eds) *Perceptions of Crime and Anti-social Behaviour: Findings from the 2008/09 British Crime Survey*. Available at: http://webarchive.nationalarchives.gov.uk/20110218135832/rds.homeoffice.gov.uk/rds/pdfs09/hosb1709.pdf.

Pickett, J., Mancini, C., Mears, D., and Gertz, M. (2014) 'Public (Mis) Understanding of Crime Policy: The Effects of Criminal Justice Experience and Media Reliance Criminal Justice Policy Review' *Criminal Justice Policy Review*, 1–23.

Prosser, J. (2011) 'Visual Methodology: Toward a More Seeing Research' in Denzin, N. and Lincoln, Y. (eds) *The Sage Handbook of Qualitative Research* (4th edn). London: Sage.

Radzinowicz, L. (1961) *In Search of Criminology*. London: Heinemann Educational Books.

Scanlon, E., McAndrew, P. and O'Shea, T. (2015) 'Designing for Educational Technology to Enhance the Experience of Learners in Distance Education: How Open Educational Resources, Learning Design and Moocs Are Influencing Learning' *Journal of Interactive Media in Education*, 2015(1), p.Art. 6

Siemens, G. (2005) 'Connectivism: A Learning Theory for the Digital Age' *International Journal of Instructional Technology and Distance Learning* 2(1): 3–10.

Thomas, C. (2010) *Are Juries Fair?* Ministry of Justice Research Series 1/10. London: Ministry of Justice.

Young, A. (2012) 'Criminal Images: The Affective Judgment of Graffiti and Street Art' *Crime Media Culture* 8(3): 297–314.

Chapter 29

Agyeman, J., Bullard, R., and Evans, B. (2003) *Just Sustainabilities: Development in an Unequal World*. Cambridge, Mass.: MIT Press.

Becker, H. (1995) 'Visual Sociology, Documentary Photography, and Photojournalism: It's (Almost) All a Matter of Context' *Visual Sociology* 10(1–2): 5–14.

BBC (2014) Editor Sacked Over 'Hoax' Photos. 14 May 2004. Available at: http://news.bbc.co.uk/1/hi/uk_politics/3716151.stm.

Brown, G. R. (2016) 'The Blue Line on Thin Ice: Police Use of Force Modifications in the Era of Cameraphones and YouTube' *British Journal of Criminology* 56(2): 293–312.

Carrabine, E. (2012) 'Just Images: Aesthetics, Ethics and Visual Criminology' *British Journal of Criminology* 52(3): 463–89.

Carrabine, E. (2014) 'Seeing Things: Violence, Voyeurism and the Camera' *Theoretical Criminology* 18(2) 134–58.

Cohen, S. (2001) *States of Denial: Knowing About Atrocities and Suffering*. Cambridge: Polity Press.

Crank, J. and Jacoby, L. (2015) *Crime, Violence and Global Warming*. Abingdon: Routledge.

Fellig, ['Weegee'] (1945) *Naked City*. New York: Da Capo Press.

Feeley, M. and Simon, J. (1992) 'The New Penology: Notes on the Emerging of Corrections and Its Implications' *Criminology* 30(4): 449–75.

Ferrell, J., Hayward, K., and Young, J. (2008) *Cultural Criminology: An Invitation*. London: Sage.

Foucault, M. (1977) *Discipline and Punish* (A. Sheridan, trans.). London: Vintage Books.

Gekoski, A., Gray, J., and Adler, J. (2012) 'What Makes A Homicide Newsworthy? UK National Tabloid Newspaper Journalists Tell All' *British Journal of Criminology* 52: 1212–32.

Greenfield, S. (2014) *Mind Change: How Digital Technologies are Leaving Their Marks on our Brains*. London: Ebury Publishing.

Hansard (2009) House of Commons, 1 April 2009, cols 267-8, WH. London: Hansard.

Hood, R. (2002) 'Criminology and penal policy: the vital role of empirical research' in Bottoms, A. and Tonry, M. (eds) *Ideology, Crime and Criminal Justice: A symposium in honour of Sir Leon Radzinowicz.* Cullompton: Willan.

Jones, P. and Wardle, C. (2008) '"No Emotion, No Sympathy": The Visual Construction of Maxine Carr' *Crime, Media and Culture* 4(1): 53–71.

Kolb, D. (1984) *Experiential Learning: Experience as the Source of Learning and Development.* New Jersey: Prentice Hall.

Kolb, D. (2015) *Experiential Learning: Experience as the Source of Learning and Development* (2nd edn). New Jersey: Pearson.

Ofqual (2015) *Qualification and Component Levels: Requirements and Guidance for All awarding Organisations and All Qualifications Level descriptors.* Available from: https://www.gov.uk/government/uploads/system/uploads/attachment_data/file/461637/qualification-and-component-levels.pdf.

Pratt, J., Brown, D., Brown, M., Hallsworth, S., and Morrison, W. (eds) (2005) *The New Punitiveness: Trends, theories, perspectives.* Cullompton: Willan.

QAA (2014) Subject Benchmark Statement UK Quality Code for Higher Education: Criminology. Available from: http://www.qaa.ac.uk/en/Publications/Documents/SBS-criminology-14.pdf (last accessed 12 January 2017).

Taylor, I., Walton, P., and Young, J. (1973) *The New Criminology: For a Social Theory of Deviance.* London: Routledge & Kegan Paul.

UNESCO (2005) *United Nations Decade of Education for Sustainable Development (2005–2014): International Implementation Scheme.* Paris: UNESCO. Available at: http://unesdoc.unesco.org/images/0014/001486/148654e.pdf.

Yorke, M. (2004, reissued 2006) *Employability in Higher Education: What it is – What it is not.* Learning and Employability Series. York: Higher Education Academy.

Chapter 30

BMG Research (2013) *Social Enterprise: Market Trends.* Available at: https://www.gov.uk/government/uploads/system/uploads/attachment_data/file/205291/Social_Enterprises_Market_Trends_-_report_v1.pdf.

Balta, M., Coughlan, J., and Hobson, P. (2012) 'Motivations And Barriers In Undergraduate Students' Decisions To Enroll In Placement Courses In The UK' *Journal of International Education Research* 8(4): 399–413.

Bowes, L. and Harvey, L. (2000) *The Impact of Sandwich Education on the Activities of Graduates Six Months Post-Graduation.* London: National Centre for Work Experience and the Centre for Research into Quality.

Brennan, J., Little, B., Connor, H., de Weert, E., Delve, S., Harris, J., Josselyn, B., Ratcliffe, N., and Scesa, A. (2006) *Towards a Strategy for Workplace Learning: Report to HEFCE by CHERI and KPMG.* Bristol: Higher Education Funding Council for England.

Brewis, G., Russell, R., and Holdsworth, C. (2010) Bursting the Bubble: Students, Volunteering and the Community. Available at: http://www.publicengagement.ac.uk/sites/default/files/publication/nccpe_bursting_the_bubble_fullreport_0_0.pdf.

Brown, P. and Hesketh, A. (2004) *The Mismanagement of Talent: Employability and Jobs in the Knowledge Economy.* Oxford: Oxford University Press.

Bureau of Labor Statistics (2012) 'Number of Jobs Held, Labor Market Activity, and Earnings Growth among the Youngest Baby Boomers: Results from a Longitudinal Survey.' Available at: www.bls.gov/news.release/pdf/nlsoy.pdf.

Cabinet Office (2014) *Community Life Survey: England, 2013–2014.* Available from: https://www.gov.uk/government/statistics/community-life-survey-2013-to-2014-statistical-analysis (last accessed 3 March 2015).

Canton, R. (2011) *Probation: Working with Offenders.* Abingdon: Routledge.

Chase, R. (2015) *Peers Inc: How People and Platforms are Inventing the Collaborative Economy and Reinventing Capitalism.* London: Headline Publishing Group.

Cole, D. and Tibby, M. (2013) *Defining and Developing your Approach to Employability: A Framework for Higher Education Institutions.* Available at: https://www.heacademy.ac.uk/resource/defining-and-developing-your-approach-employability-framework-higher-education-institutions

Crown Prosecution Service (2014) *Crown Prosecution Service Annual Report and Accounts 2013–14.* Available from: https://www.cps.gov.uk/publications/docs/annual_report_2013_14.pdf (last accessed 23 October 2015).

Frey, T. (2011) *Communicating with the Future.* Colorado: DaVinci Institute Press.

Gibbs, P. and Morris, A. (2001) 'The Accreditation of Work Experience: Whose Interests are Served?' *Learning Organization* 8(2): 82–9.

Hall, D. (1996) 'Protean Careers of the 21st Century' *The Academy of Management Executive* 10(4): 8–16.

Hall, D. (1976) *Careers in Organizations.* Pacific Palisades, CA: Goodyear.

High Fliers (2014) *The Graduate Market in 2014.* Available from: http://www.highfliers.co.uk/download/GMReport14.pdf (last accessed 27 October 2014).

Home Office (2014) *Police Workforce, England and Wales,* 31 March 2014. Available at: https://www.gov.uk/government/publications/police-workforce-england-and-wales-31-march-2014/police-workforce-england-and-wales-31-march-2014.

Howard League for Penal Reform (2014) *Media release: Public-sector prison officer numbers cut by 41 per cent.* Available at: http://www.howardleague.org/prison-officer-numbers.

House of Commons Committee of Public Accounts (2014) *Contracting out Public Services to the Private Sector, Forty-seventh Report of Session 2013-14.* Available at: http://www.publications.parliament.uk/pa/cm201314/cmselect/cmpubacc/777/777.pdf.

Keen, R. (2014) *Charities, Social Action & the Voluntary Sector: Statistics.* House of Commons Library Standard note SN05428.

Law, B. and Watts, A. (1977) *Schools, Careers and Community.* London: Church Information Office.

Little, B. and Harvey, L. (2006) *Learning Through Work Placements and Beyond.* Sheffield: Centre for Research and Evaluation.

Lowden, K., Hall, S., Elliot, D., and Lewin, J. (2011) *Employers' Perceptions of the Employability of New Graduates.* London: Edge Foundation.

Maguire, M. (2012) 'Response 1: Big Society, the Voluntary Sector and the Marketisation of Criminal Justice' *Criminology & Criminal Justice* 12(5): 483–505.

Mandilaras, A. (2004). 'Industrial Placement and Degree Performance: Evidence from a British Higher Education' *International Review of Economics Education* 3(1): 39–51.

Ministry of Justice (2015) *Community Rehabilitation Company (CRC) Workforce Information Summary Report: Quarter 3 2014/15.* Ministry of Justice: London. Available at: https://www.gov.uk/government/uploads/system/uploads/attachment_data/file/381036/crc-workforce-information-summary-report-q2-2014-15.pdf.

Ministry of Justice (2014) *Workforce Information Summary Report: Quarter 4, 2013 to 2014.* Ministry of Justice: London. Available at: https://www.gov.uk/government/uploads/system/uploads/attachment_data/file/315043/probation-service-workforce-information-summary-report-q4-2013-14.pdf.

NUS/HSBC (2011) *Student Experience Report: Employability.* Available at: http://www.nus.org.uk/PageFiles/12238/NUS-HSBC-report-Employability-web.pdf.

Oldfield, M. and Grimshaw, R. (2010) *Probation Resources, Staffing and Workloads 2001-2008*. London: Centre for Crime and Justice Studies.

Parker, N. (2013) *Independent Review of ACPO*. Available at: http://apccs.police.uk/wp-content/uploads/2013/08/Independent-review-of-ACPO.pdf.

Pegg, A., Waldock, J., Hendy-Isaac, S., and Lawton, R. (2012) *Pedagogy for Employability*. York: HEA.

Prison Service Pay Review Body (2014) *Thirteenth Report on England and Wales 2014*. Available at: https://www.gov.uk/government/uploads/system/uploads/attachment_data/file/288701/Prison_Service_13th_report.pdf.

Ridley-Duff, R. and Bull, M. (2011) *Understanding Social Enterprise: Theory & Practice*. London: Sage.

Quality Assurance Agency for Higher Education (2012) *Enterprise* and *Entrepreneurship Education: Guidance for UK Higher Education Providers*. Gloucester: QAA. Available at: http://www.qaa.ac.uk/en/Publications/Documents/enterprise-entrepreneurship-guidance.pdf.

Sadler, P. and Good, E. (2006) 'The Impact of Self- and Peer-Grading on Student Learning' *Educational Assessment* 11(1): 1–31.

Sutton Trust (2014) *Research Brief: Internship or Indenture?* London: The Sutton Trust. Available at: http://www.suttontrust.com/wp-content/uploads/2014/11/Unpaid-Internships.pdf.

Tomczak, P. (2014) 'The Penal Voluntary Sector in England and Wales: Beyond Neoliberalism?' *Criminology & Criminal Justice* 14(4): 470–86.

INDEX

abolitionism
  critical criminology 745
  left realism 489
  meaning 745
  punishment 745, 759–63
abuse of process
  criminal justice 561
academics
  careers 860
actus reus 559
adulterisation
  meaning 247, 256
adversarial justice
  'adversarial-lite' policy 582
  beyond reasonable doubt 103
  burden of proof 565
  criminal justice 103–4, 565–6
  evaluation 104–5
  HM Courts Service 568
  juries 103–4, 566
  magistrates' courts 103
  meaning 103, 565
  miscarriages of justice 104, 590
  origins 104
  Ponting case 103
  presumption of innocence 565, 566
  structures 557–8
  trials 103–4, 565–6
  'triple S agenda' 582
  victimology 203
agenda bias
  knowledge 140
  meaning 140
alcohol
  youth crime 531–4
androcentricism
  challenging 286
  feminist criminology 284, 286, 287
  meaning 35
anomie 390–1
anthropology
  criminology 34
anti-essentialism
  critical race theory 265
antisocial behaviour
  crime control 651
  critical criminology 419–21
  dispersal orders 625
  responsibilisation 651
appellate courts 557, 558
Aristotle
  justice 95–6
artefactual risk factor theories 512–17, 529
Asset 250–1, 606, 612, 647

AssetPlus 253–4, 606
assisted suicide 58
Attorney General 571
autrefois **rule** 560–1
avoidance learning 365

BAME community *see* **black and minority ethnic communities**
Beccaria, C.
  classical criminology 325–7
  death penalty 673
  deterrence 326
before and after experimental design 153
behaviour
  control of individual behaviour 57
Bentham, J.
  Bentham's Panopticon 326–7, 636
  classical criminology 325–7
biological positivism
  background 346
  biochemical influences 354–6
  black and minority ethnic communities 345
  born criminal 346–8
  brain functions 351–4
  brain structure 351–4
  central nervous system 351–3
  chemical influences 354–6
  cognitive learning 370, 371
  conclusions 359
  determinism 357, 508
  drugs 354–6
  evolutionary psychology 358–9
  facial features 348–51
  Galton, F. 348–50
  generally 35
  genetics
    adoption 356–7
    family studies 356
    twin studies 356–7
  Lombroso, C. 346–8
  meaning 344
  peripheral nervous system 351
  punishment 345
  Sheldon, W. 348
  somatotyping 348
  substance abuse 354–5
  testosterone 354–6
biopsychosocial theory 507
biosocial theory
  biopsychosocial theory 507
  meaning 507
  right realism 507
  risk factor theories 507–8

Birmingham Six 104, 589, 590, 822
black and minority ethnic communities
  see also **critical race theory**
  Acts of Parliament 266–7
  biological positivism 345
  'black' criminality 265
  crime statistics 271–3
  Crown Prosecution Service 275–6
  custodial sentences 264, 748
  Denman Inquiry 269, 275
  discrimination 266–8, 426–7, 747–9
  'ethnic penalty' 748
  inequalities 264
  institutional racism 268, 277, 655, 748
  Islam 748
  justice 84
  labelling 265
  labelling perspectives 265, 425–6
  Laming Review 270
  Lammy Review 270
  Lawrence Inquiry 268–9, 748
  legislation 266–7
  Mubarek Inquiry 269, 277
  Muslims 748
  policing 254, 266, 273–4
  positivist theories 264
  prisons 276–7
  prosecutions 275–6
  protected characteristics 269
  psychological positivism 345
  Race Review 269
  riots 270
  Scarman Inquiry 267–8
  self-interrogation 269–70
  sentencing 264, 270, 276
  State responses to inequality and discrimination 266–8
  stop and search 273–4, 426–7, 747–9
  stop and search powers 273–4, 426–7, 747–9
  Young Black People and Criminal Justice System 269
  Young Review 269
  youth crime 276
Blackstone ratio 559
blogs 47–9
Bonger, W.
  capitalism 429–30
born criminal
  crime prevention 348
  genetics 356
  positivism 346, 348
  prostitution 432
  women 432

British Crime Survey 126
broken windows 484, 632–3
burden of proof
   adversarial justice 565
   confessions 591
   criminal prosecutions 559–60
   insanity 560
   presumption of innocence 559–60
bureaucratic model of justice 89–90
butterfly effect
   causes of crime 544

Cambridge-Somerville Youth Study 622
capital punishment *see* **death penalty**
capitalism
   Bonger, W. 429–30
   crimes of the powerful 429–30
   critical criminology 428–30
   feminist criminology 294–5
   harm principle 75
   Marxism 428–9
   means of production 429
   mode of production 429
   political economy 428
   pyramid of capitalism 429
Cardiff Three 590
careers
   see also **employability**
   academics 860
   charity advocates 861–2
   civil servants 861
   community development workers 862
   community interest companies 864
   courts 851–3
   Crown Prosecution Service 853
   decision-making 845
   development learning 842, 843–4, 859
   'DOTS' approach 844–6
   employability distinguished 842
   generally 834
   legal profession 851–3
   maximising opportunities 842, 845
   people in criminal justice
      courts 851–3
      Crown Prosecution Service 853
      generally 846–7
      legal profession 851–3
      police 847–51
      prisons 856–9
      probation service 853–6
      social work 853
      youth offending teams 853–4
   police 847–51
   prisons 856–9
   probation service 853–6
   researchers 859–60
   self-employment 862–4
   self-theories 845
   social enterprise 862–4
   social work 853
   'SODT' approach 845
   summary 866
   teachers 860–1
   transferring employability to career 864–5

transition learning 846
undergraduate phase 843
victim support 861
volunteering 863
youth offending teams 853–4
categories
   general crime categories 34
   specific crime categories 34
   study of criminology 34–5
causes of crime
   anti-causal theory 542–3
   background 526
   butterfly effect 544
   cessation of crime 539–41
   chaos theory 542–5
   conclusions 545–6
   Context-Mechanisms-Outcomes
      model 541
   correlation 535
   culture of causality 529–30
   desistance 539–41
   determinism 35, 238, 357, 419, 508
   deterrence 526
   empirical research 530–1
   epistemology 526–8
   experiments 530–4, 536–9
   explanation 537–9
   fractal measurement 543
   identification of causes 538–9
   innovative evaluation methods 541
   multiple interventions 541–2
   operationalising the causes 529–30
   positivism 526–7
   proxy indicators 537
   realistic evaluation approach 541
   reasons for searching for causes 526
   relative deprivation 492
   responding to crime 539–42
   scientific experiments 530–1
   Scientific Methods Scale 536–7
   social construction 527–8
   summary 546–7
   surveys 534–5
   theory of change model 541–2
central nervous system 351–3
chaos theory
   butterfly effect 544
   causes of crime 542–5
   complexity critique 544
   fractal measurement 543
   Lorenz, E. 544
   unfractal measurement 544
charity advocates
   careers 861–2
cheating HMRC
   criminalisation 59
chemical castration 506, 649, 677
Chicago school 394–7
children
   see also **youth crime**
   abuse of children 438
   age of criminal responsibility 231, 247–8
   childhood
      developmental explanations 232

      generally 228–9
      historical development of concept 229–30
      social construction 230
   definition 229
   doli incapax 247–8, 560
   media 175
   presumption of innocence 248
**Children First, Offenders Second
   (CFOS)** 255–6
chivalry thesis 303–4
citizen journalism 193–4
civil servants
   careers 861
civil unrest 189
classical conditioning 365, 373
classical criminology
   Beccaria, C. 325–7
   Bentham, J. 325–7
   criminal trials 328
   culpability 329
   deterrence 328, 480
   generally 35
   historical context 327
   influence 327–9
   intention 329
   limitations 328–9
   Locke, J. 324–5
   meaning 143, 323
   power structures 329
   subjectivity 143
   supposition 143
   timing of punishment 329
cognitive behavioural therapy (CBT)
   rehabilitation of offenders 698–9
cognitive learning 368–71, 373
Cohen, S.
   punishment 750
communitarianism
   Currie, E. 101
   Etzioni, A. 100–1
   justice 100–2
   meaning 100
   radical communitarianism 101–2
communities
   importance 57
   individual behaviour 57
community development workers
   careers 862
community interest companies 864
community justice
   critical criminology 746, 757–9
community payback
   enhanced community punishment
      (ECP) 588
   groups 588
   introduction 587
   payback 588
   policy 588
   punishment 671
   purpose 587
   recidivism 588
   restorative justice 567–8
   retribution 588–9
community policing 640–1

Community Rehabilitation Companies 568
community service
  see also **community payback**
  adaptation of practices 586
  conditions 587
  criminal justice 586–9, 593
  levels of sentencing 587–8
  policies 586–9
  punishment 671
  recidivism 588
  restorative justice 567–8
  retribution 588–9
  sentencing 587–8
  seriousness of offence 587
  unpaid work requirement 567, 587, 671
  uses 586
companies
  community interest companies 864
  corporate power 209
  criminalisation 74
  punishment 663, 751–2
confessions
  burden of proof 591
  criminal justice 589–90, 592
  due process 589–90, 592
  human rights 592
  OUTSEX formula 590, 591
consensus theory 382–3
consent
  harm principle 65–6
consociational democracy 757
constructionism
  positivist criminology 527
constructivist pathways risk factor theories 518–19
contempt of court 790, 791
content analysis
  meaning 168
  media 167, 168
  research 168
control balance theory 510
controlling crime *see* **crime control**
convict criminology
  background 468–73
  criminal statistics 469
  generally 418
  impact on prisoners 470
  knowledge 469
  labelling 471–3
  miscarriages of justice 468
  power 469
  research 470
  'voice' of prisoners 470
  work-seeking 471
copyright
  research 788–9
corporate crime
  punishment 663
cost-benefit evaluation
  diversion 733–4
courts
  appellate courts 557, 558
  careers 851–3
  civil cases 570–1

criminal cases 570
criminal justice 569–71
magistrates' courts 103
public/private law distinction 569–70
rule of law 557
victimology 203–4
covert studies
  research 157, 158
crime
  see also **criminalisation**
  activities classified as crime 56
  deviance and 60–2
  law, definition in 56
  social construct, as 57–8
crime control
  agencies
    community, role of the 643
    generally 642
    judiciary 644–5
    planning 642–3
    private security 643–4
  antisocial behaviour 651
  assessment of approach 651–4
  Bentham's Panopticon 636
  blocking devices 648
  'Broken Windows' 632–3
  chemical castration 649
  community, role of the 643
  crime prevention distinguished 633
  criminal justice 632
  death penalty 655
  defensible space 636–7
  'designing out' crime 652–3
  detection technologies 648–9
  deterrence
    aims of crime control 637
    effectiveness 91
    generally 636, 653
    individual level deterrence 653–4
    policing 638
    population level deterrence 653
  due process 633–4
  efficiency of operation 634–5
  fairness 634–5
  geographical patterns 645–6
  identification issues 655–6
  incapacitation 637–8
  information technology 648
  institutional racism 655
  interests served by crime control 649–51
  judiciary 644–5
  juries 91, 93
  justice 91, 558
  limitations
    generally 654
    moral limitations 655–6
    practical limitations 654–5
  meaning 632
  minimising risk of reoffending 646–7
  miscarriages of justice 654, 655
  moral challenges 655–6
  objectives
    defensible space 636–7
    incapacitation 637–8

  interests served by crime control 649–51
  operating principles 635–6
  target hardening 636–7
  objects 645–7
  Offender Group Reconviction Scale (OGRS) 646–7
  operating principles 635–6
  pattern theory 646
  planning 642–3
  policing 632–3, 634–5, 638–42
  predictive tools 645–7
  presumptions of approach 632
  presuppositions 647–8
  private security 643–4
  property 645–6
  retribution 645
  right realism 483–4
  risk assessment 646–7
  rule of law 632
  stop and search powers 201, 273–4, 426–7, 639
  summary 656–7
  target hardening
    meaning 632
    objectives 636–7
  technologies 645–7, 648–9
  victims 649–51
  weapons 648
  zemiology 451
crime mapping
  crime statistics 124, 126
crime pattern theory
  situational crime prevention 617, 618
crime prevention
  adaptation of activity 622
  background 600
  born criminal 348
  categorisation of initiatives 616
  choices 614
  community models 611, 612–13, 615–16
  consequences 621–4
  Cornish Committee 604
  crime control distinguished 633
  crime pattern theory 617, 618
  crime statistics 602
  criminogenic situations 602, 603–4
  decision-making 614
  desistance 616
  deterrence 600, 610–11, 613
  development 604–6
  developmental models 611, 616, 617
  direct action 601
  displacement 622–3
  diversion from crime 611
  economic regeneration 614–15
  education 601, 611–12
  emergence 604–6
  escalation of crime 622
  fear of crime 602, 603
  framework 605–8
  gated communities 608
  generally 600
  Home Office 606–7
  human behaviour 600

crime prevention (*Cont.*)
  interest groups 613, 615–16
  Kirkholt Project 618–19
  limitations 621, 624–7
  local authorities 607
  meaning 600
  models
    community models 611, 612–13
    deterrence 610–11
    developmental models 611, 616, 617
    diversion from crime 611
    framework 606–8
    objectives 616
    potential victims 612
    rational choice perspective 600, 617,
      624
    routine activity theory 600, 618
    school based prevention 611–12
  Neighbourhood Watch 608
  objectives
    alternatives 608–13
    criminogenic situations 602, 603–4
    developmental crime prevention 616, 617
    fear of crime 603
    generally 603
    models 616
    potential offenders 602, 603
    risky places 602, 603–4
    situational crime prevention 616
    social crime prevention 616–17
    vulnerable groups 602, 603
  partnerships 615–16
  political context 604, 613–14, 626–7
  potential offenders 602, 603, 610–11
  priorities 614
  rational choice perspective 600, 617, 624
  replication, dangers of 625–6
  responsibilisation 617, 626
  responsibility for prevention 626
  retribution 613
  risk management 601
  risk mitigation 601
  risky places 602, 603–4
  routine activity theory 600, 618
  school based prevention 611–12
  situational crime prevention
    crime pattern theory 617, 618
    examples 610
    meaning 600, 609
    objectives 616
    opportunity theory 617
    potential offenders 610–12
    rational choice perspective 617, 624
    routine activity theory 617, 618
    success criteria 621
  social context 604
  social crime prevention
    community models 612–13
    examples 609
    meaning 600, 609
    objectives 616–17
    potential offenders 610–12
  strategies 600, 601–3
  success criteria 619–21

  summary 627
  targets of prevention 602, 620
  technologies 605
  transferability of measures 625–6
  value 600
  vulnerable groups 602, 603
  youth crime 600, 605, 607
crime science
  rise in use 447
crime statistics
  black and minority ethnic communities
    271–3
  categories of offence 119–20
  collection 115
  convict criminology 469
  crime mapping 124, 126
  crime prevention 602
  Crime Survey for England and Wales
    (CSEW)
    administration of survey 129
    background 126–7
    British Crime Survey 126
    categories of crime 129
    collection of crime records 115
    comparison of police recorded
      crime 129
    computer-assisted interviewing 129
    criticism 130–1
    frequency 126–7
    nature of social surveys 127
    operation of survey 127–8
    purpose 126
    sampling 129
  critical approach 131–2
  critical race theory 271–3
  custodial sentences 584
  cybercrime 817
  definition 116
  descriptive statistics
    meaning 114
  extent of offending 118–19
  feminist criminology 286–7
  generally 114–15
  hate crime 210–11, 213–14
  Home Office 118
  immigration 179–80
  importance 131
  interpretation 119
  justice gap 121–5
  knowledge of crime 114
  limitations 118–9, 271–2
  manipulation of data 117
  mass victimisation surveys 115
  Ministry of Justice 117
  National Crime Recording Standard
    (NCRS) 121
  'Newgate Calendar' 115
  notifiable offences 119
  offence categories 119–20
  Office for National Statistics 118
  officially recorded crime statistics
    abuses 126
    crime mapping 124, 126
    extent of offending 118–19

    generally 114, 115
    historical development 115–17
    interpretation 119
    limitations 118–19, 126
    modern statistics 117–18
    'Newgate Calendar' 115
    notifiable offences 119, 126
    offence categories 119–20
    patterns of offending 119–20
    police recorded crime 120–6
    social construct, crime as 119
    sources 117–18
    summary offences 119
    uses 126
  Old Bailey statistics 115
  patterns of offending 119–20
  police recorded crime
    bureaucracy 121
    civil disputes 122
    computer aided despatch 123
    crime mapping 124
    'cuffing' 124
    discretion 121
    factors affecting reporting of crime 122
    intelligence led policing 124
    justice gap 121
    National Crime Recording Standard
      (NCRS) 121
    'no crime' 122–4
    process of recording crime 122–4
    reporting crime 120–1
    reporting and recording distin-
      guished 121
    unrecorded crimes 121
    websites 124
  policy makers 126
  public health, use in 116
  punishment 121
  reasons for not reporting crime 122
  recording and reporting distin-
    guished 121
  reporting crime 120–1
  scepticism 114–15
  social construct, crime as 119
  statistical models 534
  summary 132–3
  summary offences 119
  surveys 534
  unrecorded crimes 121
  uses 119
  victimology 207–8
  websites 124
  youth crime 177
Crime Survey for England and Wales
  (CSEW)
  see also **crime statistics**
  administration of survey 129
  background 126–7
  British Crime Survey 126
  categories of crime 129
  collection of crime records 115
  comparison of police recorded crime 129
  computer-assisted interviewing 129
  criticism 130–1

frequency 126–7
interviews 129
nature of social surveys 127
operation of survey 127–8
purpose 126
sampling 129
victimology 200, 207
criminal justice
see also **justice**; **rule of law**
4 P's 554, 578, 591, 593
abuse of process 561
actus reus 559
adversarial justice 565–6
alternative models 716–7
Attorney General 571
autrefois rule 560–1
Blackstone ratio 559
burden of proof 560
challenging conventional assumptions 717
closed trials 562
codification 554
Community Rehabilitation Companies 568
community sentences 593
community service 586–9
confessions 589–90, 592
constitutional systems 554
courts 569–71
crime control 632
cross-examination 564–5
Crown Prosecution Service (CPS) 571–4
definition 554
discrimination 746–9
diversity of system 568
double jeopardy 560
due process 558–9, 589–91
fault principle 559
fundamental principles 559–61
future concerns 818–9
game change, meaning of 554
HM Courts Service 568
HM Prison Service 568, 856–9
human rights 562–5
illegitimate acquittals 561
inequality 746–9
Islam 665
judiciary 595
juries 562, 591
lex talionis 554
Local Criminal Justice Partnerships 568
mens rea 559
Ministry of Justice 568
National Offender Management Service (NOMS) 568
National Probation Service 568
open justice 561–2
penal populism 578–82
people
　4 P's 593
　adaptations 593
　common standards 593
　courts 595
　generally 593

impact 593
judiciary 595
police 593
principles and policies, merger of 593–5
privatisation 595
probation service 593
professionals 593
research 593, 594
police 568–9
policies
　'adversarial-lite' policy 582
　importance 582–4
　meaning 578
　penal populism 578–82
　public involvement 579
　public opinion 579
　punishment 579–80
　rehabilitation 580–1
　sentencing 580
politicians 819
practices
　community payback 586–9
　community service 586–9
　due process 589–91
　generally 584
　imprisonment 584
　overview 591–2
prosecuting authorities 571
reality TV 561–2
restorative justice 566–8
summary 574–5, 596–7
UK system 554–5
unified system 568
zemiology 451
criminalisation
see also **harm principle**
acceptable activities 59
alternatives 71
cheating HMRC 59
communal good 70
companies 74
cultural values 57, 59
deviance 60–2
driving offences 59, 71
drug use 59, 67–9
environment 71
euthanasia 60
frames of reference 75
freedom of choice 70–1
group interests 71
historical periods 58, 59
homosexuality 57–8, 61
human rights 58, 72
illegal substance abuse 59, 67–9
importance 62
individual freedoms 70–1
killing 60, 71, 77
limits 62
manslaughter 59
need for criminal law 73–5
parliament 58
pollution 71
power 72, 421

prostitution 66
public perceptions 58–9
purpose 70
reasons for criminalisation 70–3
rights violations 72–3
social construct, crime as a 57–8
social control 511
social rules and norms 60–1
societal values 71
state activity 58
suicide 58
summary 76–7
terrorism 58
unacceptable activities 59
values, protection of 71
victims 75
zemiology 451
criminology
academic subject, as 31–3
anthropology 34
areas of study 31–2
campaigning 820–3
categories 34–5
complexities of subject matter 30
content of degree course 34–5
crime categories 34–5
defining crime 32
diagrammatic explanations 32
explaining crime 32
future concerns 817–8
hybrid nature of subject 33–4
influences 33
issues 35
justice 88
knowledge 34
legal nature 34
meaning 31–3
media 34
methods of study 36–9
nature 33–4
objectives of study 30–1
organisations, study of 35
people, study of 35
psychology 34
public perception of crime 33
responding to crime 32–3
social policy 34
social sciences 34
sociology 34
stakeholders 33
study 34–50
subject matter 33–4
systems, study of 35
thematic study 35
theories 35
triad of criminology 31–2
critical criminology
see also **cultural criminology**; **labelling perspectives**
abolitionism 745
antisocial behaviour 419–21
capitalism 428–9, 428–30
community justice 746
convict criminology

critical criminology (*Cont.*)
    background 468–73
    crime statistics 469
    generally 418
    impact on prisoners 470
    knowledge 469
    labelling 471–3
    power 469
    research 470
    stigmatisation 471–3
    work-seeking 471
critical, meaning of 419
definition 419
deterrence 428
development
    capitalism 428–30
    'naughty schoolboys' 428–9
    'New Criminology' 430–1
    Young, J. 428–9
feminist criminology
    child abuse 438
    chivalry hypothesis 433
    double deviancy thesis 433, 434
    gender blindness 433
    gender gap 433–4
    generally 418
    intersectionality 434
    intimate personal violence 435–8
    masculinities 438–41
    meaning of feminism 432–3
    partner abuse 435–8
    physiognomy 432
    scope 432
    Smart, C. 432–3
    violence, women as victims of 434–8
    women in criminology 431–3
    young people, abuse of 438
fully social theory of deviance 430–1
generally 35
green criminology
    anthropocentric approach 457
    background 454–5
    biocentric approach 457
    citizen action 459–60
    cleaner energy 456–7
    ecological justice 457
    economically powerful groups 455
    economics 455–6
    environmental crimes 454–5, 457
    generally 418
    green crime 457–60
    'invisible hand' 455–6
    market society 455
    meaning 454–5
    natural world, interaction of humans
        with 454–5
    power 459
    price mechanism 455–6
    punishment 457
    regulation 459
    species justice 457
Marxist theories
    generally 418
meaning 418
modern political climate 446

'naughty schoolboys' 428–9
political project 447–50
positivist orthodoxy, challenging 419–21
power 421–2
punishment
    abolitionism 745, 759–63
    Cohen, S. 750
    community justice 746, 757–8
    conclusion 765
    corporate crime 751–2
    definitions 764–5
    English riots 751
    Foucault, M. 749–50
    Gramsci, A. 750–1
    hegemony 749–51
    limitations 763–5, 765
    meaning of critical perspectives 744–6
    power 754–5
    practical solutions 763–4
    privileged, crimes of the 751–2
    romanticising crime 764
    State crime 753–4
    summary 766
    transformative justice 745–6
    truth and reconciliation 755–7
    unjust punishment 746–9
    war crimes 752–3
social change 446
summary 441–2, 474–5
technology 446
theories 418–19
transformative justice 745–6
Young, J. 428–9
youth crime 242
zemiology
    background 450–4
    generally 418
critical moments
    desistance 238
    school exclusion 518
    youth crime 232, 518, 519
critical race theory
    see also **black and minority ethnic
        communities**
    anti-essentialism 265
    conclusions 278–80
    crime statistics 271–3
    criticisms 266
    development 264–6, 270–1
    equality laws 154
    generally 264
    inequality in criminal justice system 271
    interest convergence 265
    intersectionality 265
    'legal storytelling' 266
    meaning 264
    over-representation in crime
        statistics 273
    policing
        stop and search 273–5
    prisons 276–8
    recurring themes 265–6
    role 264
    sentencing 276
    uses 266, 270–8

visibility of race 266
cross-cultural comparisons
    meaning 35
cross-examination 564–5
Crown Prosecution Service (CPS)
    administrators 572
    background 571
    careers 853
    challenges 572–3
    Code for Crown Prosecutors 572
    criminal justice 571–4
    Crown Prosecutors 571
    Director of Public Prosecutions (DPP) 571
    geographical areas 571
    miscarriages of justice 571
    paralegals, role of 572
    prosecutions 275–6
    race and ethnicity 275–6
    responsibilities 571
    role 571–2
cryptocurrencies 818
cryptomarkets 818
culpability
    classical criminology 329
    corporations 459
    harm principle 66
    punishment 681, 717, 736
    rehabilitation of offenders 686
    truth and reconciliation 755
cultural criminology
    agency 464
    background 460–2
    carnival of crime 465–6
    Cohen, A.K. 399–401
    cultural inclusion 466–8
    delinquent subcultures 399–401
    deviancy 463–4
    differential opportunity 401–2
    emotions 464–5
    generally 418
    mass culture 464
    meaning of 'culture' 460
    neutralisation 402–6
    role of emotions 464–5
    scope 460–1
    structural exclusion 466–8
    subcultures 397, 463–5
    summary 460–1
    theories 397–410
    webs of meaning 460, 463
    Young, J. 466–8
    youth culture 397–9
cultural values
    criminalisation 57
    folk devils 397
Currie, E.
    communitarianism 101
custodial sentences
    alternatives 719
    black and minority ethnic communities
        264, 748
    crime statistics 584
    decarceration movement 719
    increased use 584
    policies 581–2

punishment 669–71, 681
race and ethnicity 264
recidivism 585
reduction in use 581–2
uses 676–7
youth crime 243–5
cybercrime
civil unrest 189
crime statistics 817
criminology 817–18
dark web 191
fraud 189
growth 817
hacking 189
hate crime 189
identity theft 189
Internet 189–90
meaning 189
media 189–90
pornography 189
researchers 775
terrorism 190

'dark figure' crime
defining crime 32
dark web
cryptomarkets 818
cybercrime 191
death penalty
Beccaria, C. 673
campaigning against 202, 820
crime control 655
deterrence 326
Foucault, M. 673
historical background 669
international campaigning against 202
just deserts 674
justice 83
retribution 665
Turkey 667
United States 350, 674
unjust penalty, as 83, 105
deaths in custody
Inquest 201
victimology 209–10
deductive research 151
defensible space
crime control 636–7
demand characteristics
example 156
inverted characteristics 157
meaning 156
observer effect 159
surveys 157
Denman Inquiry 269, 275
dependent variable
experiments 152, 531
descriptive theory 321
desistance
causes of crime 539–41
crime prevention 616
critical moments 238
diversion 722, 733
rehabilitation of offenders 688, 704, 706–7, 708, 710

responding to crime 539
social capital 700–1
social rehabilitation 701
turning points 238
youth crime 253
determinism
biological criminology 508
biological positivism 357, 508
causes of crime 35, 238, 357, 419, 508
generally 35, 419
hard determinism 238
meaning 35, 419
positivism 238, 357, 419
soft determinism 238
youth crime 238
deterrence
alternatives to punishment 734, 736, 738
Beccaria, C. 326
causes of crime 526
classical criminology 328, 480
crime control
aims of crime control 637
effectiveness 91
generally 636, 653
individual level deterrence 653–4
policing 638
population level deterrence 653
crime prevention 600, 610–11, 613
critical criminology 428
death penalty 326
defiance 622
future-orientated strategy 717
left realism 490
overdeterrence 622
policing 638, 639
punishment 667
rehabilitation of offenders 702
right realism 482
risk assessment 646
sentencing 567
theory 322
developmental theories
childhood 229–30, 232
crime prevention 611, 616, 617
youth crime 3, 232–5
deviance
see also **criminalisation**
amplification 245–7
crime and 60–2
cultural criminology 463–4
cultural standards 60
deviancy amplification 146, 177, 245, 246, 248
deviant reaction 431
Durkheim 61
fully social theory 430–1
homosexuality 61
immediate origins of act 431
labelling perspectives 424–5
meaning 61–2
nature of deviance 424–5
'New Criminology' 430–1
origins of act 431
primary deviance 424
secondary deviance 424

social control 60
social interactionism 424
social reaction 431
social rules and norms 60–1
stigmatisation 424–5
wider origins of act 431
youth crime 245–7
differential association 383–7
differential coercion theory 510
Director of Public Prosecutions (DPP) 571
disabled people
hate crime 215–16
medical model of disability 215–17
reporting crime 217
social model of disability 215–16
discourse analysis
media 167, 168–9
overview 169
purpose 168
research 168–9
uses 168
discrimination
black and minority ethnic communities 266–8, 426–7, 747–9
criminal justice 746–9
punishment 746–9
race and ethnicity 266–8
stop and search powers 426–7
dispersal orders 625
dissertations 43
distance learning 38
diversion
see also **punishment**
aims 721–3, 725
cost-effectiveness 733–4
crime prevention 611
desistance 722, 733
institutionalisation 727
minimum intervention 722
objective of criminal justice 716, 722
practical operation 730–2
rationale 725
restorative approaches distinguished 721
Scotland 721
secondary deviance 733
youth crime 255, 721–2, 727, 728–9
documentary analysis
see also **content analysis; secondary data analysis**
meaning 159
research 159
secondary data analysis 158–60
triangulation 160
doli incapax 247–8, 560
domestic violence
Clare's Law 293
emotional abuse 293
feminist criminology 290–4, 434–8
harm principle 72
double jeopardy 560
driving offences
criminalisation 59, 71
justice 82

drug use
  criminalisation 59
  generally 56
  harm principle 67–9
due process
  Birmingham Six 590
  Blackstone ratio 559
  Cardiff Three 590
  confessions 589–90, 592
  crime control 633–4
  criminal justice 558–9, 589–91
  custody rights 590
  fair procedure 558
  Guildford Four 590
  justice 91–2, 94
  meaning 91–2
  miscarriages of justice 590, 679
  practice, in 589–90
  presumption of innocence 92, 94
  procedural justice 92, 558
  terrorism 94
Durkheim, E.
  functionalism 382, 387–91
  justice 90
  social control 61

e-safety 190–3
ecological validity
  experiments 153
economics
  green criminology 455–6
**Edinburgh integrated pathways
    theory** 517–18
education
  crime prevention 601, 611–12
  Internet 192
either way offences
  meaning 558
empirical knowledge
  see also **experiments; surveys**
  causes of crime 530–1
  feminist criminology 295–6, 307
  generally 142
  meaning 140
  research 151
  youth crime 234–5
employability
  see also **careers**
  application of skills 839
  business awareness 837, 838
  careers 834
  communication skills 837, 838
  continuing professional development
    834
  customer awareness 837, 838
  employers' perceptions 837–9
  enterprise skills 837, 838–9
  entrepreneurship 837, 838–9
  generally 7, 834
  information technology skills 837, 838
  job market 835
  literacy skills 837, 838
  massive open online course
    (MOOC) 834

  monitoring 836–7
  multi-agency approach 845
  numeracy skills 837, 838
  open access sources 834–5
  perceptions of employers 837–9
  placements 816, 817, 841
  positive can-do attitude 837, 838
  prisons 856–9
  problem solving skills 837, 838
  producing employability 836–42
  'RARE' framework 840
  research 815–17
  self-assessment 836–7
  sharing economy 834
  skills preferred by employers 837–9
  summary 866
  transferring employability to career 864–5
  vision 834
  volunteering 841–2
  work-based learning 840–2
  work shadowing 841
**enhanced community punishment
    (ECP)** 588
**enhanced pathways risk factor
    theories** 512, 517–20
environmental crimes
  green criminology 454–5
epistemological reflexivity 140, 152,
    806–9
epistemology
  causes of crime 526–8
  constructionism 527
  feminist theories 284, 295–7, 307–8
  interpretivism 527
  knowledge 142
  meaning 142
  positivist criminology 526–7
equal treatment
  justice 82
essay questions 42
essentialism 265
ethical standards
  researchers
    copyright 788–9
    dissemination of findings 797
    importance 786–9, 791–2
    photography 786–7, 787–8
    principles of research 787–8
    visual criminology 786–7, 787–8
ethnicity *see* **black and minority ethnic
    communities**
ethnocentrism
  meaning 35
Etzioni, A.
  communitarianism 100–1
euthanasia *see* **mercy killings**
evolutionary psychology 358–9
examinations 43–4
experiments
  see also **causes of crime**
  before and after experimental
    design 153
  cause and effect 531
  causes of crime 530–4, 536–9

  control 153–4, 531
  control group 153
  dependent variable 152, 531
  design 153
  ecological validity 153
  experimental group 153
  explanation 537–9
  extraneous variables 154, 531
  independent variable 152, 531
  interventions 153, 154
  objectives 530–1
  real world 153
  reductionism 154
  reliability 153
  research 152–4
  Scientific Methods Scale 536–7
  shoplifting 153, 154
  standardisation 153
  supposition 153
  variables 152–3
  youth crime and alcohol 531–4
extraneous variables
  experiments 154, 531

fair procedure *see* **due process**
fear of crime
  subjectivity 147–8
feminist criminology
  androcentricism 284, 286, 287
  capitalism 294–5
  chivalry thesis 303–4
  concept of gender 285–6
  conclusions 308
  crime statistics 286–7
  criminal justice system
    chivalry thesis 303–4
    early explanations of female crime
      299–300
    'evil woman' hypotheses 304
    feminist explanations of female
      crime 300
    generally 299
    masculinities, study of 300–3
    offenders, women as 303–4
  critical criminology
    child abuse 438
    chivalry hypothesis 433
    double deviancy thesis 433, 434
    gender blindness 433
    gender gap 433–4
    generally 418
    intersectionality 434
    intimate personal violence 435–8
    masculinities 438–41
    meaning of feminism 432–3
    physiognomy 432
    scope 432
    Smart, C. 432–3
    violence, women as victims of 434–8
    women in criminology 431–3
    young people, abuse of 438
  criticisms
    empiricism 307
    liberal feminist criminology 304–5

Marxist feminist criminology 307
postmodern feminism 307–8
radical feminist criminology 305–6
socialist feminist criminology 307
standpoint feminism 307
definitions 285
disability feminism 302–3
domestic abuse 290–4, 434–8
emotional abuse 293
empiricism 295–6, 307
epistemologies 284, 295–7, 307–8
'evil woman' hypotheses 304
female offending 284
gender gap 433–4
hate crime 303
hegemonic masculinity 301
intersectionality 297–9
'ladette culture' 289
liberal feminist theory 288–90, 304–5
Marxist feminist theory 294–5, 307
masculinities 438–41
masculinities, study of 300–3, 438–41
offenders, women as 303–4
origins 284–5
patriarchy 290
physiognomy 432
postmodern feminism 296–7, 307–8
principles
    challenging androcentrism 286
    concept of gender 285–6
    gender dichotomy 286
    generally 285
    reversing gender blindness 285–6
    theorising the gender gap 286–7
queer feminism 302–3
radical feminism 290–4, 305–6
reversing gender blindness 285–6
sexual violence 294
Smart, C. 432–3
Smart's theory 284
socialist theory 295, 307
standpoint feminism 296, 307
summary 309–10
theoretical basis
    generally 287–8
    liberal feminist theory 288–90
    Marxist feminist theory 294–5
    radical feminism 290–4
    socialist theory 295
'third wave' 298
transfeminism 302–3
United States 284
victimology 208, 284
violence, women as victims of 290–2,
    434–8
films
    criminology in 182–5
    prison films 185
    traditional crime films 184
fines
    punishment 671–2
Fisher Inquiry 589
folk devils
    culture 397

media 182, 246
migrants 178
youth crime 397
Foucault, M.
    death penalty 673
    power 383
    prisons 669–70
    punishment 668, 673–4, 749–50
fox hunting with dogs 56
fractal measurement 543
Freud, S.
    child development 232
    psychoanalysis 360–3, 535, 691
functionalism
    Durkheim, E. 387–91
    social structural theories
        387–91

gang culture 240
gated communities 608
gender
    see also **feminist criminology**
    androcentrism 286
    biological sex distinguished 285
    concept 285–6
    dichotomy 286
    gender gap
        feminist criminology 433–4
    homogenisation 286
    liberal feminist theory 288–90
    norms 285–6
    reversing gender blindness 285–6
    theorising gender gap 286–7
globalisation 101, 391, 511
Good Lives Model (GLM) 699–700
Gramsci, A.
    hegemony 750–1
    punishment 750–1
grand theory 321–2
green criminology
    anthropocentric approach 457
    background 454–5
    biocentric approach 457
    citizen action 459–60
    cleaner energy 456–7
    ecological justice 457
    economics 455–6
    environmental crimes 454–5
    environmental justice 457
    generally 418
    green crime 457–60
    'invisible hand' 455–6
    market society 455
    meaning 454–5
    natural world, interaction of humans
        with 454–5
    power 459
    price mechanism 455–6
    punishment 457
    regulation 459
    species justice 457
group norms
    subjectivity 147
Guildford Four 104, 590

hacking 189
Haldane principle
    independence of research 789
harm principle
    see also **criminalisation**
    anxiety 64–5
    capitalism 75
    companies 74
    consent 65–6
    criminal law, need for 73
    criminalisation 58–9, 62–4
    culpability 66
    Devlin, LJ 64
    direct harm 71
    domestic violence 72
    drug use 67–9
    emotional/psychological harm 63
    Feinberg 64–5
    frames of reference 75
    harm 62–3
    hate speech 65
    homosexuality 64
    human rights 72
    illegal substance abuse 67–9
    immoral activities 64–5
    importance 63
    indirect harm 69–70
    limits of principle 70
    meaning 62
    Mill, J.S. 62
    necessary but not sufficient test 63
    non-criminal harm 73–5
    nudity 64
    omissions 63
    other non-criminal harms 73–5
    paternalism 67
    physical harm 63
    possibility or risk of harm 71
    power 72
    prostitution 66
    remote harms 69–70
    sadomasochism 66
    self, harm to 67–9
    serious offence, meaning of 65
    sexual violence 72
    summary 76–7
    usefulness of test 63–4
    victims 75
hate crime
    see also **victimology**
    crime statistics 210–11, 213–14
    definitions 210–11
    disabled people 215–16
    generally 189
    homophobia 218–19
    Islam 218, 604
    limitations in examining hate crime
        213
    meaning 210–11
    monitored strands 211, 213
    need for legislation 211–12
    online hate crime 213
    power 212
    rates 213

hate crime (*Cont.*)
　social media 213
　StopHateUK 201–2, 213, 214
　theoretical approaches 212–13
hegemony
　Gramsci, A. 750–1
　hegemonic masculinity 301
　meaning 750–1
　punishment 749–51
higher education
　see also **learning; research; researchers;**
　　students
　Higher Education Academy (HEA) 815
　Higher Education Achievement Report
　　(HEAR) 814–15
　levels 811–13
　progression 811–13
　researchers 799–800
　student unions 815
　unique selling point 815–17
Hirschi, T.
　social control 509–10
HM Courts Service
　criminal justice 568
HM Prison Service 568, 856–9
Hobbes, T. 483
Home Office
　crime prevention 606–7
　crime statistics 118
　policing 568
homophobia
　crime statistics 219–20
　hate crime 218–19
homosexuality
　criminalisation 57–8, 61
　deviance 61
　harm principle 64
　homophobic hate crime 218–19
Howard League for Penal Reform 201, 243,
　　588, 649, 820, 856
human rights
　absolute rights 563
　confessions 592
　criminal justice 562–5
　criminalisation 58, 72
　criminology 58
　criticisms 563–4
　derogations 563
　European Convention on Human Rights 72
　harm principle 72
　inhuman treatment 72
　international standards 56–7
　life sentences 580
　limited rights 563
　meaning 57
　qualified rights 563
　retroactive offences 563
　special rights 563
　types of interest protected 72–3
　violations 72–3
hybrid theories *see* **integrated theories**

identity theft 189
illegal substance abuse *see* **drug use**

immigration
　media
　　crime statistics 179–80
　　'deviant migrant', fear of the 178
　　overview 178–9
　　politics of immigration 180–2
impact evaluations 792
imprisonment *see* **custodial sentences;**
　　punishment; sentencing
independent study 38–40
independent variable
　experiments 152, 531
indeterminate sentencing 580, 581
indictable offences 558
inductive research 151
Inquest 201
inquisitorial system
　evaluation 104–5
　investigations 104
　justice 104
institutional racism 268, 277, 655, 748
integrated theories
　artefactual risk factor theories 512–17, 529
　background 504–5
　constructivist pathways risk factor
　　theories 518–19
　control balance theory 510
　differential coercion theory 510
　Edinburgh integrated pathways
　　theory 517–18
　enhanced pathways risk factor
　　theories 512, 517–20
　evolution of theories 505–6
　groups of theories 520
　hybrid theories 504
　limitations of explanatory theories 504–5
　main groups 504
　positivist theories
　　assessment 511
　　biosocial risk factor theories 507–8
　　biosocial theory 507
　　control balance theory 510
　　differential coercion theory 510
　　integrated risk theories 505
　　power control theory 510
　　right realist biosocial theory 507
　　social control theories 505, 509–11
　　socio-biological theories 505, 506–9
　power control theory 510–11
　Risk Factor Prevention Paradigm
　　(RFPP) 512
　risk factor theories
　　artefactual risk factor theories 512–17,
　　　529
　　background 511–12
　　constructivist pathways risk factor
　　　theories 518–19
　　Edinburgh integrated pathways
　　　theory 517–18
　　enhanced pathways risk factor
　　　theories 512, 517–20
　　globalisation 511
　　increase in crime 511–12
　　risk society 511

　self-control theory 510
　social control theories 505, 509–11
　summary 520–1
intelligence-led policing 640
Intensive Alternative to Custody (IAC) 676
intention
　classical criminology 329
interest groups
　crime prevention 613
Internet
　cybercrime 189–90
　dark net 191
　e-safety 190–3
　education 192
　exploitation 190–3
　risk 190–3
　social media 191
　young people, use by 190–3
internships 37, 38, 47, 841–2, 850, 851, 861
interpretivism
　knowledge 142
　meaning 323
　sociology 527
Islam
　black and minority ethnic communities
　　748
　criminal justice 665
　hate crime 218, 604
　institutional racism 748
　justice systems 104
　punishment 665
　radicalisation 241
　social rules 60

judiciary
　accountability 556–7
　apolitical 556
　appointments 556
　court structures 557–8
　criminal justice 595
　independence 556, 595
　media involvement 556
　role 557
　rule of law 556
　security of tenure 556
　sentencing 595
Jung, K. 361, 363
juries
　acquittals 791
　adversarial justice 103–4, 566
　anonymity 791
　crime control 91, 93
　criminal justice 562, 591
　punishment 669
　research 565, 790, 791–2
　role 635
　tribunal of fact 558
　visual images in deliberations 826
just deserts
　death penalty 674
justice
　see also **criminal justice; rule of law**
　adversarial systems 103–4
　Aristotle 95–6

bureaucratic model 89–90
communitarianism 100–2
core issue, as 86
crime control model 91, 558
criminal justice system 83–4, 102–5
    adversarial systems 103–4
    evaluation 104–5
    generally 102–3
    inquisitorial system 104
    Islamic justice systems 104
    miscarriages of justice 104–5
criminology 88
cultural factors 87
death penalty 83
definitions 85
descriptive models 88, 89–90
domination, maintenance of 90
drawing ideas together 105–6
driving offences 82
due process 91–2, 558–9
Durkheim 90
equal application of law 86
equal treatment 82
ethnicity 84
evaluative test 86
everyday use of term 82–3
generally 82
Hume, David 83
importance 82, 83
injustice 82
injustice, justification of 85
inquisitorial system 104
interested parties and actors 86
legalistic concept 86
maintenance of domination 90
miscarriages of justice 104–5
models
    application of normative models 92–3
    bureaucratic model 89–90
    crime control 91, 93
    descriptive models 88, 89–90
    due process 91–2, 94
    Durkheim 90
    generally 88
    normative models 88, 90–5
    power models 90
    rights 92, 94
    status passage 90
    stigmatisation 90
    Weber 89–90
narrow definition 85, 86
normative models 88, 90–5
personal factors 87
philosophical ideas
    Aristotle 95–6
    communitarianism 100–2
    generally 95
    Rawls, J. 96–8
    Sen, A. 98–100
power models 90
preliminary issues 82–5
procedural justice 92
punishment 105–6, 680–1
radical communitarianism 101–2

Rawls, J. 83, 96–8
reasons for decisions 85, 86
reasons for study 87–8
restorative justice 102
rights model 92, 94
riots 84
scales of justice 85–6
Sen, A. 83, 98–100
sentencing 105–6
social construct 83
social justice 88
sporting events 82–3, 85
status passage 90
stigmatisation 90
summary 107–9
terrorism 93
torture 93
utilitarianism 91
visual depiction 85–6
Weber 89–90
justice gap
crime statistics 121–5
meaning 121

**Key Elements of Effective Practice
    (KEEP)** 250
killing
criminalisation 60, 71, 77
intention 60, 329, 404
mercy killings 56, 60, 329, 385, 404
United States 350
women, by 301
knowledge
see also **research**; **surveys**
agenda bias 140
classicism 143
convict criminology 469
criminological theory as knowledge 143–4
criminology 34
critical criminology 144
documentary analysis 159
empirical research 140
empiricism 142
epistemology 142
fact distinguished 141
generally 140–1
interpretivism 142
meaning of knowledge about crime 141–2
media misrepresentation 146
obtaining knowledge 141
positivism 143–4
realism 142
reflexivity 140, 152
research 151–2
secondary data analysis 158–60
social construction 141
sources 141
study 143, 150–2
subjectivity
    dominant subject viewpoints 145–6
    existing knowledge 148
    external bias 144–6
    external-internal 146–7
    fear of crime 147–8

generally 140, 142
group norms 147
individual demographics 146–7
internal subjectivity 147–8
media misrepresentation 146
peer groups 147
personal experience 147–8
police, experiences with 148
professional subjectivity 144–5
social interactions 147
summary 162–3
supposition 140, 143, 148–50
unsupported opinions 140
validity 140, 141
Kolb's learning cycle 807

labelling perspectives
see also **critical criminology**
1960's radicalism 422–8
basis 419
black and minority ethnic communities
    265, 425–6
convict criminology 471–3
critique 427–8
development 422–8
deviancy 424–5
generally 418
impact of perspectives 427
minimising 717
spoilt identity 425
stop and search powers 426–7
victimless crimes 427
youth crime 242
zemiology 451
Lammy Review 270
Lawrence Inquiry 268–9, 748
learning
classical conditioning 365
cognitive learning 368–71, 373
generally 364–5
Kolb's learning cycle 807
massive open online course (MOOC) 799,
    834
operant conditioning or learning 365–7
reflexivity 806–9
social learning 367–8
theoretical approach 806–7
theories 365–71
lectures
students 36
left realism
deterrence 490
evaluation 495–6
individualism 490
key ideas 489–92
policy implications
    social exclusion 492–5
    social inclusion 492–5
    socio-economic causes of crime 492
    'square of crime' 492
relative deprivation 490–2
legal moralism 64
legal profession
careers 851–3

lex talionis 554
liberal feminist theory 288–90, 304–5
Lieber Code 752–3
life sentences
  human rights 580
  indeterminate sentences 580
  whole life orders 580
literature reviews 42–3
local authorities
  crime prevention 607
Local Criminal Justice Partnerships 568
Locke, J.
  classical criminology 324–5
Lombroso, C.
  biological positivism 346–8
Lorenz, E.
  butterfly effect 544

Macpherson Inquiry 84
magistrates' courts
  adversarial systems 103
mandatory sentencing 580, 581
manslaughter
  criminalisation 59
Marxism
  capitalism 428–9
  feminist theory 294–5, 307
masculinities
  criminal justice system 300–3
  feminist criminology 438–41
  meaning 438
massive open online course (MOOC)
  799, 834
media
  see also **Internet**
  celebrity stories 173
  Chibnall's professional imperatives 170–2
  children 175
  citizen journalism 193–4
  content analysis 167, 168
  controversy 169
  conventionalism 171–2
  crime detectives 182–4
  crime statistics 177
  cybercrime 189–90
  dark net 191
  deviancy amplification 146, 177, 245,
    246, 248
  discourse analysis 167, 168–9
  dramatisation 170, 171
  film, criminology in 183–5
  folk devils 182, 246
  future of media criminology 193–4
  gaming 187–8
  historical development 166–7
  ideology 173
  imagery 173
  immediacy 170, 171, 173–5
  immigration
    crime statistics 179–80
    'deviant migrant', fear of the 178
    overview 178–9
    politics of immigration 180–2
  individualism 173

  influence 34
  location of crime 173
  methods of analysis 167–9
  misrepresentation 146
  music 186–7
  new issues 167
  new technology
    gaming 187–8
    media effects 188–9
  news values 170–3
  newsworthiness 170–5
  novelty 172
  personalisation 170, 171
  political diversion 173
  popular entertainment 186
  predictability 172
  public anxieties 186
  public fascination with crime 166–7
  relationship between crime and media 167
  risk of crime 173
  sex offences 173
  simplification 170, 171, 172
  social media 191, 192
  structured access 172
  subjectivity 146
  summary 194–5
  television 182–4
  terrorist threat 146
  threshold for importance of story 172
  titillation 170, 171, 173
  traditional media criminology 167–9
  United States 146
  victimology 202
  violence, level of 173
  visual spectacle 173
  youth crime
    crime statistics 177
    demonisation 176
    deviancy amplification spiral 177
    education 177
    folk devils 177
    health backgrounds 177
    moral panics 177
    overview 175–6
    'presence of absence' 176–7
mens rea 559
mercy killings
  criminalisation 60
  generally 56
  intention 329, 404
  punishment 385
  social norms 60
Merton, R.K.
  strain theory 391–4
metacompetencies 843
metaskills 843
Ministry of Justice
  crime statistics 117
  criminal justice 568
miscarriages of justice
  adversarial justice 104, 590
  Birmingham Six 104, 589, 590, 822
  Blackstone ratio 559
  Cardiff Three 590

  convict criminology 468
  crime control 654, 655
  criminal justice system 104–5
  Crown Prosecution Service 571
  due process 590, 679
  Guildford Four 104, 590
  justice 104–5
  punishment 662, 677, 678–80
  reporting 169
  retribution 678
  statistics 678
  zemiology 450
moral panics
  child offenders 247
  folk devils 177, 397
  immigration 267
  youth crime 397, 464
Mubarek Inquiry 269, 277
murder *see* **killing**

National Association for Youth Justice 201
National Crime Recording Standard
    (NCRS) 121
National Offender Management Service
    (NOMS) 568
National Probation Service 568
neighbourhood policing 641–2
Neighbourhood Watch 608
neo-classical criminology 329–30
'Newgate Calendar' 115
newsworthiness
  media 170–5
non-governmental organisations
  victimology
    Howard League for Penal Reform 201
    Inquest 201
    international pressure groups 202
    National Association for Youth
      Justice 201
    role 200
    StopHateUK 201–2
    Stopwatch 201
non-participant observation 159
normative theory 88, 90–5, 321

OASys 606
observations
  research 157–8
observer effects 159
Offender Group Reconviction Scale
    (OGRS) 646–7
Office for National Statistics 118
officially recorded crime statistics
  see also **crime statistics**
  abuses 126
  extent of offending 118–19
  generally 114, 115
  historical development 115–17
  interpretation 119
  limitations 118–19, 126
  modern statistics 117–18
  'Newgate Calendar' 115
  notifiable offences 119, 126
  offence categories 119–20

police recorded crime 120–6
social construct, crime as 119
sources 117–18
summary offences 119
uses 126
Onset 251–2, 612
ontology
meaning 295
objectivist ontology 526, 527
open justice
criminal justice 561–2
reality TV 561–2
operant learning 365–7, 371, 373
opportunity theory
situational crime prevention 617
OUTSEX formula 590, 591

paralegals 572
parliamentary sovereignty 555
participant observation 157
paternalism
harm principle 67
meaning 67
pathways
constructivist pathways risk factor
theories 518–19
Edinburgh integrated pathways
theory 517–18
enhanced pathways risk factor
theories 512, 517–20
patriarchy
feminist criminology 290
power 422
pedagogy 39
peer groups
subjectivity 147
penal populism
criminal justice 578–82
peripheral nervous system 351
personal transferable skills
analytical skills 436
careers 15
employability 7, 15, 26, 37, 44, 46
postgraduates 800
presentations 45
students 7, 14, 15
Philips Commission 589–90
physiognomy
meaning 432
placements
employability 816, 817, 841
forms 38, 841
mentors 38
study 37, 41
work-based assessment 47
work-based learning 38, 841
planning
crime control 642–3
pluralism
meaning 421
Police and Crime Commissioners 568–9
policing
black and minority ethnic communities
254, 266, 273–4

careers 847–51
challenges for the police 569
Chief Constable 568
community policing 640–1
crime control 632–3, 634–5, 638–42
criminal justice 568–9
critical race theory
stop and search 273–5
deterrence 638, 639
duties 638
employers 847–9
focused deterrence 639
historical development 568
Home Office 568
intelligence-led policing 124, 640
international careers 850–1
moral guardians, police as 642
neighbourhood policing 641–2
origins of police service 568
Police and Crime Commissioners 568–9
policing by consent 200
private provision 638
private security 569
problem orientated policing 641
recorded crime 120–6
risk identification and management 638
role 569, 638–42
social control 638
specialist careers 850–1
stop and search powers 201, 273–4,
426–7, 639
strategies 638–9
subjectivity 148
targeted approach 638–9
tripartite system 568–9
zero tolerance policing 639–40
policy makers
government 578
penal populism 578–82
stakeholders, as 33
politicians
stakeholders, as 33
pollution
criminalisation 71
Ponting case 103
populist punitiveness 578–9
pornography 188, 189, 192
positivist criminology
see also **biological positivism**;
psychological positivism
born criminal 346, 348
causes of crime 526–7
challenge from critical criminology 419–20
consensus 419
constructionalism 527
determinism 35, 238, 357, 419
early positivists 346–51, 378
epistemology 526–7
knowledge 143–4
meaning 323, 344
neo-positivists 378
objectivism 526–7
punishment 344–6
rehabilitation 344–6, 419

research 143–4
scientism 419
victimology 208–9
postgraduate research 799–800
postmodern feminism 296–7, 307–8
power
conflicting groups 421
convict criminology 469
criminalisation 72, 421
critical criminology 421–2
diversity 421
evading criminalisation 421–2
green criminology 459
patriarchy 422
pluralism 421
political power 422
power control theory 510–11
punishment 754–5
relations, power 421
sociology 383
zemiology 451, 454
practitioners
stakeholders, as 33
presentations
students 44–5
presumption of innocence
burden of proof 559–60
children 248
due process 92, 94
rule of law 559
youth crime 248
prevention of crime *see* **crime prevention**
prisons
see also **custodial sentences**
black and minority ethnic communities
276–8
careers in prison service 856–9
conditions 670
convict criminology 418, 468–73
critical race theory 276–8
employability 856–9
films 185
Foucault, M. 669–70
population rates in Europe 679
punishment 669–71
retribution 669
private security
crime control 643–4
policing 569, 643–4
probation
careers in probation service 853–6
casework approach 694
correctional approach 694–5
historical development 693
professionals 693
rehabilitation of offenders 693–5
relationship between officer and
probationer 694
Scotland 694
social work career 853
youth offending teams 853–4
procedural justice
due process 92, 558
meaning 92

process evaluation 792
proportionality
  punishment 677–8
  rehabilitation of offenders 707–8
prosecutions
  black and minority ethnic communities
    275–6
  Crown Prosecution Service 275–6
prostitution
  criminalisation 66
  harm principle 66
protean
  meaning 586, 843
psychoanalysis
  defence mechanisms 362
  Freud, S. 360–3
  generally 359–60
  Jung, K. 363–4
  levels of awareness 360
  personality 360–1
  stages of development 361
psychological positivism
  behavioural psychologists 359
  black and minority ethnic communities
    345
  classical conditioning 365
  cognitive aspects 359
  evolutionary psychology 358–9
  extroversion 363–4
  introverts 363
  Jung, K. 363–4
  learning
    classical conditioning or learning 365
    cognitive learning 368–71
    generally 364–5
    operant conditioning or learning 365–7
    social learning 367–8
    theories 365–71
  meaning 344
  neuroticism 363–4
  personality traits 345
  psychoanalysis
    defence mechanisms 362
    Freud, S. 360–3
    generally 359–60
    Jung, K. 363–4
    levels of awareness 360
    personality 360–1
    stages of development 361
  psychology 359
  psychoticism 363–4
  punishment 345
  sociological theories 359
  summary 372–3
psychology
  criminology 34
public opinion
  criminalisation 58–9
  influence 33
punishment
  see also **community service; custodial**
    sentences; sentencing
  abolitionism 745, 759–63
  accountability 663–4

alternatives
  see also **diversion; restorative justice**
  assessment of impact 732–4
  challenges 728–32
  compromise, as 736
  consultative processes 723
  cost-effectiveness 733–4
  credibility 726–7
  custody, alternatives to 719
  delivery 728–32
  evidence 732–4
  generally 716
  implications 734–6
  informal processes 723
  limitations 737–9
  negotiated processes 723
  offence resolution 716–18, 719–20
  operation 725–8
  organisation 725–8
  practices 728–32
  purpose 720–3
  repeat cautioning 726
  role of State 716–17
  structure 725–8
  summary 739–40
  transformational goals 723–5
  victims 720
  wider benefits 735–6
Aquinas, T. 662
assumptions 662
biological positivism 345
bodily punishment 670
capital punishment 669, 670, 681
challenges 681–2
chemical castration 506, 649, 677
Cohen, S. 750
community justice 746, 757–9
community payback 671
consequences 677–80
corporate crime 663
crime statistics 121
criminal justice 664
critical criminology
  abolitionism 745, 759–63
  Cohen, S. 750
  community justice 746, 757–9
  conclusion 765
  corporate crime 751–2
  definitions 764–5
  English riots 751
  Foucault, M. 749–50
  Gramsci, A. 750–1
  hegemony 749–51
  limitations 763–5, 765
  meaning of critical perspectives 744–6
  power 754–5
  privileged, crimes of the 751–2
  romanticising crime 764
  State crime 753–4
  summary 766
  transformative justice 745–6
  truth and reconciliation 755–7
  unjust punishment 746–9
  war crimes 752–3

culpability 681, 717, 736
cultural differences 665
custodial sentences 669–71, 681
delivery
  fines 671–2
  generally 668
  historical background 668–9
  modern methods 671
  prisons 669–71
deterrence 667
discrimination 746–9
fines 671–2
Foucault, M. 668, 673–4, 749–50
Gramsci, A. 750–1
green criminology 457
hegemony 749–51
impact 675–7
innovations 676
intent 663–4
Islam 665
joint responsibility 664
juries 669
justice 105–6, 680–1
legitimacy 663
limitations of victim involvement 666
meaning 662–3
miscarriages of justice 662, 677, 678–80
modern methods 671
moral justification 662
moral and social order 667–8
objects 673–4
offence resolution 717–18
organisation 675–7
personal statements, victim 665–6
policies 579–80
political context 675–6, 680–1
positivist criminology 344–6
power 754–5
practices 675–7
prisons 669–71
proportionality 677–8
psychological positivism 345
public approval 680–1
purpose 664–8
rehabilitation of offenders 688
religious influences 665
resolution approach 717–18
responsibility for actions 716
restitution 664
retribution 662–4
right realism 482
social context 681–2
stakeholders 716
State crime 753–4
steps 663
subjective effect 681
summary 682–3
truth and reconciliation 755–7
unjust punishment 746–9
unpaid work requirement 567, 587,
  671
victims 665–6
war crimes 752–3
zemiology 451

radical communitarianism 101–2
radical feminist theory 290–4, 305–6
radicalisation
  youth crime 241
rape
  burglary with intent to commit rape 57
  crime, as 56
  generally 56–7
rational choice
  crime prevention 600, 617, 624
  event decisions 332–4
  generally 35
  involvement decisions 330–2
  situational crime prevention 600, 617, 624
  theory 330–4
Rawls, J.
  constitution 98
  contract-based ideas 98
  difference principle 97
  equality 97, 98
  institutions, just 98
  justice 83, 96–8
  liberty 97, 98
  original position 96–7, 98
  Sen's critique 98–9
  social contract 96
  veil of ignorance 96
realism
  see also **left realism; right realism**
  background 480–1
  emergency 480–1
  generally 35
  knowledge 142
  meaning 480
  political context 481–2
  responsibilisation 481
  riots 497–8
  summary 498–9
realistic evaluation approach 541
recidivism
  community payback 588
  community service 588
  custodial sentences 585
  rehabilitation of offenders 701–2
reductionism
  experiments 154
referral orders 727–8
reflexivity
  knowledge 140, 152
  learning 806–9
  students 806–9
rehabilitation of offenders
  assumptions
    change in circumstances 686–7
    choice 687
    community purpose 687
    culpability 687
    needs of offender 687
    success of rehabilitation 687
  cognitive behavioural therapy (CBT)
    698–9
  compulsion 708
  culpability 686
  delivery of services

cognitive behavioural therapy
  (CBT) 698–9
  Good Lives Model (GLM) 699–700
  models 698–701
  risk, need, responsivity (RNR) 699
  social rehabilitation 701
  desistance 688, 704, 706–7, 708, 710
  deterrence 702
  evaluation 701–4
  evidence 705–6
  formal rehabilitation 689–90
  generally 686
  Good Lives Model (GLM) 699–700
  impact 704–7
  judicial rehabilitation 688
  legal rehabilitation 688
  limitations 707–10
  meaning 686–8
  models
    formal rehabilitation 689–90
    judicial rehabilitation 688
    legal rehabilitation 688
    moral rehabilitation 688, 690–1
    needs of offender 691–3
    psychological rehabilitation 688, 691
    punishment 688
    scope 688, 689
    social rehabilitation 688, 690–1
  moral rehabilitation 688, 690–1
  multimodal programmes 702–3
  needs of offender 691–3
  objectives 695–8
  offender first approach 708–10
  organisation 693–5
  policies 580–1
  positivist criminology 344–6, 419
  probation 693–5
  proportionality 707–8
  psychological rehabilitation 688, 691
  punishment 688
  recidivism 701–2
  reform 687–8
  reintegration 687–8
  religious factors 695–7
  removal of barriers 689–90
  resettlement 587–8, 697–8, 705
  restoration 686
  restorative justice 566
  'rewards' 692–3
  risk, need, responsivity (RNR) 699
  self-discipline 690–1
  social rehabilitation 688, 690–1, 701
  spent convictions 689–90
  spiritual element 695–7
  success criteria 701–4
  summary 711
  treatment 691
reintegrative shaming 724–5
relative deprivation
  causes of crime 492
  left realism 490, 492
  meaning 482, 490
repeat cautioning 726
reporting crime

  see also **crime statistics**
  factors affecting reporting of crime 122
  police recorded crime 120–1
  reasons for not reporting crime 122
  recording distinguished 121
research
  see also **researchers; students**
  applied research 151
  assessment of learning 45–6
  barriers 789–93
  combination of methods 160–1
  content analysis 168
  convict criminology 470
  copyright 788–9
  covert studies 157, 158
  critical reflection 161–2
  deductive research 151
  discourse analysis 168–9
  documentary analysis 159
  empirical research 151
  evaluation 792–3
  experiments 152–4
  funding 151–2
  inductive research 151
  juries 565, 790, 791–2
  knowledge 151–2
  meaning 773
  methods 152
  mixed methods 160–1
  multi-model methods 160–1
  multiple methods 160–1
  observations 157–8
  postgraduate research 799–800
  practicality 151
  reasons to do research 772–4
  referencing research 795–6
  research posters 46
  research-based assessment 45–6
  secondary analysis 158–60
  study as 151–2
  summary 162–3
  triangulation 160
  watching, by 157–8
researchers
  see also **research; students**
  barriers 789–93
  careers 859–60
  challenges 823–9
  choice of topic 775–7, 798
  commencing research 775
  context of images 824–7
  copyright 788–9
  creative methodologies 783
  cybercrime 775
  dissemination of findings 796–9
  dissertations 775–6
  employability inspired topics 776–80
  ethical standards
    copyright 788–9
    dissemination of findings 797
    importance 786–9, 791–2
    photography 786–7, 787–8
    principles of research 787–8
    visual criminology 786–7, 787–8

researchers (*Cont.*)
  evaluation of research 792–3
  generally 772
  higher education 799–800
  independence 789–90
  knowledge producers, students as 773, 774
  legal issues 790–1
  local initiatives 776
  new methods of study 823–9
  personally inspired topics 776
  planning research
    communication methods 783–6
    creative methodologies 783
    documentary data 782
    empirical research 782
    generally 780
    historical methods 780–3
    literature reviews 780
    type of analysis 782–3
  postgraduate research 799–800
  publication of research 796–9
  reasons to do research 772–4
  referencing research 795–6
  summary 801, 829–30
  television 798–9
  theoretical background 772–3
  topic for research 775
  'triad of criminology' 775
  undergraduates, expectations from 773
  visual criminology 823–9
  writing up research
    generally 793–4
    referencing 795–6
    style of writing 794–5
responsibilisation
  antisocial behaviour 651
  children 247
  crime prevention 617, 626
  meaning 242
  realism 481
  risk assessment 252
restitution
  civil cases 570
  punishment 664
restorative justice
  see also **punishment**
  background 718, 723–4
  community payback 567–8
  community service 567–8
  cost-effectiveness 733–4
  criminal justice 566–8
  definition 566, 716
  development 566–7
  international movement 718–19
  mediation 727
  origins 718, 727
  practice in the community 723
  probation 567
  rationale 725
  referral orders 727–8
  rehabilitation of offenders 566
  reintegration 723–4
  reintegrative shaming 724–5

reparation 727
unpaid work requirement 567, 587, 671
victim-offender mediation 567
victimology 567
retribution
  alternatives to punishment 736
  atonement 670
  crime control 645
  crime prevention 613
  custodial sentences 669–71
  death penalty 665
  maintaining moral and social order 667
  meaning 326
  miscarriages of justice 678
  moral and social order 667–8
  paying back 588–9
  prisons 669
  punishment 662–4, 663, 664, 666, 668, 681, 682
  sentencing 586
right realism
  anti-intellectualism 482
  biosocial theory 507
  'chavs' 486–8
  crime control 483–4
  criticism 488–9
  deterrence 482
  evaluation 488–9
  free market economics 482
  key ideas 482–3
  neo-conservatism 482
  policy implications
    'chavs' 486–8
    crime control 483–4
    Murray, C. 484–6
    underclass 484–6
    Wilson, J.Q. 483–4
  public order 484
  punishment 482
  risk management 484
  self-interest 483
  street crime 482
  underclass 484–6
  victimology 484
riots
  English riots 751
  justice 84
  realism 497–8
Risk Factor Prevention Paradigm (RFPP) 512
  youth crime 235, 249, 250
risk factor theories
  artefactual risk factor theories 512–17, 529
  background 511–12
  constructivist pathways risk factor theories 518–19
  Edinburgh integrated pathways theory 517–18
  enhanced pathways risk factor theories 512, 517–20
  globalisation 511
  increase in crime 511–12
risk, need, responsivity (RNR) 699
routine activity theory

crime prevention 600, 618
  meaning 334–5
rule of law
  accountability of judiciary 556–7
  courts 557
  crime control 632
  historical development 555–6
  independent judiciary 556
  judiciary 556
  meaning 555
  parliamentary sovereignty 555
  presumption of innocence 559
  security of tenure of judges 556–7
  separation of powers 555–6

sadomasochism
  harm principle 66
Scarman Inquiry 267–8
scientific experiments *see* **experiments**
Scientific Methods Scale 536–7
secondary data analysis
  double subjectivity 160
  research 158–60
  triangulation 160
secondary deviance
  consequences 424
  diversion from crime 733
  meaning 424
  youth crime 242–3
security of tenure
  judges 556
seminars
  students 37
Sen, A.
  fairness 98–9
  impartial spectators 99
  justice 98–100
  procedural rules 99
  Rawls, critique of 98–9
  social choice 99
sentencing
  see also **community payback; community service; custodial sentences; punishment**
  black and minority ethnic communities 264, 270, 276
  community service 587–8
  critical race theory 276
  deterrence 567
  fairness 680–1
  Howard League for Penal Reform 201
  indeterminate sentences 580, 581
  innovations 676
  Intensive Alternative to Custody (IAC) 676
  judiciary 595
  justice 105–6
  mandatory sentences 580, 581
  policies 580
  purpose 567, 716
  referral orders 727–8
  retribution 586
  'triple S agenda' 582
  whole life orders 580

separation of powers 555–6
sexual offences
  harm principle 72
  media 173
  victimology 208–9, 294
Sheldon, W.
  biological positivism 348
shoplifting
  experiments 153, 154
situational crime prevention
  see also **crime prevention**
  crime pattern theory 617, 618
  examples 610
  meaning 600, 609
  objectives 616
  opportunity theory 617
  rational choice perspective 600, 617
  routine activity theory 617
  success criteria 621
  target hardening 636
  theory 335–6
Smart, C.
  feminist criminology 432–3
Smith, A.
  'invisible hand' 455–6
smoking 56
social conflict theories 379
social construction
  causes of crime 527–8
  childhood 230
  crime statistics 119
  justice 83
  knowledge 141
  meaning 35
social contract
  Rawls 96
social control
  21st century theories 510–11
  control balance theory 510
  criminalisation 511
  deviance 60
  differential control theory 510
  Durkheim, E. 61
  Hirschi, T. 509–10
  integrated theories 505, 509–11
  meaning 61
  power control theory 510
  self-control theory 510
  theory 509–10
  traditional theories 509–10
social crime prevention
  see also **crime prevention**
  community models 612–13
  examples 609–10
  meaning 600, 609
  objectives 616–17
  potential offenders 610–12
  victimology 612
social desirability bias
  surveys 156
social enterprise
  careers 862–4
social harm
  meaning 35

social interaction theories
  deviance 424
  differential association 383–7
  generally 379
  learned behaviour, crime as 383–7
  micro-sociological theories 383
  Sutherland, E.H. 383–7
  white-collar crime 383–5
social justice
  meaning 88
  poverty 88
social learning theory 367–8, 373
social media 191, 192
  hate crime 213
social mores 380–2
social policy
  criminology 34
social process theories 379
social sciences
  criminology 34
social structural theories
  anomie 390–1
  Chicago school 394–7
  Durkheim, E. 387–91
  functionalism 387–91
  generally 379
  Merton, R.K. 391–4
  normality of crime 387–91
  strain theory 391–4
social work
  careers 853
socialisation 382–3
socialist feminism 295, 307
sociological positivism
  generally 35, 378–9
  neo-positivists 378
sociology
  Chicago school 394–7
  consensus theory 382–3
  criminology 34
  culture theories 397–410
  interpretivism 527
  key concepts
    consensus theory 382–3
    generally 379
    power 383
    role in society 380–2
    rules and norms 380–1
    social mores 380
    socialisation 382–3
    status 380–2
  power 383
  rules and norms 380–1
  social exclusion 406–10
  social interaction theories
    differential association 383–7
    generally 379
    learned behaviour, crime as 383–7
    micro-sociological theories 383
    Sutherland, E.H. 383–7
    white-collar crime 383–5
  social mores 380–2
  social structural theories
    anomie 390–1

Chicago school 394–7
Durkheim, E. 387–91
functionalism 387–91
generally 379
Merton, R.K. 391–4
normality of crime 387–91
strain theory 391–4
socialisation 382–3
subculture theories 397–410
subject matter 378–9
summary 411–14
theories
  culture theories 397–410
  social conflict theories 379
  social interaction theories 379, 383–7
  social structural theories 379, 387–97
  types 379
underclass 406–10
white-collar crime 383–5
somatotyping 348
spent convictions 689–90
sporting events
  justice 82–3, 85
standpoint feminism 296, 307
state activity
  criminalisation 58
State crime
  punishment 753–4
statistics *see* **crime statistics**
Stephen Lawrence Inquiry 84, 85
stigmatisation
  convict criminology 471–3
  deviance 424, 424–5
  impact 424–5
  justice 90
  meaning 90
  youth crime 242
stop and search powers
  black and minority ethnic communities
    273–4, 426–7, 747–9
  crime control 201, 273–4, 426–7, 639
  discrimination 426–7
  labelling perspectives 426–7
  policing 201, 273–4, 426–7, 639
  Stopwatch 201
  strip searches 275
  traffic stops 275
StopHateUK 201–2, 213, 214
Stopwatch 201
strain theory 391–4
street crime
  right realism 482
students
  see also **careers**; **employability**; **higher**
    education; **researchers**
  academic journals 23
  academic support 10–1
  active learning 30
  additional learning needs 12
  administration office 10–11
  alternative learning materials
    blogs 24
    social media 24
  'Always Be Critical' 26, 39–40

students (*Cont.*)
arriving at university 8–9
assessment of learning
blogs 47–9
criteria 42
dissertations 43
essays 42
examinations 43–4
generally 41–2
literature reviews 42–3
peer assessment 42
presentations 44–5
research posters 46
research-based assessment 45–6
review 47
self-assessment 42
visual assessments 49–50
work-based assessment 47
autodidactic age 40
blogs 47–9
books
critical analysis 22
edited texts 22–3
monographs 22
research-based books 22
textbooks 22
choice of university 7
communication with staff 18
computing facilities 15–17
course structures 21
critical analysis texts 22
curriculum vitae 7
departments 10–11, 17–18
direct learning 36
disability needs 11, 12
dissertations 43
distance learning 38
edited texts 22–3
edupunk 40
effective study 6
engaged student, becoming 6–7
essay questions 42
examinations 43–4
goals 6
guidance 7
handbooks, programme 20
health conditions 12
independent study 38–40
indirect learning 36
international students 12–13
journals 23
learning expectations 20–1
learning experiences 36
learning journey 8–11, 26
learning resources 21–2
lectures 36
levels of higher education 811–13
libraries 15–17
literature reviews 42–3
massive open online course (MOOC) 799,
834
methods of study 36–9
monographs 22
pedagogical patterns 40–1

pedagogy 39
peer support 25
personal tutors 18–19, 37
presentations 44–5
Programme Director 17
reflexivity 806–9
relevance of studies 809–11
reports 23–4
research posters 46
research-based assessment 45–6
research-based books 22
review 47
seminars 37
societies 13–15
student unions 815
student-staff committees 19
study of criminology 34–9
subject societies and networks 24–5
support services 7, 9–10
teaching staff 18–19
textbooks 22
'travel partners' 7, 11–15
tutorials 37
university 9–10
university policies 20
virtual learning 38
Virtual Learning Environment 20
visual assessments 49–50
work-based assessment 47
work-based learning 38
subjectivity
dominant subject viewpoints 145–6
existing knowledge 148
external-internal 146–7
fear of crime 147–8
generally 140, 142
group norms 147
individual demographics 146–7
internal subjectivity 147–8
knowledge 140, 142
media misrepresentation 146
peer groups 147
personal experience 147–8
police, experiences with 148
professional subjectivity 144–5
social interactions 147
suicide
assisted suicide 58
criminalisation 58
summary offences
meaning 558
officially recorded crime statistics 119
supposition
knowledge 140, 143, 148–50
risk prediction 149–50
surveys
behaviour of participants 156
causes of crime 534–5
crime statistics 534
demand characteristics 157
examples 154
interviews 155–7
leading questions 156
objectives 154

piloting 156
purpose 154
questionnaires 154
social desirability bias 156
statistical analysis 534
validity of results 156–7
Sutherland, E.H.
social interaction theories 383–7

target hardening
meaning 632
objectives 636–7
situational crime prevention 636
teachers
careers 860–1
terrorism
criminalisation 58
cybercrime 190
due process 94
inhuman and degrading treatment 93
justice 93
media portrayal 146
rights model 94
testosterone
biological positivism 354–6
theories
accuracy 320
assessment 318
breadth of claims 319
competing theories 318
concepts 322
counterclaims 320
coverage 319
criminological theory
classicism 323, 324–9
critical criminology 324
generally 322–3
interpretivism 323
positivism 323
critical criminology 418–19
critical evaluation 320
descriptive theories 321
deterrence theory 322
empirical validity 320
grand theories 321–2
hypotheses 321
importance of understanding 316–17
integrated theories 321–2
interpretivism 323
logical consistency 319
meaning 317–18
neo-classical criminology 329–30, 336–7
normative theories 321
positivism 323
rational choice theory 330–4
relationship to other theories 320
research evidence 320
role of theories 316–17
routine activity theory 334–5
situational crime prevention 335–6
summary 337–9
testing a theory 318–20
theorist 316
types

descriptive theories 321
    generally 321
    grand theories 321–2
    hypotheses 321
    integrated theories 321–2
    normative theories 321
  uses 316–17
  verification 319
theory of change model 541–2
transformative justice
  critical criminology 745–6
  meaning 745
trials
  adversarial justice 103–4, 565–6
truth and reconciliation 755–7
turning points *see* **critical moments**
tutorials
  students 37

underclass
  right realism 484–6
United Nations
  victims, definition of 204–5
utilitarianism
  justice 91
  meaning 91

victim surveys *see* **Crime Survey for England and Wales (CSEW)**
victimless crimes
  labelling perspectives 427
victimology
  see also **hate crime**
  adversarial justice 203
  anthropological studies 203
  changing role of the victim 202–3
  corporate power 209
  court system 203–4
  crime control 649–51
  crime statistics 207–8
  Crime Survey for England and Wales (CSEW) 200, 207
  criminal trials, victims in 203–4
  criminalisation 75
  critical victimology 206, 209–10
  deaths in custody 209–10
  definition of 'victim' 204
  deserving victims 206
  dispute resolution 202–3
  fear of crime 147–8
  feminism 208
  feminist criminology 208, 284
  harm principle 75
  'hierarchy' 206
  ideal victims 206–7
  impact 204
  importance 200
  labelling 209
  meaning 34
  measuring 207–8
  measuring victimisation 207–8
  media 202
  needs of victims 208
  non-governmental organisations

Howard League for Penal Reform 201
  Inquest 201
  international pressure groups 202
  National Association for Youth Justice 201
  role 200
  StopHateUK 201–2
  Stopwatch 201
  policy reform 200
  positivism 208–9
  prevention of crime 200
  punishment 665–6
  radical victimology 206, 209–10
  relating to victims 204
  restorative justice 567
  right realism 484
  sexual offences 208–9, 294
  social crime prevention 612
  social exclusion 206
  state power 209
  summary 221–3
  theoretical approaches
    critical approach 209–10
    feminism 208
    generally 208
    positivism 208–9
    radical approaches 209–10
  undeserving victims 206
  United Nations definition 204–5
  victim blaming and shaming 207
  Victim Personal Statements (VPS) 665–6
  victim precipitation 434
  victimisation 204
  women 206, 434–8
  youth offending teams 250
virtual learning 38
visual assessments 49–50
visual criminology 823–9
volunteering
  careers 863
  employability 841–2

war crimes 752–3
Weberian sociology
  justice 89–90
  meaning 89
websites
  crime statistics 124
white-collar crime 383–5
whole life orders 580
women
  victimology 206
work shadowing 841
work-based assessment 47
work-based learning 38, 840–2

Young Black People and Criminal Justice System 269
Young, J.
  critical criminology 428–9
  cultural criminology 466–8
Young Review 269
youth crime
  age of criminal responsibility 231, 247–8

age-graded theory of informal social control 236–8
  agency 238–9
  alcohol use 531–4
  amplification of deviance 245–7
  Asset tool 250–1
  AssetPlus 253–4
  black and minority ethnic communities 276
  Bulger murder 247–8
  Cambridge Study 235–6
  childhood
    background 228–9
    developmental explanations 232
    historical development of concept 229–30
    social construct 230
  Children First, Offenders Second (CFOS) 255–6
  conclusions 257–8
  crime prevention 600, 605, 607
  crime statistics 177
  critical criminology 242
  critical moments 232, 518, 519
  custodial sentences 243–5
  definition of 'child' 229
  delinquency
    age-graded theory of informal social control 236–8
    agency 232, 238–9
    Cambridge Study 235–6
    cultural factors 239
    developmental theories 3, 233–5
    emergence, concept of 234
    empirical theories 234–5
    genetics 233
    individual attributes 232
    individualised causes 233
    mediated choice 238–9
    psychodynamic factors 232
    Risk Factor Prevention Paradigm 235
    social/structural influence 232
    theories 232
    transitions 234
  desistance 253
  determinism 238
  developmental theories 233–4
  diversion 255, 721–2, 727, 728–9
  doli incapax 247–8, 560
  early intervention 250
  experiments 531–4
  folk devils 397
  gang culture 240
  gender 233
  generally 228
  interventionist diversion 255
  Key Elements of Effective Practice (KEEP) 250
  labelling theory 242
  media
    crime statistics 177
    demonisation 176
    deviancy amplification spiral 177
    education 177

youth crime (*Cont.*)
folk devils 177
health backgrounds 177
overview 175–6
'presence of absence' 176–7
subcultures 177–8
mediated choice 238–9
moral panics 397, 464
National Association for Youth Justice 201
Onset 251–2
positive youth justice 255–7
pre-offending risk assessment 251–2
presumption of innocence 248
progressive approaches
case study 256–7
diversion 255
generally 254–5
interventionist diversion 255
positive youth justice 255–7
pre-court processes 255
radicalisation 241
reductionism of risk management 252–4
responding to offending behaviour

early intervention 250
generally 248–9
Risk Factor Prevention Paradigm 249, 250
risk-focused early intervention 250
triangle of risk-based crime reduction and prevention 249–50
responsibilisation 242
restorative justice 728–30
rights of the child 229
Risk Factor Prevention Paradigm 235, 249, 250
risk factors 250–2
scaled approach to assessment/intervention 251
secondary deviance 242–3
social construction 241–3
stigmatisation 242
summary 258–9
them and us mentality 248
triangle of risk-based crime reduction and prevention 249–50
turning points 238

victims of crime, offenders as 242
Youth Inclusion Panels 251, 252
Youth Inclusion and Support Panels 251, 252
Youth Justice Board 250

zemiology
background 450–4
crime 451
crime control 451
criminal justice system 451
criminalisation 451
critical themes 451
generally 418
labelling perspectives 451
meaning 34, 451
power 451, 454
punishment 451
'safety crimes' 452–4
seriousness of crime 451
social harm 450–1
zero tolerance policing 639–40